CW00543328

GABRIEL MANTZ

# SOUTH AMERICAN FOOTBALL INTERNATIONAL LINE-UPS & STATISTICS 1902-2013

# VOLUME 1

British Library Cataloguing in Publication Data
A catalogue record for this book is available from the British Library

ISBN 978-1-86223-287-7

Copyright © 2014, SOCCER BOOKS LIMITED (01472 696226)
72 St. Peter's Avenue, Cleethorpes, N.E. Lincolnshire, DN35 8HU, England

Web site www.soccer-books.co.uk
e-mail info@soccer-books.co.uk

All rights are reserved. No part of this publication may be reproduced, stored in a retrieval system or transmitted, in any form or by any means, electronic, mechanical, photocopying, recording, or otherwise, without the prior written permission of Soccer Books Limited.

**Printed in the UK by 4edge Ltd.**

Dear Readers,

This book is the first volume of a new series which will contain statistics for all matches played by South American national teams from the very first game played in 1902 through to the present day. There are 10 national teams in South America and the governing body of association football in South America is CONMEBOL (Confederación Sudamericana de Fútbol – The South American Football Confederation), also the oldest continental confederation in the world. With 10 member football associations, CONMEBOL has the fewest members of all continental confederations belonging to FIFA. However, the national teams belonging to CONMEBOL have won nine of 19 FIFA World Cup tournaments played between 1930 and 2010 (Brazil winning five times, Argentina and Uruguay each with two trophies). In 1916, the first South American continental championship was founded under the name Campeonato Sudamericano de Fútbol. The competition still exists to this day though it is now named the Campeonato Sudamericano Copa América or more simply the Copa América. In this, the oldest of continental football competitions, Uruguay holds the record number of victories after winning the trophy on 15 occasions between 1916 and 2011.

The first international match between two South American national teams was played on 20th July 1902 between Uruguay and Argentina, approximately 3 months earlier than the first European game played between non-British national teams (Austria played Hungary on 12th October 1902). This first volume contains the complete statistical records of the national teams of Argentina, Bolivia and Chile.

The Argentinian national football team, known as the "Albicelestes" won two FIFA World Championships (as hosts in 1978 and in Mexico in 1986) and also lost two other finals (the first World Cup in 1930 and in 1990). Argentina have also won 14 titles in the Copa América, were twice Olympic Champions (in 2004 and 2008) and were also the winners of the first FIFA Confederations Cup held in 1992.

The Bolivian national football team has enjoyed fewer successes and have only progressed through the qualifiers to the final tournament of the FIFA World Cup on three occasions. Bolivia's chief success in football came as they became South American champions in 1963 as they won the Copa América. Many of Bolivia's best results over the year are due in no small part to the fact that Bolivia play their home games at the "Hernando Siles Zuazo" stadium in la Paz which has an altitude of 3,637 metres (11,932 feet) above sea level! The rarefied atmosphere at this high altitude causes many problems for visiting teams, especially as they are often lacking enough time to acclimatise to the difficult conditions.

The Chilean national football team has played in eight World Cup final tournaments and were also hosts of the 1962 FIFA World Cup, when they won the Bronze medal after finishing in third place. They have never won the Copa América but have been runners-up in the competition on four occasions.

This book contains statistics for all the matches played by each country's "A" national team from their first match until the end of 2013. For each match played, besides the names of the players who appear you will find the number of caps and goals for each player achieved by that game. There is also information about the stadium, referee and attendance for each game and, of course, the name of the national team coach. In addition to the individual match information, a second section lists all the players to make an international appearance for each country which shows number of total caps won and goals scored, the period when the player made his international appearances and the club he was playing for at the time. A third section presents information for all the national coaches/managers and a fourth section presents head-to-head statistics for each country versus all opponents faced in international matches. I have to apologise for the lack of complete statistical data for some players, but it can be very difficult to be find this information. I hope that readers will find this work both useful and informative.

The Author

## SUMMARY



### ABBREVIATIONS

**FM/Nr** Number of first match played for the national team / Player counter
**DOB** Date of birth

### FIFA COUNTRY CODES – SOUTH AMERICA

| | |
|---|---|
| Argentina | **ARG** |
| Bolivia | **BOL** |
| Brazil | **BRA** |
| Chile | **CHI** |
| Colombia | **COL** |
| Ecuador | **ECU** |
| Paraguay | **PAR** |
| Peru | **PER** |
| Uruguay | **URU** |
| Venezuela | **VEN** |

# ARGENTINA

| The Country: |
|---|
| República Argentina (Argentine Republic) |
| Capital: Buenos Aires |
| Surface: 2,766,890 km² |
| Inhabitants: 41,660,417 |
| Time: UTC-3 |

| The FA: |
|---|
| Asociación del Fútbol Argentino |
| Viamonte 1366/76 Buenos Aires 1053 |
| Foundation date: 1893 |
| Member of FIFA since: 1912 |
| Member of CONMEBOL since: 1916 |

## NATIONAL TEAM RECORDS

| COPA AMÉRICA | |
|---|---|
| **1916** | Runners-up |
| **1917** | Runners-up |
| **1919** | 3rd Place |
| **1920** | Runners-up |
| **1921** | **Winners** |
| **1922** | 4th Place |
| **1923** | Runners-up |
| **1924** | Runners-up |
| **1925** | **Winners** |
| **1926** | Runners-up |
| **1927** | **Winners** |
| **1929** | **Winners** |
| **1935** | Runners-up |
| **1937** | **Winners** |
| **1939** | Withdrew |
| **1941** | **Winners** |
| **1942** | Runners-up |
| **1945** | **Winners** |
| **1946** | **Winners** |
| **1947** | **Winners** |
| **1949** | Withdrew |
| **1953** | Withdrew |
| **1955** | **Winners** |
| **1956** | 3rd Place |
| **1957** | **Winners** |
| **1959** | **Winners** |
| **1959E** | Runners-up |
| **1963** | 3rd Place |
| **1967** | Runners-up |
| **1975** | Group Stage |
| **1979** | Group Stage |
| **1983** | Group Stage |
| **1987** | 4th Place |
| **1989** | 3rd Place |
| **1991** | **Winners** |
| **1993** | **Winners** |
| **1995** | Quarter-Finals |
| **1997** | Quarter-Finals |
| **1999** | Quarter-Finals |
| **2001** | Withdrew |
| **2004** | Runners-up |
| **2007** | Runners-up |
| **2011** | Quarter-Finals |

| WORLD CUP | |
|---|---|
| **1930** | Final Tournament (Runners-up) |
| **1934** | Final Tournament (1st Round) |
| **1938** | Withdrew |
| **1950** | Withdrew |
| **1954** | Withdrew |
| **1958** | Final Tournament (Group Stage) |
| **1962** | Final Tournament (Group Stage) |
| **1966** | Final Tournament (Quarter-Finals) |
| **1970** | Qualifiers |
| **1974** | Final Tournament (2nd Round) |
| **1978** | **Final Tournament (Winners)** |
| **1982** | Final Tournament (2nd Round) |
| **1986** | **Final Tournament (Winners)** |
| **1990** | Final Tournament (Runners-up) |
| **1994** | Final Tournament (1/16 Finals) |
| **1998** | Final Tournament (Quarter-Finals) |
| **2002** | Final Tournament (Group Stage) |
| **2006** | Final Tournament (Quarter-Finals) |
| **2010** | Final Tournament (Quarter-Finals) |
| **2014** | Final Tournament (*to be played*) |

| OLYMPIC GAMES 1900-2012 |
|---|
| 1928 (Runners-up), 1960, 1964, 1988, 1996 (Runners-up), **2004 & 2008 (Winners)** |
| **FIFA CONFEDERATIONS CUP 1992-2013** |
| **1992 (Winners)**, 1995 (Runners-up), 2005 (Runners-up) |
| **PLAYER WITH MOST INTERNATIONAL CAPS** |
| Javier Adelmar Zanetti – 145 caps (1994-2011) |
| **PLAYER WITH MOST INTERNATIONAL GOALS** |
| Gabriel Omar Batistuta – 56 goals (78 caps, 1991-2002) |

# FULL INTERNATIONALS (1902-2013)

**1.** 20.07.1902 **URUGUAY - ARGENTINA** **0-6(0-2)**
Estadio Paso del Molino, Montevideo; Referee: Roberto Ruud (Argentina); Attendance: 8,000
**ARG:** José Laforia (1/0), William Leslie (1/0), Walter Buchanan (1/0), Eduardo Patricio Duggan (1/0), Carlos Buchanan (1/0), Ernesto Brown (1/0), Edward Morgan (1/1), Juan José Moore (1/0), Juan Anderson (1/1), Carlos Edgard Dickinson (1/1), Jorge Brown (1/1). Trainer: no.
**Goals**: Carlos Edgard Dickinson (3), Germán Arímalo (31 own goal), Edward Morgan (64), Carlos Carve Urioste (66 own goal), Juan Anderson (71), Jorge Brown (86).

**2.** 13.09.1903 **ARGENTINA - URUGUAY** **2-3(0-1)**
Estadio Sociedad Hípica, Buenos Aires; Referee: Roberto Ruud (Argentina); Attendance: 4,000
**ARG:** Jorge Howard (1/0), Carlos Brown (1/0), Walter Buchanan (2/0), Emilio Firpo (1/0), Carlos Buchanan (2/0), Ernesto Brown (2/0), Gottlob Weiss (1/0), Juan José Moore (2/0), Eugenio Moore (1/0), Carlos Edgard Dickinson (2/1), Jorge Brown (2/3). Trainer: no.
**Goals**: Jorge Brown (51, 80).

**3.** 15.08.1905 **ARGENTINA - URUGUAY** **0-0** Copa Lipton
Campo de la Sociedad Sportiva, Buenos Aires; Referee: Guillermo Jordán (Argentina); Attendance: 5,000
**ARG:** José Laforia (2/0), Carlos Brown (2/0), Jorge Brown (3/3), J. Rodman (1/0), Patricio Browne (1/0), Carlos Edgard Dickinson (3/1), Gottlob Weiss (2/0), Juan José Moore (3/0), Arthur H. Forrester (1/0), Carlos Lett (1/0), Pablo Frers (1/0). Trainer: no.

**4.** 15.08.1906 **URUGUAY - ARGENTINA** **0-2(0-1)** Copa Lipton
Estadio Parque Central, Montevideo; Referee: Guillermo McFarlane (Argentina); Attendance: 5,000
**ARG:** José Laforia (3/0), Juan Domingo Brown (1/0), Zenón Díaz (1/0), Carlos Edgard Dickinson (4/1), Carlos Buchanan (3/0), Patricio Browne (2/0), Gottlob Weiss (3/0), Alfredo Brown (1/1), Jorge Brown (4/3), Tristán González (1/1), Eliseo Brown (1/0). Trainer: no.
**Goals**: Alfredo Brown (28), Tristán González (85).

**5.** 21.10.1906 **ARGENTINA - URUGUAY** **2-1(1-0)** Copa Newton
Campo de la Sociedad Sportiva, Buenos Aires; Referee: Guillermo Jordán (Argentina); Attendance: 4,000
**ARG:** Ricardo Coulthurst (1/0), Juan Domingo Brown (2/0), Jorge Brown (5/3), Carlos Edgard Dickinson (5/1), Carlos Buchanan (4/0), Patricio Browne (3/0), Gottlob Weiss (4/0), Héctor Henman (1/0), Arnoldo Watson Hutton (1/1), Wilfredo Stocks (1/0), Eliseo Brown (2/1). Trainer: no.
**Goals**: Arnoldo Watson Hutton (15), Eliseo Brown (80).

**6.** 15.08.1907 **ARGENTINA - URUGUAY** **2-1(2-0)** Copa Lipton
Estadio Estudiantes, Buenos Aires; Referee: Guillermo Leslie (Argentina); Attendance: 7,000
**ARG:** José Laforia (4/0), Juan Domingo Brown (3/0), Jorge Brown (6/3), Armando Ginocchio (1/0), Arturo Jacobs (1/1), Haroldo M. Grant (1/0), R. Pertino (1/0), Alfredo Brown (2/1), Arnoldo Watson Hutton (2/1), Eliseo Brown (3/2), José Susán (1/0). Trainer: no.
**Goals**: Eliseo Brown, Arturo Jacobs.

**7.** 06.10.1907 **URUGUAY - ARGENTINA** **1-2(0-1)** Copa Newton
Estadio Parque Central, Montevideo; Referee: Cecil Poole (Uruguay); Attendance: 9,000
**ARG:** Carlos Tomás Wilson (1/0), Juan Domingo Brown (4/0), Colin Campbell (1/0), Guillermo Ross (1/0), Juan Antonio Murray (1/0), Juan Wood (1/0), Arthur H. Forrester (1/0), Alfredo Brown (3/1), Carlos Whalley (1/0), Arturo Jacobs (2/1), Ricardo Malbrán (1/2). Trainer: no.
**Goals**: Ricardo Malbrán 2.

**8.** 15.08.1908 **URUGUAY - ARGENTINA** **2-2(1-1)** Copa Lipton
Estadio Parque Central, Montevideo; Referee: Léon Peyrou (Uruguay); Attendance: 7,000
**ARG:** Carlos Tomás Wilson (2/0), Jorge Brown (7/3), Martín Murphy (1/0), Patricio Browne (4/0), Carlos Buchanan (5/0), Luis Vernet Amadeo (1/0), Maximiliano Susán (1/1), Alfredo Brown (4/1), Ernesto Brown (3/1), Juan Rossi (1/0), José Viale (1/0). Trainer: no.
**Goals**: Ernesto Brown, Maximiliano Susán.

**9.** 13.09.1908 **ARGENTINA - URUGUAY** **2-1(1-0)** Copa Newton
Estadio Club Gymnasia y Esgrima, Buenos Aires; Referee: Mariano Reyna (Argentina); Attendance: 7,000
**ARG:** Carlos Tomás Wilson (3/0), Juan Domingo Brown (5/0), Martín Murphy (2/0), Patricio Browne (5/0), Haroldo Ratcliff (1/0), Ernesto Brown (4/1), Gottlob Weiss (5/0), Alfredo Brown (5/1), Arnoldo Watson Hutton (3/2), Eliseo Brown (4/3), Maximiliano Susán (2/1). Trainer: no.
**Goals**: Eliseo Brown, Arnoldo Watson Hutton.

**10.** 04.10.1908 **ARGENTINA - URUGUAY** **0-1(0-0)** Premio de Honor Argentino
Estadio Club Gymnasia y Esgrima, Buenos Aires; Referee: Mariano Reyna (Argentina); Attendance: 7,000
**ARG:** Carlos Tomás Wilson (4/0), Jorge Brown (8/3), Juan Domingo Brown (6/0), Patricio Browne (6/0), Maximiliano Susán (3/1), Arturo Jacobs (3/1), Gottlob Weiss (6/0), Alfredo Brown (6/1), Arnoldo Watson Hutton (4/2), Eliseo Brown (5/3), José Susán (2/0). Trainer: no.

**11.** 15.08.1909 **ARGENTINA - URUGUAY** **2-1(2-0)** Copa Lipton
Estadio Club Gymnasia y Esgrima, Buenos Aires; Referee: Guillermo Jordán (Argentina); Attendance: 4,000
**ARG:** Carlos Tomás Wilson (5/0), Jorge Brown (9/3), Juan Domingo Brown (7/0), Patricio Browne (7/0), Ernesto Brown (5/1), Arturo Jacobs (4/1), Maximiliano Susán (4/1), Eduardo Rothschild (1/0), Arnoldo Watson Hutton (5/3), Eliseo Brown (6/4), José Viale (2/0). Trainer: no.
**Goals**: Arnoldo Watson Hutton, Eliseo Brown.

**12.** 19.09.1909 **URUGUAY - ARGENTINA** **2-2(0-2)** Copa Newton
Estadio Parque Belvedere, Montevideo; Referee: Juan Dall'Orto (Uruguay); Attendance: 9,000
**ARG:** Carlos Tomás Wilson (6/0), Jorge Brown (10/3), Juan Domingo Brown (8/0), Harold Lloyd (1/0), Juan Antonio Murray (2/0), J. Sheridan (1/0), Elías Fernández (1/0), Juan Rossi (2/0), Maximiliano Susán (5/1), Eliseo Brown (7/4), José Viale (3/1). Trainer: no.
**Goals**: José Viale, Alberto García (own goal).

**13.** 10.10.1909 **ARGENTINA - URUGUAY** **3-1(2-1)** Premio de Honor Argentino
Estadio Club Gymnasia y Esgrima, Buenos Aires; Referee: Apeles Bordabehere (Uruguay); Attendance: 6,500
**ARG:** Carlos Tomás Wilson (7/0), Jorge Brown (11/4), Juan Domingo Brown (9/0), Henry Lawrie (1/0), Maximiliano Susán (6/1), Arturo Jacobs (5/1), Elías Fernández (2/0), Alfredo Brown (7/3), Arnoldo Watson Hutton (6/3), Eliseo Brown (8/4), José Viale (4/1). Trainer: no.
**Goals**: Alfredo Brown 2, Jorge Brown (penalty).

**14.** 27.05.1910 **ARGENTINA - CHILE** **3-1(2-1)** Torneo América de Sud
Estadio Belgrano, Buenos Aires; Referee: Armando Bergalli (Chile); Attendance: 6,200
**ARG:** Enrique Rojo (1/0), Santiago Gallino (1/0), Arturo Chiappe (1/0), Luis Vernet Amadeo (2/0), Haroldo M. Grant (2/0), Armando Ginocchio (2/0), Maximiliano Susán (7/2), Elías Fernández (3/0), Juan Enrique Hayes (1/1), Manuel González (1/0), José Viale (5/2). Trainer: no.
**Goals**: José Viale (38), Maximiliano Susán (43), Juan Enrique Hayes (68).

**15.** 05.06.1910 **ARGENTINA - CHILE** **5-1(3-0)**
Estadio Club Gymnasia y Esgrima, Buenos Aires; Referee: Léon Peyrou (Uruguay); Attendance: 2,500
**ARG:** Carlos Tomás Wilson (8/0), Jorge Brown (12/4), Juan Domingo Brown (10/0), Armando Ginocchio (3/0), Ernesto Brown (6/1), Arturo Jacobs (6/1), Gottlob Weiss (7/1), Maximiliano Susán (8/3), Juan Enrique Hayes (2/3), Ricardo Malbrán (2/2), José Viale (6/3). Trainer: no.
**Goals**: José Viale, Juan Enrique Hayes 2, Gottlob Weiss, Maximiliano Susán.

**16.** 12.06.1910 **ARGENTINA - URUGUAY** **4-1(2-0)** Torneo América de Sud
Estadio Club Gymnasia y Esgrima, Buenos Aires; Referee: Armando Bergalli (Chile); Attendance: 8,000
**ARG:** Carlos Tomás Wilson (9/0), Jorge Brown (13/4), Juan Domingo Brown (11/0), Armando Ginocchio (4/0), Ernesto Brown (7/1), Arturo Jacobs (7/1), Manuel González (2/0), Maximiliano Susán (9/4), Juan Enrique Hayes (3/4), Arnoldo Watson Hutton (7/4), José Viale (7/4). Trainer: no.
**Goals**: José Viale, Juan Enrique Hayes, Arnoldo Watson Hutton, Maximiliano Susán.

**17.** 15.08.1910 **URUGUAY - ARGENTINA** **3-1(1-0)** Copa Lipton
Estadio Parque Belvedere, Montevideo; Referee: Léon Peyrou (Uruguay); Attendance: 8,000
**ARG:** Carlos Tomás Wilson (10/0), Jorge Brown (14/4), Juan Domingo Brown (12/0), Armando Ginocchio (5/0), Ernesto Brown (8/1), Haroldo M. Grant (3/0), Elías Fernández (4/0), Maximiliano Susán (10/4), Juan Enrique Hayes (4/5), Arnoldo Watson Hutton (8/4), José Viale (8/4). Trainer: no.
**Goal**: Juan Enrique Hayes.

**18.** 11.09.1910 **CHILE - ARGENTINA** **0-3(0-1)**
Estadio Sporting Club, Viña del Mar; Referee: Hamilton (Chile); Attendance: 7,000
**ARG:** Carlos Tomás Wilson (11/0), Martín Murphy (3/0), Juan Domingo Brown (13/0), J. Sheridan (2/0), Patricio Browne (8/0), Ernesto Brown (9/1), Elías Fernández (5/1), Manuel González (3/1), Juan Olegario Gil (1/0), Henry Lawrie (2/1), José Viale (9/4). Trainer: no.
**Goals**: Henry Lawrie, Elías Fernández, Manuel González.

**19.** 13.11.1910 **ARGENTINA - URUGUAY** **1-1(0-0,1-1)** Premio de Honor Argentino
Estadio Club Gymnasia y Esgrima, Buenos Aires; Referee: Héctor Alfano (Argentina); Attendance: 5,000
**ARG:** Juan José Rithner (1/0), Santiago Gallino (2/0), Juan Domingo Brown (14/0), Tomás González (1/0), Haroldo M. Grant (4/0), Luis Vernet Amadeo (3/0), Elías Fernández (6/1), Eduardo Rothschild (2/0), Arnoldo Watson Hutton (9/4), Manuel González (4/2), José Viale (10/4). Trainer: no.
**Goal**: Manuel González.

**20.** 27.11.1910 **ARGENTINA - URUGUAY** **2-6(1-5)** Premio de Honor Argentino
Estadio Club Gymnasia y Esgrima, Buenos Aires; Referee: Héctor Alfano (Argentina); Attendance: 10,000
**ARG:** Juan José Rithner (2/0), Santiago Gallino (3/0), Juan Domingo Brown (15/0), Tomás González (2/0), Haroldo M. Grant (5/0), Luis Vernet Amadeo (4/0), Elías Fernández (7/1), Eduardo Rothschild (3/0), Arnoldo Watson Hutton (10/4), Manuel González (5/3), José Viale (11/5). Trainer: no.
**Goals**: Manuel González, José Viale.

**21.** 15.08.1911 **ARGENTINA - URUGUAY** **0-2(0-0)** Copa Lipton
Estadio Club Gymnasia y Esgrima, Buenos Aires; Referee: Héctor Alfano (Argentina); Attendance: 15,000
**ARG:** Carlos Tomás Wilson (12/0), Jorge Brown (15/4), Juan Domingo Brown (16/0), Manuel Malbrán (1/0), Haroldo M. Grant (6/0), Ernesto Brown (10/1), Elías Fernández (8/1), Maximiliano Susán (11/4), Juan Enrique Hayes (5/5), Carlos Lett (2/0), José Viale (12/5). Trainer: no.

**22.** 17.09.1911 **URUGUAY - ARGENTINA** **2-3(0-1)** Copa Newton
Estadio Parque Central, Montevideo; Referee: Alvaro Saralegui (Uruguay); Attendance: 15,000
**ARG:** Carlos Tomás Wilson (13/0), Jorge Brown (16/4), Juan Domingo Brown (17/0), Alfredo Lorenzo Dickinson (1/0), Cirilo Russ (1/0), Adolfo Peel Yates (1/0), Maximiliano Susán (12/4), Alfredo Brown (8/4), Eliseo Brown (9/6), Juan Enrique Hayes (6/5), Elías Fernández (9/1). Trainer: no.
**Goals**: Alfredo Brown, Eliseo Brown 2.

**23.** 08.10.1911 **URUGUAY - ARGENTINA** **1-1(0-1,1-1)** Premio de Honor Uruguayo
Estadio Parque Central, Montevideo; Referee: Léon Peyrou (Uruguay); Attendance: 12,000
**ARG:** Carlos Tomás Wilson (14/0), Jorge Brown (17/4), Juan Domingo Brown (18/0), Alfredo Lorenzo Dickinson (2/0), Ernesto Brown (11/1), Adolfo Peel Yates (2/0), Elías Fernández (10/1), Alfredo Brown (9/4), Arnoldo Watson Hutton (11/5), Juan Enrique Hayes (7/5), Maximiliano Susán (13/4). Trainer: no.
**Goal**: Arnoldo Watson Hutton.

**24.** 22.10.1911 **ARGENTINA - URUGUAY** **2-0(2-0)** Premio de Honor Argentino
Estadio Club Gymnasia y Esgrima, Buenos Aires; Referee: Héctor Alfano (Argentina); Attendance: 18,000
**ARG:** Carlos Tomás Wilson (15/0), Jorge Brown (18/4), Juan Domingo Brown (19/0), Adolfo Peel Yates (3/0), Maximiliano Susán (14/4), Alfredo Lorenzo Dickinson (3/0), Elías Fernández (11/1), Antonio Piaggio (1/2), Eliseo Brown (10/6), Arnoldo Watson Hutton (12/5), Juan Enrique Hayes (8/5). Trainer: no.
**Goals**: Antonio Piaggio 2.

**25.** 29.10.1911 **URUGUAY - ARGENTINA** **3-0(1-0)** Premio de Honor Uruguayo
Estadio Parque Central, Montevideo; Referee: Juan Dall'Orto (Uruguay); Attendance: 15,000
**ARG:** Carlos Tomás Wilson (16/0), Jorge Brown (19/4), Juan Domingo Brown (20/0), Adolfo Peel Yates (4/0), Maximiliano Susán (15/4), Alfredo Lorenzo Dickinson (4/0), Elías Fernández (12/1), Arnoldo Watson Hutton (13/5), Antonio Piaggio (2/2), Juan Enrique Hayes (9/5), Henry Lawrie (3/1). Trainer: no.

**26.** 15.08.1912 **URUGUAY - ARGENTINA** **2-0(1-0)** Copa Lipton
Estadio Parque Central, Montevideo; Referee: Alvaro Saralegui (Uruguay); Attendance: 18,000
**ARG:** Carlos Tomás Wilson (17/0), Jorge Brown (20/4), Juan Domingo Brown (21/0), José Morroni (1/0), Maximiliano Susán (16/4), Ernesto Brown (12/1), Alberto Bernardino Ohaco (1/0), Antonio Ameal Pereyra (1/0), Guillermo Dannaher (1/0), Juan Enrique Hayes (10/5), José Viale (13/5). Trainer: no.

**27.** 25.08.1912 **URUGUAY - ARGENTINA** **3-0(2-0)** Premio de Honor Uruguayo
Estadio Parque Central, Montevideo; Referee: Alvaro Saralegui (Uruguay); Attendance: 18,000
**ARG:** Carlos Tomás Wilson (18/0), Jorge Brown (21/4), Juan Domingo Brown (22/0), Cirilo Russ (2/0), Maximiliano Susán (17/4), Ernesto Brown (13/1), Manuel González (6/3), Arnoldo Watson Hutton (14/5), Sidney Buck (1/0), Juan Enrique Hayes (11/5), José Viale (14/5). Trainer: no.

**28.** 22.09.1912 **ARGENTINA - URUGUAY** **0-1(0-0)** Premio de Honor Uruguayo
Estadio Club Gymnasia y Esgrima, Buenos Aires; Referee: Guillermo Jordán (Argentina); Attendance: 18,000
**ARG:** Juan José Rithner (3/0), Antonio Apraiz (1/0), Arturo Reparaz (1/0), Juan Johnston (1/0), Ernesto Sande (1/0), Gerónimo Badaracco (1/0), Bleo Pedro Fournol „Calomino" (1/0), A. Márquez (1/0), Antonio Piaggio (3/2), Santiago Sayanes (1/0), Pascual Polimeni (1/0). Trainer: no.

**29.** 06.10.1912 **ARGENTINA - URUGUAY** **3-3(1-2)** Copa Newton
Estadio Racing Club, Avellaneda, Buenos Aires; Referee: Héctor Alfano (Argentina); Attendance: 12,000
**ARG:** Carlos Tomás Wilson (19/0), Jorge Brown (22/4), Juan Domingo Brown (23/0), Arturo Chiappe (2/0), Cirilo Russ (3/0), Pablo Molina (1/0), Maximiliano Susán (18/4), Juan Enrique Hayes (12/5), Arnoldo Watson Hutton (15/6), Manuel González (7/3), José Viale (15/7). Trainer: no.
**Goals**: Arnoldo Watson Hutton, José Viale 2.

**30.** 01.12.1912 **URUGUAY - ARGENTINA** **1-3(1-1,1-1)** Copa Montevideo
Estadio Parque Central, Montevideo; Referee: Juan Bartolazzo (Uruguay); Attendance: 12,000
**ARG:** Carlos Pearson (1/0), Juan José Bello (1/0), Juan Domingo Brown (24/0), Arturo Chiappe (3/0), Carlos González (1/0), Alberto Olivari (1/0), Juan Hospital (1/0), Juan Manuel Rogers (1/0), Alberto Andrés Marcovecchio (1/1), Manuel González (8/4), José Viale (16/8). Trainer: no.
**Goals**: Manuel González, Alberto Andrés Marcovecchio, José Viale.

**31.** 15.06.1913 **ARGENTINA - URUGUAY** **1-1(0-1,1-1)*** Copa Presídente Roque Sáenz Peña
Estadio Racing Club, Avellaneda, Buenos Aires; Referee: Héctor Alfano (Argentina); Attendance: 12,000
**ARG:** Carlos Tomás Wilson (20/0), Arturo Chiappe (4/0), Juan Domingo Brown (25/0), Ángel Mallen (1/0), José Morroni (2/0), Arturo Jacobs (8/1), Maximiliano Susán (19/4), Manuel González (9/5), Alberto Andrés Marcovecchio (2/1), Arnoldo Watson Hutton (16/6), Francisco Taggino (1/0). Trainer: no.
**Goal**: Manuel González.
**After 17 mins extra-time, the match was stopped due to nightfall.*

**32.** 09.07.1913 **ARGENTINA - URUGUAY** **2-1(1-1)** Copa Presídente Roque Sáenz Peña
Estadio Racing Club, Avellaneda, Buenos Aires; Referee: Héctor Alfano (Argentina); Attendance: 12,000
**ARG:** Carlos Tomás Wilson (21/0), Arturo Chiappe (5/0), Juan Domingo Brown (26/0), Alberto Olivari (2/0), Ángel Mallen (2/0), Mario Luis Negri (1/0), Horacio Vignoles (1/0), Arnoldo Watson Hutton (17/6), Juan Hospital (2/0), Manuel González (10/7), Alfredo Meira (1/0). Trainer: no.
**Goals**: Manuel González 2.

**33.** 15.08.1913 **ARGENTINA - URUGUAY** **4-0(2-0)** Copa Lipton
Estadio Racing Club, Avellaneda, Buenos Aires; Referee: José Susán (Argentina); Attendance: 15,000
**ARG:** Carlos Tomás Wilson (22/0), Arturo Chiappe (6/0), Juan Domingo Brown (27/0), Ricardo Pepe (1/0), José Morroni (3/0), Alberto Olivari (3/0), Juan Manuel Rogers (2/0), Alberto Bernardino Ohaco (2/0), Maximiliano Susán (20/8), Donato Abatángelo (1/0), José Viale (17/8). Trainer: no.
**Goals**: Maximiliano Susán 4.

**34.** 31.08.1913 **ARGENTINA - URUGUAY** **2-0(0-0)** Premio de Honor Uruguayo
Estadio Club Gymnasia y Esgrima, Buenos Aires; Referee: Carlos Aerst (Argentina); Attendance: 8,500
**ARG:** Juan José Rithner (4/0), Zenón Díaz (2/0), Arturo Reparaz (2/0), Santiago Sayanes (2/0), Ernesto Sande (2/0), Gerónimo Badaracco (2/0), Juan José Lamas (1/0), Guillermo Dannaher (2/0), Juan Enrique Hayes (13/6), Carlos Guidi (1/0), Pascual Polimeni (2/1). Trainer: no.
**Goals**: Juan Enrique Hayes, Pascual Polimeni.

**35.** 05.10.1913 **URUGUAY - ARGENTINA** **1-0(0-0)** Premio de Honor Uruguayo
Estadio Parque Central, Montevideo; Referee: Hugo Gondra (Argentina); Attendance: 10,000
**ARG:** Carlos Tomás Wilson (23/0), Jorge Brown (23/4), Juan Domingo Brown (28/0), Arturo Chiappe (7/0), Ángel Mallen (3/0), Alberto Olivari (4/0), Elías Fernández (13/1), Manuel González (11/7), Maximiliano Susán (21/8), Luis Povey (1/0), José Viale (18/8). Trainer: no.

**36.** 26.10.1913 **URUGUAY - ARGENTINA** **1-0(0-0)** Copa Newton
Estadio Parque Central, Montevideo; Referee: Hugo Gondra (Argentina); Attendance: 12,000
**ARG:** Carlos Muttoni (1/0), Arturo Chiappe (8/0), Juan Domingo Brown (29/0), Heriberto Simmons (1/0), Ángel Mallen (4/0), Alberto Olivari (5/0), Juan Manuel Rogers (3/0), Juan Rossi (3/0), Maximiliano Susán (22/8), Juan Hospital (3/0), Francisco Taggino (2/0). Trainer: no.

**37.** 30.08.1914 **URUGUAY - ARGENTINA** **3-2(1-1)** Premio de Honor Uruguayo
Estadio Parque Central, Montevideo; Referee: Luis Farinasso (Uruguay); Attendance: 8,000
**ARG:** Juan José Rithner (5/0), Antonio Bruno (1/0), Rodolfo Martínez (1/0), Santiago Sayanes (3/0), Ernesto Sande (3/0), Gerónimo Badaracco (3/0), Bleo Pedro Fournol „Calomino" (2/1), Juan Cabano (1/0), Pedro Gallardo (1/0), Guillermo Dannaher (3/1), Pascual Polimeni (3/1). Trainer: no.
**Goals**: Bleo Pedro Fournol „Calomino", Guillermo Dannaher.

**38.** 13.09.1914 **ARGENTINA - URUGUAY** **2-1(1-0)** Premio de Honor Argentino
Estadio Club Gymnasia y Esgrima, Buenos Aires; Referee: Angel Landoni (Uruguay); Attendance: 12,500
**ARG:** Juan José Rithner (6/0), Diómedes Bernasconi (1/0), Carlos Galup Lanús (1/0), Ricardo Naón (1/0), Pedro Rithner (1/0), Santiago Sayanes (4/0), Juan José Lamas (2/0), Delfín Lazcano (1/1), Pedro Gallardo (2/1), Carlos Izaguirre (1/0), Francisco Crespo (1/0). Trainer: no.
**Goals**: Pedro Gallardo, Delfín Lazcano.

**39.** 20.09.1914 **ARGENTINA - BRAZIL** **3-0(1-0)**
Estadio Club Gymnasia y Esgrima, Buenos Aires; Referee: Léon Peyrou (Uruguay); Attendance: 18,000
**ARG:** Carlos Muttoni (2/0), Roberto González Escarrá (1/0), Arturo Reparaz (3/0), Mariano Aldea (1/0), Aquiles Molfino (1/1), Santiago Sayanes (5/0), Juan José Lamas (3/0), Roberto Leonardi (1/0), Antonio Piaggio (4/2), Carlos Izaguirre (2/2), Francisco Crespo (2/0). Trainer: no.
**Goals**: Carlos Izaguirre, Aquiles Molfino, Carlos Izaguirre.

**40.** 27.09.1914 **ARGENTINA - BRAZIL** **0-1(0-1)** Copa Roca
Estadio Club Gymnasia y Esgrima, Buenos Aires; Referee: Alberto Borgerth (Brazil); Attendance: 17,000
**ARG:** Juan José Rithner (7/0), Diómedes Bernasconi (2/0), Carlos Galup Lanús (2/0), Ricardo Naón (2/0), Ernesto Sande (4/0), Santiago Sayanes (6/0), Juan José Lamas (4/0), Roberto Leonardi (2/0), Antonio Piaggio (5/2), Carlos Izaguirre (3/2), Francisco Crespo (3/0). Trainer: no.

**41.** 18.07.1915 **URUGUAY - ARGENTINA** **2-3(0-1)** Premio de Honor Uruguayo
Estadio Parque Central, Montevideo; Referee: Carlos Williams (Argentina); Attendance: 12,000
**ARG:** Carlos Tomás Wilson (24/0), Arturo Chiappe (9/0), Juan Domingo Brown (30/0), Alberto Olivari (6/0), Cándido García (1/0), Gerónimo Badaracco (4/0), Elías Fernández (14/1), Juan Enrique Hayes (14/7), Alberto Andrés Marcovecchio (3/3), Ennis Hayes (1/0), Juan Nelusco Perinetti (1/0). Trainer: no.
**Goals**: Alberto Andrés Marcovecchio, Alberto Andrés Marcovecchio, Juan Enrique Hayes.

**42.** 15.08.1915 **ARGENTINA - URUGUAY** **2-1(0-1)** Copa Lipton

Estadio Club Gymnasia y Esgrima, Buenos Aires; Referee: Héctor Alfano (Argentina); Attendance: 18,000

**ARG:** Juan José Rithner (8/0), Arturo Chiappe (10/0), Juan Domingo Brown (31/0), Alberto Olivari (7/0), Cándido García (2/0), Gerónimo Badaracco (5/0), Rodolfo Fraga Petrao (1/0), Alberto Bernardino Ohaco (3/0), Juan Enrique Hayes (15/8), Alberto Andrés Marcovecchio (4/4), José Viale (19/8). Trainer: no.

**Goals**: Alberto Andrés Marcovecchio, Juan Enrique Hayes.

**43.** 12.09.1915 **URUGUAY - ARGENTINA** **2-0(1-0)** Copa Newton

Estadio Parque Central, Montevideo; Referee: Carlos Williams (Argentina); Attendance: 12,000

**ARG:** Juan José Rithner (9/0), Arturo Chiappe (11/0), Juan Domingo Brown (32/0), Ángel Betular (1/0), Cándido García (3/0), Gerónimo Badaracco (6/0), Juan José Lamas (5/0), Alberto Bernardino Ohaco (4/0), Juan Enrique Hayes (16/8), Juan Hospital (4/0), Pascual Polimeni (4/1). Trainer: no.

**44.** 06.07.1916 **ARGENTINA - CHILE** **6-1(1-1)** 1st Copa América

Estadio Club Gymnasia y Esgrima, Buenos Aires; Referee: Sidney Pullen (Brazil); Attendance: 15,000

**ARG:** Carlos Tomás Wilson (25/0), Armando Reyes (1/0), Juan Domingo Brown (33/2) (Cap), Pedro Martínez (1/0), Francisco Olazar (1/0), Gerónimo Badaracco (7/0), Adolfo Heissinger (1/0), Alberto Bernardino Ohaco (5/2), Alberto Andrés Marcovecchio (5/6), Carlos Guidi (2/0), Juan Nelusco Perinetti (2/0). Trainer: no.

**Goals**: Alberto Bernardino Ohaco (2), Juan Domingo Brown (60 penalty), Juan Domingo Brown (62 penalty), Alberto Andrés Marcovecchio (67), Alberto Bernardino Ohaco (75), Alberto Andrés Marcovecchio (89).

**45.** 10.07.1916 **ARGENTINA - BRAZIL** **1-1(1-1)** 1st Copa América

Estadio Club Gymnasia y Esgrima, Buenos Aires; Referee: Carlos Fanta Tomaszewski (Chile); Attendance: 12,000

**ARG:** Juan José Rithner (10/0), Arturo Chiappe (12/0), Juan Domingo Brown (34/2) (Cap), Pedro Martínez (2/0), Francisco Olazar (2/0), Gerónimo Badaracco (8/0), Adolfo Heissinger (2/0), José Laguna (1/1), Alberto Andrés Marcovecchio (6/6), Carlos Guidi (3/0), Claudio Bincaz (1/0). Trainer: no.

**Goal**: José Laguna (10).

**46.** 12.07.1916 **ARGENTINA - CHILE** **1-0(1-0)**

Estadio Club Gymnasia y Esgrima, Buenos Aires; Referee: Patricio MacCarthy (Argentina); Attendance: 12,000

**ARG:** Marcos Crocce (1/0), Oscar Ivanesevich (1/0), Armando Reyes (2/0), Pedro Martínez (3/0), Francisco Olazar (3/0), Gerónimo Badaracco (9/0), Adolfo Heissinger (3/1), Alberto Bernardino Ohaco (6/2), Alberto Andrés Marcovecchio (7/6), Juan Hospital (5/0), Juan Nelusco Perinetti (3/0). Trainer: no.

**Goal**: Adolfo Heissinger.

**47.** 17.07.1916 **ARGENTINA - URUGUAY** **0-0** 1st Copa América

Estadio Racing Club, Avellaneda, Buenos Aires; Referee: Carlos Fanta Tomaszewski (Chile); Attendance: 17,000

**ARG:** Carlos Isola (1/0), Zenón Díaz (3/0), Armando Reyes (3/0), Pedro Martínez (4/0), Francisco Olazar (4/0), Gerónimo Badaracco (10/0), Adolfo Heissinger (4/1), Alberto Bernardino Ohaco (7/2), Juan Enrique Hayes (17/8), Ennis Hayes (2/0), Juan Nelusco Perinetti (4/0). Trainer: no.

**48.** 15.08.1916 **ARGENTINA - URUGUAY** **3-1(0-1)** Copa Newton

Estadio Racing Club, Avellaneda, Buenos Aires; Referee: Luis Gil (Argentina); Attendance: 16,000

**ARG:** Emilio Fernández (1/0), Zenón Díaz (4/0), Armando Reyes (4/0), Santiago Sayanes (7/0), Ernesto Sande (5/0), Pedro Martínez (5/0), Zoilo Canaveri (1/0), Alberto Bernardino Ohaco (8/4), Marius Hiller (1/1), Carlos Guidi (4/0), Pascual Polimeni (5/1). Trainer: no.

**Goals**: Alberto Bernardino Ohaco, Alberto Bernardino Ohaco, Marius Hiller.

**49.** 15.08.1916 **URUGUAY - ARGENTINA** **1-2(1-1)** Copa Lipton

Estadio Parque Central, Montevideo; Referee: José Di Lucca (Argentina); Attendance: 5,000

**ARG:** Carlos Isola (2/0), Arturo Chiappe (13/0), Juan Domingo Brown (35/2), Ernesto Mattozzi (1/0), Francisco Olazar (5/0), Alberto Felisari (1/0), Antonio Blanco (1/0), José Laiolo (1/1), Juan Enrique Hayes (18/8), Ennis Hayes (3/1), Juan Nelusco Perinetti (5/0). Trainer: no.

**Goals**: Ennis Hayes, José Laiolo.

**50.** 01.10.1916 **URUGUAY - ARGENTINA** **0-1(0-1)** Premio de Honor Uruguayo

Estadio Parque Belvedere, Montevideo; Referee: Angel Minoli (Uruguay); Attendance: 7,000

**ARG:** Carlos Isola (3/0), Zenón Díaz (5/0), Armando Reyes (5/0), Ernesto Mattozzi (2/0), Francisco Olazar (6/0), Alberto Felisari (2/0), Pascual Garré (1/0), Atilio Badalini (1/1), Alberto Andrés Marcovecchio (8/6), Carlos Guidi (5/0), Juan Nelusco Perinetti (6/0). Trainer: no.

**Goal**: Atilio Badalini.

**51.** 01.10.1916 **ARGENTINA - URUGUAY** **7-2(2-0)** Copa Prensa

Estadio Racing Club, Avellaneda, Buenos Aires; Referee: Guillermo Jordán (Argentina); Attendance: 11,000

**ARG:** Emilio Fernández (2/0), Arturo Chiappe (14/0), Juan Domingo Brown (36/2), Heriberto Simmons (2/1), Cándido García (4/0), Pedro Martínez (6/0), Zoilo Canaveri (2/0), Juan Cabano (2/1), Marius Hiller (2/4), Ennis Hayes (4/3), Francisco Taggino (3/0). Trainer: no.

**Goals**: Heriberto Simmons, Marius Hiller 2, Juan Cabano, Ennis Hayes, Marius Hiller, Ennis Hayes.

**52.** 29.10.1916 **URUGUAY - ARGENTINA** **3-1(1-1)** Copa Prensa

Estadio Parque Central, Montevideo; Referee: Ricardo Vallarino (Uruguay); Attendance: 12,000

**ARG:** Carlos Isola (4/0), Zenón Díaz (6/0), Armando Reyes (6/0), Ernesto Mattozzi (3/0), Ernesto Sande (6/0), Alberto Felisari (3/0), Elías Fernández (15/1), Carlos Guidi (6/1), Juan Enrique Hayes (19/8), Ennis Hayes (5/3), Juan Nelusco Perinetti (7/0). Trainer: no.

**Goal**: Carlos Guidi.

**53.** 18.07.1917 **URUGUAY - ARGENTINA** **0-2(0-2)** Premio de Honor Uruguayo

Estadio Parque Central, Montevideo; Referee: Alvaro Saralegui (Uruguay); Attendance: 12,000

**ARG:** Carlos Isola (5/0), Antonio Ferro (1/0), Armando Reyes (7/0), Ernesto Mattozzi (4/0), Francisco Olazar (7/0), José Ventureira (1/0), Nicolás Vivaldo (1/0), Alberto Andrés Marcovecchio (9/8), Carlos Guidi (7/1), Miguel Ginevra (1/0), Juan Nelusco Perinetti (8/0). Trainer: no.

**Goals**: Alberto Andrés Marcovecchio 2.

**54.** 15.08.1917 **ARGENTINA - URUGUAY** **1-0(1-0)** Copa Lipton

Estadio Racing Club, Avellaneda, Buenos Aires; Referee: Germán Guassone (Argentina); Attendance: 11,000

**ARG:** Carlos Isola (6/0), Antonio Ferro (2/0), Armando Reyes (8/0), Ernesto Mattozzi (5/0), Francisco Olazar (8/0), José Ventureira (2/0), Bleo Pedro Fournol „Calomino" (3/2), Nicolás Vivaldo (2/0), Roberto Leonardi (3/0), Nicolás Rofrano (1/0), Juan Nelusco Perinetti (9/0). Trainer: no.

**Goal**: Bleo Pedro Fournol „Calomino".

**55.** 02.09.1917 **URUGUAY - ARGENTINA** **1-0(0-0)** Copa Newton
Estadio Parque Central, Montevideo; Referee: Ricardo Vallarino (Uruguay); Attendance: 15,000
**ARG:** Carlos Isola (7/0), Antonio Ferro (3/0), Armando Reyes (9/0), Ernesto Mattozzi (6/0), Francisco Olazar (9/0), Pedro Martínez (7/0), Bleo Pedro Fournol „Calomino" (4/2), Nicolás Vivaldo (3/0), Alberto Andrés Marcovecchio (10/8), Nicolás Rofrano (2/0), Francisco Taggino (4/0). Trainer: no.

**56.** 03.10.1917 **ARGENTINA - BRAZIL** **4-2(1-2)** 2nd Copa América
Estadio Parque Central, Montevideo (Uruguay); Referee: Carlos Fanta Tomaszewski (Chile); Attendance: 20,000
**ARG:** Carlos Isola (8/0), Antonio Ferro (4/0), Armando Reyes (10/0), Ernesto Mattozzi (7/0), Francisco Olazar (10/0), Ricardo Pepe (2/0), Bleo Pedro Fournol „Calomino" (5/3), Antonio Blanco (2/1), Alberto Bernardino Ohaco (9/6), Alfredo Martín (1/0), Juan Nelusco Perinetti (10/0). Trainer: no.
**Goals**: Bleo Pedro Fournol „Calomino" (15), Alberto Bernardino Ohaco (56, 58), Antonio Blanco (80).

**57.** 06.10.1917 **ARGENTINA - CHILE** **1-0(0-0)** 2nd Copa América
Estadio Parque Central, Montevideo (Uruguay); Referee: Alvaro Saralegui (Uruguay); Attendance: 12,000
**ARG:** Carlos Isola (9/0), Antonio Ferro (5/0), Armando Reyes (11/0), Ernesto Mattozzi (8/0), Francisco Olazar (11/0), Pedro Martínez (8/0), Antonio Blanco (3/1), Nicolás Vivaldo (4/0), Alberto Bernardino Ohaco (10/6), Alfredo Martín (2/0), Juan Nelusco Perinetti (11/0). Trainer: no.
**Goal**: Luis García (76 own goal).

**58.** 14.10.1917 **URUGUAY - ARGENTINA** **1-0(0-0)** 2nd Copa América
Estadio Parque Central, Montevideo; Referee: Juan Livingstone (Chile); Attendance: 40,000
**ARG:** Carlos Isola (10/0), Antonio Ferro (6/0), Armando Reyes (12/0), Ernesto Mattozzi (9/0), Francisco Olazar (12/0), Pedro Martínez (9/0), Bleo Pedro Fournol „Calomino" (6/3), Alberto Bernardino Ohaco (11/6), Alfredo Martín (3/0), Ennis Hayes (6/3), Juan Nelusco Perinetti (12/0). Trainer: no.

**59.** 21.10.1917 **ARGENTINA - CHILE** **1-1(0-1)**
Estadio Racing Club, Avellaneda, Buenos Aires; Referee: Germán Guassone (Argentina); Attendance: 10,000
**ARG:** Carlos Isola (11/0), A. Elordi (1/0), Armando Reyes (13/0), Ernesto Mattozzi (10/0), Francisco Olazar (13/0), M. Madero (1/0), Bleo Pedro Fournol „Calomino" (7/3), Antonio Blanco (4/1), Alberto Bernardino Ohaco (12/7), Alfredo Martín (4/0), Juan Nelusco Perinetti (13/0). Trainer: no.
**Goal**: Alberto Bernardino Ohaco.

**60.** 18.07.1918 **URUGUAY - ARGENTINA** **1-1(1-1,1-1)** Premio de Honor Uruguayo
Estadio Parque Central, Montevideo; Referee: Alvaro Saralegui (Uruguay); Attendance: 30,000
**ARG:** Carlos Isola (12/0), Antonio Ferro (7/0), Armando Reyes (14/0), Antonio Roque Cortella (1/0), Francisco Olazar (14/0), José Alfredo López (1/0), Bleo Pedro Fournol „Calomino" (8/3), José Laiolo (2/2), Juan Enrique Hayes (20/8), Nicolás Rofrano (3/0), Jaime Chavín (1/0). Trainer: no.
**Goal**: José Laiolo.
**After 39 mins extra-time, the match was stopped due to nightfall*

**61.** 28.07.1918 **URUGUAY - ARGENTINA** **3-1(2-1)** Premio de Honor Uruguayo
Estadio Parque Central, Montevideo; Referee: Angel Minoli (Uruguay); Attendance: 20,000
**ARG:** Carlos Isola (13/0), Antonio Ferro (8/0), Antonio Schiaretta (1/0), Ernesto Mattozzi (11/0), Cándido García (5/1), José Alfredo López (2/0), Bleo Pedro Fournol „Calomino" (9/3), José Laiolo (3/2), Alberto Bernardino Ohaco (13/7), Nicolás Rofrano (4/0), Alfredo Martín (5/0). Trainer: no.
**Goals**: Cándido García.

**62.** 15.08.1918 **ARGENTINA - URUGUAY** **0-0** Premio de Honor Argentino
Estadio Club Gymnasia y Esgrima, Buenos Aires; Referee: Calixto Gardi (Argentina); Attendance: 18,000
**ARG:** Carlos Isola (14/0), Roberto Castagnola (1/0), Armando Reyes (15/0), Ernesto Mattozzi (12/0), Eduardo Blanco (1/0), Gerónimo Badaracco (11/0), Bleo Pedro Fournol „Calomino" (10/3), Alfredo Martín (6/0), Edwin Clarcke (1/0), Ennis Hayes (7/3), Juan Francia (1/0). Trainer: no.

**63.** 25.08.1918 **ARGENTINA - URUGUAY** **2-1(2-1)** Premio de Honor Argentino
Estadio Club Gymnasia y Esgrima, Buenos Aires; Referee: Calixto Gardi (Argentina); Attendance: 12,000
**ARG:** Carlos Isola (15/0), Antonio Roque Cortella (2/0), Armando Reyes (16/0), Ernesto Mattozzi (13/0), Mario Busso (1/0), José Alfredo López (3/0), Bleo Pedro Fournol „Calomino" (11/3), Antonio Blanco (5/1), Alfredo Martín (7/2), Ennis Hayes (8/3), Juan Nelusco Perinetti (14/0). Trainer: no.
**Goals**: Alfredo Martín 2.

**64.** 20.09.1918 **URUGUAY - ARGENTINA** **1-1(0-0)** Copa Lipton
Estadio Parque Central, Montevideo; Referee: Emilio Scoteguazza (Uruguay); Attendance: 15,000
**ARG:** Carlos Isola (16/0), Roberto Castagnola (2/0), Armando Reyes (17/0), Ernesto Mattozzi (14/0), Eduardo Blanco (2/0), Gerónimo Badaracco (12/0), Bleo Pedro Fournol „Calomino" (12/3), Antonio Blanco (6/1), Alfredo Martín (8/2), Ennis Hayes (9/3), Jorge Calandra (1/1). Trainer: no.
**Goal**: Jorge Calandra.

**65.** 29.09.1918 **ARGENTINA - URUGUAY** **2-0(2-0)** Copa Newton
Estadio Club Gymnasia y Esgrima, Buenos Aires; Referee: Germán Guassone (Argentina); Attendance: 9,000
**ARG:** Carlos Isola (17/0), Roberto Castagnola (3/0), Armando Reyes (18/0), Ernesto Mattozzi (15/0), Francisco Olazar (15/0), Gerónimo Badaracco (13/0), Bleo Pedro Fournol „Calomino" (13/3), Antonio Blanco (7/2), Nicolás Vivaldo (5/1), Ennis Hayes (10/3), Jorge Calandra (2/1). Trainer: no.
**Goals**: Nicolás Vivaldo, Antonio Blanco.

**66.** 11.05.1919 **PARAGUAY - ARGENTINA** **1-5(1-1)**
Estadio Puerto Sajonia, Asunción; Referee: Germán Guassone (Argentina); Attendance: 8,000
**ARG:** Américo Miguel Tesorieri (1/0), Roberto Sancet (1/0), Humberto Juan Recanatini (1/0), José Alfredo López (4/0), Mario Busso (2/0), Luis Célico (1/0), Alberto Bianatti (1/0), José Laguna (2/3), Juan Carlos Adet (1/0), Alberto Ochandío (1/2), Pascual Polimeni (6/2). Trainer: no.
**Goals**: Pascual Polimeni, José Laguna 2, Alberto Ochandío 2.

**67.** 13.05.1919 **URUGUAY - ARGENTINA** **3-2(2-1)** 3rd Copa América
Estádio das Laranjeiras, Rio de Janeiro (Brazil); Referee: Robert L. Todd (England); Attendance: 18,000
**ARG:** Carlos Isola (Cap) (18/0), Antonio Roque Cortella (3/0), Armando Reyes (19/0), Ernesto Mattozzi (16/0), Eduardo Uslenghi (1/0), Pedro Martínez (10/0), Bleo Pedro Fournol „Calomino" (14/3), José Laiolo (4/2), Edwin Clarcke (2/0), Carlos Izaguirre (4/3), Juan Nelusco Perinetti (15/0). Trainer: no.
**Goals**: Carlos Izaguirre (34), Manuel Varela (79 own goal).

**68.** 15.05.1919 **PARAGUAY - ARGENTINA** **0-3(0-2)***
Estadio Puerto Sajonia, Asunción; Referee: Germán Guassone (Argentina); Attendance: 3,000
**ARG:** Américo Miguel Tesorieri (2/0), Carlos Alberto Gallo (1/0), Humberto Juan Recanatini (2/0), José Alfredo López (5/0), Mario Busso (3/0), Luis Célico (2/0), Ernesto Vieyro (1/0), Delfín Lazcano (2/2), Juan Carlos Adet (2/1), Alberto Ochandío (2/3), Pascual Polimeni (7/2). Trainer: no.
**Goals**: Delfín Lazcano, Juan Carlos Adet, Alberto Ochandío.
**Abandoned after 52 mins.*

**69.** 18.05.1919 **BRAZIL - ARGENTINA** **3-1(1-0)** 3rd Copa América
Estádio das Laranjeiras, Rio de Janeiro; Referee: Robert L. Todd (England); Attendance: 22,000
**ARG:** Carlos Isola (Cap) (19/0), Roberto Castagnola (4/0), Armando Reyes (20/0), Ernesto Mattozzi (17/0), Eduardo Uslenghi (2/0), Pedro Martínez (11/0), Bleo Pedro Fournol „Calomino“ (15/3), Carlos Izaguirre (5/4), Edwin Clarcke (3/0), Enrique Brichetto (1/0), Juan Nelusco Perinetti (16/0). Trainer: no.
**Goal**: Carlos Izaguirre (65).

**70.** 21.05.1919 **PARAGUAY - ARGENTINA** **1-2(0-0)**
Estadio Puerto Sajonia, Asunción; Referee: Francisco Andreu Balcó (Paraguay); Attendance: 5,000
**ARG:** Américo Miguel Tesorieri (3/0), Carlos Alberto Gallo (2/0), Humberto Juan Recanatini (3/0), José Alfredo López (6/0), Mario Busso (4/0), Luis Célico (3/0), Alberto Bianatti (2/0), José Laguna (3/3), Juan Carlos Adet (3/2), Alberto Ochandío (3/4), Pascual Polimeni (8/2). Trainer: no.
**Goals**: Juan Carlos Adet, Alberto Ochandío.

**71.** 22.05.1919 **ARGENTINA - CHILE** **4-1(3-1)** 3rd Copa América
Estádio das Laranjeiras, Rio de Janeiro (Brazil); Referee: Joaquim Antônio Leite de Castro (Brazil); Attendance: 15,000
**ARG:** Carlos Isola (Cap) (20/0), Roberto Castagnola (5/0), Armando Reyes (21/0), Ernesto Mattozzi (18/0), Roberto Felices (1/0), Pedro Martínez (12/0), Bleo Pedro Fournol „Calomino“ (16/3), Alfredo Martín (9/2), Edwin Clarcke (4/3), Carlos Izaguirre (6/5), Juan Nelusco Perinetti (17/0). Trainer: no.
**Goals**: Edwin Clarcke (10), Carlos Izaguirre (13), Edwin Clarcke (23, 62).

**72.** 24.05.1919 **PARAGUAY - ARGENTINA** **1-2(1-0)**
Estadio Puerto Sajonia, Asunción; Referee: Plutarco Recalde (Paraguay); Attendance: 8,000
**ARG:** Américo Miguel Tesorieri (4/0), Carlos Alberto Gallo (3/0), Ernesto Vieyro (2/0), José Alfredo López (7/0), Mario Busso (5/0), Luis Célico (4/0), Alberto Bianatti (3/1), José Laguna (4/3), Juan Carlos Adet (4/2), Alberto Ochandío (4/5), Pascual Polimeni (9/2). Trainer: no.
**Goals**: Alberto Bianatti, Alberto Ochandío.

**73.** 01.06.1919 **BRAZIL - ARGENTINA** **3-3(3-2)** Taça Roberto Cherry
Estádio das Laranjeiras, Rio de Janeiro; Referee: Angelo Minoli (Uruguay); Attendance: 17,000
**ARG:** Carlos Isola (21/0), Roberto Castagnola (6/0), Armando Reyes (22/0), Ernesto Mattozzi (19/1), Eduardo Uslenghi (3/0), Pedro Martínez (13/0), Bleo Pedro Fournol „Calomino“ (17/3), José Laiolo (5/3), Edwin Clarcke (5/4), Nicolás Rofrano (5/0), Francisco Taggino (5/0). Trainer: no.
**Goals**: Edwin Clarcke, Ernesto Mattozzi, José Laiolo.

**74.** 18.07.1919 **URUGUAY - ARGENTINA** **4-1(4-0)** Premio de Honor Uruguayo
Estadio Parque Central, Montevideo; Referee: Martín Aphesteguy (Uruguay); Attendance: 15,000
**ARG:** Guillermo Magistretti (1/0), Juan Madero (1/0), Agustín Alberti (1/0), Luis Cilley (1/0), Eduardo Uslenghi (4/0), Pedro Martínez (14/0), Adolfo Heissinger (5/1), Carlos Izaguirre (7/5), Juan Enrique Hayes (21/8), Ennis Hayes (11/4), Juan Francia (2/0). Trainer: no.
**Goal**: Ennis Hayes.

**75.** 24.08.1919 **URUGUAY - ARGENTINA** **2-1(2-0)** Copa Newton
Estadio Parque Central, Montevideo; Referee: Angel Minoli (Uruguay); Attendance: 30,000
**ARG:** Marcos Crocce (2/0), Roberto Castagnola (7/0), Humberto Juan Recanatini (4/0), Ernesto Mattozzi (20/1), Francisco Olazar (16/1), Jacobo Urso (1/0), Bleo Pedro Fournol „Calomino“ (18/3), Albérico Zabaleta (1/0), Alberto Andrés Marcovecchio (11/8), Nicolás Vivaldo (6/1), Inocencio Alzúa (1/0). Trainer: no.
**Goals**: Francisco Olazar.

**76.** 07.09.1919 **ARGENTINA - URUGUAY** **1-2(0-2)*** Copa Lipton
Estadio Club Gymnasia y Esgrima, Buenos Aires; Referee: Ricardo Palma (Argentina); Attendance: 17,000
**ARG:** Emilio Araya (1/0), Roberto Castagnola (8/0), Humberto Juan Recanatini (5/0), Ernesto Mattozzi (21/1), Francisco Olazar (17/1), Enrique Macchiavello (1/0), Bleo Pedro Fournol „Calomino“ (19/3), Atilio Badalini (2/2), Alberto Andrés Marcovecchio (12/8), Alberto Ochandío (5/5), Juan Nelusco Perinetti (18/0). Trainer: no.
**Goal**: Atilio Badalini.
**Abandoned after 86 mins.*

**77.** 19.10.1919 **ARGENTINA - URUGUAY** **6-1(1-0)** Premio de Honor Argentino
Estadio Club Gymnasia y Esgrima, Buenos Aires; Referee: Juan José Rithner (Argentina); Attendance: 18,000
**ARG:** Emilio Araya (2/0), Carlos Alberto Gallo (4/0), Humberto Juan Recanatini (6/0), Antonio Roque Cortella (4/0), Ernesto Celli (1/1), Eduardo Uslenghi (5/0), Bleo Pedro Fournol „Calomino“ (20/3), Julio Libonatti (1/3), Atilio Badalini (3/2), Nicolás Vivaldo (7/2), Jaime Chavín (2/1). Trainer: no.
**Goals**: Julio Libonatti, Ernesto Celli, Nicolás Vivaldo, Jaime Chavín, Julio Libonatti 2.

**78.** 07.12.1919 **URUGUAY - ARGENTINA** **4-2(1-0)** Copa Prensa
Estadio Parque Central, Montevideo; Referee: Ricardo Vallarino (Uruguay); Attendance: 12,000
**ARG:** Emilio Araya (3/0), Carlos Alberto Gallo (5/0), Adolfo Celli (1/0), Eduardo Uslenghi (6/0), Ernesto Celli (2/1), Pedro Martínez (15/0), Bleo Pedro Fournol „Calomino“ (21/3), Julio Libonatti (2/4), Atilio Badalini (4/3), Alfredo Martín (10/2), Jaime Chavín (3/1). Trainer: no.
**Goals**: Julio Libonatti, Atilio Badalini.

**79.** 18.07.1920 **URUGUAY - ARGENTINA** **2-0(1-0)** Premio de Honor Uruguayo
Estadio Parque Central, Montevideo; Referee: Martín Aphesteguy (Uruguay); Attendance: 25,000
**ARG:** Octavio Juan Díaz (1/0), Juan Salvador Presta (1/0), Adolfo Celli (2/0), Francisco Ballart (1/0), Antonio Sacarella (1/0), Ernesto Scoffano (1/0), Bleo Pedro Fournol „Calomino“ (22/3), Julio Libonatti (3/4), José Fausto Lucarelli (1/0), Raúl Echeverría (1/0), Jorge Calandra (3/1). Trainer: no.

**80.** 25.07.1920 **ARGENTINA - URUGUAY** **1-3(0-2)** Copa Newton
Estadio Sportivo Barracas, Buenos Aires; Referee: Calixto Gardi (Argentina); Attendance: 18,000
**ARG:** Octavio Juan Díaz (2/0), Antonio Roque Cortella (5/0), Adolfo Celli (3/0), Alberto Latorre Lelong (1/0), Juan Salvador Presta (2/0), Norberto Carabelli (1/0), Bleo Pedro Fournol „Calomino“ (23/3), Julio Libonatti (4/4), Edwin Clarcke (6/5), José Fausto Lucarelli (2/0), Antonio De Miguel (1/0). Trainer: no.

**Goal**: Edwin Clarcke.

**81.** 08.08.1920 **ARGENTINA - URUGUAY** **1-0(0-0)** Premio de Honor Argentino
Estadio Sportivo Barracas, Buenos Aires; Referee: Fernando Díez (Argentina); Attendance: 15,000
**ARG:** Ernesto Kiessel (1/0), Antonio Roque Cortella (6/0), Florindo Bearzotti (1/0), Ángel Frumento (1/0), Miguel Dellavalle (1/0), Eduardo Uslenghi (7/0), Bleo Pedro Fournol „Calomino" (24/4), Julio Libonatti (5/4), Atilio Badalini (5/3), José Fausto Lucarelli (3/0), Antonio De Miguel (2/0). Trainer: no.
**Goal**: Bleo Pedro Fournol „Calomino" (penalty).

**82.** 12.09.1920 **URUGUAY - ARGENTINA** **1-1(1-0)** 4th Copa América
Estadio Sporting Club, Valparaíso (Chile); Referee: Francisco Jiménez (Chile); Attendance: 17,000
**ARG:** Américo Miguel Tesorieri (5/0), Antonio Roque Cortella (7/0), Florindo Bearzotti (2/0), Ángel Frumento (2/0), Miguel Dellavalle (2/0), Eduardo Uslenghi (8/0), Bleo Pedro Fournol „Calomino" (25/4) (Cap), Julio Libonatti (6/4), Atilio Badalini (6/3), Raúl Echeverría (2/1), Antonio De Miguel (3/0). Trainer: no.
**Goal**: Raúl Echeverría (75).

**83.** 20.09.1920 **CHILE - ARGENTINA** **1-1(1-1)** 4th Copa América
Estadio Sporting Club, Valparaíso; Referee: João De María (Brazil); Attendance: 16,000
**ARG:** Américo Miguel Tesorieri (6/0), Antonio Roque Cortella (8/0), Florindo Bearzotti (3/0), Ángel Frumento (3/0), Miguel Dellavalle (3/1), Eduardo Uslenghi (9/0), Bleo Pedro Fournol „Calomino" (26/4) (Cap), Julio Libonatti (7/4), Atilio Badalini (7/3), José Fausto Lucarelli (4/0), Antonio De Miguel (4/0). Trainer: no.
**Goal**: Miguel Dellavalle (13).

**84.** 25.09.1920 **ARGENTINA - BRAZIL** **2-0(1-0)** 4th Copa América
Estadio Sporting Club, Valparaíso (Chile); Referee: Martín Aphesteguy (Uruguay); Attendance: 12,000
**ARG:** Américo Miguel Tesorieri (7/0), Antonio Roque Cortella (9/0), Florindo Bearzotti (4/0), Ángel Frumento (4/0), Juan Salvador Presta (3/0), Roberto Bruzzone (1/0), Bleo Pedro Fournol „Calomino" (27/4) (Cap), Julio Libonatti (8/5), Atilio Badalini (8/3), Raúl Echeverría (3/2), Antonio De Miguel (5/0). Trainer: no.
**Goals**: Raúl Echeverría (40), Julio Libonatti (73).

**85.** 07.04.1921 **PARAGUAY - ARGENTINA** **3-1(1-1)**
Estadio Parque Caballero, Asunción; Referee: Miguel Barba (Paraguay); Attendance: 6,000
**ARG:** Guillermo Magistretti (2/0), Antonio Roque Cortella (10/0), Pablo Bertolini (1/0), Odilón Lizárraga (1/0), Roberto Bruzzone (2/0), Eduardo Uslenghi (10/0), Bleo Pedro Fournol „Calomino" (28/4), Alfredo Tassín (1/0), Edwin Clarcke (7/5), Pedro Corbella (1/1), Pascual Polimeni (10/2). Trainer: no.
**Goal**: Pedro Corbella.

**86.** 14.04.1921 **PARAGUAY - ARGENTINA** **2-2(2-1)**
Estadio Parque Caballero, Asunción; Referee: Víctor Cabañas Saguier (Paraguay); Attendance: 8,000
**ARG:** Guillermo Magistretti (3/0), Antonio Roque Cortella (11/0), Pablo Bertolini (2/0), Ludovico Bidoglio (1/0), Roberto Bruzzone (3/0), Eduardo Uslenghi (11/0), Bleo Pedro Fournol „Calomino" (29/5), Pablo Bosso (1/0), Edwin Clarcke (8/6), Pedro Corbella (2/1), Pascual Polimeni (11/2). Trainer: no.
**Goals**: Edwin Clarcke, Bleo Pedro Fournol „Calomino" (penalty).

**87.** 02.10.1921 **ARGENTINA - BRAZIL** **1-0(1-0)** 5th Copa América
Estadio Sportivo Barracas, Buenos Aires; Referee: Ricardo Vallarino (Uruguay); Attendance: 20,000
**ARG:** Américo Miguel Tesorieri (8/0), Adolfo Celli (4/0), Florindo Bearzotti (5/0), José Alfredo López (8/0), Miguel Dellavalle (4/1), Emilio Solari (1/0), Bleo Pedro Fournol „Calomino" (Cap) (30/5), Julio Libonatti (9/6), Gabino Sosa (1/0), Raúl Echeverría (4/2), Jaime Chavín (4/1). Trainer: no.
**Goal**: Julio Libonatti (27).

**88.** 16.10.1921 **ARGENTINA - PARAGUAY** **3-0(1-0)** 5th Copa América
Estadio Sportivo Barracas, Buenos Aires; Referee: Ricardo Vallarino (Uruguay); Attendance: 25,000
**ARG:** Américo Miguel Tesorieri (9/0), Adolfo Celli (5/0), Florindo Bearzotti (6/0), Juan Salvador Presta (4/0), Miguel Dellavalle (5/1), Emilio Solari (2/0), Bleo Pedro Fournol „Calomino" (Cap) (31/5), Julio Libonatti (10/7), Blas Saruppo (1/1), Raúl Echeverría (5/3), Vicente González (1/0). Trainer: no.
**Goals**: Julio Libonatti (43), Blas Saruppo (71), Raúl Echeverría (76).

**89.** 30.10.1921 **ARGENTINA - URUGUAY** **1-0(0-0)** 5th Copa América
Estadio Sportivo Barracas, Buenos Aires; Referee: Carlos Pedro Santos (Brazil); Attendance: 35,000
**ARG:** Américo Miguel Tesorieri (10/0), Adolfo Celli (6/0), Florindo Bearzotti (7/0), José Alfredo López (9/0), Miguel Dellavalle (6/1), Emilio Solari (3/0), Bleo Pedro Fournol „Calomino" (Cap) (32/5), Julio Libonatti (11/8), Blas Saruppo (2/1), Raúl Echeverría (6/3), Vicente González (2/0). Trainer: no.
**Goal**: Julio Libonatti (57).

**90.** 28.09.1922 **CHILE - ARGENTINA** **0-4(0-3)** 6th Copa América
Estádio das Laranjeiras, Rio de Janeiro (Brazil); Referee: Ricardo Vallarino (Uruguay); Attendance: 2,500
**ARG:** Américo Miguel Tesorieri (Cap) (11/0), Adolfo Celli (7/0), Pedro Castoldi (1/0), Alfredo Luis Chabrolín (1/0), Miguel Dellavalle (7/1), Emilio Solari (4/0), Julio Libonatti (12/8), Ángel Domingo Chiessa (1/1), José Bruno Gaslini (1/1), Ernesto Celli (3/1), Juan Francia (3/2). Trainer: no.
**Goals**: Ángel Domingo Chiessa (10), Juan Francia (36, 41), José Bruno Gaslini (75).

**91.** 08.10.1922 **URUGUAY - ARGENTINA** **1-0(1-0)** 6th Copa América
Estádio das Laranjeiras, Rio de Janeiro (Brazil); Referee: Carlos Pedro Santos (Brazil); Attendance: 14,000
**ARG:** Américo Miguel Tesorieri (Cap) (12/0), Adolfo Celli (8/0), Pedro Castoldi (2/0), Alfredo Luis Chabrolín (2/0), Miguel Dellavalle (8/1), Emilio Solari (5/0), Julio Libonatti (13/8), Ernesto Celli (4/1), José Bruno Gaslini (2/1), Nicolás Rofrano (6/0), Juan Francia (4/2). Trainer: no.

**92.** 15.10.1922 **BRAZIL - ARGENTINA** **2-0(1-0)** 6th Copa América
Estádio das Laranjeiras, Rio de Janeiro; Referee: Francisco Andreu Balcó (Paraguay); Attendance: 25,000
**ARG:** Américo Miguel Tesorieri (Cap) (13/0), Adolfo Celli (9/0), Florencio Sarasíbar (1/0), Alfredo Luis Chabrolín (3/0), Ángel Segundo Médici (1/0), Emilio Solari (6/0), Julio Libonatti (14/8), Ángel Domingo Chiessa (2/1), José Bruno Gaslini (3/1), Julio Rivet (1/0), Juan Francia (5/2). Trainer: no.

**93.** 18.10.1922 **ARGENTINA - PARAGUAY** **2-0(0-0)***
Estádio das Laranjeiras, Rio de Janeiro; Referee: Henrique Vignal (Brazil); Attendance: 8,000
**ARG:** Américo Miguel Tesorieri (Cap) (14/0), Adolfo Celli (10/0), Pedro Castoldi (3/0), Alfredo Luis Chabrolín (4/0), Ángel Segundo Médici (2/0), Emilio Solari (7/0), Julio Rivet (2/0), Ángel Domingo Chiessa (3/1), José Bruno Gaslini (4/1), Marcelo De Césari (1/0), Juan Francia (6/4). Trainer: no.
**Goals**: Juan Francia (63, 79 penalty).
**Abandoned after 79 mins.*

**94.** 22.10.1922 **BRAZIL - ARGENTINA** **2-1(0-1)** Copa Roca
Estádio Parque Antártica, São Paulo; Referee: Antônio Carneiro de Campos (Brazil); Attendance: 12,000
**ARG:** Américo Miguel Tesorieri (15/0), Adolfo Celli (11/0), Pedro Castoldi (4/0), Alfredo Luis Chabrolín (5/0), Ángel Segundo Médici (3/0), Emilio Solari (8/0), Julio Rivet (3/0), Ángel Domingo Chiessa (4/1), José Bruno Gaslini (5/1), Marcelo De Césari (2/0), Juan Francia (7/5). Trainer: no.
**Goal**: Juan Francia.

**95.** 22.10.1922 **ARGENTINA - CHILE** **1-0(1-0)**
Estadio Sportivo Barracas, Buenos Aires; Referee: Ricardo Vallarino (Uruguay); Attendance: 6,000
**ARG:** Guillermo Magistretti (4/0), Ludovico Bidoglio (2/0), Juan Carlos Iribarren (1/0), Juan Evaristo (1/0), Santiago Power (1/0), José Salerno (1/0), Bleo Pedro Fournol „Calomino“ (33/5), Carlos Izaguirre (8/5), José Caldera (1/0), Raúl Echeverría (7/4), Cesáreo Juan Onzari (1/0). Trainer: no.
**Goal**: Raúl Echeverría.

**96.** 12.11.1922 **URUGUAY - ARGENTINA** **1-0(1-0)** Copa Lipton
Estadio Parque Central, Montevideo; Referee: Ricardo Vallarino (Uruguay); Attendance: 12,000
**ARG:** Américo Miguel Tesorieri (16/0), Pedro Castoldi (5/0), Juan Carlos Iribarren (2/0), Ángel Segundo Médici (4/0), Santiago Power (2/0), Emilio Solari (9/0), Bleo Pedro Fournol „Calomino“ (34/5), Carlos Izaguirre (9/5), Edwin Clarcke (9/6), Raúl Echeverría (8/4), Julio Rivet (4/0). Trainer: no.

**97.** 10.12.1922 **URUGUAY - ARGENTINA** **1-0(1-0)** Premio de Honor Uruguayo
Estadio Parque Central, Montevideo; Referee: Aurelio San Martín (Uruguay); Attendance: 8,000
**ARG:** Américo Miguel Tesorieri (17/0), Nicolás Vivaldo (8/2), Florindo Bearzotti (8/0), Ángel Segundo Médici (5/0), Santiago Power (3/0), Emilio Solari (10/0), Domingo Alberto Tarasconi (1/0), Sergio Varela (1/0), Gabino Sosa (2/0), Alejandro De los Santos (1/0), Julio Rivet (5/0). Trainer: no.

**98.** 17.12.1922 **ARGENTINA - URUGUAY** **2-2(2-1)** Copa Newton
Estadio Sportivo Barracas, Buenos Aires; Referee: Gerónimo Rapossi (Argentina); Attendance: 16,000
**ARG:** Américo Miguel Tesorieri (18/0), Adolfo Celli (12/0), Florindo Bearzotti (9/0), Ángel Segundo Médici (6/0), Victorio Faggiani (1/0), Emilio Solari (11/0), Bleo Pedro Fournol „Calomino“ (35/5), Julio Libonatti (15/8), Atilio Badalini (9/5), Gabino Sosa (3/0), Juan Francia (8/5). Trainer: no.
**Goals**: Atilio Badalini 2.

**99.** 20.05.1923 **ARGENTINA - PARAGUAY** **0-2(0-1)** Copa Chevallier Boutell
Estadio Sportivo Barracas, Buenos Aires; Referee: Servando Pérez (Argentina); Attendance: 25,000
**ARG:** Guillermo Magistretti (5/0), Juan Salvador Presta (5/0), Ramón Alfredo Muttis (1/0), Pedro Capalbo (1/0), Juan Vigliola (1/0), Aníbal Argañaraz (1/0), Adán Loizo (1/0), Ángel Domingo Chiessa (5/1), Blas Saruppo (3/1), Carlos Izaguirre (10/5), Benjamín Delgado (1/0). Trainer: no.

**100.** 25.05.1923 **ARGENTINA - PARAGUAY** **1-0(0-0)** Copa Chevallier Boutell
Estadio Sportivo Barracas, Buenos Aires; Referee: Manuel Lozano (Argentina); Attendance: 25,000
**ARG:** Américo Miguel Tesorieri (19/0), Carlos Nóbile (1/0), Ramón Alfredo Muttis (2/0), Roberto Seregni (1/0), Juan Vigliola (2/0), Juan Salvador Presta (6/0), Adán Loizo (2/0), Ángel Domingo Chiessa (6/1), Emilio Francisco Goin (1/0), Carlos Izaguirre (11/6), Benjamín Delgado (2/0). Trainer: no.
**Goal**: Carlos Izaguirre.

**101.** 24.06.1923 **ARGENTINA - URUGUAY** **0-0** Copa Lipton
Estadio Sportivo Barracas, Buenos Aires; Referee: Gerónimo Rapossi (Argentina); Attendance: 30,000
**ARG:** Américo Miguel Tesorieri (20/0), Ludovico Bidoglio (3/0), Ramón Alfredo Muttis (3/0), Juan Evaristo (2/0), Roberto Seregni (2/0), Emilio Solari (12/0), Bleo Pedro Fournol „Calomino“ (36/5), Blas Saruppo (4/1), Ángel Domingo Chiessa (7/1), Carlos Izaguirre (12/6), Cesáreo Juan Onzari (2/0). Trainer: no.

**102.** 15.07.1923 **ARGENTINA - URUGUAY** **2-2(1-0)** Premio de Honor Argentino
Estadio Sportivo Barracas, Buenos Aires; Referee: Héctor Alfano (Argentina); Attendance: 25,000
**ARG:** Américo Miguel Tesorieri (21/0), Ludovico Bidoglio (4/0), Juan Carlos Iribarren (3/0), Juan Evaristo (3/0), Roberto Seregni (3/0), Emilio Solari (13/0), Adán Loizo (3/0), Carlos Izaguirre (13/7), Blas Saruppo (5/1), Ángel Domingo Chiessa (8/1), Cesáreo Juan Onzari (3/1). Trainer: no.
**Goals**: Carlos Izaguirre, Cesáreo Juan Onzari.

**103.** 22.07.1923 **URUGUAY - ARGENTINA** **2-2(2-0)** Premio de Honor Uruguayo
Estadio Parque Central, Montevideo; Referee: Ricardo Vallarino (Uruguay); Attendance: 10,000
**ARG:** Américo Miguel Tesorieri (22/0), Ludovico Bidoglio (5/0), Juan Carlos Iribarren (4/0), Juan Evaristo (4/0), Roberto Seregni (4/0), Emilio Solari (14/0), Domingo Alberto Tarasconi (2/1), Carlos Izaguirre (14/7), Juan Carlos Irurieta (1/1), Alejandro De los Santos (2/0), Benjamín Delgado (3/0). Trainer: no.
**Goals**: Domingo Alberto Tarasconi, Juan Carlos Irurieta.

**104.** 30.09.1923 **URUGUAY - ARGENTINA** **0-2(0-2)** Premio de Honor Uruguayo
Estadio Parque Central, Montevideo; Referee: José Rami (Uruguay); Attendance: 7,000
**ARG:** Américo Miguel Tesorieri (23/0), Ludovico Bidoglio (6/0), Juan Carlos Iribarren (5/0), Ángel Segundo Médici (7/0), Luis Vaccaro (1/0), Emilio Solari (15/0), Adán Loizo (4/0), Blas Saruppo (6/2), Adolfo López (1/1), Antonio Rosado (1/0), Cesáreo Juan Onzari (4/1). Trainer: no.
**Goals**: Blas Saruppo, Adolfo López.

**105.** 28.10.1923 **ARGENTINA - PARAGUAY** **4-3(1-1)** 7th Copa América
Estadio Parque Central, Montevideo (Uruguay); Referee: Angel Minoli (Uruguay); Attendance: 20,000
**ARG:** Américo Miguel Tesorieri (Cap) (24/0), Ludovico Bidoglio (7/0), Juan Carlos Iribarren (6/0), Ángel Segundo Médici (8/0), Luis Vaccaro (2/0), Emilio Solari (16/0), Adán Loizo (5/0), Blas Saruppo (7/3), Vicente Aguirre (1/3), Antonio De Miguel (6/0), Cesáreo Juan Onzari (5/1). Trainer: Ángel Vásquez (1).
**Goals**: Blas Saruppo (18), Vicente Aguirre (58, 77, 86).

**106.** 18.11.1923 **ARGENTINA - BRAZIL** **2-1(1-1)** 7th Copa América
Estadio Parque Central, Montevideo (Uruguay); Referee: Miguel Barba (Paraguay); Attendance: 15,000
**ARG:** Federico Cancino (1/0), Ludovico Bidoglio (Cap) (8/0), Juan Carlos Iribarren (7/0), Ángel Segundo Médici (9/0), Luis Vaccaro (3/0), Emilio Solari (17/0), Adán Loizo (6/0), Antonio De Miguel (7/0), Blas Saruppo (8/4), Vicente Aguirre (2/3), Cesáreo Juan Onzari (6/2). Trainer: Ángel Vásquez (2).
**Goals**: Cesáreo Juan Onzari (15), Blas Saruppo (76).

**107.** 02.12.1923 **URUGUAY - ARGENTINA** **2-0(1-0)** 7th Copa América
Estadio Parque Central, Montevideo; Referee: Antônio Carneiro de Campos (Brazil); Attendance: 22,000
**ARG:** Américo Miguel Tesorieri (25/0), Ludovico Bidoglio (Cap) (9/0), Juan Carlos Iribarren (8/0), Ángel Segundo Médici (10/0), Luis Vaccaro (4/0), Emilio Solari (18/0), Adán Loizo (7/0), Antonio De Miguel (8/0), Blas Saruppo (9/4), Vicente Aguirre (3/3), Cesáreo Juan Onzari (7/2). Trainer: Ángel

Vásquez (3).

**108.** 02.12.1923 **ARGENTINA - BRAZIL** **0-2(0-1)** Taça Brasil-Argentina
Estadio Sportivo Barracas, Buenos Aires; Referee: Antônio Carneiro de Campos (Brazil); Attendance: 5,000
**ARG:** Jorge Iribarren (1/0), José Voltura (1/0), Juan Prato (1/0), G. Méndez (1/0), Roberto Seregni (5/0), Juan Bautista Scursoni (1/0), Bleo Pedro Fournol „Calomino" (37/5), Carlos Lalaurette (1/0), Nicolás Vivaldo (9/2), Luis Lázzari (1/0), José Gurutchague (1/0). Trainer: no.

**109.** 08.12.1923 **ARGENTINA - URUGUAY** **2-3(2-1)** Copa Ministro
Estadio Racing Club, Avellaneda, Buenos Aires; Referee: Pascual Gilio (Argentina); Attendance: 8,000
**ARG:** Marcos Crocce (3/0), Roberto Castagnola (9/0), Juan Van Kamenade (1/0), Ernesto Mattozzi (22/1), Cándido García (6/1), Luis Célico (5/0), Juan Natalio Perinetti (1/0), Lindolfo Acosta (1/1), Juan Anunziata (1/1), José Fortunato (1/0), Manuel Pardal (1/0). Trainer: no.
**Goals**: José Anunziata, Lindolfo Acosta.

**110.** 09.12.1923 **ARGENTINA - BRAZIL** **2-0(0-0)** Copa Roca
Estadio Sportivo Barracas, Buenos Aires; Referee: Lorenzo Muzzio (Argentina); Attendance: 15,000
**ARG:** Américo Miguel Tesorieri (26/0), Ludovico Bidoglio (10/0), Juan Carlos Iribarren (9/0), Ángel Segundo Médici (11/0), Roberto Seregni (6/0), Emilio Solari (19/0), Adán Loizo (8/0), Antonio Cerrotti (1/0), Domingo Alberto Tarasconi (3/1), Ángel Domingo Chiessa (9/1), Cesáreo Juan Onzari (8/3). Trainer: no.
**Goals**: Dino I (own goal), Cesáreo Juan Onzari.

**111.** 15.05.1924 **PARAGUAY - ARGENTINA** **1-3(0-0)** Copa Chevallier Boutell
Estadio Parque Caballero, Asunción; Referee: Francisco Andreu Balcó (Paraguay); Attendance: 10,000
**ARG:** Américo Miguel Tesorieri (27/0), Ludovico Bidoglio (11/0), Juan Carlos Iribarren (10/0), Ángel Segundo Médici (12/0), Guillermo Ronzoni (1/0), Emilio Solari (20/0), Adán Loizo (9/0), Adolfo López (2/1), Domingo Alberto Tarasconi (4/2), Manuel Seoane (1/1), Cesáreo Juan Onzari (9/4). Trainer: no.
**Goals**: Cesáreo Juan Onzari, Domingo Alberto Tarasconi, Manuel Seoane.

**112.** 18.05.1924 **PARAGUAY - ARGENTINA** **2-1(1-0)** Copa Chevallier Boutell
Estadio Parque Caballero, Asunción; Referee: Miguel Barba (Paraguay); Attendance: 8,000
**ARG:** Américo Miguel Tesorieri (28/0), Ludovico Bidoglio (12/0), Juan Bautista Scursoni (2/0), Ángel Segundo Médici (13/0), Guillermo Ronzoni (2/0), Emilio Solari (21/0), Adán Loizo (10/0), Adolfo López (3/1), Domingo Alberto Tarasconi (5/3), Manuel Seoane (2/1), Alejandro De los Santos (3/0). Trainer: no.
**Goal**: Domingo Alberto Tarasconi.

**113.** 25.05.1924 **URUGUAY - ARGENTINA** **2-0(1-0)** Copa Newton
Estadio Parque Central, Montevideo; Referee: José Rami (Uruguay); Attendance: 12,000
**ARG:** Federico Cancino (2/0), Felipe Cherro (1/0), L. Pérez (1/0), Alfredo Luis Chabrolín (6/0), Luis Vaccaro (5/0), Mario Fortunato (1/0), Alberto Bianatti (4/1), Antonio Cerrotti (2/0), Armando Stagnaro (1/0), Ernesto Celli (5/1), Dante Pertini (1/0). Trainer: no.

**114.** 25.05.1924 **ARGENTINA - URUGUAY** **4-0(3-0)** Copa Newton
Estadio Sportivo Barracas, Buenos Aires; Referee: Lorenzo Muzzio (Argentina); Attendance: 6,000
**ARG:** Bernardo Nuin (1/0), Roberto Cochrane (1/0), Natalio Molinari (1/0), Eduardo Dimare (1/0), Cándido MacCourbey (1/0), Alejandro Laurenzano (1/0), Bleo Pedro Fournol „Calomino" (38/5), Osvaldo Goicoechea (1/3), Gabino Sosa (4/0), Vicente Aguirre (4/4), José Gurutchague (2/0). Trainer: no.
**Goals**: Osvaldo Goicoechea 2, Vicente Aguirre, Osvaldo Goicoechea.

**115.** 10.08.1924 **ARGENTINA - URUGUAY** **0-0** Copa Ministro
Estadio River Plate, Buenos Aires; Referee: Vicente Vitterito (Uruguay); Attendance: 30,000
**ARG:** Marcos Crocce (4/0), Roberto Castagnola (10/0), Humberto Juan Recanatini (7/0), Pablo Bartolucci (1/0), Luis Felipe Monti (1/0), Luis Célico (6/0), Juan Natalio Perinetti (2/0), Lindolfo Acosta (2/1), Gerardo Caldás (1/0), Juan Anunziata (2/1), Raimundo Bibiani Orsi (1/0). Trainer: no.

**116.** 31.08.1924 **URUGUAY - ARGENTINA** **2-3(0-0)** Premio de Honor Uruguayo
Estadio Pocitos, Montevideo; Referee: José Galli (Argentina); Attendance: 15,000
**ARG:** Felipe Scarpone (1/0), Humberto Juan Recanatini (8/0), Pedro Omar (1/0), Pablo Bartolucci (2/0), Luis Felipe Monti (2/1), Luis Célico (7/0), Juan Natalio Perinetti (3/0), José Fausto Lucarelli (5/2), Gerardo Caldás (2/0), Luis Ravaschino (1/0), Raimundo Bibiani Orsi (2/0). Trainer: no.
**Goals**: José Fausto Lucarelli 2, Luis Felipe Monti.

**117.** 21.09.1924 **URUGUAY - ARGENTINA** **1-1(1-0)**
Estadio Parque Central, Montevideo; Referee: Servando Pérez (Argentina); Attendance: 30,000
**ARG:** Américo Miguel Tesorieri (29/0), Adolfo Celli (13/0), Florindo Bearzotti (10/0), Ángel Segundo Médici (14/0), Luis Vaccaro (6/0), Emilio Solari (22/0), Domingo Alberto Tarasconi (6/4), Osvaldo Goicoechea (2/3), Gabino Sosa (5/0), Manuel Seoane (3/1), Cesáreo Juan Onzari (10/4). Trainer: Ángel Vásquez (4).
**Goal**: Domingo Alberto Tarasconi.

**118.** 28.09.1924 **ARGENTINA - URUGUAY** **0-0***
Estadio Sportivo Barracas, Buenos Aires; Referee: Ricardo Vallarino (Uruguay); Attendance: 60,000
**ARG:** Américo Miguel Tesorieri (30/0), Adolfo Celli (14/0), Florindo Bearzotti (11/0), Ángel Segundo Médici (15/0), Mario Fortunato (2/0), Emilio Solari (23/0), Domingo Alberto Tarasconi (7/4), Ernesto Celli (6/1), Gabino Sosa (6/0), Manuel Seoane (4/1), Cesáreo Juan Onzari (11/4). Trainer: Ángel Vásquez (5).
**Abandoned after only 4 mins!*

**119.** 02.10.1924 **ARGENTINA - URUGUAY** **2-1(1-1)***
Estadio Sportivo Barracas, Buenos Aires; Referee: Ricardo Vallarino (Uruguay); Attendance: 20,000
**ARG:** Américo Miguel Tesorieri (31/0), Florindo Bearzotti (12/0), Adolfo Celli (15/0) [28.Ludovico Bidoglio (13/0)], Ángel Segundo Médici (16/0), Mario Fortunato (3/0), Emilio Solari (24/0), Domingo Alberto Tarasconi (8/5), Ernesto Celli (7/1), Gabino Sosa (7/0), Manuel Seoane (5/1), Cesáreo Juan Onzari (12/5). Trainer: Ángel Vásquez (6).
**Goals**: Cesáreo Juan Onzari, Domingo Alberto Tarasconi.
**Abandoned after 86 mins, after Uruguayan team left the field.*

**120.** 12.10.1924 **PARAGUAY - ARGENTINA** **0-0** 8th Copa América
Estadio Parque Central, Montevideo (Uruguay); Referee: Angel Minolli (Uruguay); Attendance: 8,000
**ARG:** Américo Miguel Tesorieri (Cap) (32/0), Ludovico Bidoglio (14/0), Florindo Bearzotti (13/0), Ángel Segundo Médici (17/0), Luis Vaccaro (7/0), Emilio Solari (25/0), Domingo Alberto Tarasconi (9/5), Juan Loyarte (1/0), Gabino Sosa (8/0), Manuel Seoane (6/1), Cesáreo Juan Onzari (13/5). Trainer:

Ángel Vásquez (7).

**121.** 25.10.1924 **CHILE - ARGENTINA** **0-2(0-1)** 8th Copa América
Estadio Parque Central, Montevideo (Uruguay); Referee: Angel Minolli (Uruguay); Attendance: 15,000
**ARG:** Américo Miguel Tesorieri (Cap) (33/0), Ludovico Bidoglio (15/0), Florindo Bearzotti (14/0), Ángel Segundo Médici (18/0), Mario Fortunato (4/0), Emilio Solari (26/0), Alfredo Garassini (1/0), Juan Loyarte (2/1), Gabino Sosa (9/1), Manuel Seoane (7/1), Cesáreo Juan Onzari (14/5). Trainer: Ángel Vásquez (8).
**Goals**: Gabino Sosa (5), Juan Loyarte (78).

**122.** 02.11.1924 **URUGUAY - ARGENTINA** **0-0** 8th Copa América
Estadio Parque Central, Montevideo; Referee: Carlos Fanta Tomaszewski (Chile); Attendance: 20,000
**ARG:** Américo Miguel Tesorieri (Cap) (34/0), Ludovico Bidoglio (16/0), Florindo Bearzotti (15/0), Ángel Segundo Médici (19/0), Roberto Cochrane (2/0), Emilio Solari (27/0), Domingo Alberto Tarasconi (10/5), Juan Loyarte (3/1), Gabino Sosa (10/1), Manuel Seoane (8/1), Cesáreo Juan Onzari (15/5). Trainer: Ángel Vásquez (9).

**123.** 09.07.1925 **ARGENTINA - PARAGUAY** **1-1(0-0)** Copa Chevallier Boutell
Estadio Boca Juniors, Buenos Aires; Referee: Luis Celleri (Argentina); Attendance: 20,000
**ARG:** Jorge Iribarren (2/0), Carlos Nóbile (2/0), Natalio Molinari (2/0), Juan Evaristo (5/1), César Giulidori (1/0), E. Souza (1/0), Adán Loizo (11/0), Feliciano Perducca (1/0), Juan Félix Maglio (1/0), Alejandro De los Santos (4/0), Ernesto Blanco (1/0). Trainer: Ángel Vásquez (10).
**Goal**: Juan Evaristo.

**124.** 12.07.1925 **ARGENTINA - PARAGUAY** **1-1(0-0)** Copa Chevallier Boutell
Estadio Sportivo Barracas, Buenos Aires; Referee: Gerónimo Repossi (Argentina); Attendance: 15,000
**ARG:** Jorge Iribarren (3/0), Carlos Nóbile (3/0), Natalio Molinari (3/0), Juan Evaristo (6/1), César Giulidori (2/0), Emilio Cacopardo (1/0), Adán Loizo (12/0), Nicolás Vivaldo (10/2), José Bruno Gaslini (6/2), Juan Félix Maglio (2/0), Ernesto Blanco (2/0). Trainer: Ángel Vásquez (11).
**Goal**: José Bruno Gaslini.

**125.** 29.11.1925 **ARGENTINA - PARAGUAY** **2-0(1-0)** 9th Copa América
Estadio Boca Juniors, Buenos Aires; Referee: Ricardo Vallarino (Uruguay); Attendance: 18,000
**ARG:** Américo Miguel Tesorieri (Cap) (35/0), Ludovico Bidoglio (17/0), Ramón Alfredo Muttis (4/0), Ángel Segundo Médici (20/0), Luis Vaccaro (8/0), Mario Fortunato (5/0), Domingo Alberto Tarasconi (11/5), Martín Sánchez (1/1), Juan Carlos Irurieta (2/1), Manuel Seoane (9/2), Juan Bianchi (1/0). Trainer: Ángel Vásquez (12).
**Goals**: Manuel Seoane (2), Martín Sánchez (72).

**126.** 13.12.1925 **ARGENTINA - BRAZIL** **4-1(1-1)** 9th Copa América
Estadio Sportivo Barracas, Buenos Aires; Referee: Manuel Chaparro (Paraguay); Attendance: 25,000
**ARG:** Américo Miguel Tesorieri (Cap) (36/0), Ludovico Bidoglio (18/0), Ramón Alfredo Muttis (5/0), Ángel Segundo Médici (21/0), Luis Vaccaro (9/0), Mario Fortunato (6/0), Domingo Alberto Tarasconi (12/5), Martín Sánchez (2/1), Alfredo Garassini (2/1), Manuel Seoane (10/5), Juan Bianchi (2/0). Trainer: Ángel Vásquez (13).
**Goals**: Manuel Seoane (41, 48), Alfredo Garassini (72), Manuel Seoane (74).

**127.** 20.12.1925 **ARGENTINA - PARAGUAY** **3-1(2-1)** 9th Copa América
Estadio Boca Juniors, Buenos Aires; Referee: Alfonso Leite de Castro (Brasil); Attendance: 25,000
**ARG:** Américo Miguel Tesorieri (Cap) (37/0), Ludovico Bidoglio (19/0), Ramón Alfredo Muttis (6/0), Ángel Segundo Médici (22/0), Luis Vaccaro (10/0), Mario Fortunato (7/0), Domingo Alberto Tarasconi (13/6), Martín Sánchez (3/1), Juan Carlos Irurieta (3/2), Manuel Seoane (11/6), Juan Bianchi (3/0). Trainer: Ángel Vásquez (14).
**Goals**: Domingo Alberto Tarasconi (22), Manuel Seoane (32), Juan Carlos Irurieta (63).

**128.** 25.12.1925 **ARGENTINA - BRAZIL** **2-2(1-2)** 9th Copa América
Estadio Sportivo Barracas, Buenos Aires; Referee: Manuel Chaparro (Paraguay); Attendance: 18,000
**ARG:** Américo Miguel Tesorieri (Cap) (38/0), Ludovico Bidoglio (20/0), Ramón Alfredo Muttis (7/0), Ángel Segundo Médici (23/0), Luis Vaccaro (11/0), Mario Fortunato (8/0), Domingo Alberto Tarasconi (14/6), Antonio Cerrotti (3/1), Alejandro De los Santos (5/0), Manuel Seoane (12/7), Juan Bianchi (4/0). Trainer: Ángel Vásquez (15).
**Goals**: Antonio Cerrotti (41), Manuel Seoane (55).

**129.** 29.05.1926 **ARGENTINA - PARAGUAY** **2-1(1-0)** Copa Chevallier Boutell
Estadio Boca Juniors, Buenos Aires; Referee: Francisco Andreu Balcó (Paraguay); Attendance: 6,000
**ARG:** Argento Arzeni (1/0), Felipe Cherro (2/1), Pascual Di Paola (1/0), Emilio Cacopardo (2/0), Luis Vaccaro (12/0), Emilio Solari (28/0), Juan Villagra (1/0), Renato Cesarini (1/0), Armando Stagnaro (2/1), Feliciano Perducca (2/0), Benjamín Delgado (4/0). Trainer: no.
**Goals**: Armando Stagnaro, Felipe Cherro (penalty).

**130.** 03.06.1926 **ARGENTINA - PARAGUAY** **2-1(1-0)** Copa Chevallier Boutell
Estadio Sportivo Barracas, Buenos Aires; Referee: Francisco Andreu Balcó (Paraguay); Attendance: 3,000
**ARG:** Argento Arzeni (2/0), Felipe Cherro (3/1), Pascual Di Paola (2/0), Emilio Cacopardo (3/0), Luis Vaccaro (13/0), Emilio Solari (29/0), Juan Villagra (2/1), Alberto Lucena (1/0), Renato Cesarini (2/1), Feliciano Perducca (3/0), Benjamín Delgado (5/0). Trainer: no.
**Goals**: Renato Cesarini, Juan Villagra.

**131.** 16.10.1926 **ARGENTINA - BOLIVIA** **5-0(4-0)** 10th Copa América
Estadio Sport de Nuñoa, Santiago (Chile); Referee: Aníbal Tejada (Uruguay); Attendance: 8,000
**ARG:** Octavio Juan Díaz (3/0), Ludovico Bidoglio (Cap) (21/0), Ramón Alfredo Muttis (8/0), Ángel Segundo Médici (24/0), Luis Vaccaro (14/0), Mario Fortunato (9/0), Domingo Alberto Tarasconi (15/6), Roberto Eugenio Cherro (1/2), Gabino Sosa (11/2), Antonio De Miguel (9/1), Benjamín Delgado (6/1). Trainer: no.
**Goals**: Roberto Eugenio Cherro (9, 19), Gabino Sosa (31), Benjamín Delgado (43), Antonio De Miguel (74).

**132.** 20.10.1926 **ARGENTINA - PARAGUAY** **8-0(5-0)** 10th Copa América
Estadio Sport de Nuñoa, Santiago (Chile); Referee: Francisco Jiménez (Chile); Attendance: 3,000
**ARG:** Octavio Juan Díaz (4/0), Ludovico Bidoglio (Cap) (22/0), Ramón Alfredo Muttis (9/0), Ángel Segundo Médici (25/0), Luis Vaccaro (15/0), Mario Fortunato (10/0), Domingo Alberto Tarasconi (16/6), Roberto Eugenio Cherro (2/3), Gabino Sosa (12/6), Antonio De Miguel (10/2), Benjamín Delgado (7/3). Trainer: no.
**Goals**: Gabino Sosa (11), Roberto Eugenio Cherro (16), Gabino Sosa (32), Benjamín Delgado (40, 42), Antonio De Miguel (52), Gabino Sosa (59, 87).

**133.** 24.10.1926 **URUGUAY - ARGENTINA** **2-0(1-0)** 10th Copa América
Estadio Sport de Nuñoa, Santiago (Chile); Referee: Miguel Barba (Paraguay); Attendance: 15,000
**ARG:** Octavio Juan Díaz (5/0), Ludovico Bidoglio (Cap) (23/0), Roberto Cochrane (3/0), Ángel Segundo Médici (26/0), Luis Vaccaro (16/0), Silvestre Conti (1/0), Domingo Alberto Tarasconi (17/6), Roberto Eugenio Cherro (3/3), Gabino Sosa (13/6), Antonio De Miguel (11/2), Benjamín Delgado (8/3). Trainer: no.

**134.** 31.10.1926 **CHILE - ARGENTINA** **1-1(1-1)** 10th Copa América
Estadio Sport de Nuñoa, Santiago; Referee: Miguel Barba (Paraguay); Attendance: 8,000
**ARG:** Octavio Juan Díaz (6/0), Ludovico Bidoglio (Cap) (24/0), Ramón Alfredo Muttis (10/0), Ángel Segundo Médici (27/0), Luis Vaccaro (17/0), Mario Fortunato (11/0), Domingo Alberto Tarasconi (18/7), Roberto Eugenio Cherro (4/3), Gabino Sosa (14/6), Feliciano Perducca (4/0), Benjamín Delgado (9/3). Trainer: no.
**Goal**: Domingo Alberto Tarasconi (42).

**135.** 14.07.1927 **URUGUAY - ARGENTINA** **0-1(0-0)** Copa Newton
Estadio Parque Central, Montevideo; Referee: Domingo Lombardi (Uruguay); Attendance: 12,000
**ARG:** Ángel Bossio (1/0), Pedro Omar (2/0), Humberto Juan Recanatini (9/0), Juan Evaristo (7/1), Adolfo Bernabé Zumelzú (1/0), Rodolfo Orlando Orlandini (1/0), Alfredo Carricaberry (1/1), Donato Penella (1/0), Manuel Ferreira (1/0), Roberto Bacchi (1/0), Raimundo Bibiani Orsi (3/0). Trainer: José Lago Millán (1).
**Goal**: Alfredo Carricaberry.

**136.** 30.08.1927 **ARGENTINA - URUGUAY** **0-1(0-0)** Copa Lipton
Estadio Boca Juniors, Buenos Aires; Referee: Servando Pérez (Argentina); Attendance: 25,000
**ARG:** Octavio Juan Díaz (7/0), Ludovico Bidoglio (25/0), Humberto Juan Recanatini (10/0), Ángel Segundo Médici (28/0), Saúl Calandra (1/0), Rodolfo Orlando Orlandini (2/0), Alfredo Carricaberry (1/1), Donato Penella (2/0), Gabino Sosa (15/6), Manuel Seoane (13/7), Raimundo Bibiani Orsi (4/0). Trainer: José Lago Millán (2).

**137.** 30.10.1927 **BOLIVIA - ARGENTINA** **1-7(1-5)** 11th Copa América
Estadio Nacional, Lima (Peru); Referee: Benjamín Fuentes (Peru); Attendance: 15,000
**ARG:** Octavio Juan Díaz (8/0), Ludovico Bidoglio (Cap) (26/0), Humberto Juan Recanatini (11/1), Juan Evaristo (8/1), Luis Felipe Monti (3/1), José Hipólito Fossa (1/0), Alfredo Carricaberry (3/3), Pedro Ochoa Baigorri (1/0), Manuel Ferreira (2/0), Manuel Seoane (14/9), Segundo Luna (1/2). Trainer: José Lago Millán (3).
**Goals**: Segundo Luna (18), Alfredo Carricaberry (20), Humberto Juan Recanatini (24 penalty), Manuel Seoane (29), Alfredo Carricaberry (36), Segundo Luna (56), Manuel Seoane (79).

**138.** 20.11.1927 **ARGENTINA - URUGUAY** **3-2(0-1)** 11th Copa América
Estadio Nacional, Lima (Peru); Referee: David Thurner (England); Attendance: 26,000
**ARG:** Octavio Juan Díaz (9/0), Ludovico Bidoglio (Cap) (27/0), Humberto Juan Recanatini (12/2), Juan Evaristo (9/1), Adolfo Bernabé Zumelzú (2/0), Luis Felipe Monti (4/1), Alfredo Carricaberry (4/3), Juan Félix Maglio (3/0), Manuel Ferreira (3/0), Manuel Seoane (15/9), Segundo Luna (2/3). Trainer: José Lago Millán (4).
**Goals**: Humberto Juan Recanatini (56), Segundo Luna (70), Adhemar Canavessi (85 own goal).

**139.** 27.11.1927 **PERU - ARGENTINA** **1-5(1-5)** 11th Copa América
Estadio Nacional, Lima; Referee: Victorio Gariboni (Bolivia); Attendance: 15,000
**ARG:** Ángel Bossio (2/0), Ludovico Bidoglio (Cap) (28/0), Humberto Juan Recanatini (13/2), Juan Evaristo (10/1), Adolfo Bernabé Zumelzú (3/0), Luis Felipe Monti (5/1), Alfredo Carricaberry (5/4), Juan Félix Maglio (4/2), Manuel Ferreira (4/2), Manuel Seoane (16/9), Raimundo Bibiani Orsi (5/0). Trainer: José Lago Millán (5).
**Goals**: Manuel Ferreira (1), Juan Félix Maglio (22, 25), Manuel Ferreira (30), Alfredo Carricaberry (38).

**140.** 01.04.1928 **PORTUGAL - ARGENTINA** **0-0**
Estádio do Lumiar, Lisboa; Referee: Lorenzo Martínez (Argentina); Attendance: 20,000
**ARG:** Octavio Juan Díaz (10/0), Ludovico Bidoglio (29/0), Fernando Paternóster (1/0), Ángel Segundo Médici (29/0), Saúl Calandra (2/0), Rodolfo Orlando Orlandini (3/0), Juan Natalio Perinetti (4/0), Pedro Ochoa Baigorri (2/0), Domingo Alberto Tarasconi (19/7), Roberto Eugenio Cherro (5/3), Raimundo Bibiani Orsi (6/0). Trainer: José Lago Millán (6).

**141.** 29.05.1928 **ARGENTINA – UNITED STATES** **11-2(4-0)** 9th OG. Group Stage.
Olympisch Stadion, Amsterdam (Holland); Referee: Paul Ruoff (Switzerland); Attendance: 3,800
**ARG:** Ángel Bossio (3/0), Ludovico Bidoglio (30/0), Fernando Paternóster (2/0), Ángel Segundo Médici (30/0), Saúl Calandra (3/0), Luis Felipe Monti (6/1), Alfredo Carricaberry (6/4), Domingo Alberto Tarasconi (20/11), Manuel Ferreira (5/4), Roberto Eugenio Cherro (6/6), Raimundo Bibiani Orsi (7/2). Trainer: José Lago Millán (7).
**Goals**: Manuel Ferreira, Domingo Alberto Tarasconi, Manuel Ferreira, Raimundo Bibiani Orsi, Roberto Eugenio Cherro 3, Domingo Alberto Tarasconi 2, Raimundo Bibiani Orsi, Domingo Alberto Tarasconi.

**142.** 02.06.1928 **ARGENTINA - BELGIUM** **6-3(3-2)** 9th OG.Quarter-Finals.
Olympisch Stadion, Amsterdam (Holland); Referee: Achille Da Gama Malcher (Italy); Attendance: 25,000
**ARG:** Ángel Bossio (4/0), Ludovico Bidoglio (31/0), Fernando Paternóster (3/0), Ángel Segundo Médici (31/0), Luis Felipe Monti (7/1), Rodolfo Orlando Orlandini (4/0), Alfredo Carricaberry (7/4), Domingo Alberto Tarasconi (21/15), Manuel Ferreira (6/5), Roberto Eugenio Cherro (7/6), Raimundo Bibiani Orsi (8/3). Trainer: José Lago Millán (8).
**Goals**: Domingo Alberto Tarasconi (4), Manuel Ferreira (6), Domingo Alberto Tarasconi (10, 75), Raimundo Bibiani Orsi (80), Domingo Alberto Tarasconi (88).

**143.** 06.06.1928 **ARGENTINA - EGYPT** **6-0(3-0)** 9th OG.Semi-Finals.
Olympisch Stadion, Amsterdam (Holland); Referee: Pedro Escartin (Spain); Attendance: 8,000
**ARG:** Octavio Juan Díaz (11/0), Ludovico Bidoglio (32/0), Fernando Paternóster (4/0), Ángel Segundo Médici (32/0), Luis Felipe Monti (8/1), Juan Evaristo (11/1), Alfredo Carricaberry (8/4), Domingo Alberto Tarasconi (22/18), Manuel Ferreira (7/7), Roberto Eugenio Cherro (8/7), Raimundo Bibiani Orsi (9/3). Trainer: José Lago Millán (9).
**Goals**: Roberto Eugenio Cherro, Manuel Ferreira, Domingo Alberto Tarasconi 3, Manuel Ferreira.

**144.** 10.06.1928 **URUGUAY - ARGENTINA** **1-1(1-0,1-1)** 9th OG.Final.
Olympisch Stadion, Amsterdam (Holland); Referee: Johannes Mutters (Holland); Attendance: 28,000
**ARG:** Ángel Bossio (5/0), Ludovico Bidoglio (33/0), Fernando Paternóster (5/0), Ángel Segundo Médici (33/0), Luis Felipe Monti (9/1), Juan Evaristo (12/1), Alfredo Carricaberry (9/4), Domingo Alberto Tarasconi (23/18), Manuel Ferreira (8/8), Enrique Gainzarain (1/0), Raimundo Bibiani Orsi (10/3). Trainer: José Lago Millán (10).
**Goal**: Manuel Ferreira.

**145.** 13.06.1928 **URUGUAY - ARGENTINA** **2-1(1-1)** 9th OG.Final (Replay).
Olympisch Stadion, Amsterdam (Holland); Referee: Johannes Mutters (Holland); Attendance: 28,000
**ARG:** Ángel Bossio (6/0), Ludovico Bidoglio (34/0), Fernando Paternóster (6/0), Ángel Segundo Médici (34/0), Luis Felipe Monti (10/2), Juan Evaristo (13/1), Alfredo Carricaberry (10/4), Domingo Alberto Tarasconi (24/18), Manuel Ferreira (9/8), Feliciano Perducca (5/0), Raimundo Bibiani Orsi (11/3). Trainer: José Lago Millán (11).
**Goal**: Luis Felipe Monti.

**146.** 30.08.1928 **ARGENTINA - URUGUAY** **1-0(1-0)** Copa Newton
Estadio Independiente, Avellaneda, Buenos Aires; Referee: Gerónimo Rapossi (Argentina); Attendance: 50,000
**ARG:** Ángel Bossio (7/0), Felipe Cherro (4/1), Humberto Juan Recanatini (14/2), Pablo Bartolucci (3/0), Adolfo Bernabé Zumelzú (4/0), Juan Evaristo (14/1), Leonardo Sandoval (1/0), Juan Arrillaga (1/0), Manuel Ferreira (10/8), Manuel Seoane (17/10), Raimundo Bibiani Orsi (12/3). Trainer: José Lago Millán (12).
**Goal**: Manuel Seoane.

**147.** 21.09.1928 **URUGUAY - ARGENTINA** **2-2(0-1)** Copa Lipton
Estadio Parque Central, Montevideo; Referee: Aníbal Tejada (Uruguay); Attendance: 18,000
**ARG:** Ángel Bossio (8/0), Pedro Omar (3/0), Humberto Juan Recanatini (15/2), Pablo Bartolucci (4/0), Adolfo Bernabé Zumelzú (5/0), Jorge Alonso (1/1), Carlos Desiderio Peucelle (1/0), Pedro Marassi (1/0), Gerardo Caldás (3/0), Juan Félix Maglio (5/3), Carlos Spadaro (1/0). Trainer: José Lago Millán (13).
**Goals**: Juan Félix Maglio, Jorge Alonso.

**148.** 16.06.1929 **ARGENTINA - URUGUAY** **2-0(0-0)** Copa Cámara de Diputados
Estadio Gasómetro de Boedo, Buenos Aires; Referee: Aníbal Tejada (Uruguay); Attendance: 50,000
**ARG:** Ángel Bossio (9/0), Pedro Omar (4/0), Fernando Paternóster (7/0), Juan Evaristo (15/1), Adolfo Bernabé Zumelzú (6/0), Gerardo Moreyras (1/0), Carlos Desiderio Peucelle (2/1), Alejandro Scopelli (1/1), Manuel Ferreira (11/8), Domingo Alberto Tarasconi (25/18), Marino Evaristo (1/0). Trainer: no.
**Goals**: Carlos Desiderio Peucelle, Alejandro Scopelli.

**149.** 16.06.1929 **URUGUAY - ARGENTINA** **1-1(1-0)**
Estadio Parque Central, Montevideo; Referee: José Galli (Argentina); Attendance: 30,000
**ARG:** Juan Botasso (1/0), Felipe Cherro (5/1), Juan Carlos Iribarren (11/0), Pablo Bartolucci (5/0), Carlos Volante (1/0), Rodolfo Orlando Orlandini (5/0), Leonardo Sandoval (2/0), Juan Félix Maglio (6/4), Juan Arrillaga (2/0), Esteban Kuko (1/0), Ismael Morgada (1/0). Trainer: no.
**Goal**: Juan Félix Maglio.

**150.** 20.09.1929 **URUGUAY - ARGENTINA** **2-1(1-0)** Copa Newton
Estadio Parque Central, Montevideo; Referee: Domingo Lombari (Uruguay); Attendance: 30,000
**ARG:** Ángel Bossio (10/0), Felipe Cherro (6/1), Fernando Paternóster (8/0), Juan Evaristo (16/1), Adolfo Bernabé Zumelzú (7/0), Jorge Alonso (2/1), Miguel Ángel Lauri (1/0), Alejandro Scopelli (2/1), Manuel Ferreira (12/8), Juan Félix Maglio (7/5), Ismael Morgada (2/0). Trainer: Francisco Olazar (1).
**Goal**: Juan Félix Maglio.

**151.** 28.09.1929 **ARGENTINA - URUGUAY** **0-0** Copa Lipton
Estadio Gasómetro de Boedo, Buenos Aires; Referee: Servando Pérez (Argentina); Attendance: 60,000
**ARG:** Ángel Bossio (11/0), Felipe Cherro (7/1), Fernando Paternóster (9/0), Juan Evaristo (17/1), Adolfo Bernabé Zumelzú (8/0), Luis Felipe Monti (11/2), Miguel Ángel Lauri (2/0), Alejandro Scopelli (3/1), Manuel Ferreira (13/8), Juan Félix Maglio (8/5), Carlos Spadaro (2/0). Trainer: Francisco Olazar (2).

**152.** 03.11.1929 **ARGENTINA - PERU** **3-0(2-0)** 12th Copa América
Estadio Gasómetro de Boedo, Buenos Aires; Referee: Aníbal Tejada (Uruguay); Attendance: 20,000
**ARG:** Ángel Bossio (12/0), Oscar Tarrío (1/0), Fernando Paternóster (10/0), Juan Evaristo (18/1), Adolfo Bernabé Zumelzú (9/2), Rodolfo Orlando Orlandini (6/0), Carlos Desiderio Peucelle (3/2), Juan Antonio Rivarola (1/0), Manuel Ferreira (Cap) (14/8), Manuel Seoane (18/10), Marino Evaristo (2/0). Trainer: Francisco Olazar – Juan José Tramutola (1).
**Goals**: Carlos Desiderio Peucelle (27), Adolfo Bernabé Zumelzú (38, 58).

**153.** 10.11.1929 **ARGENTINA - PARAGUAY** **4-1(2-0)** 12th Copa América
Estadio Gasómetro de Boedo, Buenos Aires; Referee: Julio Borrelli (Peru); Attendance: 20,000
**ARG:** Ángel Bossio (13/0), Oscar Tarrío (2/0), Fernando Paternóster (11/0), Juan Evaristo (19/1), Adolfo Bernabé Zumelzú (10/2), Alberto Chividini (1/0), Carlos Desiderio Peucelle (4/2), Juan Antonio Rivarola (2/0), Manuel Ferreira (Cap) (15/11), Roberto Eugenio Cherro (9/8), Marino Evaristo (3/0). Trainer: Francisco Olazar – Juan José Tramutola (2).
**Goals**: Manuel Ferreira (7, 24, 48), Roberto Eugenio Cherro (50).

**154.** 17.11.1929 **ARGENTINA - URUGUAY** **2-0(1-0)** 12th Copa América
Estadio Gasómetro de Boedo, Buenos Aires; Referee: Miguel Barba (Paraguay); Attendance: 60,000
**ARG:** Ángel Bossio (14/0), Oscar Tarrío (3/0), Fernando Paternóster (12/0), Juan Evaristo (20/1), Adolfo Bernabé Zumelzú (11/2), Alberto Chividini (2/0), Carlos Desiderio Peucelle (5/2), Juan Antonio Rivarola (3/0), Manuel Ferreira (Cap) (16/12), Roberto Eugenio Cherro (10/8), Marino Evaristo (4/1). Trainer: Francisco Olazar – Juan José Tramutola (3).
**Goals**: Manuel Ferreira (14), Marino Evaristo (77).

**155.** 25.05.1930 **ARGENTINA - URUGUAY** **1-1(1-1)** Copa Newton
Estadio Gasómetro de Boedo, Buenos Aires; Referee: Miguel Barba (Paraguay); Attendance: 60,000
**ARG:** Ángel Bossio (15/0), Oscar Tarrío (4/0), Alberto Cuello (1/0), Juan Evaristo (21/1), Adolfo Bernabé Zumelzú (12/2), Rodolfo Orlando Orlandini (7/0), Juan Natalio Perinetti (5/0), Francisco Antonio Varallo (1/1), Bernabé Ferreyra (1/0), Manuel Ferreira (17/12), Marino Evaristo (5/1). Trainer: Francisco Olazar – Juan José Tramutola (4).
**Goal**: Francisco Antonio Varallo.

**156.** 15.07.1930 **ARGENTINA - FRANCE** **1-0(0-0)** 1st FIFA WC. Group Stage.
Estadio Parque Central, Montevideo; Referee: Gilberto de Álmeida Rego (Brazil); Attendance: 15,000
**ARG:** Ángel Bossio (16/0), José Della Torre (1/0), Ramón Alfredo Muttis (11/0), Pedro Arico Suárez (1/0), Luis Felipe Monti (12/3), Juan Evaristo (22/1), Juan Natalio Perinetti (6/0), Francisco Antonio Varallo (2/1), Manuel Ferreira (Cap) (18/12), Roberto Eugenio Cherro (11/8), Marino Evaristo (6/1). Trainer: Francisco Olazar – Juan José Tramutola (5).
**Goal**: Luis Felipe Monti (81).

**157.** 19.07.1930 **ARGENTINA - MEXICO** **6-3(3-1)** 1st FIFA WC. Group Stage.
Estadio Centenario, Montevideo (Uruguay); Referee: Ulises Saucedo (Bolivia); Attendance: 50,000
**ARG:** Ángel Bossio (17/0), José Della Torre (2/0), Fernando Paternóster (13/0), Alberto Chividini (3/0), Adolfo Bernabé Zumelzú (Cap) (13/4), Rodolfo Orlando Orlandini (8/0), Carlos Desiderio Peucelle (6/2), Guillermo Stábile (1/3), Francisco Antonio Varallo (3/2), Atilio Demaría (1/0), Carlos Spadaro (3/0). Trainer: Francisco Olazar – Juan José Tramutola (6).
**Goals**: Guillermo Stábile (8), Adolfo Bernabé Zumelzú (12), Guillermo Stábile (17), Francisco Antonio Varallo (53), Adolfo Bernabé Zumelzú (55), Guillermo Stábile (80).

**158.** 22.07.1930 **ARGENTINA - CHILE** **3-1(2-1)** 1st FIFA WC. Group Stage.
Estadio Centenario, Montevideo (Uruguay); Referee: John Langenus (Belgium); Attendance: 35,000
**ARG:** Ángel Bossio (18/0), José Della Torre (3/0), Fernando Paternóster (14/0), Juan Evaristo (23/1), Luis Felipe Monti (13/3), Rodolfo Orlando Orlandini (9/0), Carlos Desiderio Peucelle (7/2), Francisco Antonio Varallo (4/2), Guillermo Stábile (2/5), Manuel Ferreira (Cap) (19/12), Marino Evaristo (7/2). Trainer: Francisco Olazar – Juan José Tramutola (7).
**Goals**: Guillermo Stábile (12, 13), Marino Evaristo (51).

**159.** 26.07.1930 **ARGENTINA – UNITED STATES** **6-1(1-0)** 1st FIFA WC.Semi-Finals.
Estadio Centenario, Montevideo (Uruguay); Referee: John Langenus (Belgium); Attendance: 50,000
**ARG:** Juan Botasso (2/0), José Della Torre (4/0), Fernando Paternóster (15/0), Juan Evaristo (24/1), Luis Felipe Monti (14/4), Rodolfo Orlando Orlandini (10/0), Carlos Desiderio Peucelle (8/4), Alejandro Scopelli (4/2), Guillermo Stábile (3/7), Manuel Ferreira (Cap) (20/12), Marino Evaristo (8/2). Trainer: Francisco Olazar – Juan José Tramutola (8).
**Goals**: Luis Felipe Monti (20), Alejandro Scopelli (56), Guillermo Stábile (69), Carlos Desiderio Peucelle (80, 85), Guillermo Stábile (87).

**160.** 30.07.1930 **URUGUAY - ARGENTINA** **4-2(1-2)** 1st FIFA WC.Final.
Estadio Centenario, Montevideo; Referee: John Langenus (Belgium); Attendance: 60,000
**ARG:** Juan Botasso (3/0), José Della Torre (5/0), Fernando Paternóster (16/0), Juan Evaristo (25/1), Luis Felipe Monti (15/4), Pedro Arico Suárez (2/0), Carlos Desiderio Peucelle (9/5), Francisco Antonio Varallo (5/2), Guillermo Stábile (4/8), Manuel Ferreira (Cap) (21/12), Marino Evaristo (9/2). Trainer: Francisco Olazar – Juan José Tramutola (9).
**Goals**: Carlos Desiderio Peucelle (20), Guillermo Stábile (37).

**161.** 03.08.1930 **ARGENTINA - YUGOSLAVIA** **3-1(3-1)**
Estadio River Plate, Buenos Aires; Referee: José Bartolomé Macías (Argentina); Attendance: 30,000
**ARG:** Eduardo Alterio (1/0), Oscar Tarrío (5/0), Juan Carlos Iribarren (12/0), Olegario Villegas (1/0), Carlos Volante (2/0), Camillo Bonelli (1/0), Leonardo Sandoval (3/0), Juan Arrillaga (3/0), Francisco Esponda (1/1), Alfredo Trujillo (1/2), Luis Gómez (1/0). Trainer: no.
**Goals**: Francisco Esponda (24), Alfredo Trujillo (27, 30).

**162.** 19.04.1931 **PARAGUAY - ARGENTINA** **0-1(0-1)**
Estadio Puerto Sajonia, Asunción; Referee: Manuel Chaparro (Paraguay); Attendance: 4,000
**ARG:** Fortunato Grimoldi (1/0), Luis Ferrario (1/0), F. Rodríguez (1/0), Mario Artel (1/0), Adolfo Lagomarsino (1/0), R. García (1/0), Sebastián Medina (1/0), Alfredo Ciriaco Devincenzi (1/0), Emilio Castro (1/0), Carlos Desiderio Peucelle (10/6), Antonio Del Felice (1/0). Trainer: no.
**Goal**: Carlos Desiderio Peucelle.

**163.** 25.04.1931 **PARAGUAY - ARGENTINA** **1-1(1-0)**
Estadio Puerto Sajonia, Asunción; Referee: Caetano Rodríguez (Paraguay); Attendance: 3,000
**ARG:** Fortunato Grimoldi (2/0), Luis Ferrario (2/0), F. Rodríguez (2/0), Mario Artel (2/0), Adolfo Lagomarsino (2/0), R. García (2/0), Carlos Bertetti (1/0), Juan Carlos Haedo (1/0), Emilio Castro (2/1), Carlos Desiderio Peucelle (11/6), Antonio Del Felice (2/0). Trainer: no.
**Goal**: Emilio Castro.

**164.** 04.07.1931 **ARGENTINA - PARAGUAY** **1-1(0-1)** Copa Chevallier Boutell
Estadio Sportivo Barracas, Buenos Aires; Referee: Domingo Salari (Argentina); Attendance: 10,000
**ARG:** Domingo Fossati (1/0), Oscar Tarrío (6/0), Humberto Juan Recanatini (16/2), Arcadio Julio López (1/0), Luis Felipe Monti (16/5), José Gargiulo (1/0), Alfredo Carricaberry (11/4), Alfredo Ciriaco Devincenzi (2/0), Juan Félix Maglio (9/5), Atilio Demaría (2/0), Carlos Spadaro (4/0). Trainer: no.
**Goal**: Luis Felipe Monti.

**165.** 09.07.1931 **ARGENTINA - PARAGUAY** **3-1(1-0)** Copa Chevallier Boutell
Estadio Sportivo Barracas, Buenos Aires; Referee: Celestino Destaillats (Paraguay); Attendance: 5,000
**ARG:** Domingo Fossati (2/0), Nicolás Pujolás (1/0), Humberto Juan Recanatini (17/2), Arcadio Julio López (2/0), Rodolfo De Jonge (1/0), José Gargiulo (2/0), Alfredo Carricaberry (12/4), Alfredo Ciriaco Devincenzi (3/0), Emilio Castro (3/3), Atilio Demaría (3/0), Carlos Spadaro (5/1). Trainer: no.
**Goals**: Emilio Castro 2, Carlos Spadaro.

**166.** 15.05.1932 **ARGENTINA - URUGUAY** **2-0(2-0)** Copa Comiteto Olimpico
Estadio Sportivo Barracas, Buenos Aires; Referee: Emilio Solari (Argentina); Attendance: 15,000
**ARG:** Atilio Patrignani (1/0), Felipe Cherro (8/1), Lucio Querido (1/0), Pablo Bartolucci (6/0), Aquilles Baglietto (1/0), Horacio Martínez (1/1), Juan Facio (1/0), Oscar Luppo (1/0) [15.Armando Zoroza (1/0)], Juan Carlos Irurieta (4/2), Roberto Eugenio Cherro (12/9), Oscar Correa (1/0). Trainer: no.
**Goals**: Horacio Martínez, Roberto Eugenio Cherro.

**167.** 19.05.1932 **URUGUAY - ARGENTINA** **1-0(0-0)** Copa Comiteto Olimpico
Estadio Centenario, Montevideo; Referee: Domingo Lombardi (Uruguay); Attendance: 30,000
**ARG:** Atilio Patrignani (2/0), Felipe Cherro (9/1), Lucio Querido (2/0), Pablo Bartolucci (7/0), Aquilles Baglietto (2/0), Horacio Martínez (2/1), Ricardo Sarco (1/0), Víctor Pérez (1/0), Juan Carlos Irurieta (5/2), Julio Ciancia (1/0), Oscar Correa (2/0). Trainer: no.

**168.** 21.01.1933 **URUGUAY - ARGENTINA** **2-1(1-0)**
Estadio Centenario, Montevideo; Referee: Aníbal Tejada (Uruguay); Attendance: 45,000
**ARG:** Atilio Herrera (1/0), José María González (1/0), José Arturo Scarcella (1/0), Alberto Viola (1/0), José María Minella (1/0), Ismael Arrese (1/0), Miguel Ángel Lauri (3/0), Juan Antonio Rivarola (4/0), Alberto Máximo Zozaya (1/0), Vicente Antonio Zito (1/0), Enrique Guaita (1/1). Trainer: no.
**Goal**: Enrique Guaita.

**169.** 05.02.1933 **ARGENTINA - URUGUAY** **4-1(1-1)**
Estadio Independiente, Avellaneda, Buenos Aires; Referee: Eduardo Forte (Argentina); Attendance: 60,000
**ARG:** Atilio Herrera (2/0), José María González (2/0), José Arturo Scarcella (2/0), Carlos Santamaría (1/0), Andrés Stagnaro (1/0), Francisco Garraffa (1/0), Miguel Ángel Lauri (4/0), Juan Antonio Rivarola (5/0), Alberto Máximo Zozaya (2/0), Roberto Eugenio Cherro (13/13), Enrique Guaita (2/1). Trainer: no.
**Goals**: Roberto Eugenio Cherro 4.

**170.** 14.12.1933 **URUGUAY - ARGENTINA** **0-1(0-0)**
Estadio Centenario, Montevideo; Referee: Martín Aphesteguy (Uruguay); Attendance: 35,000
**ARG:** Ángel Bossio (19/0), José María González (3/0), Alberto Cuello (2/0), Carlos Santamaría (2/0), José María Minella (2/0), Francisco Garraffa (2/0), Miguel Ángel Lauri (5/0), Francisco Antonio Varallo (6/3) [83.Vicente Antonio Zito (2/0)], Bernabé Ferreyra (2/0), Antonio Sastre (1/0), Arturo Arrieta (1/0). Trainer: no.
**Goal**: Francisco Antonio Varallo.

**171.** 27.05.1934 **SWEDEN - ARGENTINA** **3-2(1-1)** 2nd FIFA WC. 1st Round.
Stadio Littoriale, Bologna (Italy); Referee: Eugen Braun (Austria); Attendance: 15,000
**ARG:** Héctor Luis Freschi (1/0), Juan Carlos Pedevilla (1/0), Ernesto Antonio Bellis (1/1), José Eduardo Nehín (1/0), Constantino Urbieta Sosa (1/0), Arcadio Julio López (3/0), Francisco Rúa (1/0), Federico Wilde (1/0), Alfredo Ciriaco Devincenzi (4/0), Luis Alberto Galateo (1/1), Roberto Luis Irañeta (1/0). Trainer: Felipe Pascucci (1).
**Goals**: Ernesto Antonio Bellis (4), Luis Alberto Galateo (48).

**172.** 18.07.1934 **URUGUAY - ARGENTINA** **2-2(1-1)**
Estadio Centenario, Montevideo; Referee: Martín Aphesteguy (Uruguay); Attendance: 60,000
**ARG:** Fernando Bello (1/0), José María González (4/0), Alberto Cuello (3/0), Carlos Santamaría (3/0), José María Minella (3/0), Aarón Wergifker (1/0), Tomás González Peralta (1/1), Delfín Benítez Cáceres (1/1), Arturo Naón (1/0), Antonio Sastre (2/0), Tomás Beristain (1/0) [46.Carlos Desiderio Peucelle (12/6)]. Trainer: no.
**Goals**: Tomás González Peralta, Delfín Benítez Cáceres.

**173.** 15.08.1934 **ARGENTINA - URUGUAY** **1-0(0-0)**
Estadio Independiente, Avellaneda, Buenos Aires; Referee: Alberto Neme (Argentina); Attendance: 75,000
**ARG:** Fernando Bello (2/0), José María González (5/0), Alberto Cuello (4/0), Carlos Santamaría (4/0), José María Minella (4/0), Aarón Wergifker (2/0), Tomás González Peralta (2/1), Francisco Antonio Varallo (7/3) [46.Carlos Desiderio Peucelle (13/7)], Arturo Naón (2/0), Antonio Sastre (3/0), Arturo Arrieta (2/0). Trainer: no.
**Goal**: Carlos Desiderio Peucelle.

**174.** 06.01.1935 **ARGENTINA - CHILE** **4-1(1-1)** 13th Copa América
Estadio Nacional, Lima (Peru); Referee: Miguel Serra Hurtado (Peru); Attendance: 25,000
**ARG:** Fernando Bello (3/0), Carlos Wilson (1/0), José Arturo Scarcella (3/0), Rodolfo De Jonge (2/0), José María Minella (Cap) (5/0), Antonio De Mare (1/0), Miguel Ángel Lauri (6/1), Antonio Sastre (4/0), Herminio Masantonio (1/1), Vicente Antonio Zito (3/0) [41.Diego García (1/1)], Arturo Arrieta (3/1). Trainer: no.
**Goals**: Miguel Ángel Lauri (28), Arturo Arrieta (49), Diego García (57), Herminio Masantonio (71).

**175.** 20.01.1935 **PERU - ARGENTINA** **1-4(1-1)** 13th Copa América
Estadio Nacional, Lima; Referee: César Pioli (Uruguay); Attendance: 21,000
**ARG:** Fernando Bello (4/0), Carlos Wilson (2/0), José Arturo Scarcella (4/0), Rodolfo De Jonge (3/0), José María Minella (Cap) (6/0), Antonio De Mare (2/0), Miguel Ángel Lauri (7/1), Antonio Sastre (5/0), Herminio Masantonio (2/4), Diego García (2/2), Arturo Arrieta (4/1). Trainer: no.
**Goals**: Herminio Masantonio (10), Diego García (50), Herminio Masantonio (61, 81).

**176.** 27.01.1935 **URUGUAY - ARGENTINA** **3-0(3-0)** 13th Copa América
Estadio Nacional, Lima (Peru); Referee: Humberto Reginatto Balbo (Chile); Attendance: 30,000
**ARG:** Fernando Bello (5/0) [25.Sebastián Inocencio Gualco (1/0)], Carlos Wilson (3/0), José Arturo Scarcella (5/0), Rodolfo De Jonge (4/0), José María Minella (Cap) (7/0), Antonio De Mare (3/0) [31.Roberto Sbarra (1/0)], Miguel Ángel Lauri (8/1), Antonio Sastre (6/0), Herminio Masantonio (3/4), Diego García (3/2) [29.Vicente Antonio Zito (4/0)], Arturo Arrieta (5/1). Trainer: no.

**177.** 18.07.1935 **URUGUAY - ARGENTINA** **1-1(0-0)** Copa Héctor Gómez
Estadio Centenario, Montevideo; Referee: Martín Aphesteguy (Uruguay); Attendance: 20,000
**ARG:** Ángel Bossio (20/0), Alfredo Eleuterio Forrester (1/0), Manuel De Sáa (1/0), Carlos Santamaría (5/0), Manuel Dañil (1/0), Aarón Wergifker (3/0), Miguel Ángel Lauri (9/1), Juan Antonio Rivarola (6/0) [46.Antonio Sastre (7/0)], Francisco Antonio Varallo (8/3), Carlos Desiderio Peucelle (14/8), Enrique García (1/0). Trainer: Manuel Seoane (1).
**Goal**: Carlos Desiderio Peucelle.

**178.** 15.08.1935 **ARGENTINA - URUGUAY** **3-0(2-0)** Copa Juan Mignaburu
Estadio Independiente, Avellaneda, Buenos Aires; Referee: José Galli (Argentina); Attendance: 40,000
**ARG:** Ángel Bossio (21/0), Alfredo Eleuterio Forrester (2/0), Manuel De Sáa (2/0), Carlos Santamaría (6/0), Manuel Dañil (2/0), Aarón Wergifker (4/0), Miguel Ángel Lauri (10/1), Francisco Antonio Varallo (9/3) [79.Antonio Sastre (8/0)], Alberto Máximo Zozaya (3/2), Diego García (4/3), Enrique García (2/0). Trainer: Manuel Seoane (2).
**Goals**: Alberto Máximo Zozaya, Diego García, Alberto Máximo Zozaya.

**179.** 09.08.1936 **ARGENTINA - URUGUAY** **1-0(0-0)** Copa Juan Mignaburu
Estadio Independiente, Avellaneda, Buenos Aires; Referee: Domingo Salari (Argentina); Attendance: 40,000
**ARG:** Juan Alberto Estrada (1/0), Oscar Tarrío (7/0), Sabino Coletta (1/0), Enrique Vernières (1/0), Ernesto Lazzatti (1/0), Arcadio Julio López (4/0), Raimundo Bibiani Orsi (13/3), Antonio Sastre (9/0), Alberto Máximo Zozaya (4/3), José Manuel Moreno (1/0), Enrique García (3/0). Trainer: Manuel Seoane (3).
**Goal**: Alberto Máximo Zozaya.

**180.** 20.09.1936 **URUGUAY - ARGENTINA** **2-1(0-1)**
Estadio Centenario, Montevideo; Referee: Carlos Cerón (Uruguay); Attendance: 45,000
**ARG:** Juan Alberto Estrada (2/0), Oscar Tarrío (8/0), Alberto Cuello (5/0) [46.Sabino Coletta (2/0)], Alfredo Díaz (1/0), José María Minella (8/0), Aarón Wergifker (5/0), Rubén Cavadini (1/0), Francisco Antonio Varallo (10/3) [72.Ricardo Alarcón (1/0)], Agustín Cosso (1/0), Diego García (5/4), Enrique García (4/0). Trainer: Manuel Seoane (4).
**Goal**: Diego García.

**181.** 30.12.1936 **ARGENTINA - CHILE** **2-1(2-0)** 14th Copa América
Estadio Gasómetro de Boedo, Buenos Aires; Referee: Aníbal Tejada (Uruguay); Attendance: 35,000
**ARG:** Juan Alberto Estrada (3/0), Oscar Tarrío (9/0), Juan Carlos Iribarren (13/0), Antonio Sastre (10/0), José María Minella (Cap) (9/0), Celestino Martínez (1/0), Carlos Desiderio Peucelle (15/8), Francisco Antonio Varallo (11/5), Bernabé Ferreyra (3/0), Alejandro Scopelli (5/2) [75.Roberto Eugenio Cherro (14/13)], Enrique García (5/0). Trainer: Manuel Seoane (5).
**Goals**: Francisco Antonio Varallo (30, 43).

**182.** 09.01.1937 **ARGENTINA - PARAGUAY** **6-1(3-0)** 14th Copa América
Estadio Gasómetro de Boedo, Buenos Aires; Referee: Aníbal Tejada (Uruguay); Attendance: 42,000
**ARG:** Juan Alberto Estrada (4/0), Oscar Tarrío (10/0), Juan Carlos Iribarren (14/0) [53.Alberto Cuello (6/0)], Antonio Sastre (11/0), José María Minella (Cap) (10/0), Celestino Martínez (2/0), Carlos Desiderio Peucelle (16/8), Francisco Antonio Varallo (12/5), Alberto Máximo Zozaya (5/6), Alejandro Scopelli (6/4), Enrique García (6/1). Trainer: Manuel Seoane (6).
**Goals**: Alejandro Scopelli (5), Enrique García (8), Alberto Máximo Zozaya (33), Alejandro Scopelli (54), Alberto Máximo Zozaya (75, 82).

**183.** 16.01.1937 **ARGENTINA - PERU** **1-0(0-0)** 14th Copa América
Estadio Gasómetro de Boedo, Buenos Aires; Referee: Aníbal Tejada (Uruguay); Attendance: 40,000
**ARG:** Juan Alberto Estrada (5/0), Luis María Fazio (1/0), Juan Carlos Iribarren (15/0), Antonio Sastre (12/0) [*sent off 84**] [84.Héctor Blotto (1/0)], José María Minella (Cap) (11/0), Celestino Martínez (3/0) [80.Bartolomé Colombo (1/0)], Carlos Desiderio Peucelle (17/8), Francisco Antonio Varallo (13/5), Alberto Máximo Zozaya (6/7), Roberto Eugenio Cherro (15/13) [61.Vicente De la Mata (1/0)], Enrique García (7/1). Trainer: Manuel Seoane (7).
**Goal**: Alberto Máximo Zozaya (55).
**not authorised substitution of a player who was sent off, escaped to the referee!*

**184.** 23.01.1937 **ARGENTINA - URUGUAY** **2-3(0-1)** 14th Copa América
Estadio Gasómetro de Boedo, Buenos Aires; Referee: Alfredo Vargas Ascui (Chile); Attendance: 60,000
**ARG:** Juan Alberto Estrada (6/0), Oscar Tarrío (11/0), Juan Carlos Iribarren (16/0), Antonio Sastre (13/0), Ernesto Lazzatti (2/0) [59.José María Minella (12/0)], Celestino Martínez (4/0) [76.Bartolomé Colombo (2/0)], Carlos Desiderio Peucelle (18/8), Vicente De la Mata (2/0) [46.Alberto Máximo Zozaya (7/8)], Francisco Antonio Varallo (14/6) (Cap), Alejandro Scopelli (7/4), Enrique García (8/1). Trainer: Manuel Seoane (8).
**Goals**: Francisco Antonio Varallo (63), Alberto Máximo Zozaya (68).

**185.** 30.01.1937. **ARGENTINA - BRAZIL** **1-0(0-0)** 14th Copa América
Estadio Gasómetro de Boedo, Buenos Aires; Referee: Aníbal Tejada (Uruguay); Attendance: 65,000
**ARG:** Fernando Bello (6/0), Oscar Tarrío (12/0), Juan Carlos Iribarren (17/0) [46.Luis María Fazio (2/0)], Antonio Sastre (14/0), José María Minella (Cap) (13/0) [46.Ernesto Lazzatti (3/0)], Celestino Martínez (5/0), Enrique Guaita (3/1), Francisco Antonio Varallo (15/6), Alberto Máximo Zozaya (8/8), Alejandro Scopelli (8/4) [46.Roberto Eugenio Cherro (16/13)], Enrique García (9/2). Trainer: Manuel Seoane (9).
**Goal**: Enrique García (48).

**186.** 01.02.1937 **ARGENTINA - BRAZIL** **2-0(0-0,0-0)** 14th Copa América
Estadio Gasómetro de Boedo, Buenos Aires; Referee: Luis Angel Mirabal (Uruguay); Attendance: 60,000
**ARG:** Fernando Bello (7/0), Oscar Tarrío (13/0), Luis María Fazio (3/0), Antonio Sastre (15/0), Ernesto Lazzatti (4/0), Celestino Martínez (6/0), Enrique Guaita (4/1), Francisco Antonio Varallo (16/6) (Cap) [84.Vicente De la Mata (3/2)], Alberto Máximo Zozaya (9/8) [65.Bernabé Ferreyra (4/0)], Roberto Eugenio Cherro (17/13) [46.Carlos Desiderio Peucelle (19/8)], Enrique García (10/2). Trainer: Manuel Seoane (10).
**Goals**: Vicente De la Mata (109,112).

**187.** 10.10.1937 **URUGUAY - ARGENTINA** **0-3(0-0)** Copa Newton
Estadio Centenario, Montevideo; Referee: Aníbal Tejada (Uruguay); Attendance: 38,000
**ARG:** Atilio Herrera (3/0), Oscar Montañés (1/0), Lorenzo Gilli (1/0), Antonio Sastre (16/0), Bruno Rodolfi (1/0), Celestino Martínez (7/0), Carlos Desiderio Peucelle (20/8), Manuel Fidel (1/1), Juan Marvezzi (1/1), José Manuel Moreno (2/1), Enrique García (11/2). Trainer: no.
**Goals**: Juan Marvezzi, José Manuel Moreno, Manuel Fidel.

**188.** 11.11.1937 **ARGENTINA - URUGUAY** **5-1(2-1)** Copa Lipton
Estadio Independiente, Avellaneda, Buenos Aires; Referee: Isaac Caswell (England); Attendance: 50,000
**ARG:** Atilio Herrera (4/0), Oscar Montañés (2/0), Lorenzo Gilli (2/0), Antonio Sastre (17/0), Bruno Rodolfi (2/0), Celestino Martínez (8/0), Carlos Desiderio Peucelle (21/8), Manuel Fidel (2/2), Herminio Masantonio (4/7), José Manuel Moreno (3/1), Enrique García (12/3). Trainer: no.
**Goals**: Herminio Masantonio 2, Manuel Fidel, Herminio Masantonio, Enrique García.

**189.** 18.06.1938 **ARGENTINA - URUGUAY** **1-0(1-0)** Copa Juan Mignaburu
Estadio Monumental „Antonio Vespucio Liberti“, Buenos Aires; Referee: Alberto Neme (Argentina); Attendance: 40,000
**ARG:** Sebastián Inocencio Gualco (2/0), Oscar Montañés (3/0), Sabino Coletta (3/0), Manuel Aragüez (1/0), Héctor García (1/0), Celestino Martínez (9/0), Tomás González Peralta (3/1), Ricardo Alarcón (2/0), Herminio Masantonio (5/7), José Manuel Moreno (4/2), Enrique García (13/3). Trainer: Ángel Fernández Roca (1).
**Goal**: José Manuel Moreno.

**190.** 12.10.1938 **URUGUAY - ARGENTINA** **2-3(2-1)** Copa Héctor Gómez
Estadio Centenario, Montevideo; Referee: Aníbal Tejada (Uruguay); Attendance: 45,000
**ARG:** Fernando Bello (8/0), Oscar Montañés (4/0), Sabino Coletta (4/0) [*sent off 62*], Manuel Aragüez (2/0), José María Minella (14/0), Celestino Martínez (10/0), Rubén Cavadini (2/1), Manuel Fidel (3/2), Agustín Cosso (2/1), José Manuel Moreno (5/2), Enrique García (14/4). Trainer: Ángel Fernández Roca (2).
**Goals**: Enrique García, Agustín Cosso, Rubén Cavadini.

**191.** 15.01.1939 **BRAZIL - ARGENTINA** **1-5(0-3)** Copa Roca
Estádio São Januario, Rio de Janeiro; Referee: Carlos de Oliveira Monteiro (Brazil); Attendance: 30,000
**ARG:** Sebastián Inocencio Gualco (3/0), Oscar Montañés (5/0), Sabino Coletta (5/0), Arcadio Julio López (5/0), Bruno Rodolfi (3/0), Pedro Arico Suárez (3/0), Carlos Desiderio Peucelle (22/8), Antonio Sastre (18/0), Herminio Masantonio (6/9), José Manuel Moreno (6/4), Enrique García (15/5). Trainer: Ángel Fernández Roca (3).
**Goals**: Enrique García, Herminio Masantonio, José Manuel Moreno, Herminio Masantonio, José Manuel Moreno.

**192.** 22.01.1939 **BRAZIL - ARGENTINA** **3-2(1-2)** Copa Roca
Estádio São Januario, Rio de Janeiro; Referee: Carlos de Oliveira Monteiro (Brazil); Attendance: 27,000
**ARG:** Sebastián Inocencio Gualco (4/0), Oscar Montañés (6/0), Sabino Coletta (6/0), Arcadio Julio López (6/0), Bruno Rodolfi (4/1), Pedro Arico Suárez (4/0), Carlos Desiderio Peucelle (23/8), Antonio Sastre (19/0), Herminio Masantonio (7/9), José Manuel Moreno (7/4), Enrique García (16/6). Trainer: Ángel Fernández Roca (4).
**Goals**: Bruno Rodolfi, Enrique García.
* *Abandoned after 86.mins when the Argentinian players left the pitch in protest against the referee's decisions.*

**193.** 14.08.1939 **PARAGUAY - ARGENTINA** **0-1(0-1)** Copa Chevallier Boutell
Estadio Puerto Sajonia, Asunción; Referee: Cayetano De Nicola (Paraguay); Attendance: 20,000
**ARG:** Sebastián Inocencio Gualco (5/0), Oscar Montañés (7/0), Ignacio Díaz (1/0), Manuel Aragüez (3/0), Bruno Rodolfi (5/1), Pedro Arico Suárez (5/0), Juan Fattone (1/0), José Fabrini (1/1), Herminio Masantonio (8/9) [75.Jaime Sarlanga (1/0)], Antonio Sastre (20/0), Enrique García (17/6) [52.Aníbal Troncoso (1/0)]. Trainer: Guillermo Stábile (1).
**Goal**: José Fabrini.

**194.** 16.08.1939 **PARAGUAY - ARGENTINA** **2-2(1-0)** Copa Chevallier Boutell
Estadio Puerto Sajonia, Asunción; Referee: Arsenio Lugo (Paraguay); Attendance: 20,000
**ARG:** Sebastián Inocencio Gualco (6/0), Oscar Montañés (Cap) (8/0), Ignacio Díaz (2/0), Manuel Aragüez (4/0), Bruno Rodolfi (6/1) [51.José Toledo (1/0)], Pedro Arico Suárez (6/0) [46.Roberto Sbarra (2/0)], Jaime Sarlanga (2/1), José Fabrini (2/1), Herminio Masantonio (9/9) [71.Luis Arrieta (1/1)], Antonio Sastre (21/0), Enrique García (18/6) [71.Aníbal Troncoso (2/0)]. Trainer: Guillermo Stábile (2).
**Goals**: Jaime Sarlanga, Luis Arrieta.

**195.** 18.02.1940 **BRAZIL - ARGENTINA** **2-2(0-0,1-1)** Copa Roca
Estádio Parque Antártica, São Paulo; Referee: José Ferreira Lemos (Brazil); Attendance: 40,000
**ARG:** Sebastián Inocencio Gualco (7/0), José Salomón (1/0), Víctor Miguel Valussi (1/0), Manuel Aragüez (5/0), Ángel Perucca (1/0), Pedro Arico Suárez (Cap) (7/0), Carlos Desiderio Peucelle (24/8), Antonio Sastre (22/0), Luis Arrieta (2/1) [67.Fabio Cassán (1/1)], Emilio Baldonedo (1/1), Enrique García (19/6). Trainer: Guillermo Stábile (3).
**Goals**: Fabio Cassán (74), Emilio Baldonedo (116).

**196.** 18.02.1940 **ARGENTINA - PARAGUAY** **3-1(2-1)** Copa Chevallier Boutell
Estadio Independiente, Avellaneda, Buenos Aires; Referee: Juan José Alvarez (Argentina); Attendance: 25,000
**ARG:** Luis Bernabé Heredia (1/0), Oscar Montañés (9/0), Ignacio Díaz (3/0), Héctor Blotto (2/0) [65.Jorge Tittonel (1/0)], Raúl Osvaldo Leguizamón (1/1), Bartolomé Colombo (3/0), Juan José Maril (1/0), José Aurelio Gómez (1/0), Ángel Laferrara (1/0) [72.Juan Marvezzi (2/1)], Gabino Ballesteros (1/1), Adolfo Alfredo Pedernera (1/1). Trainer: Carlos Calocero (1) replacing Guillermo Stábile.
**Goals**: Gabino Ballesteros (12), Adolfo Alfredo Pedernera (21), Raúl Osvaldo Leguizamón (80).

**197.** 25.02.1940 **BRAZIL - ARGENTINA** **0-3(0-1)** Copa Roca
Estádio Parque Antártica, São Paulo; Referee: José Ferreira Lemos (Brazil); Attendance: 40,000
**ARG:** Sebastián Inocencio Gualco (8/0), José Salomón (2/0), Víctor Miguel Valussi (2/0), Manuel Aragüez (6/0), Ángel Perucca (2/0), Pedro Arico Suárez (Cap) (8/0), Carlos Desiderio Peucelle (25/8) [29.Juan Zorilla (1/0)], Antonio Sastre (23/1), Fabio Cassán (2/1), Emilio Baldonedo (1/2) [73.Manuel Fidel (4/3)], Enrique García (20/6). Trainer: Guillermo Stábile (4).
**Goals**: Emilio Baldonedo (35), Manuel Fidel (87), Antonio Sastre (89).

**198.** 25.02.1940 **ARGENTINA - PARAGUAY** **4-0(2-0)** Copa Chevallier Boutell
San Martín; Referee: Juan José Alvarez (Argentina); Attendance: 15,000
**ARG:** Luis Bernabé Heredia (2/0), Oscar Montañés (Cap) (10/0), Jorge Alberti (1/0), Héctor Blotto (3/0), Julio Zava (1/0), Bartolomé Colombo (4/0), Juan José Maril (2/0), José Aurelio Gómez (2/0) [46.Juan Prado (1/0)], Ángel Laferrara (2/2) [46.Herminio Masantonio (10/11)], Gabino Ballesteros (2/1), Adolfo Alfredo Pedernera (2/1). Trainer: Carlos Calocero (2) replacing Guillermo Stábile.
**Goals**: Ángel Laferrara (33, 34), Herminio Masantonio (53, 80).

**199.** 02.03.1940 **ARGENTINA - CHILE** **4-1(2-0)** Copa Presidente del Chile
Estadio Chacarita Juniors, Buenos Aires; Referee: Celestino Destaillats (Paraguay); Attendance: 40,000
**ARG:** Juan Elías Yustrich (1/0), Oscar Montañés (Cap) (11/0), Jorge Alberti (2/0), Héctor Blotto (4/0), Bruno Rodolfi (7/1), Bartolomé Colombo (5/0), Juan José Maril (3/1), Daniel Cornélio Sabio (1/0), Ángel Laferrara (3/5), Gabino Ballesteros (3/1) [88.Juan Prado (2/0)], Adolfo Alfredo Pedernera (3/1). Trainer: Guillermo Stábile (5).
**Goals**: Ángel Laferrara (44), Juan José Maril (45), Ángel Laferrara (57, 68).

**200.** 05.03.1940 **ARGENTINA - BRAZIL** **6-1(2-0)** Copa Roca
Estadio Gasómetro de Boedo, Buenos Aires; Referee: José Bartolomé Macías (Argentina); Attendance: 18,000
**ARG:** Sebastián Inocencio Gualco (9/0), José Salomón (3/0), Víctor Miguel Valussi (3/0) [70.Ernesto González (1/0)], Manuel Aragüez (7/0), Ángel Perucca (3/0), Pedro Arico Suárez (Cap) (9/0), Carlos Desiderio Peucelle (26/12), Antonio Sastre (24/1), Herminio Masantonio (11/12), Emilio Baldonedo (3/3), Enrique García (21/6). Trainer: Guillermo Stábile (6).
**Goals**: Herminio Masantonio, Carlos Desiderio Peucelle 4, Emilio Baldonedo.

**201.** 09.03.1940 **ARGENTINA - CHILE** **3-2(0-1)** Copa Presidente del Chile
Estadio Gasómetro de Boedo, Buenos Aires; Referee: Juan José Alvarez (Argentina); Attendance: 15,000
**ARG:** Juan Alberto Estrada (7/0), Oscar Montañés (Cap) (12/0), Ignacio Díaz (4/0), Héctor Blotto (5/0), Bruno Rodolfi (8/1), Bartolomé Colombo (6/0), Juan José Maril (4/1), Daniel Cornélio Sabio (2/0) [62.Juan Prado (3/0)], Ángel Laferrara (4/5) [25.Luis Arrieta (3/4)], Gabino Ballesteros (4/1), Adolfo Alfredo Pedernera (4/1). Trainer: Guillermo Stábile (7).
**Goals**: Luis Arrieta (56, 74, 83).

**202.** 10.03.1940 **ARGENTINA - BRAZIL** **2-3(1-1)** Copa Roca
Estadio Gasómetro de Boedo, Buenos Aires; Referee: José Bartolomé Macías (Argentina); Attendance: 75,000
**ARG:** Sebastián Inocencio Gualco (10/0), José Salomón (4/0), Víctor Miguel Valussi (4/0), Manuel Aragüez (8/0), Ángel Perucca (4/0), Pedro Arico Suárez (Cap) (10/0), Carlos Desiderio Peucelle (27/12), José Manuel Moreno (8/4), Herminio Masantonio (12/12) [78.Fabio Cassán (3/1)], Emilio Baldonedo (4/5), Enrique García (22/6). Trainer: Guillermo Stábile (8).
**Goals**: Emilio Baldonedo (28, 53).

**203.** 17.03.1940 **ARGENTINA - BRAZIL** **5-1(4-1)** Copa Roca
Estadio Independiente, Avellaneda, Buenos Aires; Referee: José Bartolomé Macías (Argentina); Attendance: 50,000
**ARG:** Sebastián Inocencio Gualco (11/0), José Salomón (5/0), Víctor Miguel Valussi (5/0), Manuel Aragüez (9/0) [46.Roberto Sbarra (3/0)], Raúl Osvaldo Leguizamón (2/1), Pedro Arico Suárez (Cap) (11/0), Carlos Desiderio Peucelle (28/13), Antonio Sastre (25/1), Herminio Masantonio (13/13) [63.Fabio Cassán (4/2)], Emilio Baldonedo (5/7), Enrique García (23/6). Trainer: Guillermo Stábile (9).
**Goals**: Emilio Baldonedo (3), Herminio Masantonio (9), Carlos Desiderio Peucelle (22), Emilio Baldonedo (41), Fabio Cassán (86).

**204.** 18.07.1940 **URUGUAY - ARGENTINA** **3-0(1-0)** Copa Héctor Gómez
Estadio Centenario, Montevideo; Referee: Aníbal Tejada (Uruguay); Attendance: 35,000
**ARG:** Juan Alberto Estrada (8/0), José Salomón (6/0), Víctor Miguel Valussi (6/0) [46.Jorge Alberti (3/0)], Gregorio Juan Esperón (1/0), José María Minella (15/0), Pedro Arico Suárez (Cap) (12/0), Juan Carlos Heredia (1/0) [13.Adolfo Alfredo Pedernera (5/1)], Antonio Sastre (26/1), Herminio Masantonio (14/13), Emilio Baldonedo (6/7), Enrique García (24/6). Trainer: Guillermo Stábile (10).

**205.** 15.08.1940 **ARGENTINA - URUGUAY** **5-0(1-0)** Copa Juan Mignaburu
Estadio Monumental „Antonio Vespucio Liberti“, Buenos Aires; Referee: Ubaldo Ruíz (Argentina); Attendance: 25,000
**ARG:** Juan Alberto Estrada (9/0), José Salomón (7/0) [75.Evarista De Lovo (1/0)], Jorge Alberti (4/0), Gregorio Juan Esperón (2/1), José María Minella (Cap) (16/0), José Pedro Batagliero (1/0), Alberto Edmundo Belén (1/0), José Manuel Moreno (9/5), Jaime Sarlanga (3/2) [66.Juan Marvezzi (3/3)], Bernardo José Gandulla (1/0), Gabino Arregui (1/0). Trainer: Guillermo Stábile (11).
**Goals**: Jaime Sarlanga (41), Gregorio Juan Esperón (64 penalty), José Manuel Moreno (77), Juan Marvezzi (86, 90).

**206.** 05.01.1941 **CHILE - ARGENTINA** **1-2(0-0)** Copa Presidente del Chile
Estadio Nacional, Santiago; Referee: Víctor Francisco Rivas (Chile); Attendance: 55,000
**ARG:** Juan Alberto Estrada (10/0), José Salomón (8/0), Jorge Alberti (5/0), Gregorio Juan Esperón (3/1), José María Minella (Cap) (17/0) [46.Eusebio Videla (1/0)], José Pedro Batagliero (2/0), Juan Gayol (1/0), José Manuel Moreno (10/5), Juan Marvezzi (4/3) [46.Luis Arrieta (4/4)], Rafael Sanz (1/0) [46.Antonio Sastre (27/2)], Gabino Arregui (2/1). Trainer: Guillermo Stábile (12).
**Goals**: Antonio Sastre (63), Gabino Arregui (65).

**207.** 09.01.1941 **CHILE - ARGENTINA** **2-5(1-2)** Copa Presidente del Chile
Estadio Nacional, Santiago; Referee: Alfredo Vargas Ascui (Chile); Attendance: 50,000
**ARG:** Juan Alberto Estrada (11/0), José Salomón (9/0), Jorge Alberti (6/0), Roberto Sbarra (4/0) [46.Gregorio Juan Esperón (4/1)], José María Minella (Cap) (18/0), José Pedro Batagliero (3/0), Alberto Edmundo Belén (2/0) [60.Juan Gayol (2/0)], José Manuel Moreno (11/5), Luis Arrieta (5/6), Antonio Sastre (28/4), Gabino Arregui (3/2). Trainer: Guillermo Stábile (13).
**Goals**: Antonio Sastre (7 penalty), Luis Arrieta (30), Antonio Sastre (50), Gabino Arregui (58), Luis Arrieta (65).

**208.** 19.01.1941 **PERU - ARGENTINA** **1-1(0-0)** Copa Roque Sáenz Peña
Estadio Nacional, Lima; Referee: López Torres (Argentina); Attendance: 35,000
**ARG:** Juan Alberto Estrada (12/0), José Salomón (10/0), Jorge Alberti (7/0), Roberto Sbarra (5/0), José María Minella (Cap) (19/0), José Pedro Batagliero (4/0), Alberto Edmundo Belén (3/1), José Manuel Moreno (12/5), Luis Arrieta (6/6), Antonio Sastre (29/4) [46.Rafael Sanz (2/0)], Gabino Arregui (4/2). Trainer: Guillermo Stábile (14).
**Goal**: Alberto Edmundo Belén (53).

**209.** 26.01.1941 **PERU - ARGENTINA** **1-1(1-1)** Copa Roque Sáenz Peña
Estadio Nacional, Lima; Referee: Enrique Cuenca (Peru); Attendance: 30,000
**ARG:** Juan Alberto Estrada (13/0), José Salomón (11/0), Jorge Alberti (8/0), Roberto Sbarra (6/0), José María Minella (Cap) (20/0) [46.Eusebio Videla (2/0)], José Pedro Batagliero (5/0) [46.Ricardo Alarcón (3/0)], Alberto Edmundo Belén (4/2), José Manuel Moreno (13/5), Luis Arrieta (7/6) [65.Juan Marvezzi (5/3)], Antonio Sastre (30/4), Gabino Arregui (5/2). Trainer: Guillermo Stábile (15).
**Goal**: Alberto Edmundo Belén (12).

**210.** 29.01.1941 **PERU - ARGENTINA** **0-3(0-0)** Copa Roque Sáenz Peña
Estadio Nacional, Lima; Referee: Enrique Cuenca (Peru); Attendance: 20,000
**ARG:** Juan Alberto Estrada (14/0), José Salomón (12/0), Jorge Alberti (9/0), Roberto Sbarra (7/0), José María Minella (Cap) (21/0), Eusebio Videla (3/0), Alberto Edmundo Belén (5/2), Ricardo Alarcón (4/0) [72.Antonio Sastre (31/5)], Luis Arrieta (8/6) [46.Juan Marvezzi (6/4)], José Manuel Moreno (14/6), Gabino Arregui (6/2). Trainer: Guillermo Stábile (16).
**Goals**: José Manuel Moreno (55), Antonio Sastre (75), Juan Marvezzi (89).

**211.** 12.02.1941 **ARGENTINA - PERU** **2-1(1-0)** 16th Copa América
Estadio Nacional, Santiago (Chile); Referee: Alfredo Vargas Ascui (Chile); Attendance: 45,000
**ARG:** Juan Alberto Estrada (15/0), José Salomón (13/0), Jorge Alberti (10/0), Gregorio Juan Esperón (5/1), José María Minella (Cap) (22/0), Roberto Sbarra (8/0), Alberto Edmundo Belén (6/2), Juan Marvezzi (7/4), Antonio Sastre (32/5), José Manuel Moreno (15/8), Gabino Arregui (7/2). Trainer: Guillermo Stábile (17).
**Goals**: José Manuel Moreno (2, 72).

**212.** 16.02.1941 **ARGENTINA - ECUADOR** **6-1(5-0)** 16th Copa América
Estadio Nacional, Santiago (Chile); Referee: Aníbal Tejada (Uruguay); Attendance: 70,000
**ARG:** Sebastián Inocencio Gualco (12/0), José Salomón (14/0), Jorge Alberti (11/0), Bartolomé Colombo (7/0), José María Minella (Cap) (23/0), Roberto Sbarra (9/0), Adolfo Alfredo Pedernera (6/1), José Manuel Moreno (16/9), Juan Marvezzi (8/9), Antonio Sastre (33/5), Enrique García (25/6). Trainer: Guillermo Stábile (18).
**Goals**: Juan Marvezzi (3, 17, 28), José Manuel Moreno (30), Juan Marvezzi (39, 59).

**213.** 23.02.1941 **ARGENTINA - URUGUAY** **1-0(0-0)** 16th Copa América
Estadio Nacional, Santiago (Chile); Referee: Alfredo Vargas Ascui (Chile); Attendance: 48,000
**ARG:** Juan Alberto Estrada (16/0), José Salomón (15/0) [86.Sabino Coletta (7/0)], Jorge Alberti (12/0), Roberto Sbarra (10/0), José María Minella (Cap) (24/0) [40.Eusebio Videla (4/0)], Bartolomé Colombo (8/0), Adolfo Alfredo Pedernera (7/1), José Manuel Moreno (17/9), Juan Marvezzi (9/9), Antonio Sastre (34/6), Enrique García (26/6). Trainer: Guillermo Stábile (19).
**Goal**: Antonio Sastre (53).

**214.** 04.03.1941 **CHILE - ARGENTINA** **0-1(0-0)** 16th Copa América
Estadio Nacional, Santiago; Referee: Aníbal Tejada (Uruguay); Attendance: 60,300
**ARG:** Juan Alberto Estrada (17/0), José Salomón (Cap) (16/0), Jorge Alberti (13/0), Eusebio Videla (5/0), José Pedro Batagliero (6/0), Roberto Sbarra (11/0), Adolfo Alfredo Pedernera (8/1), José Manuel Moreno (18/9), Luis Arrieta (9/6), Antonio Sastre (35/6), Enrique García (27/7). Trainer: Guillermo Stábile (20).
**Goal**: Enrique García (71).

**215.** 11.01.1942 **ARGENTINA - PARAGUAY** **4-3(2-0)** 17th Copa América
Estadio Centenario, Montevideo (Uruguay); Referee: José Ferreira Lemos (Brazil); Attendance: 20,000
**ARG:** Sebastián Inocencio Gualco (13/0), José Salomón (Cap) (17/0), Jorge Alberti (14/0), Héctor Blotto (6/0), Ángel Perucca (5/1), José Ramos (1/0), Mario Tossoni (1/0), Raimundo Sandoval (1/1), Herminio Masantonio (15/15), José Manuel Moreno (19/9), Enrique García (28/7). Trainer: Guillermo Stábile (21).
**Goals**: Raimundo Sandoval (9), Herminio Masantonio (30, 47), Ángel Perucca (88).

**216.** 17.01.1942 **ARGENTINA - BRAZIL** **2-1(2-1)** 17th Copa América
Estadio Centenario, Montevideo (Uruguay); Referee: Enrique Cuenca (Peru); Attendance: 35,000
**ARG:** Sebastián Inocencio Gualco (14/0), José Salomón (Cap) (18/0) [70.Oscar Montañés (13/0)], Jorge Alberti (15/0), Gregorio Juan Esperón (6/1), Eusebio Videla (6/0) [46.Ángel Perucca (6/1)], José Ramos (2/0), Mario Tossoni (2/0) [65.Juan Carlos Heredia (2/0)], Adolfo Alfredo Pedernera (9/1), Herminio Masantonio (16/16), José Manuel Moreno (20/9), Enrique García (29/8). Trainer: Guillermo Stábile (22).
**Goals**: Enrique García (3), Herminio Masantonio (27).

**217.** 22.01.1942 **ARGENTINA - ECUADOR** **12-0(6-0)** 17th Copa América
Estadio Centenario, Montevideo (Uruguay); Referee: Manuel Soto (Chile); Attendance: 25,000
**ARG:** Sebastián Inocencio Gualco (15/0), José Salomón (Cap) (19/0), Víctor Miguel Valussi (7/0), Gregorio Juan Esperón (7/1), Ángel Perucca (7/2), José Ramos (3/0), Juan Carlos Heredia (3/0), Adolfo Alfredo Pedernera (10/2), Herminio Masantonio (17/20), José Manuel Moreno (21/14), Enrique García (30/9). Trainer: Guillermo Stábile (23).
**Goals**: Enrique García (2), José Manuel Moreno (12, 16, 22), Adolfo Alfredo Pedernera (25), José Manuel Moreno (32), Herminio Masantonio (54, 65, 68, 70), Ángel Perucca (88), José Manuel Moreno (89).

**218.** 25.01.1942 **ARGENTINA - PERU** **3-1(1-1)** 17th Copa América
Estadio Centenario, Montevideo (Uruguay); Referee: Aníbal Tejada (Uruguay); Attendance: 12,000
**ARG:** Sebastián Inocencio Gualco (16/0), José Salomón (Cap) (20/0) [80.Oscar Montañés (14/0)], Jorge Alberti (16/0), Gregorio Juan Esperón (8/1), Ángel Perucca (8/2), José Ramos (4/0), Juan Carlos Heredia (4/1) [75.Mario Tossoni (3/0)], Adolfo Alfredo Pedernera (11/2), Herminio Masantonio (18/20) [65.Ángel Laferrara (5/5)], José Manuel Moreno (22/16), Enrique García (31/9). Trainer: Guillermo Stábile (24).
**Goals**: Juan Carlos Heredia (12), José Manuel Moreno (65, 72).

**219.** 31.01.1942 **ARGENTINA - CHILE** **0-0*** 17th Copa América
Estadio Centenario, Montevideo (Uruguay); Referee: Enrique Cuenca (Peru); Attendance: 15,000
**ARG:** Sebastián Inocencio Gualco (17/0), José Salomón (Cap) (21/0), Jorge Alberti (17/0), Gregorio Juan Esperón (9/1), Eusebio Videla (7/0), José Ramos (5/0), Juan Carlos Heredia (5/1), Adolfo Alfredo Pedernera (12/2), Ángel Laferrara (6/5), José Manuel Moreno (23/16), Enrique García (32/9). Trainer: Guillermo Stábile (25).
**After 43 mins, chilean player left the field due to badperformances from Referee Cuenca. The match was awarded as win for Argentina.*

**220.** 07.02.1942 **URUGUAY - ARGENTINA** **1-0(0-0)** 17th Copa América
Estadio Centenario, Montevideo; Referee: Mario Rojas (Paraguay); Attendance: 70,000
**ARG:** Sebastián Inocencio Gualco (18/0), José Salomón (Cap) (22/0), Víctor Miguel Valussi (8/0) [31.Oscar Montañés (15/0)], Gregorio Juan Esperón (10/1), Ángel Perucca (9/2), José Ramos (6/0), Juan Carlos Heredia (6/1) [72.Adolfo Alfredo Pedernera (13/2)], Raimundo Sandoval (2/1), Herminio Masantonio (19/20), José Manuel Moreno (24/16), Enrique García (33/9). Trainer: Guillermo Stábile (26).

**221.** 25.05.1942 **ARGENTINA - URUGUAY** **4-1(3-0)** Copa Newton
Estadio Monumental „Antonio Vespucio Liberti", Buenos Aires; Referee: Juan José Alvarez (Argentina); Attendance: 40,000
**ARG:** Sebastián Inocencio Gualco (19/0), José Salomón (Cap) (23/0), Jorge Alberti (18/1) [63.Ignacio Díaz (5/0)], Norberto Antonio Yácono (1/0), Ángel Perucca (10/2), José María Arnaldo (1/0), Juan Carlos Muñoz (1/0), José Manuel Moreno (25/16), René Alejandro Pontoni (1/2), Rinaldo Fioramonte Martino (1/1), Enrique García (34/9). Trainer: Guillermo Stábile (27).
**Goals**: Jorge Alberti (13), Rinaldo Fioramonte Martino (34), René Alejandro Pontoni (40, 61).

**222.** 25.08.1942 **URUGUAY - ARGENTINA** **1-1(0-0)** Copa Lipton
Estadio Centenario, Montevideo; Referee: Aníbal Tejada (Uruguay); Attendance: 49,850
**ARG:** Sebastián Inocencio Gualco (20/0), José Salomón (Cap) (24/0), Ignacio Díaz (6/0), Norberto Antonio Yácono (2/0), Bruno Rodolfi (9/1), Alfredo Zárraga (1/0) [68.Carlos Adolfo Sosa (1/0)], Juan Carlos Muñoz (2/1), José Manuel Moreno (26/16), Norberto José Pairoux (1/0) [58.Jaime Sarlanga (4/2)], Rinaldo Fioramonte Martino (2/1) [85.Ángel Amadeo Labruna (1/0)], Manuel Gregorio Pelegrina (1/0). Trainer: Guillermo Stábile (28).
**Goal**: Juan Carlos Muñoz (51).

**223.** 28.03.1943 **ARGENTINA - URUGUAY** **3-3(2-1)** Copa Juan Mignaburu
Estadio Monumental „Antonio Vespucio Liberti", Buenos Aires; Referee: José Bartolomé Macías (Argentina); Attendance: 40,000
**ARG:** Isaac Roberto López (1/0) [28.Fernando Bello (9/0)], José Salomón (Cap) (25/0), Jorge Alberti (19/1), Norberto Antonio Yácono (3/0) [46.Celestino Martínez (11/0)], Raúl Osvaldo Leguizamón (3/1), Jorge Tittonel (2/0), Juan Carlos Muñoz (3/1), Juan José Negri (1/0) [59.Jaime Sarlanga (5/2)], René Alejandro Pontoni (2/4), Rinaldo Fioramonte Martino (3/2), Enrique García (35/9). Trainer: Guillermo Stábile (29).
**Goals**: René Alejandro Pontoni (2, 31), Rinaldo Fioramonte Martino (89 penalty).

**224.** 04.04.1943 **URUGUAY - ARGENTINA** **0-1(0-0)** Copa Héctor Gómez

Estadio Centenario, Montevideo; Referee: Aníbal Tejada (Uruguay); Attendance: 50,320

**ARG:** Sebastián Inocencio Gualco (21/0), José Salomón (Cap) (26/0) [46.Víctor Miguel Valussi (9/0)], Juan Carlos Sobrero (1/0), Celestino Martínez (12/0), Manuel Ernesto Giúdice (1/0) [54.Salvador Grecco (1/0)], Ernesto Liztherman (1/0) [54.Jorge Tittonel (3/0)], Juan Carlos Muñoz (4/1), José Canteli (1/1), René Alejandro Pontoni (3/4), Mario Morosano (1/0), Juan Silvano Ferreyra (1/0). Trainer: Guillermo Stábile (30).

**Goal**: José Canteli (79).

**225.** 10.07.1943 **PARAGUAY - ARGENTINA** **2-5(1-2)** Copa Chevallier Boutell

Estadio Defensores del Chaco, Asunción; Referee: José Bartolomé Macías (Argentina); Attendance: 12,000

**ARG:** Sebastián Inocencio Gualco (Cap) (22/0), Eduardo Enrique Rodríguez (1/0) [46.Rubén Omar Noceda (1/0)], Ignacio Díaz (7/0) [56.Juan Carlos Sobrero (2/0)], Norberto Antonio Yácono (4/0), Salvador Grecco (2/0) [46.Enrique Espinosa (1/0)], José María Arnaldo (2/0) [46.Celestino Martínez (13/0)], Alberto Edmundo Belén (7/2), Alfredo Borgnia (1/0) [56.Vicente De la Mata (4/3)], Jaime Sarlanga (6/4) [76.Alberto Lijé (1/0)], Rinaldo Fioramonte Martino (4/3), Manuel Gregorio Pelegrina (2/1). Trainer: Guillermo Stábile (31).

**Goals**: Jaime Sarlanga (21), Manuel Gregorio Pelegrina (25), Rinaldo Fioramonte Martino (48), Jaime Sarlanga (74), Vicente De la Mata (79).

**226.** 11.07.1943 **PARAGUAY - ARGENTINA** **2-1(1-0)** Copa Chevallier Boutell

Estadio Defensores del Chaco, Asunción; Referee: Cayetano De Nicola (Paraguay); Attendance: 10,000

**ARG:** Sebastián Inocencio Gualco (Cap) (23/0), Eduardo Enrique Rodríguez (2/0) [46.Rubén Omar Noceda (2/0)], Ignacio Díaz (8/0) [46.Juan Carlos Sobrero (3/0)], Norberto Antonio Yácono (5/0) [40.Celestino Martínez (14/0)], Salvador Grecco (3/0) [*sent off 50*], José María Arnaldo (3/0), Alberto Edmundo Belén (8/2), Alfredo Borgnia (2/0) [46.Vicente De la Mata (5/3)], Jaime Sarlanga (7/5), Rinaldo Fioramonte Martino (5/3) [65.Enrique Espinosa (2/0)], Manuel Gregorio Pelegrina (3/1). Trainer: Guillermo Stábile (32).

**Goal**: Jaime Sarlanga (85).

**227.** 06.01.1945 **ARGENTINA - PARAGUAY** **5-2(3-1)** Copa Chevallier Boutell

Estadio Gasómetro de Boedo, Buenos Aires; Referee: José Bartolomé Macías (Argentina); Attendance: 45,000

**ARG:** Héctor Ricardo (1/0), José Salomón (Cap) (27/0), Roberto Justo De Zorzi (1/0), Carlos Adolfo Sosa (2/0) [74.Oscar Carlos Sastre (1/0)], Ángel Perucca (11/2), Bartolomé Colombo (9/0), Juan Carlos Muñoz (5/2), Vicente De la Mata (6/3), René Alejandro Pontoni (4/6), Rinaldo Fioramonte Martino (6/4), Félix Loustau (1/1). Trainer: Guillermo Stábile (33).

**Goals**: Juan Carlos Muñoz (3), Félix Loustau (24), René Alejandro Pontoni (36, 63), Rinaldo Fioramonte Martino (67).

**228.** 09.01.1945 **ARGENTINA - PARAGUAY** **5-3(3-2)** Copa Chevallier Boutell

Estadio Gasómetro de Boedo, Buenos Aires; Referee: Osvaldo Cossio (Argentina); Attendance: 40,000

**ARG:** Héctor Ricardo (2/0), José Salomón (Cap) (28/0), Roberto Justo De Zorzi (2/0), Carlos Adolfo Sosa (3/0) [46.Enrique Espinosa (3/0)], Ángel Perucca (12/2), Bartolomé Colombo (10/0), Juan Carlos Muñoz (6/2), Norberto Doroteo Méndez (1/0), René Alejandro Pontoni (5/10), Rinaldo Fioramonte Martino (7/5), Félix Loustau (2/1). Trainer: Guillermo Stábile (34).

**Goals**: René Alejandro Pontoni (5), Rinaldo Fioramonte Martino (18), René Alejandro Pontoni (36, 70, 87).

**229.** 18.01.1945 **ARGENTINA - BOLIVIA** **4-0(2-0)** 18th Copa América

Estadio Nacional, Santiago (Chile); Referee: Humberto Reginatto Balbo (Chile); Attendance: 35,000

**ARG:** Fernando Bello (10/0), José Salomón (Cap) (29/0), Roberto Justo De Zorzi (3/0), Carlos Adolfo Sosa (4/0), Ángel Perucca (13/2), Bartolomé Colombo (11/0), Juan Carlos Muñoz (7/2), Vicente De la Mata (7/4) [81.Armando Farro (1/0)], René Alejandro Pontoni (6/11) [81.Juan José Ferraro (1/0)], Rinaldo Fioramonte Martino (8/6), Félix Loustau (3/2). Trainer: Guillermo Stábile (35).

**Goals**: René Alejandro Pontoni (10), Rinaldo Fioramonte Martino (43), Félix Loustau (70), Vicente De la Mata (75).

**230.** 31.01.1945 **ARGENTINA - ECUADOR** **4-2(1-0)** 18th Copa América

Estadio Nacional, Santiago (Chile); Referee: Nobel Valentini (Uruguay); Attendance: 60,000

**ARG:** Fernando Bello (11/0), José Salomón (Cap) (30/0), Roberto Justo De Zorzi (4/0), Carlos Adolfo Sosa (5/0), Ángel Perucca (14/2), Bartolomé Colombo (12/0), Mario Emilio Heriberto Boyé (1/0), Vicente De la Mata (8/5) [62.Norberto Doroteo Méndez (2/0)], René Alejandro Pontoni (7/12), Rinaldo Fioramonte Martino (9/7), Manuel Gregorio Pelegrina (4/1). Trainer: Guillermo Stábile (36).

**Goals**: René Alejandro Pontoni (11), Vicente De la Mata (50), Rinaldo Fioramonte Martino (69), Manuel Gregorio Pelegrina (83).

**231.** 07.02.1945 **ARGENTINA - COLOMBIA** **9-1(6-0)** 18th Copa América

Estadio Nacional, Santiago (Chile); Referee: Nobel Valentini (Uruguay); Attendance: 60,000

**ARG:** Héctor Ricardo (3/0), José Salomón (Cap) (31/0), Roberto Justo De Zorzi (5/0), Carlos Adolfo Sosa (6/0), Ángel Perucca (15/2), Bartolomé Colombo (13/0), Mario Emilio Heriberto Boyé (2/1), Norberto Doroteo Méndez (3/2), René Alejandro Pontoni (8/14) [77.Juan José Ferraro (2/2)], Rinaldo Fioramonte Martino (10/8) [76.Armando Farro (2/0)], Félix Loustau (4/3). Trainer: Guillermo Stábile (37).

**Goals**: René Alejandro Pontoni (3, 7), Norberto Doroteo Méndez (15), Rinaldo Fioramonte Martino (27), Norberto Doroteo Méndez (39), Mario Emilio Heriberto Boyé (41), Félix Loustau (50), Juan José Ferraro (80, 81).

**232.** 11.02.1945 **CHILE - ARGENTINA** **1-1(1-0)** 18th Copa América

Estadio Nacional, Santiago; Referee: Nobel Valentini (Uruguay); Attendance: 70,000

**ARG:** Héctor Ricardo (4/0), José Salomón (Cap) (32/0), Roberto Justo De Zorzi (6/0), Carlos Adolfo Sosa (7/0), Ángel Perucca (16/2), Bartolomé Colombo (14/0), Mario Emilio Heriberto Boyé (3/1) [46.Juan Carlos Muñoz (8/2)], Norberto Doroteo Méndez (4/3), René Alejandro Pontoni (9/14), Rinaldo Fioramonte Martino (11/8), Félix Loustau (5/3). Trainer: Guillermo Stábile (38).

**Goal**: Norberto Doroteo Méndez (67).

**233.** 15.02.1945 **ARGENTINA - BRAZIL** **3-1(3-1)** 18th Copa América

Estadio Nacional, Santiago (Chile); Referee: Nobel Valentini (Uruguay); Attendance: 65,000

**ARG:** Héctor Ricardo (5/0), José Salomón (Cap) (33/0), Roberto Justo De Zorzi (7/0) [30.Nicolás Palma (1/0)], Carlos Adolfo Sosa (8/0), Ángel Perucca (17/2), Bartolomé Colombo (15/0), Juan Carlos Muñoz (9/2), Norberto Doroteo Méndez (5/6) [67.Vicente De la Mata (9/5)], René Alejandro Pontoni (10/14), Rinaldo Fioramonte Martino (12/8) [68.Armando Farro (3/0)], Félix Loustau (6/3). Trainer: Guillermo Stábile (39).

**Goals**: Norberto Doroteo Méndez (14, 20, 40).

**234.** 25.02.1945 **ARGENTINA - URUGUAY** **1-0(0-0)** 18th Copa América

Estadio Nacional, Santiago (Chile); Referee: Juan Las Heras Marrodan (Chile); Attendance: 40,000

**ARG:** Héctor Ricardo (6/0), José Salomón (Cap) (34/0), Nicolás Palma (2/0), Carlos Adolfo Sosa (9/0), Ángel Perucca (18/2), Bartolomé Colombo (16/0), Juan Carlos Muñoz (10/2) [77.Mario Emilio Heriberto Boyé (4/1)], Norberto Doroteo Méndez (6/6), Juan José Ferraro (3/2), Rinaldo Fioramonte Martino (13/9), Félix Loustau (7/3). Trainer: Guillermo Stábile (40).

**Goal**: Rinaldo Fioramonte Martino (50).

**235.** 07.07.1945 **PARAGUAY - ARGENTINA** **5-1(4-0)** Copa Chevallier Boutell
Estadio Defensores del Chaco, Asunción; Referee: Marcos Rojas (Paraguay); Attendance: 17,000
**ARG:** Héctor Ricardo (7/0), José Salomón (Cap) (35/0), Nicolás Palma (3/0), Enrique Espinosa (4/0), Oscar Carlos Sastre (2/0), Bartolomé Colombo (17/0), Juan Carlos Salvini (1/0), Norberto Doroteo Méndez (7/6) [65.Vicente De la Mata (10/5)], René Alejandro Pontoni (11/15) [65.Juan José Ferraro (4/2)], Rinaldo Fioramonte Martino (14/9) [65.Ángel Amadeo Labruna (2/0)], Félix Loustau (8/3). Trainer: Guillermo Stábile (41).
**Goal**: René Alejandro Pontoni (50).

**236.** 09.07.1945 **PARAGUAY - ARGENTINA** **1-3(1-2)** Copa Chevallier Boutell
Estadio Defensores del Chaco, Asunción; Referee: Marcos Rojas (Paraguay); Attendance: 15,000
**ARG:** Gabriel Mario Ogando (1/0), José Manuel Marante (1/0), Jorge Alberti (Cap) (20/1), Juan Carlos Fonda (1/0), León Strembel (1/0), José Pedro Batagliero (7/0), Juan Carlos Muñoz (11/2) [55.Juan Carlos Salvini (2/0)], Norberto Doroteo Méndez (8/7), Juan José Ferraro (5/2), Rinaldo Fioramonte Martino (15/10) [55.Ángel Amadeo Labruna (3/0)], Ezra Sued (1/1). Trainer: Guillermo Stábile (42).
**Goals**: Norberto Doroteo Méndez (37), Ezra Sued (40), Rinaldo Fioramonte Martino (49).

**237.** 18.07.1945 **URUGUAY - ARGENTINA** **2-2(0-2)** Copa Lipton
Estadio Centenario, Montevideo; Referee: Juan Carlos Armental (Uruguay); Attendance: 40,000
**ARG:** Gabriel Mario Ogando (2/0), José Salomón (Cap) (36/0), Nicolás Palma (4/0) [31.Jorge Alberti (21/1)], Juan Carlos Fonda (2/0), León Strembel (2/0), José Pedro Batagliero (8/0), Juan Carlos Salvini (3/0), Norberto Doroteo Méndez (9/7), Juan José Ferraro (6/2), Rinaldo Fioramonte Martino (16/11) [46.Ángel Amadeo Labruna (4/0)], Ezra Sued (2/1). Trainer: Guillermo Stábile (43).
**Goals**: Rinaldo Fioramonte Martino (6), Alfredo Young (16 own goal).

**238.** 15.08.1945 **ARGENTINA - URUGUAY** **6-2(4-1)** Copa Newton
Estadio Gasómetro de Boedo, Buenos Aires; Referee: Eduardo Forte (Argentina); Attendance: 55,000
**ARG:** Gabriel Mario Ogando (3/0), José Salomón (Cap) (37/0) [46.José Manuel Marante (2/0)], Eduardo Enrique Rodríguez (3/0) [46.Jorge Alberti (22/1)], Juan Carlos Fonda (3/0), León Strembel (3/0), José Ramos (7/0), Juan Carlos Salvini (4/0), Norberto Doroteo Méndez (10/8), Juan José Ferraro (7/3) [67.Adolfo Alfredo Pedernera (14/3)], Rinaldo Fioramonte Martino (17/13), Félix Loustau (9/4). Trainer: Guillermo Stábile (44).
**Goals**: Félix Loustau (7), Juan José Ferraro (12), Norberto Doroteo Méndez (36), Rinaldo Fioramonte Martino (43, 57), Adolfo Alfredo Pedernera (85).

**239.** 16.12.1945 **BRAZIL - ARGENTINA** **3-4(2-2)** Copa Roca
Estádio Pacaembú, São Paulo; Referee: Mário Gonçalves Vianna (Brazil); Attendance: 59,613
**ARG:** Claudio Vacca (1/0), José Salomón (Cap) (38/0), Juan Carlos Sobrero (4/0), Carlos Adolfo Sosa (10/0) [40.Juan Carlos Fonda (4/0)], Ángel Perucca (19/2), José Ramos (8/0), Norberto Doroteo Méndez (11/8) [80.Juan Carlos Salvini (5/0)], Mario Emilio Heriberto Boyé (5/2), Adolfo Alfredo Pedernera (15/4), Ángel Amadeo Labruna (5/1), Ezra Sued (3/2). Trainer: Guillermo Stábile (45).
**Goals**: Adolfo Alfredo Pedernera (14), Mario Emilio Heriberto Boyé (39), Ezra Sued (62), Ángel Amadeo Labruna (73).

**240.** 20.12.1945 **BRAZIL - ARGENTINA** **6-2(2-1)** Copa Roca
Estádio São Januario, Rio de Janeiro; Referee: Mário Gonçalves Vianna (Brazil); Attendance: 70,000
**ARG:** Claudio Vacca (2/0), José Manuel Marante (3/0), Juan Carlos Sobrero (5/0), Carlos Adolfo Sosa (11/0) [70.Juan Carlos Fonda (5/0)], Ángel Perucca (20/2), José Ramos (9/0) [70.José Pedro Batagliero (9/0)], René Alejandro Pontoni (12/15), Mario Emilio Heriberto Boyé (6/2), Adolfo Alfredo Pedernera (16/5), Rinaldo Fioramonte Martino (18/14) [70.Ángel Amadeo Labruna (6/1)], Ezra Sued (4/2). Trainer: Guillermo Stábile (46).
**Goals**: Adolfo Alfredo Pedernera (30 penalty), Rinaldo Fioramonte Martino (46).

**241.** 23.12.1945 **BRAZIL - ARGENTINA** **3-1(0-0)** Copa Roca
Estádio São Januario, Rio de Janeiro; Referee: Mário Gonçalves Vianna (Brazil); Attendance: 70,000
**ARG:** Gabriel Mario Ogando (4/0), José Salomón (Cap) (39/0), Jorge Alberti (23/1), Juan Carlos Fonda (6/0), León Strembel (4/0) [24.Ángel Perucca (21/2)], José Pedro Batagliero (10/0) [43.José Ramos (10/0)], Juan Carlos Salvini (6/0), Adolfo Alfredo Pedernera (17/5) [63.René Alejandro Pontoni (13/15)], Rinaldo Fioramonte Martino (19/15), Ángel Amadeo Labruna (7/1), Ezra Sued (5/2). Trainer: Guillermo Stábile (47).
**Goal**: Rinaldo Fioramonte Martino (64).

**242.** 12.01.1946 **ARGENTINA - PARAGUAY** **2-0(2-0)** 19th Copa América
Estadio Monumental „Antonio Vespucio Liberti", Buenos Aires; Referee: Mário Gonçalves Vianna (Brazil); Attendance: 70,000
**ARG:** Claudio Vacca (3/0), José Salomón (Cap) (40/0) [57.José Manuel Marante (4/0)], Juan Carlos Sobrero (6/0), Carlos Adolfo Sosa (12/0), León Strembel (5/0), José Ramos (11/0), Mario Emilio Heriberto Boyé (7/2) [*sent off 40*], Vicente De la Mata (11/6) [69.Norberto Doroteo Méndez (12/8)], René Alejandro Pontoni (14/15), Rinaldo Fioramonte Martino (20/16), Félix Loustau (10/4). Trainer: Guillermo Stábile (48).
**Goals**: Vicente De la Mata (6), Rinaldo Fioramonte Martino (43).

**243.** 19.01.1946 **ARGENTINA - BOLIVIA** **7-1(2-0)** 19th Copa América
Estadio Gasómetro de Boedo, Buenos Aires; Referee: Higinio Madrid (Chile); Attendance: 65,000
**ARG:** Claudio Vacca (4/0), José Salomón (Cap) (41/0), Juan Carlos Sobrero (7/0), Juan Carlos Fonda (7/0), León Strembel (6/0), Natalio Agustín Pescia (1/0), Juan Carlos Salvini (7/2), Norberto Doroteo Méndez (13/10), Adolfo Alfredo Pedernera (18/5), Ángel Amadeo Labruna (8/3), Félix Loustau (11/5). Trainer: Guillermo Stábile (49).
**Goals**: Ángel Amadeo Labruna (34), Norberto Doroteo Méndez (39, 60), Juan Carlos Salvini (75), Félix Loustau (79), Juan Carlos Salvini (84), Ángel Amadeo Labruna (89).

**244.** 26.01.1946 **ARGENTINA - CHILE** **3-1(1-0)** 19th Copa América
Estadio Monumental „Antonio Vespucio Liberti", Buenos Aires; Referee: Nobel Valentini (Uruguay); Attendance: 80,000
**ARG:** Claudio Vacca (5/0), José Salomón (Cap) (42/0), Juan Carlos Sobrero (8/0), Juan Carlos Fonda (8/0), León Strembel (7/0), Natalio Agustín Pescia (2/0), Juan Carlos Salvini (8/2) [12.René Alejandro Pontoni (15/15)], Norberto Doroteo Méndez (14/10), Adolfo Alfredo Pedernera (19/6), Ángel Amadeo Labruna (9/5), Félix Loustau (12/5). Trainer: Guillermo Stábile (50).
**Goals**: Ángel Amadeo Labruna (39, 60), Adolfo Alfredo Pedernera (65).

**245.** 02.02.1946 **ARGENTINA - URUGUAY** **3-1(1-0)** 19th Copa América
Estadio Gasómetro de Boedo, Buenos Aires; Referee: Mário Gonçalves Vianna (Brazil); Attendance: 80,000
**ARG:** Claudio Vacca (6/0), José Salomón (Cap) (43/0), Juan Carlos Sobrero (9/0), Juan Carlos Fonda (9/0) [65.Carlos Adolfo Sosa (13/0)], León Strembel (8/0), Natalio Agustín Pescia (3/0), Vicente De la Mata (12/6), Norberto Doroteo Méndez (15/11), Adolfo Alfredo Pedernera (20/7), Ángel Amadeo Labruna (10/6), Félix Loustau (13/5). Trainer: Guillermo Stábile (51).
**Goals**: Adolfo Alfredo Pedernera (32), Ángel Amadeo Labruna (46), Norberto Doroteo Méndez (72).

**246.** 10.02.1946 **ARGENTINA - BRAZIL** **2-0(1-0)*** 19th Copa América
Estadio Monumental „Antonio Vespucio Liberti", Buenos Aires; Referee: Nobel Valentini (Uruguay); Attendance: 80,000
**ARG:** Claudio Vacca (7/0), José Salomón (Cap) (44/0) [30.José Manuel Marante (5/0)], Juan Carlos Sobrero (10/0), Juan Carlos Fonda (10/0), León Strembel (9/0) [30.Saúl Ongaro (1/0)], Natalio Agustín Pescia (4/0), Vicente De la Mata (13/6) [*sent off 30*], Norberto Doroteo Méndez (16/13), Adolfo Alfredo Pedernera (21/7), Ángel Amadeo Labruna (11/6), Félix Loustau (14/5). Trainer: Guillermo Stábile (52).
**Goals**: Norberto Doroteo Méndez (38, 55).
**The match was suspended for 70 minutes after the 30th minute.*

**247.** 02.12.1947 **ARGENTINA - PARAGUAY** **6-0(3-0)** 20th Copa América
Estadio „George Capwell", Guayaquil (Ecuador); Referee: Francisco Víctor Rivas (Chile); Attendance: 20,000
**ARG:** Julio Adolfo Cozzi (1/0), José Manuel Marante (Cap) (6/0) [42.Juan Carlos Colman (1/0)], Juan Carlos Sobrero (11/0), Norberto Antonio Yácono (6/0), Ángel Perucca (22/2), Natalio Agustín Pescia (5/0), Mario Emilio Heriberto Boyé (8/2), Norberto Doroteo Méndez (17/14), René Alejandro Pontoni (16/18), José Manuel Moreno (27/17), Félix Loustau (15/6). Trainer: Guillermo Stábile (53).
**Goals**: José Manuel Moreno (10), Félix Loustau (22), René Alejandro Pontoni (40, 50, 82), Norberto Doroteo Méndez (87).

**248.** 04.12.1947 **ARGENTINA - BOLIVIA** **7-0(3-0)** 20th Copa América
Estadio „George Capwell", Guayaquil (Ecuador); Referee: Federico Muñoz Medina (Ecuador); Attendance: 30,000
**ARG:** Julio Adolfo Cozzi (2/0), Juan Carlos Colman (2/0), Nicolás Palma (5/0), Norberto Antonio Yácono (7/0) [63.Oscar Carlos Sastre (3/0)], Ángel Perucca (23/2) (Cap) [76.Néstor Raúl Rossi (1/0)], Natalio Agustín Pescia (6/0), Mario Emilio Heriberto Boyé (9/4), Norberto Doroteo Méndez (18/16), René Alejandro Pontoni (17/19) [30.Alfredo Di Stéfano (1/1)], José Manuel Moreno (28/17), Félix Loustau (16/7). Trainer: Guillermo Stábile (54).
**Goals**: Norberto Doroteo Méndez (3), René Alejandro Pontoni (22), Norberto Doroteo Méndez (44), Félix Loustau (56), Mario Emilio Heriberto Boyé (58), Alfredo Di Stéfano (62), Mario Emilio Heriberto Boyé (76).

**249.** 11.12.1947 **ARGENTINA - PERU** **3-2(1-1)** 20th Copa América
Estadio „George Capwell", Guayaquil (Ecuador); Referee: Luis Alberto Fernández (Uruguay); Attendance: 22,000
**ARG:** Julio Adolfo Cozzi (3/0), Juan Carlos Colman (3/0), Juan Carlos Sobrero (12/0), Norberto Antonio Yácono (8/0), Ángel Perucca (Cap) (24/2), Natalio Agustín Pescia (7/0), Mario Emilio Heriberto Boyé (10/5), Norberto Doroteo Méndez (19/16), Alfredo Di Stéfano (2/2), José Manuel Moreno (29/18), Félix Loustau (17/7). Trainer: Guillermo Stábile (55).
**Goals**: José Manuel Moreno (41), Alfredo Di Stéfano (55), Mario Emilio Heriberto Boyé (56).

**250.** 16.12.1947 **ARGENTINA - CHILE** **1-1(1-1)** 20th Copa América
Estadio „George Capwell", Guayaquil (Ecuador); Referee: Luis Alberto Fernández (Uruguay); Attendance: 30,000
**ARG:** Julio Adolfo Cozzi (4/0), José Manuel Marante (7/0) [76.Juan Carlos Colman (4/0)], Juan Carlos Sobrero (13/0), Norberto Antonio Yácono (9/0), Ángel Perucca (Cap) (25/2) [65.Néstor Raúl Rossi (2/0)], Natalio Agustín Pescia (8/0), Mario Emilio Heriberto Boyé (11/5), Norberto Doroteo Méndez (20/16), Alfredo Di Stéfano (3/3), José Manuel Moreno (30/18) [56.Mario Fernández (1/0)], Félix Loustau (18/7). Trainer: Guillermo Stábile (56).
**Goal**: Alfredo Di Stéfano (12).

**251.** 18.12.1947 **ARGENTINA - COLOMBIA** **6-0(3-0)** 20th Copa América
Estadio „George Capwell", Guayaquil (Ecuador); Referee: Alfredo Alvarez Fernández (Bolivia); Attendance: 12,000
**ARG:** Julio Adolfo Cozzi (5/0), Juan Carlos Colman (5/0), Nicolás Palma (6/0) [42.Juan Carlos Sobrero (14/0)], Oscar Carlos Sastre (4/0), Néstor Raúl Rossi (Cap) (3/0), Ernesto Gutiérrez (1/0), Mario Emilio Heriberto Boyé (12/6) [67.Camilo Rodolfo Cerviño (1/0)], Norberto Doroteo Méndez (21/16), Alfredo Di Stéfano (4/6), Mario Fernández (2/1) [46.Francisco Campana (1/0)], Félix Loustau (19/8). Trainer: Guillermo Stábile (57).
**Goals**: Mario Fernández (7), Alfredo Di Stéfano (30), Mario Emilio Heriberto Boyé (38), Félix Loustau (55), Alfredo Di Stéfano (62, 75).

**252.** 25.12.1947 **ECUADOR - ARGENTINA** **0-2(0-1)** 20th Copa América
Estadio „George Capwell", Guayaquil; Referee: Alfredo Alvarez Fernández (Bolivia) after 35 mins Mario Rubén Heyen (Paraguay); Attendance: 25,000
**ARG:** Obdulio Diano (1/0), José Manuel Marante (8/0), Juan Carlos Sobrero (15/0), Norberto Antonio Yácono (10/0), Ángel Perucca (Cap) (26/2) [46.Néstor Raúl Rossi (4/0)], Natalio Agustín Pescia (9/0), Mario Emilio Heriberto Boyé (13/6), Norberto Doroteo Méndez (22/17), Alfredo Di Stéfano (5/6) [65.René Alejandro Pontoni (18/19)], José Manuel Moreno (31/19), Félix Loustau (20/8). Trainer: Guillermo Stábile (58).
**Goals**: José Manuel Moreno (30), Norberto Doroteo Méndez (72).

**253.** 28.12.1947 **ARGENTINA - URUGUAY** **3-1(1-0)** 20th Copa América
Estadio „George Capwell", Guayaquil (Ecuador); Referee: Mario Rubén Heyen (Paraguay); Attendance: 25,000
**ARG:** Julio Adolfo Cozzi (6/0), José Manuel Marante (9/0), Juan Carlos Sobrero (16/0), Norberto Antonio Yácono (11/0), Néstor Raúl Rossi (Cap) (5/0), Natalio Agustín Pescia (10/0), Mario Emilio Heriberto Boyé (14/6), Norberto Doroteo Méndez (23/19) [86.Mario Fernández (3/1)], René Alejandro Pontoni (19/19) [69.Alfredo Di Stéfano (6/6)], José Manuel Moreno (32/19), Félix Loustau (21/9) [86.Ezra Sued (6/2)]. Trainer: Guillermo Stábile (59).
**Goals**: Norberto Doroteo Méndez (30, 46), Félix Loustau (85).

**254.** 25.03.1950 **ARGENTINA - PARAGUAY** **2-2** Copa Chevallier Boutell
Estadio Monumental „Antonio Vespucio Liberti", Buenos Aires; Referee: Bertley Cross (England); Attendance: 60,000
**ARG:** Miguel Ángel Rugilo (1/0), Juan Carlos Colman (6/0), Juan Manuel Filgueiras (1/0), Norberto Antonio Yácono (12/0) [46.Walter Garcerón (1/0)], César Héctor Castagno (1/0) [85.Luis Villa (1/0)], Ernesto Gutiérrez (2/0), Julio Carlos Santiago Vernazza (1/1), Norberto Doroteo Méndez (24/19) [46.José Manuel Moreno (33/19)], Rubén Norberto Bravo (Cap) (1/1) [85.Gabriel Uñate (1/0)], Ángel Amadeo Labruna (12/6), Félix Loustau (22/9). Trainer: Guillermo Stábile (60).
**Goals**: Rubén Norberto Bravo (54), Julio Carlos Santiago Vernazza (64).

**255.** 29.03.1950 **ARGENTINA - PARAGUAY** **4-0(1-0)** Copa Chevallier Boutell
Estadio Gasómetro de Boedo, Buenos Aires; Referee: Harry Artles (England); Attendance: 65,000
**ARG:** Miguel Ángel Rugilo (2/0), Juan Carlos Colman (7/0) [72.Higinio García (1/0)], Juan Manuel Filgueiras (2/0), Norberto Antonio Yácono (13/0) [60.Walter Garcerón (2/0)], César Héctor Castagno (2/0), Ernesto Gutiérrez (3/0), Julio Carlos Santiago Vernazza (2/1), Norberto Doroteo Méndez (25/19) [61.José Manuel Moreno (34/19)], Rubén Norberto Bravo (Cap) (2/1) [46.Gabriel Uñate (2/2)], Ángel Amadeo Labruna (13/8), Félix Loustau (23/9). Trainer: Guillermo Stábile (61).
**Goals**: Ángel Amadeo Labruna (14), Gabriel Uñate (67, 71), Ángel Amadeo Labruna (86).

**256.** 09.05.1951 **ENGLAND - ARGENTINA** **2-1(0-1)**
Wembley Stadium, London; Referee: Benjamin Merwyn Griffiths (Wales); Attendance: 100,000
**ARG:** Miguel Ángel Rugilo (3/0), Juan Carlos Colman (8/0) [36.Ángel Natalio Allegri (1/0)], Juan Manuel Filgueiras (3/0), Norberto Antonio Yácono (Cap) (14/0), Ubaldo Faina (1/0), Natalio Agustín Pescia (11/0), Mario Emilio Heriberto Boyé (15/7), Norberto Doroteo Méndez (26/19), Rubén Norberto Bravo (3/1), Ángel Amadeo Labruna (14/8), Félix Loustau (24/9). Trainer: Guillermo Stábile (62).
**Goal**: Mario Emilio Heriberto Boyé (18).

**257.** 13.05.1951 **REPUBLIC OF IRELAND– ARGENTINA** **0-1(0-0)**
Dalymount Park, Dublin; Referee: Reginald Leafe (England); Attendance: 42,000
**ARG:** Miguel Ángel Rugilo (4/0), Ángel Natalio Allegri (2/0), Juan Manuel Filgueiras (4/0) [39.José M. García Pérez (1/0)], Norberto Antonio Yácono (Cap) (15/0), Ubaldo Faina (2/0), Ernesto Gutiérrez (4/0), Mario Emilio Heriberto Boyé (16/7), Norberto Doroteo Méndez (27/19), Juan Armando Benavídez Rodríguez (1/0), Ángel Amadeo Labruna (15/9), Félix Loustau (25/9). Trainer: Guillermo Stábile (63).
**Goal**: Ángel Amadeo Labruna (53).

**258.** 07.12.1952 **SPAIN - ARGENTINA** **0-1(0-0)**
Estadio Chamartín, Madrid; Referee: Arthur Edward Ellis (England); Attendance: 100,000
**ARG:** Gabriel Mario Ogando (5/0) [53.Julio Elías Musimessi (1/0)], Ángel Natalio Allegri (Cap) (3/0), José M. García Pérez (2/0), Juan Francisco Lombardo (1/0), Eliseo Víctor Mouriño (1/0), Ernesto Gutiérrez (5/0), Mario Emilio Heriberto Boyé (17/7), Norberto Doroteo Méndez (28/19), Ricardo Raymundo Infante (1/1), Ángel Amadeo Labruna (16/9) [46.Ernesto Grillo (1/0)], Félix Loustau (26/9). Trainer: Guillermo Stábile (64).
**Goal**: Ricardo Raymundo Infante (58).

**259.** 14.12.1952 **PORTUGAL - ARGENTINA** **1-3(0-3)**
Estádio Nacional, Lisboa; Referee: William Ling (England); Attendance: 70,000
**ARG:** Julio Elías Musimessi (2/0), Ángel Natalio Allegri (Cap) (4/0) [46.Osvaldo Ferretti (1/0)], José M. García Pérez (3/0), Juan Francisco Lombardo (2/0), Eliseo Víctor Mouriño (2/0), Ernesto Gutiérrez (6/0), Julio Carlos Santiago Vernazza (3/1), Norberto Doroteo Méndez (29/19) [67.Ernesto Grillo (2/0)], Ricardo Raymundo Infante (2/1), Ángel Amadeo Labruna (17/11), Félix Loustau (27/10). Trainer: Guillermo Stábile (65).
**Goals**: Félix Loustau (10), Ángel Amadeo Labruna (36, 38).

**260.** 14.05.1953 **ARGENTINA - ENGLAND** **3-1(1-1)**
Estadio Monumental „Antonio Vespucio Liberti", Buenos Aires; Referee: Arthur Edward Ellis (England); Attendance: 85,483
**ARG:** Julio Elías Musimessi (3/0), Pedro Rodolfo Dellacha (1/0), José M. García Pérez (4/0), Juan Francisco Lombardo (3/0), Eliseo Víctor Mouriño (Cap) (3/0), Ernesto Gutiérrez (7/0), Rodolfo Joaquín Micheli (1/1), Carlos José Cecconato (1/0) [43.Norberto Doroteo Méndez (30/19)], Carlos Lacasia (1/0), Ernesto Grillo (3/2), Osvaldo Héctor Cruz (1/0). Trainer: Guillermo Stábile (66).
**Goals**: Ernesto Grillo (42), Rodolfo Joaquín Micheli (57), Ernesto Grillo (78).

**261.** 17.05.1953 **ARGENTINA - ENGLAND** **0-0***
Estadio Monumental „Antonio Vespucio Liberti", Buenos Aires; Referee: Arthur Edward Ellis (England); Attendance: 91,000
**ARG:** Julio Elías Musimessi (4/0), Pedro Rodolfo Dellacha (2/0), José M. García Pérez (5/0), Juan Francisco Lombardo (4/0), Eliseo Víctor Mouriño (Cap) (4/0), Ernesto Gutiérrez (8/0), Rodolfo Joaquín Micheli (2/1), Carlos José Cecconato (2/0), Carlos Lacasia (2/0), Ernesto Grillo (4/2), Osvaldo Héctor Cruz (2/0). Trainer: Guillermo Stábile (67).
**Abandoned after 21 mins due to waterlogged pitch.*

**262.** 05.07.1953 **ARGENTINA - SPAIN** **1-0(0-0)**
Estadio Monumental „Antonio Vespucio Liberti", Buenos Aires; Referee: Archer W. Luty (England); Attendance: 88,787
**ARG:** Julio Elías Musimessi (5/0), Pedro Rodolfo Dellacha (3/0), José M. García Pérez (6/0), Juan Francisco Lombardo (5/0), Eliseo Víctor Mouriño (Cap) (5/0), Ernesto Gutiérrez (9/0), Rodolfo Joaquín Micheli (3/1), Carlos José Cecconato (3/0), Carlos Lacasia (3/0), Ernesto Grillo (5/3), Osvaldo Héctor Cruz (3/0). Trainer: Guillermo Stábile (68).
**Goal**: Ernesto Grillo (86).

**263.** 28.11.1954 **PORTUGAL - ARGENTINA** **1-3(0-1)**
Estádio Nacional, Lisboa; Referee: Archer W. Luty (England); Attendance: 50,000
**ARG:** Amadeo Raúl Carrizo (1/0) [80.Roque Saverio Marrapodi (1/0)], Pedro Rodolfo Dellacha (4/0), Federico Pizarro (1/0), Juan Francisco Lombardo (6/0), Eliseo Víctor Mouriño (Cap) (6/0), Natalio Agustín Pescia (12/0), Rodolfo Joaquín Micheli (4/2), Carlos José Cecconato (4/0), Ricardo Bonelli (1/0) [80.José Borrello (1/0)], Ernesto Grillo (6/4), Osvaldo Héctor Cruz (4/1). Trainer: Guillermo Stábile (69).
**Goals**: Rodolfo Joaquín Micheli (16), Ernesto Grillo (70), Osvaldo Héctor Cruz (75).

**264.** 05.12.1954 **ITALY - ARGENTINA** **2-0(1-0)**
Stadio Olimpico, Roma; Referee: Erich Steiner (Austria); Attendance: 80,000
**ARG:** Amadeo Raúl Carrizo (2/0) [46.Roque Saverio Marrapodi (2/0)], Pedro Rodolfo Dellacha (5/0), Federico Pizarro (2/0), Juan Francisco Lombardo (7/0), Eliseo Víctor Mouriño (Cap) (7/0), Ernesto Gutiérrez (10/0), Julio Carlos Santiago Vernazza (4/1), Eliseo Prado (1/0), Ricardo Bonelli (2/0) [61.José Borrello (2/0)], Ernesto Grillo (7/4), Osvaldo Héctor Cruz (5/1). Trainer: Guillermo Stábile (70).

**265.** 02.03.1955 **ARGENTINA - PARAGUAY** **5-3(2-1)** 23rd Copa América
Estadio Nacional, Santiago; Referee: Juan Carlos Robles (Chile); Attendance: 35,000
**ARG:** Julio Elías Musimessi (6/0), Pedro Rodolfo Dellacha (6/0), Federico Vairo (1/0), Juan Francisco Lombardo (8/0), Eliseo Víctor Mouriño (Cap) (8/0), Ernesto Gutiérrez (11/0), Rodolfo Joaquín Micheli (5/6), Carlos José Cecconato (5/0), Ricardo Bonelli (3/0) [68.José Borrello (3/1)], Ernesto Grillo (8/4) [60.Ángel Amadeo Labruna (18/11)], Osvaldo Héctor Cruz (6/1). Trainer: Guillermo Stábile (71).
**Goals**: Rodolfo Joaquín Micheli (5, 18 penalty, 64), José Borrello (74), Rodolfo Joaquín Micheli (83).

**266.** 09.03.1955 **ARGENTINA - ECUADOR** **4-0(3-0)** 23rd Copa América
Estadio Nacional, Santiago; Referee: Juan Carlos Robles (Chile); Attendance: 40,000
**ARG:** Julio Elías Musimessi (7/0), Pedro Rodolfo Dellacha (7/0) [71.Juan Carlos Colman (9/0)], Federico Vairo (2/0), Juan Francisco Lombardo (9/0), Eliseo Víctor Mouriño (Cap) (9/0), Ernesto Gutiérrez (12/0), Rodolfo Joaquín Micheli (6/7), Carlos José Cecconato (6/0), Ricardo Bonelli (4/1) [65.José Borrello (4/2) [*sent off 88*]], Ernesto Grillo (9/5) [65.Ángel Amadeo Labruna (19/11)], Osvaldo Héctor Cruz (7/1). Trainer: Guillermo Stábile (72).
**Goals**: Ricardo Bonelli (11), Ernesto Grillo (24), Rodolfo Joaquín Micheli (28), José Borrello (71).

**267.** 16.03.1955 **ARGENTINA - PERU** **2-2(2-1)** 23rd Copa América
Estadio Nacional, Santiago; Referee: Washington Rodríguez (Uruguay); Attendance: 23,000
**ARG:** Julio Elías Musimessi (8/0), Juan Carlos Colman (10/0), Luis Ángel Bagnatto (1/0), Juan Francisco Lombardo (10/0), Eliseo Víctor Mouriño (Cap) (10/0), Gilberto Pascasio Sola (1/0) [73.Ernesto Gutiérrez (13/0)], Rodolfo Joaquín Micheli (7/7), Carlos José Cecconato (7/1), Ricardo Bonelli (5/1) [80.José Borrello (5/2)], Ernesto Grillo (10/6) [73.Ángel Amadeo Labruna (20/11)], Osvaldo Héctor Cruz (8/1). Trainer: Guillermo Stábile (73).
**Goals**: Ernesto Grillo (7), Carlos José Cecconato (41).

**268.** 27.03.1955 **ARGENTINA - URUGUAY** **6-1(2-1)** 23rd Copa América
Estadio Nacional, Santiago; Referee: Juan Carlos Robles (Chile); Attendance: 35,000
**ARG:** Julio Elías Musimessi (9/0), Pedro Rodolfo Dellacha (8/0), Federico Vairo (3/0), Juan Francisco Lombardo (11/0), Arnaldo Balay (1/0), Ernesto Gutiérrez (14/0), Rodolfo Joaquín Micheli (8/9) [79.Julio Carlos Santiago Vernazza (5/1)], Carlos José Cecconato (8/1), José Borrello (6/3), Ángel Amadeo Labruna (Cap) (21/14) [79.Norberto Conde (1/0)], Ernesto Bernardo Cucchiaroni (1/0). Trainer: Guillermo Stábile (74).
**Goals**: Rodolfo Joaquín Micheli (37), Ángel Amadeo Labruna (39), Rodolfo Joaquín Micheli (61), Ángel Amadeo Labruna (71), José Borrello (76), Ángel Amadeo Labruna (77).

**269.** 30.03.1955 **CHILE - ARGENTINA** **0-1(0-0)** 23rd Copa América
Estadio Nacional, Santiago; Referee: Washington Rodríguez (Uruguay); Attendance: 65,000
**ARG:** Julio Elías Musimessi (10/0), Pedro Rodolfo Dellacha (9/0), Federico Vairo (4/0), Juan Francisco Lombardo (12/0), Arnaldo Balay (2/0), Ernesto Gutiérrez (15/0), Rodolfo Joaquín Micheli (9/10) [82.Julio Carlos Santiago Vernazza (6/1)], Carlos José Cecconato (9/1), José Borrello (7/3), Ángel Amadeo Labruna (Cap) (22/14), Ernesto Bernardo Cucchiaroni (2/0). Trainer: Guillermo Stábile (75).
**Goal**: Rodolfo Joaquín Micheli (59).

**270.** 22.01.1956 **ARGENTINA - PERU** **2-1(1-0)** 24th Copa América
Estadio Centenario, Montevideo; Referee: Washington Rodríguez (Uruguay); Attendance: 16,000
**ARG:** Julio Elías Musimessi (11/0), Pedro Rodolfo Dellacha (10/0), Federico Vairo (5/1), Juan Francisco Lombardo (13/0), Eliseo Víctor Mouriño (Cap) (11/0), Ernesto Gutiérrez (16/0), Rodolfo Joaquín Micheli (10/10) [83.Luis Pentrelli (1/0)], Enrique Omar Sívori (1/1), Ricardo Bonelli (6/1) [78.Francisco Ramón Loiácono (1/0)], Ángel Amadeo Labruna (23/14), Ernesto Bernardo Cucchiaroni (3/0). Trainer: Guillermo Stábile (76).
**Goals**: Enrique Omar Sívori (43), Federico Vairo (51).

**271.** 29.01.1956 **ARGENTINA - CHILE** **2-0(1-0)** 24th Copa América
Estadio Centenario, Montevideo; Referee: João Baptista Laurito (Brazil); Attendance: 45,000
**ARG:** Julio Elías Musimessi (12/0), Juan Carlos Colman (11/0), Federico Vairo (6/1), Juan Francisco Lombardo (14/0), José Varacka (1/0) [46.Eliseo Víctor Mouriño (12/0)], Ernesto Gutiérrez (17/0), Rodolfo Joaquín Micheli (11/10), Enrique Omar Sívori (2/1) [65.Carlos José Cecconato (10/1)], Francisco Ramón Loiácono (2/0) [46.Ricardo Bonelli (7/1)], Ángel Amadeo Labruna (Cap) (24/16), Ernesto Bernardo Cucchiaroni (4/0) [*sent off 75*]. Trainer: Guillermo Stábile (77).
**Goals**: Ángel Amadeo Labruna (9, 79).

**272.** 01.02.1956 **ARGENTINA – PARAGUAY** **1-0(0-0)** 24th Copa América
Estadio Centenario, Montevideo; Referee: João Baptista Laurito (Brazil); Attendance: 20,000
**ARG:** Julio Elías Musimessi (13/0), Juan Carlos Colman (12/0), Federico Vairo (7/1), Juan Francisco Lombardo (15/0), Eliseo Víctor Mouriño (Cap) (13/0), Ernesto Gutiérrez (18/0), Rodolfo Joaquín Micheli (12/10) [46.Luis Pentrelli (2/0)], Carlos José Cecconato (11/2) [75.Ernesto Grillo (11/6)], Ricardo Bonelli (8/1), Ángel Amadeo Labruna (25/16), Ernesto Bernardo Cucchiaroni (5/0). Trainer: Guillermo Stábile (78).
**Goal**: Carlos José Cecconato (54).

**273.** 05.02.1956 **BRAZIL - ARGENTINA** **1-0(0-0)** 24th Copa América
Estadio Centenario, Montevideo; Referee: Washington Rodríguez (Uruguay); Attendance: 20,000
**ARG:** Julio Elías Musimessi (14/0), Juan Carlos Colman (13/0) [42.José M. García Pérez (7/0)], Federico Vairo (8/1), Juan Francisco Lombardo (16/0), Eliseo Víctor Mouriño (Cap) (14/0), Ernesto Gutiérrez (19/0), Luis Pentrelli (3/0), Carlos José Cecconato (12/2), Ernesto Grillo (12/6), Ángel Amadeo Labruna (26/16) [79.Enrique Omar Sívori (3/1)], Ernesto Bernardo Cucchiaroni (6/0). Trainer: Guillermo Stábile (79).

**274.** 15.02.1956 **URUGUAY - ARGENTINA** **1-0(1-0)** 24th Copa América
Estadio Centenario, Montevideo; Referee: Cayetano de Nicola (Paraguay); Attendance: 80,000
**ARG:** Julio Elías Musimessi (15/0), Pedro Rodolfo Dellacha (11/0), Federico Vairo (9/1), Juan Francisco Lombardo (17/0), Eliseo Víctor Mouriño (Cap) (15/0), Ernesto Gutiérrez (20/0), Luis Pentrelli (4/0), Enrique Omar Sívori (4/1), Ernesto Grillo (13/6), Ángel Amadeo Labruna (27/16), Roberto Héctor Zárate (1/0). Trainer: Guillermo Stábile (80).

**275.** 28.02.1956 **ARGENTINA - PERU** **0-0** Campeonato Panamericano
Estadio Olímpico de Centro Universitário, Ciudad de México (Mexico); Referee: Alberto Monard de Gama Malcher (Brazil); Attendance: 60,000
**ARG:** Rogelio Antonio Domínguez (1/0), Juan Manuel Filgueiras (5/0), Federico Vairo (10/1), Nicolás Daponte (1/0), Héctor Juan Guidi (Cap) (1/0), Natalio Sivo (1/0) [25.Ernesto Gutiérrez (21/0)], Oreste Osmar Corbatta (1/0), Humberto Dionisio Maschio (1/0) [67.Francisco Ramón Loiácono (3/0)], Benito Cejas (1/0) [*sent off 19*], Dante Homérico Lugo González (1/0) [28.Enrique Omar Sívori (5/1)], José Yudica (1/0). Trainer: Guillermo Stábile (81).

**276.** 06.03.1956 **ARGENTINA – COSTA RICA** **4-3(1-2)** Campeonato Panamericano
Estadio Olímpico de Centro Universitário, Ciudad de México (Mexico); Referee: Alberto Monard de Gama Malcher (Brazil); Attendance: 35,000
**ARG:** Rogelio Antonio Domínguez (2/0), Federico Pizarro (3/0) [53.Luis Néstor Cardoso (1/0)], Federico Vairo (11/1), Nicolás Daponte (2/0), Héctor Juan Guidi (Cap) (2/0) [53.Eliseo Víctor Mouriño (16/0)], Ernesto Gutiérrez (22/0), Luis Pentrelli (5/0), Norberto Doroteo Méndez (31/19) [54.Francisco Ramón Loiácono (4/0)], Humberto Dionisio Maschio (2/1), Enrique Omar Sívori (6/4), Ernesto Bernardo Cucchiaroni (7/0). Trainer: Guillermo Stábile (82).
**Goals**: Humberto Dionisio Maschio (27), Enrique Omar Sívori (60, 79, 85).

**277.** 11.03.1956 **ARGENTINA - CHILE** **3-0(1-0)** Campeonato Panamericano
Estadio Olímpico de Centro Universitário, Ciudad de México (Mexico); Referee: Alberto Monard de Gama Malcher (Brazil); Attendance: 40,000
**ARG:** Rogelio Antonio Domínguez (3/0), Luis Néstor Cardoso (2/0) [66.Federico Pizarro (4/0)], Federico Vairo (12/1), Nicolás Daponte (3/0), Eliseo Víctor Mouriño (17/0), Ernesto Gutiérrez (23/0) [75.Natalio Sivo (2/0)], Oreste Osmar Corbatta (2/0), Humberto Dionisio Maschio (3/3), Francisco Ramón Loiácono (5/0), Enrique Omar Sívori (7/5) [75.Dante Homérico Lugo González (2/0)], Ernesto Bernardo Cucchiaroni (8/0). Trainer: Guillermo Stábile (83).
**Goals**: Humberto Dionisio Maschio (30), Enrique Omar Sívori (50), Humberto Dionisio Maschio (65).

**278.** 13.03.1956 **MEXICO - ARGENTINA** **0-0** Campeonato Panamericano
Estadio Olímpico de Centro Universitário, Ciudad de México; Referee: Alberto Monard de Gama Malcher (Brazil); Attendance: 80,000
**ARG:** Rogelio Antonio Domínguez (4/0), Luis Néstor Cardoso (3/0), Federico Vairo (13/1) [*sent off 55*], Nicolás Daponte (4/0), Eliseo Víctor Mouriño (Cap) (18/0) [*sent off 55*], Natalio Sivo (3/0) [53.Héctor Juan Guidi (3/0)], Oreste Osmar Corbatta (3/0) [53.Juan Manuel Filgueiras (6/0)], Humberto Dionisio Maschio (4/3) [*sent off 58*], Francisco Ramón Loiácono (6/0), Dante Homérico Lugo González (3/0) [67.Enrique Omar Sívori (8/5)], Ernesto Bernardo Cucchiaroni (9/0) [*sent of 58*]. Trainer: Guillermo Stábile (84).

**279.** 18.03.1956 **BRAZIL - ARGENTINA** **2-2(1-1)** Campeonato Panamericano
Estadio Olímpico de Centro Universitário, Ciudad de México (Mexico); Referee: Cláudio Vicuña Larrain (Chile); Attendance: 80,000
**ARG:** Rogelio Antonio Domínguez (5/0), Luis Néstor Cardoso (4/0), Juan Manuel Filgueiras (7/0), Nicolás Daponte (5/0), Héctor Juan Guidi (Cap) (4/0), Natalio Sivo (4/0), Luis Pentrelli (6/0), Benito Cejas (2/0), Francisco Ramón Loiácono (7/0) [85.Oscar Di Stéfano (1/0)], Enrique Omar Sívori (9/6), José Yudica (2/1). Trainer: Guillermo Stábile (85).
**Goals**: José Yudica (36), Enrique Omar Sívori (85).

**280.** 24.06.1956 **ARGENTINA - ITALY** **1-0(0-0)**
Estadio Monumental „Antonio Vespucio Liberti", Buenos Aires; Referee: Reginald Leafe (England); Attendance: 100,000
**ARG:** Rogelio Antonio Domínguez (6/0), Pedro Rodolfo Dellacha (12/0), Federico Vairo (14/1), Juan Carlos Giménez (1/0), Héctor Juan Guidi (5/0), Alfredo Jorge Benegas (1/0), Ernesto Sansone (1/0), Norberto Conde (2/1), Humberto Dionisio Maschio (5/3), Ángel Amadeo Labruna (Cap) (28/16) [28.Ernesto Grillo (14/6)], Osvaldo Héctor Cruz (9/1) [46.José Yudica (3/1)]. Trainer: Guillermo Stábile (86).
**Goal**: Norberto Conde (65).

**281.** 01.07.1956 **URUGUAY - ARGENTINA** **1-2(0-0)** Copa Atlántico
Estadio Centenario, Montevideo; Referee: Erwin Hieger (Austria); Attendance: 51,927
**ARG:** Rogelio Antonio Domínguez (7/0), Pedro Rodolfo Dellacha (Cap) (13/0), Federico Vairo (15/1), Juan Carlos Giménez (2/0), Héctor Juan Guidi (6/0), Alfredo Jorge Benegas (2/0) [72.Néstor Raúl Rossi (6/0)], Ernesto Sansone (2/0), Norberto Conde (3/1), Francisco Ramón Loiácono (8/0) [46.Enrique Omar Sívori (10/6)], Ernesto Grillo (15/8), José Yudica (4/1). Trainer: Guillermo Stábile (87).
**Goals**: Ernesto Grillo (52, 82).

**282.** 08.07.1956 **ARGENTINA - BRAZIL** **0-0** Copa Atlántico
Estadio „Juan Domingo Perón" (Racing Club), Avellaneda, Buenos Aires; Referee: Juan Regis Brozzi (Argentina); Attendance: 80,000
**ARG:** Rogelio Antonio Domínguez (8/0), Pedro Rodolfo Dellacha (Cap) (14/0), Federico Vairo (16/1), Juan Carlos Giménez (3/0), Héctor Juan Guidi (7/0) [56.Néstor Raúl Rossi (7/0)], Natalio Sivo (5/0), Ernesto Sansone (3/0) [46.Rodolfo Joaquín Micheli (13/10)], Norberto Conde (4/1), Antonio Valentín Angelillo (1/0), Ernesto Grillo (16/8), Osvaldo Héctor Cruz (10/1). Trainer: Guillermo Stábile (88).

**283.** 15.08.1956 **PARAGUAY - ARGENTINA** **0-1(0-1)** Copa Chevallier Boutell
Estadio Puerto Sajonia, Asunción; Referee: Bertley Cross (England); Attendance: 18,000
**ARG:** Rogelio Antonio Domínguez (9/0), Pedro Rodolfo Dellacha (Cap) (15/0), Federico Vairo (17/1), Juan Francisco Lombardo (18/0), Héctor Juan Guidi (8/0), Alfredo Jorge Benegas (3/0), Ernesto Bernardo Cucchiaroni (10/0), Norberto Conde (5/2), Antonio Valentín Angelillo (2/0) [72.Enrique Omar Sívori (11/6)], Ernesto Grillo (17/8), Osvaldo Héctor Cruz (11/1). Trainer: Guillermo Stábile (89).
**Goal**: Norberto Conde (24).

**284.** 19.08.1956 **ARGENTINA - CZECHOSLOVAKIA** **1-0(0-0)**
Estadio Gasómetro de Boedo, Buenos Aires; Referee: Bertley Cross (England); Attendance: 60,000
**ARG:** Rogelio Antonio Domínguez (10/0), Pedro Rodolfo Dellacha (Cap) (16/0), Federico Vairo (18/1), Juan Francisco Lombardo (19/0), Héctor Juan Guidi (9/0) [66.Néstor Raúl Rossi (8/0)], Alfredo Jorge Benegas (4/0), Rodolfo Joaquín Micheli (14/10) [77.Ernesto Bernardo Cucchiaroni (11/0)], Norberto Conde (6/2) [66.Enrique Omar Sívori (12/6)], Antonio Valentín Angelillo (3/1), Ernesto Grillo (18/8), Osvaldo Héctor Cruz (12/1). Trainer: Guillermo Stábile (90).
**Goal**: Antonio Valentín Angelillo (81).

**285.** 10.10.1956 **URUGUAY - ARGENTINA** **1-2(1-1)**
Estadio „José Artigas", Paysandú; Referee: Erich Steiner (Austria); Attendance: 25,000
**ARG:** Antonio Roma (1/0), Pedro Rodolfo Dellacha (Cap) (17/0), Federico Vairo (19/1), Fernando Manuel Gianserra (1/0), Héctor Juan Guidi (10/0) [20.Héctor César Pederzoli (1/0)], Ángel Osvaldo Schadlein (1/0), Oreste Osmar Corbatta (4/0) [83.Luis Pentrelli (7/0)], Norberto Conde (7/2), Juan José Ferraro (8/3), Juan Nawacki (1/0) [30.Héctor Adolfo De Bourgoing (1/0)], Antonio Héctor Garabal (1/2). Trainer: Guillermo Stábile (91).
**Goal**: Antonio Héctor Garabal (7, 89).

**286.** 14.11.1956 **ARGENTINA - URUGUAY** **2-2(2-1)**
Estadio „Alberto Armando", Buenos Aires; Referee: Bertley Cross (England); Attendance: 40,000
**ARG:** Rogelio Antonio Domínguez (11/0), Pedro Rodolfo Dellacha (Cap) (18/0), Federico Vairo (20/1), Juan Francisco Lombardo (20/0), Héctor Juan Guidi (11/0) [77.Héctor César Pederzoli (2/0)], Ángel Osvaldo Schadlein (2/0), Oreste Osmar Corbatta (5/1) [65.Héctor Adolfo De Bourgoing (2/0)], Norberto Conde (8/2) [80.Héctor Molina (1/0)], Antonio Valentín Angelillo (4/2), Ernesto Grillo (19/8), Osvaldo Héctor Cruz (13/1). Trainer: Guillermo Stábile (92).
**Goals**: Oreste Osmar Corbatta (37 penalty), Antonio Valentín Angelillo (44).

**287.** 05.12.1956 **BRAZIL* - ARGENTINA** **1-2(1-0)** Copa Raúl Colombo
Estádio „Jornalista Mário Filho" (Maracanã), Rio de Janeiro; Referee: Estebán Marino (Uruguay); Attendance: 90,000
**ARG:** Antonio Roma (2/0), Federico Pizarro (5/0), Federico Vairo (21/1), Oscar Hernán Mantegari (1/0), Néstor Raúl Rossi (Cap) (9/0), Adolfo Jorge Benegas (5/0) [41.Ángel Osvaldo Schadlein (3/0)], Ernesto Sansone (4/0) [46.Roberto Jesús Puppo (1/0)], Oscar Pablo Rossi (1/0), Ricardo Raymundo Infante (3/1) [46.José Francisco Sanfilippo (1/1)], Enrique Omar Sívori (13/6), Antonio Héctor Garabal (2/3). Trainer: Guillermo Stábile (93).
**Goals**: José Francisco Sanfilippo (69), Antonio Héctor Garabal (70).
**Not official for Brazil, who played with the Guanabara State Team.*

**288.** 13.03.1957 **ARGENTINA - COLOMBIA** **8-2(4-2)** 25th Copa América
Estadio Nacional, Lima (Peru); Referee: Ronald Lynch (England); Attendance: 42,000
**ARG:** Rogelio Antonio Domínguez (12/0), Pedro Rodolfo Dellacha (Cap) (19/0), Federico Vairo (22/1), Juan Carlos Giménez (4/0), Néstor Raúl Rossi (10/0), Ángel Osvaldo Schadlein (4/0) [65.Alfredo Jorge Benegas (6/0)], Oreste Osmar Corbatta (6/2), Humberto Dionisio Maschio (6/7), Antonio Valentín Angelillo (5/4), José Francisco Sanfilippo (2/1), Osvaldo Héctor Cruz (14/2). Trainer: Guillermo Stábile (94).
**Goals**: Osvaldo Héctor Cruz (5), Antonio Valentín Angelillo (10), Humberto Dionisio Maschio (16, 23, 53), Oreste Osmar Corbatta (59), Antonio Valentín Angelillo (73), Humberto Dionisio Maschio (85).

**289.** 17.03.1957 **ARGENTINA - ECUADOR** **3-0(3-0)** 25th Copa América
Estadio Nacional, Lima (Peru); Referee: Bertley Cross (England); Attendance: 50,000
**ARG:** Rogelio Antonio Domínguez (13/0), Pedro Rodolfo Dellacha (Cap) (20/0), Federico Vairo (23/1), Juan Carlos Giménez (5/0), Néstor Raúl Rossi (11/0), Ángel Osvaldo Schadlein (5/0), Oreste Osmar Corbatta (7/2) [63.Héctor Adolfo De Bourgoing (3/0)], Humberto Dionisio Maschio (7/7) [38.José Francisco Sanfilippo (3/1)], Antonio Valentín Angelillo (6/6), Enrique Omar Sívori (14/7) [78.Juan Alberto Castro (1/0)], Osvaldo Héctor Cruz (15/2). Trainer: Guillermo Stábile (95).
**Goals**: Antonio Valentín Angelillo (5), Enrique Omar Sívori (14), Antonio Valentín Angelillo (39).

**290.** 20.03.1957 **ARGENTINA - URUGUAY** **4-0(1-0)** 25th Copa América
Estadio Nacional, Lima (Peru); Referee: Erwin Hieger (Austria); Attendance: 40,000
**ARG:** Rogelio Antonio Domínguez (14/0), Pedro Rodolfo Dellacha (Cap) (21/0), Federico Vairo (24/1), Juan Carlos Giménez (6/0), Néstor Raúl Rossi (12/0) [75.Héctor Juan Guidi (12/0)], Ángel Osvaldo Schadlein (6/0), Oreste Osmar Corbatta (8/2), Humberto Dionisio Maschio (8/9), Antonio Valentín Angelillo (7/7), Enrique Omar Sívori (15/7) [80.José Francisco Sanfilippo (4/2)], Osvaldo Héctor Cruz (16/2). Trainer: Guillermo Stábile (96).
**Goals**: Humberto Dionisio Maschio (7), Antonio Valentín Angelillo (48), Humberto Dionisio Maschio (73), José Francisco Sanfilippo (83).

**291.** 28.03.1957 **ARGENTINA - CHILE** **6-2(2-2)** 25th Copa América
Estadio Nacional, Lima (Peru); Referee: Robert Turner (England); Attendance: 50,000
**ARG:** Rogelio Antonio Domínguez (15/0), Pedro Rodolfo Dellacha (Cap) (22/0), Federico Vairo (25/1), Juan Carlos Giménez (7/0), Néstor Raúl Rossi (13/0), Ángel Osvaldo Schadlein (7/0), Oreste Osmar Corbatta (9/3), Humberto Dionisio Maschio (9/11) [80.José Francisco Sanfilippo (5/2)], Antonio Valentín Angelillo (8/9), Enrique Omar Sívori (16/8), Osvaldo Héctor Cruz (17/2). Trainer: Guillermo Stábile (97).
**Goals**: Enrique Omar Sívori (7), Antonio Valentín Angelillo (21), Humberto Dionisio Maschio (53), Antonio Valentín Angelillo (70), Humberto Dionisio Maschio (74), Oreste Osmar Corbatta (83 penalty).

**292.** 03.04.1957 **ARGENTINA - BRAZIL** **3-0(1-0)** 25th Copa América
Estadio Nacional, Lima (Peru); Referee: Robert Turner (England); Attendance: 55,000
**ARG:** Rogelio Antonio Domínguez (16/0), Pedro Rodolfo Dellacha (Cap) (23/0), Federico Vairo (26/1), Juan Carlos Giménez (8/0), Néstor Raúl Rossi (14/0), Ángel Osvaldo Schadlein (8/0), Oreste Osmar Corbatta (10/3), Humberto Dionisio Maschio (10/12), Antonio Valentín Angelillo (9/10), Enrique Omar Sívori (17/8), Osvaldo Héctor Cruz (18/3). Trainer: Guillermo Stábile (98).
**Goals**: Antonio Valentín Angelillo (23), Humberto Dionisio Maschio (87), Osvaldo Héctor Cruz (90).

**293.** 06.04.1957 **PERU - ARGENTINA** **2-1(1-0)** 25th Copa América
Estadio Nacional, Lima; Referee: Bertley Cross (England); Attendance: 50,000
**ARG:** Rogelio Antonio Domínguez (17/0) [46.Antonio Roma (3/0)], Pedro Rodolfo Dellacha (Cap) (24/0), David Carmelo Iñigo (1/0), Juan Carlos Giménez (9/0), Néstor Raúl Rossi (15/0), Ángel Osvaldo Schadlein (9/0), Oreste Osmar Corbatta (11/3), Humberto Dionisio Maschio (11/12), Antonio Valentín Angelillo (10/10), Enrique Omar Sívori (18/9), Osvaldo Héctor Cruz (19/3). Trainer: Guillermo Stábile (99).
**Goal**: Enrique Omar Sívori (50).

**294.** 09.04.1957 **PERU - ARGENTINA** **1-4(0-1)**
Estadio Nacional, Lima; Referee: Diego De Leo (Mexico); Attendance: 40,000
**ARG:** Antonio Roma (4/0), Pedro Rodolfo Dellacha (Cap) (25/0) [46.Federico Pizarro (6/0)], David Carmelo Iñigo (2/0), Oscar Hernán Mantegari (2/0), Héctor Juan Guidi (13/0), Ángel Osvaldo Schadlein (10/0), Oreste Osmar Corbatta (12/3) [46.Héctor Adolfo De Bourgoing (4/0)], Humberto Dionisio Maschio (12/12) [46.José Francisco Sanfilippo (6/2)], Antonio Valentín Angelillo (11/11) [46.Miguel Antonio Juárez (1/1)], Enrique Omar Sívori (19/9) [46.Juan Alberto Castro (2/1)], Osvaldo Héctor Cruz (20/3) [46.Roberto Leonardo Brookes (1/1)]. Trainer: Guillermo Stábile (100).
**Goals**: Antonio Valentín Angelillo (15), Miguel Antonio Juárez (55), Juan Alberto Castro (70), Roberto Leonardo Brookes (76).

**295.** 23.05.1957 **URUGUAY - ARGENTINA** **0-0** Copa Newton
Estadio Centenario, Montevideo; Referee: Erwin Hieger (Austria); Attendance: 32,764
**ARG:** Rogelio Antonio Domínguez (18/0), Pedro Rodolfo Dellacha (Cap) (26/0), Federico Vairo (27/1), Juan Carlos Giménez (10/0), Héctor Juan Guidi (14/0), Ángel Osvaldo Schadlein (11/0) [87.Juan Eulogio Urriolabeitía (1/0)], Oreste Osmar Corbatta (13/3) [70.Héctor Adolfo De Bourgoing (5/0)], Antonio Valentín Angelillo (12/11), José Francisco Sanfilippo (7/2) [70.Héctor Edelmiro Antonio (1/0)], Ángel Amadeo Labruna (29/16), Osvaldo Héctor Cruz (21/3). Trainer: Guillermo Stábile (101).

**296.** 05.06.1957 **ARGENTINA - URUGUAY** **1-1(0-0)** Copa Lipton
Estadio El Palacio, Buenos Aires; Referee: Estebán Marino (Uruguay); Attendance: 35,950
**ARG:** Rogelio Antonio Domínguez (19/0), Pedro Rodolfo Dellacha (Cap) (27/0), Federico Vairo (28/1), Juan Carlos Giménez (11/0), Héctor Juan Guidi (15/0), Ángel Osvaldo Schadlein (12/0) [57.José Varacka (2/0)], Oreste Osmar Corbatta (14/3), Antonio Valentín Angelillo (13/12), José Francisco Sanfilippo (8/2) [46.Héctor Edelmiro Antonio (2/0)], Ángel Amadeo Labruna (30/16), Osvaldo Héctor Cruz (22/3). Trainer: Guillermo Stábile (102).
**Goal**: Antonio Valentín Angelillo (64).

**297.** 07.07.1957 **BRAZIL - ARGENTINA** **1-2** Copa Roca
Estádio „Jornalista Mário Filho“ (Maracanã), Rio de Janeiro; Referee: Erwin Hieger (Austria); Attendance: 80,000
**ARG:** Amadeo Raúl Carrizo (3/0), Federico Pizarro (7/0), Federico Vairo (29/1), Fernando Manuel Gianserra (2/0), Néstor Raúl Rossi (16/0) [79.Héctor Juan Guidi (16/0)], Juan Eulogio Urriolabeitía (2/0), Oreste Osmar Corbatta (15/3), José Herrera (1/0) [70.Héctor Edelmiro Antonio (3/0)], Miguel Antonio Juárez (2/2) [79.Roberto Manuel Blanco (1/0)], Ángel Amadeo Labruna (Cap) (31/17), Ramón Moyano (1/0). Trainer: Guillermo Stábile (103).
**Goals**: Ángel Amadeo Labruna (29), Miguel Antonio Juárez (78).

**298.** 10.07.1957 **BRAZIL - ARGENTINA** **2-0** Copa Roca
Estádio Pacaembú, São Paulo; Referee: John Husband (England); Attendance: 65,000
**ARG:** Amadeo Raúl Carrizo (4/0) [66.Julio Elías Musimessi (16/0)], Juan Biagioli (1/0), Federico Vairo (30/1), Fernando Manuel Gianserra (3/0), Néstor Raúl Rossi (17/0) [66.Héctor Juan Guidi (17/0)], Juan Eulogio Urriolabeitía (3/0), Oreste Osmar Corbatta (16/3), José Herrera (2/0) [50.Héctor Edelmiro Antonio (4/0)], Miguel Antonio Juárez (3/2), Ángel Amadeo Labruna (Cap) (32/17), Alberto Sesti (1/0). Trainer: Guillermo Stábile (104).

**299.** 06.10.1957 **BOLIVIA - ARGENTINA** **2-0(1-0)** 6th FIFA WC. Qualifiers
Estadio „Hernándo Siles Zuazo“, La Paz; Referee: Paul Wyssling (Switzerland); Attendance: 25,000
**ARG:** Amadeo Raúl Carrizo (5/0), Pedro Rodolfo Dellacha (Cap) (28/0), Federico Vairo (31/1), Fernando Manuel Gianserra (4/0), Héctor Juan Guidi (18/0), Gilberto Pascasio Sola (2/0), Oreste Osmar Corbatta (17/3), Norberto Conde (9/2), Norberto Menéndez (1/0), José Francisco Sanfilippo (9/2), Roberto Héctor Zárate (2/0). Trainer: Guillermo Stábile (105).

**300.** 13.10.1957 **CHILE - ARGENTINA** **0-2(0-1)** 6th FIFA WC. Qualifiers
Estadio Nacional, Santiago; Referee: Paul Wyssling (Switzerland); Attendance: 45,000
**ARG:** Amadeo Raúl Carrizo (6/0), Pedro Rodolfo Dellacha (Cap) (29/0), Federico Vairo (32/1), Juan Francisco Lombardo (21/0), Néstor Raúl Rossi (18/0), Gilberto Pascasio Sola (3/0), Oreste Osmar Corbatta (18/3), Norberto Conde (10/3), Norberto Menéndez (2/1), Ángel Amadeo Labruna (33/17), Roberto Héctor Zárate (3/0). Trainer: Guillermo Stábile (106).
**Goals**: Norberto Menéndez (40), Norberto Conde (68).

**301.** 20.10.1957 **ARGENTINA - CHILE** **4-0(4-0)** 6th FIFA WC. Qualifiers

Estadio „Alberto Armando“, Buenos Aires; Referee: Paul Wyssling (Switzerland); Attendance: 70,000

**ARG:** Amadeo Raúl Carrizo (7/0), Pedro Rodolfo Dellacha (Cap) (30/0), Federico Vairo (33/1), Juan Francisco Lombardo (22/0), Néstor Raúl Rossi (19/0), Gilberto Pascasio Sola (4/0), Oreste Osmar Corbatta (19/5), Eliseo Prado (2/0), Norberto Menéndez (3/2), Ángel Amadeo Labruna (34/17), Roberto Héctor Zárate (4/1). Trainer: Guillermo Stábile (107).

**Goals**: Oreste Osmar Corbatta (1), Norberto Menéndez (13), Roberto Héctor Zárate (15), Oreste Osmar Corbatta (41).

**302.** 27.10.1957 **ARGENTINA - BOLIVIA** **4-0(1-0)** 6th FIFA WC. Qualifiers

Estadio Independiente, Avellaneda, Buenos Aires; Referee: Paul Wyssling (Switzerland); Attendance: 60,000

**ARG:** Amadeo Raúl Carrizo (8/0), Alfredo Ricardo Pérez (1/0), Federico Vairo (34/1), Juan Francisco Lombardo (23/0), Néstor Raúl Rossi (20/0), Gilberto Pascasio Sola (5/0) [*sent off 32*], Oreste Osmar Corbatta (20/6), Eliseo Prado (3/1), Norberto Menéndez (4/3), Ángel Amadeo Labruna (Cap) (35/17), Roberto Héctor Zárate (5/2). Trainer: Guillermo Stábile (108).

**Goals**: Roberto Héctor Zárate (8), Oreste Osmar Corbatta (62), Eliseo Prado (64), Norberto Menéndez (65).

**303.** 06.04.1958 **URUGUAY - ARGENTINA** **1-0**

Estadio Centenario, Montevideo; Referee: José María Codesal (Uruguay); Attendance: 40,000

**ARG:** Amadeo Raúl Carrizo (9/0), Alfredo Ricardo Pérez (2/0), Federico Vairo (35/1), Juan Francisco Lombardo (24/0), Eliseo Víctor Mouriño (Cap) (19/0) [46.Arnaldo Balay (3/0)], Rafael García Fierro (1/0) [46.José Varacka (3/0)], Oreste Osmar Corbatta (21/6), Norberto Constante Boggio (1/0) [46.Norberto Conde (11/3)], Norberto Menéndez (5/3), Miguel Antonio Juárez (4/2), Roberto Héctor Zárate (6/2). Trainer: Guillermo Stábile (109).

**304.** 20.04.1958 **PARAGUAY - ARGENTINA** **1-0(1-0)**

Estadio Puerto Sajonia, Asunción; Referee: Erwin Hieger (Austria); Attendance: 30,000

**ARG:** Amadeo Raúl Carrizo (10/0), Alfredo Ricardo Pérez (3/0), Federico Vairo (36/1), Juan Francisco Lombardo (25/0), Néstor Raúl Rossi (Cap) (21/0), José Varacka (4/0), Oscar Pablo Rossi (2/0) [46.Eliseo Prado (4/1)], Oreste Osmar Corbatta (22/6), Miguel Antonio Juárez (5/2), Norberto Conde (12/3), Osvaldo Héctor Cruz (23/3). Trainer: Guillermo Stábile (110).

**305.** 26.04.1958 **ARGENTINA - PARAGUAY** **2-0(1-0)**

Estadio „Juan Domingo Perón“ (Racing Club), Avellaneda, Buenos Aires; Referee: Erwin Hieger (Austria); Attendance: 60,000

**ARG:** Amadeo Raúl Carrizo (11/0), Pedro Rodolfo Dellacha (Cap) (31/0), Federico Vairo (37/1), Juan Francisco Lombardo (26/0), Néstor Raúl Rossi (22/0), Eliseo Prado (5/2) [61.Oscar Pablo Rossi (3/0)], José Varacka (5/0) [85.José Manuel Ramos Delgado (1/0)], Oreste Osmar Corbatta (23/7), Norberto Menéndez (6/3), José Francisco Sanfilippo (10/2) [70.Alfredo Hugo Rojas (1/0)], Roberto Héctor Zárate (7/2). Trainer: Guillermo Stábile (111).

**Goals**: Eliseo Prado (6), Oreste Osmar Corbatta (83).

**306.** 30.04.1958 **ARGENTINA - URUGUAY** **2-0(0-0)**

Estadio El Palacio, Buenos Aires; Referee: Robert Turner (England); Attendance: 25,000

**ARG:** Amadeo Raúl Carrizo (12/0), Pedro Rodolfo Dellacha (Cap) (32/0), Federico Vairo (38/1), Juan Francisco Lombardo (27/0), Néstor Raúl Rossi (23/0), José Varacka (6/0), Oreste Osmar Corbatta (24/7), Eliseo Prado (6/3), Norberto Menéndez (7/3) [46.Ricardo Raymundo Infante (4/2)], Alfredo Hugo Rojas (2/0) [*sent off 58*], Roberto Héctor Zárate (8/2) [*sent off 30*]. Trainer: Guillermo Stábile (112).

**Goals**: Eliseo Prado (68), Ricardo Raymundo Infante (75).

**307.** 08.06.1958 **WEST GERMANY - ARGENTINA** **3-1(2-1)** 6th FIFA WC. Group Stage.

Malmö Stadion, Malmö (Sweden); Referee: Reginald Leafe (England); Attendance: 31,156

**ARG:** Amadeo Raúl Carrizo (13/0), Pedro Rodolfo Dellacha (Cap) (33/0), Federico Vairo (39/1), Juan Francisco Lombardo (28/0), Néstor Raúl Rossi (24/0), José Varacka (7/0), Oreste Osmar Corbatta (25/8), Eliseo Prado (7/3), Norberto Menéndez (8/3), Alfredo Hugo Rojas (3/0), Osvaldo Héctor Cruz (24/3). Trainer: Guillermo Stábile (113).

**Goal**: Oreste Osmar Corbatta (3).

**308.** 11.06.1958 **NORTHERN IRELAND - ARGENTINA** **1-3(1-1)** 6th FIFA WC. Group Stage.

Orjans Vall Stadion, Halmstad (Sweden); Referee: Sten Ahlner (Sweden); Attendance: 14,174

**ARG:** Amadeo Raúl Carrizo (14/0), Pedro Rodolfo Dellacha (Cap) (34/0), Federico Vairo (40/1), Juan Francisco Lombardo (29/0), Néstor Raúl Rossi (25/0), José Varacka (8/0), Oreste Osmar Corbatta (26/9), Ludovico Héctor Avio (1/1), Norberto Menéndez (9/4), Ángel Amadeo Labruna (36/17), Norberto Constante Boggio (2/0). Trainer: Guillermo Stábile (114).

**Goals**: Oreste Osmar Corbatta (38 penalty), Norberto Menéndez (55), Ludovico Héctor Avio (60).

**309.** 15.06.1958 **CZECHOSLOVAKIA - ARGENTINA** **6-1(3-0)** 6th FIFA WC. Group Stage.

Olimpiastadion, Helsingborg (Sweden); Referee: Arthur Edward Ellis (England); Attendance: 16,481

**ARG:** Amadeo Raúl Carrizo (15/0), Pedro Rodolfo Dellacha (Cap) (35/0), Federico Vairo (41/1), Juan Francisco Lombardo (30/0), Néstor Raúl Rossi (26/0), José Varacka (9/0), Oreste Osmar Corbatta (27/10), Ludovico Héctor Avio (2/1), Norberto Menéndez (10/4), Ángel Amadeo Labruna (37/17), Norberto Constante Boggio (3/0). Trainer: Guillermo Stábile (115).

**Goal**: Oreste Osmar Corbatta (65 penalty).

**310.** 07.03.1959 **ARGENTINA - CHILE** **6-1(4-1)** 26th Copa América

Estadio Monumental „Antonio Vespucio Liberti“, Buenos Aires; Referee: Washington Rodríguez (Uruguay); Attendance: 70,000

**ARG:** Osvaldo Jorge Negri (1/0), Luis Néstor Cardoso (5/0), Julio Alberto Nuín (1/0), Carmelo Simeone (1/0), Vladislao Wenceslao Cap (1/0), José Varacka (10/0), Oreste Osmar Corbatta (28/10), Juan José Pizzuti (Cap) (1/2) [75.Osvaldo Oscar Güenzatti (1/0)], Pedro Waldemar Manfredini (1/2), Pedro Eugenio Callá (1/1) [75.Juan José Rodríguez (1/0)], Raúl Oscar Belén (1/1). Trainer: Victorio Luis Spinetto-José Della Torre-José Barreiro (1).

**Goals**: Pedro Waldemar Manfredini (5), Pedro Eugenio Callá (7), Juan José Pizzuti (17, 39), Pedro Waldemar Manfredini (50), Raúl Oscar Belén (75).

**311.** 11.03.1959 **ARGENTINA - BOLIVIA** **2-0(1-0)** 26th Copa América

Estadio Monumental „Antonio Vespucio Liberti“, Buenos Aires; Referee: Juan Carlos Robles (Chile); Attendance: 45,000

**ARG:** Osvaldo Jorge Negri (2/0), Luis Néstor Cardoso (6/0), Juan Carlos Murúa (1/0), Carmelo Simeone (2/0) [46.Juan Francisco Lombardo (31/0)], Vladislao Wenceslao Cap (2/0), José Varacka (11/0), Oreste Osmar Corbatta (29/11), Juan José Pizzuti (Cap) (2/2) [80.Osvaldo Oscar Güenzatti (2/0)], Pedro Waldemar Manfredini (2/2), Pedro Eugenio Callá (2/2), Raúl Oscar Belén (2/1). Trainer: Victorio Luis Spinetto-José Della Torre-José Barreiro (2).

**Goals**: Oreste Osmar Corbatta (2), Pedro Eugenio Callá (79).

**312.** 18.03.1959 **ARGENTINA - PERU** **3-1(2-0)** 26th Copa América

Estadio Monumental „Antonio Vespucio Liberti“, Buenos Aires; Referee: Alberto Monard de Gama Malcher (Brazil); Attendance: 70,000

**ARG:** Osvaldo Jorge Negri (3/0), Jorge Bernardo Griffa (1/0), Juan Carlos Murúa (2/0), Juan Francisco Lombardo (32/0), Vladislao Wenceslao Cap (3/0), Eliseo Víctor Mouriño (20/0), Oreste Osmar Corbatta (30/12) [78.Osvaldo Ángel Nardiello (1/0)], Juan José Pizzuti (Cap) (3/2), Pedro Waldemar Manfredini (3/2) [64.Héctor Rubén Sosa (1/1)], Pedro Eugenio Callá (3/2), Raúl Oscar Belén (3/1). Trainer: Victorio Luis Spinetto-José Della Torre-José Barreiro (3).

**Goals**: Oreste Osmar Corbatta (18 penalty), Héctor Rubén Sosa (42), Víctor Benítez (78 own goal).

**313.** 22.03.1959 **ARGENTINA - PARAGUAY** **3-1(1-1)** 26th Copa América
Estadio Monumental „Antonio Vespucio Liberti", Buenos Aires; Referee: Juan Carlos Robles (Chile); Attendance: 50,000
**ARG:** Osvaldo Jorge Negri (4/0), Jorge Bernardo Griffa (2/0), Juan Carlos Murúa (3/0), Juan Francisco Lombardo (33/0), Vladislao Wenceslao Cap (4/1), Eliseo Víctor Mouriño (21/0), Oreste Osmar Corbatta (31/13) [52.Osvaldo Ángel Nardiello (2/0)], Juan José Pizzuti (Cap) (4/2), Héctor Rubén Sosa (2/2), Pedro Eugenio Callá (4/2) [52.Juan José Rodríguez (2/0)], Raúl Oscar Belén (4/1) [86.Roberto Leonardo Brookes (2/1)]. Trainer: Victorio Luis Spinetto-José Della Torre-José Barreiro (4).
**Goals**: Oreste Osmar Corbatta (15), Héctor Rubén Sosa (63), Vladislao Wenceslao Cap (69).

**314.** 30.03.1959 **ARGENTINA - URUGUAY** **4-1(1-0)** 26th Copa América
Estadio Monumental „Antonio Vespucio Liberti", Buenos Aires; Referee: Isidro Ramírez Alvarez (Paraguay); Attendance: 80,000
**ARG:** Osvaldo Jorge Negri (5/0), Jorge Bernardo Griffa (3/0), Juan Carlos Murúa (4/0), Juan Francisco Lombardo (34/0), Vladislao Wenceslao Cap (5/1), Eliseo Víctor Mouriño (22/0), Oreste Osmar Corbatta (32/13) [46.Osvaldo Ángel Nardiello (3/0)], Juan José Pizzuti (Cap) (5/2), Héctor Rubén Sosa (3/4), Pedro Eugenio Callá (5/2) [46.Juan José Rodríguez (3/0)], Raúl Oscar Belén (5/3). Trainer: Victorio Luis Spinetto-José Della Torre-José Barreiro (5).
**Goals**: Raúl Oscar Belén (15), Héctor Rubén Sosa (55), Raúl Oscar Belén (60), Héctor Rubén Sosa (80).

**315.** 04.04.1959 **ARGENTINA - BRAZIL** **1-1(1-0)** 26th Copa América
Estadio Monumental „Antonio Vespucio Liberti", Buenos Aires; Referee: Juan Carlos Robles (Chile); Attendance: 85,000
**ARG:** Osvaldo Jorge Negri (6/0), Jorge Bernardo Griffa (4/0) [50.Luis Néstor Cardoso (7/0)], Juan Carlos Murúa (5/0), Juan Francisco Lombardo (35/0) [46.Carmelo Simeone (3/0)], Vladislao Wenceslao Cap (6/1), Eliseo Víctor Mouriño (23/0), Osvaldo Ángel Nardiello (4/0), Juan José Pizzuti (Cap) (6/3), Héctor Rubén Sosa (4/4), Pedro Eugenio Callá (6/2) [60.Juan José Rodríguez (4/0)], Raúl Oscar Belén (6/3). Trainer: Victorio Luis Spinetto-José Della Torre-José Barreiro (6).
**Goal**: Juan José Pizzuti (40).

**316.** 18.11.1959 **CHILE - ARGENTINA** **4-2(1-1)**
Estadio Nacional, Santiago; Referee: Juan Carlos Robles (Chile); Attendance: 36,581
**ARG:** Osvaldo Jorge Negri (7/0) [46-80.Vladimir Tarnawsky* (1/0)], Norberto Anido (1/0), Juan Carlos Murúa (6/0), Juan Francisco Lombardo (Cap) (36/0), Antonio Ubaldo Rattín (1/0) [46.Vladislao Wenceslao Cap (7/1)], José Varacka (12/0), Héctor Osvaldo Facundo (1/0) [46.Raúl Oscar Belén (7/3)], Miguel Ángel Ruíz (1/1) [46.Juan José Pizzuti (7/3)], Omar Higinio García (1/0) [73.Norberto Menéndez (11/4) [*sent off 89*]], José Francisco Sanfilippo (11/3), Norberto Constante Boggio (4/0). Trainer: José Manuel Moreno (1).
**Goals**: Miguel Ángel Ruíz (27), José Francisco Sanfilippo (46).
**After 80 mins Negri was comeback on the field.*

**317.** 09.12.1959 **ARGENTINA - PARAGUAY** **4-2(1-1)** 27th Copa América
Estadio Modelo, Guayaquil (Ecuador); Referee: Estebán Marino (Uruguay); Attendance: 15,000
**ARG:** Néstor Martín Errea (1/0), Norberto Anido (2/0), Juan Carlos Murúa (7/0), Juan Francisco Lombardo (37/0), Antonio Ubaldo Rattín (2/0) [69.Héctor Juan Guidi (19/0)], Eliseo Víctor Mouriño (Cap) (24/0), Héctor Osvaldo Facundo (2/0), Miguel Ángel Ruíz (2/1) [69.Juan José Pizzuti (8/4)], Omar Higinio García (2/0) [46.Héctor Rubén Sosa (5/4)], José Francisco Sanfilippo (12/6), Norberto Constante Boggio (5/0). Trainer: José Manuel Moreno (2).
**Goals**: José Francisco Sanfilippo (8, 57), Juan José Pizzuti (81), José Francisco Sanfilippo (89 penalty).

**318.** 12.12.1959 **ECUADOR - ARGENTINA** **1-1(1-0)** 27th Copa América
Estadio Modelo, Guayaquil; Referee: José María Gomes Sobrinho (Brazil); Attendance: 55,000
**ARG:** Osvaldo Jorge Negri (8/0), Carlos Alberto Arredondo (1/0), Carlos Timoteo Griguol (1/0), Juan Carlos Murúa (8/0), Héctor Juan Guidi (20/0), Eliseo Víctor Mouriño (Cap) (25/0), Héctor Osvaldo Facundo (3/0) [51.Norberto Constante Boggio (6/0)], Juan José Pizzuti (9/4) [81.Miguel Ángel Ruíz (3/1)], Héctor Rubén Sosa (6/5), José Francisco Sanfilippo (13/6) [63.Juan José Rodríguez (5/0)], Raúl Oscar Belén (8/3). Trainer: José Manuel Moreno (3).
**Goal**: Héctor Rubén Sosa (62).

**319.** 16.12.1959 **URUGUAY - ARGENTINA** **5-0(3-0)** 27th Copa América
Estadio Modelo, Guayaquil (Ecuador); Referee: José María Gomes Sobrinho (Brazil); Attendance: 50,000
**ARG:** Osvaldo Jorge Negri (9/0), Carlos Alberto Arredondo (2/0), Carlos Timoteo Griguol (2/0), Juan Carlos Murúa (9/0), Héctor Juan Guidi (21/0), Rodolfo Carlos Betinotti (1/0) [25.Antonio Ubaldo Rattín (3/0)], Norberto Constante Boggio (7/0), Juan José Pizzuti (Cap) (10/4) [*sent off 57*], Héctor Rubén Sosa (7/5) [65.Miguel Ángel Ruíz (4/1)], José Francisco Sanfilippo (14/6) [65.Juan José Rodríguez (6/0)], Raúl Oscar Belén (9/3). Trainer: José Manuel Moreno (4).

**320.** 22.12.1959 **ARGENTINA - BRAZIL** **4-1(2-1)** 27th Copa América
Estadio Modelo, Guayaquil (Ecuador); Referee: Estebán Marino (Uruguay); Attendance: 45,000
**ARG:** Osvaldo Jorge Negri (10/0), Carlos Alberto Arredondo (3/0), Norberto Anido (3/0), Juan Carlos Murúa (10/0), Héctor Juan Guidi (22/0), Eliseo Víctor Mouriño (Cap) (26/0), Héctor Osvaldo Facundo (4/0) [65.José Ángel Carbone (1/0)], Miguel Ángel Ruíz (5/1), Omar Higinio García (3/1), José Francisco Sanfilippo (15/9), Raúl Oscar Belén (10/3). Trainer: José Manuel Moreno (5).
**Goals**: Omar Higinio García (2), José Francisco Sanfilippo (27, 89, 90).

**321.** 08.03.1960 **COSTA RICA – ARGENTINA** **0-0** Campeonato Panamericano
Estadio Nacional, San José; Referee: Artur Villarinho (Brazil); Attendance: 35,000
**ARG:** Osvaldo Fabián Ocampo Ayala (1/0), Marcelo Edmundo Etchegaray (1/0), Carlos Alberto Álvarez (1/0), Rubén Marino Navarro (1/0), Héctor Juan Guidi (Cap) (23/0), José Varacka (13/0), Osvaldo Ángel Nardiello (5/0) [77.Lorenzo Alberto Dacquarti (1/0)], Pedro Eugenio Callá (7/2), Walter Antonio Jiménez (1/0), Ramón Gregorio Abeledo (1/0) [74.Ermindo Ángel Onega (1/0)], Raúl Oscar Belén (11/3) [Roberto Leonardo Brookes (3/1)]. Trainer: Guillermo Stábile (115).

**322.** 10.03.1960 **ARGENTINA - MEXICO** **3-2(2-2)** Campeonato Panamericano
Estadio Nacional, San José (Costa Rica); Referee: Artur Villarinho (Brazil); Attendance: 40,000
**ARG:** Osvaldo Fabián Ocampo Ayala (2/0), Marcelo Edmundo Etchegaray (2/0), Carlos Alberto Álvarez (2/0), Rubén Marino Navarro (2/0), Héctor Juan Guidi (Cap) (24/0) [64.Héctor César Pederzoli (3/0)], José Varacka (14/0), Osvaldo Ángel Nardiello (6/1) [48.Lorenzo Alberto Dacquarti (2/0)], Pedro Eugenio Callá (8/2) [64.Edgardo Jorge D'Ascenzo (1/0)], Walter Antonio Jiménez (2/0), Ramón Gregorio Abeledo (2/0), Raúl Oscar Belén (12/5). Trainer: Guillermo Stábile (116).
**Goals**: Raúl Oscar Belén (10), Osvaldo Ángel Nardiello (11), Raúl Oscar Belén (46).

**323.** 13.03.1960 **ARGENTINA - BRAZIL** **2-1(1-0)** Campeonato Panamericano
Estadio Nacional, San José (Costa Rica); Referee: Rafael Valenzuela (Mexico); Attendance: 40,000
**ARG:** Osvaldo Fabián Ocampo Ayala (3/0), Marcelo Edmundo Etchegaray (3/0), Carlos Alberto Álvarez (3/0), Rubén Marino Navarro (3/0), Héctor Juan Guidi (Cap) (25/0), Walter Antonio Jiménez (3/0), José Varacka (15/0) [62.Ricardo Blas Bosich (1/0)], Osvaldo Ángel Nardiello (7/2), Pedro Eugenio Callá (9/2) [42.Edgardo Jorge D'Ascenzo (2/0)], Ramón Gregorio Abeledo (3/0), Raúl Oscar Belén (13/6) [Roberto Leonardo Brookes (4/1)]. Trainer: Guillermo Stábile (117).
**Goals**: Raúl Oscar Belén (15), Osvaldo Ángel Nardiello (52).

**324.** 15.03.1960 **COSTA RICA – ARGENTINA** **0-2(0-1)** Campeonato Panamericano
Estadio Nacional, San José (Costa Rica); Referee: Rafael Valenzuela (Mexico); Attendance: 8,460
**ARG:** Osvaldo Fabián Ocampo Ayala (4/0), Marcelo Edmundo Etchegaray (4/0) [68.Silvio Marzolini (1/0)], Carlos Alberto Álvarez (4/0), Rubén Marino Navarro (4/0), Héctor Juan Guidi (Cap) (26/0), José Varacka (16/0), Walter Antonio Jiménez (4/0) [46.Juan Carlos Sarnari (1/0)], Pedro Eugenio Callá (10/3) [46.Edgardo Jorge D'Ascenzo (3/0)], Ermindo Ángel Onega (2/1), Lorenzo Alberto Dacquarti (3/0), Raúl Oscar Belén (14/6). Trainer: Guillermo Stábile (118).
**Goals**: Ermindo Ángel Onega (1), Pedro Eugenio Callá (60).

**325.** 17.03.1960 **ARGENTINA - MEXICO** **2-0(1-0)** Campeonato Panamericano
Estadio Nacional, San José (Costa Rica); Referee: Juan Soto París (Costa Rica); Attendance: 40,000
**ARG:** Osvaldo Fabián Ocampo Ayala (5/0), Carlos Alberto Álvarez (5/0), Silvio Marzolini (2/0), Rubén Marino Navarro (5/0), Héctor Juan Guidi (Cap) (27/0), José Varacka (17/0) [65.Ricardo Blas Bosich (2/0)], Pedro Eugenio Callá (11/3) [60.Edgardo Jorge D'Ascenzo (4/0)], Ramón Gregorio Abeledo (4/0) [60.Ermindo Ángel Onega (3/1)], Osvaldo Ángel Nardiello (8/3), Walter Antonio Jiménez (5/1), Raúl Oscar Belén (15/6). Trainer: Guillermo Stábile (119).
**Goals**: Walter Antonio Jiménez (21), Osvaldo Ángel Nardiello (66).

**326.** 20.03.1960 **ARGENTINA - BRAZIL** **0-1(0-0)** Campeonato Panamericano
Estadio Nacional, San José (Costa Rica); Referee: Juan Soto París (Costa Rica); Attendance: 40,000
**ARG:** Osvaldo Fabián Ocampo Ayala (6/0), Carlos Alberto Álvarez (6/0), Silvio Marzolini (3/0), Rubén Marino Navarro (Cap) (6/0), Héctor César Pederzoli (4/0), José Varacka (18/0), Pedro Eugenio Callá (12/3) [46.Edgardo Jorge D'Ascenzo (5/0)], Ramón Gregorio Abeledo (5/0) [62.Ermindo Ángel Onega (4/1)], Osvaldo Ángel Nardiello (9/3) [80.Lorenzo Alberto Dacquarti (4/0)], Walter Antonio Jiménez (6/1), Raúl Oscar Belén (16/6). Trainer: Guillermo Stábile (120).

**327.** 26.05.1960 **ARGENTINA - BRAZIL** **4-2(2-0)** Copa Roca
Estadio Monumental „Antonio Vespucio Liberti", Buenos Aires; Referee: Juan Carlos Robles (Chile); Attendance: 50,000
**ARG:** Osvaldo Fabián Ocampo Ayala (7/0), Carlos Alberto Álvarez (7/0), Marcelo Edmundo Etchegaray (5/0), Rubén Marino Navarro (7/0), Héctor Juan Guidi (Cap) (28/0) [68.Antonio Cielinsky (1/0)], José Nazionale (1/0), Martín Esteban Pando (1/0) [65.Héctor Rubén Berón (1/0)], Osvaldo Ángel Nardiello (10/5), Osvaldo Carceo (1/0), Edgardo Jorge D'Ascenzo (6/1), Raúl Oscar Belén (17/7). Trainer: Guillermo Stábile (121).
**Goals**: Osvaldo Ángel Nardiello (13, 25), Edgardo Jorge D'Ascenzo (59), Raúl Oscar Belén (89).

**328.** 29.05.1960 **ARGENTINA - BRAZIL** **1-4(0-0,0-2)** Copa Roca
Estadio Monumental „Antonio Vespucio Liberti", Buenos Aires; Referee: Juan Carlos Robles (Chile); Attendance: 60,000
**ARG:** Osvaldo Fabián Ocampo Ayala (8/0), Carlos Alberto Álvarez (8/0), Juan Carlos Murúa (11/0), Rubén Marino Navarro (8/0), Héctor Juan Guidi (Cap) (29/0), José Nazionale (2/0), Martín Esteban Pando (2/0) [80.Héctor Rubén Berón (2/0)], Osvaldo Ángel Nardiello (11/5), Osvaldo Carceo (2/0) [70.Walter Antonio Jiménez (7/1)], Edgardo Jorge D'Ascenzo (7/1) [80.Héctor Rubén Sosa (8/6)], Raúl Oscar Belén (18/7). Trainer: Guillermo Stábile (122).
**Goal**: Héctor Rubén Sosa (91).

**329.** 09.07.1960 **ARGENTINA - PARAGUAY** **1-0(0-0)** Copa Atlántico
Estadio Monumental „Antonio Vespucio Liberti", Buenos Aires; Referee: João Etzel Filho (Brazil)
**ARG:** Antonio Roma (5/0), Rubén Marino Navarro (Cap) (9/0), Miguel Ángel Vidal (1/0), Carmelo Simeone (4/0), Guillermo César Reynoso (1/0) [60.Héctor Juan Guidi (30/0)], Federico Sacchi (1/0) [46.José Varacka (19/0)], Osvaldo Ángel Nardiello (12/5), Martín Esteban Pando (3/0), Norberto Menéndez (12/4) [46.Osvaldo Carceo (3/0)], Héctor Rubén Sosa (9/7), Raúl Oscar Belén (19/7). Trainer: Guillermo Stábile (123).
**Goal**: Héctor Rubén Sosa (71).

**330.** 12.07.1960 **BRAZIL – ARGENTINA** **5-1(3-1)** Copa Atlántico
Estádio „Jornalista Mário Filho" (Maracanã), Rio de Janeiro; Referee: Juan Carlos Armental (Uruguay); Attendance: 57,874
**ARG:** Antonio Roma (6/0), Néstor Lucas Cardoso (1/0), Rubén Marino Navarro (10/0), Carmelo Simeone (5/0), Héctor Juan Guidi (Cap) (31/0), José Varacka (20/0) [*sent off*], Norberto Constante Boggio (8/0) [62.Osvaldo Carceo (4/0)], Oscar Pablo Rossi (4/0), Norberto Menéndez (13/4) [46.Federico Sacchi (2/0)], Héctor Rubén Sosa (10/8) [62.Hugo Osvaldo González (1/0)], Raúl Oscar Belén (20/7). Trainer: Guillermo Stábile (124).
**Goal**: Héctor Rubén Sosa (6).

**331.** 24.07.1960 **ARGENTINA - SPAIN** **2-0(2-0)**
Estadio Monumental „Antonio Vespucio Liberti", Buenos Aires; Referee: Juan Carlos Robles (Chile); Attendance: 70,000
**ARG:** Antonio Roma (7/0), Carmelo Simeone (6/0), Rubén Marino Navarro (11/0), Miguel Ángel Vidal (2/0), Héctor Juan Guidi (Cap) (32/0), Federico Sacchi (3/0), Norberto Constante Boggio (9/0), Oscar Pablo Rossi (5/0), Norberto Menéndez (14/4) [75.Walter Antonio Jiménez (8/1)], José Francisco Sanfilippo (16/11) [72.Ernesto Grillo (20/8)], Raúl Oscar Belén (21/7). Trainer: Victorio Luis Spinetto (1).
**Goals**: José Francisco Sanfilippo (30, 37).

**332.** 17.08.1960 **ARGENTINA - URUGUAY** **4-0(0-0)** Copa Atlántico
Estadio Monumental „Antonio Vespucio Liberti", Buenos Aires; Referee: João Etzel Filho (Brazil); Attendance: 40,000
**ARG:** Antonio Roma (8/0), Rubén Marino Navarro (Cap) (12/0), Miguel Ángel Vidal (3/0), Carmelo Simeone (7/0), Ricardo José María Ramaciotti (1/0), Juan Carlos Schneider (1/0) [46.Antonio Cielinsky (2/0)], Oscar Pablo Rossi (6/0), Oreste Osmar Corbatta (33/13), Norberto Constante Boggio (10/0) [58.Roberto Leonardo Brookes (5/1)], Walter Antonio Jiménez (9/2), José Francisco Sanfilippo (17/14). Trainer: Victorio Luis Spinetto (2).
**Goals**: José Francisco Sanfilippo (48), Walter Antonio Jiménez (53), José Francisco Sanfilippo (59, 69).

**333.** 04.12.1960 **ECUADOR - ARGENTINA** **3-6(0-4)** 7th FIFA WC. Qualifiers
Estadio Olimpico „Atahualpa", Guayaquil; Referee: Juan Carlos Robles (Chile); Attendance: 60,000
**ARG:** Antonio Roma (9/0), Carmelo Simeone (8/0), Rubén Marino Navarro (Cap) (13/0), Miguel Ángel Vidal (4/0), Ricardo José María Ramaciotti (2/1), Federico Sacchi (4/0), Oreste Osmar Corbatta (34/15), Martín Esteban Pando (4/1), Héctor Rubén Sosa (11/9), José Francisco Sanfilippo (18/15), Raúl Oscar Belén (22/7). Trainer: Victorio Luis Spinetto (3).
**Goals**: Oreste Osmar Corbatta (5 penalty), Martín Esteban Pando (12), Héctor Rubén Sosa (14), Oreste Osmar Corbatta (40), José Francisco Sanfilippo (47), Ricardo José María Ramaciotti (75).

**334.** 17.12.1960 **ARGENTINA - ECUADOR** **5-0(1-0)** 7th FIFA WC. Qualifiers
Estadio „Alberto Armando", Buenos Aires; Referee: Juan Carlos Robles (Chile); Attendance: 50,000
**ARG:** Antonio Roma (10/0), Carmelo Simeone (9/0), Rubén Marino Navarro (Cap) (14/0), Miguel Ángel Vidal (5/0), Ricardo José María Ramaciotti (3/1), Federico Sacchi (5/0), Oreste Osmar Corbatta (35/16), Martín Esteban Pando (5/2), Héctor Rubén Sosa (12/10), José Francisco Sanfilippo (19/16), Raúl Oscar Belén (23/7). Trainer: Victorio Luis Spinetto (4).
**Goals**: Romulo Gómez (6 own goal), José Francisco Sanfilippo (53), Oreste Osmar Corbatta (55 penalty), Héctor Rubén Sosa (75), Martín Esteban Pando (90).

**335.** 17.05.1961 **PARAGUAY - ARGENTINA** **0-0**
Estadio Puerto Sajonia, Asunción; Referee: Roberto Héctor Goicoechea (Argentina); Attendance: 8,000
**ARG:** Antonio Roma (11/0), Carmelo Simeone (10/0), Rubén Marino Navarro (Cap) (15/0) [30.Silvio Marzolini (4/0)], Miguel Ángel Vidal (6/0) [70.Roberto Manuel Blanco (2/0)], Ricardo José María Ramaciotti (4/1), José Rafael Albrecht (1/0), Martín Roberto Canseco (1/0) [46.Mario Luis Griguol (1/0)], Martín Esteban Pando (6/2), Luis Alfredo Artime (1/0), Ermindo Ángel Onega (5/1) [46.Oscar Pablo Rossi (7/0)], Raúl Oscar Belén (24/7) [46.Alberto Mario González (1/0)]. Trainer: Victorio Luis Spinetto (5).

**336.** 04.06.1961 **PORTUGAL - ARGENTINA** **0-2(0-0)**
Estádio Nacional, Lisboa; Referee: Manuel Asensi (Spain); Attendance: 65,000
**ARG:** Antonio Roma (12/0), Carmelo Simeone (11/0), José Manuel Ramos Delgado (2/0), Miguel Ángel Vidal (7/0), Héctor Juan Guidi (Cap) (33/0), Federico Sacchi (6/0), Oreste Osmar Corbatta (36/16), Oscar Pablo Rossi (8/0) [46.Martín Esteban Pando (7/3)], Héctor Rubén Sosa (13/10), José Francisco Sanfilippo (20/17), Alberto Mario González (2/0). Trainer: Victorio Luis Spinetto (6).
**Goals**: Martín Esteban Pando (50), José Francisco Sanfilippo (80).

**337.** 11.06.1961 **SPAIN - ARGENTINA** **2-0(0-0)**
Estadio „Ramón Sánchez Pizjuán", Sevilla; Referee: Concetto Lo Bello (Italy); Attendance: 60,000
**ARG:** Antonio Roma (13/0), Carmelo Simeone (12/0), José Manuel Ramos Delgado (3/0), Miguel Ángel Vidal (8/0) [46.Silvio Marzolini (5/0)], Héctor Juan Guidi (Cap) (34/0), Federico Sacchi (7/0) [54.José Rafael Albrecht (2/0)], Oreste Osmar Corbatta (37/16), Martín Esteban Pando (8/3), Héctor Rubén Sosa (14/10), José Francisco Sanfilippo (21/17), Alberto Mario González (3/0). Trainer: Victorio Luis Spinetto (7).

**338.** 15.06.1961 **ITALY - ARGENTINA** **4-1(3-0)**
Stadio Comunale, Firenze; Referee: Marcel Bois (France); Attendance: 36,500
**ARG:** Néstor Martín Errea (2/0) [46.Antonio Roma (14/0)], Carmelo Simeone (13/0), Silvio Marzolini (6/0), Rubén Marino Navarro (16/0), Héctor Juan Guidi (Cap) (35/0) [46.Ricardo José María Ramaciotti (5/1)], Federico Sacchi (8/1), Mario Luis Griguol (2/0), Oscar Pablo Rossi (9/0) [46.Martín Esteban Pando (9/3)], Ermindo Ángel Onega (6/1), José Francisco Sanfilippo (22/17), Alberto Mario González (4/0). Trainer: Victorio Luis Spinetto (8).
**Goal**: Federico Sacchi (67).

**339.** 19.06.1961 **CZECHOSLOVAKIA - ARGENTINA** **3-3(2-2)**
Štadion Za Lužánkami, Brno; Referee: Josef Stoll (Austria); Attendance: 40,000
**ARG:** Antonio Roma (15/0), Carmelo Simeone (14/0), José Manuel Ramos Delgado (4/0), Miguel Ángel Vidal (9/0), Héctor Juan Guidi (Cap) (36/0), Federico Sacchi (9/1) [83.José Rafael Albrecht (3/0)], Oreste Osmar Corbatta (38/16) [62.Mario Luis Griguol (3/0)], Martín Esteban Pando (10/3), Héctor Rubén Sosa (15/10) [62.Luis Alfredo Artime (2/1)], José Francisco Sanfilippo (23/19), Norberto Constante Boggio (11/0). Trainer: Victorio Luis Spinetto (9).
**Goals**: José Francisco Sanfilippo (5, 37), Luis Alfredo Artime (57).

**340.** 24.06.1961 **SOVIET UNION - ARGENTINA** **0-0**
Lenin Moskva, Moskva; Referee: Giulio Campanati (Italy); Attendance: 102,000
**ARG:** Antonio Roma (16/0), Carmelo Simeone (15/0), José Manuel Ramos Delgado (5/0), Miguel Ángel Vidal (10/0), Héctor Juan Guidi (Cap) (37/0) [53.Ricardo José María Ramaciotti (6/1)], José Rafael Albrecht (4/0), Mario Luis Griguol (4/0) [75.Oreste Osmar Corbatta (39/16)], Martín Esteban Pando (11/3), Héctor Rubén Sosa (16/10) [46.Oscar Pablo Rossi (10/0)], José Francisco Sanfilippo (24/19), Norberto Constante Boggio (12/0). Trainer: Victorio Luis Spinetto (10).

**341.** 12.10.1961 **ARGENTINA - PARAGUAY** **5-1(4-0)**
Estadio Independiente, Avellaneda, Buenos Aires; Referee: Cabrera (Paraguay); Attendance: 30,500
**ARG:** Antonio Roma (17/0) [68.Edgardo Norberto Andrada (1/0)], José Manuel Ramos Delgado (6/0), Miguel Ángel Vidal (Cap) (11/0), Carlos Alberto Sainz (1/0), Antonio Ubaldo Rattín (4/0), Antonio Cielinsky (3/0), Oreste Osmar Corbatta (40/18), Juan José Pizzuti (11/4) [63.Oscar Pablo Rossi (11/0)], Luis Alfredo Artime (3/2) [17.Marcelo Ernesto Pagani (1/1)], José Francisco Sanfilippo (25/20) [63.Alberto Mario González (5/0)], Raúl Oscar Belén (25/7). Trainer: José D'Amico (1).
**Goals**: Oreste Osmar Corbatta (6), Luis Alfredo Artime (11), Marcelo Ernesto Pagani (27), José Francisco Sanfilippo (42), Oreste Osmar Corbatta (62 penalty).

**342.** 18.11.1961 **ARGENTINA – SOVIET UNION** **1-2(0-2)**
Estadio Monumental „Antonio Vespucio Liberti", Buenos Aires; Referee: Juan Carlos Robles (Chile); Attendance: 100,000
**ARG:** Antonio Roma (18/0), José Manuel Ramos Delgado (7/0), Miguel Ángel Vidal (Cap) (12/0), Carmelo Simeone (16/0), Mario Luis Griguol (5/0) [46.Antonio Ubaldo Rattín (5/0)], Federico Sacchi (10/1), Oreste Osmar Corbatta (41/18), Juan José Pizzuti (12/4) [67.Marcelo Ernesto Pagani (2/1)], Luis Alfredo Artime (4/2) [46.Martín Esteban Pando (12/3)], José Francisco Sanfilippo (26/20), Raúl Oscar Belén (26/8). Trainer: José D'Amico (2).
**Goal**: Raúl Oscar Belén (87).

**343.** 13.03.1962 **URUGUAY - ARGENTINA** **1-1(0-1)**
Estadio Centenario, Montevideo; Referee: Sergio Bustamante (Chile); Attendance: 35,000
**ARG:** Antonio Roma (19/0), Rubén Marino Navarro (Cap) (17/0), Alberto Jorge Mariotti (1/0), Carmelo Simeone (17/0), Antonio Ubaldo Rattín (6/0) [88.Raúl Alberto Páez (1/0)], Vladislao Wenceslao Cap (8/1), Oreste Osmar Corbatta (42/18), Ramón Gregorio Abeledo (6/0) [59.Oscar Pablo Rossi (12/0)], Luis Eduardo Suárez (1/0) [58.Mario Rodríguez (1/0)], Héctor Rubén Sosa (17/10) [68.Pedro Eugenio Callá (13/3)], Raúl Oscar Belén (27/9). Trainer: Juan Carlos Lorenzo (1).
**Goal**: Raúl Oscar Belén (16).

**344.** 28.03.1962 **ARGENTINA - MEXICO** **1-0(1-0)**
Estadio Monumental „Antonio Vespucio Liberti", Buenos Aires; Referee: Carlos Nay Foino (Argentina); Attendance: 20,000
**ARG:** Antonio Roma (20/0), Rubén Marino Navarro (Cap) (18/0), Miguel Ángel Vidal (13/0), Carlos Alberto Sainz (2/0), Antonio Ubaldo Rattín (7/0), Vladislao Wenceslao Cap (9/1), Oreste Osmar Corbatta (43/18) [60.Héctor Osvaldo Facundo (5/0)], Ramón Gregorio Abeledo (7/0) [Alberto Mario González (6/0)], Luis Alfredo Artime (5/2) [60.Marcelo Ernesto Pagani (3/1)], José Francisco Sanfilippo (27/20), Raúl Oscar Belén (28/9). Trainer: Juan Carlos Lorenzo (2).
**Goal**: Arturo Chaines (21 own goal).

**345.** 30.05.1962 **ARGENTINA - BULGARIA** **1-0(1-0)** 7th FIFA WC. Group Stage.
Estadio „Braden Copper", Rancagua (Chile); Referee: Juan Gardeazábal Garay (Spain); Attendance: 7,134
**ARG:** Antonio Roma (21/0), Rubén Marino Navarro (Cap) (19/0), Silvio Marzolini (7/0), Carlos Alberto Sainz (3/0), Raúl Alberto Páez (2/0), Federico Sacchi (11/1), Héctor Osvaldo Facundo (6/1), Oscar Pablo Rossi (13/0), Marcelo Ernesto Pagani (4/1), José Francisco Sanfilippo (28/20), Raúl Oscar Belén (29/9). Trainer: Juan Carlos Lorenzo (3).
**Goal**: Héctor Osvaldo Facundo (4).

**346.** 02.06.1962 **ENGLAND - ARGENTINA** **3-1(2-0)** 7th FIFA WC. Group Stage.
Estadio „Braden Copper", Rancagua (Chile); Referee: Nikolay Latyshev (Soviet Union); Attendance: 9,749
**ARG:** Antonio Roma (22/0), Rubén Marino Navarro (Cap) (20/0), Silvio Marzolini (8/0), Vladislao Wenceslao Cap (10/1), Raúl Alberto Páez (3/0), Federico Sacchi (12/1), Antonio Ubaldo Rattín (8/0), Juan Carlos Oleniak (1/0), Héctor Rubén Sosa (18/10), José Francisco Sanfilippo (29/21), Raúl Oscar Belén (30/9). Trainer: Juan Carlos Lorenzo (4).
**Goal**: José Francisco Sanfilippo (81).

**347.** 06.06.1962 **HUNGARY - ARGENTINA** **0-0** 7th FIFA WC. Group Stage.
Estadio „Braden Copper", Rancagua (Chile); Referee: Arturo Maximo Yamasaki Maldonado (Peru); Attendance: 7,945
**ARG:** Rogelio Antonio Domínguez (20/0), José Manuel Ramos Delgado (8/0), Carlos Alberto Sainz (4/0), Silvio Marzolini (9/0), Vladislao Wenceslao Cap (11/1), Federico Sacchi (13/1), Martín Esteban Pando (Cap) (13/3), Héctor Osvaldo Facundo (7/1), Marcelo Ernesto Pagani (5/1), Juan Carlos Oleniak (2/0), Alberto Mario González (7/0). Trainer: Juan Carlos Lorenzo (5).

**348.** 15.08.1962 **ARGENTINA - URUGUAY** **3-1(1-0)** Copa Lipton
Estadio Monumental „Antonio Vespucio Liberti", Buenos Aires; Referee: Juan Regis Brozzi (Argentina); Attendance: 30,000
**ARG:** Rogelio Antonio Domínguez (21/0), José Manuel Ramos Delgado (9/0), Miguel Ángel Vidal (14/0), Carlos Alberto Sainz (5/0), Antonio Ubaldo Rattín (9/0), José Varacka (21/0), Ernesto Humberto Juárez (1/0), César Luis Menotti (1/0), Marcelo Ernesto Pagani (6/2) [46.Daniel Alberto Willington (1/1)], Ernesto Grillo (Cap) (21/8), Alberto Mario González (8/1). Trainer: Néstor Raúl Rossi (1).
**Goals**: Marcelo Ernesto Pagani (30), Daniel Alberto Willington (54), Alberto Mario González (69).

**349.** 07.11.1962 **CHILE - ARGENTINA** **1-1(1-1)** Copa Carlos Dittborn
Estadio Nacional, Santiago; Referee: Juan Carlos Robles (Chile); Attendance: 51,000
**ARG:** Edgardo Norberto Andrada (2/0), Rubén Marino Navarro (Cap) (21/0), Néstor Lucas Cardoso (2/0), Carmelo Simeone (18/0) [80.Roberto Oscar Ferreiro (1/0)], Mario Luis Griguol (6/0), Jorge Alberto Maldonado (1/0), Ernesto Humberto Juárez (2/0), César Luis Menotti (2/0) [83.Mario Rodríguez (2/0)], Luis Alfredo Artime (6/3), Oscar Pablo Rossi (14/0), Roberto Leonardo Brookes (6/1). Trainer: Alejandro Galán (1).
**Goal**: Luis Alfredo Artime (12).

**350.** 21.11.1962 **ARGENTINA - CHILE** **1-0(0-0)** Copa Carlos Dittborn
Estadio Monumental „Antonio Vespucio Liberti", Buenos Aires; Referee: Roberto Héctor Goicoechea (Argentina); Attendance: 30,000
**ARG:** Edgardo Norberto Andrada (3/0), Rubén Marino Navarro (Cap) (22/0), Néstor Lucas Cardoso (3/0), Carmelo Simeone (19/0), Mario Luis Griguol (7/0) [53.José Rafael Albrecht (5/0)], Jorge Alberto Maldonado (2/0), Ernesto Humberto Juárez (3/0), César Luis Menotti (3/0) [73.Mario Rodríguez (3/0)], Luis Alfredo Artime (7/4), Oscar Pablo Rossi (15/0), Roberto Leonardo Brookes (7/1) [53.Luis Gregorio Ciaccia (1/0)]. Trainer: Alejandro Galán (2).
**Goal**: Luis Alfredo Artime (78).

**351.** 10.03.1963 **ARGENTINA - COLOMBIA** **4-2(2-2)** 28th Copa América
Estadio „Félix Capriles", Cochabamba (Bolivia); Referee: João Etzel Filho (Brazil); Attendance: 18,000
**ARG:** Edgardo Norberto Andrada (4/0), Rubén Marino Navarro (Cap) (23/0), Néstor Lucas Cardoso (4/0), Oscar Raimundo Martín (1/0), José Rafael Albrecht (6/0) [59.Carlos Timoteo Griguol (3/0)], José Ricardo Vázquez (1/0), Ernesto Humberto Juárez (4/0), César Luis Menotti (4/0) [75.Mario Rodríguez (4/1)], Jorge Hugo Fernández (1/1) [46.Oscar Pablo Rossi (16/0)], Raúl Armando Savoy (1/0), Roberto Héctor Zárate (9/4). Trainer: Horacio Amable Torres (1).
**Goals**: Roberto Héctor Zárate (3), Jorge Hugo Fernández (11), Mario Rodríguez (87), Roberto Héctor Zárate (89).

**352.** 13.03.1963 **ARGENTINA - PERU** **1-2(0-0)** 28th Copa América
Estadio „Félix Capriles", Cochabamba (Bolivia); Referee: José Dimas Larrosa (Paraguay); Attendance: 10,000
**ARG:** Edgardo Norberto Andrada (5/0), Rubén Marino Navarro (Cap) (24/0), Mario Roque Ditro (1/0), Oscar Raimundo Martín (2/0), Carlos Timoteo Griguol (4/0), José Ricardo Vázquez (2/0), Raúl Emilio Bernao (1/0) [69.Ernesto Humberto Juárez (5/0)], César Luis Menotti (5/0), Oscar Pablo Rossi (17/0) [55.Mario Rodríguez (5/1)], Raúl Armando Savoy (2/0), Roberto Héctor Zárate (10/5) [80.Juan Carlos Lallana (1/0)]. Trainer: Horacio Amable Torres (2).
**Goal**: Roberto Héctor Zárate (57).

**353.** 20.03.1963 **ARGENTINA - ECUADOR** **4-2(1-1)** 28th Copa América
Estadio „Félix Capriles", Cochabamba (Bolivia); Referee: Arturo Maximo Yamasaki Maldonado (Peru); Attendance: 20,000
**ARG:** Edgardo Norberto Andrada (6/0), Rubén Marino Navarro (Cap) (25/0), Mario Roque Ditro (2/0) [72.Roberto Oscar Ferreiro (2/0)], Oscar Raimundo Martín (3/0), Carlos Timoteo Griguol (5/0), José Ricardo Vázquez (3/0), Ernesto Humberto Juárez (6/0), Enrique Santiago Fernández (1/0) [84.Oscar Pablo Rossi (18/0)], Mario Rodríguez (6/2), Raúl Armando Savoy (3/2), Roberto Héctor Zárate (11/6). Trainer: Horacio Amable Torres (3).
**Goals**: Raúl Armando Savoy (34), Roberto Héctor Zárate (53), Mario Rodríguez (58), Raúl Armando Savoy (90).

**354.** 24.03.1963 **ARGENTINA - BRAZIL** **3-0(2-0)** 28th Copa América
Estadio „Hernándo Siles Zuazo", La Paz (Bolivia); Referee: Arturo Maximo Yamasaki Maldonado (Peru); Attendance: 30,000
**ARG:** Edgardo Norberto Andrada (7/0), Rubén Marino Navarro (Cap) (26/0), Mario Roque Ditro (3/0) [59.Néstor Lucas Cardoso (5/0)], Oscar Raimundo Martín (4/0), Carlos Timoteo Griguol (6/0), José Ricardo Vázquez (4/0), Ernesto Humberto Juárez (7/1), Enrique Santiago Fernández (2/0), Mario Rodríguez (7/3), Raúl Armando Savoy (4/3), Roberto Héctor Zárate (12/6). Trainer: Horacio Amable Torres (4).
**Goals**: Mario Rodríguez (3), Raúl Armando Savoy (33), Ernesto Humberto Juárez (86).

**355.** 28.03.1963 **BOLIVIA - ARGENTINA** **3-2(2-2)** 28th Copa América
Estadio „Hernándo Siles Zuazo", La Paz; Referee: Arturo Maximo Yamasaki Maldonado (Peru); Attendance: 20,000
**ARG:** Edgardo Norberto Andrada (8/0), Rubén Marino Navarro (Cap) (27/0), Néstor Lucas Cardoso (6/0), Oscar Raimundo Martín (5/0) [46.Roberto Oscar Ferreiro (3/0)], Carlos Timoteo Griguol (7/0), José Ricardo Vázquez (5/0), Ernesto Humberto Juárez (8/1), Enrique Santiago Fernández (3/0) [67.Jorge Hugo Fernández (2/1)], Mario Rodríguez (8/5), Raúl Armando Savoy (5/3), Roberto Héctor Zárate (13/6). Trainer: Horacio Amable Torres (5).
**Goals**: Mario Rodríguez (27, 34).

**356.** 31.03.1963 **ARGENTINA - PARAGUAY** **1-1(0-1)** 28th Copa América
Estadio „Hernándo Siles Zuazo", La Paz (Bolivia); Referee: Arturo Maximo Yamasaki Maldonado (Peru); Attendance: 15,000
**ARG:** Edgardo Norberto Andrada (9/0), Rubén Marino Navarro (Cap) (28/0), Néstor Lucas Cardoso (7/0), Oscar Raimundo Martín (6/0), Carlos Timoteo Griguol (8/0), Norberto Claudio Bautista (1/0), Ernesto Humberto Juárez (9/1) [57.Raúl Emilio Bernao (2/0)], Enrique Santiago Fernández (4/0) [77.Oscar Pablo Rossi (19/0)], Jorge Hugo Fernández (3/1), Raúl Armando Savoy (6/3), Roberto Héctor Zárate (14/6) [57.Juan Carlos Lallana (2/1)]. Trainer: Horacio Amable Torres (6).
**Goal**: Juan Carlos Lallana (58).

**357.** 13.04.1963 **BRAZIL - ARGENTINA** **2-3(0-1)** Copa Roca
Estádio „Cicero Pompeu de Toledo" Morumbi, São Paulo; Referee: Estebán Marino (Uruguay); Attendance: 50,000
**ARG:** Edgardo Norberto Andrada (10/0), Rubén Marino Navarro (Cap) (29/0), David Carmelo Iñigo (3/0), Oscar Raimundo Martín (7/0) [82.Roberto Oscar Ferreiro (4/0)], Antonio Cielinsky (4/0) [64.José Agustín Mesiano (1/0)], José Ricardo Vázquez (6/0), Ernesto Humberto Juárez (10/2), Enrique Santiago Fernández (5/0), Julio San Lorenzo (1/0) [56.Mario Rodríguez (9/5)], Raúl Armando Savoy (7/3), Juan Carlos Lallana (3/3). Trainer: Horacio Amable Torres (7).
**Goals**: Juan Carlos Lallana (29, 47), Ernesto Humberto Juárez (63).

**358.** 16.04.1963 **BRAZIL - ARGENTINA** **5-2(x-x,4-1)** Copa Roca
Estádio „Jornalista Mário Filho" (Maracanã), Rio de Janeiro; Referee: Estebán Marino (Uruguay); Attendance:
**ARG:** Edgardo Norberto Andrada (11/0), Rubén Marino Navarro (Cap) (30/0), David Carmelo Iñigo (4/0) [85.Raúl Decaria (1/0)], Oscar Raimundo Martín (8/0), Antonio Cielinsky (5/0), José Ricardo Vázquez (7/0), Ernesto Humberto Juárez (11/2), Enrique Santiago Fernández (6/1), Julio San Lorenzo (2/0) [65.César Luis Menotti (6/0)], Raúl Armando Savoy (8/4), Juan Carlos Lallana (4/3) [85.Mario Rodríguez (10/5)]. Trainer: Horacio Amable Torres (8).
**Goals**: Enrique Santiago Fernández, Raúl Armando Savoy.

**359.** 15.10.1963 **PARAGUAY - ARGENTINA** **0-4(0-1)** Copa Chevallier Boutell
Estadio Puerto Sajonia, Asunción; Referee: Manuel Velarde (Argentina)
**ARG:** Amadeo Raúl Carrizo (16/0), Rubén Marino Navarro (Cap) (31/0), Mario Bonczuk (1/0), Roberto Oscar Ferreiro (5/0), Antonio Ubaldo Rattín (10/0) [79.José Rafael Albrecht (7/0)], José Varacka (22/0), Ernesto Humberto Juárez (12/2) [46.Daniel Alberto Willington (2/1); 79.Oscar Pablo Rossi (20/0)], Enrique Santiago Fernández (7/1), Luis Alfredo Artime (8/6), Ermindo Ángel Onega (7/2), Raúl Armando Savoy (9/5). Trainer: José D'Amico (3).
**Goals**: Luis Alfredo Artime (38, 55), Raúl Armando Savoy (82), Ermindo Ángel Onega (87).

**360.** 29.10.1963 **ARGENTINA - PARAGUAY** **2-3(1-1)** Copa Chevallier Boutell
Estadio Monumental „Antonio Vespucio Liberti", Buenos Aires; Referee: José Dimas Larrosa (Paraguay); Attendance: 40,000
**ARG:** Amadeo Raúl Carrizo (17/0) [46.Edgardo Norberto Andrada (12/0)], Rubén Marino Navarro (Cap) (32/0), Mario Bonczuk (2/0), Roberto Oscar Ferreiro (6/0), Antonio Ubaldo Rattín (11/0) [46.Federico Sacchi (14/1)], José Varacka (23/0), Ermindo Ángel Onega (8/2), Enrique Santiago Fernández (8/1) [82.Oscar Pablo Rossi (21/0)], Luis Alfredo Artime (9/7), César Luis Menotti (7/1) [46.Daniel Alberto Willington (3/1)], Raúl Oscar Belén (31/9). Trainer: José D'Amico (4).
**Goals**: César Luis Menotti (15), Luis Alfredo Artime (58).

**361.** 31.05.1964 **ARGENTINA - PORTUGAL** **2-0(0-0)** Copa des Naciones
Estádio „Jornalista Mário Filho" (Maracanã), Rio de Janeiro; Referee: Leopold Sylvain Horn (Holland); Attendance: 40,000
**ARG:** Amadeo Raúl Carrizo (18/0), José Manuel Ramos Delgado (Cap) (10/0), Miguel Ángel Vidal (15/0), Carmelo Simeone (20/0), Antonio Ubaldo Rattín (12/0), José Varacka (24/0), Ermindo Ángel Onega (9/2), Alberto Rendo (1/1), Luis Alfredo Artime (10/7), Alfredo Hugo Rojas (4/1), Adolfo Norberto Bielli (1/0). Trainer: José María Minella (1).
**Goals**: Alfredo Hugo Rojas (56), Alberto Rendo (89).

**362.** 03.06.1964 **BRAZIL - ARGENTINA** **0-3(0-1)** Copa des Naciones
Estádio Pacaembú, São Paulo; Referee: Gottfried Dienst (Switzerland); Attendance: 50,000
**ARG:** Amadeo Raúl Carrizo (19/0), José Manuel Ramos Delgado (Cap) (11/0), Abel Omar Vieytez (1/0), Carmelo Simeone (21/0), Antonio Ubaldo Rattín (13/0), José Varacka (25/0), Ermindo Ángel Onega (10/3), Alberto Rendo (2/1), Pedro Prospitti (1/0), Alfredo Hugo Rojas (5/1), José Agustín Mesiano (2/0) [27.Roberto Marcelo Telch (1/2)]. Trainer: José María Minella (2).
**Goals**: Ermindo Ángel Onega (38), Roberto Marcelo Telch (61, 89).

**363.** 06.06.1964 **ARGENTINA - ENGLAND** **1-0(0-0)** Copa des Naciones
Estádio „Jornalista Mário Filho" (Maracanã), Rio de Janeiro; Referee: Leopold Sylvain Horn (Holland); Attendance: 15,000
**ARG:** Amadeo Raúl Carrizo (20/0), José Manuel Ramos Delgado (Cap) (12/0), Miguel Ángel Vidal (16/0), Carmelo Simeone (22/0), Antonio Ubaldo Rattín (14/0), Abel Omar Vieytez (2/0), Ermindo Ángel Onega (11/3), Alberto Rendo (3/1), Pedro Prospitti (2/0) [40.Mario Norberto Chaldú (1/0)], Alfredo Hugo Rojas (6/2), Roberto Marcelo Telch (2/2). Trainer: José María Minella (3).
**Goal**: Alfredo Hugo Rojas (66).

**364.** 24.09.1964 **ARGENTINA - CHILE** **5-0(3-0)** Copa Carlos Dittborn
Estadio Monumental „Antonio Vespucio Liberti", Buenos Aires; Referee: Aurelio Domingo Bossolino (Argentina); Attendance: 30,000
**ARG:** Ediberto Luis Righi (1/0) [68.Agustín Enrique Irusta (1/0)], José Manuel Ramos Delgado (Cap) (13/0), Abel Omar Vieytez (3/0), Adolfo Vázquez (1/0), Antonio Ubaldo Rattín (15/0) [46.Roberto Marcelo Telch (3/2)], José Varacka (26/0) [59.José Agustín Mesiano (3/0)], Mario Norberto Chaldú (2/0), Alberto Rendo (4/2), Luis Alfredo Artime (11/9) [59.Daniel Alberto Willington (4/1)], Ermindo Ángel Onega (12/4), Adolfo Norberto Bielli (2/1). Trainer: José María Minella (4).
**Goals**: Luis Alfredo Artime (3), Ermindo Ángel Onega (32), Luis Alfredo Artime (42), Alberto Rendo (49), Adolfo Norberto Bielli (69).

**365.** 14.10.1964 **CHILE - ARGENTINA** **1-1(1-1)** Copa Carlos Dittborn
Estadio Nacional, Santiago; Referee: Juan Carlos Robles (Chile); Attendance: 52,160
**ARG:** Ediberto Luis Righi (2/0), José Manuel Ramos Delgado (Cap) (14/0), Abel Omar Vieytez (4/0), Adolfo Vázquez (2/0), Antonio Ubaldo Rattín (16/1), José Agustín Mesiano (4/0), Mario Norberto Chaldú (3/0) [46.José Luis Luna (1/0)], Alberto Rendo (5/2), Alfredo Hugo Rojas (7/2), Ermindo Ángel Onega (13/4) [46.Daniel Alberto Willington (5/1)], Adolfo Norberto Bielli (3/1). Trainer: José María Minella (5).
**Goal**: Antonio Ubaldo Rattín (39).

**366.** 25.11.1964 **PARAGUAY - ARGENTINA** **3-0** Copa Chevallier Boutell
Estadio Parque Caballero, Asunción; Referee: José Dimas Larrosa (Paraguay); Attendance: 25,000
**ARG:** Ediberto Luis Righi (3/0) [76.Miguel Ángel Santoro (1/0)], José Manuel Ramos Delgado (Cap) (15/0), José Bernabé Leonardi (1/0), Adolfo Vázquez (3/0), Antonio Ubaldo Rattín (17/1), José Rafael Albrecht (8/0), José Luis Luna (2/0), Daniel Alberto Willington (6/1), Alfredo Hugo Rojas (8/2) [74.Victorio Francisco Casá (1/0)], Ermindo Ángel Onega (14/4), Adolfo Norberto Bielli (4/1). Trainer: José María Minella (6).

**367.** 08.12.1964 **ARGENTINA - PARAGUAY** **8-1(4-0)** Copa Chevallier Boutell
Estadio Monumental „Antonio Vespucio Liberti“, Buenos Aires; Referee: Miguel Ángel Francisco Comesaña (Argentina); Attendance: 40,000
**ARG:** Antonio Roma (23/0), José Manuel Ramos Delgado (Cap) (16/0), Silvio Marzolini (10/0) [70.José Bernabé Leonardi (2/0)], Adolfo Vázquez (4/0), Antonio Ubaldo Rattín (18/1) [36.Roberto Marcelo Telch (4/2)], José Rafael Albrecht (9/0) [70.Raúl Horacio Madero (1/0)], José Luis Luna (3/0), Pedro Prospitti (3/2), Luis Alfredo Artime (12/13), Ermindo Ángel Onega (15/6), Adolfo Norberto Bielli (5/1). Trainer: José María Minella (7).
**Goals**: Luis Alfredo Artime (5), Ermindo Ángel Onega (12), Luis Alfredo Artime (29), Pedro Prospitti (43), Luis Alfredo Artime (79), Pedro Prospitti (81), Luis Alfredo Artime (85), Ermindo Ángel Onega (90).

**368.** 03.06.1965 **FRANCE - ARGENTINA** **0-0**
Stade Parc des Princes, Paris; Referee: John Keith Taylor (England); Attendance: 11,931
**ARG:** Antonio Roma (24/0), José Manuel Ramos Delgado (Cap) (17/0), Silvio Marzolini (11/0), Roberto Oscar Ferreiro (7/0), Antonio Ubaldo Rattín (19/1), José Rafael Albrecht (10/0), José Luis Luna (4/0) [57.Norberto Santiago Raffo (1/0)], Alberto Rendo (6/2), Daniel Alberto Willington (7/1), Alfredo Hugo Rojas (9/2), Alberto Mario González (9/1). Trainer: José María Minella (8).

**369.** 09.06.1965 **BRAZIL - ARGENTINA** **0-0**
Estádio „Jornalista Mário Filho“ (Maracanã), Rio de Janeiro; Referee: Arturo Maximo Yamasaki Maldonado (Peru); Attendance: 130,910
**ARG:** Antonio Roma (25/0), José Manuel Ramos Delgado (Cap) (18/0), José Bernabé Leonardi (3/0), Roberto Oscar Ferreiro (8/0), Federico Sacchi (15/1), José Rafael Albrecht (11/0), Mario Norberto Chaldú (4/0) [74.Luis Medina (1/0)], Antonio Ubaldo Rattín (20/1), Alberto Rendo (7/2), Daniel Alberto Willington (8/1) [61.Norberto Santiago Raffo (2/0)], Alfredo Hugo Rojas (10/2). Trainer: José María Minella (9).

**370.** 14.07.1965 **ARGENTINA - CHILE** **1-0(1-0)** Copa Carlos Dittborn
Estadio Monumental „Antonio Vespucio Liberti“, Buenos Aires; Referee: Roberto Héctor Goicoechea (Argentina); Attendance: 25,000
**ARG:** Antonio Roma (26/0), José Manuel Ramos Delgado (Cap) (19/0), José Bernabé Leonardi (4/0), Roberto Oscar Ferreiro (9/0), Antonio Ubaldo Rattín (21/1), José Rafael Albrecht (12/0), Raúl Emilio Bernao (3/0), Ángel Clemente Rojas (1/1), Ermindo Ángel Onega (16/6), Vicente De La Mata (1/0), Oscar Tomás Más (1/0). Trainer: José María Minella (10).
**Goal**: Ángel Clemente Rojas (28).

**371.** 21.07.1965 **CHILE - ARGENTINA** **1-1(1-0)** Copa Carlos Dittborn
Estadio Nacional, Santiago; Referee: Rafael Hormazábal Díaz (Chile); Attendance: 30,000
**ARG:** Antonio Roma (27/0), José Manuel Ramos Delgado (Cap) (20/0), José Bernabé Leonardi (5/0), José Enrique Diez (1/0), José Agustín Mesiano (5/0) [46.Abel Omar Vieytez (5/0)], José Rafael Albrecht (13/0), Raúl Emilio Bernao (4/0), Alberto Rendo (8/2) [39.Vicente De La Mata (2/0)], Luis Alfredo Artime (13/13), Ermindo Ángel Onega (17/6), Oscar Tomás Más (2/1). Trainer: José María Minella (11).
**Goal**: Oscar Tomás Más (67).

**372.** 01.08.1965 **ARGENTINA - PARAGUAY** **3-0(3-0)** 8th FIFA WC. Qualifiers
Estadio Monumental „Antonio Vespucio Liberti“, Buenos Aires; Referee: Pablo Vega Albergati (Uruguay); Attendance: 63,817
**ARG:** Antonio Roma (28/0), José Manuel Ramos Delgado (Cap) (21/0), José Bernabé Leonardi (6/0), Roberto Oscar Ferreiro (10/0), Antonio Ubaldo Rattín (22/1), José Rafael Albrecht (14/0), Raúl Emilio Bernao (5/0), Vicente De La Mata (3/0), Luis Alfredo Artime (14/14), Ermindo Ángel Onega (18/7), Oscar Tomás Más (3/1). Trainer: José María Minella (12).
**Goals**: Ricardo González (15 own goal), Ermindo Ángel Onega (26), Luis Alfredo Artime (35).

**373.** 08.08.1965 **PARAGUAY - ARGENTINA** **0-0** 8th FIFA WC. Qualifiers
Estadio Defensores del Chaco, Asunción; Referee: Antonio Vuig (Brazil); Attendance: 20,763
**ARG:** Antonio Roma (29/0), José Manuel Ramos Delgado (Cap) (22/0), José Bernabé Leonardi (7/0), Roberto Oscar Ferreiro (11/0), José Rafael Albrecht (15/0), José Varacka (27/0), Raúl Emilio Bernao (6/0), Vicente De La Mata (4/0), Luis Alfredo Artime (15/14), Ermindo Ángel Onega (19/7), Oscar Tomás Más (4/1). Trainer: José María Minella (13).

**374.** 17.08.1965 **ARGENTINA - BOLIVIA** **4-1(3-0)** 8th FIFA WC. Qualifiers
Estadio Monumental „Antonio Vespucio Liberti“, Buenos Aires; Referee: Estebán Marino (Uruguay); Attendance: 56,173
**ARG:** Antonio Roma (30/0), José Manuel Ramos Delgado (Cap) (23/0), Abel Omar Vieytez (6/0), Roberto Oscar Ferreiro (12/0), Antonio Ubaldo Rattín (23/1), José Rafael Albrecht (16/0), Raúl Emilio Bernao (7/2), Ángel Clemente Rojas (2/1), Ermindo Ángel Onega (20/9), Héctor Rodolfo Veira (1/0), Oscar Tomás Más (5/1). Trainer: José María Minella (14).
**Goals**: Raúl Emilio Bernao (3), Ermindo Ángel Onega (24 penalty,25), Raúl Emilio Bernao (56).

**375.** 29.08.1965 **BOLIVIA - ARGENTINA** **1-2(1-2)** 8th FIFA WC. Qualifiers
Estadio „Hernándo Siles Zuazo“, La Paz; Referee: Carlos Riveros (Peru); Attendance: 9,690
**ARG:** Antonio Roma (31/0), José Manuel Ramos Delgado (Cap) (24/0), José Bernabé Leonardi (8/0), José Enrique Diez (2/0), Antonio Ubaldo Rattín (24/1), José Varacka (28/0), José Luis Luna (5/0), José Rafael Albrecht (17/0), Luis Alfredo Artime (16/16), Ermindo Ángel Onega (21/9), Oscar Tomás Más (6/1). Trainer: José María Minella (15).
**Goals**: Luis Alfredo Artime (31, 39).

**376.** 01.12.1965 **ARGENTINA – SOVIET UNION** **1-1(0-1)**
Estadio Monumental „Antonio Vespucio Liberti“, Buenos Aires; Referee: Estebán Marino (Uruguay); Attendance: 60,000
**ARG:** Miguel Ángel Santoro (2/0), José Manuel Ramos Delgado (Cap) (25/0), Oscar Miguel Malbernat (1/0), Roberto Oscar Ferreiro (13/0), Antonio Ubaldo Rattín (25/1), José Rafael Albrecht (18/0), José Luis Luna (6/0) [68.Oscar Antonio Pianetti (1/0)], Alberto Mario González (10/1), Juan Carlos Lallana (5/3), Ermindo Ángel Onega (22/10), Oscar Tomás Más (7/1). Trainer: Osvaldo Juan Zubeldía (1).
**Goal**: Ermindo Ángel Onega.

**377.** 11.06.1966 **ARGENTINA - POLAND** **1-1(1-0)**
Estadio Monumental „Antonio Vespucio Liberti“, Buenos Aires; Referee: Roberto Héctor Goicoechea (Argentina); Attendance: 50,000
**ARG:** Antonio Roma (32/0), Roberto Alfredo Perfumo (1/0), Silvio Marzolini (12/0), Roberto Oscar Ferreiro (14/0), Antonio Ubaldo Rattín (Cap) (26/1), José Rafael Albrecht (19/0), Ermindo Ángel Onega (23/10), Vicente De La Mata (5/0) [46.Juan Carlos Sarnari (2/0)], Alfredo Hugo Rojas (11/2), Daniel Germán Onega (1/0) [60.Aníbal Roberto Tarabini (1/0)], Oscar Tomás Más (8/2). Trainer: Juan Carlos Lorenzo (6).
**Goal**: Oscar Tomás Más (10).

**378.** 22.06.1966 **ITALY - ARGENTINA** **3-0(1-0)**
Stadio Comunale, Torino; Referee: Manuel Lousada Rodriguez (Portugal); Attendance: 65,000
**ARG:** Antonio Roma (33/0), Roberto Oscar Ferreiro (15/0), Roberto Alfredo Perfumo (2/0), José Rafael Albrecht (20/0), Silvio Marzolini (Cap) (13/0) [49.Carlos Alberto Sainz (6/0) [*sent off 66*]], Juan Carlos Sarnari (3/0), Jorge Raúl Solari (1/0), Mario Norberto Chaldú (5/0), Daniel Germán Onega (2/0) [49.Ángel Clemente Rojas (3/1)], Vicente De La Mata (6/0) [21.Ermindo Ángel Onega (24/10)], Oscar Tomás Más (9/2). Trainer: Juan Carlos Lorenzo (7).

**379.** 13.07.1966 **ARGENTINA - SPAIN** **2-1(0-0)** 8th FIFA WC. Group Stage.
Villa Park Stadium, Birmingham (England); Referee: Dimitar Rumenchev (Bulgaria); Attendance: 42,783
**ARG:** Antonio Roma (34/0), Roberto Oscar Ferreiro (16/0), Roberto Alfredo Perfumo (3/0), José Rafael Albrecht (21/0), Silvio Marzolini (14/0), Jorge Raúl Solari (2/0), Antonio Ubaldo Rattín (Cap) (27/1), Alberto Mario González (11/1), Ermindo Ángel Onega (25/10), Luis Alfredo Artime (17/18), Oscar Tomás Más (10/2). Trainer: Juan Carlos Lorenzo (8).
**Goals**: Luis Alfredo Artime (65, 79).

**380.** 16.07.1966 **ARGENTINA – WEST GERMANY** **0-0** 8th FIFA WC. Group Stage.
Villa Park Stadium, Birmingham (England); Referee: Konstantin Zečević (Yugoslavia); Attendance: 46,587
**ARG:** Antonio Roma (35/0), Roberto Oscar Ferreiro (17/0), Roberto Alfredo Perfumo (4/0), José Rafael Albrecht (22/0) [*sent off 65*], Silvio Marzolini (15/0), Jorge Raúl Solari (3/0), Antonio Ubaldo Rattín (Cap) (28/1), Alberto Mario González (12/1), Ermindo Ángel Onega (26/10), Luis Alfredo Artime (18/18), Oscar Tomás Más (11/2). Trainer: Juan Carlos Lorenzo (9).

**381.** 19.07.1966 **ARGENTINA - SWITZERLAND** **2-0(0-0)** 8th FIFA WC. Group Stage.
Hillsborough Stadium, Sheffield (England); Referee: Joaquim Fernandes Campos (Portugal); Attendance: 32,127
**ARG:** Antonio Roma (36/0), Roberto Oscar Ferreiro (18/0), Roberto Alfredo Perfumo (5/0), Oscar Osvaldo Calics (1/0), Silvio Marzolini (16/0), Jorge Raúl Solari (4/0), Antonio Ubaldo Rattín (Cap) (29/1), Alberto Mario González (13/1), Ermindo Ángel Onega (27/11), Luis Alfredo Artime (19/19), Oscar Tomás Más (12/2). Trainer: Juan Carlos Lorenzo (10).
**Goals**: Luis Alfredo Artime (52), Ermindo Ángel Onega (81).

**382.** 23.07.1966 **ENGLAND - ARGENTINA** **1-0(0-0)** 8th FIFA WC.Quarter-Finals.
Wembley Stadium, London; Referee: Rudolf Kreitlein (West Germany); Attendance: 88,000
**ARG:** Antonio Roma (37/0), Roberto Oscar Ferreiro (19/0), Roberto Alfredo Perfumo (6/0), José Rafael Albrecht (23/0), Silvio Marzolini (17/0), Jorge Raúl Solari (5/0), Antonio Ubaldo Rattín (Cap) (30/1) [*sent off 35*], Alberto Mario González (14/1), Ermindo Ángel Onega (28/11), Luis Alfredo Artime (20/19), Oscar Tomás Más (13/2). Trainer: Juan Carlos Lorenzo (11).

**383.** 18.01.1967 **ARGENTINA - PARAGUAY** **4-1(1-0)** 29th Copa América
Estadio Centenario, Montevideo (Uruguay); Referee: Mario Gasc (Chile); Attendance: 12,000
**ARG:** Antonio Roma (38/0), Iselín Santos Ovejero (1/0), Oscar Osvaldo Calics (2/0), José Rafael Albrecht (Cap) (24/1), Silvio Marzolini (18/0), David Acevedo (1/0), Raúl Emilio Bernao (8/3), Alberto Mario González (15/1) [75.Juan Carlos Sarnari (4/0)], Luis Alfredo Artime (21/20), Alfredo Hugo Rojas (12/2) [75.Norberto Santiago Raffo (3/0)], Oscar Tomás Más (14/3). Trainer: Alejandro Galán (3).
**Goals**: Oscar Tomás Más (23), Raúl Emilio Bernao (71), Luis Alfredo Artime (73), José Rafael Albrecht (89 penalty).

**384.** 22.01.1967 **ARGENTINA - BOLIVIA** **1-0(0-0)** 29th Copa América
Estadio Centenario, Montevideo (Uruguay); Referee: Eunápio Gouveia de Queiroz (Brazil); Attendance: 6,000
**ARG:** Antonio Roma (39/0), Iselín Santos Ovejero (2/0), Oscar Osvaldo Calics (3/0), José Rafael Albrecht (25/1), Silvio Marzolini (19/0), David Acevedo (2/0), Raúl Emilio Bernao (9/4), Alberto Mario González (16/1), Luis Alfredo Artime (22/20), Alfredo Hugo Rojas (13/2) [65.Héctor Rodolfo Veira (2/0)], Oscar Tomás Más (15/3). Trainer: Alejandro Galán (4).
**Goal**: Raúl Emilio Bernao (67).

**385.** 25.01.1967 **ARGENTINA - VENEZUELA** **5-1(2-0)** 29th Copa América
Estadio Centenario, Montevideo (Uruguay); Referee: Mario Gasc (Chile); Attendance: 2,500
**ARG:** Antonio Roma (40/0), Iselín Santos Ovejero (3/0) [62.Sebastián Humberto Viberti (1/0)], Oscar Osvaldo Calics (4/0), José Rafael Albrecht (26/1), Silvio Marzolini (20/1), David Acevedo (3/0) [66.Antonio Rosl (1/0)], Raúl Emilio Bernao (10/4), Alberto Mario González (17/1), Luis Alfredo Artime (23/23), Juan Carlos Sarnari (5/0), Juan Carlos Carone (1/1). Trainer: Alejandro Galán (5).
**Goals**: Luis Alfredo Artime (18), Juan Carlos Carone (26), Silvio Marzolini (50), Luis Alfredo Artime (65, 88).

**386.** 28.01.1967 **ARGENTINA - CHILE** **2-0(1-0)** 29th Copa América
Estadio Centenario, Montevideo (Uruguay); Referee: Isidro Ramírez Álvarez (Paraguay); Attendance: 14,000
**ARG:** Antonio Roma (41/0), Iselín Santos Ovejero (4/0) [55.Sebastián Humberto Viberti (2/0)], Oscar Osvaldo Calics (5/0), José Rafael Albrecht (27/1), Silvio Marzolini (21/1), David Acevedo (4/0), Raúl Emilio Bernao (11/4), Alberto Mario González (18/1), Luis Alfredo Artime (24/24), Juan Carlos Sarnari (6/1), Oscar Tomás Más (16/3). Trainer: Alejandro Galán (6).
**Goals**: Juan Carlos Sarnari (36), Luis Alfredo Artime (80).

**387.** 02.02.1967 **URUGUAY - ARGENTINA** **1-0(0-0)** 29th Copa América
Estadio Centenario, Montevideo; Referee: Mario Gasc (Chile); Attendance: 65,000
**ARG:** Antonio Roma (42/0), Oscar Osvaldo Calics (6/0), José Rafael Albrecht (28/1), Silvio Marzolini (22/1), Antonio Ubaldo Rattín (Cap) (31/1), David Acevedo (5/0), Raúl Emilio Bernao (12/4) [75.Norberto Santiago Raffo (4/0)], Alberto Mario González (19/1), Luis Alfredo Artime (25/24), Juan Carlos Sarnari (7/1) [85.Alfredo Hugo Rojas (14/2)], Oscar Tomás Más (17/3) [75.Juan Carlos Carone (2/1)]. Trainer: Alejandro Galán (7).

**388.** 15.08.1967 **CHILE - ARGENTINA** **1-0(0-0)**
Estadio Nacional, Santiago; Referee: Rafael Hormazábal Díaz (Chile); Attendance: 60,000
**ARG:** José Miguel Marín (1/0), Andrés Bertolotti (1/0), Nelson Juan López (1/0), Eduardo Luján Manera (1/0), Carlos Oscar Pachamé (Cap) (1/0), Roberto Domingo Rogel (1/0), Mario Pardo (1/0), Sebastián Humberto Viberti (3/0), Narciso Horacio Doval (1/0), Omar Wehbe (1/0), Juan Carlos Carone (3/1). Trainer: Carmelo Faraone (1).

**389.** 22.08.1967 **MEXICO - ARGENTINA** **2-1(0-0)**
Estadio Azteca, Ciudad de México; Referee: Abel Aguilar (Mexico); Attendance:
**ARG:** José Miguel Marín (2/0) [77.Carlos Adolfo Buttice (1/0)], Eduardo Luján Manera (2/0), Roberto Domingo Rogel (2/0), José Rafael Albrecht (29/1), Nelson Juan López (2/0) [37.Antonio Oscar Laginestra (1/0)], Carlos Oscar Pachamé (2/0) [68.Jorge Carlos Masalis (1/0)], Mario Pardo (2/0) [30.Hugo Ángel Tedesco (1/0)], Sebastián Humberto Viberti (4/0), Rodolfo José Fischer (1/0) [61.Daniel Germán Onega (3/0)], Roberto Jaime Zywica (1/0) [61.Omar Wehbe (2/0)], Juan Carlos Carone (4/1) [46.Enzo Enrique Gennoni (1/1)]. Trainer: Carmelo Faraone (2).
**Goal**: Enzo Enrique Gennoni (62).

**390.** 13.10.1967 **PARAGUAY - ARGENTINA** **1-1**
Estadio Puerto Sajonia, Asunción; Referee: Salvador Valenzuela (Paraguay); Attendance: 18,000
**ARG:** Hugo Orlando Gatti (1/0), Eduardo Luján Manera (3/0), Miguel Ángel López (1/0), José Rafael Albrecht (30/1), Nelson Juan López (3/0), Jorge Raúl Solari (6/0) [65.Carlos Oscar Pachamé (3/0)], Raúl Armando Savoy (10/5), Mario Pardo (3/1), Rodolfo José Fischer (2/0), Ermindo Ángel Onega (Cap) (29/11) [65.Juan Miguel Echecopar (1/0)], Oscar Antonio Pianetti (2/0) [46.Aníbal Roberto Tarabini (2/0)]. Trainer: Renato Cesarini (1).
**Goal**: Mario Pardo (17).

**391.** 08.11.1967 **CHILE - ARGENTINA** **3-1(2-0)**
Estadio Nacional, Santiago; Referee: Cláudio Vicuña Larrain (Chile); Attendance: 43,232
**ARG:** Hugo Orlando Gatti (2/0), Roberto Alfredo Perfumo (7/0), José Bernabé Leonardi (9/0), Luis Gregorio Gallo (1/0), Carlos Oscar Pachamé (4/0), José Rafael Albrecht (31/1), Raúl Emilio Bernao (13/4) [67.Mario Pardo (4/1)], Juan Carlos Rulli (1/0), Juan Carlos Cárdenas (1/0) [75.Manuel Ángel Silva (1/0)], Ermindo Ángel Onega (Cap) (30/11) [46.Jorge Hugo Fernández (4/1)], Aníbal Roberto Tarabini (3/0) [46.Juan Carlos Carone (5/2)]. Trainer: Renato Cesarini (2).
**Goal**: Juan Carlos Carone (59).

**392.** 15.05.1968 **PARAGUAY - ARGENTINA** **2-0(1-0)**
Estadio Puerto Sajonia, Asunción; Referee: Rodolfo Pérez Osorio (Paraguay); Attendance: 10,000
**ARG:** Carlos Adolfo Buttice (2/0), Luis Gregorio Gallo (2/0), Roberto Alfredo Perfumo (8/0), José Rafael Albrecht (Cap) (32/1), Nelson Juan López (4/0) [46.Néstor Aníbal Sinatra (1/0)], Juan Carlos Rulli (2/0), Alberto Rendo (9/2), Héctor Salvador Minitti (1/0), Rodolfo José Fischer (3/0), Daniel Alberto Willington (9/1), Roque Alberto Avallay (1/0) [46.Oscar Tomás Más (18/3)]. Trainer: Renato Cesarini (3).

**393.** 05.06.1968 **ARGENTINA - URUGUAY** **2-0(1-0)** Copa Lipton
Estadio Monumental „Antonio Vespucio Liberti“, Buenos Aires; Referee: Guillermo Nimo (Argentina); Attendance: 20,000
**ARG:** Carlos Adolfo Buttice (3/0) [30.Rubén Omar Sánchez (1/0)], Luis Gregorio Gallo (3/0), Roberto Alfredo Perfumo (9/0), José Rafael Albrecht (Cap) (33/1), Antonio Rosl (2/0), José Demetrio Solórzano (1/0) [46.Antonio Roberto Cabrera (1/0)], Victorio Nicolás Cocco (1/0), Pedro Alexis González (1/0) [46.Mario Pardo (5/1)], Rodolfo José Fischer (4/1), Daniel Alberto Willington (10/1), Roque Alberto Avallay (2/1). Trainer: Renato Cesarini (4).
**Goals**: Roque Alberto Avallay (8), Rodolfo José Fischer (71).

**394.** 20.06.1968 **URUGUAY - ARGENTINA** **2-1(1-0)** Copa Newton
Estadio Centenario, Montevideo; Referee: Ramón Ivannoe Barreto Ruíz (Uruguay); Attendance: 9,706
**ARG:** Carlos Adolfo Buttice (4/0), Luis Gregorio Gallo (4/0), Roberto Alfredo Perfumo (Cap) (10/0), José Rafael Albrecht (34/1), Antonio Rosl (3/0), Antonio Roberto Cabrera (2/0), Victorio Nicolás Cocco (2/0) [46.Raúl Armando Savoy (11/5)], Alberto Rendo (10/2), Pedro Alexis González (2/0) [46.Mario Pardo (6/1)], Rodolfo José Fischer (5/1), Roque Alberto Avallay (3/1). Trainer: Renato Cesarini (5).
**Goal**: Pablo Forlán (60 own goal).

**395.** 07.08.1968 **BRAZIL - ARGENTINA** **4-1(2-0)**
Estádio „Jornalista Mário Filho“ (Maracanã), Rio de Janeiro; Referee: Armando Nunes Castanheiras da Rosa Marques (Brazil); Attendance: 39,375
**ARG:** Rubén Omar Sánchez (2/0), Héctor Alberto Ostúa (1/0), Roberto Alfredo Perfumo (Cap) (11/0), Alfio Rubén Basile (1/1), Oscar Miguel Malbernat (2/0), Jorge Raúl Solari (7/0) [66.Raúl Armando Savoy (12/5)], Alberto Rendo (11/2), Roberto Rodolfo Aguirre (1/0), Carlos José Veglio (1/0) [72.Héctor Salvador Minitti (2/0)], Héctor Casimiro Yazalde (1/0), Oscar Tomás Más (19/3). Trainer: José María Minella (16).
**Goal**: Alfio Rubén Basile (89).

**396.** 11.08.1968 **BRAZIL - ARGENTINA** **3-2(2-1)**
Estádio Mineirão, Belo Horizonte; Referee: Agomar Martins (Brazil); Attendance: 50,000
**ARG:** Rubén Omar Sánchez (3/0), Héctor Alberto Ostúa (2/0), Roberto Alfredo Perfumo (Cap) (12/0), Alfio Rubén Basile (2/1), Oscar Miguel Malbernat (3/0), Jorge Raúl Solari (8/0), Raúl Armando Savoy (13/5), Alberto Rendo (12/3), Carlos José Veglio (2/0) [67.Manuel Ángel Silva (2/1)], Héctor Casimiro Yazalde (2/0), Rodolfo José Fischer (6/1) [79.Héctor Salvador Minitti (3/0)]. Trainer: José María Minella (17).
**Goals**: Alberto Rendo (32), Manuel Ángel Silva (77).

**397.** 29.08.1968 **PERU - ARGENTINA** **2-2**
Estadio Nacional, Lima; Referee: Erwin Hieger (Austria); Attendance: 25,000
**ARG:** Edgardo Norberto Andrada (13/0), Héctor Alberto Ostúa (3/0) [46.Jorge Raúl Solari (9/0)], Roberto Alfredo Perfumo (13/0), José Rafael Albrecht (Cap) (35/1), Nelson Juan López (5/0), Alfio Rubén Basile (3/1) [46.Roberto Rodolfo Aguirre (2/0)], Raúl Armando Savoy (14/6), Alberto Rendo (13/3), Héctor Salvador Minitti (4/0), Héctor Casimiro Yazalde (3/1) [75.Manuel Ángel Silva (3/1)], Rodolfo José Fischer (7/1). Trainer: José María Minella (18).
**Goals**: Héctor Casimiro Yazalde (30), Raúl Armando Savoy (67).

**398.** 01.09.1968 **PERU - ARGENTINA** **1-1**
Estadio Nacional, Lima; Referee: José Varrone (Venezuela); Attendance: 30,000
**ARG:** Edgardo Norberto Andrada (14/0), Roberto Rodolfo Aguirre (3/0), Roberto Alfredo Perfumo (Cap) (14/0), José Rafael Albrecht (36/1), Nelson Juan López (6/0), Alberto Rendo (14/3) [67.Jorge Raúl Solari (10/0)], Raúl Armando Savoy (15/6), Carlos José Veglio (3/1) [85.Oscar Tomás Más (20/3)], Héctor Salvador Minitti (5/0), Héctor Casimiro Yazalde (4/1) [64.Manuel Ángel Silva (4/1)], Rodolfo José Fischer (8/1). Trainer: José María Minella (19).
**Goal**: Carlos José Veglio.

**399.** 27.11.1968 **ARGENTINA - CHILE** **4-0(2-0)** Copa Carlos Dittborn
Estadio Central, Rosario; Referee: Aurelio Domingo Bossolino (Argentina); Attendance: 20,000
**ARG:** Edgardo Norberto Andrada (15/0), Luis Gregorio Gallo (5/0) [46.Héctor Salvador Minitti (6/1)], Roberto Alfredo Perfumo (Cap) (15/0), Raúl Horacio Madero (2/0), Oscar Miguel Malbernat (4/0), Roberto Rodolfo Aguirre (4/0), Alfio Rubén Basile (4/1), Juan Carlos Rulli (3/0), Carlos José Veglio (4/2), Rodolfo José Fischer (9/3), Roberto Marcelo Salomone (1/0) [65.Manuel Ángel Silva (5/1)]. Trainer: José María Minella (20).
**Goals**: Carlos José Veglio (10), Rodolfo José Fischer (14), Héctor Salvador Minitti (79), Rodolfo José Fischer (82).

**400.** 04.12.1968 **CHILE - ARGENTINA** **2-1(1-1)** Copa Carlos Dittborn
Estadio Nacional, Santiago; Referee: Jaime Amor (Chile); Attendance: 30,000
**ARG:** Edgardo Norberto Andrada (16/0), Oscar Miguel Malbernat (5/0), Roberto Alfredo Perfumo (Cap) (16/0), Armando Oscar Ovide (1/0), Raúl Horacio Madero (3/0), Juan Carlos Rulli (4/0), Alberto Rendo (15/4) [46.Raúl Armando Savoy (16/6)], Roberto Rodolfo Aguirre (5/0), Carlos José Veglio (5/2) [46.Héctor Casimiro Yazalde (5/1)], Rodolfo José Fischer (10/3), Roberto Marcelo Salomone (2/0). Trainer: José María Minella (21).
**Goal**: Alberto Rendo (33).

**401.** 17.12.1968 **ARGENTINA - POLAND** **1-0(1-0)**
Estadio „General San Martín“, Mar del Plata; Referee: Guillermo Nimo (Argentina); Attendance: 6,000
**ARG:** Edgardo Norberto Andrada (Cap) (17/0), Oscar Miguel Malbernat (6/0), Aurelio José Pascuttini (1/0), Roberto Domingo Rogel (3/0), Armando Oscar Ovide (2/0), Alberto Pompeo Tardivo (1/0), Roberto Rodolfo Aguirre (6/0), Raúl Armando Savoy (17/7) [82.Jorge Héctor Olmedo (1/0)], Héctor Salvador Minitti (7/1), Manuel Ángel Silva (6/1), Roque Alberto Avallay (4/1) [46.Rodolfo José Fischer (11/3)]. Trainer: José María Minella (22).
**Goal**: Raúl Armando Savoy (36 penalty).

**402.** 22.12.1968 **ARGENTINA - YUGOSLAVIA** **1-1(0-1)**
Estadio „General San Martín", Mar del Plata; Referee: Miguel Ángel Francisco Comesaña (Argentina); Attendance: 3,000
**ARG:** Edgardo Norberto Andrada (Cap) (18/0), Oscar Miguel Malbernat (7/0), Aurelio José Pascuttini (2/0), Roberto Domingo Rogel (4/0), Nelson Juan López (7/0), Alberto Pompeo Tardivo (2/0), Roberto Rodolfo Aguirre (7/0), Carlos José Veglio (6/2), Pedro Alexis González (3/0) [46.Héctor Salvador Minitti (8/1)], Manuel Ángel Silva (7/1) [60.Jorge Héctor Olmedo (2/1)], Rodolfo José Fischer (12/3). Trainer: José María Minella (23).
**Goal**: Jorge Héctor Olmedo (61).

**403.** 19.03.1969 **ARGENTINA - PARAGUAY** **1-1**
El Coloso del Parque, Rosario; Referee: Rubén Cabrera (Uruguay); Attendance: 20,000
**ARG:** Edgardo Norberto Andrada (19/0), Oscar Miguel Malbernat (8/0), Roberto Alfredo Perfumo (Cap) (17/0), Raúl Horacio Madero (4/0), Nelson Juan López (8/0), Roberto Rodolfo Aguirre (8/0), Victorio Nicolás Cocco (3/1), Carlos José Veglio (7/2) [46.Juan Carlos Rulli (5/0)], Héctor Salvador Minitti (9/1) [65.Pedro Alexis González (4/0)], Héctor Casimiro Yazalde (6/1), Rodolfo José Fischer (13/3). Trainer: Humberto Dionisio Maschio (1).
**Goal**: Victorio Nicolás Cocco (54).

**404.** 09.04.1969 **PARAGUAY - ARGENTINA** **0-0**
Estadio Puerto Sajonia, Asunción; Referee: César Augusto Orozco Guerrero (Peru); Attendance: 15,000
**ARG:** Edgardo Norberto Andrada (20/0), Luis Gregorio Gallo (6/0), Roberto Alfredo Perfumo (Cap) (18/0), Raúl Horacio Madero (5/0), Oscar Miguel Malbernat (9/0), Antonio Roberto Cabrera (3/0), Alfio Rubén Basile (5/1), Victorio Nicolás Cocco (4/1), Pedro Alexis González (5/0), Roberto Marcelo Salomone (3/0), Juan Ramón Verón (1/0). Trainer: Humberto Dionisio Maschio (2).

**405.** 28.05.1969 **CHILE - ARGENTINA** **1-1(1-0)**
Estadio Nacional, Santiago; Referee: Alberto Boullosa (Uruguay); Attendance: 30,000
**ARG:** Miguel Ángel Santoro (3/0), Rubén José Suñé (1/0), Roberto Alfredo Perfumo (19/0), Antonio Ubaldo Rattín (Cap) (32/1), Silvio Marzolini (23/1), Alfio Rubén Basile (6/1), Jorge Recio (1/0), Antonio Roberto Cabrera (4/0), Omar Wehbe (3/0), Héctor Casimiro Yazalde (7/1) [57.Carlos José Veglio (8/2)], Roberto Marcelo Salomone (4/0). Trainer: Humberto Dionisio Maschio (3).
**Goal**: Alberto Quintano (56 own goal).

**406.** 11.06.1969 **ARGENTINA - CHILE** **2-1(0-0)**
Estadio Parque Independencia, La Plata; Referee: Rodolfo Pérez Osorio (Paraguay); Attendance: 25,000
**ARG:** Agustín Mario Céjas (1/0), Rubén José Suñé (2/0), Aurelio José Pascuttini (3/0), Silvio Marzolini (24/1), Antonio Ubaldo Rattín (Cap) (33/1) [25.Jorge Recio (2/0); 46.Carlos Oscar Pachamé (5/0)], Alfio Rubén Basile (7/1), Juan Carlos Rulli (6/0), Victorio Nicolás Cocco (5/1) [61.Miguel Ángel Brindisi (1/1)], Osvaldo José Lamelza (1/0), Omar Wehbe (4/0), Rodolfo José Fischer (14/4). Trainer: Humberto Dionisio Maschio (4).
**Goals**: Rodolfo José Fischer (65), Miguel Ángel Brindisi (73).

**407.** 27.07.1969 **BOLIVIA - ARGENTINA** **3-1(1-1)** 9th FIFA WC. Qualifiers
Estadio „Hernándo Siles Zuazo", La Paz; Referee: Hugo Sosa (Paraguay); Attendance: 21,267
**ARG:** Agustín Mario Céjas (2/0), Rubén José Suñé (3/0), Roberto Alfredo Perfumo (20/0), José Rafael Albrecht (37/1), Silvio Marzolini (25/1), Miguel Ángel Brindisi (2/1), Antonio Ubaldo Rattín (Cap) (34/1) [79.Carlos Oscar Pachamé (6/0)], Victorio Nicolás Cocco (6/1), Ángel Alberto Marcos (1/0), Daniel Germán Onega (4/0), Aníbal Roberto Tarabini (4/1). Trainer: Adolfo Alfredo Pedernera (1).
**Goal**: Aníbal Roberto Tarabini (43).

**408.** 03.08.1969 **PERU - ARGENTINA** **1-0(0-0)** 9th FIFA WC. Qualifiers
Estadio Nacional, Lima; Referee: Aírton Viera de Moraes (Brazil); Attendance: 43,147
**ARG:** Agustín Mario Céjas (3/0) [85.Miguel Ángel Santoro (4/0)], Luis Gregorio Gallo (7/0), Roberto Alfredo Perfumo (Cap) (21/0), Alfio Rubén Basile (8/1) [*sent off 63*], Silvio Marzolini (26/1), Miguel Ángel Brindisi (3/1), Juan Carlos Rulli (7/0), Carlos Oscar Pachamé (7/0), Raúl Emilio Bernao (14/4), Héctor Casimiro Yazalde (8/1) [71.Daniel Germán Onega (5/0)], Aníbal Roberto Tarabini (5/1). Trainer: Adolfo Alfredo Pedernera (2).

**409.** 24.08.1969 **ARGENTINA - BOLIVIA** **1-0(0-0)** 9th FIFA WC. Qualifiers
Estadio „Alberto Armando", Buenos Aires; Referee: Armando Peña Rocha (Uruguay); Attendance: 47,069
**ARG:** Agustín Mario Céjas (4/0), Rubén José Suñé (4/0), Roberto Alfredo Perfumo (Cap) (22/0), José Rafael Albrecht (38/2), Silvio Marzolini (27/1), Juan Carlos Rulli (8/0), Carlos Oscar Pachamé (8/0), Raúl Emilio Bernao (15/4), Héctor Casimiro Yazalde (9/1), Daniel Germán Onega (6/0), Oscar Tomás Más (21/3). Trainer: Adolfo Alfredo Pedernera (3).
**Goal**: José Rafael Albrecht (62 penalty).

**410.** 31.08.1969 **ARGENTINA - PERU** **2-2(0-0)** 9th FIFA WC. Qualifiers
Estadio „Alberto Armando", Buenos Aires; Referee: Rafael Hormazábal Díaz (Chile); Attendance: 53,627
**ARG:** Agustín Mario Céjas (5/0), Luis Gregorio Gallo (8/0), Roberto Alfredo Perfumo (Cap) (23/0), José Rafael Albrecht (39/3), Silvio Marzolini (28/1), Miguel Ángel Brindisi (4/1), Juan Carlos Rulli (9/0) [46.Alberto Rendo (16/5)], Carlos Oscar Pachamé (9/0), Ángel Alberto Marcos (2/0), Héctor Casimiro Yazalde (10/1), Aníbal Roberto Tarabini (6/1). Trainer: Adolfo Alfredo Pedernera (4).
**Goals**: José Rafael Albrecht (80 penalty), Alberto Rendo (85).

**411.** 04.03.1970 **BRAZIL - ARGENTINA** **0-2(0-0)**
Estádio Beira-Rio, Porto Alegre; Referee: Armando Nunes Castanheiras da Rosa Marques (Brazil); Attendance:
**ARG:** Agustín Mario Céjas (6/0), Oscar Miguel Malbernat (10/0), Roberto Alfredo Perfumo (24/0), Roberto Domingo Rogel (5/0), Rubén Osvaldo Díaz (1/0), Norberto Rubén Madurga (1/0), Miguel Ángel Brindisi (5/1), José Omar Pastoriza (1/0), Marcos Norberto Conigliaro (1/1), Rodolfo José Fischer (15/4), Oscar Tomás Más (22/4). Trainer: Juan José Pizzuti (1).
**Goals**: Oscar Tomás Más (67), Marcos Norberto Conigliaro (72).

**412.** 08.03.1970 **BRAZIL - ARGENTINA** **2-1(0-0)**
Estádio „Jornalista Mário Filho" (Maracanã), Rio de Janeiro; Referee: Aírton Vieira de Moraes (Brazil); Attendance:
**ARG:** Agustín Mario Céjas (7/0) [Miguel Ángel Santoro (5/0)], Oscar Miguel Malbernat (11/0), Roberto Alfredo Perfumo (25/0), Roberto Domingo Rogel (6/0), Rubén Osvaldo Díaz (2/0), Norberto Rubén Madurga (2/0), Miguel Ángel Brindisi (6/2), José Omar Pastoriza (2/0), Marcos Norberto Conigliaro (2/1), Rodolfo José Fischer (16/4) [Daniel Germán Onega (7/0)], Oscar Tomás Más (23/4). Trainer: Juan José Pizzuti (2).
**Goal**: Miguel Ángel Brindisi (71).

**413.** 08.04.1970 **ARGENTINA - URUGUAY** **2-1(1-1)**
Estadio „Alberto Armando“, Buenos Aires; Referee: Luis Pestarino (Argentina); Attendance:
**ARG:** Agustín Mario Céjas (8/0), Oscar Miguel Malbernat (12/0), Roberto Alfredo Perfumo (26/0) (Cap), Roberto Domingo Rogel (7/0), Rubén Osvaldo Díaz (3/0), Miguel Ángel Brindisi (7/2), Norberto Rubén Madurga (3/0), Miguel Ángel Raimondo (1/0), Marcos Norberto Conigliaro (3/2), Rodolfo José Fischer (17/4) [Daniel Germán Onega (8/0)], Oscar Tomás Más (24/5). Trainer: Juan José Pizzuti (3).
**Goals**: Marcos Norberto Conigliaro (30), Oscar Tomás Más (65).

**414.** 15.04.1970 **URUGUAY - ARGENTINA** **2-1(1-1)**
Estadio Centenario, Montevideo; Referee: Alejandro Otero (Uruguay); Attendance:
**ARG:** Agustín Mario Céjas (9/0), Oscar Miguel Malbernat (13/0), Roberto Alfredo Perfumo (27/0) (Cap), Edgardo Luis Cantú (1/0), Rubén Osvaldo Díaz (4/0), Miguel Ángel Brindisi (8/2), Miguel Ángel Raimondo (2/0) [31.Carlos José Veglio (9/2)], Roberto Marcelo Telch (5/2), Marcos Norberto Conigliaro (4/2), Rodolfo José Fischer (18/4), Luis Alberto Giribet (1/1). Trainer: Juan José Pizzuti (4).
**Goal**: Luis Alberto Giribet (44).

**415.** 22.10.1970 **PARAGUAY - ARGENTINA** **1-1(1-1)** Copa Erico
Estadio Defensores del Chaco, Asunción; Referee: Aírton Viera de Moraes (Brazil); Attendance:
**ARG:** Miguel Ángel Santoro (6/0), Oscar Miguel Malbernat (14/0) [Jorge Omar Carrascosa (1/0)], Roberto Alfredo Perfumo (28/0), César Augusto Laraignée (1/0), Antonio Rosl (4/0), Miguel Ángel Brindisi (9/3), Miguel Ángel Raimondo (3/0), Ángel Alberto Marcos (3/0), Daniel Alberto Willington (11/1) [Carlos Alberto Bianchi (1/0)], Héctor Casimiro Yazalde (11/1), Juan Ramón Verón (2/0). Trainer: Juan José Pizzuti (5).
**Goal**: Miguel Ángel Brindisi (4).

**416.** 08.01.1971 **ARGENTINA - FRANCE** **3-4(0-1)**
Estadio „Alberto Armando“, Buenos Aires; Referee: Roberto Osvaldo Barreiro (Argentina); Attendance: 4,500
**ARG:** José Miguel Marín (3/0), Rubén José Suñé (5/0), Roberto Alfredo Perfumo (29/0), César Augusto Laraignée (2/1), Jorge Omar Carrascosa (2/0), Norberto Rubén Madurga (4/0), Miguel Alberto Nicolau (1/1), Miguel Ángel Tojo (1/0) [46.Miguel Ángel Brindisi (10/4)], Roberto Artemio Gramajo (1/0) [46.Ángel Alberto Marcos (4/0)], Alfredo Domingo Obberti (1/0) [66.Carlos Alberto Bianchi (2/0)], Juan Ramón Verón (3/0). Trainer: Juan José Pizzuti (6).
**Goals**: Miguel Ángel Brindisi (55), Miguel Alberto Nicolau (73), César Augusto Laraignée (90 penalty).

**417.** 13.01.1971 **ARGENTINA - FRANCE** **2-0(1-0)**
Estadio „General San Martín“, Mar del Plata; Referee: Arturo Andrés Ithurralde (Argentina); Attendance: 18,000
**ARG:** Miguel Ángel Santoro (7/0), Rubén José Suñé (6/0), Roberto Alfredo Perfumo (30/0) [Miguel Ángel Tojo (2/0)], César Augusto Laraignée (3/2), Jorge Omar Carrascosa (3/0), Norberto Rubén Madurga (5/1), Miguel Alberto Nicolau (2/1), Miguel Ángel Brindisi (11/4), Ángel Alberto Marcos (5/0), Héctor Casimiro Yazalde (12/1), Juan Ramón Verón (4/0). Trainer: Juan José Pizzuti (7).
**Goals**: César Augusto Laraignée (4 penalty), Norberto Rubén Madurga (75).

**418.** 04.07.1971 **PARAGUAY - ARGENTINA** **1-1(0-0)** Copa Chevallier Boutell
Estadio Puerto Sajonia, Asunción; Referee: Arnaldo David César Coelho (Brazil); Attendance:
**ARG:** José Miguel Marín (4/0), Jorge Eduardo Dominichi (1/0), Ricardo Néstor Rezza (1/0), César Augusto Laraignée (4/2), Ramón Armando Heredia (1/0), José Omar Pastoriza (3/0), Ángel Antonio Landucci (1/0), Daniel Germán Onega (9/0), Ángel Alberto Marcos (6/1), Rodolfo José Fischer (19/4), Oscar Tomás Más (25/5) [46.Carlos Alberto Bianchi (3/0)]. Trainer: Juan José Pizzuti (8).
**Goal**: Ángel Alberto Marcos (51).

**419.** 09.07.1971 **ARGENTINA - PARAGUAY** **1-0(1-0)** Copa Chevallier Boutell
Estadio Central, Rosario; Referee: Lorenzo Cantillana (Argentina); Attendance: 25,000
**ARG:** José Miguel Marín (5/0), Jorge Omar Carrascosa (4/0), Ricardo Néstor Rezza (2/0), César Augusto Laraignée (5/3), Ramón Armando Heredia (2/0), José Omar Pastoriza (4/0), Ángel Antonio Landucci (2/0), Ángel Alberto Marcos (7/1), Daniel Germán Onega (10/0) [46.Norberto Rubén Madurga (6/1)], Rodolfo José Fischer (20/4) [65.Carlos Alberto Bianchi (4/0)], Oscar Tomás Más (26/5). Trainer: Juan José Pizzuti (9).
**Goal**: César Augusto Laraignée (17).

**420.** 14.07.1971 **ARGENTINA - URUGUAY** **1-0(0-0)**
Estadio „Alberto Armando“, Buenos Aires; Referee: Ramón Ivannoe Barreto Ruíz (Uruguay), Attendance: 30,000
**ARG:** Rubén Omar Sánchez (4/0), Jorge Eduardo Dominichi (2/0), Ricardo Néstor Rezza (3/0), César Augusto Laraignée (Cap) (6/3), Ramón Armando Heredia (3/0), José Omar Pastoriza (5/0), Ángel Antonio Landucci (3/0), Norberto Rubén Madurga (7/2), Rubén Hugo Ayala (1/0), Carlos Alberto Bianchi (5/0) [66.Rodolfo José Fischer (21/4)], Oscar Tomás Más (27/5). Trainer: Juan José Pizzuti (10).
**Goal**: Norberto Rubén Madurga (60).

**421.** 18.07.1971 **URUGUAY - ARGENTINA** **1-1(0-1)** Copa Lipton
Estadio Centenario, Montevideo; Referee: Luis Pestarino (Argentina), Attendance: 40,000
**ARG:** Rubén Omar Sánchez (5/0), Jorge Eduardo Dominichi (3/0), Ricardo Néstor Rezza (4/0), César Augusto Laraignée (Cap) (7/3), Ramón Armando Heredia (4/0), José Omar Pastoriza (6/0), Ángel Antonio Landucci (4/0), Miguel Ángel Brindisi (12/4), Rubén Hugo Ayala (2/0) [46.Pedro Andrés Verde (1/0)], Carlos Alberto Bianchi (6/1), Rodolfo José Fischer (22/4). Trainer: Juan José Pizzuti (11).
**Goal**: Carlos Alberto Bianchi (18).

**422.** 21.07.1971 **CHILE - ARGENTINA** **2-2(0-1)** Copa Carlos Dittborn
Estadio Nacional, Santiago; Referee: Arturo Andrés Ithurralde (Argentina); Attendance: 50,000
**ARG:** Rubén Omar Sánchez (6/0), Jorge Eduardo Dominichi (4/0), Ricardo Néstor Rezza (5/0), César Augusto Laraignée (8/3), Ramón Armando Heredia (5/0), Ángel Antonio Landucci (5/0) [José Omar Pastoriza (7/0)], Miguel Ángel Brindisi (13/4), Norberto Rubén Madurga (8/2) [Daniel Germán Onega (11/0)], Rubén Hugo Ayala (3/0), Carlos Alberto Bianchi (7/3), Rodolfo José Fischer (23/4). Trainer: Juan José Pizzuti (12).
**Goals**: Carlos Alberto Bianchi (42, 85).

**423.** 28.07.1971 **ARGENTINA - BRAZIL** **1-1(0-0)** Copa Roca
Estadio Monumental „Antonio Vespucio Liberti“, Buenos Aires; Referee: Vital Loraux (Belgium)
**ARG:** Rubén Omar Sánchez (7/0), Jorge Eduardo Dominichi (5/0), Ángel Hugo Bargas (1/0), César Augusto Laraignée (9/3), Ramón Armando Heredia (6/0), Miguel Ángel Brindisi (14/4), José Omar Pastoriza (8/0), Norberto Rubén Madurga (9/3), Rubén Hugo Ayala (4/0), Carlos Alberto Bianchi (8/3), Rodolfo José Fischer (24/4) [Pedro Andrés Verde (2/0)]. Trainer: Juan José Pizzuti (13).
**Goal**: Norberto Rubén Madurga (90).

**424.** 31.07.1971 **ARGENTINA - BRAZIL** **2-2(1-0,1-1)** Copa Roca
Estadio Monumental „Antonio Vespucio Liberti", Buenos Aires; Referee: Rudolf Scheurer (Switzerland)
**ARG:** Rubén Omar Sánchez (8/0), Jorge Eduardo Dominichi (6/0), Ángel Hugo Bargas (2/0), César Augusto Laraignée (10/3), Ramón Armando Heredia (7/0), Miguel Ángel Brindisi (15/4), José Omar Pastoriza (9/0), Norberto Rubén Madurga (10/3) [Ángel Antonio Landucci (6/0)], Rubén Hugo Ayala (5/0) [Daniel Germán Onega (12/0)], Carlos Alberto Bianchi (9/3) [Ernesto Enrique Mastrángelo (1/0)], Rodolfo José Fischer (25/6). Trainer: Juan José Pizzuti (14).
**Goals**: Rodolfo José Fischer 2.

**425.** 04.08.1971 **ARGENTINA - CHILE** **1-0(0-0)** Copa Carlos Dittborn
Estadio „Alberto Armando", Buenos Aires; Referee: Cantillana (Chile); Attendance: 30,000
**ARG:** Rubén Omar Sánchez (9/0), Jorge Eduardo Dominichi (7/0), Ángel Hugo Bargas (3/0), César Augusto Laraignée (11/3), Ramón Armando Heredia (8/0), Miguel Ángel Brindisi (16/4), José Omar Pastoriza (10/0), Norberto Rubén Madurga (11/3), Daniel Germán Onega (13/0), Carlos Alberto Bianchi (10/3), Rodolfo José Fischer (26/7). Trainer: Juan José Pizzuti (15).
**Goal**: Rodolfo José Fischer (87).

**426.** 25.05.1972 **ARGENTINA - PARAGUAY** **0-0**
Estadio Gimnasia y Tiro, Salta; Referee: Luis Pestarino (Argentina); Attendance: 18,000
**ARG:** Rubén Omar Sánchez (10/0), Jorge Eduardo Dominichi (8/0), Ángel Hugo Bargas (4/0), Osvaldo José Piazza (1/0), Rubén Osvaldo Díaz (5/0), Miguel Ángel Brindisi (17/4), Ángel Antonio Landucci (7/0), Ramón César Bóveda (1/0) [Osvaldo Rubén Potente (1/0)], Daniel Germán Onega (14/0) [Carlos Alberto Colman (1/0)], Rodolfo José Fischer (27/7), Oscar Tomás Más (28/5). Trainer: Juan José Pizzuti (16).

**427.** 31.05.1972 **CHILE - ARGENTINA** **3-4(1-1)** Copa Carlos Dittborn
Estadio Nacional, Santiago; Referee: Humberto Oreste Dellacasa (Argentina); Attendance: 45,000
**ARG:** Daniel Alberto Carnevali (1/0), Jorge Eduardo Dominichi (9/0), Ángel Hugo Bargas (5/0), Osvaldo José Piazza (2/0) [Ramón Armando Heredia (9/0)], Rubén Osvaldo Díaz (6/0), Miguel Ángel Brindisi (18/4), Miguel Ángel Raimondo (4/1), Alejandro Estanislao Semenewicz (1/0), Ernesto Enrique Mastrángelo (2/1), Rodolfo José Fischer (28/7), Oscar Tomás Más (29/7). Trainer: Juan José Pizzuti (17).
**Goals**: Oscar Tomás Más (4), Miguel Ángel Raimondo (48), Oscar Tómas Más (54), Ernesto Enrique Mastrángelo.

**428.** 22.06.1972 **ARGENTINA - COLOMBIA** **4-1(1-0)** Brazil Independence Cup
Estádio Fonte Nova, Salvador de Bahía (Brazil); Referee: Kurt Tschenscher (West Germany)
**ARG:** Daniel Alberto Carnevali (2/0), Enrique Ernesto Wolff (1/0), Ángel Hugo Bargas (6/1), Osvaldo José Piazza (3/0), Ramón Armando Heredia (10/0), Miguel Ángel Brindisi (19/4), José Omar Pastoriza (11/0) [Ángel Antonio Landucci (8/0)], Alejandro Estanislao Semenewicz (2/0), Carlos Alberto Bianchi (11/6), Rodolfo José Fischer (29/7) [Ernesto Enrique Mastrángelo (3/1)], Oscar Tomás Más (30/7). Trainer: Juan José Pizzuti (18).
**Goals**: Carlos Alberto Bianchi (14, 48), Ángel Hugo Bargas (60), Carlos Alberto Bianchi (62).

**429.** 25.06.1972 **ARGENTINA - FRANCE** **0-0** Brazil Independence Cup
Estádio Fonte Nova, Salvador de Bahía (Brazil); Referee: Armando Nunes Castanheiras da Rosa Marques (Brazil); Attendance: 6,587
**ARG:** Miguel Ángel Santoro (8/0), Enrique Ernesto Wolff (2/0), Ángel Hugo Bargas (7/1), Osvaldo José Piazza (4/0), Rubén Osvaldo Díaz (7/0), Miguel Ángel Raimondo (5/1), Alejandro Estanislao Semenewicz (3/0), José Omar Pastoriza (12/0), Carlos Alberto Bianchi (12/6), Rodolfo José Fischer (30/7), Oscar Tomás Más (31/7). Trainer: Juan José Pizzuti (19).

**430.** 29.06.1972 **PORTUGAL - ARGENTINA** **3-1(2-1)** Brazil Independence Cup
Estádio „Jornalista Mário Filho" (Maracanã), Rio de Janeiro (Brazil); Referee: Edwin Keith Walker (England)
**ARG:** Miguel Ángel Santoro (9/0), Enrique Ernesto Wolff (3/0), Ángel Hugo Bargas (8/1), Miguel Ángel López (2/0), Ramón Armando Heredia (11/0), Miguel Ángel Brindisi (20/5), Alejandro Estanislao Semenewicz (4/0), José Omar Pastoriza (Cap) (13/0), Carlos Alberto Bianchi (13/6), Rodolfo José Fischer (31/7), Oscar Tomás Más (32/7) [59.Ernesto Enrique Mastrángelo (4/1)]. Trainer: Juan José Pizzuti (20).
**Goal**: Miguel Ángel Brindisi (38).

**431.** 02.07.1972 **ARGENTINA – SOVIET UNION** **1-0(1-0)** Brazil Independence Cup
Estádio Mineirão, Belo Horizonte (Brazil); Referee: Alfonso González Archundia (Mexico); Attendance: 8,000
**ARG:** Miguel Ángel Santoro (10/0), Enrique Ernesto Wolff (4/0) [80.Jorge Eduardo Dominichi (10/0)], Ángel Hugo Bargas (9/1), Osvaldo José Piazza (5/0), Ramón Armando Heredia (12/0), Miguel Ángel Raimondo (6/1) [70.Miguel Ángel Brindisi (21/5)], Alejandro Estanislao Semenewicz (5/0), José Omar Pastoriza (14/1), Ernesto Enrique Mastrángelo (5/1), Rodolfo José Fischer (32/7), Oscar Tomás Más (33/7). Trainer: Juan José Pizzuti (21).
**Goal**: José Omar Pastoriza (26).

**432.** 06.07.1972 **ARGENTINA - URUGUAY** **1-0(0-0)** Brazil Independence Cup
Estádio Beira-Rio, Porto Alegre (Brazil); Referee: Edwin Keith Walker (England); Attendance:
**ARG:** Miguel Ángel Santoro (11/0), Enrique Ernesto Wolff (5/0) [46.Jorge Eduardo Dominichi (11/0)], Ángel Hugo Bargas (10/1), Osvaldo José Piazza (6/0), Ramón Armando Heredia (13/0), Miguel Ángel Raimondo (7/1), Alejandro Estanislao Semenewicz (6/0), José Omar Pastoriza (15/1), Ernesto Enrique Mastrángelo (6/1), Rodolfo José Fischer (33/7) [73.Roque Alberto Avallay (5/1)], Oscar Tomás Más (34/8). Trainer: Juan José Pizzuti (22).
**Goal**: Oscar Tomás Más (82).

**433.** 09.07.1972 **YUGOSLAVIA - ARGENTINA** **4-2(2-0)** Brazil Independence Cup
Estádio „Jornalista Mário Filho" (Maracanã), Rio de Janeiro (Brazil); Referee: Paul Schiller (Austria); Attendance: 120,000
**ARG:** Miguel Ángel Santoro (12/0), Jorge Eduardo Dominichi (12/0), Ángel Hugo Bargas (11/1), Osvaldo José Piazza (7/0), Ramón Armando Heredia (14/0) [71.Rubén Osvaldo Díaz (8/0)], Alejandro Estanislao Semenewicz (7/0), José Omar Pastoriza (16/1) [*sent off 79*], Miguel Ángel Raimondo (8/1) [46.Miguel Ángel Brindisi (22/7)], Ernesto Enrique Mastrángelo (7/1), Roque Alberto Avallay (6/1), Oscar Tomás Más (35/8). Trainer: Juan José Pizzuti (23).
**Goals**: Miguel Ángel Brindisi (58 penalty,89 penalty).

**434.** 27.09.1972 **ARGENTINA - CHILE** **2-0(1-0)** Copa Carlos Dittborn
Estadio „José Amalfitani", Buenos Aires; Referee: Alberto Martínez González (Chile); Attendance: 20,000
**ARG:** Daniel Alberto Carnevali (3/0), Enrique Ernesto Wolff (6/0), Ramón Armando Heredia (15/0), Ángel Hugo Bargas (12/1), Antonio Rosl (5/0), Miguel Ángel Brindisi (23/8), Roberto Marcelo Telch (6/2) [Reinaldo Carlos Merlo (1/0)], Ramón César Bóveda (2/0) [José Orlando Berta (1/0)], Rubén Hugo Ayala (6/1), Jorge Luis Ghiso (1/0), Norberto Osvaldo Alonso (1/0) [*sent off 60*]. Trainer: Enrique Omar Sívori (1).
**Goals**: Miguel Ángel Brindisi (34), Rubén Hugo Ayala (63).

**435.** 11.10.1972 **SPAIN - ARGENTINA** **1-0(1-0)** Copa Hispanidad

Estadio „Santiago Bernabéu", Madrid; Referee: Kurt Tschenscher (West Germany); Attendance: 50,000

**ARG:** Daniel Alberto Carnevali (4/0), Enrique Ernesto Wolff (7/0), Ángel Hugo Bargas (13/1), Ramón Armando Heredia (16/0), Antonio Rosl (6/0), Miguel Ángel Brindisi (24/8), Reinaldo Carlos Merlo (2/0), Juan José López (1/0), Norberto Osvaldo Alonso (2/0), Roque Alberto Avallay (7/1) [70.Ramón César Bóveda (3/0)], Rubén Hugo Ayala (7/1). Trainer: Enrique Omar Sívori (2).

**436.** 25.10.1972 **PERU - ARGENTINA** **0-2(0-1)** Copa Castilla

Estadio Nacional, Lima; Referee: Carlos Rivero (Peru); Attendance: 20,000

**ARG:** Daniel Alberto Carnevali (5/0), Enrique Ernesto Wolff (8/0), Ángel Hugo Bargas (14/1), Ramón Armando Heredia (17/0), Antonio Rosl (7/0) [Mario Estanislao Killer (1/0)], Miguel Ángel Brindisi (25/8), Reinaldo Carlos Merlo (3/0) [Roberto Mario Espósito (1/0)], Norberto Osvaldo Alonso (3/0), Ramón Héctor Ponce (1/0), Rubén Hugo Ayala (8/3), Mario Rubén Mendoza (1/0) [Jorge Luis Ghiso (2/0)]. Trainer: Enrique Omar Sívori (3).

**Goals**: Rubén Hugo Ayala (14, 85).

**437.** 06.02.1973 **MEXICO - ARGENTINA** **2-0(2-0)**

Estadio Azteca, Ciudad de México; Referee: Marco Antonio Dorantes (Mexico)

**ARG:** Daniel Alberto Carnevali (6/0), Enrique Ernesto Wolff (9/0), Jorge Alberto Buzzo (1/0), Ramón Armando Heredia (18/0) [*sent off 85*], Antonio Rosl (8/0) [46.Vicente Alberto Pernía (1/0)], Miguel Ángel Brindisi (26/8), Roberto Marcelo Telch (7/2), Norberto Osvaldo Alonso (4/0) [46.Jorge Luis Ghiso (3/0)], Ramón Héctor Ponce (2/0), Roque Alberto Avallay (8/1) [46.Carlos Manuel Morete (1/0)], Enrique Salvador Chazarreta (1/0) [46.Carlos Alberto Babington (1/0)]. Trainer: Enrique Omar Sívori (4).

**438.** 14.02.1973 **WEST GERMANY - ARGENTINA** **2-3(0-2)**

Olympiastadion, München; Referee: Concetto Lo Bello (Italy); Attendance: 55,000

**ARG:** Daniel Alberto Carnevali (7/0), Enrique Ernesto Wolff (10/0), Ángel Hugo Bargas (15/1), Ramón Armando Heredia (19/0), Antonio Rosl (9/0), Miguel Ángel Brindisi (27/9), Roberto Marcelo Telch (8/2), Norberto Osvaldo Alonso (5/1) [80.Carlos Alberto Babington (2/0)], Enrique Salvador Chazarreta (2/0), Roque Alberto Avallay (9/1), Jorge Luis Ghiso (4/1). Trainer: Enrique Omar Sívori (5).

**Goals**: Jorge Luis Ghiso (4), Norberto Osvaldo Alonso (14), Miguel Ángel Brindisi (67 penalty).

**439.** 20.02.1973 **ISRAEL - ARGENTINA** **1-1(1-1)**

Bloomfield Stadium, Jaffa; Referee: Naftali Eitan (Israel); Attendance: 16,000

**ARG:** Daniel Alberto Carnevali (8/0), Enrique Ernesto Wolff (11/0), Jorge Alberto Buzzo (2/0), Ramón Armando Heredia (20/1), Antonio Rosl (10/0), Miguel Ángel Brindisi (28/9), Roberto Marcelo Telch (9/2), Norberto Osvaldo Alonso (6/1) [68.Ramón Héctor Ponce (3/0)], Enrique Salvador Chazarreta (3/0), Roque Alberto Avallay (10/1) [68.Carlos Manuel Morete (2/0)], Jorge Luis Ghiso (5/1). Trainer: Enrique Omar Sívori (6).

**Goal**: Ramón Armando Heredia (36).

**440.** 17.05.1973 **ARGENTINA - URUGUAY** **1-1(0-1)** Copa Lipton

Estadio „José Amalfitani", Buenos Aires; Referee: Oscar Veiró (Argentina); Attendance:

**ARG:** Daniel Alberto Carnevali (9/0), Enrique Ernesto Wolff (Cap) (12/0), Jorge Alberto Buzzo (3/0) [89.Jorge Troncoso (1/0)], Hugo Pena (1/0), Antonio Rosl (11/0), Miguel Ángel Brindisi (29/10), Roberto Marcelo Telch (10/2), Carlos Alberto Babington (3/0) [77.Norberto Osvaldo Alonso (7/1)], René Orlando Houseman (1/0) [62.Ramón Héctor Ponce (4/0)], Carlos Alfredo Guerini (1/0), Rubén Hugo Ayala (9/3) [58.Roque Alberto Avallay (11/1)]. Trainer: Miguel Ignomiriello (1).

**Goal**: Miguel Ángel Brindisi (87).

**441.** 23.05.1973 **URUGUAY - ARGENTINA** **1-1(0-0)** Copa Newton

Estadio Centenario, Montevideo; Referee: Luis Gregorio Da Rosa (Uruguay), Attendance: 20,000

**ARG:** Daniel Alberto Carnevali (10/0), Enrique Ernesto Wolff (Cap) (13/0), Jorge Alberto Buzzo (4/0), Jorge Troncoso (2/0), Antonio Rosl (12/0), Miguel Ángel Brindisi (30/10), Roberto Marcelo Telch (11/2) [46.Francisco Faustino Russo (1/0) [*sent off 75*]], Ramón Héctor Ponce (5/0) [70.Mario Estanislao Killer (2/0)], Carlos Alberto Babington (4/1), Rubén Hugo Ayala (10/3), Roque Alberto Avallay (12/1). Trainer: Miguel Ignomiriello (2).

**Goal**: Carlos Alberto Babington (54 penalty).

**442.** 13.07.1973 **ARGENTINA - CHILE** **5-4(3-2)** Copa Carlos Dittborn

Estadio „Alberto Armando", Buenos Aires; Referee: Armando Nunes Castanheiras da Rosa Marques (Brazil); Attendance: 25,000

**ARG:** Daniel Alberto Carnevali (11/0), Enrique Ernesto Wolff (14/0), Ángel Hugo Bargas (16/1), Ramón Armando Heredia (21/1), Antonio Rosl (13/0) [Vicente Alberto Pernía (2/0)], Miguel Ángel Brindisi (31/12), Roberto Marcelo Telch (12/2), Norberto Osvaldo Alonso (8/1) [56.Enrique Salvador Chazarreta (4/0)], Ramón Héctor Ponce (6/0), Rubén Hugo Ayala (11/5), Carlos Alfredo Guerini (2/1). Trainer: Enrique Omar Sívori (7).

**Goals**: Carlos Alfredo Guerini (1), Rubén Hugo Ayala (19), Miguel Ángel Brindisi (33, 69), Rubén Hugo Ayala (85).

**443.** 18.07.1973 **CHILE - ARGENTINA** **3-1(2-1)** Copa Carlos Dittborn

Estadio Nacional, Santiago; Referee: Ángel Eduardo Pazos Bianchi (Uruguay); Attendance: 35,000

**ARG:** Daniel Alberto Carnevali (12/0), Enrique Ernesto Wolff (15/0), Ángel Hugo Bargas (17/1), Ramón Armando Heredia (22/1), Vicente Alberto Pernía (3/0), Miguel Ángel Brindisi (32/13), Roberto Marcelo Telch (13/2), Norberto Osvaldo Alonso (9/1) [65.Carlos Alfredo Guerini (3/1)], René Orlando Houseman (2/0) [46.Roque Alberto Avallay (13/1)], Rubén Hugo Ayala (12/5), Enrique Salvador Chazarreta (5/0). Trainer: Enrique Omar Sívori (8).

**Goal**: Miguel Ángel Brindisi (43 penalty).

**444.** 27.07.1973 **ARGENTINA - PERU** **3-1(1-1)** Copa Castilla

Estadio „Alberto Armando", Buenos Aires; Referee: Arturo Andrés Ithurralde (Argentina); Attendance:

**ARG:** Daniel Alberto Carnevali (13/0), Enrique Ernesto Wolff (16/0), Ángel Hugo Bargas (18/1), Ramón Armando Heredia (23/1) [Jorge Troncoso (3/0)], Hériberto Luis Correa (1/0), Miguel Ángel Brindisi (33/14), Roberto Marcelo Telch (14/2), Enrique Salvador Chazarreta (6/0), René Orlando Houseman (3/0) [Ramón Héctor Ponce (7/0)], Rubén Hugo Ayala (13/5), Carlos Alfredo Guerini (4/3). Trainer: Enrique Omar Sívori (9).

**Goals**: Carlos Alfredo Guerini (37, 55), Miguel Ángel Brindisi (59).

**445.** 09.09.1973 **ARGENTINA - BOLIVIA** **4-0(2-0)** 10th FIFA WC. Qualifiers

Estadio „Alberto Armando", Buenos Aires; Referee: Ángel Eduardo Pazos Bianchi (Uruguay); Attendance: 39,243

**ARG:** Daniel Alberto Carnevali (14/0), Enrique Ernesto Wolff (Cap) (17/0), Ángel Hugo Bargas (19/1), Francisco Pedro Manuel Sá (1/0), Hériberto Luis Correa (2/0), Miguel Ángel Brindisi (34/16), Roberto Marcelo Telch (15/2), Carlos Alberto Babington (5/1), Agustín Alberto Balbuena (1/0), Rubén Hugo Ayala (14/7), Carlos Alfredo Guerini (5/3). Trainer: Enrique Omar Sívori (10).

**Goals**: Miguel Ángel Brindisi (31, 43), Rubén Hugo Ayala (65, 76).

**446.** 16.09.1973 **PARAGUAY - ARGENTINA** **1-1(1-1)** 10th FIFA WC. Qualifiers
Estadio Puerto Sajonia, Asunción; Referee: Omar Delgado Piedrahita (Colombia); Attendance: 47,116
**ARG:** Daniel Alberto Carnevali (15/0), Enrique Ernesto Wolff (Cap) (18/0), Ángel Hugo Bargas (20/1), Francisco Pedro Manuel Sá (2/0), Hériberto Luis Correa (3/0), Miguel Ángel Brindisi (35/16) [87.Carlos Alberto Babington (6/1)], Roberto Marcelo Telch (16/2), Enrique Salvador Chazarreta (7/0), Agustín Alberto Balbuena (2/0), Rubén Hugo Ayala (15/8), Carlos Alfredo Guerini (6/3) [46.Roque Alberto Avallay (14/1)]. Trainer: Enrique Omar Sívori (11).
**Goal**: Rubén Hugo Ayala (33).

**447.** 23.09.1973 **BOLIVIA - ARGENTINA** **0-1(0-1)** 10th FIFA WC. Qualifiers
Estadio „Hernándo Siles Zuazo“, La Paz; Referee: Arnaldo David César Coelho (Brazil); Attendance: 19,266
**ARG:** Daniel Alberto Carnevali (16/0), Rubén Oscar Glariá (1/0), Ángel Hugo Bargas (21/1), Daniel José Tagliani (1/0), Osvaldo Roberto Cortés (1/0), Rubén Galván (1/0), Roberto Marcelo Telch (17/2) [76.Marcelo Antonio Trobbiani (1/0)], Oscar Ramón Fornari (1/1), Mario Alberto Kempes (1/0) [64.Ricardo Enrique Bochini (1/0)], Rubén Hugo Ayala (16/8), Aldo Pedro Poy (1/0). Trainer: Enrique Omar Sívori & Miguel Ignomiriello (1).
**Goal**: Oscar Ramón Fornari (17).

**448.** 07.10.1973 **ARGENTINA - PARAGUAY** **3-1(1-1)** 10th FIFA WC. Qualifiers
Estadio „Alberto Armando“, Buenos Aires; Referee: Rafael Hormozabál Díaz (Chile); Attendance: 58,657
**ARG:** Daniel Alberto Carnevali (17/0), Enrique Ernesto Wolff (19/0), Ángel Hugo Bargas (22/1), Francisco Pedro Manuel Sá (3/0), Hériberto Luis Correa (4/0), Miguel Ángel Brindisi (36/16), Roberto Marcelo Telch (18/2), Carlos Alberto Babington (7/1) [46.Agustín Alberto Balbuena (3/0)], Enrique Salvador Chazarreta (8/0), Rubén Hugo Ayala (17/10), Ramón Héctor Ponce (8/0) [53.Carlos Alfredo Guerini (7/4)]. Trainer: Enrique Omar Sívori (12).
**Goals**: Rubén Hugo Ayala (32 penalty, 57), Carlos Alfredo Guerini (89).

**449.** 22.04.1974 **ARGENTINA - ROMANIA** **2-1(0-1)**
Estadio „José Amalfitani“, Buenos Aires; Referee: Arturo Andrés Ithurralde (Argentina); Attendance: 45,000
**ARG:** Miguel Ángel Santoro (13/0), Rubén Oscar Glariá (2/0), Néstor Hugo Togneri (1/0), Francisco Pedro Manuel Sá (4/0), Alberto César Tarantini (1/0), Miguel Ángel Brindisi (37/16), Carlos Vicente Squeo (1/0), Roberto Marcelo Telch (19/2), Enrique Salvador Chazarreta (9/0) [46.René Orlando Houseman (4/1)], Agustín Alberto Balbuena (4/0), Mario Alberto Kempes (2/1). Trainer: Vladislao Wenceslao Cap (1).
**Goals**: René Orlando Houseman (57), Mario Alberto Kempes (76).

**450.** 18.05.1974 **FRANCE - ARGENTINA** **0-1(0-1)**
Stade Parc des Princes, Paris; Referee: Johannes Nicolaas Ignatius „Jan“ Keizer (Holland); Attendance: 26,735
**ARG:** Daniel Alberto Carnevali (18/0), Rubén Oscar Glariá (3/0) [46.Enrique Ernesto Wolff (20/0)], Ángel Hugo Bargas (23/1), Roberto Alberto Perfumo (Cap) (31/0), Francisco Pedro Manuel Sá (5/0), Miguel Ángel Brindisi (38/16) [75.Enrique Salvador Chazarreta (10/0)], Roberto Marcelo Telch (20/2), Carlos Vicente Squeo (2/0), René Orlando Houseman (5/1) [46.Roque Alberto Avallay (15/1)], Agustín Alberto Balbuena (5/0), Mario Alberto Kempes (3/2). Trainer: Vladislao Wenceslao Cap (2).
**Goal**: Mario Alberto Kempes (22).

**451.** 22.05.1974 **ENGLAND - ARGENTINA** **2-2(1-0)**
Wembley Stadium, London; Referee: Arturo Andrés Ithurralde (Argentina); Attendance: 68,000
**ARG:** Daniel Alberto Carnevali (19/0), Rubén Oscar Glariá (4/0) [46.Enrique Ernesto Wolff (21/0)], Ángel Hugo Bargas (24/1), Roberto Alberto Perfumo (Cap) (32/0), Francisco Pedro Manuel Sá (6/0), Miguel Ángel Brindisi (39/16) [67.René Orlando Houseman (6/1)], Roberto Marcelo Telch (21/2), Carlos Vicente Squeo (3/0), Agustín Alberto Balbuena (6/0), Rubén Hugo Ayala (18/10), Mario Alberto Kempes (4/4). Trainer: Vladislao Wenceslao Cap (3).
**Goals**: Mario Alberto Kempes (58, 89 penalty).

**452.** 26.05.1974 **HOLLAND - ARGENTINA** **4-1(2-1)**
Olympisch Stadion, Amsterdam; Referee: Adolf Prokop (East Germany); Attendance: 20,000
**ARG:** Daniel Alberto Carnevali (20/0), Enrique Ernesto Wolff (22/1), Ángel Hugo Bargas (25/1), Roberto Alberto Perfumo (Cap) (33/0) [67.Aldo Pedro Poy (2/0)], Francisco Pedro Manuel Sá (7/0), Ramón Armando Heredia (24/1), Roberto Marcelo Telch (22/2), Carlos Vicente Squeo (4/0), Héctor Casimiro Yazalde (13/1) [60.Enrique Salvador Chazarreta (11/0)], Rubén Hugo Ayala (19/10), Mario Alberto Kempes (5/4) [44.René Orlando Houseman (7/1)]. Trainer: Vladislao Wenceslao Cap (4).
**Goal**: Enrique Ernesto Wolff (34).

**453.** 15.06.1974 **POLAND - ARGENTINA** **3-2(2-0)** 10th FIFA WC. Group Stage.
Neckarstadion, Stuttgart (West Germany); Referee: Clive Thomas (Wales); Attendance: 32,700
**ARG:** Daniel Alberto Carnevali (21/0), Enrique Ernesto Wolff (23/1), Ángel Hugo Bargas (26/1) [69.Roberto Marcelo Telch (23/2)], Roberto Alberto Perfumo (Cap) (34/0), Francisco Pedro Manuel Sá (8/0), Ramón Armando Heredia (25/2), Miguel Ángel Brindisi (40/16) [46.René Orlando Houseman (8/1)], Carlos Alberto Babington (8/2), Agustín Alberto Balbuena (7/0), Rubén Hugo Ayala (20/10), Mario Alberto Kempes (6/4). Trainer: Vladislao Wenceslao Cap (5).
**Goals**: Ramón Armando Heredia (61), Carlos Alberto Babington (67).

**454.** 19.06.1974 **ARGENTINA - ITALY** **1-1(1-1)** 10th FIFA WC. Group Stage.
Neckarstadion, Stuttgart (West Germany); Referee: Pavel Kazakov (Soviet Union); Attendance: 70,100
**ARG:** Daniel Alberto Carnevali (22/0), Enrique Ernesto Wolff (24/1) [61.Rubén Oscar Glariá (5/0)], Roberto Alberto Perfumo (Cap) (35/0), Ramón Armando Heredia (26/2), Francisco Pedro Manuel Sá (9/0), Roberto Marcelo Telch (24/2), René Orlando Houseman (9/2), Carlos Alberto Babington (9/2), Rubén Hugo Ayala (21/10), Héctor Casimiro Yazalde (14/1) [78.Enrique Salvador Chazarreta (12/0)], Mario Alberto Kempes (7/4). Trainer: Vladislao Wenceslao Cap (6).
**Goal**: René Orlando Houseman (19).

**455.** 23.06.1974 **ARGENTINA - HAITI** **4-1(2-0)** 10th FIFA WC. Group Stage.
Olympiastadion, München (West Germany); Referee: Pablo Augusto Sánchez Ibáñez (Spain); Attendance: 25,900
**ARG:** Daniel Alberto Carnevali (23/0), Enrique Ernesto Wolff (25/1), Roberto Alberto Perfumo (Cap) (36/0), Ramón Armando Heredia (27/2), Francisco Pedro Manuel Sá (10/0), Roberto Marcelo Telch (25/2), René Orlando Houseman (10/3) [59.Miguel Ángel Brindisi (41/16)], Carlos Alberto Babington (10/2), Rubén Hugo Ayala (22/11), Héctor Casimiro Yazalde (15/3), Mario Alberto Kempes (8/4) [57.Agustín Alberto Balbuena (8/0)]. Trainer: Vladislao Wenceslao Cap (7).
**Goals**: Héctor Casimiro Yazalde (15), René Orlando Houseman (18), Rubén Hugo Ayala (55), Héctor Casimiro Yazalde (67).

**456.** 26.06.1974 **HOLLAND - ARGENTINA** **4-0(2-0)** 10th FIFA WC.2nd Round.
Parkstadion, Gelsenkirchen (West Germany); Referee: Robert Holley Davidson (Scotland); Attendance: 56,548
**ARG:** Daniel Alberto Carnevali (24/0), Enrique Ernesto Wolff (26/1) [46.Rubén Oscar Glariá (6/0)], Roberto Alberto Perfumo (Cap) (37/0), Ramón Armando Heredia (28/2), Francisco Pedro Manuel Sá (11/0), Roberto Marcelo Telch (26/2), Carlos Vicente Squeo (5/0), Agustín Alberto Balbuena (9/0), Rubén Hugo Ayala (23/11), Héctor Casimiro Yazalde (16/3), René Orlando Houseman (11/3) [65.Mario Alberto Kempes (9/4)]. Trainer: Vladislao Wenceslao Cap (8).

**457.** 30.06.1974 **BRAZIL - ARGENTINA** **2-1(1-1)** 10th FIFA WC.2nd Round.
Niedersachsenstadion, Hannover (West Germany); Referee: Vital Loraux (Belgium); Attendance: 39,400
**ARG:** Daniel Alberto Carnevali (25/0), Rubén Oscar Glariá (7/0), Ángel Hugo Bargas (27/1), Ramón Armando Heredia (29/2), Francisco Pedro Manuel Sá (12/0) [61.Jorge Omar Carrascosa (5/0)], Miguel Ángel Brindisi (42/17) (Cap), Carlos Vicente Squeo (6/0), Carlos Alberto Babington (11/2), Agustín Alberto Balbuena (10/0), Rubén Hugo Ayala (24/11), Mario Alberto Kempes (10/4) [46.René Orlando Houseman (12/3)]. Trainer: Vladislao Wenceslao Cap (9).
**Goal**: Miguel Ángel Brindisi (35).

**458.** 03.07.1974 **ARGENTINA – EAST GERMANY** **1-1(1-1)** 10th FIFA WC.2nd Round.
Parkstadion, Gelsenkirchen (West Germany); Referee: John Keith Taylor (England); Attendance: 54,254
**ARG:** Ubaldo Matildo Fillol (1/0), Enrique Ernesto Wolff (Cap) (27/1), Ángel Hugo Bargas (28/1), Ramón Armando Heredia (30/2), Jorge Omar Carrascosa (6/0), Miguel Ángel Brindisi (43/17), Roberto Marcelo Telch (27/2), Carlos Alberto Babington (12/2), René Orlando Houseman (13/4), Rubén Hugo Ayala (25/11), Mario Alberto Kempes (11/4). Trainer: Vladislao Wenceslao Cap (10).
**Goal**: René Orlando Houseman (21).

**459.** 12.10.1974 **ARGENTINA - SPAIN** **1-1(0-0)** Copa Hispanidád
Estadio Monumental „Antonio Vespucio Liberti“, Buenos Aires; Referee: Armando Nunes Castanheiras da Rosa Marques (Brazil); Attendance: 70,000
**ARG:** Rubén Omar Sánchez (11/0), Vicente Alberto Pernía (4/0), Jorge Paolino (1/0), Roberto Domingo Rogel (8/1), Jorge Omar Carrascosa (7/0), Miguel Ángel Brindisi (44/17) [68.Marcelo Antonio Trobbiani (2/0)], Francisco Faustino Russo (2/0), Carlos Alberto Babington (13/2) [68.Osvaldo Rubén Potente (2/0)], René Orlando Houseman (14/4), Edgardo Roberto Di Meola (1/0), Enzo Ferrero (1/0). Trainer: César Luis Menotti (1).
**Goal**: Roberto Domingo Rogel (83).

**460.** 06.11.1974 **CHILE - ARGENTINA** **0-2(0-0)** Copa Carlos Dittborn
Estadio Nacional, Santiago; Referee: Alberto Ducatelli (Argentina); Attendance: 45,000
**ARG:** Rubén Omar Sánchez (12/0), Vicente Alberto Pernía (5/0), Jorge Paolino (2/0), Jorge Omar Carrascosa (8/0), Roberto Domingo Rogel (9/1), Francisco Faustino Russo (3/0) [59.Gerónimo Luis Saccardi (1/0)], Marcelo Antonio Trobbiani (3/0), Horacio Raúl Cordero (1/0) [60.Juan José López (2/1)], Daniel Ricardo Bertoni (1/0), Ricardo Enrique Bochini (2/0), Enzo Ferrero (2/1). Trainer: César Luis Menotti (2).
**Goals**: Juan José López (78), Enzo Ferrero (86).

**461.** 20.11.1974 **ARGENTINA - CHILE** **1-1(1-1)** Copa Carlos Dittborn
Estadio „José Amalfitani“, Buenos Aires; Referee: Juan Ambrosio Silvagno Cavanna (Chile); Attendance: 20,000
**ARG:** Rubén Omar Sánchez (13/0), Vicente Alberto Pernía (6/0), Jorge Paolino (3/0), Jorge Omar Carrascosa (9/0), Roberto Domingo Rogel (10/1), Marcelo Antonio Trobbiani (4/0), Osvaldo Rubén Potente (3/0), Gerónimo Luis Saccardi (2/0) [60.Rubén Galván (2/0)], Rubén Horacio Galletti (1/1) [78.Roberto Mouzo (1/0)], Ricardo Enrique Bochini (3/0), Enzo Ferrero (3/1). Trainer: César Luis Menotti (3).
**Goal**: Rubén Horacio Galletti (43 penalty).

**462.** 18.07.1975 **URUGUAY - ARGENTINA** **2-3(0-1)** Copa Newton
Estadio Centenario, Montevideo; Referee: Néstor Gregorio Da Rosa Caraballo (Uruguay); Attendance: 40,000
**ARG:** Ricardo Antonio La Volpe (1/0), Jorge Troncoso (4/0), Rubén Galván (3/0) [46.Eduardo Miguel Solari (1/0)], Jorge Omar Carrascosa (Cap) (10/0), Mario Estanislao Killer (3/0), Juan Domingo Antonio Rocchia (1/0), Ricardo Enrique Bochini (4/0), René Orlando Houseman (15/4) [65.Jorge Alberto Francisco Valdano (1/2)], Julio Daniel Asad (1/0), Oscar Alberto Ortíz (1/0), Norberto Osvaldo Alonso (10/2). Trainer: César Luis Menotti (4).
**Goals**: Norberto Osvaldo Alonso (10), Jorge Alberto Francisco Valdano (79, 84).

**463.** 03.08.1975 **VENEZUELA - ARGENTINA** **1-5(1-3)** 30th Copa América. Group Stage.
Estadio Olímpico, Caracas; Referee: Rafael Hormozabál Díaz (Chile); Attendance: 15,000
**ARG:** Hugo Orlando Gatti (3/0), Andrés Orlando Rebottaro (1/0), José Luis Pavoni (1/0), Daniel Pedro Killer (1/0), Rafael José Eloy Pavón (1/0), Julio Daniel Asad (2/0), Américo Rubén Gallego (1/0), Mario Nicasio Zanabria (1/0) [56.Osvaldo César Ardiles (1/1)], Ramón César Bóveda (4/0), Leopoldo Jacinto Luque (1/3), Mario Alberto Kempes (12/5) [56.José Daniel Valencia (1/0)]. Trainer: César Luis Menotti (5).
**Goals**: Leopoldo Jacinto Luque (12), Mario Alberto Kempes (30), Leopoldo Jacinto Luque (34, 66), Osvaldo César Ardiles (86).

**464.** 06.08.1975 **BRAZIL - ARGENTINA** **2-1(1-1)** 30th Copa América. Group Stage.
Estádio Mineirão, Belo Horizonte; Referee: Ramón Ivannoe Barreto Ruíz (Uruguay); Attendance: 80,000
**ARG:** Hugo Orlando Gatti (4/0), Andrés Orlando Rebottaro (2/0), José Luis Pavoni (2/0), Daniel Pedro Killer (2/0), Rafael José Eloy Pavón (2/0), Osvaldo César Ardiles (2/1) [57.Mario Nicasio Zanabria (2/0)], Américo Rubén Gallego (2/0), Julio Daniel Asad (3/1), Ramón César Bóveda (5/0) [57.Jorge Alberto Francisco Valdano (2/2)], Leopoldo Jacinto Luque (2/3), Mario Alberto Kempes (13/5). Trainer: César Luis Menotti (6).
**Goal**: Julio Daniel Asad (11).

**465.** 10.08.1975 **ARGENTINA - VENEZUELA** **11-0(4-0)** 30th Copa América. Group Stage.
Estadio Cor de León, Rosario; Referee: Pedro Reyes (Peru); Attendance: 50,000
**ARG:** Hugo Orlando Gatti (5/0), Andrés Orlando Rebottaro (3/0), José Luis Pavoni (3/0), Daniel Pedro Killer (3/3), Mario Estanislao Killer (4/0), Osvaldo César Ardiles (3/2) [85.Julio Daniel Asad (4/1)], Américo Rubén Gallego (3/1), Mario Nicasio Zanabria (3/2) [76.José Daniel Valencia (2/0)], Ramón César Bóveda (6/1), Leopoldo Jacinto Luque (3/4), Mario Alberto Kempes (14/7). Trainer: César Luis Menotti (7).
**Goals**: Daniel Pedro Killer (8), Américo Rubén Gallego (14), Osvaldo César Ardiles (39), Daniel Pedro Killer (41), Mario Alberto Kempes (53), Mario Nicasio Zanabria (56), Daniel Pedro Killer (62), Mario Nicasio Zanabria (64), Ramón César Bóveda (80), Mario Alberto Kempes (81), Leopoldo Jacinto Luque (85).

**466.** 16.08.1975 **ARGENTINA - BRAZIL** **0-1(0-1)** 30th Copa América. Group Stage.
Estadio Cor de León, Rosario; Referee: Juan Carlos Robles (Chile); Attendance: 50,000
**ARG:** Hugo Orlando Gatti (6/0), Andrés Orlando Rebottaro (4/0), José Luis Pavoni (4/0), Daniel Pedro Killer (4/3), Mario Estanislao Killer (5/0), Osvaldo César Ardiles (4/2) [57.Julio Daniel Asad (5/1)], Américo Rubén Gallego (4/1), Mario Nicasio Zanabria (4/2), Ramón César Bóveda (7/1), Leopoldo Jacinto Luque (4/4), Mario Alberto Kempes (15/7). Trainer: César Luis Menotti (8).

**467.** 21.08.1975 **ARGENTINA – UNITED STATES** **6-0(3-0)** Copa Ciudad de México
Estadio Azteca, Ciudad de México (Mexico); Attendance: 1,500
**ARG:** Ricardo Antonio La Volpe (2/0) [Héctor Rodolfo Baley (1/0)], José María Suárez (1/0), Pablo de las Mecedes Cárdenas (1/1) [Enzo Héctor Trossero (1/0)], Aldo Roque Espinoza (1/0), Edgar Oscar Fernández (1/0), Américo Rubén Gallego (5/1) [Miguel Ángel Oviedo (1/0)], Osvaldo César Ardiles (5/4), José Daniel Valencia (3/1), Armando Ignacio Quinteros (1/0), Daniel Ricardo Astegiano (1/0) [Daniel Horacio Marangoni (1/0)], Hugo Oscar Coscia (1/2). Trainer: César Luis Menotti (9).
**Goals**: Osvaldo César Ardiles (19, 23), Pablo de las Mecedes Cárdenas (36), Hugo Oscar Coscia (58), José Daniel Valencia (82), Hugo Oscar Coscia (90).

**468.** 28.08.1975 **ARGENTINA – COSTA RICA** **2-0(1-0)** Copa Ciudad de México
Estadio Azteca, Ciudad de México (Mexico); Referee: Alfonso González Archundia (Mexico); Attendance:
**ARG:** Ricardo Antonio La Volpe (3/0), José María Suárez (2/0), Pablo de las Mecedes Cárdenas (2/1), Enzo Héctor Trossero (2/0) [Miguel Ángel Oviedo (2/0)], Edgar Oscar Fernández (2/0), Américo Rubén Gallego (6/1), Armando Ignacio Quinteros (2/0), Osvaldo César Ardiles (6/4), José Daniel Valencia (4/1) [Ángel Héctor Bocanelli (1/0)], Daniel Ricardo Astegiano (2/2) [Daniel Horacio Marangoni (2/0)], Hugo Oscar Coscia (2/2). Trainer: César Luis Menotti (10).
**Goals**: Daniel Ricardo Astegiano (28, 50).

**469.** 31.08.1975 **MEXICO - ARGENTINA** **1-1(1-1)** Copa Ciudad de México
Estadio Azteca, Ciudad de México; Referee: Arturo Maximo Yamasaki Maldonado (Peru); Attendance:
**ARG:** Ricardo Antonio La Volpe (4/0), José María Suárez (3/0), Pablo de las Mecedes Cárdenas (3/1), Aldo Roque Espinoza (2/0) [36.Miguel Ángel Oviedo (3/0)], Edgar Oscar Fernández (3/0), Américo Rubén Gallego (7/1), Armando Ignacio Quinteros (3/0) [61.Daniel Horacio Marangoni (3/0)], Osvaldo César Ardiles (7/4), José Daniel Valencia (5/1) [86.Ángel Héctor Bocanelli (2/0)], Daniel Ricardo Astegiano (3/2), Hugo Oscar Coscia (3/3). Trainer: César Luis Menotti (11).
**Goal**: Hugo Oscar Coscia (34).

**470.** 25.02.1976 **PARAGUAY - ARGENTINA** **2-3(1-2)** Copa Atlántico
Estadio Defensores del Chaco, Asunción; Referee: Héctor Ortíz (Paraguay); Attendance:
**ARG:** Ricardo Antonio La Volpe (5/0), Andrés Orlando Rebottaro (5/0), Pablo de las Mecedes Cárdenas (4/1), Daniel Pedro Killer (5/3), Alberto César Tarantini (2/0), Américo Rubén Gallego (8/1), Marcelo Antonio Trobbiani (5/0) [68.Julio Daniel Asad (6/1)], Ricardo Enrique Bochini (5/0), Héctor Horacio Scotta (1/3), Oscar Alberto Ortíz (2/0) [57.René Orlando Houseman (16/4)], Mario Alberto Kempes (16/7). Trainer: César Luis Menotti (12).
**Goals**: Héctor Horacio Scotta (11, 38, 52).

**471.** 27.02.1976 **ARGENTINA - BRAZIL** **1-2(0-1)** Copa Atlántico & Copa Roca
Estadio Monumental „Antonio Vespucio Liberti“, Buenos Aires; Referee: Roberto Osvaldo Barreiro (Argentina)
**ARG:** Ricardo Antonio La Volpe (6/0), Andrés Orlando Rebottaro (6/0), Pablo de las Mecedes Cárdenas (5/1), Daniel Pedro Killer (6/3), Alberto César Tarantini (3/0), Américo Rubén Gallego (9/1), Marcelo Antonio Trobbiani (6/0) [70.Julio Daniel Asad (7/1)], Ricardo Enrique Bochini (6/0), Héctor Horacio Scotta (2/3) [57.René Orlando Houseman (17/4)], Oscar Alberto Ortíz (3/0), Mario Alberto Kempes (17/8). Trainer: César Luis Menotti (13).
**Goal**: Mario Alberto Kempes (74).

**472.** 20.03.1976 **SOVIET UNION - ARGENTINA** **0-1(0-1)**
Centralniy Stadium, Kiev; Referee: Sergio Gonella (Italy); Attendance: 45,000
**ARG:** Hugo Orlando Gatti (7/0), Jorge Mario Olguín (1/0), Daniel Pedro Killer (7/3), Jorge Omar Carrascosa (11/0), Alberto César Tarantini (4/0), Américo Rubén Gallego (10/1), Osvaldo César Ardiles (8/4) [61.Daniel Alberto Passarella (1/0)], Ricardo Enrique Bochini (7/0), Marcelo Antonio Trobbiani (7/0), Leopoldo Jacinto Luque (5/4), Mario Alberto Kempes (18/9) [68.René Orlando Houseman (18/4)]. Trainer: César Luis Menotti (14).
**Goal**: Mario Alberto Kempes (43).

**473.** 24.03.1976 **POLAND - ARGENTINA** **1-2(0-0)**
Śląski Stadion, Chorzów; Referee: Ernst Dörflinger (Switzerland); Attendance: 60,000
**ARG:** Hugo Orlando Gatti (8/0), Jorge Mario Olguín (2/0), Daniel Pedro Killer (8/3), Jorge Omar Carrascosa (12/0), Alberto César Tarantini (5/0), Marcelo Antonio Trobbiani (8/0) [71.Osvaldo César Ardiles (9/4)], Américo Rubén Gallego (11/1), Ricardo Enrique Bochini (8/0), Héctor Horacio Scotta (3/4) [64.René Orlando Houseman (19/5)], Leopoldo Jacinto Luque (6/4), Mario Alberto Kempes (19/9). Trainer: César Luis Menotti (15).
**Goals**: Héctor Horacio Scotta (63), René Orlando Houseman (69).

**474.** 27.03.1976 **HUNGARY - ARGENTINA** **2-0(2-0)**
Népstadion, Budapest; Referee: Gianfranco Menegali (Italy); Attendance: 25,000
**ARG:** Hugo Orlando Gatti (9/0), Jorge Mario Olguín (3/0), Daniel Pedro Killer (9/3), Jorge Omar Carrascosa (13/0), Alberto César Tarantini (6/0), Osvaldo César Ardiles (10/4), Américo Rubén Gallego (12/1), Ricardo Enrique Bochini (9/0), Héctor Horacio Scotta (4/4) [58.René Orlando Houseman (20/5)], Leopoldo Jacinto Luque (7/4) [55.Marcelo Antonio Trobbiani (9/0)], Mario Alberto Kempes (20/9). Trainer: César Luis Menotti (16).

**475.** 08.04.1976 **ARGENTINA - URUGUAY** **4-1(1-0)** Copa Atlántico
Estadio „José Amalfitani“, Buenos Aires; Referee: Arturo Andrés Ithurralde (Argentina); Attendance:
**ARG:** Hugo Orlando Gatti (10/0), Jorge Mario Olguín (4/0), Jorge Omar Carrascosa (Cap) (14/0), Daniel Alberto Passarella (2/0), Daniel Pedro Killer (10/3), Osvaldo César Ardiles (11/4) [62.Marcelo Antonio Trobbiani (10/0)], Américo Rubén Gallego (13/1), Ricardo Enrique Bochini (10/0), René Orlando Houseman (21/5) [62.Héctor Horacio Scotta (5/5)], Leopoldo Jacinto Luque (8/5), Mario Alberto Kempes (21/11). Trainer: César Luis Menotti (17).
**Goals**: Mario Alberto Kempes (21), Leopoldo Jacinto Luque (50), Mario Alberto Kempes (57), Héctor Horacio Scotta (89).

**476.** 28.04.1976 **ARGENTINA - PARAGUAY** **2-2(0-0)** Copa Atlántico
Estadio „José Amalfitani“, Buenos Aires; Referee: Ángel Norberto Coerezza (Argentina)
**ARG:** Ricardo Antonio La Volpe (7/0), Jorge Mario Olguín (5/0), Jorge Omar Carrascosa (15/0), Alberto César Tarantini (7/0), Daniel Pedro Killer (11/3), Osvaldo César Ardiles (12/4), Américo Rubén Gallego (14/1), Ricardo Enrique Bochini (11/0), René Orlando Houseman (22/5), Leopoldo Jacinto Luque (9/5), Mario Alberto Kempes (22/13) [68.Héctor Horacio Scotta (6/5)]. Trainer: César Luis Menotti (18).
**Goals**: Mario Alberto Kempes (48, 50).

**477.** 19.05.1976 **BRAZIL - ARGENTINA** **2-0(0-0)** Copa Atlántico & Copa Roca
Estádio „Jornalista Mário Filho“ (Maracanã), Rio de Janeiro; Referee: Agomir Martins (Brazil)
**ARG:** Ricardo Antonio La Volpe (8/0), Jorge Mario Olguín (6/0), Jorge Omar Carrascosa (16/0), Daniel Alberto Passarella (3/0), Alberto César Tarantini (8/0), Marcelo Antonio Trobbiani (11/0), Américo Rubén Gallego (15/1), Ricardo Enrique Bochini (12/0) [46.Norberto Osvaldo Alonso (11/2)], René Orlando Houseman (23/5), Leopoldo Jacinto Luque (10/5) [46.José Daniel Valencia (6/1)], Mario Alberto Kempes (23/13). Trainer: César Luis Menotti (19).

**478.** 09.06.1976 **URUGUAY - ARGENTINA** **0-3(0-3)** Copa Atlántico
Estadio Centenario, Montevideo; Referee: Ramón Ivannoe Barreto Ruíz (Uruguay), Attendance: 30,000
**ARG:** Hugo Orlando Gatti (11/0) [*sent off 40*], Jorge Mario Olguín (7/0), Jorge Omar Carrascosa (Cap) (17/0), Daniel Alberto Passarella (4/0), Alberto César Tarantini (9/0), Osvaldo César Ardiles (13/4), Américo Rubén Gallego (16/1), Ricardo Enrique Bochini (13/0), René Orlando Houseman (24/6) [40.Héctor Rodolfo Baley (2/0)], Leopoldo Jacinto Luque (11/6) [46.Héctor Horacio Scotta (7/5)], Mario Alberto Kempes (24/14). Trainer: César Luis Menotti (20).
**Goals**: Leopoldo Jacinto Luque (2), Mario Alberto Kempes (11), René Orlando Houseman (28).

**479.** 13.10.1976 **ARGENTINA - CHILE** **2-0(1-0)** Copa Carlos Dittborn
Estadio „José Amalfitani“, Buenos Aires; Referee: Ramón Ivannoe Barreto Ruíz (Uruguay); Attendance: 40,000
**ARG:** Hugo Orlando Gatti (12/0), Jorge Mario Olguín (8/0), Jorge Omar Carrascosa (18/0), Daniel Pedro Killer (12/3), Alberto César Tarantini (10/0), Osvaldo César Ardiles (14/5), Américo Rubén Gallego (17/1), José Daniel Valencia (7/1), René Orlando Houseman (25/6) [Julio Ricardo Villa (1/0)], José Luis Saldaño (1/0) [Alberto Beltrán (1/0)], Ricardo Daniel Bertoni (2/1). Trainer: César Luis Menotti (21).
**Goals**: Osvaldo César Ardiles (2), Ricardo Daniel Bertoni (88).

**480.** 28.10.1976 **PERU - ARGENTINA** **1-3(1-1)** Copa Ramón Castilla
Estadio Nacional, Lima; Referee: José Ramírez (Peru)
**ARG:** Hugo Orlando Gatti (13/0), Jorge Mario Olguín (9/0), Jorge Omar Carrascosa (19/0), Daniel Alberto Passarella (5/1), Alberto César Tarantini (11/0), Osvaldo César Ardiles (15/5) [Julio Ricardo Villa (2/0)], Américo Rubén Gallego (18/1), José Daniel Valencia (8/1), René Orlando Houseman (26/7), José Luis Saldaño (2/0) [Raúl Francisco Agüero (1/0)], Ricardo Daniel Bertoni (3/1). Trainer: César Luis Menotti (22).
**Goals**: Alfredo Quesada (2 own goal), Daniel Alberto Passarella (75), René Orlando Houseman (78).

**481.** 10.11.1976 **ARGENTINA - PERU** **1-0(0-0)** Copa Ramón Castilla
Estadio „José Amalfitani“, Buenos Aires; Referee: Jorge Eduardo Romero (Argentina); Attendance: 45,000
**ARG:** Héctor Rodolfo Baley (3/0), Jorge Mario Olguín (10/0), Roberto Mouzo (2/0), Daniel Alberto Passarella (6/2), Alberto César Tarantini (12/0), Julio Ricardo Villa (3/0) [59.Osvaldo César Ardiles (16/5)], Américo Rubén Gallego (19/1), José Daniel Valencia (9/1), René Orlando Houseman (27/7), Raúl Francisco Agüero (2/0) [José Luis Saldaño (3/0)], Ricardo Daniel Bertoni (4/1). Trainer: César Luis Menotti (23).
**Goal**: Daniel Alberto Passarella (63).

**482.** 28.11.1976 **ARGENTINA – SOVIET UNION** **0-0**
Estadio Monumental „Antonio Vespucio Liberti“, Buenos Aires; Referee: José Faville Neto (Brazil); Attendance: 60,000
**ARG:** Hugo Orlando Gatti (14/0), Jorge Mario Olguín (11/0), Jorge Omar Carrascosa (20/0), Daniel Pedro Killer (13/3), Alberto César Tarantini (13/0), Osvaldo César Ardiles (17/5), Américo Rubén Gallego (20/1), José Daniel Valencia (10/1) [Juan Ramón Rocha (1/0)], René Orlando Houseman (28/7), José Luis Saldaño (4/0) [Ricardo Enrique Bochini (14/0)], Ricardo Daniel Bertoni (5/1). Trainer: César Luis Menotti (24).

**483.** 27.02.1977 **ARGENTINA - HUNGARY** **5-1(4-0)**
Estadio „Alberto Armando“, Buenos Aires; Referee: Ramón Ivanoe Barreto Ruíz (Uruguay); Attendance: 60,000
**ARG:** Hugo Orlando Gatti (15/0), Jorge Mario Olguín (12/0), Jorge Omar Carrascosa (21/0), Daniel Pedro Killer (14/3), Alberto César Tarantini (14/0), Osvaldo César Ardiles (18/5), Américo Rubén Gallego (21/1), Julio Ricardo Villa (4/0) [65.Jorge José Benítez (1/0)], René Orlando Houseman (29/7) [62.Luis Darío Felman (1/0)], Leopoldo Jacinto Luque (12/8) [62.Diego Armando Maradona (1/0)], Ricardo Daniel Bertoni (6/4). Trainer: César Luis Menotti (25).
**Goals**: Ricardo Daniel Bertoni (11, 18), Leopoldo Jacinto Luque (37), Ricardo Daniel Bertoni (44), Leopoldo Jacinto Luque (47).

**484.** 22.03.1977 **ARGENTINA - IRAN** **1-1(1-0,1-1,1-1); 5-2 on penalties** International Tournament
Estadio „Santiago Bernabéu“, Madrid; Referee: Franco Martínez (Spain); Attendance:
**ARG:** Hugo Orlando Gatti (16/0), Jorge Mario Olguín (13/0), Jorge Omar Carrascosa (22/0), Daniel Pedro Killer (15/3), Alberto César Tarantini (15/0), Osvaldo César Ardiles (19/5), Américo Rubén Gallego (22/1), Julio Ricardo Villa (5/0) [60.Jorge José Benítez (2/0)], René Orlando Houseman (30/7) [60.Oscar Alberto Ortíz (4/0)], Leopoldo Jacinto Luque (13/8), Ricardo Daniel Bertoni (7/5). Trainer: César Luis Menotti (26).
**Goal**: Ricardo Daniel Bertoni (14 penalty).
**Penalties**: Ricardo Daniel Bertoni, Jorge José Benítez, Jorge Mario Olguín, Osvaldo César Ardiles.

**485.** 29.05.1977 **ARGENTINA - POLAND** **3-1(1-1)**
Estadio „Alberto Armando“, Buenos Aires; Referee: José Romei Cañete (Paraguay); Attendance: 70,000
**ARG:** Hugo Orlando Gatti (17/0), Jorge Mario Olguín (14/0), Jorge Omar Carrascosa (23/0), Daniel Pedro Killer (16/3), Vicente Alberto Pernía (7/0), Osvaldo César Ardiles (20/5), Américo Rubén Gallego (23/1), Julio Ricardo Villa (6/0) [58.Ricardo Enrique Bochini (15/0)], Ricardo Daniel Bertoni (8/7), Leopoldo Jacinto Luque (14/9), Oscar Alberto Ortíz (5/0) [59.Omar Rubén Larrosa (1/0)]. Trainer: César Luis Menotti (27).
**Goals**: Ricardo Daniel Bertoni (41 penalty), Leopoldo Jacinto Luque (53), Ricardo Daniel Bertoni (72).

**486.** 05.06.1977 **ARGENTINA – WEST GERMANY** **1-3(0-1)**
Estadio „Alberto Armando“, Buenos Aires; Referee: Arnaldo David César Coelho (Brazil); Attendance: 60,000
**ARG:** Hugo Orlando Gatti (18/0), Jorge Mario Olguín (15/0), Jorge Omar Carrascosa (24/0) [Alberto César Tarantini (16/0)], Daniel Alberto Passarella (7/3), Vicente Alberto Pernía (8/0), Osvaldo César Ardiles (21/5), Américo Rubén Gallego (24/1), Julio Ricardo Villa (7/0) [44.Ricardo Enrique Bochini (16/0)], Ricardo Daniel Bertoni (9/7), Leopoldo Jacinto Luque (15/9), Omar Rubén Larrosa (2/0) [76.Oscar Alberto Ortíz (6/0)]. Trainer: César Luis Menotti (28).
**Goal**: Daniel Alberto Passarella (73).

**487.** 12.06.1977 **ARGENTINA - ENGLAND** **1-1(1-1)**
Estadio „Alberto Armando“, Buenos Aires; Referee: Ramón Ivanoe Barreto Ruíz (Uruguay); Attendance: 60,000
**ARG:** Héctor Rodolfo Baley (4/0), Vicente Alberto Pernía (9/0), Daniel Pedro Killer (17/3), Daniel Alberto Passarella (8/3), Alberto César Tarantini (17/0), Osvaldo César Ardiles (22/5), Américo Rubén Gallego (25/1), Ricardo Enrique Bochini (17/0) [55.Omar Rubén Larrosa (3/0)], Ricardo Daniel Bertoni (10/8) [*sent off 82*], Leopoldo Jacinto Luque (16/9), Oscar Alberto Ortíz (7/0) [55.Juan Ramón Rocha (2/0)]. Trainer: César Luis Menotti (29).
**Goal**: Ricardo Daniel Bertoni (15).

**488.** 18.06.1977 **ARGENTINA - SCOTLAND** **1-1(0-0)**
Estadio „Alberto Armando“, Buenos Aires; Referee: Romualdo Arppi Filho (Brazil); Attendance: 57,000
**ARG:** Héctor Rodolfo Baley (5/0), Vicente Alberto Pernía (10/0) [*sent off 56*], Daniel Pedro Killer (18/3), Daniel Alberto Passarella (9/4), Jorge Omar Carrascosa (Cap) (25/0), Osvaldo César Ardiles (23/5), Américo Rubén Gallego (26/1), Omar Rubén Larrosa (4/0) [70.Oscar Víctor Trossero (1/0)], Pedro Alexis González (6/0) [59.Alberto César Tarantini (18/0)], Leopoldo Jacinto Luque (17/9), René Orlando Houseman (31/7). Trainer: César Luis Menotti (30).
**Goal**: Daniel Alberto Passarella (80 penalty).

**489.** 26.06.1977 **ARGENTINA - FRANCE** **0-0**
Estadio „Alberto Armando", Buenos Aires; Referee: Edison Pérez Nuñez (Peru); Attendance: 55,000
**ARG:** Héctor Rodolfo Baley (6/0), Alberto César Tarantini (19/0), Daniel Pedro Killer (19/3) [69.Jorge Mario Olguín (16/0)], Daniel Alberto Passarella (10/4), Jorge Omar Carrascosa (Cap) (26/0), Julio Ricardo Villa (8/0), Américo Rubén Gallego (27/1), Omar Rubén Larrosa (5/0), Pedro Alexis González (7/0) [46.Osvaldo César Ardiles (24/5)], Leopoldo Jacinto Luque (18/9) [60.Oscar Víctor Trossero (2/0)], René Orlando Houseman (32/7). Trainer: César Luis Menotti (31).

**490.** 03.07.1977 **ARGENTINA - YUGOSLAVIA** **1-0(1-0)**
Estadio „Alberto Armando", Buenos Aires; Referee: Juan Ambrosio Silvagno Cavanna (Chile); Attendance: 60,000
**ARG:** Héctor Rodolfo Baley (7/0), Jorge Mario Olguín (17/0), Jorge Omar Carrascosa (Cap) (27/0), Daniel Alberto Passarella (11/5), Alberto César Tarantini (20/0), Osvaldo César Ardiles (25/5), Rubén Galván (4/0), Julio Ricardo Villa (9/0) [67.Ricardo Enrique Bochini (18/0)], René Orlando Houseman (33/7), Leopoldo Jacinto Luque (19/9) [67.Oscar Víctor Trossero (3/0)], Oscar Alberto Ortíz (8/0). Trainer: César Luis Menotti (32).
**Goal**: Daniel Alberto Passarella (32 penalty).

**491.** 12.07.1977 **ARGENTINA – EAST GERMANY** **2-0(1-0)**
Estadio „Alberto Armando", Buenos Aires; Referee: Ramón Ivanoe Barreto Ruíz (Uruguay); Attendance: 50,000
**ARG:** Héctor Rodolfo Baley (8/0), Jorge Mario Olguín (18/0), Jorge Omar Carrascosa (Cap) (28/1), Daniel Alberto Passarella (12/5), Alberto César Tarantini (21/0), Osvaldo César Ardiles (26/5) [83.Juan Ramón Rocha (3/0)], Rubén Galván (5/0), Julio Ricardo Villa (10/0), René Orlando Houseman (34/8), Leopoldo Jacinto Luque (20/9), Oscar Alberto Ortíz (9/0). Trainer: César Luis Menotti (33).
**Goals**: René Orlando Houseman (30), Jorge Omar Carrascosa (72).

**492.** 24.08.1977 **ARGENTINA - PARAGUAY** **2-1(1-1)** Copa Félix Bogado
Estadio „Alberto Armando", Buenos Aires; Referee: Ramón Ivanoe Barreto Ruíz (Uruguay)
**ARG:** Héctor Rodolfo Baley (9/0), Jorge Mario Olguín (19/0), Daniel Pedro Killer (20/3), Daniel Alberto Passarella (13/5), Jorge Omar Carrascosa (Cap) (29/1), Osvaldo César Ardiles (27/5) [46.Américo Rubén Gallego (28/1)], Luis Adolfo Galván (1/0), Julio Ricardo Villa (11/0) [60.Diego Armando Maradona (2/0)], René Orlando Houseman (35/8), Leopoldo Jacinto Luque (21/11), Ricardo Daniel Bertoni (11/8). Trainer: César Luis Menotti (34).
**Goals**: Leopoldo Jacinto Luque (10, 78).

**493.** 31.08.1977 **PARAGUAY - ARGENTINA** **2-0(0-0,2-0); 3-1 on penalties** Copa Félix Bogado
Estadio Defensores del Chaco, Asunción; Referee: Juan Ambrosio Silvagno Cavanna (Chile)
**ARG:** Héctor Rodolfo Baley (10/0), Alberto César Tarantini (22/0) [*sent off 74*], Jorge Mario Olguín (20/0), Daniel Pedro Killer (21/3), Jorge Omar Carrascosa (Cap) (30/1), Osvaldo César Ardiles (28/5), Américo Rubén Gallego (29/1), Diego Armando Maradona (3/0), René Orlando Houseman (36/8) [67.Oscar Alberto Ortíz (10/0)], Omar Pedro Roldán (1/0) [67.Leopoldo Jacinto Luque (22/11)], Ricardo Daniel Bertoni (12/8). Trainer: César Luis Menotti (35).
**Penalties**: Ricardo Daniel Bertoni, Jorge Mario Olguín (save), Diego Armando Maradona (save), Daniel Pedro Killer (save).

**494.** 19.03.1978 **ARGENTINA - PERU** **2-1(1-0)** Copa Ramón Castilla
Estadio „Alberto Armando", Buenos Aires; Referee: Juan José Fortunato (Uruguay); Attendance: 35,000
**ARG:** Ubaldo Matildo Fillol (2/0), Rubén Oscar Pagnanini (1/1), Luis Adolfo Galván (2/0), Daniel Alberto Passarella (Cap) (14/5), Víctor Alfredo Bottaniz (1/0), Osvaldo César Ardiles (29/5) [56.Omar Rubén Larrosa (6/0)], Américo Rubén Gallego (30/1) [74.Miguel Ángel Oviedo (4/0)], José Daniel Valencia (11/1), René Orlando Houseman (37/9), Leopoldo Jacinto Luque (23/11) [60.Humberto Rafael Bravo (1/0)], Oscar Alberto Ortíz (11/0). Trainer: César Luis Menotti (36).
**Goals**: René Orlando Houseman (41), Rubén Oscar Pagnanini (69).

**495.** 23.03.1978 **PERU - ARGENTINA** **1-3(0-3)** Copa Ramón Castilla
Estadio Nacional, Lima; Referee: Edison Pérez Nuñez (Peru); Attendance: 43,490
**ARG:** Ubaldo Matildo Fillol (3/0), Rubén Oscar Pagnanini (2/1), Luis Adolfo Galván (3/0), Daniel Alberto Passarella (Cap) (15/6), Víctor Alfredo Bottaniz (2/0), Osvaldo César Ardiles (30/5), Américo Rubén Gallego (31/1), José Daniel Valencia (12/1) [70.Omar Rubén Larrosa (7/0)], René Orlando Houseman (38/10) [60.Humberto Rafael Bravo (2/0)], Leopoldo Jacinto Luque (24/12), Oscar Alberto Ortíz (12/0). Trainer: César Luis Menotti (37).
**Goals**: Leopoldo Jacinto Luque (7), Daniel Alberto Passarella (25 penalty), René Orlando Houseman (30).

**496.** 29.03.1978 **ARGENTINA - BULGARIA** **3-1(2-1)**
Estadio „Alberto Armando", Buenos Aires; Referee: Roque Serillo (Uruguay); Attendance: 60,000
**ARG:** Ubaldo Matildo Fillol (4/0), Rubén Oscar Pagnanini (3/1), Luis Adolfo Galván (4/0), Daniel Alberto Passarella (Cap) (16/6), Alberto César Tarantini (23/0), Osvaldo César Ardiles (31/6) [72.Omar Rubén Larrosa (8/0)], Américo Rubén Gallego (32/2), José Daniel Valencia (13/1), René Orlando Houseman (39/10) [61.Ricardo Daniel Bertoni (13/8)], Leopoldo Jacinto Luque (25/12), Oscar Alberto Ortíz (13/1). Trainer: César Luis Menotti (38).
**Goals**: Américo Rubén Gallego (9), Oscar Alberto Ortíz (13), Osvaldo César Ardiles (66).

**497.** 05.04.1978 **ARGENTINA - ROMANIA** **2-0(2-0)**
Estadio „Alberto Armando", Buenos Aires; Referee: Juan Daniel Cardellino de San Vicente (Uruguay); Attendance: 60,000
**ARG:** Ubaldo Matildo Fillol (5/0), Jorge Mario Olguín (21/0), Luis Adolfo Galván (5/0), Daniel Alberto Passarella (Cap) (17/8), Alberto César Tarantini (24/0), Osvaldo César Ardiles (32/6), Américo Rubén Gallego (33/2), José Daniel Valencia (14/1) [63.Julio Ricardo Villa (12/0)], René Orlando Houseman (40/10), Leopoldo Jacinto Luque (26/12), Ricardo Daniel Bertoni (14/8) [68.Humberto Rafael Bravo (3/0)]. Trainer: César Luis Menotti (39).
**Goals**: Daniel Alberto Passarella (20, 33).

**498.** 19.04.1978 **ARGENTINA – REPUBLIC OF IRELAND** **3-1(1-0)**
Estadio „Alberto Armando", Buenos Aires; Referee: José Luis Martínez Bazán (Uruguay)
**ARG:** Ubaldo Matildo Fillol (6/0), Jorge Mario Olguín (22/0), Luis Adolfo Galván (6/0), Daniel Alberto Passarella (Cap) (18/8), Alberto César Tarantini (25/0), Osvaldo César Ardiles (33/6), Américo Rubén Gallego (34/2), Julio Ricardo Villa (13/1) [58.Diego Armando Maradona (4/0)], René Orlando Houseman (41/10), Leopoldo Jacinto Luque (27/13), Oscar Alberto Ortíz (14/2) [58.Ricardo Daniel Bertoni (15/8)]. Trainer: César Luis Menotti (40).
**Goals**: Leopoldo Jacinto Luque (16), Oscar Alberto Ortíz (46), Julio Ricardo Villa (55).

**499.** 25.04.1978 **URUGUAY - ARGENTINA** **2-0(0-0)**
Estadio Centenario, Montevideo; Referee: Jorge Eduardo Romero (Argentina); Attendance: 26,000
**ARG:** Héctor Rodolfo Baley (11/0), Rubén Oscar Pagnanini (4/1), Luis Adolfo Galván (7/0), Daniel Pedro Killer (Cap) (22/3), Víctor Alfredo Bottaniz (3/0), Omar Rubén Larrosa (9/0) [66.José Daniel Valencia (15/1)], Rubén Galván (6/0) [66.Miguel Ángel Oviedo (5/0)], Julio Ricardo Villa (14/1), René Orlando Houseman (42/10), Humberto Rafael Bravo (4/0), Ricardo Daniel Bertoni (16/8). Trainer: César Luis Menotti (41).

**500.** 03.05.1978 **ARGENTINA - URUGUAY** **3-0(1-0)**
Estadio „Alberto Armando", Buenos Aires; Referee: José Luis da Rosa Barbosa (Uruguay); Attendance: 60,000
**ARG:** Ubaldo Matildo Fillol (7/0), Jorge Mario Olguín (23/0), Luis Adolfo Galván (8/0), Daniel Alberto Passarella (Cap) (19/8), Alberto César Tarantini (26/0), Osvaldo César Ardiles (34/7), Américo Rubén Gallego (35/2), José Daniel Valencia (16/1) [46.Norberto Osvaldo Alonso (12/3)], René Orlando Houseman (43/10), Leopoldo Jacinto Luque (28/14) [77.Miguel Ángel Oviedo (6/0)], Oscar Alberto Ortíz (15/2) [61.Ricardo Daniel Bertoni (17/8)]. Trainer: César Luis Menotti (42).
**Goals**: Leopoldo Jacinto Luque (21), Osvaldo César Ardiles (50), Norberto Osvaldo Alonso (90).

**501.** 02.06.1978 **ARGENTINA - HUNGARY** **2-1(1-1)** 11th FIFA WC. Group Stage.
Estadio Monumental „Antonio Vespucio Liberti", Buenos Aires; Referee: Antonio Da Silva Garrido (Portugal); Attendance: 71,615
**ARG:** Ubaldo Matildo Fillol (8/0), Jorge Mario Olguín (24/0), Luis Adolfo Galván (9/0), Daniel Alberto Passarella (Cap) (20/8), Alberto César Tarantini (27/0), Osvaldo César Ardiles (35/7), Américo Rubén Gallego (36/2), José Daniel Valencia (17/1) [75.Norberto Osvaldo Alonso (13/3)], René Orlando Houseman (44/10) [67.Ricardo Daniel Bertoni (18/9)], Leopoldo Jacinto Luque (29/15), Mario Alberto Kempes (25/14). Trainer: César Luis Menotti (43).
**Goals**: Leopoldo Jacinto Luque (15), Ricardo Daniel Bertoni (84).

**502.** 06.06.1978 **ARGENTINA - FRANCE** **2-1(1-0)** 11th FIFA WC. Group Stage.
Estadio Monumental „Antonio Vespucio Liberti", Buenos Aires; Referee: Jean Dubach (Switzerland); Attendance: 71,666
**ARG:** Ubaldo Matildo Fillol (9/0), Jorge Mario Olguín (25/0), Luis Adolfo Galván (10/0), Daniel Alberto Passarella (Cap) (21/9), Alberto César Tarantini (28/0), Osvaldo César Ardiles (36/7), Américo Rubén Gallego (37/2), José Daniel Valencia (18/1) [64.Norberto Osvaldo Alonso (14/3); 71.Oscar Alberto Ortíz (16/2)], René Orlando Houseman (45/10), Leopoldo Jacinto Luque (30/16), Mario Alberto Kempes (26/14). Trainer: César Luis Menotti (44).
**Goals**: Daniel Alberto Passarella (45 penalty), Leopoldo Jacinto Luque (73).

**503.** 10.06.1978 **ARGENTINA - ITALY** **0-1(0-0)** 11th FIFA WC. Group Stage.
Estadio Monumental „Antonio Vespucio Liberti", Buenos Aires; Referee: Abraham Klein (Israel); Attendance: 71,712
**ARG:** Ubaldo Matildo Fillol (10/0), Jorge Mario Olguín (26/0), Luis Adolfo Galván (11/0), Daniel Alberto Passarella (Cap) (22/9), Alberto César Tarantini (29/0), Osvaldo César Ardiles (37/7), Américo Rubén Gallego (38/2), José Daniel Valencia (19/1), Ricardo Daniel Bertoni (19/9), Oscar Alberto Ortíz (17/2), Mario Alberto Kempes (27/14) [72.René Orlando Houseman (46/10)]. Trainer: César Luis Menotti (45).

**504.** 14.06.1978 **ARGENTINA - POLAND** **2-0(1-0)** 11th FIFA WC.2nd Round.
Estadio Central (Doctor Lisandro de la Torre), Rosario; Referee: Ulf Eriksson (Sweden); Attendance: 37,091
**ARG:** Ubaldo Matildo Fillol (11/0), Jorge Mario Olguín (27/0), Luis Adolfo Galván (12/0), Daniel Alberto Passarella (Cap) (23/9), Alberto César Tarantini (30/0), Osvaldo César Ardiles (38/7), Américo Rubén Gallego (39/2), José Daniel Valencia (20/1) [46.Julio Ricardo Villa (15/1)], Ricardo Daniel Bertoni (20/9), René Orlando Houseman (47/10) [83.Oscar Alberto Ortíz (18/2)], Mario Alberto Kempes (28/16). Trainer: César Luis Menotti (46).
**Goals**: Mario Alberto Kempes (16, 71).

**505.** 18.06.1978 **ARGENTINA - BRAZIL** **0-0** 11th FIFA WC.2nd Round.
Estadio Central (Doctor Lisandro de la Torre), Rosario; Referee: Károly Palotai (Hungary); Attendance: 37,326
**ARG:** Ubaldo Matildo Fillol (12/0), Jorge Mario Olguín (28/0), Luis Adolfo Galván (13/0), Daniel Alberto Passarella (Cap) (24/9), Alberto César Tarantini (31/0), Osvaldo César Ardiles (39/7) [46.Julio Ricardo Villa (16/1)], Américo Rubén Gallego (40/2), Mario Alberto Kempes (29/16), Ricardo Daniel Bertoni (21/9), Leopoldo Jacinto Luque (31/16), Oscar Alberto Ortíz (19/2) [60.Norberto Osvaldo Alonso (15/3)]. Trainer: César Luis Menotti (47).

**506.** 21.06.1978 **ARGENTINA - PERU** **6-0(2-0)** 11th FIFA WC.2nd Round.
Estadio Central (Doctor Lisandro de la Torre), Rosario; Referee: Robert Charles Paul Wurtz (France); Attendance: 38,000
**ARG:** Ubaldo Matildo Fillol (13/0), Jorge Mario Olguín (29/0), Luis Adolfo Galván (14/0), Daniel Alberto Passarella (Cap) (25/9), Alberto César Tarantini (32/1), Omar Rubén Larrosa (10/0), Américo Rubén Gallego (41/2) [86.Miguel Ángel Oviedo (7/0)], Mario Alberto Kempes (30/18), Ricardo Daniel Bertoni (22/9) [65.René Orlando Houseman (48/11)], Leopoldo Jacinto Luque (32/18), Oscar Alberto Ortíz (20/2). Trainer: César Luis Menotti (48).
**Goals**: Mario Alberto Kempes (21), Alberto César Tarantini (43), Mario Alberto Kempes (49), Leopoldo Jacinto Luque (50), René Orlando Houseman (67), Leopoldo Jacinto Luque (72).

**507.** 25.06.1978 **ARGENTINA - HOLLAND** **3-1(1-0,1-1)** 11th FIFA WC.Final.
Estadio Monumental „Antonio Vespucio Liberti", Buenos Aires; Referee: Sergio Gonella (Italy); Attendance: 71,483
**ARG:** Ubaldo Matildo Fillol (14/0), Jorge Mario Olguín (30/0), Luis Adolfo Galván (15/0), Daniel Alberto Passarella (Cap) (26/9), Alberto César Tarantini (33/1), Osvaldo César Ardiles (40/7) [66.Omar Rubén Larrosa (11/0)], Américo Rubén Gallego (42/2), Mario Alberto Kempes (31/20), Ricardo Daniel Bertoni (23/10), Leopoldo Jacinto Luque (33/18), Oscar Alberto Ortíz (21/2) [74.René Orlando Houseman (49/11)]. Trainer: César Luis Menotti (49).
**Goals**: Mario Alberto Kempes (38, 105), Ricardo Daniel Bertoni (115).

**508.** 25.04.1979 **ARGENTINA - BULGARIA** **2-1(1-1)**
Estadio Monumental „Antonio Vespucio Liberti", Buenos Aires; Referee: Juan José Fortunato (Uruguay); Attendance: 80,000
**ARG:** Ubaldo Matildo Fillol (15/0), Jorge Mario Olguín (31/0), Hugo Eduardo Villaverde (1/0) [Juan Ernesto Simón (1/0)], Daniel Alberto Passarella (Cap) (27/10), Jorge Alberto García (1/0), Juan Alberto Barbas (1/0) [64.José Luis Gaitán (1/0)], Américo Rubén Gallego (43/2), Diego Armando Maradona (5/0), René Orlando Houseman (50/12), José Omar Reinaldi (1/0), Oscar Alberto Ortíz (22/2) [66.Hugo Osmar Perotti (1/0)]. Trainer: César Luis Menotti (50).
**Goals**: René Orlando Houseman, Daniel Alberto Passarella.

**509.** 22.05.1979 **ARGENTINA - HOLLAND** **0-0; 8-7 on penalties**
Wankdorf Stadion, Bern; Referee: Ramón Ivanoe Barreto Ruíz (Uruguay); Attendance: 40,000
**ARG:** Ubaldo Matildo Fillol (16/0), Jorge Mario Olguín (32/0), Hugo Eduardo Villaverde (2/0), Daniel Alberto Passarella (Cap) (28/10), Alberto César Tarantini (34/1), Osvaldo César Ardiles (41/7), Américo Rubén Gallego (44/2), Diego Armando Maradona (6/0), Ricardo Daniel Bertoni (24/10) [67.René Orlando Houseman (51/12)], Leopoldo Jacinto Luque (34/18) [61.Juan Alberto Barbas (2/0)], Oscar Alberto Ortíz (23/2) [85.Enzo Héctor Trossero (3/0)]. Trainer: César Luis Menotti (51).
**Penalties**: Jorge Mario Olguín (missed), Diego Armando Maradona, Osvaldo César Ardiles (missed), Américo Rubén Gallego, Hugo Eduardo Villaverde, Alberto César Tarantini, Enzo Héctor Trossero, Daniel Alberto Passarella, René Orlando Houseman, Juan Alberto Barbas.

**510.** 26.05.1979 **ITALY - ARGENTINA** **2-2(1-1)**
Stadio Olimpico, Roma; Referee: Luis Antonio Porem (Portugal); Attendance: 59,834
**ARG:** Ubaldo Matildo Fillol (17/0), Jorge Mario Olguín (33/0), Hugo Eduardo Villaverde (3/0), Daniel Alberto Passarella (Cap) (29/11), Alberto César Tarantini (35/1), Juan Alberto Barbas (3/0) [68.Miguel Ángel Oviedo (8/0)], Américo Rubén Gallego (45/2), Diego Armando Maradona (7/0), René Orlando Houseman (52/12), Leopoldo Jacinto Luque (35/18), José Daniel Valencia (21/2). Trainer: César Luis Menotti (52).
**Goals**: José Daniel Valencia (7), Daniel Alberto Passarella (56 penalty).

**511.** 29.05.1979 **REPUBLIC OF IRELAND - ARGENTINA** **0-0**
Lansdowne Road, Dublin; Referee: Robert Bonar Valentine (Scotland); Attendance: 25,000
**ARG:** Ubaldo Matildo Fillol (18/0), Jorge Mario Olguín (34/0), Hugo Eduardo Villaverde (4/0), Enzo Héctor Trossero (4/0), Alberto César Tarantini (36/1) [81.Américo Rubén Gallego (46/2)], Juan Alberto Barbas (4/0), Miguel Ángel Oviedo (9/0), José Daniel Valencia (22/2), René Orlando Houseman (53/12), José Omar Reinaldi (2/0) [46.Norberto Daniel Outes (1/0)], Hugo Osmar Perotti (2/0) [46.Diego Armando Maradona (8/0)]. Trainer: César Luis Menotti (53).

**512.** 02.06.1979 **SCOTLAND - ARGENTINA** **1-3(0-1)**
Hampden Park, Glasgow; Referee: Patrick Partridge (England); Attendance: 61,918
**ARG:** Ubaldo Matildo Fillol (19/0), Jorge Mario Olguín (35/0), Hugo Eduardo Villaverde (5/0) [21.Enzo Héctor Trossero (5/0)], Daniel Alberto Passarella (Cap) (30/11), Alberto César Tarantini (37/1), Juan Alberto Barbas (5/0), Américo Rubén Gallego (47/2), Diego Armando Maradona (9/1), René Orlando Houseman (54/12) [56.Norberto Daniel Outes (2/0)], Leopoldo Jacinto Luque (36/20), José Daniel Valencia (23/2). Trainer: César Luis Menotti (54).
**Goals**: Leopoldo Jacinto Luque (33, 61), Diego Armando Maradona (70).

**513.** 18.07.1979 **BOLIVIA - ARGENTINA** **2-1(1-1)** 31st Copa América. Group Stage.
Estadio „Hernándo Siles Zuazo“, La Paz; Referee: Octavio Sierra Mesa (Colombia); Attendance: 40,000
**ARG:** Enrique Bernardo Vidallé (1/0), Eduardo Omar Saporiti (1/0), José Daniel Van Tuyne (1/0), Daniel Alberto Passarella (Cap) (31/11), Miguel Ángel Bordón (1/0), Jorge Osvaldo Gáspari (1/0), Pedro Omar Larraquy (1/0), Carlos Ángel López (1/1), José Antonio Castro (1/0), Sergio Élio Ángel Fortunato (1/0) [59.José Luis Gaitán (2/0)], Roberto Osvaldo Díaz (1/0) [46.Hugo Oscar Coscia (4/3)]. Trainer: César Luis Menotti (55).
**Goal**: Carlos Ángel López (5).

**514.** 02.08.1979 **BRAZIL - ARGENTINA** **2-1(1-1)** 31st Copa América. Group Stage.
Estádio „Jornalista Mário Filho“ (Maracanã), Rio de Janeiro; Referee: Edison Pérez Nuñez (Peru); Attendance: 130,000
**ARG:** Enrique Bernardo Vidallé (2/0), Juan Alberto Barbas (6/0), José Daniel Van Tuyne (2/0), Daniel Alberto Passarella (Cap) (32/11), Miguel Ángel Bordón (2/0), Jorge Osvaldo Gáspari (2/0), Pedro Omar Larraquy (2/0), José Luis Gaitán (3/0) [46.Carlos Ángel López (2/1)], Diego Armando Maradona (10/1), Hugo Oscar Coscia (5/4), Roberto Osvaldo Díaz (2/0) [62.José Antonio Castro (2/0)]. Trainer: César Luis Menotti (56).
**Goal**: Hugo Oscar Coscia (29).

**515.** 08.08.1979 **ARGENTINA - BOLIVIA** **3-0(2-0)** 31st Copa América. Group Stage.
Estadio „José Amalfitani“, Buenos Aires; Referee: Víctor Sergio Vásquez Sánchez (Chile); Attendance: 30,000
**ARG:** Enrique Bernardo Vidallé (3/0), Eduardo Omar Saporiti (2/0), José Daniel Van Tuyne (3/0), Daniel Alberto Passarella (Cap) (33/12), Miguel Ángel Bordón (3/0), Jorge Osvaldo Gáspari (3/1), Pedro Omar Larraquy (3/0) [46.Juan Alberto Barbas (7/0)], Diego Armando Maradona (11/2), Hugo Oscar Coscia (6/4), Sergio Élio Ángel Fortunato (2/0), Roberto Osvaldo Díaz (3/0). Trainer: César Luis Menotti (57).
**Goals**: Daniel Alberto Passarella (1), Jorge Osvaldo Gáspari (15), Diego Armando Maradona (65).

**516.** 23.08.1979 **ARGENTINA - BRAZIL** **2-2(1-1)** 31st Copa América. Group Stage.
Estadio Monumental „Antonio Vespucio Liberti“, Buenos Aires; Referee: Roque Tito Cerullo Giuliano (Uruguay); Attendance: 68,000
**ARG:** Enrique Bernardo Vidallé (4/0), Victorio Orlando Ocaño (1/0), José Daniel Van Tuyne (4/0), Daniel Alberto Passarella (Cap) (34/13), Miguel Ángel Bordón (4/0), Jorge Osvaldo Gáspari (4/1), Américo Rubén Gallego (48/2), Ricardo Enrique Bochini (19/0), Hugo Oscar Coscia (7/4) [59.José Daniel Valencia (24/2)], Sergio Élio Ángel Fortunato (3/0) [79.José Antonio Castro (3/0)], Roberto Osvaldo Díaz (4/1). Trainer: César Luis Menotti (58).
**Goals**: Daniel Alberto Passarella (38), Roberto Osvaldo Díaz (71).

**517.** 12.09.1979 **WEST GERMANY - ARGENTINA** **2-1(0-0)**
Olympiastadion, Berlin; Referee: Ulf Eriksson (Sweden); Attendance: 45,000
**ARG:** Enrique Bernardo Vidallé (5/0), Victorio Orlando Ocaño (2/0), José Daniel Van Tuyne (5/0), Daniel Alberto Passarella (Cap) (35/13), Juan Carlos Bujedo (1/0), Jorge Osvaldo Gáspari (5/1), Américo Rubén Gallego (49/2), Patricio José Hernández (1/0), Hugo Oscar Coscia (8/4) [54.José Antonio Castro (4/1)], Sergio Élio Ángel Fortunato (4/0) [46.Ramón Ángel Díaz (1/0)], Roberto Osvaldo Díaz (5/1) [56.Carlos Ángel López (3/1)]. Trainer: César Luis Menotti (59).
**Goal**: José Antonio Castro (84).

**518.** 16.09.1979 **YUGOSLAVIA - ARGENTINA** **4-2(1-0)**
Crvena zvezda Stadion, Beograd; Referee: Romeo Stîncan (Romania); Attendance: 20,000
**ARG:** Enrique Bernardo Vidallé (6/0), Victorio Orlando Ocaño (3/0), José Daniel Van Tuyne (6/0), Daniel Alberto Passarella (Cap) (36/14), Juan Carlos Bujedo (2/0), Patricio José Hernández (2/0), Américo Rubén Gallego (50/2), Carlos Ángel López (4/1), Hugo Oscar Coscia (9/4) [46.Ramón Ángel Díaz (2/1)], Sergio Élio Ángel Fortunato (5/0), Roberto Osvaldo Díaz (6/1) [55.José Antonio Castro (5/1)]. Trainer: César Luis Menotti (60).
**Goals**: Daniel Alberto Passarella (81), Ramón Ángel Díaz (89).

**519.** 13.05.1980 **ENGLAND - ARGENTINA** **3-1(1-0)**
Wembley Stadium, London; Referee: Brian Robert McGinlay (Scotland); Attendance: 92,000
**ARG:** Ubaldo Matildo Fillol (20/0), Jorge Mario Olguín (36/0), José Daniel Van Tuyne (7/0), Daniel Alberto Passarella (Cap) (37/15), Alberto César Tarantini (38/1), Juan Alberto Barbas (8/0) [51.Carlos Luis Ischia (1/0)], Américo Rubén Gallego (51/2), Diego Armando Maradona (12/2), Santiago Santamaría (1/0) [63.Ramón Ángel Díaz (3/1)], Leopoldo Jacinto Luque (37/20), José Daniel Valencia (25/2). Trainer: César Luis Menotti (61).
**Goal**: Daniel Alberto Passarella (55 penalty).

**520.** 16.05.1980 **REPUBLIC OF IRELAND - ARGENTINA** **0-1(0-1)**
Lansdowne Road, Dublin; Referee: George Courtney (England); Attendance: 35,000
**ARG:** Ubaldo Matildo Fillol (21/0), Jorge Mario Olguín (37/0), Juan Ernesto Simón (2/0), Daniel Alberto Passarella (Cap) (38/15), Alberto César Tarantini (39/1), Juan Alberto Barbas (9/0), Américo Rubén Gallego (52/2), Diego Armando Maradona (13/2), Santiago Santamaría (2/0), Ramón Ángel Díaz (4/1) [73.Gabriel Humberto Calderón (1/0)], José Daniel Valencia (26/3). Trainer: César Luis Menotti (62).
**Goal**: José Daniel Valencia (28).

**521.** 21.05.1980 **AUSTRIA - ARGENTINA** **1-5(1-3)**
Prater Stadion, Wien; Referee: André Daina (Switzerland); Attendance: 67,500
**ARG:** Ubaldo Matildo Fillol (22/0), Jorge Mario Olguín (38/0), José Daniel Van Tuyne (8/0), Daniel Alberto Passarella (Cap) (39/15), Alberto César Tarantini (40/1) [29.Victorio Orlando Ocaño (4/0)], Juan Alberto Barbas (10/0), Américo Rubén Gallego (53/2), Diego Armando Maradona (14/5), Santiago Santamaría (3/1) [70.Ramón Ángel Díaz (5/1)], Leopoldo Jacinto Luque (38/21), José Daniel Valencia (27/3) [70.Carlos Luis Ischia (2/0)]. Trainer: César Luis Menotti (63).
**Goals**: Santiago Santamaría (2), Leopoldo Jacinto Luque (10), Diego Armando Maradona (15, 75, 88).

**522.** 18.09.1980 **ARGENTINA - CHILE** **2-2(2-1)**
Estadio Municipal, Mendoza; Referee: Claudio Aquiles Busca (Argentina); Attendance: 35,000
**ARG:** Ubaldo Matildo Fillol (23/0), Jorge Mario Olguín (39/0), Luis Adolfo Galván (16/0), Daniel Alberto Passarella (Cap) (40/15), Alberto César Tarantini (41/1), Diego Armando Maradona (15/5), Américo Rubén Gallego (54/2), José Daniel Valencia (28/4), Santiago Santamaría (4/1), Leopoldo Jacinto Luque (39/21) [82.Carlos Daniel Tapia (1/0)], Ramón Ángel Díaz (6/2). Trainer: César Luis Menotti (64).
**Goals**: José Daniel Valencia (21), Ramón Ángel Díaz (41).

**523.** 09.10.1980 **ARGENTINA - BULGARIA** **2-0(1-0)**
Estadio Monumental „Antonio Vespucio Liberti", Buenos Aires; Referee: Claudio Aquiles Busca (Argentina); Attendance: 40,000
**ARG:** Ubaldo Matildo Fillol (24/0), Jorge Mario Olguín (40/0), Luis Adolfo Galván (17/0), Daniel Alberto Passarella (Cap) (41/15), Alberto César Tarantini (42/1), Juan Alberto Barbas (11/0), Américo Rubén Gallego (55/2), Diego Armando Maradona (16/5), Santiago Santamaría (5/2), Ramón Ángel Díaz (7/3), José Daniel Valencia (29/4). Trainer: César Luis Menotti (65).
**Goals**: Santiago Santamaría (32), Ramón Ángel Díaz (80).

**524.** 12.10.1980 **ARGENTINA - POLAND** **2-1(1-0)**
Estadio Monumental „Antonio Vespucio Liberti", Buenos Aires; Referee: Teodoro Nitti (Argentina); Attendance: 50,000
**ARG:** Ubaldo Matildo Fillol (25/0), Jorge Mario Olguín (41/0), Luis Adolfo Galván (18/0), Daniel Alberto Passarella (Cap) (42/16), Alberto César Tarantini (43/1), Juan Alberto Barbas (12/0), Américo Rubén Gallego (56/2), Diego Armando Maradona (17/6), Santiago Santamaría (6/2) [75.Leopoldo Jacinto Luque (40/21)], Ramón Ángel Díaz (8/3), José Daniel Valencia (30/4) [71.Patricio José Hernández (3/0)]. Trainer: César Luis Menotti (66).
**Goals**: Daniel Alberto Passarella (15 penalty), Diego Armando Maradona (59).

**525.** 15.10.1980 **ARGENTINA - CZECHOSLOVAKIA** **1-0(1-0)**
Estadio Monumental „Antonio Vespucio Liberti", Buenos Aires; Referee: Juan Daniel Cardellino de San Vicente (Uruguay); Attendance: 75,000
**ARG:** Ubaldo Matildo Fillol (26/0), Jorge Mario Olguín (42/0), Luis Adolfo Galván (19/0), Daniel Alberto Passarella (Cap) (43/16), Alberto César Tarantini (44/1), Juan Alberto Barbas (13/0), Américo Rubén Gallego (57/2), Diego Armando Maradona (18/6), Santiago Santamaría (7/2), Ramón Ángel Díaz (9/4), Leopoldo Jacinto Luque (41/21) [76.Patricio José Hernández (4/0)]. Trainer: César Luis Menotti (67).
**Goal**: Ramón Ángel Díaz (17).

**526.** 04.12.1980 **ARGENTINA – SOVIET UNION** **1-1(1-1)**
Estadio „José María Minella", Mar del Plata; Referee: Jorge Eduardo Romero (Argentina); Attendance: 31,598
**ARG:** Ubaldo Matildo Fillol (27/0), Jorge Mario Olguín (43/0), Luis Adolfo Galván (20/0), Daniel Alberto Passarella (Cap) (44/16), Alberto César Tarantini (45/1), Juan Alberto Barbas (14/0), Américo Rubén Gallego (58/2), Diego Armando Maradona (19/7), Jorge Carlos Cecchi (1/0) [73.Carlos Guillermo Fren (1/0)], Ramón Ángel Díaz (10/4), José Daniel Valencia (31/4). Trainer: César Luis Menotti (68).
**Goal**: Diego Armando Maradona (19).

**527.** 16.12.1980 **ARGENTINA - SWITZERLAND** **5-0(4-0)**
Estadio Chateau Carreras, Córdoba; Referee: José Luis Martínez Bazán (Uruguay); Attendance: 12,000
**ARG:** Ubaldo Matildo Fillol (28/0), Jorge Mario Olguín (44/0), Luis Adolfo Galván (21/0), Daniel Alberto Passarella (Cap) (45/17), Alberto César Tarantini (46/1), Juan Alberto Barbas (15/0), Américo Rubén Gallego (59/2) [67.José Daniel Van Tuyne (9/0)], Diego Armando Maradona (20/8), Ramón Ángel Díaz (11/5), Leopoldo Jacinto Luque (42/22) [61.Jorge Carlos Cecchi (2/0)], José Daniel Valencia (32/5) [73.Alejandro Luis Débole (1/0)]. Trainer: César Luis Menotti (69).
**Goals**: Ramón Ángel Díaz (5), Leopoldo Jacinto Luque (9), José Daniel Valencia (43), Diego Armando Maradona (45), Daniel Alberto Passarella (67 penalty).

**528.** 01.01.1981 **ARGENTINA – WEST GERMANY** **2-1(0-1)** 1st Mundialito. Group Stage.
Estadio Centenario, Montevideo; Referee: Augusto Lamo Castillo (Spain); Attendance: 55,000
**ARG:** Ubaldo Matildo Fillol (29/0), Jorge Mario Olguín (45/0), Luis Adolfo Galván (22/0), Daniel Alberto Passarella (Cap) (46/17), Alberto César Tarantini (47/1), Osvaldo César Ardiles (42/7), Américo Rubén Gallego (60/2), Diego Armando Maradona (21/8), Ricardo Daniel Bertoni (25/10) [67.Leopoldo Jacinto Luque (43/22)], Ramón Ángel Díaz (12/6), Mario Alberto Kempes (32/20) [42.José Daniel Valencia (33/5)]. Trainer: César Luis Menotti (70).
**Goals**: Manfred Kaltz (85 own goal), Ramón Ángel Díaz (88).

**529.** 04.01.1981 **BRAZIL - ARGENTINA** **1-1(0-1)** 1st Mundialito. Group Stage.
Estadio Centenario, Montevideo; Referee: Erich Linemayr (Austria); Attendance: 65,000
**ARG:** Ubaldo Matildo Fillol (30/0), Jorge Mario Olguín (46/0), Luis Adolfo Galván (23/0), Daniel Alberto Passarella (Cap) (47/17), Alberto César Tarantini (48/1), Osvaldo César Ardiles (43/7), Américo Rubén Gallego (61/2), Diego Armando Maradona (22/9), Juan Alberto Barbas (16/0) [67.Leopoldo Jacinto Luque (44/22)], Ramón Ángel Díaz (13/6), Ricardo Daniel Bertoni (26/10) [46.José Daniel Valencia (34/5)]. Trainer: César Luis Menotti (71).
**Goal**: Diego Armando Maradona (30).

**530.** 28.10.1981 **ARGENTINA - POLAND** **1-2(1-0)**
Estadio Monumental „Antonio Vespucio Liberti", Buenos Aires; Referee: Juan Daniel Cardellino de San Vicente (Uruguay); Attendance: 40,000
**ARG:** Ubaldo Matildo Fillol (31/0), Jorge Mario Olguín (47/0), Edgardo Bauza (1/0), Daniel Alberto Passarella (Cap) (48/18), Alberto César Tarantini (49/1), Juan Alberto Barbas (17/0), Américo Rubén Gallego (62/2), Luis Antonio Amuchástegui (1/0), Ricardo Alberto Gareca (1/0), Ramón Ángel Díaz (14/6), Mario Alberto Kempes (33/20) [70.José Daniel Valencia (35/5)]. Trainer: César Luis Menotti (72).
**Goal**: Daniel Alberto Passarella (42).

**531.** 11.11.1981 **ARGENTINA - CZECHOSLOVAKIA** **1-1(0-1)**
Estadio Monumental „Antonio Vespucio Liberti", Buenos Aires; Referee: Juan Ambrosio Silvagno Cavanna (Chile); Attendance: 60,000
**ARG:** Ubaldo Matildo Fillol (32/0), Jorge Mario Olguín (48/0), Luis Adolfo Galván (24/0), Daniel Alberto Passarella (Cap) (49/18), Alberto César Tarantini (50/1), Juan Alberto Barbas (18/0) [Leopoldo Jacinto Luque (45/22)], Américo Rubén Gallego (63/3), Luis Antonio Amuchástegui (2/0), José Daniel Valencia (36/5) [Patricio José Hernández (5/0)], Ramón Ángel Díaz (15/6), Mario Alberto Kempes (34/20). Trainer: César Luis Menotti (73).
**Goal**: Américo Rubén Gallego (71).

**532.** 09.03.1982 **ARGENTINA - CZECHOSLOVAKIA** **0-0**
Estadio „José María Minella", Mar del Plata; Referee: Juan Carlos Loustau (Argentina); Attendance: 25,000
**ARG:** Héctor Rodolfo Baley (12/0), Jorge Mario Olguín (49/0), José Daniel Van Tuyne (10/0), Enzo Héctor Trossero (6/0), Alberto César Tarantini (51/1), Juan Alberto Barbas (19/0), Gabriel Humberto Calderón (2/0), Diego Armando Maradona (23/9), Enzo Daniel Bulleri (1/0), José Daniel Valencia (37/5) [65.Raúl Chaparro (1/0)], Patricio José Hernández (6/0). Trainer: César Luis Menotti (74).

**533.** 24.03.1982 **ARGENTINA – WEST GERMANY** **1-1(0-1)**
Estadio Monumental „Antonio Vespucio Liberti", Buenos Aires; Referee: José Luis Martínez Bazán (Uruguay); Attendance: 69,000
**ARG:** Héctor Rodolfo Baley (13/0), Jorge Mario Olguín (50/0), Luis Adolfo Galván (25/0), Daniel Alberto Passarella (Cap) (50/18), Alberto César Tarantini (52/1), Juan Alberto Barbas (20/0), Américo Rubén Gallego (64/3), Diego Armando Maradona (24/9), Gabriel Humberto Calderón (3/1), Ramón Ángel Díaz (16/6), Mario Alberto Kempes (35/20) [78.Patricio José Hernández (7/0)]. Trainer: César Luis Menotti (75).
**Goal**: Gabriel Humberto Calderón (67).

**534.** 14.04.1982 **ARGENTINA – SOVIET UNION** **1-1(1-0)**
Estadio Monumental „Antonio Vespucio Liberti", Buenos Aires; Referee: Romualdo Arppi Filho (England); Attendance: 50,000
**ARG:** Ubaldo Matildo Fillol (33/0), Jorge Mario Olguín (51/0), Luis Adolfo Galván (26/0), Daniel Alberto Passarella (Cap) (51/18), Alberto César Tarantini (53/1), Américo Rubén Gallego (65/3), Osvaldo César Ardiles (44/7), Diego Armando Maradona (25/9), Jorge Alberto Francisco Valdano (3/2) [81.Patricio José Hernández (8/0)], Ramón Ángel Díaz (17/7), Mario Alberto Kempes (36/20). Trainer: César Luis Menotti (76).
**Goal**: Ramón Ángel Díaz (43).

**535.** 05.05.1982 **ARGENTINA - BULGARIA** **2-1(2-1)**
Estadio „José Amalfitani", Buenos Aires; Referee: Juan Carlos Loustau (Argentina); Attendance: 37,000
**ARG:** Ubaldo Matildo Fillol (34/0), Jorge Mario Olguín (52/0), Luis Adolfo Galván (27/0), Daniel Alberto Passarella (Cap) (52/19), Alberto César Tarantini (54/1), Américo Rubén Gallego (66/3), Osvaldo César Ardiles (45/7), Diego Armando Maradona (26/9), Jorge Alberto Francisco Valdano (4/2) [80.Patricio José Hernández (9/0)], Ramón Ángel Díaz (18/8) [72.José Daniel Valencia (38/5)], Mario Alberto Kempes (37/20) [48.Santiago Santamaría (8/2)]. Trainer: César Luis Menotti (77).
**Goals**: Ramón Ángel Díaz (24), Daniel Alberto Passarella (44).

**536.** 12.05.1982 **ARGENTINA - ROMANIA** **1-0(0-0)**
Estadio Central (Doctor Lisandro de la Torre), Rosario; Referee: Claudio Aquiles Busca (Argentina); Attendance: 40,000
**ARG:** Ubaldo Matildo Fillol (35/0), Jorge Mario Olguín (53/0), Luis Adolfo Galván (28/0), Daniel Alberto Passarella (Cap) (53/19), Alberto César Tarantini (55/1), Osvaldo César Ardiles (46/7) [74.Patricio José Hernández (10/0)], Américo Rubén Gallego (67/3), Diego Armando Maradona (27/9), Jorge Alberto Francisco Valdano (5/2), Ramón Ángel Díaz (19/9), Mario Alberto Kempes (38/20) [69.Juan Alberto Barbas (21/0)]. Trainer: César Luis Menotti (78).
**Goal**: Ramón Ángel Díaz (56).

**537.** 13.06.1982 **BELGIUM - ARGENTINA** **1-0(0-0)** 12th FIFA WC. Group Stage.
Estadio Camp Nou, Barcelona (Spain); Referee: Vojtech Christov (Czechoslovakia); Attendance: 95,000
**ARG:** Ubaldo Matildo Fillol (36/0), Jorge Mario Olguín (54/0), Luis Adolfo Galván (29/0), Daniel Alberto Passarella (Cap) (54/19), Alberto César Tarantini (56/1), Osvaldo César Ardiles (47/7), Américo Rubén Gallego (68/3), Diego Armando Maradona (28/9), Ricardo Daniel Bertoni (27/10), Ramón Ángel Díaz (20/9) [64.Jorge Alberto Francisco Valdano (6/2)], Mario Alberto Kempes (39/20). Trainer: César Luis Menotti (79).

**538.** 18.06.1982 **ARGENTINA - HUNGARY** **4-1(2-0)** 12th FIFA WC. Group Stage.
Estadio „José Rico Pérez", Alicante (Spain); Referee: Belaid Lacarne (Algeria); Attendance: 32,000
**ARG:** Ubaldo Matildo Fillol (37/0), Jorge Mario Olguín (55/0), Luis Adolfo Galván (30/0), Daniel Alberto Passarella (Cap) (55/19), Alberto César Tarantini (57/1) [51.Juan Alberto Barbas (22/0)], Osvaldo César Ardiles (48/8), Américo Rubén Gallego (69/3), Diego Armando Maradona (29/11), Ricardo Daniel Bertoni (28/11), Jorge Alberto Francisco Valdano (7/2) [24.Gabriel Humberto Calderón (4/1)], Mario Alberto Kempes (40/20). Trainer: César Luis Menotti (80).
**Goals**: Ricardo Daniel Bertoni (26), Diego Armando Maradona (28, 57), Osvaldo César Ardiles (60).

**539.** 23.06.1982 **ARGENTINA – EL SALVADOR** **2-0(1-0)** 12th FIFA WC. Group Stage.
Estadio „José Rico Pérez", Alicante (Spain); Referee: Luis Barrancos Alvarez (Bolivia); Attendance: 32,500
**ARG:** Ubaldo Matildo Fillol (38/0), Jorge Mario Olguín (56/0), Luis Adolfo Galván (31/0), Daniel Alberto Passarella (Cap) (56/20), Alberto César Tarantini (58/1), Osvaldo César Ardiles (49/8), Américo Rubén Gallego (70/3), Diego Armando Maradona (30/11), Ricardo Daniel Bertoni (29/12) [68.Ramón Ángel Díaz (21/9)], Gabriel Humberto Calderón (5/1) [78.Santiago Santamaría (9/2)], Mario Alberto Kempes (41/20). Trainer: César Luis Menotti (81).
**Goals**: Daniel Alberto Passarella (22 penalty), Ricardo Daniel Bertoni (52).

**540.** 29.06.1982 **ITALY - ARGENTINA** **2-1(0-0)** 12th FIFA WC.2nd Round.
Estadio Sarría, Barcelona (Spain); Referee: Nicolae Rainea (Romania); Attendance: 43,000
**ARG:** Ubaldo Matildo Fillol (39/0), Jorge Mario Olguín (57/0), Luis Adolfo Galván (32/0), Daniel Alberto Passarella (Cap) (57/21), Alberto César Tarantini (59/1), Osvaldo César Ardiles (50/8), Américo Rubén Gallego (71/3) [*sent off 84*], Diego Armando Maradona (31/11), Ricardo Daniel Bertoni (30/12), Ramón Ángel Díaz (22/9) [59.Gabriel Humberto Calderón (6/1)], Mario Alberto Kempes (42/20) [59.José Daniel Valencia (39/5)]. Trainer: César Luis Menotti (82).
**Goal**: Daniel Alberto Passarella (83).

**541.** 02.07.1982 **BRAZIL - ARGENTINA** **3-1(1-0)** 12th FIFA WC.2nd Round.
Estadio Sarría, Barcelona (Spain); Referee: Lamberto Mario Rúbio Vásquez (Mexico); Attendance: 44,000
**ARG:** Ubaldo Matildo Fillol (40/0), Jorge Mario Olguín (58/0), Luis Adolfo Galván (33/0), Daniel Alberto Passarella (Cap) (58/21), Alberto César Tarantini (60/1), Osvaldo César Ardiles (51/8), Juan Alberto Barbas (23/0), Diego Armando Maradona (32/11) [*sent off 86*], Ricardo Daniel Bertoni (31/12) [64.Santiago Santamaría (10/2)], Gabriel Humberto Calderón (7/1), Mario Alberto Kempes (43/20) [46. Ramón Ángel Díaz (23/10)]. Trainer: César Luis Menotti (83).
**Goal**: Ramón Ángel Díaz (89).

**542.** 12.05.1983 **CHILE - ARGENTINA** **2-2(1-0)**
Estadio Nacional, Santiago; Referee: Juan Daniel Cardellino de San Vicente (Uruguay); Attendance: 19,615
**ARG:** Ubaldo Matildo Fillol (41/0), Carlos Alberto Arregui (1/0), Enzo Héctor Trossero (7/0), Oscar Alfredo Ruggeri (1/0), Julio Jorge Olarticoechea (1/0), Ricardo Omar Giusti (1/0), Claudio Oscar Marangoni (1/0), Norberto Osvaldo Alonso (16/4), Jorge Luis Burruchaga (1/0) [68.Alejandro Esteban Sabella (1/0)], Gabriel Humberto Calderón (8/1) [86.Víctor Rogelio Ramos (1/0)], Ricardo Alberto Gareca (2/1). Trainer: Dr. Carlos Salvador Bilardo (1).
**Goals**: Norberto Osvaldo Alonso (57), Ricardo Alberto Gareca (80).

**543.** 23.06.1983 **ARGENTINA - CHILE** **1-0(0-0)**
Estadio „José Amalfitani", Buenos Aires; Referee: Juan Francisco Escobar Váldez (Paraguay); Attendance: 18,000
**ARG:** Ubaldo Matildo Fillol (42/0), Néstor Rolando Clausen (1/0) [89.Julio Jorge Olarticoechea (2/0)], Enzo Héctor Trossero (8/0), Oscar Alfredo Ruggeri (2/0), Oscar Alfredo Garré (1/0), Carlos Alberto Arregui (2/0) [57.Rubén Darío Insúa (1/0)], Claudio Oscar Marangoni (2/0), Gabriel Humberto Calderón (9/1), Carlos Manuel Morete (3/1) [79.Jorge Roberto Rinaldi (1/0)], Norberto Osvaldo Alonso (17/4), José Daniel Ponce (1/0). Trainer: Dr. Carlos Salvador Bilardo (2).
**Goal**: Carlos Manuel Morete (70).

**544.** 14.07.1983 **PARAGUAY - ARGENTINA** **1-0(0-0)** Copa Félix Bogado
Estadio Defensores del Chaco, Asunción; Referee: Ernesto Filippi Cavani (Uruguay); Attendance: 36,000
**ARG:** Nery Alberto Pumpido (1/0), Néstor Rolando Clausen (2/0), Enzo Héctor Trossero (9/0), Oscar Alfredo Ruggeri (3/0), Oscar Alfredo Garré (2/0), Ricardo Omar Giusti (2/0) [64.Jorge Roberto Rinaldi (2/0)], Claudio Oscar Marangoni (3/0), Gabriel Humberto Calderón (10/1), Norberto Osvaldo Alonso (18/4) [54.Jorge Luis Burruchaga (2/0)], Ricardo Alberto Gareca (3/1), Juan José Urruti (1/0) [68.Marcelo Antonio Trobbiani (12/0)]. Trainer: Dr. Carlos Salvador Bilardo (3).

**545.** 21.07.1983 **ARGENTINA - PARAGUAY** **0-0** Copa Félix Bogado
Estadio „José Amalfitani", Buenos Aires; Referee: Gastón Edmundo Castro Makuc (Chile); Attendance: 35,000
**ARG:** Nery Alberto Pumpido (2/0), Néstor Rolando Clausen (3/0), Omar Roberto Jorge (1/0), Oscar Alfredo Ruggeri (4/0), Oscar Alfredo Garré (3/0), Alejandro Esteban Sabella (2/0), Claudio Oscar Marangoni (4/0), José Daniel Ponce (2/0) [69.Jorge Luis Burruchaga (3/0)], Norberto Osvaldo Alonso (19/4) [57.Carlos Manuel Morete (4/1)], Luis Antonio Amuchástegui (3/0) [57.Víctor Rogelio Ramos (2/0)], Ricardo Alberto Gareca (4/1). Trainer: Dr. Carlos Salvador Bilardo (4).

**546.** 10.08.1983 **ECUADOR – ARGENTINA** **2-2(0-1)** 32nd Copa América. Group Stage.
Estadio Olímpico „Atahualpa", Quito; Referee: Gilberto Aristizábal Murcia (Colombia); Attendance: 50,000
**ARG:** Nery Alberto Pumpido (3/0), Néstor Rolando Clausen (4/0) [69.Juan Carlos Bujedo (3/0)], José Luis Brown (1/0), Omar Roberto Jorge (2/0), Oscar Alfredo Garré (4/0), Ricardo Omar Giusti (3/0), Miguel Ángel Russo (1/0), Alejandro Esteban Sabella (3/0), Jorge Luis Burruchaga (4/2), Víctor Rogelio Ramos (3/0) [68.Rubén Darío Insúa (2/0)], Ricardo Alberto Gareca (5/1). Trainer: Dr. Carlos Salvador Bilardo (5).
**Goals**: Jorge Luis Burruchaga (40, 51)

**547.** 24.08.1983 **ARGENTINA - BRAZIL** **1-0(0-0)** 32nd Copa América. Group Stage.
Estadio Monumental „Antonio Vespucio Liberti", Buenos Aires; Referee: Juan Daniel Cardellino de San Vicente (Uruguay); Attendance: 56,000
**ARG:** Ubaldo Matildo Fillol (43/0), Julián José Camino (1/0), Roberto Mouzo (3/0), Enzo Héctor Trossero (10/0), Oscar Alfredo Garré (5/0), José Daniel Ponce (3/0), Miguel Ángel Russo (2/0) [46.Claudio Oscar Marangoni (5/0)], Alejandro Esteban Sabella (4/0), Alberto José Márcico (1/0) [78.Víctor Rogelio Ramos (4/0)], Jorge Luis Burruchaga (5/2), Ricardo Alberto Gareca (6/2). Trainer: Dr. Carlos Salvador Bilardo (6).
**Goal**: Ricardo Alberto Gareca (55).

**548.** 07.09.1983 **ARGENTINA - ECUADOR** **2-2(0-1)** 32nd Copa América. Group Stage.
Estadio Monumental „Antonio Vespucio Liberti", Buenos Aires; Referee: Juan Daniel Cardellino de San Vicente (Uruguay); Attendance: 40,000
**ARG:** Ubaldo Matildo Fillol (44/0), Julián José Camino (2/0), Roberto Mouzo (4/0), Enzo Héctor Trossero (11/0), Oscar Alfredo Garré (6/0), José Daniel Ponce (4/0) [46.Víctor Rogelio Ramos (5/1)], Claudio Oscar Marangoni (6/0) [70.Jorge Roberto Rinaldi (3/0)], Alejandro Esteban Sabella (5/0), Alberto José Márcico (2/0), Jorge Luis Burruchaga (6/3), Ricardo Alberto Gareca (7/2). Trainer: Dr. Carlos Salvador Bilardo (7).
**Goals**: Víctor Rogelio Ramos (50), Jorge Luis Burruchaga (90 penalty).

**549.** 14.09.1983 **BRAZIL - ARGENTINA** **0-0** 32nd Copa América. Group Stage.
Estádio „Jornalista Mário Filho" (Maracanã), Rio de Janeiro; Referee: Mario Líra González (Chile); Attendance: 75,000
**ARG:** Ubaldo Matildo Fillol (45/0), Julio Jorge Olarticoechea (3/0), José Luis Brown (2/0), Enzo Héctor Trossero (12/0), Oscar Alfredo Garré (7/0), Miguel Ángel Russo (3/0), Claudio Oscar Marangoni (7/0), Alejandro Esteban Sabella (6/0) [65.Víctor Rogelio Ramos (6/1)], Alberto José Márcico (3/0) [82.José Daniel Ponce (5/0)], Jorge Luis Burruchaga (7/3), Ricardo Alberto Gareca (8/2). Trainer: Dr. Carlos Salvador Bilardo (8).

**550.** 12.01.1984 **ARGENTINA - ROMANIA** **1-0(1-0)** Nehru Cup
Eden Gardens Stadium, Calcutta (India); Referee: Alojzy Jargus (Poland)
**ARG:** Nery Alberto Pumpido (4/0), Julián José Camino (3/0), Rubén José Agüero (1/0), Héctor Raúl Cúper (1/0), Oscar Alfredo Garré (8/0), Ricardo Omar Giusti (4/0), Víctor Rogelio Ramos (7/1), José Daniel Ponce (6/0), Jorge Luis Burruchaga (8/4), Ricardo Alberto Gareca (9/2), Alberto José Márcico (4/0) [59.Jorge Carlos Alberto Domínguez (1/0)]. Trainer: Dr. Carlos Salvador Bilardo (9).
**Goal**: Jorge Luis Burruchaga (9).

**551.** 14.01.1984 **INDIA - ARGENTINA** **0-1(0-0)** Nehru Cup
Eden Gardens Stadium, Calcutta; Referee: Dan Petrescu (Romania)
**ARG:** Nery Alberto Pumpido (5/0), Julián José Camino (4/0), Rubén José Agüero (2/0), Héctor Raúl Cúper (2/0), Oscar Alfredo Garré (9/0), Ricardo Omar Giusti (5/0), Jorge Carlos Alberto Domínguez (2/0) [85.Rubén Darío Insúa (3/0)], José Daniel Ponce (7/0), Jorge Luis Burruchaga (9/4), Ricardo Alberto Gareca (10/3), Jorge Roberto Rinaldi (4/0) [57.Víctor Rogelio Ramos (8/1)]. Trainer: Dr. Carlos Salvador Bilardo (10).
**Goal**: Ricardo Alberto Gareca (79).

**552.** 17.01.1984 **ARGENTINA - POLAND** **1-1(0-0)** Nehru Cup
Eden Gardens Stadium, Calcutta (India); Referee: Károly Palotai (Hungary); Attendance: 80,000
**ARG:** Nery Alberto Pumpido (6/0), Julián José Camino (5/0), Rubén José Agüero (3/0), Héctor Raúl Cúper (3/0), Oscar Alfredo Garré (10/0), Ricardo Omar Giusti (6/0), Carlos Alberto Arregui (3/0), José Daniel Ponce (8/1) [69.Rubén Darío Insúa (4/0)], Jorge Luis Burruchaga (Cap) (10/4), Ricardo Alberto Gareca (11/3), Alberto José Márcico (5/0) [75.Víctor Rogelio Ramos (9/1)]. Trainer: Dr. Carlos Salvador Bilardo (11).
**Goal**: José Daniel Ponce (51).

**553.** 20.01.1984 **CHINA P.R. - ARGENTINA** **1-0(0-0)** Nehru Cup
Eden Gardens Stadium, Calcutta (India); Referee: Gangadharam Natajaram (India)
**ARG:** Nery Alberto Pumpido (7/0), Julián José Camino (6/0), Rubén José Agüero (4/0), Héctor Raúl Cúper (4/0), Oscar Alfredo Garré (11/0), Ricardo Omar Giusti (7/0), Carlos Alberto Arregui (4/0) [49.Rubén Darío Insúa (5/0)], José Daniel Ponce (9/1), Jorge Luis Burruchaga (11/4), Ricardo Alberto Gareca (12/3), Alberto José Márcico (6/0) [73.Jorge Carlos Alberto Domínguez (3/0)]. Trainer: Dr. Carlos Salvador Bilardo (12).

**554.** 24.01.1984 **ARGENTINA - HUNGARY** **3-0(1-0)** Nehru Cup
Eden Gardens Stadium, Calcutta (India); Referee: Dan Petrescu (Romania)
**ARG:** Nery Alberto Pumpido (8/0), Julián José Camino (7/0), Rubén José Agüero (5/0), Héctor Raúl Cúper (5/0), Oscar Alfredo Garré (12/0), Carlos Alberto Arregui (5/1), Rubén Darío Insúa (6/0), José Daniel Ponce (10/1), Jorge Luis Burruchaga (12/4), Ricardo Alberto Gareca (13/4), Alberto José Márcico (7/0) [85.Víctor Rogelio Ramos (10/1)]. Trainer: Dr. Carlos Salvador Bilardo (13).
**Goals**: László Rácz (7 own goal), Ricardo Alberto Gareca (54), Carlos Alberto Arregui (60).

**555.** 17.06.1984 **BRAZIL - ARGENTINA** **0-0**
Estádio „Cicero Pompeu de Toledo" Morumbi, São Paulo; Referee: Arturo Andrés Ithurralde (Argentina); Attendance: 32,000
**ARG:** Ubaldo Matildo Fillol (46/0), Néstor Rolando Clausen (5/0), Enzo Héctor Trossero (13/0), José Luis Brown (3/0), Oscar Alfredo Garré (13/0) [*sent off 69*], Claudio Oscar Marangoni (8/0) [62.Ricardo Omar Giusti (8/0)], Marcelo Antonio Trobbiani (13/0) [61.Jorge Roberto Rinaldi (5/0)], Alejandro Esteban Sabella (7/0), Jorge Luis Burruchaga (13/4), Ricardo Alberto Gareca (14/4), Alberto José Márcico (8/0). Trainer: Dr. Carlos Salvador Bilardo (14).

**556.** 18.07.1984 **URUGUAY - ARGENTINA** **1-0(0-0)**
Estadio Centenario, Montevideo; Referee: Edison Pérez Nuñez (Peru); Attendance: 56,000
**ARG:** Nery Alberto Pumpido (9/0), Néstor Rolando Clausen (6/0), Enzo Héctor Trossero (Cap) (14/0), José Luis Brown (4/0), Oscar Alfredo Garré (14/0), Claudio Oscar Marangoni (9/0), Miguel Ángel Russo (4/0) [71.Ricardo Omar Giusti (9/0)], Alejandro Esteban Sabella (8/0), Jorge Luis Burruchaga (14/4), Alberto José Márcico (9/0) [58.Marcelo Antonio Trobbiani (14/0)], Jorge Roberto Rinaldi (6/0) [46.Gerardo Manuel González (1/0)]. Trainer: Dr. Carlos Salvador Bilardo (15).

**557.** 02.08.1984 **ARGENTINA - URUGUAY** **0-0**
Estadio Monumental „Antonio Vespucio Liberti", Buenos Aires; Referee: Juan Francisco Escobar Váldez (Paraguay); Attendance: 15,000
**ARG:** Nery Alberto Pumpido (10/0), Eduardo Omar Saporiti (3/0), Enzo Héctor Trossero (Cap) (15/0), José Luis Brown (5/0) [42.Rubén José Agüero (6/0)], Oscar Alfredo Garré (15/0), Ricardo Omar Giusti (10/0), José Daniel Ponce (11/1), Jorge Luis Burruchaga (15/4), Gerardo Manuel González (2/0) [75.Oscar Alberto Dertycia (1/0)], Ricardo Alberto Gareca (15/4), Alberto José Márcico (10/0). Trainer: Dr. Carlos Salvador Bilardo (16).

**558.** 24.08.1984 **COLOMBIA - ARGENTINA** **1-0(0-0)**
Estadio „Nemesio Camacho" 'El Campín', Bogotá; Referee: Elías Victoriano Jácome Guerreiro (Ecuador); Attendance: 35,000
**ARG:** Nery Alberto Pumpido (11/0), Eduardo Omar Saporiti (4/0) [62.Julián José Camino (8/0)], Enzo Héctor Trossero (Cap) (16/0) [*sent off 81*], Oscar Alfredo Ruggeri (5/0), Oscar Alfredo Garré (16/0), Ricardo Omar Giusti (11/0) [*sent off 56*], José Daniel Ponce (12/1) [69.Miguel Ángel Russo (5/0)], Ricardo Enrique Bochini (20/0), Jorge Luis Burruchaga (16/4), Oscar Alberto Dertycia (2/0) [64.Jorge Roberto Rinaldi (7/0)], Ricardo Alberto Gareca (16/4) [*sent off 87*]. Trainer: Dr. Carlos Salvador Bilardo (17).

**559.** 01.09.1984 **SWITZERLAND - ARGENTINA** **0-2(0-2)**
Wankdorf Stadion, Bern; Referee: Patrick A. Kelly (Republic of Ireland); Attendance: 15,000
**ARG:** Luis Alberto Islas (1/0), Julián José Camino (9/0), Oscar Alfredo Ruggeri (6/0), José Luis Brown (6/0), Oscar Alfredo Garré (17/0), Ricardo Enrique Bochini (21/0) [88.Jorge Roberto Rinaldi (8/0)], José Daniel Ponce (13/2), Miguel Ángel Russo (6/0), Jorge Luis Burruchaga (17/4), Oscar Alberto Dertycia (3/1) [76.Gerardo Manuel González (3/0)], Marcelo Antonio Trobbiani (15/0) [65.Alberto José Márcico (11/0)]. Trainer: Dr. Carlos Salvador Bilardo (18).
**Goals**: José Daniel Ponce (6), Oscar Alberto Dertycia (34).

**560.** 05.09.1984 **BELGIUM - ARGENTINA** **0-2(0-2)**
Stade Heysel, Bruxelles; Referee: Franz Wöhrer (Austria); Attendance: 7,853
**ARG:** Luis Alberto Islas (2/0), Julián José Camino (10/0), Enzo Héctor Trossero (17/0), José Luis Brown (7/0) [68.Oscar Alfredo Garré (18/0)], Oscar Alfredo Ruggeri (7/1) [*sent off 83*], Miguel Ángel Russo (7/0), José Daniel Ponce (14/2) [51.Ricardo Omar Giusti (12/0)], Jorge Luis Burruchaga (Cap) (18/4), Ricardo Enrique Bochini (22/0) [75.Alberto José Márcico (12/0)], Ricardo Alberto Gareca (17/4), Marcelo Antonio Trobbiani (16/1) [88.Jorge Roberto Rinaldi (9/0)]. Trainer: Dr. Carlos Salvador Bilardo (19).
**Goals**: Marcelo Antonio Trobbiani (9), Oscar Alfredo Ruggeri (37).

**561.** 12.09.1984 **WEST GERMANY - ARGENTINA** **1-3(0-2)**
Rheinstadion, Düsseldorf; Referee: Robert Charles Paul Wurtz (France); Attendance: 45,000
**ARG:** Nery Alberto Pumpido (12/0), Enzo Héctor Trossero (18/0), José Luis Brown (8/0) [54.Julián José Camino (11/0)], Oscar Alfredo Garré (19/0), Miguel Ángel Russo (8/0), José Daniel Ponce (15/4), Ricardo Omar Giusti (13/0), Jorge Luis Burruchaga (Cap) (19/5), Ricardo Enrique Bochini (23/0), Ricardo Alberto Gareca (18/4), Marcelo Antonio Trobbiani (17/1) [77.Jorge Roberto Rinaldi (10/0)]. Trainer: Dr. Carlos Salvador Bilardo (20).
**Goals**: José Daniel Ponce (5, 36), Jorge Luis Burruchaga (58).

**562.** 18.09.1984 **MEXICO - ARGENTINA** **1-1(1-1)**
Estadio Universitário, Monterrey; Referee: Edward Bellion (United States); Attendance: 60,000
**ARG:** Luis Alberto Islas (3/0), Enzo Héctor Trossero (19/0), Oscar Alfredo Ruggeri (8/1), Oscar Alfredo Garré (20/0), Miguel Ángel Russo (9/0), José Daniel Ponce (16/4), Ricardo Omar Giusti (14/0), Jorge Luis Burruchaga (20/6) [89.Jorge Roberto Rinaldi (11/0)], Ricardo Enrique Bochini (24/0) [46.Alberto José Márcico (13/0)], Ricardo Alberto Gareca (19/4), Marcelo Antonio Trobbiani (18/1) [57.Oscar Alberto Dertycia (4/1)]. Trainer: Dr. Carlos Salvador Bilardo (21).
**Goal**: Jorge Luis Burruchaga (12).

**563.** 25.10.1984 **ARGENTINA - MEXICO** **1-1(1-1)***
Estadio „José Amalfitani", Buenos Aires; Referee: Juan Francisco Escobar Váldez (Paraguay)
**ARG:** Ubaldo Matildo Fillol (47/0), Julián José Camino (12/0), Enzo Héctor Trossero (20/0), Oscar Alfredo Ruggeri (9/1), Oscar Alfredo Garré (21/0), Miguel Ángel Russo (10/0), José Daniel Ponce (17/4) [70.Ricardo Omar Giusti (15/0)], Ricardo Enrique Bochini (25/0) [70.Alberto José Márcico (14/0)], Jorge Luis Burruchaga (21/6), Ricardo Alberto Gareca (20/5) [62.Oscar Alberto Dertycia (5/1)], Marcelo Antonio Trobbiani (19/1) [78.Jorge Roberto Rinaldi (12/0)]. Trainer: Dr. Carlos Salvador Bilardo (22).
**Goal**: Ricardo Alberto Gareca.
**Abandoned after 85 mins due to invasion of the field.*

**564.** 28.04.1985 **PARAGUAY - ARGENTINA** **1-0(0-0)**
Estadio Defensores del Chaco, Asunción; Referee: Ernesto Filippi Cavani (Uruguay); Attendance: 25,000
**ARG:** Ubaldo Matildo Fillol (48/0), Néstor Rolando Clausen (7/0), Oscar Alfredo Ruggeri (10/1), José Luis Brown (9/0), Oscar Alfredo Garré (22/0), Juan Alberto Barbas (24/0), Marcelo Antonio Trobbiani (20/1) [53.Ricardo Omar Giusti (16/0)], José Daniel Ponce (18/4), Alberto José Márcico (15/0) [56.Oscar Alberto Dertycia (6/1)], Ricardo Alberto Gareca (21/5), Pedro Pablo Pasculli (1/0). Trainer: Dr. Carlos Salvador Bilardo (23).

**565.** 05.05.1985 **BRAZIL - ARGENTINA** **2-1(1-1)**
Estádio Fonte Nova, Salvador; Referee: Edison Pérez Nuñez (Peru); Attendance: 77,000
**ARG:** Ubaldo Matildo Fillol (49/0), Néstor Rolando Clausen (8/0) [77.Jorge Roberto Rinaldi (13/0)], Oscar Alfredo Ruggeri (11/1), José Luis Brown (10/0), Oscar Alfredo Garré (23/0), Juan Alberto Barbas (25/0), José Daniel Ponce (19/4) [85.Mario Alberto Vanemerak (1/0)], Marcelo Antonio Trobbiani (21/1) [64.Enzo Héctor Trossero (21/0)], Jorge Luis Burruchaga (22/7), Ricardo Alberto Gareca (22/5) [53.Oscar Alberto Dertycia (7/1)], Pedro Pablo Pasculli (2/0) [*sent off 71*]. Trainer: Dr. Carlos Salvador Bilardo (24).
**Goal**: Jorge Luis Burruchaga (31).

**566.** 09.05.1985 **ARGENTINA - PARAGUAY** **1-1(1-0)**
Estadio Monumental „Antonio Vespucio Liberti", Buenos Aires; Referee: Artemio Sención (Uruguay); Attendance: 40,000
**ARG:** Ubaldo Matildo Fillol (50/0), Néstor Rolando Clausen (9/0), José Luis Brown (11/0), Daniel Alberto Passarella (59/21), Oscar Alfredo Ruggeri (12/1), Juan Alberto Barbas (26/0) [76.Jorge Roberto Rinaldi (14/0)], José Daniel Ponce (20/4) [71.Marcelo Antonio Trobbiani (22/1)], Diego Armando Maradona (Cap) (33/12), Jorge Luis Burruchaga (23/7), Ricardo Alberto Gareca (23/5), Oscar Alberto Dertycia (8/1). Trainer: Dr. Carlos Salvador Bilardo (25).
**Goal**: Diego Armando Maradona (43 penalty).

**567.** 14.05.1985 **ARGENTINA - CHILE** **2-0(1-0)**
Estadio Monumental „Antonio Vespucio Liberti", Buenos Aires; Referee: Carlos Alberto Maciel (Paraguay); Attendance: 36,000
**ARG:** Nery Alberto Pumpido (13/0), Néstor Rolando Clausen (10/0), José Luis Brown (12/0), Daniel Alberto Passarella (60/21), Oscar Alfredo Ruggeri (13/1), Miguel Ángel Russo (11/0), José Daniel Ponce (21/4) [46.Ricardo Omar Giusti (17/0)], Diego Armando Maradona (Cap) (34/13), Jorge Luis Burruchaga (24/8), Pedro Pablo Pasculli (3/0), Ricardo Alberto Gareca (24/5). Trainer: Dr. Carlos Salvador Bilardo (26).
**Goals**: Diego Armando Maradona (37 penalty), Jorge Luis Burruchaga (67).

**568.** 26.05.1985 **VENEZUELA - ARGENTINA** **2-3(1-2)** 13th FIFA WC. Qualifiers
Estadio Pueblo Nuevo, San Cristóbal; Referee: Juan Daniel Cardellino de San Vicente (Uruguay); Attendance: 30,000
**ARG:** Ubaldo Matildo Fillol (51/0), Néstor Rolando Clausen (11/0), Enzo Héctor Trossero (22/0), Daniel Alberto Passarella (61/22), Oscar Alfredo Garré (24/0), Miguel Ángel Russo (12/0), José Daniel Ponce (22/4), Diego Armando Maradona (Cap) (35/15), Jorge Luis Burruchaga (25/8), Pedro Pablo Pasculli (4/0) [82.Jorge Alberto Francisco Valdano (8/2)], Ricardo Alberto Gareca (25/5) [67.Alberto José Márcico (16/0)]. Trainer: Dr. Carlos Salvador Bilardo (27).
**Goals**: Diego Armando Maradona (2), Daniel Alberto Passarella (40), Diego Armando Maradona (58).

**569.** 02.06.1985 **COLOMBIA - ARGENTINA** **1-3(0-1)** 13th FIFA WC. Qualifiers
Estadio „Nemesio Camacho" 'El Campín', Bogotá; Referee: Arnaldo David César Coelho (Brazil); Attendance: 58,000
**ARG:** Ubaldo Matildo Fillol (52/0), Néstor Rolando Clausen (12/0), Enzo Héctor Trossero (23/0), Daniel Alberto Passarella (62/22), Oscar Alfredo Garré (25/0), Ricardo Omar Giusti (18/0), Miguel Ángel Russo (13/0), Marcelo Antonio Trobbiani (23/1) [57.Juan Alberto Barbas (27/0)], Diego Armando Maradona (Cap) (36/15), Jorge Luis Burruchaga (26/9), Pedro Pablo Pasculli (5/2) [86.Oscar Alberto Dertycia (9/1)]. Trainer: Dr. Carlos Salvador Bilardo (28).
**Goals**: Pedro Pablo Pasculli (43, 68), Jorge Luis Burruchaga (85).

**570.** 09.06.1985 **ARGENTINA - VENEZUELA** **3-0(1-0)** 13th FIFA WC. Qualifiers
Estadio Monumental „Antonio Vespucio Liberti", Buenos Aires; Referee: Gastón Edmundo Castro Makuc (Chile); Attendance: 35,000
**ARG:** Ubaldo Matildo Fillol (53/0), Néstor Rolando Clausen (13/1), Enzo Héctor Trossero (24/0), Daniel Alberto Passarella (63/22), Oscar Alfredo Garré (26/0), Ricardo Omar Giusti (19/0), Miguel Ángel Russo (14/1), Diego Armando Maradona (Cap) (37/16), Jorge Luis Burruchaga (27/9), Pedro Pablo Pasculli (6/2), Jorge Alberto Francisco Valdano (9/2). Trainer: Dr. Carlos Salvador Bilardo (29).
**Goals**: Miguel Ángel Russo (28), Néstor Rolando Clausen (87), Diego Armando Maradona (90).

**571.** 16.06.1985 **ARGENTINA - COLOMBIA** **1-0(1-0)** 13th FIFA WC. Qualifiers
Estadio Monumental „Antonio Vespucio Liberti", Buenos Aires; Referee: Gabriel González (Paraguay); Attendance: 30,000
**ARG:** Ubaldo Matildo Fillol (54/0), Néstor Rolando Clausen (14/1), Enzo Héctor Trossero (25/0), Daniel Alberto Passarella (64/22), Oscar Alfredo Garré (27/0), Ricardo Omar Giusti (20/0), Miguel Ángel Russo (15/1) [46.Juan Alberto Barbas (28/0)], Diego Armando Maradona (Cap) (38/16), Jorge Luis Burruchaga (28/9), Pedro Pablo Pasculli (7/2), Jorge Alberto Francisco Valdano (10/3). Trainer: Dr. Carlos Salvador Bilardo (30).
**Goal**: Jorge Alberto Francisco Valdano (26).

**572.** 23.06.1985 **PERU - ARGENTINA** **1-0(1-0)** 13th FIFA WC. Qualifiers
Estadio Nacional, Lima; Referee: Hernán Silva Arce (Chile); Attendance: 43,000
**ARG:** Ubaldo Matildo Fillol (55/0), Néstor Rolando Clausen (15/1) [81.Oscar Alfredo Ruggeri (14/1)], Enzo Héctor Trossero (26/0), Daniel Alberto Passarella (65/22), Oscar Alfredo Garré (28/0), Ricardo Omar Giusti (21/0), Miguel Ángel Russo (16/1) [46.Pedro Pablo Pasculli (8/2)], Juan Alberto Barbas (29/0), Diego Armando Maradona (Cap) (39/16), Jorge Luis Burruchaga (29/9), Jorge Alberto Francisco Valdano (11/3). Trainer: Dr. Carlos Salvador Bilardo (31).

**573.** 30.06.1985 **ARGENTINA - PERU** **2-2(1-2)** 13th FIFA WC. Qualifiers
Estadio Monumental „Antonio Vespucio Liberti", Buenos Aires; Referee: Romualdo Arppi Filho (Brazil); Attendance: 65,457
**ARG:** Ubaldo Matildo Fillol (56/0), Julián José Camino (13/0) [61.Ricardo Alberto Gareca (26/5)], Enzo Héctor Trossero (27/0), Daniel Alberto Passarella (66/23), Oscar Alfredo Garré (29/0), Ricardo Omar Giusti (22/0), Juan Alberto Barbas (30/0) [78.Marcelo Antonio Trobbiani (24/1)], Diego Armando Maradona (Cap) (40/16), Jorge Luis Burruchaga (30/9), Pedro Pablo Pasculli (9/3), Jorge Alberto Francisco Valdano (12/3). Trainer: Dr. Carlos Salvador Bilardo (32).
**Goals**: Pedro Pablo Pasculli (12), Daniel Alberto Passarella (81).

**574.** 14.11.1985 **ARGENTINA - MEXICO** **1-1(1-0)**
Memorial Coliseum, Los Angeles; Referee: Edward Bellion (United States); Attendance: 42,501
**ARG:** Luis Alberto Islas (4/0), Néstor Rolando Clausen (16/1), José Luis Brown (13/0), Oscar Alfredo Ruggeri (15/1), Sergio Daniel Batista (1/0), Miguel Ángel Russo (17/1), Juan Alberto Barbas (31/0), Diego Armando Maradona (Cap) (41/17), Ricardo Enrique Bochini (26/0), Pedro Pablo Pasculli (10/3) [77.Oscar Alberto Dertycia (10/1)], Claudio Daniel Borghi (1/0) [77.José Daniel Ponce (23/4)]. Trainer: Dr. Carlos Salvador Bilardo (33).
**Goal**: Diego Armando Maradona (37).

**575.** 17.11.1985 **MEXICO - ARGENTINA** **1-1(1-0)**
Estadio Cuauhtémoc, Puebla; Referee: John Meachin (Canada); Attendance: 41,000
**ARG:** Luis Alberto Islas (5/0), José Luis Cuciuffo (1/0), José Luis Brown (14/0), Oscar Alfredo Ruggeri (16/2), Sergio Daniel Batista (2/0), Ricardo Omar Giusti (23/0), Enzo Héctor Trossero (28/0) [46.Juan Alberto Barbas (32/0)], Diego Armando Maradona (Cap) (42/17), Ricardo Enrique Bochini (27/0) [46.José Daniel Ponce (24/4)], Sergio Omar Almirón (1/0) [75.Oscar Alberto Dertycia (11/1)], Claudio Daniel Borghi (2/0) [46.Pedro Pablo Pasculli (11/3)]. Trainer: Dr. Carlos Salvador Bilardo (34).
**Goal**: Oscar Alfredo Ruggeri (68).

**576.** 26.03.1986 **FRANCE - ARGENTINA** **2-0(1-0)**
Stade Parc des Princes, Paris; Referee: Franz Gächter (Switzerland); Attendance: 40,045
**ARG:** Nery Alberto Pumpido (14/0), Néstor Rolando Clausen (17/1), Oscar Alfredo Ruggeri (17/2), Daniel Alberto Passarella (67/23), Oscar Alfredo Garré (30/0), Ricardo Omar Giusti (24/0), Sergio Daniel Batista (3/0), Diego Armando Maradona (Cap) (43/17), Jorge Luis Burruchaga (31/9), Claudio Daniel Borghi (3/0) [*sent off 59*], Jorge Alberto Francisco Valdano (13/3). Trainer: Dr. Carlos Salvador Bilardo (35).

**577.** 30.04.1986 **NORWAY - ARGENTINA** **1-0(0-0)**
Ullevaal Stadion, Oslo; Referee: Erik Fredriksson (Sweden); Attendance: 15,058
**ARG:** Luis Alberto Islas (6/0), Néstor Rolando Clausen (18/1) [46.Julio Jorge Olarticoechea (4/0)], Oscar Alfredo Ruggeri (18/2), Daniel Alberto Passarella (68/23), Oscar Alfredo Garré (31/0), Ricardo Omar Giusti (25/0), Sergio Daniel Batista (4/0) [83.Héctor Adolfo Enrique (1/0)], Diego Armando Maradona (Cap) (44/17), Jorge Luis Burruchaga (32/9), Marcelo Antonio Trobbiani (25/1) [46.Pedro Pablo Pasculli (12/3)], Sergio Omar Almirón (2/0). Trainer: Dr. Carlos Salvador Bilardo (36).

**578.** 04.05.1986 **ISRAEL - ARGENTINA** **2-7(1-2)**
National Stadium, Ramat Gan, Tel Aviv; Referee: Bruno Galler (Switzerland); Attendance: 30,000
**ARG:** Nery Alberto Pumpido (15/0), Julio Jorge Olarticoechea (5/0), Oscar Alfredo Ruggeri (19/2), Daniel Alberto Passarella (69/23), Oscar Alfredo Garré (32/0), Ricardo Omar Giusti (26/0) [59.Carlos Daniel Tapia (2/1)], Sergio Daniel Batista (5/0), Diego Armando Maradona (Cap) (45/19), Jorge Luis Burruchaga (33/9) [66.Héctor Adolfo Enrique (2/0)], Claudio Daniel Borghi (4/1) [77.Pedro Pablo Pasculli (13/3)], Sergio Omar Almirón (3/3). Trainer: Dr. Carlos Salvador Bilardo (37).
**Goals**: Sergio Omar Almirón (4), Diego Armando Maradona (21), Sergio Omar Almirón (57), Claudio Daniel Borghi (58), Sergio Omar Almirón (62), Diego Armando Maradona (75), Carlos Daniel Tapia (90).

**579.** 02.06.1986 **ARGENTINA – SOUTH KOREA** **3-1(2-0)** 13th FIFA WC. Group Stage.
Estadio Olimpico'68, Ciudad de México (Mexico); Referee: Victoriano Sánchez Arminio (Spain); Attendance: 60,000
**ARG:** Nery Alberto Pumpido (16/0), Néstor Rolando Clausen (19/1), José Luis Brown (15/0), Oscar Alfredo Ruggeri (20/3), Oscar Alfredo Garré (33/0), Ricardo Omar Giusti (27/0), Sergio Daniel Batista (6/0) [75.Julio Jorge Olarticoechea (6/0)], Jorge Luis Burruchaga (34/9), Diego Armando Maradona (Cap) (46/19), Pedro Pablo Pasculli (14/3) [74.Carlos Daniel Tapia (3/1)], Jorge Alberto Francisco Valdano (14/5). Trainer: Dr. Carlos Salvador Bilardo (38).
**Goals**: Jorge Alberto Francisco Valdano (5), Oscar Alfredo Ruggeri (14), Jorge Alberto Francisco Valdano (47).

**580.** 05.06.1986 **ITALY - ARGENTINA** **1-1(1-1)** 13th FIFA WC. Group Stage.
Estadio Cuauhtémoc, Puebla (Mexico); Referee: Johannes Nicolaas Ignatius „Jan" Keizer (Holland); Attendance: 32,000
**ARG:** Nery Alberto Pumpido (17/0), José Luis Cuciuffo (2/0), José Luis Brown (16/0), Oscar Alfredo Ruggeri (21/3), Oscar Alfredo Garré (34/0), Ricardo Omar Giusti (28/0), Sergio Daniel Batista (7/0) [50.Julio Jorge Olarticoechea (7/0)], Jorge Luis Burruchaga (35/9), Diego Armando Maradona (Cap) (47/20), Claudio Daniel Borghi (5/1) [75.Héctor Adolfo Enrique (3/0)], Jorge Alberto Francisco Valdano (15/5). Trainer: Dr. Carlos Salvador Bilardo (39).
**Goal**: Diego Armando Maradona (34).

**581.** 10.06.1986 **ARGENTINA - BULGARIA** **2-0(1-0)** 13th FIFA WC. Group Stage.
Estadio Olimpico'68, Ciudad de México (Mexico); Referee: Morera Berny Ulloa (Costa Rica); Attendance: 40,000
**ARG:** Nery Alberto Pumpido (18/0), José Luis Cuciuffo (3/0), José Luis Brown (17/0), Oscar Alfredo Ruggeri (22/3), Oscar Alfredo Garré (35/0), Ricardo Omar Giusti (29/0), Sergio Daniel Batista (8/0) [46.Julio Jorge Olarticoechea (8/0)], Jorge Luis Burruchaga (36/10), Diego Armando Maradona (Cap) (48/20), Claudio Daniel Borghi (6/1) [46.Héctor Adolfo Enrique (4/0)], Jorge Alberto Francisco Valdano (16/6). Trainer: Dr. Carlos Salvador Bilardo (40).
**Goals**: Jorge Alberto Francisco Valdano (3), Jorge Luis Burruchaga (76).

**582.** 16.06.1986 **ARGENTINA - URUGUAY** **1-0(1-0)** 13th FIFA WC.2nd Round.
Estadio Cuauhtémoc, Puebla (Mexico); Referee: Luigi Agnolin (Italy); Attendance: 26,000
**ARG:** Nery Alberto Pumpido (19/0), José Luis Cuciuffo (4/0), José Luis Brown (18/0), Oscar Alfredo Ruggeri (23/3), Oscar Alfredo Garré (36/0), Ricardo Omar Giusti (30/0), Sergio Daniel Batista (9/0) [87.Julio Jorge Olarticoechea (9/0)], Jorge Luis Burruchaga (37/10), Diego Armando Maradona (Cap) (49/20), Pedro Pablo Pasculli (15/4), Jorge Alberto Francisco Valdano (17/6). Trainer: Dr. Carlos Salvador Bilardo (41).
**Goal**: Pedro Pablo Pasculli (42).

**583.** 22.06.1986 **ARGENTINA - ENGLAND** **2-1(0-0)** 13th FIFA WC. Quarter-Finals.
Estadio Azteca, Ciudad de México (Mexico); Referee: Ali Bennaceur (Tunisia); Attendance: 114,500
**ARG:** Nery Alberto Pumpido (20/0), José Luis Cuciuffo (5/0), José Luis Brown (19/0), Oscar Alfredo Ruggeri (24/3), Julio Jorge Olarticoechea (10/0), Ricardo Omar Giusti (31/0), Sergio Daniel Batista (10/0), Jorge Luis Burruchaga (38/10) [76.Carlos Daniel Tapia (4/1)], Héctor Adolfo Enrique (5/0), Diego Armando Maradona (Cap) (50/22), Jorge Alberto Francisco Valdano (18/6). Trainer: Dr. Carlos Salvador Bilardo (42).
**Goals**: Diego Armando Maradona (52, 56).

**584.** 25.06.1986 **ARGENTINA - BELGIUM** **2-0(0-0)** 13th FIFA WC. Semi-Finals.
Estadio Azteca, Ciudad de México (Mexico); Referee: Antonio Márquez (Mexico); Attendance: 110,820
**ARG:** Nery Alberto Pumpido (21/0), José Luis Cuciuffo (6/0), José Luis Brown (20/0), Oscar Alfredo Ruggeri (25/3), Julio Jorge Olarticoechea (11/0), Ricardo Omar Giusti (32/0), Sergio Daniel Batista (11/0), Jorge Luis Burruchaga (39/10) [86.Ricardo Enrique Bochini (28/0)], Héctor Adolfo Enrique (6/0), Diego Armando Maradona (Cap) (51/24), Jorge Alberto Francisco Valdano (19/6). Trainer: Dr. Carlos Salvador Bilardo (43).
**Goals**: Diego Armando Maradona (52, 63).

**585.** 29.06.1986 **ARGENTINA – WEST GERMANY** **3-2(1-0)** 13th FIFA WC. Final.
Estadio Azteca, Ciudad de México (Mexico); Referee: Romualdo Arppi Filho (Brazil); Attendance: 114,600
**ARG:** Nery Alberto Pumpido (22/0), José Luis Cuciuffo (7/0), José Luis Brown (21/1), Oscar Alfredo Ruggeri (26/3), Julio Jorge Olarticoechea (12/0), Ricardo Omar Giusti (33/0), Sergio Daniel Batista (12/0), Diego Armando Maradona (Cap) (52/24), Héctor Adolfo Enrique (7/0), Jorge Luis Burruchaga (40/11) [89.Marcelo Antonio Trobbiani (26/1)], Jorge Alberto Francisco Valdano (20/7). Trainer: Dr. Carlos Salvador Bilardo (44).
**Goals**: José Luis Brown (23), Jorge Alberto Francisco Valdano (56), Jorge Luis Burruchaga (85).

**586.** 10.06.1987 **ITALY - ARGENTINA** **3-1(2-0)**
Hardturm Stadion, Zürich (Switzerland); Referee: Joël Quiniou (France); Attendance: 30,000
**ARG:** Sergio Javier Goycochea (1/0), José Luis Cuciuffo (8/0), José Luis Brown (22/1), Oscar Alfredo Ruggeri (27/3), Oscar Alfredo Garré (37/0), Sergio Daniel Batista (13/0), Roque Raúl Alfaro (1/0) [73.Oscar Alberto Dertycia (12/1)], Diego Armando Maradona (Cap) (53/25), Julio Jorge Olarticoechea (13/0) [46.Hernán Edgardo Díaz (1/0)], Juan Gilberto Funes (1/0) [60.Pedro Pablo Pasculli (16/4)], Darío Andrés Siviski (1/0) [85.Claudio Paul Caniggia (1/0)]. Trainer: Dr. Carlos Salvador Bilardo (45).
**Goal**: Diego Armando Maradona (62).

**587.** 20.06.1987 **ARGENTINA - PARAGUAY** **0-1(0-1)**
Estadio Monumental „Antonio Vespucio Liberti", Buenos Aires; Referee: Abel Gnecco (Argentina); Attendance: 10,000
**ARG:** Luis Alberto Islas (7/0), José Luis Cuciuffo (9/0) [46.Hernán Edgardo Díaz (2/0)], José Luis Brown (23/1), Oscar Alfredo Ruggeri (28/3), Oscar Alfredo Garré (38/0), Sergio Daniel Batista (14/0), Ricardo Omar Giusti (34/0), José Alberto Percudani (1/0) [65.Oscar Alberto Dertycia (13/1)], Darío Andrés Siviski (2/0) [55.Claudio Paul Caniggia (2/0)], Carlos Daniel Tapia (5/1), Juan Gilberto Funes (2/0). Trainer: Dr. Carlos Salvador Bilardo (46).

**588.** 27.06.1987 **ARGENTINA - PERU** **1-1(0-0)** 33rd Copa América. Group Stage.
Estadio Monumental „Antonio Vespucio Liberti", Buenos Aires; Referee: Armando Pérez Hoyos (Colombia); Attendance: 40,000
**ARG:** Luis Alberto Islas (8/0), José Luis Cuciuffo (10/0), José Luis Brown (24/1), Oscar Alfredo Ruggeri (29/3), Julio Jorge Olarticoechea (14/0), Sergio Daniel Batista (15/0) [*sent off 68*], Ricardo Omar Giusti (35/0), Roque Raúl Alfaro (2/0) [80.Hernán Edgardo Díaz (3/0)], Diego Armando Maradona (Cap) (54/26), Carlos Daniel Tapia (6/1) [64.Claudio Paul Caniggia (3/0)], José Alberto Percudani (2/0). Trainer: Dr. Carlos Salvador Bilardo (47).
**Goal**: Diego Armando Maradona (47).

**589.** 02.07.1987 **ARGENTINA - ECUADOR** **3-0(0-0)** 33rd Copa América. Group Stage.
Estadio Monumental „Antonio Vespucio Liberti", Buenos Aires; Referee: Romualdo Arppi Filho (Brazil); Attendance: 30,000
**ARG:** Luis Alberto Islas (9/0), José Luis Cuciuffo (11/0), José Luis Brown (25/1), Oscar Alfredo Ruggeri (30/3), Julio Jorge Olarticoechea (15/0), Ricardo Omar Giusti (36/0), Roque Raúl Alfaro (3/0) [46.Claudio Paul Caniggia (4/1)], Hernán Edgardo Díaz (4/0) [80.Darío Andrés Siviski (3/0)], Diego Armando Maradona (Cap) (55/28), Carlos Daniel Tapia (7/1), José Alberto Percudani (3/0). Trainer: Dr. Carlos Salvador Bilardo (48).
**Goals**: Claudio Paul Caniggia (50), Diego Armando Maradona (67 penalty,85).

**590.** 09.07.1987 **ARGENTINA - URUGUAY** **0-1(0-1)** 33rd Copa América. Semi-Finals.
Estadio Monumental „Antonio Vespucio Liberti", Buenos Aires; Referee: Elías Victoriano Jácome Guerreiro (Ecuador); Attendance: 65,000
**ARG:** Luis Alberto Islas (10/0), José Luis Cuciuffo (12/0) [77.Roque Raúl Alfaro (4/0)], José Luis Brown (26/1), Oscar Alfredo Ruggeri (31/3), Julio Jorge Olarticoechea (16/0), Ricardo Omar Giusti (37/0), Sergio Daniel Batista (16/0), Diego Armando Maradona (Cap) (56/28), Carlos Daniel Tapia (8/1), Claudio Paul Caniggia (5/1), José Alberto Percudani (4/0) [46.Juan Gilberto Funes (3/0)]. Trainer: Dr. Carlos Salvador Bilardo (49).

**591.** 11.07.1987 **ARGENTINA - COLOMBIA** **1-2(0-2)** 33rd Copa América. Bronze Medal.
Estadio Monumental „Antonio Vespucio Liberti", Buenos Aires; Referee: Bernardo Corujo Darriba (Venezuela); Attendance: 15,000
**ARG:** Luis Alberto Islas (11/0), José Luis Cuciuffo (13/0), José Luis Brown (27/1), Oscar Alfredo Ruggeri (32/3), Julio Jorge Olarticoechea (17/0), Ricardo Omar Giusti (38/0), Sergio Daniel Batista (17/0), Diego Armando Maradona (Cap) (57/28), Carlos Daniel Tapia (9/1) [46.Roque Raúl Alfaro (5/0)], Claudio Paul Caniggia (6/2), José Alberto Percudani (5/0) [46.Juan Gilberto Funes (4/0)]. Trainer: Dr. Carlos Salvador Bilardo (50).
**Goal**: Claudio Paul Caniggia (86).

**592.** 16.12.1987 **ARGENTINA – WEST GERMANY** **1-0(0-0)**
Estadio „José Amalfitani", Buenos Aires; Referee: Arnaldo David César Coelho (Brazil); Attendance: 45,000
**ARG:** Nery Alberto Pumpido (23/0), José Luis Cuciuffo (14/0), José Luis Brown (28/1), Oscar Alfredo Ruggeri (33/3), Néstor Ariel Fabbri (1/0), Roberto Néstor Sensini (1/0), Sergio Daniel Batista (18/0), Diego Armando Maradona (Cap) (58/28), Jorge Luis Burruchaga (41/12) [73.Darío Andrés Siviski (4/0)], José Luis Rodríguez (1/0) [64.Pedro Antonio Troglio (1/0)], Jorge Alberto Francisco Valdano (21/7) [87.Oscar Alberto Dertycia (14/1)]. Trainer: Dr. Carlos Salvador Bilardo (51).
**Goal**: Jorge Luis Burruchaga (55).

**593.** 31.03.1988 **SOVIET UNION - ARGENTINA** **4-2(2-1)** International Tournament
Olympiastadion, West Berlin (West Germany); Referee: Joël Quiniou (France); Attendance: 10,000
**ARG:** Nery Alberto Pumpido (24/0), José Luis Cuciuffo (15/0), José Luis Brown (29/1) [72.Oscar Alfredo Garré (39/0)], Oscar Alfredo Ruggeri (34/3), Julio Jorge Olarticoechea (18/0) [Néstor Rolando Clausen (20/1)], Roberto Néstor Sensini (2/0), Ricardo Omar Giusti (39/0), Diego Armando Maradona (Cap) (59/29), Hernán Edgardo Díaz (5/0), Pedro Antonio Troglio (2/1), Claudio Paul Caniggia (7/2). Trainer: Dr. Carlos Salvador Bilardo (52).
**Goals**: Pedro Antonio Troglio (18), Diego Armando Maradona (67).

**594.** 02.04.1988 **WEST GERMANY - ARGENTINA** **1-0(1-0)** International Tournament
Olympiastadion, West Berlin; Referee: Kurt Röthlisberger (Switzerland); Attendance: 30,000
**ARG:** Nery Alberto Pumpido (25/0), Pedro Damián Monzón (1/0), José Luis Brown (30/1), Oscar Alfredo Ruggeri (35/3), Roberto Néstor Sensini (3/0) [74.José Luis Rodríguez (2/0)], Hernán Edgardo Díaz (6/0), Sergio Daniel Batista (19/0), Ricardo Omar Giusti (40/0), Diego Armando Maradona (Cap) (60/29), Pedro Antonio Troglio (3/1), Claudio Paul Caniggia (8/2). Trainer: Dr. Carlos Salvador Bilardo (53).

**595.** 06.07.1988 **ARGENTINA - SAUDI ARABIA** **2-2(1-1)** Australian Bicentenary Cup
Football Park, Adelaide (Australia); Referee: Barry Harwood (Australia); Attendance: 11,000
**ARG:** Luis Alberto Islas (12/0), Néstor Gabriel Lorenzo (1/0), Mario Bruno Lucca (1/0), Oscar Alfredo Ruggeri (36/3), Néstor Ariel Fabbri (2/0) [80.José Luis Cuciuffo (16/0)], Hernán Edgardo Díaz (7/2), Fernando Fabián Lanzidei (1/0), Ricardo Omar Giusti (41/0), Claudio Martín Cabrera (1/0), Oscar Alberto Dertycia (15/1) [58.Daniel Toribio Aquino (1/0)], José Luis Rodríguez (3/0). Trainer: Dr. Carlos Salvador Bilardo (54).
**Goals**: Hernán Edgardo Díaz (27, 49 penalty).

**596.** 10.07.1988 **BRAZIL - ARGENTINA** **0-0** Australian Bicentenary Cup
Olimpic Park, Melbourne (Australia); Referee: Donald Campbell (Australia); Attendance: 13,850
**ARG:** Luis Alberto Islas (13/0), Néstor Gabriel Lorenzo (2/0), Mario Bruno Lucca (2/0), Oscar Alfredo Ruggeri (37/3), Oscar Alfredo Garré (40/0), Ricardo Omar Giusti (42/0), Hernán Edgardo Díaz (8/2), Sergio Daniel Batista (20/0), Claudio Martín Cabrera (2/0) [80.Oscar Alberto Dertycia (16/1)], Darío Andrés Siviski (5/0) [51.Fernando Fabián Lanzidei (2/0)], José Luis Rodríguez (4/0). Trainer: Dr. Carlos Salvador Bilardo (55).

**597.** 14.07.1988 **AUSTRALIA - ARGENTINA** **4-1(2-1)** Australian Bicentenary Cup
Football Stadium, Sydney; Referee: Gary Power (Australia); Attendance: 20,000
**ARG:** Luis Alberto Islas (14/0), Néstor Gabriel Lorenzo (3/0), Mario Bruno Lucca (3/0), Oscar Alfredo Ruggeri (38/4), Oscar Alfredo Garré (41/0), Hernán Edgardo Díaz (9/2), Diego Pablo Simeone (1/0), Sergio Daniel Batista (21/0) [87.Pedro Damián Monzón (2/0)], Claudio Martín Cabrera (3/0) [63.Oscar Alberto Dertycia (17/1)], Daniel Toribio Aquino (2/0), José Luis Rodríguez (5/0). Trainer: Dr. Carlos Salvador Bilardo (56).
**Goal**: Oscar Alfredo Ruggeri (31).

**598.** 16.07.1988 **ARGENTINA – SAUDI ARABIA** **2-0(2-0)** Australian Bicentenary Cup
Bruce Stadium, Canberra (Australia); Referee: Gary Power (Australia); Attendance: 5,000
**ARG:** Luis Alberto Islas (15/0), Néstor Gabriel Lorenzo (4/0), Mario Bruno Lucca (4/0), Oscar Alfredo Ruggeri (39/4), Pedro Damián Monzón (3/0) [82.José Luis Rodríguez (6/0)], Hernán Edgardo Díaz (10/2), Ricardo Omar Giusti (43/0), Diego Pablo Simeone (2/1), Claudio Martín Cabrera (4/0), Darío Andrés Siviski (6/0) [61.Fernando Fabián Lanzidei (3/0)], Oscar Alberto Dertycia (18/2). Trainer: Dr. Carlos Salvador Bilardo (57).
**Goals**: Diego Pablo Simeone (4), Oscar Alberto Dertycia (30).

**599.** 12.10.1988 **SPAIN - ARGENTINA** **1-1(1-1)** Copa Hispanidád
Estadio „Ramón Sánchez Pizjuán", Sevilla; Referee: Carlo Longhi (Italy); Attendance: 50,000
**ARG:** Nery Alberto Pumpido (26/0), José Luis Cuciuffo (17/0), José Luis Brown (31/1), Oscar Alfredo Ruggeri (40/4), Néstor Ariel Fabbri (3/0) [55.Julio Jorge Olarticoechea (19/0)], Sergio Daniel Batista (22/0), Ricardo Omar Giusti (44/0), Diego Armando Maradona (Cap) (61/29) [75.Carlos Daniel Tapia (10/1)], Claudio Paul Caniggia (9/3) [76.Gustavo Abel Dezotti (1/0)], Pedro Antonio Troglio (4/1), Gabriel Humberto Calderón (11/1). Trainer: Dr. Carlos Salvador Bilardo (58).
**Goal**: Claudio Paul Caniggia (43).

**600.** 09.03.1989 **COLOMBIA - ARGENTINA** **1-0(1-0)**
Estadio Metropolitano „Roberto Meléndez“, Barranquilla; Referee: Guillermo Quirola (Ecuador); Attendance: 60,000
**ARG:** Julio César Falcioni (1/0), Néstor Oscar Craviotto (1/0), Pedro Damián Monzón (4/0), Hernán Edgardo Díaz (11/2), Néstor Gabriel Lorenzo (5/0), Diego Pablo Simeone (3/1), Ernesto Enrique Corti (1/0) [75.Claudio Martín Cabrera (5/0)], José Horacio Basualdo (1/0), Héctor Adolfo Enrique (Cap) (8/0), Abel Eduardo Balbo (1/0), Mauro Gabriel Airez (1/0) [65.Carlos Alejandro Alfaro Moreno (1/0)]. Trainer: Dr. Carlos Salvador Bilardo (59).

**601.** 13.04.1989 **ECUADOR - ARGENTINA** **2-2(0-2)**
Estadio „Isidro Romero Carbo“, Guayaquil; Referee: César Horacio Cachay (Peru); Attendance: 12,000
**ARG:** Luis Alberto Islas (16/0), Néstor Gabriel Lorenzo (6/0), Pedro Damián Monzón (5/0), Hernán Edgardo Díaz (12/2), Roberto Néstor Sensini (4/0), José Horacio Basualdo (2/0) [87.Ernesto Enrique Corti (2/0)], Sergio Daniel Batista (Cap) (23/0), Néstor Raúl Gorosito (1/0), Héctor Adolfo Enrique (9/0) [56.Diego Pablo Simeone (4/1)], Abel Eduardo Balbo (2/0), Carlos Alejandro Alfaro Moreno (2/1) [77.Sergio Silvano Maciel (1/0)]. Trainer: Dr. Carlos Salvador Bilardo (60).
**Goals**: Carlos Alejandro Alfaro Moreno (7, 35).

**602.** 20.04.1989 **CHILE - ARGENTINA** **1-1(0-1)**
Estadio Nacional, Santiago; Referee: Octavio Sierra Mesa (Colombia); Attendance: 11,663
**ARG:** Luis Alberto Islas (17/0), Néstor Gabriel Lorenzo (7/0), Pedro Damián Monzón (6/0), Hernán Edgardo Díaz (13/2), Roberto Néstor Sensini (5/0), José Horacio Basualdo (3/0) [60.Jorge Alberto Ortega (1/0)], Sergio Daniel Batista (Cap) (24/0), Néstor Raúl Gorosito (2/0), Héctor Adolfo Enrique (10/0) [66.Diego Pablo Simeone (5/1)], Abel Eduardo Balbo (3/0), Mauro Gabriel Airez (2/1) [76.Sergio Silvano Maciel (2/0)]. Trainer: Dr. Carlos Salvador Bilardo (61).
**Goal**: Mauro Gabriel Airez (17).

**603.** 02.07.1989 **ARGENTINA - CHILE** **1-0(0-0)** 34th Copa América. Group Stage.
Estádio Serra Dourada, Goiânia (Brazil); Referee: Arnaldo David César Coelho (Brazil); Attendance: 40,000
**ARG:** Luis Alberto Islas (18/0), Néstor Rolando Clausen (21/1) [71.José Horacio Basualdo (4/0)], José Luis Brown (32/1), Oscar Alfredo Ruggeri (41/4), Roberto Néstor Sensini (6/0), Pedro Antonio Troglio (5/1), Jorge Luis Burruchaga (42/12), Sergio Daniel Batista (25/0), Gabriel Humberto Calderón (12/1), Claudio Paul Caniggia (10/4) [67.Carlos Alejandro Alfaro Moreno (3/1)], Diego Armando Maradona (Cap) (62/29). Trainer: Dr. Carlos Salvador Bilardo (62).
**Goal**: Claudio Paul Caniggia (55).

**604.** 04.07.1989 **ARGENTINA - ECUADOR** **0-0** 34th Copa América. Group Stage.
Estádio Serra Dourada, Goiânia (Brazil); Referee: José Ramírez Calle (Peru); Attendance: 12,000
**ARG:** Luis Alberto Islas (19/0), José Luis Cuciuffo (18/0), Oscar Alfredo Ruggeri (42/4), José Luis Brown (33/1), Roberto Néstor Sensini (7/0), Néstor Rolando Clausen (22/1), Sergio Daniel Batista (26/0), Jorge Luis Burruchaga (43/12) [70.Pedro Antonio Troglio (6/1)], Gabriel Humberto Calderón (13/1), Claudio Paul Caniggia (11/4) [74.Carlos Alejandro Alfaro Moreno (4/1) [*sent off 89*]], Diego Armando Maradona (Cap) (63/29). Trainer: Dr. Carlos Salvador Bilardo (63).

**605.** 08.07.1989 **ARGENTINA - URUGUAY** **1-0(0-0)** 34th Copa América. Group Stage.
Estádio Serra Dourada, Goiânia (Brazil); Referee: Jesús Díaz Palacios (Colombia); Attendance: 18,000
**ARG:** Nery Alberto Pumpido (27/0), Néstor Rolando Clausen (23/1), Oscar Alfredo Ruggeri (43/4) [*sent off 17*], José Luis Brown (34/1), Roberto Néstor Sensini (8/0), Jorge Luis Burruchaga (44/12) [54.Claudio Paul Caniggia (12/5)], Pedro Antonio Troglio (7/1), Sergio Daniel Batista (27/0), José Horacio Basualdo (5/0), Gabriel Humberto Calderón (14/1) [80.José Luis Cuciuffo (19/0)], Diego Armando Maradona (Cap) (64/29). Trainer: Dr. Carlos Salvador Bilardo (64).
**Goal**: Claudio Paul Caniggia (69).

**606.** 10.07.1989 **ARGENTINA - BOLIVIA** **0-0** 34th Copa América. Group Stage.
Estádio Serra Dourada, Goiânia (Brazil); Referee: Nelson Rodríguez Fernández (Venezuela); Attendance: 5,000
**ARG:** Nery Alberto Pumpido (28/0), José Luis Cuciuffo (20/0), Pedro Damián Monzón (7/0), José Luis Brown (35/1), Roberto Néstor Sensini (9/0) [64.José Horacio Basualdo (6/0)], Néstor Raúl Gorosito (3/0), Héctor Adolfo Enrique (11/0), Diego Armando Maradona (Cap) (65/29), Hernán Edgardo Díaz (14/2), Claudio Paul Caniggia (13/5) [54.Pedro Antonio Troglio (8/1)], Carlos Alejandro Alfaro Moreno (5/1). Trainer: Dr. Carlos Salvador Bilardo (65).

**607.** 12.07.1989 **BRAZIL - ARGENTINA** **2-0(0-0)** 34th Copa América. Final Round.
Estádio „Jornalista Mário Filho“ (Maracanã), Rio de Janeiro; Referee: Juan Daniel Cardellino de San Vicente (Uruguay); Attendance: 100,135
**ARG:** Nery Alberto Pumpido (29/0), Néstor Rolando Clausen (24/1), Oscar Alfredo Ruggeri (44/4), José Luis Brown (36/1), Roberto Néstor Sensini (10/0), Pedro Antonio Troglio (9/1), Jorge Luis Burruchaga (45/12) [55.Claudio Paul Caniggia (14/5)], Sergio Daniel Batista (28/0), José Horacio Basualdo (7/0), Gabriel Humberto Calderón (15/1) [58.Ricardo Omar Giusti (45/0)], Diego Armando Maradona (Cap) (66/29). Trainer: Dr. Carlos Salvador Bilardo (66).

**608.** 14.07.1989 **URUGUAY - ARGENTINA** **2-0(1-0)** 34th Copa América. Final Round.
Estádio „Jornalista Mário Filho“ (Maracanã), Rio de Janeiro (Brazil); Referee: Arnaldo David César Coelho (Brazil); Attendance: 45,000
**ARG:** Nery Alberto Pumpido (30/0), Néstor Rolando Clausen (25/1), José Luis Cuciuffo (21/0) [54.Néstor Raúl Gorosito (4/0)], Oscar Alfredo Ruggeri (45/4) [*sent off 64*], Roberto Néstor Sensini (11/0), José Horacio Basualdo (8/0), Jorge Luis Burruchaga (46/12) [46.Abel Eduardo Balbo (4/0)], Sergio Daniel Batista (29/0), Pedro Antonio Troglio (10/1), Claudio Paul Caniggia (15/5), Diego Armando Maradona (Cap) (67/29). Trainer: Dr. Carlos Salvador Bilardo (67).

**609.** 16.07.1989 **ARGENTINA - PARAGUAY** **0-0** 34th Copa América. Final Round.
Estádio „Jornalista Mário Filho“ (Maracanã), Rio de Janeiro (Brazil); Referee: Jesús Díaz Palacios (Colombia); Attendance: 90,000
**ARG:** Nery Alberto Pumpido (31/0), Néstor Rolando Clausen (26/1) [63.Néstor Raúl Gorosito (5/0)], Pedro Damián Monzón (8/0), Hernán Edgardo Díaz (15/2), Roberto Néstor Sensini (12/0), Ricardo Omar Giusti (46/0), José Horacio Basualdo (9/0), Jorge Luis Burruchaga (Cap) (47/12), Pedro Antonio Troglio (11/1), Abel Eduardo Balbo (5/0), Gabriel Humberto Calderón (16/1) [46.Carlos Alejandro Alfaro Moreno (6/1)]. Trainer: Dr. Carlos Salvador Bilardo (68).

**610.** 21.12.1989 **ITALY - ARGENTINA** **0-0**
Stadio Sant'Elia, Cagliari; Referee: Alexei Spirin (Soviet Union); Attendance: 29,635
**ARG:** Nery Alberto Pumpido (32/0), Oscar Alfredo Ruggeri (46/4), Juan Ernesto Simón (3/0), José Horacio Basualdo (10/0) [39.Pedro Antonio Troglio (12/1)], Sergio Daniel Batista (30/0), Pedro Damián Monzón (9/0), Julio Jorge Olarticoechea (20/0), Jorge Luis Burruchaga (48/12), Ricardo Omar Giusti (47/0), Diego Armando Maradona (Cap) (68/29), Gustavo Abel Dezotti (2/0) [69.Claudio Paul Caniggia (16/5)]. Trainer: Dr. Carlos Salvador Bilardo (69).

**611.** 17.01.1990 **MEXICO - ARGENTINA** **2-0(1-0)**
Memorial Coliseum, Los Angeles; Referee: Vincent Mauro (United States); Attendance: 20,000
**ARG:** Sergio Javier Goycochea (2/0), Néstor Ariel Fabbri (4/0), Edgardo Bauza (2/0), Julio Jorge Olarticoechea (21/0), Pedro Damián Monzón (10/0) [82.Diego Pablo Simeone (6/1)], José Horacio Basualdo (11/0), Néstor Raúl Gorosito (6/0), Sergio Daniel Batista (31/0), Ricardo Omar Giusti (48/0), Carlos Alejandro Alfaro Moreno (7/1), Mauro Gabriel Airez (3/1). Trainer: Dr. Carlos Salvador Bilardo (70).

**612.** 28.03.1990 **SCOTLAND - ARGENTINA** **1-0(0-0)**
Hampden Park, Glasgow; Referee: Frans Houben (Holland); Attendance: 51,537
**ARG:** Nery Alberto Pumpido (Cap) (33/0), Edgardo Bauza (3/0), Roberto Néstor Sensini (13/0), Néstor Ariel Fabbri (5/0), Oscar Alfredo Ruggeri (47/4) [60.Pedro Damián Monzón (11/0)], Sergio Daniel Batista (32/0), Gabriel Humberto Calderón (17/1), José Horacio Basualdo (12/0), Jorge Luis Burruchaga (49/12) [49.Pedro Antonio Troglio (13/1)], Jorge Alberto Francisco Valdano (22/7) [46.Abel Eduardo Balbo (6/0)], Claudio Paul Caniggia (17/5). Trainer: Dr. Carlos Salvador Bilardo (71).

**613.** 03.05.1990 **AUSTRIA - ARGENTINA** **1-1(1-1)**
Prater Stadion, Wien; Referee: Alphonse Constantin (Belgium); Attendance: 57,000
**ARG:** Nery Alberto Pumpido (34/0), Juan Ernesto Simón (4/0), Oscar Alfredo Ruggeri (48/4), José Tiburcio Serrizuela (1/0), Sergio Daniel Batista (33/0), Roberto Néstor Sensini (14/0), José Horacio Basualdo (13/0), Néstor Gabriel Lorenzo (8/0) [76.Pedro Antonio Troglio (14/1)], Jorge Luis Burruchaga (50/13) [88.Ricardo Omar Giusti (49/0)], Diego Armando Maradona (69/29), Abel Eduardo Balbo (7/0) [46.Claudio Paul Caniggia (18/5)]. Trainer: Dr. Carlos Salvador Bilardo (72).
**Goal**: Jorge Luis Burruchaga (30).

**614.** 08.05.1990 **SWITZERLAND - ARGENTINA** **1-1(0-0)**
Wankdorf Stadion, Bern; Referee: Patrick Kelly (Republic of Ireland); Attendance: 10,000
**ARG:** Nery Alberto Pumpido (35/0), Juan Ernesto Simón (5/0), José Tiburcio Serrizuela (2/0), Oscar Alfredo Ruggeri (49/4), Sergio Daniel Batista (34/0), Roberto Néstor Sensini (15/0) [56.Pedro Antonio Troglio (15/1)], José Horacio Basualdo (14/0), Néstor Gabriel Lorenzo (9/0), Jorge Luis Burruchaga (51/13) [85.Claudio Paul Caniggia (19/5)], Diego Armando Maradona (70/29), Abel Eduardo Balbo (8/1) [60.Gustavo Abel Dezotti (3/0)]. Trainer: Dr. Carlos Salvador Bilardo (73).
**Goal**: Abel Eduardo Balbo (52).

**615.** 22.05.1990 **ISRAEL - ARGENTINA** **1-2(1-1)**
National Stadium, Ramat-Gan, Tel Aviv; Referee: Vojtech Christov (Czechoslovakia); Attendance: 45,000
**ARG:** Nery Alberto Pumpido (36/0), Juan Ernesto Simón (6/0), Oscar Alfredo Ruggeri (50/4), José Tiburcio Serrizuela (3/0) [80.Néstor Ariel Fabbri (6/0)], Roberto Néstor Sensini (16/0) [88.Néstor Gabriel Lorenzo (10/0)], Sergio Daniel Batista (35/0), Jorge Luis Burruchaga (52/13), José Horacio Basualdo (15/0), Gustavo Abel Dezotti (4/0) [61.Claudio Paul Caniggia (20/6)], Diego Armando Maradona (71/30), Abel Eduardo Balbo (9/1) [85.Julio Jorge Olarticoechea (22/0)]. Trainer: Dr. Carlos Salvador Bilardo (74).
**Goals**: Diego Armando Maradona (35), Claudio Paul Caniggia (68).

**616.** 08.06.1990 **CAMEROON - ARGENTINA** **1-0(0-0)** 14th FIFA WC. Group Stage.
Stadio „Giuseppe Meazza“, Milano (Italy); Referee: Michel Vautrot (France); Attendance: 73,780
**ARG:** Nery Alberto Pumpido (37/0), Juan Ernesto Simón (7/0), Oscar Alfredo Ruggeri (51/4) [46.Claudio Paul Caniggia (21/6)], Néstor Ariel Fabbri (7/0), Sergio Daniel Batista (36/0), José Horacio Basualdo (16/0), Néstor Gabriel Lorenzo (11/0), Roberto Néstor Sensini (17/0) [69.Gabriel Humberto Calderón (18/1)], Diego Armando Maradona (Cap) (72/30), Jorge Luis Burruchaga (53/13), Abel Eduardo Balbo (10/1). Trainer: Dr. Carlos Salvador Bilardo (75).

**617.** 13.06.1990 **ARGENTINA – SOVIET UNION** **2-0(1-0)** 14th FIFA WC. Group Stage.
Stadio „San Paolo“, Napoli (Italy); Referee: Erik Fredriksson (Sweden); Attendance: 55,759
**ARG:** Nery Alberto Pumpido (38/0) [11.Sergio Javier Goycochea (3/0)], Juan Ernesto Simón (8/0), José Tiburcio Serrizuela (4/0), Julio Jorge Olarticoechea (23/0), Sergio Daniel Batista (37/0), José Horacio Basualdo (17/0), Pedro Antonio Troglio (16/2), Jorge Luis Burruchaga (54/14), Claudio Paul Caniggia (22/6), Diego Armando Maradona (Cap) (73/30), Pedro Damián Monzón (12/0) [78.Néstor Gabriel Lorenzo (12/0)]. Trainer: Dr. Carlos Salvador Bilardo (76).
**Goals**: Pedro Antonio Troglio (27), Jorge Luis Burruchaga (79).

**618.** 18.06.1990 **ARGENTINA - ROMANIA** **1-1(0-0)** 14th FIFA WC. Group Stage.
Stadio „San Paolo“, Napoli (Italy); Referee: Carlos Silva Valente (Portugal); Attendance: 52,733
**ARG:** Sergio Javier Goycochea (4/0), Juan Ernesto Simón (9/0), Pedro Damián Monzón (13/1), José Tiburcio Serrizuela (5/0), Julio Jorge Olarticoechea (24/0), Sergio Daniel Batista (38/0), José Horacio Basualdo (18/0), Pedro Antonio Troglio (17/2) [53.Ricardo Omar Giusti (50/0)], Jorge Luis Burruchaga (55/14) [60.Gustavo Abel Dezotti (5/0)], Diego Armando Maradona (Cap) (74/30), Claudio Paul Caniggia (23/6). Trainer: Dr. Carlos Salvador Bilardo (77).
**Goal**: Pedro Damián Monzón (63).

**619.** 24.06.1990 **ARGENTINA - BRAZIL** **1-0(0-0)** 14th FIFA WC. 2nd Round.
Stadio „Delle Alpi“, Torino (Italy); Referee: Joël Quiniou (France); Attendance: 61,381
**ARG:** Sergio Javier Goycochea (5/0), Juan Ernesto Simón (10/0), Oscar Alfredo Ruggeri (52/4), Pedro Damián Monzón (14/1), Julio Jorge Olarticoechea (25/0), Ricardo Omar Giusti (51/0), Pedro Antonio Troglio (18/2) [63.Gabriel Humberto Calderón (19/1)], José Horacio Basualdo (19/0), Jorge Luis Burruchaga (56/14), Claudio Paul Caniggia (24/7), Diego Armando Maradona (Cap) (75/30). Trainer: Dr. Carlos Salvador Bilardo (78).
**Goal**: Claudio Paul Caniggia (80).

**620.** 30.06.1990 **ARGENTINA - YUGOSLAVIA** **0-0; 3-2 penalties** 14th FIFA WC. Quarter-Finals.
Stadio Comunale, Firenze; Referee: Kurt Röthlisberger (Switzerland); Attendance: 38,971
**ARG:** Sergio Javier Goycochea (6/0), Juan Ernesto Simón (11/0), Julio Jorge Olarticoechea (26/0) [51.Pedro Antonio Troglio (19/2)], José Tiburcio Serrizuela (6/0), Oscar Alfredo Ruggeri (53/4), José Horacio Basualdo (20/0), Jorge Luis Burruchaga (57/14), Diego Armando Maradona (Cap) (76/30), Ricardo Omar Giusti (52/0), Gabriel Humberto Calderón (20/1) [87.Gustavo Abel Dezotti (6/0)], Claudio Paul Caniggia (25/7). Trainer: Dr. Carlos Salvador Bilardo (79).
**Penalties**: José Tiburcio Serrizuela, Jorge Luis Burruchaga, Diego Armando Maradona [save], Pedro Antonio Troglio [miss], Gustavo Abel Dezotti.

**621.** 03.07.1990 **ITALY - ARGENTINA** **1-1(1-0,1-1,1-1); 3-4 penalties** 14th FIFA WC. Semi-Finals.
Stadio „San Paolo“, Napoli (Italy); Referee: Michel Vautrot (France); Attendance: 59,978
**ARG:** Sergio Javier Goycochea (7/0), Juan Ernesto Simón (12/0), Oscar Alfredo Ruggeri (54/4), Julio Jorge Olarticoechea (27/0), José Tiburcio Serrizuela (7/0), Ricardo Omar Giusti (53/0) [*sent off 103*], Jorge Luis Burruchaga (58/14), José Horacio Basualdo (21/0) [99.Sergio Daniel Batista (39/0)], Gabriel Humberto Calderón (21/1) [46.Pedro Antonio Troglio (20/2)], Claudio Paul Caniggia (26/8), Diego Armando Maradona (Cap) (77/30). Trainer: Dr. Carlos Salvador Bilardo (80).
**Goal**: Claudio Paul Caniggia (67).

**Penalties**: José Tiburcio Serrizuela, Jorge Luis Burruchaga, Julio Jorge Olarticoechea, Diego Armando Maradona.

**622.** 08.07.1990 **WEST GERMANY - ARGENTINA** **1-0(0-0)** 14th FIFA WC. Final.
Stadio Olimpico, Roma; Referee: Edgardo Codesal (Mexico); Attendance: 73,603
**ARG:** Sergio Javier Goycochea (8/0), Juan Ernesto Simón (13/0), José Tiburcio Serrizuela (8/0), Oscar Alfredo Ruggeri (55/4) [46.Pedro Damián Monzón (15/1) [*sent off 65*]], Pedro Antonio Troglio (21/2), Roberto Néstor Sensini (18/0), Jorge Luis Burruchaga (59/14) [54.Gabriel Humberto Calderón (22/1)], José Horacio Basualdo (22/0), Néstor Gabriel Lorenzo (13/0), Gustavo Abel Dezotti (7/0) [*sent off 87*], Diego Armando Maradona (Cap) (78/30). Trainer: Dr. Carlos Salvador Bilardo (81).

**623.** 19.02.1991 **ARGENTINA - HUNGARY** **2-0(1-0)**
Estadio Cordoviola, Rosario; Referee: Juan Carlos Loustau (Argentina); Attendance: 31,446
**ARG:** Sergio Javier Goycochea (9/0), Fernando Andrés Gamboa (1/0), Fabián Armando Basualdo (1/0), Oscar Alfredo Ruggeri (56/4), Carlos Alberto Enrique (1/0), David Carlos Nazareno Bisconti (1/0), José Luis Villareal (1/0), Darío Javier Franco (1/1), Diego Fernando Latorre (1/0) [84.Gerardo Daniel Martino (1/0)], Ramón Ismael Medina Bello (1/0) [72.Ariel Eduardo Boldrini (1/0)], Antonio Ricardo Mohamed (1/1) [84.Carlos Alejandro Alfaro Moreno (8/1)]. Trainer: Alfio Oscar Basile (1).
**Goals**: Darío Javier Franco (38), Antonio Ricardo Mohamed (46).

**624.** 13.03.1991 **ARGENTINA - MEXICO** **0-0**
Estadio „José Amalfitani", Buenos Aires; Referee: Ricardo Calabria (Argentina); Attendance: 40,000
**ARG:** Sergio Javier Goycochea (10/0), Fabián Armando Basualdo (2/0), Fernando Andrés Gamboa (2/0), Oscar Alfredo Ruggeri (57/4), Carlos Alberto Enrique (2/0), Leonardo Rubén Astrada (1/0), David Carlos Nazareno Bisconti (2/0) [60.Gustavo Miguel Zapata (1/0)], Darío Javier Franco (2/1), Sergio Ángel Berti (1/0) [65.Carlos Alejandro Alfaro Moreno (9/1)], Ramón Ismael Medina Bello (2/0), Víctor Hugo Ferreyra (1/0). Trainer: Alfio Oscar Basile (2).

**625.** 27.03.1991 **ARGENTINA - BRAZIL** **3-3(3-1)**
Estadio „José Amalfitani", Buenos Aires; Referee: Juan Bava (Argentina); Attendance: 40,087
**ARG:** Sergio Javier Goycochea (11/0), Néstor Oscar Craviotto (2/0) [81.Dante Rubén Unali (1/0)], Fernando Andrés Gamboa (3/0), Oscar Alfredo Ruggeri (58/4), Ricardo Daniel Altamirano (1/0), Darío Javier Franco (3/2), Miguel Ángel Ludueña (1/0) [55.Blas Armando Giunta (1/0)], David Carlos Nazareno Bisconti (3/1) [89.Sergio Fabián Vázquez (1/0)], Claudio Omar García (1/0) [*sent off 89*], Víctor Hugo Ferreyra (2/1) [65.Ariel Eduardo Boldrini (2/0)], Diego Fernando Latorre (2/0). Trainer: Alfio Oscar Basile (3).
**Goals**: Víctor Hugo Ferreyra (33), Darío Javier Franco (42), David Carlos Nazareno Bisconti (44).

**626.** 19.05.1991 **UNITED STATES - ARGENTINA** **0-1(0-1)**
Stanford Stadium, Palo Alto, San Francisco; Referee: Robert Sawtell (Canada); Attendance: 31,763
**ARG:** Sergio Javier Goycochea (12/0), Sergio Fabián Vázquez (2/0) [88.Fernando Andrés Gamboa (4/0)], Oscar Alfredo Ruggeri (59/4), Carlos Alberto Enrique (3/0), Fabián Armando Basualdo (3/0), Leonardo Rubén Astrada (2/0), Ariel Eduardo Boldrini (3/0), Darío Javier Franco (4/3), Sergio Ángel Berti (2/0), David Carlos Nazareno Bisconti (4/1) [84.Gustavo Miguel Zapata (2/0)], Carlos Alejandro Alfaro Moreno (10/1) [74.Antonio Ricardo Mohamed (2/1)]. Trainer: Alfio Oscar Basile (4).
**Goal**: Darío Javier Franco (33).

**627.** 23.05.1991 **ARGENTINA – SOVIET UNION** **1-1(1-0)** International Tournament
Old Trafford, Manchester (England); Referee: Peter Mikkelsen (Denmark); Attendance: 23,743
**ARG:** Sergio Javier Goycochea (13/0), Sergio Fabián Vázquez (3/0), Oscar Alfredo Ruggeri (60/5), Carlos Alberto Enrique (4/0), Fabián Armando Basualdo (4/0), Leonardo Rubén Astrada (3/0), Claudio Omar García (2/0), Darío Javier Franco (5/3), Diego Pablo Simeone (7/1), David Carlos Nazareno Bisconti (5/1) [70.Sergio Ángel Berti (3/0)], Carlos Alejandro Alfaro Moreno (11/1). Trainer: Alfio Oscar Basile (5).
**Goal**: Oscar Alfredo Ruggeri (44).

**628.** 25.05.1991 **ENGLAND - ARGENTINA** **2-2(1-0)** International Tournament
Wembley Stadium, London; Referee: Zoran Petrović (Yugoslavia); Attendance: 44,497
**ARG:** Sergio Javier Goycochea (14/0), Sergio Fabián Vázquez (4/0), Fernando Andrés Gamboa (5/0), Oscar Alfredo Ruggeri (61/5), Carlos Alberto Enrique (5/0), Fabián Armando Basualdo (5/0), Claudio Omar García (3/1), Darío Javier Franco (6/4), Diego Pablo Simeone (8/1), Germán Ricardo Martellotto (1/0) [59.Antonio Ricardo Mohamed (3/1)], Ariel Eduardo Boldrini (4/0). Trainer: Alfio Oscar Basile (6).
**Goals**: Claudio Omar García (65), Darío Javier Franco (70).

**629.** 27.06.1991 **BRAZIL - ARGENTINA** **1-1(0-0)**
Antônio de Couto Pereira „Pinheirão", Curitiba; Referee: Wilson Carlos dos Santos (Brazil); Attendance: 44,429
**ARG:** Sergio Javier Goycochea (15/0), Néstor Oscar Craviotto (3/0), Oscar Alfredo Ruggeri (62/5), Sergio Fabián Vázquez (5/0), Carlos Alberto Enrique (6/0) [*sent off 58*], Darío Javier Franco (7/4), Leonardo Rubén Astrada (4/0), Diego Pablo Simeone (9/1), Diego Fernando Latorre (3/0) [61.Fabián Armando Basualdo (6/0)], Claudio Paul Caniggia (27/9) [88.Claudio Omar García (4/1)], Gabriel Omar Batistuta (1/0). Trainer: Alfio Oscar Basile (7).
**Goal**: Claudio Paul Caniggia (50).

**630.** 08.07.1991 **ARGENTINA - VENEZUELA** **3-0(2-0)** 35th Copa América. Group Stage.
Estadio Regional, Concepción (Chile); Referee: Milton Villavicencio Echeverría (Ecuador); Attendance: 7,000
**ARG:** Sergio Javier Goycochea (16/0), Fabián Armando Basualdo (7/0), Sergio Fabián Vázquez (6/0), Oscar Alfredo Ruggeri (63/5), Néstor Oscar Craviotto (4/0), Leonardo Rubén Astrada (5/0), Diego Pablo Simeone (10/1), Darío Javier Franco (8/4), Diego Fernando Latorre (4/0) [79.Leonardo Adrián Rodríguez (1/0)], Gabriel Omar Batistuta (2/2), Claudio Paul Caniggia (28/10) [85.Claudio Omar García (5/1)]. Trainer: Alfio Oscar Basile (8).
**Goals**: Gabriel Omar Batistuta (28), Claudio Paul Caniggia (43), Gabriel Omar Batistuta (50 penalty).

**631.** 10.07.1991 **CHILE - ARGENTINA** **0-1(0-0)** 35th Copa América. Group Stage.
Estadio Nacional, Santiago; Referee: José Roberto Ramiz Wright (Brazil); Attendance: 70,000
**ARG:** Sergio Javier Goycochea (17/0), Fabián Armando Basualdo (8/0), Sergio Fabián Vázquez (7/0), Oscar Alfredo Ruggeri (64/5), Néstor Oscar Craviotto (5/0), Diego Pablo Simeone (11/1), Leonardo Rubén Astrada (6/0), Darío Javier Franco (9/4), Diego Fernando Latorre (5/0) [46.Leonardo Adrián Rodríguez (2/0)], Gabriel Omar Batistuta (3/3), Claudio Paul Caniggia (29/10). Trainer: Alfio Oscar Basile (9).
**Goal**: Gabriel Omar Batistuta (81).

**632.** 12.07.1991 **ARGENTINA - PARAGUAY** **4-1(1-0)** 35th Copa América. Group Stage.
Estadio Regional, Concepción (Chile); Referee: Ernesto Filippi Cavani (Uruguay); Attendance: 40,000
**ARG:** Sergio Javier Goycochea (18/0), Fabián Armando Basualdo (9/0) [72.Fernando Andrés Gamboa (6/0)], Sergio Fabián Vázquez (8/0), Oscar Alfredo Ruggeri (65/5), Carlos Alberto Enrique (7/0), Gustavo Miguel Zapata (3/0), Leonardo Rubén Astrada (7/1) [77.Blas Armando Giunta (2/0)], Diego Pablo Simeone (12/2), Leonardo Adrián Rodríguez (3/0), Claudio Paul Caniggia (30/11), Gabriel Omar Batistuta (4/4). Trainer: Alfio Oscar Basile (10).
**Goals**: Gabriel Omar Batistuta (40), Diego Pablo Simeone (61), Leonardo Rubén Astrada (70), Claudio Paul Caniggia (81).

**633.** 14.07.1991 **ARGENTINA - PERU** **3-2(1-1)** 35th Copa América. Group Stage.
Estadio Nacional, Santiago (Chile); Referee: Juan Oscar Ortubé Vargas (Bolivia); Attendance: 80,000
**ARG:** Alejandro Fabio Lanari (1/0), Ricardo Daniel Altamirano (2/0), Fernando Andrés Gamboa (7/0), Néstor Oscar Craviotto (6/1), Carlos Alberto Enrique (8/0), Gustavo Miguel Zapata (4/0), Blas Armando Giunta (3/0), Antonio Ricardo Mohamed (4/1), Diego Fernando Latorre (6/1), Claudio Omar García (6/2) [72.Leonardo Rubén Astrada (8/1)], Ramón Ismael Medina Bello (3/0) [85.Darío Javier Franco (10/4)]. Trainer: Alfio Oscar Basile (11).
**Goals**: Diego Fernando Latorre (3), Néstor Oscar Craviotto (51), Claudio Omar García (57).

**634.** 17.07.1991 **ARGENTINA - BRAZIL** **3-2(2-1)** 35th Copa América. Final Round.
Estadio Nacional, Santiago (Chile); Referee: Carlos Alberto Maciel (Paraguay); Attendance: 65,000
**ARG:** Sergio Javier Goycochea (19/0), Fabián Armando Basualdo (10/0), Sergio Fabián Vázquez (9/0), Oscar Alfredo Ruggeri (Cap) (66/5), Carlos Alberto Enrique (9/0) [*sent off 61*], Leonardo Rubén Astrada (9/1), Darío Javier Franco (11/6), Diego Pablo Simeone (13/2), Leonardo Adrián Rodríguez (4/0) [82.Blas Armando Giunta (4/0)], Gabriel Omar Batistuta (5/5), Claudio Paul Caniggia (31/11) [*sent off 31*]. Trainer: Alfio Oscar Basile (12).
**Goals**: Darío Javier Franco (1, 39), Gabriel Omar Batistuta (46).

**635.** 19.07.1991 **CHILE - ARGENTINA** **0-0** 35th Copa América. Final Round.
Estadio Nacional, Santiago; Referee: Ernesto Filippi Cavani (Uruguay); Attendance: 50,000
**ARG:** Sergio Javier Goycochea (20/0), Fabián Armando Basualdo (11/0), Oscar Alfredo Ruggeri (Cap) (67/5), Sergio Fabián Vázquez (10/0), Ricardo Daniel Altamirano (3/0), Leonardo Rubén Astrada (10/1), Darío Javier Franco (12/6), Diego Pablo Simeone (14/2), Leonardo Adrián Rodríguez (5/0) [85.Blas Armando Giunta (5/0)], Gabriel Omar Batistuta (6/5), Ramón Ismael Medina Bello (4/0). Trainer: Alfio Oscar Basile (13).

**636.** 21.07.1991 **ARGENTINA - COLOMBIA** **2-1(2-0)** 35th Copa América. Final Round.
Estadio Nacional, Santiago (Chile); Referee: Juan Francisco Escobar Váldez (Paraguay); Attendance:
**ARG:** Sergio Javier Goycochea (21/0), Fabián Armando Basualdo (12/0), Sergio Fabián Vázquez (11/0), Oscar Alfredo Ruggeri (Cap) (68/5), Ricardo Daniel Altamirano (4/0), Diego Pablo Simeone (15/3), Darío Javier Franco (13/6), Leonardo Rubén Astrada (11/1), Leonardo Adrián Rodríguez (6/0) [77.Blas Armando Giunta (6/0)], Claudio Paul Caniggia (32/11), Gabriel Omar Batistuta (7/6). Trainer: Alfio Oscar Basile (14).
**Goals**: Diego Pablo Simeone (11), Gabriel Omar Batistuta (19).

**637.** 31.05.1992 **JAPAN - ARGENTINA** **0-1(0-0)** Kirin Cup
National Stadium, Tokyo; Referee: Kil Ki-Cheol (South Korea); Attendance: 60,000
**ARG:** Sergio Javier Goycochea (22/0), Sergio Fabián Vázquez (12/0), Fabián Armando Basualdo (13/0), Oscar Alfredo Ruggeri (69/5), Néstor Oscar Craviotto (7/1), Darío Javier Franco (14/6), José Luis Villareal (2/0), Leonardo Adrián Rodríguez (7/0) [82.Leonardo Rubén Astrada (12/1)], Diego Sebastián Cagna (1/0), Claudio Paul Caniggia (33/11), Gabriel Omar Batistuta (8/7) [89.Alberto Federico Acosta (1/0)]. Trainer: Alfio Oscar Basile (15).
**Goal**: Gabriel Omar Batistuta (53).

**638.** 03.06.1992 **ARGENTINA - WALES** **1-0(0-0)** Kirin Cup
Memorial Centre, Gifu (Japan); Referee: Kichiro Tachi (Japan); Attendance: 31,000
**ARG:** Luis Alberto Islas (20/0), Fabián Armando Basualdo (14/0), Ricardo Daniel Altamirano (5/0), Sergio Fabián Vázquez (13/0), Oscar Alfredo Ruggeri (70/5), Leonardo Adrián Rodríguez (8/0) [60.Alberto Federico Acosta (2/0)], José Luis Villareal (3/0), Diego Sebastián Cagna (2/0), Darío Javier Franco (15/6), Claudio Paul Caniggia (34/11), Gabriel Omar Batistuta (9/8). Trainer: Alfio Oscar Basile (16).
**Goal**: Gabriel Omar Batistuta (87).

**639.** 18.06.1992 **ARGENTINA - AUSTRALIA** **2-0(0-0)**
Estadio Monumental „Antonio Vespucio Liberti", Buenos Aires; Referee: Eduardo Dluzniewski Takoz (Uruguay); Attendance: 35,000
**ARG:** Sergio Javier Goycochea (23/0), Sergio Fabián Vázquez (14/0), Fabián Armando Basualdo (15/0), Oscar Alfredo Ruggeri (71/5), Ricardo Daniel Altamirano (6/0) [46.Sergio Fabián Zárate (1/0)], Diego Sebastián Cagna (3/0), Darío Javier Franco (16/6), Fernando Carlos Redondo (1/0), Leonardo Adrián Rodríguez (9/0) [67.Darío Oscar Scotto (1/0)], Gabriel Omar Batistuta (10/10) [67.Claudio Omar García (7/2)], Claudio Paul Caniggia (35/11) [70.Leonardo Rubén Astrada (13/1)]. Trainer: Alfio Oscar Basile (17).
**Goals**: Gabriel Omar Batistuta (47 penalty,57).

**640.** 23.09.1992 **URUGUAY - ARGENTINA** **0-0** Copa Lipton
Estadio Centenario, Montevideo; Referee: Félix Ramón Benegas Caballero (Paraguay); Attendance: 35,000
**ARG:** Luis Alberto Islas (21/0), Fabián Armando Basualdo (Cap) (16/0), Sergio Fabián Vázquez (15/0), Fernando Gabriel Cáceres (1/0), Julio César Saldaña (1/0), Diego Sebastián Cagna (4/0) [75.Alejandro Víctor Mancuso (1/0)], José Luis Villareal (4/0), Alberto José Márcico (17/0), Néstor Raúl Gorosito (7/0) [*sent off 74*], Ramón Ismael Medina Bello (5/0), Alberto Federico Acosta (3/0). Trainer: Alfio Oscar Basile (18).

**641.** 16.10.1992 **ARGENTINA – IVORY COAST** **4-0(2-0)** King Fahd Cup
„King Fahd" International Stadium, Riyadh (Saudi Arabia); Referee: Jamal Al-Sharif (Syria); Attendance: 15,000
**ARG:** Sergio Javier Goycochea (24/0), Sergio Fabián Vázquez (16/0), Ricardo Daniel Altamirano (7/1), Fabián Armando Basualdo (17/0), Oscar Alfredo Ruggeri (72/5), Fernando Carlos Redondo (2/0), José Luis Villareal (5/0) [75.Diego Sebastián Cagna (5/0)], Diego Pablo Simeone (16/3), Leonardo Adrián Rodríguez (10/0) [67.Alberto Federico Acosta (4/1)], Claudio Paul Caniggia (36/11), Gabriel Omar Batistuta (11/12). Trainer: Alfio Oscar Basile (19).
**Goals**: Gabriel Omar Batistuta (2, 10), Ricardo Daniel Altamirano (67), Alberto Federico Acosta (81).

**642.** 20.10.1992 **SAUDI ARABIA - ARGENTINA** **1-3(0-2)** King Fahd Cup
„King Fahd" International Stadium, Riyadh; Referee: An-Yan Lim Kee Chong (Mauritius); Attendance: 75,000
**ARG:** Sergio Javier Goycochea (25/0), Sergio Fabián Vázquez (17/0), Ricardo Daniel Altamirano (8/1), Fabián Armando Basualdo (18/0), Oscar Alfredo Ruggeri (73/5), Fernando Carlos Redondo (3/0), José Luis Villareal (6/0) [81.Diego Sebastián Cagna (6/0)], Diego Pablo Simeone (17/4), Leonardo Adrián Rodríguez (11/1) [73.Alberto Federico Acosta (5/1)], Claudio Paul Caniggia (37/12), Gabriel Omar Batistuta (12/12). Trainer: Alfio Oscar Basile (20).
**Goals**: Leonardo Adrián Rodríguez (18), Claudio Paul Caniggia (24), Diego Pablo Simeone (64).

**643.** 26.11.1992 **ARGENTINA - POLAND** **2-0(1-0)**
Estadio „Alberto Armando", Buenos Aires; Referee: Renato Marsiglia (Brazil); Attendance: 35,000
**ARG:** Luis Alberto Islas (22/0), Néstor Oscar Craviotto (8/2), Oscar Alfredo Ruggeri (Cap) (74/5), Sergio Fabián Vázquez (18/0), Ricardo Daniel Altamirano (9/1), José Luis Villareal (7/0) [78.Néstor Raúl Gorosito (8/0)], Fernando Carlos Redondo (4/0), Diego Pablo Simeone (18/4), Leonardo Adrián Rodríguez (12/1) [78.Diego Sebastián Cagna (7/0)], Ramón Ismael Medina Bello (6/1) [78.Julio Alberto Zamora (1/0)], Alberto Federico Acosta (6/1). Trainer: Alfio Oscar Basile (21).
**Goals**: Néstor Oscar Craviotto (22), Ramón Ismael Medina Bello (64).

**644.** 18.02.1993 **ARGENTINA - BRAZIL** **1-1(1-0)** Copa Centenario AFA
Estadio Monumental „Antonio Vespucio Liberti", Buenos Aires; Referee: Ernesto Filippi Cavani (Uruguay); Attendance: 65,000
**ARG:** Luis Alberto Islas (23/0), Fabián Armando Basualdo (19/0), Sergio Fabián Vázquez (19/0), Oscar Alfredo Ruggeri (75/5) [*sent off 75*], Ricardo Daniel Altamirano (10/1), Darío Javier Franco (17/6) [64.Gustavo Miguel Zapata (5/0)], Alejandro Víctor Mancuso (2/1), Diego Pablo Simeone (19/4), Diego Armando Maradona (79/30), Gabriel Omar Batistuta (13/12), Claudio Paul Caniggia (38/12) [81.Alberto Federico Acosta (7/1)]. Trainer: Alfio Oscar Basile (22).
**Goal**: Alejandro Víctor Mancuso (16).

**645.** 24.02.1993 **ARGENTINA - DENMARK** **1-1(1-1,1-1); 5-4 on penalties** Copa Artemio Franchi
Estadio „José María Minella", Mar del Plata; Referee: Sándor Puhl (Hungary); Attendance: 34,683
**ARG:** Sergio Javier Goycochea (26/0), Néstor Oscar Craviotto (9/2) [113.Julio César Saldaña (2/0)], Jorge Horacio Borelli (1/0), Sergio Fabián Vázquez (20/0), Ricardo Daniel Altamirano (11/1), Diego Pablo Simeone (20/4), Alejandro Víctor Mancuso (3/1), Leonardo Adrián Rodríguez (13/1) [60.Darío Javier Franco (18/6)], Diego Armando Maradona (80/30), Claudio Paul Caniggia (39/13), Gabriel Omar Batistuta (14/12). Trainer: Alfio Oscar Basile (23).
**Goal**: Claudio Paul Caniggia (30 penalty).
**Penalties**: Diego Armando Maradona, Gabriel Omar Batistuta, Diego Pablo Simeone, Alejandro Víctor Mancuso, Claudio Paul Caniggia [save], Julio César Saldaña.

**646.** 17.06.1993 **ARGENTINA - BOLIVIA** **1-0(0-0)** 36th Copa América. Group Stage.
Estadio Nuevo de Mayo, Machala (Ecuador); Referee: Arturo A. Angeles (United States); Attendance: 16,000
**ARG:** Sergio Javier Goycochea (27/0), Néstor Oscar Craviotto (10/2), Oscar Alfredo Ruggeri (Cap) (76/5), Sergio Fabián Vázquez (21/0), Ricardo Daniel Altamirano (12/1), Darío Javier Franco (19/6) [32.Gustavo Miguel Zapata (6/0)], Fernando Carlos Redondo (5/0), Leonardo Adrián Rodríguez (14/1) [63.Néstor Raúl Gorosito (9/0)], Claudio Omar García (8/2), Gabriel Omar Batistuta (15/13), Alberto Federico Acosta (8/1). Trainer: Alfio Oscar Basile (24).
**Goal**: Gabriel Omar Batistuta (53).

**647.** 20.06.1993 **ARGENTINA - MEXICO** **1-1(1-1)** 36th Copa América. Group Stage.
Estadio „George Capwell", Guayaquil (Ecuador); Referee: Juan Francisco Escobar Váldez (Paraguay); Attendance: 16,000
**ARG:** Sergio Javier Goycochea (28/0), Fabián Armando Basualdo (20/0), Sergio Fabián Vázquez (22/0), Oscar Alfredo Ruggeri (Cap) (77/6), Néstor Oscar Craviotto (11/2), Fernando Carlos Redondo (6/0) [81.Néstor Raúl Gorosito (10/0)], Gustavo Miguel Zapata (7/0), Leonardo Adrián Rodríguez (15/1) [56.Alejandro Víctor Mancuso (4/1)], Diego Pablo Simeone (21/4), Claudio Omar García (9/2), Gabriel Omar Batistuta (16/13). Trainer: Alfio Oscar Basile (25).
**Goals**: Oscar Alfredo Ruggeri (28).

**648.** 23.06.1993 **ARGENTINA - COLOMBIA** **1-1(1-1)** 36th Copa América. Group Stage.
Estadio Monumental, Guayaquil (Ecuador); Referee: Márcio Rezende de Freitas (Brazil); Attendance: 45,000
**ARG:** Sergio Javier Goycochea (29/0), Fabián Armando Basualdo (21/0), Oscar Alfredo Ruggeri (78/6), Jorge Horacio Borelli (2/0), Ricardo Daniel Altamirano (13/1), Gustavo Miguel Zapata (8/0), Diego Pablo Simeone (22/5), Fernando Carlos Redondo (7/0) [*sent off 49*], Leonardo Adrián Rodríguez (16/1) [67.Néstor Raúl Gorosito (11/0)], Gabriel Omar Batistuta (17/13) [77.Alberto Federico Acosta (9/1)], Ramón Ismael Medina Bello (7/1). Trainer: Alfio Oscar Basile (26).
**Goal**: Diego Pablo Simeone (2).

**649.** 27.06.1993 **ARGENTINA - BRAZIL** **1-1(0-1,1-1); 6-5 on penalties** 36th Copa América. Quarter-Finals.
Estadio Monumental, Guayaquil (Ecuador); Referee: Alberto Tejada Noriega (Peru); Attendance: 25,000
**ARG:** Sergio Javier Goycochea (30/0), Fabián Armando Basualdo (22/0), Oscar Alfredo Ruggeri (Cap) (79/6), Jorge Horacio Borelli (3/0), Ricardo Daniel Altamirano (14/1), Gustavo Miguel Zapata (9/0), Diego Pablo Simeone (23/5), José Horacio Basualdo (23/0) [54.Leonardo Adrián Rodríguez (17/2)], Néstor Raúl Gorosito (12/0), Gabriel Omar Batistuta (18/13) [62.Alberto Federico Acosta (10/1)], Ramón Ismael Medina Bello (8/1). Trainer: Alfio Oscar Basile (27).
**Goal**: Leonardo Adrián Rodríguez (69).
**Penalties**: Néstor Raúl Gorosito, Diego Pablo Simeone, Leonardo Adrián Rodríguez, Alberto Federico Acosta, Ramón Ismael Medina Bello, Jorge Horacio Borelli.

**650.** 01.07.1993 **ARGENTINA - COLOMBIA** **0-0; 6-5 penalties** 36th Copa América. Semi-Finals.
Estadio Monumental, Guayaquil (Ecuador); Referee: Jorge Luis Nieves Parra (Uruguay); Attendance: 15,000
**ARG:** Sergio Javier Goycochea (31/0), Fabián Armando Basualdo (23/0), Oscar Alfredo Ruggeri (Cap) (80/6) [46.Fernando Gabriel Cáceres (2/0)], Jorge Horacio Borelli (4/0), Ricardo Daniel Altamirano (15/1), Gustavo Miguel Zapata (10/0) [69.Leonardo Adrián Rodríguez (18/2)], Diego Pablo Simeone (24/5), Fernando Carlos Redondo (8/0), Néstor Raúl Gorosito (13/0), Gabriel Omar Batistuta (19/13), Alberto Federico Acosta (11/1). Trainer: Alfio Oscar Basile (28).
**Penalties**: Néstor Raúl Gorosito, Gabriel Omar Batistuta, Diego Pablo Simeone, Leonardo Adrián Rodríguez, Alberto Federico Acosta, Jorge Horacio Borelli.

**651.** 04.07.1993 **ARGENTINA - MEXICO** **2-1(0-0)** 36th Copa América. Final.
Estadio Monumental, Guayaquil (Ecuador); Referee: Márcio Rezende de Freitas (Brazil); Attendance: 40,000
**ARG:** Sergio Javier Goycochea (32/0), Fabián Armando Basualdo (24/0), Jorge Horacio Borelli (5/0), Oscar Alfredo Ruggeri (Cap) (81/6) [40.Fernando Gabriel Cáceres (3/0)], Ricardo Daniel Altamirano (16/1), Diego Pablo Simeone (25/5), Gustavo Miguel Zapata (11/0), Fernando Carlos Redondo (9/0), Néstor Raúl Gorosito (14/0) [64.Leonardo Adrián Rodríguez (19/2)], Alberto Federico Acosta (12/1), Gabriel Omar Batistuta (20/15). Trainer: Alfio Oscar Basile (29).
**Goals**: Gabriel Omar Batistuta (63, 74).

**652.** 01.08.1993 **PERU - ARGENTINA** **0-1(0-1)** 15th FIFA WC. Qualifiers.
Estadio Nacional, Lima; Referee: Enrique Marín Gallo (Chile); Attendance: 27,000
**ARG:** Sergio Javier Goycochea (33/0), Jorge Horacio Borelli (6/0), Fabián Armando Basualdo (25/0), Ricardo Daniel Altamirano (17/1), Oscar Alfredo Ruggeri (82/6), Gustavo Miguel Zapata (12/0), Leonardo Adrián Rodríguez (20/2) [61.José Horacio Basualdo (24/0)], Diego Pablo Simeone (26/5), Fernando Carlos Redondo (10/0), Gabriel Omar Batistuta (21/16), Alberto Federico Acosta (13/1) [77.Claudio Omar García (10/2)]. Trainer: Alfio Oscar Basile (30).
**Goal**: Gabriel Omar Batistuta (29).

**653.** 08.08.1993 **PARAGUAY - ARGENTINA** **1-3(1-1)** 15th FIFA WC. Qualifiers

Estadio Defensores del Chaco, Asunción; Referee: Ernesto Filippi Cavani (Uruguay); Attendance: 46,500

**ARG:** Sergio Javier Goycochea (34/0), Fabián Armando Basualdo (26/0), Jorge Horacio Borelli (7/0), Oscar Alfredo Ruggeri (83/6) [*sent off 43*], Ricardo Daniel Altamirano (18/1), José Luis Villareal (8/0) [46.José Horacio Basualdo (25/0)], Fernando Carlos Redondo (11/1), Leonardo Adrián Rodríguez (21/2) [46.Fernando Gabriel Cáceres (4/0)], Diego Pablo Simeone (27/5), Gabriel Omar Batistuta (22/16) [*sent off 27*], Ramón Ismael Medina Bello (9/3). Trainer: Alfio Oscar Basile (31).

**Goals**: Ramón Ismael Medina Bello (15), Fernando Carlos Redondo (65), Ramón Ismael Medina Bello (78).

**654.** 15.08.1993 **COLOMBIA - ARGENTINA** **2-1(1-0)** 15th FIFA WC. Qualifiers

Estadio Metropolitano „Roberto Meléndez", Barranquilla; Referee: José Aparecido de Oliveira (Brazil); Attendance: 60,000

**ARG:** Sergio Javier Goycochea (35/0), Fabián Armando Basualdo (27/0), Jorge Horacio Borelli (8/0), Fernando Gabriel Cáceres (5/0), Ricardo Daniel Altamirano (19/1), Fernando Carlos Redondo (12/1), Gustavo Miguel Zapata (13/0), José Horacio Basualdo (26/0) [46.Julio Alberto Zamora (2/0)], Diego Pablo Simeone (28/5) [*sent off 77*], Alberto Federico Acosta (14/1) [82.Leonardo Adrián Rodríguez (22/2)], Ramón Ismael Medina Bello (10/4). Trainer: Alfio Oscar Basile (32).

**Goal**: Ramón Ismael Medina Bello (87).

**655.** 22.08.1993 **ARGENTINA - PERU** **2-1(2-0)** 15th FIFA WC. Qualifiers

Estadio Monumental „Antonio Vespucio Liberti", Buenos Aires; Referee: Jorge Luis Nieves Parra (Uruguay); Attendance: 60,000

**ARG:** Sergio Javier Goycochea (36/0), Jorge Horacio Borelli (9/0), Néstor Oscar Craviotto (12/2), Oscar Alfredo Ruggeri (84/6), Fernando Gabriel Cáceres (6/0) [72.Ricardo Daniel Altamirano (20/1)], Gustavo Miguel Zapata (14/0), Fernando Carlos Redondo (13/1), Néstor Raúl Gorosito (15/0), Leonardo Adrián Rodríguez (23/2) [71.José Horacio Basualdo (27/0)], Gabriel Omar Batistuta (23/17), Ramón Ismael Medina Bello (11/5). Trainer: Alfio Oscar Basile (33).

**Goals**: Gabriel Omar Batistuta (32), Ramón Ismael Medina Bello (37).

**656.** 29.08.1993 **ARGENTINA - PARAGUAY** **0-0** 15th FIFA WC. Qualifiers

Estadio Monumental „Antonio Vespucio Liberti", Buenos Aires; Referee: Jorge Orellana (Ecuador); Attendance: 47,000

**ARG:** Sergio Javier Goycochea (37/0), Fabián Armando Basualdo (28/0), Jorge Horacio Borelli (10/0), Oscar Alfredo Ruggeri (85/6), Ricardo Daniel Altamirano (21/1), Fernando Carlos Redondo (14/1) [63.Leonardo Adrián Rodríguez (24/2)], Gustavo Miguel Zapata (15/0), Néstor Raúl Gorosito (16/0) [71.Julio Alberto Zamora (3/0)], Diego Pablo Simeone (29/5), Gabriel Omar Batistuta (24/17), Ramón Ismael Medina Bello (12/5). Trainer: Alfio Oscar Basile (34).

**657.** 05.09.1993 **ARGENTINA - COLOMBIA** **0-5(0-1)** 15th FIFA WC. Qualifiers

Estadio Monumental „Antonio Vespucio Liberti", Buenos Aires; Referee: Ernesto Filippi Cavani (Uruguay); Attendance: 53,000

**ARG:** Sergio Javier Goycochea (38/0), Julio César Saldaña (3/0), Oscar Alfredo Ruggeri (86/6), Jorge Horacio Borelli (11/0), Ricardo Daniel Altamirano (22/1), Leonardo Adrián Rodríguez (25/2) [53.Claudio Omar García (11/2)], Diego Pablo Simeone (30/5), Fernando Carlos Redondo (15/1) [70.Alberto Federico Acosta (15/1)], Gustavo Miguel Zapata (16/0), Gabriel Omar Batistuta (25/17), Ramón Ismael Medina Bello (13/5). Trainer: Alfio Oscar Basile (35).

**658.** 31.10.1993 **AUSTRALIA - ARGENTINA** **1-1(1-1)** 15th FIFA WC.Qual. (Play-offs)

Sydney Football Stadium, Sydney; Referee: Sándor Puhl (Hungary); Attendance: 43,967

**ARG:** Sergio Javier Goycochea (39/0), Jorge Horacio Borelli (12/0), Sergio Fabián Vázquez (23/0), José Antonio Chamot (1/0), Carlos Javier MacAllister (1/0), Hugo Leonardo Pérez (1/0), Fernando Carlos Redondo (16/1), José Horacio Basualdo (28/0) [70.Gustavo Miguel Zapata (17/0)], Diego Armando Maradona (81/30), Gabriel Omar Batistuta (26/17), Abel Eduardo Balbo (11/2) [89.Fernando Gabriel Cáceres (7/0)]. Trainer: Alfio Oscar Basile (36).

**Goal**: Abel Eduardo Balbo (37).

**659.** 17.11.1993 **ARGENTINA - AUSTRALIA** **1-0(0-0)** 15th FIFA WC.Qual. (Play-offs)

Estadio Monumental „Antonio Vespucio Liberti", Buenos Aires; Referee: Peter Mikkelsen (Denmark); Attendance: 59,768

**ARG:** Sergio Javier Goycochea (40/0), José Antonio Chamot (2/0), Sergio Fabián Vázquez (24/0), Oscar Alfredo Ruggeri (87/6), Carlos Javier MacAllister (2/0), Hugo Leonardo Pérez (2/0), Fernando Carlos Redondo (17/1), Diego Pablo Simeone (31/5), Diego Armando Maradona (Cap) (82/30), Gabriel Omar Batistuta (27/18), Abel Eduardo Balbo (12/2) [70.Gustavo Miguel Zapata (18/0)]. Trainer: Alfio Oscar Basile (37).

**Goal**: Gabriel Omar Batistuta (59).

**660.** 15.12.1993 **ARGENTINA - GERMANY** **2-1(1-1)**

Orange Bowl, Miami (United States); Referee: Philip Don (England); Attendance: 35,221

**ARG:** Sergio Javier Goycochea (41/0), Hernán Edgardo Díaz (16/3), Sergio Fabián Vázquez (25/0) [87.Jorge Horacio Borelli (13/0)], Oscar Alfredo Ruggeri (88/6), Carlos Javier MacAllister (3/0), Hugo Leonardo Pérez (3/0), Alejandro Víctor Mancuso (5/1), Leonardo Adrián Rodríguez (26/2) [89.Roberto Carlos Monserrat (1/0)], Diego Sebastián Cagna (8/0), Abel Eduardo Balbo (13/3), Ramón Ismael Medina Bello (14/5) [90.Ariel Arnaldo Ortega (1/0)]. Trainer: Alfio Oscar Basile (38).

**Goals**: Hernán Edgardo Díaz (5), Abel Eduardo Balbo (65).

**661.** 23.03.1994 **BRAZIL - ARGENTINA** **2-0(1-0)**

Estádio Arruda, Recife; Referee: Wilson Souza Mendonça (Brazil); Attendance: 85,000

**ARG:** Sergio Javier Goycochea (42/0), Hernán Edgardo Díaz (17/3), Sergio Fabián Vázquez (26/0), Fernando Gabriel Cáceres (8/0), José Antonio Chamot (3/0), Fernando Carlos Redondo (18/1), Diego Pablo Simeone (32/5), Diego Sebastián Cagna (9/0) [61.Roberto Carlos Monserrat (2/0)], Leonardo Adrián Rodríguez (27/2) [77.Ariel Arnaldo Ortega (2/0)], Claudio Omar García (12/2), Gabriel Omar Batistuta (28/18). Trainer: Alfio Oscar Basile (39).

**662.** 20.04.1994 **ARGENTINA - MOROCCO** **3-1(1-0)** Copa Salta

Estadio Gimnasia y Tiro, Salta; Referee: Oscar Velásquez Alvarenga (Paraguay); Attendance: 35,000

**ARG:** Luis Alberto Islas (24/0), José Antonio Chamot (4/0), Oscar Alfredo Ruggeri (89/6), Hernán Edgardo Díaz (18/3), Sergio Fabián Vázquez (27/0) [31.Juan José Borrelli (1/0)], Alejandro Víctor Mancuso (6/1), Diego Pablo Simeone (33/5), Diego Sebastián Cagna (10/0) [46.Hugo Leonardo Pérez (4/1)], Diego Armando Maradona (83/31) [75.Ariel Arnaldo Ortega (3/0)], Abel Eduardo Balbo (14/4), Gabriel Omar Batistuta (29/18) [86.Roberto Carlos Monserrat (3/0)]. Trainer: Alfio Oscar Basile (40).

**Goals**: Abel Eduardo Balbo (13), Diego Armando Maradona (55 penalty), Hugo Leonardo Pérez (81).

**663.** 18.05.1994 **CHILE - ARGENTINA** **3-3(1-1)**

Estadio Nacional, Santiago; Referee: Eduardo Dluzniewski Takoz (Uruguay); Attendance: 51,193

**ARG:** Luis Alberto Islas (25/0), Roberto Néstor Sensini (19/0), Jorge Horacio Borelli (15/0), Oscar Alfredo Ruggeri (90/7), José Antonio Chamot (5/1), Diego Pablo Simeone (34/5), José Horacio Basualdo (29/0) [46.Hugo Leonardo Pérez (5/1)], Alejandro Víctor Mancuso (7/1) [46.Fernando Carlos Redondo (19/1)], Diego Armando Maradona (84/31) [87.Darío Javier Franco (20/6)], Gabriel Omar Batistuta (30/18) [77.Ramón Ismael Medina Bello (15/5)], Abel Eduardo Balbo (15/5). Trainer: Alfio Oscar Basile (41).

**Goals**: José Antonio Chamot (9), Abel Eduardo Balbo (68), Oscar Alfredo Ruggeri (82).

**664.** 25.05.1994 **ECUADOR - ARGENTINA** **1-0(0-0)**
Estadio Monumental, Guayaquil; Referee: Jorge Orellana (Ecuador); Attendance: 35,000
**ARG:** Sergio Javier Goycochea (43/0), José Antonio Chamot (6/1), Roberto Néstor Sensini (20/0), Oscar Alfredo Ruggeri (91/7), Sergio Fabián Vázquez (28/0), Diego Armando Maradona (85/31), Darío Javier Franco (21/6) [66.Leonardo Adrián Rodríguez (28/2)], Fernando Carlos Redondo (20/1), Diego Pablo Simeone (35/5), Abel Eduardo Balbo (16/5) [72.Gabriel Omar Batistuta (31/18)], Claudio Paul Caniggia (40/13). Trainer: Alfio Oscar Basile (42).

**665.** 31.05.1994 **ISRAEL - ARGENTINA** **0-3(0-1)**
National Stadium, Ramat-Gan, Tel Aviv; Referee: Loizos Loizou (Cyprus); Attendance: 35,000
**ARG:** Luis Alberto Islas (26/0), Roberto Néstor Sensini (21/0), Sergio Fabián Vázquez (29/0), Oscar Alfredo Ruggeri (92/7), José Antonio Chamot (7/1), Fernando Carlos Redondo (21/1), Diego Pablo Simeone (36/5), Diego Armando Maradona (86/31) [78.Darío Javier Franco (22/6)], Claudio Paul Caniggia (41/14) [81.Ariel Arnaldo Ortega (4/0)], Abel Eduardo Balbo (17/5), Gabriel Omar Batistuta (32/20). Trainer: Alfio Oscar Basile (43).
**Goals**: Gabriel Omar Batistuta (27, 49), Claudio Paul Caniggia (53).

**666.** 04.06.1994 **CROATIA - ARGENTINA** **0-0**
Maksimir Stadion, Zagreb; Referee: Gerd Grabher (Austria); Attendance: 40,000
**ARG:** Sergio Javier Goycochea (44/0), Sergio Fabián Vázquez (30/0) [87.Fernando Gabriel Cáceres (9/0)], José Antonio Chamot (8/1), Roberto Néstor Sensini (22/0), Fernando Carlos Redondo (22/1), Oscar Alfredo Ruggeri (93/7), Claudio Paul Caniggia (42/14) [83.Ariel Arnaldo Ortega (5/0)], Diego Pablo Simeone (37/5), Gabriel Omar Batistuta (33/20), Diego Armando Maradona (87/31), Abel Eduardo Balbo (18/5) [70.Alejandro Víctor Mancuso (8/1)]. Trainer: Alfio Oscar Basile (44).

**667.** 21.06.1994 **ARGENTINA - GREECE** **4-0(2-0)** 15th FIFA WC. Group Stage.
Foxboro Stadium, Boston (United States); Referee: Arturo A. Angeles (United States); Attendance: 53,644
**ARG:** Luis Alberto Islas (27/0), Roberto Nestor Sensini (23/0), Fernando Gabriel Cáceres (10/0), Oscar Alfredo Ruggeri (94/7), José Antonio Chamot (9/1), Diego Pablo Simeone (38/5), Fernando Carlos Redondo (23/1), Diego Armando Maradona (Cap) (88/32) [83.Ariel Arnaldo Ortega (6/0)], Abel Eduardo Balbo (19/5) [79.Alejandro Víctor Mancuso (9/1)], Claudio Paul Caniggia (43/14), Gabriel Omar Batistuta (34/23). Trainer: Alfio Oscar Basile (45).
**Goals**: Gabriel Omar Batistuta (2, 45), Diego Armando Maradona (60), Gabriel Omar Batistuta (90 penalty).

**668.** 25.06.1994 **ARGENTINA - NIGERIA** **2-1(2-1)** 15th FIFA WC. Group Stage.
Foxboro Stadium, Boston (United States); Referee: Bo Karlsson (Sweden); Attendance: 54,453
**ARG:** Luis Alberto Islas (28/0), Roberto Néstor Sensini (24/0) [87.Hernán Edgardo Díaz (19/3)], Fernando Gabriel Cáceres (11/0), Oscar Alfredo Ruggeri (95/7), José Antonio Chamot (10/1), Diego Pablo Simeone (39/5), Fernando Carlos Redondo (24/1), Diego Armando Maradona (Cap) (89/32), Abel Eduardo Balbo (20/5) [71.Alejandro Víctor Mancuso (10/1)], Claudio Paul Caniggia (44/16), Gabriel Omar Batistuta (35/23). Trainer: Alfio Oscar Basile (46).
**Goals**: Claudio Paul Caniggia (22, 29).

**669.** 30.06.1994 **BULGARIA - ARGENTINA** **2-0(0-0)** 15th FIFA WC. Group Stage.
Cotton Bowl, Dallas (United States); Referee: Neji Jouini (Tunisia); Attendance: 63,998
**ARG:** Luis Alberto Islas (29/0), Hernán Edgardo Díaz (20/3), Fernando Gabriel Cáceres (12/0), Oscar Alfredo Ruggeri (Cap) (96/7), José Antonio Chamot (11/1), Diego Pablo Simeone (40/5), Fernando Carlos Redondo (25/1), Abel Eduardo Balbo (21/5), Leonardo Adrián Rodríguez (29/2) [67.Ramón Ismael Medina Bello (16/5)], Claudio Paul Caniggia (45/16) [26.Ariel Arnaldo Ortega (7/0)], Gabriel Omar Batistuta (36/23). Trainer: Alfio Oscar Basile (47).

**670.** 03.07.1994 **ROMANIA - ARGENTINA** **3-2(2-1)** 15th FIFA WC. 2nd Round.
Memorial Coliseum, Los Angeles (United States); Referee: Pierluigi Pairetto (Italy); Attendance: 90,469
**ARG:** Luis Alberto Islas (30/0), Roberto Néstor Sensini (25/0) [62.Ramón Ismael Medina Bello (17/5)], Fernando Gabriel Cáceres (13/0), Oscar Alfredo Ruggeri (Cap) (97/7), José Antonio Chamot (12/1), Ariel Arnaldo Ortega (8/0), José Horacio Basualdo (30/0), Diego Pablo Simeone (41/5), Fernando Carlos Redondo (26/1), Abel Eduardo Balbo (22/6), Gabriel Omar Batistuta (37/24). Trainer: Alfio Oscar Basile (48).
**Goals**: Gabriel Omar Batistuta (15 penalty), Abel Eduardo Balbo (73).

**671.** 16.11.1994 **CHILE - ARGENTINA** **0-3(0-2)**
Estadio Nacional, Santiago; Referee: José Joaquín Torres Cadena (Colombia); Attendance: 21,842
**ARG:** Carlos Gustavo Bossio (1/0), Javier Adelmar Zanetti (1/0), Roberto Fabián Ayala (1/0), Néstor Ariel Fabbri (8/0), Rodolfo Martín Arruabarrena (1/0), Marcelo Alejandro Escudero (1/1) [81.Nelson David Vivas (1/0)], Hugo Leonardo Pérez (6/1), Cristián Gustavo Bassedas (1/0), Marcelo Fabián Espina (1/1) [86.Marcelo Daniel Gallardo (1/0)], Ariel Arnaldo Ortega (9/0) [80.Luis Alberto Carranza (1/0)], Sebastián Pascual Rambert (1/1) [85.José Oscar Flores (1/0)]. Trainer: Daniel Alberto Passarella (1).
**Goals**: Sebastián Pascual Rambert (5), Marcelo Fabián Espina (23), Marcelo Alejandro Escudero (79).

**672.** 21.12.1994 **ARGENTINA – ROMANIA LEAGUE XI** **1-0(0-0)**
Estadio „José Amalfitani", Buenos Aires; Referee: Iván Enrique Guerrero Levancini (Chile); Attendance: 35,000
**ARG:** Carlos Gustavo Bossio (2/0), Javier Adelmar Zanetti (2/0), Roberto Fabián Ayala (2/0), Néstor Ariel Fabbri (9/0), Rodolfo Martín Arruabarrena (2/0), Marcelo Alejandro Escudero (2/1) [67.José Oscar Flores (2/0)], Hugo Leonardo Pérez (7/2), Cristián Gustavo Bassedas (2/0), Marcelo Fabián Espina (2/1) [67.Gustavo Adrián López (1/0)], Ariel Arnaldo Ortega (10/0) [82.Marcelo Daniel Gallardo (2/0)], Sebastián Pascual Rambert (2/1). Trainer: Daniel Alberto Passarella (2).
**Goal**: Hugo Leonardo Pérez (77).

**673.** 27.12.1994 **ARGENTINA - YUGOSLAVIA** **1-0(1-0)**
Estadio Monumental „Antonio Vespucio Liberti", Buenos Aires; Referee: Jorge Luis Nieves Parra (Uruguay); Attendance: 20,000
**ARG:** Carlos Gustavo Bossio (3/0), Javier Adelmar Zanetti (3/0), Roberto Fabián Ayala (3/0), Néstor Ariel Fabbri (10/0), Rodolfo Martín Arruabarrena (3/0), Marcelo Alejandro Escudero (3/1), Hugo Leonardo Pérez (8/2), Cristián Gustavo Bassedas (3/0), Marcelo Fabián Espina (3/1) [68.Gustavo Adrián López (2/0)], Ariel Arnaldo Ortega (11/1), Sebastián Pascual Rambert (3/1). Trainer: Daniel Alberto Passarella (3).
**Goal**: Ariel Arnaldo Ortega (21).

**674.** 08.01.1995 **ARGENTINA - JAPAN** **5-1(2-0)** King Fahd Cup
„King Fahd" International Stadium, Riyadh (Saudi Arabia); Referee: Rodrigo Badilla Sequeira (Costa Rica); Attendance: 10,000
**ARG:** Carlos Gustavo Bossio (4/0), Javier Adelmar Zanetti (4/0), Néstor Ariel Fabbri (11/0), Roberto Fabián Ayala (Cap) (4/0), José Antonio Chamot (13/2), Hugo Leonardo Pérez (9/2), Ariel Arnaldo Ortega (12/2) [67.Marcelo Daniel Gallardo (3/0)], Marcelo Alejandro Escudero (4/1) [55.Gustavo Adrián López (3/0)], Gabriel Omar Batistuta (38/26), Sebastián Pascual Rambert (4/2), Cristián Gustavo Bassedas (4/0). Trainer: Daniel Alberto Passarella (4).
**Goals**: Sebastián Pascual Rambert (31), Ariel Arnaldo Ortega (45), Gabriel Omar Batistuta (47), José Antonio Chamot (54), Gabriel Omar Batistuta (86 penalty).

**675.** 10.01.1995 **ARGENTINA - NIGERIA** **0-0** King Fahd Cup

„King Fahd" International Stadium, Riyadh (Saudi Arabia); Referee: Ali Mohammed Bujsaim (United Arab Emirates); Attendance: 20,000

**ARG:** Carlos Gustavo Bossio (5/0), Javier Adelmar Zanetti (5/0), Néstor Ariel Fabbri (12/0), Roberto Fabián Ayala (Cap) (5/0), José Antonio Chamot (14/2), Hugo Leonardo Pérez (10/2), Ariel Arnaldo Ortega (13/2), Marcelo Alejandro Escudero (5/1), Gabriel Omar Batistuta (39/26), Sebastián Pascual Rambert (5/2), Cristián Gustavo Bassedas (5/0). Trainer: Daniel Alberto Passarella (5).

**676.** 13.01.1995 **DENMARK - ARGENTINA** **2-0(1-0)** King Fahd Cup

„King Fahd" International Stadium, Riyadh (Saudi Arabia); Referee: Ali Mohammed Bujsaim (United Arab Emirates); Attendance: 35,000

**ARG:** Claudio Gustavo Bossio (6/0), Javier Adelmar Zanetti (6/0), Néstor Ariel Fabbri (13/0), Roberto Fabián Ayala (Cap) (6/0), José Antonio Chamot (15/2), Jorge Rubén Jiménez (1/0) [65.Gustavo Adrián López (4/0)], Marcelo Alejandro Escudero (6/1), Ariel Arnaldo Ortega (14/2), Gabriel Omar Batistuta (40/26), Sebastián Pascual Rambert (6/2) [75.Marcelo Fabián Espina (4/1)], Cristián Gustavo Bassedas (6/0). Trainer: Daniel Alberto Passarella (6).

**677.** 14.02.1995 **ARGENTINA - BULGARIA** **4-1(2-0)**

Estadio Malvinas Argentinas, Mendoza; Referee: Eduardo Gamboa Martínez (Chile); Attendance: 42,615

**ARG:** Carlos Gustavo Bossio (7/0), Javier Adelmar Zanetti (7/0), Pablo Oscar Rotchen (1/0), Roberto Fabián Ayala (7/0), Rodolfo Martín Arruabarrena (4/0) [72.Juan Pablo Sorín (1/0)], Cristián Gustavo Bassedas (7/0), Marcelo Daniel Gallardo (4/2) [60.Daniel Oscar Garnero (1/0)], Jorge Rubén Jiménez (2/0), Roberto Carlos Monserrat (4/0), Ariel Arnaldo Ortega (15/2) [66.Guillermo Gustavo Barros Schelotto (1/0)], Sebastián Pascual Rambert (7/4) [66.Hernán Jorge Crespo (1/0)]. Trainer: Daniel Alberto Passarella (7).

**Goals**: Marcelo Daniel Gallardo (33 penalty,36 penalty), Sebastián Pascual Rambert (55, 65).

**678.** 13.05.1995 **SOUTH AFRICA - ARGENTINA** **1-1(1-0)** Nelson Mandela Cup

Ellis Park, Johannesburg; Referee: Philip Don (England); Attendance: 50,000

**ARG:** Carlos Gustavo Bossio (8/0), Nelson David Vivas (2/0) [46.Cristián Gustavo Bassedas (8/0)], Roberto Fabián Ayala (8/0), Néstor Ariel Fabbri (14/0), Juan Pablo Sorín (2/0) [68.Claudio Javier López (1/0)], Leonardo Rubén Astrada (14/1), Sergio Ángel Berti (4/0), Marcelo Daniel Gallardo (5/3), Javier Adelmar Zanetti (8/0), Omar Andrés Asad (1/0) [88.Gabriel Francisco Schurrer (1/0)], Ariel Arnaldo Ortega (16/2). Trainer: Daniel Alberto Passarella (8).

**Goal**: Marcelo Daniel Gallardo (80 penalty).

**679.** 31.05.1995 **ARGENTINA - PERU** **1-0(1-0)** Copa de Municipalidad Córdoba

Estadio Olímpico, Córdoba; Referee: Daniel Bello Rotunno (Uruguay); Attendance: 15,000

**ARG:** Germán Adrián Ramón Burgos (1/0), Javier Adelmar Zanetti (9/0), Roberto Fabián Ayala (9/0) [42.Juan Pablo Sorín (3/0)], Néstor Ariel Fabbri (15/1), Gabriel Francisco Schurrer (2/0), Leonardo Rubén Astrada (15/1), Marcelo Daniel Gallardo (6/3), Cristián Gustavo Bassedas (9/0) [59.Marcelo Alejandro Escudero (7/1)], Sergio Ángel Berti (5/0) [74.Omar Andrés Asad (2/0)], Ariel Arnaldo Ortega (17/2), Claudio Javier López (2/0). Trainer: Daniel Alberto Passarella (9).

**Goal**: Néstor Ariel Fabbri (23).

**680.** 14.06.1995 **ARGENTINA - PARAGUAY** **2-1(1-1)**

Estadio Cordiviola (Central), Rosario; Referee: Carlos Manuel Robles Mella (Chile); Attendance: 14,000

**ARG:** Germán Adrián Ramón Burgos (2/0), Javier Adelmar Zanetti (10/0), Ricardo Daniel Altamirano (23/1), Néstor Ariel Fabbri (16/1) [36.Fernando Gabriel Cáceres (14/0)], Gabriel Francisco Schurrer (3/0), Sergio Ángel Berti (6/1), Marcelo Alejandro Escudero (8/1) [78.Cristián Gustavo Bassedas (10/0)], Marcelo Daniel Gallardo (7/3), Marcelo Adrián Gómez (1/0) [62.Leonardo Rubén Astrada (16/1)], Alberto Federico Acosta (16/2), Abel Eduardo Balbo (23/6). Trainer: Daniel Alberto Passarella (10).

**Goals**: Sergio Ángel Berti (29), Alberto Federico Acosta (75).

**681.** 22.06.1995 **ARGENTINA – SLOVAKIA LEAGUE XI** **6-0(0-0)**

Estadio Malvinas Argentinas, Mendoza; Referee: Mario Fernando Sánchez Yanten (Chile); Attendance: 35,000

**ARG:** Rolando Hernándo Cristante (1/0), Roberto Fabián Ayala (10/0), Fernando Gabriel Cáceres (15/0), José Antonio Chamot (16/2), Javier Adelmar Zanetti (11/1), Leonardo Rubén Astrada (16/1), Cristián Gustavo Bassedas (11/0) [46.Sergio Ángel Berti (7/1); 71.Ariel Arnaldo Ortega (18/2)], Marcelo Fabián Espina (5/1) [46.Marcelo Daniel Gallardo (8/5)], Diego Pablo Simeone (42/6), Abel Eduardo Balbo (24/6), Gabriel Omar Batistuta (41/28). Trainer: Daniel Alberto Passarella (11).

**Goals**: Marcelo Daniel Gallardo (58), Javier Adelmar Zanetti (61), Gabriel Omar Batistuta (68), Marcelo Daniel Gallardo (69 penalty), Diego Pablo Simeone (80), Gabriel Omar Batistuta (89).

**682.** 30.06.1995 **ARGENTINA - AUSTRALIA** **2-0(1-0)**

Estadio Centenario, Quilmes; Referee: Ubaldo Aquino Valenzano (Paraguay); Attendance: 18,000

**ARG:** Rolando Hernándo Cristante (2/0), Leonardo Rubén Astrada (18/1), Roberto Fabián Ayala (11/0), Fernando Gabriel Cáceres (16/0), José Antonio Chamot (17/2), Javier Adelmar Zanetti (12/1), Sergio Ángel Berti (8/1), Marcelo Daniel Gallardo (9/5) [77.Ariel Arnaldo Ortega (19/2)], Diego Pablo Simeone (43/6), Abel Eduardo Balbo (25/7), Gabriel Omar Batistuta (42/29). Trainer: Daniel Alberto Passarella (12).

**Goals**: Abel Eduardo Balbo (7), Gabriel Omar Batistuta (90).

**683.** 08.07.1995 **ARGENTINA - BOLIVIA** **2-1(0-0)** 37th Copa América. Group Stage.

Estadio Parque „General Artigas", Paysandú (Uruguay); Referee: Eduardo Dluzniewski Takoz (Uruguay); Attendance: 20,000

**ARG:** Rolando Hernándo Cristante (3/0), Javier Adelmar Zanetti (13/1), Roberto Fabián Ayala (12/0), Fernando Gabriel Cáceres (17/0), José Antonio Chamot (18/2), Diego Pablo Simeone (44/6), Hugo Leonardo Pérez (11/2) [46.Leonardo Rubén Astrada (19/1)], Juan José Borrelli (2/0), Marcelo Daniel Gallardo (10/5) [46.Ariel Arnaldo Ortega (20/2)], Abel Eduardo Balbo (26/8) [82.Alberto Federico Acosta (17/2)], Gabriel Omar Batistuta (43/30). Trainer: Daniel Alberto Passarella (13).

**Goals**: Gabriel Omar Batistuta (70), Abel Eduardo Balbo (81).

**684.** 11.07.1995 **ARGENTINA - CHILE** **4-0(2-0)** 37th Copa América. Group Stage.

Estadio Parque „General Artigas", Paysandú (Uruguay); Referee: Arturo Pablo Brizio Carter (Mexico); Attendance: 16,000

**ARG:** Rolando Hernándo Cristante (4/0), Javier Adelmar Zanetti (14/1), Roberto Fabián Ayala (13/0) [59.Néstor Ariel Fabbri (17/1)], Fernando Gabriel Cáceres (18/0), José Antonio Chamot (19/2) [46.Ricardo Daniel Altamirano (24/1)], Juan José Borrelli (3/0), Leonardo Rubén Astrada (20/1) [59.Hugo Leonardo Pérez (12/2)], Diego Pablo Simeone (45/7), Ariel Arnaldo Ortega (21/2), Abel Eduardo Balbo (27/9), Gabriel Omar Batistuta (44/32). Trainer: Daniel Alberto Passarella (14).

**Goals**: Gabriel Omar Batistuta (1), Diego Pablo Simeone (6), Gabriel Omar Batistuta (51), Abel Eduardo Balbo (54).

**685.** 14.07.1995 **UNITED STATES - ARGENTINA** **3-0(2-0)** 37th Copa América. Group Stage.

Estadio Parque „General Artigas", Paysandú (Uruguay); Referee: Márcio Rezende de Freitas (Brazil); Attendance: 8,000

**ARG:** Carlos Gustavo Bossio (9/0), Ricardo Daniel Altamirano (25/1), Roberto Fabián Ayala (14/0), Néstor Ariel Fabbri (18/1), Gabriel Francisco Schurrer (4/0), Marcelo Alejandro Escudero (9/1) [46.Diego Pablo Simeone (46/7)], Hugo Leonardo Pérez (13/2), Marcelo Fabián Espina (6/1) [46.Ariel Arnaldo Ortega (22/2)], Marcelo Daniel Gallardo (11/5), Alberto Federico Acosta (18/2) [65.Abel Eduardo Balbo (28/9)], Gabriel Omar Batistuta (45/32). Trainer:

Daniel Alberto Passarella (15).

**686.** 17.07.1995 **ARGENTINA - BRAZIL** **2-2(1-2,2-2); 2-4 penalties** 37th Copa América. Quarter-Finals.
Estadio „Atilio Paiva Olivera", Rivera (Uruguay); Referee: Alberto Tejada Noriega (Peru); Attendance: 24,000
**ARG:** Rolando Hernándo Cristante (5/0), Javier Adelmar Zanetti (15/1), Néstor Ariel Fabbri (19/1), Fernando Gabriel Cáceres (19/0), José Antonio Chamot (20/2), Diego Pablo Simeone (47/7), Leonardo Rubén Astrada (21/1) [*sent off 45*], Juan José Borrelli (4/0), Ariel Arnaldo Ortega (23/2) [46.Hugo Leonardo Pérez (14/2)], Abel Eduardo Balbo (29/10) [76.Alberto Federico Acosta (19/2)], Gabriel Omar Batistuta (46/33) [60.Roberto Fabián Ayala (15/0)]. Trainer: Daniel Alberto Passarella (16).
**Goals**: Abel Eduardo Balbo (2), Gabriel Omar Batistuta (29).
**Penalties**: Hugo Leonardo Pérez, Alberto Federico Acosta, Diego Pablo Simeone [save], Néstor Ariel Fabbri [save].

**687.** 20.09.1995 **SPAIN - ARGENTINA** **2-1(1-0)**
Estadio „Vicente Calderón", Madrid; Referee: Sotiris Vorgias (Greece); Attendance: 50,000
**ARG:** Germán Adrián Ramón Burgos (3/0), Javier Adelmar Zanetti (16/1), Roberto Fabián Ayala (16/0), Fernando Gabriel Cáceres (20/0), José Antonio Chamot (21/2), Leonardo Rubén Astrada (22/1), Juan José Borrelli (5/0) [58.Marcelo Daniel Gallardo (12/5)], Ariel Arnaldo Ortega (24/3), Diego Pablo Simeone (48/7), Abel Eduardo Balbo (30/10), Gabriel Omar Batistuta (47/33). Trainer: Daniel Alberto Passarella (17).
**Goal**: Ariel Arnaldo Ortega (80).

**688.** 11.10.1995 **ARGENTINA - COLOMBIA** **0-0**
Estadio Monumental „Antonio Vespucio Liberti", Buenos Aires; Referee: Eduardo Dluzniewski Takoz (Uruguay); Attendance: 25,000
**ARG:** Germán Adrián Ramón Burgos (4/0), Javier Adelmar Zanetti (17/1), Néstor Ariel Fabbri (20/1), Roberto Luis Trotta (1/0), José Antonio Chamot (22/2), Leonardo Rubén Astrada (23/1), José Horacio Basualdo (31/0), Juan José Borrelli (6/0) [82.Cristián Gustavo Bassedas (12/0)], Ariel Arnaldo Ortega (25/3), Marcelo Alejandro Delgado (1/0), Sebastián Pascual Rambert (8/4) [80.Hugo Norberto Castillo (1/0)]. Trainer: Daniel Alberto Passarella (18).

**689.** 08.11.1995 **ARGENTINA - BRAZIL** **0-1(0-0)** Copa 50imo Aniversário Clarín
Estadio Monumental „Antonio Vespucio Liberti", Buenos Aires; Referee: Ernesto Cavani Filippi (Uruguay); Attendance: 64,000
**ARG:** Rolando Hernándo Cristante (6/0), Fernando Gabriel Cáceres (21/0), Roberto Luis Trotta (2/0), Ricardo Daniel Altamirano (26/1), Javier Adelmar Zanetti (18/1), Leonardo Rubén Astrada (24/1), Diego Pablo Simeone (49/7) [82.Cristián Alberto González (1/0) [*sent off 84*]], Sergio Ángel Berti (9/1) [46.Gustavo Adrián López (5/0)], Marcelo Daniel Gallardo (13/5) [46.Ariel Arnaldo Ortega (26/3)], Gabriel Omar Batistuta (48/33), Abel Eduardo Balbo (31/10). Trainer: Daniel Alberto Passarella (19).

**690.** 21.12.1995 **ARGENTINA - VENEZUELA** **6-0(5-0)**
Estadio Malvinas Argentinas, Mendoza; Referee: Eduardo Gamboa Martínez (Chile); Attendance: 5,000
**ARG:** Oscar Fernando Passet (1/0), Roberto Fabián Ayala (17/0) [76.Roberto Luis Trotta (3/0)], Hernán Edgardo Díaz (21/3), Juan Carlos Ramírez (1/0), Roberto Néstor Sensini (26/0), Rodolfo Esteban Cardoso (1/1), Fernando Edgar Galetto (1/0), Gustavo Adrián López (6/2) [61.Ariel Arnaldo Ortega (27/3)], Carlos Javier Netto (1/1), Claudio Darío Biaggio (1/0), Juan Eduardo Esnáider (1/2) [77.Marcelo Alejandro Delgado (2/0)]. Trainer: Daniel Alberto Passarella (20).
**Goals**: Juan Eduardo Esnáider (2), Gustavo Adrián López (18 penalty), Rodolfo Esteban Cardoso (24), Gustavo Adrián López (28 penalty), Juan Eduardo Esnáider (32), Carlos Javier Netto (83).

**691.** 24.04.1996 **ARGENTINA - BOLIVIA** **3-1(2-1)** 16th FIFA WC. Qualifiers
Estadio Monumental „Antonio Vespucio Liberti", Buenos Aires; Referee: Mario Fernando Sánchez Yanten (Chile); Attendance: 49,750
**ARG:** Oscar Fernando Passet (2/0), Javier Adelmar Zanetti (19/1), Roberto Fabián Ayala (18/0), Matías Jesús Almeyda (1/0), José Antonio Chamot (23/2), Roberto Néstor Sensini (27/0), Claudio Paul Caniggia (46/16) [75.Abel Eduardo Balbo (32/10)], Diego Pablo Simeone (50/7), Gabriel Omar Batistuta (49/34) [86.Claudio Javier López (3/0)], Ariel Arnaldo Ortega (28/5), Hugo Alberto Morales (1/0). Trainer: Daniel Alberto Passarella (21).
**Goals**: Ariel Arnaldo Ortega (8, 18), Gabriel Omar Batistuta (59).

**692.** 02.06.1996 **ECUADOR - ARGENTINA** **2-0(0-0)** 16th FIFA WC. Qualifiers
Estadio Olimpico „Atahualpa", Quito; Referee: Armando Pérez Hoyos (Colombia); Attendance: 41,500
**ARG:** Carlos Gustavo Bossio (10/0), Javier Adelmar Zanetti (20/1), Matías Jesús Almeyda (2/0), Fernando Gabriel Cáceres (22/0), Roberto Néstor Sensini (28/0), José Antonio Chamot (24/2), Diego Pablo Simeone (51/7), Hugo Alberto Morales (2/0) [76.Claudio Javier López (4/0)], Ariel Arnaldo Ortega (29/5), Claudio Paul Caniggia (47/16), Gabriel Omar Batistuta (50/34) [75.Hernán Jorge Crespo (2/0)]. Trainer: Daniel Alberto Passarella (22).

**693.** 20.06.1996 **ARGENTINA – POLAND LEAGUE XI** **2-0(0-0)**
Estadio „San Martín", Tucumán; Referee: Horacio Marcelo Elizondo (Argentina); Attendance: 18,000
**ARG:** Carlos Gustavo Bossio (11/0), Javier Adelmar Zanetti (21/1), Roberto Fabián Ayala (19/0), José Antonio Chamot (25/2) [81.Héctor Mauricio Pineda (1/0)], Roberto Néstor Sensini (29/0), Gustavo Adrián López (7/2), Hugo Alberto Morales (3/0), Diego Pablo Simeone (52/8), Juan Sebastián Verón (1/0) [81.Cristián Gustavo Bassedas (13/0)], Marcelo Alejandro Delgado (3/0) [46.Abel Eduardo Balbo (33/11)], Claudio Javier López (5/0). Trainer: Daniel Alberto Passarella (23).
**Goals**: Abel Eduardo Balbo (73), Diego Pablo Simeone (77).

**694.** 07.07.1996 **PERU - ARGENTINA** **0-0** 16th FIFA WC. Qualifiers
Estadio Nacional, Lima; Referee: Wilson Souza Mendonça (Brazil); Attendance: 43,675
**ARG:** Germán Adrián Ramón Burgos (5/0), Javier Adelmar Zanetti (22/1), Roberto Fabián Ayala (20/0), Roberto Néstor Sensini (30/0), José Antonio Chamot (26/2), Diego Pablo Simeone (53/8), Matías Jesús Almeyda (3/0), Hugo Alberto Morales (4/0) [46.Cristián Gustavo Bassedas (14/0)], Ariel Arnaldo Ortega (30/5) [89.Gustavo Adrián López (8/2)], Claudio Paul Caniggia (48/16) [72.Pablo Ariel Paz (1/0)], Abel Eduardo Balbo (34/11) [*sent off 29*]. Trainer: Daniel Alberto Passarella (24).

**695.** 01.09.1996 **ARGENTINA - PARAGUAY** **1-1(1-1)** 16th FIFA WC. Qualifiers
Estadio Monumental „Antonio Vespucio Liberti", Buenos Aires; Referee: Antonio Pereira Da Silva (Brazil); Attendance: 65,500
**ARG:** Germán Adrián Ramón Burgos (6/0), Javier Adelmar Zanetti (23/1) [87.José Fabián Albornóz (1/0)], Roberto Fabián Ayala (21/0), Fernando Gabriel Cáceres (23/0), José Antonio Chamot (27/2), Cristián Gustavo Bassedas (15/0) [52.Juan Sebastián Verón (2/0)], Matías Jesús Almeyda (4/0), Hugo Alberto Morales (5/0), Ariel Arnaldo Ortega (31/5), Guillermo Gustavo Barros Schelotto (2/0) [52.Claudio Javier López (6/0)], Gabriel Omar Batistuta (51/35). Trainer: Daniel Alberto Passarella (25).
**Goal**: Gabriel Omar Batistuta (27).

**696.** 09.10.1996 **VENEZUELA - ARGENTINA** **2-5(1-1)** 16th FIFA WC. Qualifiers
Estadio Pueblo Nuevo, San Cristóbal; Referee: Eduardo Dluzniewski Takoz (Uruguay); Attendance: 30,000
**ARG:** Pablo Oscar Cavallero (1/0), Roberto Fabián Ayala (22/0), Juan Pablo Sorín (4/1), Hernán Edgardo Díaz (22/3), Matías Jesús Almeyda (5/0), Eduardo Magnolo Berizzo (1/0), José Fabián Albornóz (2/1), Diego Pablo Simeone (54/9) [87.Roberto Antonio Molina (1/0)], Gabriel Omar Batistuta (52/35), Ariel Arnaldo Ortega (32/6) [87.Claudio Javier López (7/0)], Hugo Alberto Morales (6/1). Trainer: Daniel Alberto Passarella (26).
**Goals**: Ariel Arnaldo Ortega (35), Juan Pablo Sorín (68), Diego Pablo Simeone (77), Hugo Alberto Morales (86), José Fabián Albornóz (90).

**697.** 15.12.1996 **ARGENTINA - CHILE** **1-1(0-0)** 16th FIFA WC. Qualifiers
Estadio Monumental „Antonio Vespucio Liberti", Buenos Aires; Referee: Ubaldo Aquino Valenzano (Paraguay); Attendance: 59,870
**ARG:** Pablo Oscar Cavallero (2/0), Nelson David Vivas (3/0) [46.Gustavo Adrián López (9/2)], Roberto Fabián Ayala (23/0) [*sent off 60*], Eduardo Magnolo Berizzo (2/0), Juan Pablo Sorín (5/1), Javier Adelmar Zanetti (24/1), Matías Jesús Almeyda (6/0), Hugo Alberto Morales (7/1) [67.Patricio Alejandro Camps (1/0)], José Fabián Albornóz (3/1) [37.Abel Eduardo Balbo (35/11)], Ariel Arnaldo Ortega (33/6), Gabriel Omar Batistuta (53/36). Trainer: Daniel Alberto Passarella (27).
**Goal**: Gabriel Omar Batistuta (76 penalty).

**698.** 27.12.1996 **ARGENTINA - YUGOSLAVIA** **2-3(1-1)**
Estadio 13 de Julio, Mar del Plata; Referee: Ángel Osvaldo Sánches (Argentina); Attendance: 19,683
**ARG:** Roberto Oscar Bonano (1/0), Nelson David Vivas (4/0), Víctor Hugo Sotomayor (1/0), Néstor Ariel Fabbri (21/1), Eduardo Magnolo Berizzo (3/0), Diego Pablo Simeone (55/9), Leonardo Rubén Astrada (25/1), Guillermo Carlos Morigi (1/0) [46.Hernán Jorge Crespo (3/0)], Patricio Alejandro Camps (2/0) [46.Hugo Alberto Morales (8/2)], Ariel Arnaldo Ortega (34/6), Juan Eduardo Esnáider (2/3). Trainer: Daniel Alberto Passarella (28).
**Goals**: Juan Eduardo Esnáider (43 penalty), Hugo Alberto Morales (62).

**699.** 12.01.1997 **URUGUAY - ARGENTINA** **0-0** 16th FIFA WC. Qualifiers
Estadio Centenario, Montevideo; Referee: Márcio Rezende de Freitas (Brazil); Attendance: 62,000
**ARG:** Ignacio Carlos González (1/0), Nelson David Vivas (5/0), Roberto Néstor Sensini (31/0), Pablo Ariel Paz (2/0), José Antonio Chamot (28/2), Diego Pablo Simeone (56/9), Matías Jesús Almeyda (7/0), Cristián Gustavo Bassedas (16/0), Néstor Raúl Gorosito (17/0) [56.Hernán Jorge Crespo (4/0)], Ariel Arnaldo Ortega (35/6), Gabriel Omar Batistuta (54/36). Trainer: Daniel Alberto Passarella (29).

**700.** 12.02.1997 **COLOMBIA - ARGENTINA** **0-1(0-1)** 16th FIFA WC. Qualifiers
Estadio Metropolitano „Roberto Meléndez", Barranquilla; Referee: Antônio Pereira Da Silva (Brazil); Attendance: 47,000
**ARG:** Ignacio Carlos González (2/0), Hernán Edgardo Díaz (23/3), Roberto Néstor Sensini (32/0), Eduardo Magnolo Berizzo (4/0) [*sent off 42*], Pablo Ariel Paz (3/0), Diego Pablo Simeone (57/9), Gustavo Miguel Zapata (19/0), Juan Sebastián Verón (3/0), Ariel Arnaldo Ortega (36/6), Claudio Javier López (8/1) [87.Juan Pablo Sorín (6/1)], Hernán Jorge Crespo (5/0) [44.Nelson David Vivas (6/0)]. Trainer: Daniel Alberto Passarella (30).
**Goal**: Claudio Javier López (10).

**701.** 02.04.1997 **BOLIVIA - ARGENTINA** **2-1(1-1)** 16th FIFA WC. Qualifiers
Estadio „Hernándo Siles Zuazo", La Paz; Referee: Marinho Dos Santos Sidrack (Brazil); Attendance: 44,372
**ARG:** Ignacio Carlos González (3/0), Nelson David Vivas (7/0) [*sent off 66*], Roberto Néstor Sensini (33/0), Pablo Ariel Paz (4/0), Juan Pablo Sorín (7/1), Hernán Edgardo Díaz (24/3), Gustavo Miguel Zapata (20/0) [*sent off 81*], Diego Sebastián Cagna (11/0) [51.Ariel Arnaldo Ortega (37/6)], Néstor Raúl Gorosito (18/1) [46.Juan Sebastián Verón (4/0)], Marcelo Alejandro Delgado (4/0) [71.José Luis Calderón (1/0)], Julio Ricardo Cruz (1/0). Trainer: Daniel Alberto Passarella (31).
**Goal**: Néstor Raúl Gorosito (41).

**702.** 30.04.1997 **ARGENTINA - ECUADOR** **2-1(2-0)** 16th FIFA WC. Qualifiers
Estadio Monumental „Antonio Vespucio Liberti", Buenos Aires; Referee: Félix Ramón Benegas Caballero (Paraguay); Attendance: 62,300
**ARG:** Carlos Ángel Roa (1/0), Pablo Ariel Paz (5/0), Roberto Fabián Ayala (24/0), José Antonio Chamot (29/2), Diego Pablo Simeone (58/9), Matías Jesús Almeyda (8/0), Sergio Ángel Berti (10/1) [76.Hugo Alberto Morales (9/2)], Juan Sebastián Verón (5/0), Ariel Arnaldo Ortega (38/7), Hernán Jorge Crespo (6/1), Claudio Javier López (9/1) [76.Eduardo Magnolo Berizzo (5/0)]. Trainer: Daniel Alberto Passarella (32).
**Goals**: Ariel Arnaldo Ortega (18), Hernán Jorge Crespo (30).

**703.** 08.06.1997 **ARGENTINA - PERU** **2-0(1-0)** 16th FIFA WC. Qualifiers
Estadio Monumental „Antonio Vespucio Liberti", Buenos Aires; Referee: Claudio Vinicius Cerdeira (Brazil); Attendance: 56,069
**ARG:** Carlos Ángel Roa (2/0), Hernán Edgardo Díaz (25/3), Roberto Fabián Ayala (25/0), Roberto Néstor Sensini (34/0), José Antonio Chamot (30/2), Diego Pablo Simeone (59/10), Matías Jesús Almeyda (9/0), Sergio Ángel Berti (11/1) [69.Juan José Borrelli (7/0)], Ariel Arnaldo Ortega (39/7) [52.Cristián Gustavo Bassedas (17/0)], Claudio Javier López (10/1), Hernán Jorge Crespo (7/2) [85.José Luis Calderón (2/0)]. Trainer: Daniel Alberto Passarella (33).
**Goals**: Hernán Jorge Crespo (44), Diego Pablo Simeone (46).

**704.** 11.06.1997 **ARGENTINA - ECUADOR** **0-0** 38th Copa América. Group Stage.
Estadio „Félix Capriles", Cochabamba (Bolivia); Referee: Jorge Luis Nieves Parra (Uruguay); Attendance: 17,000
**ARG:** Ignacio Carlos González (4/0), Jorge Daniel Martínez (1/0), Pablo Oscar Rotchen (2/0), Mauricio Andrés Pellegrino (1/0), Raúl Ernesto Cardozo (1/0), Gustavo Miguel Zapata (21/0), Claudio Daniel Husaín (1/0), Rodolfo Esteban Cardoso (2/1), Gustavo Adrián López (10/2) [46.Marcelo Daniel Gallardo (14/5)], Marcelo Alejandro Delgado (5/0), Julio Ricardo Cruz (2/0) [61.José Luis Calderón (3/0)]. Trainer: Daniel Alberto Passarella (34).

**705.** 14.06.1997 **ARGENTINA - CHILE** **2-0(0-0)** 38th Copa América. Group Stage.
Estadio „Félix Capriles", Cochabamba (Bolivia); Referee: Antônio Pereira Da Silva (Brazil); Attendance: 9,000
**ARG:** Marcelo Leonardo Ojeda (1/0), Jorge Daniel Martínez (2/0), Pablo Oscar Rotchen (3/0), Mauricio Andrés Pellegrino (2/0), Raúl Ernesto Cardozo (2/0), Cristián Gustavo Bassedas (18/0) [80.Claudio Daniel Husaín (2/0)], Gustavo Miguel Zapata (22/0), Rodolfo Esteban Cardoso (3/1) [68.Sergio Ángel Berti (12/2)], Marcelo Daniel Gallardo (15/6), Marcelo Alejandro Delgado (6/0), José Luis Calderón (4/0) [70.Julio Ricardo Cruz (3/0)]. Trainer: Daniel Alberto Passarella (35).
**Goals**: Sergio Ángel Berti (83), Marcelo Daniel Gallardo (86).

**706.** 17.06.1997 **ARGENTINA - PARAGUAY** **1-1(0-0)** 38th Copa América. Group Stage.
Estadio „Félix Capriles", Cochabamba (Bolivia); Referee: Jorge Luis Nieves Parra (Uruguay); Attendance: 8,000
**ARG:** Carlos Ángel Roa (3/0), Nelson David Vivas (8/0), Pablo Oscar Rotchen (4/0) [*sent off 86*], Mauricio Andrés Pellegrino (3/0), Raúl Ernesto Cardozo (3/0), Cristián Gustavo Bassedas (19/0) [80.Martín Andrés Posse (1/0)], Gustavo Miguel Zapata (23/0), Rodolfo Esteban Cardoso (4/1) [78.Sergio Ángel Berti (13/2)], Marcelo Daniel Gallardo (16/7), Marcelo Alejandro Delgado (7/0), José Luis Calderón (5/0) [54.Julio Ricardo Cruz (4/0)]. Trainer: Daniel Alberto Passarella (36).
**Goals**: Marcelo Daniel Gallardo (90 penalty).

**707.** 21.06.1997 **PERU - ARGENTINA** **2-1(1-0)** 38th Copa América.Quarter-Finals.
Estadio Olímpico Patria, Sucre (Bolivia); Referee: Byron Aldemar Moreno Ruales (Ecuador); Attendance: 9,000
**ARG:** Carlos Ángel Roa (4/0), Nelson David Vivas (9/0), Héctor Mauricio Pineda (2/0), Eduardo Magnolo Berizzo (6/0) [*sent off 67*], Raúl Ernesto Cardozo (4/0) [46.Jorge Daniel Martínez (3/0)], Cristián Gustavo Bassedas (20/0), Gustavo Miguel Zapata (24/0) [*sent off 82*], Marcelo Daniel Gallardo (17/8) [*sent off 67*], Rodolfo Esteban Cardoso (5/1) [46.Sergio Ángel Berti (14/2)], Marcelo Alejandro Delgado (8/0), Julio Ricardo Cruz (5/0) [46.Martín Andrés Posse (2/0)]. Trainer: Daniel Alberto Passarella (37).
**Goal**: Marcelo Daniel Gallardo (66 penalty).

**708.** 06.07.1997 **PARAGUAY - ARGENTINA** **1-2(0-2)** 16th FIFA WC. Qualifiers
Estadio Defensores del Chaco, Asunción; Referee: Márcio Rezende de Freitas (Brazil); Attendance: 30,000
**ARG:** Carlos Ángel Roa (5/0), Hernán Edgardo Díaz (26/3) [*sent off 86*], Roberto Fabián Ayala (26/0), Roberto Néstor Sensini (35/0), José Antonio Chamot (31/2), Diego Pablo Simeone (60/10), Matías Jesús Almeyda (10/0), Juan Sebastián Verón (6/1) [51.Javier Adelmar Zanetti (25/1)], Marcelo Daniel Gallardo (18/9) [85.Pablo Ariel Paz (6/0)], Claudio Javier López (11/1), Hernán Jorge Crespo (8/2) [78.Sergio Ángel Berti (15/2)]. Trainer: Daniel Alberto Passarella (38).
**Goals**: Marcelo Daniel Gallardo (30), Juan Sebastián Verón (41).

**709.** 20.07.1997 **ARGENTINA - VENEZUELA** **2-0(1-0)** 16th FIFA WC. Qualifiers
Estadio Monumental „Antonio Vespucio Liberti", Buenos Aires; Referee: Wilson Souza Mendonça (Brazil); Attendance: 48,000
**ARG:** Carlos Ángel Roa (6/0), Leonardo Rubén Astrada (26/1), Javier Adelmar Zanetti (26/1), Roberto Fabián Ayala (27/0) [52.Pablo Ariel Paz (7/1)], Roberto Néstor Sensini (36/0), José Antonio Chamot (32/2), Diego Pablo Simeone (61/10), Juan Sebastián Verón (7/1), Marcelo Daniel Gallardo (19/9) [57.Ariel Arnaldo Ortega (40/7)], Hernán Jorge Crespo (9/3), Claudio Javier López (12/1) [76.Sergio Ángel Berti (16/2)]. Trainer: Daniel Alberto Passarella (39).
**Goals**: Hernán Jorge Crespo (31), Pablo Ariel Paz (58).

**710.** 10.09.1997 **CHILE - ARGENTINA** **1-2(1-1)** 16th FIFA WC. Qualifiers
Estadio Nacional, Santiago; Referee: Francisco Mourão Dacildo (Brazil); Attendance: 73,644
**ARG:** Carlos Ángel Roa (7/0), Pablo Ariel Paz (8/1), Roberto Fabián Ayala (28/0), Roberto Néstor Sensini (37/0), Diego Pablo Simeone (62/10), Matías Jesús Almeyda (11/0), Juan Sebastián Verón (8/1), Marcelo Daniel Gallardo (20/10) [86.Javier Adelmar Zanetti (27/1)], Ariel Arnaldo Ortega (41/7), Hernán Jorge Crespo (10/3) [71.Sergio Ángel Berti (17/2)], Claudio Javier López (13/2). Trainer: Daniel Alberto Passarella (40).
**Goals**: Marcelo Daniel Gallardo (25), Claudio Javier López (86).

**711.** 12.10.1997 **ARGENTINA - URUGUAY** **0-0** 16th FIFA WC. Qualifiers
Estadio Monumental „Antonio Vespucio Liberti", Buenos Aires; Referee: Claudio Vinicius Cerdeira (Brazil); Attendance: 52,000
**ARG:** Carlos Ángel Roa (8/0), Roberto Néstor Sensini (38/0), Pablo Ariel Paz (9/1), Roberto Fabián Ayala (29/0), Javier Adelmar Zanetti (28/1) [64.Sergio Ángel Berti (18/2)], Juan Sebastián Verón (9/1), Diego Pablo Simeone (Cap) (63/10), Matías Jesús Almeyda (12/0), Hernán Jorge Crespo (11/3) [69.Juan Eduardo Esnáider (3/3)], Ariel Arnaldo Ortega (42/7), Claudio Javier López (14/2) [74.Martín Andrés Posse (3/0)]. Trainer: Daniel Alberto Passarella (41).

**712.** 16.11.1997 **ARGENTINA - COLOMBIA** **1-1(0-1)** 16th FIFA WC. Qualifiers
Estadio „Alberto Armando", Buenos Aires; Referee: Márcio Rezende de Freitas (Brazil); Attendance: 40,000
**ARG:** Carlos Ángel Roa (9/0), Fernando Gabriel Cáceres (24/1), Roberto Fabián Ayala (30/0), Roberto Néstor Sensini (39/0), Diego Pablo Simeone (64/10), Leonardo Rubén Astrada (27/1) [82.Gustavo Miguel Zapata (25/0)], Juan Sebastián Verón (10/1), Marcelo Daniel Gallardo (21/10) [80.Juan Román Riquelme (1/0)], Ariel Arnaldo Ortega (43/7), Claudio Javier López (15/2) [56.Hernán Jorge Crespo (12/3)], Gabriel Omar Batistuta (55/36). Trainer: Daniel Alberto Passarella (42).
**Goal**: Fernando Gabriel Cáceres (69).

**713.** 19.02.1998 **ARGENTINA – ROMANIA LEAGUE XI** **2-1(1-0)**
Estadio Malvinas Argentinas, Mendoza; Referee: Guido Aros Alvarado (Chile); Attendance: 23,715
**ARG:** Germán Adrián Ramón Burgos (7/0), Nelson David Vivas (10/1), Roberto Fabián Ayala (31/1), José Antonio Chamot (33/2), Leonardo Rubén Astrada (28/1) [73.Gustavo Miguel Zapata (26/0)], Hernán Edgardo Díaz (27/3), Marcelo Daniel Gallardo (22/10) [73.Marcelo Alejandro Delgado (9/0)], Diego Pablo Simeone (65/10), Juan Sebastián Verón (11/1), Hernán Jorge Crespo (13/3), Ariel Arnaldo Ortega (44/7). Trainer: Daniel Alberto Passarella (43).
**Goals**: Nelson David Vivas (9), Roberto Fabián Ayala (52).

**714.** 24.02.1998 **ARGENTINA - YUGOSLAVIA** **3-1(1-0)**
Estadio „José María Minella", Mar del Plata; Referee: Ubaldo Aquino Valenzano (Paraguay); Attendance: 35,000
**ARG:** Germán Adrián Ramón Burgos (8/0) [90.Pablo Oscar Cavallero (3/0)], Hernán Edgardo Díaz (28/3), Roberto Fabián Ayala (32/1), José Antonio Chamot (34/2), Eduardo Magnolo Berizzo (7/0), Juan Sebastián Verón (12/1), Leonardo Rubén Astrada (29/1), Diego Pablo Simeone (66/10), Marcelo Daniel Gallardo (23/10), Ariel Arnaldo Ortega (45/7), Hernán Jorge Crespo (14/6). Trainer: Daniel Alberto Passarella (44).
**Goals**: Hernán Jorge Crespo (45 penalty,85,89).

**715.** 10.03.1998 **ARGENTINA - BULGARIA** **2-0(1-0)**
Estadio „José Amalfitani", Buenos Aires; Referee: Gustavo Méndez González (Uruguay); Attendance: 21,291
**ARG:** Pablo Oscar Cavallero (4/0), Roberto Fabián Ayala (33/1) [77.Eduardo Magnolo Berizzo (8/0)], Gustavo Adrián Lombardi (1/0), José Antonio Chamot (35/2), Héctor Mauricio Pineda (3/0), Rodolfo Esteban Cardoso (6/1), Marcelo Daniel Gallardo (24/10) [46.Sergio Ángel Berti (19/2)], Juan Sebastián Verón (13/1), Gustavo Miguel Zapata (27/0), Gabriel Omar Batistuta (56/37) [65.Marcelo Alejandro Delgado (10/0)], Claudio Javier López (16/3). Trainer: Daniel Alberto Passarella (45).
**Goals**: Gabriel Omar Batistuta (36), Claudio Javier López (86).

**716.** 15.04.1998 **ISRAEL - ARGENTINA** **2-1(0-0)**
„Teddy Kollek" Stadium, Jerusalem; Referee: Kostas Kapitanis (Cyprus); Attendance: 14,000
**ARG:** Germán Adrián Ramón Burgos (9/0), Gustavo Adrián Lombardi (2/0) [66.Sergio Ángel Berti (20/2)], Roberto Néstor Sensini (40/0), Pablo Ariel Paz (10/1), Héctor Mauricio Pineda (4/0), Diego Sebastián Cagna (12/1), Matías Jesús Almeyda (13/0), Marcelo Daniel Gallardo (25/10), Rodolfo Esteban Cardoso (7/1) [46.Ariel Arnaldo Ortega (46/7)], Gabriel Omar Batistuta (57/37), Claudio Javier López (17/3). Trainer: Daniel Alberto Passarella (46).
**Goal**: Diego Sebastián Cagna (77).

**717.** 22.04.1998 **REPUBLIC OF IRELAND - ARGENTINA** **0-2(0-2)**
Lansdowne Road, Dublin; Referee: Stuart Dougal (Scotland); Attendance: 38,500
**ARG:** Germán Adrián Ramón Burgos (10/0), Nelson David Vivas (11/1), Roberto Fabián Ayala (34/1), Roberto Néstor Sensini (41/0), Matías Jesús Almeyda (14/0), Sergio Ángel Berti (21/2) [63.Héctor Mauricio Pineda (5/0)], Ariel Arnaldo Ortega (47/8), Diego Pablo Simeone (Cap) (67/10), Juan Sebastián Verón (14/1), Gabriel Omar Batistuta (58/38), Claudio Javier López (18/3) [84.Marcelo Alejandro Delgado (11/0)]. Trainer: Daniel Alberto Passarella (47).
**Goals**: Gabriel Omar Batistuta (26), Ariel Arnaldo Ortega (40).

**718.** 29.04.1998 **BRAZIL - ARGENTINA** **0-1(0-0)**
Estádio „Jornalista Mário Filho" (Maracanã), Rio de Janeiro; Referee: Alain Sars (France); Attendance: 99,697
**ARG:** Germán Adrián Ramón Burgos (11/0), Nelson David Vivas (12/1), Roberto Fabián Ayala (35/1), Roberto Néstor Sensini (42/0), Matías Jesús Almeyda (15/0), Javier Adelmar Zanetti (29/1), Ariel Arnaldo Ortega (48/8) [75.Marcelo Alejandro Delgado (12/0)], Diego Pablo Simeone (68/10), Juan Sebastián Verón (15/1), Gabriel Omar Batistuta (59/38), Claudio Javier López (19/4) [88.Héctor Mauricio Pineda (6/0)]. Trainer: Daniel Alberto Passarella (48).
**Goal**: Claudio Javier López (84).

**719.** 14.05.1998 **ARGENTINA – BOSNIA-HERZEGOVINA** **5-0(2-0)**
Estadio Olímpico, Córdoba; Referee: Luis Mariano Peña Catalán (Chile); Attendance: 44,243
**ARG:** Carlos Ángel Roa (10/0) [50.Germán Adrián Ramón Burgos (12/0)], Pablo Ariel Paz (11/1), Roberto Fabián Ayala (36/1), Roberto Néstor Sensini (43/0), Javier Adelmar Zanetti (30/2), Matías Jesús Almeyda (16/0) [90.Leonardo Rubén Astrada (30/1)], Ariel Arnaldo Ortega (49/9) [83.Marcelo Alejandro Delgado (13/0)], Diego Pablo Simeone (69/10) [65.Marcelo Daniel Gallardo (26/10)], Juan Sebastián Verón (16/1), Gabriel Omar Batistuta (60/41), Claudio Javier López (20/4). Trainer: Daniel Alberto Passarella (49).
**Goals**: Gabriel Omar Batistuta (6, 24), Javier Adelmar Zanetti (55), Ariel Arnaldo Ortega (61), Gabriel Omar Batistuta (80).

**720.** 19.05.1998 **ARGENTINA - CHILE** **1-0(0-0)**
Estadio Malvinas Argentinas, Mendoza; Referee: Ubaldo Aquino Valenzano (Paraguay); Attendance: 43,864
**ARG:** Germán Adrián Ramón Burgos (13/0), Pablo Ariel Paz (12/1), Roberto Fabián Ayala (37/1), Roberto Néstor Sensini (44/0), Javier Adelmar Zanetti (31/2), Matías Jesús Almeyda (17/0), Diego Pablo Simeone (70/10) [74.Marcelo Daniel Gallardo (27/10)], Juan Sebastián Verón (17/1), Ariel Arnaldo Ortega (50/9) [76.Héctor Mauricio Pineda (7/0)], Gabriel Omar Batistuta (61/42), Claudio Javier López (21/4) [74.Marcelo Alejandro Delgado (14/0)]. Trainer: Daniel Alberto Passarella (50).
**Goal**: Gabriel Omar Batistuta (46).

**721.** 25.05.1998 **ARGENTINA – SOUTH AFRICA** **2-0(0-0)**
Estadio Monumental „Antonio Vespucio Liberti", Buenos Aires; Referee: Gustavo Méndez González (Uruguay); Attendance: 40,000
**ARG:** Germán Adrián Ramón Burgos (14/0), Roberto Fabián Ayala (38/1) [79.Nelson David Vivas (13/1)], Roberto Néstor Sensini (45/0), Pablo Ariel Paz (13/1), Javier Adelmar Zanetti (32/2), Matías Jesús Almeyda (18/0), Diego Pablo Simeone (71/10), Juan Sebastián Verón (18/1), Ariel Arnaldo Ortega (51/10), Gabriel Omar Batistuta (62/43), Claudio Javier López (22/4). Trainer: Daniel Alberto Passarella (51).
**Goals**: Gabriel Omar Batistuta (49), Ariel Arnaldo Ortega (90).

**722.** 14.06.1998 **ARGENTINA - JAPAN** **1-0(1-0)** 16th FIFA WC. Group Stage.
Stade Municipal, Toulouse (France); Referee: Mario van der Ende (Holland); Attendance: 33,400
**ARG:** Carlos Ángel Roa (11/0), Roberto Fabián Ayala (39/1), Roberto Néstor Sensini (46/0) [74.José Antonio Chamot (36/2)], Nelson David Vivas (14/1), Javier Adelmar Zanetti (33/2), Matías Jesús Almeyda (19/0), Diego Pablo Simeone (Cap) (72/10), Juan Sebastián Verón (19/1), Ariel Arnaldo Ortega (52/10), Claudio Javier López (23/4) [62.Abel Eduardo Balbo (36/11)], Gabriel Omar Batistuta (63/44). Trainer: Daniel Alberto Passarella (52).
**Goal**: Gabriel Omar Batistuta (28).

**723.** 21.06.1998 **ARGENTINA - JAMAICA** **5-0(1-0)** 16th FIFA WC. Group Stage.
Stade Parc des Princes, Paris (France); Referee: Rune Pedersen (Norway); Attendance: 48,000
**ARG:** Carlos Ángel Roa (12/0), Roberto Fabián Ayala (40/1), Roberto Néstor Sensini (47/0) [25.Nelson David Vivas (15/1)], José Antonio Chamot (37/2), Javier Adelmar Zanetti (34/2), Matías Jesús Almeyda (20/0), Diego Pablo Simeone (Cap) (73/10) [80.Héctor Mauricio Pineda (8/0)], Ariel Arnaldo Ortega (53/12), Juan Sebastián Verón (20/1), Claudio Javier López (24/4) [75.Marcelo Daniel Gallardo (28/10)], Gabriel Omar Batistuta (64/47). Trainer: Daniel Alberto Passarella (53).
**Goals**: Ariel Arnaldo Ortega (32, 55), Gabriel Omar Batistuta (72, 79, 83 penalty).

**724.** 26.06.1998 **ARGENTINA - CROATIA** **1-0(1-0)** 16th FIFA WC. Group Stage.
Stade Lescure, Bordeaux (France); Referee: Said Belqola (Morocco); Attendance: 36,500
**ARG:** Carlos Ángel Roa (13/0), Roberto Fabián Ayala (41/1), Nelson David Vivas (16/1), Pablo Ariel Paz (14/1), Javier Adelmar Zanetti (35/2) [68.Diego Pablo Simeone (74/10)], Matías Jesús Almeyda (21/0), Héctor Mauricio Pineda (9/1), Juan Sebastián Verón (21/1), Ariel Arnaldo Ortega (54/12) [53.Claudio Javier López (25/4)], Marcelo Daniel Gallardo (29/10) [81.Sergio Ángel Berti (22/2)], Gabriel Omar Batistuta (65/47) (Cap). Trainer: Daniel Alberto Passarella (54).
**Goal**: Héctor Mauricio Pineda (34).

**725.** 30.06.1998 **ARGENTINA - ENGLAND** **2-2(2-2,2-2); 4-3 on penalties** 16th FIFA WC. 2nd Round.
Stade „Geoffroy Guichard", Saint-Etienne (France); Referee: Kim Milton Nielsen (Denmark); Attendance: 36,000
**ARG:** Carlos Ángel Roa (14/0), Roberto Fabián Ayala (42/1), Matías Jesús Almeyda (22/0), José Antonio Chamot (38/2), Ariel Arnaldo Ortega (55/12), Nelson David Vivas (17/1), Diego Pablo Simeone (Cap) (75/10) [91.Sergio Ángel Berti (23/2)], Juan Sebastián Verón (22/1), Javier Adelmar Zanetti (36/3), Claudio Javier López (26/4) [68.Marcelo Daniel Gallardo (30/10)], Gabriel Omar Batistuta (66/48) [68.Hernán Jorge Crespo (15/6)]. Trainer: Daniel Alberto Passarella (55).
**Goals**: Gabriel Omar Batistuta (5 penalty), Javier Adelmar Zanetti (45).
**Penalties**: Sergio Ángel Berti, Hernán Jorge Crespo [save], Juan Sebastián Verón, Marcelo Daniel Gallardo, Roberto Fabián Ayala.

**726.** 04.07.1998 **HOLLAND - ARGENTINA** **2-1(1-1)** 16th FIFA WC. Quarter-Finals.
Stade Vélodrome, Marseille (France); Referee: Arturo Pablo Brizio Carter (Mexico); Attendance: 55,000
**ARG:** Carlos Ángel Roa (15/0), Roberto Néstor Sensini (48/0), Roberto Fabián Ayala (43/1), José Antonio Chamot (39/2) [90.Abel Eduardo Balbo (37/11)], Javier Adelmar Zanetti (37/3), Matías Jesús Almeyda (23/0) [67.Héctor Mauricio Pineda (10/1)], Diego Pablo Simeone (Cap) (76/10), Juan Sebastián Verón (23/1), Ariel Arnaldo Ortega (56/12) [*sent off 87*], Claudio Javier López (27/5), Gabriel Omar Batistuta (67/48). Trainer: Daniel Alberto Passarella (56).
**Goal**: Claudio Javier López (18).

**727.** 03.02.1999 **VENEZUELA - ARGENTINA** **0-2(0-0)**
Estadio „José 'Pachencho' Romero", Maracaibo; Referee: Fernando Panesso (Colombia); Attendance: 32,000
**ARG:** Germán Adrián Ramón Burgos (15/0), Hugo Benjamín Ibarra (1/0) [23.Claudio Daniel Husaín (3/0)], Eduardo Magnolo Berizzo (9/0), Walter Adrián Samuel (1/1), Juan Pablo Sorín (8/1), Diego Sebastián Cagna (13/1), Leonardo Rubén Astrada (31/1), Cristián Gustavo Bassedas (21/0), Marcelo Daniel Gallardo (31/11), Guillermo Gustavo Barros Schelotto (3/0) [90.Juan Ramón Fernández (1/0)], Martín Palermo (1/0). Trainer: Marcelo Alberto Bielsa (1).
**Goals**: Walter Adrián Samuel (46), Marcelo Daniel Gallardo (68).

**728.** 10.02.1999 **ARGENTINA - MEXICO** **1-0(0-0)**
Memorial Coliseum, Los Angeles (United States); Referee: Richard Grady (United States); Attendance: 91,585
**ARG:** Germán Adrián Ramón Burgos (16/0), Claudio Daniel Husaín (4/0), Eduardo Magnolo Berizzo (10/0), Walter Adrián Samuel (2/1), Juan Pablo Sorín (9/2), Diego Sebastián Cagna (14/1), Leonardo Rubén Astrada (32/1), Cristián Gustavo Bassedas (22/0) [81.Sebastián Ariel Méndez (1/0)], Marcelo Daniel Gallardo (32/11) [90.Jorge Héctor San Esteban (1/0)], Guillermo Gustavo Barros Schelotto (4/0), Martín Palermo (2/0). Trainer: Marcelo Alberto Bielsa (2).
**Goal**: Juan Pablo Sorín (66).

**729.** 31.03.1999 **HOLLAND - ARGENTINA** **1-1(1-0)**
ArenA, Amsterdam; Referee: Graham Poll (England); Attendance: 55,132
**ARG:** Carlos Ángel Roa (16/0), Roberto Néstor Sensini (49/0) [79.Gustavo Adrián López (11/2)], Roberto Fabián Ayala (44/1), Mauricio Roberto Pochettino (1/0), Javier Adelmar Zanetti (38/3), Fernando Carlos Redondo (27/1), Nelson David Vivas (18/1), Juan Sebastián Verón (24/1), Ariel Arnaldo Ortega (Cap) (57/12) [46.Andrés Guglielminpietro (1/0); 81.Hernán Jorge Crespo (16/6)], Gabriel Omar Batistuta (68/49), Claudio Javier López (28/5). Trainer: Marcelo Alberto Bielsa (3).
**Goal**: Gabriel Omar Batistuta (82).

**730.** 09.06.1999 **ARGENTINA - MEXICO** **2-2(1-1)** Copa Reebok
Soldier Field, Chicago (United States); Referee: Richard Grady (United States); Attendance: 64,433
**ARG:** Germán Adrián Ramón Burgos (17/0), Hugo Benjamín Ibarra (2/0) [83.Pablo César Aimar Giordano (1/0)], Roberto Fabián Ayala (45/1), Mauricio Roberto Pochettino (2/0), Juan Pablo Sorín (10/2), Javier Adelmar Zanetti (39/3), Fernando Daniel Pandolfi (1/0) [46.Andrés Guglielminpietro (2/0)], Diego Pablo Simeone (77/10), Gustavo Adrián López (12/3), Julio Ricardo Cruz (6/1) [73.Sebastián Ariel Méndez (2/0)], Cristián Alberto González (2/0) [65.Claudio Daniel Husaín (5/0)]. Trainer: Marcelo Alberto Bielsa (4).
**Goals**: Julio Ricardo Cruz (19), Gustavo Adrián López (52).

**731.** 13.06.1999 **UNITED STATES - ARGENTINA** **1-0(0-0)**
„Robert F. Kennedy" Memorial Stadium, Washington; Referee: Rodrigo Badilla Sequeira (Costa Rica); Attendance: 40,119
**ARG:** Germán Adrián Ramón Burgos (18/0), Javier Adelmar Zanetti (40/3), Roberto Fabián Ayala (Cap) (46/1), Mauricio Roberto Pochettino (3/0), Hugo Benjamín Ibarra (3/0), Claudio Daniel Husaín (6/0), Diego Pablo Simeone (78/10), Andrés Guglielminpietro (3/0), Pablo César Aimar Giordano (2/0) [60.Cristián Alberto González (3/0)], Gustavo Adrián López (13/3), Julio Ricardo Cruz (7/1) [78.Fernando Daniel Pandolfi (2/0)]. Trainer: Marcelo Alberto Bielsa (5).

**732.** 26.06.1999 **ARGENTINA - LITHUANIA** **0-0**
Estadio „José Amalfitani", Buenos Aires; Referee: Daniel Bello Rotunno (Uruguay); Attendance: 11,314
**ARG:** Germán Adrián Ramón Burgos (19/0), Roberto Fabián Ayala (47/1), Juan Pablo Sorín (11/2) [67.Diego Sebastián Cagna (15/1)], Hugo Benjamín Ibarra (4/0), Diego Pablo Simeone (79/10), Walter Adrián Samuel (3/1), Javier Adelmar Zanetti (41/3), Martín Palermo (3/0), Ariel Arnaldo Ortega (58/12) [46.Guillermo Gustavo Barros Schelotto (5/0)], Gustavo Adrián López (14/3) [60.Cristián Alberto González (4/0)], Juan Román Riquelme (2/0). Trainer: Marcelo Alberto Bielsa (6).

**733.** 01.07.1999 **ARGENTINA - ECUADOR** **3-1(1-0)** 39th Copa América. Group Stage.
Estadio „Feliciano Cáceres", Luque (Paraguay); Referee: Gilberto Hidalgo Zamora (Peru); Attendance: 18,000
**ARG:** Germán Adrián Ramón Burgos (20/0), Hugo Benjamín Ibarra (5/0), Roberto Fabián Ayala (48/1), Walter Adrián Samuel (4/1), Javier Adelmar Zanetti (42/3), Diego Pablo Simeone (80/11), Juan Pablo Sorín (12/2), Juan Román Riquelme (3/0) [90.Diego Sebastián Cagna (16/1)], Gustavo Adrián López (15/3) [67.Andrés Guglielminpietro (4/0)], Guillermo Gustavo Barros Schelotto (6/0) [75.Cristián Alberto González (5/0)], Martín Palermo (4/2). Trainer: Marcelo Alberto Bielsa (7).
**Goals**: Diego Pablo Simeone (12), Martín Palermo (55, 61).

**734.** 04.07.1999 **COLOMBIA - ARGENTINA** **3-0(1-0)** 39th Copa América. Group Stage.
Estadio „Feliciano Cáceres", Luque (Paraguay); Referee: Ubaldo Aquino Valenzano (Paraguay); Attendance: 22,000
**ARG:** Germán Adrián Ramón Burgos (21/0), Nelson David Vivas (19/1) [61.Hugo Benjamín Ibarra (6/0)], Roberto Fabián Ayala (49/1), Walter Adrián Samuel (5/1), Juan Pablo Sorín (13/2) [46.Diego Sebastián Cagna (17/1)], Javier Adelmar Zanetti (43/3) [*sent off 69*], Diego Pablo Simeone (81/11), Juan Román Riquelme (4/0), Guillermo Gustavo Barros Schelotto (7/0) [68.Andrés Guglielminpietro (5/0)], Martín Palermo (5/2), Cristián Alberto González (6/0). Trainer: Marcelo Alberto Bielsa (8).

**735.** 07.07.1999 **ARGENTINA - URUGUAY** **2-0(1-0)** 39th Copa América. Group Stage.
Estadio „Feliciano Cáceres", Luque (Paraguay); Referee: Gilberto Hidalgo Zamora (Peru); Attendance: 18,000
**ARG:** Germán Adrián Ramón Burgos (22/0), Nelson David Vivas (20/1) [*sent off 73*], Roberto Fabián Ayala (Cap) (50/1), Walter Adrián Samuel (6/1), Juan Pablo Sorín (14/2), Diego Pablo Simeone (82/11), Diego Sebastián Cagna (18/1) [85.Claudio Daniel Husaín (7/0)], Juan Román Riquelme (5/0), Cristián Alberto González (7/1), Guillermo Gustavo Barros Schelotto (8/0) [76.Mauricio Roberto Pochettino (4/0)], Martín Palermo (6/3) [78.Gustavo Adrián López (16/3)]. Trainer: Marcelo Alberto Bielsa (9).
**Goals**: Cristián Alberto González (1), Martín Palermo (56).

**736.** 11.07.1999 **BRAZIL - ARGENTINA** **2-1(1-1)** 39th Copa América. Quarter-Finals.
Estadio „Antonio Oddone Sarubbi", Ciudad del Este (Paraguay); Referee: Gustavo Méndez González (Uruguay); Attendance: 26,000
**ARG:** Germán Adrián Ramón Burgos (23/0), Mauricio Roberto Pochettino (5/0), Roberto Fabián Ayala (51/1), Walter Adrián Samuel (7/1), Juan Pablo Sorín (15/3) [69.Gustavo Adrián López (17/3)], Javier Adelmar Zanetti (44/3), Diego Pablo Simeone (83/11) [69.Diego Sebastián Cagna (19/1)], Juan Román Riquelme (6/0), Ariel Arnaldo Ortega (59/12), Martín Palermo (7/3), Cristián Alberto González (8/1). Trainer: Marcelo Alberto Bielsa (10).
**Goal**: Juan Pablo Sorín (10).

**737.** 04.09.1999 **ARGENTINA - BRAZIL** **2-0(1-0)** Copa Zero Hora
Estadio Monumental „Antonio Vespucio Liberti“, Buenos Aires; Referee: Gustavo Méndez González (Uruguay); Attendance: 60,000
**ARG:** Roberto Oscar Bonano (2/0), Roberto Fabián Ayala (52/1), Nelson David Vivas (21/1), Walter Adrián Samuel (8/1), Javier Adelmar Zanetti (45/3), Fernando Carlos Redondo (28/1), Juan Pablo Sorín (16/3), Juan Sebastián Verón (25/2) [86.Diego Pablo Simeone (84/11)], Ariel Arnaldo Ortega (60/12) [74.Marcelo Daniel Gallardo (33/11)], Hernán Jorge Crespo (17/7) [89.Eduardo Magnolo Berizzo (11/0)], Claudio Javier López (29/5) [46.Cristián Alberto González (9/1)]. Trainer: Marcelo Alberto Bielsa (11).
**Goals**: Juan Sebastián Verón (29), Hernán Jorge Crespo (57).

**738.** 07.09.1999 **BRAZIL - ARGENTINA** **4-2(2-1)** Copa Zero Hora
Estádio Beira-Rio, Porto Alegre; Referee: Oscar Julián Ruiz Acosta (Colombia); Attendance: 75,000
**ARG:** Roberto Oscar Bonano (3/0), Roberto Fabián Ayala (53/2), Walter Adrián Samuel (9/1), Nelson David Vivas (22/1) [71.Claudio Daniel Husaín (8/0)], Fernando Carlos Redondo (29/1) [59.Diego Pablo Simeone (85/11)], Juan Pablo Sorín (17/3), Juan Sebastián Verón (26/2) [55.Guillermo Gustavo Barros Schelotto (9/0)], Javier Adelmar Zanetti (46/3), Hernán Jorge Crespo (18/7) [79.Claudio Javier López (30/5)], Ariel Arnaldo Ortega (61/13), Cristián Alberto González (10/1) [46.Marcelo Daniel Gallardo (34/11)]. Trainer: Marcelo Alberto Bielsa (12).
**Goals**: Roberto Fabián Ayala (45), Ariel Arnaldo Ortega (88).

**739.** 13.10.1999 **ARGENTINA - COLOMBIA** **2-1(1-0)**
Estadio Olímpico, Córdoba; Referee: Mario Fernando Sánchez Yanten (Chile); Attendance: 42,000
**ARG:** Roberto Oscar Bonano (4/0), Roberto Néstor Sensini (50/0), Roberto Fabián Ayala (54/2), Walter Adrián Samuel (10/1), Claudio Daniel Husaín (9/0), Diego Pablo Simeone (86/11), Javier Adelmar Zanetti (47/3), Juan Sebastián Verón (27/2), Ariel Arnaldo Ortega (62/14), Gabriel Omar Batistuta (69/50), Andrés Guglielminpietro (6/0) [66.Guillermo Gustavo Barros Schelotto (10/0); 90.Nelson David Vivas (23/1)]. Trainer: Marcelo Alberto Bielsa (13).
**Goals**: Gabriel Omar Batistuta (6), Ariel Arnaldo Ortega (70).

**740.** 17.11.1999 **SPAIN - ARGENTINA** **0-2(0-0)**
Estadio Olimpico La Cartuja, Sevilla; Referee: Giorgios Psychomanys (Greece); Attendance: 65,000
**ARG:** Germán Adrián Ramón Burgos (24/0), Roberto Néstor Sensini (51/0), Roberto Fabián Ayala (55/2), Mauricio Roberto Pochettino (6/1), Nelson David Vivas (24/1), Diego Pablo Simeone (87/11), Javier Adelmar Zanetti (48/3), Cristián Alberto González (11/2), Ariel Arnaldo Ortega (63/14) [87.Santiago Hernán Solari (1/0)], Hernán Jorge Crespo (19/7) [90.Eduardo Magnolo Berizzo (12/0)], Claudio Javier López (31/5) [77.Gustavo Adrián López (18/3)]. Trainer: Marcelo Alberto Bielsa (14).
**Goals**: Cristián Alberto González (63), Mauricio Roberto Pochettino (75).

**741.** 23.02.2000 **ENGLAND - ARGENTINA** **0-0**
Wembley Stadium, London; Referee: Dr. Markus Merk (Germany); Attendance: 74,008
**ARG:** Pablo Oscar Cavallero (5/0), Roberto Fabián Ayala (56/2), Rodolfo Martín Arruabarrena (5/0) [68.Nelson David Vivas (25/1)], Roberto Néstor Sensini (52/0) [35.Mauricio Roberto Pochettino (7/1)], Diego Pablo Simeone (88/11), José Antonio Chamot (40/2), Cristián Alberto González (12/2), Javier Adelmar Zanetti (49/3), Juan Sebastián Verón (28/2), Gabriel Omar Batistuta (70/50) [56.Hernán Jorge Crespo (20/7)], Ariel Arnaldo Ortega (64/14) [90.Gustavo Adrián López (19/3)]. Trainer: Marcelo Alberto Bielsa (15).

**742.** 29.03.2000 **ARGENTINA - CHILE** **4-1(2-1)** 17th FIFA WC. Qualifiers
Estadio Monumental „Antonio Vespucio Liberti“, Buenos Aires; Referee: Byron Aldemar Moreno Ruales (Ecuador); Attendance: 46,374
**ARG:** Roberto Oscar Bonano (5/0), Mauricio Roberto Pochettino (8/1), Roberto Fabián Ayala (57/2), Walter Adrián Samuel (11/1), Javier Adelmar Zanetti (50/3), Diego Pablo Simeone (89/11), Juan Sebastián Verón (29/4), Cristián Alberto González (13/2), Claudio Javier López (32/6) [88.Gustavo Adrián López (20/3)], Ariel Arnaldo Ortega (65/14) [84.Roberto Néstor Sensini (53/0)], Gabriel Omar Batistuta (71/51) [88.Hernán Jorge Crespo (21/7)]. Trainer: Marcelo Alberto Bielsa (16).
**Goals**: Gabriel Omar Batistuta (10), Juan Sebastián Verón (33, 71 penalty), Claudio Javier López (88).

**743.** 26.04.2000 **VENEZUELA - ARGENTINA** **0-4(0-2)** 17th FIFA WC. Qualifiers
Estadio „José 'Pachencho' Romero“, Maracaibo; Referee: Carlos Amarilla Demarqui (Paraguay); Attendance: 19,355
**ARG:** Roberto Oscar Bonano (6/0), Roberto Néstor Sensini (54/0), Roberto Fabián Ayala (58/3), Walter Adrián Samuel (12/1), Javier Adelmar Zanetti (51/3), Diego Pablo Simeone (90/11), Juan Sebastián Verón (30/4), Cristián Alberto González (14/2), Ariel Arnaldo Ortega (66/16) [78.Marcelo Daniel Gallardo (35/11)], Hernán Jorge Crespo (22/8), Claudio Javier López (33/6) [68.Gustavo Adrián López (21/3)]. Trainer: Marcelo Alberto Bielsa (17).
**Goals**: Roberto Fabián Ayala (8), Ariel Arnaldo Ortega (23, 77), Hernán Jorge Crespo (89).

**744.** 04.06.2000 **ARGENTINA - BOLIVIA** **1-0(0-0)** 17th FIFA WC. Qualifiers
Estadio Monumental „Antonio Vespucio Liberti“, Buenos Aires; Referee: Márcio Rezende de Freitas (Brazil); Attendance: 50,669
**ARG:** Roberto Oscar Bonano (7/0), Roberto Néstor Sensini (55/0), Roberto Fabián Ayala (59/3), Walter Adrián Samuel (13/1), Javier Adelmar Zanetti (52/3) [71.Gustavo Adrián López (22/4)], Diego Pablo Simeone (91/11), Cristián Alberto González (15/2), Juan Sebastián Verón (31/4), Ariel Arnaldo Ortega (67/16) [83.Pablo César Aimar Giordano (3/0)], Gabriel Omar Batistuta (72/51), Claudio Javier López (34/6) [88.Matías Jesús Almeyda (24/0)]. Trainer: Marcelo Alberto Bielsa (18).
**Goal**: Gustavo Adrián López (85).

**745.** 29.06.2000 **COLOMBIA - ARGENTINA** **1-3(1-2)** 17th FIFA WC. Qualifiers
Estadio „Nemesio Camacho“ 'El Campín', Bogotá; Referee: Jorge Larrionda Pietrafiesa (Uruguay); Attendance: 43,426
**ARG:** Roberto Oscar Bonano (8/0), Roberto Fabián Ayala (60/3), Roberto Néstor Sensini (56/0), Walter Adrián Samuel (14/1), Javier Adelmar Zanetti (53/3), Diego Pablo Simeone (92/11), Cristián Alberto González (16/2), Juan Sebastián Verón (32/4) [67.Gustavo Adrián López (23/4)], Ariel Arnaldo Ortega (68/16) [86.Juan Pablo Sorín (18/3)], Gabriel Omar Batistuta (73/53) [67.Hernán Jorge Crespo (23/9)], Claudio Javier López (35/6). Trainer: Marcelo Alberto Bielsa (19).
**Goals**: Gabriel Omar Batistuta (25, 45), Hernán Jorge Crespo (75).

**746.** 19.07.2000 **ARGENTINA - ECUADOR** **2-0(1-0)** 17th FIFA WC. Qualifiers
Estadio Monumental „Antonio Vespucio Liberti“, Buenos Aires; Referee: Daniel Bello Rotunno (Uruguay); Attendance: 44,199
**ARG:** Roberto Oscar Bonano (9/0), Roberto Fabián Ayala (61/3), Roberto Néstor Sensini (57/0), Walter Adrián Samuel (15/1), Javier Adelmar Zanetti (54/3), Diego Pablo Simeone (93/11), Cristián Alberto González (17/2) [76.Juan Pablo Sorín (19/3)], Juan Sebastián Verón (33/4), Ariel Arnaldo Ortega (69/16), Hernán Jorge Crespo (24/10) [76.Pablo César Aimar Giordano (4/0)], Claudio Javier López (36/7). Trainer: Marcelo Alberto Bielsa (20).
**Goals**: Hernán Jorge Crespo (23), Claudio Javier López (50).

**747.** 26.07.2000 **BRAZIL - ARGENTINA** **3-1(2-1)** 17th FIFA WC. Qualifiers
Estádio „Cicero Pompeu de Toledo“ Morumbi, São Paulo; Referee: Gustavo Méndez González (Uruguay); Attendance: 80,000
**ARG:** Roberto Oscar Bonano (10/0), Roberto Fabián Ayala (62/3), Roberto Néstor Sensini (58/0), Walter Adrián Samuel (16/1), Javier Adelmar Zanetti (55/3) [38.Matías Jesús Almeyda (25/1)], Diego Pablo Simeone (94/11), Cristián Alberto González (18/2) [71.Juan Pablo Sorín (20/3)], Juan Sebastián Verón (34/4), Ariel Arnaldo Ortega (70/16) [71.Gustavo Adrián López (24/4)], Hernán Jorge Crespo (25/10), Claudio Javier López (37/7). Trainer: Marcelo Alberto Bielsa (21).
**Goal**: Matías Jesús Almeyda (45).

**748.** 16.08.2000 **ARGENTINA - PARAGUAY** **1-1(0-0)** 17th FIFA WC. Qualifiers
Estadio Monumental „Antonio Vespucio Liberti“, Buenos Aires; Referee: Antônio Pereira Da Silva (Brazil); Attendance: 46,000
**ARG:** Roberto Oscar Bonano (11/0), Roberto Néstor Sensini (59/0), Roberto Fabián Ayala (63/3), Walter Adrián Samuel (17/1), Juan Sebastián Verón (35/4), Diego Pablo Simeone (95/11) [71.Nelson David Vivas (26/1)], Cristián Alberto González (19/2) [46.Juan Pablo Sorín (21/3)], Pablo César Aimar Giordano (5/1), Ariel Arnaldo Ortega (71/16), Hernán Jorge Crespo (26/10), Gustavo Adrián López (25/4) [75.Javier Pedro Saviola (1/0)]. Trainer: Marcelo Alberto Bielsa (22).
**Goal**: Pablo César Aimar Giordano (66).

**749.** 03.09.2000 **PERU - ARGENTINA** **1-2(0-2)** 17th FIFA WC. Qualifiers
Estadio Nacional, Lima; Referee: Oscar Julián Ruíz Acosta (Colombia); Attendance: 43,951
**ARG:** Roberto Oscar Bonano (12/0), Roberto Néstor Sensini (60/0), Roberto Fabián Ayala (64/3), Walter Adrián Samuel (18/1), Juan Pablo Sorín (22/3), Juan Sebastián Verón (36/5), Diego Pablo Simeone (96/11) [80.Nelson David Vivas (27/1)], Pablo César Aimar Giordano (6/1), Ariel Arnaldo Ortega (72/16) [73.Claudio Daniel Husaín (10/0)], Hernán Jorge Crespo (27/11), Claudio Javier López (38/7) [84.Gustavo Adrián López (26/4)]. Trainer: Marcelo Alberto Bielsa (23).
**Goals**: Hernán Jorge Crespo (25), Juan Sebastián Verón (37).

**750.** 08.10.2000 **ARGENTINA - URUGUAY** **2-1(2-0)** 17th FIFA WC. Qualifiers
Estadio Monumental „Antonio Vespucio Liberti“, Buenos Aires; Referee: Márcio Rezende de Freitas (Brazil); Attendance: 48,792
**ARG:** Germán Adrián Ramón Burgos (25/0), Roberto Fabián Ayala (65/3), Nelson David Vivas (28/1), Walter Adrián Samuel (19/1), Diego Pablo Simeone (97/11), Claudio Daniel Husaín (11/0), Juan Pablo Sorín (23/3), Marcelo Daniel Gallardo (36/12) [78.Marcelo Alejandro Delgado (15/0)], Claudio Javier López (39/7) [73.Gustavo Adrián López (27/4)], Gabriel Omar Batistuta (74/54), Cristián Alberto González (20/2). Trainer: Marcelo Alberto Bielsa (24).
**Goals**: Marcelo Daniel Gallardo (28), Gabriel Omar Batistuta (42).

**751.** 15.11.2000 **CHILE - ARGENTINA** **0-2(0-1)** 17th FIFA WC. Qualifiers
Estadio Nacional, Santiago; Referee: Carlos Amarilla Demarqui (Paraguay); Attendance: 56,529
**ARG:** Germán Adrián Ramón Burgos (26/0) [72.Roberto Oscar Bonano (13/0)], Roberto Fabián Ayala (66/3), Nelson David Vivas (29/1), Walter Adrián Samuel (20/1), Claudio Daniel Husaín (12/1), Matías Jesús Almeyda (26/1), Juan Pablo Sorín (24/3), Juan Sebastián Verón (37/5) [51.Pablo César Aimar Giordano (7/1)], Ariel Arnaldo Ortega (73/17), Julio Ricardo Cruz (8/1) [83.Eduardo Magnolo Berizzo (13/0)], Cristián Alberto González (21/2). Trainer: Marcelo Alberto Bielsa (25).
**Goals**: Ariel Arnaldo Ortega (27), Claudio Daniel Husaín (89).

**752.** 20.12.2000 **ARGENTINA - MEXICO** **2-0(1-0)** Copa Reebok
Memorial Coliseum, Los Angeles (United States); Referee: Kevin Scott (United States); Attendance: 65,000
**ARG:** Germán Adrián Ramón Burgos (27/0), Nelson David Vivas (30/1), Diego Sebastián Crosa (1/0), Gabriel Alejandro Milito (1/0) [75.Leandro Damián Cufré (1/0)], Lucas Martín Castromán (1/0), Diego Pablo Simeone (98/11), Esteban Matías Cambiasso Deleau (1/0), Diego Rodolfo Placente (1/0), Ariel Arnaldo Ortega (74/17) [77.Luciano Martín Galletti (1/1)], Marcelo Alejandro Delgado (16/0) [85.Bernardo Daniel Romeo (1/0)], Santiago Hernán Solari (2/1). Trainer: Marcelo Alberto Bielsa (26).
**Goals**: Santiago Hernán Solari (12), Luciano Martín Galletti (81).

**753.** 28.02.2001 **ITALY - ARGENTINA** **1-2(1-1)**
Stadio Olimpico, Roma; Referee: Alain Sars (France); Attendance: 20,000
**ARG:** Germán Adrián Ramón Burgos (28/0), Nelson David Vivas (31/1), Roberto Fabián Ayala (Cap) (67/3) [81.Mauricio Roberto Pochettino (9/1)], Walter Adrián Samuel (21/1), Javier Adelmar Zanetti (56/3), Juan Sebastián Verón (38/5) [73.Claudio Daniel Husaín (13/1)], Diego Pablo Simeone (99/11), Juan Pablo Sorín (25/3), Pablo César Aimar Giordano (8/1) [81.Marcelo Daniel Gallardo (37/12)], Hernán Jorge Crespo (28/12) [90.Julio Ricardo Cruz (9/1)], Cristián Alberto González (22/3) [85.Gustavo Adrián López (28/4)]. Trainer: Marcelo Alberto Bielsa (27).
**Goals**: Cristián Alberto González (36), Hernán Jorge Crespo (48).

**754.** 28.03.2001 **ARGENTINA - VENEZUELA** **5-0(2-0)** 17th FIFA WC. Qualifiers
Estadio Monumental „Antonio Vespucio Liberti“, Buenos Aires; Referee: Gilberto Hidalgo Zamora (Peru); Attendance: 32,000
**ARG:** Germán Adrián Ramón Burgos (29/0), Juan Pablo Sorín (26/4) [62.Javier Adelmar Zanetti (57/3)], Nelson David Vivas (32/1), Mauricio Roberto Pochettino (10/1), Walter Adrián Samuel (22/2), Hernán Jorge Crespo (29/13), Ariel Arnaldo Ortega (75/17) [69.Gustavo Adrián López (29/4)], Juan Sebastián Verón (39/6), Diego Pablo Simeone (**100**/11), Cristián Alberto González (23/3), Marcelo Daniel Gallardo (38/13) [75.Claudio Javier López (40/7)]. Trainer: Marcelo Alberto Bielsa (28).
**Goals**: Hernán Jorge Crespo (13), Juan Pablo Sorín (31), Juan Sebastián Verón (51), Marcelo Daniel Gallardo (60), Walter Adrián Samuel (85).

**755.** 25.04.2001 **BOLIVIA - ARGENTINA** **3-3(1-1)** 17th FIFA WC. Qualifiers
Estadio „Hernándo Siles Zuazo“, La Paz; Referee: Oscar Julián Ruíz Acosta (Colombia); Attendance: 28,872
**ARG:** Germán Adrián Ramón Burgos (30/0), Roberto Fabián Ayala (68/3), Juan Pablo Sorín (27/5), Nelson David Vivas (33/1), Walter Adrián Samuel (23/2), Javier Adelmar Zanetti (58/3) [61.Ariel Arnaldo Ortega (76/17)], Juan Sebastián Verón (40/6), Diego Pablo Simeone (101/11), Pablo César Aimar Giordano (9/1) [57.Marcelo Daniel Gallardo (39/13)], Hernán Jorge Crespo (30/15), Gustavo Adrián López (30/4) [46.Claudio Javier López (41/7)]. Trainer: Marcelo Alberto Bielsa (29).
**Goals**: Hernán Jorge Crespo (43, 88), Juan Pablo Sorín (90).

**756.** 03.06.2001 **ARGENTINA - COLOMBIA** **3-0(3-0)** 17th FIFA WC. Qualifiers
Estadio Monumental „Antonio Vespucio Liberti“, Buenos Aires; Referee: Mario Fernando Sánchez Yanten (Chile); Attendance: 46,500
**ARG:** Pablo Oscar Cavallero (6/0), Roberto Fabián Ayala (69/3), Juan Pablo Sorín (28/5), Nelson David Vivas (34/1), Mauricio Roberto Pochettino (11/1), Claudio Javier López (42/8) [79.Pablo César Aimar Giordano (10/1)], Javier Adelmar Zanetti (59/3), Juan Sebastián Verón (41/6) [81.Marcelo Daniel Gallardo (40/13)], Diego Pablo Simeone (102/11), Hernán Jorge Crespo (31/16) [65.Marcelo Alejandro Delgado (17/0)], Cristián Alberto González (24/4). Trainer: Marcelo Alberto Bielsa (30).
**Goals**: Cristián Alberto González (22), Claudio Javier López (35), Hernán Jorge Crespo (38).

**757.** 15.08.2001 **ECUADOR - ARGENTINA** **0-2(0-2)** 17th FIFA WC. Qualifiers
Estadio Olimpico „Atahualpa", Quito; Referee: Stefano Braschi (Italy); Attendance: 38,156
**ARG:** Germán Adrián Ramón Burgos (31/0), Roberto Fabián Ayala (70/3), Juan Pablo Sorín (29/5), Nelson David Vivas (35/1), Walter Adrián Samuel (24/2), Javier Adelmar Zanetti (60/3), Juan Sebastián Verón (42/7), Diego Pablo Simeone (103/11) [67.Matías Jesús Almeyda (27/1)], Pablo César Aimar Giordano (11/1) [59.Ariel Arnaldo Ortega (77/17)], Hernán Jorge Crespo (32/17), Cristián Alberto González (25/4) [84.Claudio Javier López (43/8)]. Trainer: Marcelo Alberto Bielsa (31).
**Goals**: Juan Sebastián Verón (19), Hernán Jorge Crespo (34 penalty).

**758.** 05.09.2001 **ARGENTINA - BRAZIL** **2-1(0-1)** 17th FIFA WC. Qualifiers
Estadio Monumental „Antonio Vespucio Liberti", Buenos Aires; Referee: Urs Meier (Switzerland); Attendance: 51,000
**ARG:** Germán Adrián Ramón Burgos (32/0), Roberto Fabián Ayala (71/3), Nelson David Vivas (36/1), Walter Adrián Samuel (25/2), Diego Rodolfo Placente (2/0) [46.Ariel Arnaldo Ortega (78/17)], Claudio Javier López (44/8) [87.Matías Jesús Almeyda (28/1)], Javier Adelmar Zanetti (61/3), Diego Pablo Simeone (104/11), Pablo César Aimar Giordano (12/1) [64.Marcelo Daniel Gallardo (41/14)], Hernán Jorge Crespo (33/17), Cristián Alberto González (26/4). Trainer: Marcelo Alberto Bielsa (32).
**Goals**: Marcelo Daniel Gallardo (76), Cris (84 own goal).

**759.** 07.10.2001 **PARAGUAY - ARGENTINA** **2-2(0-0)** 17th FIFA WC. Qualifiers
Estadio Defensores del Chacho, Asunción; Referee: Gilberto Hidalgo Zamora (Peru); Attendance: 45,000
**ARG:** Pablo Oscar Cavallero (7/0), Roberto Fabián Ayala (72/3), Mauricio Roberto Pochettino (12/2), Walter Adrián Samuel (26/2), Juan Pablo Sorín (30/5) [63.Claudio Javier López (45/8)], Javier Adelmar Zanetti (62/3), Matías Jesús Almeyda (29/1), Ariel Arnaldo Ortega (79/17) [80.Pablo César Aimar Giordano (13/1)], Juan Sebastián Verón (43/7), Gabriel Omar Batistuta (75/55) [90.Julio Ricardo Cruz (10/1)], Cristián Alberto González (27/4). Trainer: Marcelo Alberto Bielsa (33).
**Goals**: Mauricio Roberto Pochettino (67), Gabriel Omar Batistuta (73).

**760.** 08.11.2001 **ARGENTINA - PERU** **2-0(0-0)** 17th FIFA WC. Qualifiers
Estadio Monumental „Antonio Vespucio Liberti", Buenos Aires; Referee: Jorge Larrionda Pietrafiesa (Uruguay); Attendance: 18,901
**ARG:** Germán Adrián Ramón Burgos (33/0), Roberto Fabián Ayala (73/3), Mauricio Roberto Pochettino (13/2), Walter Adrián Samuel (27/3), Juan Pablo Sorín (31/5), Matías Jesús Almeyda (30/1), Javier Adelmar Zanetti (63/3), Julio Ricardo Cruz (11/1) [46.Claudio Javier López (46/9)], Ariel Arnaldo Ortega (80/17) [73.Pablo César Aimar Giordano (14/1)], Juan Sebastián Verón (44/7), Cristián Alberto González (28/4) [87.Bernardo Daniel Romeo (2/0)]. Trainer: Marcelo Alberto Bielsa (34).
**Goals**: Walter Adrián Samuel (46), Claudio Javier López (84).

**761.** 14.11.2001 **URUGUAY - ARGENTINA** **1-1(1-1)** 17th FIFA WC. Qualifiers
Estadio Centenario, Montevideo; Referee: Dr. Markus Merk (Germany); Attendance: 48,100
**ARG:** Germán Adrián Ramón Burgos (34/0), Roberto Fabián Ayala (74/3), Mauricio Roberto Pochettino (14/2), Walter Adrián Samuel (28/3), Juan Pablo Sorín (32/5), Matías Jesús Almeyda (31/1), Claudio Javier López (47/10), Javier Adelmar Zanetti (64/3), Juan Sebastián Verón (45/7), Pablo César Aimar Giordano (15/1) [82.Diego Rodolfo Placente (3/0)], Ariel Arnaldo Ortega (81/17) [46.Julio Ricardo Cruz (12/1)]. Trainer: Marcelo Alberto Bielsa (35).
**Goal**: Claudio Javier López (44).

**762.** 13.02.2002 **WALES - ARGENTINA** **1-1(1-0)**
Millennium Stadium, Cardiff; Referee: Paul McKeon (Republic of Ireland); Attendance: 61,738
**ARG:** Sebastián Diego Saja (1/0), Nelson David Vivas (37/1), José Antonio Chamot (41/2), Diego Rodolfo Placente (4/0), Claudio Daniel Husaín (14/1), Juan Román Riquelme (7/0) [73.Pablo César Aimar Giordano (16/1)], Juan Pablo Sorín (33/5), Julio Ricardo Cruz (13/2) [73.Javier Pedro Saviola (2/0)], Juan Sebastián Verón (Cap) (46/7), Claudio Paul Caniggia (49/16) [90.Luciano Martín Galletti (2/1)], Cristián Alberto González (29/4). Trainer: Marcelo Alberto Bielsa (36).
**Goal**: Julio Ricardo Cruz (62).

**763.** 27.03.2002 **ARGENTINA - CAMEROON** **2-2(1-1)**
Stade Charmilles, Genève; Referee: Urs Meier (Switzerland); Attendance: 7,660
**ARG:** Germán Adrián Ramón Burgos (35/0), José Antonio Chamot (42/2), Mauricio Roberto Pochettino (15/2), Walter Adrián Samuel (29/3), Javier Adelmar Zanetti (65/3) [46.Matías Jesús Almeyda (32/1)], Juan Sebastián Verón (47/8), Pablo César Aimar Giordano (17/2), Juan Pablo Sorín (34/5) [76.Diego Rodolfo Placente (5/0)], Claudio Paul Caniggia (50/16) [89.Santiago Hernán Solari (3/1)], Claudio Javier López (48/10), Cristián Alberto González (30/4). Trainer: Marcelo Alberto Bielsa (37).
**Goals**: Juan Sebastián Verón (17 penalty), Pablo César Aimar Giordano (65).

**764.** 17.04.2002 **GERMANY - ARGENTINA** **0-1(0-0)**
„Gottlieb-Daimler" Stadion, Stuttgart; Referee: Manuel Enrique Mejuto González (Spain); Attendance: 54,570
**ARG:** Pablo Oscar Cavallero (8/0), Facundo Hernán Quiroga (1/0), Walter Adrián Samuel (30/3), Mauricio Roberto Pochettino (16/2), Javier Adelmar Zanetti (66/3), Matías Jesús Almeyda (33/1), Gustavo Adrián López (31/4) [77.Javier Pedro Saviola (3/0)], Juan Pablo Sorín (35/6), Pablo César Aimar Giordano (18/2) [31.Marcelo Daniel Gallardo (42/14); 62.Santiago Hernán Solari (4/1)], Claudio Javier López (49/10), Cristián Alberto González (31/4) [89.Diego Rodolfo Placente (6/0)]. Trainer: Marcelo Alberto Bielsa (38).
**Goal**: Juan Pablo Sorín (48).

**765.** 02.06.2002 **ARGENTINA - NIGERIA** **1-0(0-0)** 17th FIFA WC. Group Stage.
Kashima Stadium, Ibaraki (Japan); Referee: Gilles Veissière (France); Attendance: 34,050
**ARG:** Pablo Oscar Cavallero (9/0), Javier Adelmar Zanetti (67/3), Mauricio Roberto Pochettino (17/2), Walter Adrián Samuel (31/3), Juan Pablo Sorín (36/6), Diego Pablo Simeone (105/11), Ariel Arnaldo Ortega (82/17), Juan Sebastián Verón (Cap) (48/8) [78.Pablo César Aimar Giordano (19/2)], Diego Rodolfo Placente (7/0), Gabriel Omar Batistuta (76/56) [81.Hernán Jorge Crespo (34/17)], Claudio Javier López (50/10) [46.Cristián Alberto González (32/4)]. Trainer: Marcelo Alberto Bielsa (39).
**Goal**: Gabriel Omar Batistuta (63).

**766.** 07.06.2002 **ENGLAND - ARGENTINA** **1-0(1-0)** 17th FIFA WC. Group Stage.
Sapporo Dome, Sapporo (Japan); Referee: Pierluigi Collina (Italy); Attendance: 35,927
**ARG:** Pablo Oscar Cavallero (10/0), Mauricio Roberto Pochettino (18/2), Walter Adrián Samuel (32/3), Juan Pablo Sorín (37/6), Javier Adelmar Zanetti (68/3), Diego Pablo Simeone (106/11), Juan Sebastián Verón (Cap) (49/8) [46.Pablo César Aimar Giordano (20/2)], Ariel Arnaldo Ortega (83/17), Diego Rodolfo Placente (8/0), Gabriel Omar Batistuta (77/56) [60.Hernán Jorge Crespo (35/17)], Cristián Alberto González (33/4) [64.Claudio Javier López (51/10)]. Trainer: Marcelo Alberto Bielsa (40).

**767.** 12.06.2002 **ARGENTINA - SWEDEN** **1-1(0-0)** 17th FIFA WC. Group Stage.
Miyagi Stadium, Miyagi (Japan); Referee: Ali Mohammed Bujsaim (United Arab Emirates); Attendance: 45,777
**ARG:** Pablo Oscar Cavallero (11/0), Mauricio Roberto Pochettino (19/2), Walter Adrián Samuel (33/3), José Antonio Chamot (43/2), Juan Pablo Sorín (38/6) [63.Cristián Alberto González (34/4)], Javier Adelmar Zanetti (69/3), Matías Jesús Almeyda (34/1) [63.Juan Sebastián Verón (50/8)], Ariel Arnaldo Ortega (84/17), Pablo César Aimar Giordano (21/2), Claudio Javier López (52/10), Gabriel Omar Batistuta (Cap) (78/56) [58.Hernán Jorge Crespo (36/18)]. Trainer: Marcelo Alberto Bielsa (41). (Claudio Paul Caniggia was sent off from the substitutes bench at 45 mins).
**Goal**: Hernán Jorge Crespo (88).

**768.** 20.11.2002 **JAPAN - ARGENTINA** **0-2(0-0)**
Saitama World Cup Stadium, Saitama; Referee: Saad Kameel Mane (Kuwait); Attendance: 61,816
**ARG:** Pablo Oscar Cavallero (12/0), Roberto Fabián Ayala (75/3), Facundo Hernán Quiroga (2/0) [89.Mauricio Roberto Pochettino (20/2)], Walter Adrián Samuel (34/3), Juan Pablo Sorín (39/7), Javier Adelmar Zanetti (70/3), Matías Jesús Almeyda (35/1), Ariel Arnaldo Ortega (85/17) [73.Javier Pedro Saviola (4/0)], Juan Sebastián Verón (Cap) (51/8), Claudio Javier López (53/10) [65.Cristián Alberto González (35/4)], Hernán Jorge Crespo (37/19) [83.Santiago Hernán Solari (5/1)]. Trainer: Marcelo Alberto Bielsa (42).
**Goals**: Juan Pablo Sorín (47), Hernán Jorge Crespo (49).

**769.** 31.01.2003 **HONDURAS - ARGENTINA** **1-3(1-1)**
Estadio Olímpico Metropolitano, San Pedro Sula; Referee: Neftalí Recinos (El Salvador); Attendance: 20,000
**ARG:** Sebastián Diego Saja (2/0), Ariel Hernán Garcé (1/0) [*sent off 79*], Nicolás Andrés Burdisso (1/0), Gabriel Alejandro Milito (2/0) [*sent off 73*], Pablo Horacio Guiñazú (1/0), Luis Oscar González (1/2), Leonardo Daniel Ponzio (1/0) [46.Sebastián Alejandro Battaglia (1/0)], Andrés Nicolás D'Alessandro (1/0), Federico Insúa (1/0) [80.Javier Gonzálo Rodríguez (1/0)], Mariano Nicolás González (1/0) [85.Clemente Juan Rodríguez (1/0)], Diego Alberto Milito (1/1) [88.César Andrés Carignano (1/0)]. Trainer: Marcelo Alberto Bielsa (43).
**Goals**: Diego Alberto Milito (15), Luis Oscar González (53, 56).

**770.** 04.02.2003 **ARGENTINA - MEXICO** **1-0(1-0)**
Memorial Coliseum, Los Angeles (United States); Referee: Kevin Stott (United States); Attendance: 65,000
**ARG:** Sebastián Diego Saja (3/0), Nicolás Andrés Burdisso (2/0), Javier Gonzálo Rodríguez (2/1), Leonardo Daniel Ponzio (2/0), Pablo Horacio Guiñazú (2/0), Sebastián Alejandro Battaglia (2/0), Mariano Nicolás González (2/0) [85.César Andrés Carignano (2/0)], Luis Oscar González (2/2), Andrés Nicolás D'Alessandro (2/0), Federico Insúa (2/0), Diego Alberto Milito (2/1) [55.Clemente Juan Rodríguez (2/0)]. Trainer: Marcelo Alberto Bielsa (44).
**Goal**: Javier Gonzálo Rodríguez (13).

**771.** 08.02.2003 **UNITED STATES - ARGENTINA** **0-1(0-1)**
Orange Bowl, Miami; Referee: Carlos Batres (Guatemala); Attendance: 27,196
**ARG:** Sebastián Diego Saja (4/0), Ariel Hernán Garcé (2/0), Nicolás Andrés Burdisso (3/0), Gabriel Alejandro Milito (3/0), Pablo Horacio Guiñazú (3/0), Luis Oscar González (3/3), Sebastián Alejandro Battaglia (3/0), Andrés Nicolás D'Alessandro (3/0) [*sent off 90*], Federico Insúa (3/0) [77.Leandro Attilio Romagnoli (1/0)], Mariano Nicolás González (3/0) [46.César Andrés Carignano (3/0)], Diego Alberto Milito (3/1) [85.Clemente Juan Rodríguez (3/0)]. Trainer: Marcelo Alberto Bielsa (45).
**Goal**: Luis Oscar González (8).

**772.** 12.02.2003 **HOLLAND - ARGENTINA** **1-0(0-0)**
ArenA, Amsterdam; Referee: Kim Milton Nielsen (Denmark); Attendance: 40,090
**ARG:** Pablo Oscar Cavallero (13/0), Roberto Fabián Ayala (76/3), Facundo Hernán Quiroga (3/0), Walter Adrián Samuel (35/3), Juan Pablo Sorín (40/7), Javier Adelmar Zanetti (71/3), Juan Sebastián Verón (52/8) [74.Esteban Matías Cambiasso Deleau (2/0)], Pablo César Aimar Giordano (22/2), Ariel Arnaldo Ortega (86/17) [63.Marcelo Daniel Gallardo (43/14)], Claudio Javier López (54/10) [81.Santiago Hernán Solari (6/1)], Gustavo Adrián López (32/4) [58.Javier Pedro Saviola (5/0)]. Trainer: Marcelo Alberto Bielsa (46).

**773.** 30.04.2003 **LIBYA - ARGENTINA** **1-3(0-1)**
Stade 11th June, Tripoli; Referee: Abdel Zahmul (Tunisia); Attendance: 70,000
**ARG:** Pablo Oscar Cavallero (14/0), Facundo Hernán Quiroga (4/0), Fabricio Coloccini (1/0), Diego Rodolfo Placente (9/0), Juan Pablo Sorín (41/7) [46.Gabriel Iván Heinze (1/0)], Lucas Martín Castromán (2/0) [46.Juan Román Riquelme (8/1)], Esteban Matías Cambiasso Deleau (3/0), Pablo César Aimar Giordano (23/3), Santiago Hernán Solari (7/1) [46.Marcelo Daniel Gallardo (44/14)], Luciano Martín Galletti (3/1), Javier Pedro Saviola (6/1) [72.Lionel Sebastián Scaloni (1/0)]. Trainer: Marcelo Alberto Bielsa (47).
**Goals**: Javier Pedro Saviola (22), Juan Román Riquelme (67), Pablo César Aimar Giordano (89).

**774.** 08.06.2003 **JAPAN - ARGENTINA** **1-4(0-2)** Kirin Cup
Nagai Stadium, Osaka; Referee: Herbert Fandel (Germany); Attendance: 42,508
**ARG:** Pablo Oscar Cavallero (15/0), Facundo Hernán Quiroga (5/0), Fabricio Coloccini (2/0), Diego Rodolfo Placente (10/0), Javier Adelmar Zanetti (72/4), Lucas Martín Castromán (3/0) [36.Gabriel Iván Heinze (2/0)], Esteban Matías Cambiasso Deleau (4/0), Pablo César Aimar Giordano (24/3) [63.Juan Román Riquelme (9/1)], Santiago Hernán Solari (8/1) [75.Maximiliano Rubén Rodríguez (1/1)], Luciano Martín Galletti (4/1), Javier Pedro Saviola (7/2) [72.Bernardo Daniel Romeo (3/1)]. Trainer: Marcelo Alberto Bielsa (48).
**Goals**: Javier Pedro Saviola (30), Javier Adelmar Zanetti (45), Bernardo Daniel Romeo (78), Maximiliano Rubén Rodríguez (82).

**775.** 11.06.2003 **SOUTH KOREA - ARGENTINA** **0-1(0-1)**
Sangam World Cup Stadium, Seoul; Referee: Rungklay Mungkol (Thailand); Attendance: 30,000
**ARG:** Pablo Oscar Cavallero (16/0), Facundo Hernán Quiroga (6/0), Fabricio Coloccini (3/0), Diego Rodolfo Placente (11/0), Gabriel Iván Heinze (3/0), Javier Adelmar Zanetti (73/4), Esteban Matías Cambiasso Deleau (5/0), Pablo César Aimar Giordano (25/3) [78.Juan Román Riquelme (10/1)], Santiago Hernán Solari (9/1) [82.Lucas Martín Castromán (4/0)], Luciano Martín Galletti (5/1) [34.Maximiliano Rubén Rodríguez (2/1)], Javier Pedro Saviola (8/3) [85.Bernardo Daniel Romeo (4/1)]. Trainer: Marcelo Alberto Bielsa (49).
**Goal**: Javier Pedro Saviola (44).

**776.** 16.07.2003 **ARGENTINA - URUGUAY** **2-2(2-2)**
Estadio Unico Ciudad de La Plata, La Plata; Referee: Epifanio González Chávez (Paraguay); Attendance: 35,000
**ARG:** Franco Costanzo (1/0), Clemente Juan Rodríguez (4/0), Daniel Alberto Díaz (1/0), Gabriel Alejandro Milito (Cap) (4/0), Federico Hernán Domínguez (1/0), Luis Oscar González (4/3), Javier Alejandro Mascherano (1/0), Andrés Nicolás D'Alessandro (4/0), César Fabián Delgado (1/0) [77.Mariano Nicolás González (4/0)], Diego Alberto Milito (4/3), Federico Insúa (4/0) [70.Pablo Horacio Guiñazú (4/0)]. Trainer: Marcelo Alberto Bielsa (50).
**Goals**: Diego Alberto Milito (4, 9).

**777.** 20.08.2003 **URUGUAY - ARGENTINA** **2-3(1-1)**
Stadio „Artemio Franchi", Firenze (Italy); Referee: Massimo De Santis (Italy); Attendance: 8,000
**ARG:** Pablo Oscar Cavallero (17/0), Javier Adelmar Zanetti (74/4), Roberto Fabián Ayala (Cap) (77/3), Walter Adrián Samuel (36/4), Diego Rodolfo Placente (12/0), Juan Sebastián Verón (53/9) [64.Javier Pedro Saviola (9/3)], Matías Jesús Almeyda (36/1), Pablo César Aimar Giordano (26/3), Diego Alberto Milito (5/3) [46.Cristián Alberto González (36/4)], Hernán Jorge Crespo (38/19) [82.Luis Oscar González (5/3)], Claudio Javier López (55/10) [64.Andrés Nicolás D'Alessandro (5/1)]. Trainer: Marcelo Alberto Bielsa (51).
**Goals**: Juan Sebastián Verón (45), Walter Adrián Samuel (81), Andrés Nicolás D'Alessandro (85).

**778.** 06.09.2003 **ARGENTINA - CHILE** **2-2(2-0)** 18th FIFA WC. Qualifiers
Estadio Monumental „Antonio Vespucio Liberti", Buenos Aires; Referee: Ubaldo Aquino Valenzano (Paraguay); Attendance: 35,372
**ARG:** Pablo Oscar Cavallero (18/0), Javier Adelmar Zanetti (75/4), Roberto Fabián Ayala (78/3), Walter Adrián Samuel (37/4) [*sent off 87*], Nelson David Vivas (38/1), Andrés Nicolás D'Alessandro (6/1), Juan Sebastián Verón (54/9) [69.Matías Jesús Almeyda (37/1)], Pablo César Aimar Giordano (27/4), Cristián Alberto González (37/5), César Fabián Delgado (2/0), Hernán Jorge Crespo (39/19) [72.Javier Pedro Saviola (10/3)]. Trainer: Marcelo Alberto Bielsa (52).
**Goals**: Cristián Alberto González (32), Pablo César Aimar Giordano (36).

**779.** 09.09.2003 **VENEZUELA - ARGENTINA** **0-3(0-3)** 18th FIFA WC. Qualifiers
Olimpico „Ciudad Universitaria", Caracas; Referee: Martín Emilio Vázquez Broquetas (Uruguay); Attendance: 24,783
**ARG:** Pablo Oscar Cavallero (19/0), Javier Adelmar Zanetti (76/4), Nelson David Vivas (39/1), Roberto Fabián Ayala (79/3), Diego Rodolfo Placente (13/0), Andrés Nicolás D'Alessandro (7/1) [85.Luis Oscar González (6/3)], Juan Sebastián Verón (55/9), Pablo César Aimar Giordano (28/5) [63.Gabriel Iván Heinze (4/0)], Cristián Alberto González (38/5), César Fabián Delgado (3/1) [81.Matías Jesús Almeyda (38/1)], Hernán Jorge Crespo (40/20). Trainer: Marcelo Alberto Bielsa (53).
**Goals**: Pablo César Aimar Giordano (7), Hernán Jorge Crespo (25), César Fabián Delgado (32).

**780.** 15.11.2003 **ARGENTINA - BOLIVIA** **3-0(0-0)** 18th FIFA WC. Qualifiers
Estadio Monumental „Antonio Vespucio Liberti", Buenos Aires; Referee: Gilberto Hidalgo Zamora (Peru); Attendance: 30,042
**ARG:** Pablo Oscar Cavallero (20/0), Javier Adelmar Zanetti (77/4), Roberto Fabián Ayala (80/3), Walter Adrián Samuel (38/4), Facundo Hernán Quiroga (7/0), Andrés Nicolás D'Alessandro (8/2) [84.Juan Pablo Sorín (42/7)], Matías Jesús Almeyda (39/1) [89.Esteban Matías Cambiasso Deleau (6/0)], Pablo César Aimar Giordano (29/6), Cristián Alberto González (39/5), Hernán Jorge Crespo (41/21) [80.Javier Pedro Saviola (11/3)], César Fabián Delgado (4/1). Trainer: Marcelo Alberto Bielsa (54).
**Goals**: Andrés Nicolás D'Alessandro (57), Hernán Jorge Crespo (61), Pablo César Aimar Giordano (63).

**781.** 19.11.2003 **COLOMBIA - ARGENTINA** **1-1(0-1)** 18th FIFA WC. Qualifiers
Estadio Metropolitano „Roberto Meléndez", Barranquilla; Referee: Carlos Eugenio Simón (Brazil); Attendance: 19,034
**ARG:** Pablo Oscar Cavallero (21/0), Facundo Hernán Quiroga (8/0), Roberto Fabián Ayala (81/3), Walter Adrián Samuel (39/4), Diego Rodolfo Placente (14/0), Javier Adelmar Zanetti (78/4), Matías Jesús Almeyda (40/1), Pablo César Aimar Giordano (30/6) [71.Andrés Nicolás D'Alessandro (9/2)], Cristián Alberto González (40/5), César Fabián Delgado (5/1) [46.Juan Sebastián Verón (56/9)], Hernán Jorge Crespo (42/22) [71.Javier Pedro Saviola (12/3)]. Trainer: Marcelo Alberto Bielsa (55).
**Goal**: Hernán Jorge Crespo (28).

**782.** 30.03.2004 **ARGENTINA - ECUADOR** **1-0(0-0)**
Estadio Monumental „Antonio Vespucio Liberti", Buenos Aires; Referee: Martín Emilio Vázquez Broquetas (Uruguay); Attendance: 55,000
**ARG:** Pablo Oscar Cavallero (22/0), Clemente Juan Rodríguez (5/0), Roberto Fabián Ayala (82/3), Gabriel Iván Heinze (5/0), Juan Pablo Sorín (43/7), Pablo César Aimar Giordano (31/6) [56.Juan Román Riquelme (11/1)], Luis Oscar González (7/3), Andrés Nicolás D'Alessandro (10/2), César Fabián Delgado (6/1) [66.Nicolás Andrés Burdisso (4/0)], Hernán Jorge Crespo (43/23), Mariano Nicolás González (5/0) [46.Carlos Alberto Tévez (1/0)]. Trainer: Marcelo Alberto Bielsa (56).
**Goal**: Hernán Jorge Crespo (61).

**783.** 28.04.2004 **MOROCCO - ARGENTINA** **0-1(0-0)**
Stade „Mohammed V", Casablanca; Referee: Falla Ndoye (Senegal); Attendance: 65,000
**ARG:** Pablo Oscar Cavallero (23/0), Facundo Hernán Quiroga (9/0), Roberto Fabián Ayala (83/3), Walter Adrián Samuel (40/4), Javier Adelmar Zanetti (79/4), Andrés Nicolás D'Alessandro (11/2), Esteban Matías Cambiasso Deleau (7/0), Santiago Hernán Solari (10/1) [46.Juan Román Riquelme (12/1)], Cristián Alberto González (41/6) [90.Gabriel Alejandro Milito (5/0)], César Fabián Delgado (7/1), Hernán Jorge Crespo (44/23) [88.Diego Rodolfo Placente (15/0)]. Trainer: Marcelo Alberto Bielsa (57).
**Goal**: Cristián Alberto González (53).

**784.** 02.06.2004 **BRAZIL - ARGENTINA** **3-1(1-0)** 18th FIFA WC. Qualifiers
Estádio Mineirão, Belo Horizonte; Referee: Oscar Julián Ruíz Acosta (Colombia); Attendance: 60,000
**ARG:** Pablo Oscar Cavallero (24/0), Facundo Hernán Quiroga (10/0), Walter Adrián Samuel (41/4), Gabriel Iván Heinze (6/0), Juan Pablo Sorín (44/8), Javier Adelmar Zanetti (80/4), Javier Alejandro Mascherano (2/0), Luis Oscar González (8/3) [61.Pablo César Aimar Giordano (32/6)], Cristián Alberto González (42/6), César Fabián Delgado (8/1) [36.Mauro Damián Rosales (1/0); 61.Javier Pedro Saviola (13/3)], Hernán Jorge Crespo (45/23). Trainer: Marcelo Alberto Bielsa (58).
**Goal**: Juan Pablo Sorín (80).

**785.** 06.06.2004 **ARGENTINA - PARAGUAY** **0-0** 18th FIFA WC. Qualifiers
Estadio Monumental „Antonio Vespucio Liberti", Buenos Aires; Referee: Carlos Eugênio Simón (Brazil); Attendance: 37,000
**ARG:** Roberto Carlos Abbondanzieri (1/0), Roberto Fabián Ayala (84/3), Walter Adrián Samuel (42/4), Gabriel Iván Heinze (7/0), Juan Pablo Sorín (45/8), Luis Oscar González (9/3) [68.Mauro Damián Rosales (2/0)], Javier Alejandro Mascherano (3/0), Carlos Alberto Tévez (2/0), Cristián Alberto González (43/6), Hernán Jorge Crespo (46/23), Javier Pedro Saviola (14/3). Trainer: Marcelo Alberto Bielsa (59).

**786.** 27.06.2004 **COLOMBIA - ARGENTINA** **2-0(0-0)**
Orange Bowl, Miami (United States); Referee: Kevin Terry (United States); Attendance: 30,000
**ARG:** Pablo Oscar Cavallero (25/0), Facundo Hernán Quiroga (11/0) [46.Mariano Nicolás González (6/0)], Roberto Fabián Ayala (85/3), Gabriel Iván Heinze (8/0), Juan Pablo Sorín (46/8) [79.Diego Rodolfo Placente (16/0)], Javier Adelmar Zanetti (81/4), Fabricio Coloccini (4/0), Andrés Nicolás D'Alessandro (12/2) [*sent off 67*], Cristián Alberto González (44/6) [76.Luciano Gabriel Figueroa (1/0)], Mauro Damián Rosales (3/0), Javier Pedro Saviola (15/3). Trainer: Marcelo Alberto Bielsa (60).

**787.** 30.06.2004 **ARGENTINA - PERU** **2-1(1-1)**
Giants Stadium, East Rutherford, New York (United States); Referee: Kevin Stott (United States); Attendance: 41,013
**ARG:** Pablo Oscar Cavallero (26/0), Facundo Hernán Quiroga (12/0), Roberto Fabián Ayala (86/3), Gabriel Iván Heinze (9/0), Juan Pablo Sorín (47/8), Javier Adelmar Zanetti (82/4), Fabricio Coloccini (5/0), Cristián Alberto González (45/7) [90.Diego Rodolfo Placente (17/0)], Mauro Damián Rosales (4/0), Javier Pedro Saviola (16/4) [88.Luciano Gabriel Figueroa (2/0)], Mariano Nicolás González (7/0). Trainer: Marcelo Alberto Bielsa (61).
**Goals**: Cristián Alberto González (25 penalty), Javier Pedro Saviola (72).

**788.** 07.07.2004 **ARGENTINA - ECUADOR** **6-1(1-0)** 41st Copa América. Group Stage.
Estadio „Elías Aguirre", Chiclayo (Peru); Referee: Carlos Amarilla Demarqui (Paraguay); Attendance: 24,000
**ARG:** Roberto Carlos Abbondanzieri (2/0), Javier Adelmar Zanetti (83/4), Roberto Fabián Ayala (87/3), Gabriel Iván Heinze (10/0), Juan Pablo Sorín (48/8), Luis Oscar González (10/4), Javier Alejandro Mascherano (4/0), Andrés Nicolás D'Alessandro (13/3), Cristián Alberto González (46/8) [87.Clemente Juan Rodríguez (6/0)], César Fabián Delgado (9/1) [70.Mauro Damián Rosales (5/0)], Javier Pedro Saviola (17/7) [83.Carlos Alberto Tévez (3/0)]. Trainer: Marcelo Alberto Bielsa (62).
**Goals**: Cristián Alberto González (5 penalty), Javier Pedro Saviola (64, 74, 79), Andrés Nicolás D'Alessandro (84), Luis Oscar González (90).

**789.** 10.07.2004 **MEXICO - ARGENTINA** **1-0(1-0)** 41st Copa América. Group Stage.
Estadio „Elías Aguirre", Chiclayo (Peru); Referee: Márcio Rezende de Freitas (Brazil); Attendance: 25,000
**ARG:** Roberto Carlos Abbondanzieri (3/0), Javier Adelmar Zanetti (84/4), Roberto Fabián Ayala (88/3), Gabriel Iván Heinze (11/0), Juan Pablo Sorín (49/8) [77.Luciano Gabriel Figueroa (3/0)], Luis Oscar González (11/4) [66.Carlos Alberto Tévez (4/0)], Javier Alejandro Mascherano (5/0), Andrés Nicolás D'Alessandro (14/3), Cristián Alberto González (47/8), César Fabián Delgado (10/1) [66.Mauro Damián Rosales (6/0)], Javier Pedro Saviola (18/7). Trainer: Marcelo Alberto Bielsa (63).

**790.** 13.07.2004 **ARGENTINA - URUGUAY** **4-2(2-0)** 41st Copa América. Group Stage.
Estadio „Miguel Grau", Piura (Peru); Referee: Rubén Selman (Chile); Attendance: 19,865
**ARG:** Roberto Carlos Abbondanzieri (4/0), Javier Adelmar Zanetti (85/4), Roberto Fabián Ayala (89/4), Gabriel Iván Heinze (12/0), Clemente Juan Rodríguez (7/0) [46.Mariano Nicolás González (8/0)], Luis Oscar González (12/4) [80.Javier Pedro Saviola (19/7)], Javier Alejandro Mascherano (6/0), Andrés Nicolás D'Alessandro (15/3), Cristián Alberto González (48/9), César Fabián Delgado (11/1) [77.Carlos Alberto Tévez (5/0)], Luciano Gabriel Figueroa (4/2). Trainer: Marcelo Alberto Bielsa (64).
**Goals**: Cristián Alberto González (20 penalty), Luciano Gabriel Figueroa (21), Roberto Fabián Ayala (81), Luciano Gabriel Figueroa (90).

**791.** 17.07.2004 **PERU -ARGENTINA** **0-1(0-0)** 41st Copa América. Quarter-Finals.
Estadio „Elías Aguirre", Chiclayo; Referee: Carlos Amarilla Demarqui (Paraguay); Attendance: 25,000
**ARG:** Roberto Carlos Abbondanzieri (5/0), Javier Adelmar Zanetti (86/4), Roberto Fabián Ayala (90/4), Gabriel Iván Heinze (13/0), Juan Pablo Sorín (50/8), Luis Oscar González (13/4), Fabricio Coloccini (6/0), Andrés Nicolás D'Alessandro (16/3) [58.Carlos Alberto Tévez (6/1)], Cristián Alberto González (49/9), César Fabián Delgado (12/1) [77.Mauro Damián Rosales (7/0)], Luciano Gabriel Figueroa (5/2) [84.Facundo Hernán Quiroga (13/0)]. Trainer: Marcelo Alberto Bielsa (65).
**Goal**: Carlos Alberto Tévez (61).

**792.** 20.07.2004 **ARGENTINA - COLOMBIA** **3-0(1-0)** 41st Copa América. Semi-Finals.
Estadio Nacional, Lima (Peru); Referee: Gilberto Hidalgo Zamora (Peru); Attendance: 22,000
**ARG:** Roberto Carlos Abbondanzieri (6/0), Javier Adelmar Zanetti (87/4), Fabricio Coloccini (7/0), Gabriel Iván Heinze (14/0), Juan Pablo Sorín (51/9), Luis Oscar González (14/5), Javier Alejandro Mascherano (7/0), Carlos Alberto Tévez (7/2), Cristián Alberto González (50/9) [85.Diego Rodolfo Placente (18/0)], César Fabián Delgado (13/1) [61.Mauro Damián Rosales (8/0)], Luciano Gabriel Figueroa (6/2) [65.Facundo Hernán Quiroga (14/0)]. Trainer: Marcelo Alberto Bielsa (66).
**Goals**: Carlos Alberto Tévez (33), Luis Oscar González (50), Juan Pablo Sorín (80).

**793.** 25.07.2004 **ARGENTINA - BRAZIL** **2-2(1-1,2-2,2-2); 2-4 on penalties** 41st Copa América. Final.
Estadio Nacional, Lima (Peru); Referee: Carlos Amarilla Demarqui (Paraguay); Attendance: 43,000
**ARG:** Roberto Carlos Abbondanzieri (7/0), Fabricio Coloccini (8/0), Roberto Fabián Ayala (91/4), Gabriel Iván Heinze (15/0), Juan Pablo Sorín (52/9), Javier Adelmar Zanetti (88/4), Javier Alejandro Mascherano (8/0), Luis Oscar González (15/5) [75.Andrés Nicolás D'Alessandro (17/3)], Cristián Alberto González (51/10), Mauro Damián Rosales (9/0) [64.César Fabián Delgado (14/2)], Carlos Alberto Tévez (8/2) [90.Facundo Hernán Quiroga (15/0)]. Trainer: Marcelo Alberto Bielsa (67).
**Goals**: Cristián Alberto González (21 penalty), César Fabián Delgado (87).
**Penalties:** Andrés Nicolás D'Alessandro (saved), Gabriel Iván Heinze (miss), Cristián Alberto González, Juan Pablo Sorín.

**794.** 18.08.2004 **JAPAN - ARGENTINA** **1-2(0-2)**
ECOPA Stadium, Shizuoka; Referee: Yun Lu (China); Attendance: 48,721
**ARG:** Leonardo Franco Neorén (1/0), Facundo Hernán Quiroga (16/0), Walter Adrián Samuel (43/4), Gabriel Alejandro Milito (6/0), Diego Rodolfo Placente (19/0), Lionel Sebastián Scaloni (2/0), Lucas Martín Ademar Bernardi (1/0), Juan Román Riquelme (13/1), Mario Alberto Santana (1/1) [61.Maximiliano Rubén Rodríguez (3/1)], Diego Alberto Milito (6/3) [85.Leonardo Daniel Ponzio (3/0)], Luciano Martín Galletti (6/2) [65.Ariel Miguel Santiago Ibagaza (1/0)]. Trainer: Marcelo Alberto Bielsa (68).
**Goals**: Luciano Martín Galletti (4), Mario Alberto Santana (40).

**795.** 04.09.2004 **PERU - ARGENTINA** **1-3(0-1)** 18th FIFA WC. Qualifiers
Estadio Monumental „Teodoro Fernández", Lima; Referee: Carlos Eugenio Simón (Brazil); Attendance: 28,000
**ARG:** Roberto Carlos Abbondanzieri (8/0), Javier Adelmar Zanetti (89/4), Fabricio Coloccini (9/1), Gabriel Iván Heinze (16/0), Gabriel Alejandro Milito (7/0), Javier Alejandro Mascherano (9/0), Andrés Nicolás D'Alessandro (18/3) [65.Diego Alberto Milito (7/3)], Cristián Alberto González (52/10) [*sent off 45*], Mauro Damián Rosales (10/1), Carlos Alberto Tévez (9/2) [84.Nicolás Rubén Medina (1/0)], César Fabián Delgado (15/2) [71.Juan Pablo Sorín (53/10)]. Trainer: Marcelo Alberto Bielsa (69).
**Goals**: Mauro Damián Rosales (14), Fabricio Coloccini (67), Juan Pablo Sorín (90).

**796.** 09.10.2004 **ARGENTINA - URUGUAY** **4-2(3-0)** 18th FIFA WC. Qualifiers
Estadio Monumental „Antonio Vespucio Liberti", Buenos Aires; Referee: Wilson Souza Mendonça (Brazil); Attendance: 50,000
**ARG:** Roberto Carlos Abbondanzieri (9/0), Walter Adrián Samuel (44/4), Javier Adelmar Zanetti (90/5), Fabricio Coloccini (10/1), Gabriel Iván Heinze (17/0), Juan Pablo Sorín (54/10), Luis Oscar González (16/6) [68.Maximiliano Rubén Rodríguez (4/1)], Esteban Matías Cambiasso Deleau (8/0), Juan Román Riquelme (14/1), Javier Pedro Saviola (20/7), Luciano Gabriel Figueroa (7/4) [81.Federico Insúa (5/0)]. Trainer: José Néstor Pekerman (1).
**Goals**: Luis Oscar González (6), Luciano Gabriel Figueroa (32), Javier Adelmar Zanetti (45), Luciano Gabriel Figueroa (54).

**797.** 13.10.2004 **CHILE - ARGENTINA** **0-0** 18th FIFA WC. Qualifiers
Estadio Nacional, Santiago; Referee: Carlos Amarilla Demarqui (Paraguay); Attendance: 57,671
**ARG:** Roberto Carlos Abbondanzieri (10/0), Fabricio Coloccini (11/1), Walter Adrián Samuel (45/4), Gabriel Iván Heinze (18/0), Juan Pablo Sorín (55/10), Javier Adelmar Zanetti (91/5), Esteban Matías Cambiasso Deleau (9/0), Juan Román Riquelme (15/1), Luis Oscar González (17/6) [46.Javier Alejandro Mascherano (10/0)], Luciano Gabriel Figueroa (8/4) [63.Carlos Alberto Tévez (10/2)], Javier Pedro Saviola (21/7) [77.Andrés Nicolás D'Alessandro (19/3)]. Trainer: José Néstor Pekerman (2).

**798.** 17.11.2004 **ARGENTINA - VENEZUELA** **3-2(2-1)** 18th FIFA WC. Qualifiers
Estadio Monumental „Antonio Vespucio Liberti", Buenos Aires; Referee: Gilberto Hidalgo Zamora (Peru); Attendance: 30,000
**ARG:** Roberto Carlos Abbondanzieri (11/0), Javier Adelmar Zanetti (92/5), Javier Gonzálo Rodríguez (3/1), Gabriel Alejandro Milito (8/0), Juan Pablo Sorín (56/10), Javier Alejandro Mascherano (11/0), Juan Román Riquelme (16/2), Esteban Matías Cambiasso Deleau (10/0) [80.Diego Rodolfo Placente (20/0)], Santiago Hernán Solari (11/1) [66.Luis Oscar González (18/6)], César Fabián Delgado (16/2) [58.Javier Pedro Saviola (22/8)], Luciano Gabriel Figueroa (9/4). Trainer: José Néstor Pekerman (3).
**Goals**: José Manuel Rey (4 own goal), Juan Román Riquelme (45), Javier Pedro Saviola (66).

**799.** 09.02.2005 **GERMANY - ARGENTINA** **2-2(2-1)**
LTU-Arena, Düsseldorf; Referee: Stefano Farina (Italy); Attendance: 52,000
**ARG:** Roberto Carlos Abbondanzieri (12/0), Javier Adelmar Zanetti (93/5), Nicolás Andrés Burdisso (5/0), Gabriel Alejandro Milito (9/0) [46.Esteban Matías Cambiasso Deleau (11/0)], Gabriel Iván Heinze (19/0), Lionel Sebastián Scaloni (3/0) [46.Maximiliano Rubén Rodríguez (5/1)], Juan Román Riquelme (17/2), Aldo Pedro Duscher (1/0) [77.Luciano Martín Galletti (7/2)], Juan Pablo Sorín (57/10), Javier Pedro Saviola (23/8), Hernán Jorge Crespo (47/25). Trainer: José Néstor Pekerman (4).
**Goals**: Hernán Jorge Crespo (40 penalty, 81).

**800.** 09.03.2005 **ARGENTINA - MEXICO** **1-1(0-1)**
Memorial Coliseum, Los Angeles (United States); Referee: Brian Hall (United States); Attendance: 51,345
**ARG:** Germán Darío Lux (1/0), Federico Insúa (6/0) [60.Lisandro López (1/0)], Eduardo Nicolás Tuzzio (1/0), Fabricio Fabio Fuentes (1/0), Daniel Alberto Díaz (2/0), Martín Andrés Romagnoli (1/0), Rodrigo Sebastián Palacio (1/0) [80.José Ernesto Sosa (1/0)], Javier Alejandro Mascherano (12/0), Víctor Eduardo Zapata (1/0), Lucas Martín Castromán (5/0) [46.Fernando Daniel Belluschi (1/0)], Rolando David Zárate (1/1) [74.Sebastián Ariel Romero (1/0)]. Trainer: José Néstor Pekerman (5).
**Goal**: Rolando David Zárate (67).

**801.** 26.03.2005 **BOLIVIA - ARGENTINA** **1-2(0-0)** 18th FIFA WC. Qualifiers
Estadio „Hernándo Siles Zuazo", La Paz; Referee: Jorge Larrionda Pietrafiesa (Uruguay); Attendance: 25,000
**ARG:** Roberto Carlos Abbondanzieri (13/0), Leandro Damián Cufré (2/0), Nicolás Andrés Burdisso (6/0), Gabriel Alejandro Milito (10/0), Clemente Juan Rodríguez (8/0), Aldo Pedro Duscher (2/0), Esteban Matías Cambiasso Deleau (12/0), Maximiliano Rubén Rodríguez (6/1) [65.Leonardo Daniel Ponzio (4/0)], Lionel Sebastián Scaloni (4/0), Luciano Gabriel Figueroa (10/5) [75.Rolando David Zárate (2/1)], Luciano Martín Galletti (8/3) [83.Rodrigo Sebastián Palacio (2/0)]. Trainer: José Néstor Pekerman (6).
**Goals**: Luciano Gabriel Figueroa (57), Luciano Martín Galletti (63).

**802.** 30.03.2005 **ARGENTINA - COLOMBIA** **1-0(0-0)** 18th FIFA WC. Qualifiers
Estadio Monumental „Antonio Vespucio Liberti", Buenos Aires; Referee: Carlos Amarilla Demarqui (Paraguay); Attendance: 40,000
**ARG:** Roberto Carlos Abbondanzieri (14/0), Javier Adelmar Zanetti (94/5), Roberto Fabián Ayala (92/4), Gabriel Iván Heinze (20/0), Juan Pablo Sorín (58/10), Luis Oscar González (19/6), Javier Alejandro Mascherano (13/0) [55.Luciano Martín Galletti (9/3)], Esteban Matías Cambiasso Deleau (13/0), Juan Román Riquelme (18/2), Javier Pedro Saviola (24/8) [79.Diego Rodolfo Placente (21/0)], Hernán Jorge Crespo (48/26). Trainer: José Néstor Pekerman (7).
**Goal**: Hernán Jorge Crespo (65).

**803.** 04.06.2005 **ECUADOR - ARGENTINA** **2-0(0-0)** 18th FIFA WC. Qualifiers
Estadio Olimpico „Atahualpa", Quito; Referee: Rubén Selman (Chile); Attendance: 37,583
**ARG:** Leonardo Franco Neorén (3/0), Javier Adelmar Zanetti (95/5), Fabricio Coloccini (12/1), Walter Adrián Samuel (46/4), Gabriel Alejandro Milito (11/0) [68.Luciano Gabriel Figueroa (11/5)], Aldo Pedro Duscher (3/0) [31.Carlos Alberto Tévez (11/2)], Cristián Alberto González (53/10), Esteban Matías Cambiasso Deleau (14/0) [*sent off 88*], Pablo César Aimar Giordano (33/6) [74.Andrés Nicolás D'Alessandro (20/3)], Luciano Martín Galletti (10/3), Maximiliano Rubén Rodríguez (7/1). Trainer: José Néstor Pekerman (8).

**804.** 08.06.2005 **ARGENTINA - BRAZIL** **3-1(3-0)** 18th FIFA WC. Qualifiers
Estadio Monumental „Antonio Vespucio Liberti", Buenos Aires; Referee: Gustavo Méndez González (Uruguay); Attendance: 49,497
**ARG:** Roberto Carlos Abbondanzieri (15/0), Fabricio Coloccini (13/1), Roberto Fabián Ayala (93/4), Gabriel Iván Heinze (21/0), Luis Oscar González (20/6) [71.Javier Adelmar Zanetti (96/5)], Javier Alejandro Mascherano (14/0), Juan Pablo Sorín (59/10), Cristián Alberto González (54/10), Juan Román Riquelme (19/3), Javier Pedro Saviola (25/8) [82.Carlos Alberto Tévez (12/2)], Hernán Jorge Crespo (49/28). Trainer: José Néstor Pekerman (9).
**Goals**: Hernán Jorge Crespo (3), Juan Román Riquelme (18), Hernán Jorge Crespo (40).

**805.** 15.06.2005 **ARGENTINA - TUNISIA** **2-1(1-0)** 5th Confed. Cup. Group Stage.
FIFA-WM Stadion (RheinEnergie), Köln (Germany); Referee: Roberto Rosetti (Italy); Attendance: 28,033
**ARG:** Germán Darío Lux (2/0), Fabricio Coloccini (14/1), Javier Gonzálo Rodríguez (4/1), Gabriel Iván Heinze (22/0), Juan Pablo Sorín (60/10) [79.Javier Adelmar Zanetti (97/5)], Mario Alberto Santana (2/1), Juan Román Riquelme (20/4), Lucas Martín Ademar Bernardi (2/0), Maximiliano Rubén Rodríguez (8/1), Javier Pedro Saviola (26/9) [66.Carlos Alberto Tévez (13/2)], Luciano Martín Galletti (11/3). Trainer: José Néstor Pekerman (10).
**Goals**: Juan Román Riquelme (33 penalty), Javier Pedro Saviola (57).

**806.** 18.06.2005 **ARGENTINA - AUSTRALIA** **4-2(2-0)** 5th Confed. Cup. Group Stage.
Frankenstadion, Nürnberg (Germany); Referee: Shamsul Maldin (Singapore); Attendance: 25,658
**ARG:** Germán Darío Lux (3/0), Walter Adrián Samuel (47/4), Fabricio Coloccini (15/1) [86.Javier Gonzálo Rodríguez (5/1)], Gabriel Iván Heinze (23/0), Juan Pablo Sorín (61/10), Javier Adelmar Zanetti (98/5), Mario Alberto Santana (3/1) [66.Esteban Matías Cambiasso Deleau (15/0)], Juan Román Riquelme (21/5), Lucas Martín Ademar Bernardi (3/0), Javier Pedro Saviola (27/9) [73.Pablo César Aimar Giordano (34/6)], Luciano Gabriel Figueroa (12/8). Trainer: José Néstor Pekerman (11).
**Goals**: Luciano Gabriel Figueroa (12), Juan Román Riquelme (32 penalty), Luciano Gabriel Figueroa (53, 89).

**807.** 21.06.2005 **GERMANY - ARGENTINA** **2-2(1-1)** 5th Confed. Cup. Group Stage.
Frankenstadion, Nürnberg; Referee: Luboš Michel (Slovakia); Attendance: 42,088
**ARG:** Germán Darío Lux (4/0), Javier Adelmar Zanetti (99/5), Fabricio Coloccini (16/1), Walter Adrián Samuel (48/4) [62.Mario Alberto Santana (4/1)], Gabriel Iván Heinze (24/0), Lucas Martín Ademar Bernardi (4/0) [53.Pablo César Aimar Giordano (35/6)], Esteban Matías Cambiasso Deleau (16/1), Juan Román Riquelme (22/6), Juan Pablo Sorín (62/10), Carlos Alberto Tévez (14/2) [80.César Fabián Delgado (17/2)], Luciano Gabriel Figueroa (13/8). Trainer: José Néstor Pekerman (12).
**Goals**: Juan Román Riquelme (32), Esteban Matías Cambiasso Deleau (74).

**808.** 26.06.2005 **ARGENTINA – MEXICO** **1-1(0-0,0-0,1-1); 6-5 on penalties** 5th Confed. Cup. Semi-Finals.
FIFA-WM Stadion (AWD-Arena), Hannover (Germany); Referee: Roberto Rosetti (Italy); Attendance: 43,667
**ARG:** Germán Darío Lux (5/0), Javier Adelmar Zanetti (**100**/5), Fabricio Coloccini (17/1), Gabriel Alejandro Milito (12/0) [66.Maximiliano Rubén Rodríguez (9/1)], Gabriel Iván Heinze (25/0), Mario Alberto Santana (5/1) [76.Pablo César Aimar Giordano (36/6)], Esteban Matías Cambiasso Deleau (17/1), Juan Román Riquelme (23/6), Juan Pablo Sorín (63/10), Javier Pedro Saviola (28/9) [*sent off 90*], Luciano Gabriel Figueroa (14/9) [116.Luciano Martín Galletti (12/3)]. Trainer: José Néstor Pekerman (13).
**Goal**: Luciano Gabriel Figueroa (110).
**Penalties**: Juan Román Riquelme, Maximiliano Rubén Rodríguez, Pablo César Aimar Giordano, Luciano Martín Galletti, Juan Pablo Sorín, Esteban Matías Cambiasso Deleau.

**809.** 29.06.2005 **BRAZIL - ARGENTINA** **4-1(2-0)** 5th Confed. Cup. Final.
Waldstadion, Frankfurt/Main (Germany); Referee: Luboš Michel (Slovakia); Attendance: 45,591
**ARG:** Germán Darío Lux (6/0), Fabricio Coloccini (18/1), Gabriel Iván Heinze (26/0), Diego Rodolfo Placente (22/0), Javier Adelmar Zanetti (101/5), Lucas Martín Ademar Bernardi (5/0), Esteban Matías Cambiasso Deleau (18/1) [55.Pablo César Aimar Giordano (37/7)], Juan Román Riquelme (24/6), Juan Pablo Sorín (64/10), Luciano Gabriel Figueroa (15/9) [71.Carlos Alberto Tévez (15/2)], César Fabián Delgado (18/2) [79.Luciano Martín Galletti (13/3)]. Trainer: José Néstor Pekerman (14).
**Goal**: Pablo César Aimar Giordano (65).

**810.** 17.08.2005 **HUNGARY - ARGENTINA** **1-2(1-1)**
„Puskás Ferenc“ Stadion, Budapest; Referee: Dr. Markus Merk (Germany); Attendance: 22,000
**ARG:** Leonardo Franco Neorén (3/0), Lionel Sebastián Scaloni (5/0), Roberto Fabián Ayala (94/4), Gabriel Iván Heinze (27/1), Lucas Martín Ademar Bernardi (6/0), Andrés Nicolás D'Alessandro (21/3) [90.Mario Alberto Santana (6/1)], Luis Oscar González (21/6) [82.Pablo Javier Zabaleta Girod (1/0)], Maximiliano Rubén Rodríguez (10/2), Juan Pablo Sorín (65/10), Lisandro López (2/0) [64.Lionel Andrés Messi (1/0) [*sent off 65*]], Hernán Jorge Crespo (50/28). Trainer: José Néstor Pekerman (15).
**Goals**: Maximiliano Rubén Rodríguez (19), Gabriel Iván Heinze (62).

**811.** 03.09.2005 **PARAGUAY - ARGENTINA** **1-0(1-0)** 18th FIFA WC. Qualifiers
Estadio Defensores del Chaco, Asunción; Referee: Carlos Eugênio Simón (Brazil); Attendance: 32,000
**ARG:** Roberto Carlos Abbondanzieri (16/0), Fabricio Coloccini (19/1), Roberto Fabián Ayala (95/4), Gabriel Iván Heinze (28/1) [*sent off 56*], Pablo Javier Zabaleta Girod (2/0), Luis Oscar González (22/6), Esteban Matías Cambiasso Deleau (19/1), Juan Pablo Sorín (66/10), Juan Román Riquelme (25/6) [71.Andrés Nicolás D'Alessandro (22/3)], César Fabián Delgado (19/2) [61.Lionel Andrés Messi (2/0)], Ernesto Antonio Farías (1/0). Trainer: José Néstor Pekerman (16).

**812.** 09.10.2005 **ARGENTINA - PERU** **2-0(0-0)** 18th FIFA WC. Qualifiers
Estadio Monumental „Antonio Vespucio Liberti“, Buenos Aires; Referee: Carlos Torres (Paraguay); Attendance: 36,977
**ARG:** Roberto Carlos Abbondanzieri (17/0), Fabricio Coloccini (20/1), Roberto Fabián Ayala (96/4), Gabriel Alejandro Milito (13/0), Juan Pablo Sorín (67/10), Sebastián Alejandro Battaglia (4/0), Luis Oscar González (23/6), Cristián Alberto González (55/10) [58.Carlos Alberto Tévez (16/2)], Juan Román Riquelme (26/7) [84.Mario Alberto Santana (7/1)], Hernán Jorge Crespo (51/28), Lionel Andrés Messi (3/0). Trainer: José Néstor Pekerman (17).
**Goals**: Juan Román Riquelme (80 penalty), Luis Guadalupe (90 own goal).

**813.** 12.10.2005 **URUGUAY - ARGENTINA** **1-0(0-0)** 18th FIFA WC. Qualifiers
Estadio Centenario, Montevideo; Referee: Wilson Souza Mendonça (Brazil); Attendance: 55,000
**ARG:** Roberto Carlos Abbondanzieri (18/0), Roberto Fabián Ayala (97/4), Walter Adrián Samuel (49/4), Leonardo Daniel Ponzio (5/0), Juan Pablo Sorín (68/10), Sebastián Alejandro Battaglia (5/0), Luis Oscar González (24/6) [79.Lionel Andrés Messi (4/0)], Cristián Alberto González (56/10) [61.Pablo César Aimar Giordano (38/7)], Juan Román Riquelme (27/7), Carlos Alberto Tévez (17/2), Hernán Jorge Crespo (52/28) [61.César Fabián Delgado (20/2)]. Trainer: José Néstor Pekerman (18).

**814.** 12.11.2005 **ENGLAND - ARGENTINA** **3-2(1-1)**
Stade de Suisse, Genève (Switzerland); Referee: Philippe Leuba (Switzerland); Attendance: 29,000
**ARG:** Roberto Carlos Abbondanzieri (19/0), Javier Adelmar Zanetti (102/5), Roberto Fabián Ayala (98/4) [74.Fabricio Coloccini (21/1)], Walter Adrián Samuel (50/5), Juan Pablo Sorín (69/10), Martín Gastón Demichelis (1/0), Esteban Matías Cambiasso Deleau (20/1), Maximiliano Rubén Rodríguez (11/2), Juan Román Riquelme (28/7) [84.Luis Oscar González (25/6)], Carlos Alberto Tévez (18/2) [86.Julio Ricardo Cruz (14/2)], Hernán Jorge Crespo (53/29) [70.Javier Pedro Saviola (29/9)]. Trainer: José Néstor Pekerman (19).
**Goals**: Hernán Jorge Crespo (34), Walter Adrián Samuel (53).

**815.** 16.11.2005 **QATAR - ARGENTINA** **0-3(0-0)**
Al-Ittihad Stadium, Doha; Referee: Al-Fadhli (Kuwait)
**ARG:** Roberto Carlos Abbondanzieri (20/0), Roberto Fabián Ayala (99/5), Walter Adrián Samuel (51/5) [81.Gabriel Alejandro Milito (14/0)], Juan Pablo Sorín (70/10), Martín Gastón Demichelis (2/0) [46.Fabricio Coloccini (22/1)], Maximiliano Rubén Rodríguez (12/2), Sebastián Alejandro Battaglia (6/0), Daniel Rubén Bilos (1/0) [60.Luis Oscar González (26/6)], Juan Román Riquelme (29/8), Lionel Andrés Messi (5/0) [81.Carlos Alberto Tévez (19/2)], Javier Pedro Saviola (30/9) [60.Julio Ricardo Cruz (15/3)]. Trainer: José Néstor Pekerman (20).
**Goals**: Juan Román Riquelme (70), Julio Ricardo Cruz (72), Roberto Fabián Ayala (73).

**816.** 01.03.2006 **CROATIA - ARGENTINA** **3-2(1-2)**
St. Jakob-Park, Basel (Switzerland); Referee: Markus Nobs (Switzerland); Attendance: 13,138
**ARG:** Roberto Carlos Abbondanzieri (21/0), Fabricio Coloccini (23/1) [60.Luis Oscar González (27/6)], Nicolás Andrés Burdisso (7/0), Walter Adrián Samuel (52/5), Leonardo Daniel Ponzio (6/0), Martín Gastón Demichelis (3/0), Esteban Matías Cambiasso Deleau (21/1), Lionel Andrés Messi (6/1), Juan Román Riquelme (30/8), Carlos Alberto Tévez (20/3) [68.Pablo César Aimar Giordano (39/7)], Hernán Jorge Crespo (54/29) [75.Diego Alberto Milito (8/3)]. Trainer: José Néstor Pekerman (21).
**Goals**: Carlos Alberto Tévez (4), Lionel Andrés Messi (8).

**817.** 30.05.2006 **ARGENTINA - ANGOLA** **2-0(2-0)**
Stadio Arechi, Salerno (Italy); Referee: Stefano Farina (Italy); Attendance: 7,000
**ARG:** Roberto Carlos Abbondanzieri (22/0), Nicolás Andrés Burdisso (8/0) [82.Leandro Damián Cufré (3/0)], Roberto Fabián Ayala (**100**/5), Gabriel Iván Heinze (29/1) [64.Gabriel Alejandro Milito (15/0)], Juan Pablo Sorín (71/11), Maximiliano Rubén Rodríguez (13/3) [77.Pablo César Aimar Giordano (40/7)], Javier Alejandro Mascherano (15/0), Esteban Matías Cambiasso Deleau (22/1) [77.Carlos Alberto Tévez (21/3)], Juan Román Riquelme (31/8) [64.Lionel Sebastián Scaloni (6/0)], Javier Pedro Saviola (31/9) [64.Lionel Andrés Messi (7/1)], Hernán Jorge Crespo (55/29). Trainer: José Néstor Pekerman (22).
**Goals**: Maximiliano Rubén Rodríguez (28), Juan Pablo Sorín (36).

**818.** 10.06.2006 **ARGENTINA – IVORY COAST** **2-1(2-0)** 18th FIFA WC. Group Stage.
FIFA World Cup Stadium (AOL-Arena), Hamburg (Germany); Referee: Frank De Bleeckere (Belgium); Attendance: 45,442
**ARG:** Roberto Carlos Abbondanzieri (23/0), Nicolás Andrés Burdisso (9/0), Roberto Fabián Ayala (101/5), Gabriel Iván Heinze (30/1), Juan Pablo Sorín (Cap) (72/11), Maximiliano Rubén Rodríguez (14/3), Javier Alejandro Mascherano (16/0), Esteban Matías Cambiasso Deleau (23/1), Juan Román Riquelme (32/8) [90+3.Pablo César Aimar Giordano (41/7)], Javier Pedro Saviola (32/10) [76.Luis Oscar González (28/6)], Hernán Jorge Crespo (56/30) [64.Rodrigo Sebastián Palacio (3/0)]. Trainer: José Néstor Pekerman (23).
**Goals**: Hernán Jorge Crespo (24), Javier Pedro Saviola (38).

**819.** 16.06.2006 **ARGENTINA – SERBIA & MONTENEGRO** **6-0(3-0)** 18th FIFA WC. Group Stage.
FIFA World Cup Stadium (Veltins-Arena), Gelsenkirchen (Germany); Referee: Roberto Rosetti (Italy); Attendance: 52,000
**ARG:** Roberto Carlos Abbondanzieri (24/0), Nicolás Andrés Burdisso (10/0), Roberto Fabián Ayala (102/5), Gabriel Iván Heinze (31/1), Juan Pablo Sorín (Cap) (73/11), Luis Oscar González (29/6) [17.Esteban Matías Cambiasso Deleau (24/2)], Javier Alejandro Mascherano (17/0), Juan Román Riquelme (33/8), Maximiliano Rubén Rodríguez (15/5) [75.Lionel Andrés Messi (8/2)], Javier Pedro Saviola (33/10) [59.Carlos Alberto Tévez (22/4)], Hernán Jorge Crespo (57/31). Trainer: José Néstor Pekerman (24).
**Goals**: Maximiliano Rubén Rodríguez (6), Esteban Matías Cambiasso Deleau (31), Maximiliano Rubén Rodríguez (41), Hernán Jorge Crespo (78), Carlos Alberto Tévez (84), Lionel Andrés Messi (88).

**820.** 21.06.2006 **HOLLAND - ARGENTINA** **0-0** 18th FIFA WC. Group Stage.
FIFA World Cup Stadium (Wald), Frankfurt/Main (Germany); Referee: Luis Medina Cantalejo (Spain); Attendance: 48,000
**ARG:** Roberto Carlos Abbondanzieri (25/0), Nicolás Andrés Burdisso (11/0) [24.Fabricio Coloccini (24/1)], Roberto Fabián Ayala (Cap) (103/5), Gabriel Alejandro Milito (16/0), Leandro Damián Cufré (4/0), Maximiliano Rubén Rodríguez (16/5), Javier Alejandro Mascherano (18/0), Esteban Matías Cambiasso Deleau (25/2), Juan Román Riquelme (34/8) [80.Pablo César Aimar Giordano (42/7)], Lionel Andrés Messi (9/2) [70.Julio Ricardo Cruz (16/3)], Carlos Alberto Tévez (23/4). Trainer: José Néstor Pekerman (25).

**821.** 24.06.2006 **ARGENTINA - MEXICO** **2-1(1-1,1-1)** 18th FIFA WC. 2nd Round.
Zentralstadion, Leipzig (Germany); Referee: Massimo Busacca (Switzerland); Attendance: 43,000
**ARG:** Roberto Carlos Abbondanzieri (26/0), Lionel Sebastián Scaloni (7/0), Roberto Fabián Ayala (104/5), Gabriel Iván Heinze (32/1), Juan Pablo Sorín (Cap) (74/11), Esteban Matías Cambiasso Deleau (26/2) [76.Pablo César Aimar Giordano (43/7)], Javier Alejandro Mascherano (19/0), Juan Román Riquelme (35/8), Maximiliano Rubén Rodríguez (17/6), Javier Pedro Saviola (34/10) [84.Lionel Andrés Messi (10/2)], Hernán Jorge Crespo (58/32) [75.Carlos Alberto Tévez (24/4)]. Trainer: José Néstor Pekerman (26).
**Goals**: Hernán Jorge Crespo (9), Maximiliano Rubén Rodríguez (98).

**822.** 30.06.2006 **GERMANY - ARGENTINA** **1-1(0-0,1-1,1-1); 4-2 on penalties** 18th FIFA WC. Quarter-Finals.
Olympiastadion, Berlin; Referee: Ľuboš Michel (Slovakia); Attendance: 72,000
**ARG:** Roberto Carlos Abbondanzieri (27/0) [71.Leonardo Neorén Franco (4/0)], Fabricio Coloccini (25/1), Roberto Fabián Ayala (105/6), Gabriel Iván Heinze (33/1), Juan Pablo Sorín (Cap) (75/11), Luis Oscar González (30/6), Javier Alejandro Mascherano (20/0), Maximiliano Rubén Rodríguez (18/6), Juan Román Riquelme (36/8) [72.Esteban Matías Cambiasso Deleau (27/2)], Hernán Jorge Crespo (59/32) [79.Julio Ricardo Cruz (17/3)], Carlos Alberto Tévez (25/4). Trainer: José Néstor Pekerman (27).
**Goal**: Roberto Fabián Ayala (49).
**Penalties**: Julio Ricardo Cruz, Roberto Fabián Ayala (save), Maximiliano Rubén Rodríguez, Esteban Matías Cambiasso Deleau (save).
**After the penalty-shoot-out, reserve player Leandro Damián Cufré was sent off due to unsportlike behaviour.*

**823.** 03.09.2006 **BRAZIL - ARGENTINA** **3-0(1-0)**
Emirates Stadium, London (England); Referee: Stephen Bennett (England); Attendance: 59,032
**ARG:** Roberto Carlos Abbondanzieri (28/0), Pablo Javier Zabaleta Girod (3/0), Fabricio Coloccini (26/1), Gabriel Alejandro Milito (17/0), Clemente Juan Rodríguez (9/0) [46.Walter Adrián Samuel (53/5)], Luis Oscar González (31/6), Javier Alejandro Mascherano (21/0) [46.Leandro Daniel Somoza (1/0)], Juan Román Riquelme (Cap) (37/8), Daniel Rubén Bilos (2/0) [72.Federico Insúa (7/0)], Lionel Andrés Messi (11/2), Carlos Alberto Tévez (26/4) [66.Sergio Leonel Agüero del Castillo (1/0)]. Trainer: Alfio Oscar Basile (49).

**824.** 11.10.2006 **SPAIN - ARGENTINA** **2-1(1-1)**
Estadio La Nueva Condomina, Murcia; Referee: Laurent Duhamel (France); Attendance: 31,000
**ARG:** Roberto Carlos Abbondanzieri (29/0), Pablo Javier Zabaleta Girod (4/0), Roberto Fabián Ayala (Cap) (106/6), Gabriel Alejandro Milito (18/0), Rodolfo Martín Arruabarrena (6/0), Luis Oscar González (32/6) [46.Leandro Daniel Somoza (2/0)], Javier Alejandro Mascherano (22/0), Maximiliano Rubén Rodríguez (19/6) [16.Daniel Rubén Bilos (3/1)], Federico Insúa (8/0) [56.Pablo César Aimar Giordano (44/7)], Lionel Andrés Messi (12/2) [61.Javier Pedro Saviola (35/10)], Carlos Alberto Tévez (27/4) [71.Sergio Leonel Agüero del Castillo (2/0)]. Trainer: Alfio Oscar Basile (50).
**Goal**: Daniel Rubén Bilos (35).

**825.** 07.02.2007 **FRANCE - ARGENTINA** **0-1(0-1)**
Stade de France, Saint-Denis, Paris; Referee: Damir Skomina (Slovenia); Attendance: 79,862
**ARG:** Roberto Carlos Abbondanzieri (30/0), Nicolás Andrés Burdisso (12/0), Roberto Fabián Ayala (Cap) (107/6), Gabriel Alejandro Milito (19/0), Gabriel Iván Heinze (34/1), Javier Adelmar Zanetti (103/5), Fernando Rubén Gago (1/0), Esteban Matías Cambiasso Deleau (28/2), Luis Oscar González (33/6) [78.Jonás Manuel Gutiérrez (1/0)], Hernán Jorge Crespo (60/32) [78.Diego Alberto Milito (9/3)], Javier Pedro Saviola (36/11) [83.Sergio Leonel Agüero del Castillo (3/0)]. Trainer: Alfio Oscar Basile (51).
**Goal**: Javier Pedro Saviola (15).

**826.** 18.04.2007 **ARGENTINA - CHILE** **0-0**
Estadio Malvinas Argentinas, Mendoza; Referee: Martín Emilio Vázquez Broquetas (Uruguay); Attendance: 38,000
**ARG:** Juan Pablo Carrizo (1/0), Hugo Benjamín Ibarra (Cap) (7/0), Eduardo Nicolás Tuzzio (2/0), Daniel Alberto Díaz (3/0), Jonathan Bottinelli (1/0), Fernando Daniel Belluschi (2/0) [81.Leonardo Daniel Ponzio (7/0)], Cristian Raúl Ledesma (1/0), José Ernesto Sosa (2/0) [81.Pablo Martín Ledesma (1/0)], Daniel Gastón Montenegro (1/0) [63.Neri Raúl Cardozo (1/0)], Rodrigo Sebastián Palacio (4/0) [63.Ezequiel Iván Lavezzi (1/0)], Hugo Mariano Pavone (1/0). Trainer: Alfio Oscar Basile (52).

**827.** 02.06.2007 **SWITZERLAND - ARGENTINA** **1-1(0-0)**
St.Jakob-Park, Basel; Referee: Domenico Messina (Italy); Attendance: 29,000
**ARG:** Roberto Carlos Abbondanzieri (31/0), Javier Adelmar Zanetti (104/5), Roberto Fabián Ayala (Cap) (108/6), Gabriel Alejandro Milito (20/0), Gabriel Iván Heinze (35/1), Luis Oscar González (34/6) [67.Javier Alejandro Mascherano (23/0)], Fernando Rubén Gago (2/0), Esteban Matías Cambiasso Deleau (29/2), Lionel Andrés Messi (13/2) [89.Javier Pedro Saviola (37/11)], Hernán Jorge Crespo (61/32) [67.Diego Alberto Milito (10/3)], Carlos Alberto Tévez (28/5) [79.Pablo César Aimar Giordano (45/7)]. Trainer: Alfio Oscar Basile (53).
**Goal**: Carlos Alberto Tévez (49).

**828.** 05.06.2007 **ARGENTINA - ALGERIA** **4-3(1-2)**
Estadio Camp Nou, Barcelona (Spain); Referee: Alfonso Álvarez Izquierdo (Spain); Attendance: n/a
**ARG:** Roberto Carlos Abbondanzieri (32/0), Nicolás Andrés Burdisso (13/0) [46.Luis Oscar González (35/6)], Roberto Fabián Ayala (Cap) (109/6), Gabriel Alejandro Milito (21/0), Javier Horacio Pinola (1/0), Javier Adelmar Zanetti (105/5), Fernando Rubén Gago (3/0) [46.Javier Alejandro Mascherano (24/0)], Esteban Matías Cambiasso Deleau (30/3), Lionel Andrés Messi (14/4), Carlos Alberto Tévez (29/6) [67.Pablo César Aimar Giordano (46/7)], Diego Alberto Milito (11/3) [60.Hernán Jorge Crespo (62/32)]. Trainer: Alfio Oscar Basile (54).
**Goals**: Carlos Alberto Tévez (1 penalty), Lionel Andrés Messi (54 penalty), Esteban Matías Cambiasso Deleau (58), Lionel Andrés Messi (73).

**829.** 28.06.2007 **ARGENTINA – UNITED STATES** **4-1(1-1)** 42nd Copa América. Group Stage.
Estadio "José Encarnación 'Pachencho' Romero", Maracaibo (Venezuela); Referee: Carlos Luis Chandía Alarcón (Chile); Attendance: 34,500
**ARG:** Roberto Carlos Abbondanzieri (33/0), Javier Adelmar Zanetti (106/5), Roberto Fabián Ayala (Cap) (110/6), Gabriel Alejandro Milito (22/0), Gabriel Iván Heinze (36/1), Javier Alejandro Mascherano (25/0), Juan Sebastián Verón (57/9) [86.Fernando Rubén Gago (4/0)], Juan Román Riquelme (38/8), Esteban Matías Cambiasso Deleau (31/3) [58.Pablo César Aimar Giordano (47/8)], Lionel Andrés Messi (15/4) [79.Carlos Alberto Tévez (30/7)], Hernán Jorge Crespo (63/34). Trainer: Alfio Oscar Basile (55).
**Goals**: Hernán Jorge Crespo (11, 64), Pablo César Aimar Giordano (78), Carlos Alberto Tévez (85).

**830.** 02.07.2007 **ARGENTINA - COLOMBIA** **4-2(3-1)** 42nd Copa América. Group Stage.
Estadio "José Encarnación 'Pachencho' Romero", Maracaibo (Venezuela); Referee: Carlos Eugênio Simon (Brazil); Attendance: 35,000
**ARG:** Roberto Carlos Abbondanzieri (34/0), Javier Adelmar Zanetti (107/5), Roberto Fabián Ayala (Cap) (111/6), Gabriel Alejandro Milito (23/0), Gabriel Iván Heinze (37/1), Javier Alejandro Mascherano (26/0), Juan Sebastián Verón (58/9) [80.Luis Oscar González (36/6)], Juan Román Riquelme (39/10), Esteban Matías Cambiasso Deleau (32/3), Lionel Andrés Messi (16/4) [84.Carlos Alberto Tévez (31/7)], Hernán Jorge Crespo (64/35) [21.Diego Alberto Milito (12/4)]. Trainer: Alfio Oscar Basile (56).
**Goals**: Hernán Jorge Crespo (20 penalty), Juan Román Riquelme (34, 45), Diego Alberto Milito (90).

**831.** 05.07.2007 **ARGENTINA - PARAGUAY** **1-0(0-0)** 42nd Copa América. Group Stage.
Estadio Metropolitano de Fútbol de Lara, Barquisimeto (Venezuela); Referee: Jorge Larrionda Pietrafesa (Uruguay); Attendance: 37,000
**ARG:** Roberto Carlos Abbondanzieri (35/0), Hugo Benjamín Ibarra (8/0), Nicolás Andrés Burdisso (14/0), Daniel Alberto Díaz (4/0), Javier Adelmar Zanetti (Cap) (108/5), Fernando Rubén Gago (5/0), Luis Oscar González (37/6) [67.Javier Alejandro Mascherano (27/1)], Pablo César Aimar Giordano (48/8) [85.Roberto Fabián Ayala (112/6)], Esteban Matías Cambiasso Deleau (33/3) [67.Lionel Andrés Messi (17/4)], Rodrígo Sebastián Palacio (5/0), Carlos Alberto Tévez (32/7). Trainer: Alfio Oscar Basile (57).
**Goal**: Javier Alejandro Mascherano (79).

**832.** 08.07.2007 **ARGENTINA - PERU** **4-0(0-0)** 42nd Copa América. Quarter-Finals.
Estadio Metropolitano de Fútbol de Lara, Barquisimeto (Venezuela); Referee: Carlos Eugênio Simon (Brazil); Attendance: 37,000
**ARG:** Roberto Carlos Abbondanzieri (36/0), Javier Adelmar Zanetti (109/5), Roberto Fabián Ayala (Cap) (113/6), Gabriel Alejandro Milito (24/0), Gabriel Iván Heinze (38/1), Javier Alejandro Mascherano (28/2), Juan Sebastián Verón (59/9) [71.Fernando Rubén Gago (6/0)], Juan Román Riquelme (40/12), Esteban Matías Cambiasso Deleau (34/3) [83.Pablo César Aimar Giordano (49/8)], Lionel Andrés Messi (18/5), Diego Alberto Milito (13/4) [46.Carlos Alberto Tévez (33/7)]. Trainer: Alfio Oscar Basile (58).
**Goals**: Juan Román Riquelme (47), Lionel Andrés Messi (61), Javier Alejandro Mascherano (75), Juan Román Riquelme (86).

**833.** 11.07.2007 **ARGENTINA - MEXICO** **3-0(1-0)** 42nd Copa América. Semi-Finals.
Estadio Polideportivo Cachamay, Puerto Ordaz (Venezuela); Referee: Carlos Luis Chandía Alarcón (Chile); Attendance: 40,000
**ARG:** Roberto Carlos Abbondanzieri (37/0), Javier Adelmar Zanetti (110/5), Roberto Fabián Ayala (Cap) (114/6), Gabriel Alejandro Milito (25/0), Gabriel Iván Heinze (39/2), Javier Alejandro Mascherano (29/2), Juan Sebastián Verón (60/9) [78.Fernando Rubén Gago (7/0)], Juan Román Riquelme (41/13) [87.Pablo César Aimar Giordano (50/8)], Esteban Matías Cambiasso Deleau (35/3), Lionel Andrés Messi (19/6), Carlos Alberto Tévez (34/7) [78.Rodrígo Sebastián Palacio (6/0)]. Trainer: Alfio Oscar Basile (59).
**Goals**: Gabriel Iván Heinze (45), Lionel Andrés Messi (61), Juan Román Riquelme (66 penalty).

**834.** 15.07.2007 **BRAZIL - ARGENTINA** **3-0(2-0)** 42nd Copa América. Final.
Estadio "José Encarnación 'Pachencho' Romero", Maracaibo (Venezuela); Referee: Carlos Arencio Amarilla Demarqui (Paraguay); Attendance: 42,000
**ARG:** Roberto Carlos Abbondanzieri (38/0), Javier Adelmar Zanetti (111/5), Roberto Fabián Ayala (Cap) (115/6), Gabriel Alejandro Milito (26/0), Gabriel Iván Heinze (40/2), Javier Alejandro Mascherano (30/2), Juan Sebastián Verón (61/9) [67.Luis Oscar González (38/6)], Juan Román Riquelme (42/13), Esteban Matías Cambiasso Deleau (36/3) [59.Pablo César Aimar Giordano (51/8)], Lionel Andrés Messi (20/6), Carlos Alberto Tévez (35/7). Trainer: Alfio Oscar Basile (60).

**835.** 22.08.2007 **NORWAY - ARGENTINA** **2-1(1-0)**
Ullevaal Stadion, Oslo; Referee: Darko Čeferin (Slovenia); Attendance: 23,932
**ARG:** Oscar Alfredo Ustari (1/0), Javier Adelmar Zanetti (Cap) (112/5), Ezequiel Marcelo Garay González (1/0), Nicolás Andrés Burdisso (15/0), Gabriel Alejandro Milito (27/0), Javier Alejandro Mascherano (31/2), Maximiliano Rubén Rodríguez (20/7), Luis Oscar González (39/6) [46.Federico Insúa (9/0)], Ezequiel Iván Lavezzi (2/0) [46.Javier Pedro Saviola (38/11)], Diego Alberto Milito (14/4) [79.Fernando Rubén Gago (8/0)], Lionel Andrés Messi (21/6). Trainer: Alfio Oscar Basile (61).
**Goal**: Maximiliano Rubén Rodríguez (84).

**836.** 11.09.2007 **AUSTRALIA - ARGENTINA** **0-1(0-0)**
Cricket Ground, Melbourne; Referee: Michael Dean (England); Attendance: 70,171
**ARG:** Roberto Carlos Abbondanzieri (39/0), Nicolás Andrés Burdisso (16/0), Martín Gastón Demichelis (4/1), Gabriel Alejandro Milito (28/0), Gabriel Iván Heinze (41/2), Javier Adelmar Zanetti (Cap) (113/5), Javier Alejandro Mascherano (32/2), Jonás Manuel Gutiérrez (2/0) [72.Fernando Rubén Gago (9/0)], Federico Insúa (10/0) [82.Cristian Raúl Ledesma (2/0)], Lionel Andrés Messi (22/6) [90+1.Sergio Leonel Agüero del Castillo (4/0)], Carlos Alberto Tévez (36/7) [85.Javier Pedro Saviola (39/11)]. Trainer: Alfio Oscar Basile (62).
**Goal**: Martín Gastón Demichelis (49).

**837.** 13.10.2007 **ARGENTINA - CHILE** **2-0(2-0)** 19th FIFA WC. Qualifiers
Estadio Monumental „Antonio Vespucio Liberti", Buenos Aires; Referee: Martín Emilio Vázquez Broquetas (Uruguay); Attendance: 55,000
**ARG:** Roberto Carlos Abbondanzieri (40/0), Javier Adelmar Zanetti (Cap) (114/5), Martín Gastón Demichelis (5/1), Gabriel Alejandro Milito (29/0), Gabriel Iván Heinze (42/2), Javier Alejandro Mascherano (33/2), Esteban Matías Cambiasso Deleau (37/3), Maximiliano Rubén Rodríguez (21/7) [68.Fernando Rubén Gago (10/0)], Juan Román Riquelme (43/15), Lionel Andrés Messi (23/6) [84.Javier Pedro Saviola (40/11)], Carlos Alberto Tévez (37/7) [74.Sergio Leonel Agüero del Castillo (5/0)]. Trainer: Alfio Oscar Basile (63).
**Goals**: Juan Román Riquelme (27, 45).

**838.** 16.10.2007 **VENEZUELA - ARGENTINA** **0-2(0-2)** 19th FIFA WC. Qualifiers
Estadio "José Encarnación 'Pachencho' Romero", Maracaibo; Referee: Carlos Eugênio Simon (Brazil); Attendance: 35,000
**ARG:** Roberto Carlos Abbondanzieri (41/0), Hugo Benjamín Ibarra (9/0) [64.Fernando Rubén Gago (11/0)], Martín Gastón Demichelis (6/1), Gabriel Alejandro Milito (30/1), Nicolás Andrés Burdisso (17/0) [74.Daniel Alberto Díaz (5/0)], Javier Adelmar Zanetti (Cap) (115/5), Javier Alejandro Mascherano (34/2), Esteban Matías Cambiasso Deleau (38/3), Juan Román Riquelme (44/15), Lionel Andrés Messi (24/7), Carlos Alberto Tévez (38/7) [81.Germán Gustavo Denis (1/0)]. Trainer: Alfio Oscar Basile (64).
**Goals**: Gabriel Alejandro Milito (16), Lionel Andrés Messi (43).

**839.** 17.11.2007 **ARGENTINA - BOLIVIA** **3-0(1-0)** 19th FIFA WC. Qualifiers
Estadio Monumental „Antonio Vespucio Liberti", Buenos Aires; Referee: Víctor Hugo Rivera (Peru); Attendance: 43,308
**ARG:** Roberto Carlos Abbondanzieri (42/0), Javier Adelmar Zanetti (Cap) (116/5), Martín Gastón Demichelis (7/1), Gabriel Alejandro Milito (31/1), Hugo Benjamín Ibarra (10/0), Javier Alejandro Mascherano (35/2), Esteban Matías Cambiasso Deleau (39/3) [69.Fernando Rubén Gago (12/0)], Juan Román Riquelme (45/17), Lionel Andrés Messi (25/7), Sergio Leonel Agüero del Castillo (6/1) [75.Maximiliano Rubén Rodríguez (22/7)], Carlos Alberto Tévez (39/7) [83.Germán Gustavo Denis (2/0)]. Trainer: Alfio Oscar Basile (65).
**Goals**: Sergio Leonel Agüero del Castillo (41), Juan Román Riquelme (57, 74).

**840.** 20.11.2007 **COLOMBIA - ARGENTINA** **2-1(0-1)** 19th FIFA WC. Qualifiers
Estadio „Nemesio Camacho" ‚El Campín', Bogotá; Referee: Jorge Larrionda Pietrafesa (Uruguay); Attendance: 41,700
**ARG:** Roberto Carlos Abbondanzieri (43/0), Javier Adelmar Zanetti (Cap) (117/5), Martín Gastón Demichelis (8/1), Gabriel Alejandro Milito (32/1), Hugo Benjamín Ibarra (11/0), Javier Alejandro Mascherano (36/2), Esteban Matías Cambiasso Deleau (40/3) [75.Maximiliano Rubén Rodríguez (23/7)], Juan Román Riquelme (46/17), Fernando Rubén Gago (13/0), Lionel Andrés Messi (26/8), Carlos Alberto Tévez (40/7) [*sent off 25*]. Trainer: Alfio Oscar Basile (66).
**Goal**: Lionel Andrés Messi (36).

**841.** 26.03.2008 **EGYPT - ARGENTINA** **0-2(0-0)**
National Stadium, Cairo; Referee: Jamal Hemody (Algeria); Attendance: n/a
**ARG:** Roberto Carlos Abbondanzieri (44/0), Javier Adelmar Zanetti (Cap) (118/5), Martín Gastón Demichelis (9/1) [83.Fabricio Coloccini (27/1)], Nicolás Andrés Burdisso (18/1), Gabriel Iván Heinze (43/2), Javier Alejandro Mascherano (37/2), Fernando Rubén Gago (14/0), Maximiliano Rubén Rodríguez (24/7) [89.Pablo Javier Zabaleta Girod (5/0)], Luis Oscar González (40/6), Sergio Leonel Agüero del Castillo (7/2) [86.Lisandro López (3/0)], Julio Ricardo Cruz (18/3) [69.Fernando Ezequiel Cavenaghi (1/0)]. Trainer: Alfio Oscar Basile (67).
**Goals**: Sergio Leonel Agüero del Castillo (66), Nicolás Andrés Burdisso (85).

**842.** 04.06.2008 **MEXICO - ARGENTINA** **1-4(0-3)**
Qualcomm Stadium, San Diego (United States); Referee: Mauricio Navarro (Canada); Attendance: 68,498
**ARG:** Roberto Carlos Abbondanzieri (45/0), Javier Adelmar Zanetti (119/5), Martín Gastón Demichelis (10/1), Nicolás Andrés Burdisso (19/2), Fabricio Coloccini (28/1), Javier Alejandro Mascherano (38/2), Fernando Rubén Gago (15/0) [79.Éver Maximiliano David Banega (1/0)], Maximiliano Rubén Rodríguez (25/8) [73.Jonás Manuel Gutiérrez (3/0)], Sergio Leonel Agüero del Castillo (8/3) [85.José Ernesto Sosa (3/0)], Julio Ricardo Cruz (19/3) [60.Fernando Ezequiel Cavenaghi (2/0)], Lionel Andrés Messi (27/9) [85.Lisandro López (4/0)]. Trainer: Alfio Oscar Basile (68).
**Goals**: Nicolás Andrés Burdisso (11), Lionel Andrés Messi (18), Maximiliano Rubén Rodríguez (29), Sergio Leonel Agüero del Castillo (71).

**843.** 08.06.2008 **UNITED STATES - ARGENTINA** **0-0**
Giants Stadium, East Rutherford; Referee: Joel Aguilar (El Salvador); Attendance: 78,682
**ARG:** Roberto Carlos Abbondanzieri (46/0), Javier Gonzalo Rodríguez (6/1), Nicolás Andrés Burdisso (20/2) [46.Martín Gastón Demichelis (11/1)], Gabriel Iván Heinze (44/2), Pablo Javier Zabaleta Girod (6/0) [77.Javier Adelmar Zanetti (120/5)], Fernando Rubén Gago (16/0), Maximiliano Rubén Rodríguez (26/8) [74.Fernando Ezequiel Cavenaghi (3/0)], Javier Alejandro Mascherano (39/2), Julio Ricardo Cruz (20/3) [64.Lisandro López (5/0)], Sergio Leonel Agüero del Castillo (9/3) [88.Éver Maximiliano David Banega (2/0)], Lionel Andrés Messi (28/9) [46.José Ernesto Sosa (4/0)]. Trainer: Alfio Oscar Basile (69).

**844.** 15.06.2008 **ARGENTINA - ECUADOR** **1-1(0-0)** 19th FIFA WC. Qualifiers
Estadio Monumental „Antonio Vespucio Liberti", Buenos Aires; Referee: René Ortubé Betancourt (Bolivia); Attendance: 41,167
**ARG:** Roberto Carlos Abbondanzieri (47/0), Nicolás Andrés Burdisso (21/2), Martín Gastón Demichelis (12/1), Gabriel Iván Heinze (45/2), Javier Adelmar Zanetti (121/5), Javier Alejandro Mascherano (40/2) [63.Julio Ricardo Cruz (21/3)], Juan Sebastián Verón (62/9) [89.Rodrigo Sebastián Palacio (7/1)], Maximiliano Rubén Rodríguez (27/8) [46.Fernando Rubén Gago (17/0)], Juan Román Riquelme (47/17), Sergio Leonel Agüero del Castillo (10/3), Lionel Andrés Messi (29/9). Trainer: Alfio Oscar Basile (70).
**Goal**: Rodrigo Sebastián Palacio (89).

**845.** 18.06.2008 **BRAZIL - ARGENTINA** **0-0** 19th FIFA WC. Qualifiers
Estádio „Governador Magalhães Pinto", Belo Horizonte; Referee: Óscar Julián Ruiz Acosta (Colombia); Attendance: 65,000
**ARG:** Roberto Carlos Abbondanzieri (48/0), Javier Adelmar Zanetti (122/5), Nicolás Andrés Burdisso (22/2), Fabricio Coloccini (29/1), Gabriel Iván Heinze (46/2), Javier Alejandro Mascherano (41/2), Fernando Rubén Gago (18/0), Jonás Manuel Gutiérrez (4/0), Juan Román Riquelme (48/17) [84.Sebastián Alejandro Battaglia (7/0)], Lionel Andrés Messi (30/9) [90+2.Rodrigo Sebastián Palacio (8/1)], Julio Ricardo Cruz (22/3) [67.Sergio Leonel Agüero del Castillo (11/3)]. Trainer: Alfio Oscar Basile (71).

**846.** 20.08.2008 **BELARUS - ARGENTINA** **0-0**
Dinamo Stadium, Minsk; Referee: Stanislav Sukhina (Russia); Attendance: 20,000
**ARG:** Juan Pablo Carrizo (2/0), Javier Adelmar Zanetti (123/5), Nicolás Andrés Burdisso (23/2), Fabricio Coloccini (30/1), Gabriel Iván Heinze (47/2), Pablo Martín Ledesma (2/0) [64.Fernando Ezequiel Cavenaghi (4/0)], Esteban Matías Cambiasso Deleau (41/3), Luis Oscar González (41/6), Jonás Manuel Gutiérrez (5/0), Carlos Alberto Tévez (41/7) [79.Lisandro López (6/0)], Germán Gustavo Denis (3/0) [64.Mariano Nicolás González (9/0)]. Trainer: Alfio Oscar Basile (72).

**847.** 06.09.2008 **ARGENTINA - PARAGUAY** **1-1(0-1)** 19th FIFA WC. Qualifiers
Estadio Monumental „Antonio Vespucio Liberti", Buenos Aires; Referee: Carlos Eugênio Simon (Brazil); Attendance: 46,250
**ARG:** Roberto Carlos Abbondanzieri (49/0) [14.Juan Pablo Carrizo (3/0)], Fabricio Coloccini (31/1), Martín Gastón Demichelis (13/1), Gabriel Iván Heinze (48/2) [46.Daniel Alberto Díaz (6/0)], Javier Adelmar Zanetti (124/5), Javier Alejandro Mascherano (42/2), Esteban Matías Cambiasso Deleau (42/3), Ángel Fabián di María (1/0) [46.Sergio Leonel Agüero del Castillo (12/4)], Juan Román Riquelme (49/17), Lionel Andrés Messi (31/9), Carlos Alberto Tévez (42/7) [*sent off 30*]. Trainer: Alfio Oscar Basile (73).
**Goal**: Sergio Leonel Agüero del Castillo (60).

**848.** 10.09.2008 **PERU - ARGENTINA** **1-1(0-0)** 19th FIFA WC. Qualifiers
Estadio Monumental, Lima; Referee: Carlos Arecio Amarilla Demarqui (Paraguay); Attendance: 40,000
**ARG:** Juan Pablo Carrizo (4/0), Fabricio Coloccini (32/1), Daniel Alberto Díaz (7/0), Martín Gastón Demichelis (14/1), Javier Adelmar Zanetti (125/5), Esteban Matías Cambiasso Deleau (43/4) [87.Pablo Javier Zabaleta Girod (7/0)], Fernando Rubén Gago (19/0), Juan Román Riquelme (50/17), Jonás Manuel Gutiérrez (6/0) [16.Sebastián Alejandro Battaglia (8/0)], Lionel Andrés Messi (32/9), Sergio Leonel Agüero del Castillo (13/4) [63.Germán Gustavo Denis (4/0)]. Trainer: Alfio Oscar Basile (74).
**Goal**: Esteban Matías Cambiasso Deleau (82).

**849.** 11.10.2008 **ARGENTINA - URUGUAY** **2-1(2-1)** 19th FIFA WC. Qualifiers
Estadio Monumental „Antonio Vespucio Liberti", Buenos Aires; Referee: Carlos Manuel Torres (Paraguay); Attendance: 42,421
**ARG:** Juan Pablo Carrizo (5/0), Javier Adelmar Zanetti (126/5), Martín Gastón Demichelis (15/1), Nicolás Andrés Burdisso (24/2), Gabriel Iván Heinze (49/2), Javier Alejandro Mascherano (43/2), Esteban Matías Cambiasso Deleau (44/4), Juan Román Riquelme (51/17) [72.Cristian Raúl Ledesma (3/0)], Sergio Leonel Agüero del Castillo (14/5) [71.Diego Alberto Milito (15/4)], Lionel Andrés Messi (33/10) [88.Daniel Alberto Díaz (8/0)], Carlos Alberto Tévez (43/7). Trainer: Alfio Oscar Basile (75).
**Goals**: Lionel Andrés Messi (6), Sergio Leonel Agüero del Castillo (13).

**850.** 15.10.2008 **CHILE - ARGENTINA** **1-0(1-0)** 19th FIFA WC. Qualifiers
Estadio Nacional, Santiago; Referee: Óscar Julián Ruiz Acosta (Colombia); Attendance: 65,000
**ARG:** Juan Pablo Carrizo (6/0), Javier Adelmar Zanetti (127/5), Nicolás Andrés Burdisso (25/2) [20.Daniel Alberto Díaz (9/0)], Martín Gastón Demichelis (16/1), Gabriel Iván Heinze (50/2), Javier Alejandro Mascherano (44/2), Esteban Matías Cambiasso Deleau (45/4) [83.José Gustavo Sand (1/0)], Cristian Raúl Ledesma (4/0), Lionel Andrés Messi (34/10), Diego Alberto Milito (16/4) [46.Gonzalo Rubén Bergessio (1/0)], Sergio Leonel Agüero del Castillo (15/5). Trainer: Alfio Oscar Basile (76).

**851.** 19.11.2008 **SCOTLAND - ARGENTINA** **0-1(0-1)**
Hampden Park, Glasgow; Referee: Felix Brych (Germany); Attendance: 32,492
**ARG:** Juan Pablo Carrizo (7/0), Javier Adelmar Zanetti (128/5), Martín Gastón Demichelis (17/1), Gabriel Iván Heinze (51/2), Jonás Manuel Gutiérrez (7/0) [71.Luis Oscar González (42/6)], Maximiliano Rubén Rodríguez (28/9) [90.José Ernesto Sosa (5/0)], Emiliano Ramiro Papa (1/0) [86.Daniel Alberto Díaz (10/0)], Javier Alejandro Mascherano (45/2), Fernando Rubén Gago (20/0), Ezequiel Iván Lavezzi (3/0) [75.Germán Gustavo Denis (5/0)], Carlos Alberto Tévez (44/7). Trainer: Diego Armando Maradona (1).
**Goals**: Maximiliano Rubén Rodríguez (8).

**852.** 11.02.2009 **FRANCE - ARGENTINA** **0-2(0-1)**
Stade Vélodrome, Marseille; Referee: Jonas Eriksson (Sweden); Attendance: 60,000
**ARG:** Juan Pablo Carrizo (8/0), Javier Adelmar Zanetti (129/5), Martín Gastón Demichelis (18/1), Gabriel Iván Heinze (52/2), Emiliano Ramiro Papa (2/0), Maximiliano Rubén Rodríguez (29/9) [80.Marcos Alberto Angeleri (1/0)], Javier Alejandro Mascherano (46/2), Fernando Rubén Gago (21/0), Jonás Manuel Gutiérrez (8/1), Lionel Andrés Messi (35/11), Sergio Leonel Agüero del Castillo (16/5) [80.Carlos Alberto Tévez (45/7)]. Trainer: Diego Armando Maradona (2).
**Goals**: Jonás Manuel Gutiérrez (41), Lionel Andrés Messi (83).

**853.** 28.03.2009 **ARGENTINA - VENEZUELA** **4-0(1-0)** 19th FIFA WC. Qualifiers
Estadio Monumental „Antonio Vespucio Liberti", Buenos Aires; Referee: Victor Hugo Rivera (Peru); Attendance: 46,085
**ARG:** Juan Pablo Carrizo (9/0), Javier Adelmar Zanetti (130/5), Marcos Alberto Angeleri (2/0), Gabriel Iván Heinze (53/2), Maximiliano Rubén Rodríguez (30/10) [74.Ángel Fabián di María (2/0)], Javier Alejandro Mascherano (47/2), Fernando Rubén Gago (22/0), Jonás Manuel Gutiérrez (9/1), Lionel Andrés Messi (36/12), Sergio Leonel Agüero del Castillo (17/6) [78.Diego Alberto Milito (17/4)], Carlos Alberto Tévez (46/8) [70.Juan Sebastián Verón (63/9)]. Trainer: Diego Armando Maradona (3).
**Goals**: Lionel Andrés Messi (26), Carlos Alberto Tévez (47), Maximiliano Rubén Rodríguez (51), Sergio Leonel Agüero del Castillo (73).

**854.** 01.04.2009 **BOLIVIA - ARGENTINA** **6-1(3-1)** 19th FIFA WC. Qualifiers
Estadio „Hernando Siles Zuazo", La Paz; Referee: Martín Vásquez (Uruguay); Attendance: 30,487
**ARG:** Juan Pablo Carrizo (10/0), Javier Adelmar Zanetti (131/5), Martín Gastón Demichelis (19/1), Gabriel Iván Heinze (54/2), Emiliano Ramiro Papa (3/0), Luis Oscar González (43/7) [68.Marcos Alberto Angeleri (3/0)], Fernando Rubén Gago (23/0), Javier Alejandro Mascherano (48/2), Maximiliano Rubén Rodríguez (31/10) [56.Ángel Fabián di María (3/0) [*sent off 64*]], Carlos Alberto Tévez (47/8) [74.Daniel Gastón Montenegro (2/0)], Lionel Andrés Messi (37/12). Trainer: Diego Armando Maradona (4).
**Goal**: Luis Oscar González (24).

**855.** 20.05.2009 **ARGENTINA - PANAMA** **3-1(2-1)**
Estadio „Brigadier General Estanislao López", Santa Fé; Referee: Jorge Joaquín Antequera Castedo (Bolivia)
**ARG:** Diego Raúl Pozo (1/0) [72.Cristian Daniel Campestrini (1/0)], Alexis Javier Ferrero (1/0) [67.Ignacio Canuto (1/0)], Matías Nicolás Caruzzo (1/0), Nicolás Hernán Gonzalo Otamendi (1/0), Hernán Darío Bernardello (1/0) [46.Leonardo Sebastián Prediguer (1/0)], Fabián Andrés Rinaudo (1/0) [58.Franco Zuculini (1/0)], Matias Adrián Defederico (1/1) [46.Emiliano Ramiro Papa (4/0)], Daniel Gastón Montenegro (Cap) (3/0), Eduardo Antonio Salvio (1/0) [59.Sebastián Marcelo Blanco (1/0)], José Gustavo Sand (2/0) [46.Oscar Esteban Fuertes (1/0)], Gonzalo Rubén Bergessio (2/2). Trainer: Diego Armando Maradona (5).
**Goals**: Matias Adrián De Federico (27), Gonzalo Rubén Bergessio (39, 84).

**856.** 06.06.2009 **ARGENTINA - COLOMBIA** **1-0(1-0)** 19th FIFA WC. Qualifiers
Estadio Monumental „Antonio Vespucio Liberti", Buenos Aires; Referee: René Ortubé Betancourt (Bolivia); Attendance: 55,000
**ARG:** Mariano Gonzalo Andújar (1/0), Martín Gastón Demichelis (20/1), Daniel Alberto Díaz (11/1), Gabriel Iván Heinze (55/2), Fernando Rubén Gago (24/0) [46.Javier Adelmar Zanetti (132/5)], Javier Alejandro Mascherano (49/2), Jonás Manuel Gutiérrez (10/1), Juan Sebastián Verón (64/9), Lionel Andrés Messi (38/12), Sergio Leonel Agüero del Castillo (18/6) [40.Diego Alberto Milito (18/4)], Carlos Alberto Tévez (48/8) [83.Nicolás Andrés Burdisso (26/2)]. Trainer: Diego Armando Maradona (6).
**Goal**: Daniel Alberto Díaz (55).

**857.** 10.06.2009 **ECUADOR - ARGENTINA** **2-0(0-0)** 19th FIFA WC. Qualifiers
Estadio Olímpico „Atahualpa", Quito; Referee: Carlos Chandía Alarcón (Chile); Attendance: 36,359
**ARG:** Mariano Gonzalo Andújar (2/0), Javier Adelmar Zanetti (133/5), Martín Gastón Demichelis (21/1), Nicolás Hernán Gonzalo Otamendi (2/0), Gabriel Iván Heinze (56/2) [83.Diego Alberto Milito (19/4)], Maximiliano Rubén Rodríguez (32/10), Sebastián Alejandro Battaglia (9/0), Fernando Rubén Gago (25/0) [75.Juan Sebastián Verón (65/9)], Jonás Manuel Gutiérrez (11/1), Lionel Andrés Messi (39/12), Carlos Alberto Tévez (49/8) [67.Gonzalo Rubén Bergessio (3/2)]. Trainer: Diego Armando Maradona (7).

**858.** 12.08.2009 **RUSSIA - ARGENTINA** **2-3(1-1)**
Lokomotiv Stadium, Moskva; Referee: Frank De Bleeckere (Belgium); Attendance: 28,000
**ARG:** Mariano Gonzalo Andújar (3/0), Javier Adelmar Zanetti (134/5), Nicolás Andrés Burdisso (27/2) [46.Daniel Alberto Díaz (12/1)], Nicolás Hernán Gonzalo Otamendi (3/0) [46.Emiliano Ramiro Papa (5/0)], Gabriel Iván Heinze (57/2), Maximiliano Rubén Rodríguez (33/10) [58.Jesús Alberto Dátolo (1/1)], Javier Alejandro Mascherano (50/2), Mario Ariel Bolatti (1/0) [66.Sebastián Alejandro Battaglia (10/0)], Jonás Manuel Gutiérrez (12/1), Diego Alberto Milito (20/4) [46.Lisandro López (7/1)], Sergio Leonel Agüero del Castillo (19/7) [63.Ezequiel Iván Lavezzi (4/0)]. Trainer: Diego Armando Maradona (8).
**Goals**: Sergio Leonel Agüero del Castillo (45), Lisandro López (46), Jesús Alberto Dátolo (59).

**859.** 05.09.2009 **ARGENTINA - BRAZIL** **1-3(0-2)** 19th FIFA WC. Qualifiers
Estadio Gigante de Arroyito, Rosario; Referee: Óscar Julián Ruiz Acosta (Colombia); Attendance: 37,000
**ARG:** Mariano Gonzalo Andújar (4/0), Javier Adelmar Zanetti (135/5), Sebastián Enrique Domínguez (1/0), Nicolás Hernán Gonzalo Otamendi (4/0), Gabriel Iván Heinze (58/2), Maximiliano Rubén Rodríguez (34/10) [46.Sergio Leonel Agüero del Castillo (20/7)], Javier Alejandro Mascherano (51/2), Juan Sebastián Verón (66/9), Jesús Alberto Dátolo (2/2), Lionel Andrés Messi (40/12), Carlos Alberto Tévez (50/8) [68.Diego Alberto Milito (21/4)]. Trainer: Diego Armando Maradona (9).
**Goal**: Jesús Alberto Dátolo (65).

**860.** 09.09.2009 **PARAGUAY - ARGENTINA** **1-0(1-0)** 19th FIFA WC. Qualifiers
Estadio Defensores del Chaco, Asunción; Referee: Sálvio Spínola Fagundes Filho (Brazil); Attendance: 38,000
**ARG:** Sergio Germán Romero (1/0), Javier Adelmar Zanetti (136/5), Sebastián Enrique Domínguez (2/0) [80.Rolando Carlos Schiavi (1/0)], Gabriel Iván Heinze (59/2), Emiliano Ramiro Papa (6/0), Juan Sebastián Verón (67/9) [*sent off 53*], Javier Alejandro Mascherano (52/2), Fernando Rubén Gago (26/0), Jesús Alberto Dátolo (3/2) [46.Ezequiel Iván Lavezzi (5/0)], Lionel Andrés Messi (41/12), Sergio Leonel Agüero del Castillo (21/7) [59.Martín Palermo (8/3)]. Trainer: Diego Armando Maradona (10).

**861.** 30.09.2009 **ARGENTINA - GHANA** **2-0(2-0)**
Estadio Olímpico de Córdoba, Córdoba; Referee: Enrique Roberto Ossés Zencovich (Chile)
**ARG:** Diego Raúl Pozo (2/0), Ignacio Canuto (2/0), Rolando Carlos Schiavi (2/0) [46.Juan Manuel Insaurralde (1/0)], Matías Nicolás Caruzzo (2/0), Luciano Fabián Monzón (1/0), Enzo Nicolás Pérez (1/0) [46.Jesús Davíd José Méndez (1/0)], Mario Ariel Bolatti (2/0) [66.Rodrigo Braña (1/0)], Leonel Jesús Vangioni (1/0), Federico Insúa (11/0) [66.Osvaldo Nicolás Fabián Gaitán (1/0)], Gabriel Agustín Hauche (1/0) [57.Luis Miguel Rodríguez (1/0)], Martín Palermo (9/5) [57.Mauro Boselli (1/0)]. Trainer: Diego Armando Maradona (11).
**Goals**: Martín Palermo (28, 39).

**862.** 10.10.2009 **ARGENTINA - PERU** **2-1(0-0)** 19th FIFA WC. Qualifiers
Estadio Monumental „Antonio Vespucio Liberti", Buenos Aires; Referee: René Ortubé Betancourt (Bolivia); Attendance: 38,019
**ARG:** Sergio Germán Romero (2/0), Jonás Manuel Gutiérrez (13/1), Rolando Carlos Schiavi (3/0), Gabriel Iván Heinze (60/2), Emiliano Adrián Insúa Zapata (1/0), Enzo Nicolás Pérez (2/0) [46.Martín Palermo (10/6)], Javier Alejandro Mascherano (53/2), Ángel Fabián di María (4/0), Pablo César Aimar Giordano (52/8) [75.Federico Insúa (12/0)], Lionel Andrés Messi (42/12), Gonzalo Gerardo Higuaín (1/1) [67.Martín Gastón Demichelis (22/1)]. Trainer: Diego Armando Maradona (12).
**Goals**: Gonzalo Gerardo Higuaín (48), Martín Palermo (90+2).

**863.** 14.10.2009 **URUGUAY - ARGENTINA** **0-1(0-0)** 19th FIFA WC. Qualifiers
Estadio Centenario, Montevideo; Referee: Carlos Arecio Amarilla Demarqui (Paraguay); Attendance: 60,000
**ARG:** Sergio Germán Romero (3/0), Nicolás Hernán Gonzalo Otamendi (5/0), Martín Gastón Demichelis (23/1), Rolando Carlos Schiavi (4/0), Gabriel Iván Heinze (61/2), Jonás Manuel Gutiérrez (14/1), Javier Alejandro Mascherano (54/2), Juan Sebastián Verón (68/9), Ángel Fabián di María (5/0) [75.Luciano Fabián Monzón (2/0)], Lionel Andrés Messi (43/12) [85.Carlos Alberto Tévez (51/8)], Gonzalo Gerardo Higuaín (2/1) [79.Mario Ariel Bolatti (3/1)]. Trainer: Diego Armando Maradona (13).
**Goal**: Mario Ariel Bolatti (84).

**864.** 14.11.2009 **SPAIN - ARGENTINA** **2-1(1-0)**
Estadio „Vicente Calderón", Madrid; Referee: Alan Kelly (Republic of Ireland); Attendance: 54,000
**ARG:** Sergio Germán Romero (4/0), Fabricio Coloccini (33/1), Martín Gastón Demichelis (24/1), Gabriel Iván Heinze (62/2), Cristian Daniel Ansaldi (1/0), Maximiliano Rubén Rodríguez (35/10) [83.Diego Perotti (1/0)], Javier Alejandro Mascherano (55/2), Fernando Rubén Gago (27/0) [74.Esteban Matías Cambiasso Deleau (46/4)], Ángel Fabián di María (6/0), Lionel Andrés Messi (44/13) [83.Ezequiel Iván Lavezzi (6/0)], Gonzalo Gerardo Higuaín (3/1) [58.Carlos Alberto Tévez (52/8)]. Trainer: Diego Armando Maradona (14).
**Goal**: Lionel Andrés Messi (61 penalty).

**865.** 26.01.2010 **ARGENTINA – COSTA RICA** **3-2(2-1)**
Estadio „Hilario Sánchez", San Juan; Referee: Carlos Arecio Amarilla Demarqui (Paraguay)
**ARG:** Cristian Daniel Campestrini (2/0), Guillermo Enio Burdisso (1/1), Carlos Javier Matheu (1/0) [5.Matías Nicolás Caruzzo (3/0)], Luciano Fabián Monzón (3/0), Clemente Juan Rodríguez (10/0), Juan Ignacio Mercier (1/0) [68.Franco Razzotti (1/0)], José Ernesto Sosa (6/1), Walter Daniel Erviti Roldán (1/0) [46.Federico Insúa (13/0)], Osvaldo Nicolás Fabián Gaitán (2/0) [46.Enzo Nicolás Pérez (3/0)], Gabriel Agustín Hauche (2/0) [61.Franco Daniel Jara (1/1)], Martín Palermo (11/6) [73.Mauro Boselli (2/0)]. Trainer: Diego Armando Maradona (15).
**Goals**: José Ernesto Sosa (10), Guillermo Enio Burdisso (38), Franco Daniel Jara (79).

**866.** 10.02.2010 **ARGENTINA - JAMAICA** **2-1(0-0)**
Estadio „José María Minella", Mar del Plata; Referee: Víctor Hugo Rivera Chávez (Peru)
**ARG:** Nelson Martín Ibáñez (1/0), Gabriel Iván Mercado (1/0) [89.Ignacio Canuto (3/1)], Mariano Raúl Echevarría (1/0) [71.Matías Nicolás Caruzzo (4/0)], Leonel Galeano (1/0) [54.Osvaldo Nicolás Fabián Gaitán (3/0)], Luciano Fabián Monzón (4/0), Patricio Daniel Toranzo (1/0), Juan Ignacio Mercier (2/0), Walter Aníbal Acevedo (1/0) [60.Jesús Davíd José Méndez (2/0)], Federico Insúa (14/0), Franco Daniel Jara (2/1) [46.Gabriel Agustín Hauche (3/0)], Martín Palermo (12/7). Trainer: Diego Armando Maradona (16).
**Goals**: Martín Palermo (77), Ignacio Canuto (90+3).

**867.** 03.03.2010 **GERMANY - ARGENTINA** **0-1(0-1)**
Allianz-Arena, München; Referee: Martin Atkinson (England); Attendance: 65,152
**ARG:** Sergio Germán Romero (5/0), Nicolás Hernán Gonzalo Otamendi (6/0), Martín Gastón Demichelis (25/1) [46.Nicolás Andrés Burdisso (28/2)], Wálter Adrián Samuel (54/5), Gabriel Iván Heinze (63/2) [47.Clemente Juan Rodríguez (11/0)], Javier Alejandro Mascherano (Cap) (56/2), Jonás Manuel Gutiérrez (15/1), Juan Sebastián Verón (69/9) [90.Mario Ariel Bolatti (4/1)], Ángel Fabián di María (7/0), Lionel Andrés Messi (45/13), Gonzalo Gerardo Higuaín (4/2) [62.Carlos Alberto Tévez (53/8)]. Trainer: Diego Armando Maradona (17).
**Goal**: Gonzalo Gerardo Higuaín (45).

**868.** 05.05.2010 **ARGENTINA - HAITI** **4-0(2-0)**
Estadio Coloso del Ruca Quimey, Cutral Có; Referee: Enrique Roberto Osses Zencovich (Chile) ; Attendance: 16,500
**ARG:** Diego Raúl Pozo (3/0) [46.Adrián José Gabbarini (1/0)], Ariel Hernán Garcé (3/0), Paolo Duval Goltz (1/0) [69.Matías Nicolás Caruzzo (5/0)], Juan Manuel Insaurralde (2/0), Cristian Carlos Villagra (1/0), Patricio Daniel Toranzo (2/0), Juan Ignacio Mercier (3/0) [62.Nicolás Andrés Olmedo (1/0)], Sebastián Marcelo Blanco (2/1), Facundo Daniel Bertoglio (1/2) [70.Franco Daniel Jara (3/1)], Arnaldo Ariel Ortega (87/17) [60.José Luis Fernández (1/0)], Martín Palermo (13/8) [64.Juan Pablo Pereyra (1/0)]. Trainer: Diego Armando Maradona (18).
**Goals**: Facundo Daniel Bertoglio (33), Martín Palermo (42), Sebastián Marcelo Blanco (50), Facundo Daniel Bertoglio (56).

**869.** 24.05.2010 **ARGENTINA - CANADA** **5-0(3-0)**
Estadio Monumental „Antonio Vespucio Liberti“, Buenos Aires; Referee: Víctor Hugo Rivera Chávez (Peru); Attendance: 60,000
**ARG:** Sergio Germán Romero (6/0), Jonás Manuel Gutiérrez (16/1), Nicolás Andrés Burdisso (29/2), Nicolás Hernán Gonzalo Otamendi (7/0), Gabriel Iván Heinze (64/2) [59.Clemente Juan Rodríguez (12/0)], Maximiliano Rubén Rodríguez (36/12) [46.Juan Sebastián Verón (70/9)], Javier Alejandro Mascherano (57/2) [59.Mario Ariel Bolatti (5/1)], Ángel Fabián di María (8/1), Javier Matías Pastore (1/0) [74.Ariel Hernán Garcé (4/0)], Gonzalo Gerardo Higuaín (5/2) [68.Martín Palermo (14/8)], Carlos Alberto Tévez (54/9) [70.Sergio Leonel Agüero del Castillo (22/8)]. Trainer: Diego Armando Maradona (19).
**Goals**: Maximiliano Rubén Rodríguez (15, 31), Ángel Fabián di María (36), Carlos Alberto Tévez (62), Sergio Leonel Agüero del Castillo (74).

**870.** 12.06.2010 **ARGENTINA – NIGERIA** **1-0(1-0)** 19th FIFA WC. Group Stage.
Ellis Park Stadium, Johannesburg (South Africa); Referee: Wolfgang Stark (Germany); Attendance: 55,686
**ARG:** Sergio Germán Romero (7/0), Jonás Manuel Gutiérrez (17/1), Martín Gastón Demichelis (26/1), Walter Adrián Samuel (55/5), Gabriel Iván Heinze (65/3), Javier Alejandro Mascherano (Cap) (58/2), Juan Sebastián Verón (71/9) [74.Maximiliano Rubén Rodríguez (37/12)], Ángel Fabián di María (9/1) [85.Nicolás Andrés Burdisso (30/2)], Lionel Andrés Messi (46/13), Carlos Alberto Tévez (55/9), Gonzalo Gerardo Higuaín (6/2) [79.Diego Alberto Milito (22/4)]. Trainer: Diego Armando Maradona (20).
**Goal**: Gabriel Iván Heinze (6).

**871.** 17.06.2010 **ARGENTINA - SOUTH KOREA** **4-1(2-1)** 19th FIFA WC. Group Stage.
Soccer City, Johannesburg (South Africa); Referee: Frank De Bleeckere (Belgium); Attendance: 82,174
**ARG:** Sergio Germán Romero (8/0), Jonás Manuel Gutiérrez (18/1), Martín Gastón Demichelis (27/1), Walter Adrián Samuel (56/5) [23.Nicolás Andrés Burdisso (31/2)], Gabriel Iván Heinze (66/3), Javier Alejandro Mascherano (Cap) (59/2), Maximiliano Rubén Rodríguez (38/12), Ángel Fabián di María (10/1), Lionel Andrés Messi (47/13), Gonzalo Gerardo Higuaín (7/5) [82.Mario Ariel Bolatti (6/1)], Carlos Alberto Tévez (56/9) [75.Sergio Leonel Agüero del Castillo (23/8)]. Trainer: Diego Armando Maradona (21).
**Goals**: Park Chu-Young (17 own goal), Gonzalo Gerardo Higuaín (33, 76, 80).

**872.** 22.06.2010 **GREECE - ARGENTINA** **0-2(0-0)** 19th FIFA WC. Group Stage.
„Peter Mokaba“ Stadium, Polokwane (South Africa); Referee: Ravshan Irmatov (Uzbekistan); Attendance: 38,891
**ARG:** Sergio Germán Romero (9/0), Nicolás Andrés Burdisso (32/2), Martín Gastón Demichelis (28/2), Nicolás Hernán Gonzalo Otamendi (8/0), Clemente Juan Rodríguez (13/0), Juan Sebastián Verón (72/9), Mario Ariel Bolatti (7/1), Maximiliano Rubén Rodríguez (39/12) [63.Ángel Fabián di María (11/1)], Lionel Andrés Messi (Cap) (48/13), Sergio Leonel Agüero del Castillo (24/8) [77.Javier Matías Pastore (2/0)], Diego Alberto Milito (23/4) [80.Martín Palermo (15/9)]. Trainer: Diego Armando Maradona (22).
**Goals**: Martín Gastón Demichelis (77), Martín Palermo (89).

**873.** 27.06.2010 **ARGENTINA - MEXICO** **3-1(2-0)** 19th FIFA WC. 2nd Round.
Soccer City, Johannesburg (South Africa); Referee: Roberto Rosetti (Italy); Attendance: 84,377
**ARG:** Sergio Germán Romero (10/0), Nicolás Hernán Gonzalo Otamendi (9/0), Martín Gastón Demichelis (29/2), Nicolás Andrés Burdisso (33/2), Gabriel Iván Heinze (67/3), Javier Alejandro Mascherano (Cap) (60/2), Maximiliano Rubén Rodríguez (40/12) [87.Javier Matías Pastore (3/0)], Ángel Fabián di María (12/1) [79.Jonás Manuel Gutiérrez (19/1)], Lionel Andrés Messi (49/13), Carlos Alberto Tévez (57/11) [69.Juan Sebastián Verón (73/9)], Gonzalo Gerardo Higuaín (8/6). Trainer: Diego Armando Maradona (23).
**Goals**: Carlos Alberto Tévez (26), Gonzalo Gerardo Higuaín (33), Carlos Alberto Tévez (52).

**874.** 03.07.2010 **ARGENTINA - GERMANY** **0-4(0-1)** 19th FIFA WC. Quarter-Finals.
Cape Town Stadium, Cape Town (South Africa); Referee: Ravshan Irmatov (Uzbekistan); Attendance: 64,100
**ARG:** Sergio Germán Romero (11/0), Nicolás Hernán Gonzalo Otamendi (10/0) [70.Javier Matías Pastore (4/0)], Martín Gastón Demichelis (30/2), Nicolás Andrés Burdisso (34/2), Gabriel Iván Heinze (68/3), Maximiliano Rubén Rodríguez (41/12), Javier Alejandro Mascherano (Cap) (61/2), Ángel Fabián di María (13/1) [75.Sergio Leonel Agüero del Castillo (25/8)], Lionel Andrés Messi (50/13), Carlos Alberto Tévez (58/11), Gonzalo Gerardo Higuaín (9/6). Trainer: Diego Armando Maradona (24).

**875.** 11.08.2010 **REPUBLIC OF IRELAND - ARGENTINA** **0-1(0-1)**
Aviva Stadium, Dublin; Referee: Peter Rasmussen (Denmark); Attendance: 49,500
**ARG:** Sergio Germán Romero (12/0), Nicolás Andrés Burdisso (35/2) [46.Pablo Javier Zabaleta Girod (8/0)], Gabriel Iván Heinze (69/3) [72.Emiliano Adrián Insúa Zapata (2/0)], Walter Adrián Samuel (57/5) [83.Fabricio Coloccini (34/1)], Martín Gastón Demichelis (31/2), Fernando Rubén Gago (28/0), Javier Alejandro Mascherano (Cap) (62/2), Éver Maximiliano David Banega (3/0), Ángel Fabián di María (14/2) [75.Jonás Manuel Gutiérrez (20/1)], Gonzalo Gerardo Higuaín (10/6) [46.Diego Alberto Milito (24/4)], Lionel Andrés Messi (51/13) [58.Ezequiel Iván Lavezzi (7/0)]. Trainer: Sergio Daniel Batista (1).
**Goal**: Ángel Fabián di María (20).

**876.** 07.09.2010 **ARGENTINA - SPAIN** **4-1(3-0)**
Estadio Monumental „Antonio Vespucio Liberti“, Buenos Aires; Referee: Óscar Julián Ruiz Acosta (Colombia); Attendance: 53,000
**ARG:** Sergio Germán Romero (13/0), Javier Adelmar Zanetti (137/5), Martín Gastón Demichelis (32/2), Gabriel Alejandro Milito (33/1), Gabriel Iván Heinze (70/3), Éver Maximiliano David Banega (4/0), Javier Alejandro Mascherano (Cap) (63/2), Esteban Matías Cambiasso Deleau (47/4), Lionel Andrés Messi (52/14) [89.Andrés Nicolás D'Alessandro (23/3)], Gonzalo Gerardo Higuaín (11/7) [68.Sergio Leonel Agüero del Castillo (26/9)], Carlos Alberto Tévez (59/12) [59.Ángel Fabián di María (15/2)]. Trainer: Sergio Daniel Batista (2).
**Goals**: Lionel Andrés Messi (10), Gonzalo Gerardo Higuaín (13), Carlos Alberto Tévez (34), Sergio Leonel Agüero del Castillo (90+1).

**877.** 08.10.2010 **JAPAN - ARGENTINA** **1-0(1-0)**

NACK5 Stadium, Ōmiya; Referee: Pawel Gil (Poland); Attendance: 57,735

**ARG:** Sergio Germán Romero (14/0), Nicolás Andrés Burdisso (36/2) [78.Ezequiel Iván Lavezzi (8/0)], Martín Gastón Demichelis (33/2), Gabriel Alejandro Milito (34/1), Gabriel Iván Heinze (71/3), Javier Alejandro Mascherano (Cap) (64/2), Esteban Matías Cambiasso Deleau (48/4) [44.Mario Ariel Bolatti (8/1); 84.Ángel Fabián di María (16/2)], Andrés Nicolás D'Alessandro (24/3) [59.Javier Matías Pastore (5/0)], Lionel Andrés Messi (53/14), Carlos Alberto Tévez (60/12), Diego Alberto Milito (25/4) [33.Gonzalo Gerardo Higuaín (12/7)]. Trainer: Sergio Daniel Batista (3).

**878.** 17.11.2010 **ARGENTINA - BRAZIL** **1-0(0-0)**

Khalifa International Stadium, Doha (Qatar); Referee: Abdullah Dor Mohammed Balideh (Qatar); Attendance: 50,000

**ARG:** Sergio Germán Romero (15/0), Nicolás Andrés Burdisso (37/2), Gabriel Iván Heinze (72/3), Nicolás Martín Pareja (1/0), Javier Adelmar Zanetti (138/5), Javier Alejandro Mascherano (Cap) (65/2), Éver Maximiliano David Banega (5/0), Ángel Fabián di María (17/2), Javier Matías Pastore (6/0) [69.Andrés Nicolás D'Alessandro (25/3)], Gonzalo Gerardo Higuaín (13/7) [46.Ezequiel Iván Lavezzi (9/0)], Lionel Andrés Messi (54/15). Trainer: Sergio Daniel Batista (4).

**Goal**: Lionel Andrés Messi (90+1).

**879.** 09.02.2011 **ARGENTINA - PORTUGAL** **2-1(1-1)**

Stade de Genève, Genève (Switzerland); Referee: Massimo Busacca (Switzerland); Attendance: 30,000

**ARG:** Sergio Germán Romero (16/0), Nicolás Andrés Burdisso (38/2), Gabriel Alejandro Milito (35/1), Faustino Marcos Alberto Rojo (1/0), Javier Adelmar Zanetti (139/5) [61.Pablo Javier Zabaleta Girod (9/0)], Javier Alejandro Mascherano (66/2), Esteban Matías Cambiasso Deleau (49/4) [78.Lucas Rodrigo Biglia (1/0)], Éver Maximiliano David Banega (6/0) [62.Fernando Rubén Gago (29/0)], Ángel Fabián di María (18/3) [65.Javier Matías Pastore (7/0)], Ezequiel Iván Lavezzi (10/0) [83.Juan Manuel Martínez (1/0)], Lionel Andrés Messi (55/16). Trainer: Sergio Daniel Batista (5).

**Goals**: Ángel Fabián di María (13), Lionel Andrés Messi (89 penalty).

**880.** 16.03.2011 **ARGENTINA - VENEZUELA** **4-1(2-1)**

Estadio del Bicentenario, San Juan; Referee: Claudio Alfredo Puga Briones (Chile); Attendance: 25,000

**ARG:** Javier Hernán García (1/0) [46.Agustín Federico Marchesín (1/0)], Iván Alexis Pillud (1/0) [46.Gastón Ricardo Díaz (1/0)], Lisandro Ezequiel López (1/0), Jonathan Ramón Maidana (1/0), Ariel Mauricio Rojas (1/0) [32.Luciano Fabián Monzón (5/0)], Cristian Manuel Chávez (1/1), Maximiliano Nicolás Moralez (1/0) [55.Luciano Román Aued (1/1)], Claudio Ariel Yacob (1/0) [61.Fabián Andrés Rinaudo (2/0)], Diego Hernán Valeri (1/0), Matías Adrián Defederico (2/1) [46.Mauricio Ezequiel Sperdutti (1/0)], Pablo Nicolás Mouche (1/2). Trainer: Sergio Daniel Batista (6).

**Goals**: Cristian Manuel Chávez (20), Pablo Nicolás Mouche (35, 53), Luciano Román Aued (75).

**881.** 26.03.2011 **UNITED STATES - ARGENTINA** **1-1(0-1)**

New Meadowlands Stadium, East Rutherford, New Jersey; Referee: Roberto García Orozco (Mexico); Attendance: 78,986

**ARG:** Mariano Gonzalo Andújar (5/0), Nicolás Andrés Burdisso (39/2), Gabriel Alejandro Milito (36/1), Faustino Marcos Alberto Rojo (2/0), Javier Adelmar Zanetti (140/5), Javier Alejandro Mascherano (67/2), Éver Maximiliano David Banega (7/0), Esteban Matías Cambiasso Deleau (50/5) [75.Lucas Rodrigo Biglia (2/0)], Ezequiel Iván Lavezzi (11/0), Lionel Andrés Messi (56/16), Ángel Fabián di María (19/3). Trainer: Sergio Daniel Batista (7).

**Goal**: Esteban Matías Cambiasso Deleau (42).

**882.** 29.03.2011 **COSTA RICA - ARGENTINA** **0-0**

Estadio Nacional, San José; Referee: Marco Antonio Rodríguez Moreno (Mexico); Attendance: 35,000

**ARG:** Mariano Gonzalo Andújar (6/0), Marcos Alberto Angeleri (4/0), Ezequiel Marcelo Garay González (2/0), Gabriel Alejandro Milito (37/1) [46.Nicolás Hernán Gonzalo Otamendi (11/0)], Faustino Marcos Alberto Rojo (3/0), José Ernesto Sosa (7/1) [66.Eduardo Antonio Salvio (2/0)], Javier Alejandro Mascherano (68/2) [46.Mario Ariel Bolatti (9/1)], Éver Maximiliano David Banega (8/0) [46.Fernando Daniel Belluschi (3/0)], Lucas Rodrigo Biglia (3/0), Osvaldo Nicolás Fabián Gaitán (4/0), Javier Matías Pastore (8/0). Trainer: Sergio Daniel Batista (8).

**883.** 20.04.2011 **ARGENTINA - ECUADOR** **2-2(2-1)**

Estadio "José María Minella", Mar del Plata; Referee: Roberto Carlos Silvera (Uruguay); Attendance: n/a

**ARG:** Juan Pablo Carrizo (11/0), Federico Fernández (1/0) [46.Ismael Alberto Quílez (1/0)], Jonathan Ramón Maidana (2/0), Iván Alexis Pillud (2/0) [46.Julián Alberto Velázquez (1/0)], Cristian Manuel Chávez (2/1), Enzo Nicolás Pérez (4/0) [69.Mauricio Ezequiel Sperdutti (2/0)], Ariel Mauricio Rojas (2/0) [65.Luciano Fabián Monzón (6/0)], Diego Hernán Valeri (2/0), Claudio Ariel Yacob (2/1) [43.Lucas Ezequiel Viatri (1/0)], Gabriel Agustín Hauche (4/1) [46.Luciano Román Aued (2/1)], Pablo Nicolás Mouche (2/2). Trainer: Sergio Daniel Batista (9).

**Goals**: Claudio Ariel Yacob (32), Gabriel Agustín Hauche (34).

**884.** 25.05.2011 **ARGENTINA - PARAGUAY** **4-2(3-1)**

Estadio Centenario del Club Atlético Sarmiento, Resistencia; Referee: Roberto Carlos Silvera (Uruguay); Attendance: n/a

**ARG:** Juan Pablo Carrizo (12/0), Federico Fernández (2/1), Lisandro Ezequiel López (2/0) [74.Jonathan Pablo Bottinelli (1/0)], Iván Alexis Pillud (3/0) [65.Ismael Alberto Quílez (2/0)], Luciano Fabián Monzón (7/0), Cristian Manuel Chávez (3/1), Enzo Nicolás Pérez (5/1) [77.Lucas Ezequiel Viatri (2/0)], Fabián Andrés Rinaudo (3/0), Diego Hernán Valeri (3/0) [86.Ariel Mauricio Rojas (3/0)], Erik Manuel Lamela (1/0) [58.Pablo Nicolás Mouche (3/2)], Gabriel Agustín Hauche (5/3) [65.Diego Alberto Morales (1/0)]. Trainer: Sergio Daniel Batista (10).

**Goals**: Gabriel Agustín Hauche (9), Federico Fernández (37), Gabriel Agustín Hauche (45), Enzo Nicolás Pérez (74).

**885.** 01.06.2011 **NIGERIA - ARGENTINA** **4-1(3-0)**

Abuja International Stadium, Abuja; Referee: Ibrahim Chaibou (Niger); Attendance: 30,000

**ARG:** Adrián José Gabbarini (2/0), Pablo Javier Zabaleta Girod (10/0), Federico Julián Fazio (1/0), Ezequiel Marcelo Garay González (3/0) [64.Mateo Pablo Musacchio (1/0)], Emiliano Adrián Insúa Zapata (3/0), Mario Ariel Bolatti (10/1), Fernando Daniel Belluschi (4/0) [61.Nicolás Santiago Bertolo (1/0)], Alberto Facundo Costa (1/0) [57.Alejandro Ariel Cabral (1/0)], Osvaldo Nicolás Fabián Gaitán (5/0), Diego Perotti (2/0) [69.Franco Daniel Jara (4/1)], Mauro Boselli (3/1). Trainer: Sergio Daniel Batista (11).

**Goal**: Mauro Boselli (90+8 penalty).

**886.** 05.06.2011 **POLAND - ARGENTINA** **2-1(1-0)**

Stadion Wojska Polskiego, Warszawa; Referee: Manuel Gräfe (Germany); Attendance: 12,000

**ARG:** Adrián José Gabbarini (3/0), Pablo Javier Zabaleta Girod (11/0) [46.Jonathan Pablo Bottinelli (3/0)], Mateo Pablo Musacchio (2/0), Federico Julián Fazio (2/0) [46.Emiliano Adrián Insúa Zapata (4/0)], Cristian Daniel Ansaldi (2/0), Mario Ariel Bolatti (11/1), Nicolás Santiago Bertolo (2/0) [46.Fernando Daniel Belluschi (5/0)], Alejandro Ariel Cabral (2/0) [68.Mauro Abel Formica (1/0)], Pablo Daniel Piatti (1/0) [78.Osvaldo Nicolás Fabián Gaitán (6/0)], Jonathan Ezequiel Cristaldo (1/0), Marco Gastón Ruben Rodríguez (1/1). Trainer: Sergio Daniel Batista (13).

**Goal**: Marco Gastón Ruben Rodríguez (46).

**887.** 20.06.2011 **ARGENTINA - ALBANIA** **4-0(2-0)**
Estadio Monumental „Antonio Vespucio Liberti“, Buenos Aires; Referee: Jorge Luis Larrionda Pietrafesa (Uruguay); Attendance: 21,000
**ARG:** Sergio Germán Romero (17/0), Nicolás Andrés Burdisso (40/2), Gabriel Alejandro Milito (38/1), Faustino Marcos Alberto Rojo (4/0) [46.Pablo Javier Zabaleta Girod (12/0)], Javier Alejandro Mascherano (69/2), Javier Adelmar Zanetti (141/5), Éver Maximiliano David Banega (9/0), Lucas Rodrigo Biglia (4/0) [46.Fernando Rubén Gago (30/0)], Ezequiel Iván Lavezzi (12/1) [61.Sergio Leonel Agüero del Castillo (27/10)], Ángel Fabián di María (20/3) [46.Carlos Alberto Tévez (61/13)], Lionel Andrés Messi (57/17). Trainer: Sergio Daniel Batista (12).
**Goals**: Ezequiel Iván Lavezzi (5), Lionel Andrés Messi (42), Sergio Leonel Agüero del Castillo (74), Carlos Alberto Tévez (89).

**888.** 01.07.2011 **ARGENTINA - BOLIVIA** **1-1(0-0)** 43rd Copa América. Group Stage.
Estadio Ciudad de La Plata, La Plata; Referee: Roberto Carlos Silvera Calcerrada (Uruguay); Attendance: 52,700
**ARG:** Sergio Germán Romero (18/0), Javier Adelmar Zanetti (142/5), Nicolás Andrés Burdisso (41/2), Gabriel Alejandro Milito (39/1), Faustino Marcos Alberto Rojo (5/0), Éver Maximiliano David Banega (10/0), Javier Alejandro Mascherano (70/2), Esteban Matías Cambiasso Deleau (51/5) [46.Ángel Fabián di María (21/3)], Ezequiel Iván Lavezzi (13/1) [71.Sergio Leonel Agüero del Castillo (28/11)], Lionel Andrés Messi (58/17), Carlos Alberto Tévez (62/13). Trainer: Sergio Daniel Batista (14).
**Goal**: Sergio Leonel Agüero del Castillo (75).

**889.** 06.07.2011 **ARGENTINA - COLOMBIA** **0-0** 43rd Copa América. Group Stage.
Estadio "Brigadier General Estanislao López", Santa Fe; Referee: Sálvio Spínola Fagundes Filho (Brazil); Attendance: 47,000
**ARG:** Sergio Germán Romero (19/0), Pablo Javier Zabaleta Girod (13/0), Nicolás Andrés Burdisso (42/2), Gabriel Alejandro Milito (40/1), Javier Adelmar Zanetti (143/5), Éver Maximiliano David Banega (11/0) [72.Gonzalo Gerardo Higuaín (14/7)], Javier Alejandro Mascherano (71/2), Esteban Matías Cambiasso Deleau (52/5) [60.Fernando Rubén Gago (31/0)], Ezequiel Iván Lavezzi (14/1) [60.Sergio Leonel Agüero del Castillo (29/11)], Lionel Andrés Messi (59/17), Carlos Alberto Tévez (63/13). Trainer: Sergio Daniel Batista (15).

**890.** 11.07.2011 **ARGENTINA – COSTA RICA** **3-0(1-0)** 43rd Copa América. Group Stage.
Estadio „Mario Alberto Kempes“, Córdoba; Referee: Víctor Hugo Rivera Chávez (Peru); Attendance: n/a
**ARG:** Sergio Germán Romero (20/0), Pablo Javier Zabaleta Girod (14/0), Nicolás Andrés Burdisso (43/2), Gabriel Alejandro Milito (41/1), Javier Adelmar Zanetti (144/5), Fernando Rubén Gago (32/0), Javier Alejandro Mascherano (72/2), Lionel Andrés Messi (60/17), Ángel Fabián di María (22/4) [80.Lucas Rodrigo Biglia (5/0)], Sergio Leonel Agüero del Castillo (30/13) [85.Ezequiel Iván Lavezzi (15/1)], Gonzalo Gerardo Higuaín (15/7) [80.Javier Matías Pastore (9/0)]. Trainer: Sergio Daniel Batista (16).
**Goals**: Sergio Leonel Agüero del Castillo (45, 52), Ángel Fabián di María (63).

**891.** 16.07.2011 **ARGENTINA - URUGUAY** **1-1(1-1,1-1,1-1); 4-5 on penalties** 43rd Copa América. Quarter-Finals.
Estadio „Brigadier Estanislao López“, Santa Fé; Referee: Carlos Arecio Amarilla Demarqui (Paraguay), Attendance: 37,000
**ARG:** Sergio Germán Romero (21/0), Pablo Javier Zabaleta Girod (15/0), Nicolás Andrés Burdisso (44/2), Gabriel Alejandro Milito (42/1), Javier Adelmar Zanetti (145/5), Javier Alejandro Mascherano (73/2) [*sent off 86*], Fernando Rubén Gago (33/0) [96.Lucas Rodrigo Biglia (6/0)], Lionel Andrés Messi (61/17), Ángel Fabián di María (23/4) [72.Javier Matías Pastore (10/0)], Sergio Leonel Agüero del Castillo (31/13) [83.Carlos Alberto Tévez (64/13)], Gonzalo Gerardo Higuaín (16/8). Trainer: Sergio Daniel Batista (17).
**Goal**: Gonzalo Gerardo Higuaín (17).
**Penalties**: Lionel Andrés Messi, Nicolás Andrés Burdisso, Carlos Alberto Tévez (saved), Javier Matías Pastore, Gonzalo Gerardo Higuaín.

**892.** 02.09.2011 **VENEZUELA - ARGENTINA** **0-1(0-0)**
Yuba Bharati Krirangan (Salt Lake Stadium), Calcutta (India); Referee: Dinesh Nair (India); Attendance: 90,000
**ARG:** Sergio Germán Romero (22/0), Nicolás Hernán Gonzalo Otamendi (12/1), Faustino Marcos Alberto Rojo (6/0), Pablo Javier Zabaleta Girod (16/0) [83.Federico Fernández (3/1)], Martín Gastón Demichelis (34/2), Javier Alejandro Mascherano (74/2), Ricardo Gabriel Álvarez (1/0) [60.Javier Matías Pastore (11/0)], Luis Óscar González (44/7) [73.José Ernesto Sosa (8/1)], Ángel Fabián di María (24/4), Lionel Andrés Messi (62/17), Gonzalo Gerardo Higuaín (17/8) [77.Sergio Leonel Agüero del Castillo (32/13)]. Trainer: Alejandro Sabella (1).
**Goal**: Nicolás Hernán Gonzalo Otamendi (70).

**893.** 06.09.2011 **ARGENTINA - NIGERIA** **3-1(2-0)**
Bangabandhu National Stadium, Dhaka (Bangladesh); Referee: Akbar Bakhshizadeh (Iran); Attendance: 32,000
**ARG:** Sergio Germán Romero (23/0), Nicolás Andrés Burdisso (45/2), Nicolás Hernán Gonzalo Otamendi (13/1), Faustino Marcos Alberto Rojo (7/0) [68.Jonás Manuel Gutiérrez (21/1)], Pablo Javier Zabaleta Girod (17/0) [83.Federico Fernández (4/1)], Martín Gastón Demichelis (35/2), Javier Alejandro Mascherano (75/2), José Ernesto Sosa (9/1) [89.Ricardo Gabriel Álvarez (2/0)], Ángel Fabián di María (25/5) [76.Éver Maximiliano David Banega (12/0)], Gonzalo Gerardo Higuaín (18/9) [77.Sergio Leonel Agüero del Castillo (33/13)], Lionel Andrés Messi (63/17). Trainer: Alejandro Sabella (2).
**Goals**: Gonzalo Gerardo Higuaín (24), Ángel Fabián di María (26), Uwa Elderson Echiéjilé (66 own goal).

**894.** 14.09.2011 **ARGENTINA - BRAZIL** **0-0**
Estadio „Mario Alberto Kempes“, Córdoba; Referee: Enrique Roberto Osses Zencovich (Chile); Attendance: 50,000
**ARG:** Agustín Ignacio Orión (1/0), Christian Ariel Cellay (1/0), Sebastián Enrique Domínguez (3/0), Iván Alexis Pillud (4/0), Emiliano Ramiro Papa (7/0), Leandro Desábato (1/0), Héctor Canteros (1/0), Víctor Eduardo Zapata (1/0), Augusto Matías Fernández (1/0) [87.Cristian Manuel Chávez (4/1)], Mauro Boselli (4/1) [23.Emmanuel Gigliotti (1/0)], Juan Manuel Martínez (1/0) [58.Pablo Nicolás Mouche (4/2)]. Trainer: Alejandro Sabella (3).

**895.** 28.09.2011 **BRAZIL - ARGENTINA** **2-0(0-0)**
Estádio Mangueirão, Belém; Referee: Jorge Luis Larrionda Pietrafiesa (Uruguay); Attendance: 43,038
**ARG:** Agustín Ignacio Orión (2/0), Christian Ariel Cellay (2/0), Sebastián Enrique Domínguez (4/0), Iván Alexis Pillud (5/0) [78.Pablo Nicolás Mouche (5/2)], Emiliano Ramiro Papa (8/0), Leandro Desábato (2/0), Héctor Canteros (2/0) [60.Mario Ariel Bolatti (12/1)], Pablo Horacio Guiñazú (5/0), Augusto Matías Fernández (2/0), Walter Damián Montillo (1/0), Lucas Ezequiel Viatri (3/0). Trainer: Alejandro Sabella (4).

**896.** 07.10.2011 **ARGENTINA - CHILE** **4-1(2-0)** 20th FIFA WC. Qualifiers
Estadio Monumental „Antonio Vespucio Liberti“, Buenos Aires; Referee: Wilmar Alexander Roldán Pérez (Colombia); Attendance: 26,161
**ARG:** Mariano Gonzalo Andújar (7/0), Nicolás Andrés Burdisso (46/2), Nicolás Hernán Gonzalo Otamendi (14/1), Faustino Marcos Alberto Rojo (8/0), Pablo Javier Zabaleta Girod (18/0), Éver Maximiliano David Banega (13/0) [72.Fabián Andrés Rinaudo (4/0)], Rodrigo Braña (2/0), José Ernesto Sosa (10/1) [80.Eduardo Antonio Salvio (3/0)], Ángel Fabián di María (26/5) [85.Jonás Manuel Gutiérrez (22/1)], Lionel Andrés Messi (64/18), Gonzalo Gerardo Higuaín (19/12). Trainer: Alejandro Sabella (5).
**Goals**: Gonzalo Gerardo Higuaín (7), Lionel Andrés Messi (25), Gonzalo Gerardo Higuaín (51, 62).

**897.** 11.10.2011 **VENEZUELA - ARGENTINA** **1-0(0-0)** 20th FIFA WC. Qualifiers

Estadio „José Antonio Anzoátegui", Puerto La Cruz; Referee: Roberto Carlos Silvera Calcerrada (Uruguay); Attendance: 35,600

**ARG:** Mariano Gonzalo Andújar (8/0), Nicolás Andrés Burdisso (47/2), Nicolás Hernán Gonzalo Otamendi (15/1), Faustino Marcos Alberto Rojo (9/0), Pablo Javier Zabaleta Girod (19/0) [66.Éver Maximiliano David Banega (14/0)], Martín Gastón Demichelis (36/2), Javier Alejandro Mascherano (76/2), José Ernesto Sosa (11/1) [74.Rodrigo Sebastián Palacio (1/0)], Ángel Fabián di María (27/5) [84.Javier Matías Pastore (12/0)], Lionel Andrés Messi (65/18), Gonzalo Gerardo Higuaín (20/12). Trainer: Alejandro Sabella (6).

**898.** 11.11.2011 **ARGENTINA - BOLIVIA** **1-1(0-0)** 20th FIFA WC. Qualifiers

Estadio Monumental „Antonio Vespucio Liberti", Buenos Aires; Referee: Carlos Alfredo Vera Rodríguez (Ecuador); Attendance: 27,592

**ARG:** Sergio Germán Romero (24/0), Nicolás Andrés Burdisso (48/2), Clemente Juan Rodríguez (14/0), Pablo Javier Zabaleta Girod (20/0), Martín Gastón Demichelis (37/2), Javier Alejandro Mascherano (77/2) [82.José Ernesto Sosa (12/1)], Fernando Rubén Gago (34/0), Ricardo Gabriel Álvarez (3/0) [59.Ezequiel Iván Lavezzi (16/2)], Javier Matías Pastore (13/0), Lionel Andrés Messi (66/18), Gonzalo Gerardo Higuaín (21/12). Trainer: Alejandro Sabella (7).

**Goal**: Ezequiel Iván Lavezzi (60).

**899.** 15.11.2011 **COLOMBIA - ARGENTINA** **1-2(1-0)** 20th FIFA WC. Qualifiers

Estadio Metropolitano "Roberto Meléndez", Barranquilla; Referee: Sálvio Spínola Fagundes Filho (Brazil); Attendance: 49,600

**ARG:** Sergio Germán Romero (25/0), Nicolás Andrés Burdisso (49/2) [37.Leandro Desábato (3/0)], Federico Fernández (5/1), Clemente Juan Rodríguez (15/0), Pablo Javier Zabaleta Girod (21/0), Javier Alejandro Mascherano (78/2), Rodrigo Braña (3/0), Pablo Horacio Guiñazú (6/0) [46.Sergio Leonel Agüero del Castillo (34/14)], José Ernesto Sosa (13/1), Lionel Andrés Messi (67/19), Gonzalo Gerardo Higuaín (22/12) [86.Fernando Rubén Gago (35/0)]. Trainer: Alejandro Sabella (8).

**Goals**: Lionel Andrés Messi (61), Sergio Leonel Agüero del Castillo (84).

**900.** 29.02.2012 **SWITZERLAND - ARGENTINA** **1-3(0-1)**

Stade de Suisse-Wankdorf, Bern; Referee: Florian Meyer (Germany); Attendance: 30,250

**ARG:** Sergio Germán Romero (26/0), Hugo Armando Campagnaro (1/0), Ezequiel Marcelo Garay González (4/0), Federico Fernández (6/1), Pablo Javier Zabaleta Girod (22/0), Maximiliano Rubén Rodríguez (1/0) [70.Eduardo Antonio Salvio (4/0)], Javier Alejandro Mascherano (79/2), Rodrigo Braña (4/0) [46.Fernando Rubén Gago (36/0)], José Ernesto Sosa (14/1) [80.Gonzalo Gerardo Higuaín (23/12)], Lionel Andrés Messi (68/22), Sergio Leonel Agüero del Castillo (35/14). Trainer: Alejandro Sabella (9).

**Goals**: Lionel Andrés Messi (20, 88, 90+3).

**901.** 02.06.2012 **ARGENTINA - ECUADOR** **4-0(3-0)** 20th FIFA WC. Qualifiers

Estadio Monumental „Antonio Vespucio Liberti", Buenos Aires; Referee: Víctor Hugo Rivera Chávez (Peru); Attendance: 50,000

**ARG:** Sergio Germán Romero (27/0), Pablo Javier Zabaleta Girod (23/0), Federico Fernández (7/1), Ezequiel Marcelo Garay González (5/0), Clemente Juan Rodríguez (16/0), Fernando Rubén Gago (37/0), Javier Alejandro Mascherano (80/2), Ángel Fabián di María (28/6) [83.Maximiliano Rubén Rodríguez (43/12)], Lionel Andrés Messi (69/23), Sergio Leonel Agüero del Castillo (36/15) [63.José Ernesto Sosa (15/1)], Gonzalo Gerardo Higuaín (24/13) [74.Ezequiel Iván Lavezzi (17/2)]. Trainer: Alejandro Sabella (10).

**Goals**: Sergio Leonel Agüero del Castillo (19), Gonzalo Gerardo Higuaín (29), Lionel Andrés Messi (31), Ángel Fabián di María (76).

**902.** 09.06.2012 **BRAZIL - ARGENTINA** **3-4(1-2)**

MetLife Stadium, East Rutherford, New Jersey (United States); Referee: Jair Marrufo (United States); Attendance: 81,994

**ARG:** Sergio Germán Romero (28/0), Pablo Javier Zabaleta Girod (24/0), Ezequiel Marcelo Garay González (6/0), Clemente Juan Rodríguez (17/0) [88.Hugo Armando Campagnaro (2/0)], Federico Fernández (8/2), Javier Alejandro Mascherano (81/2), Fernando Rubén Gago (38/0), José Ernesto Sosa (16/1) [61.Pablo Horacio Guiñazú (7/0)], Ángel Fabián di María (29/6) [74.Sergio Leonel Agüero del Castillo (37/15)], Lionel Andrés Messi (70/26), Gonzalo Gerardo Higuaín (25/13) [88.Ezequiel Iván Lavezzi (18/2) [*sent off 90+1*]]. Trainer: Alejandro Sabella (11).

**Goals**: Lionel Andrés Messi (31, 34), Federico Fernández (76), Lionel Andrés Messi (85).

**903.** 15.08.2012 **GERMANY - ARGENTINA** **1-3(0-1)**

Commerzbank Arena, Frankfurt; Referee: Jonas Eriksson (Sweden); Attendance: 48,808

**ARG:** Sergio Germán Romero (29/0), Federico Fernández (9/2), Ezequiel Marcelo Garay González (7/0), Faustino Marcos Alberto Rojo (10/0), Pablo Javier Zabaleta Girod (25/0) [65.Hugo Armando Campagnaro (3/0)], Javier Alejandro Mascherano (82/2) [79.Rodrigo Braña (5/0)], Fernando Rubén Gago (39/0), José Ernesto Sosa (17/1) [46.Sergio Leonel Agüero del Castillo (38/15)], Ángel Fabián di María Hernández (30/7) [73.Pablo Horacio Guiñazú (8/0)], Gonzalo Gerardo Higuaín (26/13), Lionel Andrés Messi (71/27). Trainer: Alejandro Sabella (12).

**Goals**: Sami Khedira (45 own goal), Lionel Andrés Messi (52), Ángel Fabián di María Hernández (73).

**904.** 07.09.2012 **ARGENTINA - PARAGUAY** **3-1(2-1)** 20th FIFA WC. Qualifiers

Estadio "Mario Alberto Kempes", Córdoba; Referee: Wilson Luiz Seneme (Brazil); Attendance: 57,000

**ARG:** Sergio Germán Romero (30/0), Hugo Armando Campagnaro (4/0), Federico Fernández (10/2), Ezequiel Marcelo Garay González (8/0), Faustino Marcos Alberto Rojo (11/0), Fernando Rubén Gago (40/0), Rodrigo Braña (6/0) [87.Lucas Rodrigo Biglia (7/0)], Ezequiel Iván Lavezzi (19/2) [65.Rodrigo Sebastián Palacio (10/1)], Lionel Andrés Messi (72/28), Ángel Fabián di María Hernández (31/8) [79.Pablo Horacio Guiñazú (9/0)], Gonzalo Gerardo Higuaín (27/14). Trainer: Alejandro Sabella (13).

**Goals**: Ángel Fabián di María Hernández (2), Gonzalo Gerardo Higuaín (31), Lionel Andrés Messi (63).

**905.** 11.09.2012 **PERU - ARGENTINA** **1-1(1-1)** 20th FIFA WC. Qualifiers

Estadio Nacional, Lima; Referee: Wilmar Alexander Roldán Pérez (Colombia); Attendance: 34,111

**ARG:** Sergio Germán Romero (31/0), Hugo Armando Campagnaro (5/0), Federico Fernández (11/2), Ezequiel Marcelo Garay González (9/0), Faustino Marcos Alberto Rojo (12/0), Fernando Rubén Gago (41/0) [61.Pablo Horacio Guiñazú (10/0)], Javier Alejandro Mascherano (83/2), Ezequiel Iván Lavezzi (20/2) [74.Enzo Nicolás Pérez (6/1)], Ángel Fabián di María Hernández (32/8) [89.Maximiliano Rubén Rodríguez (44/12)], Lionel Andrés Messi (73/28), Gonzalo Gerardo Higuaín (28/15). Trainer: Alejandro Sabella (14).

**Goal**: Gonzalo Gerardo Higuaín (37).

**906.** 19.09.2012 **BRAZIL - ARGENTINA** **2-1(1-1)** Superclásico de las Américas

Estádio Serra Dourada, Goiânia; Referee: Carlos Arecio Amarilla Demarqui (Paraguay); Attendance: 37,781

**ARG:** Oscar Alfredo Ustari (2/0), Lisandro Ezequiel López (3/0) [72.Santiago Vergini (1/0)], Sebastián Enrique Domínguez (5/0), Leandro Desábato (4/0), Gino Peruzzi Lucchetti (1/0), Maximiliano Rubén Rodríguez (45/12), Rodrigo Braña (7/0), Pablo Horacio Guiñazú (11/0), Clemente Juan Rodríguez (18/0), Juan Manuel Martínez (3/1) [87.Leandro Daniel Somoza (3/0)], Hernán Barcos (1/0) [76.Rogelio Gabriel Funes Mori (1/0)]. Trainer: Alejandro Sabella (15).

**Goals**: Juan Manuel Martínez (20).

**907.** 12.10.2012 **ARGENTINA - URUGUAY** **3-0(0-0)** 20th FIFA WC. Qualifiers

Estadio Malvinas Argentinas, Mendoza; Referee: Leandro Pedro Vuaden (Brazil); Attendance: 31,997

**ARG:** Sergio Germán Romero (32/0), Pablo Javier Zabaleta Girod (26/0), Federico Fernández (12/2), Ezequiel Marcelo Garay González (10/0), Faustino Marcos Alberto Rojo (13/0) [67.Hugo Armando Campagnaro (6/0)], Fernando Rubén Gago (42/0), Javier Alejandro Mascherano (84/2), Ángel Fabián di María Hernández (33/8), Lionel Andrés Messi (74/30), Sergio Leonel Agüero del Castillo (39/16) [79.Pablo Horacio Guiñazú (12/0)], Gonzalo Gerardo Higuaín (29/15) [83.Hernán Barcos (2/0)]. Lionel Andrés Messi (66), Sergio Leonel Agüero del Castillo (75), Lionel Andrés Messi (80). Trainer: Alejandro Sabella (16).

**Goals**: Lionel Andrés Messi (66), Sergio Leonel Agüero del Castillo (75), Lionel Andrés Messi (80).

**908.** 16.10.2012 **CHILE - ARGENTINA** **1-2(0-2)** 20th FIFA WC. Qualifiers

Estadio Nacional, Santiago; Referee: Antonio Arias Alvarenga (Paraguay); Attendance: 45,000

**ARG:** Sergio Germán Romero (33/0), Hugo Armando Campagnaro (7/0), Federico Fernández (13/2), Ezequiel Marcelo Garay González (11/0), Pablo Javier Zabaleta Girod (27/0), Fernando Rubén Gago (43/0), Javier Alejandro Mascherano (85/2), Lionel Andrés Messi (75/31), Ángel Fabián di María Hernández (34/8) [77.José Ernesto Sosa (18/1)], Gonzalo Gerardo Higuaín (30/16) [61.Pablo Horacio Guiñazú (13/0)], Sergio Leonel Agüero del Castillo (40/16) [82.Hernán Barcos (3/0)]. Trainer: Alejandro Sabella (17).

**Goals**: Lionel Andrés Messi (28), Gonzalo Gerardo Higuaín (31).

**909.** 14.11.2012 **SAUDI ARABIA - ARGENTINA** **0-0**

"King Fahd" International Stadium, Riyadh; Referee: Ali Abdulnabi (Bahrain); Attendance: 51,000

**ARG:** Sergio Germán Romero (34/0), Fabricio Coloccini (35/1), Federico Fernández (14/2), Faustino Marcos Alberto Rojo (14/0), Pablo Javier Zabaleta Girod (28/0), Javier Alejandro Mascherano (86/2), Alberto Facundo Costa (2/0) [46.Augusto Matías Fernández (3/0)], Eduardo Antonio Salvio (5/0) [46.Franco Matías Di Santo (1/0)], Ángel Fabián di María Hernández (35/8), Sergio Leonel Agüero del Castillo (41/16), Lionel Andrés Messi (76/31). Trainer: Alejandro Sabella (18).

**910.** 21.11.2012 **ARGENTINA - BRAZIL** **2-1(0-0); 3-4 on penalties** Superclásico de las Américas

Estadio "Alberto J. Armando ", Buenos Aires; Referee: Enrique Roberto Osses Zencovich (Chile); Attendance: 20,000

**ARG:** Agustín Ignacio Orión (3/0), Sebastián Enrique Domínguez (6/0), Lisandro Ezequiel López (4/0), Gino Peruzzi Lucchetti (2/0), Leandro Desábato (5/0), Leonel Jesús Vangioni (2/0), Francisco Cerro (1/0) [88.Oscar Adrián Ahumada (1/0)], Pablo Horacio Guiñazú (14/0), Walter Damián Montillo (2/0), Hernán Barcos (4/0) [69.Ignacio Martín Scocco (1/2)], Juan Manuel Martínez (4/1). Trainer: Alejandro Sabella (19).

**Goals**: Ignacio Martín Scocco (82 penalty, 90).

**911.** 06.02.2013 **SWEDEN - ARGENTINA** **2-3(1-3)**

Friends Arena, Stockholm; Referee: Antony Gautier (France); Attendance: 49,646

**ARG:** Sergio Germán Romero (35/0), Hugo Armando Campagnaro (8/0), Federico Fernández (15/2), Ezequiel Marcelo Garay González (12/0) [87.Fabricio Coloccini (36/1)], Pablo Javier Zabaleta Girod (29/0) [60.Cristian Daniel Ansaldi (3/0)], Javier Alejandro Mascherano (87/2), Fernando Rubén Gago (44/0) [67.Éver Maximiliano David Banega (15/0)], Ángel Fabián di María Hernández (36/8) [46.Walter Damián Montillo (3/0)], Lionel Andrés Messi (77/31), Sergio Leonel Agüero del Castillo (42/17) [75.Ezequiel Iván Lavezzi (21/2)], Gonzalo Gerardo Higuaín (31/18) [90.Franco Matías Di Santo (2/0)]. Trainer: Alejandro Sabella (20).

**Goals**: Gonzalo Gerardo Higuaín (3), Sergio Leonel Agüero del Castillo (19), Gonzalo Gerardo Higuaín (23).

**912.** 22.03.2013 **ARGENTINA - VENEZUELA** **3-0(2-0)** 20th FIFA WC. Qualifiers

Estadio Monumental "Antonio Vespucio Liberti", Buenos Aires; Referee: Víctor Hugo Carrillo (Peru); Attendance: 40,000

**ARG:** Sergio Germán Romero (36/0), Pablo Javier Zabaleta Girod (30/0), Federico Fernández (16/2), Ezequiel Marcelo Garay González (13/0), Faustino Marcos Alberto Rojo (15/0), Fernando Rubén Gago (45/0) [62.Éver Maximiliano David Banega (16/0)], Javier Alejandro Mascherano (88/2), Walter Damián Montillo (4/0), Lionel Andrés Messi (78/32), Ezequiel Iván Lavezzi (22/2) [83.Maximiliano Rubén Rodríguez (46/12)], Gonzalo Gerardo Higuaín (32/20) [80.Rodrigo Sebastián Palacio (11/1)]. Trainer: Alejandro Sabella (21).

**Goals**: Gonzalo Gerardo Higuaín (29), Lionel Andrés Messi (43 penalty), Gonzalo Gerardo Higuaín (59).

**913.** 26.03.2013 **BOLIVIA - ARGENTINA** **1-1(1-1)** 20th FIFA WC. Qualifiers

Estadio "Hernando Siles Zuazo", La Paz; Referee: Enrique Roberto Osses Zencovich (Chile); Attendance: 35,000

**ARG:** Sergio Germán Romero (37/0), José María Basanta (1/0), Hugo Armando Campagnaro (9/0), Sebastián Enrique Domínguez (7/0), Gino Peruzzi Lucchetti (3/0), Clemente Juan Rodríguez (19/0), Javier Alejandro Mascherano (89/2), Éver Maximiliano David Banega (17/1) [62.Leonardo Daniel Ponzio (8/0)], Ángel Fabián di María Hernández (37/8) [90.Pablo Horacio Guiñazú (15/0)], Lionel Andrés Messi (79/32), Rodrigo Sebastián Palacio (12/1) [86.Franco Matías Di Santo (3/0)]. Trainer: Alejandro Sabella (22).

**Goals**: Éver Maximiliano David Banega (44).

**914.** 07.06.2013 **ARGENTINA - COLOMBIA** **0-0** 20th FIFA WC. Qualifiers

Estadio Monumental "Antonio Vespucio Liberti", Buenos Aires; Referee: Marlon Escalante Álvarez (Venezuela); Attendance: 44,807

**ARG:** Sergio Germán Romero (38/0), Pablo Javier Zabaleta Girod (31/0), Ezequiel Marcelo Garay González (14/0), Federico Fernández (17/2), Faustino Marcos Alberto Rojo (16/0), Javier Alejandro Mascherano (90/2), Lucas Rodrigo Biglia (8/0), Ángel Fabián di María Hernández (38/8), Walter Damián Montillo (5/0) [58.Lionel Andrés Messi (80/32)], Sergio Leonel Agüero del Castillo (43/17) [81.Ezequiel Iván Lavezzi (23/2)], Gonzalo Gerardo Higuaín (33/20) [*sent off 26*]. Trainer: Alejandro Sabella (23).

**915.** 11.06.2013 **ECUADOR - ARGENTINA** **1-1(1-1)** 20th FIFA WC. Qualifiers

Estadio Olímpico Atahualpa, Quito; Referee: Enrique Cáceres Villafante (Paraguay); Attendance: 35,000

**ARG:** Sergio Germán Romero (39/0), Ezequiel Marcelo Garay González (15/0), José María Basanta (2/0), Federico Fernández (18/2), Faustino Marcos Alberto Rojo (17/0), Gino Peruzzi Lucchetti (4/0), Javier Alejandro Mascherano (91/2) [*sent off 86*], Ángel Fabián di María Hernández (39/8), Éver Maximiliano David Banega (18/1) [76.Lucas Rodrigo Biglia (9/0)], Rodrigo Sebastián Palacio (13/1) [90+1.Rodrigo Braña (8/0)], Sergio Leonel Agüero del Castillo (44/18) [61.Lionel Andrés Messi (81/32)]. Trainer: Alejandro Sabella (24).

**Goals**: Sergio Leonel Agüero del Castillo (4 penalty).

**916.** 14.06.2013 **GUATEMALA - ARGENTINA** **0-4(0-3)**

Estadio "Mateo Flores", Ciudad de Guatemala; Referee: Armando Isai Castro Oviedo (Honduras); Attendance: 23,000

**ARG:** Mariano Gonzalo Andújar (9/0), Fabricio Coloccini (37/1), José María Basanta (3/0) [64.Javier Alejandro Mascherano (92/2)], Hugo Armando Campagnaro (10/0), Clemente Juan Rodríguez (20/0), Lucas Rodrigo Biglia (10/0) [46.Rodrigo Braña (9/0)], Pablo Horacio Guiñazú (16/0) [71.Éver Maximiliano David Banega (19/1)], Augusto Matías Fernández (4/1), Lionel Andrés Messi (82/35) [68.Rodrigo Sebastián Palacio (14/1)], Sergio Leonel Agüero del Castillo (45/18) [46.Erik Manuel Lamela (2/0)], Ezequiel Iván Lavezzi (24/2) [79.Walter Damián Montillo (6/0)]. Trainer: Alejandro Sabella (25).

**Goals**: Lionel Andrés Messi (15), Augusto Matías Fernández (36), Lionel Andrés Messi (40, 49).

**917.** 14.08.2013 **ITALY - ARGENTINA** **1-2(0-1)**
Stadio Olimpico, Roma; Referee: Wolfgang Stark (Germany); Attendance: 35,000
**ARG:** Mariano Gonzalo Andújar (10/0), Ezequiel Marcelo Garay González (16/0) [72.Fabricio Coloccini (38/1)], José María Basanta (4/0), Hugo Armando Campagnaro (11/0), Federico Fernández (19/2), Javier Alejandro Mascherano (93/2) [76.Maximiliano Rubén Rodríguez (47/12)], Lucas Rodrigo Biglia (11/0), Ángel Fabián di María Hernández (40/8) [81.Ricardo Gabriel Álvarez (4/0)], Rodrigo Sebastián Palacio (15/1) [89.Augusto Matías Fernández (5/1)], Gonzalo Gerardo Higuaín (34/21) [61.Ezequiel Iván Lavezzi (25/2)], Erik Manuel Lamela (3/0) [46.Éver Maximiliano David Banega (20/2)]. Trainer: Alejandro Sabella (26).
**Goals**: Gonzalo Gerardo Higuaín (21), Éver Maximiliano David Banega (49).

**918.** 11.09.2013 **PARAGUAY - ARGENTINA** **2-5(1-2)** 20th FIFA WC. Qualifiers
Estadio Defensores del Chaco, Asunción; Referee: Enrique Roberto Osses Zencovich (Chile); Attendance: 27,000
**ARG:** Sergio Germán Romero (40/0), Fabricio Coloccini (39/1), Pablo Javier Zabaleta Girod (32/0), José María Basanta (5/0), Hugo Armando Campagnaro (12/0), Lucas Rodrigo Biglia (12/0), Fernando Rubén Gago (46/0) [86.Maximiliano Rubén Rodríguez (48/13)], Ángel Fabián di María Hernández (41/9), Rodrigo Sebastián Palacio (16/1) [65.Ezequiel Iván Lavezzi (26/2)], Lionel Andrés Messi (83/37), Sergio Leonel Agüero del Castillo (46/19) [77.Éver Maximiliano David Banega (21/2)]. Trainer: Alejandro Sabella (27).
**Goals**: Lionel Andrés Messi (12 penalty), Sergio Leonel Agüero del Castillo (32), Ángel Fabián di María Hernández (50), Lionel Andrés Messi (53 penalty), Maximiliano Rubén Rodríguez (90).

**919.** 11.10.2013 **ARGENTINA - PERU** **3-1(2-1)** 20th FIFA WC. Qualifiers
Estadio Monumental „Antonio Vespucio Liberti“, Buenos Aires; Referee: Carlos Alfredo Vera Rodríguez (Ecuador); Attendance: 28,977
**ARG:** Sergio Germán Romero (41/0), Pablo Javier Zabaleta Girod (33/0), Ezequiel Marcelo Garay González (17/0), Federico Fernández (20/2), Faustino Marcos Alberto Rojo (18/0), Lucas Rodrigo Biglia (13/0), Ángel Fabián di María Hernández (42/9) [90+1.Leandro Daniel Somoza (4/0)], Éver Maximiliano David Banega (22/2), Rodrigo Sebastián Palacio (17/2) [80.Erik Manuel Lamela (4/0)], Sergio Leonel Agüero del Castillo (47/19), Ezequiel Iván Lavezzi (27/4) [87.Maximiliano Rubén Rodríguez (49/13)]. Trainer: Alejandro Sabella (28).
**Goals**: Ezequiel Iván Lavezzi (23, 35), Rodrigo Sebastián Palacio (47).

**920.** 15.10.2013 **URUGUAY - ARGENTINA** **3-2(2-2)** 20th FIFA WC. Qualifiers
Estadio Centenario, Montevideo; Referee: Marcelo de Lima Henrique (Brazil); Attendance: 55,000
**ARG:** Sergio Germán Romero (42/0), Sebastián Enrique Domínguez (8/0), José María Basanta (6/0), Hugo Armando Campagnaro (13/0), Federico Fernández (21/2), Maximiliano Rubén Rodríguez (50/15), Lucas Rodrigo Biglia (14/0), Augusto Matías Fernández (6/1) [82.Mauro Emanuel Icardi Rivero (1/0)], Éver Maximiliano David Banega (23/2) [68.Leandro Daniel Somoza (5/0)], Rodrigo Sebastián Palacio (18/2), Erik Manuel Lamela (5/0) [76.José Ernesto Sosa (19/1)]. Trainer: Alejandro Sabella (29).
**Goals**: Maximiliano Rubén Rodríguez (14, 41).

**921.** 15.11.2013 **ECUADOR - ARGENTINA** **0-0**
MetLife Stadium, East Rutherford, New Jersey (United States); Referee: Silviu Petrescu (Canada); Attendance: n/a
**ARG:** Sergio Germán Romero (43/0), Ezequiel Marcelo Garay González (18/0), Facundo Sebastián Roncaglia (1/0) [63.Pablo Javier Zabaleta Girod (34/0)], Federico Fernández (22/2), Lucas Alfonso Orbán (1/0), Javier Alejandro Mascherano (94/2), Ángel Fabián di María Hernández (43/9), Éver Maximiliano David Banega (24/2) [69.Lucas Rodrigo Biglia (15/0)], Ricardo Gabriel Álvarez (5/0) [79.Maximiliano Rubén Rodríguez (51/15)], Gonzalo Gerardo Higuaín (35/21) [71.Rodrigo Sebastián Palacio (19/2)], Ezequiel Iván Lavezzi (28/4) [63.Sergio Leonel Agüero del Castillo (48/19)]. Trainer: Alejandro Sabella (30).

**922.** 18.11.2013 **ARGENTINA – BOSNIA-HERZEGOVINA** **2-0(1-0)**
Busch Stadium, St. Louis (United States); Referee: Edwin Jurisevic (United States); Attendance: n/a
**ARG:** Sergio Germán Romero (44/0), Pablo Javier Zabaleta Girod (35/0), José María Basanta Pavone (7/0), Federico Fernández (23/2), Nicolás Hernán Gonzalo Otamendi (16/1), Faustino Marcos Alberto Rojo (19/0), Javier Alejandro Mascherano (95/2), Maximiliano Rubén Rodríguez (52/15) [72.Lucas Rodrigo Biglia (16/0)], Ángel Fabián di María Hernández (44/9) [86.Augusto Matías Fernández (7/1)], Rodrigo Sebastián Palacio (20/2), Sergio Leonel Agüero del Castillo (49/21) [77.Erik Manuel Lamela (6/0)]. Trainer: Alejandro Sabella (31).
**Goals**: Sergio Leonel Agüero del Castillo (40, 66).

# INTERNATIONAL PLAYERS

| FM/Nr | Name | DOB | Caps | Goals | Period, Club |
|---|---|---|---|---|---|
| (33/095) | ABATÁNGELO Donato | | 1 | 0 | 1913, CA Boca Juniors Buenos Aires (1/0). |
| (785/1125) | ABBONDANZIERI Roberto Carlos | 19.08.1972 | 49 | 0 | 2004-2008, CA Boca Juniors Buenos Aires (27/0), Getafe CF (22/0). |
| (321/630) | ABELEDO Ramón Gregorio | 29.04.1937 | 7 | 0 | 1960-1962, CA Independiente Avellaneda (7/0). |
| (383/710) | ACEVEDO David | 20.02.1937 | 5 | 0 | 1967, CA Independiente Avellaneda (5/0). |
| (866/1217) | ACEVEDO Walter Aníbal | 16.02.1982 | 1 | 0 | 2010, CA Independiente Avellaneda (1/0). |
| (637/1002) | ACOSTA Alberto Federico | 23.08.1966 | 19 | 2 | 1992-1995, CA San Lorenzo de Almagro Buenos Aires (6/1), CA Boca Juniors Buenos Aires (9/0), CD Universidad Católica Santiago (4/1). |
| (109/249) | ACOSTA Lindolfo | | 2 | 1 | 1923-1924, CA San Lorenzo de Almagro Buenos Aires (2/1). |
| (66/162) | ADET Juan Carlos | | 4 | 2 | 1919, Club Sportivo Almagro Buenos Aires (4/2). |
| (823/1150) | AGÜERO DEL CASTILLO Sergio Leonel | 02.06.1988 | 49 | 21 | 2006-2013, Club Atlético de Madrid (31/13), Manchester City FC (18/8). |
| (480/867) | AGÜERO Raúl Francisco | 10.10.1952 | 2 | 0 | 1976, CA Rosario Central (2/0). |
| (550/933) | AGÜERO Rubén José | 20.02.1960 | 6 | 0 | 1984, CA Estudiantes de La Plata (6/0). |
| (395/747) | AGUIRRE Roberto Rodolfo | 10.02.1942 | 8 | 0 | 1968-1969, CA Newell'S Old Boys Rosario (7/0), Racing Club Avellaneda (1/0). |
| (105/237) | AGUIRRE Vicente | | 4 | 4 | 1923-1924, Club Central Córdoba Rosario (4/4). |
| (910/1274) | AHUMADA Oscar Adrián | 31.08.1982 | 1 | 0 | 2012, CA All Boys Buenos Aires (1/0). |
| (730/1087) | AIMAR GIORDANO Pablo César | 03.11.1979 | 52 | 8 | 1999-2009, CA River Plate Buenos Aires (7/1), Valencia CF (36/6), Real Zaragoza CD (8/1), Sport Lisboa e Benfica (1/0). |
| (600/970) | AIREZ Mauro Gabriel | 26.10.1968 | 3 | 1 | 1989-1990, Club Gimnasia y Esgrima La Plata (3/1). |
| (180/410) | ALARCÓN Ricardo | 12.01.1914 | 4 | 0 | 1936-1941, CA San Lorenzo de Almagro Buenos Aires (2/0), CA Boca Juniors Buenos Aires (2/0). |
| (74/171) | ALBERTI Agustín | | 1 | 0 | 1919, CA Huracán Buenos Aires (1/0). |
| (198/444) | ALBERTI Jorge | 18.05.1912 | 23 | 1 | 1940-1945, CA Huracán Buenos Aires (23/1). |
| (695/1058) | ALBORNÓZ José Fabián | 19.07.1970 | 3 | 1 | 1996, CA Independiente Avellaneda (3/1). |
| (335/649) | ALBRECHT José Rafael | 23.08.1941 | 39 | 3 | 1961-1969, CA Estudiantes de La Plata (5/0), CA San Lorenzo de Almagro (34/3). |
| (39/113) | ALDEA Mariano | | 1 | 0 | 1914, Club Hispano Argentino Buenos Aires (1/0). |
| (600/971) | ALFARO MORENO Carlos Alejandro | 18.10.1964 | 11 | 1 | 1989-1991, CA Independiente Avellaneda (11/1). |
| (586/947) | ALFARO Roque Raúl | 15.08.1956 | 5 | 0 | 1987, CA River Plate Buenos Aires (5/0). |
| (256/524) | ALLEGRI Ángel Natalio | 26.12.1926 | 4 | 0 | 1951-1952, CA Vélez Sarsfield (4/0). |
| (691/1053) | ALMEYDA Matías Jesús | 21.12.1973 | 40 | 1 | 1996-2003, CA River Plate Buenos Aires (3/0), Sevilla CF (6/0), SS Lazio Roma (16/1), AC Parma (9/0), Internazionale FC Milano (6/0). |
| (575/944) | ALMIRÓN Sergio Omar | 18.11.1958 | 3 | 3 | 1985-1986, CA Newell's Old Boys Rosario (3/3). |
| (147/307) | ALONSO Jorge | | 2 | 1 | 1928-1929, Club San Fernando (2/1). |
| (434/792) | ALONSO Norberto Osvaldo | 04.01.1953 | 19 | 4 | 1972-1983, CA River Plate Buenos Aires (15/3), CA San Lorenzo de Almagro Buenos Aires (4/1). |
| (625/991) | ALTAMIRANO Ricardo Daniel | 12.12.1965 | 26 | 1 | 1991-1995, CA Independiente Avellaneda (4/0), CA River Plate Buenos Aires (12/1), 1993-94 (6/0), CA River Plate Buenos Aires (4/0). |
| (161/329) | ALTERIO Eduardo | | 1 | 0 | 1930, CA Chacarita Juniors Buenos Aires (1/0). |
| (321/627) | ÁLVAREZ Carlos Alberto | 02.03.1933 | 8 | 0 | 1960, CA Rosario Central (8/0). |
| (892/1259) | ÁLVAREZ Ricardo Gabriel | 12.04.1988 | 5 | 0 | 2011-2013, Internazionale FC Milano (5/0). |
| (75/175) | ALZÚA Inocencio | | 1 | 0 | 1919, Club Atlético San Isidro (1/0). |
| (8/044) | AMADEO Luis Vernet | | 4 | 0 | 1908-1910, Club Atlético San Isidro (1/0), Club Gymnasia y Esgrima Buenos Aires (3/0). |
| (530/909) | AMUCHÁSTEGUI Luis Antonio | 12.12.1960 | 3 | 0 | 1981-1983, CA Racing de Córdoba (3/0). |
| (1/009) | ANDERSON Juan | | 1 | 1 | 1902, Lomas AC (1/1). |
| (341/656) | ANDRADA Edgardo Norberto | 02.01.1939 | 20 | 0 | 1961-1969, CA Rosario Central (20/0). |
| (856/1186) | ANDÚJAR Mariano Gonzalo | 30.07.1983 | 10 | 0 | 2009-2013, Club Estudiantes de La Plata (2/0), Calcio Catania (8/0). |
| (852/1171) | ANGELERI Marcos Alberto | 07.04.1983 | 4 | 0 | 2009-2011, Club Estudiantes de La Plata (3/0), Sunderland AFC (1/0). |
| (282/569) | ANGELILLO Antonio Valentín | 05.09.1937 | 13 | 12 | 1956-1957, CA Boca Juniors Buenos Aires (13/12). |
| (316/614) | ANIDO Norberto | 08.02.1933 | 3 | 0 | 1959, Racing Club Avellaneda (3/0). |
| (864/1204) | ANSALDI Cristian Daniel | 20.09.1986 | 3 | 0 | 2009-2013, FK Rubin Kazan (3/0). |
| (295/586) | ANTONIO Héctor Edelmiro | 09.07.1929 | 4 | 0 | 1957, CA Estudiantes de La Plata (4/0). |
| (109/250) | ANUNZIATA José | | 2 | 1 | 1923-1924, CA San Isidro (2/1). |
| (28/072) | APRAIZ Antonio | | 1 | 0 | 1912, Club Gimnasia y Esgrima Buenos Aires (1/0). |
| (595/962) | AQUINO Daniel Toribio | 09.06.1965 | 2 | 0 | 1988, CA Banfield (2/0). |
| (189/421) | ARAGÜEZ Manuel | 30.11.1914 | 9 | 0 | 1938-1940, Club Argentino de Rosario (2/0), CA Chacarita Juniors Buenos Aires (7/0). |
| (76/176) | ARAYA Emilio | | 3 | 0 | 1919, Club Gimnasia y Esgrima Rosario (3/0). |
| (464/847) | ARDILES Osvaldo César | 03.08.1952 | 51 | 8 | 1975-1982, CA Huracán Buenos Aires (40/7), Tottenham Hotspur FC London (11/1). |
| (99/227) | ARGAÑARAZ Aníbal | | 1 | 0 | 1923, CA Platense Buenos Aires (1/0). |
| (221/464) | ARNALDO José María | 07.12.1923 | 3 | 0 | 1942-1943, CA San Lorenzo de Almagro Buenos Aires (3/0). |
| (318/621) | ARREDONDO Carlos Alberto | 26.10.1933 | 3 | 0 | 1959, CA Huracán Buenos Aires (3/0). |
| (542/913) | ARREGUI Carlos Alberto | 07.11.1954 | 5 | 1 | 1983-1984, CA Independiente Avellaneda (2/0), Club Ferro Carril Oeste (3/1). |
| (205/455) | ARREGUI Gabino | 07.11.1914 | 7 | 2 | 1940-1941, Club Gimnasia y Esgrima La Plata (7/2). |
| (168/368) | ARRESE Ismael | | 1 | 0 | 1933, CA Platense Buenos Aires (1/0). |
| (170/376) | ARRIETA Arturo | 12.07.1911 | 5 | 1 | 1933-1935, CA San Lorenzo de Almagro Buenos Aires (5/1). |
| (194/429) | ARRIETA Luis | | 9 | 6 | 1939-1941, CA Lanús (9/6). |
| (146/306) | ARRILLAGA Juan | | 3 | 0 | 1928-1930, Quilmes AC (3/0). |
| (671/1020) | ARRUABARRENA Rodolfo Martín | 20.07.1975 | 6 | 0 | 1994-2006, CA Newell's Old Boys Rosario (3/0), CA Boca Juniors Buenos Aires (2/0), Villarreal CF (1/0). |

| | | | | | |
|---|---|---|---|---|---|
| (162/338) | ARTEL Mario | | **2** | **0** | 1931, CA El Porvenir Gerli (2/0). |
| (335/651) | ARTIME Luis Alfredo | 02.12.1939 | **25** | **24** | 1961-1967, CA Atlanta Buenos Aires (4/2), CA River Plate Buenos Aires (12/14) CA Independiente Avellaneda (9/8). |
| (129/285) | ARZENI Argento | | **2** | **0** | 1926, CA Sportsman Buenos Aires (2/0). |
| (462/836) | ASAD Julio Daniel | 07.06.1953 | **7** | **1** | 1975-1976, CA Vélez Sarsfield (7/1). |
| (678/1036) | ASAD Omar Andrés | 09.04.1971 | **2** | **0** | 1995, CA Vélez Sarsfield (2/0). |
| (467/854) | ASTEGIANO Daniel Ricardo | 27.08.1952 | **3** | **2** | 1975, Atlético Ingenio Ledesma de Jujuy (3/2). |
| (624/987) | ASTRADA Leonardo Rubén | 06.01.1970 | **32** | **1** | 1991-1999, CA River Plate Buenos Aires (32/1). |
| (880/1243) | AUED Luciano Román | 01.03.1987 | **2** | **1** | 2011, Club Gimnasia y Esgrima La Plata (2/1). |
| (392/738) | AVALLAY Roque Alberto | 14.12.1945 | **15** | **1** | 1968-1974, CA Newell's Old Boys Rosario (3/1), CA Independiente Avellaneda (1/0), CA Huracán Buenos Aires (11/0). |
| (308/599) | AVIO Ludovico Héctor | 06.10.1932 | **2** | **1** | 1958, CA Vélez Sarsfield (2/1). |
| (321/625) | AYALA Osvaldo Fabián Ocampo | 05.08.1938 | **8** | **0** | 1960, CA Boca Juniors Buenos Aires (8/0). |
| (671/1019) | AYALA Roberto Fabián | 14.04.1973 | **115** | **6** | 1994-2007, CA River Plate Buenos Aires (3/0), AC Parma (12/0), SSC Napoli (28/1), Milan AC (21/2), Valencia CF (51/3). |
| (420/780) | AYALA Rubén Hugo | 05.01.1950 | **25** | **11** | 1971-1974, CA San Lorenzo de Almagro Buenos Aires (10/3), Club Atlético de Madrid (15/8). |

| | | | | | |
|---|---|---|---|---|---|
| (437/804) | BABINGTON Carlos Alberto | 20.09.1949 | **13** | **2** | 1973-1974, CA Huracán Buenos Aires (13/2). |
| (135/298) | BACCHI Roberto | | **1** | **0** | 1927, Club Gimnasia y Esgrima Buenos Aires (1/0). |
| (50/138) | BADALINI Atilio | | **9** | **5** | 1916-1922, CA Newell's Old Boys Rosario (9/5). |
| (28/076) | BADARACCO Gerónimo | | **13** | **0** | 1912-1918, CA Argentino Quilmes Buenos Aires (3/0), Club Atlético San Isidro (10/0). |
| (166/354) | BAGLIETTO Aquilles | | **2** | **0** | 1932, CA All Boys Buenos Aires (2/0). |
| (267/545) | BAGNATTO Luis Ángel | 10.05.1924 | **1** | **0** | 1955, CA Banfield (1/0). |
| (268/547) | BALAY Arnaldo | 02.09.1928 | **3** | **0** | 1955-1958, Racing Club Avellaneda (3/0). |
| (600/969) | BALBO Abel Eduardo | 01.06.1966 | **37** | **11** | 1989-1998, CA River Plate Buenos Aires (5/0), Udinese Calcio (5/1), AS Roma (27/10). |
| (445/812) | BALBUENA Agustín Alberto | 01.09.1945 | **10** | **0** | 1973-1974, CA Independiente Avellaneda (10/0). |
| (195/433) | BALDONEDO Emilio | 23.06.1916 | **6** | **7** | 1940, CA Huracán Buenos Aires (6/7). |
| (467/856) | BALEY Héctor Rodolfo | 16.11.1950 | **13** | **0** | 1975-1982, CA Colón de Santa Fe (1/0), CA Huracán Buenos Aires (10/0), CA Talleres de Córdoba (2/0). |
| (79/183) | BALLART Francisco | | **1** | **0** | 1920, Tiro Federal Rosario (1/0). |
| (196/440) | BALLESTEROS Gabino | | **4** | **1** | 1940, CA San Lorenzo de Almagro Buenos Aires (4/1). |
| (842/1166) | BANEGA Éver Maximiliano David | 29.06.1988 | **24** | **2** | 2008-2013, Valencia CF (24/2). |
| (508/881) | BARBAS Juan Alberto | 23.08.1959 | **32** | **0** | 1979-1985, Racing Club Avellaneda (23/0), Real Zaragoza CD (7/0), US Lecce (2/0). |
| (906/1270) | BARCOS Hernán | 11.04.1984 | **4** | **0** | 2012-2013, SE Palmeiras São Paulo (4/0). |
| (423/782) | BARGAS Ángel Hugo | 29.10.1946 | **28** | **1** | 1971-1974, CA Chacarita Juniors Buenos Aires (14/1), FC Nantes (14/0). |
| (677/1033) | BARROS SCHELOTTO Gustavo Guillermo | 04.05.1973 | **10** | **0** | 1995-1999, Club Gimnasia y Esgrima La Plata (2/0), CA Boca Juniors Buenos Aires (8/0). |
| (115/268) | BARTOLUCCI Pablo | | **6** | **0** | 1924-1932, CS Sportivo Buenos Aires (2/0), CA Huracán Buenos Aires (3/0), Club Sportivo Barracas (2/0). |
| (913/1276) | BASANTA PAVONE José María | 03.04.1984 | **7** | **0** | 2013, CF Monterrey (7/0). |
| (395/746) | BASILE Alfio Rubén | 01.11.1943 | **8** | **1** | 1968-1969, Racing Club Avellaneda (8/1). |
| (671/1022) | BASSEDAS Cristián Gustavo | 16.02.1973 | **22** | **0** | 1994-1999, CA Vélez Sarsfield (22/0). |
| (623/977) | BASUALDO Fabián Armando | 26.02.1964 | **28** | **0** | 1991-1993, CA River Plate Buenos Aires (28/0). |
| (600/968) | BASUALDO José Horacio | 20.06.1963 | **31** | **0** | 1989-1995, Club Deportivo Mandiyú (9/0), VfB Stuttgart (13/0), CA Vélez Sarsfield (9/0). |
| (205/452) | BATAGLIERO José Pedro | | **10** | **0** | 1940-1945, CA Atlanta Buenos Aires (6/0), CA Independiente Avellaneda (4/0). |
| (574/941) | BATISTA Sergio Daniel | 09.11.1962 | **39** | **0** | 1985-1990, AA Argentinos Juniors Buenos Aires (21/0), CA River Plate Buenos Aires (18/0). |
| (629/998) | BATISTUTA Gabriel Omar | 01.02.1969 | **78** | **56** | 1991-2002, CA Boca Juniors Buenos Aires (7/6), AC Fiorentina Firenze (66/47), AS Roma (5/3). |
| (769/1109) | BATTAGLIA Sebastián Alejandro | 08.11.1980 | **10** | **0** | 2003-2009, CA Boca Juniors Buenos Aires (10/0). |
| (356/676) | BAUTISTA Norberto Claudio | 30.12.1940 | **1** | **0** | 1963, CA Rosario Central (1/0). |
| (530/908) | BAUZA Edgardo | 26.01.1958 | **3** | **0** | 1981-1990, CA Rosario Central (1/0), CD Veracruz (2/0). |
| (81/192) | BEARZOTTI Florindo | | **15** | **0** | 1920-1924, CA Belgrano Rosario (15/0). |
| (205/453) | BELÉN Alberto Edmundo | 22.06.1917 | **8** | **2** | 1940-1943, Club Gimnasia y Esgrima La Plata (1/0), CA Newell's Old Boys Rosario (7/2). |
| (310/607) | BELÉN Raúl Oscar | 01.07.1931 | **31** | **9** | 1959-1963, Racing Club Avellaneda (31/9). |
| (171/379) | BELLIS Ernesto Antonio | 01.02.1909 | **1** | **1** | 1934, CA Defensores de Belgrano (1/1). |
| (172/386) | BELLO Fernando | 29.11.1910 | **11** | **0** | 1934-1945, CA Independiente Avellaneda (11/0). |
| (30/083) | BELLO Juan José | | **1** | **0** | 1912, Club Atlético San Isidro (1/0). |
| (800/1140) | BELLUSCHI Fernando Daniel | 10.09.1983 | **5** | **0** | 2005-2011, CA Newell's Old Boys Rosario (1/0), CA River Plate Buenos Aires (1/0), FC do Porto (3/0). |
| (479/866) | BELTRÁN Alberto | 03.02.1947 | **1** | **0** | 1976, CA River Plate Buenos Aires (1/0). |
| (257/525) | BENAVÍDEZ RODRÍGUEZ Juan Armando | 20.10.1927 | **1** | **0** | 1951, CA San Lorenzo de Almagro Buenos Aires (1/0). |
| (280/567) | BENEGAS Alfredo Jorge | 30.11.1922 | **6** | **0** | 1956-1957, CA San Lorenzo de Almagro Buenos Aires (6/0). |
| (172/389) | BENÍTEZ CÁCERES Delfín | 26.09.1910 | **1** | **1** | 1934, CA Boca Juniors Buenos Aires (1/1). |
| (483/871) | BENÍTEZ Jorge José | 03.06.1950 | **2** | **0** | 1977, CA Boca Juniors Buenos Aires (2/0). |
| (850/1168) | BERGESSIO Gonzalo Rubén | 20.07.1984 | **3** | **2** | 2008-2009, CA San Lorenzo de Almagro Buenos Aires (3/2). |
| (172/391) | BERISTAIN Tomás | | **1** | **0** | 1934, CA Platense Buenos Aires (1/0). |
| (696/1060) | BERIZZO Eduardo Magnolo | 13.11.1969 | **13** | **0** | 1996-2000, CA River Plate Buenos Aires (10/0), Olympique de Marseille (2/0), CA River Plate Buenos Aires (1/0). |
| (352/673) | BERNAO Raúl Emilio | 05.11.1941 | **15** | **4** | 1963-1969, CA Independiente Avellaneda (15/4). |
| (855/1176) | BERNARDELLO Hernán Darío | 03.08.1986 | **1** | **0** | 2009, CA Newell's Old Boys Rosario (1/0). |
| (794/1128) | BERNARDI Lucas Martín Ademar | 27.09.1977 | **6** | **0** | 2004-2005, AS Monaco (6/0). |

| | | | | | |
|---|---|---|---|---|---|
| (38/105) | BERNASCONI Diómedes | | 2 | 0 | 1914, CA Estudiantes de La Plata (2/0). |
| (327/640) | BERÓN Héctor Rubén | 16.06.1932 | 2 | 0 | 1960, Club Ferro Carril Oeste (2/0). |
| (434/794) | BERTA José Orlando | 19.04.1952 | 1 | 0 | 1972, CA Newell's Old Boys Rosario (1/0). |
| (163/345) | BERTETTI Carlos | | 1 | 0 | 1931, CA Banfield (1/0). |
| (624/988) | BERTI Sergio Ángel | 17.02.1969 | 23 | 2 | 1991-1998, CA River Plate Buenos Aires (23/2). |
| (868/1220) | BERTOGLIO Facundo Daniel | 30.06.1990 | 1 | 2 | 2010, CA Colón de Santa Fé (1/2). |
| (85/196) | BERTOLINI Pablo | | 2 | 0 | 1921, Club Sportivo Palermo Buenos Aires (2/0). |
| (885/1253) | BERTOLO Nicolás Santiago | 02.01.1986 | 2 | 0 | 2011, Real Zaragoza (2/0). |
| (388/715) | BERTOLOTTI Andrés | 19.09.1943 | 1 | 0 | 1967, Quilmes AC (1/0). |
| (460/830) | BERTONI Daniel Ricado | 14.03.1955 | 31 | 12 | 1974-1982, CA Independiente Avellaneda (23/10), Sevilla CF (1/0), AC Fiorentina Firenze (7/2). |
| (319/623) | BETINOTTI Rodolfo Carlos | 07.10.1932 | 1 | 0 | 1959, CA Atlanta Buenos Aires (1/0). |
| (43/120) | BETULAR Ángel | | 1 | 0 | 1915, Racing Club Avellaneda (1/0). |
| (690/1051) | BIAGGIO Claudio Darío | 02.07.1967 | 1 | 0 | 1995, CA San Lorenzo de Almagro Buenos Aires (1/0). |
| (298/591) | BIAGIOLI Juan | | 1 | 0 | 1957, CA Rosario Central (1/0). |
| (66/161) | BIANATTI Alberto | | 4 | 1 | 1919-1924, CA Eureka Buenos Aires (3/1), Club Sportivo Barracas Buenos Aires (1/0). |
| (415/771) | BIANCHI Carlos Alberto | 26.04.1949 | 13 | 6 | 1970-1972, CA Vélez Sarsfield (13/6). |
| (125/284) | BIANCHI Juan | | 4 | 0 | 1925, CSD Progresista Gerli (4/0). |
| (86/200) | BIDOGLIO Ludovico | 05.02.1900 | 34 | 0 | 1921-1928, Club Sportivo Palermo Buenos Aires (2/0), CA Boca Juniors Buenos Aires (32/0). |
| (361/682) | BIELLI Adolfo Norberto | 15.06.1940 | 5 | 1 | 1964, CA Estudiantes de La Plata (5/1). |
| (879/1228) | BIGLIA Lucas Rodrigo | 30.01.1986 | 16 | 0 | 2011-2013, RSC Anderlecht Bruxelles (10/0), SS Lazio Roma (6/0). |
| (815/1148) | BILOS Daniel Rubén | 03.09.1980 | 3 | 1 | 2005-2006, CA Boca Juniors Buenos Aires (1/0), AS St. Etienne (2/1). |
| (45/126) | BINCAZ Claudio | | 1 | 0 | 1916, Club Atlético San Isidro (1/0). |
| (623/978) | BISCONTI David Carlos Nazareno | 22.09.1968 | 5 | 1 | 1991, CA Rosario Central (5/1). |
| (49/135) | BLANCO Antonio | | 7 | 2 | 1916-1918, CA Rosario Central (7/2). |
| (62/152) | BLANCO Eduardo | | 2 | 0 | 1918, CA Rosario Central (2/0). |
| (123/281) | BLANCO Ernesto | | 2 | 0 | 1925, Club Del Plata Buenos Aires (2/0). |
| (297/590) | BLANCO Roberto Manuel | 26.11.1938 | 2 | 0 | 1957-1961, Racing Club Avellaneda (2/0). |
| (855/1183) | BLANCO Sebastián Marcelo | 15.03.1988 | 2 | 1 | 2009-2010, CA Lanús (2/1). |
| (183/415) | BLOTTO Héctor | | 6 | 0 | 1937-1942, CA Estudiantes de La Plata (6/0). |
| (468/860) | BOCANELLI Ángel Héctor | 22.01.1954 | 2 | 0 | 1975, CA Talleres de Córdoba (2/0). |
| (447/820) | BOCHINI Ricardo Enrique | 25.01.1954 | 28 | 0 | 1973-1986, CA Independiente Avellaneda (28/0). |
| (303/596) | BOGGIO Norberto Constante | 11.08.1931 | 12 | 0 | 1958-1961, CA San Lorenzo de Almagro Buenos Aires (12/0). |
| (858/1187) | BOLATTI Mario Ariel | 17.02.1985 | 12 | 1 | 2009-2011, CA Huracán Buenos Aires (3/1), AC Fiorentina Firenze (5/0), SC Internacional Porto Alegre (4/0). |
| (623/985) | BOLDRINI Ariel Eduardo | 26.07.1965 | 4 | 0 | 1991, CA Newell's Old Boys Rosario (4/0). |
| (698/1063) | BONANO Roberto Oscar | 24.01.1970 | 13 | 0 | 1996-2000, CA River Plate Buenos Aires (13/0). |
| (359/680) | BONCZUK Mario | 22.10.1939 | 2 | 0 | 1963, CA Atlanta Buenos Aires (2/0). |
| (161/331) | BONELLI Camillo | | 1 | 0 | 1930, CA River Plate Buenos Aires (1/0). |
| (263/540) | BONELLI Ricardo | 28.10.1932 | 8 | 1 | 1954-1956, CA Independiente Avellaneda (8/1). |
| (513/890) | BORDÓN Miguel Ángel | 27.10.1952 | 4 | 0 | 1979, CA Boca Juniors Buenos Aires (4/0). |
| (645/1010) | BORELLI Jorge Horacio | 02.11.1964 | 14 | 0 | 1993-1994, Racing Club Avellaneda (14/0). |
| (574/942) | BORGHI Claudio Daniel | 28.09.1964 | 6 | 1 | 1985-1986, AA Argentinos Juniors Buenos Aires (6/1). |
| (225/483) | BORGNIA Alfredo | | 2 | 0 | 1943, CA San Lorenzo de Almagro Buenos Aires (2/0). |
| (662/1016) | BORRELLI Juan José | 09.11.1970 | 7 | 0 | 1994-1997, Panathinaïkos AO Athína (7/0). |
| (263/542) | BORRELLO José | 24.11.1929 | 7 | 3 | 1954-1955, CA Boca Juniors Buenos Aires (7/3). |
| (861/1199) | BOSELLI Mauro | 22.05.1985 | 4 | 1 | 2009-2011, Club Estusiantes de La Plata (4/1). |
| (323/634) | BOSICH Ricardo Blas | 16.07.1932 | 2 | 0 | 1960, CA Vélez Sarsfield (2/0). |
| (135/292) | BOSSIO Ángel | 05.05.1905 | 21 | 0 | 1927-1935, CA Talleres Remedios de Escalada (19/0), CA River Plate Buenos Aires (2/0). |
| (671/1017) | BOSSIO Carlos Gustavo | 01.12.1973 | 11 | 0 | 1994-1996, CA Estudiantes de La Plata (11/0). |
| (86/201) | BOSSO Pablo | | 1 | 0 | 1921, CA Boca Juniors Buenos Aires (1/0). |
| (149/314) | BOTASSO Juan | 23.10.1905 | 3 | 0 | 1929-1930, CA Argentino Quilmes (3/0). |
| (494/877) | BOTTANIZ Víctor Alfredo | 12.05.1953 | 3 | 0 | 1978, Unión Santa Fe (3/0). |
| (826/1154) | BOTTINELLI Jonathan Pablo | 14.09.1984 | 3 | 0 | 2007-2011, CA San Lorenzo de Almagro Buenos Aires (3/0). |
| (426/785) | BÓVEDA Ramón César | 18.03.1949 | 7 | 1 | 1972-1975, CA Rosario Central (7/1). |
| (230/494) | BOYÉ Mario Emilio Heriberto | 22.07.1922 | 17 | 7 | 1945-1952, CA Boca Juniors Buenos Aires (14/6), Racing Club Avellaneda (3/1). |
| (861/1200) | BRAÑA Rodrigo | 07.03.1979 | 9 | 0 | 2009-2013, Club Estudiantes de La Plata (9/0). |
| (494/878) | BRAVO Humberto Rafael | 02.02.1951 | 4 | 0 | 1978, CA Talleres de Córdoba (4/0). |
| (254/518) | BRAVO Rubén Norberto | 16.11.1923 | 3 | 1 | 1950-1951, Racing Club Avellaneda (3/1). |
| (69/167) | BRICHETTO Enrique | | 1 | 0 | 1919, CA Boca Juniors Buenos Aires (1/0). |
| (406/760) | BRINDISI Miguel Ángel | 08.10.1950 | 44 | 17 | 1969-1974, CA Huracán Buenos Aires (44/17). |
| (294/585) | BROOKES Roberto Leonardo | | 7 | 1 | 1957-1962, CA Chacarita Juniors Buenos Aires (7/1). |
| (4/024) | BROWN Alfredo | | 9 | 4 | 1906-1911, Club Alumni AC Buenos Aires (9/4). |
| (2/013) | BROWN Carlos | | 2 | 0 | 1903-1905, Club Alumni AC Buenos Aires (2/0). |
| (4/026) | BROWN Eliseo | | 10 | 6 | 1906-1911, Club Alumni AC Buenos Aires (10/6). |
| (1/006) | BROWN Ernesto | | 13 | 1 | 1902-1912, Club Alumni AC Buenos Aires (11/1), Quilmes AC (2/0). |
| (1/011) | BROWN Jorge | | 23 | 4 | 1902-1913, Club Alumni AC Buenos Aires (19/4), Quilmes AC (4/0). |
| (546/929) | BROWN José Luis | 10.11.1956 | 36 | 1 | 1983-1989, Club Atlético Nacional Medellín (8/0), CA Boca Juniors Buenos Aires (6/0), Club Deportivo Española Buenos Aires (7/1), Brest Armorique FC (6/0), CF Real Murcia (9/0). |
| (4/022) | BROWN Juan Domingo | 21.06.1888 | 36 | 2 | 1906-1916, Club Alumni AC Buenos Aires (20/0), Quilmes AC (16/2). |
| (3/018) | BROWNE Patricio | | 8 | 0 | 1905-1910, Club Alumni AC Buenos Aires (8/0). |
| (37/101) | BRUNO Antonio | | 1 | 0 | 1914, Club Gimnasia y Esgrima Buenos Aires (1/0). |
| (84/195) | BRUZZONE Roberto | | 3 | 0 | 1920-1921, Club Sportivo Palermo Buenos Aires (1/0), Club Del Plata Buenos Aires (2/0). |

| | | | | | |
|---|---|---|---|---|---|
| (1/005) | BUCHANAN Carlos | | **5** | **0** | 1902-1908, Club Alumni AC Buenos Aires (5/0). |
| (1/003) | BUCHANAN Walter | | **2** | **0** | 1902-1903, Club Alumni AC Buenos Aires (2/0). |
| (27/071) | BUCK Sidney | | **1** | **0** | 1912, Quilmes AC (1/0). |
| (517/898) | BUJEDO Juan Carlos | 08.03.1956 | **3** | **0** | 1979-1983, Racing Club Avellaneda (2/0), CA Vélez Sarsfield (1/0). |
| (532/911) | BULLERI Enzo Daniel | 03.11.1956 | **1** | **0** | 1982, CA River Plate Buenos Aires (1/0). |
| (865/1206) | BURDISSO Guillermo Enio | 24.04.1988 | **1** | **1** | 2010, CA Rosario Central (1/1). |
| (769/1101) | BURDISSO Nicolás Andrés | 12.04.1981 | **49** | **2** | 2003-2011, CA Boca Juniors Buenos Aires (4/0), Internazionale FC Milano (23/2), AS Roma (22/0). |
| (679/1039) | BURGOS Germán Adrián Ramón | 16.04.1969 | **35** | **0** | 1995-2002, CA River Plate Buenos Aires (23/0), RCD Mallorca (7/0), Club Atlético de Madrid (5/0). |
| (542/918) | BURRUCHAGA Jorge Luis | 09.10.1962 | **59** | **14** | 1983-1990, CA Independiente Avellaneda (30/9), FC Nantes (29/5). |
| (63/155) | BUSSO Mario | | **5** | **0** | 1918-1919, CA Atlanta Buenos Aires (1/0), CA Boca Juniors Buenos Aires (4/0). |
| (389/729) | BUTTICE Carlos Adolfo | 15.03.1935 | **4** | **0** | 1967-1968, CA San Lorenzo de Almagro Buenos Aires (4/0). |
| (437/800) | BUZZO Jorge Alberto | 02.09.1946 | **4** | **0** | 1973, CA Chacarita Juniors Buenos Aires (4/0). |
| | | | | | |
| (37/103) | CABANO Juan | | **2** | **1** | 1914-1916, CA Argentino Quilmes Buenos Aires (2/1). |
| (885/1252) | CABRAL Alejandro Ariel | 11.09.1987 | **2** | **0** | 2011, KP Legia Warszawa (2/0). |
| (393/744) | CABRERA Antonio Roberto | 17.10.1943 | **3** | **0** | 1968-1969, CA Boca Juniors Buenos Aires (4/0). |
| (595/961) | CABRERA Claudio Martín | 20.11.1963 | **5** | **0** | 1988-1989, CA Vélez Sarsfield (5/0). |
| (640/1006) | CÁCERES Fernando Gabriel | 07.02.1969 | **24** | **1** | 1992-1997, CA River Plate Buenos Aires (3/0), Real Zaragoza CD (19/0), CA Boca Juniors Buenos Aires (2/1). |
| (124/282) | CACOPARDO Emilio | | **3** | **0** | 1925-1926, CA Porteño Buenos Aires (3/0). |
| (637/1001) | CAGNA Diego Sebastián | 19.04.1970 | **19** | **1** | 1992-1999, AA Argentinos Juniors Buenos Aires (3/0), CA Independiente (7/0), CA Boca Juniors Buenos Aires (9/1). |
| (64/156) | CALANDRA Jorge | | **3** | **1** | 1918-1920, CA Estudiantes de La Plata (3/1). |
| (136/299) | CALANDRA Saúl | | **3** | **0** | 1927-1928, CA Estudiantes de La Plata (3/0). |
| (115/270) | CALDÁS Gerardo | | **3** | **0** | 1924-1928, CA Defensores de Belgrano (3/0). |
| (95/218) | CALDERA José | | **1** | **0** | 1922, CA Huracán Buenos Aires (1/0). |
| (520/903) | CALDERÓN Gabriel Humberto | 07.02.1960 | **22** | **1** | 1980-1990, Racing Club Avellaneda (1/0), CA Independiente Avellaneda (9/1), Paris St.Germain FC (12/0). |
| (701/1068) | CALDERÓN José Luis | 24.10.1970 | **5** | **0** | 1997, CA Independiente Avellaneda (5/0). |
| (381/708) | CALICS Oscar Osvaldo | 18.11.1939 | **6** | **0** | 1966-1967, CA San Lorenzo de Almagro Buenos Aires (6/0). |
| (310/606) | CALLÁ Pedro Eugenio | 01.01.1934 | **13** | **3** | 1959-1963, AA Argentinos Juniors Buenos Aires (6/2), CA Vélez Sarsfield (6/1), CA Boca Juniors Buenos Aires (1/0). |
| (752/1093) | CAMBIASSO DELEAU Esteban Matías | 18.08.1980 | **52** | **5** | 2000-2011, CA Independiente Avellaneda (1/0), Real Madrid CF (6/0), Internazionale FC Milano (45/5). |
| (547/931) | CAMINO Julián José | 02.05.1961 | **13** | **0** | 1983-1985, CA Estudiantes de La Plata (13/0). |
| (900/1267) | CAMPAGNARO Hugo Armando | 27.06.1980 | **13** | **0** | 2012-2013, SSC Napoli (10/0), FC Internazionale Milano (3/0). |
| (251/511) | CAMPANA Francisco | 09.05.1925 | **1** | **0** | 1947, CA Chacarita Juniors Buenos Aires (1/0). |
| (7/037) | CAMPBELL Colin | | **1** | **0** | 1907, CA Estudiantes Buenos Aires (1/0). |
| (855/1185) | CAMPESTRINI Cristian Daniel | 16.06.1980 | **2** | **0** | 2009-2010, Arsenal FC de Sarandí (2/0). |
| (697/1062) | CAMPS Patricio Alejandro | 22.01.1972 | **2** | **0** | 1996, CA Vélez Sarsfield (2/0). |
| (48/131) | CANAVERI Zoilo | | **2** | **0** | 1916, Racing Club Avellaneda (2/0). |
| (106/238) | CANCINO Federico | | **2** | **0** | 1923-1924, Alvear Buenos Aires (2/0). |
| (586/951) | CANIGGIA Claudio Paul | 09.01.1967 | **50** | **16** | 1987-2002, CA River Plate Buenos Aires (8/3), Hellas Verona (7/2), Atalanta Calcio Bergamo (20/6), AS Roma (10/5), CA Boca Juniors Buenos Aires (3/0), Glasgow Rangers FC (2/0). |
| (335/650) | CANSECO Martín Roberto | 14.09.1935 | **1** | **0** | 1961, AA Argentinos Juniors Buenos Aires (1/0). |
| (224/478) | CANTELI José | 31.05.1917 | **1** | **1** | 1943, CA Newell's Old Boys Rosario (1/1). |
| (894/1263) | CANTEROS Héctor | 15.03.1989 | **2** | **0** | 2011, CA Vélez Sarsfield (2/0). |
| (414/767) | CANTÚ Edgardo Luis | 21.02.1947 | **1** | **0** | 1970, CA Huracán Buenos Aires (1/0). |
| (855/1184) | CANUTO Ignacio | 20.02.1986 | **3** | **1** | 2009-2010, AA Argentinos Juniors Buenos Aires (3/1). |
| (310/603) | CAP Vladislao Wenceslao | 05.07.1934 | **11** | **1** | 1959-1962, Racing Club Avellaneda (7/1), CA River Plate Buenos Aires (4/0). |
| (99/225) | CAPALBO Pedro | | **1** | **0** | 1923, Club Sportivo Barracas (1/0). |
| (80/189) | CARABELLI Norberto | | **1** | **0** | 1920, CA Huracán Buenos Aires (1/0). |
| (320/624) | CARBONE José Ángel | 15.09.1930 | **1** | **0** | 1959, CA Independiente Avellaneda (1/0). |
| (327/639) | CARCEO Osvaldo | | **4** | **0** | 1960, AA Argentinos Juniors Buenos Aires (4/0). |
| (391/735) | CÁRDENAS Juan Carlos | 25.07.1945 | **1** | **0** | 1967, Racing Club Avellaneda (1/0). |
| (467/850) | CÁRDENAS Pablo de las Mercedes | 15.01.1949 | **5** | **1** | 1975-1976, CA Unión de Santa Fe (5/1). |
| (276/564) | CARDOSO Luis Néstor | 18.07.1930 | **7** | **0** | 1956-1959, CA Boca Juniors Buenos Aires (7/0). |
| (330/645) | CARDOSO Néstor Lucas | 17.11.1935 | **7** | **0** | 1960-1963, CA Rosario Central (7/0). |
| (690/1048) | CARDOSO Rodolfo Esteban | 17.10.1968 | **7** | **1** | 1995-1998, SV Werder Bremen (1/1), Hamburger SV (4/0), CA Boca Juniors Buenos Aires (2/0). |
| (826/1158) | CARDOZO Neri Raúl | 08.08.1986 | **1** | **0** | 2007, CA Boca Juniors Buenos Aires (1/0). |
| (704/1072) | CARDOZO Raúl Ernesto | 28.10.1967 | **4** | **0** | 1997, CA Vélez Sarsfield (4/0). |
| (769/1112) | CARIGNANO César Andrés | 28.09.1982 | **3** | **0** | 2003, CA Colón de Santa Fe (3/0). |
| (427/788) | CARNEVALI Daniel Alberto | 04.12.1946 | **25** | **0** | 1972-1974, CA Chacarita Juniors Buenos Aires (10/0), UD Las Palmas (15/0). |
| (385/711) | CARONE Juan Carlos | 18.05.1942 | **5** | **2** | 1967-1968, CA Vélez Sarsfield (5/2). |
| (671/1025) | CARRANZA Luis Alberto | 15.06.1972 | **1** | **0** | 1994, CA Boca Juniors Buenos Aires (1/0). |
| (415/770) | CARRASCOSA Jorge Omar | 15.08.1948 | **30** | **1** | 1970-1977, CA Rosario Central (4/0), CA Huracán Buenos Aires (26/1). |
| (135/295) | CARRICABERRY Alfredo D. | | **12** | **4** | 1927-1931, CA San Lorenzo de Almagro Buenos Aires (10/4), Club Sportivo Palermo Buenos Aires (2/0). |
| (263/538) | CARRIZO Amadeo Raúl | 12.05.1926 | **20** | **0** | 1954-1964, CA River Plate Buenos Aires (20/0). |
| (826/1153) | CARRIZO Juan Pablo | 06.05.1984 | **12** | **0** | 2007-2011, CA River Plate Buenos Aires (1/0), SS Lazio Roma (9/0), CA River Plate Buenos Aires (2/0). |
| (855/1174) | CARUZZO Matías Nicolás | 15.08.1984 | **5** | **0** | 2009-2010, AA Argentinos Juniors Buenos Aires (5/0). |
| (366/693) | CASÁ Victorio Francisco | 28.10.1943 | **1** | **0** | 1964, CA San Lorenzo de Almagro Buenos Aires (1/0). |

| | | | | | |
|---|---|---|---|---|---|
| (195/434) | CASSÁN Fabio | | 4 | 2 | 1940, CA Chacarita Juniors Buenos Aires (4/2). |
| (254/516) | CASTAGNO César Héctor | 22.12.1924 | 2 | 0 | 1950, CA River Plate Buenos Aires (2/0). |
| (62/151) | CASTAGNOLA Roberto | | 10 | 0 | 1918-1924, Racing Club Avellaneda (10/0). |
| (688/1044) | CASTILLO Hugo Norberto | 17.03.1971 | 1 | 0 | 1995, CD Deportivo Español Buenos Aires (1/0). |
| (90/206) | CASTOLDI Pedro | | 5 | 0 | 1922, Club Sportivo Barracas (5/0). |
| (162/343) | CASTRO Emilio | | 3 | 3 | 1931, CA Banfield (3/3). |
| (513/894) | CASTRO José Antonio | 15.10.1955 | 5 | 1 | 1979, CA Vélez Sarsfield (5/1). |
| (289/582) | CASTRO Juan Alberto | 30.11.1932 | 2 | 1 | 1957, CA Rosario Central (2/1). |
| (752/1092) | CASTROMÁN Lucas Martín | 02.10.1980 | 5 | 0 | 2000-2005, CA Vélez Sarsfield (1/0), SS Lazio Roma (3/0), CA Vélez Sarsfield (1/0). |
| (180/408) | CAVADINI Rubén | | 2 | 1 | 1936-1938, CA San Lorenzo de Almagro Buenos Aires (2/1). |
| (696/1059) | CAVALLERO Pablo Oscar | 13.04.1974 | 26 | 0 | 1996-2004, CA Vélez Sarsfield (4/0), RCD Espanyol Barcelona (1/0), RC Celta de Vigo (21/0). |
| (841/1165) | CAVENAGHI Fernando Ezequiel | 21.09.1983 | 4 | 0 | 2007-2008, Girondins de Bordeaux (1/0). |
| (526/905) | CECCHI Jorge Carlos | 15.05.1963 | 2 | 0 | 1980, CA Boca Juniors Buenos Aires (2/0). |
| (260/535) | CECCONATO Carlos José | 27.01.1930 | 12 | 2 | 1953-1956, CA Independiente Avellaneda (12/2). |
| (406/758) | CÉJAS Agustín Mario | 22.03.1945 | 9 | 0 | 1969-1970, Racing Club Avellaneda (9/0). |
| (275/561) | CEJAS Benito | 03.02.1934 | 2 | 0 | 1956, CA Lanús (2/0). |
| (66/160) | CÉLICO Luis | | 7 | 0 | 1919-1924, CA Atlanta Buenos Aires (7/0). |
| (894/1261) | CELLAY Christian Ariel | 05.09.1981 | 2 | 0 | 2011, Club Estudiantes de La Plata (2/0). |
| (78/180) | CELLI Adolfo | | 15 | 0 | 1919-1924, CA Newell's Old Boys Rosario (15/0). |
| (77/178) | CELLI Ernesto | | 7 | 1 | 1919-1924, CA Newell's Old Boys Rosario (7/1). |
| (910/1273) | CERRO Francisco | 09.02.1988 | 1 | 0 | 2012, CA Vélez Sarsfield (1/0). |
| (110/253) | CERROTTI Antonio | | 3 | 1 | 1923-1925, CA Boca Juniors Buenos Aires (3/1). |
| (251/512) | CERVIÑO Camilo Rodolfo | 21.03.1926 | 1 | 0 | 1947, CA Independiente Avellaneda (1/0). |
| (129/288) | CESARINI Renato | 11.04.1906 | 2 | 1 | 1926, CA Chacarita Juniors Buenos Aires (2/1). |
| (90/207) | CHABROLÍN Alfredo Luis | | 6 | 0 | 1922-1924, CA Newell's Old Boys Rosario (6/0). |
| (363/686) | CHALDÚ Mario Norberto | 06.06.1942 | 5 | 0 | 1964-1966, CA Banfield (4/0), CA San Lorenzo de Almagro Buenos Aires (1/0). |
| (658/1011) | CHAMOT José Antonio | 17.05.1969 | 43 | 2 | 1993-2002, Foggia Calcio (12/1), SS Lazio Roma (27/1), Milan AC (4/0). |
| (532/912) | CHAPARRO Raúl | 03.05.1953 | 1 | 0 | 1982, Instituto AC de Córdoba (1/0). |
| (880/1235) | CHÁVEZ Cristian Manuel | 16.06.1986 | 4 | 1 | 2011, CA Boca Juniors Buenos Aires (4/1). |
| (60/149) | CHAVÍN Jaime | | 4 | 1 | 1918-1921, CA Huracán Buenos Aires (4/1). |
| (437/801) | CHAZARRETA Enrique Salvador | 29.07.1947 | 12 | 0 | 1973-1974, CA San Lorenzo de Almagro Buenos Aires (12/0). |
| (113/256) | CHERRO Felipe | | 9 | 1 | 1924-1932, Club Sportivo Barracas (9/1). |
| (131/290) | CHERRO Roberto Eugenio | 23.10.1907 | 17 | 13 | 1926-1937, CA Boca Juniors Buenos Aires (11/8), Club Sportivo Barracas (1/1), CA Boca Juniors Buenos Aires (5/4). |
| (14/056) | CHIAPPE Arturo | | 14 | 0 | 1910-1916, CA River Plate Buenos Aires (14/0). |
| (90/208) | CHIESSA Ángel Domingo | | 9 | 1 | 1922-1923, CA Huracán Buenos Aires (9/1). |
| (153/321) | CHIVIDINI Alberto | 23.09.1907 | 3 | 0 | 1929-1930, Club Central Norte Tucumán (3/0). |
| (350/667) | CIACCIA Luis Gregorio | | 1 | 0 | 1962, Club Gimnasia y Esgrima La Plata (1/0). |
| (167/362) | CIANCIA Julio | | 1 | 0 | 1932, CA Talleres Remedios de Escalada (10). |
| (327/641) | CIELINSKY Antonio | | 5 | 0 | 1960-1963, CA Vélez Sarsfield (5/0). |
| (74/172) | CILLEY Luis | | 1 | 0 | 1919, Club Atlético San Isidro (1/0). |
| (62/153) | CLARCKE Edwin | | 9 | 6 | 1918-1921, CA Rosario Central (1/0), CA Porteño Buenos Aires (5/5), Club Sportivo Palermo Buenos Aires (3/1). |
| (543/921) | CLAUSEN Néstor Rolando | 29.09.1962 | 26 | 1 | 1983-1989, CA Independiente Avellaneda (20/1), FC Sion (6/0). |
| (393/741) | COCCO Victorio Nicolás | 23.03.1946 | 6 | 1 | 1968-1969, CA San Lorenzo de Almagro Buenos Aires (6/1). |
| (114/262) | COCHRANE Roberto | | 3 | 0 | 1924-1926, CA Rosario Central (2/0), Tiro Federal Rosario (1/0). |
| (179/403) | COLETTA Sabino | 12.05.1914 | 7 | 0 | 1936-1941, CA Independiente Avellaneda (7/0). |
| (426/787) | COLMAN Carlos Alberto | 02.09.1945 | 1 | 0 | 1972, CA Rosario Central (1/0). |
| (247/506) | COLMAN Juan Carlos | 15.12.1922 | 13 | 0 | 1947-1956, CA Newell's Old Boys Rosario (5/0), CA Boca Juniors Buenos Aires (8/0). |
| (773/1114) | COLOCCINI Fabricio | 22.01.1982 | 39 | 1 | 2003-2013, Club Atlético de Madrid (3/0), Villarreal CF (5/1), Milan AC (3/0), RC Deportivo La Coruña (18/0), Newcastle United FC (10/0). |
| (183/414) | COLOMBO Bartolomé | 24.08.1916 | 17 | 0 | 1937-1945, AA Argentinos Juniors Buenos Aires (2/0), CA San Lorenzo de Almagro Buenos Aires (15/0). |
| (268/549) | CONDE Norberto | 14.03.1931 | 12 | 3 | 1955-1958, CA Vélez Sarsfield (12/3). |
| (411/765) | CONIGLIARO Marcos Norberto | 09.12.1942 | 4 | 2 | 1970, CA Estudiantes de La Plata (4/2). |
| (133/291) | CONTI Silvestre | | 1 | 0 | 1926, Club Nacional Rosario (1/0). |
| (275/559) | CORBATTA Oreste Osmar | 11.03.1936 | 43 | 18 | 1956-1962, Racing Club Avellaneda (43/18). |
| (85/199) | CORBELLA Pedro | | 2 | 1 | 1921, Club Sportivo Palermo Buenos Aires (2/1). |
| (460/828) | CORDERO Horacio Raúl | 22.05.1950 | 1 | 0 | 1974, AA Argentinos Juniors Buenos Aires (1/0). |
| (444/810) | CORREA Hériberto Luis | 16.03.1949 | 4 | 0 | 1973, CA Vélez Sarsfield (4/0). |
| (166/358) | CORREA Oscar | | 2 | 0 | 1932, CA Almagro Buenos Aires (2/0). |
| (60/147) | CORTELLA Antonio Roque | | 11 | 0 | 1918-1921, CA Defensores de Belgrano Buenos Aires (3/0), CA Boca Juniors Buenos Aires (8/0). |
| (447/815) | CORTÉS Osvaldo Roberto | 06.06.1950 | 1 | 0 | 1973, CA Atlanta Buenos Aires (1/0). |
| (600/967) | CORTI Ernesto Enrique | 21.03.1963 | 2 | 0 | 1989, CA River Plate Buenos Aires (2/0). |
| (467/855) | COSCIA Hugo Oscar | 12.10.1952 | 9 | 4 | 1975-1979, CA Colón de Santa Fe (3/3), CA San Lorenzo de Almagro Buenos Aires (6/1). |
| (180/409) | COSSO Agustín | 10.09.1909 | 2 | 1 | 1936-1938, CA Vélez Sarsfield (1/0), CA San Lorenzo de Almagro Buenos Aires (1/1). |
| (885/1251) | COSTA Alberto Facundo | 09.01.1985 | 2 | 0 | 2011-2012, Valencia CF (2/0). |
| (776/1118) | COSTANZO Franco | 05.09.1980 | 1 | 0 | 2003, CA River Plate Buenos Aires (1/0). |
| (5/027) | COULTHURST Ricardo | | 1 | 0 | 1906, Quilmes AC (1/0). |
| (247/505) | COZZI Julio Adolfo | 14.07.1922 | 6 | 0 | 1947, CA Platense Buenos Aires (6/0). |
| (600/966) | CRAVIOTTO Néstor Oscar | 03.10.1963 | 12 | 2 | 1989-1993, CA Estudiantes de La Plata (1/0), CA Independiente Avellaneda (11/2). |

| | | | | | |
|---|---|---|---|---|---|
| (38/111) | CRESPO Francisco | | **3** | **0** | 1914, CA Tigre (3/0). |
| (677/1034) | CRESPO Hernán Jorge | 05.07.1975 | **64** | **35** | 1995-2007, CA River Plate Buenos Aires (2/0), AC Parma (23/10), SS Lazio Roma (11/8), Internazionale FC Milano (2/1), Chelsea FC London (8/4), Milan AC (3/5), Chelsea FC London (10/4), Internazionale FC Milano (5/3). |
| (886/1256) | CRISTALDO Jonathan Ezequiel | 05.03.1989 | **1** | **0** | 2011, FK Metalist Kharkiv (1/0). |
| (681/1041) | CRISTANTE Rolando Hernándo | 16.09.1969 | **6** | **0** | 1995, CA Platense Buenos Aires (5/0), CD Toluca (1/0). |
| (46/127) | CROCCE Marcos | | **4** | **0** | 1916-1924, Racing Club Avellaneda (4/0). |
| (752/1090) | CROSA Diego Sebastián | 18.04.1976 | **1** | **0** | 2000, CA Vélez Sarsfield (1/0). |
| (701/1067) | CRUZ Julio Ricardo | 10.10.1974 | **22** | **3** | 1997-2008, CA River Plate Buenos Aires (5/0), SC Feyenoord Rotterdam (2/1), Bologna FC (6/1), Internazionale FC Milano (9/1). |
| (260/537) | CRUZ Osvaldo Héctor | 29.05.1931 | **24** | **3** | 1953-1958, CA Independiente Avellaneda (24/3). |
| (268/548) | CUCCHIARONI Ernesto Bernardo | 11.04.1906 | **11** | **0** | 1955-1956, CA Boca Juniors Buenos Aires (11/0). |
| (575/943) | CUCIUFFO José Luis | 01.02.1961 | **21** | **0** | 1985-1989, CA Vélez Sarsfield Buenos Aires (14/0), CA Boca Juniors Buenos Aires (7/0). |
| (155/322) | CUELLO Alberto | 23.09.1908 | **6** | **0** | 1930-1937, CA Tigre (1/0), CA River Plate Buenos Aires (5/0). |
| (752/1095) | CUFRÉ Leandro Damián | 09.05.1978 | **4** | **0** | 2000-2006, Club Gimnasia y Esgrima La Plata (1/0), AS Roma (3/0). |
| (550/934) | CÚPER Héctor Raúl | 16.11.1955 | **5** | **0** | 1984, Club Ferro Carril Oeste (5/0). |
| (769/1105) | D'ALESSANDRO Andrés Nicolás | 15.04.1981 | **25** | **3** | 2003-2010, CA River Plate Buenos Aires (4/0), VfL Wolfsburg (18/3), SC Internacional Porto Alegre (3/0). |
| (322/633) | D'ASCENZO Edgardo Jorge | 17.06.1937 | **7** | **1** | 1960, CA Nueva Chicago Buenos Aires (5/0), Independiente Avellaneda (2/1). |
| (321/631) | DACQUARTI Lorenzo Alberto | 15.12.1934 | **4** | **0** | 1960, CA Nueva Chicago Buenos Aires (4/0). |
| (177/400) | DAÑIL Manuel | | **2** | **0** | 1935, Racing Club Avellaneda (2/0). |
| (26/070) | DANNAHER Guillermo | | **3** | **1** | 1912-1914, Tiro Federal Rosario (1/0), CA Argentino Quilmes Buenos Aires (2/1). |
| (275/556) | DAPONTE Nicolás | | **5** | **0** | 1956, CA Lanús (5/0). |
| (858/1188) | DÁTOLO Jesús Alberto | 19.05.1984 | **3** | **2** | 2009, SSC Napoli (3/2). |
| (285/576) | DE BOURGOING Héctor Adolfo | 23.07.1934 | **5** | **0** | 1956-1957, CA Tigre (2/0), CA River Plate Buenos Aires (3/0). |
| (93/213) | DE CÉSARI Marcelo | | **2** | **0** | 1922, CA Boca Juniors Buenos Aires (2/0). |
| (165/351) | DE JONGE Rodolfo | | **4** | **0** | 1931-1935, CA Defensores de Belgrano (1/0), CA Independiente Avellaneda (1/0). |
| (183/413) | DE LA MATA Vicente | 15.01.1918 | **13** | **6** | 1937-1946, Club Central Cordóba Rosario (2/0), CA Independiente Avellaneda (11/6). |
| (370/698) | DE LA MATA Vicente | 02.07.1944 | **6** | **0** | 1965-1966, CA Independiente Avellaneda (6/0). |
| (97/222) | DE LOS SANTOS Alejandro | | **5** | **0** | 1922-1925, Club Sportivo Dock Sud Buenos Aires (1/0), CA El Porvenir Gerli (4/0). |
| (205/456) | DE LOVO Evarista | | **1** | **0** | 1940, Club Gimnasia y Esgrima La Plata (1/0). |
| (174/393) | DE MARE Antonio | | **3** | **0** | 1935, Racing Club Avellaneda (3/0). |
| (80/190) | DE MIGUEL Antonio | | **11** | **2** | 1920-1926, CA Newell's Old Boys Rosario (5/0), Tiro Federal Rosario (6/2). |
| (177/399) | DE SÁA Manuel | | **2** | **0** | 1935, CA Vélez Sarsfield (2/0). |
| (227/488) | DE ZORZI Roberto Justo | 27.07.1921 | **7** | **0** | 1945, CA Boca Juniors Buenos Aires (7/0). |
| (527/907) | DÉBOLE Alejandro Luis | 08.12.1962 | **1** | **0** | 1980, Club Ferro Carril Oeste (1/0). |
| (358/679) | DECARIA Raúl | 22.05.1939 | **1** | **0** | 1963, CA Independiente Avellaneda (1/0). |
| (855/1178) | DEFEDERICO Matías Adrián | 23.08.1989 | **2** | **1** | 2009-2011, CA Huracán Buenos Aires (1/1), CA Independiente Avellaneda (1/0). |
| (162/344) | DEL FELICE Antonio | | **2** | **0** | 1931, CA Belgrano Rosario (2/0). |
| (99/229) | DELGADO Benjamín | | **9** | **3** | 1923-1926, Club San Fernando (2/0), CA Boca Juniors Buenos Aires (7/3). |
| (776/1122) | DELGADO César Fabián | 18.08.1981 | **20** | **2** | 2003-2005, CA Rosario Central (1/0), CDS Cruz Azul Ciudad de México (19/2). |
| (688/1043) | DELGADO Marcelo Alejandro | 24.03.1973 | **17** | **0** | 1995-2001, Racing Club Avellaneda (14/0), CA Boca Juniors Buenos Aires (3/0). |
| (156/325) | DELLA TORRE José | 26.03.1906 | **5** | **0** | 1930, Racing Club Avellaneda (5/0). |
| (260/533) | DELLACHA Pedro Rodolfo | 09.07.1926 | **35** | **0** | 1953-1958, Racing Club Avellaneda (35/0). |
| (81/194) | DELLAVALLE Miguel | | **8** | **1** | 1920-1922, Atlético Central Córdoba (3/1), CA Talleres de Córdoba (5/0). |
| (157/328) | DEMARÍA Atilio | 10.03.1909 | **3** | **0** | 1930-1931, CA Estudiantil Porteño Buenos Aires (3/0). |
| (814/1147) | DEMICHELIS Martín Gastón | 20.12.1980 | **37** | **2** | 2005-2011, FC Bayern München (33/2), Málaga CF (4/0). |
| (838/1164) | DENIS Germán Gustavo | 10.09.1981 | **5** | **0** | 2007-2008, CA Independiente Avellaneda (2/0), SSC Napoli (3/0). |
| (557/937) | DERTYCIA Oscar Alberto | 03.03.1965 | **18** | **2** | 1984-1988, CA Instituto de Córdoba (18/2). |
| (894/1262) | DESÁBATO Leandro | 24.01.1979 | **5** | **0** | 2011-2012, Club Estudiantes de La Plata (5/0). |
| (162/342) | DEVINCENZI Alfredo Ciriaco | 09.06.1907 | **4** | **0** | 1931-1934, CA Estudiantil Porteño Buenos Aires (4/0). |
| (599/964) | DEZOTTI Gustavo Abel | 14.02.1964 | **7** | **0** | 1988-1990, SS Lazio Roma (1/0), Cremonese US (6/0). |
| (847/1167) | DI MARÍA Ángel Fabián | 14.02.1988 | **44** | **9** | 2008-2013, Sport Lisboa e Benfica (13/1), Real Madrid CF (31/8). |
| (459/827) | DI MEOLA Edgardo Roberto | 23.09.1950 | **1** | **0** | 1974, Club Gimnasia y Esgrima La Plata (1/0). |
| (129/286) | DI PAOLA Pascual | | **2** | **0** | 1926, AA Argentinos Juniors Buenos Aires (2/0). |
| (909/1272) | DI SANTO Franco Matías | 07.04.1989 | **3** | **0** | 2012-2013, Wigan Athletic FC (3/0). |
| (248/507) | DI STÉFANO Alfredo S. | 04.07.1926 | **6** | **6** | 1947, CA River Plate Buenos Aires (6/6). |
| (279/565) | DI STÉFANO Oscar | 29.12.1929 | **1** | **0** | 1956, AA Argentinos Juniors Buenos Aires (1/0). |
| (252/513) | DIANO Obdulio | 27.10.1919 | **1** | **0** | 1947, CA Boca Juniors Buenos Aires (1/0). |
| (180/407) | DÍAZ Alfredo | | **1** | **0** | 1936, CA Newell's Old Boys Rosario (1/0). |
| (776/1119) | DÍAZ Daniel Alberto | 13.03.1979 | **12** | **1** | 2003-2009, CA Rosario Central (1/0), CA Boca Juniors Buenos Aires (3/0), Getafe CF (8/1). |
| (880/1241) | DÍAZ Gastón Ricardo | 13.03.1988 | **1** | **0** | 2011, CA Vélez Sarsfield (1/0). |
| (586/950) | DÍAZ Hernán Edgardo | 26.02.1965 | **28** | **3** | 1987-1998, CA Rosario Central (15/3), CA River Plate Buenos Aires (13/0). |
| (193/423) | DÍAZ Ignacio | | **8** | **0** | 1939-1943, CA Rosario Central (4/0), CA San Lorenzo de Almagro Buenos Aires (4/0). |

| | | | | | |
|---|---|---|---|---|---|
| (79/181) | DÍAZ Octavio Juan | | 11 | 0 | 1920-1928, CA Rosario Central (11/0). |
| (517/900) | DÍAZ Ramón Ángel | 29.08.1959 | 23 | 10 | 1979-1982, CA River Plate Buenos Aires (23/10). |
| (513/896) | DÍAZ Roberto Osvaldo | 03.03.1953 | 6 | 1 | 1979, Racing Club Avellaneda (6/1). |
| (411/762) | DÍAZ Rubén Osvaldo | 08.01.1946 | 8 | 0 | 1970-1972, Racing Club Avellaneda (8/0). |
| (4/023) | DÍAZ Zenón | | 6 | 0 | 1906-1916, CA Rosario Central (6/0). |
| (22/063) | DICKINSON Alfredo Lorenzo | | 4 | 0 | 1911, Club Alumni AC Buenos Aires (4/0). |
| (1/010) | DICKINSON Carlos Edgard | | 5 | 1 | 1902-1906, Belgrano AC Buenos Aires (5/1). |
| (371/700) | DIEZ José Enrique | 21.04.1942 | 2 | 0 | 1965, AA Argentinos Juniors Buenos Aires (2/0). |
| (114/264) | DIMARE Eduardo | | 1 | 0 | 1924, Club Del Plata Buenos Aires (1/0). |
| (352/672) | DITRO Mario Roque | 17.08.1936 | 3 | 0 | 1963, CA River Plate Buenos Aires (3/0). |
| (776/1120) | DOMÍNGUEZ Federico Hernán | 13.08.1976 | 1 | 0 | 2003, CA Independiente Avellaneda (1/0). |
| (550/935) | DOMÍNGUEZ Jorge Carlos Alberto | 07.03.1959 | 3 | 0 | 1984, CA Boca Juniors Buenos Aires (3/0). |
| (275/555) | DOMÍNGUEZ Rogelio Antonio | 09.03.1931 | 21 | 0 | 1956-1962, Racing Club Avellaneda (19/0), CA River Plate Buenos Aires (2/0). |
| (859/1189) | DOMÍNGUEZ Sebastián Enrique | 29.07.1980 | 8 | 0 | 2009-2013, CA Vélez Sarsfield (8/0). |
| (418/776) | DOMINICHI Jorge Eduardo | 31.03.1947 | 12 | 0 | 1971-1972, CA River Plate Buenos Aires (12/0). |
| (388/721) | DOVAL Narciso Horacio | 04.01.1944 | 1 | 0 | 1967, CA San Lorenzo de Almagro Buenos Aires (1/0). |
| (1/004) | DUGGAN Eduardo Patricio | | 1 | 0 | 1902, Belgrano AC Buenos Aires (1/0). |
| (799/1132) | DUSCHER Aldo Pedro | 22.03.1979 | 3 | 0 | 2005, RC Deportivo La Coruña (3/0). |
| | | | | | |
| (390/732) | ECHECOPAR Juan Miguel | 16.10.1946 | 1 | 0 | 1967, CA Estudiantes de La Plata (1/0). |
| (866/1214) | ECHEVARRÍA Mariano Raúl | 27.05.1981 | 1 | 0 | 2010, CA Chacarita Juniors San Martín (1/0). |
| (79/187) | ECHEVERRÍA Raúl | | 8 | 4 | 1920-1922, CA Estudiantes de La Plata (8/4). |
| (59/145) | ELORDI A. | | 1 | 0 | 1917, CA Estudiantes Buenos Aires (1/0). |
| (623/977) | ENRIQUE Carlos Alberto | 12.12.1963 | 9 | 0 | 1991, CA River Plate Buenos Aires (9/0). |
| (577/945) | ENRIQUE Héctor Adolfo | 26.04.1962 | 11 | 0 | 1986-1989, CA River Plate Buenos Aires (11/0). |
| (317/620) | ERREA Néstor Martín | 27.04.1939 | 2 | 0 | 1959-1961, CA Atlanta Buenos Aires (2/0). |
| (865/1209) | ERVITI ROLDÁN Walter Daniel | 12.06.1980 | 1 | 0 | 2010, CA Banfield (1/0). |
| (671/1021) | ESCUDERO Marcelo Alejandro | 25.07.1972 | 9 | 1 | 1994-1995, CA Newell's Old Boys Rosario (9/1). |
| (690/1052) | ESNÁIDER Juan Eduardo | 05.03.1973 | 3 | 3 | 1995-1997, Real Madrid CF (1/2), Club Atlético de Madrid (1/1), RCD Espanyol Barcelona (1/0). |
| (204/450) | ESPERÓN Gregorio Juan | 15.02.1917 | 10 | 1 | 1940-1942, CA Platense Buenos Aires (10/1). |
| (671/1023) | ESPINA Marcelo Fabián | 28.04.1967 | 6 | 1 | 1994-1995, CA Platense Buenos Aires (3/1), CSD Colo Colo Santiago (3/0). |
| (225/485) | ESPINOSA Enrique | | 4 | 0 | 1943-1945, CA Atlanta Buenos Aires (4/0). |
| (467/851) | ESPINOZA Aldo Roque | 05.01.1955 | 2 | 0 | 1975, CA Huracán Buenos Aires (2/0). |
| (161/332) | ESPONDA Francisco | | 1 | 1 | 1930, Club Ferro Carril Oeste (1/1). |
| (436/799) | ESPÓSITO Roberto Mario | 21.12.1950 | 1 | 0 | 1972, CA San Lorenzo de Almagro Buenos Aires (1/0). |
| (179/402) | ESTRADA Juan Alberto | 28.10.1912 | 17 | 0 | 1936-1941, CA Huracán Buenos Aires (6/0), CA Boca Juniors Buenos Aires (11/0). |
| (321/626) | ETCHEGARAY Marcelo Edmundo | 11.02.1935 | 5 | 0 | 1960, CA River Plate Buenos Aires (5/0). |
| (95/215) | EVARISTO Juan | 20.06.1902 | 25 | 1 | 1922-1930, Club Sportivo Palermo Buenos Aires (4/0), CA Huracán Buenos Aires (2/1), Club Sportivo Palermo Buenos Aires (14/0), Club Sportivo Barracas (5/0). |
| (148/313) | EVARISTO Marino "Mario" | 10.12.1904 | 9 | 2 | 1929-1930, Club Sportivo Palermo Buenos Aires (4/1), CA Boca Juniors Buenos Aires (5/1). |
| | | | | | |
| (592/953) | FABBRI Néstor Ariel | 29.04.1968 | 21 | 1 | 1987-1996, Racing Club Avellaneda (7/0), CA Boca Juniors Buenos Aires (14/1). |
| (193/425) | FABRINI José | | 2 | 1 | 1939, CA Newell's Old Boys Rosario (2/1). |
| (166/356) | FACIO Juan | | 1 | 0 | 1932, CA Defensores de Belgrano (1/0). |
| (316/616) | FACUNDO Héctor Osvaldo | 27.11.1937 | 7 | 1 | 1959-1962, CA San Lorenzo de Almagro Buenos Aires (7/1). |
| (98/223) | FAGGIANI Victorio | | 1 | 0 | 1922, Tiro Federal Rosario (1/0). |
| (256/523) | FAINA Ubaldo | 30.11.1927 | 2 | 0 | 1951, CA Newell's Old Boys Rosario (2/0). |
| (600/965) | FALCIONI Julio César | 20.07.1956 | 1 | 0 | 1989, CA Vélez Sarsfield (1/0). |
| (811/1146) | FARÍAS Ernesto Alberto | 29.05.1980 | 1 | 0 | 2005, CA River Plate Buenos Aires (1/0). |
| (229/492) | FARRO Armando | 20.12.1922 | 3 | 0 | 1945, CA Banfield (3/0). |
| (193/424) | FATTONE Juan | | 1 | 0 | 1939, CA Tigre (1/0). |
| (885/1250) | FAZIO Federico Julián | 17.03.1987 | 2 | 0 | 2011, Sevilla FC (2/0). |
| (183/412) | FAZIO Luis María | 23.04.1911 | 3 | 0 | 1937, CA Independiente Avellaneda (3/0). |
| (71/168) | FELICES Roberto | | 1 | 0 | 1919, Club Gimnasia y Esgrima La Plata (1/0). |
| (49/134) | FELISARI Alberto | | 3 | 0 | 1916, CA Platense Buenos Aires (3/0). |
| (483/869) | FELMAN Luis Darío | 25.10.1951 | 1 | 0 | 1977, CA Boca Juniors Buenos Aires (1/0). |
| (894/1264) | FERNÁNDEZ Augusto Matías | 10.04.1986 | 7 | 1 | 2011-2013, CA Vélez Sarsfield (2/0), Real Club Celta de Vigo (5/1). |
| (467/852) | FERNÁNDEZ Edgar Oscar | 21.02.1952 | 3 | 0 | 1975, CA Colón de Santa Fe (3/0). |
| (12/052) | FERNÁNDEZ Elías | | 15 | 1 | 1909-1916, CA River Plate Buenos Aires (12/1), Club Atlético San Isidro (3/0). |
| (48/130) | FERNÁNDEZ Emilio | | 2 | 0 | 1916, Club Gimnasia y Esgrima La Plata (2/0). |
| (353/675) | FERNÁNDEZ Enrique Santiago | 21.03.1944 | 8 | 1 | 1963, CA Rosario Central (8/1). |
| (883/1244) | FERNÁNDEZ Federico | 21.02.1989 | 23 | 2 | 2011-2013, Club Estudiantes La Plata (2/1), SSC Napoli (12/1), Getafe CF (4/0), SSC Napoli (5/0). |
| (351/670) | FERNÁNDEZ Jorge Hugo | 24.02.1942 | 4 | 1 | 1963-1967, CA Atlanta Buenos Aires (4/1). |
| (868/1222) | FERNÁNDEZ José Luis | 26.10.1987 | 1 | 0 | 2010, Racing Club de Avellaneda (1/0). |
| (727/1081) | FERNÁNDEZ Juan Ramón | 05.03.1980 | 1 | 0 | 1999, CA Estudiantes de La Plata (1/0). |
| (250/509) | FERNÁNDEZ Mario | | 3 | 1 | 1947, CA Independiente Avellaneda (3/1). |
| (162/336) | FERRARIO Luis | | 2 | 0 | 1931, CA Argentino Quilmes (2/0). |
| (229/493) | FERRARO Juan José | 05.09.1923 | 8 | 3 | 1945-1956, CA Vélez Sarsfield (8/3). |
| (135/297) | FERREIRA Manuel | 22.10.1905 | 21 | 12 | 1927-1930, CA Estudiantes de La Plata (21/12). |
| (349/666) | FERREIRO Roberto Oscar | 25.04.1935 | 19 | 0 | 1962-1966, CA Independiente Avellaneda (19/0). |
| (855/1173) | FERRERO Alexis Javier | 31.03.1979 | 1 | 0 | 2009, CA Colón de Santa Fé (1/0). |
| (459/828) | FERRERO Enzo | 03.01.1953 | 3 | 1 | 1974, CA Boca Juniors Buenos Aires (3/1). |

| | | | | | |
|---|---|---|---|---|---|
| (259/532) | FERRETTI Osvaldo | | **1** | **0** | 1952, CA Banfield (1/0). |
| (155/324) | FERREYRA Bernabé | 12.02.1909 | **4** | **0** | 1930-1937, CA Tigre (1/0), CA River Plate Buenos Aires (3/0). |
| (224/480) | FERREYRA Juan Silvano | | **1** | **0** | 1943, CA Newell's Old Boys Rosario (1/0). |
| (624/989) | FERREYRA Víctor Hugo | 24.02.1964 | **2** | **1** | 1991, CA San Lorenzo de Almagro Buenos Aires (2/1). |
| (53/139) | FERRO Antonio | | **8** | **0** | 1917-1918, CA Independiente Avellaneda (8/0). |
| (187/419) | FIDEL Manuel | | **4** | **3** | 1937-1940, Club Gimnasia y Esgrima La Plata (4/3). |
| (786/1126) | FIGUEROA Luciano Gabriel | 19.05.1981 | **15** | **9** | 2004-2005, CDS Cruz Azul Ciudad de México (9/4), Villarreal CF (6/5). |
| (254/515) | FILGUEIRAS Juan Manuel | 11.01.1927 | **7** | **0** | 1950-1956, CA Huracán Buenos Aires (7/0). |
| (458/825) | FILLOL Ubaldo Matildo | 21.07.1950 | **56** | **0** | 1974-1985, CA River Plate Buenos Aires (42/0), AA Argentinos Juniors Buenos Aires (3/0), CR Flamengo Rio de Janeiro (11/0). |
| (2/014) | FIRPO Emilio | | **1** | **0** | 1903, Barracas AC Lanús (1/0). |
| (389/723) | FISCHER Rodolfo José | 02.04.1944 | **33** | **7** | 1967-1972, CA San Lorenzo de Almagro Buenos Aires (33/7). |
| (671/1027) | FLORES José Oscar | 16.05.1971 | **2** | **0** | 1994, CA Vélez Sarsfield (2/0). |
| (236/499) | FONDA Juan Carlos | 15.10.1919 | **10** | **0** | 1945-1946, CA Platense Buenos Aires (10/0). |
| (886/1258) | FORMICA Mauro Abel | 04.04.1988 | **1** | **0** | 2011, CA Newell's Old Boys Rosario (1/0). |
| (447/817) | FORNARI Oscar Ramón | 15.03.1950 | **1** | **1** | 1973, CA Vélez Sarsfield (1/1). |
| (177/398) | FORRESTER Alfredo Eleuterio | | **2** | **0** | 1935, CA Vélez Sarsfield (2/0). |
| (3/019) | FORRESTER Arthur H. | | **2** | **0** | 1905-1907, Belgrano AC Buenos Aires (2/0). |
| (109/251) | FORTUNATO José | | **1** | **0** | 1923, CA Barracas Central Buenos Aires (1/0). |
| (113/258) | FORTUNATO Mario | | **11** | **0** | 1924-1926, CA Huracán Buenos Aires (11/0). |
| (513/895) | FORTUNATO Sergio Élio Ángel | 23.10.1956 | **5** | **0** | 1979, CA Estudiantes de La Plata (5/0). |
| (137/300) | FOSSA José Hipólito | | **1** | **0** | 1927, CA San Lorenzo de Almagro Buenos Aires (1/0). |
| (164/347) | FOSSATI Domingo | | **2** | **0** | 1931, Club Sportivo Palermo Buenos Aires (2/0). |
| (28/077) | FOURNOL Bleo Pedro "Calomino" | 13.03.1892 | **38** | **5** | 1912-1924, CA Argentino Quilmes Buenos Aires (2/1), CA Boca Juniors Buenos Aires (36/4). |
| (42/119) | FRAGA PETRAO Rodolfo | | **1** | **0** | 1915, CA River Plate Buenos Aires (1/0). |
| (62/154) | FRANCIA Juan | | **8** | **5** | 1918-1922, CA Newell's Old Boys Rosario (2/0), Tiro Federal Rosario (6/5). |
| (623/981) | FRANCO Darío Javier | 17.01.1969 | **22** | **6** | 1991-1994, CA Newell's Old Boys Rosario (13/6), Real Zaragoza CD (9/0). |
| (794/1127) | FRANCO Leonardo "Leo" Neorén | 20.05.1977 | **4** | **0** | 2004-2006, Club Atlético de Madrid (4/0). |
| (526/906) | FREN Carlos Guillermo | 27.12.1954 | **1** | **0** | 1980, CA Independiente Avellaneda (1/0). |
| (3/021) | FRERS Pablo | | **1** | **0** | 1905, Belgrano AC Buenos Aires (1/0). |
| (171/377) | FRESCHI Héctor Luis | 22.05.1911 | **1** | **0** | 1934, CA Sarmiento Resistencia Chaco (1/0). |
| (81/193) | FRUMENTO Ángel | | **4** | **0** | 1920, Club Argentino de Banfield (4/0). |
| (800/1135) | FUENTES Fabricio Fabio | 13.10.1976 | **1** | **0** | 2005, CA Vélez Sarsfield (1/0). |
| (855/1181) | FUERTES Oscar Esteban | 26.12.1972 | **1** | **0** | 2009, CA Colón de Santa Fé (1/0). |
| (586/948) | FUNES Juan Gilberto | 08.03.1963 | **4** | **0** | 1987, CA River Plate Buenos Aires (4/0). |
| (906/1271) | FUNES MORI Rogelio Gabriel | 05.03.1991 | **1** | **0** | 2012, CA River Plate Buenos Aires (1/0). |

| | | | | | |
|---|---|---|---|---|---|
| (868/1221) | GABBARINI Adrián José | 10.10.1985 | **3** | **0** | 2010-2011, CA Independiente Avellaneda (3/0). |
| (825/1151) | GAGO Fernando Rubén | 10.04.1986 | **46** | **0** | 2007-2013, Real Madrid CF (33/0), AS Roma (5/0), Valencia CF (5/0), CA Vélez Sarsfield (2/0), CA Boca Juniors Buenos Aires (1/0). |
| (144/304) | GAINZARAIN Enrique | | **1** | **0** | 1928, Club Ferro Carril Oeste (1/0). |
| (508/884) | GAITÁN José Luis | 07.09.1957 | **3** | **0** | 1979, CA Rosario Central (3/0). |
| (861/1201) | GAITÁN Osvaldo Nicolás Fabián | 23.02.1988 | **6** | **0** | 2009-2011, CA Boca Juniors Buenos Aires (3/0), Sport Lisboa e Benfica (3/0). |
| (171/384) | GALATEO Luis Alberto | | **1** | **1** | 1934, CA Unión Santa Fe (1/1). |
| (866/1215) | GALEANO Leonel | 02.08.1991 | **1** | **0** | 2010, CA Independiente Avellaneda (1/0). |
| (690/1049) | GALETTO Fernando Edgar | 13.04.1971 | **1** | **0** | 1995, CA San Lorenzo de Almagro Buenos Aires (1/0). |
| (671/1028) | GALLARDO Marcelo Daniel | 18.01.1976 | **44** | **14** | 1994-2003, CA River Plate Buenos Aires (32/11), AS Monaco (12/2). |
| (37/104) | GALLARDO Pedro | | **2** | **1** | 1914, CA Independiente Campana (2/1). |
| (464/844) | GALLEGO Américo Rubén | 25.04.1955 | **71** | **3** | 1975-1982, CA Newell's Old Boys Rosario (61/2), CA River Plate Buenos Aires (10/1). |
| (752/1096) | GALLETTI Luciano Martín | 09.04.1980 | **13** | **3** | 2000-2005, CA Estudiantes de La Plata (1/1), Real Zaragoza CD (12/2). |
| (461/832) | GALLETTI Rubén Horacio | 18.09.1952 | **1** | **1** | 1974, CA Estudiantes de La Plata (1/1). |
| (14/055) | GALLINO Santiago | | **3** | **0** | 1910, Club Gimnasia y Esgrima Buenos Aires (3/0). |
| (68/165) | GALLO Carlos Alberto | | **5** | **0** | 1919, CA Estudiantes de La Plata (5/0). |
| (391/733) | GALLO Luis Gregorio | 10.04.1945 | **8** | **0** | 1967-1968, CA Vélez Sarsfield (8/0). |
| (38/106) | GALUP LANÚS Carlos | | **2** | **0** | 1914, CA Estudiantes de La Plata (2/0). |
| (492/874) | GALVÁN Luis Adolfo | 24.02.1948 | **33** | **0** | 1977-1982, CA Talleres de Córdoba (33/0). |
| (447/816) | GALVÁN Rubén | 07.04.1952 | **6** | **0** | 1973-1978, CA Independiente Avellaneda (6/0). |
| (623/976) | GAMBOA Fernando Andrés | 28.10.1970 | **7** | **0** | 1991, CA Newell's Old Boys Rosario (7/0). |
| (205/454) | GANDULLA Bernardo José | 01.03.1916 | **1** | **0** | 1940, CA Boca Juniors Buenos Aires (1/0). |
| (285/574) | GARABAL Antonio Héctor | 17.10.1934 | **2** | **3** | 1956, Club Ferro Carril Oeste (2/3). |
| (121/276) | GARASSINI Alfredo | | **2** | **1** | 1924-1925, CA Boca Juniors Buenos Aires (2/1). |
| (835/1163) | GARAY GONZÁLEZ Ezequiel Marcelo | 10.10.1986 | **18** | **0** | 2007-2013, Real Racing Club de Santander (1/0), Real Madrid CF (2/0), Sport Lisboa e Benfica (15/0). |
| (769/1100) | GARCÉ Ariel Hernán | 14.07.1979 | **4** | **0** | 2003-2010, CA River Plate Buenos Aires (2/0), CA Colón de Santa Fé (2/0). |
| (254/519) | GARCERÓN Walter | 29.06.1920 | **2** | **0** | 1950, CA Estudiantes de La Plata (2/0). |
| (41/116) | GARCÍA Cándido | | **6** | **1** | 1915-1923, CA River Plate Buenos Aires (6/1). |
| (625/993) | GARCÍA Claudio Omar | 24.08.1963 | **12** | **2** | 1991-1994, Racing Club Avellaneda (12/2). |
| (174/395) | GARCÍA Diego | 23.01.1907 | **5** | **4** | 1935-1937, CA San Lorenzo de Almagro Buenos Aires (5/4). |
| (177/401) | GARCÍA Enrique | 30.11.1912 | **35** | **9** | 1935-1943, Racing Club Avellaneda (35/9). |
| (303/595) | GARCÍA FIERRO Rafael | 30.11.1929 | **1** | **0** | 1958, CA Vélez Sarsfield (1/0). |
| (189/422) | GARCÍA Héctor | | **1** | **0** | 1938, CA Huracán Buenos Aires (1/0). |
| (255/522) | GARCÍA Higinio | | **1** | **0** | 1950, Racing Club Avellaneda (1/0). |
| (880/1230) | GARCÍA Javier Hernán | 29.01.1987 | **1** | **0** | 2011, CA Boca Juniors Buenos Aires (1/0). |

| | | | | | |
|---|---|---|---|---|---|
| (508/880) | GARCÍA Jorge Alberto | 12.11.1956 | 1 | 0 | 1979, CA Rosario Central (1/0). |
| (316/618) | GARCÍA Omar Higinio | 12.09.1937 | 3 | 1 | 1959, CA San Lorenzo de Almagro Buenos Aires (3/1). |
| (257/526) | GARCÍA PÉREZ José M. | 03.12.1921 | 7 | 0 | 1951-1957, Racing Club Avellaneda (7/0). |
| (162/340) | GARCÍA R. | | 2 | 0 | 1931, CA Belgrano Rosario (2/0). |
| (530/910) | GARECA Ricardo Alberto | 10.02.1958 | 26 | 5 | 1981-1985, CA Sarmiento de Junín (1/0), CA Boca Juniors Buenos Aires (25/5). |
| (164/349) | GARGIULO José | | 2 | 0 | 1931, CA Estudiantil Porteño Buenos Aires (2/0). |
| (677/1032) | GARNERO Daniel Oscar | 01.04.1969 | 1 | 0 | 1995, CA Independiente Avellaneda (1/0). |
| (169/374) | GARRAFFA Francisco | 17.05.1910 | 2 | 0 | 1933, Racing Club Avellaneda (2/0). |
| (543/922) | GARRÉ Oscar Alfredo | 09.12.1956 | 41 | 0 | 1983-1988, Club Ferro Carril Oeste (41/0). |
| (50/137) | GARRÉ Pascual | | 1 | 0 | 1916, CA Independiente Avellaneda (1/0). |
| (90/209) | GASLINI José Bruno | | 6 | 2 | 1922-1925, Alvear Buenos Aires (5/1), CA Chacarita Juniors Buenos Aires San Martín (1/1). |
| (513/891) | GÁSPARI Jorge Osvaldo | 03.11.1958 | 5 | 1 | 1979, Quilmes AC (5/1). |
| (390/730) | GATTI Hugo Orlando | 19.08.1944 | 18 | 0 | 1967-1977, CA River Plate Buenos Aires (2/0), CA Unión Santa Fe (4/0), CA Boca Juniors Buenos Aires (12/0). |
| (206/457) | GAYOL Juan | | 2 | 0 | 1941, CA Newell's Old Boys Rosario (2/0). |
| (389/727) | GENNONI Enzo Enrique | 27.04.1943 | 1 | 1 | 1967, CA Rosario Central (1/1). |
| (434/791) | GHISO Jorge Luis | 21.06.1951 | 5 | 1 | 1972-1973, CA River Plate Buenos Aires (5/1). |
| (285/571) | GIANSERRA Fernando Manuel | 05.10.1931 | 4 | 0 | 1956-1957, CA Tigre (4/0). |
| (894/1265) | GIGLIOTTI Emmanuel | 20.05.1987 | 1 | 0 | 2011, CA San Lorenzo de Almagro (1/0). |
| (18/059) | GIL Juan Olegario | | 1 | 0 | 1910, Club Atlético San Isidro (1/0). |
| (187/417) | GILLI Lorenzo | 28.05.1905 | 2 | 0 | 1937, CA San Lorenzo de Almagro Buenos Aires (2/0). |
| (280/566) | GIMÉNEZ Juan Carlos | 16.02.1927 | 11 | 0 | 1956-1957, Racing Club Avellaneda (11/0). |
| (53/142) | GINEVRA Miguel | | 1 | 0 | 1917, CA Huracán Buenos Aires (1/0). |
| (6/031) | GINOCCHIO Armando | | 5 | 0 | 1907-1910, CA Estudiantes Buenos Aires (1/0), CA Newell's Old Boys Rosario (4/0). |
| (414/768) | GIRIBET Luis Alberto | 08.12.1946 | 1 | 1 | 1970, CA Huracán Buenos Aires (1/1). |
| (224/476) | GIÚDICE Manuel Ernesto | 10.12.1917 | 1 | 0 | 1943, CA Huracán Buenos Aires (1/0). |
| (123/277) | GIULIDORI César | | 2 | 0 | 1925, CA Palermo Buenos Aires (2/0). |
| (625/994) | GIUNTA Blas Armando | 06.09.1963 | 6 | 0 | 1991, CA Boca Juniors Buenos Aires (6/0). |
| (542/916) | GIUSTI Ricardo Omar | 11.12.1956 | 53 | 0 | 1983-1990, CA Independiente Avellaneda (53/0). |
| (447/813) | GLARIÁ Rubén Oscar | 10.03.1948 | 7 | 0 | 1973-1974, CA San Lorenzo de Almagro Buenos Aires (7/0). |
| (114/267) | GOICOECHEA Osvaldo | | 2 | 3 | 1924, CA Belgrano Rosario (2/3). |
| (100/232) | GOIN Emilio Francisco | | 1 | 0 | 1923, CA Porteño Buenos Aires (1/0). |
| (868/1218) | GOLTZ Paolo Duval | 12.05.1985 | 1 | 0 | 2010, CA Huracán Buenos Aires (1/0). |
| (196/438) | GÓMEZ José Aurelio | | 2 | 0 | 1940, CA Estudiantes de La Plata (2/0). |
| (161/334) | GÓMEZ Luis | | 1 | 0 | 1930, CA Chacarita Juniors Buenos Aires (1/0). |
| (680/1040) | GÓMEZ Marcelo Adrián | 08.12.1970 | 1 | 0 | 1995, CA Vélez Sarsfield (1/0). |
| (335/653) | GONZÁLEZ Alberto Mario | 21.08.1941 | 19 | 1 | 1961-1967, CA Atlanta Buenos Aires (5/0), CA Boca Juniors Buenos Aires (14/1). |
| (30/084) | GONZÁLEZ Carlos | | 1 | 0 | 1912, CA Newell's Old Boys Rosario (1/0). |
| (689/1045) | GONZÁLEZ Cristián Alberto "Kily" | 04.08.1974 | 56 | 10 | 1995-2005, CA Boca Juniors Buenos Aires (1/0), Real Zaragoza CD (7/1), Valencia CF (32/5), Internazionale FC Milano (16/4). |
| (200/449) | GONZÁLEZ Ernesto | | 1 | 0 | 1940, CA San Lorenzo de Almagro Buenos Aires (1/0). |
| (39/112) | GONZÁLEZ ESCARRÁ Roberto | | 1 | 0 | 1914, CA Porteño Buenos Aires (1/0). |
| (556/936) | GONZÁLEZ Gerardo Manuel | 17.08.1959 | 3 | 0 | 1984, CA Rosario Central (3/0). |
| (330/646) | GONZÁLEZ Hugo Osvaldo | 30.11.1934 | 1 | 0 | 1960, AA Argentinos Juniors Buenos Aires (1/0). |
| (699/1066) | GONZÁLEZ Ignacio Carlos | 17.12.1971 | 4 | 0 | 1997, Racing Club Avellaneda (4/0). |
| (168/364) | GONZÁLEZ José María | | 5 | 0 | 1933-1934, Racing Club Avellaneda (5/0). |
| (769/1103) | GONZÁLEZ Luis Oscar | 19.01.1981 | 44 | 7 | 2003-2011, CA River Plate Buenos Aires (20/6), FC do Porto (23/1), Olympique de Marseille (1/0). |
| (14/058) | GONZÁLEZ Manuel | | 11 | 7 | 1910-1913, CA Newell's Old Boys Rosario (11/7). |
| (769/1107) | GONZÁLEZ Mariano Nicolás | 05.05.1981 | 9 | 0 | 2003-2008, Racing Club Avellaneda (8/0), FC do Porto (1/0). |
| (393/742) | GONZÁLEZ Pedro Alexis | 10.03.1946 | 7 | 0 | 1968-1977, CA San Lorenzo de Almagro Buenos Aires (5/0), CA River Plate Buenos Aires (2/0). |
| (172/388) | GONZÁLEZ PERALTA Tomás | 26.04.1903 | 3 | 1 | 1934-1938, Club Gimnasia y Esgrima La Plata (3/1). |
| (19/061) | GONZÁLEZ Tomás | | 2 | 0 | 1910, Club Alumni AC Buenos Aires (2/0). |
| (4/025) | GONZÁLEZ Tristán | | 1 | 1 | 1906, CA Estudiantes Buenos Aires (1/1). |
| (88/205) | GONZÁLEZ Vicente | | 2 | 0 | 1921, Club Gimnasia y Esgrima Mendoza (2/0). |
| (601/972) | GOROSITO Néstor Raúl | 14.05.1964 | 18 | 1 | 1989-1997, CA San Lorenzo de Almagro Buenos Aires (5/0), FC Tirol Innsbruck (1/0), CA San Lorenzo de Almagro Buenos Aires (12/1). |
| (586/946) | GOYCOCHEA Sergio Javier | 17.10.1963 | 44 | 0 | 1987-1994, CA River Plate Buenos Aires (1/0), CD Los Millonarios Bogotá (7/0), Racing Club Avellaneda (13/0), Club Cerro Porteno Asunción (2/0), Club Olimpia Asunción (3/0), CA River Plate Buenos Aires (18/0). |
| (416/774) | GRAMAJO Roberto Artemio | 28.07.1947 | 1 | 0 | 1971, CA Rosario Central (1/0). |
| (6/033) | GRANT Haroldo M. | | 6 | 0 | 1907-1911, Belgrano AC Buenos Aires (6/0). |
| (224/481) | GRECCO Salvador | 21.01.1922 | 3 | 0 | 1943-1945, CA San Lorenzo de Almagro Buenos Aires (3/0). |
| (312/611) | GRIFFA Jorge Bernardo | 07.09.1935 | 4 | 0 | 1959, CA Newell's Old Boys Rosario (4/0). |
| (318/622) | GRIGUOL Carlos Timoteo | 04.09.1936 | 8 | 0 | 1959-1963, CA Atlanta Buenos Aires (8/0). |
| (335/652) | GRIGUOL Mario Luis | 04.04.1937 | 7 | 0 | 1961-1962, CA Atlanta Buenos Aires (7/0). |
| (258/530) | GRILLO Ernesto | 01.10.1929 | 21 | 8 | 1952-1962, CA Independiente Avellaneda (19/8), CA Boca Juniors (2/0). |
| (162/335) | GRIMOLDI Fortunato | | 2 | 0 | 1931, CA Excursionistas Buenos Aires (2/0). |
| (168/371) | GUAITA Enrique | 15.07.1910 | 4 | 1 | 1933-1937, CA Estudiantes de La Plata (2/1), Racing Club Avellaneda (2/0). |
| (176/396) | GUALCO Sebastián Inocencio | 26.04.1912 | 23 | 0 | 1935-1943, CA San Lorenzo de Almagro Buenos Aires (11/0), Club Ferro Carril Oeste (12/0). |
| (310/608) | GÜENZATTI Osvaldo Oscar | | 2 | 0 | 1959, CA Atlanta Buenos Aires (2/0). |

| | | | | | |
|---|---|---|---|---|---|
| (440/807) | GUERINI Carlos Alfredo | 10.03.1949 | **7** | **4** | 1973, CA Boca Juniors Buenos Aires (1/0), Club Belgrano de Córdoba (6/4). |
| (729/1085) | GUGLIELMINPIETRO Andrés | 10.04.1974 | **6** | **0** | 1999, Milan AC (6/0). |
| (34/097) | GUIDI Carlos | | **7** | **1** | 1913-1917, Tiro Federal Rosario (7/1). |
| (275/557) | GUIDI Héctor Juan | 14.07.1930 | **37** | **0** | 1956-1961, CA Lanús (37/0). |
| (769/1102) | GUIÑAZÚ Pablo Horacio | 26.08.1978 | **16** | **0** | 2003-2013, CA Independiente Avellaneda (4/0), SC Internacional Porto Alegre (10/0), Club Libertad Asunción (2/0). |
| (108/246) | GURUTCHAGUE José | | **2** | **0** | 1923-1924, CA El Porvenir Gerli (2/0). |
| (251/510) | GUTIÉRREZ Ernesto | 09.11.1927 | **23** | **0** | 1947-1956, Racing Club Avellaneda (23/0). |
| (825/1152) | GUTIÉRREZ Jonás Manuel | 07.05.1983 | **22** | **1** | 2007-2011, RCD Mallorca (4/0), Newcastle United FC (18/1). |
| (163/346) | HAEDO Juan Carlos | | **1** | **0** | 1931, CA Tigre (1/0). |
| (861/1195) | HAUCHE Gabriel Agustín | 27.11.1986 | **5** | **3** | 2009-2011, AA Argentinos Juniors Buenos Aires (1/0), Racing Club de Avellaneda (4/3). |
| (41/117) | HAYES Ennis | | **11** | **4** | 1915-1919, CA Rosario Central (11/4). |
| (14/057) | HAYES Juan Enrique | | **21** | **8** | 1910-1919, CA Rosario Central (21/8). |
| (773/1115) | HEINZE Gabriel Iván | 19.03.1978 | **72** | **3** | 2003-2010, Paris St.Germain FC (7/0), Manchester United FC (33/2), Real Madrid CF (16/0), Olympique de Marseille (16/1). |
| (44/124) | HEISSINGER Adolfo | | **5** | **1** | 1916-1919, CA Tigre (5/1). |
| (5/028) | HENMAN Héctor | | **1** | **0** | 1906, Club Alumni AC Buenos Aires (1/0). |
| (204/451) | HEREDIA Juan Carlos | | **6** | **1** | 1940-1942, CA Rosario Central (6/1). |
| (196/435) | HEREDIA Luis Bernabé | | **2** | **0** | 1940, CA Newell's Old Boys Rosario (2/0). |
| (418/778) | HEREDIA Ramón Armando | 26.02.1951 | **30** | **2** | 1971-1974, CA San Lorenzo de Almagro Buenos Aires (23/1), Club Atlético de Madrid (7/1). |
| (517/899) | HERNÁNDEZ Patricio José | 16.08.1956 | **10** | **0** | 1979-1982, CA Estudiantes de La Plata (10/0). |
| (168/363) | HERRERA Atilio | 03.12.1911 | **4** | **0** | 1933-1937, Club Gimnasia y Esgrima La Plata (4/0). |
| (297/588) | HERRERA José | 27.04.1937 | **2** | **0** | 1957, CA San Lorenzo de Almagro Buenos Aires (2/0). |
| (862/1203) | HIGUAÍN Gonzalo Gerardo | 10.12.1987 | **35** | **21** | 2009-2013, Real Madrid CF (25/13), SSC Napoli (10/8). |
| (48/132) | HILLER Marius | 05.08.1892 | **2** | **4** | 1916, Club Gimnasia y Esgrima La Plata (2/4). |
| (30/086) | HOSPITAL Juan | | **5** | **0** | 1912-1916, Racing Club Avellaneda (5/0). |
| (440/806) | HOUSEMAN René Orlando | 19.07.1953 | **54** | **12** | 1973-1979, CA Huracán Buenos Aires (54/12). |
| (2/012) | HOWARD Jorge | | **1** | **0** | 1903, Belgrano AC Buenos Aires (1/0). |
| (704/1073) | HUSAÍN Claudio Daniel | 20.11.1974 | **14** | **1** | 1997-2002, CA Vélez Sarsfield (9/0), CA River Plate Buenos Aires (1/0), SSC Napoli (3/1), CA River Plate Buenos Aires (1/0). |
| (794/1130) | IBAGAZA Ariel Miguel Santiago | 27.10.1976 | **1** | **0** | 2004, Club Atlético de Madrid (1/0). |
| (866/1212) | IBÁÑEZ Nelson Martín | 19.01.1981 | **1** | **0** | 2010, CD Godoy Cruz (1/0). |
| (727/1078) | IBARRA Hugo Benjamín | 01.04.1974 | **11** | **0** | 1999-2007, CA Boca Juniors Buenos Aires (11/0). |
| (920/1277) | ICARDI RIVERO Mauro Emanuel | 19.02.1993 | **1** | **0** | 2013, FC Internazionale Milano (1/0). |
| (258/529) | INFANTE Ricardo Raymundo | 21.06.1924 | **4** | **2** | 1952-1958, CA Estudiantes de La Plata (2/1), CA Huracán Buenos Aires (1/0), CA Estudiantes de La Plata (1/1). |
| (293/583) | IÑIGO David Carmelo | | **4** | **0** | 1957-1963, CA San Lorenzo de Almagro Buenos Aires (2/0), CA Chacarita Juniors Buenos Aires (2/0). |
| (861/1196) | INSAURRALDE Juan Manuel | 03.10.1984 | **2** | **0** | 2009-2010, CA Newell's Old Boys Rosario (2/0). |
| (769/1106) | INSÚA Federico | 03.01.1980 | **14** | **0** | 2003-2010, CA Independiente Avellaneda (6/0), VfL Borussia Mönchengladbach (2/0), CF América Ciudad de México (2/0), CA Boca Juniors Buenos Aires (4/0). |
| (543/924) | INSÚA Rubén Darío | 17.04.1961 | **6** | **0** | 1983-1984, CA San Lorenzo de Almagro Buenos Aires (6/0). |
| (862/1202) | INSÚA ZAPATA Emiliano Adrián | 07.01.1989 | **4** | **0** | 2009-2011, Liverpool FC (1/0), Galatasaray SK Istanbul (3/0). |
| (171/385) | IRAÑETA Roberto Luis | 21.03.1915 | **1** | **0** | 1934, Club Gimnasia y Esgrima Mendoza (1/0). |
| (108/239) | IRIBARREN Jorge | | **3** | **0** | 1923-1925, AA Argentinos Juniors Buenos Aires (1/0), CA Villa Urquiza San Martín (2/0). |
| (95/214) | IRIBARREN Juan Carlos | 27.05.1901 | **17** | **0** | 1922-1937, AA Argentino Juniors Buenos Aires (11/0), CA River Plate Buenos Aires (1/0), CA Chacarita Juniors Buenos Aires (5/0). |
| (103/233) | IRURIETA Juan Carlos | | **5** | **2** | 1923-1932, CA Estudiantes de La Plata (1/1), CA Argentino Quilmes (2/1), CA All Boys Buenos Aires (2/0). |
| (364/689) | IRUSTA Agustín Enrique | 27.03.1938 | **1** | **0** | 1964, CA San Lorenzo de Almagro Buenos Aires (1/0). |
| (519/902) | ISCHIA Carlos Luis | 28.10.1956 | **2** | **0** | 1980, CA Vélez Sarsfield (2/0). |
| (559/938) | ISLAS Luis Alberto | 22.12.1965 | **30** | **0** | 1984-1994, CA Estudiantes de La Plata (6/0), CA Independiente Avellaneda (9/0), CD Logroñés (2/0), Club Atlético de Madrid (3/0), CA Independiente Avellaneda (10/0). |
| (47/129) | ISOLA Carlos | | **21** | **0** | 1916-1919, CA River Plate Buenos Aires (21/0). |
| (46/128) | IVANESEVICH Oscar | | **1** | **0** | 1916, CA Estudiantes Buenos Aires (1/0). |
| (38/110) | IZAGUIRRE Carlos | | **14** | **7** | 1914-1923, CA Porteño Buenos Aires (7/5), Club Sportivo Palermo Buenos Aires (7/2). |
| (6/032) | JACOBS Arturo | | **8** | **1** | 1907-1913, Club Alumni AC Buenos Aires (7/1), Belgrano AC Buenos Aires (1/0). |
| (865/1210) | JARA Franco Daniel | 15.07.1988 | **4** | **1** | 2010-2011, Arsenal FC de Sarandí (3/1), Sport Lisboa e Benfica (1/0). |
| (676/1030) | JIMÉNEZ Jorge Rubén | 07.04.1970 | **2** | **0** | 1995, CA Banfield (2/0). |
| (321/629) | JIMÉNEZ Walter Antonio | 25.05.1939 | **9** | **2** | 1960, CA Independiente Avellaneda (9/2). |
| (28/074) | JOHNSTON Juan | | **1** | **0** | 1912, CA Argentino Quilmes Buenos Aires (1/0). |
| (545/928) | JORGE Omar Roberto | 30.08.1956 | **2** | **0** | 1983, CA Vélez Sarsfield (2/0). |
| (348/662) | JUÁREZ Ernesto Humberto | | **12** | **2** | 1962-1963, CA Huracán Buenos Aires (11/2), CA River Plate Buenos Aires (1/0). |
| (294/584) | JUÁREZ Miguel Antonio | 30.11.1931 | **5** | **2** | 1957-1958, CA Rosario Central (5/2). |
| (447/818) | KEMPES Mario Alberto | 15.07.1954 | **43** | **20** | 1973-1982, Instituto AC de Córdoba (1/0), CA Rosario Central (23/14), Valencia CF (8/6), CA River Plate Buenos Aires (11/0). |
| (81/191) | KIESSEL Ernesto | | **1** | **0** | 1920, CA Huracán Buenos Aires (1/0). |
| (464/842) | KILLER Daniel Pedro | 21.12.1949 | **22** | **3** | 1975-1978, CA Rosario Central (13/3), Racing Club Avellaneda (9/0). |

| | | | | | |
|---|---|---|---|---|---|
| (436/798) | KILLER Mario Estanislao | 15.08.1951 | 5 | 0 | 1972-1975, CA Rosario Central (5/0). |
| (149/316) | KUKO Esteban | 04.11.1907 | 1 | 0 | 1929, CA Boca Juniors Buenos Aires (1/0). |
| (462/834) | LA VOLPE Ricardo Antonio | 06.02.1952 | 8 | 0 | 1975-1976, CA Banfield (4/0), CA San Lorenzo de Almagro Buenos Aires (4/0). |
| (222/472) | LABRUNA Ángel Amadeo | 28.09.1918 | 37 | 17 | 1942-1958, CA River Plate Buenos Aires (37/17). |
| (260/536) | LACASIA Carlos | 02.05.1926 | 3 | 0 | 1953, CA Independiente Avellaneda (3/0). |
| (196/439) | LAFERRARA Ángel R. | 27.03.1917 | 6 | 5 | 1940-1942, CA Estudiantes de La Plata (6/5). |
| (1/001) | LAFORIA José | | 4 | 0 | 1902-1907, Barracas AC Lanús (1/0), Club Alumni Buenos Aires (3/0). |
| (389/726) | LAGINESTRA Antonio Oscar | 25.08.1943 | 1 | 0 | 1967, Quilmes AC (1/0). |
| (162/339) | LAGOMARSINO Adolfo | | 2 | 0 | 1931, CA Banfield (2/0). |
| (45/125) | LAGUNA José | | 4 | 3 | 1916-1919, CA Huracán Buenos Aires (4/3). |
| (49/136) | LAIOLO José | | 5 | 3 | 1916-1919, CA Rosario Central (1/1), CA River Plate Buenos Aires (4/2). |
| (108/244) | LALAURETTE Carlos | | 1 | 0 | 1923, CSD Progresista Gerli (1/0). |
| (352/674) | LALLANA Juan Carlos | 24.12.1938 | 5 | 3 | 1963-1965, AA Argentinos Juniors Buenos Aires (4/3), CA River Plate Buenos Aires (1/0). |
| (34/096) | LAMAS Juan José | | 5 | 0 | 1913-1915, CA Estudiantes de La Plata (5/0). |
| (884/1248) | LAMELA Erik Manuel | 04.03.1992 | 6 | 0 | 2011-2013, CA River Plate Buenos Aires (1/0), AS Roma (2/0), Tottenham Hotspur FC London (3/0). |
| (406/759) | LAMELZA Osvaldo José | 08.05.1944 | 1 | 0 | 1969, Racing Club Avellaneda (1/0). |
| (633/1000) | LANARI Alejandro Fabio | 02.05.1960 | 1 | 0 | 1991, CA Rosario Central (1/0). |
| (418/779) | LANDUCCI Ángel Antonio | 23.01.1948 | 8 | 0 | 1971-1972, CA Rosario Central (8/0). |
| (595/960) | LANZIDEI Fernando Fabián | 30.06.1965 | 3 | 0 | 1988, CA Rosario Central (3/0). |
| (415/769) | LARAIGNÉE César Augusto | 10.02.1949 | 11 | 3 | 1970-1971, CA River Plate Buenos Aires (11/3). |
| (513/892) | LARRAQUY Pedro Omar | 13.06.1956 | 3 | 0 | 1979, CA Vélez Sarsfield (3/0). |
| (485/872) | LARROSA Omar Rubén | 18.11.1947 | 11 | 0 | 1977-1978, CA Independiente Avellaneda (11/0). |
| (623/982) | LATORRE Diego Fernando | 04.08.1969 | 6 | 1 | 1991, CA Boca Juniors Buenos Aires (6/1). |
| (80/188) | LATORRE LELONG Alberto | | 1 | 0 | 1920, CA Estudiantes de La Plata (1/0). |
| (114/266) | LAURENZANO Alejandro | | 1 | 0 | 1924, CA Temperley (1/0). |
| (150/318) | LAURI Miguel Ángel | 29.08.1908 | 10 | 1 | 1929-1935, CA Estudiantes de La Plata (10/1). |
| (826/1159) | LAVEZZI Ezequiel Iván | 03.05.1985 | 28 | 4 | 2007-2013, CA San Lorenzo de Almagro Buenos Aires (1/0), SSC Napoli (17/2), Paris Saint-Germain FC (10/2). |
| (13/053) | LAWRIE Henry | | 3 | 1 | 1909-1911, Club Alumni AC Buenos Aires (3/1). |
| (38/109) | LAZCANO Delfín | | 2 | 2 | 1914-1919, CA Estudiantes de La Plata (2/2). |
| (108/245) | LÁZZARI Luis | | 1 | 0 | 1923, Alvear Buenos Aires (1/0). |
| (179/405) | LAZZATTI Ernesto | 25.09.1915 | 4 | 0 | 1936-1937, CA Boca Juniors Buenos Aires (4/0). |
| (826/1155) | LEDESMA Cristian Raúl | 29.12.1978 | 4 | 0 | 2007-2008, CA San Lorenzo de Almagro Buenos Aires (1/0), Olympiacos SFP Peiraiás (1/0), CA San Lorenzo de Almagro Buenos Aires (2/0). |
| (826/1160) | LEDESMA Pablo Martín | 04.02.1984 | 2 | 0 | 2007-2008, CA Boca Juniors Buenos Aires (1/0), Calcio Catania (1/0). |
| (196/436) | LEGUIZAMÓN Raúl Osvaldo | | 3 | 1 | 1940-1943, CA Independiente Avellaneda (3/1). |
| (366/691) | LEONARDI José Bernabé | 11.06.1939 | 9 | 0 | 1964-1967, Club Ferro Carril Oeste (9/0). |
| (39/115) | LEONARDI Roberto | | 3 | 0 | 1914-1917, CA Estudiantes de La Plata (3/0). |
| (1/002) | LESLIE William | | 1 | 0 | 1902, Quilmes AC (1/0). |
| (3/020) | LETT Carlos | | 2 | 0 | 1905-1911, Club Alumni AC Buenos Aires (2/0). |
| (77/179) | LIBONATTI Julio | 05.07.1901 | 15 | 8 | 1919-1922, CA Newell's Old Boys Rosario (15/8). |
| (225/486) | LIJÉ Alberto | 02.02.1920 | 1 | 0 | 1943, Club Ferro Carril Oeste (1/0). |
| (85/197) | LIZÁRRAGA Odilón | | 1 | 0 | 1921, Club Sportivo Palermo Buenos Aires (1/0). |
| (224/477) | LIZTHERMAN Ernesto | 22.03.1914 | 1 | 0 | 1943, CA Chacarita Juniors Buenos Aires (1/0). |
| (12/050) | LLOYD Harold | | 1 | 0 | 1909, Quilmes AC (1/0). |
| (270/551) | LOIÁCONO Francisco Ramón | 12.12.1935 | 8 | 0 | 1956, Club Gimnasia y Esgrima La Plata (8/0). |
| (99/228) | LOIZO Adán | | 12 | 0 | 1923-1925, CA Huracán Buenos Aires (12/0). |
| (715/1077) | LOMBARDI Gustavo Adrián | 10.09.1975 | 2 | 0 | 1998, UD Salamanca (2/0). |
| (258/527) | LOMBARDO Juan Francisco | 11.06.1925 | 37 | 0 | 1952-1959, CA Boca Juniors Buenos Aires (37/0). |
| (104/235) | LÓPEZ Adolfo | | 3 | 1 | 1923-1924, Club Argentino de Banfield (3/1). |
| (164/348) | LÓPEZ Arcadio Julio | 15.09.1910 | 6 | 0 | 1931-1939, CS Sportivo Buenos Aires (3/0), Club Ferro Carril Oeste (1/0), CA Boca Juniors Buenos Aires (2/0). |
| (513/893) | LÓPEZ Carlos Ángel | 17.07.1952 | 4 | 1 | 1979, Racing Club Avellaneda (4/1). |
| (678/1037) | LÓPEZ Claudio Javier | 17.07.1974 | 55 | 10 | 1995-2003, Racing Club Avellaneda (5/0), Valencia CF (30/6), SS Lazio Roma (20/4). |
| (672/1029) | LÓPEZ Gustavo Adrián | 13.04.1973 | 32 | 4 | 1994-2003, CA Independiente Avellaneda (6/2), Real Zaragoza CD (11/1), RC Celta de Vigo (15/1). |
| (223/473) | LÓPEZ Isaac Roberto | 30.11.1917 | 1 | 0 | 1943, CA Chacarita Juniors Buenos Aires (1/0). |
| (60/148) | LÓPEZ José Alfredo | | 9 | 0 | 1918-1921, CA Boca Juniors Buenos Aires (9/0). |
| (435/795) | LÓPEZ Juan José | 31.10.1950 | 2 | 1 | 1972-1974, CA River Plate Buenos Aires (2/1). |
| (800/1141) | LÓPEZ Lisandro | 02.03.1983 | 7 | 1 | 2005-2009, Racing Club Avellaneda (1/0), FC do Porto (5/0), Olympique Lyonnais (1/1). |
| (880/1232) | LÓPEZ Lisandro Ezequiel | 01.09.1989 | 4 | 0 | 2011-2012, Arsenal FC de Sarandí (4/0). |
| (390/731) | LÓPEZ Miguel Ángel | 01.03.1942 | 2 | 0 | 1967-1972, Club Ferro Carril Oeste (1/0), CA Independiente Avellaneda (1/0). |
| (388/716) | LÓPEZ Nelson Juan | 24.06.1941 | 8 | 0 | 1967-1968, CA Banfield (8/0). |
| (595/958) | LORENZO Néstor Gabriel | 28.02.1966 | 13 | 0 | 1988-1990, AA Argentinos Juniors Buenos Aires (7/0), AS Bari (6/0). |
| (227/489) | LOUSTAU Félix | 25.12.1922 | 27 | 10 | 1945-1952, CA River Plate Buenos Aires (27/10). |
| (120/275) | LOYARTE Juan | | 3 | 1 | 1924, CA Colón de Santa Fe (3/1). |
| (79/186) | LUCARELLI José Fausto | | 5 | 2 | 1920-1924, Club Argentino de Banfield (4/0), CS Sportivo Buenos Aires (1/2). |
| (595/959) | LUCCA Mario Bruno | 06.08.1961 | 4 | 0 | 1988, CA Vélez Sarsfield (4/0). |
| (130/289) | LUCENA Alberto | | 1 | 0 | 1926, CA Sportsman Buenos Aires (1/0). |

| | | | | | |
|---|---|---|---|---|---|
| (625/992) | LUDUEÑA Miguel Ángel | 06.02.1958 | 1 | 0 | 1991, CA Independiente Avellaneda (1/0). |
| (275/562) | LUGO GONZÁLEZ Dante Homérico | 28.08.1932 | 3 | 0 | 1956, CA Lanús (3/0). |
| (365/690) | LUNA José Luis | 30.10.1940 | 6 | 0 | 1964-1965, CA Atlanta Buenos Aires (6/0). |
| (137/302) | LUNA Segundo | | 2 | 3 | 1927, Liga Cultural de Santiago del Estero (2/3). |
| (166/357) | LUPPO Oscar | | 1 | 0 | 1932, CA Defensores de Belgrano (1/0). |
| (464/846) | LUQUE Leopoldo Jacinto | 03.05.1949 | 45 | 22 | 1975-1981, Unión Santa Fe (4/4), CA River Plate Buenos Aires (40/18), Unión Santa Fe (1/0). |
| (800/1133) | LUX Germán Darío | 07.06.1982 | 6 | 0 | 2005, CA River Plate Buenos Aires (6/0). |
| (658/1012) | MacALLISTER Carlos Javier | 06.03.1968 | 3 | 0 | 1993, CA Boca Juniors Buenos Aires (3/0). |
| (76/177) | MACCHIAVELLO Enrique | | 1 | 0 | 1919, Racing Club Avellaneda (1/0). |
| (114/265) | MacCOURBEY Cándido | | 1 | 0 | 1924, Club Sportivo Barracas (1/0). |
| (601/973) | MACIEL Sergio Silvano | 07.02.1965 | 2 | 0 | 1989, Club Deportivo Armenio (2/0). |
| (74/170) | MADERO Juan | | 1 | 0 | 1919, CA Estudiantes Buenos Aires (1/0). |
| (59/146) | MADERO M. | | 1 | 0 | 1917, CA Estudiantes Buenos Aires (1/0). |
| (367/694) | MADERO Raúl Horacio | 21.05.1939 | 5 | 0 | 1964-1969, CA Estudiantes de La Plata (5/0). |
| (411/763) | MADURGA Norberto Rubén | 29.12.1944 | 11 | 3 | 1970-1971, CA Boca Juniors Buenos Aires (11/3). |
| (74/169) | MAGISTRETTI Guillermo | | 5 | 0 | 1919-1923, CA Tigre (1/0), Club Sportivo Palermo Buenos Aires (4/0). |
| (123/280) | MAGLIO Juan Félix | | 9 | 5 | 1925-1931, CA Nueva Chicago Buenos Aires (2/0), CA San Lorenzo de Almagro Buenos Aires (6/5), Club Ferrocarriles del Estado Buenos Aires (1/0). |
| (880/1233) | MAIDANA Jonathan Ramón | 29.07.1985 | 2 | 0 | 2011, CA River Plate Buenos Aires (2/0). |
| (376/702) | MALBERNAT Oscar Miguel | 02.02.1944 | 14 | 0 | 1965-1970, CA Estudiantes de La Plata (14/0). |
| (21/062) | MALBRÁN Manuel | | 1 | 0 | 1911, Club Atlético San Isidro (1/0). |
| (7/042) | MALBRÁN Ricardo | | 2 | 2 | 1907-1915, Club Atlético San Isidro (2/2). |
| (349/665) | MALDONADO Jorge Alberto | 05.05.1929 | 2 | 0 | 1962, CA Independiente Avellaneda (2/0). |
| (31/089) | MALLEN Ángel | | 4 | 0 | 1913, Belgrano AC Buenos Aires (4/0). |
| (640/1008) | MANCUSO Alejandro Víctor | 04.09.1968 | 10 | 1 | 1992-1994, CA Vélez Sarsfield (1/0), CA Boca Juniors Buenos Aires (9/1). |
| (388/717) | MANERA Eduardo Luján | 22.08.1944 | 3 | 0 | 1967, CA Estudiantes de La Plata (3/0). |
| (310/605) | MANFREDINI Pedro Waldemar | 07.09.1935 | 3 | 2 | 1959, Racing Club Avellaneda (3/2). |
| (287/578) | MANTEGARI Oscar Hernán | 20.10.1928 | 2 | 0 | 1956-1957, CA River Plate Buenos Aires (2/0). |
| (483/870) | MARADONA Diego Armando | 30.10.1960 | 89 | 32 | 1977-1994, AA Argentinos Juniors Buenos Aires (22/9), CA Boca Juniors Buenos Aires (10/2), SSC Napoli (46/19), Sevilla CF (2/0), CA Newell's Old Boys Rosario (2/0), no club (7/2). |
| (542/917) | MARANGONI Claudio Oscar | 17.11.1954 | 9 | 0 | 1983-1984, CA Independiente Avellaneda (9/0). |
| (467/859) | MARANGONI Daniel Horacio | 19.08.1951 | 3 | 0 | 1975, CA Chacarita Juniors Buenos Aires (3/0). |
| (236/498) | MARANTE José Manuel | 27.02.1915 | 9 | 0 | 1945-1947, CA Boca Juniors Buenos Aires (9/0). |
| (147/309) | MARASSI Pedro | | 1 | 0 | 1928, Club Sportivo Barracas (1/0). |
| (880/1240) | MARCHESÍN Agustín Federico | 16.03.1988 | 1 | 0 | 2011, CA Lanús (1/0). |
| (547/932) | MÁRCICO Alberto José | 13.05.1960 | 17 | 0 | 1983-1992, Club Ferro Carril Oeste (16/0), CA Boca Juniors Buenos Aires (1/0). |
| (407/761) | MARCOS Ángel Alberto | 07.04.1943 | 7 | 1 | 1969-1971, CA Chacarita Juniors Buenos Aires (7/1). |
| (30/088) | MARCOVECCHIO Alberto Andrés | | 12 | 8 | 1912-1919, Racing Club Avellaneda (12/8). |
| (196/437) | MARIL Juan José | | 4 | 1 | 1940, CA Independiente Avellaneda (4/1). |
| (388/714) | MARÍN José Miguel | 15.05.1945 | 5 | 0 | 1967-1971, CA Vélez Sarsfield (5/0). |
| (343/657) | MARIOTTI Alberto Jorge | 23.08.1935 | 1 | 0 | 1962, CA San Lorenzo de Almagro Buenos Aires (1/0). |
| (28/078) | MÁRQUEZ A. | | 1 | 0 | 1912, CA Porteño Buenos Aires (1/0). |
| (263/541) | MARRAPODI Roque Saverio | 18.06.1929 | 2 | 0 | 1954, Club Ferro Carril Oeste (2/0). |
| (628/997) | MARTELLOTTO Germán Ricardo | 16.11.1962 | 1 | 0 | 1991, (1/0). |
| (56/144) | MARTÍN Alfredo | | 10 | 2 | 1917-1919, CA Tigre (5/0), CA Boca Juniors Buenos Aires (5/2). |
| (351/668) | MARTÍN Oscar Raimundo | 23.06.1934 | 8 | 0 | 1963, CA Chacarita Juniors Buenos Aires (6/0), Racing Club Avellaneda (2/0). |
| (181/411) | MARTÍNEZ Celestino | | 14 | 0 | 1937-1943, CA Independiente Avellaneda (14/0). |
| (166/355) | MARTÍNEZ Horacio | | 2 | 1 | 1932, CA Estudiantil Porteño Buenos Aires (2/1). |
| (704/1070) | MARTÍNEZ Jorge Daniel | 20.06.1973 | 3 | 0 | 1997, CA Independiente Avellaneda (3/0). |
| (879/1229) | MARTÍNEZ Juan Manuel | 25.10.1985 | 4 | 1 | 2011-2012, CA Vélez Sarsfield (2/0), SC Corinthians Paulista São Paulo (2/1). |
| (44/122) | MARTÍNEZ Pedro | 19.05.1893 | 15 | 0 | 1916-1919, CA Huracán Buenos Aires (15/0). |
| (37/102) | MARTÍNEZ Rodolfo | | 1 | 0 | 1914, CA Argentino Quilmes Buenos Aires (1/0). |
| (623/986) | MARTINO Gerardo Daniel | 22.11.1962 | 1 | 0 | 1991, CA Newell's Old Boys Rosario (1/0). |
| (221/467) | MARTINO Rinaldo Fioramonte | 06.10.1921 | 20 | 16 | 1942-1946, CA San Lorenzo de Almagro Buenos Aires (20/16). |
| (187/420) | MARVEZZI Juan | 16.11.1915 | 9 | 9 | 1937-1941, CA Tigre (9/9). |
| (324/636) | MARZOLINI Silvio | 04.10.1940 | 28 | 1 | 1960-1969, Club Ferro Carril Oeste (3/0), CA Boca Juniors Buenos Aires (25/1). |
| (370/699) | MÁS Oscar Tomás | 29.10.1946 | 35 | 8 | 1965-1972, CA River Plate Buenos Aires (35/8). |
| (389/728) | MASALIS Jorge Carlos | 10.03.1945 | 1 | 0 | 1967, CA Banfield (1/0). |
| (174/394) | MASANTONIO Herminio | 05.08.1910 | 19 | 20 | 1935-1942, CA Huracán Buenos Aires (19/20). |
| (776/1121) | MASCHERANO Javier Alejandro | 08.06.1984 | 95 | 2 | 2003-2013, CA River Plate Buenos Aires (14/0), SC Corinthians São Paulo (6/0), West Ham United FC London (2/0), Liverpool FC (39/2), FC Barcelona (34/0). |
| (275/560) | MASCHIO Humberto Dionisio | 20.02.1933 | 12 | 12 | 1956-1957, Racing Club Avellaneda (12/12). |
| (424/783) | MASTRÁNGELO Ernesto Enrique | 05.07.1948 | 7 | 1 | 1971-1972, CA Atlanta Buenos Aires (1/0), CA River Plate Buenos Aires (6/1). |
| (865/1207) | MATHEU Carlos Javier | 13.05.1985 | 1 | 0 | 2010, CA Independiente Avellaneda (1/0). |
| (49/133) | MATTOZZI Ernesto | | 22 | 1 | 1916-1923, Club Estudiantil Porteño Buenos Aires (22/1). |
| (92/211) | MÉDICI Ángel Segundo | 20.12.1897 | 34 | 0 | 1922-1928, CA Boca Juniors Buenos Aires (34/0). |
| (623/983) | MEDINA BELLO Ramón Ismael | 29.04.1966 | 17 | 5 | 1991-1994, CA River Plate Buenos Aires (14/5), Yokohama Marinos (3/0). |
| (369/696) | MEDINA Luis | 10.10.1940 | 1 | 0 | 1965, CA All Boys Buenos Aires (1/0). |

| | | | | | |
|---|---|---|---|---|---|
| (795/1131) | MEDINA Nicolás Rubén | 17.02.1982 | 1 | 0 | 2004, CA Rosario Central (1/0). |
| (162/341) | MEDINA Sebastián | | 1 | 0 | 1931, Club Central Córdoba Rosario (1/0). |
| (32/093) | MEIRA Alfredo | | 1 | 0 | 1913, Clun Atlético San Isidro (1/0). |
| (108/242) | MÉNDEZ G. | | 1 | 0 | 1923, Club San Fernando (1/0). |
| (861/1197) | MÉNDEZ Jesús Davíd José | 01.08.1984 | 2 | 0 | 2009-2010, CA Rosario Central (1/0), CA Boca Juniors Buenos Aires (1/0). |
| (228/491) | MÉNDEZ Norberto Doroteo | 05.01.1923 | 31 | 19 | 1945-1956, CA Huracán Buenos Aires (23/19), Racing Club Avellaneda (7/0), CA Tigre (1/0). |
| (728/1082) | MÉNDEZ Sebastián Ariel | 04.07.1977 | 2 | 0 | 1999, CA Vélez Sarsfield (2/0). |
| (436/797) | MENDOZA Mario Rubén | 19.01.1949 | 1 | 0 | 1972, CA Newell's Old Boys Rosario (1/0). |
| (299/593) | MENÉNDEZ Norberto | 14.12.1936 | 14 | 4 | 1957-1960, CA River Plate Buenos Aires (14/4). |
| (348/663) | MENOTTI César Luis | 05.11.1938 | 7 | 1 | 1962-1963, CA Rosario Central (7/1). |
| (866/1213) | MERCADO Gabriel Iván | 18.03.1987 | 1 | 0 | 2010, Racing Club de Avellaneda (1/0). |
| (865/1208) | MERCIER Juan Ignacio | 02.02.1980 | 3 | 0 | 2010, AA Argentinos Juniors Buenos Aires (3/0). |
| (434/793) | MERLO Reinaldo Carlo | 20.05.1950 | 3 | 0 | 1972, CA River Plate Buenos Aires (3/0). |
| (357/678) | MESIANO José Agustín | 01.05.1942 | 5 | 0 | 1963-1965, AA Argentinos Juniors Buenos Aires (4/0), CA Rosario Central (1/0). |
| (810/1144) | MESSI Lionel Andrés | 24.06.1987 | 83 | 37 | 2005-2013, FC Barcelona (83/37). |
| (260/534) | MICHELI Rodolfo Joaquín | 24.04.1930 | 14 | 10 | 1953-1956, CA Independiente Avellaneda (14/10). |
| (769/1108) | MILITO Diego Alberto | 12.06.1979 | 25 | 4 | 2003-2010, Racing Club Avellaneda (5/3), Genoa 1893 Genova (2/0), Real Zaragoza CD (7/1), Genoa CFC (5/0), Internazionale FC Milano (6/0). |
| (752/1091) | MILITO Gabriel Alejandro | 07.09.1980 | 42 | 1 | 2000-2011, CA Independiente Avellaneda (4/0), Real Zaragoza CD (22/0), FC Barcelona (16/1). |
| (168/367) | MINELLA José María | 30.11.1908 | 24 | 0 | 1933-1941, Club Gimnasia y Esgrima La Plata (7/0), CA River Plate Buenos Aires (16/0). |
| (392/737) | MINITTI Héctor Salvador | 06.05.1943 | 9 | 1 | 1968-1969, CA Lanús (8/1), CA River Plate Buenos Aires (1/0). |
| (623/984) | MOHAMED Antonio Ricardo | 02.04.1970 | 4 | 1 | 1991, CA Huracán Buenos Aires (4/1). |
| (39/114) | MOLFINO Aquiles | | 1 | 1 | 1914, Club Gimnasia y Esgrima Buenos Aires (1/1). |
| (286/577) | MOLINA Héctor | | 1 | 0 | 1956, CA Estudiantes de La Plata (1/0). |
| (29/081) | MOLINA Pablo | | 1 | 0 | 1912, CA Rosario Central (1/0). |
| (696/1061) | MOLINA Roberto Antonio | 28.10.1971 | 1 | 0 | 1996, CA Independiente Avellaneda (1/0). |
| (114/263) | MOLINARI Natalio | | 3 | 0 | 1924-1925, CA Belgrano Rosario (3/0). |
| (660/1014) | MONSERRAT Roberto Carlos | 13.09.1968 | 4 | 0 | 1993-1995, CA San Lorenzo de Almagro Buenos Aires (4/0). |
| (187/416) | MONTAÑÉS Oscar | 14.08.1912 | 15 | 0 | 1937-1942, Club Gimnasia y Esgrima La Plata (15/0). |
| (826/1156) | MONTENEGRO Daniel Gastón | 28.03.1979 | 3 | 0 | 2007-2009, CA Independiente Avellaneda (3/0). |
| (115/269) | MONTI Luis Felipe | 15.05.1901 | 16 | 5 | 1924-1931, CA San Lorenzo de Almagro Buenos Aires (15/4), Club Sportivo Palermo (1/1). |
| (895/1266) | MONTILLO Walter Damián | 14.04.1984 | 6 | 0 | 2011-2013, Cruzeiro EC Belo Horizonte (3/0), Santos FC (3/0). |
| (861/1192) | MONZÓN Luciano Fabián | 13.04.1987 | 7 | 0 | 2009-2011, CA Boca Juniors Buenos Aires (7/0). |
| (594/957) | MONZÓN Pedro Damián | 23.02.1962 | 15 | 1 | 1988-1990, CA Independiente Avellaneda (15/1). |
| (2/016) | MOORE Eugenio | | 1 | 0 | 1903, Club Alumni AC Buenos Aires (1/0). |
| (1/008) | MOORE Juan José | | 3 | 0 | 1902-1905, Club Alumni AC Buenos Aires (3/0). |
| (884/1249) | MORALES Diego Alberto | 29.11.1986 | 1 | 0 | 2011, CA Tigre (1/0). |
| (691/1054) | MORALES Hugo Alberto | 30.07.1974 | 9 | 2 | 1996-1997, Lanús AC (9/2). |
| (880/1236) | MORALEZ Maximiliano Nicolás | 26.02.1987 | 1 | 0 | 2011, CA Vélez Sarsfield (1/0). |
| (179/406) | MORENO José Manuel | 03.08.1916 | 34 | 19 | 1936-1950, CA River Plate Buenos Aires (32/19), CA Boca Juniors Buenos Aires (2/0). |
| (437/803) | MORETE Carlos Manuel | 14.01.1952 | 4 | 1 | 1973-1983, CA River Plate Buenos Aires (2/0), CA Independiente Avellaneda (2/1). |
| (148/311) | MOREYRAS Gerardo | | 1 | 0 | 1929, CA Boca Juniors Buenos Aires (1/0). |
| (149/317) | MORGADA Ismael | | 2 | 0 | 1929, Club Gimnasia y Esgrima La Plata (2/0). |
| (1/007) | MORGAN Edward | | 1 | 1 | 1902, Quilmes AC (1/1). |
| (698/1065) | MORIGI Guillermo Carlos | 01.03.1974 | 1 | 0 | 1996, CA Vélez Sarsfield (1/0). |
| (224/479) | MOROSANO Mario | 30.11.1917 | 1 | 0 | 1943, CA Newell's Old Boys Rosario (1/0). |
| (26/067) | MORRONI José | | 3 | 0 | 1912-1913, Club Atlético San Isidro (3/0). |
| (880/1239) | MOUCHE Pablo Nicolás | 11.10.1987 | 5 | 2 | 2011, CA Boca Juniors Buenos Aires (5/2). |
| (258/528) | MOURIÑO Eliseo Víctor | 03.06.1927 | 26 | 0 | 1952-1959, CA Banfield (2/0), CA Boca Juniors (24/0). |
| (461/833) | MOUZO Roberto | 08.01.1953 | 4 | 0 | 1974-1983, CA Boca Juniors Buenos Aires (4/0). |
| (297/588) | MOYANO Ramón | 30.11.1925 | 1 | 0 | 1957, CA Lanús (1/0). |
| (221/465) | MUÑOZ Juan Carlos | 04.03.1919 | 11 | 2 | 1942-1945, CA River Plate Buenos Aires (11/2). |
| (8/043) | MURPHY Martín | | 3 | 0 | 1908-1910, Belgrano AC Buenos Aires (3/0). |
| (7/039) | MURRAY Juan Antonio | | 2 | 0 | 1907-1909, Quilmes AC (2/0). |
| (311/610) | MURÚA Juan Carlos | 17.07.1935 | 11 | 0 | 1959-1960, Racing Club Avellaneda (11/0). |
| (885/1254) | MUSACCHIO Mateo Pablo | 26.08.1990 | 2 | 0 | 2011, Villarreal CF (2/0). |
| (258/531) | MUSIMESSI Julio Elías | 09.07.1823 | 16 | 0 | 1952-1957, CA Newell's Old Boys Rosario (2/0), CA Boca Juniors Buenos Aires (14/0). |
| (99/224) | MUTTIS Ramón Alfredo | 12.03.1899 | 11 | 0 | 1923-1930, CA Boca Juniors Buenos Aires (11/0). |
| (36/099) | MUTTONI Carlos | | 2 | 0 | 1913-1914, Racing Club Avellaneda (1/0), CA Independiente Avellaneda (1/0). |

| | | | | | |
|---|---|---|---|---|---|
| (172/390) | NAÓN Arturo | | 2 | 0 | 1934, Club Gimnasia y Esgrima La Plata (2/0). |
| (38/107) | NAÓN Ricardo | | 2 | 0 | 1914, CA Estudiantes de La Plata (2/0). |
| (312/613) | NARDIELLO Osvaldo Ángel | 31.08.1936 | 12 | 5 | 1959-1960, CA Boca Juniors Buenos Aires (12/5). |
| (321/628) | NAVARRO Rubén Marino | 30.03.1933 | 32 | 0 | 1960-1963, CA Independiente Avellaneda (32/0). |
| (285/573) | NAWACKI Juan | | 1 | 0 | 1956, AA Argentinos Juniors Buenos Aires (1/0). |
| (327/637) | NAZIONALE José | 30.03.1927 | 2 | 0 | 1960, CA Lanús (2/0). |
| (223/474) | NEGRI Juan José | 08.03.1920 | 1 | 0 | 1943, CA Estudiantes de La Plata (1/0). |
| (32/091) | NEGRI Mario Luis | | 1 | 0 | 1913, Club Estudiantil Porteño Buenos Aires (1/0). |
| (310/600) | NEGRI Osvaldo Jorge | 30.11.1932 | 10 | 0 | 1959, Racing Club Avellaneda (10/0). |
| (171/380) | NEHÍN José Eduardo | 13.10.1905 | 1 | 0 | 1934, Club Sportivo Desamparados San Juan (1/0). |

| | | | | | |
|---|---|---|---|---|---|
| (690/1050) | NETTO Carlos Javier | 24.07.1970 | **1** | **1** | 1995, CA San Lorenzo de Almagro Buenos Aires (1/1). |
| (416/772) | NICOLAU Miguel Alberto | 20.06.1946 | **2** | **1** | 1971, CA Boca Juniors Buenos Aires (2/1). |
| (100/230) | NÓBILE Carlos | | **3** | **0** | 1923-1925, CA Huracán Buenos Aires (3/0). |
| (225/484) | NOCEDA Rubén Omar | | **2** | **0** | 1943, Club Ferro Carril Oeste (2/0). |
| (114/261) | NUIN Bernardo | | **1** | **0** | 1924, CA Newell's Old Boys Rosario (1/0). |
| (310/601) | NUÍN Julio Alberto | | **1** | **0** | 1959, CA River Plate Buenos Aires (1/0). |
| | | | | | |
| (416/775) | OBBERTI Alfredo Domingo | 12.08.1945 | **1** | **0** | 1971, CA Newell's Old Boys Rosario (1/0). |
| (516/897) | OCAÑO Victorio Orlando | 09.06.1954 | **4** | **0** | 1979-1980, CA Talleres de Córdoba (4/0). |
| (66/163) | OCHANDÍO Alberto | | **5** | **5** | 1919, CA Estudiantes Buenos Aires (5/5). |
| (137/301) | OCHOA BAIGORRI Pedro | | **2** | **0** | 1927-1928, Racing Club Avellaneda (2/0). |
| (236/497) | OGANDO Gabriel Mario | 22.08.1921 | **5** | **0** | 1945-1952, CA Estudiantes de La Plata (5/0). |
| (26/068) | OHACO Alberto Bernardino | | **13** | **7** | 1912-1918, Racing Club Avellaneda (13/7). |
| (705/1074) | OJEDA Marcelo Leonardo | 08.12.1968 | **1** | **0** | 1997, CD Tenerife (1/0). |
| (542/915) | OLARTICOECHEA Julio Jorge | 18.10.1958 | **27** | **0** | 1983-1990, CA River Plate Buenos Aires (3/0), CA Boca Juniors Buenos Aires (9/0), AA Argentinos Juniors Buenos Aires (6/0), Racing Club Avellaneda (9/0). |
| (44/123) | OLAZAR Francisco | 10.07.1885 | **17** | **1** | 1916-1919, Racing Club Avellaneda (17/1). |
| (346/661) | OLENIAK Juan Carlos | 04.03.1942 | **2** | **0** | 1962, AA Argentinos Juniors Buenos Aires (2/0). |
| (472/862) | OLGUÍN Jorge Mario | 17.05.1952 | **58** | **0** | 1976-1982, CA San Lorenzo de Almagro Buenos Aires (38/0), CA Independiente Avellaneda (20/0). |
| (30/085) | OLIVARI Alberto | | **7** | **0** | 1912-1915, Club Atlético San Isidro (7/0). |
| (401/754) | OLMEDO Jorge Héctor | 09.02.1944 | **2** | **1** | 1968, CA Huracán Buenos Aires (2/1). |
| (868/1223) | OLMEDO Nicolás Andrés | 10.03.1983 | **1** | **0** | 2010, CD Godoy Cruz (1/0). |
| (116/273) | OMAR Pedro | | **4** | **0** | 1924-1929, CA San Lorenzo de Almagro Buenos Aires (4/0). |
| (377/705) | ONEGA Daniel Germán | 17.03.1945 | **14** | **0** | 1966-1972, CA River Plate Buenos Aires (13/0), Racing Club Avellaneda (1/0). |
| (321/632) | ONEGA Ermindo Ángel | 30.04.1940 | **30** | **11** | 1960-1967, CA River Plate Buenos Aires (30/11). |
| (246/504) | ONGARO Saúl F. | 24.08.1916 | **1** | **0** | 1946, CA Estudiantes de La Plata (1/0). |
| (95/219) | ONZARI Cesáreo Juan | 1903 | **15** | **5** | 1922-1924, CA Huracán Buenos Aires (15/5). |
| (921/1279) | ORBÁN Lucas Alfonso | 03.02.1989 | **1** | **0** | 2013, Girondins de Bordeaux (1/0). |
| (894/1260) | ORIÓN Agustín Ignacio | 26.07.1981 | **3** | **0** | 2011-2012, CA Boca Juniors Buenos Aires (3/0). |
| (135/294) | ORLANDINI Rodolfo Orlando | 01.01.1905 | **10** | **0** | 1927-1930, CS Sportivo Buenos Aires (10/0). |
| (115/271) | ORSI Raimundo Bibiani | 02.12.1901 | **13** | **3** | 1924-1936, CA Independiente Avellaneda (13/3). |
| (660/1015) | ORTEGA Ariel Arnaldo | 04.03.1974 | **87** | **17** | 1993-2010, CA River Plate Buenos Aires (34/6), Valencia CF (22/6), Sampdoria UC Genova (3/0), AC Parma (12/4), CA River Plate Buenos Aires (13/1), Fenerbahçe SK Istanbul (2/0), CA River Plate Buenos Aires (1/0). |
| (602/974) | ORTEGA Jorge Alberto | | **1** | **0** | 1989, Club Deportivo Español Buenos Aires (1/0). |
| (462/837) | ORTÍZ Oscar Alberto | 08.04.1953 | **23** | **2** | 1975-1979, CA San Lorenzo de Almagro Buenos Aires (3/0), CA River Plate Buenos Aires (20/2). |
| (395/745) | OSTÚA Héctor Alberto | 11.09.1945 | **3** | **0** | 1968, CA Lanús (3/0). |
| (855/1175) | OTAMENDI Nicolás Hernán | 12.02.1988 | **16** | **1** | 2009-2013, CA Vélez Sarsfield (10/0), FC do Porto (6/1). |
| (511/886) | OUTES Norberto Daniel | 10.10.1953 | **2** | **0** | 1979, CA Independiente Avellaneda (20). |
| (383/709) | OVEJERO Iselín Santos | 16.10.1945 | **4** | **0** | 1967, CA Vélez Sarsfield (4/0). |
| (400/751) | OVIDE Armando Oscar | 03.09.1947 | **2** | **0** | 1968, CA Boca Juniors Buenos Aires (2/0). |
| (467/858) | OVIEDO Miguel Ángel | 12.10.1950 | **9** | **0** | 1975-1979, CA Talleres de Córdoba (9/0). |
| | | | | | |
| (388/718) | PACHAMÉ Carlos Oscar | 25.02.1944 | **9** | **0** | 1967-1969, CA Estudiantes de La Plata (9/0). |
| (343/660) | PÁEZ Raúl Alberto | 25.06.1937 | **3** | **0** | 1962, CA San Lorenzo de Almagro Buenos Aires (3/0). |
| (341/655) | PAGANI Marcelo Ernesto | 19.08.1941 | **6** | **2** | 1961-1962, CA Rosario Central (2/1), CA River Plate Buenos Aires (4/1). |
| (494/876) | PAGNANINI Rubén Oscar | 31.01.1949 | **4** | **1** | 1978, CA Independiente Avellaneda (4/1). |
| (222/469) | PAIROUX Norberto José | | **1** | **0** | 1942, CA Atlanta Buenos Aires (1/0). |
| (800/1137) | PALACIO Rodrigo Sebastián | 05.02.1982 | **20** | **2** | 2005-2013, CA Boca Juniors Buenos Aires (8/1), Genoa CFC (1/0), FC Internazionale Milano (11/1). |
| (727/1080) | PALERMO Martín | 07.11.1973 | **15** | **9** | 1999-2010, CA Boca Juniors Buenos Aires (15/9). |
| (233/495) | PALMA Nicolás | | **6** | **0** | 1945-1947, CA Estudiantes de La Plata (4/0), Racing Club Avellaneda (2/0). |
| (327/638) | PANDO Martín Esteban | 26.12.1834 | **13** | **3** | 1960-1962, AA Argentinos Juniors Buenos Aires (12/3), CA River Plate Buenos Aires (1/0). |
| (730/1086) | PANDOLFI Fernando Daniel | 29.05.1974 | **2** | **0** | 1999, CA Vélez Sarsfield (2/0). |
| (459/826) | PAOLINO Jorge | 12.07.1949 | **3** | **0** | 1974, CA Huracán Buenos Aires (3/0). |
| (851/1170) | PAPA Emiliano Ramiro | 19.04.1982 | **8** | **0** | 2008-2011, CA Vélez Sarsfield (8/0). |
| (109/252) | PARDAL Manuel | | **1** | **0** | 1923, CA Platense Buenos Aires (1/0). |
| (388/720) | PARDO Mario | 01.06.1943 | **6** | **1** | 1967-1968, Club Gimnasia y Esgrima La Plata (6/1). |
| (878/1226) | PAREJA Nicolás Martín | 19.01.1984 | **1** | **0** | 2010, FK Spartak Moskva (1/0). |
| (564/939) | PASCULLI Pedro Pablo | 17.05.1960 | **16** | **4** | 1985-1987, AA Argentinos Juniors Buenos Aires (9/3), US Lecce (7/1). |
| (401/752) | PASCUTTINI Aurelio José | 19.03.1944 | **3** | **0** | 1968-1969, CA Rosario Central (3/0). |
| (472/863) | PASSARELLA Daniel Alberto | 25.05.1953 | **69** | **23** | 1976-1986, CA River Plate Buenos Aires (58/21), AC Fiorentina Firenze (11/2). |
| (690/1046) | PASSET Oscar Fernando | 12.10.1965 | **2** | **0** | 1995-1996, CA San Lorenzo de Almagro Buenos Aires (2/0). |
| (869/1225) | PASTORE Javier Matías | 20.06.1989 | **13** | **0** | 2010-2011, US Città di Palermo (10/0), Paris Saint-Germain FC (3/0). |
| (411/764) | PASTORIZA José Omar | 23.05.1942 | **16** | **1** | 1970-1972, CA Independiente Avellaneda (16/1). |
| (140/303) | PATERNÓSTER Fernando | 24.05.1903 | **16** | **0** | 1928-1930, Racing Club Avellaneda (16/0). |
| (166/352) | PATRIGNANI Atilio | | **2** | **0** | 1932, Club All Boys Buenos Aires (2/0). |
| (464/843) | PAVÓN Rafael Eloy Tomás | 04.11.1953 | **2** | **0** | 1975, CA Belgrano Córdoba (2/0). |
| (826/1157) | PAVONE Hugo Mariano | 27.05.1982 | **1** | **0** | 2007, CA Estudiantes de La Plata (1/0). |
| (463/841) | PAVONI José Luis | 23.05.1954 | **4** | **0** | 1975, CA Newell's Old Boys Rosario (4/0). |
| (694/1057) | PAZ Pablo Ariel | 27.01.1973 | **14** | **1** | 1996-1998, CA Banfield (1/0), CD Tenerifa (13/1). |

| | | | | | |
|---|---|---|---|---|---|
| (30/082) | PEARSON Carlos | | **1** | **0** | 1912, Quilmes AC (1/0). |
| (196/441) | PEDERNERA Adolfo Alfredo | 15.11.1918 | **21** | **7** | 1940-1946, CA River Plate Buenos Aires (21/7). |
| (285/575) | PEDERZOLI Héctor César | | **4** | **0** | 1956-1960, AA Argentinos Juniors Buenos Aires (2/0), CA River Plate Buenos Aires (2/0). |
| (171/378) | PEDEVILLA Juan Carlos | 06.06.1909 | **1** | **0** | 1934, CA Estudiantil Porteño Buenos Aires (1/0). |
| (222/470) | PELEGRINA Manuel Gregorio | 29.11.1919 | **4** | **1** | 1942-1945, CA Estudiantes de La Plata (4/1). |
| (704/1071) | PELLEGRINO Mauricio Andrés | 05.10.1971 | **3** | **0** | 1997, CA Vélez Sarsfield (3/0). |
| (440/805) | PENA Hugo | 28.11.1951 | **1** | **0** | 1973, AA Argentinos Juniors Buenos Aires (1/0). |
| (135/296) | PENELLA Donato | | **2** | **0** | 1927, CA Boca Juniors Buenos Aires (2/0). |
| (270/552) | PENTRELLI Luis | 15.06.1932 | **7** | **0** | 1956, Club Gimnasia y Esgrima La Plata (7/0). |
| (33/094) | PEPE Ricardo | | **2** | **0** | 1913-1917, Racing Club Avellaneda (2/0). |
| (587/952) | PERCUDANI José Alberto | 22.03.1965 | **5** | **0** | 1987, CA Independiente Avellaneda (5/0). |
| (123/279) | PERDUCCA Feliciano | | **5** | **0** | 1925-1928, CA Temperley (3/0), CA Boca Alumni Buenos Aires (2/0). |
| (26/069) | PEREYRA Antonio Ameal | | **1** | **0** | 1912, CA River Plate Buenos Aires (1/0). |
| (868/1224) | PEREYRA Juan Pablo | 30.05.1984 | **1** | **0** | 2010, Club Atlético Tucumán (1/0). |
| (302/594) | PÉREZ Alfredo Ricardo | 10.04.1929 | **3** | **0** | 1957-1958, CA River Plate Buenos Aires (3/0). |
| (861/1193) | PÉREZ Enzo Nicolás | 22.06.1986 | **6** | **1** | 2009-2012, Club Estudiantes de La Plata (5/1), Sport Lisboa e Benfica (1/0). |
| (658/1013) | PÉREZ Hugo Leonardo | 06.09.1968 | **14** | **2** | 1993-1995, CA Independiente Avellaneda (5/1), Real Sporting Gijón (9/1). |
| (113/257) | PÉREZ L. | | **1** | **0** | 1924, Club San Fernando (1/0). |
| (167/361) | PÉREZ Víctor | | **1** | **0** | 1932, CA Almagro Buenos Aires (1/0). |
| (377/704) | PERFUMO Roberto Alfredo | 03.10.1942 | **37** | **0** | 1966-1974, Racing Club Avellaneda (30/0), Cruzeiro EC Belo Horizonte (7/0). |
| (109/248) | PERINETTI Juan Natalio | 28.12.1900 | **6** | **0** | 1923-1930, Racing Club Avellaneda (6/0). |
| (41/118) | PERINETTI Juan Nelusco | | **18** | **0** | 1915-1919, Racing Club Avellaneda (18/0). |
| (437/802) | PERNÍA Vicente Alberto | 25.05.1949 | **10** | **0** | 1973-1977, CA Boca Juniors Buenos Aires (10/0). |
| (864/1205) | PEROTTI Diego | 26.07.1988 | **2** | **0** | 2009-2011, Sevilla FC (2/0). |
| (508/885) | PEROTTI Hugo Osmar | 06.03.1959 | **2** | **0** | 1979, CA Boca Juniors Buenos Aires (2/0). |
| (113/260) | PERTINI Dante | | **1** | **0** | 1924, CA Boca Juniors Buenos Aires (1/0). |
| (6/034) | PERTINO R. | | **1** | **0** | 1907, CA Porteño Buenos Aires (1/0). |
| (195/432) | PERUCCA Ángel | 19.08.1918 | **26** | **2** | 1940-1947, CA Newell's Old Boys Rosario (26/2). |
| (906/1269) | PERUZZI LUCCHETTI Gino | 09.06.1992 | **4** | **0** | 2012-2013, CA Vélez Sarsfield (4/0). |
| (243/503) | PESCIA Natalio Agustín | 01.01.1922 | **12** | **0** | 1946-1954, CA Boca Juniors Buenos Aires (12/0). |
| (147/308) | PEUCELLE Carlos Desiderio | 13.09.1908 | **28** | **13** | 1928-1940, CS Sportivo Buenos Aires (11/6), CA River Plate Buenos Aires (17/7). |
| (24/066) | PIAGGIO Antonio | | **5** | **2** | 1911-1914, CA Porteño Buenos Aires (5/2). |
| (376/703) | PIANETTI Oscar Antonio | 01.10.1942 | **2** | **0** | 1965-1967, CA Boca Juniors Buenos Aires (2/0). |
| (886/1255) | PIATTI Pablo Daniel | 31.03.1989 | **1** | **0** | 2011, UD Almería (1/0). |
| (426/784) | PIAZZA Osvaldo José | 06.04.1947 | **7** | **0** | 1972, CA Lanús (7/0). |
| (880/1231) | PILLUD Iván Alexis | 24.04.1986 | **5** | **0** | 2011, Racing Club de Avellaneda (5/0). |
| (693/1056) | PINEDA Héctor Mauricio | 13.07.1975 | **10** | **1** | 1996-1998, CA Huracán Buenos Aires (1/0), CA Boca Juniors Buenos Aires (1/0), Udinese Calcio (8/1). |
| (828/1161) | PINOLA Javier Horacio | 24.02.1983 | **1** | **0** | 2007, 1.FC Nürnberg (1/0). |
| (263/539) | PIZARRO Federico A. | 17.01.1927 | **7** | **0** | 1954-1957, CA Chacarita Juniors Buenos Aires (2/0), CA San Lorenzo de Almagro Buenos Aires (5/0). |
| (310/604) | PIZZUTI Juan José | 09.05.1927 | **12** | **4** | 1959-1961, Racing Club Avellaneda (12/4). |
| (752/1094) | PLACENTE Diego Rodolfo | 24.04.1977 | **22** | **0** | 2000-2005, CA River Plate Buenos Aires (1/0), TSV Bayer 04 Leverkusen (21/0). |
| (729/1084) | POCHETTINO Mauricio Roberto | 02.03.1973 | **20** | **2** | 1999-2002, CD Espanyol Barcelona (8/1), Paris St.Germain FC (12/1). |
| (28/080) | POLIMENI Pascual | | **11** | **2** | 1912-1921, CA Argentino Quilmes Buenos Aires (4/1), CA Porteño Buenos Aires (5/1), Club Sportivo Palermo Buenos Aires (2/0). |
| (543/923) | PONCE José Daniel | 26.06.1962 | **24** | **4** | 1983-1985, CA Estudiantes de La Plata (24/4). |
| (436/796) | PONCE Ramón Héctor | 05.07.1948 | **8** | **0** | 1972-1973, CA Boca Juniors Buenos Aires (8/0). |
| (221/466) | PONTONI René Alejandro | 18.05.1920 | **19** | **19** | 1942-1947, CA Newell's Old Boys Rosario (3/4), CA San Lorenzo de Almagro Buenos Aires (16/15). |
| (769/1104) | PONZIO Leonardo Daniel | 29.01.1982 | **8** | **0** | 2003-2013, CA Newell's Old Boys Rosario (2/0), Real Zaragoza CD (4/0), CA River Plate Buenos Aires (2/0). |
| (706/1075) | POSSE Martín Andrés | 02.08.1975 | **3** | **0** | 1997, CA Vélez Sarsfield (3/0). |
| (426/786) | POTENTE Osvaldo Rubén | 16.11.1951 | **3** | **0** | 1972-1974, CA Boca Juniors Buenos Aires (3/0). |
| (35/098) | POVEY Luis | | **1** | **0** | 1913, CA Newell's Old Boys Rosario (1/0). |
| (95/216) | POWER Santiago | | **3** | **0** | 1922, Club Sportivo Dock Sud Buenos Aires (3/0). |
| (447/819) | POY Aldo Pedro | 14.09.1945 | **2** | **0** | 1973-1974, CA Rosario Central (2/0). |
| (855/1172) | POZO Diego Raúl | 16.02.1978 | **3** | **0** | 2009-2010, CA Colón de Santa Fé (3/0). |
| (264/543) | PRADO Eliseo | 17.09.1929 | **7** | **3** | 1954-1958, CA River Plate Buenos Aires (7/3). |
| (198/446) | PRADO Juan | | **3** | **0** | 1940, CA Platense Buenos Aires (3/0). |
| (108/241) | PRATO Juan | 06.06.1903 | **1** | **0** | 1923, CA Huracán Buenos Aires (1/0). |
| (855/1180) | PREDIGUER Leonardo Sebastián | 04.09.1986 | **1** | **0** | 2009, CA Colón de Santa Fé (1/0). |
| (79/182) | PRESTA Juan Salvador | | **6** | **0** | 1920-1923, CA Porteño Buenos Aires (6/0). |
| (362/684) | PROSPITTI Pedro | 24.07.1941 | **3** | **2** | 1964, CA Independiente Avellaneda (3/2). |
| (165/350) | PUJOLÁS Nicolás | | **1** | **0** | 1931, CA Estudiantil Porteño Buenos Aires (1/0). |
| (544/926) | PUMPIDO Nery Alberto | 30.07.1957 | **38** | **0** | 1983-1990, CA Vélez Sarsfield (8/0), CA River Plate Buenos Aires (17/0), Real Betis Balompié Sevilla (13/0). |
| (287/580) | PUPPO Roberto Jesús | | **1** | **0** | 1956, CA Newell's Old Boys Rosario (1/0). |

| | | | | | |
|---|---|---|---|---|---|
| (166/353) | QUERIDO Lucio | | **2** | **0** | 1932, CA Defensores de Belgrano (2/0). |
| (883/1245) | QUÍLEZ Ismael Alberto | 02.10.1988 | **2** | **0** | 2011, CA Colón de Santa Fé (2/0). |
| (467/853) | QUINTEROS Armando Ignacio | 28.03.1955 | **3** | **0** | 1975, CA Vélez Sarsfield (3/0). |

| | | | | | |
|---|---|---|---|---|---|
| (764/1099) | QUIROGA Facundo Hernán | 10.01.1978 | **16** | **0** | 2002-2004, Sporting Clube de Portugal Lisboa (12/0), VfL Wolfsburg (4/0). |
| (368/695) | RAFFO Norberto Santiago | 12.04.1939 | **4** | **0** | 1965-1967, CA Banfield (2/0), Racing Club Avellaneda (2/0). |
| (413/766) | RAIMONDO Miguel Ángel | 12.12.1943 | **8** | **1** | 1970-1972, CA Independiente Avellaneda (8/1). |
| (332/647) | RAMACIOTTI Ricardo José María | | **6** | **1** | 1960-1961, AA Argentinos Juniors Buenos Aires (6/1). |
| (671/1024) | RAMBERT Sebastián Pascual | 30.01.1974 | **8** | **4** | 1994-1995, CA Independiente Avellaneda (7/4), Internazionale FC Milano (1/0). |
| (690/1047) | RAMÍREZ Juan Carlos | 07.03.1975 | **1** | **0** | 1995, CA Independiente Avellaneda (1/0). |
| (305/598) | RAMOS DELGADO José Manuel | 25.08.1935 | **25** | **0** | 1958-1965, CA Lanús (1/0), CA River Plate Buenos Aires (24/0). |
| (215/460) | RAMOS José | | **11** | **0** | 1942-1946, CA River Plate Buenos Aires (11/0). |
| (542/920) | RAMOS Víctor Rogelio | 04.09.1958 | **10** | **1** | 1983-1984, CA Newell's Old Boys Rosario (10/1). |
| (9/048) | RATCLIFF Haroldo | | **1** | **0** | 1908, Belgrano AC Buenos Aires (1/0). |
| (316/615) | RATTÍN Antonio Ubaldo | 16.05.1937 | **34** | **1** | 1959-1969, CA Boca Juniors Buenos Aires (34/1). |
| (116/274) | RAVASCHINO Luis | | **1** | **0** | 1924, CA Independiente Avellaneda (1/0). |
| (865/1211) | RAZZOTTI Franco | 06.02.1985 | **1** | **0** | 2010, CA Vélez Sarsfield (1/0). |
| (463/840) | REBOTTARO Andrés Orlando | 05.09.1952 | **6** | **0** | 1975-1976, CA Newell's Old Boys Rosario (6/0). |
| (66/159) | RECANATINI Humberto Juan | | **17** | **2** | 1919-1931, Club Sportivo Almagro Buenos Aires (17/2). |
| (405/757) | RECIO Jorge | 02.01.1942 | **2** | **0** | 1969, CA River Plate Buenos Aires (2/0). |
| (639/1003) | REDONDO Fernando Carlos | 06.06.1969 | **29** | **1** | 1992-1999, CD Tenerife (26/1), Real Madrid CF (3/0). |
| (508/882) | REINALDI José Omar | 21.05.1949 | **2** | **0** | 1979, CA Talleres de Córdoba (2/0). |
| (361/681) | RENDO Alberto | 03.01.1940 | **16** | **5** | 1964-1969, CA Huracán Buenos Aires (5/2), CA San Lorenzo de Almagro Buenos Aires (11/3). |
| (28/073) | REPARAZ Arturo | | **3** | **0** | 1912-1914, Club Gimnasia y Esgrima Buenos Aires (3/0). |
| (44/121) | REYES Armando | | **22** | **0** | 1916-1919, Racing Club Avellaneda (22/0). |
| (329/643) | REYNOSO Guillermo César | 19.08.1933 | **1** | **0** | 1960, CA San Lorenzo de Almagro Buenos Aires (1/0). |
| (418/777) | REZZA Ricardo Néstor | 04.07.1948 | **5** | **0** | 1971, CA San Lorenzo de Almagro Buenos Aires (5/0). |
| (227/487) | RICARDO Héctor | 10.02.1925 | **7** | **0** | 1945, CA Rosario Central (7/0). |
| (364/687) | RIGHI Ediberto Luis | 15.06.1936 | **3** | **0** | 1964, CA Banfield (3/0). |
| (543/925) | RINALDI Jorge Roberto | 23.03.1963 | **14** | **0** | 1983-1985, CA San Lorenzo de Almagro Buenos Aires (14/0). |
| (855/1177) | RINAUDO Fabián Andrés | 15.05.1987 | **4** | **0** | 2009-2011, Club de Gimnasia y Esgrima La Plata (3/0), Sporting Clube de Portugal Lisboa (1/0). |
| (712/1076) | RIQUELME Juan Román | 24.06.1978 | **51** | **17** | 1997-2008, CA Boca Juniors Buenos Aires (7/0), FC Barcelona (3/1), Villarreal CF (27/7), CA Boca Juniors Buenos Aires (5/5), Villarreal CF (4/4), CA Boca Juniors Buenos Aires (5/0). |
| (19/060) | RITHNER Juan José | | **10** | **0** | 1910-1916, CA Porteño Buenos Aires (10/0). |
| (38/108) | RITHNER Pedro | | **1** | **0** | 1914, Club Baradero (1/0). |
| (152/320) | RIVAROLA Juan Antonio | | **6** | **0** | 1929-1935, CA Colón de Santa Fe (3/0), CA Huracán Buenos Aires (3/0). |
| (92/212) | RIVET Julio | | **5** | **0** | 1922, Club Del Plata Buenos Aires (5/0). |
| (702/1069) | ROA Carlos Ángel | 15.08.1969 | **16** | **0** | 1997-1999, Lanús AC (6/0), RCD Mallorca (10/0). |
| (462/835) | ROCCHIA Juan Domingo Antonio | 13.06.1951 | **1** | **0** | 1975, Club Ferro Carril Oeste (1/0). |
| (482/868) | ROCHA Juan Ramón | 08.03.1954 | **3** | **0** | 1976-1977, CA Newell's Old Boys Rosario (3/0). |
| (3/017) | RODMAN J. | | **1** | **0** | 1905, Quilmes AC (1/0). |
| (187/418) | RODOLFI Bruno | 26.04.1915 | **9** | **1** | 1937-1942, CA River Plate Buenos Aires (9/1). |
| (769/1111) | RODRÍGUEZ Clemente Juan | 31.07.1981 | **20** | **0** | 2003-2013, CA Boca Juniors Buenos Aires (7/0), FK Spartak Moskva (2/0), Club Estudiantes de La Plata (4/0), CA Boca Juniors Buenos Aires (7/0). |
| (225/482) | RODRÍGUEZ Eduardo Enrique | 20.05.1918 | **3** | **0** | 1943-1945, CA Estudiantes de La Plata (2/0), CA River Plate Buenos Aires (1/0). |
| (162/337) | RODRÍGUEZ F. | | **2** | **0** | 1931, CA Banfield (2/0). |
| (769/1110) | RODRÍGUEZ Javier Gonzálo | 10.04.1984 | **6** | **1** | 2003-2008, CA San Lorenzo de Almagro Buenos Aires (2/1), Villarreal CF (4/0). |
| (592/955) | RODRÍGUEZ José Luis | 21.07.1963 | **6** | **0** | 1987-1988, Club Deportivo Español Buenos Aires (6/0). |
| (310/609) | RODRÍGUEZ Juan José | 11.01.1937 | **6** | **0** | 1959, CA Boca Juniors Buenos Aires (6/0). |
| (630/999) | RODRÍGUEZ Leonardo Adrián | 27.08.1966 | **29** | **2** | 1991-1994, CA San Lorenzo de Almagro Buenos Aires (6/0), SC Toulon (3/0), Atalanta Calcio Bergamo (17/2), BVB Borussia Dortmund (3/0). |
| (861/1198) | RODRÍGUEZ Luis Miguel | 01.01.1985 | **1** | **0** | 2009, Club Atlético Tucumán (1/0). |
| (343/659) | RODRÍGUEZ Mario | | **10** | **5** | 1962-1963, CA Chacarita Juniors Buenos Aires (10/5). |
| (774/1117) | RODRÍGUEZ Maximiliano Rubén | 02.01.1981 | **52** | **15** | 2003-2013, RCD Espanyol Barcelona (9/1), Club Atlético de Madrid (32/11), Liverpool FC (2/0), CA Newell's Old Boys (9/3). |
| (54/143) | ROFRANO Nicolás | | **6** | **0** | 1917-1922, CA River Plate Buenos Aires (5/0), Alvear Buenos Aires (1/0). |
| (388/719) | ROGEL Roberto Domingo | 20.07.1944 | **10** | **1** | 1967-1974, Club Gimnasia y Esgrima La Plata (2/0), CA Boca Juniors Buenos Aires (8/1). |
| (30/087) | ROGERS Juan Manuel | | **3** | **0** | 1912-1913, Provincial Rosario (3/0). |
| (305/597) | ROJAS Alfredo Hugo | 20.02.1937 | **14** | **2** | 1957-1967, CA Lanús (3/0), Club Gimnasia y Esgrima La Plata (5/2), CA Boca Juniors Buenos Aires (6/0). |
| (370/697) | ROJAS Ángel Clemente | 28.08.1944 | **3** | **1** | 1965-1966, CA Boca Juniors Buenos Aires (3/1). |
| (880/1234) | ROJAS Ariel Mauricio | 16.01.1986 | **3** | **0** | 2011, CD Godoy Cruz Mendoza (3/0). |
| (14/054) | ROJO Enrique | | **1** | **0** | 1910, CA Estudiantes Buenos Aires (1/0). |
| (879/1227) | ROJO Faustino Marcos Alberto | 20.03.1990 | **19** | **0** | 2011-2013, FK Spartak Moskva (9/0), Sporting Clube de Portugal Lisboa (10/0). |
| (493/875) | ROLDÁN Omar Pedro | 10.09.1949 | **1** | **0** | 1977, CA Vélez Sarsfield (1/0). |
| (285/570) | ROMA Antonio | 13.07.1932 | **42** | **0** | 1956-1967, Club Ferro Carril Oeste (4/0), CA Boca Juniors Buenos Aires (38/0). |
| (771/1113) | ROMAGNOLI Leandro Attilio | 17.03.1981 | **1** | **0** | 2003, CA San Lorenzo de Almagro Buenos Aires (1/0). |
| (800/1136) | ROMAGNOLI Martín Andrés | 30.01.1977 | **1** | **0** | 2005, CA Colón de Santa Fe (1/0). |
| (752/1097) | ROMEO Bernardo Daniel | 10.09.1977 | **4** | **1** | 2000-2003, CA San Lorenzo de Almagro Buenos Aires (2/0), Hamburger SV (2/1). |

| | | | | | |
|---|---|---|---|---|---|
| (800/1142) | ROMERO Sebastián Ariel | 27.04.1978 | 1 | 0 | 2005, Racing Club Avellaneda (1/0). |
| (860/1190) | ROMERO Sergio Germán | 22.02.1987 | 44 | 0 | 2009-2013, AZ'67 Alkmaar (21/0), UC Sampdoria Genova (18/0), AS Monaco (5/0). |
| (921/1278) | RONCAGLIA Facundo Sebastián | 10.02.1987 | 1 | 0 | 2013, AC Fiorentina Firenze (1/0). |
| (111/254) | RONZONI Guillermo | | 2 | 0 | 1924, CA El Porvenir Gerli (2/0). |
| (104/236) | ROSADO Antonio | | 1 | 0 | 1923, Club Sportivo Barracas (1/0). |
| (784/1124) | ROSALES Mauro Damián | 24.02.1981 | 10 | 1 | 2004, CA Newell's Old Boys Rosario (10/1). |
| (385/713) | ROSL Antonio | 21.03.1944 | 13 | 0 | 1967-1973, Club Gimnasia y Esgrima La Plata (3/0), CA San Lorenzo de Almagro Buenos Aires (10/0). |
| (7/038) | ROSS Guillermo | | 1 | 0 | 1907, Club Alumni CA Buenos Aires (1/0). |
| (8/046) | ROSSI Juan | | 3 | 0 | 1908-1913, Club Atlético San Isidro (3/0). |
| (248/508) | ROSSI Néstor Raúl | 10.05.1925 | 26 | 0 | 1947-1958, CA River Plate Buenos Aires (26/0). |
| (287/579) | ROSSI Oscar Pablo | 20.07.1930 | 21 | 0 | 1956-1963, CA Huracán Buenos Aires (3/0), CA San Lorenzo de Almagro Buenos Aires (18/0). |
| (677/1031) | ROTCHEN Pablo Oscar | 23.04.1973 | 4 | 0 | 195-1997, CA Independiente Avellaneda (4/0). |
| (11/049) | ROTHSCHILD Eduardo | | 3 | 0 | 1909-1910, Club Atlético San Isidro (1/0), Club Gimnasia y Esgrima Buenos Aires (2/0). |
| (171/382) | RÚA Francisco | 04.02.1911 | 1 | 0 | 1934, Club Sportivo Dock Sud Buenos Aires (1/0). |
| (886/1257) | RUBEN RODRÍGUEZ Marco Gastón | 26.10.1986 | 1 | 1 | 2011, Villarreal CF (1/1). |
| (542/914) | RUGGERI Oscar Alfredo | 26.01.1962 | 97 | 7 | 1983-1994, CA Boca Juniors Buenos Aires (9/1), CA River Plate Buenos Aires (30/3), CD Logroñés (6/0), Real Madrid CF (10/0), CA Vélez Sarsfield (16/1), Ancona Calcio (3/0), CF América Ciudad de México (14/1), CA San Lorenzo de Almagro Buenos Aires (9/1). |
| (254/514) | RUGILO Miguel Ángel | 19.01.1919 | 4 | 0 | 1950-1951, CA Vélez Sarsfield (4/0). |
| (316/617) | RUÍZ Miguel Ángel | 01.10.1934 | 5 | 1 | 1959, CA San Lorenzo de Almagro Buenos Aires (5/1). |
| (391/734) | RULLI Juan Carlos | 11.04.1937 | 9 | 0 | 1967-1969, Racing Club Avellaneda (9/0). |
| (22/064) | RUSS Cirilo | | 3 | 0 | 1911-1912, Quilmes AC (3/0). |
| (441/809) | RUSSO Francisco Faustino | 22.10.1944 | 3 | 0 | 1973-1974, CA Huracán Buenos Aires (3/0). |
| (546/930) | RUSSO Miguel Ángel | 09.04.1956 | 17 | 1 | 1983-1985, CA Estudiantes de La Plata (17/1). |

| | | | | | |
|---|---|---|---|---|---|
| (445/811) | SÁ Francisco Pedro Manuel | 25.10.1945 | 12 | 0 | 1973-1974, CA Independiente Avellaneda (12/0). |
| (542/919) | SABELLA Alejandro Esteban | 05.11.1954 | 8 | 0 | 1983-1984, CA Estudiantes de La Plata (8/0). |
| (199/448) | SABIO Daniel Cornélio | | 2 | 0 | 1940, Club Gimnasia y Esgrima La Plata (2/0). |
| (79/184) | SACARELLA Antonio | | 1 | 0 | 1920, CA Lanús (1/0). |
| (460/831) | SACCARDI Gerónimo Luis | 01.10.1949 | 2 | 0 | 1974, Club Ferro Carril Oeste (2/0). |
| (329/644) | SACCHI Federico | 04.09.1936 | 15 | 1 | 1960-1965, CA Newell's Old Boys Rosario (5/0), Racing Club Avellaneda (9/1), CA Boca Juniors Buenos Aires (1/0). |
| (341/654) | SAINZ Carlos Alberto | 13.12.1937 | 6 | 0 | 1961-1966, AA Argentinos Juniors Buenos Aires (1/0), CA River Plate Buenos Aires (5/0). |
| (762/1098) | SAJA Sebastián Diego | 05.06.1979 | 4 | 0 | 2002-2003, CA San Lorenzo de Almagro Buenos Aires (4/0). |
| (640/1007) | SALDAÑA Julio César | 14.11.1967 | 3 | 0 | 1992-1993, CA Newell's Old Boys Rosario (2/0), CA Boca Juniors Buenos Aires (1/0). |
| (479/864) | SALDAÑO José Luis | 20.10.1948 | 4 | 0 | 1976, CA Colón de Santa Fe (4/0). |
| (95/217) | SALERNO José | | 1 | 0 | 1922, CA El Porvenir Gerli (1/0). |
| (195/430) | SALOMÓN José | 09.07.1916 | 44 | 0 | 1940-1946, Racing Club Avellaneda (44/0). |
| (399/750) | SALOMONE Roberto Marcelo | 16.01.1944 | 4 | 0 | 1968-1969, Racing Club Avellaneda (4/0). |
| (235/496) | SALVINI Juan Carlos | | 8 | 2 | 1945-1946, CA Huracán Buenos Aires (8/2). |
| (855/1179) | SALVIO Eduardo Antonio | 13.07.1990 | 5 | 0 | 2009-2012, CA Lanús (1/0), Sport Lisboa e Benfica (1/0), Club Atlético de Madrid (2/0), Sport Lisboa e Benfica (1/0). |
| (727/1079) | SAMUEL Walter Adrián | 22.03.1978 | 57 | 5 | 1999-2010, CA Boca Juniors Buenos Aires (16/1), AS Roma (26/3), Real Madrid CF (6/0), Internazionale FC Milano (9/1). |
| (728/1083) | SAN ESTEBAN Jorge Héctor | 28.06.1972 | 1 | 0 | 1999, Club Gimnasia y Esgrima La Plata (1/0). |
| (357/677) | SAN LORENZO Julio | 30.11.1933 | 2 | 0 | 1963, Racing Club Avellaneda (2/0). |
| (66/158) | SANCET Roberto | | 1 | 0 | 1919, Club Gimnasia y Esgrima La Plata (1/0). |
| (125/283) | SÁNCHEZ Martín | | 3 | 1 | 1925, CA Colón de Santa Fe (3/1). |
| (393/743) | SÁNCHEZ Rubén Omar | 29.07.1945 | 13 | 0 | 1968-1974, CA Boca Juniors Buenos Aires (13/0). |
| (850/1169) | SAND José Gustavo | 17.07.1980 | 2 | 0 | 2008-2009, CA Lanús (2/0). |
| (28/075) | SANDE Ernesto | | 6 | 0 | 1912-1916, CA Independiente Avellaneda (6/0). |
| (146/305) | SANDOVAL Leonardo | | 3 | 0 | 1928-1930, Quilmes AC (3/0). |
| (215/462) | SANDOVAL Raimundo | | 2 | 1 | 1942, CA Tigre (2/1). |
| (287/581) | SANFILIPPO José Francisco | 04.05.1935 | 29 | 21 | 1956-1962, CA San Lorenzo de Almagro Buenos Aires (29/21). |
| (280/568) | SANSONE Ernesto | 08.01.1933 | 4 | 0 | 1956, CA Vélez Sarsfield (4/0). |
| (169/372) | SANTAMARÍA Carlos | | 6 | 0 | 1933-1935, CA River Plate Buenos Aires (6/0). |
| (519/901) | SANTAMARÍA Santiago | 23.10.1953 | 10 | 2 | 1980-1982, CA Newell's Old Boys Rosario (10/2). |
| (794/1129) | SANTANA Mario Alberto | 25.12.1981 | 7 | 1 | 2004-2005, Palermo US (7/1). |
| (366/692) | SANTORO Miguel Ángel | 27.02.1942 | 13 | 0 | 1964-1974, CA Independiente Avellaneda (13/0). |
| (206/458) | SANZ Rafael | 02.05.1915 | 2 | 0 | 1941, CA Banfield (2/0). |
| (513/888) | SAPORITI Eduardo Omar | 29.12.1954 | 4 | 0 | 1979-1984, CA River Plate Buenos Aires (4/0). |
| (92/210) | SARASÍBAR Florencio | | 1 | 0 | 1922, CA Rosario Central (1/0). |
| (167/360) | SARCO Ricardo | | 1 | 0 | 1932, Club Sportivo Barracas (1/0). |
| (193/427) | SARLANGA Jaime | 24.02.1916 | 7 | 5 | 1939-1943, Club Ferro Carril Oeste (2/1), CA Boca Juniors Buenos Aires (5/4). |
| (324/635) | SARNARI Juan Carlos | 22.01.1942 | 7 | 1 | 1960-1967, CA River Plate Buenos Aires (7/1). |
| (88/204) | SARUPPO Blas | | 9 | 4 | 1921-1923, Club Sportivo Barracas (9/4). |
| (170/375) | SASTRE Antonio | 27.04.1911 | 35 | 6 | 1933-1941, CA Independiente Avellaneda (35/6). |
| (227/490) | SASTRE Oscar Carlos | 25.12.1920 | 4 | 0 | 1945-1947, CA Independiente Avellaneda (4/0). |
| (748/1089) | SAVIOLA Javier Pedro | 11.12.1981 | 40 | 11 | 2000-2007, CA River Plate Buenos Aires (1/0), FC Barcelona (18/7), AS Monaco (9/2), Sevilla FC (6/1), FC Barcelona (3/1), Real Madrid CF (3/0). |
| (351/671) | SAVOY Raúl Armando | 15.07.1938 | 17 | 7 | 1963-1968, CA Chacarita Juniors Buenos Aires (9/5), CA Independiente Avellaneda (8/2). |

| | | | | | |
|---|---|---|---|---|---|
| (28/079) | SAYANES Santiago | | **7** | **0** | 1912-1916, Club Gimnasia y Esgrima Buenos Aires (6/0), Club Ferro Carril Oeste (1/0). |
| (176/397) | SBARRA Roberto | | **11** | **0** | 1935-1941, CA Estudiantes de La Plata (11/0). |
| (773/1116) | SCALONI Lionel Sebastián | 16.05.1978 | **7** | **0** | 2003-2006, RC Deportivo La Coruña (5/0), West Ham United FC London (2/0). |
| (168/365) | SCARCELLA José Arturo | | **5** | **0** | 1933-1935, Racing Club Avellaneda (5/0). |
| (116/272) | SCARPONE Felipe | | **1** | **0** | 1924, Club Gimnasia y Esgrima La Plata (1/0). |
| (285/572) | SCHADLEIN Ángel Osvaldo | 1934 | **12** | **0** | 1956-1957, Club Gimnasia y Esgrima La Plata (12/0). |
| (61/150) | SCHIARETTA Antonio | | **1** | **0** | 1918, Club Sportivo Barracas Buenos Aires (1/0). |
| (860/1191) | SCHIAVI Rolando Carlos | 18.01.1973 | **4** | **0** | 2009, CA Newell's Old Boys Rosario (4/0). |
| (332/648) | SCHNEIDER Juan Carlos | | **1** | **0** | 1960, CA River Plate Buenos Aires (1/0). |
| (678/1038) | SCHURRER Gabriel Francisco | 16.08.1971 | **4** | **0** | 1995, Lanús AC (4/0). |
| (910/1275) | SCOCCO Ignacio Martín | 29.05.1985 | **1** | **2** | 2012, CA Newell's Old Boys Rosario (1/2). |
| (79/185) | SCOFFANO Ernesto | | **1** | **0** | 1920, CA Lanús (1/0). |
| (148/312) | SCOPELLI Alejandro | 12.05.1908 | **8** | **4** | 1929-1937, CA Estudiantes de La Plata (4/2), Racing Club Avellaneda (4/2). |
| (470/861) | SCOTTA Héctor Horacio | 27.09.1950 | **7** | **5** | 1976, CA San Lorenzo de Almagro Buenos Aires (7/5). |
| (639/1005) | SCOTTO Darío Oscar | 01.09.1969 | **1** | **0** | 1992, CA Platense Buenos Aires (1/0). |
| (108/243) | SCURSONI Juan Bautista | | **2** | **0** | 1923-1924, CA Huracán Buenos Aires (2/0). |
| (427/789) | SEMENEWICZ Alejandro Estanislao | 01.06.1949 | **7** | **0** | 1972, CA Independiente Avellaneda (7/0). |
| (592/954) | SENSINI Roberto Néstor | 12.10.1966 | **60** | **0** | 1987-2000, CA Newell's Old Boys Rosario (12/0), Udinese Calcio (6/0), AC Parma (31/0), SS Lazio Roma (11/0). |
| (111/255) | SEOANE Manuel | 19.03.1902 | **18** | **10** | 1924-1928, CA El Porvenir Gerli (12/7), CA Independiente Avellaneda (6/3). |
| (100/231) | SEREGNI Roberto | | **6** | **0** | 1923, Club Del Plata Buenos Aires (6/0). |
| (613/975) | SERRIZUELA José Tiburcio | 16.06.1962 | **8** | **0** | 1990, CA River Plate Buenos Aires (8/0). |
| (298/592) | SESTI Alberto | 20.10.1929 | **1** | **0** | 1957, CA Idependiente Avellaneda (1/0). |
| (12/051) | SHERIDAN J. | | **2** | **0** | 1909-1910, CA Porteño Buenos Aires (2/0). |
| (391/736) | SILVA Manuel Ángel | 05.03.1942 | **7** | **1** | 1967-1968, CA Lanús (7/1). |
| (310/602) | SIMEONE Carmelo | 22.09.1933 | **22** | **0** | 1959-1964, CA Vélez Sarsfield (16/0), CA Boca Juniors Buenos Aires (6/0). |
| (597/963) | SIMEONE Diego Pablo | 28.04.1970 | **106** | **11** | 1988-2002, CA Vélez Sarsfield (6/1), Pisa Calcio (9/2), Sevilla FC (26/2), Club Atlético de Madrid (20/5), Internazionale FC Milano (22/1), SS Lazio Roma (23/0). |
| (36/100) | SIMMONS Heriberto | | **2** | **1** | 1913-1916, CA River Plate Buenos Aires (2/1). |
| (508/883) | SIMÓN Juan Ernesto | 02.03.1960 | **13** | **0** | 1979-1990, CA Newell's Old Boys Rosario (2/0), CA Boca Juniors Buenos Aires (11/0). |
| (392/739) | SINATRA Néstor Aníbal | 07.10.1946 | **1** | **0** | 1968, CA Vélez Sarsfield (1/0). |
| (586/949) | SIVISKI Darío Andrés | 20.12.1962 | **6** | **0** | 1987-1988, CA San Lorenzo de Almagro Buenos Aires (6/0). |
| (275/558) | SIVO Natalio | 02.02.1936 | **5** | **0** | 1956, Racing Club Avellaneda (5/0). |
| (270/550) | SÍVORI Enrique Omar | 02.10.1935 | **19** | **9** | 1956-1957, CA River Plate Buenos Aires (19/9). |
| (224/475) | SOBRERO Juan Carlos | | **16** | **0** | 1943-1947, CA Newell's Old Boys Rosario (16/0). |
| (267/546) | SOLA Gilberto Pascasio | 08.11.1928 | **5** | **0** | 1955-1957, CA River Plate Buenos Aires (5/0). |
| (462/838) | SOLARI Eduardo Miguel | 12.10.1950 | **1** | **0** | 1975, CA Rosario Central 1/0). |
| (87/202) | SOLARI Emilio | | **29** | **0** | 1921-1926, CA Nueva Chicago Buenos Aires (19/0), Club Sportivo Barracas (8/0), Club Sportivo Dock Sud Buenos Aires (2/0). |
| (378/707) | SOLARI Jorge Raúl | 10.11.1941 | **10** | **0** | 1966-1968, CA River Plate Buenos Aires (10/0). |
| (740/1088) | SOLARI Santiago Hernán | 07.10.1976 | **11** | **1** | 1999-2004, Club Atlético de Madrid (1/0), Real Madrid CF (10/1). |
| (393/740) | SOLÓRZANO José Demetrio | 28.02.1941 | **1** | **0** | 1968, CA Vélez Sarsfield (1/0). |
| (823/1149) | SOMOZA Leandro Daniel | 26.01.1981 | **5** | **0** | 2006-2013, Villarreal CF (2/0), CA Boca Juniors Buenos Aires (1/0), CA Lanús (2/0). |
| (677/1035) | SORÍN Juan Pablo | 05.05.1976 | **75** | **11** | 1995-2006, AA Argentinos Juniors Buenos Aires (3/0), CA River Plate Buenos Aires (14/3), Cruzeiro EC Belo Horizonte (21/3), SS Lazio Roma (2/1), FC Barcelona (1/0), Paris St.Germain FC (11/2), Cruzeiro EC Belo Horizonte (3/1), Villarreal CF (20/1). |
| (222/471) | SOSA Carlos Adolfo | | **13** | **0** | 1942-1946, CA Boca Juniors Buenos Aires (13/0). |
| (87/203) | SOSA Gabino | | **15** | **6** | 1921-1927, Club Central Córdoba Rosario (15/6). |
| (312/612) | SOSA Héctor Rubén | 14.11.1936 | **18** | **10** | 1959-1962, Racing Club Avellaneda (18/10). |
| (800/1143) | SOSA José Ernesto | 19.06.1985 | **19** | **1** | 2005-2013, CA Estudiantes de La Plata (2/0), FC Bayern München (3/0), CA Estudiantes de La Plata (1/1), SSC Napoli (1/0), FK Metalist Kharkiv (12/0). |
| (698/1064) | SOTOMAYOR Víctor Hugo | 21.01.1968 | **1** | **0** | 1996, CA Vélez Sarsfield (1/0). |
| (123/278) | SOUZA E. | | **1** | **0** | 1925, Club Del Plata Buenos Aires (1/0). |
| (147/310) | SPADARO Carlos | 05.02.1902 | **5** | **1** | 1928-1931, CA Lanús (3/0), CA Estudiantil Porteño Buenos Aires (2/1). |
| (880/1242) | SPERDUTTI Mauricio Ezequiel | 16.02.1986 | **2** | **0** | 2011, CA Newell's Old Boys Rosario (2/0). |
| (449/824) | SQUEO Carlos Vicente | 04.06.1948 | **6** | **0** | 1974, Racing Club Avellaneda (6/0). |
| (157/327) | STÁBILE Guillermo | 17.01.1906 | **4** | **8** | 1930, CA Huracán Buenos Aires (4/8). |
| (169/373) | STAGNARO Andrés | 19.11.1907 | **1** | **0** | 1933, Racing Club Avellaneda (1/0). |
| (113/259) | STAGNARO Armando | | **2** | **1** | 1924-1926, CA Palermo Buenos Aires (2/1). |
| (5/030) | STOCKS Wilfredo | | **1** | **0** | 1906, Belgrano AC Buenos Aires (1/0). |
| (236/500) | STREMBEL León | | **9** | **0** | 1945-1946, Racing Club Avellaneda (9/0). |
| (467/849) | SUÁREZ José María | 01.05.1952 | **3** | **0** | 1975, CA Boca Juniors Buenos Aires (3/0). |
| (343/658) | SUÁREZ Luis Eduardo | 15.07.1938 | **1** | **0** | 1962, CA Independiente Avellaneda (1/0). |
| (156/326) | SUÁREZ Pedro Arico | 05.06.1908 | **12** | **0** | 1930-1940, CA Boca Juniors Buenos Aires (12/0). |
| (236/501) | SUED Ezra | 07.06.1923 | **6** | **2** | 1945-1947, Racing Club Avellaneda (6/2). |
| (405/756) | SUÑÉ Rubén José | 07.03.1947 | **6** | **0** | 1969-1971, CA Boca Juniors Buenos Aires (6/0). |
| (6/035) | SUSÁN José | | **2** | **0** | 1907-1908, CA Estudiantes Buenos Aires (2/0). |
| (8/045) | SUSÁN Maximiliano | | **22** | **8** | 1908-1913, CA Estudiantes Buenos Aires (11/4), Club Alumni AC Buenos Aires (4/0), CA Estudiantes Buenos Aires (7/4). |

| | | | | | |
|---|---|---|---|---|---|
| (31/090) | TAGGINO Francisco | | 5 | 0 | 1913-1919, CA Boca Juniors Buenos Aires (2/0), CA River Plate Buenos Aires (3/0). |
| (447/814) | TAGLIANI Daniel José | 11.10.1946 | 1 | 0 | 1973, CA Vélez Sarsfield (1/0). |
| (522/904) | TAPIA Carlos Daniel | 20.08.1962 | 10 | 1 | 1980-1988, CA River Plate Buenos Aires (1/0), CA Boca Juniors Buenos Aires (9/1). |
| (377/706) | TARABINI Aníbal Roberto | 04.08.1941 | 6 | 1 | 1966-1969, CA Independiente Avellaneda (6/1). |
| (449/823) | TARANTINI Alberto César | 03.12.1955 | 60 | 1 | 1974-1982, CA Boca Juniors Buenos Aires (22/0), no club (11/1), CA Talleres de Córdoba (7/0), CA River Plate Buenos Aires (20/0). |
| (97/220) | TARASCONI Domingo Alberto | | 25 | 18 | 1922-1929, CA Boca Juniors Buenos Aires (25/18). |
| (401/753) | TARDIVO Alberto Pompeo | 13.01.1946 | 2 | 0 | 1968, CA Colón de Santa Fe (2/0). |
| (316/619) | TARNAWSKY Vladimir | 19.08.1939 | 1 | 0 | 1959, CA Newell's Old Boys Rosario (1/0). |
| (152/319) | TARRÍO Oscar | | 13 | 0 | 1929-1937, CA San Lorenzo de Almagro Buenos Aires (5/0), Club Ferrocarriles del Estado Buenos Aires (1/0), CA San Lorenzo de Almagro (7/0). |
| (85/198) | TASSÍN Alfredo | | 1 | 0 | 1921, Club Sportivo Palermo Buenos Aires (1/0). |
| (389/725) | TEDESCO Hugo Ángel | 20.02.1947 | 1 | 0 | 1967, CA Huracán Buenos Aires (1/0). |
| (362/685) | TELCH Roberto Marcelo | 28.10.1943 | 27 | 2 | 1964-1974, CA San Lorenzo de Almagro Buenos Aires (27/2). |
| (66/157) | TESORIERI Amérci Miguel | 18.03.1899 | 38 | 0 | 1919-1925, CA Boca Juniors Buenos Aires (38/0). |
| (782/1123) | TÉVEZ Carlos Alberto | 05.02.1984 | 64 | 13 | 2004-2011, CA Boca Juniors Buenos Aires (10/2), SC Corinthians São Paulo (15/2), West Ham United FC London (10/3), Manchester United FC (14/1), Manchester City FC (15/5). |
| (196/442) | TITTONEL Jorge | 30.09.1914 | 3 | 0 | 1940-1943, CA Huracán Buenos Aires (3/0). |
| (449/822) | TOGNERI Néstor Hugo | 27.11.1942 | 1 | 0 | 1974, CA Estudiantes de La Plata (1/0). |
| (416/773) | TOJO Miguel Ángel | 09.07.1943 | 2 | 0 | 1971, CA San Lorenzo de Almagro Buenos Aires (2/0). |
| (194/428) | TOLEDO José | | 1 | 0 | 1939, CA Platense Buenos Aires (1/0). |
| (866/1216) | TORANZO Patricio Daniel | 19.03.1982 | 2 | 0 | 2010, CA Huracán Buenos Aires (2/0). |
| (215/461) | TOSSONI Mario | 30.11.1917 | 3 | 0 | 1942, CA Tigre (3/0). |
| (447/821) | TROBBIANI Marcelo Antonio | 17.02.1955 | 26 | 1 | 1973-1986, CA Boca Juniors Buenos Aires (11/0), CA Estudiantes de La Plata (14/1), CD Elche (1/0). |
| (592/956) | TROGLIO Pedro Antonio | 28.07.1965 | 21 | 2 | 1987-1990, CA River Plate Buenos Aires (3/1), Hellas Verona (8/0), SS Lazio Roma (10/1). |
| (193/426) | TRONCOSO Aníbal | | 2 | 0 | 1939, CA Tigre (2/0). |
| (440/808) | TRONCOSO Jorge | 16.07.1950 | 4 | 0 | 1973-1975, CA Vélez Sarsfield (4/0). |
| (467/857) | TROSSERO Enzo Héctor | 03.05.1953 | 28 | 0 | 1975-1985, CA Independiente Avellaneda (27/0), CD Toluca (1/0). |
| (488/873) | TROSSERO Oscar Víctor | 15.09.1953 | 3 | 0 | 1977, Unión Santa Fe (3/0). |
| (688/1042) | TROTTA Roberto Luis | 28.01.1969 | 3 | 0 | 1995, CA Vélez Sarsfield (3/0). |
| (161/333) | TRUJILLO Alfredo | | 1 | 2 | 1930, CA Boca Juniors Buenos Aires (1/2). |
| (800/1134) | TUZZIO Eduardo Nicolás | 31.07.1974 | 2 | 0 | 2005-2007, CA River Plate Buenos Aires (2/0). |

| | | | | | |
|---|---|---|---|---|---|
| (625/995) | UNALI Dante Rubén | 10.12.1966 | 1 | 0 | 1991, Club Deportivo Mandiyú (1/0). |
| (254/521) | UÑATE Gabriel | | 2 | 2 | 1950, CA San Lorenzo de Almagro Buenos Aires (2/2). |
| (171/381) | URBIETA SOSA Constantino | 12.08.1907 | 1 | 0 | 1934, CA Godoy Cruz Mendoza (1/0). |
| (295/587) | URRIOLABEITÍA Juan Eulogio | 30.11.1929 | 3 | 0 | 1957, CA River Plate Buenos Aires (3/0). |
| (544/927) | URRUTI Juan José | 24.05.1962 | 1 | 0 | 1983, CA Racing de Córdoba (1/0). |
| (75/173) | URSO Jacobo | | 1 | 0 | 1919, CA San Lorenzo de Almagro Buenos Aires (1/0). |
| (67/164) | USLENGHI Eduardo | | 11 | 0 | 1919-1921, CA Porteño Buenos Aires (9/0), Club Sportivo Palermo Buenos Aires (2/0). |
| (835/1162) | USTARI Oscar Alfredo | 03.07.1986 | 2 | 0 | 2007-2012, Getafe CF (1/0), CA Boca Juniors Buenos Aires (1/0). |

| | | | | | |
|---|---|---|---|---|---|
| (239/502) | VACCA Claudio | 24.10.1915 | 7 | 0 | 1945-1946, CA Boca Juniors Buenos Aires (7/0). |
| (104/234) | VACCARO Luis | | 17 | 0 | 1923-1926, AA Argentinos Juniors Buenos Aires (17/0). |
| (265/544) | VAIRO Federico | 23.02.1930 | 41 | 1 | 1955-1958, CA River Plate Buenos Aires (41/1). |
| (462/838) | VALDANO Jorge Alberto Francisco | 04.10.1955 | 22 | 7 | 1975-1990, CA Newell's Old Boys Rosario (2/2), Real Zaragoza CD (5/0), Real Madrid CF (15/5). |
| (464/848) | VALENCIA José Daniel | 03.10.1955 | 39 | 5 | 1975-1982, CA Talleres de Córdoba (39/5). |
| (880/1238) | VALERI Diego Hernán | 01.05.1986 | 3 | 0 | 2011, CA Lanús (3/0). |
| (195/431) | VALUSSI Víctor Miguel | 08.05.1912 | 9 | 0 | 1940-1943, CA Boca Juniors Buenos Aires (9/0). |
| (109/247) | VAN KAMENADE Juan | | 1 | 0 | 1923, CA Estudiantes Buenos Aires (1/0). |
| (513/889) | VAN TUYNE José Daniel | 13.12.1954 | 10 | 0 | 1979-1982, CA Rosario Central (8/0), CA Talleres de Córdoba (1/0), Racing Club Avellaneda (1/0). |
| (565/940) | VANEMERAK Mario Alberto | 21.10.1963 | 1 | 0 | 1985, CA Vélez Sarsfield (1/0). |
| (861/1194) | VANGIONI Leonel Jesús | 05.05.1987 | 2 | 0 | 2009-2011, CA Newell's Old Boys Rosario (2/0). |
| (271/553) | VARACKA José | 27.05.1932 | 28 | 0 | 1956-1965, CA Independiente Avellaneda (12/0), CA River Plate Buenos Aires (16/0). |
| (155/323) | VARALLO Francisco Antonio | 05.02.1910 | 16 | 6 | 1930-1937, Club Gimnasia y Esgrima La Plata (5/2), CA Boca Juniors Buenos Aires (11/4). |
| (97/221) | VARELA Sergio | | 1 | 0 | 1922, CA Nueva Chicago Buenos Aires (1/0). |
| (364/688) | VÁSQUEZ Adolfo | | 4 | 0 | 1964, CA Banfield (4/0). |
| (351/669) | VÁZQUEZ José Ricardo | 07.12.1940 | 7 | 0 | 1963, CA Chacarita Juniors Buenos Aires (7/0). |
| (625/996) | VÁZQUEZ Sergio Fabián | 23.11.1965 | 30 | 0 | 1991-1994, Club Ferro Carril Oeste (11/0), CD Universidad Católica Santiago (19/0). |
| (395/748) | VEGLIO Carlos José | 27.08.1946 | 9 | 2 | 1968-1970, CA San Lorenzo de Almagro Buenos Aires (9/2). |
| (374/701) | VEIRA Héctor Rodolfo | 29.05.1946 | 2 | 0 | 1965-1967, CA San Lorenzo de Almagro Buenos Aires (2/0). |
| (883/1247) | VELÁSQUEZ Julián Alberto | 23.10.1990 | 1 | 0 | 2011, CA Independiente Avellaneda (1/0). |
| (53/140) | VENTUREIRA José | | 2 | 0 | 1917, CA Independiente Avellaneda (2/0). |
| (421/781) | VERDE Pedro Andrés | 12.03.1952 | 2 | 0 | 1971, CA Estudiantes de La Plata (2/0). |
| (906/1268) | VERGINI Santiago | 03.08.1988 | 1 | 0 | 2012, CA Newell's Old Boys Rosario (1/0). |
| (254/517) | VERNAZZA Julio Carlos Santiago | 29.12.1928 | 6 | 1 | 1950-1955, CA Platense Buenos Aires (2/1), CA River Plate Buenos Aires (4/0). |
| (179/404) | VERNIÈRES Enrique | 28.07.1909 | 1 | 0 | 1936, CA Boca Juniors Buenos Aires (1/0). |
| (404/755) | VERÓN Juan Ramón | 17.03.1944 | 4 | 0 | 1969-1971, CA Estudiantes de La Plata (4/0). |

| | | | | | |
|---|---|---|---|---|---|
| (693/1055) | VERÓN Juan Sebastián | 09.03.1975 | 73 | 9 | 1996-2010, CA Boca Juniors Buenos Aires (1/0), Sampdoria UC Genova (22/1), AC Parma (1/0), SS Lazio Roma (17/5), Manchester United FC (11/2), Chelsea FC London (4/1), CA Estudiantes de La Plata (17/0). |
| (8/047) | VIALE José | | 19 | 8 | 1908-1915, CA Newell's Old Boys Rosario (19/8). |
| (883/1246) | VIATRI Lucas Ezequiel | 29.03.1987 | 3 | 0 | 2011, CA Boca Juniors Buenos Aires (3/0). |
| (385/712) | VIBERTI Sebastián Humberto | 05.05.1944 | 4 | 0 | 1967, CA Huracán Buenos Aires (4/0). |
| (329/642) | VIDAL Miguel Ángel | 17.08.1934 | 16 | 0 | 1960-1964, CA Huracán Buenos Aires (16/0). |
| (513/887) | VIDALLÉ Enrique Bernardo | 07.05.1952 | 6 | 0 | 1979, Club Gimnasia y Esgrima La Plata (6/0). |
| (206/459) | VIDELA Eusebio | | 7 | 0 | 1941-1942, CA Tigre (7/0). |
| (68/166) | VIEYRO Ernesto | | 2 | 0 | 1919, Columbian Buenos Aires (2/0). |
| (362/683) | VIEYTEZ Abel Omar | 07.12.1942 | 6 | 0 | 1964-1965, AA Argentinos Juniors Buenos Aires (6/0). |
| (99/226) | VIGLIOLA Juan | | 2 | 0 | 1923, Alvear Buenos Aires (2/0). |
| (32/092) | VIGNOLES Horacio | | 1 | 0 | 1913, Belgrano AC Buenos Aires (1/0). |
| (479/865) | VILLA Julio Ricardo | 18.08.1952 | 16 | 1 | 1976-1978, Club Atlético de Tucumán (3/0), Racing Club Avellaneda (13/1). |
| (254/520) | VILLA Luis | | 1 | 0 | 1950, CA Estudiantes de La Plata (1/0). |
| (868/1219) | VILLAGRA Cristian Carlos | 27.12.1985 | 1 | 0 | 2010, CA River Plate Buenos Aires (1/0). |
| (129/287) | VILLAGRA Juan | | 2 | 1 | 1926, CA Nueva Chicago Buenos Aires (2/1). |
| (623/980) | VILLAREAL José Luis | 17.03.1966 | 8 | 0 | 1991-1993, CA Boca Juniors Buenos Aires (8/0). |
| (508/879) | VILLAVERDE Hugo Eduardo | 27.01.1954 | 5 | 0 | 1979, CA Independiente Avellaneda (5/0). |
| (161/330) | VILLEGAS Olegario | | 1 | 0 | 1930, CA Talleres Remedios de Escalada (1/0). |
| (168/366) | VIOLA Alberto | | 1 | 0 | 1933, CA Estudiantes de La Plata (1/0). |
| (53/141) | VIVALDO Nicolás | | 10 | 2 | 1917-1925, Racing Club Avellaneda (6/2), CA Porteño Buenos Aires (4/0). |
| (671/1026) | VIVAS Nelson David | 18.10.1969 | 39 | 1 | 1994-2003, CA Boca Juniors Buenos Aires (9/0), FC Lugano (8/1), Arsenal FC London (7/0), RC Celta de Vigo (1/0), Arsenal FC London (9/0), Internazionale FC Milano (3/0), CA River Plate Buenos Aires (2/0). |
| (149/315) | VOLANTE Carlos | 05.11.1905 | 2 | 0 | 1929-1930, CA Platense Buenos Aires (2/0). |
| (108/240) | VOLTURA José | | 1 | 0 | 1923, CA Nueva Chicago Buenos Aires (1/0). |
| (5/029) | WATSON HUTTON Arnoldo | | 17 | 6 | 1906-1913, Club Alumni AC Buenos Aires (13/5), Belgrano AC Buenos Aires (4/1). |
| (388/722) | WEHBE Omar | 15.08.1944 | 4 | 0 | 1967-1969, CA Vélez Sarsfield (4/0). |
| (2/015) | WEISS Gottlob | | 7 | 1 | 1903-1910, Barracas AC Lanús (1/0), Club Alumni AC Buenos Aires (6/1). |
| (172/387) | WERGIFKER Aarón | 15.08.1914 | 5 | 0 | 1934-1936, CA River Plate Buenos Aires (5/0). |
| (7/041) | WHALLEY Carlos | | 1 | 0 | 1907, Belgrano AC Buenos Aires (1/0). |
| (171/383) | WILDE Federico | 1909 | 1 | 0 | 1934, CA Unión Santa Fe (1/0). |
| (348/664) | WILLINGTON Daniel Alberto | 01.09.1942 | 11 | 1 | 1962-1970, CA Vélez Sarsfield (11/1). |
| (174/392) | WILSON Carlos | | 3 | 0 | 1935, CA Talleres Remedios de Escalada (3/0). |
| (7/036) | WILSON Carlos Tomás | | 25 | 0 | 1907-1916, Club Atlético San Isidro (25/0). |
| (428/790) | WOLFF Enrique Ernesto | 21.02.1949 | 27 | 1 | 1972-1974, Racing Club Avellaneda (8/0), CA River Plate Buenos Aires (19/1). |
| (7/040) | WOOD Juan | | 1 | 0 | 1907, Belgrano AC Buenos Aires (1/0). |
| (880/1237) | YACOB Claudio Ariel | 18.07.1987 | 2 | 1 | 2011, Racing Club de Avellaneda (2/1). |
| (221/463) | YÁCONO Norberto Antonio | 08.01.1919 | 15 | 0 | 1942-1951, CA River Plate Buenos Aires (15/0). |
| (22/065) | YATES Adolfo Peel | | 4 | 0 | 1911, Club Alumni AC Buenos Aires (4/0). |
| (395/749) | YAZALDE Héctor Casimiro | 29.05.1946 | 16 | 3 | 1968-1974, CA Independiente Avellaneda (12/1), Sportig Clube de Portugal Lisboa (4/2). |
| (275/563) | YUDICA José | 07.12.1936 | 4 | 1 | 1956, CA Newell's Old Boys Rosario (4/1). |
| (199/447) | YUSTRICH Juan Elías | 09.07.1909 | 1 | 0 | 1940, CA Lanús (1/0). |
| (75/174) | ZABALETA Albérico | | 1 | 0 | 1919, Racing Club Avellaneda (1/0). |
| (810/1145) | ZABALETA GIROD Pablo Javier | 16.01.1985 | 35 | 0 | 2005-2013, RCD Espanyol Barcelona (6/0), Manchester City FC (29/0). |
| (643/1009) | ZAMORA Julio Alberto | 11.03.1966 | 3 | 0 | 1992-1993, CA Newell's Old Boys Rosario (3/0). |
| (464/845) | ZANABRIA Mario Nicasio | 01.10.1948 | 4 | 2 | 1975, CA Newell's Old Boys Rosario (4/2). |
| (671/1018) | ZANETTI Javier Adelmar | 10.08.1973 | 145 | 5 | 1994-2011, CA Banfield (12/1), Internazionale FC Milano (133/4). |
| (624/990) | ZAPATA Gustavo Miguel | 15.10.1967 | 27 | 0 | 1991-1998, CA River Plate Buenos Aires (18/0), CA San Lorenzo de Almagro Buenos Aires (9/0). |
| (800/1138) | ZAPATA Víctor Eduardo | 20.01.1979 | 2 | 0 | 2005-2011, CA River Plate Buenos Aires (1/0), CA Vélez Sarsfield (1/0). |
| (274/554) | ZÁRATE Roberto Héctor | 15.12.1932 | 14 | 6 | 1956-1963, CA River Plate Buenos Aires (8/2), CA Banfield (6/4). |
| (800/1139) | ZÁRATE Rolando David | 06.08.1978 | 2 | 1 | 2005, CA Vélez Sarsfield (2/1). |
| (639/1004) | ZÁRATE Sergio Fabián | 14.01.1969 | 1 | 0 | 1992, 1.FC Nürnberg (1/0). |
| (222/468) | ZÁRRAGA Alfredo | | 1 | 0 | 1942, CA Boca Juniors Buenos Aires (1/0). |
| (198/445) | ZAVA Julio | | 1 | 0 | 1940, CA Chacarita Juniors Buenos Aires (1/0). |
| (168/370) | ZITO Vicente Antonio | 24.11.1912 | 4 | 0 | 1933-1935, Quilmes AC (2/0), Racing Club Avellaneda (2/0). |
| (197/443) | ZORILLA Juan | | 1 | 0 | 1940, CA Independiente Avellaneda (1/0). |
| (166/359) | ZOROZA Armando | | 1 | 0 | 1932, Club Argentino de Temperley (1/0). |
| (168/369) | ZOZAYA Alberto Máximo | 10.04.1908 | 9 | 8 | 1933-1937, CA Estudiantes de La Plata (9/8). |
| (855/1182) | ZUCULINI Franco | 05.09.1990 | 1 | 0 | 2009, Racing Club de Avellaneda (1/0). |
| (135/293) | ZUMELZÚ Adolfo Bernabé | 05.01.1902 | 13 | 4 | 1927-1930, Club Sportivo Palermo Buenos Aires (13/4). |
| (389/724) | ZYWICA Roberto Jaime | 21.01.1947 | 1 | 0 | 1967, CA River Plate Buenos Aires (1/0). |

**<u>Player who won caps for another countries</u>:**

| Name | Country | Period | Caps | Goals |
|---|---|---|---|---|
| ANGELILLO Antonio Valentín | Italy | 1960-1961 | 2 | 1 |
| BENÍTEZ CÁCERES Delfín | Paraguay | 1929-1931 | 8 | 1 |
| CESARINI Renato | Italy | 1931-1934 | 11 | 3 |
| DE BOURGOING Héctor Adolfo | France | 1962-1966 | 3 | 2 |
| DEMARIA Atilio (Attilio) | Italy | 1932-1940 | 13 | 3 |
| DI STÉFANO Alfredo | Spain | 1957-1961 | 31 | 23 |
| GUAITA Enrique (Enrico) | Italy | 1934-1935 | 10 | 5 |
| HILLER (III) Marius | Germany | 1910-1911 | 3 | 1 |
| INFANTE Ricardo Raimundo | Chile | 1947-1950 | 12 | 3 |
| LIBONATTI Julio | Italy | 1926-1931 | 17 | 15 |
| LOIÁCONO Francisco Ángel (LOJACONO) | Italy | 1959-1961 | 8 | 5 |
| MARTINO Rinaldo Fioramonte | Italy | 1949 | 1 | 0 |
| MASCHIO Humberto Dionisio | Italy | 1962 | 2 | 0 |
| MONTI Luis Felipe (Luigi) | Italy | 1932-1935 | 18 | 1 |
| ORSI Raimundo Bibiani | Italy | 1929-1935 | 35 | 13 |
| SCOPELLI Alejandro | Italy | 1935 | 1 | 0 |
| SÍVORI Omar Enrique | Italy | 1961-1962 | 9 | 8 |

# NATIONAL COACHES

| Name | Period | Matches | P | W | D | L | GF | - | GA | |
|---|---|---|---|---|---|---|---|---|---|---|
| Ángel VÁSQUEZ | 28.10.1923 – 02.12.1023 | [105-107] | 3 | 2 | 0 | 1 | 6 | - | 6 | 66.66 % |
| Ángel VÁSQUEZ | 21.09.1924 – 25.12.1925 | [117-128] | 12 | 5 | 7 | 0 | 18 | - | 8 | 70.83 % |
| José Lago MILLÁN | 14.07.1927 – 21.09.1928 | [135-147] | 13 | 8 | 3 | 2 | 44 | - | 15 | 73.07 % |
| Francisco OLAZAR | 20.09.1929 – 28.09.1929 | [150-151] | 2 | 0 | 1 | 1 | 1 | - | 2 | 25.00 % |
| Francisco OLAZAR – Juan José TRAMUTOLA | 03.11.1929 – 30.07.1930 | [152-160] | 9 | 7 | 1 | 1 | 28 | - | 11 | 83.33 % |
| Felipe PASCUCCI (*Italy*) | 27.05.1934 | [171] | 1 | 0 | 0 | 1 | 2 | - | 3 | 0.00 % |
| Manuel SEOANE | 18.07.1935 – 01.02.1937 | [177-186] | 10 | 7 | 1 | 2 | 20 | - | 8 | 75.00 % |
| Ángel FERNÁNDEZ ROCA | 18.06.1938 – 22.01.1939 | [189-192] | 4 | 3 | 0 | 1 | 11 | - | 6 | 75.00 % |
| Guillermo STÁBILE | 14.08.1939 – 15.07.1958 | [193-310] | 115 | 77 | 20 | 18 | 300 | - | 130 | 75.65 % |
| Carlos CALOCERO | 18.02.1940 – 25.02.1940 | [196,198] | 2 | 2 | 0 | 0 | 7 | - | 1 | 100.00 % |
| Victorio Luis SPINETTO – José DELLA TORRE – José BARREIRO | 07.03.1959 – 04.04.1959 | [311-316] | 6 | 5 | 1 | 0 | 19 | - | 5 | 91.66 % |
| José Manuel MORENO | 18.11.1959 – 22.12.1959 | [316-320] | 5 | 2 | 1 | 2 | 11 | - | 13 | 50.00 % |
| Guillermo STÁBILE | 08.03.1960 – 12.07.1960 | [321-330] | 10 | 6 | 1 | 3 | 16 | - | 15 | 65.00 % |
| Victorio Luis SPINETTO | 24.07.1960 – 24.06.1961 | [331-340] | 10 | 5 | 3 | 2 | 23 | - | 12 | 65.00 % |
| José D'AMICO | 12.10.1961 – 18.11.1961 | [341-342] | 2 | 1 | 0 | 1 | 6 | - | 3 | 50.00 % |
| Juan Carlos LORENZO | 13.03.1962 – 06.06.1962 | [343-347] | 5 | 2 | 2 | 1 | 4 | - | 4 | 60.00 % |
| Néstor Raúl ROSSI | 15.08.1962 | [348] | 1 | 1 | 0 | 0 | 3 | - | 1 | 100.00 % |
| Alejandro GALÁN „Jim Lopes“ | 07.11.1962 – 21.11.1962 | [349-350] | 2 | 1 | 1 | 0 | 2 | - | 1 | 75.00 % |
| Horácio Amable TORRES | 10.03.1963 – 16.04.1963 | [351-358] | 8 | 4 | 1 | 3 | 20 | - | 17 | 56.25 % |
| José D'AMICO | 15.10.1963 – 29.10.1963 | [359-360] | 2 | 1 | 0 | 1 | 6 | - | 3 | 50.00 % |
| José María MINELLA | 31.05.1964 – 29.08.1965 | [361-375] | 15 | 9 | 5 | 1 | 31 | - | 8 | 76.66 % |
| Ôsvaldo Juan ZUBELDÍA | 01.12.1965 | [376] | 1 | 0 | 1 | 0 | 1 | - | 1 | 50.00 % |
| Juan Carlos LORENZO | 11.06.1966 – 23.07.1966 | [377-382] | 6 | 2 | 2 | 2 | 5 | - | 6 | 50.00 % |
| Alejandro GALÁN „Jim Lopes“ | 18.01.1967 – 02.02.1967 | [383-387] | 5 | 4 | 0 | 1 | 12 | - | 3 | 80.00 % |
| Carmelo FARAONE | 15.08.1967 – 22.08.1967 | [388-389] | 2 | 0 | 0 | 2 | 1 | - | 3 | 0.00 % |
| Renato CESARINI | 13.10.1967 – 20.06.1968 | [390-394] | 5 | 1 | 1 | 3 | 5 | - | 8 | 30.00 % |
| José María MINELLA | 07.08.1968 – 22.12.1968 | [395-402] | 8 | 2 | 3 | 3 | 13 | - | 13 | 43.75 % |
| Humberto Dionisio MASCHIO | 19.03.1969 – 11.06.1969 | [403-406] | 4 | 1 | 3 | 0 | 4 | - | 3 | 62.50 % |
| Adolfo Alfredo PEDERNERA | 27.07.1969 – 31.08.1969 | [407-410] | 4 | 1 | 1 | 2 | 4 | - | 6 | 37.50 % |
| Juan José PIZZUTI | 04.03.1970 – 09.07.1972 | [411-433] | 23 | 10 | 8 | 5 | 35 | - | 28 | 60.86 % |
| Enrique Omar SÍVORI | 27.09.1972 – 20.02.1973 | [434-439] | 6 | 3 | 1 | 2 | 8 | - | 6 | 58.33 % |
| Miguel IGNOMIRIELLO | 17.05.1973 – 23.05.1973 | [440-441] | 2 | 0 | 2 | 0 | 2 | - | 2 | 50.00 % |
| Enrique Omar SÍVORI – Miguel IGNOMIRIELLO | 23.09.1973 | [447] | 1 | 1 | 0 | 0 | 1 | - | 0 | 100.00 % |
| Enrique Omar SÍVORI | 13.07.1973 – 07.10.1973 | [442-448] | 6 | 4 | 1 | 1 | 17 | - | 10 | 75.00 % |
| Vladislao Wenceslao CAP | 22.04.1974 – 03.07.1974 | [449-458] | 10 | 3 | 3 | 4 | 15 | - | 19 | 45.00 % |
| César Luis MENOTTI [1] | 12.10.1974 – 02.07.1982 | [459-541] | 83 | 44 | 21 | 18 | 158 | - | 82 | 65.66 % |
| Dr. Carlos Salvador BILARDO | 12.05.1983 – 08.07.1990 | [542-622] | 81 | 28 | 30 | 23 | 91 | - | 74 | 53.08 % |
| Alfio Oscar BASILE [2] | 19.02.1991 – 03.07.1994 | [623-670] | 48 | 25 | 17 | 6 | 75 | - | 44 | 69.78 % |
| Daniel Alberto PASSARELLA | 16.11.1994 – 04.07.1998 | [671-726] | 56 | 33 | 13 | 10 | 101 | - | 42 | 70.53 % |
| Marcelo Alberto BIELSA | 03.02.1999 – 04.09.2004 | [727-795] | 69 | 44 | 15 | 10 | 127 | - | 61 | 74.63 % |
| José Néstor PEKERMAN | 09.10.2004 – 30.06.2006 | [796-822] | 27 | 14 | 7 | 6 | 50 | - | 33 | 64.81 % |
| Alfio Oscar BASILE | 03.09.2006 – 28.03.2008 | [823-850] | 28 | 14 | 8 | 6 | 44 | - | 25 | 64.28 % |
| Diego Armando MARADONA | 19.11.2008 – 03.07.2010 | [851-874] | 24 | 18 | 0 | 6 | 47 | - | 27 | 75.00 % |
| Sergia Daniel BATISTA | 11.08.2010 – 25.05.2011 | [875-891] | 17 | 9 | 6 | 2 | 30 | - | 17 | 70.58 % |
| Alejandro SABELLA | 02.09.2011 -> | [892-> | 31 | 19 | 8 | 4 | 63 | - | 29 | 74.19 % |

Argentina played without national coach in following matches: [1-104], [108-116],[129-134],[148-149],[161-170],[172-176],[187-188].
[1] Matches 468-470 assisted by Miguel Antonio Juárez; Match 518 assisted by Federico Sacchi.
[2] Match 655 - assisted by Reinaldo Carlos Merlo.

**National coaches several times in charge:**

| Name | How often | Matches | M | W | D | L | GF | - | GA | |
|---|---|---|---|---|---|---|---|---|---|---|
| Ángel VÁSQUEZ | 2x | [105-107],[117-128] | 15 | 7 | 7 | 1 | 24 | - | 14 | 70.00 % |
| Guillermo STÁBILE | 2x | [193-310],[321-330] | 125 | 83 | 21 | 21 | 316 | - | 145 | 74.80 % |
| José D'AMICO | 2x | [341-342],[359-360] | 4 | 2 | 0 | 2 | 12 | - | 6 | 50.00 % |
| Juan Carlos LORENZO | 2x | [343-347],[377-382] | 11 | 4 | 4 | 3 | 9 | - | 10 | 54.54 % |
| Alejandro GALÁN „Jim Lopes“ | 2x | [349-350],[383-387] | 7 | 5 | 1 | 1 | 14 | - | 4 | 78.57 % |
| José María MINELLA | 2x | [361-375],[395-402] | 23 | 11 | 8 | 4 | 44 | - | 21 | 65.21 % |
| Enrique Omar SÍVORI | 2x | [434-439],[442-448, without 447] | 12 | 7 | 2 | 3 | 25 | - | 16 | 66.66 % |
| Alfio Oscar BASILE | 2x | [623-670],[823-850] | 76 | 39 | 25 | 12 | 119 | - | 69 | 67.76 % |

# HEAD-TO-HEAD STATISTICS

| | HOME | | | | | AWAY | | | | | NEUTRAL | | | | | TOTAL | | | | |
|---|---|---|---|---|---|---|---|---|---|---|---|---|---|---|---|---|---|---|---|---|
| Albania | 1 | 1 | 0 | 0 | 4 : 0 | | | | | | | | | | | 1 | 1 | 0 | 0 | 4 : 0 |
| Algeria | | | | | | | | | | | 1 | 1 | 0 | 0 | 4 : 3 | 1 | 1 | 0 | 0 | 4 : 3 |
| Australia | 3 | 3 | 0 | 0 | 5 : 0 | 3 | 1 | 1 | 1 | 3 : 5 | 1 | 1 | 0 | 0 | 4 : 2 | 7 | 5 | 1 | 1 | 12 : 7 |
| Austria | | | | | | 2 | 1 | 1 | 0 | 6 : 2 | | | | | | 2 | 1 | 1 | 0 | 6 : 2 |
| Belarus | | | | | | 1 | 0 | 1 | 0 | 0 : 0 | | | | | | 1 | 0 | 1 | 0 | 0 : 0 |
| Belgium | | | | | | 1 | 1 | 0 | 0 | 2 : 0 | 3 | 2 | 0 | 1 | 8 : 4 | 4 | 3 | 0 | 1 | 10 : 4 |
| Bolivia | 13 | 11 | 3 | 0 | 37 : 3 | 11 | 3 | 2 | 6 | 15 : 24 | 8 | 7 | 1 | 0 | 27 : 2 | 32 | 21 | 5 | 6 | 79 : 31 |
| Bosnia-Herzegovina | 1 | 1 | 0 | 0 | 5 : 0 | | | | | | 1 | 1 | 0 | 0 | 2 : 0 | 2 | 2 | 0 | 0 | 7 : 0 |
| Angola | | | | | | | | | | | 1 | 1 | 0 | 0 | 2 : 0 | 1 | 1 | 0 | 0 | 2 : 0 |
| Brazil | 34 | 15 | 11 | 8 | 58 : 38 | 39 | 9 | 7 | 23 | 53 : 80 | 27 | 13 | 6 | 8 | 46 : 39 | 100 | 37 | 24 | 39 | 157 : 157 |
| Bulgaria | 6 | 6 | 0 | 0 | 15 : 4 | | | | | | 3 | 2 | 0 | 1 | 3 : 2 | 9 | 8 | 0 | 1 | 18 : 6 |
| Cameroon | | | | | | | | | | | 2 | 0 | 1 | 1 | 2 : 3 | 2 | 0 | 1 | 1 | 2 : 3 |
| Canada | 1 | 1 | 0 | 0 | 5 : 0 | | | | | | | | | | | 1 | 1 | 0 | 0 | 5 : 0 |
| Chile | 32 | 26 | 6 | 0 | 82 : 23 | 32 | 13 | 13 | 6 | 50 : 37 | 15 | 13 | 2 | 0 | 39 : 6 | 79 | 52 | 21 | 6 | 171 : 66 |
| China P.R. | | | | | | | | | | | 1 | 0 | 0 | 1 | 0 : 1 | 1 | 0 | 0 | 1 | 0 : 1 |
| Colombia | 11 | 5 | 4 | 2 | 10 : 9 | 9 | 4 | 1 | 4 | 12 : 10 | 12 | 8 | 2 | 2 | 41 : 15 | 32 | 17 | 7 | 8 | 63 : 34 |
| Costa Rica | 2 | 2 | 0 | 0 | 6 : 2 | 3 | 1 | 2 | 0 | 2 : 0 | 2 | 2 | 0 | 0 | 6 : 3 | 7 | 5 | 2 | 0 | 14 : 5 |
| Croatia | | | | | | 1 | 0 | 1 | 0 | 0 : 0 | 2 | 1 | 0 | 1 | 3 : 3 | 3 | 1 | 1 | 1 | 3 : 3 |
| Czechoslovakia | 4 | 2 | 2 | 0 | 3 : 1 | 1 | 0 | 1 | 0 | 3 : 3 | 1 | 0 | 0 | 1 | 1 : 6 | 6 | 2 | 3 | 1 | 7 : 10 |
| Denmark | 1 | 0 | 1 | 0 | 1 : 1 | | | | | | 1 | 0 | 0 | 1 | 0 : 2 | 2 | 0 | 1 | 1 | 1 : 3 |
| East Germany | 1 | 1 | 0 | 0 | 2 : 0 | | | | | | 1 | 0 | 1 | 0 | 1 : 1 | 2 | 1 | 1 | 0 | 3 : 1 |
| Ecuador | 9 | 6 | 3 | 0 | 22 : 6 | 11 | 3 | 4 | 4 | 16 : 16 | 11 | 8 | 3 | 0 | 42 : 7 | 31 | 17 | 10 | 4 | 80 : 29 |
| Egypt | | | | | | 1 | 1 | 0 | 0 | 2 : 0 | 1 | 1 | 0 | 0 | 6 : 0 | 2 | 2 | 0 | 0 | 8 : 0 |
| El Salvador | | | | | | | | | | | 1 | 1 | 0 | 0 | 2 : 0 | 1 | 1 | 0 | 0 | 2 : 0 |
| England | 3 | 1 | 2 | 0 | 4 : 2 | 6 | 0 | 3 | 3 | 6 : 10 | 6 | 2 | 1 | 3 | 8 : 10 | 15 | 3 | 6 | 6 | 18 : 22 |
| France | 4 | 2 | 1 | 1 | 7 : 5 | 5 | 3 | 1 | 1 | 4 : 2 | 2 | 1 | 1 | 0 | 1 : 0 | 11 | 6 | 3 | 2 | 12 : 7 |
| Germany | 3 | 1 | 1 | 1 | 3 : 4 | 10 | 5 | 3 | 2 | 17 : 12 | 7 | 3 | 1 | 3 | 8 : 12 | 20 | 9 | 5 | 6 | 28 : 28 |
| Ghana | 1 | 1 | 0 | 0 | 2 : 0 | | | | | | | | | | | 1 | 1 | 0 | 0 | 2 : 0 |
| Greece | | | | | | | | | | | 2 | 2 | 0 | 0 | 6 : 0 | 2 | 2 | 0 | 0 | 6 : 0 |
| Guatemala | | | | | | 1 | 1 | 0 | 0 | 4 : 0 | | | | | | 1 | 1 | 0 | 0 | 4 : 0 |
| Haiti | 1 | 1 | 0 | 0 | 4 : 0 | | | | | | 1 | 1 | 0 | 0 | 4 : 1 | 2 | 2 | 0 | 0 | 8 : 1 |
| Holland | 1 | 1 | 0 | 0 | 3 : 1 | 3 | 0 | 1 | 2 | 2 : 6 | 4 | 0 | 2 | 2 | 1 : 6 | 8 | 1 | 3 | 4 | 6 : 13 |
| Honduras | | | | | | 1 | 1 | 0 | 0 | 3 : 1 | | | | | | 1 | 1 | 0 | 0 | 3 : 1 |
| Hungary | 3 | 3 | 0 | 0 | 9 : 2 | 2 | 1 | 0 | 1 | 2 : 3 | 3 | 2 | 1 | 0 | 7 : 1 | 8 | 6 | 1 | 1 | 18 : 6 |
| India | | | | | | 1 | 1 | 0 | 0 | 1 : 0 | | | | | | 1 | 1 | 0 | 0 | 1 : 0 |
| Iran | | | | | | | | | | | 1 | 0 | 1 | 0 | 1 : 1 | 1 | 0 | 1 | 0 | 1 : 1 |
| Israel | | | | | | 5 | 3 | 1 | 1 | 14 : 6 | | | | | | 5 | 3 | 1 | 1 | 14 : 6 |
| Italy | 2 | 1 | 0 | 1 | 1 : 1 | 8 | 2 | 3 | 3 | 8 : 14 | 4 | 0 | 2 | 2 | 4 : 7 | 14 | 3 | 5 | 6 | 13 : 22 |
| Ivory Coast | | | | | | | | | | | 2 | 2 | 0 | 0 | 6 : 1 | 2 | 2 | 0 | 0 | 6 : 1 |
| Jamaica | 1 | 1 | 0 | 0 | 2 : 1 | | | | | | 1 | 1 | 0 | 0 | 5 : 0 | 2 | 2 | 0 | 0 | 7 : 1 |
| Japan | | | | | | 4 | 3 | 0 | 1 | 8 : 3 | 3 | 3 | 0 | 0 | 7 : 1 | 7 | 6 | 0 | 1 | 15 : 4 |
| Libya | | | | | | 1 | 1 | 0 | 0 | 3 : 1 | | | | | | 1 | 1 | 0 | 0 | 3 : 1 |
| Lithuania | 1 | 0 | 1 | 0 | 0 : 0 | | | | | | | | | | | 1 | 0 | 1 | 0 | 0 : 0 |
| Mexico | 3 | 1 | 2 | 0 | 2 : 1 | 8 | 0 | 6 | 2 | 7 : 10 | 16 | 11 | 3 | 2 | 33 : 16 | 27 | 12 | 11 | 4 | 42 : 27 |
| Morocco | 1 | 1 | 0 | 0 | 3 : 1 | 1 | 1 | 0 | 0 | 1 : 0 | | | | | | 2 | 2 | 0 | 0 | 4 : 1 |
| Nigeria | | | | | | 1 | 0 | 0 | 1 | 1 : 4 | 5 | 4 | 1 | 0 | 7 : 2 | 6 | 4 | 1 | 1 | 8 : 6 |
| Northern Ireland | | | | | | | | | | | 1 | 1 | 0 | 0 | 3 : 1 | 1 | 1 | 0 | 0 | 3 : 1 |
| Norway | | | | | | 2 | 0 | 0 | 2 | 1 : 3 | | | | | | 2 | 0 | 0 | 2 | 1 : 3 |
| Panama | 1 | 1 | 0 | 0 | 1 : 0 | | | | | | | | | | | 1 | 1 | 0 | 0 | 1 : 0 |
| Paraguay | 43 | 26 | 14 | 3 | 94 : 39 | 39 | 17 | 10 | 12 | 62 : 48 | 15 | 11 | 4 | 0 | 45 : 15 | 97 | 54 | 28 | 15 | 201 : 102 |
| Peru | 17 | 14 | 3 | 0 | 38 : 11 | 21 | 11 | 7 | 3 | 39 : 18 | 11 | 7 | 2 | 2 | 23 : 14 | 49 | 32 | 12 | 5 | 100 : 43 |
| Poland | 7 | 5 | 1 | 1 | 12 : 5 | 2 | 1 | 0 | 1 | 3 : 3 | 2 | 0 | 1 | 1 | 3 : 4 | 11 | 6 | 2 | 3 | 18 : 12 |
| Poland League XI | 1 | 1 | 0 | 0 | 2 : 0 | | | | | | | | | | | 1 | 1 | 0 | 0 | 2 : 0 |
| Portugal | | | | | | 4 | 3 | 1 | 0 | 8 : 2 | 3 | 2 | 0 | 1 | 5 : 4 | 7 | 5 | 1 | 1 | 13 : 6 |
| Qatar | | | | | | 1 | 1 | 0 | 0 | 3 : 0 | | | | | | 1 | 1 | 0 | 0 | 3 : 0 |
| Republic of Ireland | 1 | 1 | 0 | 0 | 3 : 1 | 5 | 4 | 1 | 0 | 5 : 0 | | | | | | 6 | 5 | 1 | 0 | 8 : 1 |
| Romania | 3 | 3 | 0 | 0 | 5 : 1 | | | | | | 3 | 1 | 1 | 1 | 4 : 4 | 6 | 4 | 1 | 1 | 9 : 5 |
| Romania League XI | 2 | 2 | 0 | 0 | 3 : 1 | | | | | | | | | | | 2 | 2 | 0 | 0 | 3 : 1 |
| Russia | | | | | | 1 | 1 | 0 | 0 | 3 : 2 | | | | | | 1 | 1 | 0 | 0 | 3 : 2 |
| Saudi Arabia | | | | | | 2 | 1 | 1 | 0 | 3 : 1 | 2 | 1 | 1 | 0 | 4 : 2 | 4 | 2 | 2 | 0 | 7 : 3 |
| Scotland | 1 | 0 | 1 | 0 | 1 : 1 | 3 | 2 | 0 | 1 | 4 : 2 | | | | | | 4 | 2 | 1 | 1 | 5 : 3 |
| Serbia & Montenegro | 6 | 4 | 1 | 1 | 11 : 6 | 1 | 0 | 0 | 1 | 2 : 4 | 3 | 1 | 1 | 1 | 8 : 4 | 10 | 5 | 2 | 3 | 21 : 14 |
| Slovakia League XI | 1 | 1 | 0 | 0 | 6 : 0 | | | | | | | | | | | 1 | 1 | 0 | 0 | 6 : 0 |
| South Africa | 1 | 1 | 0 | 0 | 2 : 0 | 1 | 0 | 1 | 0 | 1 : 1 | | | | | | 2 | 1 | 1 | 0 | 3 : 1 |
| South Korea | | | | | | 1 | 1 | 0 | 0 | 1 : 0 | 2 | 2 | 0 | 0 | 7 : 2 | 3 | 3 | 0 | 0 | 8 : 2 |
| Soviet Union | 5 | 0 | 4 | 1 | 4 : 5 | 2 | 1 | 1 | 0 | 1 : 0 | 4 | 2 | 1 | 1 | 6 : 5 | 11 | 3 | 6 | 2 | 11 : 10 |
| Spain | 4 | 3 | 1 | 0 | 8 : 2 | 8 | 2 | 1 | 5 | 7 : 10 | 1 | 1 | 0 | 0 | 2 : 1 | 13 | 6 | 2 | 5 | 17 : 13 |
| Sweden | | | | | : | 1 | 1 | 0 | 0 | 3 : 2 | 2 | 0 | 1 | 1 | 3 : 4 | 3 | 1 | 1 | 1 | 6 : 6 |
| Switzerland | 1 | 1 | 0 | 0 | 5 : 0 | 4 | 2 | 2 | 0 | 7 : 3 | 1 | 1 | 0 | 0 | 2 : 0 | 6 | 4 | 2 | 0 | 14 : 3 |
| Tunisia | | | | | | | | | | | 1 | 1 | 0 | 0 | 2 : 1 | 1 | 1 | 0 | 0 | 2 : 1 |
| United States | | | | | | 5 | 2 | 2 | 1 | 3 : 2 | 5 | 4 | 0 | 1 | 27 : 8 | 10 | 6 | 2 | 2 | 30 : 10 |
| Uruguay | 81 | 49 | 21 | 11 | 164 : 75 | 77 | 21 | 20 | 36 | 90 : 111 | 22 | 12 | 3 | 7 | 35 : 28 | 180 | 82 | 44 | 54 | 289 : 214 |
| Venezuela | 9 | 9 | 0 | 0 | 41 : 3 | 8 | 7 | 0 | 1 | 24 : 6 | 3 | 3 | 0 | 0 | 9 : 1 | 20 | 19 | 0 | 1 | 74 : 10 |
| Wales | | | | | | 1 | 0 | 1 | 0 | 1 : 1 | 1 | 1 | 0 | 0 | 1 : 0 | 2 | 1 | 1 | 0 | 2 : 1 |
| **TOTAL** | **327** | **215** | **82** | **30** | **695 : 257** | **361** | **137** | **100** | **124** | **516 : 468** | **234** | **145** | **44** | **45** | **526 : 255** | **922** | **497** | **226** | **199** | **1737 : 980** |

# BOLIVIA

| The Country: |
|---|
| Estado Plurinacional de Bolivia<br>(Plurinational State of Bolivia)<br>Capital: Sucre<br>Surface: 1,098,581 km²<br>Inhabitants: 10,461,053<br>Time: UTC-4 |

| The FA: |
|---|
| Federación Boliviana de Fútbol<br><br>Av. Libertador Bolívar 1168, Cochabamba<br>Year of Formation: 1925<br>Member of FIFA since: 1926<br>Member of CONMEBOL since: 1926 |

**NATIONAL TEAM RECORDS**

| COPA AMÉRICA | |
|---|---|
| **1916** | Did not enter |
| **1917** | Did not enter |
| **1919** | Did not enter |
| **1920** | Did not enter |
| **1921** | Did not enter |
| **1922** | Did not enter |
| **1923** | Did not enter |
| **1924** | Did not enter |
| **1925** | Did not enter |
| **1926** | 5th Place |
| **1927** | 4th Place |
| **1929** | Withdrew |
| **1935** | Withdrew |
| **1937** | Withdrew |
| **1939** | Withdrew |
| **1941** | Withdrew |
| **1942** | Withdrew |
| **1945** | 6th Place |
| **1946** | 6th Place |
| **1947** | 7th Place |
| **1949** | 4th Place |
| **1953** | 6th Place |
| **1955** | Withdrew |
| **1956** | Withdrew |
| **1957** | Withdrew |
| **1959** | 7th Place |
| **1959E** | Withdrew |
| **1963** | Winners |
| **1967** | 6th Place |
| **1975** | Group Stage |
| **1979** | Group Stage |
| **1983** | Group Stage |
| **1987** | Group Stage |
| **1989** | Group Stage |
| **1991** | Group Stage |
| **1993** | Group Stage |
| **1995** | Quarter-Final |
| **1997** | Runners-up |
| **1999** | Group Stage |
| **2001** | Group Stage |
| **2004** | Group Stage |
| **2007** | Group Stage |
| **2011** | Group Stage |

| WORLD CUP | |
|---|---|
| **1930** | Final Tournament (Group Stage) |
| **1934** | Did not enter |
| **1938** | Did not enter |
| **1950** | Final Tournament (Group Stage) |
| **1954** | Did not enter |
| **1958** | Did not enter |
| **1962** | Qualifiers |
| **1966** | Qualifiers |
| **1970** | Qualifiers |
| **1974** | Qualifiers |
| **1978** | Qualifiers |
| **1982** | Qualifiers |
| **1986** | Qualifiers |
| **1990** | Qualifiers |
| **1994** | Final Tournament (Group Stage) |
| **1998** | Qualifiers |
| **2002** | Qualifiers |
| **2006** | Qualifiers |
| **2010** | Qualifiers |
| **2014** | Qualifiers |

| OLYMPIC GAMES 1900-2012 |
|---|
| None |
| **FIFA CONFEDERATIONS CUP 1992-2013** |
| 1999 |
| **PLAYER WITH MOST INTERNATIONAL CAPS** |
| Marco Antonio Sandy Sansusty – 93 caps (1993-2003) |
| **PLAYER WITH MOST INTERNATIONAL GOALS** |
| Joaquín Botero Vaca – 20 goals (48 caps; 1999-2009) |

# FULL INTERNATIONALS (1926-2013)

**1.** 12.10.1926 **CHILE – BOLIVIA** **7-1** 10th Copa América
Estadio Sport de Nuñoa, Santiago; Referee: Norberto Luis Gallieri (Argentina); Attendance: 8,560
**BOL:** Jesús Bermúdez Tórrez (1/0), Casiano José Chavarría (1/0), Diógenes Lara (1/0), Jorge Soto (1/0), Renato Sáinz (1/0), Eliseo Angulo (1/0), Carlos Soto (1/0), Rafael Méndez (1/0), Teófilo Aguilar (1/1), José Bustamante (1/0), Mario Mauricio Alborta Velasco (1/0). Trainer: no.
**Goal**: Teófilo Aguilar.

**2.** 16.10.1926 **ARGENTINA – BOLIVIA** **5-0(4-0)** 10th Copa América
Estadio Sport de Nuñoa, Santiago; Referee: Aníbal Tejada (Uruguay); Attendance: 8,000
**BOL:** Jesús Bermúdez Tórrez (2/0), Diógenes Lara (2/0), Renato Sáinz (2/0), Alberto Urriolagoitía (1/0), Jorge Soto (2/0), Jorge Luis Balderrama (1/0), Carlos Soto (2/0), Rafael Méndez (2/0), Teófilo Aguilar (2/1), José Bustamante (2/0), Mario Mauricio Alborta Velasco (2/0). Trainer: no.

**3.** 23.10.1926 **PARAGUAY – BOLIVIA** **6-1** 10th Copa América
Estadio Sport de Nuñoa, Santiago; Referee: Aníbal Tejada (Uruguay); Attendance: 2,000
**BOL:** Jesús Bermúdez Tórrez (3/0), Casiano José Chavarría (2/0), Diógenes Lara (3/0), Jorge Soto (3/0), Renato Sáinz (3/0), Jorge Luis Balderrama (2/0), Carlos Soto (3/1), Rafael Méndez (3/0), Teófilo Aguilar (3/1), José Bustamante (3/0), Mario Mauricio Alborta Velasco (3/0). Trainer: no.
**Goal:** Carlos Soto.

**4.** 28.10.1926 **URUGUAY – BOLIVIA** **6-0(4-0)** 10th Copa América
Estadio Sport de Nuñoa, Santiago; Referee: Juan Pedro Barbera (Argentina); Attendance: 8,000
**BOL:** Hernán Araníbar López (1/0), Casiano José Chavarría (3/0), Diógenes Lara (4/0), Jorge Soto (4/0), Renato Sáinz (4/0), Jorge Luis Balderrama (3/0), Carlos Soto (4/1), Rafael Méndez (4/0), Teófilo Aguilar (4/1), José Bustamante (4/0), Mario Mauricio Alborta Velasco (4/0). Trainer: no.

**5.** 30.10.1927 **ARGENTINA – BOLIVIA** **7-1(5-1)** 11th Copa América
Estadio Nacional, Lima; Referee: Benjamín Fuentes (Peru); Attendance: 15,000
**BOL:** Jesús Bermúdez Tórrez (4/0), Diógenes Lara (5/0), Casiano José Chavarría (4/0), Jorge Soto (5/0), Armando Renjel (1/0), Jorge Luis Balderrama (4/0), Carlos Soto (5/1), Rafael Méndez (5/0), Renato Sáinz (5/0), José Bustamante (5/0), Mario Mauricio Alborta Velasco (5/1). Trainer: Jorge Luis Valderrama (1).
**Goal:** Mario Mauricio Alborta Velasco (42).

**6.** 06.11.1927 **URUGUAY – BOLIVIA** **9-0(3-0)** 11th Copa América
Estadio Nacional, Lima; Referee: Consolato Nay Foino (Argentina); Attendance: 6,000
**BOL:** Jesús Bermúdez Tórrez (5/0), Diógenes Lara (6/0), Casiano José Chavarría (5/0), Froilán Pinilla (1/0), Armando Renjel (2/0), Jorge Soto (6/0), Carlos Soto (6/1), Rafael Méndez (6/0), José Toro (1/0), José Bustamante (6/0), Mario Mauricio Alborta Velasco (6/1). Trainer: Jorge Luis Valderrama (2).

**7.** 13.11.1927 **PERU – BOLIVIA** **3-2(3-2)** 11th Copa América
Estadio Nacional, Lima; Referee: Consolato Nay Foino (Argentina); Attendance: 14,000
**BOL:** Jesús Bermúdez Tórrez (6/0), Diógenes Lara (7/0), Casiano José Chavarría (6/0), Jorge Soto (7/0), Armando Renjel (3/0), Jorge Luis Balderrama (5/0), N. Malpartida (1/0), Rafael Méndez (7/0), José Toro (2/0), José Bustamante (7/2), Mario Mauricio Alborta Velasco (7/1). Trainer: Jorge Luis Valderrama (3).
**Goals:** José Bustamante (13, 14).

**8.** 17.07.1930 **YUGOSLAVIA – BOLIVIA** **4-0(0-0)** 1st FIFA WC. Group Stage
Estadio Parque Central, Montevideo (Uruguay); Referee: Francisco Matteucci (Uruguay); Attendance: 18,306
**BOL:** Jesús Bermúdez Tórrez (7/0), Segundo Durandal (1/0), Casiano José Chavarría (7/0), Juan Jorge Argote (1/0), Diógenes Lara (8/0), Jorge Luis Balderrama (6/0), Gumercindo Gómez (1/0), José Bustamante (8/2), Rafael Mendéz (Cap) (8/0), Mario Mauricio Alborta Velasco (8/1), René Fernández (1/0). Trainer: Ulrico Saucedo (1).

**9.** 20.07.1930 **BRAZIL – BOLIVIA** **4-0(1-0)** 1st FIFA WC. Group Stage
Estadio Centenario, Montevideo (Uruguay); Referee: Georges Balway (France); Attendance: 25,466
**BOL:** Jesús Bermúdez Tórrez (8/0), Segundo Durandal (2/0), Casiano José Chavarría (8/0), Renato Sáinz (6/0), Diógenes Lara (9/0), Jorge Luis Balderrama (7/0), Eduardo Reyes Ortíz (1/0), José Bustamante (9/2), Rafael Mendéz (Cap) (9/0), Mario Mauricio Alborta Velasco (9/1), René Fernández (2/0). Trainer: Ulrico Saucedo (2).

**10.** 08.08.1938 **BOLIVIA - ECUADOR** **1-1** 1st Juegos Bolivarianos
Estadio Universitario, Bogotá
**BOL:** Vicente Arraya (1/0), Segundo Durandal (3/0), Conrado Angulo (1/0), Carlos Richter (1/0), Remberto Ferrel (1/0), Zenón González (1/0), Luis Montoya (1/0), Hugo Gamarra (1/0), Mario Mauricio Alborta Velasco (10/2), José Toro (3/0), Rodolfo Plaza (1/0). Trainer: Julio Borelli (1).
**Goal:** Mario Mauricio Alborta Velasco.

**11.** 11.08.1938 **BOLIVIA - VENEZUELA** **3-1(1-1)** 1st Juegos Bolivarianos
Estadio Universitario, Bogotá
**BOL:** Vicente Arraya (2/0), Segundo Durandal (4/0), Conrado Angulo (2/0), Roberto Soto (1/0), Gerardo Peláez (1/0), Zenón González (2/0), Luis Montoya (2/1), Hugo Gamarra (2/2), Mario Mauricio Alborta Velasco (11/2), Alfredo Molina (1/0), Rodolfo Plaza (2/0). Trainer: Julio Borelli (2).
**Goals:** Luis Montoya (35), Hugo Gamarra (48, 85).

**12.** 14.08.1938 **PERU - BOLIVIA** **3-0** 1st Juegos Bolivarianos
Estadio Universitario, Bogotá
**BOL:** Vicente Arraya (3/0), Segundo Durandal (5/0), Conrado Angulo (3/0), Hernán Rojas (1/0), Gerardo Peláez (2/0), Zenón González (3/0), Luis Montoya (3/1), Alfredo Molina (2/0), Mario Mauricio Alborta Velasco (12/2), José Toro (4/0), Rodolfo Plaza (3/0). Trainer: Julio Borelli (3).

**13.** 16.08.1938 **BOLIVIA - COLOMBIA** **2-1** 1st Juegos Bolivarianos
Estadio Universitario, Bogotá
**BOL:** Vicente Arraya (4/0), Conrado Angulo (4/0), Segundo Durandal (6/0), Carlos Richter (2/0), Remberto Ferrel (2/0), Vargas (1/0), Luis Montoya (4/2), Hugo Gamarra (3/2), Mario Mauricio Alborta Velasco (13/2), Alfredo Molina (3/1), Severo Orgaz (1/0). Trainer: Julio Borelli (4).
**Goals:** Luis Montoya, Alfredo Molina.

**14.** 22.08.1938 **BOLIVIA - ECUADOR** **2-1** 1st Juegos Bolivarianos
Estadio Universitario, Bogotá
**BOL:** Vicente Arraya (5/0), Segundo Durandal (7/0), Conrado Angulo (5/0), Roberto Soto (2/0), Remberto Ferrel (3/0), Zenón González (4/0), Luis Montoya (5/2), Hugo Gamarra (4/2), Mario Mauricio Alborta Velasco (14/2), Ciro Noguera (1/0), Rodolfo Plaza (4/2). Trainer: Julio Borelli (5).
**Goals:** Rodolfo Plaza 2.

**15.** 18.01.1945 **ARGENTINA - BOLIVIA** **4-0(2-0)** 18th Copa América
Estadio Nacional, Santiago; Referee: Humberto Reginatto Balbo (Chile); Attendance: 35,000
**BOL:** Vicente Arraya (6/0), Hernán Rojas (2/0) [Nicolás Prieto (1/0)], Alberto Figueroa de Achá (1/0), Manuel Gutiérrez (1/0), Raúl Fernández (1/0), Exequiel Calderón (1/0), Zenón González (5/0), Roque Romero (1/0), Armando Tapia (1/0), Walter Orozco (1/0) [Adrián Ortega (1/0)], Severo Orgaz (2/0). Trainer: Julio Borelli (6).

**16.** 24.01.1945 **CHILE - BOLIVIA** **5-0(3-0)** 18th Copa América
Estadio Nacional, Santiago; Referee: Nobel Valentini (Uruguay); Attendance: 70,000
**BOL:** Vicente Arraya (7/0), Nicolás Prieto (2/0), Alberto Figueroa de Achá (2/0), Manuel Gutiérrez (2/0), Raúl Fernández (2/0), Exequiel Calderón (2/0), Zenón González (6/0), Adrián Ortega (2/0) [Miguel Peredo (1/0)], Armando Tapia (2/0) [Donato Medrano (1/0)], Walter Orozco (2/0), Severo Orgaz (3/0). Trainer: Julio Borelli (7).

**17.** 28.01.1945 **BRAZIL - BOLIVIA** **2-0(0-0)** 18th Copa América
Estadio Nacional, Santiago; Referee: José Bartolomé Macías (Argentina); Attendance: 28,000
**BOL:** Vicente Arraya (8/0), Nicolás Prieto (3/0), Alberto Figueroa de Achá (3/0), Martín Saavedra (1/0), Raúl Fernández (3/0), Exequiel Calderón (3/0), Zenón González (7/0), Adrián Ortega (3/0), Donato Medrano (2/0) [Armando Tapia (3/0); Ruperto Inchausti (1/0)], Walter Orozco (3/0), Severo Orgaz (4/0) [*sent off*]. Trainer: Julio Borelli (8).

**18.** 11.02.1945 **ECUADOR - BOLIVIA** **0-0** 18th Copa América
Estadio Nacional, Santiago; Referee: Mário Gonçalves Vianna (Brazil); Attendance: 70,000
**BOL:** Vicente Arraya (9/0), Nicolás Prieto (4/0), Alberto Figueroa de Achá (4/0), Martín Saavedra (2/0), Raúl Fernández (4/0), Exequiel Calderón (4/0), Zenón González (8/0), Roque Romero (2/0), Armando Tapia (4/0) [Ruperto Inchausti (2/0)], Walter Orozco (4/0) [Adrián Ortega (4/0)], Severo Orgaz (5/0). Trainer: Julio Borelli (9).

**19.** 15.02.1945 **URUGUAY - BOLIVIA** **2-0(1-0)** 18th Copa América
Estadio Nacional, Santiago; Referee: Mário Gonçalves Vianna (Brazil); Attendance: 65,000
**BOL:** Vicente Arraya (10/0), Nicolás Prieto (5/0), Alberto Figueroa de Achá (5/0) [*sent off*], Martín Saavedra (3/0) [*sent off*], Raúl Fernández (5/0), Exequiel Calderón (5/0), Ruperto Inchausti (3/0), Roque Romero (3/0), Donato Medrano (3/0) [Miguel Peredo (2/0)], Walter Orozco (5/0), Severo Orgaz (6/0). Trainer: Julio Borelli (10).

**20.** 21.02.1945 **COLOMBIA - BOLIVIA** **3-3** 18th Copa América
Estadio Nacional, Santiago; Referee: Juan Las Heras Marrodan (Chile); Attendance: 22,000
**BOL:** Vicente Arraya (11/0) [Cleto Prieto (1/0)], Alberto Figueroa de Achá (6/0), Nicolás Prieto (6/0), Martín Saavedra (4/0), Raúl Fernández (6/1) [Ruperto Inchausti (4/0)], Exequiel Calderón (6/0), Manuel Gutiérrez (3/0), Zenón González (9/1), Roque Romero (4/0), Walter Orozco (6/0), Severo Orgaz (7/1). Trainer: Julio Borelli (11).
**Goals:** Raúl Fernández, Zenón González, Severo Orgaz.

**21.** 16.01.1946 **BRAZIL - BOLIVIA** **3-0(0-0)** 19th Copa América
Estadio Gasómetro de Boedo, Buenos Aires; Referee: José Bartolomé Macías (Argentina); Attendance: 50,000
**BOL:** Vicente Arraya (12/0), Alberto Figueroa de Achá (7/0), José Bustamante Nava (1/0), Exequiel Calderón (7/0), Raúl Fernández (7/1), Leonardo Ferrel (1/0), Zenón González (10/1), Adrián Ortega (5/0), Armando Tapia (5/0) [Rosenberg (1/0)], Miguel Peredo (3/0) [Félix Garzón (1/0)], Severo Orgaz (8/1). Trainer: Diógenes Lara (1).

**22.** 19.01.1946 **ARGENTINA - BOLIVIA** **7-1(2-0)** 19th Copa América
Estadio Gasómetro de Boedo, Buenos Aires; Referee: Higinio Madrid (Chile); Attendance: 65,000
**BOL:** Vicente Arraya (13/0), Alberto Figueroa de Achá (8/0), José Bustamante Nava (2/0), Exequiel Calderón (8/0), Raúl Fernández (8/1), Raúl Vargas (1/0), Zenón González (11/1), Adrián Ortega (6/0), Armando Tapia (6/0) [Ruperto Inchausti (5/0)], Miguel Peredo (4/1), Severo Orgaz (9/1) [Félix Garzón (2/0)]. Trainer: Diógenes Lara (2).
**Goal:** Miguel Peredo (67).

**23.** 26.01.1946 **PARAGUAY - BOLIVIA** **4-2** 19th Copa América
Estadio Monumental „Antonio Vespucio Liberti", Buenos Aires; Referee: José Bartolomé Macías (Argentina); Attendance: 80,000
**BOL:** Vicente Arraya (14/0), Alberto Figueroa de Achá (9/0), José Bustamante Nava (3/0), Exequiel Calderón (9/0), Raúl Fernández (9/1), Raúl Vargas (2/0), Zenón González (12/2), Adrián Ortega (7/0), Serapio Vega Saavedra (1/0), Miguel Peredo (5/1), Severo Orgaz (10/1). Trainer: Diógenes Lara (3).
**Goals:** Doroteo Coronel (own goal), Zenón González.

**24.** 29.01.1946 **URUGUAY - BOLIVIA** **5-0(3-0)** 19th Copa América
Estadio Independiente, Avellaneda, Buenos Aires; Referee: Higinio Madrid (Chile); Attendance: 30,000
**BOL:** Vicente Arraya (15/0), Alberto Figueroa de Achá (10/0), Nicolás Prieto (7/0), Exequiel Calderón (10/0), Raúl Fernández (10/1), Raúl Vargas (3/0), Zenón González (13/2) [Juan Peñaloza (1/0)], Adrián Ortega (8/0), Serapio Vega Saavedra (2/0), Miguel Peredo (6/1), Severo Orgaz (11/1). Trainer: Diógenes Lara (4).

**25.** 08.02.1946 **CHILE - BOLIVIA** **4-1** 19th Copa América
Estadio Gasómetro de Boedo, Buenos Aires; Referee: José Bartolomé Macías (Argentina); Attendance: 18,000
**BOL:** Vicente Arraya (16/0) [Guillermo Navarro (1/0)], Alberto Figueroa de Achá (11/0), José Bustamante Nava (4/0) [Leonardo Ferrel (2/0)], Rodolfo Maida (1/0) [Exequiel Calderón (11/0)], Raúl Fernández (11/1), Raúl Vargas (4/0), Juan Peñaloza (2/0), Serapio Vega Saavedra (3/0), Miguel Peredo (7/2), Adrián Ortega (9/0), Severo Orgaz (12/1). Trainer: Diógenes Lara (5).
**Goal:** Miguel Peredo.

**26.** 30.11.1947 **ECUADOR - BOLIVIA** **2-2(2-2)** 20th Copa América
Estadio „George Capwell", Guayaquil; Referee: Luis Alberto Fernández (Uruguay); Attendance: 30,000
**BOL:** Vicente Arraya (17/0), Alberto Figueroa de Achá (12/0), José Bustamante Nava (5/0), Leonardo Ferrel (3/0), Juan Guerra (1/0), Raúl Vargas (5/0), Zenón González (14/2), Víctor Agustín Ugarte Oviedo (1/0) [Arturo Tardío (1/0)], Armando Tapia (7/0), Benigno Gutiérrez Valdivia (1/2), Benjamín Maldonado (1/0). Trainer: Diógenes Lara (6).

**Goals:** Benigno Gutiérrez Valdivia (26, 44).

**27.** 04.12.1947 **ARGENTINA - BOLIVIA** **7-0(3-0)** 20th Copa América
Estadio „George Capwell", Guayaquil; Referee: Federico Muñoz Medina (Ecuador); Attendance: 30,000
**BOL:** Vicente Arraya (18/0) [Eduardo Gutiérrez Valdivia (1/0)], Alberto Figueroa de Achá (13/0) [Duberty Aráoz (1/0)], José Bustamante Nava (6/0), Leonardo Ferrel (4/0), Juan Guerra (2/0), Raúl Vargas (6/0), Zenón González (15/2), Víctor Agustín Ugarte Oviedo (2/0), Armando Tapia (8/0), Benigno Gutiérrez Valdivia (2/2), Benjamín Maldonado (2/0) [Severo Orgaz (13/1)]. Trainer: Diógenes Lara (7).

**28.** 09.12.1947 **URUGUAY - BOLIVIA** **3-0(1-0)** 20th Copa América
Estadio „George Capwell", Guayaquil; Referee: Mario Rubén Heyn (Paraguay); Attendance: 15,000
**BOL:** Vicente Arraya (19/0), Alberto Figueroa de Achá (14/0) [Duberty Aráoz (2/0)], José Bustamante Nava (7/0), Rodolfo Maida (2/0), Juan Guerra (3/0), Raúl Vargas (7/0), Zenón González (16/2), Víctor Agustín Ugarte Oviedo (3/0), Armando Tapia (9/0), Benigno Gutiérrez Valdivia (3/2), Severo Orgaz (14/1). Trainer: Diógenes Lara (8).

**29.** 13.12.1947 **COLOMBIA - BOLIVIA** **0-0** 20th Copa América
Estadio „George Capwell", Guayaquil; Referee: Luis Alberto Fernández (Uruguay); Attendance: 18,000
**BOL:** Vicente Arraya (20/0), Alberto Figueroa de Achá (15/0) [Duberty Aráoz (3/0)], José Bustamante Nava (8/0), Exequiel Calderón (12/0), Juan Guerra (4/0), Raúl Vargas (8/0), Zenón González (17/2), Víctor Agustín Ugarte Oviedo (4/0), Armando Tapia (10/0), Benigno Gutiérrez Valdivia (4/2) [Serapio Vega Saavedra (4/0)], Severo Orgaz (15/1). Trainer: Diógenes Lara (9).

**30.** 18.12.1947 **PARAGUAY - BOLIVIA** **3-1** 20th Copa América
Estadio „George Capwell", Guayaquil; Referee: Juan José Alvarez (Uruguay); Attendance: 12,000
**BOL:** Vicente Arraya (21/0) [Eduardo Gutiérrez Valdivia (2/0)], Alberto Figueroa de Achá (16/0) [Duberty Aráoz (4/0)], José Bustamante Nava (9/0), Exequiel Calderón (13/0), Juan Guerra (5/0), Raúl Vargas (9/0), Zenón González (18/3), Arturo Tardío (2/0), Armando Tapia (11/0), Serapio Vega Saavedra (5/0), Severo Orgaz (16/1). Trainer: Diógenes Lara (10).
**Goal:** Zenón González.

**31.** 27.12.1947 **PERU - BOLIVIA** **2-0(0-0)** 20th Copa América
Estadio „George Capwell", Guayaquil; Referee: Mario Rubén Heyn (Paraguay); Attendance: 5,000
**BOL:** Eduardo Gutiérrez Valdivia (3/0), Duberty Aráoz (5/0), José Bustamante Nava (10/0), Exequiel Calderón (14/0), Juan Guerra (6/0), Raúl Vargas (10/0), Zenón González (19/3) [Benjamín Maldonado (3/0)], Víctor Agustín Ugarte Oviedo (5/0), Benigno Gutiérrez Valdivia (5/2) [Serapio Vega Saavedra (6/0)], Armando Tapia (12/0), Severo Orgaz (17/1). Trainer: Diógenes Lara (11).

**32.** 31.12.1947 **CHILE - BOLIVIA** **4-3** 20th Copa América
Estadio „George Capwell", Guayaquil; Referee: Federico Muñoz Medina (Ecuador); Attendance: 5,000
**BOL:** Eduardo Gutiérrez Valdivia (4/0), Duberty Aráoz (6/0), José Bustamante Nava (11/0), Exequiel Calderón (15/0), Juan Guerra (7/0), Raúl Vargas (11/0), Zenón González (20/3), Víctor Agustín Ugarte Oviedo (6/0), Armando Tapia (13/1), Arturo Tardío (3/1), Severo Orgaz (18/2). Trainer: Diógenes Lara (12).
**Goals:** Arturo Tardío, Armando Tapia, Severo Orgaz.

**33.** 05.01.1948 **BOLIVIA - VENEZUELA** **2-2** Juegos Bolivarianos
Lima; Referee: Juan Honores (Peru)
**BOL:** Eduardo Gutiérrez Valdivia (5/0), Duberty Aráoz (7/0), José Bustamante Nava (12/0), Rodolfo Maida (3/0), Juan Guerra (8/0), Leonardo Ferrel (5/0) [Gustavo Ríos (1/0)], Zenón González (21/4), Serapio Vega Saavedra (7/0), Armando Tapia (14/2), Arturo Tardío (4/1), Severo Orgaz (19/2). Trainer: Félix Deheza (1).
**Goals:** Armando Tapia, Zenón González.

**34.** 08.01.1948 **PERU – BOLIVIA** **1-0** Juegos Bolivarianos
Lima; Referee: Waldemar Silva (Brazil)
**BOL:** Eduardo Gutiérrez Valdivia (6/0), Duberty Aráoz (8/0), José Bustamante Nava (13/0), Exequiel Calderón (16/0), Leonardo Ferrel (6/0) [Juan Guerra (9/0)], Raúl Vargas (12/0), Zenón González (22/4), Víctor Agustín Ugarte Oviedo (7/0), Armando Tapia (15/2) [Gustavo Ríos (2/0)], Benigno Gutiérrez Valdivia (6/2), Severo Orgaz (20/2). Trainer: Félix Deheza (2).

**35.** 06.04.1949 **BOLIVIA – CHILE** **3-2(0-1)** 21th Copa América
Estádio Pacaembú, São Paulo (Brazil); Referee: Cyril John Barrick (England); Attendance: 30,000
**BOL:** Eduardo Gutiérrez Valdivia (7/0), Alberto Figueroa de Achá (17/0), José Bustamante Nava (14/0), René Cabrera (1/0) [Humberto Montaño (1/0)], Antonio José Valencia (1/0), Leonardo Ferrel (7/0), Víctor Celestino Algarañaz (1/0) [Benjamín Maldonado (4/0)], Víctor Agustín Ugarte Oviedo (8/1), Mario Mena Lema (1/0) [Nemesio Rojas (1/0)], Benigno Gutiérrez Valdivia (7/3), Benedicto Godoy Véizaga (1/1). Trainer: Félix Deheza (3).
**Goals:** Víctor Agustín Ugarte Oviedo (59), Benedicto Godoy Véizaga (77), Benigno Gutiérrez Valdivia (79).

**36.** 10.04.1949 **BRAZIL – BOLIVIA** **10-1(4-0)** 21th Copa América
Estádio Pacaembú, São Paulo; Referee: Cyril John Barrick (England); Attendance: 40,000
**BOL:** Eduardo Gutiérrez Valdivia (8/0) [Vicente Arraya (22/0)], Alberto Figueroa de Achá (18/0), José Bustamante Nava (15/0), René Cabrera (2/0), Antonio José Valencia (2/0), Leonardo Ferrel (8/0), Humberto Montaño (2/0), Mario Mena Lema (2/0), Víctor Agustín Ugarte Oviedo (9/2), Benigno Gutiérrez Valdivia (8/3), Benedicto Godoy Véizaga (2/1) [Benjamín Maldonado (5/0)]. Trainer: Félix Deheza (4).
**Goal:** Víctor Agustín Ugarte Oviedo (75).

**37.** 17.04.1949 **BOLIVIA – URUGUAY** **3-2(0-0)** 21th Copa América
Estádio São Januario, Rio de Janeiro; Referee: Alberto Monard da Gama Malcher (Brazil); Attendance: 8,000
**BOL:** Vicente Arraya (23/0), Alberto Figueroa de Achá (19/0), José Bustamante Nava (16/0), René Cabrera (3/0), Antonio José Valencia (3/0), Leonardo Ferrel (9/0), Víctor Celestino Algarañaz (2/1), Mario Mena Lema (3/0) [Nemesio Rojas (2/0)], Víctor Agustín Ugarte Oviedo (10/3), Benigno Gutiérrez Valdivia (9/4), Benedicto Godoy Véizaga (3/1). Trainer: Félix Deheza (5).
**Goals:** Víctor Agustín Ugarte Oviedo (47 penalty), Víctor Celestino Algarañaz (57), Benigno Gutiérrez Valdivia (66).

**38.** 24.04.1949 **BOLIVIA – ECUADOR** **2-0(2-0)** 21th Copa América
Estádio Pacaembú, São Paulo; Referee: Mario Gardelli (Brazil); Attendance: 14,000
**BOL:** Vicente Arraya (24/0), Alberto Figueroa de Achá (20/0), José Bustamante Nava (17/0), René Cabrera (4/0), Antonio José Valencia (4/0), Humberto Montaño (3/0) [Leonardo Ferrel (10/0)], Víctor Celestino Algarañaz (3/1), Víctor Agustín Ugarte Oviedo (11/5), Mario Mena Lema (4/0), Benigno Gutiérrez Valdivia (10/4), Benedicto Godoy Véizaga (4/1) [Armando Tapia (16/2)]. Trainer: Félix Deheza (6).
**Goals:** Víctor Agustín Ugarte Oviedo (6, 14 penalty).

**39.** 27.04.1949 **PERU – BOLIVIA** **3-0(1-0)** 21th Copa América

Estádio Villa Belmiro, Santos; Referee: Alberto Monard da Gama Malcher (Brazil); Attendance: 12,000

**BOL:** Eduardo Gutiérrez Valdivia (9/0), Alberto Figueroa de Achá (21/0), José Bustamante Nava (18/0), René Cabrera (5/0), Antonio José Valencia (5/0), Leonardo Ferrel (11/0), Víctor Celestino Algarañaz (4/1), Víctor Agustín Ugarte Oviedo (12/5), Mario Mena Lema (5/0), Benigno Gutiérrez Valdivia (11/4), Benedicto Godoy Véizaga (5/1). Trainer: Félix Deheza (7).

**40.** 30.04.1949 **PARAGUAY – BOLIVIA** **7-0(3-0)** 21th Copa América

Estádio São Januario, Rio de Janeiro; Referee: Cyril John Barrick (England); Attendance: 45,000

**BOL:** Vicente Arraya (25/0) [Eduardo Gutiérrez Valdivia (10/0)], Alberto Figueroa de Achá (22/0) [N. Delgadillo (1/0)], José Bustamante Nava (19/0), René Cabrera (6/0) [*sent off*], Antonio José Valencia (6/0), Leonardo Ferrel (12/0), Víctor Celestino Algarañaz (5/1), Víctor Agustín Ugarte Oviedo (13/5), Mario Mena Lema (6/0) [Nemesio Rojas (3/0)], Benigno Gutiérrez Valdivia (12/4) [Armando Tapia (17/2)], Benedicto Godoy Véizaga (6/1). Trainer: Félix Deheza (8).

**41.** 06.05.1949 **BOLIVIA – COLOMBIA** **4-0(1-0)** 21th Copa América

Estádio Botafogo, Rio de Janeiro; Referee: Cyril John Barrick (England); Attendance: 12,000

**BOL:** Eduardo Gutiérrez Valdivia (11/0), Alberto Figueroa de Achá (23/0) [N. Delgadillo (2/0)], José Bustamante Nava (20/0), René Cabrera (7/0), Antonio José Valencia (7/0), Leonardo Ferrel (13/0), Víctor Celestino Algarañaz (6/1), Víctor Agustín Ugarte Oviedo (14/6), Mario Mena Lema (7/0) [Nemesio Rojas (4/1)], Benigno Gutiérrez Valdivia (13/5), Benedicto Godoy Véizaga (7/2) [Benjamín Maldonado (6/0)]. Trainer: Félix Deheza (9).

**Goals:** Benedicto Godoy Véizaga (10), Benigno Gutiérrez Valdivia (55), Nemesio Rojas (77), Víctor Agustín Ugarte Oviedo (81).

**42.** 26.02.1950 **BOLIVIA – CHILE** **2-0(0-0)**

Estadio „Hernándo Siles Zuazo", La Paz; Referee: Alfredo Alvarez Fernández (Bolivia); Attendance: 25,000

**BOL:** Eduardo Gutiérrez Valdivia (12/0), Duberty Aráoz (9/0), José Bustamante Nava (21/0), René Cabrera (8/0), Antonio José Valencia (8/0), Leonardo Ferrel (14/1), Víctor Celestino Algarañaz (7/1) [Víctor Brown Rojas (1/0)], Víctor Agustín Ugarte Oviedo (15/6), Mario Mena Lema (8/1), Benigno Gutiérrez Valdivia (14/5), Valdez (1/0) [Benedicto Godoy Véizaga (8/2)]. Trainer: no.

**Goals:** Mario Mena Lema (52), Leonardo Ferrel (64).

**43.** 12.03.1950 **CHILE – BOLIVIA** **5-0(3-0)**

Estadio Nacional, Santiago; Referee: Alejandro Gálvez (Chile); Attendance: 40,000

**BOL:** Eduardo Gutiérrez Valdivia (13/0) [Vicente Arraya (26/0)], Duberty Aráoz (10/0), José Bustamante Nava (22/0), René Cabrera (9/0) [Carlos Arias (1/0)], Antonio José Valencia (9/0), Leonardo Ferrel (15/1), Benedicto Godoy Véizaga (9/2), Víctor Agustín Ugarte Oviedo (16/6), Mario Mena Lema (9/1), Benigno Gutiérrez Valdivia (15/5), Víctor Brown Rojas (2/0) [Víctor Celestino Algarañaz (8/1)]. Trainer: no.

**44.** 02.07.1950 **URUGUAY – BOLIVIA** **8-0(4-0)** 4th FIFA WC. Group Stage.

Estádio Independencia, Belo Horizonte; Referee: George Reader (England); Attendance: 5,284

**BOL:** Eduardo Gutiérrez Valdivia (14/0), Alberto Figueroa de Achá (24/0), José Bustamante Nava (Cap) (23/0), Antonio Greco (1/0), Antonio José Valencia (10/0), Leonardo Ferrel (16/1), Víctor Celestino Algarañaz (9/1), Víctor Agustín Ugarte Oviedo (17/6), Roberto Caparelli Coringrato (1/0), Benigno Gutiérrez Valdivia (16/5), Benjamín Maldonado (7/0). Trainer: Mario Pretto (1).

**45.** 22.02.1953 **PERU– BOLIVIA** **0-1(0-0)** 22nd Copa América

Estadio Nacional, Lima; Referee: George Rhoden (England); Attendance: 50,000

**BOL:** Eduardo Gutiérrez Valdivia (15/0), Eduardo González (1/0), José Bustamante Nava (24/0), René Cabrera (10/0), Ramón Guillermo Santos Brizuela (1/0), Edgar Vargas Romero (1/0), Víctor Brown Rojas (3/0), Mario Mena Lema (10/1), Víctor Agustín Ugarte Oviedo (18/7), Hilarión López (1/0), Ricardo Alcón (1/0). Trainer: César Vicino (1).

**Goal:** Víctor Agustín Ugarte Oviedo (53).

**46.** 25.02.1953 **URUGUAY – BOLIVIA** **2-0(1-0)** 22nd Copa América

Estadio Nacional, Lima; Referee: Charles Dean (England); Attendance: 45,000

**BOL:** Eduardo Gutiérrez Valdivia (16/0), Eduardo González (2/0), José Bustamante Nava (25/0), René Cabrera (11/0), Ramón Guillermo Santos Brizuela (2/0), Edgar Vargas Romero (2/0), Víctor Brown Rojas (4/0) [Ricardo Sánchez (1/0)], Mario Mena Lema (11/1), Víctor Agustín Ugarte Oviedo (19/7), Hilarión López (2/0) [Benigno Gutiérrez Valdivia (17/5)], Ricardo Alcón (2/0). Trainer: César Vicino (2).

**47.** 01.03.1953 **BRAZIL – BOLIVIA** **8-1(6-0)** 22nd Copa América

Estadio Nacional, Lima; Referee: Richard Maddison (England); Attendance: 45,000

**BOL:** Eduardo Gutiérrez Valdivia (17/0), Eduardo González (3/0), José Bustamante Nava (26/0), René Cabrera (12/0), Antonio José Valencia (11/0) [Ramón Guillermo Santos Brizuela (3/0)], Edgar Vargas Romero (3/0), Víctor Brown Rojas (5/0), Mario Mena Lema (12/1), Víctor Agustín Ugarte Oviedo (20/8), Hilarión López (3/0) [Delfin Díaz (1/0)], Ricardo Alcón (3/0). Trainer: César Vicino (3).

**Goal:** Víctor Agustín Ugarte Oviedo (73 penalty).

**48.** 08.03.1953 **BOLIVIA – ECUADOR** **1-1(1-1)** 22nd Copa América

Estadio Nacional, Lima; Referee: Charles McKenna (England); Attendance: 45,000

**BOL:** Eduardo Gutiérrez Valdivia (18/0), Eduardo González (4/0), José Bustamante Nava (27/0), René Cabrera (13/0), Ramón Guillermo Santos Brizuela (4/0), Edgar Vargas Romero (4/0), Víctor Brown Rojas (6/0), Mario Mena Lema (13/1), Víctor Agustín Ugarte Oviedo (21/9), Delfin Díaz (2/0), Ricardo Alcón (4/0) [Hilarión López (4/0)]. Trainer: César Vicino (4).

**Goal:** Víctor Agustín Ugarte Oviedo (25).

**49.** 16.03.1953 **PARAGUAY – BOLIVIA** **2-1(2-0)** 22nd Copa América

Estadio Nacional, Lima; Referee: David Gregory (England); Attendance: 15,000

**BOL:** Eduardo Gutiérrez Valdivia (19/0), Eduardo González (5/0), José Bustamante Nava (28/0), René Cabrera (14/0) [Arturo Miranda (1/0)], Ramón Guillermo Santos Brizuela (5/0), Edgar Vargas Romero (5/0), Víctor Brown Rojas (7/0), Mario Mena Lema (14/1), Víctor Agustín Ugarte Oviedo (22/9), Hilarión López (5/0), Ricardo Alcón (5/0). Trainer: César Vicino (5).

**Goal:** Ramón Guillermo Santos Brizuela (76).

**50.** 28.03.1953 **BOLIVIA – CHILE** **2-2*** 22nd Copa América

Estadio Nacional, Lima; Referee: Richard Maddison (England); Attendance: 45,000

**BOL:** Raúl Reynoso (1/0) [Eduardo Gutiérrez Valdivia (20/0)], Eduardo González (6/0), José Bustamante Nava (29/0), Arturo Miranda (2/0), Ramón Guillermo Santos Brizuela (6/2), Edgar Vargas Romero (6/0), Víctor Brown Rojas (8/0) [*sent off*], Mario Mena Lema (15/1), Víctor Agustín Ugarte Oviedo (23/9), Hilarión López (6/0), Ricardo Alcón (6/1). Trainer: César Vicino (6).

**Goal:** Ramón Guillermo Santos Brizuela (15), Ricardo Alcón (49).

**The match was interrupted after 66 mins due to unsportsmanlike behaviour of bolivian players.*

**51.** 10.06.1957 **PARAGUAY - BOLIVIA** **5-2** Copa Páz del Chaco
Asunción; Referee: Jorge Saavedra (Bolivia)
**BOL:** Eustaquio Ortuno (1/0), Silvano Valdivia (1/0), Miguel Burgos Suárez (1/0) [José Rocabado Montaño (1/0)], Edgar Vargas Romero (7/0) [Arturo Miranda (3/0)], Oscar Claure (1/0) [Máximo Ramírez Burgos (1/0)], Ramón Guillermo Santos Brizuela (7/2), César Sánchez (1/0) [Víctor Brown Rojas (9/0)], Armando Escobar (1/0), Víctor Agustín Ugarte Oviedo (24/10) [Máximo Alcócer (1/0)], Ausberto García (1/1), Vicente Moreno (1/0).
**Goals:** Ausberto García, Víctor Agustín Ugarte Oviedo.

**52.** 12.06.1957 **PARAGUAY - BOLIVIA** **0-1** Copa Páz del Chaco
Asunción; Referee: Jorge Saavedra (Bolivia)
**BOL:** Eustaquio Ortuno (2/0), Silvano Valdivia (2/0) [Arturo Miranda (4/0)], Miguel Burgos Suárez (2/0), Edgar Vargas Romero (8/0) [José Rocabado Montaño (2/0)], Oscar Claure (2/0), Ramón Guillermo Santos Brizuela (8/2), Víctor Brown Rojas (10/0) [Máximo Ramírez Burgos (2/0)], Armando Escobar (2/0) [César Sánchez (2/0)], Víctor Agustín Ugarte Oviedo (25/11), Máximo Alcócer (2/0), Vicente Moreno (2/0).
**Goal:** Víctor Agustín Ugarte Oviedo.

**53.** 18.08.1957 **BOLIVIA - PARAGUAY** **3-3** Copa Páz del Chaco
La Paz; Referee: Wenceslau Zárate (Paraguay)
**BOL:** Eustaquio Ortuno (3/0), Miguel Burgos Suárez (3/0), Ramón Guillermo Santos Brizuela (9/2), Edgar Vargas Romero (9/0) [Máximo Ramírez Burgos (3/0)], Wilfredo Camacho (1/0) [Oscar Claure (3/0)], Arturo Miranda (5/0), Víctor Brown Rojas (11/0), Máximo Alcócer (3/1), Víctor Agustín Ugarte Oviedo (26/12), Mario Mena Lema (16/2) [Armando Escobar (3/0)], Ricardo Alcón (7/1).
**Goals:** Víctor Agustín Ugarte Oviedo, Mario Mena Lema, Máximo Alcócer.

**54.** 21.08.1957 **BOLIVIA - PARAGUAY** **2-1** Copa Páz del Chaco
Estadio „Hernándo Siles Zuazo", La Paz; Referee: Roberto González (Paraguay)
**BOL:** Eustaquio Ortuno (4/0), Miguel Burgos Suárez (4/0), Ramón Guillermo Santos Brizuela (10/2), Máximo Ramírez Burgos (4/0), Wilfredo Camacho (2/0), Oscar Claure (4/0) [Edgar Vargas Romero (10/0)], Víctor Brown Rojas (12/1), Máximo Alcócer (4/1), Víctor Agustín Ugarte Oviedo (27/13), Ausberto García (2/1) [Mario Mena Lema (17/2)], Ricardo Alcón (8/1).
**Goals:** Víctor Agustín Ugarte Oviedo, Víctor Brown Rojas.

**55.** 22.09.1957 **CHILE - BOLIVIA** **2-1(1-1)** 6th FIFA WC. Qualifiers
Estadio Nacional, Santiago; Referee: Paul Wyssling (Switzerland); Attendance: 37,071
**BOL**: Eustaquio Ortuno (5/0), Miguel Burgos Suárez (5/0), Oscar Claure (5/0), Ramón Guillermo Santos Brizuela (11/2), Wilfredo Camacho (3/1), Máximo Ramírez Burgos (5/0), Víctor Brown Rojas (13/1), Víctor Agustín Ugarte Oviedo (Cap) (28/13), Mario Mena Lema (18/2), Máximo Alcócer (5/1), Ricardo Alcón (9/1).
**Goal:** Wilfredo Camacho (38).

**56.** 29.09.1957 **BOLIVIA - CHILE** **3-0(1-0)** 6th FIFA WC. Qualifiers
Estadio „Hernándo Siles Zuazo", La Paz; Referee: Paul Wyssling (Switzerland)
**BOL:** Eustaquio Ortuno (6/0), Miguel Burgos Suárez (6/0), Oscar Claure (6/0), Ramón Guillermo Santos Brizuela (12/2), Wilfredo Camacho (4/0), Máximo Ramírez Burgos (6/0), Víctor Brown Rojas (14/1), Víctor Agustín Ugarte Oviedo (Cap) (29/13), Ausberto García (3/2), Máximo Alcócer (6/3), Ricardo Alcón (10/1).
**Goals:** Ausberto García (28), Máximo Alcócer (63, 87).

**57.** 06.10.1957 **BOLIVIA - ARGENTINA** **2-0(1-0)** 6th FIFA WC. Qualifiers
Estadio „Hernándo Siles Zuazo", La Paz; Referee: Paul Wyssling (Switzerland); Attendance: 25,000
**BOL**: Eustaquio Ortuno (7/0), Miguel Burgos Suárez (7/0), Oscar Claure (7/0), Ramón Guillermo Santos Brizuela (13/2), Wilfredo Camacho (5/0), Máximo Ramírez Burgos (7/1), Víctor Brown Rojas (15/1), Víctor Agustín Ugarte Oviedo (Cap) (30/13), Mario Mena Lema (19/2), Máximo Alcócer (7/4), Ricardo Alcón (11/1).
**Goals:** Máximo Alcócer (13), Máximo Ramírez Burgos (62).

**58.** 27.10.1957 **ARGENTINA - BOLIVIA** **4-0(1-0)** 6th FIFA WC. Qualifiers
Estadio Independiente, Avellaneda, Buenos Aires; Referee: Paul Wyssling (Switzerland); Attendance: 70,000
**BOL:** Eustaquio Ortuno (8/0), Miguel Burgos Suárez (8/0), Oscar Claure (8/0), Ramón Guillermo Santos Brizuela (14/2), Wilfredo Camacho (6/0), Máximo Ramírez Burgos (8/1), Víctor Brown Rojas (16/1), Víctor Agustín Ugarte Oviedo (Cap) (31/13), Ausberto García (4/2), Máximo Alcócer (8/4), Ricardo Alcón (12/1).

**59.** 08.03.1959 **URUGUAY - BOLIVIA** **7-0(3-0)** 26th Copa América
Estadio Monumental „Antonio Vespucio Liberti", Buenos Aires; Referee: Alberto Monard da Gama Malcher (Brazil); Attendance: 35,000
**BOL:** Oscar Soliz Barba (1/0) [Arturo López (1/0)], Miguel Burgos Suárez (9/0), Oscar Claure (9/0), Ramón Guillermo Santos Brizuela (15/2), Edgar Vargas Romero (11/0) [Máximo Ramírez Burgos (9/1)], César Sánchez (3/0), Wilfredo Camacho (7/0), Víctor Agustín Ugarte Oviedo (32/13), Ausberto García (5/2), Renán López (1/0), Ricardo Alcón (13/1) [Antonio Atilio Aguirre (1/0)]. Trainer: Vicente Arraya (1).

**60.** 11.03.1959 **ARGENTINA - BOLIVIA** **2-0(1-0)** 26th Copa América
Estadio Monumental „Antonio Vespucio Liberti", Buenos Aires; Referee: Juan Carlos Robles (Chile); Attendance: 45,000
**BOL:** Arturo López (2/0), Miguel Burgos Suárez (10/0), Oscar Claure (10/0), Ramón Guillermo Santos Brizuela (16/2), Wilfredo Camacho (8/0), Máximo Ramírez Burgos (10/1), César Sánchez (4/0) [Abdul Aramayo Mendizábal (1/0)], Renán López (2/0) [Víctor Agustín Ugarte Oviedo (33/13)], Mario Mena Lema (20/2) [Ausberto García (6/2)), Máximo Alcócer (9/4), Antonio Atilio Aguirre (2/0). Trainer: Vicente Arraya (2).

**61.** 15.03.1959 **PARAGUAY - BOLIVIA** **5-0** 26th Copa América
Estadio Monumental „Antonio Vespucio Liberti", Buenos Aires; Referee: Alberto Monard da Gama Malcher (Brazil); Attendance: 40,000
**BOL:** Arturo López (3/0), Oscar Claure (11/0), Miguel Burgos Suárez (11/0) [Jorge Montes (1/0)], Ramón Guillermo Santos Brizuela (17/2), Wilfredo Camacho (9/0), Máximo Ramírez Burgos (11/1), Abdul Aramayo Mendizábal (2/0), Víctor Agustín Ugarte Oviedo (34/13), Máximo Alcócer (10/4), Renán López (3/0), Ricardo Alcón (14/1) [Mario Mena Lema (21/2)]. Trainer: Vicente Arraya (3).

**62.** 21.03.1959 **BRAZIL - BOLIVIA** **4-2(3-2)** 26th Copa América
Estadio Monumental „Antonio Vespucio Liberti", Buenos Aires; Referee: Luis Antonio Ventre (Argentina); Attendance: 25,000
**BOL:** Arturo López (4/0), Oscar Claure (12/0), Ramón Guillermo Santos Brizuela (18/3), Miguel Burgos Suárez (12/0), Wilfredo Camacho (10/0), Máximo Ramírez Burgos (12/1), Abdul Aramayo Mendizábal (3/1), Víctor Agustín Ugarte Oviedo (35/13), Mario Mena Lema (22/2) [Ausberto García (7/2)], Renán López (4/0), Ricardo Alcón (15/2). Trainer: Vicente Arraya (4).
**Goals:** Ramón Guillermo Santos Brizuela (12), Abdul Aramayo Mendizábal (22).

**63.** 26.03.1959 **CHILE – BOLIVIA** **5-2** 26th Copa América
Estadio Monumental „Antonio Vespucio Liberti“, Buenos Aires; Referee: Luis Antonio Ventre (Argentina); Attendance: 70,000
**BOL:** Arturo López (5/0), Oscar Claure (13/0) [Raymundo Centeno (1/0)], Miguel Burgos Suárez (13/0), Ramón Guillermo Santos Brizuela (19/3), Wilfredo Camacho (11/0), Máximo Ramírez Burgos (13/1) [Edgar Vargas Romero (12/0)], Abdul Aramayo Mendizábal (4/1), Víctor Agustín Ugarte Oviedo (36/13) [Freddy Valda García (1/0)], Máximo Alcócer (11/6), Renán López (5/0), Antonio Atilio Aguirre (3/0). Trainer: Vicente Arraya (5).
**Goals:** Máximo Alcócer 2.

**64.** 29.03.1959 **PERU – BOLIVIA** **0-0** 26th Copa América
Estadio Monumental „Antonio Vespucio Liberti“, Buenos Aires; Referee: Washington Rodríguez (Uruguay); Attendance: 40,000
**BOL:** Arturo López (6/0), Raymundo Centeno (2/0), Jorge Montes (2/0), Ramón Guillermo Santos Brizuela (20/3), Wilfredo Camacho (12/0), Edgar Vargas Romero (13/0), Abdul Aramayo Mendizábal (5/1) [Víctor Agustín Ugarte Oviedo (37/13)], Máximo Alcócer (12/6), Ausberto García (8/2), Renán López (6/0) [Freddy Valda García (2/0)], Antonio Atilio Aguirre (4/0). Trainer: Vicente Arraya (6).

**65.** 15.07.1961 **BOLIVIA – URUGUAY** **1-1(0-1)** 7th FIFA WC. Qualifiers
Estadio „Hernándo Siles Zuazo“, La Paz; Referee: Juan Carlos Robles (Chile)
**BOL:** Griseldo Cobo Salvatierra (1/0), Roberto Cainzo Ocaranza (1/0), Mario Zabalaga (1/0), Wilfredo Camacho (13/0), Máximo Ramírez Burgos (14/1), Alberto Torres Vargas (1/0), Abdul Aramayo Mendizábal (6/1), Máximo Alcócer (13/7), Alberto Quiroga Martínez (1/0), Renán López (7/0), Antonio Atilio Aguirre (5/0).
**Goal:** Máximo Alcócer (53).

**66.** 30.07.1961 **URUGUAY – BOLIVIA** **2-1(2-0)** 7th FIFA WC. Qualifiers
Estadio Centenario, Montevideo; Referee: Juan Carlos Robles (Chile),
**BOL:** Griseldo Cobo Salvatierra (2/0), Roberto Cainzo Ocaranza (2/0), Mario Zabalaga (2/0), Wilfredo Camacho (14/1), Máximo Ramírez Burgos (15/1), Alberto Torres Vargas (2/0), César Sánchez (5/0), Máximo Alcócer (14/7), Alberto Quiroga Martínez (2/0), Armando Escobar (4/0), Antonio Atilio Aguirre (6/0).
**Goal:** Wilfredo Camacho (62).

**67.** 10.08.1962 **BOLIVIA – PARAGUAY** **3-1** Copa Páz del Chaco
Estadio „Félix Capriles“, Cochabamba; Referee: Luis Farina Flores (Bolivia)
**BOL:** Griseldo Cobo Salvatierra (3/0), Roberto Cainzo Ocaranza (3/0), Alberto Torres Vargas (3/0), Máximo Ramírez Burgos (16/1), Wilfredo Camacho (15/1), Eulogio Ramón Vargas (1/0) [Eduardo Espinoza Larosa (1/0)], Abdul Aramayo Mendizábal (7/1) [Fortunato Castillo Andia (1/0)], Máximo Alcócer (15/8), César Sánchez (6/0), Renán López (8/2) [Ausberto García (9/2)], Antonio Atilio Aguirre (7/0).
**Goals:** Renán López 2, Máximo Alcócer.

**68.** 12.08.1962 **BOLIVIA – PARAGUAY** **3-2** Copa Páz del Chaco
Estadio „Félix Capriles“, Cochabamba; Referee: Luis Farina Flores (Bolivia)
**BOL:** Arturo López (7/0), Roberto Cainzo Ocaranza (4/0), Alberto Torres Vargas (4/0), Eulogio Ramón Vargas (2/0), Máximo Ramírez Burgos (17/1), Wilfredo Camacho (16/1), Abdul Aramayo Mendizábal (8/1), Máximo Alcócer (16/8) [Mario Dimeglio Camporiale (1/0)], Víctor Agustín Ugarte Oviedo (38/13) [Armando Escobar (5/1)], Milton Flores Vargas (1/1) [Ausberto García (10/2)], Antonio Atilio Aguirre (8/1).
**Goals:** Milton Flores Vargas, Armando Escobar, Antonio Atilio Aguirre.

**69.** 17.02.1963 **PARAGUAY – BOLIVIA** **3-0** Copa Páz del Chaco
Estadio Defensores del Chaco, Asunción; Referee: Tomas Antruejo (Paraguay)
**BOL:** Arturo López (8/0), Roberto Cainzo Ocaranza (5/0), Eduardo Espinoza Larosa (2/0), Mario Zabalaga (3/0), Alberto Torres Vargas (5/0), Wilfredo Camacho (17/1) [Mario Dimeglio Camporiale (2/0)], Ramiro Blacutt Rodríguez (1/0), Abdul Aramayo Mendizábal (9/1), Milton Flores Vargas (2/1) [Víctor Agustín Ugarte Oviedo (39/13)], Ausberto García (11/2), Antonio Atilio Aguirre (9/1) [Julio Torres Vargas (1/0)].

**70.** 19.02.1963 **PARAGUAY – BOLIVIA** **5-1** Copa Páz del Chaco
Estadio Defensores del Chaco, Asunción; Referee: Tomas Antruejo (Paraguay)
**BOL:** Arturo López (9/0), Roberto Cainzo Ocaranza (6/0), Eduardo Espinoza Larosa (3/0), Mario Zabalaga (4/0) [Villarosa (1/0)], Wilfredo Camacho (18/1), Alberto Torres Vargas (6/0) [Hugo Palenque (1/0)], Ramiro Blacutt Rodríguez (2/0), Abdul Aramayo Mendizábal (10/1) [Luis Aguillera Campos (1/0)], Ausberto García (12/2), Víctor Agustín Ugarte Oviedo (40/14) [Milton Flores Vargas (3/1)], Mario Dimeglio Camporiale (3/0).
**Goal:** Víctor Agustín Ugarte Oviedo.

**71.** 10.03.1963 **BOLIVIA – ECUADOR** **4-4(2-2)** 28th Copa América
Estadio „Hernándo Siles Zuazo“, La Paz; Referee: Arturo Maximo Yamasaki Maldonado (Peru); Attendance: 15,000
**BOL:** Arturo López (10/0), Alberto Torres Vargas (7/0), Roberto Cainzo Ocaranza (7/0), Wilfredo Camacho (19/2), Eulogio Ramón Vargas (3/0), Eduardo Espinoza Larosa (4/0), Víctor Agustín Ugarte Oviedo (41/14), Fortunato Castillo Andia (2/1), Máximo Alcócer (17/9), Renán López (9/3) [Abdul Aramayo Mendizábal (11/1)], Edgar Quinteros Guarda (1/0). Trainer: Danilo Alvim (1).
**Goals:** Renán López (16), Fortunato Castillo Andia (27), Máximo Alcócer (55), Wilfredo Camacho (80).

**72.** 17.03.1963 **BOLIVIA – COLOMBIA** **2-1(2-1)** 28th Copa América
Estadio „Félix Capriles“, Cochabamba; Referee: Arturo Maximo Yamasaki Maldonado (Peru); Attendance: 18,000
**BOL:** Arturo López (11/0), Eduardo Espinoza Larosa (5/0), Hugo Palenque (2/0), Wilfredo Camacho (20/2), Eulogio Ramón Vargas (4/0), Máximo Ramírez Burgos (18/1), Ausberto García (13/2), Abdul Aramayo Mendizábal (12/1) [Fortunato Castillo Andia (3/1)], Máximo Alcócer (18/11), Renán López (10/3), Antonio Atilio Aguirre (10/1). Trainer: Danilo Alvim (2).
**Goal:** Máximo Alcócer (22, 40).

**73.** 21.03.1963 **BOLIVIA – PERU** **3-2(1-1)** 28th Copa América
Estadio „Hernándo Siles Zuazo“, La Paz; Referee: João Etzel Filho (Brazil); Attendance: 20,000
**BOL:** Arturo López (12/0), Roberto Cainzo Ocaranza (8/0), Jesús Herbas Reyes (1/0), Eulogio Ramón Vargas (5/0), Máximo Ramírez Burgos (19/1), Wilfredo Camacho (21/3), Ramiro Blacutt Rodríguez (3/0) [Abdul Aramayo Mendizábal (13/1)], Máximo Alcócer (19/12), Víctor Agustín Ugarte Oviedo (42/14), Ausberto García (14/3), Fortunato Castillo Andia (4/1). Trainer: Danilo Alvim (3).
**Goal:** Wilfredo Camacho (14), Máximo Alcócer (49), Ausberto García (57).

**74.** 24.03.1963 **BOLIVIA – PARAGUAY** **2-0(1-0)** 28th Copa América
Estadio „Félix Capriles“, Cochabamba; Referee: José Dimas Larrosa (Paraguay); Attendance: 18,000
**BOL:** Arturo López (13/0), Roberto Cainzo Ocaranza (9/0), Jesús Herbas Reyes (2/0), Máximo Ramírez Burgos (20/1), Wilfredo Camacho (22/3), Mario Zabalaga (5/0), Ausberto García (15/4), Abdul Aramayo Mendizábal (14/1) [Ramiro Blacutt Rodríguez (4/0)], Máximo Alcócer (20/12), Víctor Agustín Ugarte Oviedo (43/14) [Renán López (11/3)], Fortunato Castillo Andia (5/2). Trainer: Danilo Alvim (4).

**Goals:** Fortunato Castillo Andia (17), Ausberto García (88).

**75.** 28.03.1963 **BOLIVIA - ARGENTINA** **3-2(2-2)** 28th Copa América
Estadio „Hernándo Siles Zuazo", La Paz; Referee: Arturo Maximo Yamasaki Maldonado (Peru); Attendance: 20,000
**BOL:** Arturo López (14/0), Roberto Cainzo Ocaranza (10/0), Jesús Herbas Reyes (3/0), Wilfredo Camacho (23/4), Máximo Ramírez Burgos (21/1) [Jaime Herbas Reyes (1/0)], Máximo Alcócer (21/12), Eulogio Ramón Vargas (6/0), Ramiro Blacutt Rodríguez (5/1), Ausberto García (16/4), Víctor Agustín Ugarte Oviedo (44/14), Fortunato Castillo Andia (6/3). Trainer: Danilo Alvim (5).
**Goals:** Fortunato Castillo Andia (12), Ramiro Blacutt Rodríguez (32), Wilfredo Camacho (88).

**76.** 31.03.1963 **BOLIVIA - BRAZIL** **5-4(2-2)** 28th Copa América
Estadio „Félix Capriles", Cochabamba; Referee: Ovidio Orrego (Colombia); Attendance: 25,000
**BOL:** Arturo López (15/0), Roberto Cainzo Ocaranza (11/0), Eduardo Espinoza Larosa (6/0), Máximo Ramírez Burgos (22/1), Wilfredo Camacho (24/5), Eulogio Ramón Vargas (7/0), Ramiro Blacutt Rodríguez (6/1), Máximo Alcócer (22/13), Víctor Agustín Ugarte Oviedo (45/16), Ausberto García (17/5), Fortunato Castillo Andia (7/3). Trainer: Danilo Alvim (6).
**Goals:** Víctor Agustín Ugarte Oviedo (15), Wilfredo Camacho (25), Víctor Agustín Ugarte Oviedo (58), Ausberto García (62), Máximo Alcócer (86).

**77.** 25.07.1965 **PARAGUAY - BOLIVIA** **2-0(1-0)** 8th FIFA WC. Qualifiers
Estadio "Manuel Ferreira", Asunción; Referee: José Antonio Sundheim (Colombia); Attendance: 18,398
**BOL:** Arturo López (16/0), Roberto Cainzo Ocaranza (12/0), Oscar Quiroga (1/0), Mario Zabalaga (6/0), Alberto Torres Vargas (8/0), Máximo Ramírez Burgos (23/1), Ramiro Blacutt Rodríguez (7/1), Ausberto García (18/5), Adolfo Flores Espinoza (2/0), Rolando Vargas Romero (1/0), Antonio Atilio Aguirre (11/1). Trainer: Freddy Valda García (1).

**78.** 17.08.1965 **ARGENTINA - BOLIVIA** **4-1(3-0)** 8th FIFA WC. Qualifiers
Estadio Monumental „Antonio Vespucio Liberti", Buenos Aires; Referee: Estebán Marino (Uruguay); Attendance: 56,173
**BOL:** Arturo López (17/0), Roberto Cainzo Ocaranza (13/0), Oscar Quiroga (2/0), Valenzio Castro (1/0), Alberto Torres Vargas (9/0), Máximo Ramírez Burgos (24/1), Ramiro Blacutt Rodríguez (8/1), Jesús Herbas Reyes (4/0), Ausberto García (19/5), Rolando Vargas Romero (2/1), Fortunato Castillo Andia (8/3). Trainer: Freddy Valda García (2).
**Goal:** Rolando Vargas Romero (55).

**79.** 22.08.1965 **BOLIVIA - PARAGUAY** **2-1(1-1)** 8th FIFA WC. Qualifiers
Estadio „Hernándo Siles Zuazo", La Paz; Referee: Eduardo Rendon (Ecuador); Attendance: 7,000
**BOL:** Isaac Álvarez Moscoso (1/0), Roberto Cainzo Ocaranza (14/0), Oscar Quiroga (3/0), Mario Zabalaga (7/0), Alberto Torres Vargas (10/0), Máximo Ramírez Burgos (25/1), Ramiro Blacutt Rodríguez (9/1), Ramón Quevedo (1/1), Ausberto García (20/5), Rolando Vargas Romero (3/1), Fortunato Castillo Andia (9/4). Trainer: Freddy Valda García (3).
**Goal:** Ramón Quevedo (29), Fortunato Castillo Andia (75).

**80.** 29.08.1965 **BOLIVIA - ARGENTINA** **1-2(1-2)** 8th FIFA WC. Qualifiers
Estadio „Hernándo Siles Zuazo", La Paz; Referee: Carlos Riveros (Peru); Attendance: 9,690
**BOL:** Isaac Álvarez Moscoso (2/0), Roberto Cainzo Ocaranza (15/0), Oscar Quiroga (4/0), Mario Zabalaga (8/0), Alberto Torres Vargas (11/0), Máximo Ramírez Burgos (26/1), Ramiro Blacutt Rodríguez (10/1), Ausberto García (21/5), Adolfo Flores Espinoza (3/0), Rolando Vargas Romero (4/1), Antonio Atilio Aguirre (12/1). Trainer: Freddy Valda García (4).
**Goal:** José Ramos Delgado (35 own goal)

**81.** 17.01.1967 **URUGUAY - BOLIVIA** **4-0(2-0)** 29th Copa América
Estadio Centenario, Montevideo; Referee: Isidro Ramírez Álvarez (Paraguay); Attendance: 15,000
**BOL:** Griseldo Cobo Salvatierra (4/0), Isaac Maldonado (1/0), Roberto Troncoso (1/0), Mario Zabalaga (9/0), Oscar Quiroga (5/0), Jaime Herbas Reyes (2/0), Ramiro Blacutt Rodríguez (11/1), Wilfredo Camacho (25/5) [Rolando Vargas Romero (5/1)], Guery Agreda Cañedo (1/0), Renán López (12/3) [Edgar Quinteros Guarda (2/0)], Rómulo Cortéz (1/0). Trainer: Carlos Trigo (1).

**82.** 22.01.1967 **ARGENTINA - BOLIVIA** **1-0(0-0)** 29th Copa América
Estadio Centenario, Montevideo; Referee: Eunápio Gouveia de Queiroz (Brazil); Attendance: 6,000
**BOL:** José Issa (1/0), Hugo Palenque (3/0), Oscar Quiroga (6/0), Mario Zabalaga (10/0), Guery Agreda Cañedo (2/0), Jesús Herbas Reyes (5/0), Ramiro Blacutt Rodríguez (12/1), Rolando Vargas Romero (6/1), Ausberto García (22/5), Renán López (13/3), Edgar Quinteros Guarda (3/0). Trainer: Carlos Trigo (2).

**83.** 25.01.1967 **PARAGUAY - BOLIVIA** **1-0(0-0)** 29th Copa América
Estadio Centenario, Montevideo; Referee: Estebán Marino (Uruguay); Attendance: 5,000
**BOL:** José Issa (2/0), Hugo Palenque (4/0) [Isaac Maldonado (2/0)], Oscar Quiroga (7/0), Mario Zabalaga (11/0), Guery Agreda Cañedo (3/0) [Jesús Herbas Reyes (6/0)], Jaime Herbas Reyes (3/0), Ramiro Blacutt Rodríguez (13/1), Rolando Vargas Romero (7/1), Ausberto García (23/5), Renán López (14/3), Edgar Quinteros Guarda (4/0). Trainer: Carlos Trigo (3).

**84.** 28.01.1967 **VENEZUELA - BOLIVIA** **3-0(0-0)** 29th Copa América
Estadio Centenario, Montevideo; Referee: Mario Gasc (Chile); Attendance: 11,000
**BOL:** José Issa (3/0) [Griseldo Cobo Salvatierra (5/0)], Guery Agreda Cañedo (4/0), Oscar Quiroga (8/0), Mario Zabalaga (12/0), Wilfredo Camacho (26/5), Jaime Herbas Reyes (4/0), Ramiro Blacutt Rodríguez (14/1) [Jorge Urdinínea (1/0)], Adolfo Flores Espinoza (1/0), Ausberto García (24/5), Rolando Vargas Romero (8/1), César Sánchez (7/0) [Edgar Quinteros Guarda (5/0)]. Trainer: Carlos Trigo (4).

**85.** 01.02.1967 **CHILE - BOLIVIA** **0-0** 29th Copa América
Estadio Centenario, Montevideo; Referee: Roberto Héctor Goicoechea (Argentina); Attendance: 1,500
**BOL:** José Issa (4/0), Oscar Quiroga (9/0), Guery Agreda Cañedo (5/0), Mario Zabalaga (13/0), Wilfredo Camacho (27/5), Jesús Herbas Reyes (7/0), César Sánchez (8/0), Ramiro Blacutt Rodríguez (15/1), Ausberto García (25/5) [Jorge Urdinínea (2/0)], Rolando Vargas Romero (9/1), Jaime Herbas Reyes (5/0), Rómulo Cortéz (2/0). Trainer: Carlos Trigo (5).

**86.** 27.07.1969 **BOLIVIA - ARGENTINA** **3-1(1-1)** 9th FIFA WC. Qualifiers
Estadio „Hernándo Siles Zuazo", La Paz; Referee: Hugo Sosa (Paraguay); Attendance: 21,267
**BOL:** José Issa (5/0), Isaac Maldonado (3/0), Guery Agreda Cañedo (6/0), Raúl Álvarez Aparicio (1/1), Mario Rojas Arias (1/0), Jesús Herbas Reyes (8/0), Ramiro Blacutt Rodríguez (16/2), Remberto González Pérez (1/0), Juan Américo Díaz Cruz (1/1), René Rada Calderón (1/0), Juan P. Farías Salazar (1/0). Trainer: Freddy Valda García (5).
**Goals:** Juan Américo Díaz Cruz (18), Ramiro Blacutt Rodríguez (51), Raúl Álvarez Aparicio (70).

**87.** 10.08.1969 **BOLIVIA – PERU** **2-1(0-0)** 9th FIFA WC. Qualifiers

Estadio „Hernándo Siles Zuazo", La Paz; Referee: Sergio Chechelov (Venezuela); Attendance: 20,670

**BOL:** José Issa (6/0), Isaac Maldonado (4/0), Guery Agreda Cañedo (7/0), Raúl Álvarez Aparicio (2/2), Mario Rojas Arias (2/0), Jesús Herbas Reyes (9/0), Ramiro Blacutt Rodríguez (17/2), Remberto González Pérez (2/0) [Limbert Cabrera Rivero (1/0)], Juan Américo Díaz Cruz (2/1), René Rada Calderón (2/0), Juan P. Farías Salazar (2/0). Trainer: Freddy Valda García (6).

**Goals:** Raúl Álvarez Aparicio (69), Héctor Eduardo Chumpitaz González (80 own goal).

**88.** 17.08.1969 **PERU – BOLIVIA** **3-0(2-0)** 9th FIFA WC. Qualifiers

Estadio Nacional, Lima; Referee: Guillermo Velázquez Ramírez (Colombia); Attendance: 43,148

**BOL:** José Issa (7/0), Isaac Maldonado (5/0), Julio Díaz Gutiérrez (1/0), Raúl Álvarez Aparicio (3/2), Mario Rojas Arias (3/0), Jesús Herbas Reyes (10/0), Ramiro Blacutt Rodríguez (18/2), Alberto Torres Vargas (12/0), Juan Américo Díaz Cruz (3/1), René Rada Calderón (3/0), Limbert Cabrera Rivero (2/0) [Genaro Hurtado (1/0)]. Trainer: Freddy Valda García (7).

**89.** 24.08.1969 **ARGENTINA – BOLIVIA** **1-0(0-0)** 9th FIFA WC. Qualifiers

Estadio „Alberto J. Armando", Buenos Aires; Referee: Armando Peña Rocha (Uruguay); Attendance: 47,069

**BOL:** Griseldo Cobo Salvatierra (6/0), Isaac Maldonado (6/0), Guery Agreda Cañedo (8/0), Raúl Álvarez Aparicio (4/2), Mario Rojas Arias (4/0), Jesús Herbas Reyes (11/0), Ramiro Blacutt Rodríguez (19/2), Remberto González Pérez (3/0), Juan Américo Díaz Cruz (4/1), René Rada Calderón (4/0), Limbert Cabrera Rivero (3/0). Trainer: Freddy Valda García (8).

**90.** 11.06.1972 **PERU – BOLIVIA** **3-0** Copa Independencia de Brasil

Estádio Belfort Duarta, Curitiba; Referee: Keith Edwin Walker (England)

**BOL:** Erwin Frey (1/0), Jaime Carlos Olivera Jiménez (1/0), Miguel Antelo (1/0), Jesús Herbas Reyes (12/0), Félix Chávez (1/0), Jaime Rimazza Vargas (1/0), Jorge Moreno (1/0) [Porfirio Jiménez (1/0)], Nemesio Leanos (1/0), Ramiro Blacutt Rodríguez (20/2) [Mario Ovidio Mezza Soruco (1/0)], Nicolás Linares Saibury (1/0), Arturo Saucedo Landa (1/0). Trainer: Freddy Valda García (9).

**91.** 18.06.1972 **BOLIVIA – YUGOSLAVIA** **1-1(0-1)** Copa Independencia de Brasil

Estádio „Pedro Pedrosian", Campo Grande; Referee: Abraham Klein (Israel); Attendance: 15,000

**BOL:** Erwin Frey (2/0), Jaime Carlos Olivera Jiménez (2/0), Jesús Herbas Reyes (13/0), Guery Agreda Cañedo (9/0), Félix Chávez (2/0), Nemesio Leanos (2/0), Gerson Balcazar (1/0), Ramiro Blacutt Rodríguez (21/2), Nicolás Linares Saibury (2/0), Mario Pariente (1/1), Juan Carlos Fernández Velarde (1/0). Trainer: Freddy Valda García (10).

**Goal:** Mario Pariente (89).

**92.** 21.06.1972 **BOLIVIA – VENEZUELA** **2-2** Copa Independencia de Brasil

Estádio Vivaldo Lima, Manaus; Referee: Hwa Po Dei (Malaysia)

**BOL:** Erwin Frey (3/0), Jaime Carlos Olivera Jiménez (3/0), Miguel Antelo (2/0), Hugo Pérez (1/0), Félix Chávez (3/0), Jaime Rimazza Vargas (2/1), Ramiro Blacutt Rodríguez (22/3), Arturo Saucedo Landa (2/0), Mario Pariente (2/1) [Nicolás Linares Saibury (3/0)], Mario Ovidio Mezza Soruco (2/0), Juan Carlos Fernández Velarde (2/0). Trainer: Freddy Valda García (11).

**Goals:** Jaime Rimazza Vargas, Ramiro Blacutt Rodríguez.

**93.** 25.06.1972 **PARAGUAY – BOLIVIA** **6-1** Copa Independencia de Brasil

Estádio Vivaldo Lima, Manaus; Referee: Arnaldo David César Coelho (Brazil)

**BOL:** Erwin Frey (4/0), Jaime Carlos Olivera Jiménez (4/0), Miguel Antelo (3/0), Hugo Pérez (2/0), Félix Chávez (4/0), Jaime Rimazza Vargas (3/1) [Gerson Balcazar (2/0)], Arturo Saucedo Landa (3/0), Nemesio Leanos (3/0), Ramiro Blacutt Rodríguez (23/3) [Porfirio Jiménez (2/0)], Nicolás Linares Saibury (4/0), Mario Ovidio Mezza Soruco (3/0). Trainer: Freddy Valda García (12).

**Goal:** Pedro Ernesto Molina (own goal).

**94.** 24.03.1973 **PERU – BOLIVIA** **2-0** Copa Mariscal Sucre

Estadio Nacional, Lima; Referee: Pedro Reyes (Peru)

**BOL:** Griseldo Cobo Salvatierra (7/0), Hernán Cayo Thames (1/0), Luis Iriondo Angola (1/0), Guery Agreda Cañedo (10/0), Félix Chávez (5/0), Arturo Saucedo Landa (4/0), Jorge Jiménez Orellana (1/0), David Rocha (1/0), Nicolás Linares Saibury (5/0), Juan Carlos Fernández Velarde (3/0), Mario Ovidio Mezza Soruco (4/0). Trainer: Freddy Valda García (13).

**95.** 31.03.1973 **BOLIVIA – PARAGUAY** **1-1**

Estadio „Hernándo Siles Zuazo", La Paz; Referee: Carlos Riveros (Peru)

**BOL:** Griseldo Cobo Salvatierra (8/0), Hernán Cayo Thames (2/0), Luis Iriondo Angola (2/0), Guery Agreda Cañedo (11/0), Félix Chávez (6/0), Arturo Saucedo Landa (5/0), David Rocha (2/0), Mario Pariente (3/1), Juan Carlos Fernández Velarde (4/0) [Nicolás Linares Saibury (6/0)], Mario Ovidio Mezza Soruco (5/1), Jorge Jiménez Orellana (2/0). Trainer: Freddy Valda García (14).

**Goal:** Mario Ovidio Mezza Soruco.

**96.** 29.04.1973 **BOLIVIA – ECUADOR** **3-3**

Estadio „Hernándo Siles Zuazo", La Paz; Referee: Juan Oscar Ortubé Vargas (Bolivia)

**BOL:** Griseldo Cobo Salvatierra (9/0), Jaime Carlos Olivera Jiménez (5/0), Guery Agreda Cañedo (12/0), Miguel Antelo (4/0), Luis Iriondo Angola (3/0), Jaime Rimazza Vargas (4/1), Freddy Vargas Orozco (1/0), Nicolás Linares Saibury (7/1) [Mario Pariente (4/1)], Juan Carlos Fernández Velarde (5/1), Mario Ovidio Mezza Soruco (6/1), Juan Carlos Sánchez Frias (1/0) [Jorge Jiménez Orellana (3/1)]. Trainer: Freddy Valda García (15).

**Goals:** Nicolás Linares Saibury, Juan Carlos Fernández Velarde, Jorge Jiménez Orellana.

**97.** 06.05.1973 **ECUADOR – BOLIVIA** **0-0**

Estadio Olimpico, Quito; Referee: René Torres (Ecuador)

**BOL:** Carlos Conrado Jiménez Hurtado (1/0), Jaime Carlos Olivera Jiménez (6/0), Miguel Antelo (5/0), Guery Agreda Cañedo (13/0), Luis Iriondo Angola (4/0), Jaime Rimazza Vargas (5/1), Freddy Vargas Orozco (2/0), Nicolás Linares Saibury (8/1), Juan Carlos Fernández Velarde (6/1), Mario Ovidio Mezza Soruco (7/1) [Juan Carlos Sánchez Frias (2/0)], Jorge Jiménez Orellana (4/1). Trainer: Freddy Valda García (16).

**98.** 27.05.1973 **BRAZIL – BOLIVIA** **5-0**

Estádio „Jornalista Mario Filho" (Maracanã), Rio de Janeiro; Referee: Armando Nunes Castanheiras da Rosa Marques (Brazil)

**BOL:** Griseldo Cobo Salvatierra (10/0) [Carlos Conrado Jiménez Hurtado (2/0)], Hernán Cayo Thames (3/0) [Jaime Carlos Olivera Jiménez (7/0)], Miguel Antelo (6/0), Guery Agreda Cañedo (14/0), Félix Chávez (7/0) [Luis Iriondo Angola (5/0)], Hugo Pérez (3/0), Freddy Vargas Orozco (3/0), Nicolás Linares Saibury (9/1), Juan Carlos Fernández Velarde (7/1), Mario Ovidio Mezza Soruco (8/1) [Juan Carlos Sánchez Frias (3/0); Jorge Jiménez Orellana (5/1)]. Trainer: Freddy Valda García (17).

**99.** 15.07.1973 **BOLIVIA – PERU** **2-0** Copa Mariscal Sucre
Estadio „Hernándo Siles Zuazo", La Paz; Referee: Juan Oscar Ortubé Vargas (Bolivia)
**BOL:** Carlos Conrado Jiménez Hurtado (3/0), Jaime Carlos Olivera Jiménez (8/0), Hugo Pérez (4/0), Limbert Cabrera Bucett (1/0), Luis Iriondo Angola (6/0), Walter Costa Rojas (1/0), Juan Carlos Sánchez Frias (4/0) [Raúl Morales Gonzáles (1/0)], Freddy Vargas Orozco (4/0), Limbert Cabrera Rivero (4/0), Mario Pariente (5/1), Juan Carlos Fernández Velarde (8/1). Sustitute: Mario Ovidio Mezza Soruco (9/3). Trainer: Freddy Valda García (18).
**Goals:** Mario Ovidio Mezza Soruco 2.

**100.** 24.07.1973 **CHILE – BOLIVIA** **3-0(1-0)** Copa Leoncio Provoste
Estadio Nacional, Santiago; Referee: Arturo Maximo Yamasaki Maldonado (Peru); Attendance: 33,060
**BOL:** Carlos Conrado Jiménez Hurtado (4/0), Jaime Carlos Olivera Jiménez (9/0), Hugo Pérez (5/0), Miguel Antelo (7/0), Luis Iriondo Angola (7/0), Freddy Vargas Orozco (5/0), Limbert Cabrera Rivero (5/0), Walter Costa Rojas (2/0), Nicolás Linares Saibury (10/1) [Raúl Morales Gonzáles (2/0)], Mario Pariente (6/1), Mario Ovidio Mezza Soruco (10/3) [Juan Carlos Fernández Velarde (9/1)]. Trainer: Freddy Valda García (19).

**101.** 02.09.1973 **BOLIVIA – PARAGUAY** **1-2(1-1)** 10th FIFA WC. Qualifiers
Estadio „Hernándo Siles Zuazo", La Paz; Referee: Eduardo Rendón Villacis (Ecuador); Attendance: 19,384
**BOL:** Carlos Conrado Jiménez Hurtado (5/0), Jaime Carlos Olivera Jiménez (10/0), Hugo Pérez (6/0), Limbert Cabrera Bucett (2/0), Miguel Antelo (8/0), Walter Costa Rojas (3/0), Juan Carlos Fernández Velarde (10/1) [Adolfo Rocabado (1/0)], Freddy Vargas Orozco (6/0), Limbert Cabrera Rivero (6/0), Mario Ovidio Mezza Soruco (11/3), Raúl Morales Gonzáles (3/1). Trainer: Carlos Trigo (6).
**Goal:** Raúl Morales Gonzáles (30).

**102.** 09.09.1973 **ARGENTINA – BOLIVIA** **4-0(2-0)** 10th FIFA WC. Qualifiers
Estadio „Alberto J. Armando", Buenos Aires; Referee: Angel Eduardo Pazos Bianchi (Uruguay); Attendance: 39,243
**BOL:** Carlos Conrado Jiménez Hurtado (6/0), Luis Iriondo Angola (8/0), Jaime Carlos Olivera Jiménez (11/0), Hugo Pérez (7/0), Miguel Antelo (9/0), Arturo Saucedo Landa (6/0) [67.Adolfo Rocabado (2/0)], Juan Carlos Fernández Velarde (11/1), Freddy Vargas Orozco (7/0), Eduardo Angulo Torme (1/0), Mario Ovidio Mezza Soruco (12/3) [46.Porfirio Jiménez (3/0)], Limbert Cabrera Rivero (7/0). Trainer: Carlos Trigo (7).

**103.** 23.09.1973 **BOLIVIA – ARGENTINA** **0-1(0-1)** 10th FIFA WC. Qualifiers
Estadio „Hernándo Siles Zuazo", La Paz; Referee: Arnaldo David César Coelho (Brazil); Attendance: 19,266
**BOL:** Carlos Conrado Jiménez Hurtado (7/0), Luis Iriondo Angola (9/0), Walter Costa Rojas (4/0) [75.Jaime Carlos Olivera Jiménez (12/0)], Hugo Pérez (8/0), Miguel Antelo (10/0), Juan Carlos Fernández Velarde (12/1), Freddy Vargas Orozco (8/0), Eduardo Angulo Torme (2/0), Mario Ovidio Mezza Soruco (13/3), Raul Alberto Morales (4/1) [66.Jorge Llado (1/0)], Nicolás Linares Saibury (11/1). Trainer: Carlos Trigo (8).

**104.** 30.09.1973 **PARAGUAY – BOLIVIA** **4-0(3-0)** 10th FIFA WC. Qualifiers
Estadio Puerto Sajonia, Asunción; Referee: Alberto Tejada Burga (Peru); Attendance: 24,268
**BOL:** Carlos Conrado Jiménez Hurtado (8/0), Luis Iriondo Angola (10/0), Jaime Carlos Olivera Jiménez (13/0), Hugo Pérez (9/0), Limbert Cabrera Bucett (3/0), Miguel Antelo (11/0), Juan Carlos Fernández Velarde (13/1), Freddy Vargas Orozco (9/0), Eduardo Angulo Torme (3/0), Mario Ovidio Mezza Soruco (14/3), Jorge Jiménez Orellana (6/1) [40.Raul Alberto Morales (5/1)]. Trainer: Carlos Trigo (9).

**105.** 27.06.1975 **BOLIVIA – ARGENTINA** **1-2(0-1)** Copa Saavedra
Estadio „Félix Capriles", Cochabamba; Referee: Miguel Aliaga (Bolivia)
**BOL:** René Bilbao (1/0), Windsor Del Llano Suárez (1/0), Mario Rojas Arias (5/0), Jaime Lima Guardia (1/0), Luis Iriondo Angola (11/0), Edgar Góngora Saavedra (1/0), Luis Liendo Moreno (1/0), Mario Ovidio Mezza Soruco (15/3), Juan Carlos Sánchez Frias (5/0), Nicolás Linares Saibury (12/1), Dario Veyzaga (1/0). Trainer: Freddy Valda García (20).
**Goal:** Rafael José Eloy Pavón (55 own goal)

**106.** 07.07.1975 **BOLIVIA – PARAGUAY** **1-2**
Estadio „Félix Capriles", Cochabamba
**BOL:** Carlos Conrado Jiménez Hurtado (9/0), Eduardo Angulo Torme (4/0), Mario Rojas Arias (6/0), Jaime Lima Guardia (2/0), Windsor Del Llano Suárez (2/0), Edgar Góngora Saavedra (2/0) [Jaime Rimazza Vargas (6/1)], Nemesio Leanos (4/0), Mario Ovidio Mezza Soruco (16/3), Raúl Morales Gonzáles (4/1) [Juan Américo Díaz Cruz (5/2)], Mario Pariente (7/1), Juan Carlos Fernández Velarde (14/1) [Porfirio Jiménez (4/0)]. Trainer: Freddy Valda García (21).
**Goal:** Juan Américo Díaz Cruz.

**107.** 09.07.1975 **BOLIVIA – ECUADOR** **1-0**
Estadio „Félix Capriles", Cochabamba; Referee: Alberto Albornoz (Bolivia)
**BOL:** Carlos Conrado Jiménez Hurtado (10/0), Eduardo Angulo Torme (5/0), Mario Rojas Arias (7/0), Jaime Lima Guardia (3/0), Windsor Del Llano Suárez (3/0), Mario Ovidio Mezza Soruco (17/3), Porfirio Jiménez (5/1), Luis Liendo Moreno (2/0), Juan Carlos Sánchez Frias (6/0) [Raúl Morales Gonzáles (5/1)], Nicolás Linares Saibury (13/1), Mario Pariente (8/1). Trainer: Freddy Valda García (22).
**Goal:** Porfirio Jiménez.

**108.** 20.07.1975 **BOLIVIA – CHILE** **2-1** 30th Copa América
Estadio „Jesús Bermúdez", Oruro; Referee: Héctor Froilán Ortíz Ramírez (Paraguay); Attendance: 18,000
**BOL:** Carlos Conrado Jiménez Hurtado (11/0), Eduardo Angulo Torme (6/0), Mario Rojas Arias (8/0), Jaime Lima Guardia (4/0), Windsor Del Llano Suárez (4/0), Luis Liendo Moreno (3/0), Mario Ovidio Mezza Soruco (18/5), Nicolás Linares Saibury (14/1) [Freddy Vargas Orozco (10/0)], Raúl Morales Gonzáles (6/1), Porfirio Jiménez (6/1), Mario Pariente (9/1) [Juan Américo Díaz Cruz (6/2)]. Trainer: Freddy Valda García (23).
**Goals:** Mario Ovidio Mezza Soruco 2.

**109.** 27.07.1975 **BOLIVIA – PERU** **0-1(0-1)** 30th Copa América
Estadio „Jesús Bermúdez", Oruro; Referee: Alberto Ducatelli (Argentina); Attendance: 18,000
**BOL:** Carlos Conrado Jiménez Hurtado (12/0), Eduardo Angulo Torme (7/0), Mario Rojas Arias (9/0), Jaime Lima Guardia (5/0), Luis Iriondo Angola (12/0), Luis Liendo Moreno (4/0), Freddy Vargas Orozco (11/0) [Jaime Rimazza Vargas (7/1)], Mario Ovidio Mezza Soruco (19/5), Raúl Morales Gonzáles (7/1), Juan Américo Díaz Cruz (7/2), Porfirio Jiménez (7/1) [Juan P. Farías Salazar (3/0)]. Trainer: Freddy Valda García (24).

**110.** 07.08.1975 **PERU – BOLIVIA** **3-1(2-0)** 30th Copa América
Estadio Nacional, Lima; Referee: Romualdo Arppi Filho (Brazil); Attendance: 40,000
**BOL:** Carlos Conrado Jiménez Hurtado (13/0), Eduardo Angulo Torme (8/0), Jaime Lima Guardia (6/0), Luis Iriondo Angola (13/0), Freddy Vargas Orozco (12/0), Luis Liendo Moreno (5/0), Mario Ovidio Mezza Soruco (20/6), Raúl Morales Gonzáles (8/1), Juan Américo Díaz Cruz (8/2), Porfirio Jiménez (8/1), Juan Carlos Fernández Velarde (15/1) [Juan P. Farías Salazar (4/0)]. Trainer: Freddy Valda García (25).
**Goal:** Mario Ovidio Mezza Soruco (58 penalty).

**111.** 13.08.1975 **CHILE - BOLIVIA** **4-0(1-0)** 30th Copa América
Estadio Nacional, Santiago; Referee: Arturo Andrés Ithurralde (Argentina); Attendance: 15,000
**BOL:** Carlos Conrado Jiménez Hurtado (14/0), Eduardo Angulo Torme (9/0), Mario Rojas Arias (10/0), Jaime Lima Guardia (7/0), Luis Iriondo Angola (14/0), Porfirio Jiménez (9/1), Jaime Rimazza Vargas (8/1), Nicolás Linares Saibury (15/1), Mario Ovidio Mezza Soruco (21/6), Juan Carlos Sánchez Frias (7/0), Juan Carlos Fernández Velarde (16/1) [Juan Américo Díaz Cruz (9/2)]. Trainer: Freddy Valda García (26).

**112.** 06.02.1977 **BOLIVIA - PARAGUAY** **0-1** Copa Páz del Chaco
Estadio „Hernándo Siles Zuazo", La Paz; Referee: Juan Oscar Ortubé Vargas (Bolivia)
**BOL:** Carlos Conrado Jiménez Hurtado (15/0), Windsor Del Llano Suárez (5/0), Jorge Campos (1/0), Jaime Lima Guardia (8/0), Pablo Baldivieso Fernández (1/0), Raúl Morales Gonzáles (9/1) [Arturo Saucedo Landa (7/0)], Carlos Aragonés Espinosa (1/0), Edgar Góngora Saavedra (3/0) [Eduardo Angulo Torme (10/0)], Erwin Romero Escudero (1/0), Jesús Reynaldo Hurtado (1/0) [Porfirio Jiménez (10/1)], Miguel Aguilar (1/0). Trainer: Wilfredo Camacho (1).

**113.** 09.02.1977 **BOLIVIA - PARAGUAY** **2-2** Copa Páz del Chaco
Estadio „Félix Capriles", Cochabamba; Referee: Luis Barrancos Alvarez (Bolivia)
**BOL:** Carlos Conrado Jiménez Hurtado (16/0), Windsor Del Llano Suárez (6/0), Jaime Rimazza Vargas (9/1) [Jorge Campos (2/1)], Jaime Lima Guardia (9/0), Pablo Baldivieso Fernández (2/0), Arturo Saucedo Landa (8/0), Erwin Espinoza (1/0) [Eduardo Angulo Torme (11/0)], Erwin Romero Escudero (2/0), Porfirio Jiménez (11/2), Jesús Reynaldo Hurtado (2/0), Miguel Aguilar (2/0). Trainer: Wilfredo Camacho (2).
**Goals:** Porfirio Jiménez, Jorge Campos.

**114.** 27.02.1977 **BOLIVIA - URUGUAY** **1-0(0-0)** 11th FIFA WC. Qualifiers
Estadio "Libertador Simón Bolívar", La Paz; Referee: Romualdo Arppi (Brazil); Attendance: 20,306
**BOL:** Carlos Conrado Jiménez Hurtado (17/0), Jorge Campos (3/1), Jaime Lima Guardia (10/0), Pablo Baldivieso Fernández (3/0), Jaime Rimazza Vargas (10/1), Raúl Morales Gonzáles (10/1), Carlos Aragonés Espinosa (2/0), Eduardo Angulo Torme (12/0), Mario Ovidio Mezza Soruco (22/6), Porfirio Jiménez (12/3) [73.Jesús Reynaldo Hurtado (3/0)], Miguel Aguilar (3/0). Trainer: Wilfredo Camacho (3).
**Goal:** Porfirio Jiménez (48).

**115.** 06.03.1977 **VENEZUELA - BOLIVIA** **1-3(0-1)** 11th FIFA WC. Qualifiers
Estadio „Brígido Iriarte", Caracas; Referee: Juan Ambrosio Silvagno Cavanna (Chile); Attendance: 5,034
**BOL:** Carlos Conrado Jiménez Hurtado (18/0), Jorge Campos (4/1), Jaime Rimazza Vargas (11/1), Jaime Lima Guardia (11/0), Pablo Baldivieso Fernández (4/0), Arturo Saucedo Landa (9/0) [59.Raúl Morales Gonzáles (11/1)], Carlos Aragonés Espinosa (3/0), Eduardo Angulo Torme (13/0) [62.Erwin Romero Escudero (3/0)], Mario Ovidio Mezza Soruco (23/7), Porfirio Jiménez (13/4), Miguel Aguilar (4/1). Trainer: Wilfredo Camacho (4).
**Goals:** Mario Ovidio Mezza Soruco (7), Porfirio Jiménez (76), Miguel Aguilar (80).

**116.** 13.03.1977 **BOLIVIA - VENEZUELA** **2-0(2-0)** 11th FIFA WC. Qualifiers
Estadio „Libertador Simón Bolívar", La Paz; Referee: Edison Pérez Nuñez (Peru); Attendance: 21,217
**BOL:** Carlos Conrado Jiménez Hurtado (19/0), Jorge Campos (5/1), Jaime Lima Guardia (12/0), Pablo Baldivieso Fernández (5/0), Jaime Rimazza Vargas (12/1), Raúl Morales Gonzáles (12/1) [61.Arturo Saucedo Landa (10/0)], Eduardo Angulo Torme (14/0), Carlos Aragonés Espinosa (4/1), Mario Ovidio Mezza Soruco (24/7) [61.Erwin Romero Escudero (4/0)], Porfirio Jiménez (14/5), Miguel Aguilar (5/1). Trainer: Wilfredo Camacho (5).
**Goals:** Porfirio Jiménez (17), Carlos Aragonés Espinosa (43)

**117.** 27.03.1977 **URUGUAY - BOLIVIA** **2-2(1-1)** 11th FIFA WC. Qualifiers
Estadio Centenario, Montevideo; Referee: Arturo Andrés Ithurralde (Argentina); Attendance: 7,477
**BOL:** Carlos Conrado Jiménez Hurtado (20/0), Jorge Campos (6/1), Jaime Lima Guardia (13/0), Pablo Baldivieso Fernández (6/0), Jaime Rimazza Vargas (13/1), Eduardo Angulo Torme (15/0), Arturo Saucedo Landa (11/0) [46.Raúl Morales Gonzáles (13/1)], Erwin Romero Escudero (5/0), Carlos Aragonés Espinosa (5/1), Porfirio Jiménez (15/5), Miguel Aguilar (6/3). Trainer: Wilfredo Camacho (6).
**Goals:** Miguel Aguilar (25, 59).

**118.** 12.06.1977 **BOLIVIA - POLAND** **1-2(1-1)**
Estadio „Libertador Simón Bolívar", La Paz; Referee: Juan Oscar Ortubé Vargas (Bolivia); Attendance: 20,000
**BOL:** Ismael Peinado Lino (1/0), Jorge Campos (7/1) [Windsor Del Llano Suárez (7/0)], Jaime Lima Guardia (14/0), Jaime Rimazza Vargas (14/1), Pablo Baldivieso Fernández (7/0), Eduardo Angulo Torme (16/0), Carlos Aragonés Espinosa (Cap) (6/1), Mario Ovidio Mezza Soruco (25/7) [Erwin Romero Escudero (6/0)], Raúl Morales Gonzáles (14/1), Luis Alberto Tamayo (1/0), Porfirio Jiménez (16/6) [Jesús Reynaldo Hurtado (4/0)]. Trainer: Wilfredo Camacho (7).
**Goal:** Porfirio Jiménez (21).

**119.** 14.07.1977 **BRAZIL - BOLIVIA** **8-0(4-0)** 11th FIFA WC. Qualifiers
Estadio "Pascual Guerrero", Cali (Colombia); Referee: Juan Ambrosio Silvagno Cavanna (Chile); Attendance: 38,037
**BOL:** Carlos Conrado Jiménez Hurtado (21/0) [12.Ismael Peinado Lino (2/0)], Windsor Del Llano Suárez (8/0), Jaime Rimazza Vargas (15/1), Jaime Lima Guardia (15/0), Pablo Baldivieso Fernández (8/0), Raúl Morales Gonzáles (15/1) [66.Arturo Saucedo Landa (12/0)], Carlos Aragonés Espinosa (7/1), Eduardo Angulo Torme (17/0), Erwin Romero Escudero (7/0), Porfirio Jiménez (17/6), Miguel Aguilar (7/3). Trainer: Wilfredo Camacho (8).

**120.** 17.07.1977 **PERU - BOLIVIA** **5-0(2-0)** 11th FIFA WC. Qualifiers
Estadio "Pascual Guerrero", Cali (Colombia); Referee: Ramón Ivanoe Barreto Ruíz (Uruguay); Attendance: 32,511
**BOL:** Ismael Peinado Lino (3/0), Jorge Campos (8/1), Jaime Rimazza Vargas (16/1), Jaime Lima Guardia (16/0), Pablo Baldivieso Fernández (9/0), Windsor Del Llano Suárez (9/0), Carlos Aragonés Espinosa (8/1) [57.Raúl Morales Gonzáles (16/1)], Eduardo Angulo Torme (18/0), Erwin Romero Escudero (8/0), Porfirio Jiménez (18/6), Miguel Aguilar (8/3). Trainer: Wilfredo Camacho (9).

**121.** 29.10.1977 **HUNGARY - BOLIVIA** **6-0(5-0)** 11th FIFA WC. Qualifiers
Népstadion, Budapest; Referee: Ramón Ivanoe Barreto Ruíz (Uruguay); Attendance: 65,000
**BOL:** Arturo Galarza Mayereger (1/0), Windsor Del Llano Suárez (10/0), Víctor Jaime Villalon (1/0), Pablo Baldivieso Fernández (10/0), René Domingo Tarritolay Tester (1/0), Carlos Aragonés Espinosa (9/1), Erwin Romero Escudero (9/0), Eduardo Angulo Torme (19/0), Mario Ovidio Mezza Soruco (26/7) [79.Freddy Vargas Orozco (13/0)], Luis Fernando Bastida Pascual (1/0) [46.Juan Carlos Sánchez Frias (8/0)], Miguel Aguilar (9/3). Trainer: Wilfredo Camacho (10).

**122.** 30.11.1977 **BOLIVIA - HUNGARY** **2-3(1-2)** 11th FIFA WC. Qualifiers
Estadio „Libertador Simón Bolívar", La Paz; Referee: Charles George Rainier Corver (Holland); Attendance: 26,983
**BOL:** Luis Galarza Mayereger (1/0), Jorge Campos (9/1), Windsor Del Llano Suárez (11/0), Víctor Jaime Villalon (2/0), René Domingo Tarritolay Tester (2/0), Carlos Aragonés Espinosa (10/3), Erwin Romero Escudero (10/0), Eduardo Angulo Torme (20/0) [30.Erwin Espinoza (2/0)], Mario Ovidio Mezza Soruco (27/7), Luis Fernando Bastida Pascual (2/0) [46.Juan Carlos Sánchez Frias (9/0)], Miguel Aguilar (10/3). Trainer: Wilfredo Camacho (11).
**Goals:** Carlos Aragonés Espinosa (45 penalty, 90).

**123.** 10.07.1979 **BOLIVIA – PARAGUAY** **3-1** Copa Páz del Chaco
Estadio „Hernándo Siles Zuazo", La Paz; Referee: Jorge Antequera (Bolivia)
**BOL:** Carlos Conrado Jiménez Hurtado (22/0), Aldo Fierro Banegas (1/0), Edgar Vaca Barbosa (1/0), Erwin Espinoza (3/1), Windsor Del Llano Suárez (12/0), Carlos Fernando Borja (1/0), Carlos Aragonés Espinosa (11/4), Eduardo Angulo Torme (21/0) [Mario Ovidio Mezza Soruco (28/7)], Erwin Romero Escudero (11/0), Jesús Reynaldo Hurtado (5/0) [David Paniagua Yepez (1/0)], Silvio Rojas (1/0) [Miguel Aguilar (11/4)]. Trainer: Ramiro Blacutt Rodríguez (1).
**Goals:** Erwin Espinoza, Miguel Aguilar, Carlos Aragonés Espinosa.

**124.** 12.07.1979 **BOLIVIA – PARAGUAY** **1-1**
Estadio „Félix Capriles", Cochabamba; Referee: Jorge Pabón (Bolivia)
**BOL:** Carlos Conrado Jiménez Hurtado (23/0), Aldo Fierro Banegas (2/0), Edgar Vaca Barbosa (2/0), Erwin Espinoza (4/1), Windsor Del Llano Suárez (13/0), Carlos Aragonés Espinosa (12/4), Mario Ovidio Mezza Soruco (29/7), Eduardo Angulo Torme (22/0), Erwin Romero Escudero (12/0), David Paniagua Yepez (2/0) [Jesús Reynaldo Hurtado (6/1)], Miguel Aguilar (12/4). Trainer: Ramiro Blacutt Rodríguez (2).
**Goal:** Jesús Reynaldo Hurtado.

**125.** 18.07.1979 **BOLIVIA – ARGENTINA** **2-1(1-1)** 31st Copa América
Estadio „Hernándo Siles Zuazo", La Paz; Referee: Octavio Sierra Mesa (Colombia)
**BOL:** Carlos Conrado Jiménez Hurtado (24/0), Aldo Fierro Banegas (3/0), Edgar Vaca Barbosa (3/0), Erwin Espinoza (5/1), Windsor Del Llano Suárez (14/0), Carlos Fernando Borja (2/0), Carlos Aragonés Espinosa (13/4), Eduardo Angulo Torme (23/0), Erwin Romero Escudero (13/0), Jesús Reynaldo Hurtado (7/3) [67.Mario Ovidio Mezza Soruco (30/7)], Miguel Aguilar (13/4). Trainer: Ramiro Blacutt Rodríguez (3).
**Goals:** Jesús Reynaldo Hurtado (29, 66).

**126.** 26.07.1979 **BOLIVIA – BRAZIL** **2-1(1-1)** 31st Copa América
Estadio „Hernándo Siles Zuazo", La Paz; Referee: Orlando Sánchez (Colombia); Attendance: 40,000
**BOL:** Carlos Conrado Jiménez Hurtado (25/0), Ramiro Vargas Ríos (1/0), Erwin Espinoza (6/1), Edgar Vaca Barbosa (4/0), Windsor Del Llano Suárez (15/0), Carlos Fernando Borja (3/0), Carlos Aragonés Espinosa (14/6), Eduardo Angulo Torme (24/0) [Pablo Baldivieso Fernández (11/0)], Erwin Romero Escudero (14/0) [David Paniagua Yepez (3/0)], Jesús Reynaldo Hurtado (8/3), Miguel Aguilar (14/4). Trainer: Ramiro Blacutt Rodríguez (4).
**Goals:** Carlos Aragonés Espinosa (36 penalty,63).

**127.** 01.08.1979 **PARAGUAY – BOLIVIA** **2-0** Copa Páz del Chaco
Estadio Defensores del Chaco, Asunción; Referee: Carlos Alberto Maciel (Paraguay)
**BOL:** Carlos Conrado Jiménez Hurtado (26/0) [Hebert Hoyos (1/0)], Ramiro Vargas Ríos (2/0), Erwin Espinoza (7/1), Ronald Garrido (1/0) [Edgar Vaca Barbosa (5/0)], Windsor Del Llano Suárez (16/0), Carlos Fernando Borja (4/0), Mario Ovidio Mezza Soruco (31/7) [David Paniagua Yepez (4/0)], Luis González (1/0), Erwin Romero Escudero (15/0), Jesús Reynaldo Hurtado (9/3), Silvio Rojas (2/0). Trainer: Ramiro Blacutt Rodríguez (5).

**128.** 08.08.1979 **ARGENTINA – BOLIVIA** **3-0(2-0)** 31st Copa América
Estadio „José Amalfitani", Buenos Aires; Referee: Víctor Sergio Vásquez Sánchez (Chile); Attendance: 30,000
**BOL:** Hebert Hoyos (2/0), Ramiro Vargas Ríos (3/0), Edgar Vaca Barbosa (6/0), Erwin Espinoza (8/1), Windsor Del Llano Suárez (17/0), Carlos Fernando Borja (5/0), Carlos Aragonés Espinosa (15/6), Eduardo Angulo Torme (25/0) [*sent off 89*], Erwin Romero Escudero (16/0), Jesús Reynaldo Hurtado (10/3) [38.Mario Ovidio Mezza Soruco (32/7)], Miguel Aguilar (15/4). Trainer: Ramiro Blacutt Rodríguez (6).

**129.** 16.08.1979 **BRAZIL – BOLIVIA** **2-0(0-0)** 31st Copa América
Estádio Morumbi, São Paulo; Referee: José Antonio Vergara Guerrero (Venezuela); Attendance: 50,000
**BOL:** Carlos Conrado Jiménez Hurtado (27/0), Ramiro Vargas Ríos (4/0), Edgar Vaca Barbosa (7/0) [Rogelio Delfín Valdéz (1/0)], Erwin Espinoza (9/1), Windsor Del Llano Suárez (18/0), Carlos Fernando Borja (6/0), Carlos Aragonés Espinosa (16/6), Luis González (2/0), Erwin Romero Escudero (17/0), Jesús Reynaldo Hurtado (11/3), Miguel Aguilar (16/4). Trainer: Ramiro Blacutt Rodríguez (7).

**130.** 02.07.1980 **BOLIVIA – POLAND** **0-1(0-0)**
Estadio "Willy Bendeck", Santa Cruz de la Sierra; Referee: Jorge Antequera (Bolivia); Attendance: 20,000
**BOL:** Carlos Conrado Jiménez Hurtado (28/0), Juan Carlos Trigo (1/0), Edgar Vaca Barbosa (8/0), Erwin Espinoza (10/1), Andrés Gallardo (1/0), Simón Martínez (1/0) [33.David Paniagua Yepez (5/0)], Windsor Del Llano Suárez (19/0), Eduardo Angulo Torme (Cap) (26/0), Miguel Aguilar (17/4) [70.Luis Gutiérrez (1/0)], Jesús Reynaldo Hurtado (12/3), Silvio Rojas (3/0). Trainer: Ramiro Blacutt Rodríguez (8).

**131.** 26.08.1980 **BOLIVIA – PARAGUAY** **1-1** Copa Páz del Chaco
La Paz; Referee: Juan Oscar Ortubé Vargas (Bolivia)
**BOL:** Hebert Hoyos (3/0), Juan Carlos Trigo (2/0), Edgar Vaca Barbosa (9/0), Simón Martínez (2/0), Aldo Fierro Banegas (4/0), Carlos Aragonés Espinosa (17/7), Eduardo Angulo Torme (27/0) [Luis González (3/0)], Windsor Del Llano Suárez (20/0) [Silvio Rojas (4/0)], David Paniagua Yepez (6/0), Gastón Taborga (1/0), Miguel Aguilar (18/4). Trainer: Ramiro Blacutt Rodríguez (9).
**Goal:** Carlos Aragonés Espinosa.

**132.** 28.08.1980 **BOLIVIA – PARAGUAY** **1-3**
Estadio „Ramón 'Tahuichi' Aguilera", Santa Cruz de la Sierra; Referee: Luis Barrancos Alvarez (Bolivia)
**BOL:** Hebert Hoyos (4/0), Juan Carlos Trigo (3/0), Edgar Vaca Barbosa (10/0), Andrés Gallardo (2/0), Aldo Fierro Banegas (5/0), Eduardo Angulo Torme (28/0), Luis González (4/0), Carlos Aragonés Espinosa (18/7), David Paniagua Yepez (7/0), Gastón Taborga (2/0), Miguel Aguilar (19/5). Trainer: Ramiro Blacutt Rodríguez (10).
**Goal:** Miguel Aguilar.

**133.** 18.09.1980 **PARAGUAY – BOLIVIA** **2-1** Copa Páz del Chaco
Estadio Defensores del Chaco, Asunción; Referee: Carlos Alberto Maciel (Paraguay)
**BOL:** Hebert Hoyos (5/0), Juan Carlos Trigo (4/0), Edgar Vaca Barbosa (11/0), Andrés Gallardo (3/0), Ramiro Vargas Ríos (5/0), Jorge Camacho (1/0) [David Paniagua Yepez (8/0)], Omar Delgadillo (1/0) [Luis González (5/0)], Carlos Aragonés Espinosa (19/7), Windsor Del Llano Suárez (21/0), Gastón Taborga (3/0), Miguel Aguilar (20/6). Trainer: Ramiro Blacutt Rodríguez (11).
**Goal:** Miguel Aguilar.

**134.** 09.11.1980 **BOLIVIA – URUGUAY** **1-3**
Estadio „Félix Capriles", Cochabamba; Referee: Luis Barrancos Alvarez (Bolivia)
**BOL:** Hebert Hoyos (6/0), Juan Carlos Trigo (5/0), Edgar Vaca Barbosa (12/0), Simón Martínez (3/0), Ramiro Vargas Ríos (6/0), Jorge Camacho (2/0), Eduardo Angulo Torme (29/0), Luis González (6/0) [65.Omar Delgadillo (2/0)], Carlos Aragonés Espinosa (20/8), Gastón Taborga (4/0), Miguel Aguilar (21/6) [77.Silvio Rojas (5/0)]. Trainer: Ramiro Blacutt Rodríguez (12).
**Goal:** Carlos Aragonés Espinosa.

**135.** 30.11.1980 **BOLIVIA – FINLAND** **3-0(1-0)**
La Paz; Referee: Jorge Antequera (Bolivia); Attendance: 8,000
**BOL:** Hebert Hoyos (7/0), Juan Carlos Trigo (6/0), Simón Martínez (4/0), Edgar Vaca Barbosa (13/0), Ramiro Vargas Ríos (7/0), Jorge Camacho (3/0), Carlos Fernando Borja (7/0), Carlos Aragonés Espinosa (21/8), José Milton Melgar (1/0), Gastón Taborga (5/0), Miguel Aguilar (22/7). Substitute: Windsor Del Llano Suárez (22/1). Trainer: Ramiro Blacutt Rodríguez (13).
**Goals:** Miguel Aguilar, ???, Windsor Del Llano Suárez.

**136.** 04.12.1980 **BOLIVIA – FINLAND** **2-2(1-1)**
Santa Cruz de la Sierra; Referee: Luis Barrancos Alvarez (Bolivia); Attendance: 20,000
**BOL:** Hebert Hoyos (8/0), Aldo Fierro Banegas (6/0), Edgar Vaca Barbosa (14/0), Jorge Campos (10/1), Ramiro Vargas Ríos (8/0), Miguel Melgar (2/0), Luis González (7/0), Carlos Fernando Borja (8/0), Carlos Aragonés Espinosa (22/8), Gastón Taborga (6/0), Miguel Aguilar (23/8). Trainer: Ramiro Blacutt Rodríguez (14).
**Goal:** ??? (11 penalty), Miguel Aguilar (88).

**137.** 11.12.1980 **URUGUAY – BOLIVIA** **5-0**
Campo Municipal, Maldonado; Referee: Artemio Sención (Uruguay)
**BOL:** Hebert Hoyos (9/0), Juan Carlos Trigo (7/0), Edgar Vaca Barbosa (15/0), Simón Martínez (5/0) [46.Jorge Campos (11/1)], Aldo Fierro Banegas (7/0) [46.Ramiro Vargas Ríos (9/0)], Carlos Fernando Borja (9/0), Luis González (8/0) [57.Windsor Del Llano Suárez (23/1)], Carlos Aragonés Espinosa (23/8), José Milton Melgar (3/0), Miguel Aguilar (24/8), Silvio Rojas (6/0) [65.Gastón Taborga (7/0)]. Trainer: Ramiro Blacutt Rodríguez (15).

**138.** 25.01.1981 **BOLIVIA – CZECHOSLOVAKIA** **2-1**
Estadio „Hernándo Siles Zuazo“, La Paz; Referee: Tito Villarreal (Bolivia)
**BOL:** Carlos Conrado Jiménez Hurtado (29/0), Juan Carlos Trigo (8/0), Edgar Vaca Barbosa (16/0), Erwin Espinoza (11/1), Windsor Del Llano Suárez (24/1), Johnny Villarroel Delgadillo (1/0), Erwin Romero Escudero (18/0), Carlos Aragonés Espinosa (24/9), Carlos Fernando Borja (10/0), Gastón Taborga (8/1), Silvio Rojas (7/0). Trainer: Ramiro Blacutt Rodríguez (16).
**Goals:** Carlos Aragonés Espinosa, Gastón Taborga.

**139.** 29.01.1981 **BOLIVIA – CZECHOSLOVAKIA** **2-5**
Santa Cruz de la Sierra; Referee: Luis Barrancos Alvarez (Bolivia)
**BOL:** Carlos Conrado Jiménez Hurtado (30/0), Juan Carlos Trigo (9/0), Edgar Vaca Barbosa (17/0), Erwin Espinoza (12/1), Windsor Del Llano Suárez (25/1), Eduardo Angulo Torme (30/0), Johnny Villarroel Delgadillo (2/0), Erwin Romero Escudero (19/0), Carlos Aragonés Espinosa (25/10), Miguel Aguilar (25/8), Silvio Rojas (8/1). Trainer: Ramiro Blacutt Rodríguez (17).
**Goals:** Carlos Aragonés Espinosa, Silvio Rojas.

**140.** 01.02.1981 **BOLIVIA – BULGARIA** **1-3(1-2)**
Estadio „Hernándo Siles Zuazo“, La Paz; Referee: Juan Oscar Ortubé Vargas (Bol); Attendance: 20,000
**BOL:** Carlos Conrado Jiménez Hurtado (31/0), Juan Carlos Trigo (10/0), Luis González (9/0), Ramiro Vargas Ríos (10/0), Erwin Espinoza (13/1), Johnny Villarroel Delgadillo (3/0), Carlos Fernando Borja (11/0) [Eduardo Angulo Torme (31/0)], Gastón Taborga (9/1) [Silvio Rojas (9/1)], Erwin Romero Escudero (20/0), Carlos Aragonés Espinosa (26/11), Miguel Aguilar (26/8). Trainer: Ramiro Blacutt Rodríguez (18).
**Goal:** Carlos Aragonés Espinosa (8).

**141.** 09.02.1981 **BOLIVIA – ROMANIA "U 21"** **1-1(1-1)**
La Paz
**BOL:** Carlos Conrado Jiménez Hurtado (32/0), Juan Carlos Trigo (11/0), Simón Martínez (6/0), Erwin Espinoza (14/1), Windsor Del Llano Suárez (26/1), Eduardo Angulo Torme (32/0), Erwin Romero Escudero (21/0), Carlos Aragonés Espinosa (27/11), Carlos Fernando Borja (12/0), Gastón Taborga (10/1), Miguel Aguilar (27/9). Trainer: Ramiro Blacutt Rodríguez Rodríguez (19).
**Goal:** Miguel Aguilar (3).

**142.** 15.02.1981 **BOLIVIA – VENEZUELA** **3-0(1-0)** 12th FIFA WC. Qualifiers
Estadio „Hernándo Siles Zuazo“, La Paz; Referee: Juan Francisco Escobar Váldez (Paraguay), At: 40,000
**BOL:** Carlos Conrado Jiménez Hurtado (33/0), Juan Carlos Trigo (12/0), Edgar Vaca Barbosa (18/0), Erwin Espinoza (15/1), Windsor Del Llano Suárez (27/1), Carlos Fernando Borja (13/0), Eduardo Angulo Torme (33/0) [*sent off 83*], Carlos Aragonés Espinosa (28/12), Erwin Romero Escudero (22/0), Gastón Taborga (11/1) [32.Jesús Reynaldo Hurtado (13/4)], Miguel Aguilar (28/10). Trainer: Ramiro Blacutt Rodríguez (20).
**Goals:** Miguel Aguilar (38), Carlos Aragonés Espinosa (67), Jesús Reynaldo Hurtado (84).

**143.** 22.02.1981 **BOLIVIA – BRAZIL** **1-2(1-1)** 12th FIFA WC. Qualifiers
Estadio „Hernándo Siles Zuazo“, La Paz; Referee: Enrique Labó Revoredo (Peru); Attendance: 50,000
**BOL:** Carlos Conrado Jiménez Hurtado (34/0), Juan Carlos Trigo (13/0), Edgar Vaca Barbosa (19/0), Erwin Espinoza (16/1) [67.Silvio Rojas (10/1)], Windsor Del Llano Suárez (28/1), Carlos Fernando Borja (14/0), Johnny Villarroel Delgadillo (4/0) [16.Aldo Fierro Banegas (8/0)], Carlos Aragonés Espinosa (29/13), Erwin Romero Escudero (23/0), Jesús Reynaldo Hurtado (14/4), Miguel Aguilar (29/10). Trainer: Ramiro Blacutt Rodríguez (21).
**Goal:** Carlos Aragonés Espinosa (27).

**144.** 15.03.1981 **VENEZUELA – BOLIVIA** **1-0(1-0)** 12th FIFA WC. Qualifiers
Estadio Olímpico, Caracas; Referee: Elías Victoriano Jácome Guerreiro (Ecuador); Attendance: 25,000
**BOL:** Carlos Conrado Jiménez Hurtado (35/0), Juan Carlos Trigo (14/0), Edgar Vaca Barbosa (20/0), Erwin Espinoza (17/1), Windsor Del Llano Suárez (29/1), Carlos Fernando Borja (15/0), Johnny Villarroel Delgadillo (5/0), Carlos Aragonés Espinosa (30/13) [75.José Milton Melgar (4/0)], Erwin Romero Escudero (24/0) [85.Jorge Camacho (4/0)], Gastón Taborga (12/1), Miguel Aguilar (30/10). Trainer: José Saldanha (1).

**145.** 22.03.1981 **BRAZIL – BOLIVIA** **3-1(1-0)** 12th FIFA WC. Qualifiers
Estádio „Jornalista Mario Filho“ (Maracanã), Rio de Janeiro; Referee: Gastón Edmundo Castro Makuc (Chile); Attendance: 121,750
**BOL:** Carlos Conrado Jiménez Hurtado (36/0), Juan Carlos Trigo (15/0), Edgar Vaca Barbosa (21/0), Erwin Espinoza (18/1), Windsor Del Llano Suárez (30/1), Luis González (10/0), Johnny Villarroel Delgadillo (6/0), Carlos Aragonés Espinosa (31/14), Erwin Romero Escudero (25/0), Gastón Taborga (13/1) [46.Carlos Fernando Borja (16/0)], Miguel Aguilar (31/10). Trainer: José Saldanha (2).
**Goal:** Carlos Aragonés Espinosa (67).

**146.** 19.07.1983 **BOLIVIA – CHILE** **1-2**
Estadio „Hernándo Siles Zuazo“, La Paz; Referee: Jorge Pabón (Bolivia); Attendance: 20,156
**BOL:** Eduardo Terrazas (1/0), Ramiro Vargas Ríos (11/0), Carlos Urizar (1/0), Rolando Coimbra (1/0), Carlos Arias (1/0), Carlos Fernando Borja (17/1) [Reynaldo Zambrano (1/0)], Johnny Villarroel Delgadillo (7/0), José Milton Melgar (5/0), Erwin Romero Escudero (26/0), Gastón Taborga (14/1) [Jesús Reynaldo Hurtado (15/4)], Miguel Aguilar (32/10) [Silvio Rojas (11/1)]. Trainer: Wilfredo Camacho (12).

**Goal:** Carlos Fernando Borja.

**147.** 03.08.1983 **BOLIVIA – PARAGUAY** **2-1(0-0)**
Estadio „Hernándo Siles Zuazo", La Paz; Referee: Juan Oscar Ortubé Vargas (Bolivia)
**BOL:** Eduardo Terrazas (2/0), Ramiro Vargas Ríos (12/0), Edgar Vaca Barbosa (22/0), Carlos Urizar (2/0), Roberto Pérez (1/0), Carlos Fernando Borja (18/1) [David Paniagua Yepez (9/0)], Johnny Villarroel Delgadillo (8/0), José Milton Melgar (6/0) [Jorge Camacho (5/1)], Erwin Romero Escudero (27/0), Jesús Reynaldo Hurtado (16/4) [Gastón Taborga (15/2)], Miguel Aguilar (33/10). Trainer: Wilfredo Camacho (13).
**Goals:** Gastón Taborga (78), Jorge Camacho (86).

**148.** 05.08.1983 **BOLIVIA – PARAGUAY** **1-3**
Ramón 'Tahuichi' Aguilera, Santa Cruz de la Sierra; Referee: Jorge Antequera (Bolivia)
**BOL:** Eduardo Terrazas (3/0), Ramiro Vargas Ríos (13/0), Edgar Vaca Barbosa (23/0), Carlos Urizar (3/0), Roberto Pérez (2/0), Carlos Fernando Borja (19/1), Johnny Villarroel Delgadillo (9/0), José Milton Melgar (7/0) [Jorge Camacho (6/1)], Erwin Romero Escudero (28/0), Jesús Reynaldo Hurtado (17/4) [Gastón Taborga (16/2)], Silvio Rojas (12/2). Trainer: Wilfredo Camacho (14).
**Goal:** Silvio Rojas.

**149.** 14.08.1983 **BOLIVIA – COLOMBIA** **0-1(0-0)** 32nd Copa América
Estadio „Hernándo Siles Zuazo", La Paz; Referee: Gabriel González Roa (Paraguay); Attendance: 40,000
**BOL:** Eduardo Terrazas (4/0), Ramiro Vargas Ríos (14/0), Carlos Urizar (4/0), Edgar Vaca Barbosa (24/0), Roberto Pérez (3/0), Carlos Fernando Borja (20/1) [Fernando Salinas (1/0)], Jorge Camacho (7/1), Johnny Villarroel Delgadillo (10/0), Erwin Romero Escudero (29/0), Mario Ovidio Mezza Soruco (33/7), Miguel Aguilar (34/10) [Silvio Rojas (13/2)]. Trainer: Wilfredo Camacho (15).

**150.** 21.08.1983 **BOLIVIA – PERU** **1-1(0-0)** 32nd Copa América
Estadio „Hernándo Siles Zuazo", La Paz; Referee: Jorge Eduardo Romero (Argentina); Attendance: 45,000
**BOL:** Eduardo Terrazas (5/0), Ramiro Vargas Ríos (15/0), Carlos Urizar (5/0), Rolando Coimbra (2/0), Carlos Arias (2/0), José Milton Melgar (8/0), Edgar Castillo (1/0), Mario Ovidio Mezza Soruco (34/7), Erwin Romero Escudero (30/1), David Paniagua Yepez (10/0), Silvio Rojas (14/2). Trainer: Wilfredo Camacho (16).
**Goal:** Erwin Romero Escudero (66).

**151.** 24.08.1983 **CHILE – BOLIVIA** **4-2(4-1)**
Estadio "Carlos Dittborn", Arica; Referee: Víctor Ojeda (Chile); Attendance: 18,000
**BOL:** Hebert Hoyos (10/0) [Eduardo Terrazas (6/0)], Ramiro Vargas Ríos (16/0), Carlos Urizar (6/0), Rolando Coimbra (3/0), Carlos Arias (3/0), José Milton Melgar (9/0), Edgar Castillo (2/0), Mario Ovidio Mezza Soruco (35/8), Erwin Romero Escudero (31/1), Fernando Salinas (2/1), Silvio Rojas (15/2). Trainer: Wilfredo Camacho (17).
**Goals:** Mario Ovidio Mezza Soruco (35 penalty), Fernando Salinas (50).

**152.** 31.08.1983 **COLOMBIA – BOLIVIA** **2-2(1-0)** 32nd Copa América
Estadio „Nemesio Camacho 'El Campín'", Bogotá; Referee: José Antonio Vergara Guerrero (Venezuela); Attendance: 45,000
**BOL:** Eduardo Terrazas (7/0), Edgar Vaca Barbosa (25/0), Carlos Urizar (7/0), Rolando Coimbra (4/0), Carlos Arias (4/0), José Milton Melgar (10/1), Edgar Castillo (3/0), Mario Ovidio Mezza Soruco (36/8) [Carlos Fernando Borja (21/1)], Erwin Romero Escudero (32/1), David Paniagua Yepez (11/0) [Silvio Rojas (16/3)], Fernando Salinas (3/1). Trainer: Wilfredo Camacho (18).
**Goals:** José Milton Melgar (78), Silvio Rojas (80).

**153.** 04.09.1983 **PERU – BOLIVIA** **2-1(2-0)** 32nd Copa América
Estadio Nacional, Lima; Referee: Guillermo Budge Aguirre (Chile) ; Attendance: 50,000
**BOL:** Eduardo Terrazas (8/0), Edgar Vaca Barbosa (26/0), Carlos Urizar (8/0), Rolando Coimbra (5/0), Carlos Arias (5/0), José Milton Melgar (11/1), Edgar Castillo (4/0), Erwin Romero Escudero (33/1), David Paniagua Yepez (12/1), Fernando Salinas (4/1) [64.Mario Ovidio Mezza Soruco (37/8)], Silvio Rojas (17/3). Trainer: Wilfredo Camacho (19).
**Goal:** David Paniagua Yepez (47).

**154.** 03.02.1985 **BOLIVIA – EAST GERMANY** **2-1**
Estadio „Hernándo Siles Zuazo", La Paz, Juan Oscar Ortubé Vargas (Bolivia); Attendance: 9,000
**BOL:** Hebert Hoyos (11/0), Johnny Herrera (1/0), Eduardo Andres Villegas Camara (1/0), Roberto Pérez (4/0), Miguel Ángel Noro (1/0), Carlos Fernando Borja (22/1), Reynaldo Zambrano (2/0), Erwin Romero Escudero (34/2), Oscar Ramírez (1/0) [Augusto Guillen (1/0)], Víctor Hugo Antelo (1/1), Eliseo Ayaviri (1/0) [Mario Daniel Pinedo (1/0)]. Trainer: Carlos Rodríguez (1).
**Goals:** Víctor Hugo Antelo (7), Erwin Romero Escudero (32).

**155.** 06.02.1985 **BOLIVIA – URUGUAY** **0-1(0-0)**
Estadio „Félix Capriles", Cochabamba; Referee: Armando Aliaga (Bolivia); Attendance: 20,000
**BOL:** Hebert Hoyos (12/0), Johnny Herrera (2/0), Eduardo Andres Villegas Camara (2/0), Roberto Pérez (5/0), Miguel Ángel Noro (2/0), Carlos Fernando Borja (23/1), Reynaldo Zambrano (3/0), Erwin Romero Escudero (35/2), Oscar Ramírez (2/0), Víctor Hugo Antelo (2/1) [Mario Daniel Pinedo (2/0)], Eliseo Ayaviri (2/0) [Augusto Guillen (2/0)]. Trainer: Carlos Rodríguez (2).

**156.** 17.02.1985 **PERU – BOLIVIA** **3-0(2-0)**
Estadio Nacional, Lima; Referee: Enrique Labó Revoredo (Peru)
**BOL:** Hebert Hoyos (13/0), Johnny Herrera (3/0), Miguel Ángel Noro (3/0), Eduardo Andres Villegas Camara (3/0), Roberto Pérez (6/0), Carlos Fernando Borja (24/1), Edgar Castillo (5/0), Erwin Romero Escudero (36/2), Oscar Ramírez (3/0) [68.Augusto Guillen (3/0)], Víctor Hugo Antelo (3/1) [46.Reynaldo Zambrano (4/0)], Mario Daniel Pinedo (3/0). Trainer: Carlos Rodríguez (3).

**157.** 21.02.1985 **ECUADOR – BOLIVIA** **3-0**
Estadio Olimpico "Atahualpa", Quito; Referee: Alfredo Rodas (Ecuador)
**BOL:** Hebert Hoyos (14/0), Johnny Herrera (4/0), Miguel Ángel Noro (4/0), Eduardo Andres Villegas Camara (4/0), Roberto Pérez (7/0), Carlos Fernando Borja (25/1), Edgar Castillo (6/0), Erwin Romero Escudero (37/2), Oscar Ramírez (4/0), Mario Daniel Pinedo (4/0) [Víctor Hugo Antelo (4/1)], Fernando Salinas (5/1) [Augusto Guillen (4/0)]. Trainer: Carlos Rodríguez (4).

**158.** 24.02.1985 **VENEZUELA – BOLIVIA** **5-0**
Caracas; Referee: Bernardo Corujo Darríba (Venezuela); Attendance: 4,000
**BOL:** Hebert Hoyos (15/0), Johnny Herrera (5/0), Miguel Ángel Noro (5/0) [Marciano Saldías (1/0)], Eduardo Andres Villegas Camara (5/0), Roberto Pérez (8/0), Carlos Fernando Borja (26/1), Edgar Castillo (7/0), Erwin Romero Escudero (38/2), Oscar Ramírez (5/0), Víctor Hugo Antelo (5/1), Fernando Salinas (6/1). Trainer: Carlos Rodríguez (5).

**159.** 21.04.1985 **BOLIVIA - VENEZUELA** **4-1**
Estadio „Ramón 'Tahuichi' Aguilera", Santa Cruz de la Sierra; Referee: Luis Barrancos Alvarez (Bolivia) ; Attendance: 25,000
**BOL:** Luis Galarza Mayereger (2/0), César Enríquez (1/0) [Johnny Herrera (6/0)], Edgar Vaca Barbosa (27/0), Rolando Coimbra (6/0) [Eduardo Andres Villegas Camara (6/0)], Marciano Saldías (2/0), José Milton Melgar (12/1), José Wilson Avila (1/0), Erwin Romero Escudero (39/4) [David Paniagua Yepez (13/1)], Rolando Paniagua (1/1) [Oscar Ramírez (6/0)], Víctor Hugo Antelo (6/2), Silvio Rojas (18/3). Trainer: Carlos Rodríguez (6).
**Goals:** Víctor Hugo Antelo, Erwin Romero Escudero 2, Rolando Paniagua.

**160.** 01.05.1985 **BOLIVIA - PERU** **0-0**
Estadio „Ramón 'Tahuichi' Aguilera", Santa Cruz de la Sierra; Referee: Jorge Antequera (Bolivia); Attendance: 20,000
**BOL:** Luis Galarza Mayereger (3/0), Johnny Herrera (7/0), Edgar Vaca Barbosa (28/0) [68.Miguel Ángel Noro (6/0)], Rolando Coimbra (7/0), Roberto Pérez (9/0), Carlos Fernando Borja (27/1), José Milton Melgar (13/1), Erwin Romero Escudero (40/4), Rolando Paniagua (2/1) [59.David Paniagua Yepez (14/1)], Juan Carlos Sánchez (1/0), Silvio Rojas (19/3). Trainer: Carlos Rodríguez (7).

**161.** 26.05.1985 **BOLIVIA - PARAGUAY** **1-1(1-0)** 13th FIFA WC. Qualifiers
Estadio „Ramón 'Tahuichi' Aguilera", Santa Cruz de la Sierra; Referee: Referee: Elías Victoriano Jácome Guerreiro (Ecuador); Attendance: 20,000
**BOL:** Luis Galarza Mayereger (4/0), Johnny Herrera (8/0), Edgar Vaca Barbosa (29/0), Rolando Coimbra (8/0), Marciano Saldías (3/0), José Milton Melgar (14/1), Edgar Castillo (8/0), Erwin Romero Escudero (41/4) [Carlos Fernando Borja (28/1)], Rolando Paniagua (3/1) [David Paniagua Yepez (15/1)], Juan Carlos Sánchez (2/0), Silvio Rojas (20/4). Trainer: Carlos Rodríguez (8).
**Goal:** Silvio Rojas (9).

**162.** 02.06.1985 **BOLIVIA - BRAZIL** **0-2(0-0)** 13th FIFA WC. Qualifiers
Estadio „Ramón 'Tahuichi' Aguilera", Santa Cruz de la Sierra; Referee: Jorge Eduardo Romero (Argentina); Attendance: 25,000
**BOL:** Luis Galarza Mayereger (5/0), Johnny Herrera (9/0), Edgar Vaca Barbosa (30/0) [51.Miguel Ángel Noro (7/0)], Rolando Coimbra (9/0), Roberto Pérez (10/0), José Milton Melgar (15/1), Edgar Castillo (9/0), Erwin Romero Escudero (42/4), Rolando Paniagua (4/1), Juan Carlos Sánchez (3/0), Silvio Rojas (21/4). Trainer: Carlos Rodríguez (9).

**163.** 09.06.1985 **PARAGUAY - BOLIVIA** **3-0(2-0)** 13th FIFA WC. Qualifiers
Estadio Defensores del Chaco, Asunción; Referee: Gilberto Aristizábal Murcia (Colombia); Attendance: 40,000
**BOL:** Luis Galarza Mayereger (6/0), José Wilson Avila (2/0), Miguel Ángel Noro (8/0), Rolando Coimbra (10/0), Roberto Pérez (11/0), José Milton Melgar (16/1), Edgar Castillo (10/0), Erwin Romero Escudero (43/4), Rolando Paniagua (5/1), Erwin Cespedes (1/0) [Carlos Fernando Borja (29/1)], Silvio Rojas (22/4) [Juan Carlos Sánchez (4/0)]. Trainer: Carlos Rodríguez (10).

**164.** 30.06.1985 **BRAZIL - BOLIVIA** **1-1(1-0)** 13th FIFA WC. Qualifiers
Estádio Morumbi, São Paulo; Referee: Enrique Labó Revoredo (Peru); Attendance: 90,709
**BOL:** Luis Galarza Mayereger (7/0), José Wilson Avila (3/0), Erwin Espinoza (19/1), Rolando Coimbra (11/0), Marciano Saldías (4/0), José Milton Melgar (17/1), Edgar Castillo (11/0), Erwin Romero Escudero (44/4), Rolando Paniagua (6/1) [David Paniagua Yepez (16/1)], Juan Carlos Sánchez (5/1), Silvio Rojas (23/4) [Carlos Fernando Borja (30/1)]. Trainer: Carlos Rodríguez (11).
**Goal:** Juan Carlos Sánchez (75).

**165.** 14.06.1987 **BOLIVIA - PARAGUAY** **0-2**
Estadio „Ramón 'Tahuichi' Aguilera", Santa Cruz de la Sierra; Referee: Jorge Antequera (Bolivia)
**BOL:** Marco Antonio Barrero (1/0), José Wilson Avila (4/0), Romer Antonio Roca (1/0), Rolando Coimbra (12/0), Félix Vera (1/0), Carlos Fernando Borja (31/1), Federico Justiniano (1/0), Juan Mauricio Ramos (1/0), Carlos Arias (6/0), Rolando Paniagua (7/1), Víctor Hugo Antelo (7/2). Trainer: Osvaldo Veiga (1).

**166.** 23.06.1987 **URUGUAY - BOLIVIA** **2-1(1-1)**
Estadio Centenario, Montevideo; Referee: Roberto Otelo (Uruguay); Attendance: 8,000
**BOL:** Marco Antonio Barrero (2/0), José Wilson Avila (5/0), Rolando Coimbra (13/0), Miguel Ángel Noro (9/0), Marciano Saldías (5/0), Carlos Fernando Borja (32/1), Eduardo Andres Villegas Camara (7/0), Antonio Revuelta (1/0) [46.Federico Justiniano (2/0)], Carlos Arias (7/0), Rolando Paniagua (8/1) [60.Silvio Rojas (24/5)], Álvaro Guillermo Peña (1/0). Trainer: Osvaldo Veiga (2).
**Goal:** Silvio Rojas (22).

**167.** 28.06.1987 **PARAGUAY - BOLIVIA** **0-0** 33rd Copa América
Estadio Gigante de Arroyito, Rosario (Argentina); Referee: Enrique Labó Revoredo (Peru); Attendance: 5,000
**BOL:** Marco Antonio Barrero (3/0), José Wilson Avila (6/0), Rolando Coimbra (14/0), Miguel Ángel Noro (10/0), Félix Vera (2/0), Carlos Fernando Borja (33/1), José Milton Melgar (18/1) [46.Federico Justiniano (3/0)], Eduardo Andres Villegas Camara (8/0), Carlos Arias (8/0), Rolando Paniagua (9/1) [78.Oscar Ramírez (7/0)], Álvaro Guillermo Peña (2/0). Trainer: Osvaldo Veiga (3).

**168.** 01.07.1987 **COLOMBIA - BOLIVIA** **2-0(1-0)** 33rd Copa América
Estadio Gigante de Arroyito, Rosario (Argentina); Referee: Gastón Makuc Castro (Chile); Attendance: 5,000
**BOL:** Marco Antonio Barrero (4/0) [46.Luis Galarza Mayereger (8/0)], José Wilson Avila (7/0), Rolando Coimbra (15/0) [*sent off 81*], Miguel Ángel Noro (11/0), Félix Vera (3/0), Carlos Fernando Borja (34/1), Eduardo Andres Villegas Camara (9/0), Carlos Arias (9/0), Rolando Paniagua (10/1) [*sent off 86*], Álvaro Guillermo Peña (3/0), Gastón Taborga (17/2) [62.Oscar Ramírez (8/0)]. Trainer: Osvaldo Veiga (4).

**169.** 25.05.1989 **BOLIVIA - PARAGUAY** **3-2(2-0)**
Cochabamba; Referee: Juan Oscar Ortubé Vargas (Bolivia); Attendance: 30,000
**BOL:** Luis Galarza Mayereger (9/0) [Mauricio Ronald Soria Portillo (1/0)], Romer Antonio Roca (2/0), Carlos Arias (10/0), Miguel Ángel Rimba (1/0), Eligio Martínez (1/0), Carlos Fernando Borja (35/1), Vladimir Soria (1/0), José Milton Melgar (19/1), Erwin Sánchez (1/0) [Francisco Takeo (1/0)], Álvaro Guillermo Peña (4/1) [Fernando Salinas (7/1)], Arturo García (1/2) [Rolando Paniagua (11/1)]. Trainer: Jorge Habegger (1).
**Goals:** Álvaro Guillermo Peña (19), Arturo García (38, 50).

**170.** 01.06.1989 **PARAGUAY - BOLIVIA** **2-0(2-0)**
Asunción; Referee: Gabriel González (Paraguay)
**BOL:** Luis Galarza Mayereger (10/0), Romer Antonio Roca (3/0), Ricardo Fontana (1/0), Eligio Martínez (2/0), Marciano Saldías (6/0), Carlos Fernando Borja (36/1), Vladimir Soria (2/0), Carlos Arias (11/0), Erwin Sánchez (2/0), Álvaro Guillermo Peña (5/1), Arturo García (2/2). Trainer: Jorge Habegger (2).

**171.** 08.06.1989 **BOLIVIA - URUGUAY** **0-0**
Estadio „Ramón 'Tahuichi' Aguilera", Santa Cruz de la Sierra; Referee: Pablo Peña (Bolivia)
**BOL:** Marco Antonio Barrero (5/0), Ricardo Fontana (2/0), Romer Antonio Roca (4/0), Miguel Ángel Rimba (2/0), Eligio Martínez (3/0), Marciano Saldías (7/0), Eduardo Andres Villegas Camara (10/0) [Vladimir Soria (3/0)], Carlos Arias (12/0), Francisco Takeo (2/0) [Erwin Sánchez (3/0)], Álvaro Guillermo Peña (6/1), Fernando Salinas (8/1) [Arturo García (3/2)]. Trainer: Jorge Habegger (3).

**172.** 14.06.1989 **URUGUAY - BOLIVIA** **1-0(1-0)**
Estadio Centenario, Montevideo; Referee: Roberto Otelo (Uruguay); Attendance: 10,000
**BOL:** Luis Galarza Mayereger (11/0), Ricardo Fontana (3/0), William Ibáñez (1/0), Carlos Fernando Borja (37/1), Eligio Martínez (4/0), Marciano Saldías (8/0), Eduardo Andres Villegas Camara (11/0), Carlos Arias (13/0), Francisco Takeo (3/0) [Fernando Salinas (9/1)], Álvaro Guillermo Peña (7/1), Arturo García (4/2). Trainer: Jorge Habegger (4).

**173.** 22.06.1989 **BOLIVIA - CHILE** **0-1(0-1)**
Estadio „Ramón 'Tahuichi' Aguilera", Santa Cruz de la Sierra; Referee: Armando Aliaga (Bolivia); Attendance: 25,000
**BOL:** Marco Antonio Barrero (6/0), Romer Antonio Roca (5/0), Ricardo Fontana (4/0), Eligio Martínez (5/0), Marciano Saldías (9/0), José Milton Melgar (20/1) [Fernando Salinas (10/1)], Carlos Arias (14/0), Erwin Sánchez (4/0), Marco Antonio Etcheverry (1/0), Rolando Paniagua (12/1) [Álvaro Guillermo Peña (8/1)], Arturo García (5/2). Trainer: Jorge Habegger (5).

**174.** 27.06.1989 **CHILE - BOLIVIA** **2-1(2-0)**
Estadio Nacional, Santiago; Referee: Salvador Imperatore (Chile); Attendance: 16,092
**BOL:** Marco Antonio Barrero (7/0), Romer Antonio Roca (6/0), Ricardo Fontana (5/0), Eligio Martínez (6/0), Marciano Saldías (10/0), Carlos Fernando Borja (38/1), Eduardo Andres Villegas Camara (12/0), Carlos Arias (15/0), Erwin Sánchez (5/0), Álvaro Guillermo Peña (9/1) [60.Arturo García (6/3)], Marco Antonio Etcheverry (2/0) [60.Fernando Salinas (11/1)]. Trainer: Jorge Habegger (6).
**Goal:** Arturo García (90).

**175.** 04.07.1989 **URUGUAY - BOLIVIA** **3-0(2-0)** 34th Copa América. Group Stage
Estádio Serra Dourada, Goiânia; Referee: Arnaldo David César Coelho (Brazil); Attendance: 8,000
**BOL:** Marco Antonio Barrero (8/0), Romer Antonio Roca (7/0) [*sent off 26*], Ricardo Fontana (6/0), Eligio Martínez (7/0), Marciano Saldías (11/0), Carlos Fernando Borja (39/1), José Milton Melgar (21/1), Eduardo Andres Villegas Camara (13/0), Marco Antonio Etcheverry (3/0) [34.Ramiro Castillo Salinas (1/0)], Arturo García (7/3), Erwin Sánchez (6/0). Trainer: Jorge Habegger (7).

**176.** 06.07.1989 **ECUADOR - BOLIVIA** **0-0** 34th Copa América. Group Stage
Estádio Serra Dourada, Goiânia; Referee: Jesús Díaz Palacios (Colombia); Attendance: 3,000
**BOL:** Marco Antonio Barrero (9/0), Ricardo Fontana (7/0), Carlos Fernando Borja (40/1), Carlos Arias (16/0), Eligio Martínez (8/0), Miguel Ángel Rimba (3/0), José Milton Melgar (22/1), Eduardo Andres Villegas Camara (14/0), Ramiro Castillo Salinas (2/0), Arturo García (8/3) [68.Erwin Sánchez (7/0)], Álvaro Guillermo Peña (10/1) [77.Fernando Salinas (12/1)]. Trainer: Jorge Habegger (8).

**177.** 08.07.1989 **CHILE - BOLIVIA** **5-0(2-0)** 34th Copa América. Group Stage
Estádio Serra Dourada, Goiânia; Referee: Arnaldo David César Coelho (Brazil); Attendance: 3,000
**BOL:** Marco Antonio Barrero (10/0), Ricardo Fontana (8/0), Carlos Fernando Borja (41/1), Carlos Arias (17/0), Eligio Martínez (9/0), Miguel Ángel Rimba (4/0), José Milton Melgar (23/1), Eduardo Andres Villegas Camara (15/0), Erwin Sánchez (8/0) [46.Francisco Takeo (4/0)], Rolando Paniagua (13/1), Álvaro Guillermo Peña (11/1). Trainer: Jorge Habegger (9).

**178.** 10.07.1989 **ARGENTINA - BOLIVIA** **0-0** 34th Copa América. Group Stage
Estádio Serra Dourada, Goiânia; Referee: Nelson Rodríguez Fernández (Venezuela); Attendance: 5,000
**BOL:** Luis Galarza Mayereger (12/0), Romer Antonio Roca (8/0), Ricardo Fontana (9/0), Eligio Martínez (10/0), Marciano Saldías (12/0), Carlos Fernando Borja (42/1), José Milton Melgar (24/1), Carlos Arias (18/0), Francisco Takeo (5/0), Álvaro Guillermo Peña (12/1), Marco Antonio Etcheverry (4/0). Trainer: Jorge Habegger (10).

**179.** 20.08.1989 **BOLIVIA - PERU** **2-1(1-1)** 14th FIFA WC. Qualifiers
Estadio „Hernándo Siles Zuazo", La Paz; Referee: Armando Pérez Hoyos (Colombia); Attendance: 43,000
**BOL:** Luis Galarza Mayereger (13/0), Carlos Fernando Borja (43/1), Ricardo Fontana (10/0), Eligio Martínez (11/0), Roberto Pérez (12/0), José Milton Melgar (25/2), Vladimir Soria (4/0), Francisco Takeo (6/0) [46.Erwin Sánchez (9/0)], Erwin Romero Escudero (45/4), Álvaro Guillermo Peña (13/1), Luis William Ramallo (1/1) [75.Romer Antonio Roca (9/0)]. Trainer: Jorge Habegger (11).
**Goals:** José Milton Melgar (45 penalty), Luis William Ramallo (53).

**180.** 03.09.1989 **BOLIVIA - URUGUAY** **2-1(1-1)** 14th FIFA WC. Qualifiers
Estadio „Hernándo Siles Zuazo", La Paz; Referee: José Antonio Vergara Guerrero (Venezuela); Attendance: 52,000
**BOL:** Luis Galarza Mayereger (14/0), Marco Ferrufino (1/0), Ricardo Fontana (11/0), Eligio Martínez (12/0), Roberto Pérez (13/0), Carlos Fernando Borja (44/1), José Milton Melgar (26/2), Vladimir Soria (5/0), Erwin Romero Escudero (46/4), Álvaro Guillermo Peña (14/2) [62.Erwin Sánchez (10/0)], Luis William Ramallo (2/1). Trainer: Jorge Habegger (12).
**Goals:** Alfonso Domínguez (38 own goal), Álvaro Guillermo Peña (47).

**181.** 10.09.1989 **PERU - BOLIVIA** **1-2(0-1)** 14th FIFA WC. Qualifiers
Estadio Nacional, Lima; Referee: Carlos Alberto Maciel (Paraguay); Attendance: 9,500
**BOL:** Carlos Leonel Trucco (1/0), Ricardo Fontana (12/0), Tito Montaño (1/1), Marco Ferrufino (2/0), Eligio Martínez (13/0), Ramiro Vargas Ríos (17/0), José Milton Melgar (27/2), Vladimir Soria (6/0), Luis Héctor Cristaldo (1/0), Luis William Ramallo (3/1), Erwin Romero Escudero (47/4) [59.Erwin Sánchez (11/1)]. Trainer: Jorge Habegger (13).
**Goals:** Tito Montaño (45), Erwin Sánchez (77).

**182.** 17.09.1989 **URUGUAY - BOLIVIA** **2-0(2-0)** 14th FIFA WC. Qualifiers
Estadio Centenario, Montevideo; Referee: Gastón Castro Makuc (Chile); Attendance: 70,000
**BOL:** Carlos Leonel Trucco (2/0), Ricardo Fontana (13/0) [*sent off 77*], Tito Montaño (2/1) [46.Erwin Sánchez (12/1) [*sent off 55*], Marco Ferrufino (3/0), Eligio Martínez (14/0), Ramiro Vargas Ríos (18/0), José Milton Melgar (28/2), Carlos Fernando Borja (45/1), Eduardo Andres Villegas Camara (16/0), Erwin Romero Escudero (48/4) [46.Álvaro Guillermo Peña (15/2)], Luis William Ramallo (4/1). Trainer: Jorge Habegger (14).

**183.** 14.06.1991 **BOLIVIA - PARAGUAY** **0-1(0-0)** Copa Páz del Chaco
Estadio „Ramón 'Tahuichi' Aguilera", Santa Cruz de la Sierra; Referee: Jorge Antequera (Bolivia); Attendance: 8,000
**BOL:** Marco Antonio Barrero (11/0), Miguel Ángel Rimba (5/0), José Milton Melgar (29/2), Eduardo Jiguchi (1/0), Carlos Fernando Borja (46/1) [Juan Manuel Peña Montaño (1/0)], Ramiro Castillo Salinas (3/0), Julio César Baldivieso (1/0), Modesto Molina (1/0), Marco Antonio Etcheverry (5/0), Marciano Saldías (13/0), Marco Ferrufino (4/0). Trainer: Ramiro Blacutt Rodríguez (22).

**184.** 16.06.1991 **PARAGUAY – BOLIVIA** **0-0** Copa Páz del Chaco

Asunción; Referee: Mateo Corvalán Verdun Efigenio (Paraguay); Attendance: 8,000

**BOL:** Marco Antonio Barrero (12/0), Miguel Ángel Rimba (6/0), Eduardo Jiguchi (2/0) [*sent off*], Marco Ferrufino (5/0), Marciano Saldías (14/0), Carlos Fernando Borja (47/1), José Milton Melgar (30/2) [Juan Carlos Chávez (1/0)], Sergio Rivero (1/0), Ramiro Castillo Salinas (4/0) [José Luis Medrano (1/0)], Juan Berthy Suárez (1/0) [Modesto Molina (2/0], Modesto Soruco (1/0). Trainer: Ramiro Blacutt Rodríguez (23).

**185.** 07.07.1991 **URUGUAY – BOLIVIA** **1-1(0-1)** 35th Copa América. Group Stage

Estadio Playa Ancha, Valparaíso; Referee: Carlos Alberto Maciel (Paraguay); Attendance: 15,000

**BOL:** Víctor Hugo Aragón (1/0), Miguel Ángel Rimba (7/0), Marco Ferrufino (6/0), Marciano Saldías (15/0), Sergio Rivero (2/0), Carlos Fernando Borja (48/1), Erwin Sánchez (13/1) [82.Julio César Baldivieso (2/0)], José Milton Melgar (31/2), Ramiro Castillo Salinas (5/0), Marco Antonio Etcheverry (6/0), Juan Berthy Suárez (2/1) [82.Modesto Soruco (2/0)]. Trainer: Ramiro Blacutt Rodríguez (24).

**Goal:** Juan Berthy Suárez (16).

**186.** 09.07.1991 **BRAZIL – BOLIVIA** **2-1(1-0)** 35th Copa América. Group Stage

Estadio Sausalito, Viña del Mar (Chile); Referee: José Francisco Ramírez Calle (Peru); Attendance: 18,000

**BOL:** Víctor Hugo Aragón (2/0), Miguel Ángel Rimba (8/0), Eduardo Jiguchi (3/0), Marco Ferrufino (7/0), Marciano Saldías (16/0), Carlos Fernando Borja (49/1) [60.Álvaro Guillermo Peña (16/2)], José Milton Melgar (32/2), Ramiro Castillo Salinas (6/0), Erwin Sánchez (14/2), Marco Antonio Etcheverry (7/0), Juan Berthy Suárez (3/1) [46.Julio César Baldivieso (3/0)]. Trainer: Ramiro Blacutt Rodríguez (25).

**Goal:** Erwin Sánchez (89 penalty).

**187.** 11.07.1991 **COLOMBIA – BOLIVIA** **0-0** 35th Copa América. Group Stage

Estadio Sausalito, Viña del Mar (Chile); Referee: Francisco Farías d'Abreu (Venezuela); Attendance: 15,000

**BOL:** Marco Antonio Barrero (13/0), Miguel Ángel Rimba (9/0), Marco Ferrufino (8/0), Eduardo Jiguchi (4/0), Marciano Saldías (17/0), Julio César Baldivieso (4/0), José Milton Melgar (33/2), Ramiro Castillo Salinas (7/0) [71.Erwin Sánchez (15/2)], Marco Antonio Etcheverry (8/0), Juan Berthy Suárez (4/1), Jaime Moreno Morales (1/0) [70.Carlos Fernando Borja (50/1)]. Trainer: Ramiro Blacutt Rodríguez (26).

**188.** 13.07.1991 **ECUADOR – BOLIVIA** **4-0(2-0)** 35th Copa América. Group Stage

Estadio Sausalito, Viña del Mar (Chile); Referee: Gastón Castro Makuc (Chile); Attendance: 19,000

**BOL:** Marco Antonio Barrero (14/0), Eduardo Jiguchi (5/0) [*sent off 63*], Marco Ferrufino (9/0), Marciano Saldías (18/0), José Milton Melgar (34/2), Miguel Ángel Rimba (10/0), Modesto Molina (3/0), Carlos Fernando Borja (51/1), Ramiro Castillo Salinas (8/0) [75.José Luis Medrano (2/0)], Marco Antonio Etcheverry (9/0), Jaime Moreno Morales (2/0) [46.Julio César Baldivieso (5/0)]. Trainer: Ramiro Blacutt Rodríguez (27).

**189.** 19.01.1993 **NORTH KOREA – BOLIVIA** **2-1** Nehru Cup

"Jawaharlal Nehru" Stadium, Madras

**BOL:** Marco Antonio Barrero (15/0), Miguel Ángel Noro (12/0), William Ibáñez (2/0), Sergio Rivero (3/0), Rafael Salguero Siles (1/0), Roberto Pérez (14/0), Freddy Cossío (1/0), Mario Daniel Pinedo (5/0), Juan Mauricio Ramos (2/0), Francisco Takeo (7/1), Víctor Hugo Antelo (8/2).

**Goal:** Francisco Takeo.

**190.** 23.01.1993 **ROMANIA "B" – BOLIVIA** **2-0(1-0)** Nehru Cup

"Jawaharlal Nehru" Stadium, Madras; Referee: Kar Gautam (India)

**BOL:** Marco Antonio Barrero (16/0), Jorge Monasterio (1/0), Sergio Rivero (4/0), William Ibáñez (3/0), Miguel Ángel Noro (13/0), Freddy Cossío (2/0), Mario Daniel Pinedo (6/0), Modesto Soruco (3/0), Francisco Takeo (8/1), Roberto Pérez (15/0), Víctor Hugo Antelo (9/2).

**191.** 25.01.1993 **RUSSIA "B" – BOLIVIA** **2-1(2-1)** Nehru Cup

"Jawaharlal Nehru" Stadium, Madras; Referee: A.K. Mammukova (India)

**BOL:** Marco Antonio Barrero (17/0), Jorge Monasterio (2/0), Sergio Rivero (5/0), William Ibáñez (4/0), Freddy Cossío (3/0), Mario Daniel Pinedo (7/0), Modesto Soruco (4/0), Francisco Takeo (9/1), Roberto Pérez (16/0), Víctor Hugo Antelo (10/3), Modesto Molina (4/0).

**Goal:** Víctor Hugo Antelo (39).

**192.** 29.01.1993 **BOLIVIA – HONDURAS** **3-1(1-1)**

Estadio „Félix Capriles", Cochabamba; Referee: Armando Aliaga (Bolivia)

**BOL:** Carlos Leonel Trucco (3/0) [46.Rubén Darío Rojas (1/0)], Juan Manuel Peña Montaño (2/0), Miguel Ángel Rimba (11/0) [46.Eduardo Jiguchi (6/0)], Gustavo Domingo Quinteros (1/1), Marco Antonio Sandy Sansusty (1/0), Carlos Fernando Borja (52/1), Vladimir Soria (7/0), José Milton Melgar (35/2) [46.Luis William Ramallo (5/1)], José María Romero (1/0) [46.Johnny Villarroel (1/2)], Julio César Baldivieso (6/0), Álvaro Guillermo Peña (17/2) [46.Jaime Moreno Morales (3/0)]. Trainer: Francisco Xabier Azcargorta Uriarte (1).

**Goals:** Gustavo Domingo Quinteros (4), Johnny Villarroel (57, 75).

**193.** 03.03.1993 **PARAGUAY – BOLIVIA** **1-0(0-0)** Copa Páz del Chaco

Estadio Defensores del Chaco, Asunción; Referee: Julio Alcides Matto Estoceres (Uruguay); Attendance: 938

**BOL:** Rubén Darío Rojas (2/0), Modesto Soruco (5/0) [46.Rafael Salguero Siles (2/0)], Juan Manuel Peña Montaño (3/0), Sergio Rivero (6/0), Marcos Francisquini (1/0), Luis Héctor Cristaldo (2/0), Francisco Takeo (10/1) [Mario Daniel Pinedo (8/0)], José Milton Melgar (36/2), Johnny Villarroel (2/2) [46.Juan Carlos Ríos (1/0)], Ramiro Castillo Salinas (9/0), Jaime Moreno Morales (4/0) [62.Modesto Molina (5/0)]. Trainer: Francisco Xabier Azcargorta Uriarte (2).

**194.** 12.03.1993 **EL SALVADOR – BOLIVIA** **2-2(1-1)**

Estadio Cuscatlán, San Salvador; Referee: José Antonio Gómez Santos (El Salvador)

**BOL:** Rubén Darío Rojas (3/0), Modesto Soruco (6/0), Juan Manuel Peña Montaño (4/0), Sergio Rivero (7/0), Marcos Francisquini (2/0), Luis Héctor Cristaldo (3/0), Francisco Takeo (11/1) [79.Mario Daniel Pinedo (9/0)], José Milton Melgar (37/2), Johnny Villarroel (3/3) [52.Juan Carlos Ríos (2/0)], Ramiro Castillo Salinas (10/1), Modesto Molina (6/0) [60.Serafin Gareca (1/0)]. Trainer: Francisco Xabier Azcargorta Uriarte (3).

**Goals:** Johnny Villarroel (33), Ramiro Castillo Salinas (88).

**195.** 14.03.1993 **HONDURAS – BOLIVIA** **0-0**

San Pedro Sula; Referee: Argelio Sabillón (Honduras)

**BOL:** Rubén Darío Rojas (4/0), Modesto Soruco (7/0), Juan Manuel Peña Montaño (5/0), Sergio Rivero (8/0), Marcos Francisquini (3/0), Luis Héctor Cristaldo (4/0), Francisco Takeo (12/1) [46.Juan Carlos Ríos (3/0)], José Milton Melgar (38/2), Johnny Villarroel (4/3) [15.Serafin Gareca (2/0)], Ramiro Castillo Salinas (11/1), Modesto Molina (7/0) [70.Mario Daniel Pinedo (10/0)]. Trainer: Francisco Xabier Azcargorta Uriarte (4).

**196.** 16.03.1993 **HONDURAS – BOLIVIA** **0-0**
Tegucigalpa; Referee: Ramírez (Honduras)
**BOL:** Rubén Darío Rojas (5/0) [46.Marcelo Eduardo Torrico (1/0)], Modesto Soruco (8/0), Juan Manuel Peña Montaño (6/0), Sergio Rivero (9/0), Marcos Francisquini (4/0), Luis Héctor Cristaldo (5/0) [70. Johnny Villarroel (5/3)], Francisco Takeo (13/1), José Milton Melgar (39/2) [62.Modesto Molina (8/0)], Serafin Gareca (3/0), Juan Carlos Ríos (4/0), Mario Daniel Pinedo (11/0). Trainer: Francisco Xabier Azcargorta Uriarte (5).

**197.** 31.03.1993 **CHILE – BOLIVIA** **2-1(0-0)**
Estadio "Carlos Dittborn", Arica; Referee: Enrique Marín Gallo (Chile); Attendance: 9,580
**BOL:** Rubén Darío Rojas (6/0), Juan Manuel Peña Montaño (7/0), Sergio Rivero (10/0), Gustavo Domingo Quinteros (2/1), Modesto Soruco (9/0), José Milton Melgar (40/2), Luis Héctor Cristaldo (6/0), Erwin Sánchez (16/2) [60.Jaime Moreno Morales (5/0)], Juan Carlos Ríos (5/1), Pastor Aramayo (1/0) [60.Francisco Takeo (14/1)], Álvaro Guillermo Peña (18/2) [Luis William Ramallo (6/1)]. Trainer: Francisco Xabier Azcargorta Uriarte (6).
**Goal:** Juan Carlos Ríos (61).

**198.** 23.05.1993 **UNITED STATES – BOLIVIA** **0-0**
Fullerton Stadium, Fullerton; Referee: Brian Hall (United States); Attendance: 9,578
**BOL:** Carlos Leonel Trucco (4/0), Marco Antonio Sandy Sansusty (2/0), Juan Manuel Peña Montaño (8/0), Miguel Ángel Rimba (12/0), Gustavo Domingo Quinteros (3/1), Luis Héctor Cristaldo (7/0), Julio César Baldivieso (7/0) [89.Vladimir Soria (8/0)], José Milton Melgar (41/2), Carlos Fernando Borja (53/1) [46.Juan Carlos Ríos (6/1)], Marco Antonio Etcheverry (10/0), Jaime Moreno Morales (6/0) [73.Johnny Villarroel (6/3)]. Trainer: Francisco Xabier Azcargorta Uriarte (7).

**199.** 27.05.1993 **BOLIVIA – PARAGUAY** **2-1(1-0,2-1); 5-4 on penalties** Copa Páz del Chaco
Estadio „Félix Capriles", Cochabamba; Referee: Enrique Marín Gallo (Chile); Attendance: 10,500
**BOL:** Carlos Leonel Trucco (5/0), Juan Manuel Peña Montaño (9/0), Marco Antonio Sandy Sansusty (3/0), Miguel Ángel Rimba (13/0) [46.Modesto Soruco (10/0)], Gustavo Domingo Quinteros (4/1), Luis Héctor Cristaldo (8/0) [58.Iván Sabino Castillo (1/0)], Julio César Baldivieso (8/0) [58.Johnny Villarroel (7/3)], Carlos Fernando Borja (54/1), José Milton Melgar (42/2), Marco Antonio Etcheverry (11/0) [46.Juan Carlos Ríos (7/2)], Jaime Moreno Morales (7/1) [80.Luis William Ramallo (7/1)]. Trainer: Francisco Xabier Azcargorta Uriarte (8).
**Goals:** Jaime Moreno Morales (21), Juan Carlos Ríos (87).
**Penalties:** Johnny Villarroel, Juan Carlos Ríos, Carlos Fernando Borja, Luis William Ramallo, José Milton Melgar.

**200.** 06.06.1993 **PERU – BOLIVIA** **1-0(1-0)**
Estadio Nacional, Lima; Referee: Luis Seminario (Peru)
**BOL:** Carlos Leonel Trucco (6/0) [Rubén Darío Rojas (7/0)], Carlos Fernando Borja (55/1), Marco Antonio Sandy Sansusty (4/0), Miguel Ángel Noro (14/0), Juan Manuel Peña Montaño (10/0), Modesto Soruco (11/0), José Milton Melgar (43/2), Ramiro Castillo Salinas (12/1) [Juan Carlos Ríos (8/2)], Julio César Baldivieso (9/0) [Johnny Villarroel (8/3)], Marco Antonio Etcheverry (12/0), Álvaro Guillermo Peña (19/2) [Jaime Moreno Morales (8/1)]. Trainer: Francisco Xabier Azcargorta Uriarte (9).

**201.** 13.06.1993 **BOLIVIA – CHILE** **1-3(0-2)**
Estadio „Hernándo Siles Zuazo", La Paz; Referee: René Marcelo Ortubé Betancourt (Bolivia); Attendance: 17,165
**BOL:** Rubén Darío Rojas (8/0), Juan Manuel Peña Montaño (11/0) [21.Modesto Soruco (12/0)], Gustavo Domingo Quinteros (5/1), Marco Antonio Sandy Sansusty (5/1), Roberto Pérez (17/0) [46.Juan Carlos Ríos (9/2)], Miguel Ángel Rimba (14/0), Carlos Fernando Borja (56/1), José Milton Melgar (44/2), Marco Antonio Etcheverry (13/0) [60.Johnny Villarroel (9/3)], Julio César Baldivieso (10/0) [60.Álvaro Guillermo Peña (20/2)], Jaime Moreno Morales (9/1) [60.Luis William Ramallo (8/1)]. Trainer: Francisco Xabier Azcargorta Uriarte (10).
**Goal:** Marco Antonio Sandy Sansusty (48).

**202.** 17.06.1993 **ARGENTINA – BOLIVIA** **1-0(0-0)** 36th Copa América. Group Stage
Estadio Neuve de Mayo, Machala (Ecuador); Referee: Arturo Angeles (United States); Attendance: 16,000
**BOL:** Rubén Darío Rojas (9/0), Juan Manuel Peña Montaño (12/0), Gustavo Domingo Quinteros (6/1), Marco Antonio Sandy Sansusty (6/1), Miguel Ángel Rimba (15/0), Carlos Fernando Borja (57/1), José Milton Melgar (45/2), Marco Antonio Etcheverry (14/0), Julio César Baldivieso (11/0), Ramiro Castillo Salinas (13/1), Jaime Moreno Morales (10/1) [64.Álvaro Guillermo Peña (21/2)]. Trainer: Francisco Xabier Azcargorta Uriarte (11).

**203.** 20.06.1993 **COLOMBIA – BOLIVIA** **1-1(1-1)** 36th Copa América. Group Stage
Estadio Neuve de Mayo, Machala (Ecuador); Referee: Márcio Rezende de Freitas (Brazil); Attendance: 11,000
**BOL:** Rubén Darío Rojas (10/0), Juan Manuel Peña Montaño (13/0), Gustavo Domingo Quinteros (7/1), Marco Antonio Sandy Sansusty (7/1), Miguel Ángel Rimba (16/0) [52.Modesto Soruco (13/0)], Carlos Fernando Borja (58/1), José Milton Melgar (46/2), Ramiro Castillo Salinas (14/1), Julio César Baldivieso (12/0) [46.Luis Héctor Cristaldo (9/0)], Jaime Moreno Morales (11/1), Marco Antonio Etcheverry (15/1). Trainer: Francisco Xabier Azcargorta Uriarte (12).
**Goal:** Marco Antonio Etcheverry (14).

**204.** 23.06.1993 **MEXICO – BOLIVIA** **0-0** 36th Copa América. Group Stage
Estadio Reales Tamarindos, Portoviejo; Referee: Jorge Luis Nieves Parra (Uruguay); Attendance: 20,000
**BOL:** Rubén Darío Rojas (11/0), Carlos Fernando Borja (59/1), Juan Manuel Peña Montaño (14/0), Marco Antonio Sandy Sansusty (8/1), Gustavo Domingo Quinteros (8/1), Luis Héctor Cristaldo (10/0), Ramiro Castillo Salinas (15/1) [56.Erwin Sánchez (17/2)], José Milton Melgar (47/2), Julio César Baldivieso (13/0), Marco Antonio Etcheverry (16/1), Álvaro Guillermo Peña (22/2) [71.Jaime Moreno Morales (12/1)]. Trainer: Francisco Xabier Azcargorta Uriarte (13).

**205.** 18.07.1993 **VENEZUELA – BOLIVIA** **1-7(1-3)** 15th FIFA WC. Qualifiers
Estadio Polideportivo Cachamay, Puerto Ordaz; Referee: Morera Benny Ulloa (Costa Rica); Attendance: 12,000
**BOL:** Rubén Darío Rojas (12/0), Miguel Ángel Rimba (17/0), Gustavo Domingo Quinteros (9/1), Luis Héctor Cristaldo (11/1), Marco Antonio Sandy Sansusty (9/1), Erwin Sánchez (18/5), Carlos Fernando Borja (60/1), José Milton Melgar (48/2), Julio César Baldivieso (14/0), Marco Antonio Etcheverry (17/1) [85.Ramiro Castillo Salinas (16/1)], Luis William Ramallo (9/4) [76.Álvaro Guillermo Peña (23/2)]. Trainer: Francisco Xabier Azcargorta Uriarte (14).
**Goals:** Erwin Sánchez (25), Luis William Ramallo (37), Erwin Sánchez (39), Luis William Ramallo (61), Luis Héctor Cristaldo (64), Luis William Ramallo (68), Erwin Sánchez (70).

**206.** 25.07.1993 **BOLIVIA – BRAZIL** **2-0(0-0)** 15th FIFA WC. Qualifiers
Estadio „Hernándo Siles Zuazo", La Paz; Referee: Juan Francisco Escobar Valdéz (Paraguay); Attendance: 5,000
**BOL:** Carlos Leonel Trucco (7/0), Miguel Ángel Rimba (18/0), Gustavo Domingo Quinteros (10/1), Marco Antonio Sandy Sansusty (10/1), Carlos Fernando Borja (61/1), Luis Héctor Cristaldo (12/1), José Milton Melgar (49/2), Julio César Baldivieso (15/0), Marco Antonio Etcheverry (18/2), Erwin Sánchez (19/5) [83.Ramiro Castillo Salinas (17/1)], Luis William Ramallo (10/4) [57.Álvaro Guillermo Peña (24/3)]. Trainer: Francisco Xabier Azcargorta Uriarte (15).
**Goals:** Marco Antonio Etcheverry (88), Álvaro Guillermo Peña (89).

**207.** 08.08.1993 **BOLIVIA – URUGUAY** **3-1(0-0)** 15th FIFA WC. Qualifiers

Estadio „Hernándo Siles Zuazo", La Paz; Referee: Iván Enrique Guerrero Levancini (Chile); Attendance: 45,000

**BOL:** Carlos Leonel Trucco (8/0), Carlos Fernando Borja (62/1), Miguel Ángel Rimba (19/0), Gustavo Domingo Quinteros (11/1), Marco Antonio Sandy Sansusty (11/1), Luis Héctor Cristaldo (13/1), Julio César Baldivieso (16/0), José Milton Melgar (Cap) (50/3), Ramiro Castillo Salinas (18/1) [53.Marco Antonio Etcheverry (19/3)], Erwin Sánchez (20/6), Luis William Ramallo (11/4) [83.Álvaro Guillermo Peña (25/3)]. Trainer: Francisco Xabier Azcargorta Uriarte (16).

**Goals:** Erwin Sánchez (71), Marco Antonio Etcheverry (81), José Milton Melgar (86).

**208.** 15.08.1993 **BOLIVIA – ECUADOR** **1-0(1-0)** 15th FIFA WC. Qualifiers

Estadio „Hernándo Siles Zuazo", La Paz; Referee: Hernán Silva Arce (Chile); Attendance: 48,000

**BOL:** Carlos Leonel Trucco (9/0), Carlos Fernando Borja (63/1), Gustavo Domingo Quinteros (12/1), Marco Antonio Sandy Sansusty (12/1), Luis Héctor Cristaldo (14/1), Miguel Ángel Rimba (20/0), José Milton Melgar (51/3), Marco Antonio Etcheverry (20/3) [82.Johnny Villarroel (10/3)], Julio César Baldivieso (17/0), Luis William Ramallo (12/5) [70.Álvaro Guillermo Peña (26/3)], Erwin Sánchez (21/6). Trainer: Francisco Xabier Azcargorta Uriarte (17).

**Goal:** Luis William Ramallo (18).

**209.** 22.08.1993 **BOLIVIA – VENEZUELA** **7-0(1-0)** 15th FIFA WC. Qualifiers

Estadio „Hernándo Siles Zuazo", La Paz; Referee: Sabino Farina Cespedes (Paraguay); Attendance: 40,000

**BOL:** Carlos Leonel Trucco (10/0), Carlos Fernando Borja (64/1), Gustavo Domingo Quinteros (13/1), Marco Antonio Sandy Sansusty (13/2), Miguel Ángel Rimba (21/0), Luis Héctor Cristaldo (15/1), José Milton Melgar (52/5), Johnny Villarroel (11/3) [78.Iván Sabino Castillo (2/0)], Marco Antonio Etcheverry (21/5), Erwin Sánchez (22/7), Luis William Ramallo (13/6) [67.Álvaro Guillermo Peña (27/3)]. Trainer: Francisco Xabier Azcargorta Uriarte (18).

**Goals:** Luis William Ramallo (8), José Milton Melgar (58), Erwin Sánchez (69), Marco Antonio Sandy Sansusty (75), Marco Antonio Etcheverry (78, 82), José Milton Melgar (90).

**210.** 29.08.1993 **BRAZIL – BOLIVIA** **6-0(5-0)** 15th FIFA WC. Qualifiers

Estádio Arruda, Recife; Referee: Oscar Velásquez Alvarenga (Paraguay); Attendance: 72,000

**BOL:** Carlos Leonel Trucco (11/0), Miguel Ángel Rimba (22/0), Gustavo Domingo Quinteros (14/1), Marco Antonio Sandy Sansusty (14/2), Luis Héctor Cristaldo (16/1), Carlos Fernando Borja (65/1), José Milton Melgar (53/5), Julio César Baldivieso (18/0), Erwin Sánchez (23/7), Marco Antonio Etcheverry (22/5) [41.Juan Manuel Peña Montaño (15/0)], Luis William Ramallo (14/6) [71.Álvaro Guillermo Peña (28/3)]. Trainer: Francisco Xabier Azcargorta Uriarte (19).

**211.** 12.09.1993 **URUGUAY – BOLIVIA** **2-1(1-1)** 15th FIFA WC. Qualifiers

Estadio Centenario, Montevideo; Referee: Armando Pérez Hoyos (Colombia); Attendance: 58,000

**BOL:** Carlos Leonel Trucco (12/0), Miguel Ángel Rimba (23/0), Sergio Rivero (11/0), Gustavo Domingo Quinteros (15/1), Juan Manuel Peña Montaño (16/0) [*sent off 45*], Luis Héctor Cristaldo (17/1), Carlos Fernando Borja (66/1), José Milton Melgar (Cap) (54/5), Julio César Baldivieso (19/0) [82.Mario Daniel Pinedo (12/0)], Erwin Sánchez (24/7), Luis William Ramallo (15/7) [63.Álvaro Guillermo Peña (29/3)]. Trainer: Francisco Xabier Azcargorta Uriarte (20).

**Goal:** Luis William Ramallo (23).

**212.** 19.09.1993 **ECUADOR – BOLIVIA** **1-1(0-1)** 15th FIFA WC. Qualifiers

Estadio "Isidro Romero", Guayaquil; Referee: John Jairo Toro Rendón (Colombia); Attendance: 5,000

**BOL:** Carlos Leonel Trucco (13/0), Modesto Soruco (14/0) [78.Mario Daniel Pinedo (13/0)], Marco Antonio Sandy Sansusty (15/2), Gustavo Domingo Quinteros (16/1), Luis Héctor Cristaldo (18/1), Juan Rivero (1/0), Carlos Fernando Borja (67/1), José Milton Melgar (55/5), Julio César Baldivieso (20/0), Erwin Sánchez (25/7), Luis William Ramallo (16/8) [58.Marco Antonio Etcheverry (23/5)]. Trainer: Francisco Xabier Azcargorta Uriarte (21).

**Goal:** Luis William Ramallo (45).

**213.** 18.02.1994 **UNITED STATES – BOLIVIA** **1-1(0-1)** Joe Robbie Cup

Orange Bowl, Miami; Referee: Gilberto Acala Piñeda (Mexico); Attendance: 15,676

**BOL:** Carlos Leonel Trucco (14/0), Marco Antonio Sandy Sansusty (16/2), Miguel Ángel Rimba (24/0), Gustavo Domingo Quinteros (17/1), Robert Arteaga (1/0), José Milton Melgar (56/5), Álvaro Guillermo Peña (30/3) [70.Luis William Ramallo (17/8)], Juan Mauricio Ramos (3/0) [81.Ramiro Castillo Salinas (19/1)], Jaime Moreno Morales (13/2), Luis Héctor Cristaldo (19/1), Julio César Baldivieso (21/0). Trainer: Francisco Xabier Azcargorta Uriarte (22).

**Goal:** Jaime Moreno Morales (44).

**214.** 20.02.1994 **COLOMBIA – BOLIVIA** **2-0(1-0)** Joe Robbie Cup

Orange Bowl, Miami (United States); Referee: Jack d'Aquila (United States); Attendance: 20,171

**BOL:** Carlos Leonel Trucco (15/0), Marco Antonio Sandy Sansusty (17/2), Miguel Ángel Rimba (25/0), Gustavo Domingo Quinteros (18/1), Luis Héctor Cristaldo (20/1), Carlos Fernando Borja (68/1), José Milton Melgar (57/5), Juan Mauricio Ramos (4/0) [79.Wilson Rueda (1/0)], Juan Carlos Ríos (10/2) [46.Álvaro Guillermo Peña (31/3)], Luis William Ramallo (18/8) [46.Jaime Moreno Morales (14/2)], Julio César Baldivieso (22/0) [57.Juan Carlos Chávez (2/0)]. Trainer: Francisco Xabier Azcargorta Uriarte (23).

**215.** 26.03.1994 **UNITED STATES – BOLIVIA** **2-2(1-1)**

Cotton Bowl, Dallas; Referee: Hugh Dallas (Scotland); Attendance: 26,835

**BOL:** Carlos Leonel Trucco (16/0), Marco Antonio Sandy Sansusty (18/2), Miguel Ángel Rimba (26/0), Modesto Soruco (15/0), Luis Héctor Cristaldo (21/1), Vladimir Soria (9/0), Iván Sabino Castillo (3/0) [72.Mario Daniel Pinedo (14/1)], Julio César Baldivieso (23/1), Juan Carlos Chávez (3/0), Jaime Moreno Morales (15/2) [76.Richard Cueto (1/0)], Luis William Ramallo (19/8) [64.Álvaro Guillermo Peña (32/3)]. Trainer: Francisco Xabier Azcargorta Uriarte (24).

**Goals:** Julio César Baldivieso (12), Mario Daniel Pinedo (76).

**216.** 07.04.1994 **COLOMBIA – BOLIVIA** **0-1(0-0)**

Villavicencio; Referee: Felipe Eduardo Russi Páez (Colombia); Attendance: 15,500

**BOL:** Carlos Leonel Trucco (17/0), Marco Antonio Sandy Sansusty (19/2), Miguel Ángel Rimba (27/0), Modesto Soruco (16/0) [87.Ramiro Castillo Salinas (20/1)], Luis Héctor Cristaldo (22/1), Vladimir Soria (10/0), Mario Daniel Pinedo (15/2) [65.Carlos Fernando Borja (69/1)], Julio César Baldivieso (24/1), Juan Carlos Chávez (4/0), Luis William Ramallo (20/8) [65.Álvaro Guillermo Peña (33/3)], Jaime Moreno Morales (16/2) [76.Juan Carlos Ríos (11/2)]. Trainer: Francisco Xabier Azcargorta Uriarte (25).

**Goal:** Mario Daniel Pinedo (52).

**217.** 20.04.1994 **ROMÂNIA – BOLIVIA** **3-0(1-0)**

Stadionul Steaua, Bucureşti; Referee: Ion Crăciunescu (România); Attendance: 15,000

**BOL:** Carlos Leonel Trucco (18/0) [76.Rubén Darío Rojas (13/0)], Juan Carlos Chávez (5/0), Marco Antonio Sandy Sansusty (20/2), Óscar Carmelo Sánchez (1/0), Miguel Ángel Rimba (Cap) (28/0), Luis Héctor Cristaldo (23/1), Vladimir Soria (11/0), Erwin Sánchez (26/7) [46.Mario Daniel Pinedo (16/2)], Julio César Baldivieso (25/1) [73.Álvaro Guillermo Peña (34/3)], Jaime Moreno Morales (17/2) [62.José Milton Melgar (58/5)], Luis William Ramallo (21/8) [46.Modesto Soruco (17/0)]. Trainer: Francisco Xabier Azcargorta Uriarte (26).

**218.** 04.05.1994 **BOLIVIA – SAUDI ARABIA** **1-0(0-0)**
Cannes (France); Referee: Philippe Leduc (France); Attendance: 700
**BOL:** Rubén Darío Rojas (14/0), Carlos Fernando Borja (70/1), Miguel Ángel Rimba (29/0), Óscar Carmelo Sánchez (2/0), Marco Antonio Sandy Sansusty (21/2), Mario Daniel Pinedo (17/2) [Jaime Moreno Morales (18/2)], Juan Mauricio Ramos (5/0), José Milton Melgar (59/5), Julio César Baldivieso (26/1) [Vladimir Soria (12/0)], Erwin Sánchez (27/8), Luis William Ramallo (22/8) [Ramiro Castillo Salinas (21/1)]. Trainer: Francisco Xabier Azcargorta Uriarte (27).
**Goal:** Erwin Sánchez (77).

**219.** 11.05.1994 **BOLIVIA – CAMEROON** **1-1(0-1)** Greece Tournament
Karaiskaki Stadio, Peiraiás; Referee: Karl Finzinger (Austria); Attendance: 600
**BOL:** Rubén Darío Rojas (15/0), Juan Manuel Peña Montaño (17/0), Miguel Ángel Rimba (30/0), Óscar Carmelo Sánchez (3/0) [46.Vladimir Soria (13/0)], Marco Antonio Sandy Sansusty (22/2), Luis Héctor Cristaldo (24/1), José Milton Melgar (60/5), Julio César Baldivieso (27/1) [73.Mario Daniel Pinedo (18/2)], Ramiro Castillo Salinas (22/1) [46.Jaime Moreno Morales (19/2)], Juan Mauricio Ramos (6/0), Álvaro Guillermo Peña (35/4) [75.Luis William Ramallo (23/8)]. Trainer: Francisco Xabier Azcargorta Uriarte (28).
**Goal:** Álvaro Guillermo Peña (62).

**220.** 13.05.1994 **GREECE – BOLIVIA** **0-0** Greece Tournament
Karaiskaki Stadio, Peiraiás; Referee: Alfred Wieser (Austria); Attendance: 3,500
**BOL:** Rubén Darío Rojas (16/0), Juan Manuel Peña Montaño (18/0), Miguel Ángel Rimba (31/0), Vladimir Soria (14/0), Marco Antonio Sandy Sansusty (23/2), José Milton Melgar (61/5), Julio César Baldivieso (28/1) [63.Mario Daniel Pinedo (19/2)], Juan Mauricio Ramos (7/0) [72.Iván Sabino Castillo (4/0)], Luis Héctor Cristaldo (25/1), Jaime Moreno Morales (20/2) [82.Carlos Fernando Borja (71/1)], Álvaro Guillermo Peña (36/4) [58.Luis William Ramallo (24/8)]. Trainer: Francisco Xabier Azcargorta Uriarte (29).

**221.** 19.05.1994 **ICELAND – BOLIVIA** **1-0(0-0)**
Laugardalsvöllur Stadium, Reykjavík; Referee: Lars Gerner (Denmark); Attendance: 2,707
**BOL:** Rubén Darío Rojas (17/0), Juan Manuel Peña Montaño (19/0), Miguel Ángel Rimba (32/0), Modesto Soruco (18/0), Luis Héctor Cristaldo (26/1), Vladimir Soria (15/0), Mario Daniel Pinedo (20/2), Juan Carlos Chávez (6/0) [58.Luis William Ramallo (25/8)], José Milton Melgar (62/5), Álvaro Guillermo Peña (37/4), Juan Mauricio Ramos (8/0) [77.Ramiro Castillo Salinas (23/1)]. Trainer: Francisco Xabier Azcargorta Uriarte (30).

**222.** 24.05.1994 **REPUBLIC OF IRELAND – BOLIVIA** **1-0(0-0)**
Lansdowne Road, Dublin; Referee: Alan Howells (Wales); Attendance: 32,500
**BOL:** Carlos Leonel Trucco (19/0), Gustavo Domingo Quinteros (19/1), Modesto Soruco (19/0) [87.Juan Manuel Peña Montaño (20/0)], Miguel Ángel Rimba (33/0), Marco Antonio Sandy Sansusty (24/2), José Milton Melgar (63/5), Luis Héctor Cristaldo (27/1), Mario Daniel Pinedo (21/2) [55.Carlos Fernando Borja (72/1)], Julio César Baldivieso (29/1), Juan Mauricio Ramos (9/0), Álvaro Guillermo Peña (38/4) [46.Ramiro Castillo Salinas (24/1)]. Trainer: Francisco Xabier Azcargorta Uriarte (31).

**223.** 08.06.1994 **BOLIVIA – PERU** **0-0**
Estadio „Ramón 'Tahuichi' Aguilera", Santa Cruz de la Sierra; Referee: Pedro Saucedo Rodríguez (Bolivia); Attendance: 35,000
**BOL:** Carlos Leonel Trucco (20/0), Miguel Ángel Rimba (34/0), Marco Antonio Sandy Sansusty (25/2), Gustavo Domingo Quinteros (20/1), Luis Héctor Cristaldo (28/1), Carlos Fernando Borja (73/1) [Modesto Soruco (20/0)], José Milton Melgar (64/5), Julio César Baldivieso (30/1) [Juan Mauricio Ramos (10/0)], Erwin Sánchez (28/8), Álvaro Guillermo Peña (39/4) [Luis William Ramallo (26/8)], Jaime Moreno Morales (21/2) [Ramiro Castillo Salinas (25/1)]. Trainer: Francisco Xabier Azcargorta Uriarte (32).

**224.** 11.06.1994 **BOLIVIA – SWITZERLAND** **0-0**
Stade "Claude Robillard", Montréal (Canada); Referee: Stephen Lodge (England); Attendance: 4,655
**BOL:** Carlos Leonel Trucco (21/0), Gustavo Domingo Quinteros (21/1), Miguel Ángel Rimba (35/0), Carlos Fernando Borja (74/1) [67.Modesto Soruco (21/0)], Marco Antonio Sandy Sansusty (26/2), José Milton Melgar (65/5), Luis Héctor Cristaldo (29/1), Vladimir Soria (16/0), Erwin Sánchez (29/8) [81.Juan Mauricio Ramos (11/0)], Luis William Ramallo (27/8) [76.Jaime Moreno Morales (22/2)], Julio César Baldivieso (31/1). Trainer: Francisco Xabier Azcargorta Uriarte (33).

**225.** 17.06.1994 **GERMANY – BOLIVIA** **1-0(0-0)** 15th FIFA WC. Group Stage
Soldier Field Stadium, Chicago; Referee: Arturo Pablo Brizio Carter (Mexico); Attendance: 63,117
**BOL:** Carlos Leonel Trucco (22/0), Carlos Fernando Borja (Cap) (75/1), Gustavo Domingo Quinteros (22/1), Miguel Ángel Rimba (36/0), Marco Antonio Sandy Sansusty (27/2), Luis Héctor Cristaldo (30/1), Vladimir Soria (17/0), José Milton Melgar (66/5), Erwin Sánchez (30/8), Julio César Baldivieso (32/1) [66.Jaime Moreno Morales (23/2)], Luis William Ramallo (28/8) [79.Marco Antonio Etcheverry (24/5) [*sent off 84*]]. Trainer: Francisco Xabier Azcargorta Uriarte (34).

**226.** 23.06.1994 **BOLIVIA – SOUTH KOREA** **0-0** 15th FIFA WC. Group Stage
Foxboro Stadium, Foxboro; Referee: Leslie Mottram (Scotland); Attendance: 54,453
**BOL:** Carlos Leonel Trucco (23/0), Carlos Fernando Borja (Cap) (76/1), Miguel Ángel Rimba (37/0), Gustavo Domingo Quinteros (23/1), Marco Antonio Sandy Sansusty (28/2), Luis Héctor Cristaldo (31/1) [*sent off 82*], Vladimir Soria (18/0), Julio César Baldivieso (33/1), José Milton Melgar (67/5), Luis William Ramallo (29/8) [69.Álvaro Guillermo Peña (40/4)], Erwin Sánchez (31/8). Trainer: Francisco Xabier Azcargorta Uriarte (35).

**227.** 27.06.1994 **SPAIN – BOLIVIA** **3-1(1-0)** 15th FIFA WC. Group Stage
Soldier Field Stadium, Chicago; Referee: Rodrigo Badilla Sequeira (Costa Rica); Attendance: 63,089
**BOL:** Carlos Leonel Trucco (24/0), Carlos Fernando Borja (77/1), Miguel Ángel Rimba (38/0), Marco Antonio Sandy Sansusty (29/2), Juan Manuel Peña Montaño (21/0), Vladimir Soria (19/0) [63.Ramiro Castillo Salinas (26/1)], José Milton Melgar (Cap) (68/5), Modesto Soruco (22/0), Erwin Sánchez (32/9), Juan Mauricio Ramos (12/0) [46.Jaime Moreno Morales (24/2)], Luis William Ramallo (30/8). Trainer: Francisco Xabier Azcargorta Uriarte (36).
**Goal:** Erwin Sánchez (67)

**228.** 21.09.1994 **CHILE – BOLIVIA** **1-2(0-1)**
Estadio Nacional, Santiago; Referee: Francisco Oscar Lamolina (Argentina); Attendance: 12,072
**BOL:** Rubén Darío Rojas (18/0), Juan Manuel Peña Montaño (22/0), Marco Antonio Sandy Sansusty (30/2), Carlos Fernando Borja (78/1) [65.Modesto Soruco (23/0)], Miguel Ángel Rimba (39/0), Vladimir Soria (20/0), José Milton Melgar (69/5), Juan Carlos Guzmán (1/0) [57.Mario Daniel Pinedo (22/3)], Óscar Carmelo Sánchez (4/0), Julio César Baldivieso (34/1) [85.Henry Vaca (1/0)], Luis William Ramallo (31/9) [80.Raúl Gutiérrez (1/0)]. Trainer: Francisco Xabier Azcargorta Uriarte (37).
**Goal:** Luis William Ramallo (27), Mario Daniel Pinedo (80).

**229.** 03.04.1995 **BOLIVIA – VENEZUELA** **0-0**
Estadio Patria del Morro, Sucre; Referee: Pedro Saucedo Rodríguez (Bolivia)
**BOL:** Mauricio Ronald Soria Portillo (2/0), Juan Carlos Ruíz (1/0), Miguel Ángel Rimba (40/0), Marco Antonio Sandy Sansusty (31/2), Luis Héctor Cristaldo (32/1), José Milton Melgar (70/5), Vladimir Soria (21/0), Juan Carlos Chávez (7/0) [Juan Carlos Ríos (12/2)], Johnny Villarroel (12/3) [Franklin Flores (1/0)], Hebert Arandía (1/0) [Raúl Gutiérrez (2/0)], Luis William Ramallo (32/9) [Demetrio Angola (1/0)]. Trainer: Antonio López (1).

**230.** 14.05.1995 **BOLIVIA – PARAGUAY** **1-1(0-0)** Copa Páz del Chaco
Estadio „Félix Capriles“, Cochabamba; Referee: Luis Ángel Seminario Maura (Peru); Attendance: 35,000
**BOL:** Mauricio Ronald Soria Portillo (3/0), Carlos Fernando Borja (79/1), Miguel Ángel Rimba (41/0), Marco Antonio Sandy Sansusty (32/2), Luis Héctor Cristaldo (33/1), Vladimir Soria (22/0), Juan Carlos Chávez (8/0) [Tomás Gutiérrez (1/0)], José Milton Melgar (71/6), Julio César Baldivieso (35/1), Luis William Ramallo (33/9) [Hebert Arandía (2/0)], Raúl Gutiérrez (3/0) [Demetrio Angola (2/0)]. Trainer: Antonio López (2).
**Goal:** José Milton Melgar (75).

**231.** 09.06.1995 **PARAGUAY – BOLIVIA** **0-0; 4-3 on penalties** Copa Páz del Chaco
Estadio “Manuel Ferreira”, Asunción; Referee: Jorge Luis Nieves Parra (Uruguay); Attendance: 7,000
**BOL:** Mauricio Ronald Soria Portillo (4/0), Óscar Carmelo Sánchez (5/0), Miguel Ángel Rimba (42/0), Robert Arteaga (2/0), Marco Antonio Sandy Sansusty (33/2), Luis Héctor Cristaldo (34/1), Carlos Fernando Borja (80/1), José Milton Melgar (72/6), Juan Mauricio Ramos (13/0), Miguel Ángel Mercado (1/0) [63.Juan Berthy Suárez (5/1)], Jaime Moreno Morales (25/2) [63.Iván Sabino Castillo (5/0)]. Trainer: Antonio López (3).

**232.** 18.06.1995 **VENEZUELA – BOLIVIA** **1-3(1-1)**
Estadio “Luis Loreta Lira”, Valera; Referee: Raul Pirez (Venezuela); Attendance: 14,000
**BOL:** Mauricio Ronald Soria Portillo (5/0), Robert Arteaga (3/0), Luis Héctor Cristaldo (35/2), Marco Antonio Sandy Sansusty (34/2), Miguel Ángel Rimba (43/0), José Milton Melgar (73/6), Julio César Baldivieso (36/2) [81.Carlos Fernando Borja (81/1)], Óscar Carmelo Sánchez (6/0), Juan Mauricio Ramos (14/0) [46.Iván Sabino Castillo (6/0)], Juan Berthy Suárez (6/1) [60.Demetrio Angola (3/1)], Jaime Moreno Morales (26/2) [46.Raúl Medeiros (1/0)]. Trainer: Antonio López (4).
**Goals:** Luis Héctor Cristaldo (26), Demetrio Angola (75), Julio César Baldivieso (82).

**233.** 01.07.1995 **PERU – BOLIVIA** **4-1(2-1)**
Estadio Universidad de San Marcos, Lima; Referee: José Antonio Arana Villamonte (Peru); Attendance: 6,362
**BOL:** Carlos Leonel Trucco (25/0), Juan Carlos Ruíz (2/0), Marco Antonio Sandy Sansusty (35/3), Miguel Ángel Rimba (44/0), Luis Héctor Cristaldo (36/2), Julio César Baldivieso (37/2), José Milton Melgar (74/6), Marco Antonio Etcheverry (25/5), Juan Manuel Peña Montaño (23/0), Demetrio Angola (4/1), Álvaro Guillermo Peña (41/4). Trainer: Antonio López (5).
**Goal:** Marco Antonio Sandy Sansusty (17).

**234.** 08.07.1995 **ARGENTINA – BOLIVIA** **2-1(0-0)** 37th Copa América. Group Stage
Estadio Parque “General Artigas”, Paysandú (Uruguay); Referee: Eduardo Dluzniewski Takoz (Uruguay); Attendance: 20,000
**BOL:** Carlos Leonel Trucco (26/0), Gustavo Domingo Quinteros (24/1), Miguel Ángel Rimba (45/0), Marco Antonio Sandy Sansusty (36/3), Carlos Fernando Borja (82/1), Juan Manuel Peña Montaño (24/0), José Milton Melgar (75/6), Luis Héctor Cristaldo (37/2), Julio César Baldivieso (38/2), Marco Antonio Etcheverry (26/5), Miguel Ángel Mercado (2/0) [65.Demetrio Angola (5/2)]. Trainer: Antonio López (6).
**Goal:** Demetrio Angola (75).

**235.** 11.07.1995 **BOLIVIA – UNITED STATES** **1-0(1-0)** 37th Copa América. Group Stage
Estadio Parque “General Artigas”, Paysandú (Uruguay); Referee: Paolo Borgosano (Venezuela); Attendance: 16,000
**BOL:** Carlos Leonel Trucco (27/0), Juan Manuel Peña Montaño (25/0), Marco Antonio Sandy Sansusty (37/3), Miguel Ángel Rimba (46/0), Carlos Fernando Borja (83/1), Julio César Baldivieso (39/2) [71.Óscar Carmelo Sánchez (7/0)], José Milton Melgar (76/6), Luis Héctor Cristaldo (38/2), Juan Berthy Suárez (7/1) [45.Demetrio Angola (6/2)], Marco Antonio Etcheverry (27/6), Miguel Ángel Mercado (3/0) [56.Juan Mauricio Ramos (15/0)]. Trainer: Antonio López (7).
**Goal:** Marco Antonio Etcheverry (23).

**236.** 14.07.1995 **BOLIVIA – CHILE** **2-2(0-0)** 37th Copa América. Group Stage
Estadio Parque “General Artigas”, Paysandú (Uruguay); Referee: Alberto Tejada Noriega (Peru); Attendance: 11,000
**BOL:** Carlos Leonel Trucco (28/0), Juan Manuel Peña Montaño (26/0), Miguel Ángel Rimba (47/0), Marco Antonio Sandy Sansusty (38/3), Carlos Fernando Borja (84/1), Óscar Carmelo Sánchez (8/0) [69.Juan Mauricio Ramos (16/1)], José Milton Melgar (77/6), Luis Héctor Cristaldo (39/2), Julio César Baldivieso (40/2), Demetrio Angola (7/2) [69.Miguel Ángel Mercado (4/1)], Marco Antonio Etcheverry (28/6). Trainer: Antonio López (8).
**Goals:** Miguel Ángel Mercado (78), Juan Mauricio Ramos (87).

**237.** 16.07.1995 **URUGUAY – BOLIVIA** **2-1(2-0)** 37th Copa América. Quarter-Finals
Estadio Centenario, Montevideo; Referee: Alfredo Rodas (Ecuador); Attendance: 45,000
**BOL:** Carlos Leonel Trucco (29/0), Miguel Ángel Rimba (48/0), Óscar Carmelo Sánchez (9/1) [88.Demetrio Angola (8/2)], Marco Antonio Sandy Sansusty (39/3), Luis Héctor Cristaldo (40/2), Carlos Fernando Borja (85/1) [56.Juan Carlos Ruíz (3/0)], Juan Manuel Peña Montaño (27/0), José Milton Melgar (78/6), Julio César Baldivieso (41/2), Marco Antonio Etcheverry (29/6), Miguel Ángel Mercado (5/1) [46.Álvaro Guillermo Peña (42/4)]. Trainer: Antonio López (9).
**Goal:** Óscar Carmelo Sánchez (71).

**238.** 25.10.1995 **BOLIVIA – ECUADOR** **2-2(2-1)**
Estadio “Ramón ‘Tahuichi’ Aguilera”, Santa Cruz de la Sierra; Referee: Pablo Peña Duran (Bolivia); Attendance: 32,000
**BOL:** Carlos Leonel Trucco (30/0), Juan Manuel Peña Montaño (28/0), Miguel Ángel Rimba (49/0), Miguel Ángel Parabá (1/0), Ramiro Castillo Salinas (27/1), Luis Héctor Cristaldo (41/2) [Juan Carlos Ruíz (4/0)], Rubén Darío Tufiño (1/0), Julio César Baldivieso (42/2), Marco Antonio Etcheverry (30/7) [Juan Mauricio Ramos (17/1)], Erwin Sánchez (33/10), Rolando Paniagua (14/1) [Demetrio Angola (9/2)]. Trainer: Antonio López (10).
**Goals:** Marco Antonio Etcheverry (2), Erwin Sánchez (29).

30.01.1996 **BOLIVIA – SLOVAKIA “U 23”** **2-0(2-0)**
Estadio „Ramón ‘Tahuichi’ Aguilera“, Santa Cruz de la Sierra; Referee: Pablo Peña Duran (Bolivia); Attendance: 35,000
**BOL:** Marco Antonio Barrero [46.Mauricio Ronald Soria Portillo], Miguel Ángel Rimba, Óscar Carmelo Sánchez, Freddy Cossío, Miguel Ángel Parabá, Luis Héctor Cristaldo, Rolando Paniagua [80.Juan Mauricio Ramos], Rubén Darío Tufiño [57.Gaspar Monte; 73.Juan Carlos Ríos], Julio César Baldivieso, Marco Antonio Etcheverry [52.Ramiro Castillo Salinas], Juan Berthy Suárez. Trainer: Dušan Drašković.
**Goal:** Rubén Darío Tufiño (10), Rolando Paniagua (35).
*(It's given many doubts about this match to be considered as a FIFA full international)*

**239.** 03.02.1996 **BOLIVIA - CHILE** **1-1(1-0)**
Estadio „Félix Capriles", Cochabamba; Referee: Armando Aliaga (Bolivia); Attendance: 24,130
**BOL:** Marcelo Eduardo Torrico (2/0) [Marco Antonio Barrero (18/0)], Freddy Cossío (4/0), Miguel Ángel Rimba (50/0), Miguel Ángel Parabá (2/0), Óscar Carmelo Sánchez (10/1), Luis Héctor Cristaldo (42/2), Rubén Darío Tufiño (2/0), Ramiro Castillo Salinas (28/1) [Juan Carlos Ruíz (5/0)], Julio César Baldivieso (43/2), Rolando Paniagua (15/1) [Demetrio Angola (10/2)], Juan Berthy Suárez (8/2) [Juan Mauricio Ramos (18/1)]. Trainer: Dušan Drašković (1).
**Goal:** Juan Berthy Suárez (31).

**240.** 11.02.1996 **PERU - BOLIVIA** **1-3(0-1)**
Estadio Nacional, Lima; Referee: José Antonio Arana Villamonte (Peru); Attendance: 10,000
**BOL:** Marco Antonio Barrero (19/0), Miguel Ángel Rimba (51/0), Freddy Cossío (5/0), Óscar Carmelo Sánchez (11/1), Miguel Ángel Parabá (3/0), Rubén Darío Tufiño (3/0), Julio César Baldivieso (44/3), Ramiro Castillo Salinas (29/2) [Luis Héctor Cristaldo (43/2)], Juan Mauricio Ramos (19/1), Juan Berthy Suárez (9/2), Rolando Paniagua (16/2) [Rodolfo Céspedes (1/0)]. Trainer: Dušan Drašković (2).
**Goal:** Julio César Baldivieso (27 penalty), Rolando Paniagua (54), Ramiro Castillo Salinas (75).

**241.** 14.02.1996 **BOLIVIA - PARAGUAY** **4-1(1-0)**
Estadio Patria del Morro, Sucre; Referee: Juan Carlos Lugoñes Antezana (Bolivia); Attendance: 8,000
**BOL:** Marco Antonio Barrero (20/0), Óscar Carmelo Sánchez (12/1), Miguel Ángel Parabá (4/0), Freddy Cossío (6/0), Miguel Ángel Rimba (52/0), Julio César Baldivieso (45/3), Rubén Darío Tufiño (4/1), Juan Mauricio Ramos (20/1), Ramiro Castillo Salinas (30/3) [José Milton Melgar (79/6)], Juan Berthy Suárez (10/3) [Marco Antonio Etcheverry (31/8)], Rolando Paniagua (17/2) [Hebert Arandía (3/0)]. Trainer: Dušan Drašković (3).
**Goals:** Ramiro Castillo Salinas (8), Rubén Darío Tufiño (57), Juan Berthy Suárez (62), Marco Antonio Etcheverry (85)

**242.** 07.03.1996 **BOLIVIA - PERU** **2-0(0-0)**
Estadio „Ramón 'Tahuichi' Aguilera", Santa Cruz de la Sierra; Referee: Juan Luna Humerez (Bolivia); Attendance: 8,000
**BOL:** Marco Antonio Barrero (21/0), Miguel Ángel Rimba (53/0), Marco Antonio Herrera (1/0) [Luis Héctor Cristaldo (44/2)], Miguel Ángel Parabá (5/0), Freddy Cossío (7/0), Rubén Darío Tufiño (5/1), Juan Mauricio Ramos (21/1), Óscar Carmelo Sánchez (13/1), Ramiro Castillo Salinas (31/3) [Hebert Arandía (4/0)], Milton Coimbra Suizer (1/2) [Juan Berthy Suárez (11/3)], Rolando Paniagua (18/2) [Marco Antonio Etcheverry (32/8)]. Trainer: Dušan Drašković (4).
**Goals:** Milton Coimbra Suizer (46, 51).

**243.** 28.03.1996 **COLOMBIA - BOLIVIA** **4-1(4-1)**
Estadio "Atanasio Girardot", Medellín; Referee: Felipe Eduardo Russi Páez (Colombia); Attendance: 25,500
**BOL:** Marco Antonio Barrero (22/0), Rafael Salguero Siles (3/0), Miguel Ángel Parabá (6/0), Freddy Cossío (8/0), Iván Sabino Castillo (7/0), Luis Héctor Cristaldo (45/2), Óscar Carmelo Sánchez (14/2), Rubén Darío Tufiño (6/1), Ramiro Castillo Salinas (32/3), Milton Coimbra Suizer (2/2), Demetrio Angola (11/2) [46.Rolando Paniagua (19/2)]. Trainer: Dušan Drašković (5).
**Goal:** Óscar Carmelo Sánchez (10).

**244.** 24.04.1996 **ARGENTINA - BOLIVIA** **3-1(2-1)** 16th FIFA WC. Qualifiers
Estadio Monumental „Antonio Vespucio Liberti", Buenos Aires; Referee: Mario Fernando Sánchez Yanten (Chile); Attendance: 49,750
**BOL:** Marco Antonio Barrero (23/0), Juan Manuel Peña Montaño (29/0), Miguel Ángel Parabá (7/0), Miguel Ángel Rimba (54/0), Óscar Carmelo Sánchez (15/2), Juan Mauricio Ramos (22/1) [80.Iván Sabino Castillo (8/0)], Milton Coimbra Suizer (3/2) [77.Rolando Paniagua (20/2)], Rubén Darío Tufiño (7/1), Julio César Baldivieso (46/4), Marco Antonio Etcheverry (33/8) [79.Juan Berthy Suárez (12/3)], Ramiro Castillo Salinas (33/3). Trainer: Dušan Drašković (6).
**Goal:** Julio César Baldivieso (42).

**245.** 05.05.1996 **BOLIVIA - EL SALVADOR** **1-1(1-0)**
"Robert F. Kennedy" Memorial Stadium, Washington (United States); Referee: Esfandiar Baharmast (United States); Attendance: 13,100
**BOL:** Marco Antonio Barrero (24/0) [46.Mauricio Ronald Soria Portillo (6/0)], Eduardo Jiguchi (7/0), Óscar Carmelo Sánchez (16/2), Miguel Ángel Parabá (8/0), Miguel Ángel Rimba (55/0), Rubén Darío Tufiño (8/1), Julio César Baldivieso (47/4), Ramiro Castillo Salinas (34/3), Luis Héctor Cristaldo (46/2), Milton Coimbra Suizer (4/2), Juan Berthy Suárez (13/4) [46.Demetrio Angola (12/2)]. Trainer: Dušan Drašković (7).
**Goal:** Juan Berthy Suárez (6).

**246.** 26.05.1996 **CHILE - BOLIVIA** **2-0(2-0)**
Estadio Nacional, Santiago; Referee: Luis Héctor Olivetto (Argentina); Attendance: 24,307
**BOL:** Marco Antonio Barrero (25/0), Freddy Cossío (9/0), Óscar Carmelo Sánchez (17/2), Miguel Ángel Parabá (9/0), Miguel Ángel Rimba (56/0), Luis Héctor Cristaldo (47/2) [71.Sergio Castillo (1/0)], Mauricio Ronald Soria Portillo (7/0), Juan Mauricio Ramos (23/1), Ramiro Castillo Salinas (35/3), Milton Coimbra Suizer (5/2), Rolando Paniagua (21/2) [69.Jaime Moreno Morales (27/2)]. Trainer: Dušan Drašković (8).

**247.** 08.06.1996 **MEXICO - BOLIVIA** **1-0(0-0)** US Cup
Cotton Bowl, Dallas (United States); Referee: Brian Hall (United States); Attendance: 14,000
**BOL:** Mauricio Ronald Soria Portillo (8/0), Juan Manuel Peña Montaño (30/0), Marco Antonio Sandy Sansusty (40/3), Óscar Carmelo Sánchez (18/2), Miguel Ángel Rimba (57/0), Julio César Baldivieso (48/4), Luis Héctor Cristaldo (48/2), Marco Antonio Etcheverry (34/8), Vladimir Soria (23/0), Ramiro Castillo Salinas (36/3), Juan Berthy Suárez (14/4) [64.Milton Coimbra Suizer (6/2)]. Trainer: Dušan Drašković (9).

**248.** 12.06.1996 **UNITED STATES - BOLIVIA** **0-2(0-1)** US Cup
"Robert F. Kennedy" Memorial Stadium, Washington; Referee: Dino Bucci (Canada); Attendance: 19,350
**BOL:** Marco Antonio Barrero (26/0), Juan Manuel Peña Montaño (31/0), Óscar Carmelo Sánchez (19/2), Miguel Ángel Rimba (58/0), Marco Antonio Sandy Sansusty (41/3), Julio César Baldivieso (49/4), Juan Mauricio Ramos (24/1), Freddy Cossío (10/0), Marco Antonio Etcheverry (35/8) [46.Rolando Paniagua (22/2)], Jaime Moreno Morales (28/3) [46.Ramiro Castillo Salinas (37/3)], Milton Coimbra Suizer (7/3). Trainer: Dušan Drašković (10).
**Goals:** Jaime Moreno Morales (2), Milton Coimbra Suizer (88).

**249.** 15.06.1996 **REPUBLIC OF IRELAND - BOLIVIA** **3-0(3-0)** US Cup
Giants Stadium, East Rutherford (United States); Referee: Esfandiar Baharmast (United States); Attendance: 14,624
**BOL:** Mauricio Ronald Soria Portillo (9/0), Juan Manuel Peña Montaño (32/0), Óscar Carmelo Sánchez (20/2), Miguel Ángel Rimba (59/0), Ramiro Castillo Salinas (38/3), Julio César Baldivieso (50/4), Marco Antonio Etcheverry (36/8), Juan Mauricio Ramos (25/1) [41.Luis Héctor Cristaldo (49/2)], Freddy Cossío (11/0), Marco Antonio Sandy Sansusty (42/3), Jaime Moreno Morales (29/3) [46.Milton Coimbra Suizer (8/3)]. Trainer: Dušan Drašković (11).

**250.** 07.07.1996 **BOLIVIA - VENEZUELA** **6-1(2-0)** 16th FIFA WC. Qualifiers

Estadio „Hernándo Siles Zuazo", La Paz; Referee: José Luis Da Rosa Varela (Uruguay); Attendance: 43,822

**BOL:** Carlos Leonel Trucco (31/0), Juan Manuel Peña Montaño (33/0), Marco Antonio Sandy Sansusty (43/4), Miguel Ángel Rimba (60/0), Óscar Carmelo Sánchez (21/2), Milton Coimbra Suizer (9/4) [68.Jaime Moreno Morales (30/3)], Luis Héctor Cristaldo (50/2), Julio César Baldivieso (51/5), Marco Antonio Etcheverry (37/9) [74.Juan Berthy Suárez (15/5)], Ramiro Castillo Salinas (39/3) [75.Rolando Paniagua (23/3)], Gustavo Domingo Quinteros (25/1). Trainer: Dušan Drašković (12).

**Goals:** Marco Antonio Sandy Sansusty (4), Marco Antonio Etcheverry (41), Julio César Baldivieso (61), Milton Coimbra Suizer (67), Juan Berthy Suárez (78), Rolando Paniagua (85).

**251.** 26.07.1996 **PARAGUAY - BOLIVIA** **2-0(1-0)**

Estadio Olla Azulgrana, Asunción; Referee: Epifanio González Chávez (Paraguay); Attendance: 8,000

**BOL:** Mauricio Ronald Soria Portillo (10/0), Eduardo Jiguchi (8/0), Marco Antonio Sandy Sansusty (44/4), Sergio Castillo (2/0), Óscar Carmelo Sánchez (22/2), Freddy Cossío (12/0), Rolando Paniagua (24/3) [Juan Berthy Suárez (16/5)], Julio César Baldivieso (52/5), Álvaro Guillermo Peña (43/4), José Milton Melgar (80/6) [Miguel Ángel Parabá (10/0)], Luis Héctor Cristaldo (51/2). Trainer: Dušan Drašković (13).

**252.** 01.09.1996 **BOLIVIA - PERU** **0-0** 16th FIFA WC. Qualifiers

Estadio „Hernándo Siles Zuazo", La Paz; Referee: Oscar Velázquez Alvarenga (Paraguay); Attendance: 48,304

**BOL:** Carlos Leonel Trucco (32/0), Juan Manuel Peña Montaño (34/0), Marco Antonio Sandy Sansusty (45/4), Miguel Ángel Rimba (61/0), Óscar Carmelo Sánchez (23/2), Erwin Sánchez (34/10) [84.Rolando Paniagua (25/3)], Milton Coimbra Suizer (10/4) [63.Jaime Moreno Morales (31/3)], Iván Sabino Castillo (9/0), Julio César Baldivieso (53/5), Marco Antonio Etcheverry (38/9), Ramiro Castillo Salinas (40/3). Trainer: Dušan Drašković (14).

**253.** 08.10.1996 **URUGUAY - BOLIVIA** **1-0(0-0)** 16th FIFA WC. Qualifiers

Estadio Centenario, Montevideo; Referee: Paolo Borgosano (Venezuela); Attendance: 60,000

**BOL:** Carlos Leonel Trucco (33/0), Juan Manuel Peña Montaño (35/0), Marco Antonio Sandy Sansusty (46/4), Óscar Carmelo Sánchez (24/2), Vladimir Soria (24/0) [32.Rubén Darío Tufiño (9/1)], Luis Héctor Cristaldo (52/2), Sergio Castillo (3/0) [*sent off 79*], José Milton Melgar (81/6), Ramiro Castillo Salinas (41/3), Julio César Baldivieso (54/5) [81.Milton Coimbra Suizer (11/4)], Jaime Moreno Morales (32/3). Trainer: Antonio López (11).

**254.** 10.11.1996 **BOLIVIA - COLOMBIA** **2-2(2-1)** 16th FIFA WC. Qualifiers

Estadio „Hernándo Siles Zuazo", La Paz; Referee: José Antonio Arana Villamonte (Peru); Attendance: 43,173

**BOL:** Carlos Leonel Trucco (34/0), Juan Manuel Peña Montaño (36/0), Marco Antonio Sandy Sansusty (47/5), Óscar Carmelo Sánchez (25/2), Luis Héctor Cristaldo (53/2), Fernando Ochoaizpur (1/0), José Milton Melgar (82/6) [68.Vladimir Soria (25/0)], Marco Antonio Etcheverry (39/9), Ramiro Castillo Salinas (42/3), Luis William Ramallo (34/9) [77.Milton Coimbra Suizer (12/4)], Jaime Moreno Morales (33/4). Trainer: Antonio López (12).

**Goals:** Marco Antonio Sandy Sansusty (15), Jaime Moreno Morales (44).

**255.** 15.12.1996 **BOLIVIA - PARAGUAY** **0-0** 16th FIFA WC. Qualifiers

Estadio „Hernándo Siles Zuazo", La Paz; Referee: Jorge Luis Nieves Parra (Uruguay)

**BOL:** Carlos Leonel Trucco (35/0), Juan Manuel Peña Montaño (37/0), Marco Antonio Sandy Sansusty (48/5), Miguel Ángel Rimba (62/0), Iván Sabino Castillo (10/0), Luis William Ramallo (35/9) [46.Vladimir Soria (26/0)], Fernando Ochoaizpur (2/0), Rubén Darío Tufiño (10/1) [46.Roger Suárez (1/0)], Marco Antonio Etcheverry (40/9), Ramiro Castillo Salinas (43/3), Jaime Moreno Morales (34/4) [62.Juan Berthy Suárez (17/5)]. Trainer: Antonio López (13).

**256.** 12.01.1997 **BOLIVIA - ECUADOR** **2-0(2-0)** 16th FIFA WC. Qualifiers

Estadio „Hernándo Siles Zuazo", La Paz; Referee: Oscar Julián Ruíz Acosta (Colombia); Attendance: 39,968

**BOL:** Carlos Leonel Trucco (36/0), Juan Manuel Peña Montaño (38/0), Marco Antonio Sandy Sansusty (49/5), Julio César Baldivieso (55/5) [65.José Milton Melgar (83/6)], Óscar Carmelo Sánchez (26/2), Luis Héctor Cristaldo (54/2), Vladimir Soria (27/0), Fernando Ochoaizpur (3/0), Ramiro Castillo Salinas (44/3) [65.Limberg Gutiérrez Mariscal (1/0)], Marco Antonio Etcheverry (41/10), Jaime Moreno Morales (35/5) [73.Luis William Ramallo (36/9)]. Trainer: Antonio López (14).

**Goals:** Jaime Moreno Morales (7), Marco Antonio Etcheverry (12).

**257.** 02.02.1997 **BOLIVIA - SLOVAKIA** **0-1(0-0)**

Estadio „Félix Capriles", Cochabamba; Referee: Juan Carlos Lugoñes Antezana (Bolivia); Attendance: 30,000

**BOL:** José Carlos Fernández (1/0), Miguel Ángel Rimba (63/0), Óscar Carmelo Sánchez (27/2), Marco Antonio Sandy Sansusty (50/5), Luis Héctor Cristaldo (55/2) [65.Iván Sabino Castillo (11/0)], Ramiro Castillo Salinas (45/3) [68.José Milton Melgar (84/6)], Rubén Darío Tufiño (11/1), Vladimir Soria (28/0), Sergio Castillo (4/0), Jaime Moreno Morales (36/5) [65.Juan Berthy Suárez (18/5)], Limberg Gutiérrez Mariscal (2/0) [75.Richard Cueto (2/0]. Trainer: Antonio López (15).

**258.** 12.02.1997 **BOLIVIA - CHILE** **1-1(1-1)** 16th FIFA WC. Qualifiers

Estadio „Hernándo Siles Zuazo", La Paz; Referee: Alberto Tejada Burga (Peru); Attendance: 41,908

**BOL:** Carlos Leonel Trucco (37/0), Juan Manuel Peña Montaño (39/0), Marco Antonio Sandy Sansusty (51/5), Óscar Carmelo Sánchez (28/2), Vladimir Soria (29/1), Fernando Ochoaizpur (4/0) [46.Sergio Castillo (5/0)], Marco Antonio Etcheverry (42/10), Luis Héctor Cristaldo (56/2), Rubén Darío Tufiño (12/1), Ramiro Castillo Salinas (46/3) [46.Limberg Gutiérrez Mariscal (3/0)], Jaime Moreno Morales (37/5). Trainer: Antonio López (16).

**Goal:** Vladimir Soria (28).

**259.** 23.03.1997 **BOLIVIA - JAMAICA** **6-0(3-0)**

Estadio „Jesús Bermúdez", Oruro; Referee: René Marcelo Ortubé Betancourt (Bolivia); Attendance: 5,000

**BOL:** Mauricio Ronald Soria Portillo (11/0), Iván Sabino Castillo (12/0), Marco Antonio Sandy Sansusty (52/5) [46.Rafael Salguero Siles (4/0)], Miguel Ángel Rimba (64/0), Óscar Carmelo Sánchez (29/4), Sergio Castillo (6/0) [46.Demetrio Angola (13/2)], José Milton Melgar (85/6), Mauro Blanco (1/2), Limberg Gutiérrez Mariscal (4/0) [46.Gonzalo Germán Galindo Sánchez (1/0)], Juan Berthy Suárez (19/7), Miguel Ángel Mercado (6/1). Trainer: Antonio López (17).

**Goals:** Óscar Carmelo Sánchez (13), Mauro Blanco (23), Juan Berthy Suárez (26), Óscar Carmelo Sánchez (63), Juan Berthy Suárez (78), Mauro Blanco (86).

**260.** 02.04.1997 **BOLIVIA - ARGENTINA** **2-1(1-1)** 16th FIFA WC. Qualifiers

Estadio „Hernándo Siles Zuazo", La Paz; Referee: Sidrack Marinho Dos Santos (Brazil); Attendance: 44,372

**BOL:** Carlos Leonel Trucco (38/0), Óscar Carmelo Sánchez (30/4), Marco Antonio Sandy Sansusty (53/6), Miguel Ángel Rimba (65/0), Vladimir Soria (30/1), Fernando Ochoaizpur (5/1) [88.José Milton Melgar (86/6)], Jaime Moreno Morales (38/5) [71.Demetrio Angola (14/2)], Limberg Gutiérrez Mariscal (5/0) [51.Mauro Blanco (2/2)], Sergio Castillo (7/0), Iván Sabino Castillo (13/0), Ramiro Castillo Salinas (47/3). Trainer: Antonio López (18).

**Goals:** Marco Antonio Sandy Sansusty (8), Fernando Ochoaizpur (48).

**261.** 08.06.1997 **VENEZUELA – BOLIVIA** **1-1(0-0)** 16th FIFA WC. Qualifiers

Estadio"Luis Loreto Lira", Valera; Referee: Fernando Panesso Zuluaga (Colombia); Attendance: 3,352

**BOL:** Carlos Leonel Trucco (39/0), Óscar Carmelo Sánchez (31/4), Marco Antonio Sandy Sansusty (54/6), Vladimir Soria (31/1), Luis Héctor Cristaldo (57/2), Juan Manuel Peña Montaño (40/0), Marco Antonio Etcheverry (43/10), Sergio Castillo (8/0) [62.Iván Sabino Castillo (14/0)], Ramiro Castillo Salinas (48/4) [*sent off 84*], Julio César Baldivieso (56/5) [46.Limberg Gutiérrez Mariscal (6/0)], Jaime Moreno Morales (39/5) [46.Milton Coimbra Suizer (13/4)]. Trainer: Antonio López (19).

**Goal:** Ramiro Castillo Salinas (80).

**262.** 12.06.1997 **BOLIVIA – VENEZUELA** **1-0(0-0)** 38th Copa América. Group Stage

Estadio „Hernándo Siles Zuazo", La Paz; Referee: Byron Aldemar Moreno Ruales (Ecuador); Attendance: 40,000

**BOL:** Carlos Leonel Trucco (40/0), Miguel Ángel Rimba (66/0), Juan Manuel Peña Montaño (41/0) [*sent off 59*], Marco Antonio Sandy Sansusty (55/6), Sergio Castillo (9/0) [46.Erwin Sánchez (35/10)], Iván Sabino Castillo (15/0), Luis Héctor Cristaldo (58/2), Vladimir Soria (32/1), Ramiro Castillo Salinas (49/4), Limberg Gutiérrez Mariscal (7/0) [66.José Milton Melgar (87/6)], Milton Coimbra Suizer (14/5) [70.Jaime Moreno Morales (40/5)]. Trainer: Antonio López (20).

**Goal:** Milton Coimbra Suizer (60).

**263.** 15.06.1997 **BOLIVIA – PERU** **2-0(1-0)** 38th Copa América. Group Stage

Estadio „Hernándo Siles Zuazo", La Paz; Referee: Rodrigo Badilla Sequeira (Costa Rica); Attendance: 20,000

**BOL:** Carlos Leonel Trucco (41/0), Óscar Carmelo Sánchez (32/4), Marco Antonio Sandy Sansusty (56/6), Miguel Ángel Rimba (67/0), Iván Sabino Castillo (16/0) [46.Ramiro Castillo Salinas (50/4)], Julio César Baldivieso (57/6), Luis Héctor Cristaldo (59/2), Mauro Blanco (3/2) [46.Erwin Sánchez (36/10)], Vladimir Soria (33/1), Marco Antonio Etcheverry (44/11), Milton Coimbra Suizer (15/5) [56.Limberg Gutiérrez Mariscal (8/0)]. Trainer: Antonio López (21).

**Goals:** Marco Antonio Etcheverry (45), Julio César Baldivieso (50).

**264.** 18.06.1997 **BOLIVIA - URUGUAY** **1-0(1-0)** 38th Copa América. Group Stage

Estadio „Hernándo Siles Zuazo", La Paz; Referee: Antonio Marrufo Mendóza (Mexico); Attendance: 30,000

**BOL:** Carlos Leonel Trucco (42/0), Miguel Ángel Rimba (68/0), Juan Manuel Peña Montaño (42/0) [46.Sergio Castillo (10/0)], Marco Antonio Sandy Sansusty (57/6), Óscar Carmelo Sánchez (33/4), Vladimir Soria (34/1), Luis Héctor Cristaldo (60/2), Julio César Baldivieso (58/7) [89.Jaime Moreno Morales (41/5)], Marco Antonio Etcheverry (45/11), Milton Coimbra Suizer (16/5) [61.Erwin Sánchez (37/10)], Ramiro Castillo Salinas (51/4). Trainer: Antonio López (22).

**Goal:** Julio César Baldivieso (29).

**265.** 21.06.1997 **BOLIVIA – COLOMBIA** **2-1(2-0)** 38th Copa América. Quarter-Finals

Estadio „Hernándo Siles Zuazo", La Paz; Referee: Horacio Marcelo Elizondo (Argentina); Attendance: 30,000

**BOL:** Carlos Leonel Trucco (43/0), Óscar Carmelo Sánchez (34/4), Marco Antonio Sandy Sansusty (58/6), Juan Manuel Peña Montaño (43/0), Sergio Castillo (11/0), Luis Héctor Cristaldo (61/2), Vladimir Soria (35/1), Julio César Baldivieso (59/7), Ramiro Castillo Salinas (52/4) [71.José Milton Melgar (88/6)], Erwin Sánchez (38/11) [75.Jaime Moreno Morales (42/5)], Marco Antonio Etcheverry (46/12). Trainer: Antonio López (23).

**Goals:** Marco Antonio Etcheverry (3), Erwin Sánchez (24).

**266.** 25.06.1997 **BOLIVIA – MEXICO** **3-1(2-1)** 38th Copa América. Semi-Finals

Estadio „Hernándo Siles Zuazo", La Paz; Referee: Epifanio González Chávez (Paraguay); Attendance: 40,000

**BOL:** Carlos Leonel Trucco (44/0), Óscar Carmelo Sánchez (35/4), Juan Manuel Peña Montaño (44/0), Marco Antonio Sandy Sansusty (59/6), Sergio Castillo (12/0), Julio César Baldivieso (60/7), Vladimir Soria (36/1), Erwin Sánchez (39/12) [59.Jaime Moreno Morales (43/6), 76.Mauro Blanco (4/2)], Ramiro Castillo Salinas (53/5) [73.José Milton Melgar (89/6)], Marco Antonio Etcheverry (47/12). Trainer: Antonio López (24).

**Goals:** Erwin Sánchez (27), Ramiro Castillo Salinas (39), Jaime Moreno Morales (79).

**267.** 29.06.1997 **BOLIVIA – BRAZIL** **1-3(1-1)** 38th Copa América. Final

Estadio „Hernándo Siles Zuazo", La Paz; Referee: Jorge Luis Nieves Parra (Uruguay); Attendance: 46,000

**BOL:** Carlos Leonel Trucco (45/0), Juan Manuel Peña Montaño (45/0), Sergio Castillo (13/0), Óscar Carmelo Sánchez (36/4), Marco Antonio Sandy Sansusty (60/6), Luis Héctor Cristaldo (62/2), Julio César Baldivieso (61/7), Vladimir Soria (37/1), Erwin Sánchez (40/13), Marco Antonio Etcheverry (48/12), Jaime Moreno Morales (44/6) [74.Milton Coimbra Suizer (17/5)]. Trainer: Antonio López (25).

**Goal:** Erwin Sánchez (45).

**268.** 06.07.1997 **PERU – BOLIVIA** **2-1(1-0)** 16th FIFA WC. Qualifiers

Estadio Nacional, Lima; Referee: Wilson Mendonça Souza (Brazil); Attendance: 31,489

**BOL:** Carlos Leonel Trucco (46/0), Sergio Castillo (14/0), Óscar Carmelo Sánchez (37/4), Marco Antonio Sandy Sansusty (61/6), Julio César Baldivieso (62/7), Vladimir Soria (38/1), Juan Manuel Peña Montaño (46/0), Marco Antonio Etcheverry (49/12), Luis Héctor Cristaldo (63/3), Erwin Sánchez (41/13), Jaime Moreno Morales (45/6) [74.Limberg Gutiérrez Mariscal (9/0)]. Trainer: Antonio López (26).

**Goal:** Luis Héctor Cristaldo (56).

**269.** 20.07.1997 **BOLIVIA – URUGUAY** **1-0(0-0)** 16th FIFA WC. Qualifiers

Estadio „Hernándo Siles Zuazo", La Paz; Referee: Arturo Pablo Brizio Carter (Mexico); Attendance: 27,874

**BOL:** Carlos Leonel Trucco (47/0), Óscar Carmelo Sánchez (38/4), Marco Antonio Sandy Sansusty (62/6), Miguel Ángel Rimba (69/0), Iván Sabino Castillo (17/0), Rubén Darío Tufiño (13/1) [59.Jaime Moreno Morales (46/6)], Erwin Sánchez (42/13), Marco Antonio Etcheverry (50/13) [87.Mauro Blanco (5/2)], Sergio Castillo (15/0), Luis Héctor Cristaldo (64/3), Milton Coimbra Suizer (18/5) [46.Demetrio Angola (15/2)]. Trainer: Antonio López (27).

**Goal:** Marco Antonio Etcheverry (75).

**270.** 20.08.1997 **COLOMBIA – BOLIVIA** **3-0(2-0)** 16th FIFA WC. Qualifiers

Estadio Metropolitano, Barranquila; Referee: Cláudio Vinícius Cerdeira (Brazil),.Attendance: 25,912

**BOL:** Carlos Leonel Trucco (48/0), Juan Manuel Peña Montaño (47/0), Marco Antonio Sandy Sansusty (63/6), Óscar Carmelo Sánchez (39/4), Fernando Ochoaizpur (6/1) [*sent off 82*], Sergio Castillo (16/0), Rubén Darío Tufiño (14/1) [46.Milton Coimbra Suizer (19/5)], Marco Antonio Etcheverry (51/13), Jaime Moreno Morales (47/6) [67.Demetrio Angola (16/2)], Luis Héctor Cristaldo (65/3), Erwin Sánchez (43/13). Trainer: Antonio López (28).

**271.** 10.09.1997 **PARAGUAY – BOLIVIA** **2-1(2-0)** 16th FIFA WC. Qualifiers

Estadio Defensores del Chaco, Asunción; Referee: Benito Armando Archundia Téllez (Mexico); Attendance: 40,341

**BOL:** Carlos Leonel Trucco (49/0), Juan Manuel Peña Montaño (48/0), Marco Antonio Sandy Sansusty (64/6), Óscar Carmelo Sánchez (40/4), Miguel Ángel Rimba (70/0), Sergio Castillo (17/0), Vladimir Soria (39/1), Marco Antonio Etcheverry (52/13), José Luis Ortíz (1/0) [65.Milton Coimbra Suizer (20/5)], Mauro Blanco (6/2) [46.Juan Berthy Suárez (20/8)], Demetrio Angola (17/2) [46.Ramiro Castillo Salinas (54/5)]. Trainer: Antonio López (29).

**Goal:** Juan Berthy Suárez (58).

**272.** 12.10.1997 **ECUADOR - BOLIVIA** **1-0(1-0)** 16th FIFA WC. Qualifiers
Estadio "Isidro Romero", Guayaquil; Referee: Arturo Brizio Carter (Mexico); Attendance: 14,568
**BOL:** Carlos Leonel Trucco (50/0), Fernando Ochoaizpur (7/1), Juan Berthy Suárez (21/8) [61.Limberg Gutiérrez Mariscal (10/0)], Miguel Ángel Rimba (71/0), Iván Sabino Castillo (18/0), Eduardo Jiguchi (9/0), Sergio Castillo (18/0) [61.Mauro Blanco (7/2)], Rubén Darío Tufiño (15/1), Luis Héctor Cristaldo (66/3), Marco Antonio Etcheverry (53/13), Ramiro Castillo Salinas (55/5) [75.José Luis Ortíz (2/0)]. Trainer: Antonio López (30).

**273.** 16.11.1997 **CHILE - BOLIVIA** **3-0(2-0)** 16th FIFA WC. Qualifiers
Estadio Nacional, Santiago; Referee: Wilson Mendonça Souza (Brazil); Attendance: 74,777
**BOL:** Carlos Leonel Trucco (51/0), Marco Antonio Sandy Sansusty (65/6), Fernando Ochoaizpur (8/1) [*sent off 62*], Miguel Ángel Rimba (72/0), Óscar Carmelo Sánchez (41/4) [*sent off 85*], Sergio Castillo (19/0) [46.Vladimir Soria (40/1)], Rubén Darío Tufiño (16/1), Luis Héctor Cristaldo (67/3), Marco Antonio Etcheverry (54/13), Jaime Moreno Morales (48/6) [70.Iván Sabino Castillo (19/0)], Julio César Baldivieso (63/7) [*sent off 55*]. Trainer: Antonio López (31).

**274.** 24.01.1999 **BOLIVIA - UNITED STATES** **0-0**
Estadio „Ramón 'Tahuichi' Aguilera", Santa Cruz de la Sierra; Referee: Juan Carlos Paniagua Arandia (Bolivia); Attendance: 39,000
**BOL:** José Carlos Fernández (2/0), Sergio Castillo (20/0), Eduardo Jiguchi (10/0), Ronald Arana (1/0), Lorgio Álvarez Roca (1/0), Rubén Darío Tufiño (Cap) (17/1), Miguel Raúl Justiniano Abella (1/0), Raúl Gutiérrez (4/0) [46.Luis Liendo (1/0)], Juan Mauricio Ramos (26/1) [68.Gonzalo Germán Galindo Sánchez (2/0)], Jefferson Gottardi (1/0) [68.Juan Berthy Suárez (22/8)], Limberg Gutiérrez Mariscal (11/0) [68.Roger Suárez (2/0)]. Trainer: Héctor Veira (1).

**275.** 03.03.1999 **BOLIVIA - JAMAICA** **0-0** Copa de la Paz
Estadio "Mateo Flores", Ciudad de Guatemala; Attendance: 15,000
**BOL:** Marco Antonio Barrero (27/0), Fernando Ochoaizpur (9/1) [Richard Uriona (1/0)], Marco Antonio Sandy Sansusty (66/6), Miguel Ángel Rimba (73/0), Óscar Carmelo Sánchez (42/4), Vladimir Soria (41/1), Juan Mauricio Ramos (27/1) [Marco Antonio Etcheverry (55/13)], Milton Coimbra Suizer (21/5), Sergio Castillo (21/0), Iván Sabino Castillo (20/0), Roger Suárez (3/0) [Jaime Moreno Morales (49/6)]. Trainer: Héctor Veira (2).

**276.** 05.03.1999 **GUATEMALA - BOLIVIA** **0-3(0-1)** Copa de la Paz
Estadio "Mateo Flores", Ciudad de Guatemala; Referee: Rafael Rodríguez (El Salvador); Attendance: 10,000
**BOL:** Marco Antonio Barrero (28/0), Fernando Ochoaizpur (10/2), Marco Antonio Sandy Sansusty (67/6), Miguel Ángel Rimba (74/0), Óscar Carmelo Sánchez (43/5), Richard Uriona (2/0) [Vladimir Soria (42/1)], Sergio Castillo (22/0), Jaime Moreno Morales (50/6) [Juan Mauricio Ramos (28/1)], Iván Sabino Castillo (21/0), Milton Coimbra Suizer (22/6), Marco Antonio Etcheverry (56/13) [Luis Liendo (2/0)]. Trainer: Héctor Veira (3).
**Goals:** Fernando Ochoaizpur (8), Milton Coimbra Suizer (57), Óscar Carmelo Sánchez (63).

**277.** 07.03.1999 **PARAGUAY - BOLIVIA** **3-0(1-0)** Copa de la Paz
Estadio "Mateo Flores", Ciudad de Guatemala; Referee: Freddy Burgos Escobar (Guatemala); Attendance: 10,000
**BOL:** Marco Antonio Barrero (29/0), Fernando Ochoaizpur (11/2) [Juan Mauricio Ramos (29/1)], Marco Antonio Sandy Sansusty (68/6), Miguel Ángel Rimba (75/0), Óscar Carmelo Sánchez (44/5), Vladimir Soria (43/1), Sergio Castillo (23/0), Jaime Moreno Morales (51/6), Marco Antonio Etcheverry (57/13) [Juan Berthy Suárez (23/8)], Iván Sabino Castillo (22/0), Milton Coimbra Suizer (23/6) [Richard Uriona (3/0)]. Trainer: Héctor Veira (4).

**278.** 11.03.1999 **MEXICO - BOLIVIA** **2-1(0-1)** US Cup
Memorial Coliseum, Los Angeles (United States); Referee: Timothy Weyland (United States); Attendance: 34,154
**BOL:** Marco Antonio Barrero (30/0), Fernando Ochoaizpur (12/3) [90.Richard Uriona (4/0)], Marco Antonio Sandy Sansusty (69/6), Iván Sabino Castillo (23/0), Óscar Carmelo Sánchez (45/5), Juan Manuel Peña Montaño (49/0), Sergio Castillo (24/0) [81.Juan Mauricio Ramos (30/1)], Luis Héctor Cristaldo (68/3), Jaime Moreno Morales (52/6) [77.Juan Berthy Suárez (24/8)], Marco Antonio Etcheverry (58/13), Milton Coimbra Suizer (24/6). Trainer: Héctor Veira (5).
**Goal:** Fernando Ochoaizpur (3).

**279.** 13.03.1999 **GUATEMALA - BOLIVIA** **2-1(2-0)** US Cup
Qualcomm Stadium, San Diego (United States); Referee: Brian Hall (United States); Attendance: 50,324
**BOL:** Marco Antonio Barrero (31/0), Marco Antonio Sandy Sansusty (70/6) [46.Juan Carlos Farah (1/1)], Luis Héctor Cristaldo (69/3), Sergio Castillo (25/0) [46.Juan Mauricio Ramos (31/1)], Marco Antonio Etcheverry (59/13), Milton Coimbra Suizer (25/6), Luis Liendo (3/0) [85.Rolando Rea (1/0)], Juan Manuel Peña Montaño (50/0), Eduardo Jiguchi (11/0) [81.Richard José Rojas Gúzman (1/0)], Juan Berthy Suárez (25/8), Iván Sabino Castillo (24/0) [46.Richard Uriona (5/0)]. Trainer: Héctor Veira (6).
**Goal:** Juan Carlos Farah (49).

**280.** 28.04.1999 **BOLIVIA - CHILE** **1-1(1-0)**
Estadio „Félix Capriles", Cochabamba; Referee: José Antonio Arana Villamonte (Peru); Attendance: 3,000
**BOL:** José Carlos Fernández (3/0), Lorgio Álvarez Roca (2/0) [46.Sergio Castillo (26/0)], Ronald Arana (2/0), Marco Antonio Sandy Sansusty (71/6), Iván Sabino Castillo (25/0), Rubén Darío Tufiño (18/1), Miguel Raúl Justiniano Abella (2/0) [75.Luis Liendo (4/0)], Luis Héctor Cristaldo (70/3) [12.Gonzalo Germán Galindo Sánchez (3/0)], Limberg Gutiérrez Mariscal (12/0) [70.Raúl Gutiérrez (5/0)], José Martín Menacho (1/0) [63.Milton Coimbra Suizer (26/6)], Víctor Hugo Antelo (11/4). Trainer: Héctor Veira (7).
**Goal:** Víctor Hugo Antelo (15 penalty).

**281.** 20.06.1999 **CHILE - BOLIVIA** **1-0(1-0)**
Estadio Nacional, Santiago; Referee: Jorge Larrionda Pietrafiesa (Uruguay); Attendance: 25,000
**BOL:** José Carlos Fernández (4/0), Renny Ribera (1/0), Marco Antonio Sandy Sansusty (72/6), Juan Manuel Peña Montaño (51/0), Iván Sabino Castillo (26/0), Fernando Ochoaizpur (13/3) [46.Miguel Raúl Justiniano Abella (3/0)], Rubén Darío Tufiño (19/1), Marco Antonio Etcheverry (60/13) [71.Milton Coimbra Suizer (27/6)], Luis Liendo (5/0) [67.Raúl Gutiérrez (6/0)], Limberg Gutiérrez Mariscal (13/0), Víctor Hugo Antelo (12/4). Trainer: Héctor Veira (8).

**282.** 29.06.1999 **PARAGUAY - BOLIVIA** **0-0** 39th Copa América. Group Stage
Estadio Defensores del Chaco, Asunción; Referee: Mario Fernando Sánchez Yanten (Chile); Attendance: 42,000
**BOL:** José Carlos Fernández (5/0), Renny Ribera (2/0), Juan Manuel Peña Montaño (52/0), Marco Antonio Sandy Sansusty (73/6), Iván Sabino Castillo (27/0), Luis Héctor Cristaldo (71/3), Vladimir Soria (44/1), Rubén Darío Tufiño (20/1), Erwin Sánchez (44/13) [79.Milton Coimbra Suizer (28/6)], Limberg Gutiérrez Mariscal (14/0) [67.Jaime Moreno Morales (53/6)], Víctor Hugo Antelo (13/4) [45.Marco Antonio Etcheverry (61/13)]. Trainer: Héctor Veira (9).

**283.** 02.07.1999 **PERU - BOLIVIA** **1-0(0-0)** 39th Copa América. Group Stage
Estadio Defensores del Chaco, Asunción; Referee: Luis Solórzano (Venezuela); Attendance: 30,000
**BOL:** José Carlos Fernández (6/0), Renny Ribera (3/0), Juan Manuel Peña Montaño (53/0), Marco Antonio Sandy Sansusty (74/6), Iván Sabino Castillo (28/0), Luis Héctor Cristaldo (72/3) [65.Fernando Ochoaizpur (14/3)], Vladimir Soria (45/1), Rubén Darío Tufiño (21/1), Erwin Sánchez (45/13) [82.Luis Liendo (6/0)], Limberg Gutiérrez Mariscal (15/0) [61.Marco Antonio Etcheverry (62/13)], Jaime Moreno Morales (54/6). Trainer: Héctor Veira (10).

**284.** 05.07.1999 **BOLIVIA – JAPAN** **1-1(0-0)** 39th Copa América. Group Stage
Río Paraití, Pedro Juan Caballero (Paraguay); Referee: Byron Moreno (Ecuador); Attendance: 20,000
**BOL:** José Carlos Fernández (7/0), Renny Ribera (4/0) [87.Fernando Ochoaizpur (15/3)], Juan Manuel Peña Montaño (54/0), Óscar Carmelo Sánchez (46/5) [*sent off 44*], Iván Sabino Castillo (29/0) [75.Marco Antonio Etcheverry (63/13)], Luis Héctor Cristaldo (73/3), Rubén Darío Tufiño (22/1), Erwin Sánchez (46/14), Limberg Gutiérrez Mariscal (16/0), Víctor Hugo Antelo (14/4), Jaime Moreno Morales (55/6) [45.Gustavo Domingo Quinteros (26/1)]. Trainer: Héctor Veira (11).
**Goal:** Erwin Sánchez (52).

**285.** 25.07.1999 **BOLIVIA – EGYPT** **2-2(2-1)** 2nd Confederations Cup. Group Stage
Estadio Azteca, Ciudad de México; Referee: Anders Frisk (Sweden); Attendance: 85,000
**BOL:** José Carlos Fernández (8/0), Juan Manuel Peña Montaño (55/0), Ronald Arana (3/0), Limberg Gutiérrez Mariscal (17/1) [71.Marco Antonio Etcheverry (64/13)], Rubén Darío Tufiño (23/1), Gonzalo Germán Galindo Sánchez (4/0) [60.Vladimir Soria (46/1)], Joaquín Botero Vaca (1/0) [46.José Martín Menacho (2/0], Erwin Sánchez (Cap) (47/14), Miguel Raúl Justiniano Abella (4/0), Iván Sabino Castillo (30/0), Renny Ribera (5/1). Trainer: Héctor Veira (12).
**Goals:** Limberg Gutiérrez Mariscal (21), Renny Ribera (40).

**286.** 27.07.1999 **BOLIVIA – SAUDI ARABIA** **0-0** 2nd Confederations Cup. Group Stage
Estadio Azteca, Ciudad de México; Referee: Brian Hall (United States); Attendance: 65,000
**BOL:** José Carlos Fernández (9/0), Renny Ribera (6/1), Ronald Arana (4/0), Lorgio Álvarez Roca (3/0), Óscar Carmelo Sánchez (47/5), Rubén Darío Tufiño (24/1), Jaime Moreno Morales (56/6) [73.Joaquín Botero Vaca (2/0)], Marco Antonio Etcheverry (65/13) [53.Gonzalo Germán Galindo Sánchez (5/0)], Erwin Sánchez (48/14) [46.Limberg Gutiérrez Mariscal (18/1)], José Martín Menacho (3/0), Vladimir Soria (47/1). Trainer: Héctor Veira (13).

**287.** 29.07.1999 **MEXICO – BOLIVIA** **1-0(0-0)** 2nd Confederations Cup. Group Stage
Estadio Azteca, Ciudad de México; Referee: Oscar Julián Ruíz Acosta (Colombia); Attendance: 55,000
**BOL:** José Carlos Fernández (10/0), Ronald Arana (5/0), Óscar Carmelo Sánchez (48/5), Luis Héctor Cristaldo (74/3), Rubén Darío Tufiño (25/1), Jaime Moreno Morales (57/6) [78.Joaquín Botero Vaca (3/0)], Erwin Sánchez (Cap) (49/14), José Martín Menacho (4/0) [66.Marco Antonio Etcheverry (66/13)], Vladimir Soria (48/1) [46.Limberg Gutiérrez Mariscal (19/1)], Iván Sabino Castillo (31/0), Renny Ribera (7/1). Trainer: Héctor Veira (14).

**288.** 25.08.1999 **BOLIVIA – VENEZUELA** **0-0**
Estadio Patria del Morro, Sucre; Referee: Alfred Bernal (Bolivia); Attendance: 11,376
**BOL:** José Carlos Fernández (11/0), Renny Ribera (8/1), Ronald Arana (6/0), Percy Gil (1/0), Lorgio Álvarez Roca (4/0), Sergio Castillo (27/0) [Richard Uriona (6/0)], Raúl Gutiérrez (7/0) [Carlos Cárdenas Rodríguez (1/0)], Gonzalo Germán Galindo Sánchez (6/0), Rubén Darío Tufiño (26/1), Líder Paz Colodro (1/0) [Roger Suárez (4/0)], Milton Coimbra Suizer (29/6). Trainer: Héctor Veira (15).

**289.** 03.11.1999 **BOLIVIA – PARAGUAY** **0-0** Copa Páz del Chaco
Estadio Deportivo Español, Buenos Aires (Argentina); Referee: Horacio Marcelo Elizondo (Argentina); Attendance: 12,000
**BOL:** José Carlos Fernández (12/0), Wilder Arévalo Ramírez (1/0), Óscar Carmelo Sánchez (49/5), Marco Antonio Sandy Sansusty (75/6), Cléver Méndez (1/0), Sergio Castillo (28/0), Richard Uriona (7/0) [Franz Alvaro Calustro (1/0)], Juan Mauricio Ramos (32/1) [Darwin Peña Arce (1/0)], Líder Paz Colodro (2/0) [Roger Suárez (5/0)], Milton Coimbra Suizer (30/6) [Joselito Vaca Velasco (1/0)], Gonzalo Germán Galindo Sánchez (7/0) [Nicolás Suárez Vaca (1/0)]. Trainer: Héctor Veira (16).

**290.** 05.03.2000 **BOLIVIA – HAITI** **9-2(4-0)**
Estadio „Hernándo Siles Zuazo“, La Paz; Referee: René Marcelo Ortubé Betancourt (Bolivia); Attendance: 18,620
**BOL:** Mauricio Ronald Soria Portillo (12/0), Luis Gatty Ribeiro Roca (1/0), Marcelo Antonio Carballo Cadima (1/1), Iván Sabino Castillo (32/0), Vladimir Soria (49/1) [Miguel Raúl Justiniano Abella (5/0)], Sergio Castillo (29/0) [Percy Colque Paredes (1/0)], Gonzalo Germán Galindo Sánchez (8/0) [Richard José Rojas Gúzman (2/0)], Roger Suárez (6/4), Julio César Baldivieso (64/8), Tomás Gutiérrez (2/0), Joaquín Botero Vaca (4/3). Trainer: Carlos Aragonés Espinosa (1).
**Goals:** Roger Suárez (2, 7) Julio César Baldivieso (39), Roger Suárez (42), Joaquín Botero Vaca (64), Marcelo Antonio Carballo Cadima (68), Joaquín Botero Vaca (70), Roger Suárez (73), Joaquín Botero Vaca (88).

**291.** 16.03.2000 **VENEZUELA – BOLIVIA** **0-0**
Estadio "José 'Pachenco' Romero", Maracaibo; Referee: Jorge Manzur (Venezuela); Attendance: 8,000
**BOL:** Mauricio Ronald Soria Portillo (13/0), Renny Ribera (9/1), Óscar Carmelo Sánchez (50/5), Miguel Ángel Rimba (76/0), Marcelo Antonio Carballo Cadima (2/1), Richard José Rojas Gúzman (3/0), Miguel Raúl Justiniano Abella (6/0), Gonzalo Germán Galindo Sánchez (9/0) [80.Sergio Castillo (30/0)], Raúl Gutiérrez (8/0), Limberg Gutiérrez Mariscal (20/1) [57.Tomás Gutiérrez (3/0)], Roger Suárez (7/4). Trainer: Carlos Aragonés Espinosa (2).

**292.** 29.03.2000 **URUGUAY – BOLIVIA** **1-0(1-0)** 17th FIFA WC. Qualifiers
Estadio Centenario, Montevideo; Referee: Antônio Pereira Da Silva (Brazil); Attendance: 49,811
**BOL:** José Carlos Fernández (13/0), Renny Ribera (10/1), Juan Manuel Peña Montaño (56/0), Óscar Carmelo Sánchez (51/5), Marco Antonio Sandy Sansusty (76/6) [75.Miguel Ángel Rimba (77/0)], Iván Sabino Castillo (33/0), Luis Héctor Cristaldo (75/3), Miguel Raúl Justiniano Abella (7/0), Erwin Sánchez (50/14), Limberg Gutiérrez Mariscal (21/1) [59.Roger Suárez (8/4)], Jaime Moreno Morales (58/6) [69.Joaquín Botero Vaca (5/3)]. Trainer: Carlos Aragonés Espinosa (3).

**293.** 26.04.2000 **BOLIVIA – COLOMBIA** **1-1(1-1)** 17th FIFA WC. Qualifiers
Estadio „Hernándo Siles Zuazo“, La Paz; Referee: José Antonio Arana Villamonte (Peru); Attendance: 35,500
**BOL:** José Carlos Fernández (14/0), Juan Manuel Peña Montaño (57/0), Marco Antonio Sandy Sansusty (77/6) [32.Miguel Ángel Rimba (78/0)], Luis Gatty Ribeiro Roca (2/0), Iván Sabino Castillo (34/0), Vladimir Soria (50/1), Luis Héctor Cristaldo (76/3), Raúl Gutiérrez (9/0) [63.Gonzalo Germán Galindo Sánchez (10/0)], Erwin Sánchez (51/15), Víctor Antelo (15/4) [45.Roger Suárez (9/4)], Jaime Moreno Morales (59/6). Trainer: Carlos Aragonés Espinosa (4).
**Goal:** Erwin Sánchez (17).

**294.** 04.06.2000 **ARGENTINA – BOLIVIA** **1-0(1-0)** 17th FIFA WC. Qualifiers
Estadio Monumental „Antonio Vespucio Liberti“, Buenos Aires; Referee: Márcio Rezende de Freitas (Brazil); Attendance: 50,669
**BOL:** José Carlos Fernández (15/0), Marcelo Antonio Carballo Cadima (3/1) [*sent off 62*], Juan Manuel Peña Montaño (58/0), Marco Antonio Sandy Sansusty (78/6), Iván Sabino Castillo (35/0), Renny Ribera (11/1), Julio César Baldivieso (65/8), Luis Héctor Cristaldo (77/3), Marco Antonio Etcheverry (67/13) [78.Gonzalo Germán Galindo Sánchez (11/0)], Roger Suárez (10/4) [65.Ronald Lázaro García Justiniano (1/0)], Joaquín Botero Vaca (6/3) [83.Milton Coimbra Suizer (31/6)]. Trainer: Carlos Aragonés Espinosa (5).

**295.** 14.06.2000 **SLOVAKIA - BOLIVIA** **2-0(2-0)** Kirin Cup

Tosu Stadium, Saga (Japan); Referee: Masayoshi Okada (Japan); Attendance: 8,037

**BOL:** Sergio Daniel Galarza Solíz (1/0), Miguel Ángel Parabá (11/0), Renny Ribera (12/1), José Loayza Pedraza (1/0), Luis Camacho (1/0), Juan Rivero (2/0) [46.Ricardo Torrico (1/0)], Juan Mauricio Ramos (33/1), Luis Héctor Cristaldo (78/3) [46.Miguel Raúl Justiniano Abella (8/0)], Richard José Rojas Gúzman (4/0), Limberg Gutiérrez Mariscal (22/1) [Raúl Gutiérrez (10/0)], Tomas Gutiérrez (3/0) [Herlán Sánchez (1/0)]. Trainer: Carlos Aragonés Espinosa (6).

**296.** 18.06.2000 **JAPAN - BOLIVIA** **2-0(2-0)** Kirin Cup

International Stadium, Yokohama; Referee: Baojie Sun (China P.R.); Attendance: 65,073

**BOL:** José Carlos Fernández (16/0), Renny Ribera (13/1), Luis Camacho (2/0), José Loayza Pedraza (2/0), Ricardo Torrico (2/0), Richard José Rojas Gúzman (5/0), Raúl Gutiérrez (11/0), Miguel Raúl Justiniano Abella (9/0) [46.Franz Alvaro Calustro (2/0)], Miguel Ángel Parabá (12/0), Tomás Gutiérrez (4/0) [87.Walter Anez (1/0)], Herlán Sánchez (2/0) [46.Limberg Gutiérrez Mariscal (23/1)]. Trainer: Carlos Aragonés Espinosa (7).

**297.** 28.06.2000 **VENEZUELA - BOLIVIA** **4-2(2-0)** 17th FIFA WC. Qualifiers

Estadio Puerto Nuevo, San Cristóbal; Referee: Roger Zambrano Alcivar (Ecuador); Attendance: 7,000

**BOL:** José Carlos Fernández (17/0), Renny Ribera (14/1), Marco Antonio Etcheverry (68/13) [80.Gonzalo Germán Galindo Sánchez (12/0)], Juan Manuel Peña Montaño (59/0), Marco Antonio Sandy Sansusty (79/6), Iván Sabino Castillo (36/0), Luis Héctor Cristaldo (79/3) [*sent off 69*], Erwin Sánchez (52/15), Julio César Baldivieso (66/9), Roger Suárez (11/4) [73.Ronald Lázaro García Justiniano (2/0)], Joaquín Botero Vaca (7/3) [46.Jaime Moreno Morales (60/7)]. Trainer: Carlos Aragonés Espinosa (8).

**Goals:** Jaime Moreno Morales (49), Julio César Baldivieso (59).

**298.** 19.07.2000 **BOLIVIA - CHILE** **1-0(0-0)** 17th FIFA WC. Qualifiers

Estadio „Hernándo Siles Zuazo“, La Paz; Referee: John Jairo Toro Rendón (Colombia); Attendance: 35,412

**BOL:** Mauricio Ronald Soria Portillo (14/0), Luis Gatty Ribeiro Roca (3/0), Juan Manuel Peña Montaño (60/0), Marco Antonio Sandy Sansusty (80/6), Marcelo Antonio Carballo Cadima (4/1) [43.Miguel Ángel Rimba (79/0)], Gonzalo Germán Galindo Sánchez (13/0) [65.Percy Colque Paredes (2/0)], Ronald Lázaro García Justiniano (3/0), Franz Alvaro Calustro (3/0), Julio César Baldivieso (67/9), Roger Suárez (12/5), Joaquín Botero Vaca (8/3) [55.Tomás Gutiérrez (5/0)]. Trainer: Carlos Aragonés Espinosa (9).

**Goal:** Roger Suárez (84).

**299.** 27.07.2000 **BOLIVIA - PARAGUAY** **0-0** 17th FIFA WC. Qualifiers

Estadio „Hernándo Siles Zuazo“, La Paz; Referee: Luciano Almeida (Brazil); Attendance: 39,142

**BOL:** Mauricio Ronald Soria Portillo (15/0), Luis Gatty Ribeiro Roca (4/0), Juan Manuel Peña Montaño (61/0), Marco Antonio Sandy Sansusty (81/6), Miguel Ángel Rimba (80/0) [38.Juan Carlos Paz García (1/0)], Percy Colque Paredes (3/0), Roger Suárez (13/5), Ronald Lázaro García Justiniano (4/0), Julio César Baldivieso (68/9), Franz Alvaro Calustro (4/0) [72.Carlos Cárdenas Rodríguez (2/0)], Joaquín Botero Vaca (9/3) [52.Limberg Gutiérrez Mariscal (24/1)]. Trainer: Carlos Aragonés Espinosa (10).

**300.** 16.08.2000 **ECUADOR - BOLIVIA** **2-0(1-0)** 17th FIFA WC. Qualifiers

Estadio Casa Blanca, Quito; Referee: Luis Solórzano Torres (Venezuela); Attendance: 25,000

**BOL:** Mauricio Ronald Soria Portillo (16/0), Gonzalo Germán Galindo Sánchez (14/0), Ronald Arana (7/0), Juan Carlos Paz García (2/0), Luis Gatty Ribeiro Roca (5/0), Sergio Castillo (31/0), Marco Antonio Sandy Sansusty (82/6), Ronald Lázaro García Justiniano (5/0), Franz Alvaro Calustro (5/0) [74.Joselito Vaca Velasco (2/0)], Julio César Baldivieso (69/9) [46.Milton Coimbra Suizer (32/6)], Róger Suárez (13/5). Trainer: Carlos Aragonés Espinosa (11).

**301.** 03.09.2000 **BRAZIL - BOLIVIA** **5-0(1-0)** 17th FIFA WC. Qualifiers

Estádio „Jornalista Mario Filho“ (Maracanã), Rio de Janeiro; Referee: Guido Aros Alvarado (Chile); Attendance: 55,000

**BOL:** Mauricio Ronald Soria Portillo (17/0), Marco Antonio Sandy Sansusty (83/6), Luis Gatty Ribeiro Roca (6/0), Juan Carlos Paz García (3/0), Óscar Carmelo Sánchez (52/5), Luis Héctor Cristaldo (80/3), Lorgio Álvarez Roca (5/0), Ronald Lázaro García Justiniano (6/0) [74.Limberg Gutiérrez Mariscal (25/1)], Julio César Baldivieso (70/9), Marco Antonio Etcheverry (69/13), Jaime Moreno Morales (61/7) [27.Líder Paz Colodro (3/0)]. Trainer: Carlos Aragonés Espinosa (12).

**302.** 27.09.2000 **MEXICO - BOLIVIA** **1-0(0-0)**

Spartano Stadium, San José (United States); Referee: Ricardo A. Valenzuela (United States); Attendance: 30,154

**BOL:** Mauricio Ronald Soria Portillo (18/0), Sergio Castillo (32/0), Marco Antonio Sandy Sansusty (84/6), Juan Carlos Paz García (4/0), Óscar Carmelo Sánchez (53/5), Franz Alvaro Calustro (6/0), Ronald Lázaro García Justiniano (7/0), Percy Colque Paredes (4/0), Joselito Vaca Velasco (3/0), Milton Coimbra Suizer (33/6), Líder Paz Colodro (4/0). Trainer: Carlos Aragonés Espinosa (13).

**303.** 08.10.2000 **BOLIVIA - PERU** **1-0(1-0)** 17th FIFA WC. Qualifiers

Estadio „Hernándo Siles Zuazo“, La Paz; Referee: José Patricio Carpio Guevara (Ecuador); Attendance: 21,791

**BOL:** Mauricio Ronald Soria Portillo (19/0), Óscar Carmelo Sánchez (54/5), Juan Manuel Peña Montaño (62/0), Juan Carlos Paz García (5/0), Percy Colque Paredes (5/0), Luis Gatty Ribeiro Roca (7/0), Franz Alvaro Calustro (6/0), Joselito Vaca Velasco (4/0) [66.Raúl Gutiérrez (12/0)], Líder Paz Colodro (5/0) [46.Jaime Moreno Morales (62/7)], Ronald Lázaro García Justiniano (8/0), Roger Suárez (14/6) [80.Gonzalo Germán Galindo Sánchez (15/0)]. Trainer: Carlos Aragonés Espinosa (14).

**Goal:** Roger Suárez (4).

**304.** 15.11.2000 **BOLIVIA - URUGUAY** **0-0** 17th FIFA WC. Qualifiers

Estadio „Hernándo Siles Zuazo“, La Paz; Referee: Horacio Marcelo Elizondo (Argentina); Attendance: 29,112

**BOL:** Mauricio Ronald Soria Portillo (20/0), Luis Gatty Ribeiro Roca (8/0), Óscar Carmelo Sánchez (55/5), Juan Carlos Paz García (6/0) [80.Joselito Vaca Velasco (5/0)], Marco Antonio Sandy Sansusty (85/6), Percy Colque Paredes (6/0), Ronald Lázaro García Justiniano (9/0) [*sent off 85*], Franz Alvaro Calustro (8/0), Erwin Sánchez (53/15), José Martín Menacho (5/0), Roger Suárez (15/6) [65.Líder Paz Colodro (6/0)]. Trainer: Carlos Aragonés Espinosa (15).

**305.** 26.01.2001 **JAMAICA - BOLIVIA** **3-0(1-0)**

Orange Bowl, Miami (United States); Referee: Kevin Terry (United States); Attendance: 9,000

**BOL:** Mauricio Ronald Soria Portillo (21/0), José Loayza Pedraza (3/0) [46.Juan Carlos Farah (2/1)], Percy Gil (2/0), Sergio Castillo (33/0), Marcos Francisquini (5/0), Lorgio Álvarez Roca (6/0), Miguel Raúl Justiniano Abella (10/0), Franz Alvaro Calustro (9/0), Raúl Gutiérrez (13/0), José Martín Menacho (6/0), Líder Paz Colodro (7/0). Trainer: Carlos Aragonés Espinosa (16).

**306.** 27.03.2001 **COLOMBIA - BOLIVIA** **2-0(0-0)** 17th FIFA WC. Qualifiers
Estadio "Nemesio Camacho 'El Campín'", Bogotá; Referee: Wilson Souza Mendonça (Brazil); Attendance: 29,998
**BOL:** José Carlos Fernández (18/0), Juan Manuel Peña Montaño (63/0), Marco Antonio Sandy Sansusty (86/6), Ronald Arana (8/0), Richard José Rojas Gúzman (6/0), Luis Gatty Ribeiro Roca (9/0), Miguel Raúl Justiniano Abella (11/0), Milton Coimbra Suizer (34/6) [78.Líder Paz Colodro (8/0)], Joselito Vaca Velasco (6/0), Carlos Cárdenas Rodríguez (3/0) [58.Roger Suárez (16/6)], Percy Colque Paredes (7/0). Trainer: Carlos Aragonés Espinosa (17).

**307.** 25.04.2001 **BOLIVIA - ARGENTINA** **3-3(1-1)** 17th FIFA WC. Qualifiers
Estadio „Hernándo Siles Zuazo", La Paz; Referee: Oscar Julián Ruíz Acosta (Colombia); Attendance: 28,872
**BOL:** José Carlos Fernández (19/0), Juan Manuel Peña Montaño (64/0), Marco Antonio Sandy Sansusty (87/6), Juan Carlos Paz García (7/0), Miguel Raúl Justiniano Abella (12/0), Luis Gatty Ribeiro Roca (10/0), Joselito Vaca Velasco (7/0) [58.Richard José Rojas Gúzman (7/0)], Joaquín Botero Vaca (10/4), Julio César Baldivieso (71/9), Líder Paz Colodro (9/1) [74.Carlos Cárdenas Rodríguez (4/0)], Percy Colque Paredes (8/1). Trainer: Carlos Aragonés Espinosa (18).
**Goals:** Líder Paz Colodro (39), Percy Colque Paredes (55), Joaquín Botero Vaca (81).

**308.** 03.06.2001 **BOLIVIA - VENEZUELA** **5-0(3-0)** 17th FIFA WC. Qualifiers
Estadio „Hernándo Siles Zuazo", La Paz; Referee: José Patricio Carpio Guevara (Ecuador); Attendance: 25,000
**BOL:** Carlos Erwin Arias Égüez (1/0), Juan Manuel Peña Montaño (65/0), Miguel Raúl Justiniano Abella (13/1) [85.Richard José Rojas Gúzman (8/0)], Luis Gatty Ribeiro Roca (11/0), Franz Alvaro Calustro (10/0), Joaquín Botero Vaca (11/6), Julio César Baldivieso (72/11) [88.Darwin Peña Arce (2/0)], Líder Paz Colodro (10/1) [72.Carlos Cárdenas Rodríguez (5/0)], Juan Carlos Paz García (8/0), Ronald Raldes Balcázar (1/0), Percy Colque Paredes (9/1). Trainer: Carlos Aragonés Espinosa (19).
**Goals:** Julio César Baldivieso (32), Joaquín Botero Vaca (35), Miguel Raúl Justiniano Abella (38), Joaquín Botero Vaca (50), Julio César Baldivieso (68).

**309.** 13.07.2001 **URUGUAY - BOLIVIA** **1-0(0-0)** 40th Copa América. Group Stage
Estadio "Atanasio Girardot", Medellín; Referee: Mauricio Navarro (Canada); Attendance: 20,027
**BOL:** Carlos Erwin Arias Égüez (2/0), Luis Gatty Ribeiro Roca (12/0), Eduardo Jiguchi (12/0), Marco Antonio Sandy Sansusty (88/6), Ronald Raldes Balcázar (2/0), Lorgio Álvarez Roca (7/0), Franz Alvaro Calustro (11/0), Julio César Baldivieso (73/11), Limberg Gutiérrez Mariscal (26/1) [73.Ronald Lázaro García Justiniano (10/0)], Joaquín Botero Vaca (12/6), Milton Coimbra Suizer (35/6) [73.Líder Paz Colodro (11/1)]. Trainer: Carlos Aragonés Espinosa (20).

**310.** 16.07.2001 **HONDURAS - BOLIVIA** **2-0(0-0)** 40th Copa América. Group Stage
Estadio „Atanasio Girardot", Medellín; Referee: John Jairo Toro Rendón (Colombia); Attendance: 17,273
**BOL:** Carlos Erwin Arias Égüez (3/0), Luis Gatty Ribeiro Roca (13/0), Eduardo Jiguchi (13/0), Marco Antonio Sandy Sansusty (89/6) [*sent off 73*], Lorgio Álvarez Roca (8/0), Ronald Raldes Balcázar (3/0) [46.Limberg Gutiérrez Mariscal (27/1)], Franz Alvaro Calustro (12/0), Julio César Baldivieso (74/11) [78.Marcelo Antonio Carballo Cadima (5/1)], Joaquín Botero Vaca (13/6), Ronald Lázaro García Justiniano (11/0), Líder Paz Colodro (12/1) [66.Milton Coimbra Suizer (36/6) [*sent off 81*]]. Trainer: Carlos Aragonés Espinosa (21).

**311.** 19.07.2001 **COSTA RICA - BOLIVIA** **4-0(1-0)** 40th Copa América. Group Stage
Estadio „Atanasio Girardot", Medellín; Referee: Luis Solórzano Torres (Venezuela); Attendance: 20,233
**BOL:** Carlos Erwin Arias Égüez (4/0), Luis Gatty Ribeiro Roca (14/0), Ronald Raldes Balcázar (4/0), Eduardo Jiguchi (14/0), Marcelo Antonio Carballo Cadima (6/1), Percy Colque Paredes (10/1) [46.Lorgio Álvarez Roca (9/0)], Miguel Raúl Justiniano Abella (14/1), Julio César Baldivieso (75/11), Roger Suárez (17/6), Limberg Gutiérrez Mariscal (28/1), Joaquín Botero Vaca (14/6). Trainer: Carlos Aragonés Espinosa (22).

**312.** 14.08.2001 **CHILE - BOLIVIA** **2-2(1-1)** 17th FIFA WC. Qualifiers
Estadio Nacional, Santiago; Referee: Daniel Orlando Giménez (Argentina); Attendance: 36,409
**BOL:** Mauricio Ronald Soria Portillo (22/0), Marcelo Antonio Carballo Cadima (7/1), Ronald Raldes Balcázar (5/0), Óscar Carmelo Sánchez (56/5), Juan Manuel Peña Montaño (66/0), Miguel Raúl Justiniano Abella (15/1), Líder Paz Colodro (13/1) [58.Percy Colque Paredes (11/1)], Richard José Rojas Gúzman (9/0), Milton Coimbra Suizer (37/7), Julio César Baldivieso (76/12), Gonzalo Germán Galindo Sánchez (16/0). Trainer: Jorge Habegger (15).
**Goals:** Julio César Baldivieso (19 penalty), Milton Coimbra Suizer (71).

**313.** 05.09.2001 **PARAGUAY - BOLIVIA** **5-1(2-1)** 17th FIFA WC. Qualifiers
Estadio Defensores del Chaco, Asunción; Referee: Luis Solórzano Torres (Venezuela); Attendance: 25,000
**BOL:** Carlos Erwin Arias Égüez (5/0), Juan Manuel Peña Montaño (67/0), Luis Alberto Reyes Zabala (1/0), Juan Carlos Paz García (9/0), Miguel Raúl Justiniano Abella (16/1), Líder Paz Colodro (14/2) [78.Franz Alvaro Calustro (13/0)], Richard José Rojas Gúzman (10/0) [*sent off 76*], Julio César Baldivieso (77/12), Ronald Raldes Balcázar (6/0), José Alfredo Castillo Parada (1/0) [61.Augusto Andaveris Iriondo (1/0)], Gonzalo Germán Galindo Sánchez (17/0). Trainer: Jorge Habegger (16).
**Goal:** Líder Paz Colodro (15).

**314.** 06.10.2001 **BOLIVIA - ECUADOR** **1-5(0-2)** 17th FIFA WC. Qualifiers
Estadio „Hernándo Siles Zuazo", La Paz; Referee: Ángel Osvaldo Sánchez (Argentina); Attendance: 8,000
**BOL:** Carlos Erwin Arias Égüez (6/0), Sergio Castillo (34/0) [32.Doyle Vaca (1/0)], Ronald Raldes Balcázar (7/0), Eduardo Jiguchi (15/0), Luis Alberto Reyes Zabala (2/0), Marcelo Antonio Carballo Cadima (8/1) [*sent off 27*], Miguel Raúl Justiniano Abella (17/1), Gonzalo Germán Galindo Sánchez (18/1), Franz Alvaro Calustro (14/0), Líder Paz Colodro (15/2), Augusto Andaveris Iriondo (2/0) [46.José Alfredo Castillo Parada (2/0)]. Trainer: Jorge Habegger (17).
**Goal:** Gonzalo Germán Galindo Sánchez (59).

**315.** 07.11.2001 **BOLIVIA - BRAZIL** **3-1(1-1)** 17th FIFA WC. Qualifiers
Estadio „Hernándo Siles Zuazo", La Paz; Referee: Luis Solórzano Torres (Venezuela); Attendance: 32,574
**BOL:** Mauricio Ronald Soria Portillo (23/0), Juan Manuel Peña Montaño (68/0), Juan Carlos Paz García (10/0), Percy Colque Paredes (12/1) [67.Óscar Carmelo Sánchez (57/5)], Edgar Rolando Olivares Burgoa (1/0), Luis Gatty Ribeiro Roca (15/0), Richard José Rojas Gúzman (11/0), Joaquín Botero Vaca (15/6), Julio César Baldivieso (78/14), Líder Paz Colodro (16/3) [74.José Alfredo Castillo Parada (3/0)], Gonzalo Germán Galindo Sánchez (19/1) [54.Limberg Gutiérrez Mariscal (29/1)]. Trainer: Carlos Leonel Trucco (1).
**Goals:** Líder Paz Colodro (42), Julio César Baldivieso (70, 89 penalty).

**316.** 14.11.2001 **PERU - BOLIVIA** **1-1(1-0)** 17th FIFA WC. Qualifiers
Estadio Monumental, Lima; Referee: Héctor Baldassi (Argentina); Attendance: 2,374
**BOL:** José Carlos Fernández (20/0), Luis Alberto Reyes Zabala (3/0), Juan Carlos Paz García (11/0), Óscar Carmelo Sánchez (58/5) [54.Luis Gatty Ribeiro Roca (16/0)], Edgar Rolando Olivares Burgoa (2/0), Richard José Rojas Gúzman (12/0), Joaquín Botero Vaca (16/6) [63.José Alfredo Castillo Parada (4/1)], Milton Coimbra Suizer (38/7), Líder Paz Colodro (17/3) [90.Miguel Raúl Justiniano Abella (18/1)], Darwin Peña Arce (3/0), Gonzalo Germán Galindo Sánchez (20/1). Trainer: Carlos Leonel Trucco (2).
**Goal**: José Alfredo Castillo Parada (87).

**317.** 31.01.2002 **BRAZIL – BOLIVIA** **6-0(1-0)**
Estádio Serra Dourada, Goiânia; Referee: Antônio Pereira da Silva (Brazil); Attendance: 45,000
**BOL:** José Carlos Fernández (21/0), Miguel Ángel Hoyos Guzmán (1/0), Óscar Carmelo Sánchez (59/5), Marco Antonio Sandy Sansusty (90/6), Percy Colque Paredes (13/1) [65.José Luis Algarañaz (1/0)], Edgar Rolando Olivares Burgoa (3/0) [55.Miguel Raúl Justiniano Abella (19/1)], Joselito Vaca Velasco (8/0) [71.Darwin Peña Arce (4/0)], Armando Ibáñez Correa (1/0), Gonzalo Germán Galindo Sánchez (21/1) [80.Roberto Torres (1/0)], José Alfredo Castillo Parada (5/1), Joaquín Botero Vaca (17/6) [59.Roger Suárez (18/6)]. Trainer: Carlos Leonel Trucco (3).

**318.** 13.02.2002 **PARAGUAY – BOLIVIA** **2-2(1-2)**
Monumental, Lima "Antonio Oddone Sarubbi", Ciudad del Este; Referee: Ubaldo Aquino (Paraguay); Attendance: 22,000
**BOL:** Mauricio Ronald Soria Portillo (24/0), Wilson Escalante (1/0) [55.José Luis Algarañaz (2/0)], Marco Antonio Sandy Sansusty (91/6), Óscar Carmelo Sánchez (60/5), Percy Colque Paredes (14/2), Edgar Rolando Olivares Burgoa (4/0), Gonzalo Germán Galindo Sánchez (22/1) [90.Franz Alvaro Calustro (15/0)], Raúl Gutiérrez (14/0), Diego Didier Bengolea Vargas (1/0), Miguel Ángel Mercado (7/1) [81.Armando Ibáñez Correa (2/0)], Augusto Andaveris Iriondo (3/1) [67.Diego Aroldo Cabrera Flores (1/0)]. Trainer: Carlos Leonel Trucco (4).
**Goals:** Percy Colque Paredes (44), Augusto Andaveris Iriondo (45).

**319.** 27.03.2002 **SENEGAL – BOLIVIA** **2-1(1-0)**
Stade "Leopold Sénghor", Dakar; Referee: Modou Sowe (Gambia); Attendance: 50,000
**BOL:** Carlos Erwin Arias Égüez (7/0), Wilson Escalante (2/0), Eduardo Jiguchi (16/0), Neil Rivero (1/0), Johnny Nay (1/0), Franz Alvaro Calustro (16/0) [46.Luis Camacho (3/0)], Carlos Suárez (1/0) [61.Adrián Cuéllar (1/0)], Raúl Gutiérrez (15/0), Diego Didier Bengolea Vargas (2/1), Augusto Andaveris Iriondo (4/1) [90.Juan Carlos Melgar (1/0)], Javier Guzmán (1/0) [77.Percy Gil (3/0)]. Trainer: Carlos Leonel Trucco (5).
**Goal:** Diego Didier Bengolea Vargas (48).

**320.** 16.05.2002 **MEXICO – BOLIVIA** **1-0(0-0)**
San Francisco (United States); Referee: Michael Kennedy (United States); Attendance: 37,127
**BOL:** Carlos Erwin Arias Égüez (8/0), Miguel Ángel Hoyos Guzmán (2/0), Eduardo Jiguchi (17/0), Óscar Carmelo Sánchez (61/5), Percy Colque Paredes (15/2), Raúl Gutiérrez (16/0), Edgar Rolando Olivares Burgoa (5/0) [43.Líder Paz Colodro (18/3)], Diego Didier Bengolea Vargas (3/1), Gonzalo Germán Galindo Sánchez (23/1) [46.Rubén Darío Tufiño (27/1)], Limberg Gutiérrez Mariscal (30/1) [82.Javier Guzmán (2/0)], Augusto Andaveris Iriondo (5/1) [76.José Alfredo Castillo Parada (6/1)]. Trainer: Carlos Leonel Trucco (6).

**321.** 21.08.2002 **VENEZUELA – BOLIVIA** **2-0(2-0)**
Estadio Olímpico, Caracas; Referee: Edison Ibarra (Venezuela); Attendance: 25,000
**BOL:** Carlos Erwin Arias Égüez (9/0), Luis Gatty Ribeiro Roca (17/0) [46.Richard José Rojas Gúzman (13/0)], Eduardo Jiguchi (18/0) [46.Miguel Ángel Hoyos Guzmán (3/0)], Marco Antonio Sandy Sansusty (92/6), Óscar Carmelo Sánchez (62/5), Percy Colque Paredes (16/2), Rubén Darío Tufiño (28/1), Limberg Gutiérrez Mariscal (31/1), Marco Antonio Etcheverry (70/13) [Gonzalo Germán Galindo Sánchez (24/1)], Joaquín Botero Vaca (18/6), José Alfredo Castillo Parada (7/1). Trainer: Vladimir Soria (1).

**322.** 19.03.2003 **MEXICO – BOLIVIA** **2-0(1-0)**
Texas Stadium, Irving (United States); Referee: Kevin Terry (United States); Attendance: 40,000
**BOL:** Hugo Suárez Vaca (1/0), Wilson Escalante (3/0), Ronald Arana (9/0), Ronald Raldes Balcázar (8/0), Johnny Nay (2/0) [46.Joselito Vaca Velasco (9/0)], Raúl Gutiérrez (17/0) [80.Carlos Suárez (2/0)], Lorgio Álvarez Roca (10/0), Richard José Rojas Gúzman (14/0), Diego Didier Bengolea Vargas (4/1) [46.Gualberto Mojica Olmos (1/0)], Roger Suárez (19/6), José Alfredo Castillo Parada (8/1). Trainer: Wálter Roque (1).

**323.** 10.06.2003 **PORTUGAL – BOLIVIA** **4-0(3-0)**
Estádio Nacional, Lisboa; Referee: Asaf Kenam (Israel); Attendance: 10,000
**BOL:** Hugo Suárez Vaca (2/0), Miguel Ángel Hoyos Guzmán (4/0), Juan Manuel Peña Montaño (69/0), Ronald Raldes Balcázar (9/0), Ronald Arana (10/0), Lorgio Álvarez Roca (11/0), Franz Alvaro Calustro (17/0) [89.José Loayza Pedraza (4/0)], Ronald Lázaro García Justiniano (12/0), Gualberto Mojica Olmos (2/0) [46.Richard José Rojas Gúzman (15/0)], Roger Suárez (20/6) [68.Darwin Peña Arce (5/0)], José Alfredo Castillo Parada (9/1) [62.Augusto Andaveris Iriondo (6/1)]. Trainer: Dalcio Giovagnoli (1).

**324.** 31.08.2003 **BOLIVIA – PANAMA** **3-0(1-0)**
Estadio „Hernándo Siles Zuazo", La Paz; Referee: René Marcelo Ortubé Betancourt (Bolivia); Attendance: 8,048
**BOL:** José Carlos Fernández (22/0), Juan Carlos Paz García (12/0), Luis Gatty Ribeiro Roca (18/0), Óscar Carmelo Sánchez (63/5), Álvaro Ricaldi (1/1), Diego Didier Bengolea Vargas (5/1) [62.Limberg Morejón (1/0)], Richard José Rojas Gúzman (16/0), Julio César Baldivieso (79/14) [84.Darwin Cuéllar (1/0)], Luis Héctor Cristaldo (81/3) [67.Miguel Raúl Justiniano Abella (20/1)], Limberg Méndez Justiniano (1/1), Augusto Andaveris Iriondo (7/1) [77.Limberg Gutiérrez Mariscal (32/2)]. Trainer: Nelson Bonifacio Acosta López (1).
**Goals:** Limberg Méndez Rocha (21), Álvaro Ricaldi (52), Limberg Gutiérrez Mariscal (84)

**325.** 07.09.2003 **URUGUAY – BOLIVIA** **5-0(2-0)** 18th FIFA WC. Qualifiers
Estadio Centenario, Montevideo; Referee: Gilberto Hidalgo Zamora (Peru); Attendance: 39,253
**BOL:** Leonardo Fernández (1/0), Miguel Ángel Hoyos Guzmán (5/0) [63.Joaquín Botero Vaca (19/6)], Óscar Carmelo Sánchez (64/5), Juan Manuel Peña Montaño (70/0), Álvaro Ricaldi (2/1) [*sent off 67*], Luis Gatty Ribeiro Roca (19/0) [46.Julio César Baldivieso (80/14)], Richard José Rojas Gúzman (17/0), Luis Héctor Cristaldo (82/3), Limberg Morejón (2/0) [46.Miguel Raúl Justiniano Abella (21/1)], Limberg Méndez Justiniano (2/1), José Alfredo Castillo Parada (10/1). Trainer: Nelson Bonifacio Acosta López (2).

**326.** 10.09.2003 **BOLIVIA – COLOMBIA** **4-0(2-0)** 18th FIFA WC. Qualifiers
Estadio „Hernándo Siles Zuazo", La Paz; Referee: Paulo César Oliveira (Brazil); Attendance: 23,200
**BOL:** Leonardo Fernández (2/0) [46.José Carlos Fernández (23/0)], Juan Manuel Peña Montaño (71/0), Luis Gatty Ribeiro Roca (20/0), Juan Carlos Paz García (13/0), Óscar Carmelo Sánchez (65/5), Roger Suárez (21/6) [63.Miguel Raúl Justiniano Abella (22/1)], Richard José Rojas Gúzman (18/0) [75.Ronald Lázaro García Justiniano (13/0)], Luis Héctor Cristaldo (83/3), Julio César Baldivieso (81/15), Limberg Méndez Justiniano (3/1), Joaquín Botero Vaca (20/9). Trainer: Nelson Bonifacio Acosta López (3).
**Goals:** Julio César Baldivieso (12 penalty), Joaquín Botero Vaca (28, 49, 59).

**327.** 11.10.2003 **BOLIVIA – HONDURAS** **1-0(0-0)**
"Robert F. Kennedy" Memorial Stadium, Washington (United States); Referee: Michael Kennedy (United States); Attendance: 20,000
**BOL:** José Carlos Fernández (24/0), Luis Gatty Ribeiro Roca (21/0), Juan Manuel Peña Montaño (72/1), Óscar Carmelo Sánchez (66/5), Álvaro Ricaldi (3/1), Ronald Raldes Balcázar (10/0), Leonel Alfredo Reyes Saravia (1/0), Miguel Raúl Justiniano Abella (23/1), Joselito Vaca Velasco (10/0) [72.Gualberto Mojica Olmos (3/0)], Carlos Suárez (3/0) [55.Limberg Gutiérrez Mariscal (33/2)], Roger Suárez (22/6). Trainer: Nelson Bonifacio Acosta López (4).
**Goal:** Juan Manuel Peña Montaño (89).

**328.** 15.11.2003 **ARGENTINA - BOLIVIA** **3-0(0-0)** 18th FIFA WC. Qualifiers

Estadio Monumental „Antonio Vespucio Liberti“, Buenos Aires; Referee: Gilberto Hidalgo Zamora (Peru); Attendance: 30,042

**BOL:** Leonardo Fernández (3/0), Juan Carlos Paz García (14/0), Luis Gatty Ribeiro Roca (22/0), Óscar Carmelo Sánchez (67/5), Álvaro Ricaldi (4/1), Ronald Raldes Balcázar (11/0), Miguel Raúl Justiniano Abella (24/1), Leonel Alfredo Reyes Saravia (2/0), Roger Suárez (23/6) [69.Marco Antonio Etcheverry (71/13)], Miguel Ángel Mercado (8/1) [64.José Alfredo Castillo Parada (11/1)], Joaquín Botero Vaca (21/9) [64.Limberg Méndez Justiniano (4/1)]. Trainer: Nelson Bonifacio Acosta López (5).

**329.** 18.11.2003 **VENEZUELA - BOLIVIA** **2-1(0-0)** 18th FIFA WC. Qualifiers

Estadio "José 'Pachenco' Romero", Maracaibo; Referee: Mauricio Reinoso Fabara (Ecuador); Attendance: 30,000

**BOL:** Leonardo Fernández (4/0), Juan Carlos Paz García (15/0), Luis Gatty Ribeiro Roca (23/0), Ronald Raldes Balcázar (12/0) [80.Marco Antonio Sandy Sansusty (93/6)], Óscar Carmelo Sánchez (68/5), Lorgio Álvarez Roca (12/0), Miguel Raúl Justiniano Abella (25/1), Leonel Alfredo Reyes Saravia (3/0), Roger Suárez (24/6) [70.Limberg Méndez Justiniano (5/1)], Miguel Ángel Mercado (9/1) [65.Joselito Vaca Velasco (11/0)], Joaquín Botero Vaca (22/10). Trainer: Nelson Bonifacio Acosta López (6).

**Goal:** Joaquín Botero Vaca (60).

**330.** 30.03.2004 **BOLIVIA - CHILE** **0-2(0-1)** 18th FIFA WC. Qualifiers

Estadio „Hernándo Siles Zuazo“, La Paz; Referee: Claudio Mario Martín (Argentina); Attendance: 40,000

**BOL:** José Carlos Fernández (25/0), Óscar Carmelo Sánchez (69/5), Limbert Pizarro Vaca (1/0), Juan Manuel Peña Montaño (73/1), Danner Jesús Pachi Bozo (1/0), Leonel Alfredo Reyes Saravia (4/0) [62.Joselito Vaca Velasco (12/0)], Carmelo Angulo (1/0), Alex Da Rosa (1/0), José Alfredo Castillo Parada (12/1), Joaquín Botero Vaca (23/10) [46.Limberg Méndez Justiniano (6/1)], Roger Suárez (25/6) [46.Luis Gatty Ribeiro Roca (24/0)]. Trainer: Nelson Bonifacio Acosta López (7).

**331.** 01.06.2004 **BOLIVIA - PARAGUAY** **2-1(1-1)** 18th FIFA WC. Qualifiers

Estadio „Hernándo Siles Zuazo“, La Paz; Referee: Márcio Rezende de Freitas (Brazil); Attendance: 23,013

**BOL:** Leonardo Fernández (5/0), Luis Gatty Ribeiro Roca (25/0) [90.Hernán Soliz (1/0)], Ronald Raldes Balcázar (13/0), Sergio Jáuregui (1/0), Lorgio Álvarez Roca (13/0) [60.Roger Suárez (26/7)], Óscar Carmelo Sánchez (70/5), Julio César Baldivieso (82/15), Juan Manuel Peña Montaño (74/1) [*sent off 69*], Luis Héctor Cristaldo (84/4), Joaquín Botero Vaca (24/10), Limberg Gutiérrez Mariscal (34/2) [86.Carmelo Angulo (2/0)]. Trainer: Ramiro Blacutt Rodríguez (28).

**Goals:** Luis Héctor Cristaldo (8), Roger Suárez (71).

**332.** 05.06.2004 **ECUADOR - BOLIVIA** **3-2(3-0)** 18th FIFA WC. Qualifiers

Estadio Olímpico „Atahualpa“, Quito; Referee: Gustavo Brand (Venezuela); Attendance: 30,020

**BOL:** Leonardo Fernández (6/0), Hernán Soliz (2/0) [46.Luis Gatty Ribeiro Roca (26/0)], Ronald Raldes Balcázar (14/0), Sergio Jáuregui (2/0), Lorgio Álvarez Roca (14/0), Óscar Carmelo Sánchez (71/5), Julio César Baldivieso (83/15), Carmelo Angulo (3/0) [46.Gonzalo Germán Galindo Sánchez (25/1)], Limberg Gutiérrez Mariscal (35/3), Roger Suárez (27/7) [67.José Alfredo Castillo Parada (13/2)], Joaquín Botero Vaca (25/10). Trainer: Ramiro Blacutt Rodríguez (29).

**Goals:** Limberg Gutiérrez Mariscal (58), José Alfredo Castillo Parada (75).

**333.** 06.07.2004 **PERU - BOLIVIA** **2-2(0-1)** 41st Copa América. Group Stage

Estadio Nacional „José Díaz“, Lima; Referee: Héctor Baldassi (Argentina); Attendance: 45,000

**BOL:** Leonardo Fernández (7/0), Sergio Jáuregui (3/0), Ronald Raldes Balcázar (15/0), Ronald Arana (11/0), Lorgio Álvarez Roca (15/1), Rubén Darío Tufiño (29/1), Limbert Pizarro Vaca (2/0) [85.Juan Carlos Arce Justiniano (1/0)], Limberg Gutiérrez Mariscal (36/3) [63.Gonzalo Germán Galindo Sánchez (26/1)], Luis Héctor Cristaldo (85/4), Miguel Ángel Mercado (10/1) [73.Richard José Rojas Gúzman (19/0)], Joaquín Botero Vaca (26/11). Trainer: Ramiro Blacutt Rodríguez (30).

**Goals:** Joaquín Botero Vaca (36), Lorgio Álvarez Roca (57).

**334.** 09.07.2004 **COLOMBIA - BOLIVIA** **1-0(0-0)** 41st Copa América. Group Stage

Estadio Nacional „José Díaz“, Lima (Peru); Referee: Pedro Ramos (Uruguay); Attendance: 35,000

**BOL:** Leonardo Fernández (8/0), Sergio Jáuregui (4/0), Ronald Raldes Balcázar (16/0), Ronald Arana (12/0), Lorgio Álvarez Roca (16/1), Rubén Darío Tufiño (30/1), Limbert Pizarro Vaca (3/0), Limberg Gutiérrez Mariscal (37/3), Luis Héctor Cristaldo (86/4) [35.Wálter Alberto Flores Condarco (1/0)], Miguel Ángel Mercado (11/1) [65.Roger Suárez (28/7)], Joaquín Botero Vaca (27/11). Trainer: Ramiro Blacutt Rodríguez (31).

**335.** 12.07.2004 **BOLIVIA - VENEZUELA** **1-1(1-1)** 41st Copa América. Group Stage

Estadio Mansiche, Trujillo (Peru); Referee: William Mattus (Costa Rica); Attendance: 25,000

**BOL:** Leonardo Fernández (9/0), Sergio Jáuregui (5/0), Ronald Raldes Balcázar (17/0), Ronald Arana (13/0), Lorgio Álvarez Roca (17/1), Gonzalo Germán Galindo Sánchez (27/2), Limberg Gutiérrez Mariscal (38/3), Limbert Pizarro Vaca (4/0) [22.Rubén Darío Tufiño (31/1)], Miguel Ángel Mercado (12/1) [60.Juan Carlos Arce Justiniano (2/0)], Joaquín Botero Vaca (28/11), Roger Suárez (29/7) [71.Wálter Alberto Flores Condarco (2/0)]. Trainer: Ramiro Blacutt Rodríguez (32).

**Goal:** Gonzalo Germán Galindo Sánchez (33).

**336.** 05.09.2004 **BRAZIL - BOLIVIA** **3-1(3-0)** 18th FIFA WC. Qualifiers

Estádio Morumbí, São Paulo; Referee: Héctor Baldassi (Argentina); Attendance: 56,099

**BOL:** Leonardo Fernández (10/0), Luis Gatty Ribeiro Roca (27/0) [46.Ronald Arana (14/0)], Ronald Raldes Balcázar (18/0), Juan Manuel Peña Montaño (75/1), Lorgio Álvarez Roca (18/1), Óscar Carmelo Sánchez (72/5), Limbert Pizarro Vaca (5/0), Luis Héctor Cristaldo (87/5), Percy Colque Paredes (17/2) [46.Rubén Darío Tufiño (32/1)], Joaquín Botero Vaca (29/11), Limberg Gutiérrez Mariscal (39/3) [77.Milton Coimbra Suizer (39/7)]. Trainer: Ramiro Blacutt Rodríguez (33).

**Goal:** Luis Héctor Cristaldo (49).

**337.** 09.10.2004 **BOLIVIA - PERU** **1-0(0-0)** 18th FIFA WC. Qualifiers

Estadio „Hernándo Siles Zuazo“, La Paz; Referee: Mauricio Reynoso (Ecuador); Attendance: 23,729

**BOL:** Leonardo Fernández (11/0), Luis Gatty Ribeiro Roca (28/0) [*sent off 82*], Ronald Raldes Balcázar (19/0), Ronald Arana (15/0), Percy Colque Paredes (18/2), Erwin Sánchez (54/15) [86.Rubén Darío Tufiño (33/1)], Óscar Carmelo Sánchez (73/5), Ronald Lázaro García Justiniano (14/0), Luis Héctor Cristaldo (88/5), Limberg Gutiérrez Mariscal (40/3) [90.Gonzalo Germán Galindo Sánchez (28/2)], Joaquín Botero Vaca (30/12). Trainer: Ramiro Blacutt Rodríguez (34).

**Goal:** Joaquín Botero Vaca (56).

**338.** 12.10.2004 **BOLIVIA - URUGUAY** **0-0** 18th FIFA WC. Qualifiers

Estadio „Hernándo Siles Zuazo“, La Paz; Referee: Márcio Rezende de Freitas (Brazil); Attendance: 24,349

**BOL:** Leonardo Fernández (12/0), Marcelo Antonio Carballo Cadima (9/1) [65.Percy Colque Paredes (19/2)], Ronald Raldes Balcázar (20/0), Ronald Arana (16/0), Lorgio Álvarez Roca (19/1) [76.Gonzalo Germán Galindo Sánchez (29/2)], Ronald Lázaro García Justiniano (15/0) [46.Diego Aroldo Cabrera Flores (2/0)], Erwin Sánchez (55/15), Óscar Carmelo Sánchez (74/5), Luis Héctor Cristaldo (89/5), Joaquín Botero Vaca (31/12), Limberg Gutiérrez Mariscal (41/3). Trainer: Ramiro Blacutt Rodríguez (35).

**339.** 13.11.2004 **GUATEMALA - BOLIVIA** **1-0(1-0)**

"Robert F. Kennedy" Memorial Stadium, Washington (United States); Referee: Arkadiusz Prus (United States); Attendance: 18,000

**BOL:** Leonardo Fernández (13/0), Sergio Jáuregui (6/0), Limbert Pizarro Vaca (6/0), Ronald Arana (17/0), Lorgio Álvarez Roca (20/1), Rubén Darío Tufiño (34/1) [42.Richard José Rojas Gúzman (20/0)], Getulio Vaca Diez (1/0), Limberg Gutiérrez Mariscal (42/3), Luis Héctor Cristaldo (90/5) [46.Gonzalo Germán Galindo Sánchez (30/2)], Juan Carlos Arce Justiniano (3/0), Milton Coimbra Suizer (40/7). Trainer: Ramiro Blacutt Rodríguez (36).

**340.** 17.11.2004 **COLOMBIA - BOLIVIA** **1-0(1-0)** 18th FIFA WC. Qualifiers

Estadio Metropolitano „Roberto Meléndez“, Barranquilla; Referee: Carlos Torres (Paraguay); Attendance: 25,000

**BOL:** Leonardo Fernández (14/0), Sergio Jáuregui (7/0), Ronald Raldes Balcázar (21/0), Ronald Arana (18/0), Lorgio Álvarez Roca (21/1), Rubén Darío Tufiño (35/1) [76.Getulio Vaca Diez (2/0)], Limberg Gutiérrez Mariscal (43/3), Juan Manuel Peña Montaño (76/1) [80.Juan Carlos Arce Justiniano (4/0)], Luis Héctor Cristaldo (91/5), Joaquín Botero Vaca (32/12), Milton Coimbra Suizer (41/7) [46.Gonzalo Germán Galindo Sánchez (31/2)]. Trainer: Ramiro Blacutt Rodríguez (37).

**341.** 26.03.2005 **BOLIVIA - ARGENTINA** **1-2(0-0)** 18th FIFA WC. Qualifiers

Estadio „Hernándo Siles Zuazo“, La Paz; Referee: Jorge Larrionda Pietrafiesa (Uruguay); Attendance: 22,000

**BOL:** Leonardo Fernández (15/0), Lorgio Álvarez Roca (22/1), Ronald Raldes Balcázar (22/0), Óscar Carmelo Sánchez (75/5), Percy Colque Paredes (20/2) [46.Danner Jesús Pachi Bozo (2/0)], Carmelo Angulo (4/0) [69.Diego Aroldo Cabrera Flores (3/0)], Limbert Pizarro Vaca (7/0), Gonzalo Germán Galindo Sánchez (32/2) [85.Ronald Lázaro García Justiniano (16/0)], Erwin Sánchez (56/15), Joaquín Botero Vaca (33/12), José Alfredo Castillo Parada (14/3). Trainer: Mario Ovidio Mezza Soruco (1).

**Goal:** José Alfredo Castillo Parada (49).

**342.** 29.03.2005 **BOLIVIA - VENEZUELA** **3-1(2-0)** 18th FIFA WC. Qualifiers

Estadio „Hernándo Siles Zuazo“, La Paz; Referee: Eduardo Lecca (Peru); Attendance: 15,000

**BOL:** Leonardo Fernández (16/0), Sergio Jáuregui (8/0), Ronald Raldes Balcázar (23/0), Óscar Carmelo Sánchez (76/5), Lorgio Álvarez Roca (23/1), Limbert Pizarro Vaca (8/0), Gonzalo Germán Galindo Sánchez (33/2), Ronald Lázaro García Justiniano (17/0) [21.Joselito Vaca Velasco (13/1)], Erwin Sánchez (57/15) [80.Danner Jesús Pachi Bozo (3/0)], José Alfredo Castillo Parada (15/4) [59.Diego Aroldo Cabrera Flores (4/0)], Joaquín Botero Vaca (34/12). Trainer: Mario Ovidio Mezza Soruco (2).

**Goals:** Alejandro Cichero (2 own goal), José Alfredo Castillo Parada (26), Joselito Vaca Velasco (83).

**343.** 04.06.2005 **CHILE - BOLIVIA** **3-1(2-0)** 18th FIFA WC. Qualifiers

Estadio Nacional, Santiago; Referee: Referee: Márcio Rezende de Freitas (Brazil)); Attendance: 46,729

**BOL:** Leonardo Fernández (17/0), Sergio Jáuregui (9/0) [80.Enrique Parada Salvatierra (1/0)], Ronald Raldes Balcázar (24/0), Ronald Arana (19/0), Danner Jesús Pachi Bozo (4/0) [46.Juan Carlos Arce Justiniano (5/0)], Lorgio Álvarez Roca (24/1), Ronald Lázaro García Justiniano (18/0) [34.Joselito Vaca Velasco (14/1)], Miguel Raúl Justiniano Abella (26/1), Limberg Gutiérrez Mariscal (44/3), Milton Coimbra Suizer (42/7), José Alfredo Castillo Parada (16/5). Trainer: Mario Ovidio Mezza Soruco (3).

**Goal:** José Alfredo Castillo Parada (83 penalty).

**344.** 08.06.2005 **PARAGUAY - BOLIVIA** **4-1(1-1)** 18th FIFA WC. Qualifiers

Estadio Defensores del Chaco, Asunción; Referee: Gustavo Brand (Venezuela); Attendance: 12,000

**BOL:** Sergio Daniel Galarza Solíz (2/0), Wálter Alberto Flores Condarco (3/0), Ronald Raldes Balcázar (25/0), Sergio Jáuregui (10/0), Lorgio Álvarez Roca (25/1), Edward Mauro Zenteno Álvarez (1/0), Gualberto Mojica Olmos (4/0) [78.Joselito Vaca Velasco (15/1)], Gonzalo Germán Galindo Sánchez (34/3), Limberg Gutiérrez Mariscal (45/3), Enrique Parada Salvatierra (2/0) [46.Milton Coimbra Suizer (43/7)], José Alfredo Castillo Parada (17/5) [65.Juan Carlos Arce Justiniano (6/0)]. Trainer: Mario Ovidio Mezza Soruco (4).

**Goal:** Gonzalo Germán Galindo Sánchez (30).

**345.** 03.09.2005 **BOLIVIA - ECUADOR** **1-2(1-1)** 18th FIFA WC. Qualifiers

Estadio „Hernándo Siles Zuazo“, La Paz; Referee: Héctor Walter Baldassi (Argentina); Attendance: 11,000

**BOL:** Carlos Erwin Arias Égüez (10/0), Doyle Vaca (2/1), Ronald Raldes Balcázar (26/0), Sergio Jáuregui (11/0), Danner Jesús Pachi Bozo (5/0) [54.Joselito Vaca Velasco (16/1)], Lorgio Álvarez Roca (26/1), Wálter Alberto Flores Condarco (4/0) [66.Juan Carlos Arce Justiniano (7/0)], Alejandro Jesús Gómez (1/0), Gonzalo Germán Galindo Sánchez (35/3), Limberg Méndez Justiniano (7/1) [54.Líder Paz Colodro (19/3)], Joaquín Botero Vaca (35/12). Trainer: Mario Ovidio Mezza Soruco (5).

**Goal:** Doyle Vaca (41).

**346.** 09.10.2005 **BOLIVIA - BRAZIL** **1-1(0-1)** 18th FIFA WC. Qualifiers

Estadio „Hernándo Siles Zuazo“, La Paz; Referee: Jorge Larrionda Pietrafiesa (Uruguay); Attendance: 22,725

**BOL:** Carlos Erwin Arias Égüez (11/0), Sergio Jáuregui (12/0), Doyle Vaca (3/1), Ronald Raldes Balcázar (27/0), Miguel Ángel Hoyos Guzmán (6/0) [46.Danner Jesús Pachi Bozo (6/0)], Carmelo Angulo (5/0), Luis Héctor Cristaldo (92/5), Julio César Baldivieso (84/15), Gonzalo Germán Galindo Sánchez (36/3), Limberg Gutiérrez Mariscal (46/3) [46.José Alfredo Castillo Parada (18/6)], Joaquín Botero Vaca (36/12) [76.Líder Paz Colodro (20/3)]. Trainer: Mario Ovidio Mezza Soruco (6).

**Goal:** José Alfredo Castillo Parada (50).

**347.** 12.10.2005 **PERU - BOLIVIA** **4-1(3-0)** 18th FIFA WC. Qualifiers

Estadio Modelo "Jorge Basarde", Tacna; Referee: Oscar Sequeira (Argentina); Attendance: 14,744

**BOL:** Carlos Erwin Arias Égüez (12/0), Doyle Vaca (4/1), Danner Jesús Pachi Bozo (7/0), Ronald Raldes Balcázar (28/0), Sergio Jáuregui (13/0), Alejandro Jesús Gómez (2/0) [63.Líder Paz Colodro (21/3)], Gonzalo Germán Galindo Sánchez (37/3) [83.Joselito Vaca Velasco (17/1)], José Alfredo Castillo Parada (19/6), Carmelo Angulo (6/0), Julio César Baldivieso (85/15) [46.Limberg Gutiérrez Mariscal (47/4) [*sent off 74*], Joaquín Botero Vaca (37/12). Trainer: Mario Ovidio Mezza Soruco (7).

**Goal:** Limberg Gutiérrez Mariscal (41).

**348.** 15.11.2006 **BOLIVIA – EL SALVADOR** **5-1(3-0)**
Estadio „Hernándo Siles Zuazo", La Paz; Referee: René Marcelo Ortubé Betancourt (Bolivia); Attendance: 25,000
**BOL:** Sergio Daniel Galarza Solíz (3/0) [Hugo Suárez Vaca (3/0)], Nicolás Suárez Vaca (2/0), Óscar Carmelo Sánchez (77/6), Luis Javier Méndez Moza (1/0), Pedro Zabala (1/0), Leonel Alfredo Reyes Saravia (5/1) [Wálter Alberto Flores Condarco (5/0)], Sacha Silvestro Lima Castedo (1/0) [Carmelo Angulo (1/0)], Joselito Vaca Velasco (18/1) [Danner Jesús Pachi Bozo (8/0)], Gonzalo Germán Galindo Sánchez (38/3) [Darwin Peña Arce (6/1)], Juan Carlos Arce Justiniano (8/1), Nelson Sossa Chávez (1/1) [Pablo Antonio Salinas Menacho (1/0)]. Trainer: Erwin Sánchez Freking (1).
**Goals:** Nelson Sossa Chávez (29), Juan Carlos Arce Justiniano (33), Óscar Carmelo Sánchez (41), Leonel Alfredo Reyes Saravia (82), Darwin Peña Arce (90).

**349.** 28.03.2007 **SOUTH AFRICA - BOLIVIA** **0-1(0-1)**
First National Bank Stadium, Johannesburg; Referee: Tebogo Ramocha (Botswana); Attendance: 5,000
**BOL:** Sergio Daniel Galarza Solíz (4/0), Juan Manuel Peña Montaño (77/1) [71.Ronald Arana (20/0)], Limbert Méndez Rocha (1/0), Lorgio Álvarez Roca (27/1), Miguel Ángel Hoyos Guzmán (7/0), Ronald Lázaro García Justiniano (19/0), Gualberto Mojica Olmos (5/0), Joselito Vaca Velasco (19/2) [76.Sacha Silvestro Lima Castedo (2/0)], Gonzalo Germán Galindo Sánchez (39/3) [87.Jorge Antonio Ortíz (1/0)], Pablo Antonio Salinas Menacho (2/0) [63.Gustavo Pinedo (1/0)], Nelson Sossa Chávez (2/1). Trainer: Erwin Sánchez Freking (2).
**Goal:** Joselito Vaca Velasco (19).

**350.** 26.05.2007 **BOLIVIA – REPUBLIC OF IRELAND** **1-1(1-1)**
Gillette Stadium, Foxboro (United States); Referee: n/a; Attendance: n/a
**BOL:** Hugo Suárez Vaca (4/0), Miguel Ángel Hoyos Guzmán (8/1), Juan Manuel Peña Montaño (78/1), Lorgio Álvarez Roca (28/1), Ronald Lázaro García Justiniano (20/0) [61.Sacha Silvestro Lima Castedo (3/0)], Gualberto Mojica Olmos (6/0), Leonel Alfredo Reyes Saravia (6/1) [82.Limbert Pizarro Vaca (9/0)], Joselito Vaca Velasco (20/2) [74.Gonzalo Germán Galindo Sánchez (40/3)], Limbert Méndez Rocha (2/0), Jaime Moreno Morales (63/7) [46.Diego Aroldo Cabrera Flores (5/0)], Juan Carlos Arce Justiniano (9/1) [69.Gustavo Pinedo (2/0)]. Trainer: Erwin Sánchez Freking (3).
**Goal:** Miguel Ángel Hoyos Guzmán (14).

**351.** 20.06.2007 **BOLIVIA - PARAGUAY** **0-0** Copa Paz del Chaco
Estadio „Ramón 'Tahuichi' Aguilera", Santa Cruz de la Sierra; Referee: Joaquín Antequera (Bolivia); Attendance: 31,000
**BOL:** Sergio Daniel Galarza Solíz (5/0), Miguel Ángel Hoyos Guzmán (9/1), Ronald Raldes Balcázar (Cap) (29/0), Limbert Méndez Rocha (3/0) [66.Edemir Rodríguez Mercado (1/0)], Lorgio Álvarez Roca (29/1), Leonel Alfredo Reyes Saravia (7/1), Gualberto Mojica Olmos (7/0) [75.Sacha Silvestro Lima Castedo (4/0)], Jhasmani Campos Dávalos (1/0) [46.Darwin Peña Arce (7/1)], Joselito Vaca Velasco (21/2) [81.Gonzalo Germán Galindo Sánchez (41/3)], Jaime Moreno Morales (64/7) [59.Diego Aroldo Cabrera Flores (6/0); 86.Augusto Andaveris Iriondo (8/1)], Juan Carlos Arce Justiniano (10/1) [60.Nelson Sossa Chávez (3/1)]. Trainer: Erwin Sánchez Freking (4).

**352.** 26.06.2007 **VENEZUELA - BOLIVIA** **2-2(1-1)** 42nd Copa América. Group Stage
Estadio Polideportivo de Pueblo Nuevo, San Cristóbal (Venezuela); Referee: Mauricio Reinoso (Ecuador); Attendance: 42,000
**BOL:** Sergio Daniel Galarza Solíz (6/0), Miguel Ángel Hoyos Guzmán (10/1), Ronald Raldes Balcázar (30/0), Juan Manuel Peña Montaño (Cap) (79/1), Lorgio Álvarez Roca (30/1), Ronald Lázaro García Justiniano (21/0), Leonel Alfredo Reyes Saravia (8/1) [60.Darwin Peña Arce (8/1)], Gualberto Mojica Olmos (8/0), Joselito Vaca Velasco (22/2) [71.Gonzalo Germán Galindo Sánchez (42/3)], Juan Carlos Arce Justiniano (11/2), Jaime Moreno Morales (65/8) [74.Diego Aroldo Cabrera Flores (7/0)]. Trainer: Erwin Sánchez Freking (5).
**Goals:** Jaime Moreno Morales (39), Juan Carlos Arce Justiniano (84).

**353.** 30.06.2007 **URUGUAY - BOLIVIA** **1-0(0-0)** 42nd Copa América. Group Stage
Estadio Polideportivo de Pueblo Nuevo, San Cristóbal (Venezuela); Referee: Baldomero Toledo (United States); Attendance: 18,000
**BOL:** Sergio Daniel Galarza Solíz (7/0), Miguel Ángel Hoyos Guzmán (11/1), Ronald Raldes Balcázar (31/0), Juan Manuel Peña Montaño (Cap) (80/1), Lorgio Álvarez Roca (31/1), Ronald Lázaro García Justiniano (22/0) [29.Sacha Silvestre Lima Saucedo (5/0)], Leonel Alfredo Reyes Saravia (9/1) [71.Darwin Peña Arce (9/1)], Gualberto Mojica Olmos (9/0), Joselito Vaca Velasco (23/2) [62.Diego Aroldo Cabrera Flores (8/0)], Juan Carlos Arce Justiniano (12/2), Jaime Moreno Morales (66/8). Trainer: Erwin Sánchez Freking (6).

**354.** 03.07.2007 **BOLIVIA - PERU** **2-2(2-1)** 42nd Copa América. Group Stage
Estadio Metropolitano, Mérida (Venezuela); Referee: Carlos Luis Chandía Alarcón (Chile); Attendance: 35,000
**BOL:** Hugo Suárez Vaca (5/0), Miguel Ángel Hoyos Guzmán (12/1), Ronald Raldes Balcázar (32/0), Juan Manuel Peña Montaño (Cap) (81/1), Lorgio Álvarez Roca (32/1), Gualberto Mojica Olmos (10/0) [80.Jorge Antonio Ortíz (2/0)], Leonel Alfredo Reyes Saravia (10/1), Jhasmani Campos Dávalos (2/1) [67.Gonzalo Germán Galindo Sánchez (43/3)], Joselito Vaca Velasco (24/2), Augusto Andaveris Iriondo (9/1) [57.Juan Carlos Arce Justiniano (13/2)], Jaime Moreno Morales (67/9). Trainer: Erwin Sánchez Freking (7).
**Goals:** Jaime Moreno Morales (24), Jhasmani Campos Dávalos (45)

**355.** 22.08.2007 **ECUADOR - BOLIVIA** **1-0(1-0)**
Estadio Olímpico „Atahualpa", Quito; Referee: Alberto Duarte (Colombia); Attendance: 18,000
**BOL:** Sergio Daniel Galarza Solíz (8/0), Miguel Ángel Hoyos Guzmán (13/1), Ronald Raldes Balcázar (Cap) (33/0), Limbert Méndez Rocha (4/0), Pedro Zabala (2/0), Gualberto Mojica Olmos (11/0) [79.Sacha Silvestro Lima Castedo (6/0)], Leonel Alfredo Reyes Saravia (11/1) [57.Darwin Peña Arce (10/1)], Jhasmani Campos Dávalos (3/1) [46.Ronald Lázaro García Justiniano (23/0)], Joselito Vaca Velasco (25/2) [81.Nicolás Suárez Vaca (3/0)], Augusto Andaveris Iriondo (10/1) [68.Carlos Enrique Saucedo Urgel (1/0)], Juan Carlos Arce Justiniano (14/2) [46.Enrique Parada Salvatierra (3/0)]. Trainer: Erwin Sánchez Freking (8).

**356.** 12.09.2007 **PERU - BOLIVIA** **2-0(2-0)**
Estadio Monumental, Lima; Referee: Víctor Hugo Rivera (Peru); Attendance: 20,000
**BOL:** Hugo Suárez Vaca (6/0), Miguel Ángel Hoyos Guzmán (14/1) [56.Nicolás Suárez Vaca (4/0)], Ronald Raldes Balcázar (Cap) (34/0), Edemir Rodríguez Mercado (2/0), Lorgio Álvarez Roca (33/1), Gualberto Mojica Olmos (12/0) [65.Sacha Silvestro Lima Castedo (7/0)], Ronald Lázaro García Justiniano (24/0) [77.Alejandro Jesús Gómez (3/0)], Darwin Peña Arce (11/1) [46.Jhasmani Campos Dávalos (4/1)], Joselito Vaca Velasco (26/2), Jaime Moreno Morales (68/9) [61.Augusto Andaveris Iriondo (11/1)], Marcelo Moreno Martins (1/0) [76.Carlos Enrique Saucedo Urgel (2/0)]. Trainer: Erwin Sánchez Freking (9).

**357.** 13.10.2007 **URUGUAY - BOLIVIA** **5-0(2-0)** 19th FIFA WC. Qualifiers
Estadio Centenario, Montevideo; Referee: Rubén Selmán Albornoz (Chile); Attendance: 25,200
**BOL:** Sergio Daniel Galarza Solíz (9/0), Miguel Ángel Hoyos Guzmán (15/1) [75.Nicolás Suárez Vaca (5/0)], Ronald Raldes Balcázar (Cap) (35/0), Santos Amador Quispe (1/0), Lorgio Álvarez Roca (34/1), Sacha Silvestro Lima Castedo (8/0), Hermán Solíz Salvatierra (1/0) [46.Diego Aroldo Cabrera Flores (9/0)], Ronald Lázaro García Justiniano (25/0) [*sent off 42*], Joselito Vaca Velasco (27/2), Jaime Moreno Morales (69/9) [59.Jaime Cardozo (1/0)], Marcelo Moreno Martins (2/0). Trainer: Erwin Sánchez Freking (10).

**358.** 17.10.2007 **BOLIVIA - COLOMBIA** **0-0** 19th FIFA WC. Qualifiers

Estadio „Hernándo Siles Zuazo", La Paz; Referee: Mauricio Reinoso Fabara (Ecuador); Attendance: 19,469

**BOL:** Sergio Daniel Galarza Solíz (10/0), Luis Gatty Ribeiro Roca (29/0), Ronald Raldes Balcázar (Cap) (36/0), Santos Amador Quispe (2/0), Ricardo Verdúguez (1/0), Gualberto Mojica Olmos (13/0), Leonel Alfredo Reyes Saravia (12/1) [*sent off 69*], Jhasmani Campos Dávalos (5/1) [46.Joselito Vaca Velasco (28/2)], Limberg Gutiérrez Mariscal (48/4), Augusto Andaveris Iriondo (12/1) [55.Diego Aroldo Cabrera Flores (10/0)], Juan Carlos Arce Justiniano (15/2) [72.Ronald Gutiérrez Flores (1/0)]. Trainer: Erwin Sánchez Freking (11).

**359.** 17.11.2007 **ARGENTINA - BOLIVIA** **3-0(1-0)** 19th FIFA WC. Qualifiers

Estadio Monumental „Antonio Vespucio Liberti", Buenos Aires; Referee: Víctor Hugo Rivera (Peru); Attendance: 43,308

**BOL:** Carlos Erwin Arias Égüez (13/0), Miguel Ángel Hoyos Guzmán (16/1), Ronald Raldes Balcázar (Cap) (37/0), Limbert Méndez Rocha (5/0), Luis Alberto Gutiérrez Herrera (1/0), Ronald Lázaro García Justiniano (26/0), Nicolás Suárez Vaca (6/0), Limberg Gutiérrez Mariscal (49/4) [61.Juan Carlos Arce Justiniano (16/2)], Joselito Vaca Velasco (29/2), Jaime Moreno Morales (70/9) [60.Ronald Gutiérrez Flores (2/0)], Diego Aroldo Cabrera Flores (11/0) [79.Marcelo Moreno Martins (3/0)]. Trainer: Erwin Sánchez Freking (12).

**360.** 20.11.2007 **VENEZUELA - BOLIVIA** **5-3(2-2)** 19th FIFA WC. Qualifiers

Estadio Polideportivo de Pueblo Nuevo, San Cristóbal; Referee: Sálvio Fagundes Filho (Brazil); Attendance: 24,000

**BOL:** Carlos Erwin Arias Égüez (14/0), Luis Gatty Ribeiro Roca (30/0), Ronald Raldes Balcázar (Cap) (38/0), Limbert Méndez Rocha (6/0), Luis Alberto Gutiérrez Herrera (2/0), Ronald Lázaro García Justiniano (27/0), Alejandro Jesús Gómez (4/0), Gualberto Mojica Olmos (14/0) [70.Limberg Gutiérrez Mariscal (50/4)], Joselito Vaca Velasco (30/2) [46.Sacha Silvestro Lima Castedo (9/0)], Juan Carlos Arce Justiniano (17/3), Marcelo Moreno Martins (4/2) [82.Jaime Moreno Morales (71/9)]. Trainer: Erwin Sánchez Freking (13).

**Goals:** Marcelo Moreno Martins (19), Juan Carlos Arce Justiniano (27), Marcelo Moreno Martins (78).

**361.** 06.02.2008 **BOLIVIA - PERU** **2-1(0-0)**

Estadio „Hernándo Siles Zuazo", La Paz; Referee: René Ortube Betancourt (Bolivia); Attendance: 35,000

**BOL:** Sergio Daniel Galarza Solíz (11/0), Abdón Reyes Cardozo (1/0), Ronald Raldes Balcázar (Cap) (39/0), Leonel Alfredo Reyes Saravia (13/2), Rolando Rivera (1/0) [54.Jaime Cardozo (2/0)], Danner Jesús Pachi Bozo (9/0) [62.Mauricio Saucedo Guardia (1/0)], Limberg Gutiérrez Mariscal (51/4) [79.Nelson Sossa Chávez (4/1)], Limbert Méndez Rocha (7/0), Enrique Parada Salvatierra (4/0), Joaquín Botero Vaca (38/12) [35.Pablo Antonio Salinas Menacho (3/0)], Ricardo Pedriel Suárez (1/1) [90.Edemir Rodríguez Mercado (3/0)]. Trainer: Erwin Sánchez Freking (14).

**Goals:** Ricardo Pedriel Suárez (65), Leonel Alfredo Reyes Saravia (88).

**362.** 26.03.2008 **VENEZUELA - BOLIVIA** **0-1(0-0)**

Estadio"General José Antonio Anzoátegui", Puerto La Cruz; Referee: José Buitrago (Colombia); Attendance: 16,000

**BOL:** Sergio Daniel Galarza Solíz (12/0) [46.José Carlos Fernández (26/0)], Miguel Ángel Hoyos Guzmán (17/1), Limbert Méndez Rocha (8/0), Ronald Raldes Balcázar (Cap) (40/0), Limberg Gutiérrez Mariscal (52/4), Leonel Alfredo Reyes Saravia (14/2), Jhasmani Campos Dávalos (6/1) [46.Lorgio Álvarez Rocha (35/1)], Gualberto Mojica Olmos (15/0) [56.Sacha Silvestro Lima Castedo (10/0)], Joselito Vaca Velasco (31/2) [77.Mauricio Saucedo Guardia (2/0)], Joaquín Botero Vaca (39/12) [80.Ricardo Pedriel Suárez (2/1)], Marcelo Moreno Martins (5/2). Trainer: Erwin Sánchez Freking (15).

**Goal:** Gabriel Cichero Konarek (80 own goal).

**363.** 15.06.2008 **BOLIVIA - CHILE** **0-2(0-1)** 19th FIFA WC. Qualifiers

Estadio „Hernándo Siles Zuazo", La Paz; Referee: Victor Hugo Rivera (Peru); Attendance: 27,722

**BOL:** Sergio Daniel Galarza Solíz (13/0), Miguel Ángel Hoyos Guzmán (18/1) [78.Mauricio Saucedo Guardia (3/0)], Ronald Raldes Balcázar (41/0), Luis Alberto Gutiérrez Herrera (3/0), Abdón Reyes Cardozo (2/0), Leonel Alfredo Reyes Saravia (15/2), Lorgio Álvarez Roca (36/1) [46.Luis Gatty Ribeiro Roca (31/0)], Jhasmani Campos Dávalos (7/1) [65.Joaquín Botero Vaca (40/12)], Limberg Gutiérrez Mariscal (53/4), Juan Carlos Arce Justiniano (18/3), Marcelo Moreno Martins (6/2). Trainer: Erwin Sánchez Freking (16).

**364.** 18.06.2008 **BOLIVIA - PARAGUAY** **4-2(2-0)** 19th FIFA WC. Qualifiers

Estadio „Hernándo Siles Zuazo", La Paz; Referee: Leonardo Gaciba da Silva (Brazil); Attendance: 8,561

**BOL:** Carlos Erwin Arias Égüez (15/0), Leonel Alfredo Reyes Saravia (16/2), Ronald Raldes Balcázar (42/0), Luis Alberto Gutiérrez Herrera (4/0), Abdón Reyes Cardozo (3/0) [67.Ronald Taylor Rivero Khun (1/0)], Luis Gatty Ribeiro Roca (32/0), Ronald Lázaro García Justiniano (28/1) [46.Ronald Gutiérrez Flores (3/0)], Didí Torrico Camacho (1/0), Joselito Vaca Velasco (32/2), Marcelo Moreno Martins (7/3), Joaquín Botero Vaca (41/14) [73.Mauricio Saucedo Guardia (4/0)]. Trainer: Erwin Sánchez Freking (17).

**Goals:** Joaquín Botero Vaca (23), Ronald Lázaro García Justiniano (25), Joaquín Botero Vaca (70), Marcelo Moreno Martins (76).

**365.** 06.08.2008 **GUATEMALA - BOLIVIA** **3-0(0-0)**

"Robert F. Kennedy" Memorial Stadium, Washington D.C. (United States); Referee: n/a; Attendance: 15,000

**BOL:** Hugo Suárez Vaca (7/0), Luis Gatty Ribeiro Roca (33/0), Limbert Méndez Rocha (9/0), Ronald Taylor Rivero Khun (2/0), Luis Alberto Gutiérrez Herrera (5/0), Didí Torrico Camacho (2/0) [46.Danner Jesús Pachi Bozo (10/0)], Jaime Robles Céspedes (1/0) [82.Edgar Rolando Olivares Burgoa (6/0)], Mauricio Saucedo Guardia (5/0) [62.José Luis Chávez Sánchez (1/0)], Joselito Vaca Velasco (33/2) [52.Jaime Cardozo Tahua (1/0)], Joaquín Botero Vaca (42/14) [55.Ricardo Pedriel Suárez (3/1)], Jaime Moreno Morales (72/9) [66.Nelson Sossa Chávez (5/1)]. Trainer: Erwin Sánchez Freking (18).

**366.** 20.08.2008 **BOLIVIA - PANAMA** **1-0(0-0)**

Estadio "Ramón 'Tahuichi' Aguilera", Santa Cruz de la Sierra; Referee: Joaquín Antequera (Bolivia); Attendance: 20,000

**BOL:** Carlos Erwin Arias Égüez (16/0), Miguel Ángel Hoyos Guzmán (19/1), Ronald Taylor Rivero Khun (3/0), Limbert Méndez Rocha (10/0), Luis Alberto Gutiérrez Herrera (6/0) [46.Ignacio Awad García Justiniano (1/0)], Leonel Alfredo Reyes Saravia (17/2), Ronald Lázaro García Justiniano (29/1) [68.Mauricio Saucedo Guardia (6/0)], Didí Torrico Camacho (3/0) [68.Jhasmani Campos Dávalos (8/1)], Pablo Daniel Escobar Olivetti (1/0) [80.Jaime Robles Céspedes (2/0)], Ricardo Pedriel Suárez (4/1) [46.Joaquín Botero Vaca (43/14)], Marcelo Moreno Martins (8/3) [60.Diego Aroldo Cabrera Flores (12/1)]. Trainer: Erwin Sánchez Freking (19).

**Goal:** Diego Aroldo Cabrera Flores (78).

**367.** 06.09.2008 **ECUADOR - BOLIVIA** **3-1(1-1)** 19th FIFA WC. Qualifiers

Estadio Olímpico "Atahualpa", Quito; Referee: Pablo Antonio Pozo Quinteros (Chile); Attendance: 28,000

**BOL:** Carlos Erwin Arias Égüez (17/0), Miguel Ángel Hoyos Guzmán (20/1), Ronald Raldes Balcázar (43/0), Ronald Taylor Rivero Khun (4/0), Ignacio Awad García Justiniano (2/0), Jesús Alejandro Gómez Lanza (1/0) [*sent off 18*], Ronald Lázaro García Justiniano (30/1), Jaime Robles Céspedes (3/0), Pablo Daniel Escobar Olivetti (2/0) [67.Darwin Peña Arce (12/1)], Joselito Vaca Velasco (34/2) [88.Mauricio Saucedo Guardia (7/0)], Joaquín Botero Vaca (44/15) [64.Marcelo Moreno Martins (9/3)]. Trainer: Erwin Sánchez Freking (20).

**Goal:** Joaquín Botero Vaca (20).

**368.** 10.09.2008 **BRAZIL - BOLIVIA** **0-0** 19th FIFA WC. Qualifiers
Estádio Olímpico „João Havelange“, Rio de Janeiro; Referee: Alfredo Intriago (Ecuador); Attendance: 31,422
**BOL:** Carlos Erwin Arias Égüez (18/0), Miguel Ángel Hoyos Guzmán (21/1), Ronald Raldes Balcázar (44/0), Ronald Taylor Rivero Khun (5/0), Ignacio Awad García Justiniano (3/0), Wálter Alberto Flores Condarco (6/0), Ronald Lázaro García Justiniano (31/1), Jaime Robles Céspedes (4/0), Joselito Vaca Velasco (35/2) [89.Diego Aroldo Cabrera Flores (13/1)], Jaime Moreno Morales (73/9) [56.Luis Alberto Gutiérrez Herrera (7/0)], Marcelo Moreno Martins (10/3) [78.Pablo Daniel Escobar Olivetti (3/0)]. Trainer: Erwin Sánchez Freking (21).

**369.** 11.10.2008 **BOLIVIA - PERU** **3-0(2-0)** 19th FIFA WC. Qualifiers
Estadio „Hernándo Siles Zuazo“, La Paz; Referee: José Hernando Buitrago Arango (Colombia); Attendance: 23,147
**BOL:** Carlos Erwin Arias Égüez (19/0), Christian Israel Vargas Claros (1/0), Ronald Raldes Balcázar (45/0) [83.Luis Alberto Gutiérrez Herrera (8/0)], Ronald Taylor Rivero Khun (6/0), Abdón Reyes Cardozo (4/0), Wálter Alberto Flores Condarco (7/0), Ronald Lázaro García Justiniano (32/2), Joselito Vaca Velasco (36/2) [81.Didí Torrico Camacho (4/0)], Jaime Robles Céspedes (5/0), Joaquín Botero Vaca (45/17), Marcelo Moreno Martins (11/3) [64.Pablo Daniel Escobar Olivetti (4/0)]. Trainer: Erwin Sánchez Freking (22).
**Goals:** Joaquín Botero Vaca (3, 16), Ronald Lázaro García Justiniano (81).

**370.** 14.10.2008 **BOLIVIA - URUGUAY** **2-2(2-0)** 19th FIFA WC. Qualifiers
Estadio „Hernándo Siles Zuazo“, La Paz; Referee: Héctor Walter Baldassi (Argentina); Attendance: 21,075
**BOL:** Carlos Erwin Arias Égüez (20/0), Christian Israel Vargas Claros (2/0), Ronald Raldes Balcázar (46/0), Ronald Taylor Rivero Khun (7/0), Abdón Reyes Cardozo (5/0), Wálter Alberto Flores Condarco (8/0), Ronald Lázaro García Justiniano (33/2), Joselito Vaca Velasco (37/2) [64.Didí Torrico Camacho (5/0)], Jaime Robles Céspedes (6/0), Joaquín Botero Vaca (46/17) [71.Pablo Daniel Escobar Olivetti (5/0)], Marcelo Moreno Martins (12/5) [88.Enrique Parada Salvatierra (5/0)]. Trainer: Erwin Sánchez Freking (23).
**Goals:** Marcelo Moreno Martins (15, 41).

**371.** 22.10.2008 **BOLIVIA – EL SALVADOR** **0-2(0-1)**
“Robert F. Kennedy” Memorial Stadium, Washington D.C. (United States); Referee: Paul Warde (Canada); Attendance: n/a
**BOL:** Carlos Erwin Arias Égüez (21/0) [*sent off 33*], Miguel Ángel Hoyos Guzmán (22/1), Luis Alberto Gutiérrez Herrera (9/0), Ronald Taylor Rivero Khun (8/0), Abdón Reyes Cardozo (6/0), Jaime Robles Céspedes (7/0), Wálter Alberto Flores Condarco (9/0) [72.Jaime Moreno Morales (74/9)], Enrique Parada Salvatierra (6/0) [46.Nelson Sossa Chávez (6/1)], Mauricio Saucedo Guardia (8/0), Darwin Peña Arce (13/1), Ricardo Pedriel Suárez (5/1) [35.Sergio Daniel Galarza Solíz (14/0)]. Trainer: Erwin Sánchez Freking (24).

**372.** 11.03.2009 **BOLIVIA - MEXICO** **1-5(0-2)**
Dick‘s Sporting Goods Park, Denver (United States); Referee: Baldomero Toledo (United States); Attendance: n/a
**BOL:** Carlos Erwin Arias Égüez (22/0), Luis Gatty Ribeiro Roca (34/0) [34.Santos Amador Quispe (3/0)], Juan Manuel Peña Montaño (82/1) [*sent off 30*], Edemir Rodríguez Mercado (4/0), Miguel Ángel Hoyos Guzmán (23/1) [84.Jesús Alejandro Gómez Lanza (2/0)], Ignacio Awad García Justiniano (4/0), Wálter Alberto Flores Condarco (10/0) [46.Lorgio Álvarez Roca (37/1)], Leonel Alfredo Reyes Saravia (18/2) [75.Jaime Robles Céspedes (8/0)], Joselito Vaca Velasco (38/2) [61.Didí Torrico Camacho (6/1)], Álex Rodrigo da Rosa Dornelles (1/0), José Alfredo Castillo Parada (20/6) [46.Joaquín Botero Vaca (47/17)]. Trainer: Erwin Sánchez Freking (25).
**Goal:** Didí Torrico Camacho (68).

**373.** 28.03.2009 **COLOMBIA - BOLIVIA** **2-0(1-0)** 19th FIFA WC. Qualifiers
Estadio „Nemesio Camacho“ El Campín, Bogotá; Referee: Alfredo Intriago (Ecuador); Attendance: 22,044
**BOL:** Carlos Erwin Arias Égüez (23/0), Luis Alberto Gutiérrez Herrera (10/0), Juan Manuel Peña Montaño (83/1), Ronald Taylor Rivero Khun (9/0), Miguel Ángel Hoyos Guzmán (24/1), Wálter Alberto Flores Condarco (11/0), Ronald Lázaro García Justiniano (34/2), Jaime Robles Céspedes (9/0) [46.Didí Torrico Camacho (7/1)], Joselito Vaca Velasco (39/2) [77.Julio César Hurtado (1/0)], Pablo Daniel Escobar Olivetti (6/0), Diego Aroldo Cabrera Flores (14/1) [67.José Alfredo Castillo Parada (21/6) [*sent off 90*]]. Trainer: Erwin Sánchez Freking (26).

**374.** 01.04.2009 **BOLIVIA - ARGENTINA** **6-1(3-1)** 19th FIFA WC. Qualifiers
Estadio „Hernándo Siles Zuazo“, La Paz; Referee: Martín Emilio Vázquez Broquetas (Uruguay); Attendance: 30,487
**BOL:** Carlos Erwin Arias Égüez (24/0), Luis Gatty Ribeiro Roca (35/0), Juan Manuel Peña Montaño (84/1), Ronald Taylor Rivero Khun (10/0), Ronald Lázaro García Justiniano (35/2) [79.Wálter Alberto Flores Condarco (12/0)], Abdón Reyes Cardozo (7/0) [55.Ignacio Awad García Justiniano (5/0)], Leonel Alfredo Reyes Saravia (19/2), Didí Torrico Camacho (8/2), Álex Rodrigo da Rosa Dornelles (2/1) [69.Mauricio Saucedo Guardia (9/0)], Joaquín Botero Vaca (48/20), Marcelo Moreno Martins (13/6). Trainer: Erwin Sánchez Freking (27).
**Goals:** Marcelo Moreno Martins (12), Joaquín Botero Vaca (34 penalty), Álex Rodrigo da Rosa Dornelles (45), Joaquín Botero Vaca (55, 66), Didí Torrico Camacho (87).

**375.** 06.06.2009 **BOLIVIA - VENEZUELA** **0-1(0-1)** 19th FIFA WC. Qualifiers
Estadio „Hernándo Siles Zuazo“, La Paz; Referee: Carlos Vera (Ecuador); Attendance: 23,427
**BOL:** Carlos Erwin Arias Égüez (25/0), Ronald Raldes Balcázar (47/0), Ronald Taylor Rivero Khun (11/0), Miguel Ángel Hoyos Guzmán (25/1), Abdón Reyes Cardozo (8/0), Ronald Lázaro García Justiniano (36/2) [77.Gilbert Álvarez (1/0)], Leonel Alfredo Reyes Saravia (20/2) [*sent off 92*], Joselito Vaca Velasco (40/2) [63.Pablo Daniel Escobar Olivetti (7/0)], Álex Rodrigo da Rosa Dornelles (3/1), Diego Aroldo Cabrera Flores (15/1) [46.César Gerardo Yacerotte (1/0)], Marcelo Moreno Martins (14/6) [*sent off 80*]. Trainer: Erwin Sánchez Freking (28).

**376.** 10.06.2009 **CHILE - BOLIVIA** **4-0(1-0)** 19th FIFA WC. Qualifiers
Estadio Nacional „Julio Martínez Prádanos“, Santiago; Referee: Roberto Carlos Silvera (Uruguay); Attendance: 60,124
**BOL:** Carlos Erwin Arias Égüez (26/0), Juan Manuel Peña Montaño (85/1), Ronald Raldes Balcázar (48/0), Ronald Taylor Rivero Khun (12/0), Christian Israel Vargas Claros (3/0), Ignacio Awad García Justiniano (6/0) [*sent off 72*], Ronald Lázaro García Justiniano (37/2), Didí Torrico Camacho (9/2) [57.Abdón Reyes Cardozo (9/0)], Jaime Robles Céspedes (10/0) [84.Joselito Vaca Velasco (41/2)], Álex Rodrigo da Rosa Dornelles (4/1) [46.César Gerardo Yacerotte (2/0)], Pablo Daniel Escobar Olivetti (8/0). Trainer: Erwin Sánchez Freking (29).

**377.** 05.09.2009 **PARAGUAY - BOLIVIA** **1-0(1-0)** 19th FIFA WC. Qualifiers
Estadio Defensores del Chaco, Asunción; Referee: Victor Hugo Carrillo (Peru); Attendance: 25,094
**BOL:** Hugo Suárez Vaca (8/0), Luis Alberto Gutiérrez Herrera (11/0), Marvin Orlando Bejarano Jiménez (1/0), Luis Palacios (1/0), Edemir Rodríguez Mercado (5/0), Enrique Parada Salvatierra (7/0), Wálter Alberto Flores Condarco (13/0) [53.Danner Jesús Pachi Bozo (11/0)], Ronald Lázaro García Justiniano (38/2) [83.Joselito Vaca Velasco (42/2)], Jesús Alejandro Gómez Lanza (3/0), Pablo Daniel Escobar Olivetti (9/0) [75.Diego Aroldo Cabrera Flores (16/1)], Marcelo Moreno Martins (15/6). Trainer: Erwin Sánchez Freking (30).

**378.** 09.09.2009 **BOLIVIA - ECUADOR** **1-3(0-1)** 19th FIFA WC. Qualifiers

Estadio „Hernándo Siles Zuazo“, La Paz; Referee: Héctor Walter Baldassi (Argentina); Attendance: 10,200

**BOL:** Hugo Suárez Vaca (9/0), Marvin Orlando Bejarano Jiménez (2/0), Luis Gatty Ribeiro Roca (36/0), Ronald Taylor Rivero Khun (13/0), Edemir Rodríguez Mercado (6/0), Danner Jesús Pachi Bozo (12/0), Wálter Alberto Flores Condarco (14/0) [46.Abdón Reyes Cardozo (10/0)], Ronald Lázaro García Justiniano (39/2) [64.Helmut Enrique Gutiérrez (1/0)], Limberg Gutiérrez Mariscal (54/4), Diego Aroldo Cabrera Flores (17/1) [51.César Gerardo Yacerotte (3/1)], Marcelo Moreno Martins (16/6). Trainer: Erwin Sánchez Freking (31).

**Goal:** César Gerardo Yacerotte (85).

**379.** 11.10.2009 **BOLIVIA - BRAZIL** **2-1(2-0)** 19th FIFA WC. Qualifiers

Estadio „Hernándo Siles Zuazo“, La Paz; Referee: Pablo Antonio Pozo Quinteros (Chile); Attendance: 16,557

**BOL:** Carlos Erwin Arias Égüez (27/0), Ronald Raldes Balcázar (49/0), Ronald Taylor Rivero Khun (14/0), Wilder Zabala Perrogón (1/0), Ignacio Awad García Justiniano (7/0), Helmut Enrique Gutiérrez (2/0), Edgar Rolando Olivares Burgoa (7/1), Leonel Alfredo Reyes Saravia (21/2), Abdón Reyes Cardozo (11/0) [74.Joselito Vaca Velasco (43/2)], Juan Carlos Arce Justiniano (19/3) [79.Danner Jesús Pachi Bozo (13/0)], Marcelo Moreno Martins (17/7) [81.Ricardo Pedriel Suárez (6/1)]. Trainer: Erwin Sánchez Freking (32).

**Goal:** Edgar Rolando Olivares Burgoa (10), Marcelo Moreno Martins (32).

**380.** 14.10.2009 **PERU - BOLIVIA** **1-0(0-0)** 19th FIFA WC. Qualifiers

Estadio „Alejandro Villanueva“, Lima; Referee: Juan Soto (Venezuela); Attendance: 4,373

**BOL:** Carlos Erwin Arias Égüez (28/0), Ronald Taylor Rivero Khun (15/0), Edemir Rodríguez Mercado (7/0), Wilder Zabala Perrogón (2/0), Ignacio Awad García Justiniano (8/0), Jesús Alejandro Gómez Lanza (4/0) [81.José Luis Chávez Sánchez (2/0)], Edgar Rolando Olivares Burgoa (8/1) [77.Pablo Daniel Escobar Olivetti (10/0)], Leonel Alfredo Reyes Saravia (22/2), Rosauro Rivero Céspedes (1/0) [*sent off 39*], Joselito Vaca Velasco (44/2) [81.Ricardo Pedriel Suárez (7/1)], Marcelo Moreno Martins (18/7). Trainer: Erwin Sánchez Freking (33).

**381.** 24.02.2010 **BOLIVIA - MEXICO** **0-5(0-4)**

Candlestick Park, San Francisco (United States); Referee: Terry Vaughn (United States); Attendance: n/a

**BOL:** Daniel Vaca Tasca (1/0) [65.Carlos Emilio Lampe Porras (1/0)], Marvin Orlando Bejarano Jiménez (3/0), Ronald Eguino Segovia (1/0), Edemir Rodríguez Mercado (8/0), Santos Amador Quispe (4/0), Helmut Enrique Gutiérrez (3/0) [22.Nicolás Suárez Vaca (7/0)], Edgar Rolando Olivares Burgoa (9/1) [46.Augusto Andaveris Iriondo (13/1)], Rolando Ribera Menacho (1/0) [65.Jair Torrico Camacho (1/0)], Samuel Galindo Suheiro (1/0), Gilbert Álvarez (2/0), Wálter Veizaga Argote (1/0). Trainer: Eduardo Andres Villegas Camara (1).

**382.** 11.08.2010 **BOLIVIA - COLOMBIA** **1-1(0-1)**

Estadio „Hernándo Siles Zuazo“, La Paz; Referee: Gabriel Norberto Favale (Argentina); Attendance: 6,310

**BOL:** Daniel Vaca Tasca (2/0) [46.Carlos Emilio Lampe Porras (2/0)], Miguel Ángel Hoyos Guzmán (26/1), Edemir Rodríguez Mercado (9/0), Luis Alberto Gutiérrez Herrera (12/0), Ignacio Awad García Justiniano (9/0), Nicolás Suárez Vaca (8/0), Jaime Robles Céspedes (11/0) [46.Wálter Alberto Flores Condarco (15/0)], Joselito Vaca Velasco (45/2), Rudy Alejandro Cardozo Fernández (1/0) [46.Roberto Galindo Sánchez (1/1)], Álex Rodrigo da Rosa Dornelles (5/1) [79.Amílcar Álvaro Sánchez Gúzman (1/0)], Alcides Peña Jiménez (1/0) [46.Diego Aroldo Cabrera Flores (18/1); 49.Abdón Reyes Cardozo (12/0)]. Trainer: Eduardo Andres Villegas Camara (2).

**Goal:** Roberto Galindo Sánchez (64).

**383.** 07.10.2010 **BOLIVIA - VENEZUELA** **1-3(0-3)**

Estadio „Ramón 'Tahuichi' Aguilera“, Santa Cruz de la Sierra; Referee: Ibrahim Chaibou (Niger); Attendance: 18,000

**BOL:** Carlos Emilio Lampe Porras (3/0) [46.Daniel Vaca Tasca (3/0)], Luis Alberto Gutiérrez Herrera (13/0), Ronald Raldes Balcázar (50/0), Miguel Ángel Hoyos Guzmán (27/1), Jhasmani Campos Dávalos (9/1), Ronald Lázaro García Justiniano (40/2) [77.José Luis Chávez Sánchez (3/0)], Ignacio Awad García Justiniano (10/0) [24.Marvin Orlando Bejarano Jiménez (4/0)], Joselito Vaca Velasco (46/2), Roberto Galindo Sánchez (2/1) [46.Sacha Silvestre Lima Castedo (11/0)], Marcelo Moreno Martins (19/8) [83.José Alfredo Castillo Parada (22/6)], Wálter Veizaga Argote (2/0) [46.Mauricio Saucedo Guardia (10/0)]. Trainer: Eduardo Andres Villegas Camara (3).

**Goal:** Marcelo Moreno Martins (32).

**384.** 09.02.2011 **BOLIVIA - LATVIA** **1-2(0-1)**

Mardan Stadyumu, Antalya (Turkey); Referee: Krisztián Selmeczi (Hungary); Attendance: n/a

**BOL:** Carlos Erwin Arias Égüez (29/0), Luis Alberto Gutiérrez Herrera (14/0), Ronald Raldes Balcázar (51/0), Ronald Taylor Rivero Khun (16/0) [86.Marvin Orlando Bejarano Jiménez (5/0)], Miguel Ángel Hoyos Guzmán (28/1), Jhasmani Campos Dávalos (10/1) [46.Juan Carlos Arce Justiniano (20/4)], Wálter Alberto Flores Condarco (16/0) [74.Ricardo Pedriel Suárez (8/1)], Jaime Robles Céspedes (12/0), Joselito Vaca Velasco (47/2), Mauricio Saucedo Guardia (11/0) [65.Rudy Alejandro Cardozo Fernández (2/0)], Marcelo Moreno Martins (20/8). Trainer: Gustavo Domingo Quinteros Desabato (1).

**Goal:** Juan Carlos Arce Justiniano (55 penalty).

**385.** 25.03.2011 **PANAMA - BOLIVIA** **2-0(1-0)**

Estadio „Rommel Fernández“, Ciudad de Panamá; Referee: Walter Alexander López Castellanos (Guatemala); Attendance: 10,000

**BOL:** Carlos Erwin Arias Égüez (30/0), Ronald Raldes Balcázar (52/0), Ronald Taylor Rivero Khun (17/0), Edemir Rodríguez Mercado (10/0), Lorgio Álvarez Roca (38/1) [46.Marvin Orlando Bejarano Jiménez (6/0)], Rudy Alejandro Cardozo Fernández (3/0), Wálter Alberto Flores Condarco (17/0), Ronald Lázaro García Justiniano (41/2) [83.Jesús Alejandro Gómez Lanza (5/0)], Miguel Oswaldo Loaiza Tardio (1/0) [70.Jaime Robles Céspedes (13/0)], José Alfredo Castillo Parada (23/6), Ricardo Pedriel Suárez (9/1) [77.Augusto Andaveris Iriondo (14/1)]. Trainer: Gustavo Domingo Quinteros Desabato (2).

**386.** 28.03.2011 **GUATEMALA - BOLIVIA** **1-1(1-0)**

Estadio „Carlos Salazar Hijo“, Mazatenango; Referee: Joel Antonio Aguilar Chicas (El Salvador); Attendance: 6,154

**BOL:** Carlos Erwin Arias Égüez (31/0) [64.Sergio Daniel Galarza Solíz (15/0)], Luis Alberto Gutiérrez Herrera (15/0), Ronald Raldes Balcázar (53/0), Ronald Taylor Rivero Khun (18/0), Edemir Rodríguez Mercado (11/0), Rudy Alejandro Cardozo Fernández (4/0), Jhasmani Campos Dávalos (11/1), Wálter Alberto Flores Condarco (18/0), Jaime Robles Céspedes (14/0), Joselito Vaca Velasco (48/2), José Alfredo Castillo Parada (24/6) [56.Ricardo Pedriel Suárez (10/2)]. Trainer: Gustavo Domingo Quinteros Desabato (3).

**Goal:** Ricardo Pedriel Suárez (72).

**387.** 04.06.2011 **BOLIVIA - PARAGUAY** **0-2(0-1)** Copa Paz del Chaco

Estadio „Ramón Aguilera Costas“, Santa Cruz de la Sierra; Referee: Manuel Garay Evia (Peru); Attendance: 30,000

**BOL:** Carlos Erwin Arias Égüez (32/0), Ronald Raldes Balcázar (54/0), Ronald Taylor Rivero Khun (19/0), Lorgio Álvarez Roca (39/1), Luis Alberto Gutiérrez Herrera (16/0), Rudy Alejandro Cardozo Fernández (5/0) [56.Jhasmani Campos Dávalos (12/1)], Wálter Alberto Flores Condarco (19/0), Jaime Robles Céspedes (15/0) [65.Ronald Lázaro García Justiniano (42/2)], Joselito Vaca Velasco (49/2) [56.Edivaldo Rojas Hermoza (1/0)], Marcelo Moreno Martins (21/8), Alcides Peña Jiménez (2/0). Trainer: Gustavo Domingo Quinteros Desabato (4).

**388.** 07.06.2011 **PARAGUAY - BOLIVIA** **0-0** Copa Paz del Chaco
Estadio „Feliciano Cáceres“, Luque; Referee: Heber Roberto Lopes (Brazil); Attendance: 20,000
**BOL:** Carlos Erwin Arias Égüez (33/0), Ronald Raldes Balcázar (55/0), Ronald Taylor Rivero Khun (20/0), Lorgio Álvarez Roca (40/1), Luis Alberto Gutiérrez Herrera (17/0), Jhasmani Campos Dávalos (13/1) [76.Rudy Alejandro Cardozo Fernández (6/0)], Wálter Alberto Flores Condarco (20/0), Ignacio Awad García Justiniano (11/0) [56.José Luis Chávez Sánchez (4/0)], Jaime Robles Céspedes (16/0), Edivaldo Rojas Hermoza (2/0) [86.Mauricio Saucedo Guardia (12/0)], Marcelo Moreno Martins (22/8) [78.Ricardo Pedriel Suárez (11/2)]. Trainer: Gustavo Domingo Quinteros Desabato (5).

**389.** 01.07.2011 **ARGENTINA - BOLIVIA** **1-1(0-0)** 43rd Copa América. Group Stage
Estadio Ciudad de La Plata, La Plata; Referee: Roberto Carlos Silvera Calcerrada (Uruguay); Attendance: 52,700
**BOL:** Carlos Erwin Arias Égüez (34/0), Ronald Raldes Balcázar (56/0), Lorgio Álvarez Roca (41/1), Ronald Taylor Rivero Khun (21/0), Luis Alberto Gutiérrez Herrera (18/0), Joselito Vaca Velasco (50/2) [64.José Luis Chávez Sánchez (5/0)], Jaime Robles Céspedes (17/0), Wálter Alberto Flores Condarco (21/0), Jhasmani Campos Dávalos (14/1) [80.Juan Carlos Arce Justiniano (21/4)], Edivaldo Rojas Hermoza (3/1) [90.Rudy Alejandro Cardozo Fernández (7/0)], Marcelo Moreno Martins (23/8). Trainer: Gustavo Domingo Quinteros Desabato (6).
**Goal:** Edivaldo Rojas Hermoza (47).

**390.** 07.07.2011 **BOLIVIA – COSTA RICA** **0-2(0-0)** 43rd Copa América. Group Stage
Estadio 23 de Agosto, Jujuy (Argentina); Referee: Carlos Alfredo Vera Rodríguez (Ecuador); Attendance: 23,000
**BOL:** Carlos Erwin Arias Égüez (35/0), Lorgio Álvarez Roca (42/1), Ronald Raldes Balcázar (57/0), Ronald Taylor Rivero Khun (22/0) [*sent off 71*], Luis Alberto Gutiérrez Herrera (19/0), Jaime Robles Céspedes (18/0) [68.Alcides Peña Jiménez (3/0)], Wálter Alberto Flores Condarco (22/0) [*sent off 76*], Jhasmani Campos Dávalos (15/1) [80.Ronald Lázaro García Justiniano (43/2)], Edivaldo Rojas Hermoza (4/1) [68.José Luis Chávez Sánchez (6/0)], Juan Carlos Arce Justiniano (22/4), Marcelo Moreno Martins (24/8). Trainer: Gustavo Domingo Quinteros Desabato (7).

**391.** 10.07.2011 **COLOMBIA - BOLIVIA** **2-0(2-0)** 43rd Copa América. Group Stage
Estadio „Brigadier General Estanislao López“, Santa Fe (Argentina); Referee: Francisco Chacón Gutiérrez (Mexico); Attendance: n/a
**BOL:** Carlos Erwin Arias Égüez (36/0), Christian Israel Vargas Claros (4/0), Santos Amador Quispe (5/0), Ronald Raldes Balcázar (58/0), Lorgio Álvarez Roca (43/1), Juan Carlos Arce Justiniano (23/4) [71.Ricardo Pedriel Suárez (12/2)], Ronald Lázaro García Justiniano (44/2), Jaime Robles Céspedes (19/0), Jhasmani Campos Dávalos (16/1), Edivaldo Rojas Hermoza (5/1) [46.Joselito Vaca Velasco (51/2)], Marcelo Moreno Martins (25/8) [61.Alcides Peña Jiménez (4/0)]. Trainer: Gustavo Domingo Quinteros Desabato (8).

**392.** 10.08.2011 **BOLIVIA - PANAMA** **1-3(1-0)**
Estadio „Ramón ‚Tahuichi‘ Aguilera“, Santa Cruz de la Sierra; Referee: Víctor Hugo Carrillo Casanova (Peru); Attendance: 10,000
**BOL:** Sergio Daniel Galarza Solíz (16/0), Ronald Raldes Balcázar (59/0) [*sent off 80*], Lorgio Álvarez Roca (44/1), Luis Alberto Gutiérrez Herrera (20/0), Christian Israel Vargas Claros (5/0), Rudy Alejandro Cardozo Fernández (8/0) [70.Diego Aroldo Cabrera Flores (19/1)], Ronald Lázaro García Justiniano (45/2) [78.Ronald Lorgio Suárez Saucedo (1/0)], Jaime Robles Céspedes (20/0), Joselito Vaca Velasco (52/2), Juan Carlos Arce Justiniano (24/5) [70.Samuel Galindo Suheiro (2/0)], Alcides Peña Jiménez (5/0) [*sent off 51*]. Trainer: Gustavo Domingo Quinteros Desabato (9).
**Goals:** Juan Carlos Arce Justiniano (6).

**393.** 02.09.2011 **PERU - BOLIVIA** **2-2(1-1)**
Estadio Nacional „José Díaz“, Lima; Referee: Juan Ernesto Soto Arevalo (Venezuela); Attendance: 35,000
**BOL:** Sergio Daniel Galarza Solíz (17/0), Luis Javier Méndez Moza (2/0), Ronald Taylor Rivero Khun (23/0), Luis Alberto Gutiérrez Herrera (21/0), Christian Israel Vargas Claros (6/0), José Luis Chávez Sánchez (7/0), Rudy Alejandro Cardozo Fernández (9/1), Wálter Alberto Flores Condarco (23/0), Pablo Daniel Escobar Olivetti (11/1) [62.Mauricio Saucedo Guardia (13/0)], Edivaldo Rojas Hermoza (6/1) [75.Jaime Robles Céspedes (21/0)], Marcelo Moreno Martins (26/8) [90.Darwin Ríos Pinto (1/0)]. Trainer: Gustavo Domingo Quinteros Desabato (10).
**Goals:** Pablo Daniel Escobar Olivetti (5), Rudy Alejandro Cardozo Fernández (70).

**394.** 05.09.2011 **BOLIVIA - PERU** **0-0**
Estadio „Hernándo Siles Zuazo“, La Paz; Referee: Julio César Quintana Rodríguez (Paraguay); Attendance: n/a
**BOL:** Daniel Vaca Tasca (4/0), Enrique Parada Salvatierra (8/0), Ronald Raldes Balcázar (60/0), Ronald Taylor Rivero Khun (24/0), Luis Alberto Gutiérrez Herrera (22/0) [61.Mauricio Saucedo Guardia (14/0)], Rudy Alejandro Cardozo Fernández (10/1), Wálter Alberto Flores Condarco (24/0) [77.Alejandro Saúl Chumacero Bracamonte (1/0)], Jaime Robles Céspedes (22/0), Joselito Vaca Velasco (53/2) [82.José Luis Chávez Sánchez (8/0)], Juan Carlos Arce Justiniano (25/5), Marcelo Moreno Martins (27/8) [46.Alcides Peña Jiménez (6/0)]. Trainer: Gustavo Domingo Quinteros Desabato (11).

**395.** 07.10.2011 **URUGUAY - BOLIVIA** **4-2(3-1)** 20th FIFA WC. Qualifiers
Estadio Centenario, Montevideo; Referee: Víctor Hugo Carrillo Casanova (Peru); Attendance: 25,500
**BOL:** Carlos Erwin Arias Égüez (37/0), Ronald Raldes Balcázar (61/0), Ronald Taylor Rivero Khun (25/0), Luis Alberto Gutiérrez Herrera (23/0), Christian Israel Vargas Claros (7/0), Rudy Alejandro Cardozo Fernández (11/2), Wálter Alberto Flores Condarco (25/0) [81.José Luis Chávez Sánchez (9/0)], Jaime Robles Céspedes (23/0), Mauricio Saucedo Guardia (15/0) [46.Alcides Peña Jiménez (7/0)], Edivaldo Rojas Hermoza (7/1) [60.Joselito Vaca Velasco (54/2)], Marcelo Moreno Martins (28/9). Trainer: Gustavo Domingo Quinteros Desabato (12).
**Goals:** Rudy Alejandro Cardozo Fernández (18), Marcelo Moreno Martins (86).

**396.** 11.10.2011 **BOLIVIA - COLOMBIA** **1-2(0-0)** 20th FIFA WC. Qualifiers
Estadio „Hernándo Siles Zuazo“, La Paz; Referee: Carlos Arecio Amarilla Demarqui (Paraguay); Attendance: 33,155
**BOL:** Daniel Vaca Tasca (5/0), Ronald Raldes Balcázar (62/0), Ronald Taylor Rivero Khun (26/0), Lorgio Álvarez Roca (45/1) [76.José Luis Chávez Sánchez (10/0)], Luis Alberto Gutiérrez Herrera (24/0) [71.Jhasmani Campos Dávalos (17/1)], Rudy Alejandro Cardozo Fernández (12/2), Wálter Alberto Flores Condarco (26/1), Jaime Robles Céspedes (24/0), Pablo Daniel Escobar Olivetti (12/1), Juan Carlos Arce Justiniano (26/5), Marcelo Moreno Martins (29/9) [71.Augusto Andaveris Iriondo (15/1)]. Trainer: Gustavo Domingo Quinteros Desabato (13).
**Goals:** Wálter Alberto Flores Condarco (85).

**397.** 11.11.2011 **ARGENTINA - BOLIVIA** **1-1(0-0)** 20th FIFA WC. Qualifiers
Estadio Monumental „Antonio Vespucio Liberti“, Buenos Aires; Referee: Carlos Alfredo Vera Rodríguez (Ecuador); Attendance: 27,592
**BOL:** Carlos Erwin Arias Égüez (38/0), Luis Javier Méndez Moza (3/0), Ronald Taylor Rivero Khun (27/0), Luis Alberto Gutiérrez Herrera (25/0), Rudy Alejandro Cardozo Fernández (13/2), Christian Israel Vargas Claros (8/0), Wálter Alberto Flores Condarco (27/1), Jaime Robles Céspedes (25/0), Pablo Daniel Escobar Olivetti (13/1) [84.José Luis Chávez Sánchez (11/0)], Edivaldo Rojas Hermoza (8/1) [54.Ronald Segovia Calzadilla (1/0)], Marcelo Moreno Martins (30/10) [77.Augusto Andaveris Iriondo (16/1)]. Trainer: Gustavo Domingo Quinteros Desabato (14).
**Goals:** Marcelo Moreno Martins (56).

**398.** 15.11.2011 **VENEZUELA - BOLIVIA** **1-0(1-0)** 20th FIFA WC. Qualifiers
Estadio Pueblo Nuevo, San Cristóbal; Referee: Georges Buckley De Maritens (Peru); Attendance: 33,351
**BOL:** Carlos Erwin Arias Égüez (39/0), Ronald Raldes Balcázar (63/0), Ronald Taylor Rivero Khun (28/0), Luis Alberto Gutiérrez Herrera (26/0), Christian Israel Vargas Claros (9/0), Rudy Alejandro Cardozo Fernández (14/2) [77.Augusto Andaveris Iriondo (17/1)], José Luis Chávez Sánchez (12/0), Jaime Robles Céspedes (26/0), Ronald Segovia Calzadilla (2/0) [58.Jhasmani Campos Dávalos (18/1)], Pablo Daniel Escobar Olivetti (14/1) [58.Juan Carlos Arce Justiniano (27/5)], Marcelo Moreno Martins (31/10). Trainer: Gustavo Domingo Quinteros Desabato (15).

**399.** 29.02.2012 **BOLIVIA - CUBA** **1-0(0-0)**
Estadio „Félix Capriles“, Cochabamba; Referee: Enrique Cáceres (Paraguay); Attendance: 20,000
**BOL:** Daniel Vaca Tasca (6/0) [46.Sergio Daniel Galarza Solíz (18/0)], Luis Javier Méndez Moza (4/0), Ronald Taylor Rivero Khun (29/0), Luis Alberto Gutiérrez Herrera (27/0) [80.Abdón Reyes Cardozo (13/0)], Christian Israel Vargas Claros (10/0) [25.Óscar Añez Urachata (1/0)], Rudy Alejandro Cardozo Fernández (15/2), José Luis Chávez Sánchez (13/0) [46.Alejandro Saúl Chumacero Bracamonte (2/0)], Wálter Alberto Flores Condarco (28/1), Juan Carlos Arce Justiniano (28/5) [60.Gerardo César Yecerotte Soruco (1/0)], Marcelo Moreno Martins (32/10), Ricardo Pedriel Suárez (13/3) [70.Augusto Andaveris Iriondo (18/1)]. Trainer: Gustavo Domingo Quinteros Desabato (16).
**Goal:** Ricardo Pedriel Suárez (52).

**400.** 02.06.2012 **BOLIVIA - CHILE** **0-2(0-1)** 20th FIFA WC. Qualifiers
Estadio „Hernándo Siles Zuazo“, La Paz; Referee: Alfredo Stalin Intriago Ortega (Ecuador); Attendance: 34,389
**BOL:** Daniel Vaca Tasca (7/0), Luis Alberto Gutiérrez Herrera (28/0) [*sent off 54*], Luis Javier Méndez Moza (5/0), Christian Israel Vargas Claros (11/0), Ronald Taylor Rivero Khun (30/0), Jhasmani Campos Dávalos (19/1) [57.Rudy Alejandro Cardozo Fernández (16/2)], Alejandro Saúl Chumacero Bracamonte (3/0), Pablo Daniel Escobar Olivetti (15/1) [73.Alcides Peña Jiménez (8/0)], Wálter Alberto Flores Condarco (29/1), Juan Carlos Arce Justiniano (29/5), Ricardo Pedriel Suárez (14/3) [70.Augusto Andaveris Iriondo (19/1)]. Trainer: Gustavo Domingo Quinteros Desabato (17).

**401.** 09.06.2012 **BOLIVIA - PARAGUAY** **3-1(1-0)** 20th FIFA WC. Qualifiers
Estadio „Hernándo Siles Zuazo“, La Paz; Referee: Roberto Carlos Silvera Calcerrada (Uruguay); Attendance: n/a
**BOL:** Sergio Daniel Galarza Solíz (19/0), Christian Israel Vargas Claros (12/0), Ronny Jiménez Mendonza (1/0), Juan Gabriel Valverde Rivera (1/0), José Carlos Barba Paz (1/0), Gualberto Mojica Olmos (16/0) [73.José Luis Chávez Sánchez (14/0)], Alejandro Saúl Chumacero Bracamonte (4/0), Pablo Daniel Escobar Olivetti (16/3) [85.Rudy Alejandro Cardozo Fernández (17/2)], Wálter Alberto Flores Condarco (30/1), Marcelo Moreno Martins (33/10) [84.Augusto Andaveris Iriondo (20/1)], Alcides Peña Jiménez (9/1). Trainer: Gustavo Domingo Quinteros Desabato (18).
**Goals:** Alcides Peña Jiménez (10), Pablo Daniel Escobar Olivetti (70, 80).

**402.** 15.08.2012 **BOLIVIA - GUYANA** **2-0(0-0)**
Estadio "Ramón 'Tahuichi' Aguilera", Santa Cruz de la Sierra; Referee: Enrique Cáceres Villafane (Paraguay); Attendance: 11,000
**BOL:** Hugo Suárez Vaca (10/0), Carlos Hugo Tordoya Pizarro (1/0), Christian Israel Vargas Claros (13/0) [78.Ronald Segovia Calzadilla (3/0)], Marvin Orlando Bejarano Jiménez (7/0) [21.José Carlos Barba Paz (2/0)], Ronny Jiménez Mendonza (2/0), Jhasmani Campos Dávalos (20/1) [56.Miguel Gerardo Suárez Savino (1/1)], Gualberto Mojica Olmos (17/1), José Luis Chávez Sánchez (15/0), Marcelo Moreno Martins (34/10), Diego Aroldo Cabrera Flores (20/1) [65.Alcides Peña Jiménez (10/1)], Pedro Jesús Azogue Rojas (1/0) [51.Alejandro Saúl Chumacero Bracamonte (5/0)]. Trainer: Francisco Xabier Azcargorta Uriarte (38).
**Goals:** Gualberto Mojica Olmos (87), Miguel Gerardo Suárez Savino (90).

**403.** 07.09.2012 **ECUADOR - BOLIVIA** **1-0(0-0)** 20th FIFA WC. Qualifiers
Estadio Olímpico Atahualpa, Quito; Referee: Juan Ernesto Soto Arevalo (Venezuela); Attendance: 32,213
**BOL:** Hugo Suárez Vaca (11/0), Ronald Raldes Balcázar (64/0), Luis Alberto Gutiérrez Herrera (29/0), Luis Javier Méndez Moza (6/0), Christian Israel Vargas Claros (14/0), José Carlos Barba Paz (3/0), Gualberto Mojica Olmos (18/1) [84.Diego Aroldo Cabrera Flores (21/1)], Mauricio Saucedo Guardia (16/0) [46.Alcides Peña Jiménez (11/1)], José Luis Chávez Sánchez (16/0) [77.Alejandro Saúl Chumacero Bracamonte (6/0)], Marcelo Moreno Martins (35/10), Pedro Jesús Azogue Rojas (2/0). Trainer: Francisco Xabier Azcargorta Uriarte (39).

**404.** 12.10.2012 **BOLIVIA - PERU** **1-1(0-1)** 20th FIFA WC. Qualifiers
Estadio "Hernando Siles Zuazo", La Paz; Referee: Carlos Alfredo Vera Rodríguez (Ecuador); Attendance: 36,500
**BOL:** Hugo Suárez Vaca (12/0), Ronald Raldes Balcázar (65/0), Luis Javier Méndez Moza (7/0), Christian Israel Vargas Claros (15/0) [46.Marcelo Moreno Martins (36/10)], Juan Gabriel Valverde Rivera (2/0), Jhasmani Campos Dávalos (21/1), Alejandro Saúl Chumacero Bracamonte (7/1), Wálter Alberto Flores Condarco (31/1), Rudy Alejandro Cardozo Fernández (18/2), Juan Carlos Arce Justiniano (30/5) [75.Miguel Gerardo Suárez Savino (2/1)], Alcides Peña Jiménez (12/1) [46.Ronald Segovia Calzadilla (4/0)]. Trainer: Francisco Xabier Azcargorta Uriarte (40).
**Goal:** Alejandro Saúl Chumacero Bracamonte (51).

**405.** 16.10.2012 **BOLIVIA - URUGUAY** **4-1(2-0)** 20th FIFA WC. Qualifiers
Estadio "Hernando Siles Zuazo", La Paz; Referee: Víctor Hugo Rivera Chávez (Peru); Attendance: 25,402
**BOL:** Sergio Daniel Galarza Solíz (20/0), Ronald Raldes Balcázar (66/0), Edward Mauro Zenteno Álvarez (2/0), Luis Alberto Gutiérrez Herrera (30/0), Marvin Orlando Bejarano Jiménez (8/0), Gualberto Mojica Olmos (19/2) [69.Jhasmani Campos Dávalos (22/1)], Alejandro Saúl Chumacero Bracamonte (8/1), Rudy Alejandro Cardozo Fernández (19/2), Marcelo Moreno Martins (37/10) [58.Juan Carlos Arce Justiniano (31/5)], Carlos Enrique Saucedo Urgel (3/3), Pedro Jesús Azogue Rojas (3/0) [73.Alejandro Meleán Villarroel (1/0)]. Trainer: Francisco Xabier Azcargorta Uriarte (41).
**Goals:** Carlos Enrique Saucedo Urgel (6), Gualberto Mojica Olmos (27), Carlos Enrique Saucedo Urgel (51, 55).

**406.** 14.11.2012 **BOLIVIA - COSTA RICA** **1-1(0-0)**
Estadio "Ramón 'Tahuichi' Aguilera", Santa Cruz de la Sierra; Referee: Marcelo de Lima Henrique (Brazil); Attendance: 14,000
**BOL:** Sergio Daniel Galarza Solíz (21/0), Ronald Raldes Balcázar (67/0), Edward Mauro Zenteno Álvarez (3/0), Luis Alberto Gutiérrez Herrera (31/0), Gualberto Mojica Olmos (20/2) [55.Jhasmani Campos Dávalos (23/1)], Alejandro Saúl Chumacero Bracamonte (9/1) [80.Miguel Gerardo Suárez Savino (3/1)], Rudy Alejandro Cardozo Fernández (20/2) [59.Luis Enrique Hurtado Badani (1/0)], Diego Bejarano Ibañez (1/0) [57.Ronald Segovia Calzadilla (5/0)], Juan Carlos Arce Justiniano (32/5) [46.Darwin Ríos Pinto (2/0)], Carlos Enrique Saucedo Urgel (4/4), Pedro Jesús Azogue Rojas (4/0) [46.José Luis Chávez Sánchez (17/0)]. Trainer: Francisco Xabier Azcargorta Uriarte (42).
**Goal:** Carlos Enrique Saucedo Urgel (90+1).

**407.** 06.02.2013 **BOLIVIA - HAITI** **2-1(1-1)**
Estadio "Ramón 'Tahuichi' Aguilera", Santa Cruz de la Sierra; Referee: Ulises Luius Arnaldo Mereles Abraham (Paraguay); Attendance: 8,000
**BOL:** Carlos Erwin Arias Égüez (40/0), Ronald Raldes Balcázar (68/0), Luis Alberto Gutiérrez Herrera (32/0), Marvin Orlando Bejarano Jiménez (9/0), Ronny Jiménez Mendonza (3/0) [76.Ronald Segovia Calzadilla (6/0)], Ronald Lázaro García Justiniano (46/2) [74.Alejandro Meleán Villarroel (2/0)], Alejandro Saúl Chumacero Bracamonte (10/1) [54.Gualberto Mojica Olmos (21/3)], José Luis Chávez Sánchez (18/0), Rudy Alejandro Cardozo Fernández (21/2) [72.Danny Brayhan Bejarano Yañez (1/0)], Marcelo Moreno Martins (38/10) [84.Rodrigo Mauricio Vargas Castillo (1/0)], Carlos Enrique Saucedo Urgel (5/5) [46.Juan Eduardo Fierro Ribera (1/0)]. Trainer: Francisco Xabier Azcargorta Uriarte (43).
**Goals:** Carlos Enrique Saucedo Urgel (33), Gualberto Mojica Olmos (58).

**408.** 22.03.2013 **COLOMBIA - BOLIVIA** **5-0(1-0)** 20th FIFA WC. Qualifiers

Estadio Metropolitano "Roberto Meléndez", Barranquilla; Referee: Carlos Alfredo Vera Rodríguez (Ecuador); Attendance: 40,478

**BOL:** Carlos Erwin Arias Égüez (41/0) [46.Sergio Daniel Galarza Solíz (22/0)], Edward Mauro Zenteno Álvarez (4/0), Luis Alberto Gutiérrez Herrera (33/0), Marvin Orlando Bejarano Jiménez (10/0), Ronny Jiménez Mendonza (4/0), Ronald Lázaro García Justiniano (47/2) [57.Juan Carlos Arce Justiniano (33/5)], Gualberto Mojica Olmos (22/3), Alejandro Saúl Chumacero Bracamonte (11/1), Marcelo Moreno Martins (39/10), Carlos Enrique Saucedo Urgel (6/5) [46.Rudy Alejandro Cardozo Fernández (22/2)], Wálter Veizaga Argote (3/0). Trainer: Francisco Xabier Azcargorta Uriarte (44).

**409.** 26.03.2013 **BOLIVIA - ARGENTINA** **1-1(1-1)** 20th FIFA WC. Qualifiers

Estadio "Hernando Siles Zuazo", La Paz; Referee: Enrique Roberto Osses Zencovich (Chile); Attendance: 35,000

**BOL:** Sergio Daniel Galarza Solíz (23/0), Ronald Raldes Balcázar (69/0), Edward Mauro Zenteno Álvarez (5/0), Luis Alberto Gutiérrez Herrera (34/0), Jair Torrico Camacho (2/0) [46.Marvin Orlando Bejarano Jiménez (11/0)], Alejandro Saúl Chumacero Bracamonte (12/1), Rudy Alejandro Cardozo Fernández (23/2) [73.Gualberto Mojica Olmos (23/3)], Diego Bejarano Ibañez (2/0) [65.Juan Carlos Arce Justiniano (34/5)], Marcelo Moreno Martins (40/11), Carlos Enrique Saucedo Urgel (7/5), Wálter Veizaga Argote (4/0). Trainer: Francisco Xabier Azcargorta Uriarte (45).

**Goal:** Marcelo Moreno Martins (25).

**410.** 06.04.2013 **BOLIVIA - BRAZIL** **0-4(0-3)**

Estadio "Ramón 'Tahuichi' Aguilera", Santa Cruz de la Sierra; Referee: Patricio Loustau (Argentina); Attendance: 41,000

**BOL:** Sergio Daniel Galarza Solíz (24/0), Ronald Eguino Segovia (2/0), Edward Mauro Zenteno Álvarez (6/0), Marvin Orlando Bejarano Jiménez (12/0) [46.Jair Torrico Camacho (3/0)], Alejandro Meleán Villarroel (3/0) [46.Ronald Lázaro García Justiniano (48/2)], Jhasmani Campos Dávalos (24/1) [80.Diego Bejarano Ibañez (3/0)], Danny Brayhan Bejarano Yañez (2/0) [46.Ronny Jiménez Mendonza (5/0)], Marcelo Moreno Martins (41/11), Juan Carlos Arce Justiniano (35/5) [67.Rodrigo Mauricio Vargas Castillo (2/0)], Edivaldo Rojas Hermoza (9/1), Wálter Veizaga Argote (5/0) [46.Alejandro Saúl Chumacero Bracamonte (13/1)]. Trainer: Francisco Xabier Azcargorta Uriarte (46).

**411.** 07.06.2013 **BOLIVIA - VENEZUELA** **1-1(0-0)** 20th FIFA WC. Qualifiers

Estadio "Hernando Siles Zuazo", La Paz; Referee: Patricio Loustau (Argentina); Attendance: 10,155

**BOL:** Sergio Daniel Galarza Solíz (25/0), Ronald Raldes Balcázar (70/0) [74.Jhasmani Campos Dávalos (25/2)], Ronald Eguino Segovia (3/0), Edward Mauro Zenteno Álvarez (7/0), Alejandro Saúl Chumacero Bracamonte (14/1), Rudy Alejandro Cardozo Fernández (24/2), Wálter Veizaga Argote (6/0), Daniel Andrés Chávez Betancourt (1/0) [46.Gualberto Mojica Olmos (24/3)], Juan Carlos Arce Justiniano (36/5), Carlos Enrique Saucedo Urgel (8/5), Marcelo Moreno Martins (42/11) [64.Juan Eduardo Fierro Ribera (2/0)]. Trainer: Francisco Xabier Azcargorta Uriarte (47).

**Goal:** Jhasmani Campos Dávalos (86).

**412.** 11.06.2013 **CHILE - BOLIVIA** **3-1(2-1)** 20th FIFA WC. Qualifiers

Estadio Nacional, Santiago; Referee: Darío Agustín Ubriaco (Uruguay); Attendance: 45,000

**BOL:** Sergio Daniel Galarza Solíz (26/0), Ronald Raldes Balcázar (71/0), Edward Mauro Zenteno Álvarez (8/0), Luis Alberto Gutiérrez Herrera (35/0), Gualberto Mojica Olmos (25/3), Alejandro Saúl Chumacero Bracamonte (15/1) [46.Rudy Alejandro Cardozo Fernández (25/2)], Vicente Arze Camacho (1/0) [70.Jhasmani Campos Dávalos (26/2)], Diego Bejarano Ibáñez (4/0), Wálter Veizaga Argote (7/0), Daniel Andrés Chávez Betancourt (2/0) [46.Edivaldo Rojas Hermoza (10/1)], Marcelo Moreno Martins (43/12). Trainer: Francisco Xabier Azcargorta Uriarte (48).

**Goal:** Marcelo Moreno Martins (32).

**413.** 15.08.2013 **VENEZUELA - BOLIVIA** **2-2(1-1)**

Estadio Polideportivo de Pueblo Nuevo, San Cristóbal; Referee: Imer Lemuel Machado Barrera (Colombia); Attendance: 24,700

**BOL:** Sergio Daniel Galarza Solíz (27/0) [46.Daniel Vaca Tasca (8/0)], Ronald Raldes Balcázar (72/0), Edemir Rodríguez Mercado (12/0), Edward Mauro Zenteno Álvarez (9/0), Marvin Orlando Bejarano Jiménez (13/0), Abraham Cabrera Scapin (1/0), José Luis Chávez Sánchez (19/1) [77.Miguel Ríos (1/0)], Rudy Alejandro Cardozo Fernández (26/3) [88.Vladimir Castellón Colque (1/0)], Juan Carlos Arce Justiniano (37/5) [80.Rodrigo Luis Ramallo Cornejo (1/0)], Wálter Veizaga Argote (8/0) [55.Danny Brayhan Bejarano Yañez (3/0)], Pedro Jesús Azogue Rojas (5/0) [62.Jaime Darío Arrascaita Iriondo (1/0)]. Trainer: Francisco Xabier Azcargorta Uriarte (49).

**Goals:** Rudy Alejandro Cardozo Fernández (18), José Luis Chávez Sánchez (71).

**414.** 07.09.2013 **PARAGUAY - BOLIVIA** **4-0(1-0)** 20th FIFA WC. Qualifiers

Estadio Defensores del Chaco, Asunción; Referee: Víctor Hugo Carrillo (Peru); Attendance: 20,000

**BOL:** Sergio Daniel Galarza Solíz (28/0), Ronald Raldes Balcázar (73/0), Edemir Rodríguez Mercado (13/0), Edward Mauro Zenteno Álvarez (10/0) [46.Rudy Alejandro Cardozo Fernández (27/3)], Luis Alberto Gutiérrez Herrera (36/0), Abraham Cabrera Scapin (2/0), José Luis Chávez Sánchez (20/1) [68.Leandro Marcelo Maygua Ríos (1/0)], Vicente Arze Camacho (2/0) [46.Juan Carlos Arce Justiniano (38/5)], Danny Brayhan Bejarano Yañez (4/0), Marcelo Moreno Martins (44/12), Pedro Jesús Azogue Rojas (6/0). Trainer: Francisco Xabier Azcargorta Uriarte (50).

**415.** 10.09.2013 **BOLIVIA - ECUADOR** **1-1(0-0)** 20th FIFA WC. Qualifiers

Estadio "Hernando Siles Zuazo", La Paz; Referee: Paulo César de Oliveira (Brazil); Attendance: 12,043

**BOL:** Romel Javier Quiñónez Suárez (1/0), Ronald Raldes Balcázar (74/0), Edward Mauro Zenteno Álvarez (11/0), Marvin Orlando Bejarano Jiménez (14/0) [46.Jaime Darío Arrascaita Iriondo (2/1)], Alejandro Saúl Chumacero Bracamonte (16/1) [74.Leandro Marcelo Maygua Ríos (2/0)], Rudy Alejandro Cardozo Fernández (28/3), Diego Bejarano Ibañez (5/1), Juan Carlos Arce Justiniano (39/5), Diego Aroldo Cabrera Flores (22/1), Wálter Veizaga Argote (9/0), Pedro Jesús Azogue Rojas (7/0) [46.Marcelo Moreno Martins (45/12)]. Trainer: Francisco Xabier Azcargorta Uriarte (51).

**Goal:** Jaime Darío Arrascaita Iriondo (47).

**416.** 16.10.2013 **PERU - BOLIVIA** **1-1(1-1)** 20th FIFA WC. Qualifiers

Estadio Nacional, Lima; Referee: Enrique Cáceres Villafante (Paraguay); Attendance: *played behind closed doors*

**BOL:** Romel Javier Quiñónez Suárez (2/0), Ronald Raldes Balcázar (75/0), Edward Mauro Zenteno Álvarez (12/0), Luis Alberto Gutiérrez Herrera (37/0), Marvin Orlando Bejarano Jiménez (15/0), José Luis Chávez Sánchez (21/1), Diego Bejarano Ibáñez (6/1) [86.Edemir Rodríguez Mercado (14/0)], Danny Brayhan Bejarano Yañez (5/0) [46.Juan Carlos Arce Justiniano (40/5)], Marcelo Moreno Martins (46/12), Edivaldo Rojas Hermoza (11/1) [74.Jaime Darío Arrascaita Iriondo (3/1)], Wálter Veizaga Argote (10/0). Trainer: Francisco Xabier Azcargorta Uriarte (52).

**Goal:** Diego Bejarano Ibáñez (45).

# INTERNATIONAL PLAYERS

| FM/Nr | Name | DOB | Caps | Goals | Period, Club |
|---|---|---|---|---|---|
| (81/137) | AGREDA CAÑEDO Guery | 19.01.1944 | 14 | 0 | 1967-1973 |
| (112/190) | AGUILAR Miguel | | 34 | 10 | 1977-1983, Club The Strongest La Paz, Club Oriente Petrolero Santa Cruz de la Sierra |
| (1/009) | AGUILAR Teófilo | | 4 | 1 | 1926 |
| (70/126) | AGUILLERA CAMPOS Luis | 27.06.1932 | 1 | 0 | 1963 |
| (59/107) | AGUIRRE Antonio Atilio | | 12 | 1 | 1959-1965, Club Deportivo Municipal La Paz |
| (1/011) | ALBORTA VELASCO Mario Mauricio | 19.09.1910 | 14 | 2 | 1926-1938, Club Bolívar Independiente Unificada La Paz |
| (51/102) | ALCÓCER Máximo | 15.04.1933 | 22 | 13 | 1957-1963, Club Jorge Wilstermann Cochabamba |
| (45/087) | ALCÓN Ricardo | | 15 | 2 | 1953-1959 |
| (317/357) | ALGARAÑAZ José Luis | 03.11.1982 | 2 | 0 | 2002, Club Universidad Iberoamericana La Paz Bolívar (2/0). |
| (35/072) | ALGARAÑAZ Víctor Celestino | 06.04.1924 | 9 | 1 | 1949-1950, Club Deportivo Litoral La Paz |
| (86/142) | ÁLVAREZ APARICIO Raúl | 19.07.1936 | 4 | 2 | 1969 |
| (375/422) | ÁLVAREZ Gilbert | 07.04.1992 | 2 | 0 | 2009-2010, Callejas (2/0). |
| (79/133) | ÁLVAREZ MOSCOSO Isaac | 16.07.1933 | 2 | 0 | 1965, 31 de Octubre Obrajes |
| (274/317) | ÁLVAREZ ROCA Lorgio | 29.06.1978 | 45 | 1 | 1999-2011, CSCD Blooming Santa Cruz de la Sierra (9/0), CD Oriente Petrolero Santa Cruz de la Sierra (12/1), CA Independiente Avellaneda (5/0), Club Cerro Porteño Asunción (10/0), Club Libertad Asunción (1/0), Club Bolívar Independiente Unificada La Paz (8/0). |
| (357/401) | AMADOR QUISPE Santos | 06.04.1982 | 5 | 0 | 2007-2011, Club Bamin Real Potosí (2/0), Club Jorge Wilstermann Cochabamba (1/0), Club The Strongest La Paz (2/0). |
| (313/352) | ANDAVERIS IRIONDO Augusto | 05.05.1979 | 20 | 1 | 2001-2012, Club Universidad Iberoamericana La Paz (2/0), Club Jorge Wilstermann Cochabamba (3/1), Club San José Oruro (2/0), La Paz FC (5/0), Club Bamin Real Potosí (2/0), Club Aurora Cochabamba (6/0). |
| (399/446) | ÁÑEZ URACHATA Óscar | 23.07.1990 | 1 | 0 | 2012, CD Universitario Sucre (1/0). |
| (296/346) | ANEZ Walter | 31.05.1976 | 1 | 0 | 2000, Club Real Santa Cruz de la Sierra (1/0). |
| (229/299) | ANGOLA Demetrio | 22.06.1965 | 17 | 2 | 1995-1997, Club Jorge Wilstermann Cochabamba (17/2). |
| (330/378) | ANGULO Carmelo | 23.05.1980 | 6 | 0 | 2004-2005, Club Aurora Cochabamba (6/0). |
| (348/392) | ANGULO Carmelo | 23.05.1980 | 1 | 0 | 2006, Club Bolívar Independiente Unificada La Paz (1/0). |
| (10/025) | ANGULO Conrado | | 5 | 0 | 1938 |
| (1/006) | ANGULO Eliseo | 1902 | 1 | 0 | 1926 |
| (102/177) | ANGULO TORME Eduardo | 02.03.1953 | 33 | 0 | 1973-1981, Club The Strongest La Paz |
| (90/153) | ANTELO Miguel | 26.01.1951 | 11 | 0 | 1972-1973 |
| (154/230) | ANTELO Víctor Hugo | 02.11.1964 | 15 | 4 | 1985-2000, Club Oriente Petrolero Santa Cruz de la Sierra |
| (185/272) | ARAGÓN Víctor Hugo | 23.12.1966 | 2 | 0 | 1991, Club The Strongest La Paz (2/0). |
| (112/187) | ARAGONÉS ESPINOSA Carlos | 16.12.1956 | 31 | 14 | 1977-1981, Club Bolívar Independiente Unificada La Paz |
| (60/108) | ARAMAYO MENDIZÁBAL Abdul | 04.09.1934 | 14 | 1 | 1959-1963, CD Chaco Petrolero La Paz |
| (197/286) | ARAMAYO Pastor | 25.12.1966 | 1 | 0 | 1993, Club The Strongest La Paz (1/0). |
| (274/316) | ARANA Ronald | 18.01.1977 | 20 | 0 | 1999-2007, CD Oriente Petrolero Santa Cruz de la Sierra (1/0), Club The Strongest La Paz (5/0), CD Oriente Petrolero Santa Cruz de la Sierra (12/0), CA Rosario Central (1/0), CD Oriente Petrolero Santa Cruz de la Sierra (1/0). |
| (229/297) | ARANDIA Hebert | 09.11.1970 | 4 | 0 | 1995-1996, CSCD Blooming Santa Cruz de la Sierra (4/0). |
| (4/014) | ARANÍBAR LÓPEZ Hernán | 1907 | 1 | 0 | 1926 |
| (27/067) | ARÁOZ Duberty | 21.12.1920 | 10 | 0 | 1947-1950, Club Deportivo Litoral La Paz |
| (333/382) | ARCE JUSTINIANO Juan Carlos | 10.04.1985 | 40 | 5 | 2004-2012, CD Oriente Petrolero Santa Cruz de la Sierra (8/1), SC Corinthians Paulista São Paulo (9/2), Al-Arabi SC Doha (1/0), Sport CD Oriente Petrolero Santa Cruz de la Sierra (8/1), Club Bolívar Independiente Unificada La Paz (14/0). |
| (289/331) | ARÉVALO RAMÍREZ Wilder | 30.04.1980 | 1 | 0 | 1999, Club Jorge Wilstermann Cochabamba (1/0). |
| (8/020) | ARGOTE Juan Jorge | 1906 | 1 | 0 | 1930, Club Bolívar Independiente Unificada La Paz (1/0) |
| (146/221) | ARIAS Carlos | 26.08.1956 | 18 | 0 | 1983-1989, Club Bolívar Independiente Unificada La Paz |
| (43/080) | ARIAS Carlos | | 1 | 0 | 1950 |
| (308/348) | ARIAS ÉGÜEZ Carlos Erwin | 27.04.1982 | 41 | 0 | 2001-2013, CSCD Blooming Santa Cruz de la Sierra (9/0), Club The Strongest La Paz (3/0), CSCD Blooming Santa Cruz de la Sierra (2/0), Club Bolívar Independiente Unificada La Paz (14/0), Maccabi Netanya FC (8/0), Córdoba CF (3/0), CD Oriente Petrolero Santa Cruz de la Sierra (2/0). |
| (413/463) | ARRASCAITA IRIONDO Jaime Darío | 02.09.1991 | 3 | 1 | 2013, Club Bolívar La Paz (3/1). |
| (10/024) | ARRAYA CASTRO Vicente | 25.01.1922 | 26 | 0 | 1938-1950, Ferroviario La Paz |
| (213/289) | ARTEAGA Robert | 10.02.1973 | 3 | 0 | 1994-1995, Club The Strongest La Paz (3/0). |
| (412/461) | ARZE CAMACHO Vicente | 22.11.1985 | 2 | 0 | 2013, R Charleroi SC (2/0). |
| (159/236) | AVILA José Wilson | 19.04.1960 | 7 | 0 | 1985-1987, Club Oriente Petrolero Santa Cruz de la Sierra |
| (154/231) | AYAVIRI Eliseo | 05.02.1957 | 2 | 0 | 1985 |
| (402/453) | AZOGUE ROJAS Pedro Jesús | 06.12.1994 | 7 | 0 | 2012-2013, CD Oriente Petrolero Santa Cruz de la Sierra (7/0). |
| (91/162) | BALCAZAR Gerson | | 2 | 0 | 1972 |
| (2/013) | BALDERRAMA Jorge Luis | 12.02.1906 | 7 | 0 | 1926-1930, CD Oruro Royal |
| (112/186) | BALDIVIESO FERNÁNDEZ Pablo | 30.06.1949 | 11 | 0 | 1977-1979, Club Deportivo Municipal La Paz |

| | | | | | |
|---|---|---|---|---|---|
| (183/264) | BALDIVIESO Julio César | 02.12.1971 | **85** | **15** | 1991-2004, Club Jorge Wilstermann Cochabamba (5/0), Club Bolívar Independiente Unificada La Paz (29/1), CA Newell's Old Boys Rosario (20/4), Yokohama Marinos (9/2), Club Bolívar Independiente Unificada La Paz (7/2), CD Cobreola Calama (7/3), Al Nassr Riyadh (1/2), Club Aurora Cochabamba (3/1), Al Wakra Sports (2/0), Caracas FC (2/0). |
| (401/450) | BARBA PAZ José Carlos | 21.04.1985 | **3** | **0** | 2012, Club Aurora Cochabamba (1/0), Club Bolívar La Paz (2/0). |
| (165/240) | BARRERO Marco Antonio | 26.01.1962 | **31** | **0** | 1987-1999, Club Jorge Wilstermann Cochabamba (4/0), Club Bolívar Independiente Unificada La Paz (10/0), Club Guabirá Santa Cruz de la Sierra (3/0), CD Oriente Petrolero Santa Cruz de la Sierra (10/0), Club The Strongest La Paz (4/0). |
| (121/197) | BASTIDA PASCUAL Luis Fernando | 08.07.1948 | **2** | **0** | 1977, Club The Strongest La Paz |
| (406/456) | BEJARANO IBAÑEZ Diego | 24.08.1991 | **6** | **1** | 2012-2013, Club The Strongest La Paz (6/1). |
| (377/424) | BEJARANO JIMÉNEZ Marvin Orlando | 06.03.1988 | **15** | **0** | 2009-2013, CD Universitario Sucre (6/0), CD Oriente Petrolero Santa Cruz de la Sierra (9/0). |
| (407/457) | BEJARANO YAÑEZ Danny Brayhan | 03.01.1994 | **5** | **0** | 2013, CD Oriente Petrolero Santa Cruz de la Sierra (5/0). |
| (318/360) | BENGOLEA VARGAS Diego Didier | 07.12.1979 | **5** | **1** | 2002-2003, Club San José Oruro (5/1). |
| (1/001) | BERMÚDEZ TÓRREZ Jesús | 1902 | **8** | **0** | 1926-1930, CD Oruro Royal |
| (105/179) | BILBAO René | 03.04.1950 | **1** | **0** | 1975 |
| (69/122) | BLACUTT RODRÍGUEZ Ramiro | 03.01.1944 | **23** | **3** | 1963-1972, Club Bolívar Independiente Unificada La Paz |
| (259/313) | BLANCO Mauro | 25.11.1967 | **7** | **2** | 1997, Club The Strongest La Paz (7/2). |
| (123/201) | BORJA Carlos Fernando | 25.12.1956 | **85** | **1** | 1979-1995, Club Bolívar Independiente Unificada La Paz |
| (285/327) | BOTERO VACA Joaquín | 10.12.1977 | **48** | **20** | 1999-2009, Club Bolívar Independiente Unificada La Paz (18/6), UNAM "Los Pumas" Ciudad de México (19/6), Club Bolívar Independiente Unificada La Paz (11/8). |
| (42/079) | BROWN ROJAS Víctor | 07.03.1927 | **16** | **1** | 1950-1957, Club Deportivo Litoral La Paz |
| (51/094) | BURGOS SUÁREZ Miguel | 04.09.1929 | **13** | **0** | 1957-1959 |
| (1/010) | BUSTAMANTE José | 1907 | **9** | **2** | 1926-1930, Club Deportivo Litoral La Paz |
| (21/053) | BUSTAMANTE NAVA José | 1921 | **29** | **0** | 1946-1953, Club Deportivo Litoral La Paz |

| | | | | | |
|---|---|---|---|---|---|
| (99/173) | CABRERA BUCETT Limbert | 1947 | **3** | **0** | 1973 |
| (318/361) | CABRERA FLORES Diego Aroldo | 13.08.1982 | **22** | **1** | 2002-2011, CSCD Blooming Santa Cruz de la Sierra (1/0), Club The Strongest La Paz (1/0), Club Bolívar Independiente Unificada La Paz (2/0), Club Aurora Cochabamba (4/0), CN Cúcuta Deportivo (5/1), CD Independiente Medellín (2/0), CD Oriente Petrolero Santa Cruz de la Sierra (2/0), Asociación Deportivo Pasto (1/0), CC Deportes Tolima (1/0), Independiente Santa Fe (2/0), CD San José Oruro (1/0). |
| (35/070) | CABRERA René | | **14** | **0** | 1949-1953, Club Jorge Wilstermann Cochabamba |
| (413/462) | CABRERA SCAPIN Abraham | 20.02.1991 | **2** | **0** | 2013, Club The Strongest La Paz (2/0). |
| (65/113) | CAINZO OCARANZA Roberto | 13.04.1931 | **15** | **0** | 1961-1965, Club Deportivo Municipal La Paz |
| (15/042) | CALDERÓN Exequiel | | **16** | **0** | 1945-1948, Club Deportivo Litoral La Paz |
| (289/333) | CALUSTRO Franz Alvaro | 09.03.1974 | **17** | **0** | 1999-2003, Club Unión Central Tarija (8/0), CD Oriente Petrolero Santa Cruz de la Sierra (6/0), Club Unión Central Tarija (2/0), Club Jorge Wilstermann Cochabamba (1/0). |
| (133/214) | CAMACHO Jorge | 13.03.1956 | **7** | **1** | 1980-1983, Petrolero Cochabamba |
| (295/343) | CAMACHO Luis | 02.05.1977 | **3** | **0** | 2000-2002, CD Oriente Petrolero Santa Cruz de la Sierra (2/0), CSCD Blooming Santa Cruz de la Sierra (1/0). |
| (53/103) | CAMACHO Wilfredo | 21.06.1935 | **27** | **5** | 1957-1967, Club Deportivo Municipal La Paz |
| (351/397) | CAMPOS DÁVALOS Jhasmani | 10.05.1988 | **26** | **2** | 2007-2013, CD Oriente Petrolero Santa Cruz de la Sierra (16/1), Club Bolívar Independiente Unificada La Paz (7/0), FK Alania Vladikavkaz (3/1). |
| (112/185) | CAMPOS Jorge | 11.08.1955 | **11** | **1** | 1977-1980 |
| (44/082) | CAPARELLI CORINGRATO Roberto | 18.11.1921 | **1** | **0** | 1950, Club The Strongest La Paz (1/0). |
| (290/338) | CARBALLO CADIMA Marcelo Antonio | 07.12.1974 | **9** | **1** | 2000-2004, Club Jorge Wilstermann Cochabamba (9/1). |
| (288/330) | CÁRDENAS RODRÍGUEZ Carlos | 05.10.1976 | **5** | **0** | 1999-2001, Club Jorge Wilstermann Cochabamba (5/0). |
| (382/436) | CARDOZO FERNÁNDEZ Rudy Alejandro | 14.02.1990 | **28** | **3** | 2010-2013, Club Bolívar Independiente Unificada La Paz (28/3). |
| (357/403) | CARDOZO Jaime | 14.03.1982 | **2** | **0** | 2007-2008, Club The Strongest La Paz (2/0). |
| (365/414) | CARDOZO TAHUA Jaime | 16.10.1981 | **1** | **0** | 2008, Club The Strongest La Paz (1/0). |
| (413/466) | CASTELLÓN COLQUE Vladimir | 12.08.1989 | **1** | **0** | 2013, Club Aurora Cochabamba (1/0). |
| (67/119) | CASTILLO ANDIA Fortunato | 16.03.1939 | **9** | **4** | 1962-1965, CD Chaco Petrolero La Paz |
| (150/225) | CASTILLO Edgar | 17.04.1957 | **11** | **0** | 1983-1985, CSCD Blooming Santa Cruz de la Sierra |
| (199/287) | CASTILLO Iván Sabino | 11.07.1970 | **36** | **0** | 1993-2000, Club Bolívar Independiente Unificada La Paz (19/0), Club Gimnasia y Esgrima Jujuy (12/0), Club Bolívar Independiente Unificada La Paz (5/0). |
| (313/351) | CASTILLO PARADA José Alfredo | 09.02.1983 | **24** | **6** | 2001-2011, CD Oriente Petrolero Santa Cruz de la Sierra (7/1), Club Universidad Autonoma de Guadalajara (4/0), Club Bolívar Independiente Unificada La Paz (2/1), CA Rosario Central (6/4), CD Oriente Petrolero Santa Cruz de la Sierra (2/0), CSCD Blooming Santa Cruz de la Sierra (1/0), CF Estudiantes Guadalajara (2/0). |
| (175/257) | CASTILLO SALINAS Ramiro | 27.03.1966 | **55** | **5** | 1989-1997, AA Argentinos Juniors Buenos Aires (2/0), CA River Plate Buenos Aires (6/0), Club The Strongest La Paz (10/1), CA Platense Buenos Aires (8/0), Club Bolívar Independiente Unificada La Paz (29/4). |
| (246/308) | CASTILLO Sergio | 29.09.1970 | **34** | **0** | 1996-2001, Club The Strongest La Paz (19/0), CD Oriente Petrolero Santa Cruz de la Sierra (9/0), Club Guabirá Santa Cruz de la Sierra (6/0). |
| (78/132) | CASTRO Valenzio | | **1** | **0** | 1965 |
| (94/166) | CAYO THAMES Hernán | 19.08.1946 | **3** | **0** | 1973 |
| (63/110) | CENTENO Raymundo | | **2** | **0** | 1959 |

| | | | | | |
|---|---|---|---|---|---|
| (163/239) | CESPEDES Erwin | 11.09.1958 | **1** | **0** | 1985 |
| (240/305) | CÉSPEDES Rodolfo | 24.10.1968 | **1** | **0** | 1996, Club Guabirá Santa Cruz de la Sierra (1/0). |
| (1/002) | CHAVARRÍA Casiano José | 1902 | **8** | **0** | 1926-1930, CD Calavera La Paz |
| (411/460) | CHÁVEZ BETANCOURT Daniel Andrés | 13.01.1990 | **2** | **0** | 2013, Club The Strongest La Paz (2/0). |
| (90/154) | CHÁVEZ Félix | 01.01.1948 | **7** | **0** | 1972-1973 |
| (184/270) | CHÁVEZ Juan Carlos | 11.12.1972 | **8** | **0** | 1991-1995, CSCD Blooming Santa Cruz de la Sierra (8/0). |
| (365/415) | CHÁVEZ SÁNCHEZ José Luis | 18.05.1986 | **21** | **1** | 2008-2013, CD Universitario Sucre (1/0), CSCD Blooming Santa Cruz de la Sierra (16/0), Club Atlas de Guadalajara (4/1). |
| (394/444) | CHUMACERO BRACAMONTE Alejandro Saúl | 22.04.1991 | **16** | **1** | 2011-2013, Club The Strongest La Paz (15/1), Sport Club do Recife (1/0). |
| (51/095) | CLAURE Oscar | 18.01.1933 | **13** | **0** | 1957-1959 |
| (65/112) | COBO SALVATIERRA Griseldo | 27.01.1938 | **10** | **0** | 1961-1973, |
| (146/220) | COIMBRA Rolando | 25.02.1960 | **15** | **0** | 1983-1987, Club Guabirá Santa Cruz de la Sierra, CSCD Blooming Santa Cruz de la Sierra |
| (242/307) | COIMBRA SUIZER Milton | 04.05.1975 | **43** | **7** | 1996-2005, CD Oriente Petrolero Santa Cruz de la Sierra (12/4), CA Lanús (8/1), CD Oriente Petrolero Santa Cruz de la Sierra (18/2), no club (1/0), CD Oriente Petrolero Santa Cruz de la Sierra (2/0), Ionikos Nikea (2/0). |
| (290/339) | COLQUE PAREDES Percy | 23.10.1976 | **20** | **2** | 2000-2005, Club The Strongest La Paz (10/1), CD "Los Tigres" Nuevo Leon (2/0), Club Bolívar Independiente Unificada La Paz (8/1). |
| (81/138) | CORTÉZ Rómulo | | **2** | **0** | 1967 |
| (189/275) | COSSÍO Freddy | 01.03.1967 | **12** | **0** | 1996, Club San José Oruro (12/0). |
| (99/174) | COSTA ROJAS Walter | 23.12.1943 | **4** | **0** | 1973 |
| (181/262) | CRISTALDO Luis Héctor | 31.08.1969 | **92** | **5** | 1989-2005, CD Oriente Petrolero Santa Cruz de la Sierra (1/0), Club Bolívar Independiente Unificada La Paz (66/3), Real Sporting Gijón CF (7/0), Cerro Porteño Asunción (8/0), Club The Strongest La Paz (12/2). |
| (319/366) | CUÉLLAR Adrián | 08.09.1982 | **1** | **0** | 2002, Club Guabirá Santa Cruz de la Sierra (1/0). |
| (324/373) | CUÉLLAR Darwin | 22.10.1979 | **1** | **0** | 2003, Club Universidad Iberoamericana La Paz Bolívar (1/0). |
| (215/291) | CUETO Richard | 22.11.1970 | **2** | **0** | 1994-1997, Club Bolívar Independiente Unificada La Paz (2/0). |
| (330/379) | DA ROSA Alex | 01.06.1976 | **1** | **0** | 2004, Club The Strongest La Paz (1/0). |
| (372/420) | DA ROSA DORNELLES Álex Rodrigo | 01.06.1976 | **5** | **1** | 2009-2010, CD San José Oruro (4/1), Club Bolívar Independiente Unificada La Paz (1/0). |
| (105/180) | DEL LLANO SUÁREZ Windsor | 17.08.1949 | **30** | **1** | 1975-1981, Club Jorge Wilstermann Cochabamba, Club The Strongest La Paz |
| (129/208) | DELFÍN VALDÉZ Rogelio | 04.09.1953 | **1** | **0** | 1979, Always Ready La Paz (1/0) |
| (40/077) | DELGADILLO N. | | **2** | **0** | 1949 |
| (133/215) | DELGADILLO Omar | 19.10.1953 | **2** | **0** | 1980 |
| (86/145) | DÍAZ CRUZ Juan Américo | 12.11.1944 | **9** | **2** | 1969-1975, Club Bolívar Independiente Unificada La Paz |
| (47/089) | DÍAZ Delfin | | **2** | **0** | 1953 |
| (88/149) | DÍAZ GUTIÉRREZ Julio | 22.09.1940 | **1** | **0** | 1969 |
| (68/121) | DIMEGLIO CAMPORIALE Mario | 28.11.1932 | **3** | **0** | 1963 |
| (8/019) | DURANDAL Segundo | 17.03.1907 | **7** | **0** | 1930-1938, Club San José Oruro |
| (381/430) | EGUINO SEGOVIA Ronald | 20.02.1988 | **3** | **0** | 2010-2013, Club Bamin Real Potosí (1/0), Club Bolívar La Paz (2/0). |
| (159/235) | ENRÍQUEZ César | 18.05.1956 | **1** | **0** | 1985 |
| (318/359) | ESCALANTE Wilson | 06.05.1977 | **3** | **0** | 2002-2003, Club Unión Central Tarija (2/0), CD Oriente Petrolero Santa Cruz de la Sierra (1/0). |
| (51/097) | ESCOBAR Armando | 11.07.1932 | **5** | **1** | 1957-1961 |
| (366/416) | ESCOBAR OLIVETTI Pablo Daniel | 23.02.1979 | **16** | **3** | 2008-2012, Club The Strongest La Paz (1/0), Ipatinga FC (4/0), Esporte Clube Santo André (5/0), Club The Strongest La Paz (6/3). |
| (113/191) | ESPINOZA Erwin | 27.02.1954 | **19** | **1** | 1977-1985, Club Oriente Petrolero Santa Cruz de la Sierra |
| (67/118) | ESPINOZA LAROSA Eduardo | 09.01.1934 | **6** | **0** | 1962-1963, 31 de Octubre Obrajes |
| (173/256) | ETCHEVERRY Marco Antonio | 26.09.1970 | **71** | **13** | 1989-2003, Club Destroyers Santa Cruz de la Sierra (4/0), Club Bolívar Independiente Unificada La Paz (5/0), CSD Colo Colo Santiago (15/5), CD America Cali (6/2), Washington DC United (41/6). |
| (279/322) | FARAH Juan Carlos | 08.03.1969 | **2** | **1** | 1999-2001, CD Oriente Petrolero Santa Cruz de la Sierra (1/1), Club Independiente Petrolero Sucre (1/0). |
| (86/147) | FARÍAS SALAZAR Juan P. | 08.03.1941 | **4** | **0** | 1969-1975, Club The Strongest La Paz |
| (257/312) | FERNÁNDEZ José Carlos | 24.01.1971 | **26** | **0** | 1997-2008, Club Destroyers Santa Cruz de la Sierra (1/0), CSCD Blooming Santa Cruz de la Sierra (11/0), CD Veracruz SA (5/0), Córdoba CF (2/0), New England Revolution Boston (1/0), Club Bolívar Independiente Unificada La Paz (5/0), José Gálvez FC Chimbote 1/0). |
| (325/374) | FERNÁNDEZ Leonardo | 13.01.1974 | **17** | **0** | 2003-2005, CD Oriente Petrolero Santa Cruz de la Sierra (4/0), CA Chacarita Juniors Buenos Aires (5/0), CD Oriente Petrolero Santa Cruz de la Sierra (5/0), CA Rosario Central (3/0). |
| (15/041) | FERNÁNDEZ Raúl | | **11** | **1** | 1945-1946 |
| (8/022) | FERNÁNDEZ René | 1906 | **2** | **0** | 1930, Alianza Oruro (2/0) |
| (91/164) | FERNÁNDEZ VELARDE Juan Carlos | 25.10.1946 | **16** | **1** | 1972-1975, Club Bolívar Independiente Unificada La Paz |
| (21/054) | FERREL Leonardo | 07.07.1923 | **16** | **1** | 1946-1950, Club The Strongest La Paz |
| (10/027) | FERREL Remberto | 23.02.1907 | **3** | **0** | 1938 |
| (180/259) | FERRUFINO Marco | 25.04.1963 | **9** | **0** | 1989-1991, Club Bolívar Independiente Unificada La Paz (9/0). |
| (123/199) | FIERRO BANEGAS Aldo | 19.06.1958 | **8** | **0** | 1979-1981, Club Bolívar Independiente Unificada La Paz |
| (407/459) | FIERRO RIBERA Juan Eduardo | 23.06.1988 | **2** | **0** | 2013, FK Vojvodina Novi Sad (2/0). |

| | | | | | |
|---|---|---|---|---|---|
| (15/039) | FIGUEROA DE ACHÁ Alberto | 03.04.1920 | **24** | **0** | 1945-1950, Club The Strongest La Paz |
| (334/383) | FLORES CONDARCO Wálter Alberto | 29.10.1978 | **31** | **1** | 2004-2012, Club San José Oruro (4/0), Club Bamin Real Potosí (1/0), Club The Strongest La Paz (4/0), Club Bolívar Independiente Unificada La Paz (22/1). |
| (84/140) | FLORES ESPINOZA Adolfo | 12.02.1942 | **3** | **0** | 1967 |
| (229/298) | FLORES Franklin | 14.07.1969 | **1** | **0** | 1995, |
| (68/120) | FLORES VARGAS Milton | 27.02.1939 | **3** | **1** | 1963 |
| (170/254) | FONTANA Ricardo | 17.10.1950 | **13** | **0** | 1989, Club The Strongest La Paz (13/0). |
| (193/282) | FRANCISQUINE Marcos | 21.11.1966 | **5** | **0** | 1993-2001, Club The Strongest La Paz (4/0), Club Real Santa Cruz de la Sierra (1/0). |
| (90/151) | FREY Erwin | 26.09.1943 | **4** | **0** | 1972 |
| | | | | | |
| (121/194) | GALARZA MAYEREGER Arturo | 07.09.1944 | **1** | **0** | 1977 |
| (122/198) | GALARZA MAYEREGER Luis Esteban | 26.12.1950 | **14** | **0** | 1977-1989, Club The Strongest La Paz (8/0), Club Bolívar Independiente Unificada La Paz (6). |
| (295/341) | GALARZA SOLÍZ Sergio Daniel | 25.08.1975 | **28** | **0** | 2000-2013, CSCD Blooming Santa Cruz de la Sierra (1/0), Club Jorge Wilstermann Cochabamba (1/0), CD Oriente Petrolero Santa Cruz de la Sierra (12/0), CSCD Blooming Santa Cruz de la Sierra (12/0), Club Sport Boys Warnes (2/0). |
| (259/314) | GALINDO SÁNCHEZ Gonzalo Germán | 20.10.1974 | **43** | **3** | 1997-2007, Club Jorge Wilstermann Cochabamba (20/1), Club Bolívar Independiente Unificada La Paz (11/1), Club Sport Emelec Guayaquil (6/1), Club Bolívar Independiente Unificada (1/0), Club The Strongest La Paz (5/0). |
| (382/438) | GALINDO SÁNCHEZ Roberto | 14.10.1980 | **2** | **1** | 2010, CD Universitario Sucre (2/1). |
| (381/432) | GALINDO SUHEIRO Samuel | 18.04.1992 | **2** | **0** | 2010-2011, Arsenal FC London (1/0), Club Gimnàstic de Tarragona (1/0). |
| (130/210) | GALLARDO Andrés | 16.03.1956 | **3** | **0** | 1980 |
| (10/030) | GAMARRA Hugo | | **4** | **2** | 1938 |
| (169/251) | GARCÍA Arturo | 14.05.1965 | **8** | **3** | 1989, CD Oriente Petrolero Santa Cruz de la Sierra (8/3). |
| (51/098) | GARCÍA Ausberto | 09.02.1934 | **25** | **5** | 1957-1967, Club Jorge Wilstermann Cochabamba |
| (366/417) | GARCÍA JUSTINIANO Ignacio Awad | 20.08.1986 | **11** | **0** | 2008-2011, Club Bolívar La Paz (8/0), Club Aurora Cochabamba (2/0), CSCD Blooming Santa Cruz de la Sierra (1/0). |
| (294/340) | GARCÍA JUSTINIANO Ronald Lázaro | 17.12.1980 | **48** | **2** | 2000-2013, Club Bolívar Independiente Unificada La Paz (9/0), FC de Alverca (4/0), CSCD Blooming Santa Cruz de la Sierra (5/0), PAR Aris Thessaloníki FC (21/2), Anorthósis Famagusta FC (1/0), Club Bolívar Independiente Unificada La Paz (4/0), PAR Aris Thessaloníki (1/0), CD Oriente Petrolero Santa Cruz de la Sierra (3/0). |
| (194/284) | GARECA Serafin | 11.11.1969 | **3** | **0** | 1993, Club The Strongest La Paz (3/0). |
| (127/205) | GARRIDO Ronald | 14.04.1958 | **1** | **0** | 1979 |
| (21/056) | GARZÓN Félix | | **2** | **0** | 1946 |
| (288/328) | GIL Percy | 01.11.1976 | **3** | **0** | 1999-2002, Club Guabirá Santa Cruz de la Sierra (1/0), CSCD Blooming Santa Cruz de la Sierra (2/0). |
| (35/074) | GODOY VÉIZAGA Benedicto | | **9** | **2** | 1949-1950, Ferroviario La Paz |
| (345/387) | GÓMEZ Alejandro Jesús | 18.07.1979 | **4** | **0** | 2005-2007, CSCD Blooming Santa Cruz de la Sierra (2/0), Club San José Oruro (2/0). |
| (8/021) | GÓMEZ Gumercindo | 1907 | **1** | **0** | 1930, CD Oruro Royal (1/0) |
| (367/418) | GÓMEZ LANZA Jesús Alejandro | 18.07.1979 | **5** | **0** | 2008-2011, CSCD Blooming Santa Cruz de la Sierra (5/0). |
| (105/182) | GÓNGORA SAAVEDRA Edgar | 04.01.1955 | **3** | **0** | 1975-1977 |
| (45/083) | GONZÁLEZ Eduardo | | **6** | **0** | 1953 |
| (127/206) | GONZÁLEZ Luis | 30.01.1958 | **10** | **0** | 1979-1981, Club Oriente Petrolero Santa Cruz de la Sierra |
| (86/144) | GONZÁLEZ PÉREZ Remberto | 10.08.1944 | **3** | **0** | 1969 |
| (10/028) | GONZÁLEZ Zenón | | **22** | **4** | 1938-1948, Ferroviario La Paz |
| (274/319) | GOTTARDI Jefferson | 13.01.1976 | **1** | **0** | 1999, Club Bolívar Independiente Unificada La Paz (1/0). |
| (44/081) | GRECO Antonio | 1923 | **1** | **0** | 1950, Club Deportivo Litoral La Paz |
| (26/062) | GUERRA Juan | | **9** | **0** | 1947-1948, Ferroviario La Paz |
| (154/232) | GUILLEN Augusto | 12.10.1965 | **4** | **0** | 1985 |
| (27/068) | GUTIÉRREZ Eduardo | 17.01.1925 | **20** | **0** | 1947-1953, Ingavi La Paz |
| (358/405) | GUTIÉRREZ FLORES Ronald | 02.12.1979 | **3** | **0** | 2007-2008, La Paz FC (2/0), Bursaspor Kulübü (1/0). |
| (378/426) | GUTIÉRREZ Helmut Enrique | 02.07.1987 | **3** | **0** | 2009-2010, La Paz FC (2/0), Club Bamin Real Potosi (1/0). |
| (359/406) | GUTIÉRREZ HERRERA Luis Alberto | 15.01.1985 | **37** | **0** | 2007-2013, CD Oriente Petrolero Santa Cruz de la Sierra (9/0), Hapoel Ironi Kiryat-Shmona FC (2/0), CD Oriente Petrolero Santa Cruz de la Sierra (15/0), EC Bahia Salvador (1/0), CA Patronado de la Juventud Católica Paraná (7/0), Club Bolívar La Paz (2/0). |
| (130/212) | GUTIÉRREZ Luis | | **1** | **0** | 1980 |
| (15/040) | GUTIÉRREZ Manuel | | **3** | **0** | 1945 |
| (256/311) | GUTIÉRREZ MARISCAL Limberg | 19.11.1977 | **54** | **4** | 1997-2009, CSCD Blooming Santa Cruz de la Sierra (25/1), Club Nacional de Football Montevideo (4/0), CSCD Blooming Santa Cruz de la Sierra (2/0), Club Bolívar Independiente Unificada La Paz (16/3), CSCD Blooming Santa Cruz de la Sierra (3/0), CD Oriente Petrolero Santa Cruz de la Sierra (3/0), Club The Strongest La Paz (1/0). |
| (228/294) | GUTIÉRREZ Raúl | 08.01.1976 | **17** | **0** | 1994-2003, Libertad Santa Cruz de la Sierra (3/0), CSCD Blooming Santa Cruz de la Sierra (14/0). |
| (230/300) | GUTIÉRREZ Tomás | 01.02.1973 | **5** | **0** | 1995-2000, Club Independiente Petrolero Sucre (5/0). |
| (26/064) | GUTIÉRREZ VALDIVIA Benigno | 1925 | **17** | **5** | 1947-1953, Ferroviario La Paz, Club Deportivo Litoral La Paz |
| (319/365) | GUZMÁN Javier | 23.05.1985 | **2** | **0** | 2002, Club Jorge Wilstermann Cochabamba (2/0). |
| (228/293) | GUZMÁN Juan Carlos | 07.12.1976 | **1** | **0** | 1994, Club Destroyers Santa Cruz de la Sierra (1/0). |
| | | | | | |
| (75/129) | HERBAS REYES Jaime | 25.09.1941 | **5** | **0** | 1963-1967, Club Jorge Wilstermann Cochabamba |
| (73/128) | HERBAS REYES Jesús | 02.01.1940 | **13** | **0** | 1963-1972, Club Jorge Wilstermann Cochabamba |
| (154/226) | HERRERA Johnny | 09.05.1959 | **9** | **0** | 1985 |

| | | | | | |
|---|---|---|---|---|---|
| (242/306) | HERRERA Marco Antonio | 09.08.1971 | **1** | **0** | 1996, Club Real Santa Cruz de la Sierra (1/0). |
| (317/355) | HOYOS GUZMÁN Miguel Ángel | 11.03.1981 | **28** | **1** | 2002-2011, CD Oriente Petrolero Santa Cruz de la Sierra (6/0), Club The Strongest La Paz (10/1), CD Oriente Petrolero Santa Cruz de la Sierra (6/0), Club Bolívar Independiente Unificada la Paz (3/0), CD Oriente Petrolero Santa Cruz de la Sierra (3/0). |
| (127/207) | HOYOS Hebert | 29.04.1956 | **15** | **0** | 1979-1985, Club Oriente Petrolero Santa Cruz de la Sierra |
| (406/455) | HURTADO BADANI Luis Enrique | 27.09.1993 | **1** | **0** | 2012, CSCD Blooming Santa Cruz de la Sierra (1/0). |
| (88/150) | HURTADO Genaro | | **1** | **0** | 1969 |
| (373/421) | HURTADO Julio César | 25.12.1983 | **1** | **0** | 2009, Club Aurora Cochabamba (1/0). |

| | | | | | |
|---|---|---|---|---|---|
| (317/356) | IBÁÑEZ CORREA Armando | 04.03.1973 | **2** | **0** | 2002, CD Oriente Petrolero Santa Cruz de la Sierra (2/0) |
| (172/255) | IBÁÑEZ William | 25.06.1963 | **4** | **0** | 1989-1993, Club Jorge Wilstermann Cochabamba (4/0). |
| (17/051) | INCHAUSTI Ruperto | | **5** | **0** | 1945-1946 |
| (94/167) | IRIONDO ANGOLA Luis | 15.12.1952 | **14** | **0** | 1973-1975, Club The Strongest La Paz |
| (82/139) | ISSA José | 28.01.1942 | **7** | **0** | 1967-1969 |

| | | | | | |
|---|---|---|---|---|---|
| (331/380) | JÁUREGUI Sergio | 12.03.1981 | **13** | **0** | 2004-2005, CSCD Blooming Santa Cruz de la Sierra (10/0), Yverdon-Sport (3/0). |
| (183/263) | JIGUCHI Eduardo | 04.08.1970 | **18** | **0** | 1991-2002, CD Oriente Petrolero Santa Cruz de la Sierra (5/0), Club Bolívar Independiente Unificada La Paz (10/0), Club Jorge Wilstermann Cochabamba (3/0). |
| (97/172) | JIMÉNEZ HURTADO Carlos Conrado | 10.02.1948 | **36** | **0** | 1973-1981, Club Bolívar Independiente Unificada La Paz |
| (90/160) | JIMÉNEZ HURTADO Porfirio | 16.02.1952 | **18** | **6** | 1972-1977, Club Guabirá Santa Cruz de la Sierra |
| (401/448) | JIMÉNEZ MENDONZA Ronny | 12.04.1989 | **5** | **0** | 2012-2013, Club Bamin Real Potosí (5/0). |
| (94/168) | JIMÉNEZ ORELLANA Jorge | 23.03.1945 | **6** | **1** | 1973 |
| (274/318) | JUSTINIANO ABELLA Miguel Raúl | 29.09.1977 | **26** | **1** | 1999-2005, CSCD Blooming Santa Cruz de la Sierra (19/1), CD Oriente Petrolero Santa Cruz de la Sierra (7/0). |
| (165/243) | JUSTINIANO Federico | 18.07.1964 | **3** | **0** | 1987, Club Destroyers Santa Cruz de la Sierra |

| | | | | | |
|---|---|---|---|---|---|
| (381/434) | LAMPE PORRAS Carlos Emilio | 17.03.1987 | **3** | **0** | 2010, CD Universitario Sucre (3/0). |
| (1/003) | LARA Diógenes | 1902 | **9** | **0** | 1926-1930, Bolívar Paz Jayla Cochabamba |
| (90/157) | LEANOS Nemesio | | **4** | **0** | 1972-1975 |
| (274/320) | LIENDO Luis | 25.02.1978 | **6** | **0** | 1999, CA Boca Juniors Buenos Aires (1/0), Club Bolívar Independiente Unificada La Paz (5/0). |
| (105/183) | LIENDO MORENO Luis | 18.04.1946 | **5** | **0** | 1975, Club Bolívar Independiente Unificada La Paz |
| (348/390) | LIMA CASTEDO Sacha Silvestro | 17.08.1981 | **11** | **0** | 2006-2010, Club Korge Wilsterman Cochabamba (9/0), Club The Strongest La Paz (1/0), CD Universitario Sucre (1/0). |
| (105/181) | LIMA GUARDIA Jaime | 02.11.1950 | **16** | **0** | 1975-1977 |
| (90/158) | LINARES SAIBURY Nicolás | 06.12.1945 | **15** | **1** | 1972-1975, Club Deportivo Municipal La Paz |
| (103/178) | LLADO Jorge | 1947 | **1** | **0** | 1973 |
| (385/440) | LOAIZA TARDIO Miguel Oswaldo | 13.01.1983 | **1** | **0** | 2011, Club Bamin Real Potosí (1/0). |
| (295/342) | LOAYZA PEDRAZA José | 09.09.1976 | **4** | **0** | 2000-2001, CSCD Blooming Santa Cruz de la Sierra (2/0), Club Jorge Wilstermann Cochabamba (1/0), CSCD Blooming Santa Cruz de la Sierra (1/0). |
| (59/106) | LÓPEZ LÓPEZ Arturo | 20.05.1936 | **17** | **0** | 1959-1965, CD Chaco Petrolero La Paz |
| (45/086) | LÓPEZ LÓPEZ Hilarión | 21.10.1932 | **6** | **0** | 1953 |
| (59/105) | LÓPEZ Renán | 31.10.1939 | **14** | **3** | 1959-1967, Club Jorge Wilstermann Cochabamba |

| | | | | | |
|---|---|---|---|---|---|
| (25/060) | MAIDA Rodolfo | | **3** | **0** | 1946-1948 |
| (26/065) | MALDONADO Benjamín | 1928 | **7** | **0** | 1947-1950, Veltze Cochabamba |
| (81/135) | MALDONADO Isaac | | **6** | **0** | 1967-1969 |
| (7/018) | MALPARTIDA N. | | **1** | **0** | 1927 |
| (169/248) | MARTÍNEZ Eligio | 21.07.1955 | **14** | **0** | 1989, Club The Strongest La Paz (14/0). |
| (130/211) | MARTÍNEZ Simón | 28.10.1954 | **6** | **0** | 1980 |
| (414/467) | MAYGUA RÍOS Leandro Marcelo | 12.09.1992 | **2** | **0** | 2013, Club Bolívar La Paz (2/0). |
| (232/302) | MEDEIROS Raúl | 02.02.1975 | **1** | **0** | 1995, BK Häcken Göteborg (1/0). |
| (16/049) | MEDRANO Donato | | **3** | **0** | 1945 |
| (184/271) | MEDRANO José Luis | 16.05.1968 | **2** | **0** | 1991, CD Oriente Petrolero Santa Cruz de la Sierra (2/0). |
| (405/454) | MELEÁN VILLARROEL Alejandro | 16.06.1987 | **3** | **0** | 2012-2013, CD Oriente Petrolero Santa Cruz de la Sierra (3/0). |
| (135/216) | MELGAR José Milton | 20.09.1959 | **89** | **6** | 1980-1997, CSCD Blooming Santa Cruz de la Sierra, CA Boca Juniors Buenos Aires, Club Bolívar Independiente Unificada La Paz, CSCD Blooming Santa Cruz de la Sierra, Club The Strongest La Paz, Club Bolívar Independiente Unificada La Paz, CSCD Blooming Santa Cruz de la Sierra. |
| (319/367) | MELGAR Juan Carlos | 07.02.1984 | **1** | **0** | 2002, Academia Tahuichi Aguilera (1/0). |
| (35/073) | MENA LEMA Mario | 28.02.1927 | **22** | **2** | 1949-1959, Club Bolívar Independiente Unificada La Paz |
| (280/325) | MENACHO José Martín | 07.08.1973 | **6** | **0** | 1999-2001, CSCD Blooming Santa Cruz de la Sierra (4/0), CD Oriente Petrolero Santa Cruz de la Sierra (2/0). |
| (289/332) | MÉNDEZ Cléver | 15.09.1978 | **1** | **0** | 1999, CD Oriente Petrolero Santa Cruz de la Sierra (1/0). |
| (324/371) | MÉNDEZ JUSTINIANO Limberg | 18.09.1973 | **7** | **1** | 2003-2005, Club The Strongest La Paz (6/1), Club Aurora Cochabamba (1/0). |
| (348/388) | MÉNDEZ MOZA Luis Javier | 12.07.1985 | **7** | **0** | 2006-2012, CD Oriente Petrolero Santa Cruz de la Sierra (1/0), Club The Strongest La Paz (6/0). |
| (1/008) | MÉNDEZ Rafael | 1902 | **9** | **0** | 1926-1930, CD Universitario La Paz |
| (349/394) | MÉNDEZ ROCHA Limbert | 18.08.1982 | **10** | **0** | 2006-2010, Club Jorge Wilsterman Cochabamba (10/0). |
| (231/301) | MERCADO Miguel Ángel | 30.08.1975 | **12** | **1** | 1995-2004, Club Bolívar Independiente Unificada La Paz ( |
| (90/161) | MEZZA SORUCO Mario Ovidio | 12.12.1951 | **37** | **8** | 1972-1983, Club Bolívar Independiente Unificada La Paz, Club The Strongest La Paz |
| (49/090) | MIRANDA Arturo | 12.11.1930 | **5** | **0** | 1953-1957 |

| | | | | | |
|---|---|---|---|---|---|
| (322/369) | MOJICA OLMOS Gualberto | 07.10.1984 | **25** | **3** | 2003-2013, Club Jorge Wilstermann Cochabamba (3/0), CSCD Blooming Santa Cruz de la Sierra (1/0), FC Paços de Ferreira (6/0), CFR 1907 Cluj (4/0), CSCD Blooming Santa Cruz de la Sierra (1/0), CD Oriente Petrolero Santa Cruz de la Sierra (5/2), FC Petrolul Ploieşti (5/1). |
| (11/034) | MOLINA Alfredo | | **3** | **1** | 1938 |
| (183/265) | MOLINA Modesto | 12.09.1967 | **8** | **0** | 1991-1993, CD Oriente Petrolero Santa Cruz de la Sierra (8/0). |
| (189/276) | MONASTERIO Jorge | 08.05.1968 | **2** | **0** | 1993, CD Oriente Petrolero Santa Cruz de la Sierra (2/0). |
| (35/075) | MONTAÑO Humberto | | **3** | **0** | 1949 |
| (181/261) | MONTAÑO Tito | 11.09.1963 | **2** | **1** | 1989, |
| (61/109) | MONTES Jorge | | **2** | **0** | 1959 |
| (10/029) | MONTOYA Luis | | **5** | **2** | 1938 |
| (99/175) | MORALES GONZÁLES Raúl | 04.06.1942 | **16** | **1** | 1973-1977, Club Bolívar Independiente Unificada La Paz |
| (324/372) | MOREJÓN Limberg | 24.12.1976 | **2** | **0** | 2003, Club The Strongest La Paz (2/0). |
| (90/156) | MORENO Jorge | | **1** | **0** | 1972 |
| (356/400) | MORENO MARTINS Marcelo | 18.06.1987 | **46** | **12** | 2007-2013, Cruzeiro EC Belo Horizonte (5/2), FK Shakhtar Donetsk (9/4), SV Werder Bremen (4/1), FK Shakhtar Donetsk (13/3), Grêmio Foot-Ball Porto Alegrense (6/0), CR Flamengo Rio de Janeiro (9/2). |
| (187/273) | MORENO MORALES Jaime | 19.01.1974 | **74** | **9** | 1991-2008, CSCD Blooming Santa Cruz de la Sierra (24/2), Middlesbrough FC (2/0), Washington DC United (48/7). |
| (51/099) | MORENO Vicente | 02.07.1932 | **2** | **0** | 1957 |
| | | | | | |
| (25/061) | NAVARRO Guillermo | | **1** | **0** | 1946 |
| (319/363) | NAY Johnny | 22.04.1975 | **2** | **0** | 2002-2003, Club Jorge Wilstermann Cochabamba (1/0), Club Aurora Cochabamba (1/0). |
| (14/038) | NOGUERA Ciro | | **1** | **0** | 1938 |
| (154/228) | NORO Miguel Angel | 22.08.1961 | **14** | **0** | 1985-1993, CSCD Blooming Santa Cruz de la Sierra, Club Destroyers Santa Cruz de la Sierra |
| | | | | | |
| (254/309) | OCHOAIZPUR Fernando | 18.03.1971 | **15** | **3** | 1996-1999, Club Bolívar Independiente Unificada La Paz (2/0), Deportivo Universitario (6/1), San Luis de Fútbol Potosí (7/2). |
| (315/354) | OLIVARES BURGOA Edgar Rolando | 25.01.1977 | **9** | **1** | 2001-2010, Club Jorge Wilstermann Cochabamba (2/0), Club Bolívar Independiente Unificada La Paz (3/0), La Paz FC (1/0), Club Jorge Wilstermann Cochabamba (3/1). |
| (90/152) | OLIVERA JIMÉNEZ Jaime Carlos | 06.03.1950 | **13** | **0** | 1972-1973 |
| (13/037) | ORGAZ Severo | | **20** | **2** | 1938-1948 |
| (15/045) | OROZCO Walter | | **6** | **0** | 1945 |
| (15/047) | ORTEGA Adrián | | **9** | **0** | 1945-1946 |
| (271/315) | ORTÍZ José Luis | 18.12.1972 | **2** | **0** | 1997, CSCD Blooming Santa Cruz de la Sierra (2/0). |
| (349/396) | ORTÍZ ORTÍZ Jorge Antonio | 01.06.1984 | **2** | **0** | 2007, CSCD Blooming Santa Cruz de la Sierra (2/0). |
| (51/092) | ORTUNO Eustaquio | | **8** | **0** | 1957 |
| | | | | | |
| (330/377) | PACHI BOZO Daner Jesús | 01.01.1984 | **13** | **0** | 2004-2009, Club Bolívar Independiente Unificada La Paz (10/0), LDU Portoviejo (3/0). |
| (377/425) | PALACIOS Luis | 13.07.1977 | **1** | **0** | 2009, CD San José Oruro (1/0). |
| (70/125) | PALENQUE Hugo | 01.12.1937 | **4** | **0** | 1963-1967, 31 de Octubre Obrajes |
| (159/237) | PANIAGUA Rolando | 14.11.1966 | **25** | **3** | 1985-1996, CSCD Blooming Santa Cruz de la Sierra, Club San José Oruro |
| (123/203) | PANIAGUA YEPEZ David | 30.04.1959 | **16** | **1** | 1979-1985, Club The Strongest La Paz, CSCD Blooming Santa Cruz de la Sierra |
| (238/303) | PARABÁ Miguel Ángel | 02.08.1971 | **12** | **0** | 1995-2000, CD Oriente Petrolero Santa Cruz de la Sierra (10/0), Club Independiente Petrolero Sucre (2/0). |
| (343/385) | PARADA SALVATIERRA Enrique | 04.11.1981 | **8** | **0** | 2005-2011, Club San José Oruro (7/0), Club The Strongest La Paz (1/0). |
| (91/163) | PARIENTE Mario | 15.01.1949 | **9** | **1** | 1972-1975, Club The Strongest La Paz |
| (288/329) | PAZ COLODRO Líder | 02.12.1974 | **21** | **3** | 1999-2005, Club Guabirá Santa Cruz de la Sierra (7/0), Club The Strongest La Paz (10/3), CD Oriente Petrolero Santa Cruz de la Sierra (1/0), Club The Strongest La Paz (3/0). |
| (299/347) | PAZ GARCÍA Juan Carlos | 14.04.1970 | **15** | **0** | 2000-2003, Club The Strongest La Paz (15/0). |
| (361/409) | PEDRIEL SUÁREZ Ricardo | 19.01.1987 | **14** | **3** | 2008-2012, Club Jorge Wilsterman Cochabamba (4/1), FC Steaua Bucureşti (1/0), Giresunspor Kulübü (2/0), Sivasspor (7/2). |
| (118/192) | PEINADO LINO Ismael | 12.09.1954 | **3** | **0** | 1977 |
| (11/033) | PELÁEZ Gerardo | | **2** | **0** | 1938 |
| (166/246) | PEÑA Álvaro Guillermo | 11.02.1965 | **43** | **4** | 1987-1996, CSCD Blooming Santa Cruz de la Sierra (15/2), CD Oriente Petrolero Santa Cruz de la Sierra (1/0), Club de Deportes Temuco (24/2), CC Deportivo Tulua (2/0), Club Real Santa Cruz de la Sierra (1/0). |
| (289/334) | PEÑA ARCE Darwin | 08.08.1977 | **13** | **1** | 1999-2008, Club Bamin Real Potosí (11/1), Club San José Oruro (2/0). |
| (382/437) | PEÑA JIMÉNEZ Alcides | 14.01.1989 | **12** | **1** | 2010-2012, CD Oriente Petrolero Santa Cruz de la Sierra (12/1). |
| (183/266) | PEÑA MONTAÑO Juan Manuel | 17.01.1973 | **85** | **1** | 1991-2009, CSCD Blooming Santa Cruz de la Sierra (22/0), Club Independiente Santa Fé (5/0), Real Valladolid CF (48/1), Villarreal CF (6/0), RC Celta de Vigo (4/0). |
| (24/059) | PEÑALOZA Juan | | **2** | **0** | 1946 |
| (16/048) | PEREDO Miguel | | **7** | **2** | 1945-1946 |
| (92/165) | PÉREZ Hugo | 04.07.1948 | **9** | **0** | 1972-1973 |
| (147/223) | PÉREZ Roberto | 17.04.1960 | **17** | **0** | 1983-1993, Club Guabirá Santa Cruz de la Sierra, Club San José Oruro |
| (349/395) | PINEDO Gustavo | 18.09.1988 | **2** | **0** | 2007, Cádiz CF (1/0). |
| (154/233) | PINEDO Mario Daniel | 09.01.1964 | **22** | **3** | 1985-1994, Club Oriente Petrolero Santa Cruz de la Sierra |
| (6/016) | PINILLA Froilán | | **1** | **0** | 1927 |

| | | | | | |
|---|---|---|---|---|---|
| (330/376) | PIZARRO VACA Limbert | 16.07.1976 | **9** | **0** | 2004-2007, Club Bolívar Independiente Unificada La Paz (8/0), Club San José Oruro (1/0). |
| (10/031) | PLAZA Rodolfo | | **4** | **2** | 1938 |
| (20/052) | PRIETO Cleto | | **1** | **0** | 1945 |
| (15/046) | PRIETO Nicolás | 03.02.1914 | **7** | **0** | 1945-1946 |
| | | | | | |
| (79/134) | QUEVEDO Ramón | 31.12.1943 | **1** | **1** | 1965 |
| (415/468) | QUIÑÓNEZ SUÁREZ Romel Javier | 25.06.1992 | **2** | **0** | 2013, Club Bolívar La Paz (2/0). |
| (71/127) | QUINTEROS GUARDA Edgar | 19.07.1940 | **5** | **0** | 1963-1967, Club San José Oruro |
| (192/277) | QUINTEROS Gustavo Domingo | 15.02.1965 | **26** | **1** | 1993-1999, Club San José Oruro (8/1), Club The Strongest La Paz (15/0), CA San Lorenzo de Almagro Buenos Aires (2/0), AA Argentinos Juniors Buenos Aires (1/0). |
| (65/116) | QUIROGA MARTÍNEZ Alberto | 20.08.1932 | **2** | **0** | 1961 |
| (77/130) | QUIROGA Oscar | | **9** | **0** | 1965-1967 |
| | | | | | |
| (86/146) | RADA CALDERÓN René | 02.10.1940 | **4** | **0** | 1969 |
| (308/349) | RALDES BALCÁZAR Ronald | 20.04.1981 | **75** | **0** | 2001-2013, CD Oriente Petrolero Santa Cruz de la Sierra (12/0), CA Rosario Central (30/0), Al Hilal FC Riyadh (4/0), CDSC Cruz Azul Ciudad de México (2/0), Maccabi Tel Aviv FC (1/0), CA Colón de Santa Fé (26/0). |
| (413/465) | RAMALLO CORNEJO Rodrigo Luis | 14.10.1990 | **1** | **0** | 2013, Club Jorge Wilstermann Cochabamba (1/0). |
| (179/258) | RAMALLO Luis William | 04.07.1963 | **36** | **9** | 1989-1997, Club Destroyers Santa Cruz de la Sierra, Club Oriente Petrolero Santa Cruz de la Sierra, Club Jorge Wilstermann Cochabamba. |
| (51/101) | RAMÍREZ BURGOS Máximo | 09.06.1933 | **26** | **1** | 1957-1965, Club The Strongest La Paz |
| (154/229) | RAMÍREZ Oscar | 29.07.1961 | **8** | **0** | 1985-1987, Club Oriente Petrolero Santa Cruz de la Sierra |
| (165/244) | RAMOS Juan Mauricio | 23.09.1969 | **33** | **1** | 1987-2000, Club Florida Santa Cruz de la Sierra (1/0), Club Guabirá Santa Cruz de la Sierra (1/0), Club Destroyers Santa Cruz de la Sierra (10/0), Club Bolívar Independiente Unificada La Paz (13/1), Tampa Bay Mutiny (7/0), New England Revolution Boston (1/0). |
| (279/324) | REA Rolando | 22.10.1977 | **1** | **0** | 1999, Club The Strongest La Paz (1/0). |
| (5/015) | RENJEL Armando | | **3** | **0** | 1927 |
| (166/245) | REVUELTA Antonio | 02.03.1966 | **1** | **0** | 1987 |
| (361/407) | REYES CARDOZO Abdón | 07.11.1981 | **13** | **0** | 2008-2012, Club Bolívar Independiente Unificada La Paz (13/0). |
| (9/023) | REYES ORTÍZ Eduardo | 1907 | **1** | **0** | 1930, Club The Strongest La Paz (1/0) |
| (327/375) | REYES SARAVIA Leonel Alfredo | 19.11.1976 | **22** | **2** | 2003-2009, Club Universidad Iberoamericana La Paz Bolívar (3/0), Club Bolívar Independiente Unificada La Paz (19/2). |
| (313/350) | REYES ZABALA Luis Alberto | 08.04.1976 | **3** | **0** | 2001, Club Jorge Wilstermann Cochabamba (3/0). |
| (112/189) | REYNALDO HURTADO Jesús | 22.05.1954 | **17** | **4** | 1977-1983, Club Bolívar Independiente Unificada La Paz |
| (50/091) | REYNOSO Raúl | | **1** | **0** | 1953 |
| (290/337) | RIBEIRO ROCA Luis Gatty | 01.11.1979 | **36** | **0** | 2000-2009, Club Bolívar Independiente Unificada La Paz (28/0), Club Bamin Real Potosí (8/0). |
| (381/431) | RIBERA MENACHO Rolando | 13.03.1983 | **1** | **0** | 2010, CD Universitario Sucre (1/0). |
| (281/326) | RIBERA Renny | 30.01.1974 | **14** | **1** | 1999-2000, CSCD Blooming Santa Cruz de la Sierra (14/1). |
| (324/370) | RICALDI Álvaro | 28.04.1982 | **4** | **1** | 2003, Club Jorge Wilstermann Cochabamba (4/1). |
| (10/026) | RICHTER Carlos | | **2** | **0** | 1938 |
| (90/155) | RIMAZZA VARGAS Jaime | 12.12.1946 | **16** | **1** | 1972-1977, Club Deportivo Municipal La Paz |
| (169/247) | RIMBA Miguel Ángel | 01.11.1967 | **80** | **0** | 1989-2000, Club Bolívar Independiente Unificada La Paz (72/0), Club Atlético Tucumán (3/0), CD Oriente Petrolero Santa Cruz de la Sierra (5/0). |
| (33/069) | RÍOS Gustavo | | **2** | **0** | 1948 |
| (193/283) | RÍOS Juan Carlos | 11.05.1972 | **12** | **2** | 1993-1995, Club Ciclón de la Pampa Tarija (11/2), Club The Strongest La Paz (1/0). |
| (413/464) | RÍOS Miguel | 08.02.1988 | **1** | **0** | 2013, Club Deportivo Guabirá Montero (1/0). |
| (393/443) | RÍOS PINTO Darwin | 25.04.1991 | **2** | **0** | 2011-2012, CD Guabirá (1/0), CSCD Blooming Santa Cruz de la Sierra (1/0). |
| (361/408) | RIVERA Rolando | 13.03.1983 | **1** | **0** | 2008, Club San José Oruro (1/0). |
| (380/428) | RIVERO CÉSPEDES Rosauro | 08.09.1982 | **1** | **0** | 2009, Club The Strongest La Paz (1/0). |
| (212/288) | RIVERO Juan | 10.03.1966 | **1** | **0** | 1993, CSCD Blooming Santa Cruz de la Sierra (1/0), Club Real Santa Cruz de la Sierra (1/0). |
| (364/411) | RIVERO KHUN Ronald Taylor | 29.01.1980 | **30** | **0** | 2008-2012, CD Universitario Sucre (15/0), Club Bolívar Independiente Unificada La Paz (7/0), Shenzhen Ruby FC (6/0), CSCD Blooming Santa Cruz de la Sierra (2/0). |
| (87/148) | RIVERO Limbert Cabrera | 23.01.1948 | **7** | **0** | 1969-1973 |
| (319/362) | RIVERO Neil | 03.06.1969 | **1** | **0** | 2002, Club Guabirá Santa Cruz de la Sierra (1/0). |
| (184/268) | RIVERO Sergio | 06.12.1963 | **11** | **0** | 1991-1993, CD Oriente Petrolero Santa Cruz de la Sierra (11/0). |
| (365/413) | ROBLES CÉSPEDES Jaime | 02.02.1978 | **26** | **0** | 2008-2011, CSCD Blooming Santa Cruz de la Sierra (10/0), Club Aurora Cochabamba (16/0). |
| (165/241) | ROCA Romer Antonio | 01.07.1966 | **9** | **0** | 1987-1989, Club Oriente Petrolero Santa Cruz de la Sierra |
| (101/176) | ROCABADO Adolfo | 15.08.1946 | **2** | **0** | 1973 |
| (51/100) | ROCABADO MONTAÑO José | 27.10.1935 | **2** | **0** | 1957 |
| (94/169) | ROCHA David | | **2** | **0** | 1973 |
| (351/398) | RODRÍGUEZ MERCADO Edemir | 21.10.1984 | **14** | **0** | 2007-2013, Club Bamin Real Potosí (9/0), Club Bolívar Independiente Unificada La Paz (5/0). |
| (86/143) | ROJAS ARIAS Mario | 08.09.1941 | **10** | **0** | 1969-1975, Club Bolívar Independiente Unificada La Paz |
| (279/323) | ROJAS GUZMÁN Richard José | 22.02.1975 | **20** | **0** | 1999-2004, Club The Strongest La Paz (13/0), Club San José Oruro (5/0), Club The Strongest La Paz (2/0). |
| (387/441) | ROJAS HERMOZA Edivaldo | 17.11.1985 | **11** | **1** | 2011-2013, Associação Naval 1º de Maio Figueira da Foz (8/1), Shonan Bellmare (2/0), Muanghtongh United FC (1/0). |
| (12/035) | ROJAS Hernán | | **2** | **0** | 1938-1945 |
| (35/076) | ROJAS Nemesio | | **4** | **1** | 1949 |

| | | | | | |
|---|---|---|---|---|---|
| (192/280) | ROJAS Rubén Darío | 20.01.1961 | **18** | **0** | 1993-1994, CD Oriente Petrolero Santa Cruz de la Sierra (18/0). |
| (123/202) | ROJAS Silvio | 03.11.1959 | **24** | **5** | 1979-1987, CSCD Blooming Santa Cruz de la Sierra |
| (112/188) | ROMERO ESCUDERO Erwin | 27.07.1957 | **48** | **4** | 1977-1989, Club Oriente Petrolero Santa Cruz de la Sierra, Club Bolívar Independiente Unificada La Paz |
| (192/279) | ROMERO José María | 08.10.1964 | **1** | **0** | 1993, CD Chaco Petrolero La Paz (1/0). |
| (15/043) | ROMERO Roque | | **4** | **0** | 1945 |
| (21/055) | ROSENBERG | | **1** | **0** | 1946 |
| (214/290) | RUEDA Wilson | 17.03.1973 | **1** | **0** | 1994, |
| (229/296) | RUÍZ Juan Carlos | 14.08.1968 | **5** | **0** | 1995-1996, Club Bolívar Independiente Unificada La Paz (5/0). |
| (17/050) | SAAVEDRA Martín | | **4** | **0** | 1945 |
| (1/005) | SÁINZ Renato | 1904 | **6** | **0** | 1926-1930, Club The Strongest La Paz |
| (158/234) | SALDÍAS Marciano | 25.04.1966 | **18** | **0** | 1985-1991, Club Oriente Petrolero Santa Cruz de la Sierra |
| (189/274) | SALGUERO SILES Rafael | 17.02.1969 | **4** | **0** | 1993-1997, Club Jorge Wilstermann Cochabamba (3/0), Club Bolívar Independiente Unificada La Paz (1/0). |
| (149/224) | SALINAS Fernando | 18.05.1960 | **12** | **1** | 1983-1989, Club Bolívar Independiente Unificada La Paz |
| (348/393) | SALINAS MENACHO Pablo Antonio | 07.08.1979 | **3** | **0** | 2006-2008, Club The Strongest La Paz (3/0). |
| (51/096) | SÁNCHEZ César | | **8** | **0** | 1957-1967 |
| (169/250) | SÁNCHEZ Erwin | 19.10.1969 | **57** | **15** | 1989-2005, Club Bolívar Independiente Unificada La Paz (12/1), Sport Lisboa e Benfica (3/1), Boavista FC do Porto (25/11), Sport Lisboa e Benfica (3/0), Boavista FC do Porto (10/2), CD Oriente Petrolero Santa Cruz de la Sierra (4/0). |
| (96/171) | SÁNCHEZ FRIAS Juan Carlos | 01.09.1956 | **9** | **0** | 1973-1977, Club Jorge Wilstermann Cochabamba |
| (382/439) | SÁNCHEZ GÚZMAN Amílcar Álvaro | 23.01.1991 | **1** | **0** | 2010, Club Jorge Wilstermann Cochabamba (1/0). |
| (295/345) | SÁNCHEZ Herlán | 01.08.1972 | **2** | **0** | 2000, CD Tachira San Cristóbal (2/0). |
| (160/238) | SÁNCHEZ Juan Carlos | 12.04.1951 | **5** | **1** | 198 |
| (217/292) | SÁNCHEZ Óscar Carmelo | 16.07.1971 | **77** | **6** | 1994-2006, Club The Strongest La Paz (41/4), CA Independiente Avellaneda (8/1), Club The Strongest La Paz (9/0), Club Bolívar Independiente Unificada La Paz (27/1). |
| (46/088) | SÁNCHEZ Ricardo | | **1** | **0** | 1953 |
| (192/278) | SANDY SANSUSTY Marco Antonio | 29.08.1971 | **93** | **6** | 1993-2003, Club Bolívar Independiente Unificada La Paz (65/6), Club Gimnasia y Esgrima Jujuy (19/0), Club Bolívar Independiente Unificada La Paz (9/0). |
| (45/084) | SANTOS BRIZUELA Ramón Guillermo | 17.03.1927 | **20** | **3** | 1953-1959 |
| (361/410) | SAUCEDO GUARDIA Mauricio | 14.08.1985 | **16** | **0** | 2008-2012, Club San José Oruro (8/0), CD Universitario San Francisco Xavier Sucre (1/0), CD Oriente Petrolero Santa Cruz de la Sierra (3/0), Vitória SC Guimarães (3/0), Club Atlético Bragantino (1/0). |
| (90/159) | SAUCEDO LANDA Arturo | 04.07.1951 | **12** | **0** | 1972-1977 |
| (355/399) | SAUCEDO URGEL Carlos Enrique | 11.09.1979 | **8** | **5** | 2007-2013, Club Bolívar Independiente Unificada La Paz (2/0), CD San José Oruro (6/5). |
| (397/445) | SEGOVIA CALZADILLA Ronald | 17.01.1985 | **6** | **0** | 2011-2012, Club Aurora Cochabamba (2/0), CSCD Blooming Santa Cruz de la Sierra (4/0). |
| (59/104) | SOLIZ BARBA Oscar | 14.05.1935 | **1** | **0** | 1959 |
| (331/381) | SOLIZ Hernán | 14.07.1982 | **2** | **0** | 2004, Club The Strongest La Paz (2/0). |
| (357/402) | SOLÍZ SALVATIERRA Her | 31.12.1969 | **1** | **0** | 2007, Club The Strongest La Paz (1/0). |
| (169/252) | SORIA PORTILLO Mauricio Ronald | 10.06.1966 | **24** | **0** | 1989-2002, Club The Strongest La Paz (1/0), Club Bolívar Independiente Unificada La Paz (9/0), Club Jorge Wilstermann Cochabamba (14/0). |
| (169/249) | SORIA Vladimir | 15.07.1961 | **50** | **1** | 1989-2000, Club Bolívar Independiente Unificada La Paz (50/1). |
| (184/269) | SORUCO Modesto | 12.02.1966 | **23** | **0** | 1991-1994, CSCD Blooming Santa Cruz de la Sierra (23/0). |
| (348/391) | SOSSA CHÁVEZ Nelson | 14.03.1986 | **6** | **1** | 2006-2008, Club Jorge Wilsterman Cochabamba (6/1). |
| (1/007) | SOTO Carlos | | **6** | **1** | 1926-1927 |
| (1/004) | SOTO Jorge | 1902 | **7** | **0** | 1926-1927 |
| (11/032) | SOTO Roberto | | **2** | **0** | 1938 |
| (319/364) | SUÁREZ Carlos | 28.11.1984 | **3** | **0** | 2002-2003, CSCD Blooming Santa Cruz de la Sierra (3/0). |
| (184/267) | SUÁREZ Juan Berthy | 24.06.1969 | **25** | **8** | 1991-1999, CSCD Blooming Santa Cruz de la Sierra (4/1), Club Guabirá Santa Cruz de la Sierra (3/0), Washington DC United (10/4), Club The Strongest La Paz (8/3). |
| (255/310) | SUÁREZ Roger | 02.04.1977 | **29** | **7** | 1996-2004, CD Oriente Petrolero Santa Cruz de la Sierra (24/6), Club Bolívar Independiente Unificada La Paz (5/1). |
| (393/442) | SUÁREZ SAUCEDO Ronald Lorgio | 05.12.1990 | **1** | **0** | 2011, CSCD Blooming Santa Cruz de la Sierra (1/0). |
| (402/452) | SUÁREZ SAVINO Miguel Gerardo | 01.06.1993 | **3** | **1** | 2012, Club Bolívar La Paz (3/1). |
| (322/368) | SUÁREZ VACA Hugo | 07.02.1982 | **12** | **0** | 2003-2012, Club Jorge Wilstermann Cochabamba (6/0), Club Bamin Real Potosí (1/0), Club Jorge Wilstermann Cochabamba (2/0), CD Oriente Petrolero Santa Cruz de la Sierra (3/0). |
| (289/336) | SUÁREZ VACA Nicolás | 23.12.1978 | **8** | **0** | 1999-2010, Club Guabirá Santa Cruz de la Sierra (1/0), Club Bamin Real Potosí (5/0), CD Oriente Petrolero Santa Cruz de la Sierra (2/0). |
| (131/213) | TABORGA Gastón | 11.11.1960 | **17** | **2** | 1980-1987, CSCD Blooming Santa Cruz de la Sierra |
| (169/253) | TAKEO Francisco | 13.05.1966 | **14** | **1** | 1989-1993, Club Destroyers Santa Cruz de la Sierra (6/1), CD Oriente Petrolero Santa Cruz de la Sierra (8/0). |
| (118/193) | TAMAYO Luis Alberto | | **1** | **0** | 1977 |
| (15/044) | TAPIA Armando | 22.01.1922 | **17** | **2** | 1945-1949 |
| (26/066) | TARDÍO Arturo | | **4** | **1** | 1947-1948 |
| (121/196) | TARRITOLAY TESTER René Domingo | 26.01.1943 | **2** | **0** | 1977 |
| (146/218) | TERRAZAS Eduardo | 06.03.1962 | **8** | **0** | 1983, CSCD Blooming Santa Cruz de la Sierra (8/0) |
| (402/451) | TORDOYA PIZARRO Carlos Hugo | 31.07.1987 | **1** | **0** | 2012, CD San José Oruro (1/0). |

| | | | | | |
|---|---|---|---|---|---|
| (6/017) | TORO José | | **4** | **0** | 1927-1938 |
| (317/358) | TORRES Roberto | 17.08.1980 | **1** | **0** | 2002, CD Oriente Petrolero Santa Cruz de la Sierra (1/0). |
| (65/115) | TORRES VARGAS Alberto | 21.12.1939 | **12** | **0** | 1961-1969, Club Deportivo Municipal La Paz |
| (69/123) | TORRES VARGAS Julio | 28.12.1943 | **1** | **0** | 1963 |
| (364/412) | TORRICO CAMACHO Didí | 18.05.1988 | **9** | **2** | 2008-2009, Club Jorge Wilstermann Cochabamba (9/2). |
| (381/435) | TORRICO CAMACHO Jair | 12.08.1988 | **3** | **0** | 2010-2013, Club Jorge Wilstermann Cochabamba (1/0), Club The Strongest La Paz (2/0). |
| (196/285) | TORRICO Marcelo Eduardo | 11.01.1972 | **2** | **0** | 1993-1996, Club The Strongest La Paz (2/0). |
| (295/344) | TORRICO Ricardo | 31.04.1969 | **2** | **0** | 2000, Club Mariscal Braun La Paz (2/0). |
| (130/209) | TRIGO Juan Carlos | 14.06.1956 | **15** | **0** | 1980-1981 |
| (81/136) | TRONCOSO Roberto | | **1** | **0** | 1967 |
| (181/260) | TRUCCO Carlos Leonel | 11.08.1957 | **51** | **0** | 1989-1997, Club Bolívar Independiente Unificada La Paz (24/0), Club Atlético Hidalgo Pachuca (6/0), Club Cruz Azul Hidalgo (21/0). |
| (238/304) | TUFIÑO Rubén Darío | 09.01.1970 | **35** | **1** | 1995-2004, CD Oriente Petrolero Santa Cruz de la Sierra (16/1), CSCD Blooming Santa Cruz de la Sierra (10/0), Club Bolívar Independiente Unificada La Paz (9/0). |

| | | | | | |
|---|---|---|---|---|---|
| (26/063) | UGARTE OVIEDO Víctor Agustín | 06.06.1926 | **45** | **16** | 1947-1963, Club Bolívar Independiente Unificada La Paz |
| (84/141) | URDININEA Jorge | | **2** | **0** | 1967 |
| (274/321) | URIONA Richard | 28.03.1973 | **7** | **0** | 1999, CD Oriente Petrolero Santa Cruz de la Sierra (7/0). |
| (146/219) | URIZAR Carlos | 16.01.1957 | **8** | **0** | 1983, Club Bolívar Independiente Unificada La Paz (8/0) |
| (2/012) | URRIOLAGOITÍA Alberto | 1902 | **1** | **0** | 1926 |

| | | | | | |
|---|---|---|---|---|---|
| (123/200) | VACA BARBOSA Edgar | 02.05.1956 | **30** | **0** | 1979-1985, CSCD Blooming Santa Cruz de la Sierra, Club Guabirá Santa Cruz de la Sierra |
| (339/384) | VACA DIEZ Getulio | 24.10.1984 | **2** | **0** | 2004, CSCD Blooming Santa Cruz de la Sierra (2/0). |
| (314/353) | VACA Doyle | 08.10.1979 | **4** | **1** | 2001-2005, Club The Strongest La Paz (1/0), Club Bamin Real Potosí (3/1). |
| (228/295) | VACA Henry | 07.01.1976 | **1** | **0** | 1994, CD Oriente Petrolero Santa Cruz de la Sierra (1/0). |
| (381/428) | VACA TASCA Daniel | 03.11.1989 | **8** | **0** | 2010-2013, Club Jorge Wilstermann Cochabamba (3/0), Club The Strongest La Paz (5/0). |
| (289/335) | VACA VELASCO Joselito | 12.08.1982 | **54** | **2** | 1999-2011, CD Oriente Petrolero Santa Cruz de la Sierra (5/0), Dallas Burns (6/0), New York/New Jersey MetroStars (1/0), CSCD Blooming Santa Cruz de la Sierra (25/2), CD Oriente Petrolero Santa Cruz de la Sierra (17/0). |
| (63/111) | VALDA GARCÍA Freddy | 23.03.1932 | **2** | **0** | 1959 |
| (42/078) | VALDEZ | | **1** | **0** | 1950 |
| (51/093) | VALDIVIA Silvano | | **2** | **0** | 1957 |
| (35/071) | VALENCIA Antonio José | 10.05.1925 | **11** | **0** | 1949-1953, Club Deportivo Litoral La Paz |
| (401/449) | VALVERDE RIVERA Juan Gabriel | 24.06.1990 | **2** | **0** | 2012, Club Bolívar Independiente Unificada La Paz (2/0). |
| (13/036) | VARGAS | | **1** | **0** | 1938 |
| (407/458) | VARGAS CASTILLO Rodrigo Mauricio | 19.10.1994 | **2** | **0** | 2013, CD Oriente Petrolero Santa Cruz de la Sierra (2/0). |
| (369/419) | VARGAS CLAROS Christian Israel | 08.09.1983 | **12** | **0** | 2008-2012, Club The Strongest La Paz (2/0), CSCD Blooming Santa Cruz de la Sierra (1/0), CD San José Oruro (12/0). |
| (67/117) | VARGAS Eulogio Ramón | 21.03.1931 | **7** | **0** | 1962-1963, CD Chaco Petrolero La Paz |
| (96/170) | VARGAS OROZCO Freddy | 13.01.1951 | **13** | **0** | 1973-1977, Club Jorge Wilstermann Cochabamba |
| (22/057) | VARGAS Raúl | | **12** | **0** | 1946-1948, Ferroviario La Paz |
| (126/204) | VARGAS RÍOS Ramiro | 22.10.1958 | **18** | **0** | 1979-1989, Club Bolívar Independiente Unificada La Paz |
| (45/085) | VARGAS ROMERO Edgar | 10.08.1929 | **13** | **0** | 1953-1959 |
| (77/131) | VARGAS ROMERO Rolando | 10.04.1939 | **9** | **1** | 1965-1967 |
| (23/058) | VEGA SAAVEDRA Serapio | 23.03.1920 | **7** | **0** | 1946-1948 |
| (381/433) | VEIZAGA ARGOTE Wálter | 22.04.1986 | **10** | **0** | 2010-2013, Club Jorge Wilstermann Cochabamba (2/0), Club The Strongest La Paz (8/0). |
| (165/242) | VERA Félix | | **3** | **0** | 1987, Club Jorge Wilstermann Cochabamba |
| (358/404) | VERDÚGUEZ Ricardo | 28.07.1989 | **1** | **0** | 2007, CSCD Blooming Santa Cruz de la Sierra (1/0). |
| (105/184) | VEYZAGA Dario | | **1** | **0** | 1975 |
| (121/195) | VILLALON Víctor Jaime | 25.10.1950 | **2** | **0** | 1977 |
| (192/281) | VILLAROEL Johnny | 11.10.1968 | **12** | **3** | 1993-1995, Club The Strongest La Paz (12/3). |
| (70/124) | VILLAROSA | | **1** | **0** | 1963 |
| (138/217) | VILLARROEL DELGADILLO Johnny | 05.04.1955 | **10** | **0** | 1981-1983, Club Jorge Wilstermann Cochabamba |
| (154/227) | VILLEGAS CAMARA Eduardo Andres | 29.03.1964 | **16** | **0** | 1985-1989, Club The Strongest La Paz |

| | | | | | |
|---|---|---|---|---|---|
| (375/423) | YACEROTTE César Gerardo | 28.08.1988 | **3** | **1** | 2009, Club Bamin Real Potosí (3/1). |
| (399/447) | YECEROTTE SORUCO Gerardo César | 08.08.1985 | **1** | **0** | 2012, Club Bamin Real Potosí (1/0). |

| | | | | | |
|---|---|---|---|---|---|
| (348/389) | ZABALA Pedro | 25.07.1983 | **2** | **0** | 2006-2007, Club Universitario Sucre (2/0). |
| (379/427) | ZABALA PERROGÓN Wilder | 31.12.1982 | **2** | **0** | 2009, CD Oriente Petrolero Santa Cruz de la Sierra (2/0). |
| (65/114) | ZABALAGA Mario | 04.03.1938 | **13** | **0** | 1961-1967, Club Jorge Wilstermann Cochabamba |
| (146/222) | ZAMBRANO Reynaldo | 20.07.1957 | **4** | **0** | 1983-1985 |
| (344/386) | ZENTENO ÁLVAREZ Edward Mauro | 05.12.1984 | **12** | **0** | 2005-2013, Club Jorge Wilstermann Cochabamba (12/0). |

# NATIONAL COACHES

| Name | Period | Matches | P | W | D | L | | GF | - | GA | |
|---|---|---|---|---|---|---|---|---|---|---|---|
| Jorge Luis VALDERRAMA | 30.10.1927 – 13.11.2007 | [5-7] | 3 | 0 | 0 | 3 | | 3 | - | 19 | 0.00 % |
| Ulrico SAUCEDO | 17.03.1930 – 20.07.1930 | [8-9] | 2 | 0 | 0 | 2 | | 0 | - | 8 | 0.00 % |
| Julio BORELLI | 08.08.1938 – 21.02.1945 | [10-20] | 11 | 3 | 3 | 5 | | 11 | - | 23 | 40.90 % |
| Diógenes LARA | 16.01.1946 – 31.12.1947 | [21-32] | 12 | 0 | 2 | 10 | | 10 | - | 44 | 8.33 % |
| Félix DEHEZA | 05.01.1948 – 06.05.1949 | [33-41] | 9 | 4 | 1 | 4 | | 15 | - | 27 | 50.00 % |
| Mario PRETTO (*Italy*) | 02.07.1950 | [44] | 1 | 1 | 0 | 0 | | 0 | - | 8 | 0.00 % |
| César VICINO | 22.02.1950 – 28.03.1953 | [45-50] | 6 | 1 | 2 | 3 | | 6 | - | 15 | 33.33 % |
| Vicente ARRAYA | 08.03.1959 – 29.03.1959 | [59-64] | 6 | 0 | 1 | 5 | | 4 | - | 23 | 8.33 % |
| DANILO Alvim (*Brazil*) | 10.03.1963 – 31.03.1963 | [71-76] | 6 | 5 | 1 | 0 | | 19 | - | 13 | 91.66 % |
| Freddy VALDA GARCÍA | 25.07.1965 – 29.08.1965 | [77-80] | 4 | 1 | 0 | 3 | | 4 | - | 9 | 25.00 % |
| Carlos TRIGO | 17.01.1967 – 01.02.1967 | [81-85] | 5 | 0 | 1 | 4 | | 0 | - | 9 | 10.00 % |
| Freddy VALDA GARCÍA | 27.07.1969 – 24.07.1973 | [86-100] | 15 | 3 | 5 | 7 | | 15 | - | 32 | 36.66 % |
| Carlos TRIGO | 02.09.1973 – 30.09.1973 | [101-104] | 4 | 0 | 0 | 4 | | 1 | - | 11 | 0.00 % |
| Freddy VALDA GARCÍA | 27.06.1975 – 13.08.1975 | [105-111] | 7 | 2 | 0 | 5 | | 6 | - | 13 | 28.57 % |
| Wilfredo CAMACHO | 06.02.1977 – 30.11.1977 | [112-122] | 11 | 3 | 2 | 6 | | 13 | - | 30 | 36.36 % |
| Ramiro BLACUTT RODRÍGUEZ | 10.07.1979 – 22.02.1981 | [123-143] | 21 | 6 | 4 | 11 | | 26 | - | 40 | 38.09 % |
| José SALDANHA | 15.03.1981 – 22.03.1981 | [144-145] | 2 | 0 | 0 | 2 | | 1 | - | 4 | 0.00 % |
| Wilfredo CAMACHO | 19.07.1983 – 04.09.1983 | [146-153] | 8 | 1 | 2 | 5 | | 10 | - | 16 | 25.00 % |
| Carlos RODRÍGUEZ (*Argentina*) | 03.02.1985 – 30.06.1985 | [154-164] | 11 | 2 | 3 | 6 | | 8 | - | 21 | 31.81 % |
| Osvaldo VEIGA (*Argentina*) | 14.06.1987 – 01.07.1987 | [165-168] | 4 | 0 | 1 | 3 | | 1 | - | 6 | 12.50 % |
| Jorge HABEGGER (*Argentina*) | 25.05.1989 – 17.09.1989 | [169-182] | 14 | 4 | 3 | 7 | | 11 | - | 27 | 39.28 % |
| Ramiro BLACUTT RODRÍGUEZ | 14.06.1991 – 13.07.1991 | [183-188] | 6 | 0 | 3 | 3 | | 2 | - | 8 | 25.00 % |
| Francisco Xabier AZCARGORTA URIARTE (*Spain*) | 29.01.1993 – 21.09.1994 | [192-228] | 37 | 9 | 15 | 13 | | 39 | - | 39 | 44.59 % |
| Antonio LÓPEZ (*Spain*) | 03.04.1995 – 16.07.1995 | [229-238] | 10 | 2 | 5 | 3 | | 12 | - | 14 | 45.00 % |
| Dušan DRAŠKOVIĆ (*Yugoslavia*) | 03.02.1996 – 01.09.1996 | [239-252] | 14 | 5 | 3 | 6 | | 21 | - | 20 | 46.42 % |
| Antonio LÓPEZ (*Spain*) | 08.10.1996 – 16.11.1997 | [253-273] | 21 | 9 | 4 | 8 | | 27 | - | 23 | 52.38 % |
| Héctor VEIRA (*Argentina*) | 24.01.1999 – 03.11.1999 | [274-289] | 16 | 1 | 9 | 6 | | 9 | - | 14 | 34.37 % |
| Carlos ARAGONÉS ESPINOSA (*Spain*) | 05.03.2000 – 19.07.2001 | [290-311] | 22 | 4 | 5 | 13 | | 22 | - | 36 | 29.54 % |
| Jorge HABEGGER (*Argentina*) | 14.08.2001 – 16.10.2001 | [312-314] | 3 | 0 | 1 | 2 | | 4 | - | 12 | 16.66 % |
| Carlos Leonel TRUCCO | 07.11.2001 – 16.05.2002 | [315-320] | 6 | 1 | 2 | 3 | | 7 | - | 13 | 33.33 % |
| Vladimir SORIA | 21.08.2002 | [321] | 1 | 0 | 0 | 1 | | 0 | - | 2 | 0.00 % |
| Wálter ROQUE (*Uruguay*) | 19.03.2003 | [322] | 1 | 0 | 0 | 1 | | 0 | - | 2 | 0.00 % |
| Dalcio GIOVAGNOLI (*Argentina*) | 10.06.2003 | [323] | 1 | 0 | 0 | 1 | | 0 | - | 4 | 0.00 % |
| Nelson Bonifacio ACOSTA LÓPEZ (*Uruguay/Chile*) | 31.08.2003 – 30.03.2004 | [324-330] | 7 | 3 | 0 | 4 | | 9 | - | 12 | 42.85 % |
| Ramiro BLACUTT RODRÍGUEZ | 01.06.2004 – 17.11.2004 | [331-340] | 10 | 3 | 3 | 4 | | 10 | - | 12 | 45.00 % |
| Mario Ovidio MEZZA SORUCO | 26.03.2005 – 12.10.2005 | [341-347] | 7 | 1 | 1 | 5 | | 9 | - | 17 | 21.42 % |
| Erwin SÁNCHEZ FREKING | 15.11.2006 – 14.10.2009 | [348-380] | 33 | 9 | 7 | 17 | | 38 | - | 57 | 53.03 % |
| Eduardo Andres VILLEGAS Camara | 24.02.2010 – 07.10.2010 | [381-383] | 3 | 0 | 1 | 2 | | 2 | - | 9 | 16.66 % |
| Gustavo Domingo QUINTEROS DESABATO | 09.02.2011 – 06.06.2012 | [384-401] | 18 | 2 | 6 | 10 | | 14 | - | 28 | 27.77 % |
| Francisco Xabier AZCARGORTA URIARTE (*Spain*) | 15.08.2012 -> | [402-> | 15 | 3 | 7 | 5 | | 17 | - | 27 | 43.33 % |

Bolivia played without national coach in following matches: [1-4], [42-43].
Trainer not known for following matches: [51-58],[65-70],[189-191]

**National coaches several times in charge:**

| Name | How often | Matches | M | W | D | L | | GF | - | GA | |
|---|---|---|---|---|---|---|---|---|---|---|---|
| Freddy VALDA GARCÍA | 3x | [77-80], [86-100], [105-111] | 26 | 6 | 5 | 15 | | 25 | - | 54 | 32.69 % |
| Carlos TRIGO | 2x | [81-85], [101-104] | 9 | 0 | 1 | 8 | | 1 | - | 20 | 5.55 % |
| Wilfredo CAMACHO | 2x | [112-122], [146-153] | 19 | 4 | 4 | 11 | | 23 | - | 46 | 31.57 % |
| Ramiro BLACUTT RODRÍGUEZ | 3x | [123-143], [183-188], [331-340] | 37 | 9 | 10 | 18 | | 38 | - | 60 | 37.83 % |
| Jorge HABEGGER (*Argentina*) | 2x | [169-182], [312-314] | 17 | 4 | 4 | 9 | | 15 | - | 39 | 35.29 % |
| Antonio LÓPEZ (*Spain*) | 2x | [229-238],[253-273] | 31 | 11 | 9 | 11 | | 39 | - | 37 | 50.00 % |
| Francisco Xabier AZCARGORTA URIARTE (*Spain*) | 2x | [192-228], [402-> | 52 | 12 | 22 | 18 | | 56 | - | 66 | 44.23 % |

# HEAD-TO-HEAD STATISTICS

| | HOME | | | | | | | AWAY | | | | | | | NEUTRAL | | | | | | | TOTAL | | | | | | |
|---|---|---|---|---|---|---|---|---|---|---|---|---|---|---|---|---|---|---|---|---|---|---|---|---|---|---|---|---|
| Argentina | 12 | 6 | 2 | 4 | 25 | : | 16 | 13 | 0 | 2 | 11 | 5 | : | 37 | 8 | 0 | 1 | 7 | 2 | : | 27 | 33 | 6 | 5 | 22 | 32 | : | 80 |
| Bulgaria | 1 | 0 | 0 | 1 | 1 | : | 3 | | | | | | | | | | | | | | | 1 | 0 | 0 | 1 | 1 | : | 3 |
| Brazil | 10 | 5 | 1 | 4 | 17 | : | 19 | 10 | 0 | 2 | 8 | 4 | : | 41 | 7 | 0 | 0 | 7 | 4 | : | 31 | 27 | 5 | 3 | 19 | 25 | : | 91 |
| Cameroon | | | | | | | | | | | | | | | 1 | 0 | 1 | 0 | 1 | : | 1 | 1 | 0 | 1 | 0 | 1 | : | 1 |
| Chile | 13 | 4 | 3 | 6 | 13 | : | 16 | 17 | 1 | 1 | 15 | 12 | : | 53 | 8 | 1 | 3 | 4 | 13 | : | 24 | 38 | 6 | 7 | 25 | 38 | : | 93 |
| Colombia | 9 | 3 | 4 | 2 | 13 | : | 9 | 9 | 2 | 1 | 6 | 6 | : | 20 | 9 | 1 | 4 | 4 | 8 | : | 11 | 27 | 6 | 9 | 12 | 27 | : | 40 |
| Costa Rica | 1 | 0 | 1 | 0 | 1 | : | 1 | | | | | | | | 2 | 0 | 0 | 2 | 0 | : | 6 | 3 | 0 | 1 | 2 | 1 | : | 7 |
| Cuba | 1 | 1 | 0 | 0 | 1 | : | 0 | | | | | | | | | | | | | | | 1 | 1 | 0 | 0 | 1 | : | 0 |
| Czechoslovakia | 2 | 1 | 0 | 1 | 4 | : | 6 | | | | | | | | | | | | | | | 2 | 1 | 0 | 1 | 4 | : | 6 |
| East Germany | 1 | 1 | 0 | 0 | 2 | : | 1 | | | | | | | | | | | | | | | 1 | 1 | 0 | 0 | 2 | : | 1 |
| Ecuador | 10 | 3 | 4 | 3 | 17 | : | 20 | 9 | 0 | 2 | 7 | 6 | : | 17 | 8 | 2 | 5 | 1 | 6 | : | 7 | 27 | 5 | 11 | 11 | 29 | : | 44 |
| Egypt | | | | | | | | | | | | | | | 1 | 0 | 1 | 0 | 2 | : | 2 | 1 | 0 | 1 | 0 | 2 | : | 2 |
| El Salvador | 1 | 1 | 0 | 0 | 5 | : | 1 | 1 | 0 | 1 | 0 | 2 | : | 2 | 2 | 0 | 1 | 1 | 1 | : | 3 | 4 | 1 | 2 | 1 | 8 | : | 6 |
| Finland | 2 | 1 | 1 | 0 | 5 | : | 2 | | | | | | | | | | | | | | | 2 | 1 | 1 | 0 | 5 | : | 2 |
| Germany | | | | | | | | | | | | | | | 1 | 0 | 0 | 1 | 0 | : | 1 | 1 | 0 | 0 | 1 | 0 | : | 1 |
| Guatemala | | | | | | | | 2 | 1 | 1 | 0 | 4 | : | 1 | 3 | 0 | 0 | 3 | 1 | : | 6 | 5 | 1 | 1 | 3 | 5 | : | 7 |
| Haiti | 2 | 2 | 0 | 0 | 11 | : | 3 | | | | | | | | | | | | | | | 2 | 2 | 0 | 0 | 11 | : | 3 |
| Honduras | 1 | 1 | 0 | 0 | 3 | : | 1 | 2 | 0 | 2 | 0 | 0 | : | 0 | 2 | 1 | 0 | 1 | 1 | : | 2 | 5 | 2 | 2 | 1 | 4 | : | 3 |
| Jamaica | 1 | 1 | 0 | 0 | 6 | : | 0 | | | | | | | | 2 | 0 | 1 | 1 | 0 | : | 3 | 3 | 1 | 1 | 1 | 6 | : | 3 |
| Latvia | | | | | | | | | | | | | | | 1 | 0 | 0 | 1 | 1 | : | 2 | 1 | 0 | 0 | 1 | 1 | : | 2 |
| Mexico | 1 | 1 | 0 | 0 | 3 | : | 1 | 1 | 0 | 0 | 1 | 0 | : | 1 | 8 | 0 | 1 | 7 | 2 | : | 17 | 10 | 1 | 1 | 8 | 5 | : | 19 |
| Greece | | | | | | | | 1 | 0 | 1 | 0 | 0 | : | 0 | | | | | | | | 1 | 0 | 1 | 0 | 0 | : | 0 |
| Guyana | 1 | 1 | 0 | 0 | 2 | : | 0 | | | | | | | | | | | | | | | 1 | 1 | 0 | 0 | 2 | : | 0 |
| Hungary | 1 | 0 | 0 | 1 | 2 | : | 3 | 1 | 0 | 0 | 1 | 0 | : | 6 | | | | | | | | 2 | 0 | 0 | 2 | 2 | : | 9 |
| Iceland | | | | | | | | 1 | 0 | 0 | 1 | 0 | : | 1 | | | | | | | | 1 | 0 | 0 | 1 | 0 | : | 1 |
| Japan | | | | | | | | 1 | 0 | 0 | 1 | 0 | : | 2 | 1 | 0 | 1 | 0 | 1 | : | 1 | 2 | 0 | 1 | 1 | 1 | : | 3 |
| North Korea | | | | | | | | | | | | | | | 1 | 0 | 0 | 1 | 1 | : | 2 | 1 | 0 | 0 | 1 | 1 | : | 2 |
| South Korea | | | | | | | | | | | | | | | 1 | 0 | 1 | 0 | 0 | : | 0 | 1 | 0 | 1 | 0 | 0 | : | 0 |
| Panama | 3 | 2 | 0 | 1 | 5 | : | 3 | 1 | 0 | 0 | 1 | 0 | : | 2 | | | | | | | | 4 | 2 | 0 | 2 | 5 | : | 5 |
| Paraguay | 31 | 13 | 10 | 8 | 49 | : | 41 | 22 | 1 | 5 | 16 | 10 | : | 49 | 11 | 0 | 2 | 9 | 6 | : | 37 | 64 | 14 | 17 | 33 | 65 | : | 127 |
| Peru | 17 | 10 | 6 | 1 | 22 | : | 8 | 20 | 3 | 4 | 13 | 19 | : | 39 | 8 | 0 | 2 | 6 | 2 | : | 19 | 45 | 13 | 12 | 20 | 43 | : | 66 |
| Poland | 2 | 0 | 0 | 2 | 1 | : | 3 | | | | | | | | | | | | | | | 2 | 0 | 0 | 2 | 1 | : | 3 |
| Portugal | | | | | | | | 1 | 0 | 0 | 1 | 0 | : | 4 | | | | | | | | 1 | 0 | 0 | 1 | 0 | : | 4 |
| Rep of Ireland | | | | | | | | 1 | 0 | 0 | 1 | 0 | : | 1 | 2 | 0 | 1 | 1 | 1 | : | 4 | 3 | 0 | 1 | 2 | 1 | : | 5 |
| Romania | | | | | | | | 1 | 0 | 0 | 1 | 0 | : | 3 | | | | | | | | 1 | 0 | 0 | 1 | 0 | : | 3 |
| Romania "B" | | | | | | | | | | | | | | | 1 | 0 | 0 | 1 | 0 | : | 2 | 1 | 0 | 0 | 1 | 0 | : | 2 |
| Romania "U21" | 1 | 0 | 1 | 0 | 1 | : | 1 | | | | | | | | | | | | | | | 1 | 0 | 1 | 0 | 1 | : | 1 |
| Russia "B" | | | | | | | | | | | | | | | 1 | 0 | 0 | 1 | 1 | : | 2 | 1 | 0 | 0 | 1 | 1 | : | 2 |
| Saudi Arabia | | | | | | | | | | | | | | | 2 | 1 | 1 | 0 | 1 | : | 0 | 2 | 1 | 1 | 0 | 1 | : | 0 |
| Senegal | | | | | | | | 1 | 0 | 0 | 1 | 1 | : | 2 | | | | | | | | 1 | 0 | 0 | 1 | 1 | : | 2 |
| Slovakia | 1 | 0 | 0 | 1 | 0 | : | 1 | | | | | | | | 1 | 0 | 0 | 1 | 0 | : | 2 | 2 | 0 | 0 | 2 | 0 | : | 3 |
| Spain | | | | | | | | | | | | | | | 1 | 0 | 0 | 1 | 1 | : | 3 | 1 | 0 | 0 | 1 | 1 | : | 3 |
| South Africa | | | | | | | | 1 | 1 | 0 | 0 | 1 | : | 0 | | | | | | | | 1 | 1 | 0 | 0 | 1 | : | 0 |
| Switzerland | | | | | | | | | | | | | | | 1 | 0 | 1 | 0 | 0 | : | 0 | 1 | 0 | 1 | 0 | 0 | : | 0 |
| United States | 1 | 0 | 1 | 0 | 0 | : | 0 | 4 | 1 | 3 | 0 | 5 | : | 3 | 1 | 1 | 0 | 0 | 1 | : | 0 | 6 | 2 | 4 | 0 | 6 | : | 3 |
| Uruguay | 13 | 6 | 5 | 2 | 16 | : | 10 | 14 | 0 | 1 | 13 | 8 | : | 38 | 13 | 1 | 1 | 11 | 4 | : | 50 | 40 | 7 | 7 | 26 | 28 | : | 98 |
| Venezuela | 13 | 8 | 3 | 2 | 33 | : | 8 | 15 | 4 | 4 | 7 | 25 | : | 28 | 5 | 1 | 3 | 1 | 8 | : | 9 | 33 | 13 | 10 | 10 | 66 | : | 45 |
| Yugoslavia | | | | | | | | | | | | | | | 2 | 0 | 1 | 1 | 1 | : | 5 | 2 | 0 | 1 | 1 | 1 | : | 5 |
| **TOTAL** | **152** | **71** | **42** | **39** | **258** | **:** | **177** | **149** | **14** | **30** | **105** | **108** | **:** | **350** | **115** | **9** | **32** | **74** | **70** | **:** | **279** | **416** | **94** | **104** | **218** | **436** | **:** | **806** |

# CHILE

| The Country: |
| --- |
| República de Chile (Republic of Chile)<br>Capital: Santiago<br><br>Surface: 756,950 km²<br>Inhabitants: 17,402,630<br>Time: UTC-4 |

| The FA: |
| --- |
| Federación de Fútbol de Chile<br>Avenida Quilín No. 5635 - Comuna Peñalolén, Casilla No. 3733 Central de Casillas, Santiago<br>Year of Formation: 1895<br>Member of FIFA since: 1913<br>Member of CONMEBOL since: 1916 |

**NATIONAL TEAM RECORDS**

| COPA AMÉRICA | |
| --- | --- |
| **1916** | 4th Place |
| **1917** | 4th Place |
| **1919** | 4th Place |
| **1920** | 4th Place |
| **1921** | Withdrew |
| **1922** | 5th Place |
| **1923** | Withdrew |
| **1924** | 4th Place |
| **1925** | Withdrew |
| **1926** | 3rd Place |
| **1927** | Withdrew |
| **1929** | Withdrew |
| **1935** | 4th Place |
| **1937** | 5th Place |
| **1939** | 4th Place |
| **1941** | 3rd Place |
| **1942** | 6th Place |
| **1945** | 3rd Place |
| **1946** | 5th Place |
| **1947** | 4th Place |
| **1949** | 5th Place |
| **1953** | 4th Place |
| **1955** | Runners-up |
| **1956** | Runners-up |
| **1957** | 6th Place |
| **1959** | 5th Place |
| **1959E** | Withdrew |
| **1963** | Withdrew |
| **1967** | 3rd Place |
| **1975** | Round 1 |
| **1979** | Runners-up |
| **1983** | Round 1 |
| **1987** | Runners-up |
| **1989** | Round 1 |
| **1991** | 3rd Place |
| **1993** | Round 1 |
| **1995** | Round 1 |
| **1997** | Round 1 |
| **1999** | 4th Place |
| **2001** | Quarter-Finals |
| **2004** | Round 1 |
| **2007** | Quarter-Finals |
| **2011** | Quarter-Finals |

| WORLD CUP | |
| --- | --- |
| **1930** | Final Tournament (1st Round) |
| **1934** | Withdrew |
| **1938** | Withdrew |
| **1950** | Final Tournament (1st Round) |
| **1954** | Qualifiers |
| **1958** | Qualifiers |
| **1962** | Final Tournament (3rd Place) |
| **1966** | Final Tournament (1st Round) |
| **1970** | Qualifiers |
| **1974** | Final Tournament (1st Round) |
| **1978** | Qualifiers |
| **1982** | Final Tournament (1st Round) |
| **1986** | Qualifiers |
| **1990** | Disqualified by the FIFA |
| **1994** | Banned by the FIFA |
| **1998** | Final Tournament (2nd Round) |
| **2002** | Qualifiers |
| **2006** | Qualifiers |
| **2010** | Final Tournament (2nd Round) |
| **2014** | Final Tournament (*to be played*) |

| OLYMPIC GAMES 1900-2012 |
| --- |
| 1952, 1984, 2000 (3rd Place) |
| **FIFA CONFEDERATIONS CUP 1992-2013** |
| None |
| **PLAYER WITH MOST INTERNATIONAL CAPS** |
| Leonel Guillermo Sánchez Lineros - 84 caps (1955-1968) |
| **PLAYER WITH MOST INTERNATIONAL GOALS** |
| José Marcelo Salas Melinao - 37 goals / 71 caps (1994-2007) |

## FULL INTERNATIONALS (1910-2013)

**1.** 27.05.1910 **ARGENTINA - CHILE** **3-1(2-1)**
Estadio Belgrano, Buenos Aires; Referee: Armando Bergalli (Chile); Attendance: 6,200
**CHI:** L.C. Gibson (1/0), Carlos Hormazábal (1/0), Luis Barriga (1/0), Andrés Hoyl (1/0), Henry Allen (1/0), Próspero González (1/0), Arturo Acuña (1/0), Frank Simmons (1/1), Colin Campbell (1/0), J.P. Davidson (1/0), J.H. Hamilton (1/0). Trainer: no.
**Goal**: Frank Simmons (11).

**2.** 29.05.1910 **URUGUAY - CHILE** **3-0(1-0)** International Tournament
Estadio Colegiales, Buenos Aires; Referee: Susán (Argentina); Attendance: 6,000
**CHI:** L.C. Gibson (2/0), E.F. Ashe (1/0), J. McWilliams (1/0), Carlos Hormazábal (2/0), Henry Allen (2/0), Próspero González (2/0), Joseph Robson (1/0), Frank Simmons (2/1), Colin Campbell (2/0), J.H. Hamilton (2/0), Arturo Acuña (2/0). Trainer: no.

**3.** 05.06.1910 **ARGENTINA - CHILE** **5-1(3-0)** International Tournament
Estadio Club Gymnasia y Esgrima, Buenos Aires; Referee: Léon Peyrou (Uruguay); Attendance: 2,500
**CHI:** L.C. Gibson (3/0), E.F. Ashe (2/0), J. McWilliams (2/0), Carlos Hormazábal (3/0), Henry Allen (3/0), Próspero González (3/0), Joseph Robson (2/0), Colin Campbell (3/1), Heriberto Sturgess (1/0), J.H. Hamilton (3/0), J.P. Davidson (2/0). Trainer: no.
**Goal**: Colin Campbell (50).

**4.** 21.09.1913 **CHILE - ARGENTINA** **0-2(0-2)**
Estadio Sporting Club, Valparaíso; Referee: Jamieson (Chile); Attendance: 7,000
**CHI:** Roy Lester (1/0), Otto Ernst (1/0), Enrique Cárdenas (1/0), Carlos González (1/0), Harold Dean (1/0), Agustín Elgueta (1/0), Manuel Geldes (1/0), Primedio Brito (1/0), Alexander Skewes (1/0), Enrique Teuche (1/0), J. Johnston (1/0). Trainer: no.

**5.** 02.07.1916 **URUGUAY - CHILE** **4-0(1-0)** 1st Copa América
Estadio Club Gymnasia y Esgrima, Buenos Aires; Referee: Hugo Gronda (Argentina); Attendance: 3,000
**CHI:** Manuel Guerrero (1/0), Enrique Cárdenas (2/0), Marcos Wittke (1/0), Enrique Abello (1/0), Enrique Teuche (2/0), Ramón Unzaga (1/0), Enrique Hernando Salazar (1/0), Eufemio Fuentes (1/0), Enrique Gutiérrez (1/0), Rubén Moreno (1/0), Manuel Geldes (2/0). Trainer: Carlos Fanta Tomaszewski (1).

**6.** 06.07.1916 **ARGENTINA - CHILE** **6-1(1-1)** 1st Copa América
Estadio Club Gymnasia y Esgrima, Buenos Aires; Referee: Sidney Pullen (Brazil); Attendance: 15,000
**CHI:** Manuel Guerrero (2/0), Enrique Cárdenas (3/0), Marcos Wittke (2/0), Enrique Abello (2/0), Enrique Teuche (3/0), Ramón Unzaga (2/0), Ángel Báez (1/1), Eufemio Fuentes (2/0), Enrique Gutiérrez (2/0), Alfredo France (1/0), Manuel Geldes (3/0). Trainer: Carlos Fanta Tomaszewski (2).
**Goal**: Ángel Báez (44).

**7.** 08.07.1916 **BRAZIL - CHILE** **1-1(1-0)** 1st Copa América
Estadio Club Gymnasia y Esgrima, Buenos Aires; Referee: Léon Peyrou (Uruguay); Attendance: 15,000
**CHI:** Manuel Guerrero (3/0), Enrique Cárdenas (4/0), Marcos Wittke (3/0), Enrique Abello (3/0), Enrique Teuche (4/0), Ramón Unzaga (3/0), Ángel Báez (2/1), Rubén Moreno (2/0), Enrique Hernando Salazar (2/1), Alfredo France (2/0), Manuel Geldes (4/0). Trainer: Carlos Fanta Tomaszewski (3).
**Goal**: Enrique Hernando Salazar (85).

**8.** 12.07.1916 **ARGENTINA - CHILE** **1-0(1-0)**
Estadio Club Gymnasia y Esgrima, Buenos Aires; Referee: Patricio MacCarthy (Argentina); Attendance: 12,000
**CHI:** Jorge Paredes (1/0), Enrique Cárdenas (5/0), Marcos Wittke (4/0), Enrique Abello (4/0), Próspero González (4/0), Ramón Unzaga (4/0), Eufemio Fuentes (3/0), Enrique Teuche (5/0), Ángel Báez (3/1), Erasmo Vásquez (1/0), Alfredo France (3/0). Trainer: Carlos Fanta Tomaszewski (4).

**9.** 14.07.1916 **URUGUAY - CHILE** **4-1(2-0)**
Estadio Parque Central, Montevideo; Referee: Angel Minoli (Uruguay); Attendance: 6,000
**CHI:** Jorge Paredes (2/0), Enrique Cárdenas (6/0), Marcos Wittke (5/0), Enrique Abello (5/0), Próspero González (5/0), Ramón Unzaga (5/0), Manuel Geldes (5/0), Enrique Teuche (6/0), Ángel Báez (4/1), Rubén Moreno (3/0), Alfredo France (4/1). Trainer: Carlos Fanta Tomaszewski (5).
**Goal**: Alfredo France (48).

**10.** 30.09.1917 **URUGUAY - CHILE** **4-0(2-0)** 2nd Copa América
Estadio Parque Central, Montevideo; Referee: Germán Guassone (Argentina); Attendance: 23,000
**CHI:** Manuel Guerrero (4/0), Francisco Gatica (1/0), Enrique Cárdenas (7/0), Luis Alberto García (1/0), Héctor Baeza (1/0), Guillermo Cisternas (1/0), Manuel Geldes (6/0), Rodolfo Rojas (1/0), Bartolomé Muñoz (1/0), Luis Encina (1/0), Julio Paredes (1/0). Trainer: Julián Bertola (1).

**11.** 06.10.1917 **ARGENTINA - CHILE** **1-0(0-0)** 2nd Copa América
Estadio Parque Central, Montevideo; Referee: Alvaro Saralegui (Uruguay); Attendance: 12,000
**CHI:** Manuel Guerrero (5/0), Francisco Gatica (2/0), Enrique Cárdenas (8/0), Luis Alberto García (2/0), Norberto Guevara (1/0), Juan Alvarado (1/0), Horacio Muñoz (1/0), Rodolfo Rojas (2/0), Bartolomé Muñoz (2/0), Hernando Bolados (1/0), Julio Paredes (2/0). Trainer: Julián Bertola (2).

**12.** 12.10.1917 **BRAZIL - CHILE** **5-0(4-0)** 2nd Copa América
Estadio Parque Central, Montevideo; Referee: Ricardo Villariño (Uruguay); Attendance: 10,000
**CHI:** Manuel Guerrero (6/0), Francisco Gatica (3/0), Enrique Cárdenas (9/0), Luis Alberto García (3/0), Norberto Guevara (2/0), Juan Alvarado (2/0), Horacio Muñoz (2/0), Rodolfo Rojas (3/0), Bartolomé Muñoz (3/0), Hernando Bolados (2/0), Julio Paredes (3/0). Trainer: Julián Bertola (3).

**13.** 21.10.1917 **ARGENTINA - CHILE** **1-1(0-1)**
Estadio Racing Club, Avellaneda, Buenos Aires; Referee: Germán Guassone (Argentina); Attendance: 10,000
**CHI:** Luis Alberto García (4/0), Francisco Gatica (4/0), Rodolfo Rojas (4/0), Héctor Baeza (2/0), Guillermo Cisternas (2/0), Juan Alvarado (3/0), Manuel Geldes (7/0), Hernando Bolados (3/0), Horacio Muñoz (3/0), Bartolomé Muñoz (4/1), Julio Paredes (4/0). Trainer: Julián Bertola (4).
**Goal**: Bartolomé Muñoz.

**14.** 11.05.1919 **BRAZIL - CHILE** **6-0(3-0)** 3rd Copa América
Estádio das Laranjeiras, Rio de Janeiro; Referee: Juan Pedro Barbera (Argentina); Attendance: 20,000
**CHI:** Manuel Guerrero (7/0), Pedro Gatica (1/0), Ulises Poirier (1/0), Héctor Baeza (3/0), Carlos González (2/0), Aurelio Domínguez (1/0), Telésforo Segundo Báez (1/0), Eufemio Fuentes (4/0), Alfredo France (5/1), Horacio Muñoz (4/0), Víctor Varas (1/0). Trainer: Héctor Parra (1).

**15.** 17.05.1919 **URUGUAY - CHILE** **2-0(2-0)** 3rd Copa América
Estádio das Laranjeiras, Rio de Janeiro; Referee: Adilon Ponteado (Brazil); Attendance: 7,000
**CHI:** Manuel Guerrero (8/0), Francisco Gatica (5/0), Ulises Poirier (2/0), Héctor Baeza (4/0), Carlos González (3/0), Aurelio Domínguez (2/0), Carlos Del Río (1/0), Telésforo Segundo Báez (2/0), Eufemio Fuentes (5/0), Alfredo France (6/1), Víctor Varas (2/0). Trainer: Héctor Parra (2).

**16.** 22.05.1919 **ARGENTINA - CHILE** **4-1(3-1)** 3rd Copa América
Estádio das Laranjeiras, Rio de Janeiro; Referee: Joaquim Antônio Leite de Castro (Brazil); Attendance: 15,000
**CHI:** Manuel Guerrero (9/0), Pedro Gatica (2/0), Ulises Poirier (3/0), Héctor Baeza (5/0), Carlos González (4/0), Aurelio Domínguez (3/0), Carlos Del Río (2/0), Horacio Muñoz (5/0) [Telésforo Segundo Báez (3/0)], Eufemio Fuentes (6/0), Alfredo France (7/2), Guillermo Frez (1/0). Trainer: Héctor Parra (3).
**Goal**: Alfredo France (33).

**17.** 11.09.1920 **CHILE - BRAZIL** **0-1(0-0)** 4th Copa América
Estadio Sporting Club, Valparaíso; Referee: Martín Aphesteguy (Uruguay); Attendance: 15,000
**CHI:** Manuel Guerrero (10/0), Pedro Vergara (1/0), Ulises Poirier (4/0), Humberto Elgueta (1/0), Víctor Toro (1/0), Ramón Unzaga (6/0), Víctor Varas (3/0), Aurelio Domínguez (4/0), Blas Parra (1/0), Alfredo France (8/2), Horacio Muñoz (6/0). Trainer: Juan Carlos Bertone (1).

**18.** 17.09.1920 **CHILE - ARGENTINA** **1-1(1-1)** 4th Copa América
Estadio Sporting Club, Valparaíso; Referee: João De María (Brazil); Attendance: 16,000
**CHI:** Manuel Guerrero (11/0), Pedro Vergara (2/0), Ulises Poirier (5/0), Humberto Elgueta (2/0), Víctor Toro (2/0), Ramón Unzaga (7/0), Víctor Varas (4/0), Aurelio Domínguez (5/0), Hernando Bolados (4/1), Alfredo France (9/2), Horacio Muñoz (7/0). Trainer: Juan Carlos Bertone (2).
**Goal**: Hernando Bolados (30).

**19.** 26.09.1920 **CHILE - URUGUAY** **1-2(0-1)** 4th Copa América
Estadio Sporting Club, Valparaíso; Referee: Carlos Fanta Tomaszewski (Chile); Attendance: 16,000
**CHI:** Manuel Guerrero (12/0), Pedro Vergara (3/0), Ulises Poirier (6/0), Humberto Elgueta (3/0), Víctor Toro (3/0), Ramón Unzaga (8/0), Víctor Varas (5/0), Aurelio Domínguez (6/0), Hernando Bolados (5/2), Alfredo France (10/2), Horacio Muñoz (8/0). Trainer: Juan Carlos Bertone (3).
**Goal**: Hernando Bolados (60).

**20.** 17.09.1922 **BRAZIL - CHILE** **1-1(1-0)** 6th Copa América
Estádio das Laranjeiras, Rio de Janeiro; Referee: Ricardo Vallarino (Uruguay); Attendance: 30,000
**CHI:** Guillermo Bernal (1/0), Pedro Vergara (4/0), Ulises Poirier (7/0), Humberto Elgueta (4/0), Manuel Catalán (1/0), Oscar González (1/0), Enrique Abello (6/0), Aurelio Domínguez (7/0), Manuel Bravo (1/1), Luis Encina (2/0), Víctor Varas (6/0).Trainer: Juan Carlos Bertone (4).
**Goal**: Manuel Bravo (40).

**21.** 23.09.1922 **URUGUAY - CHILE** **2-0(2-0)** 6th Copa América
Estádio das Laranjeiras, Rio de Janeiro; Referee: Francisco Andreu Balcó (Paraguay); Attendance: 6,000
**CHI:** René Balbontín (1/0), Pedro Vergara (5/0), Ulises Poirier (8/0), Humberto Elgueta (5/0), Manuel Catalán (2/0), Oscar González (2/0), Enrique Abello (7/0), Aurelio Domínguez (8/0), Manuel Bravo (2/1), Luis Encina (3/0), Víctor Varas (7/0). Trainer: Juan Carlos Bertone (5).

**22.** 28.09.1922 **ARGENTINA - CHILE** **4-0(3-0)** 6th Copa América
Estádio das Laranjeiras, Rio de Janeiro; Referee: Ricardo Vallarino (Uruguay); Attendance: 2,500
**CHI:** René Balbontín (2/0), Pedro Vergara (6/0), Ulises Poirier (9/0), Humberto Elgueta (6/0), Manuel Catalán (3/0), Oscar González (3/0), Enrique Abello (8/0), Aurelio Domínguez (9/0), Manuel Bravo (3/1), Manuel Ramírez (1/0), Víctor Varas (8/0). Trainer: Juan Carlos Bertone (6).

**23.** 05.10.1922 **PARAGUAY - CHILE** **3-0** 6th Copa América
Estádio das Laranjeiras, Rio de Janeiro; Referee: Servando Pérez (Argentina); Attendance: 1,000
**CHI:** Guillermo Bernal (2/0), Víctor Zavala (1/0), Ulises Poirier (10/0), Humberto Elgueta (7/0), Manuel Catalán (4/0), Oscar González (4/0), Enrique Abello (9/0), Aurelio Domínguez (10/0), Luis Encina (4/0), Manuel Ramírez (2/0), Víctor Varas (9/0). Trainer: Juan Carlos Bertone (7).

**24.** 22.10.1922 **ARGENTINA - CHILE** **1-0(1-0)**
Estadio Sportivo Barracas, Buenos Aires; Referee: Ricardo Vallarino (Uruguay); Attendance: 6,000
**CHI:** Guillermo Bernal (3/0), Pedro Vergara (7/0), Ulises Poirier (11/0), Humberto Elgueta (8/0), Manuel Catalán (5/0), Enrique Abello (10/0), Aurelio Domínguez (11/0), Manuel Bravo (4/1), Luis Encina (5/0), Manuel Ramírez (3/0), Víctor Varas (10/0). Trainer: Carlos Acuña (1).

**25.** 19.10.1924 **URUGUAY - CHILE** **5-0(1-0)** 8th Copa América
Estadio Parque Central, Montevideo; Referee: Eduardo Jara (Paraguay); Attendance: 15,000
**CHI:** Aníbal Ramírez (1/0), Otto Ernst (2/0), Jorge Hamablet (1/0), Francisco Arellano (1/0), Víctor Toro (4/0), Víctor Morales Sales (1/0), Heriberto Abarzúa (1/0), Germán Reyes (1/0), Aurelio Domínguez (12/0), Oscar Molina (1/0), José Miguel Olguín (1/0).Trainer: Carlos Acuña (2).

**26.** 25.10.1924 **ARGENTINA - CHILE** **2-0(1-0)** 8th Copa América
Estadio Parque Central, Montevideo; Referee: Angel Minolli (Uruguay); Attendance: 15,000
**CHI:** Alberto Robles (1/0), Otto Ernst (3/0), Jorge Hamablet (2/0), Francisco Arellano (2/0), Víctor Toro (5/0), David Arellano (1/0), Heriberto Abarzúa (2/0), Germán Reyes (2/0), Aurelio Domínguez (13/0), Víctor Morales Sales (2/0), José Miguel Olguín (2/0). Trainer: Carlos Acuña (3).

**27.** 01.11.1924 **PARAGUAY - CHILE** **3-1** 8th Copa América
Estadio Parque Central, Montevideo; Referee: Servando Pérez (Argentina); Attendance: 1,000
**CHI:** Aníbal Ramírez (2/0), Otto Ernst (4/0), Jorge Hamablet (3/0), Francisco Arellano (3/0), Víctor Toro (6/0), David Arellano (2/0), Heriberto Abarzúa (3/0), Germán Reyes (3/0), Aurelio Domínguez (14/1), Víctor Morales Sales (3/0), José Miguel Olguín (3/0). Trainer: Carlos Acuña (4).
**Goals**: Aurelio Domínguez (6).

**28.** 12.10.1926 **CHILE - BOLIVIA** **7-1(4-?)** 10th Copa América
Estadio Sport de Nuñoa, Santiago; Referee: Norberto Luis Gallieri (Argentina); Attendance: 12,000
**CHI:** Carlos Hill (1/0), Leoncio Veloso (1/0), Ulises Poirier (12/0), Francisco Sánchez (1/0), Guillermo Saavedra Tapia (1/0), Oscar González (5/0), Carlos Luis García (1/0), Guillermo Subiabre Astorga (1/1), Manuel Ramírez (4/1), David Arellano (3/4), Humberto Moreno (1/1). Trainer: José Rosetti (1).
**Goals**: Manuel Ramírez (10), Guillermo Subiabre Astorga (14), David Arellano (15, 41), Humberto Moreno (47), David Arellano (80, 84).

**29.** 17.10.1926 **CHILE - URUGUAY** **1-3(0-2)** 10th Copa América

Estadio Sport de Nuñoa, Santiago; Referee: Pedro José Malbrán (Chile); Attendance: 11,152

**CHI:** Roberto Cortés (1/0), Leoncio Veloso (2/0), Ulises Poirier (13/0), Francisco Sánchez (2/0), Guillermo Saavedra Tapia (2/0), Oscar González (6/0), Carlos Luis García (2/0), Guillermo Subiabre Astorga (2/2), José Miguel Olguín (4/0), David Arellano (4/4), Humberto Moreno (2/1). Trainer: José Rosetti (2).

**Goal**: Guillermo Subiabre Astorga (65 penalty).

**30.** 31.10.1926 **CHILE - ARGENTINA** **1-1(1-1)** 10th Copa América

Estadio Sport de Nuñoa, Santiago; Referee: Miguel Barba (Paraguay); Attendance: 8,000

**CHI:** Roberto Cortés (2/0), Leoncio Veloso (3/0), Ulises Poirier (14/0), Víctor Toro (7/0), Guillermo Saavedra Tapia (3/1), Oscar González (7/0), Horacio Muñoz (9/0), Guillermo Subiabre Astorga (3/2), José Miguel Olguín (5/0), David Arellano (5/4), Manuel Ramírez (5/1). Trainer: José Rosetti (3).

**Goal**: Guillermo Saavedra Tapia (25).

**31.** 03.11.1926 **CHILE - PARAGUAY** **5-1(2-?)** 10th Copa América

Estadio Sport de Nuñoa, Santiago; Referee: Aníbal Tejada (Uruguay); Attendance: 6,097

**CHI:** Roberto Cortés (3/0), Manuel Figueroa (1/0), Ulises Poirier (15/0), Víctor Morales Sales (4/0), Guillermo Saavedra Tapia (4/1), Oscar González (8/0), Humberto Moreno (3/1), Guillermo Subiabre Astorga (4/2), José Miguel Olguín (6/0), David Arellano (6/7), Manuel Ramírez (6/3). Trainer: José Rosetti (4).

**Goals**: David Arellano (21), Manuel Ramírez (42), David Arellano (64, 71), Manuel Ramírez (82).

**32.** 10.12.1927 **CHILE - URUGUAY** **2-3(1-1)**

Estadio Valparaíso, Viña del Mar; Referee: Sabugo (Chile); Attendance: 8,000

**CHI:** Juan Ibacache (1/0), Víctor Urrejola (1/0), Víctor Morales Sales (5/0), Manuel Ramírez (7/3), Humberto Elgueta (9/0), Oscar Alfaro (1/2), Francisco Sánchez (3/0), Carlos Schneeberger (1/0), Carlos Luis García (3/0), Carlos Eduardo Román (1/0), Humberto Contreras (1/0). Trainer: José Rosetti (5).

**Goals**: Oscar Alfaro (35, 70).

**33.** 27.05.1928 **PORTUGAL - CHILE** **4-2(2-2)** 9th OG. Group Stage.

Olympisch Stadion, Amsterdam (Holland); Referee: Mohamed Youssof (Egypt); Attendance: 2,309

**CHI:** Juan Ibacache (2/0), Ernesto Chaparro Esqivel (1/0), Víctor Morales Sales (6/0), Arturo Torres Carrasco (1/0), Guillermo Saavedra Tapia (5/1), Humberto Contreras (2/0), Carlos Schneeberger (2/0), Oscar Alfaro (2/2), Guillermo Subiabre Astorga (5/3), Alejandro Carbonell (1/1), José Miguel Olguín (7/0). Trainer: Frank Powell (1).

**Goals**: Guillermo Subiabre Astorga (15), Alejandro Carbonell (30).

**34.** 05.06.1928 **CHILE - MEXICO** **3-1(1-1)** 9th OG.Consolation Tnmt.

Monnikenhuize Stadion, Arnhem (Holland); Referee: Michal Foltynski (Dutch Antilles); Attendance: 2,309

**CHI:** Juan Ibacache (3/0), Guillermo Arturo Riveros (1/0), Ernesto Chaparro Esqivel (2/0), Arturo Torres Carrasco (2/0), Guillermo Saavedra Tapia (6/1), Víctor Morales Sales (7/0), Carlos Schneeberger (3/0), José del Carmen Arias (1/0), Guillermo Subiabre Astorga (6/5), Oscar Alfaro (3/3), José Miguel Olguín (8/0). Trainer: Frank Powell (2).

**Goals**: Guillermo Subiabre Astorga 2, Oscar Alfaro.

**35.** 08.06.1928 **HOLLAND - CHILE** **2-2(0-0)** 9th OG.Consolation Tnmt.

Spangen Stadion, Rotterdam (Holland); Referee: Guillermo Camorera (Spain); Attendance: 18,000

**CHI:** Juan Ibacache (4/0), Jorge Lindford (1/0), Ernesto Chaparro Esqivel (3/0), Guillermo Arturo Riveros (2/0), Arturo Torres Carrasco (3/0), Víctor Morales Sales (8/0), José del Carmen Arias (2/0), Guillermo Subiabre Astorga (7/5), Manuel Bravo (5/2), Oscar Alfaro (4/4), Alejandro Carbonell (2/1).Trainer: Frank Powell (3).

**Goals**: Manuel Bravo, Oscar Alfaro.

**36.** 16.07.1930 **CHILE - MEXICO** **3-0(1-0)** 1st FIFA WC. Group Stage.

Estadio Parque Central, Montevideo (Uruguay); Referee: Henri Cristophe (Belgium); Attendance: 7,000

**CHI:** Roberto Cortés (4/0), Ulises Poirier (16/0), Víctor Morales Sales (9/0), Arturo Torres Carrasco (4/0), Guillermo Saavedra Tapia (7/1), Humberto Elgueta (10/0), Tomás Ojeda (1/0), Guillermo Subiabre Astorga (8/5), Eberardo Villalobos (1/0), Carlos Vidal (1/2), Carlos Schneeberger (4/0). Trainer: György Orth (1).

**Goals**: Carlos Vidal (3), Manuel Rosas (52 own goal), Carlos Vidal (65).

**37.** 19.07.1930 **CHILE - FRANCE** **1-0(0-0)** 1st FIFA WC. Group Stage.

Estadio Centenario, Montevideo (Uruguay); Referee: Aníbal Tejada (Uruguay); Attendance: 50,000

**CHI:** Roberto Cortés (5/0), Ernesto Chaparro Esqivel (4/0), Guillermo Arturo Riveros (3/0), Arturo Torres Carrasco (5/0), Guillermo Saavedra Tapia (8/1), Casimiro Luis Torres (1/0), Tomás Ojeda (2/0), Guillermo Subiabre Astorga (9/6), Eberardo Villalobos (2/0), Carlos Vidal (2/2), Carlos Schneeberger (5/0). Trainer: György Orth (2).

**Goal**: Guillermo Subiabre Astorga (65).

**38.** 22.07.1930 **ARGENTINA - CHILE** **3-1(2-1)** 1st FIFA WC. Group Stage.

Estadio Centenario, Montevideo (Uruguay); Referee: John Langenus (Belgium); Attendance: 35,000

**CHI:** Roberto Cortés (6/0), Ernesto Chaparro Esqivel (5/0), Víctor Morales Sales (10/0), Arturo Torres Carrasco (6/0), Guillermo Saavedra Tapia (9/1), Casimiro Luis Torres (2/0), Guillermo Arellano (1/1), Guillermo Subiabre Astorga (10/6), Eberardo Villalobos (3/0), Carlos Vidal (3/2), Juan Aguilera (1/0). Trainer: György Orth (3).

**Goal**: Guillermo Arellano (15).

**39.** 06.01.1935 **ARGENTINA - CHILE** **4-1(1-1)** 13th Copa América

Estadio Nacional, Lima (Peru); Referee: Miguel Serra Hurtado (Peru); Attendance: 25,000

**CHI:** Roberto Cortés (7/0), Conrado Welsh (1/0), Ascanio Cortés (1/0), Guillermo Gornall (1/0), Guillermo Arturo Riveros (4/0), Enrique Araneda (1/0), Andrés Carlos Aranda (1/0), Carlos Giudice (1/0), Arturo Carmona (1/1) [Enrique Sorrel (1/0)], Carlos Vidal (4/2), Moisés Avilés (1/0). Trainer: Joaquín Morales (1).

**Goal**: Arturo Carmona (8).

**40.** 18.01.1935 **URUGUAY - CHILE** **2-1(1-0)** 13th Copa América

Estadio Nacional, Lima (Peru); Referee: José Artemio Serra (Peru); Attendance: 13,000

**CHI:** Roberto Cortés (8/0) [Isaías Azzerman (1/0)], Conrado Welsh (2/0), Ascanio Cortés (2/0), Guillermo Gornall (2/0), Guillermo Arturo Riveros (5/0) [Arturo Torres Carrasco (7/0)], Enrique Araneda (2/0), Andrés Carlos Aranda (2/0), Carlos Giudice (2/1), Arturo Carmona (2/1), Carlos Vidal (5/2), José Avendaño (1/0). Trainer: Joaquín Morales (2).

**Goal**: Carlos Giudice (54).

**41.** 26.01.1935 **PERU - CHILE** **1-0(1-0)** 13th Copa América
Estadio Nacional, Lima; Referee: Eduardo Forte (Argentina); Attendance: 12,000
**CHI:** Roberto Cortés (9/0), Conrado Welsh (3/0) [Quintín Vargas (1/0)], Ascanio Cortés (3/0), Guillermo Gornall (3/0), Arturo Torres Carrasco (8/0), Enrique Araneda (3/0), Andrés Carlos Aranda (3/0), Carlos Giudice (3/1), Arturo Carmona (3/1), Carlos Vidal (6/2), José Avendaño (2/0) [Eduardo Schneeberger (1/0)]. Trainer: Joaquín Morales (3).

**42.** 30.12.1936 **ARGENTINA - CHILE** **2-1(2-0)** 14th Copa América
Estadio Gasómetro de Boedo, Buenos Aires; Referee: Aníbal Tejada (Uruguay); Attendance: 35,000
**CHI:** Luis Cabrera (1/0), Ascanio Cortés (4/0), Jorge Córdova (1/0) [Mario Baeza (1/0)], Juan Montero (1/0), Guillermo Arturo Riveros (6/0), Eduardo Schneeberger (2/0), Guillermo Torres (1/0), Arturo Carmona (4/1), Raúl Julio Toro (1/1), José Avendaño (3/0), Tomás Ojeda (3/0). Trainer: Pedro Mazullo (1).
**Goal**: Raúl Julio Toro (75).

**43.** 03.01.1937 **BRAZIL - CHILE** **6-4(5-3)** 14th Copa América
Estadio Boca Juniors, Buenos Aires (Argentina); Referee: José Bartolomé Macías (Argentina); Attendance: 20,000
**CHI:** Luis Cabrera (2/0) [Eugenio Soto (1/0)], Ascanio Cortés (5/0), Jorge Córdova (2/0) [Mario Baeza (2/0)], Juan Montero (2/0), Guillermo Arturo Riveros (7/1), Eduardo Schneeberger (3/0), Guillermo Torres (2/0), Arturo Carmona (5/1), Raúl Julio Toro (2/3), José Avendaño (4/1), Tomás Ojeda (4/0). Trainer: Pedro Mazullo (2).
**Goals**: José Avendaño (19), Raúl Julio Toro (25), Guillermo Arturo Riveros (40), Raúl Julio Toro (73).

**44.** 10.01.1937 **CHILE - URUGUAY** **3-0(1-0)** 14th Copa América
Estadio Gasómetro de Boedo, Buenos Aires (Argentina); Referee: José Bartolomé Macías (Argentina); Attendance: 18,000
**CHI:** Luis Cabrera (3/0), Ascanio Cortés (6/0), Jorge Córdova (3/0), Juan Montero (3/0), Guillermo Arturo Riveros (8/1), Luis Ponce (1/0), Guillermo Torres (3/0), Arturo Carmona (6/1) [Tomás Ojeda (5/0)], Raúl Julio Toro (3/5), José Avendaño (5/1), Moisés Avilés (2/0) [Manuel Arancibia (1/1)]. Trainer: Pedro Mazullo (3).
**Goals**: Raúl Julio Toro (17), Manuel Arancibia (59), Raúl Julio Toro (83).

**45.** 17.01.1937 **PARAGUAY - CHILE** **3-2(?-2)** 14th Copa América
Estadio Gasómetro de Boedo, Buenos Aires (Argentina); Referee: Aníbal Tejada (Uruguay); Attendance: 12,000
**CHI:** Luis Cabrera (4/0), Ascanio Cortés (7/0), Jorge Córdova (4/0), Juan Montero (4/0) [Guillermo Gornall (4/0)], Guillermo Arturo Riveros (9/1), Luis Ponce (2/0), Guillermo Torres (4/0), Manuel Arancibia (2/1) [Arturo Carmona (7/1)], Raúl Julio Toro (4/7), José Avendaño (6/1), Tomás Ojeda (6/0). Trainer: Pedro Mazullo (4).
**Goals**: Raúl Julio Toro (8, 32).

**46.** 21.01.1937 **CHILE - PERU** **2-2(1-2)** 14th Copa América
Estadio Gasómetro de Boedo, Buenos Aires (Argentina); Referee: José Bartolomé Macías (Argentina); Attendance: 12,000
**CHI:** Luis Cabrera (5/0), Ascanio Cortés (8/0), Jorge Córdova (5/0), Juan Montero (5/0), Guillermo Arturo Riveros (10/1), Luis Ponce (3/0), Guillermo Torres (5/1), Manuel Arancibia (3/2) [Arturo Carmona (8/1)], Raúl Julio Toro (5/7), José Avendaño (7/1) [Moisés Avilés (3/0)], Tomás Ojeda (7/0). Trainer: Pedro Mazullo (5).
**Goals**: Guillermo Torres (16), Manuel Arancibia (70).

**47.** 15.01.1939 **PARAGUAY - CHILE** **5-1(?-1)** 15th Copa América
Estadio Nacional, Lima (Peru); Referee: Alberto March (Ecuador); Attendance: 10,000
**CHI:** Eduardo Simián (1/0), Humberto Roa (1/0), Jorge Córdova (6/0), Juan Montero (6/0), Guillermo Arturo Riveros (11/1), Luis Ponce (4/0) [Julio Córdova (1/0)], Enrique Sorrel (2/1), Raúl Julio Toro (6/7), Alfonso Domínguez (1/0), Voltaire Carvajal (1/0), José Avendaño (8/1) [Roberto Luco (1/0)]. Trainer: Pedro Mazullo (6).
**Goal**: Enrique Sorrel (8).

**48.** 22.01.1939 **PERU - CHILE** **3-1(0-0)** 15th Copa América
Estadio Nacional, Lima; Referee: Carlos Puyol (Uruguay); Attendance: 6,000
**CHI:** Augusto Lobos (1/0), Ascanio Cortés (9/0), Jorge Córdova (7/0), Juan Montero (7/0), Felipe Mediavilla (1/0), Luis Ponce (5/0), Enrique Sorrel (3/1), Raúl Julio Toro (7/7) [Alfonso Domínguez (2/1)], Gustavo Pizarro (1/0), Voltaire Carvajal (2/0), Raúl Muñoz (1/0). Trainer: Pedro Mazullo (7).
**Goal**: Alfonso Domínguez (75).

**49.** 29.01.1939 **URUGUAY - CHILE** **3-2(2-2)** 15th Copa América
Estadio Nacional, Lima (Peru); Referee: Enrique Cuenca (Peru); Attendance: 15,000
**CHI:** Augusto Lobos (2/0) [Eduardo Simián (2/0)], Ascanio Cortés (10/0), Jorge Córdova (8/0), Julio Córdova (2/0), Guillermo Arturo Riveros (12/1) [Felipe Mediavilla (2/0)], Luis Ponce (6/0), Enrique Sorrel (4/1) [Roberto Luco (2/1)], Alfonso Domínguez (3/1), Gustavo Pizarro (2/0), José Avendaño (9/1), Raúl Muñoz (2/1). Trainer: Pedro Mazullo (8).
**Goals**: Raúl Muñoz (3), Roberto Luco (39).

**50.** 05.02.1939 **CHILE - ECUADOR** **4-1(3-1)** 15th Copa América
Estadio Nacional, Lima (Peru); Referee: Carlos Puyol (Uruguay); Attendance: 10,000
**CHI:** Eduardo Simián (3/0), Ascanio Cortés (11/0), Jorge Córdova (9/0), Julio Córdova (3/0), Guillermo Arturo Riveros (13/1), Luis Ponce (7/0), Enrique Sorrel (5/2), Raúl Julio Toro (8/8), Gustavo Pizarro (3/0), José Avendaño (10/3), Roberto Luco (3/1) [Raúl Muñoz (3/1)]. Trainer: Pedro Mazullo (9).
**Goals**: Raúl Julio Toro (6), José Avendaño (15), Enrique Sorrel (19 penalty), José Avendaño (79).

**51.** 26.02.1939 **CHILE - PARAGUAY** **4-2**
Estadio Nacional, Santiago; Attendance: 40,000
**CHI:** Augusto Lobos (3/0), Ascanio Cortés (12/0), Jorge Córdova (10/0), Julio Córdova (4/0), Guillermo Arturo Riveros (14/1) [Felipe Mediavilla (3/0)], Luis Ponce (8/0), Enrique Sorrel (6/3), Gustavo Pizarro (4/0), Alfonso Domínguez (4/1), José Avendaño (11/3) [Raúl Julio Toro (9/11)], Raúl Muñoz (4/1).Trainer: Pedro Mazullo (10).
**Goals**: Raúl Julio Toro 3, Enrique Sorrel.

**52.** 02.02.1941 **CHILE - ECUADOR** **5-0(4-0)** 16th Copa América
Estadio Nacional, Santiago; Referee: José Bartolomé Macías (Argentina); Attendance: 40,000
**CHI:** Sergio Roberto Livingstone Pohlhammer (1/0), Humberto Roa (2/0), Oscar Ellis (1/0), Manuel Arancibia (4/3), Roberto Cabrera (1/0) [Oscar Sánchez (1/0)], José Pastene (1/0), Enrique Sorrel (7/5), Osvaldo Carvajal (1/0), Raúl Julio Toro (10/12), Armando Contreras (1/1), Raúl Pérez (1/0). Trainer: Máximo Garay (1).
**Goals**: Raúl Julio Toro (10), Enrique Sorrel (18), Manuel Arancibia (25), Armando Contreras (43), Enrique Sorrel (78).

**53.** 09.02.1941 **CHILE - PERU** **1-0(1-0)** 16th Copa América
Estadio Nacional, Santiago; Referee: José Bartolomé Macías (Argentina); Attendance: 51,709
**CHI:** Sergio Roberto Livingstone Pohlhammer (2/0), Humberto Roa (3/0), Luis Vidal (1/0), Segundo Flores (1/0), Roberto Cabrera (2/0) [Oscar Sánchez (2/0)], Héctor Trejos (1/0) [José Pastene (2/0)], Enrique Sorrel (8/5), Alfonso Domínguez (5/1) [Osvaldo Carvajal (2/0)], Raúl Julio Toro (11/12), David Ruíz (1/0), Raúl Pérez (2/1). Trainer: Máximo Garay (2).
**Goal**: Raúl Pérez (23).

**54.** 16.02.1941 **CHILE – URUGUAY** **0-2(0-1)** 16th Copa América
Estadio Nacional, Santiago; Referee: José Bartolomé Macías (Argentina); Attendance: 70,000
**CHI:** Sergio Roberto Livingstone Pohlhammer (3/0), Humberto Roa (4/0), Luis Vidal (2/0) [46.Ascanio Cortés (13/0)], Segundo Flores (2/0), Roberto Cabrera (3/0), Héctor Trejos (2/0), Enrique Sorrel (9/5), Alfonso Domínguez (6/1) [46.Osvaldo Carvajal (3/0)], Raúl Julio Toro (12/12), David Ruíz (2/0), Desiderio Medina (1/0) [46.José Avendaño (12/3)]. Trainer: Máximo Garay (3).

**55.** 04.03.1941 **CHILE - ARGENTINA** **0-1(0-0)** 16th Copa América
Estadio Nacional, Santiago; Referee: Aníbal Tejada (Uruguay); Attendance: 60,300
**CHI:** Sergio Roberto Livingstone Pohlhammer (4/0), Humberto Roa (5/0), Luis Vidal (3/0), Segundo Flores (3/0), Roberto Cabrera (4/0), Héctor Trejos (3/0) [José Pastene (3/0)], Juan Muñoz (1/0) [Enrique Sorrel (10/5)], Osvaldo Carvajal (4/0), Raúl Julio Toro (13/12), Armando Contreras (2/1), Raúl Pérez (3/1). Trainer: Máximo Garay (4).

**56.** 10.01.1942 **URUGUAY - CHILE** **6-1(4-1)** 17th Copa América
Estadio Centenario, Montevideo; Referee: José Bartolomé Macías (Argentina); Attendance: 40,000
**CHI:** Mario Ibáñez (1/0) [Hernán Fernández (1/0)], Santiago Salfate (1/0), Humberto Roa (6/0) [Manuel Arancibia (5/3)], Francisco Las Heras (1/0), José Pastene (4/0), Oscar Medina (1/0), Benito Armingol (1/0), Guillermo Casanova (1/0) [Carlos Arancibia (1/0)], Alfonso Domínguez (7/1), Armando Contreras (3/2), Guillermo Torres (6/1). Trainer: Ferenc Platkó (1).
**Goal**: Armando Contreras (1).

**57.** 14.01.1942 **BRAZIL - CHILE** **6-1(2-1)** 17th Copa América
Estadio Centenario, Montevideo (Uruguay); Referee: Aníbal Tejada (Uruguay); Attendance: 10,000
**CHI:** Hernán Fernández (2/0), Santiago Salfate (2/0), Humberto Roa (7/0), Francisco Las Heras (2/0) [*sent off*], José Pastene (5/0), Oscar Medina (2/0), Benito Armingol (2/0), Guillermo Casanova (2/0) [Manuel Arancibia (6/3)], Alfonso Domínguez (8/2) [Florencio Barrera (1/0)], Armando Contreras (4/2), Guillermo Torres (7/1) [Raúl Pérez (4/1)]. Trainer: Ferenc Platkó (2).
**Goal**: Alfonso Domínguez (35).

**58.** 22.01.1942 **PARAGUAY - CHILE** **2-0(1-0)** 17th Copa América
Estadio Centenario, Montevideo (Uruguay); Referee: José Ferreira Lemos (Brazil); Attendance: 25,000
**CHI:** Sergio Roberto Livingstone Pohlhammer (5/0), Santiago Salfate (3/0), Humberto Roa (8/0), Roberto Cabrera (5/0), José Pastene (6/0), Oscar Medina (3/0), Benito Armingol (3/0), Alfonso Domínguez (9/2), Florencio Barrera (2/0), Armando Contreras (5/2) [Carlos Arancibia (2/0); Guillermo Casanova (3/0)], Fernando Riera Bauza (1/0). Trainer: Ferenc Platkó (3).

**59.** 31.01.1942 **ARGENTINA - CHILE** **0-0*** 17th Copa América
Estadio Centenario, Montevideo (Uruguay); Referee: Enrique Cuenca (Peru); Attendance: 15,000
**CHI:** Sergio Roberto Livingstone Pohlhammer (6/0), Santiago Salfate (4/0), Humberto Roa (9/0), Roberto Cabrera (6/0), José Pastene (7/0), Oscar Medina (4/0), Benito Armingol (4/0) [Guillermo Torres (8/1)], Alfonso Domínguez (10/2), Florencio Barrera (3/0), Armando Contreras (6/2) [Carlos Arancibia (3/0)], Fernando Riera Bauza (2/0). Trainer: Ferenc Platkó (4).
**After 43 mins, chilean player left the field due to badperformances from Referee Cuenca. The match was awarded as win for Argentina.*

**60.** 05.02.1942 **CHILE - ECUADOR** **2-1(2-1)** 17th Copa América
Estadio Centenario, Montevideo (Uruguay); Referee: Mario Rojas (Paraguay); Attendance: 15,000
**CHI:** Sergio Roberto Livingstone Pohlhammer (7/0), Santiago Salfate (5/0), Humberto Roa (10/0), Roberto Cabrera (7/0), José Pastene (8/0), Oscar Medina (5/0), Benito Armingol (5/1), Alfonso Domínguez (11/3), Florencio Barrera (4/0) [Guillermo Casanova (4/0)], Armando Contreras (7/2), Fernando Riera Bauza (3/0) [Guillermo Torres (9/1)]. Trainer: Ferenc Platkó (5).
**Goals**: Alfonso Domínguez (20), Benito Armingol (42).

**61.** 07.02.1942 **CHILE - PERU** **0-0** 17th Copa América
Estadio Centenario, Montevideoč (Uruguay); Referee: José Bartolomé Macías (Argentina); Attendance: 70,000
**CHI:** Sergio Roberto Livingstone Pohlhammer (8/0), Santiago Salfate (6/0), Humberto Roa (11/0), Roberto Cabrera (8/0), José Pastene (9/0), Oscar Medina (6/0), Benito Armingol (6/1), Alfonso Domínguez (12/3), Guillermo Casanova (5/0), Armando Contreras (8/2), Fernando Riera Bauza (4/0). Trainer: Ferenc Platkó (6).

**62.** 14.01.1945 **CHILE - ECUADOR** **6-3(3-2)** 18th Copa América
Estadio Nacional, Santiago; Referee: José Bartolomé Macías (Argentina); Attendance: 65,000
**CHI:** Sergio Roberto Livingstone Pohlhammer (9/0), Florencio Barrera (5/0), Víctor Klein (1/0), Francisco Las Heras (3/0), Francisco Hormazábal (1/1), Carlos Ataglich (1/0), Manuel Piñeiro (1/0), Guillermo Clavero (1/1), Juan Alcántara (1/3), Armando Contreras (9/2) [Erasmo Vera (1/1)], Desiderio Medina (2/0).Trainer: Ferenc Platkó (7).
**Goals**: Juan Alcántara (28), Erasmo Vera (29), Francisco Hormazábal (45), Juan Alcántara (59), Guillermo Clavero (70), Juan Alcántara (81).

**63.** 24.01.1945 **CHILE - BOLIVIA** **5-0(3-0)** 18th Copa América
Estadio Nacional, Santiago; Referee: Nobel Valentini (Uruguay); Attendance: 70,000
**CHI:** Sergio Roberto Livingstone Pohlhammer (10/0), Florencio Barrera (6/0), Jorge Vásquez (1/0), Francisco Las Heras (4/0), José Pastene (10/0), Carlos Ataglich (2/0) [Miguel Busquets (1/0)], Manuel Piñeiro (2/0), Guillermo Clavero (2/3), Juan Alcántara (2/5) [Armando Contreras (10/2)], Erasmo Vera (2/1), Desiderio Medina (3/1). Trainer: Ferenc Platkó (8).
**Goals**: Guillermo Clavero (13, 27), Desiderio Medina (39), Juan Alcántara (75, 79).

**64.** 31.01.1945 **CHILE - COLOMBIA** **2-0(1-0)** 18th Copa América
Estadio Nacional, Santiago; Referee: José Bartolomé Macías (Argentina); Attendance: 56,143
**CHI:** Sergio Roberto Livingstone Pohlhammer (11/0), Florencio Barrera (7/0), Jorge Vásquez (2/0) [Humberto Roa (12/0)], Francisco Las Heras (5/0), José Pastene (11/0), Miguel Busquets (2/0), Manuel Piñeiro (3/1), Guillermo Clavero (3/3), Juan Alcántara (3/5), Armando Contreras (11/2) [Atilio Cremaschi (1/0)], Desiderio Medina (4/2). Trainer: Ferenc Platkó (9).
**Goals**: Desiderio Medina (29), Manuel Piñeiro (80).

**65.** 11.02.1945 **CHILE - ARGENTINA** **1-1(1-0)** 18th Copa América
Estadio Nacional, Santiago; Referee: Nobel Valentini (Uruguay); Attendance: 70,000
**CHI:** Sergio Roberto Livingstone Pohlhammer (12/0), Florencio Barrera (8/0), Jorge Vásquez (3/0), Francisco Las Heras (6/0), José Pastene (12/0), Miguel Busquets (3/0), Manuel Piñeiro (4/1) [Benito Armingol (7/1)], Guillermo Clavero (4/3), Francisco Hormazábal (2/1), Erasmo Vera (3/1) [Carlos Varela (1/0)], Desiderio Medina (5/3) [Armando Contreras (12/2)]. Trainer: Ferenc Platkó (10).
**Goal**: Desiderio Medina (3).

**66.** 18.02.1945 **CHILE - URUGUAY** **1-0(1-0)** 18th Copa América
Estadio Nacional, Santiago; Referee: José Bartolomé Macías (Argentina); Attendance: 53,663
**CHI:** Sergio Roberto Livingstone Pohlhammer (13/0), Florencio Barrera (9/0), Jorge Vásquez (4/0), Francisco Las Heras (7/0), José Pastene (13/0) [Carlos Ataglich (3/0)], Miguel Busquets (4/0), Manuel Piñeiro (5/1), Guillermo Clavero (5/3), Francisco Hormazábal (3/1), Armando Contreras (13/2) [Erasmo Vera (4/1)], Desiderio Medina (6/4) [Mario Castro (1/0)]. Trainer: Ferenc Platkó (11).
**Goal**: Desiderio Medina (8).

**67.** 28.02.1945 **CHILE - BRAZIL** **0-1(0-1)** 18th Copa América
Estadio Nacional, Santiago; Referee: Nobel Valentini (Uruguay); Attendance: 56,814
**CHI:** Sergio Roberto Livingstone Pohlhammer (14/0), Florencio Barrera (10/0), Jorge Vásquez (5/0), Francisco Las Heras (8/0), José Pastene (14/0), Miguel Busquets (5/0), Manuel Piñeiro (6/1) [Benito Armingol (8/1)], Guillermo Clavero (6/3), Francisco Hormazábal (4/1) [Carlos Ataglich (4/0)], Erasmo Vera (5/1) [Armando Contreras (14/2)], Desiderio Medina (7/4). Trainer: Ferenc Platkó (12).

**68.** 16.01.1946 **URUGUAY - CHILE** **1-0(1-0)** 19th Copa América
Estadio Gasómetro de Boedo, Buenos Aires (Argentina); Referee: Mário Gonçalves Vianna (Brazil); Attendance: 50,000
**CHI:** Hernán Fernández (3/0), Santiago Salfate (7/0), Domingo Pino (1/0), Francisco Las Heras (9/0), José Sepúlveda (1/0), Hernán Carvallo Castro (1/0), Mario Castro (2/0), Atilio Cremaschi (2/0), Jorge Araya (1/0) [Osvaldo Sáez (1/0)], Erasmo Vera (6/1) [Rodolfo Clavería (1/0)], Desiderio Medina (8/4) [Domingo Romo (1/0)]. Trainer: Luis Tirado (1).

**69.** 19.01.1946 **CHILE - PARAGUAY** **2-1** 19th Copa América
Estadio Gasómetro de Boedo, Buenos Aires (Argentina); Referee: Nobel Valentini (Uruguay); Attendance: 60,000
**CHI:** Hernán Fernández (4/0), Santiago Salfate (8/0) [Guilermo Fuenzalida (1/0)], José López (1/0), Francisco Las Heras (10/0), José Sepúlveda (2/0), Hernán Carvallo Castro (2/0), Mario Castro (3/0), Atilio Cremaschi (3/1), Jorge Araya (2/0) [Luis Víctor Mansilla (1/0)], Erasmo Vera (7/1), Desiderio Medina (9/5). Trainer: Luis Tirado (2).
**Goals**: Deziderio Medina (48), Atilio Cremaschi (68).

**70.** 26.01.1946 **ARGENTINA - CHILE** **3-1(1-0)** 19th Copa América
Estadio Monumental „Antonio Vespucio Liberti", Buenos Aires; Referee: Nobel Valentini (Uruguay); Attendance: 80,000
**CHI:** Hernán Fernández (5/0), Santiago Salfate (9/0), José López (2/0), Francisco Las Heras (11/0), José Sepúlveda (3/0), Hernán Carvallo Castro (3/0), Mario Castro (4/0) [Juan Alcántara (4/6)], Atilio Cremaschi (4/1), Luis Víctor Mansilla (2/0) [Jorge Araya (3/0)], Erasmo Vera (8/1) [Jorge Peñaloza (1/0)], Desiderio Medina (10/5). Trainer: Luis Tirado (3).
**Goal**: Juan Alcántara (85).

**71.** 03.02.1946 **BRAZIL - CHILE** **5-1(2-0)** 19th Copa América
Estadio Gasómetro de Boedo, Buenos Aires (Argentina); Referee: Nobel Valentini (Uruguay); Attendance: 22,000
**CHI:** Hernán Fernández (6/0), Santiago Salfate (10/1), José López (3/0), Rodolfo Clavería (2/0), Guilermo Fuenzalida (2/0) [Francisco Las Heras (12/0)], Hernán Carvallo Castro (4/0), Mario Castro (5/0), Atilio Cremaschi (5/1), Osvaldo Sáez (2/0) [Luis Víctor Mansilla (3/0)], Jorge Peñaloza (2/0) [Erasmo Vera (9/1)], Desiderio Medina (11/5). Trainer: Luis Tirado (4).
**Goal**: Santiago Salfate (84 penalty).

**72.** 08.02.1946 **CHILE - BOLIVIA** **4-1** 19th Copa América
Estadio Gasómetro de Boedo, Buenos Aires (Argentina); Referee: José Bartolomé Macías (Argentina); Attendance: 18,000
**CHI:** Hernán Fernández (7/0), Santiago Salfate (11/1), José López (4/0), Francisco Las Heras (13/0), José Sepúlveda (4/0), Hernán Carvallo Castro (5/0), Mario Castro (6/0) [Juan Alcántara (5/6)], Atilio Cremaschi (6/3), Francisco Ruíz (1/0), Jorge Araya (4/2), Desiderio Medina (12/5) [Domingo Romo (2/0)]. Trainer: Luis Tirado (5).
**Goals**: Jorge Araya (9, 39), Atilio Cremaschi (49, 78).

**73.** 06.12.1947 **URUGUAY - CHILE** **6-0(3-0)** 20th Copa América
Estadio Capwell, Guayaquil (Ecuador); Referee: Juan José Alvarez (Argentina); Attendance: 20,000
**CHI:** Sergio Roberto Livingstone Pohlhammer (15/0), Francisco Urroz (1/0), Manuel Alvarez (1/0) [Juan Negri (1/0)], Manuel Machuca Berríos (1/0), Freddy Wood (1/0), Miguel Busquets (6/0), Fernando Riera Bauza (5/0), Andrés Prieto (1/0) [Osvaldo Sáez (3/0)], Jorge Araya (5/2) [Ricardo Raimundo Infante (1/0)], Jorge Peñaloza (3/0), Pedro Hugo López (1/0). Trainer: Luis Tirado (6).

**74.** 09.12.1947 **CHILE - PERU** **2-1(1-0)** 20th Copa América
Estadio Capwell, Guayaquil (Ecuador); Referee: Juan José Alvarez (Argentina); Attendance: 15,000
**CHI:** Sergio Roberto Livingstone Pohlhammer (16/0), Mario Baeza (3/0), Juan Negri (2/0), Manuel Machuca Berríos (2/0), José Sepúlveda (5/0) [Juan Manuel Acuña (1/0)], Miguel Busquets (7/0), Fernando Riera Bauza (6/0), Carlos Varela (2/1), Osvaldo Sáez (4/1), Jorge Peñaloza (4/0), Pedro Hugo López (2/0). Trainer: Luis Tirado (7).
**Goals**: Carlos Varela (25), Osvaldo Sáez (71).

**75.** 11.12.1947 **ECUADOR - CHILE** **0-3(0-0)** 20th Copa América
Estadio Capwell, Guayaquil; Referee: Juan José Alvarez (Argentina); Attendance: 22,000
**CHI:** Sergio Roberto Livingstone Pohlhammer (17/0), Francisco Urroz (2/0), Juan Negri (3/0), Manuel Machuca Berríos (3/0), José Sepúlveda (6/0), Miguel Busquets (8/0) [Juan Manuel Acuña (2/0)], José Balbuena (1/0), Carlos Varela (3/1), Osvaldo Sáez (5/1) [Jorge Araya (6/2)], Jorge Peñaloza (5/1) [Andrés Prieto (2/0)], Pedro Hugo López (3/2). Trainer: Luis Tirado (8).
**Goals**: Jorge Peñaloza (51), Pedro Hugo López (62, 72).

**76.** 16.12.1947 **ARGENTINA - CHILE** **1-1(1-1)** 20th Copa América
Estadio Capwell, Guayaquil (Ecuador); Referee: Luis Alberto Fernández (Uruguay); Attendance: 30,000
**CHI:** Sergio Roberto Livingstone Pohlhammer (18/0), Francisco Urroz (3/0), Juan Negri (4/0), Manuel Machuca Berríos (4/0), José Sepúlveda (7/0) [Juan Manuel Acuña (3/0)], Miguel Busquets (9/0) [Fernando Iván Campos (1/0)], Fernando Riera Bauza (7/1), Carlos Varela (4/1), Ricardo Raimundo Infante (2/0) [Jorge Araya (7/2)], Jorge Peñaloza (6/1), Pedro Hugo López (4/2). Trainer: Luis Tirado (9).
**Goal**: Fernando Riera Bauza (37).

**77.** 23.12.1947 **PARAGUAY - CHILE** **1-0(0-0)** 20th Copa América

Estadio Capwell, Guayaquil (Ecuador); Referee: Juan José Alvarez (Argentina); Attendance: 5,000

**CHI:** Sergio Roberto Livingstone Pohlhammer (19/0), Mario Baeza (4/0), Juan Negri (5/0), Manuel Machuca Berríos (5/0), José Sepúlveda (8/0) [Juan Manuel Acuña (4/0)], Miguel Busquets (10/0), Fernando Riera Bauza (8/1), Carlos Varela (5/1) [Ricardo Raimundo Infante (3/0)], Osvaldo Sáez (6/1), Jorge Peñaloza (7/1), Pedro Hugo López (5/2). Trainer: Luis Tirado (10).

**78.** 29.12.1947 **CHILE - COLOMBIA** **4-1(1-0)** 20th Copa América

Estadio Capwell, Guayaquil (Ecuador); Referee: Juan José Alvarez (Argentina); Attendance: 5,000

**CHI:** Sergio Roberto Livingstone Pohlhammer (20/0), Francisco Urroz (4/0), Juan Negri (6/0), Manuel Machuca Berríos (6/0), José Sepúlveda (9/0), Juan Manuel Acuña (5/0), Fernando Riera Bauza (9/2), Carlos Varela (6/1) [Jorge Peñaloza (8/1)], Jorge Araya (8/2) [Ricardo Raimundo Infante (4/1)], Andrés Prieto (3/1) [Osvaldo Sáez (7/2)], Pedro Hugo López (6/2). Trainer: Luis Tirado (11).

**Goals**: Andrés Prieto (28), Osvaldo Sáez (75), Fernando Riera Bauza (78), Ricardo Raimundo Infante (88).

**79.** 31.12.1947 **CHILE - BOLIVIA** **4-3** 20th Copa América

Estadio Capwell, Guayaquil (Ecuador); Referee: Federico Muñoz Medina (Ecuador); Attendance: 5,000

**CHI:** Sergio Roberto Livingstone Pohlhammer (21/0), Francisco Urroz (5/0) [Juan Manuel Acuña (6/0)], Manuel Alvarez (2/0), Manuel Machuca Berríos (7/0), José Sepúlveda (10/0), Freddy Wood (2/0), Fernando Riera Bauza (10/2), Carlos Varela (7/1), Ricardo Raimundo Infante (5/3), Osvaldo Sáez (8/3) [Andrés Prieto (4/1)], Pedro Hugo López (7/3). Trainer: Luis Tirado (12).

**Goals**: Ricardo Raimundo Infante (30), Osvaldo Sáez (44), Ricardo Raimundo Infante (50), Pedro Hugo López (51).

**80.** 06.04.1949 **BOLIVIA - CHILE** **3-2** 21st Copa América

Estádio Pacaembú, São Paulo (Brazil); Referee: Cyril John Barrick (England); Attendance: 30,000

**CHI:** Sergio Roberto Livingstone Pohlhammer (Cap) (22/0), Francisco Urroz (6/0), Manuel Alvarez (3/0), Manuel Machuca Berríos (8/0), Ulises Ramos (1/0), Gilberto Muñoz (1/0), Fernando Riera Bauza (11/3), Manuel Salamanca (1/1), Carlos Rodolfo Rojas (1/0) [Ricardo Raimundo Infante (6/3)], Atilio Cremaschi (7/3), Mario Castro (7/0) [Pedro Hugo López (8/3)]. Trainer: Luis Tirado (13).

**Goals**: Fernando Riera Bauza (30), Manuel Salamanca (71).

**81.** 13.04.1949 **BRAZIL - CHILE** **2-1(2-0)** 21st Copa América

Estádio Pacaembú, São Paulo; Referee: Juan Carlos Armental (Uruguay); Attendance: 35,000

**CHI:** Sergio Roberto Livingstone Pohlhammer (23/0), Francisco Urroz (7/0), Juan Negri (7/0), Manuel Machuca Berríos (9/0), Miguel Flores (1/0), Miguel Busquets (11/0), Fernando Riera Bauza (12/3), Ricardo Raimundo Infante (7/3) [Ulises Ramos (2/0)], Carlos Varela (8/1), Pedro Hugo López (9/4), Andrés Prieto (5/1) [Luis López (1/0)].Trainer: Luis Tirado (14).

**Goal**: Pedro Hugo López (89 penalty).

**82.** 17.04.1949 **CHILE - ECUADOR** **1-0(1-0)** 21st Copa América

Estádio São Januário, Rio de Janeiro (Brazil); Referee: Cyril John Barrick (England); Attendance: 8,000

**CHI:** Sergio Roberto Livingstone Pohlhammer (24/0), Francisco Urroz (8/0), Juan Negri (8/0), Manuel Machuca Berríos (10/0), Gilberto Muñoz (2/0) [Ulises Ramos (3/0)], Miguel Busquets (12/0), Mario Castro (8/0), Atilio Cremaschi (8/3) [Manuel Salamanca (2/1)], Carlos Rodolfo Rojas (2/1), Carlos Varela (9/1) [Ricardo Raimundo Infante (8/3)], Pedro Hugo López (10/4). Trainer: Luis Tirado (15).

**Goal**: Carlos Rodolfo Rojas (4).

**83.** 20.04.1949 **CHILE - COLOMBIA** **1-1(1-0)** 21st Copa América

Estádio São Januário, Rio de Janeiro (Brazil); Referee: Mario Gardelli (Brazil); Attendance: 7,000

**CHI:** Sergio Roberto Livingstone Pohlhammer (25/0), Francisco Urroz (9/0) [Ulises Ramos (4/0)], Juan Negri (9/0), Manuel Machuca Berríos (11/0), Gilberto Muñoz (3/0), Miguel Busquets (13/0), Fernando Riera Bauza (13/3), Manuel Salamanca (3/1), Ricardo Raimundo Infante (9/3) [Carlos Rodolfo Rojas (3/1)], Luis López (2/0), Pedro Hugo López (11/5). Trainer: Luis Tirado (16).

**Goals**: Pedro Hugo López (8).

**84.** 27.04.1949 **PARAGUAY - CHILE** **4-2** 21st Copa América

Estádio Pacaembú, São Paulo (Brazil); Referee: Mario Gardelli (Brazil); Attendance: 1,000

**CHI:** Sergio Roberto Livingstone Pohlhammer (26/0), Juan Negri (10/0) [Pablo Hormazábal (1/0)], Francisco Urroz (10/0) [Ulises Ramos (5/1)], Manuel Machuca Berríos (12/0), Gilberto Muñoz (4/0), Miguel Busquets (14/0), Fernando Riera Bauza (14/3), Atilio Cremaschi (9/4), Ricardo Raimundo Infante (10/3), Carlos Varela (10/1) [Luis López (3/0)], Pedro Hugo López (12/5). Trainer: Luis Tirado (17).

**Goals**: Atilio Cremaschi (8), Ulises Ramos (72).

**85.** 30.04.1949 **PERU - CHILE** **3-0(1-0)** 21st Copa América

Estádio Pacaembú, São Paulo (Brazil); Referee: Mario Gardelli (Brazil); Attendance: 1,000

**CHI:** Sergio Roberto Livingstone Pohlhammer (27/0), Miguel Flores (2/0), Juan Negri (11/0) [Pablo Hormazábal (2/0)], Manuel Machuca Berríos (13/0), Gilberto Muñoz (5/0), Ulises Ramos (6/1), Carlos Rodolfo Rojas (4/1), Atilio Cremaschi (10/4), Fernando Riera Bauza (15/3) [Mario Castro (9/0)], Andrés Prieto (6/1), Carlos Varela (11/1) [Pedro Hugo López (13/5)]. Trainer: Luis Tirado (18).

**86.** 08.05.1949 **CHILE - URUGUAY** **3-1(0-1)*** 21st Copa América

Estádio América, Belo Horizonte (Brazil); Referee: Mario Gardelli (Brazil); Attendance: 5,000

**CHI:** Sergio Roberto Livingstone Pohlhammer (28/0), Juan Negri (12/0), Miguel Flores (3/0), Manuel Machuca Berríos (14/0), Gilberto Muñoz (6/0), Miguel Busquets (15/0), Mario Castro (10/0), Atilio Cremaschi (11/5), Andrés Prieto (7/1) [Ricardo Raimundo Infante (11/5)], Carlos Rodolfo Rojas (5/1), Pedro Hugo López (14/5) [Carlos Varela (12/1)]. Trainer: Luis Tirado (19).

**Goals**: Ricardo Raimundo Infante (75, 83 penalty), Atilio Cremaschi (88).

**The uruguayan players left the field after 83 mins.*

**87.** 26.02.1950 **BOLIVIA - CHILE** **2-0(0-0)**

Estadio „Hernando Siles Zuazo“, La Paz; Referee: Alfredo Alvarez Fernández (Bolivia); Attendance: 25,000

**CHI:** Sergio Roberto Livingstone Pohlhammer (29/0), Manuel Machuca Berríos (15/0), Manuel Arriagada (1/0), Juan Negri (13/0) [Mariano Román (1/0)], Osvaldo Sáez (9/3), José López (5/0) [Arturo Farías (1/0)], Mario Castro (11/0) [José Fernández (1/0)], Atilio Cremaschi (12/5) [Fernando Iván Campos (2/0)], Mario Lorca (1/0) [Reinaldo Rebello (1/0)], Andrés Prieto (8/1), Guillermo Díaz Zambrano (1/0) [Enrique Daniel Hormazábal Silva (1/0)]. Trainer: Ferenc Platkó (13).

**88.** 12.03.1950 **CHILE - BOLIVIA** **5-0(3-0)**
Estadio Nacional, Santiago; Referee: Alejandro Gálvez (Chile); Attendance: 40,000
**CHI:** Sergio Roberto Livingstone Pohlhammer (30/0), Manuel Machuca Berríos (16/0) [Mariano Román (2/0)], Manuel Arriagada (2/0) [Juan Negri (14/0)], Arturo Farías (2/0) [José López (6/0)], Enrique Daniel Hormazábal Silva (2/1) [Adelmo Yori (1/0)], Fernando Iván Campos (3/1) [José Fernández (2/0)], Atilio Cremaschi (13/5), Mario Lorca (2/0) [Ricardo Raimundo Infante (12/5)], Mario Castro (12/0), Andrés Prieto (9/2), Guillermo Díaz Zambrano (2/2).Trainer: Ferenc Platkó (14).
**Goals**: Guillermo Díaz Zambrano (4), Fernando Iván Campos (9), Guillermo Díaz Zambrano (34), Andrés Prieto (60), Enrique Daniel Hormazábal Silva (79).

**89.** 07.04.1950 **CHILE - URUGUAY** **1-5(1-3)**
Estadio Nacional, Santiago; Referee: Mario Gardelli (Brazil); Attendance: 40,000
**CHI:** Hernán Fernández (8/0), Manuel Machuca Berríos (17/0), Daniel Morales (1/0) [Juan Negri (15/0)], Arturo Farías (3/0), Osvaldo Sáez (10/3), José López (6/0), Enrique Daniel Hormazábal Silva (3/1), Fernando Iván Campos (4/2), Mario Lorca (3/0), René Meléndez (1/0) [José Fernández (3/0)], Guillermo Díaz Zambrano (3/2).Trainer: Ferenc Platkó (15).
**Goal**: Fernando Iván Campos (18).

**90.** 09.04.1950 **CHILE - URUGUAY** **2-1(2-1)**
Estadio Nacional, Santiago; Referee: Mario Gardelli (Brazil); Attendance: 40,000
**CHI:** René Quitral (1/0), Juan Negri (16/0), Francisco Urroz (11/0), Arturo Farías (4/0), Osvaldo Sáez (11/3), Adelmo Yori (2/0), Enrique Daniel Hormazábal Silva (4/1) [Manuel Machuca Berríos (18/0)], Fernando Iván Campos (5/3), José Fernández (4/0), René Meléndez (2/0) [Manuel Muñoz (1/0)], Guillermo Díaz Zambrano (4/3).Trainer: Ferenc Platkó (16).
**Goals**: Fernando Iván Campos (1 penalty), Guillermo Díaz Zambrano (9).

**91.** 25.06.1950 **ENGLAND - CHILE** **2-0(1-0)** 4th FIFA WC. Group Stage
Estádio „Jornalista Mario Filho" (Maracanã), Rio de Janeiro (Brazil); Referee: Karel van der Meer (Holland); Attendance: 29,703
**CHI:** Sergio Roberto Livingstone Pohlhammer (31/0), Arturo Farías (5/0), Fernando Roldán (1/0), Manuel Alvarez (4/0), Miguel Busquets (16/0), Hernán Carvallo Castro (6/0), Luis Lindorfo Mayanés (1/0), Atilio Cremaschi (14/5), Jorge Robledo (1/0), Manuel Muñoz (2/0), Guillermo Díaz Zambrano (5/3). Trainer: Alberto Buccicardi (1).

**92.** 29.06.1950 **SPAIN - CHILE** **2-0(2-0)** 4th FIFA WC. Group Stage
Estádio „Jornalista Mario Filho" (Maracanã), Rio de Janeiro (Brazil); Referee: Alberto Monard da Gama Malcher (Brazil); Attendance: 19,790
**CHI:** Sergio Roberto Livingstone Pohlhammer (32/0), Arturo Farías (6/0), Fernando Roldán (2/0), Manuel Alvarez (5/0), Miguel Busquets (17/0), Hernán Carvallo Castro (7/0), Andrés Prieto (10/2), Atilio Cremaschi (15/5), Jorge Robledo (2/0), Manuel Muñoz (3/0), Guillermo Díaz Zambrano (6/3). Trainer: Alberto Buccicardi (2).

**93.** 02.07.1950 **CHILE – UNITED STATES** **5-2(2-0)** 4th FIFA WC. Group Stage
Estádio Ilha do Retiro (Esporte Clube), Recife (Brazil); Referee: Mario Gardelli (Brazil); Attendance: 8,000
**CHI:** Sergio Roberto Livingstone Pohlhammer (33/0), Arturo Farías (7/0), Manuel Machuca Berríos (19/0), Manuel Alvarez (6/0), Miguel Busquets (18/0), Carlos Rodolfo Rojas (6/1), Andrés Prieto (11/3), Atilio Cremaschi (16/7), Jorge Robledo (3/1), Fernando Riera Bauza (16/4), Carlos Ibáñez (1/0). Trainer: Alberto Buccicardi (3).
**Goals**: Jorge Robledo (16), Atilio Cremaschi (33), Andrés Prieto (54), Atilio Cremaschi (60), Fernando Riera Bauza (82).

**94.** 16.03.1952 **CHILE - PANAMA** **6-1** Panamerican Championship
Estadio Nacional, Santiago; Attendance: 40,000
**CHI:** Hernán Fernández (9/0), Adelmo Yori (3/0), Arturo Farías (8/0), Fernando Roldán (3/0), Osvaldo Sáez (12/3), Ramiro Cortés (1/0), Enrique Daniel Hormazábal Silva (5/2), Andrés Prieto (12/6), René Meléndez (3/1) [Mario Lorca (4/0)], Manuel Muñoz (4/1), Guillermo Díaz Carmona (1/0). Trainer: Luis Tirado (20).
**Goals**: Andrés Prieto 3, Enrique Daniel Hormazábal Silva, René Meléndez, Manuel Muñoz.

**95.** 26.03.1952 **CHILE - MEXICO** **4-0(2-0)** Panamerican Championship
Estadio Nacional, Santiago; Referee: Godfrey Sunderland (England); Attendance: 50,000
**CHI:** Sergio Roberto Livingstone Pohlhammer (34/0), Adelmo Yori (4/0), Arturo Farías (9/0), Fernando Roldán (4/0), Osvaldo Sáez (13/3) [Carlos Rodolfo Rojas (7/1)], Ramiro Cortés (2/0), Enrique Daniel Hormazábal Silva (6/3) Andrés Prieto (13/7), Mario Lorca (5/0), Carlos Tello (1/0), Guillermo Díaz Carmona (2/2). Trainer: Luis Tirado (21).
**Goals**: Enrique Daniel Hormazábal Silva (20), Andrés Prieto (30), Guillermo Díaz Carmona (82, 86).

**96.** 02.04.1952 **CHILE - PERU** **3-2** Panamerican Championship
Estadio Nacional, Santiago; Attendance: 47,000
**CHI:** Hernán Fernández (10/0) [Sergio Roberto Livingstone Pohlhammer (35/0)], Adelmo Yori (5/0), Arturo Farías (10/0), Fernando Roldán (5/0), Osvaldo Sáez (14/3), Ramiro Cortés (3/0), Enrique Daniel Hormazábal Silva (7/3), Andrés Prieto (14/8) [Atilio Cremaschi (17/8)], René Meléndez (4/2), Carlos Tello (2/0) [Manuel Muñoz (5/1)], Guillermo Díaz Carmona (3/2).Trainer: Luis Tirado (22).
**Goals**: Andrés Prieto, René Meléndez, Atilio Cremaschi.

**97.** 13.04.1952 **CHILE - URUGUAY** **2-0(1-0)** Panamerican Championship
Estadio Nacional, Santiago; Referee: Charles Dean (England); Attendance: 50,000
**CHI:** Sergio Roberto Livingstone Pohlhammer (36/0), Adelmo Yori (6/0), Arturo Farías (11/0), Fernando Roldán (6/0), Osvaldo Sáez (15/3), Ramiro Cortés (4/0), Enrique Daniel Hormazábal Silva (8/3), Atilio Cremaschi (18/9), René Meléndez (5/2), Manuel Muñoz (6/2), Guillermo Díaz Carmona (4/2) [Pedro Hugo López (15/5)]. Trainer: Luis Tirado (23).
**Goals**: Atilio Cremaschi (5), Manuel Muñoz (84).

**98.** 20.04.1952 **CHILE - BRAZIL** **0-3** Panamerican Championship
Estadio Nacional, Santiago; Referee: Charles Dean (England); Attendance: 50,000
**CHI:** Sergio Roberto Livingstone Pohlhammer (37/0), Adelmo Yori (7/0), Arturo Farías (12/0), Fernando Roldán (7/0), Osvaldo Sáez (16/3), Ramiro Cortés (5/0) [Carlos Rodolfo Rojas (8/1)], Enrique Daniel Hormazábal Silva (9/3), Atilio Cremaschi (19/9), Mario Lorca (6/0) [René Meléndez (6/2)], Manuel Muñoz (7/2), Guillermo Díaz Carmona (5/2) [Pedro Hugo López (16/5)]. Trainer: Luis Tirado (24).

**99.** 25.02.1953 **PARAGUAY - CHILE** **3-0(0-0)** 22nd Copa América
Estadio Nacional, Lima; Referee: Richard Maddison (England); Attendance: 38,243
**CHI:** Sergio Roberto Livingstone Pohlhammer (38/0), Arturo Farías (13/0), Ramiro Cortés (6/0), Manuel Alvarez (7/0), Fernando Roldán (8/0), Augusto Arenas (1/0) [Osvaldo Sáez (17/3)], Enrique Daniel Hormazábal Silva (10/3), Atilio Cremaschi (20/9) [Oscar Carrasco (1/0)], René Meléndez (7/2), Francisco Molina (1/0), Guillermo Díaz Carmona (6/2). Trainer: Luis Tirado (25).

**100.** 01.03.1953 **CHILE - URUGUAY** **3-2(1-0)** 22nd Copa América
Estadio Nacional, Lima; Referee: Charles Dean (England); Attendance: 38,591
**CHI:** Sergio Roberto Livingstone Pohlhammer (39/0), Fernando Roldán (9/0), Arturo Farías (14/0), Ramiro Cortés (7/0), Manuel Alvarez (8/0), Osvaldo Sáez (18/3), Enrique Daniel Hormazábal Silva (11/3) [Oscar Carrasco (2/0)], Atilio Cremaschi (21/9), René Meléndez (8/2), Francisco Molina (2/3) [Carlos Tello (3/0)], Fernando Hurtado (1/0). Trainer: Luis Tirado (26).
**Goals**: Francisco Molina (5, 55, 67).

**101.** 04.03.1953 **PERU - CHILE** **0-0** 22nd Copa América
Estadio Nacional, Lima; Referee: Richard Maddison (England); Attendance: 42,737
**CHI:** Sergio Roberto Livingstone Pohlhammer (40/0), Arturo Farías (15/0), Manuel Alvarez (9/0), Valentín Beperet (1/0) [Fernando Roldán (10/0)], Osvaldo Sáez (19/3) [Carlos Rodolfo Rojas (9/1)], Ramiro Cortés (8/0), Oscar Carrasco (3/0) [Sergio Espinoza (1/0)], Atilio Cremaschi (22/9), René Meléndez (9/2), Francisco Molina (3/3), Guillermo Díaz Carmona (7/2). Trainer: Luis Tirado (27).

**102.** 19.03.1953 **CHILE - ECUADOR** **3-0(1-0)** 22nd Copa América
Estadio Nacional, Lima; Referee: Richard Maddison (England); Attendance: 44,415
**CHI:** Sergio Roberto Livingstone Pohlhammer (41/0), Fernando Roldán (11/0), Manuel Alvarez (10/0), Ramiro Cortés (9/0), Arturo Farías (16/0), Carlos Rodolfo Rojas (10/1), Oscar Carrasco (4/0), Atilio Cremaschi (23/10), Osvaldo Sáez (20/3) [René Meléndez (10/2)], Francisco Molina (4/5), Guillermo Díaz Carmona (8/2) [Fernando Hurtado (2/0)]. Trainer: Luis Tirado (28).
**Goals**: Francisco Molina (33, 47), Atilio Cremaschi (70).

**103.** 23.03.1953 **BRAZIL - CHILE** **3-2(1-0)** 22nd Copa América
Estadio Nacional, Lima; Referee: Richard Maddison (England); Attendance: 35,000
**CHI:** Sergio Roberto Livingstone Pohlhammer (42/0), Fernando Roldán (12/0) [Alfredo Olivos (1/0)], Manuel Alvarez (11/0), Ramiro Cortés (10/0), Arturo Farías (17/0), Osvaldo Sáez (21/3), Carlos Rodolfo Rojas (11/1), Atilio Cremaschi (24/10), René Meléndez (11/2), Francisco Molina (5/7), Oscar Carrasco (5/0) [Fernando Hurtado (3/0)].Trainer: Luis Tirado (29).
**Goals**: Francisco Molina (62, 76).

**104.** 28.03.1953 **CHILE - BOLIVIA** **2-2*** 22nd Copa América
Estadio Nacional, Lima; Referee: Richard Maddison (England); Attendance: 45,000
**CHI:** Sergio Roberto Livingstone Pohlhammer (Cap) (43/0), Arturo Farías (18/0), Manuel Alvarez (12/0), Fernando Roldán (13/0), Carlos Rodolfo Rojas (12/1), Ramiro Cortés (11/0), Oscar Carrasco (6/0), Atilio Cremaschi (25/10), René Meléndez (12/2), Francisco Molina (6/7) [Carlos Tello (4/0)], Guillermo Díaz Carmona (9/4). Trainer: Luis Tirado (30).
**Goals**: Guillermo Díaz Carmona (28, 52).
**The match was interrupted after 66 mins due to unsportsmanlike behaviour of Bolivian players.*

**105.** 24.05.1953 **CHILE - ENGLAND** **1-2(0-0)**
Estadio Nacional, Santiago; Referee: Arthur Edward Ellis (England); Attendance: 56,398
**CHI:** Sergio Roberto Livingstone Pohlhammer (44/0), Manuel Alvarez (13/0), Arturo Farías (19/0), Rogelio Núñez (1/0), Carlos Rodolfo Rojas (13/1), Ramiro Cortés (12/0), Sergio Alvarez (1/0), Atilio Cremaschi (26/10), René Meléndez (13/2), Manuel Muñoz (8/2), Guillermo Díaz Carmona (10/4). Trainer: Luis Tirado (31).
**Goal**: Alfred Ernest Ramsey (86 own goal).

**106.** 12.07.1953 **CHILE - SPAIN** **1-2(0-2)**
Estadio Nacional, Santiago; Referee: Ralph Tarratt (England); Attendance: 50,000
**CHI:** Misael Escuti (1/0), Manuel Alvarez (14/0), Arturo Farías (20/0), Rogelio Núñez (2/0), Antonio Valjalo (1/0), Ramiro Cortés (13/0), Enrique Daniel Hormazábal Silva (12/3), Atilio Cremaschi (27/10), Jorge Robledo (4/1), Manuel Muñoz (9/3), Mario Castro (13/0). Trainer: Ferenc Platkó (17).
**Goal**: Manuel Muñoz (84).

**107.** 26.07.1953 **PERU - CHILE** **1-2(1-1)** Copa del Pacífico
Estadio Nacional, Lima; Attendance: 33,175
**CHI:** Sergio Roberto Livingstone Pohlhammer (45/0), Manuel Alvarez (15/0), Arturo Farías (21/0), Fernando Roldán (14/0), Carlos Rodolfo Rojas (14/1), Ramiro Cortés (14/0), Enrique Daniel Hormazábal Silva (13/4), Atilio Cremaschi (28/10), Jorge Robledo (5/2), Manuel Muñoz (10/3) [José Fernández (5/0)], Guillermo Díaz Zambrano (7/3). Trainer: Ferenc Platkó (18).
**Goals**: Enrique Daniel Hormazábal Silva (44), Jorge Robledo (86).

**108.** 28.07.1953 **PERU - CHILE** **5-0(2-0)** Copa del Pacífico
Estadio Nacional, Lima; Attendance: 29,377
**CHI:** Sergio Roberto Livingstone Pohlhammer (46/0), Manuel Alvarez (16/0), Arturo Farías (22/0), Fernando Roldán (15/0), Carlos Rodolfo Rojas (15/1), Ramiro Cortés (15/0), Enrique Daniel Hormazábal Silva (14/4), Atilio Cremaschi (29/10), Jorge Robledo (6/2), Manuel Muñoz (11/3) [Horacio Cisternas (1/0); José Fernández (6/0)], Guillermo Díaz Zambrano (8/3). Trainer: Ferenc Platkó (19).

**109.** 14.02.1954 **PARAGUAY - CHILE** **4-0(1-0)** 5th FIFA WC. Qualifiers
Estadio Libertad, Asunción; Referee: Erich Steiner (Austria); Attendance: 15,000
**CHI:** Sergio Roberto Livingstone Pohlhammer (47/0), Isaac Carrasco (1/0), Arturo Farías (23/0), Fernando Roldán (16/0), Ramiro Cortés (16/0), Eduardo Robledo (1/0), Enrique Daniel Hormazábal Silva (15/4), Atilio Cremaschi (30/10), Jorge Robledo (7/2), Manuel Muñoz (12/3), José Valdés (1/0). Trainer: Luis Tirado (32).

**110.** 21.02.1954 **CHILE - PARAGUAY** **1-3(1-1)** 5th FIFA WC. Qualifiers
Estadio Nacional, Santiago; Referee: Raymond Vincenti (France); Attendance: 42,130
**CHI:** Sergio Roberto Livingstone Pohlhammer (48/0), Caupolicán Peña (1/0) [Isaac Carrasco (2/0)], Arturo Farías (24/0), Fernando Roldán (17/0), Osvaldo Sáez (22/3), Eduardo Robledo (2/0), Enrique Daniel Hormazábal Silva (16/4), Atilio Cremaschi (31/10), Jorge Robledo (8/3), Manuel Muñoz (13/3), Bernardo Bello (1/0). Trainer: Luis Tirado (33).
**Goal**: Jorge Robledo (16).

**111.** 28.02.1954 **CHILE - BRAZIL** **0-2(0-1)** 5th FIFA WC. Qualifiers
Estadio Nacional, Santiago; Referee: Raymond Vincenti (France); Attendance: 25,085
**CHI:** Sergio Roberto Livingstone Pohlhammer (49/0), Manuel Alvarez (17/0), Rodolfo Almeyda (1/0), Isaac Carrasco (3/0), Ramiro Cortés (17/0), Eduardo Robledo (3/0), Enrique Daniel Hormazábal Silva (17/4), José Valdés (2/0) [Carlos Rodolfo Rojas (16/1)], Jorge Robledo (9/3), René Meléndez (14/2), Manuel Muñoz (14/3). Trainer: Luis Tirado (34).

**112.** 14.03.1954 **BRAZIL - CHILE** **1-0(1-0)** 5th FIFA WC. Qualifiers
Estádio „Jornalista Mario Filho" (Maracanã), Rio de Janeiro; Referee: Erich Steiner (Austria); Attendance: 112,809
**CHI:** Sergio Roberto Livingstone Pohlhammer (50/0), Manuel Alvarez (18/0), Rodolfo Almeyda (2/0), Isaac Carrasco (4/0), Ramiro Cortés (18/0), Eduardo Robledo (4/0), Enrique Daniel Hormazábal Silva (18/4), Atilio Cremaschi (32/10) [Manuel Muñoz (15/3)], Carlos Rodolfo Rojas (17/1), Jorge Robledo (10/3), René Meléndez (15/2). Trainer: Luis Tirado (35).

**113.** 17.09.1954 **CHILE - PERU** **2-1(1-1)** Copa del Pacífico
Estadio Nacional, Santiago; Referee: Juan Carlos Robles (Chile); Attendance: 21,116
**CHI:** Sergio Roberto Livingstone Pohlhammer (51/0), Manuel Alvarez (19/0), Mario Torres (1/0), Isaac Carrasco (5/0), Luis Vera (1/0), Ramiro Cortés (19/0), Braulio Musso (1/1), Enrique Daniel Hormazábal Silva (19/4), René Meléndez (16/3), Carlos Tello (5/0) [Mario Lorca (7/0)], Jaime Caupolicán Ramírez Banda (1/0). Trainer: Selection Comittee.
**Goals**: René Meléndez (30), Braulio Musso (68).

**114.** 19.09.1954 **CHILE - PERU** **2-4(1-4)** Copa del Pacífico
Estadio Nacional, Santiago; Referee: Juan Carlos Robles (Chile); Attendance: 21,051
**CHI:** Sergio Roberto Livingstone Pohlhammer (52/0), Manuel Alvarez (20/0), Mario Torres (2/0), Isaac Carrasco (6/0), Luis Vera (2/0) [Carlos Cubillos (1/0)], Ramiro Cortés (20/0), Braulio Musso (2/1), Enrique Daniel Hormazábal Silva (20/4), René Meléndez (17/5) [Carlos Tello (6/0)], Mario Lorca (8/0) [Sergio Espinoza (2/0)], Jaime Caupolicán Ramírez Banda (2/0). Trainer: Selection Comittee.
**Goals**: René Meléndez (37, 60).

**115.** 27.02.1955 **CHILE - ECUADOR** **7-1(4-0)** 23rd Copa América
Estadio Nacional, Santiago; Referee: Washington Rodríguez (Uruguay); Attendance: 32,450
**CHI:** Misael Escuti (2/0), Rodolfo Almeyda (3/0), Manuel Alvarez (21/0), Ramiro Cortés (21/0), Luis Vera (3/0) [Eduardo Robledo (5/0)], Isaac Carrasco (7/0), Enrique Daniel Hormazábal Silva (21/7), René Meléndez (18/6), Jorge Robledo (11/4), Sergio Espinoza (3/0) [Hernán Rodríguez (1/0)], Guillermo Díaz Zambrano (9/5). Trainer: Luis Tirado (36).
**Goals**: Enrique Daniel Hormazábal Silva (27), Guillermo Díaz Zambrano (31), René Meléndez (33), Guillermo Díaz Zambrano (35), Enrique Daniel Hormazábal Silva (47, 53), Jorge Robledo (55).

**116.** 06.03.1955 **CHILE - PERU** **5-4(2-1)** 23rd Copa América
Estadio Nacional, Santiago; Referee: Harry Dykes (England); Attendance: 42,833
**CHI:** Misael Escuti (3/0), Rodolfo Almeyda (4/0), Manuel Alvarez (22/0), Ramiro Cortés (22/0), Eduardo Robledo (6/0) [Antonio Valjalo (2/0)], Isaac Carrasco (8/0), Enrique Daniel Hormazábal Silva (22/8), René Meléndez (19/6), Jorge Robledo (12/6), Manuel Muñoz (16/4) [Jaime Caupolicán Ramírez Banda (3/1)], Guillermo Díaz Zambrano (10/5). Trainer: Luis Tirado (37).
**Goals**: Manuel Muñoz (9), Jorge Robledo (13), Enrique Daniel Hormazábal Silva (52), Jorge Robledo (57), Jaime Caupolicán Ramírez Banda (84).

**117.** 13.03.1955 **CHILE - URUGUAY** **2-2(1-2)** 23rd Copa América
Estadio Nacional, Santiago; Referee: Juan Regis Brozzi (Argentina); Attendance: 44,238
**CHI:** Misael Escuti (4/0), Rodolfo Almeyda (5/0), Manuel Alvarez (23/0), Ramiro Cortés (23/0), Isaac Carrasco (9/0), Eduardo Robledo (7/0), Enrique Daniel Hormazábal Silva (23/9), Jaime Caupolicán Ramírez Banda (4/1) [Guillermo Díaz Zambrano (11/5)], Jorge Robledo (13/6), Manuel Muñoz (17/5) [René Meléndez (20/6)], Guillermo Díaz Carmona (11/4). Trainer: Luis Tirado (38).
**Goals**: Manuel Muñoz (30), Enrique Daniel Hormazábal Silva (72).

**118.** 20.03.1955 **CHILE - PARAGUAY** **5-0(1-0)** 23rd Copa América
Estadio Nacional, Santiago; Referee: Washington Rodríguez (Uruguay); Attendance: 45,623
**CHI:** Misael Escuti (5/0), Rodolfo Almeyda (6/0), Manuel Alvarez (24/0), Ramiro Cortés (24/0), Eduardo Robledo (8/0), Isaac Carrasco (10/0), Enrique Daniel Hormazábal Silva (24/10), Jaime Caupolicán Ramírez Banda (5/1), Jorge Robledo (14/6), Manuel Muñoz (18/7), René Meléndez (21/8) [Guillermo Díaz Zambrano (12/5)]. Trainer: Luis Tirado (39).
**Goals**: René Meléndez (10, 52), Manuel Muñoz (77, 79), Enrique Daniel Hormazábal Silva (82).

**119.** 30.03.1955 **CHILE - ARGENTINA** **0-1(0-0)** 23rd Copa América
Estadio Nacional, Santiago; Referee: Washington Rodríguez (Uruguay); Attendance: 65,000
**CHI:** Misael Escuti (6/0), Rodolfo Almeyda (7/0), Manuel Alvarez (25/0), Ramiro Cortés (25/0), Eduardo Robledo (9/0), Isaac Carrasco (11/0), Enrique Daniel Hormazábal Silva (25/10), Jaime Caupolicán Ramírez Banda (6/1), Jorge Robledo (15/6), Manuel Muñoz (19/7) [Guillermo Díaz Zambrano (13/5)], René Meléndez (22/8) [Sergio Espinoza (4/0)]. Trainer: Luis Tirado (40).

**120.** 18.09.1955 **BRAZIL - CHILE** **1-1(1-1)** Copa Bernardo O'Higgins
Estádio „Jornalista Mario Filho" (Maracanã), Rio de Janeiro; Referee: Frederick Williams (England); Attendance: 70,000
**CHI:** Misael Escuti (7/0), Manuel Alvarez (26/0), Isaac Carrasco (12/0), Ramiro Cortés (26/0), Rodolfo Almeyda (8/0), Carlos Cubillos (2/0), Jaime Caupolicán Ramírez Banda (7/2), Enrique Daniel Hormazábal Silva (26/10) [Jorge Robledo (16/6)], René Meléndez (23/8), José Fernández (7/0), Leonel Guillermo Sánchez Lineros (1/0). Trainer: Luis Tirado (41).
**Goal**: Jaime Caupolicán Ramírez Banda (39).

**121.** 20.09.1955 **BRAZIL - CHILE** **2-1(2-1)** Copa Bernardo O'Higgins
Estádio Pacaembú, São Paulo; Referee: Harry Davis (England); Attendance: 60,000
**CHI:** Misael Escuti (8/0), Manuel Alvarez (27/0), Isaac Carrasco (13/0), Ramiro Cortés (27/0), Rodolfo Almeyda (9/0), Carlos Cubillos (3/0), Enrique Daniel Hormazábal Silva (27/11), Jorge Robledo (17/6), René Meléndez (24/8), José Fernández (8/0) [Leonel Guillermo Sánchez Lineros (2/0)], Jaime Caupolicán Ramírez Banda (8/2). Trainer: Luis Tirado (42).
**Goal**: Enrique Daniel Hormazábal Silva (33).

**122.** 24.01.1956 **CHILE - BRAZIL** **4-1(1-1)** 24th Copa América
Estadio Centenario, Montevideo (Uruguay); Referee: Juan Regis Brozzi (Argentina); Attendance: 11,514
**CHI:** Misael Escuti (9/0), Rodolfo Almeyda (10/0), Manuel Alvarez (28/0), Ramiro Cortés (28/0), Carlos Cubillos (4/0), Isaac Carrasco (14/0), Enrique Daniel Hormazábal Silva (28/13), René Meléndez (25/9), Jaime Caupolicán Ramírez Banda (9/2), Manuel Muñoz (20/7), Leonel Guillermo Sánchez Lineros (3/1). Trainer: Luis Tirado (43).
**Goals**: Enrique Daniel Hormazábal Silva (8), René Meléndez (65), Leonel Guillermo Sánchez Lineros (71), Enrique Daniel Hormazábal Silva (83).

**123.** 29.01.1956 **ARGENTINA - CHILE** **2-0(1-0)** 24th Copa América

Estadio Centenario, Montevideo (Uruguay); Referee: João Baptista Laurito (Brazil); Attendance: 45,000

**CHI:** Misael Escuti (10/0), Rodolfo Almeyda (11/0), Manuel Alvarez (29/0), Ramiro Cortés (29/0), Carlos Cubillos (5/0), Isaac Carrasco (15/0), Jaime Caupolicán Ramírez Banda (10/2), Enrique Daniel Hormazábal Silva (29/13), René Meléndez (26/9), Manuel Muñoz (21/7), Leonel Guillermo Sánchez Lineros (4/1). Trainer: Luis Tirado (44).

**124.** 06.02.1956 **URUGUAY - CHILE** **2-1(1-0)** 24th Copa América

Estadio Centenario, Montevideo; Referee: Juan Regis Brozzi (Argentina); Attendance: 61,204

**CHI:** Misael Escuti (11/0), Rodolfo Almeyda (12/0), Manuel Alvarez (30/0), Ramiro Cortés (30/0), Carlos Cubillos (6/0), Isaac Carrasco (16/0), Enrique Daniel Hormazábal Silva (30/13), René Meléndez (27/9), Jaime Caupolicán Ramírez Banda (11/3) [José Fernández (9/0)], Manuel Muñoz (22/7), Leonel Guillermo Sánchez Lineros (5/1). Trainer: Luis Tirado (45).

**Goal**: Jaime Caupolicán Ramírez Banda (59).

**125.** 09.02.1956 **CHILE - PERU** **4-3(2-1)** 24th Copa América

Estadio Centenario, Montevideo (Uruguay); Referee: Juan Regis Brozzi (Argentina); Attendance: 5,000

**CHI:** Carlos Espinoza (1/0), Manuel Alvarez (31/0) [Sergio Goity (1/0)], Isaac Carrasco (17/0), Rodolfo Almeyda (13/0), Ramiro Cortés (31/0), Mario Ortíz (1/0)], Enrique Daniel Hormazábal Silva (31/14), Sergio Espinoza (5/0) [José Fernández (10/1)], Jaime Caupolicán Ramírez Banda (12/3), Manuel Muñoz (23/8), Leonel Guillermo Sánchez Lineros (6/2) Trainer: Luis Tirado (46).

**Goals**: Enrique Daniel Hormazábal Silva (10), Manuel Muñoz (23), José Fernández (70), Leonel Guillermo Sánchez Lineros (86).

**126.** 12.02.1956 **CHILE - PARAGUAY** **2-0** 24th Copa América

Estadio Centenario, Montevideo (Uruguay); Referee: Washington Rodríguez (Uruguay); Attendance: 4,000

**CHI:** Carlos Espinoza (2/0), Rodolfo Almeyda (14/0), Manuel Alvarez (32/0), Ramiro Cortés (32/0), Carlos Cubillos (7/0), Isaac Carrasco (18/0), Enrique Daniel Hormazábal Silva (32/15), Jaime Caupolicán Ramírez Banda (13/4), Manuel Muñoz (24/8) [José Fernández (11/1)], René Meléndez (28/9), Leonel Guillermo Sánchez Lineros (7/2). Trainer: Luis Tirado (47).

**Goals**: Enrique Daniel Hormazábal Silva, Jaime Caupolicán Ramírez Banda.

**127.** 01.03.1956 **BRAZIL - CHILE** **2-1(2-1)** Panamerican Championship

Estadio Olímpico de Centro Universitário, Ciudad de México (Mexico); Referee: Alfredo Rossi (Argentina)

**CHI:** Misael Escuti (12/0), Manuel Alvarez (33/0) [Sergio Goity (2/0)], Rodolfo Almeyda (15/0), Isaac Carrasco (19/0), Ramiro Cortés (33/0), Carlos Cubillos (8/0), Jaime Çaupolicán Ramírez Banda (14/4), Enrique Daniel Hormazábal Silva (33/15) [Carlos Tello (7/1)], Jorge Robledo (18/6), Manuel Muñoz (25/8) [José Fernández (12/1)], Leonel Guillermo Sánchez Lineros (8/2). Trainer: Luis Tirado (48).

**Goal**: Carlos Tello (29).

**128.** 08.03.1956 **COSTA RICA - CHILE** **2-1(2-1)** Panamerican Championship

Estadio Olímpico de Centro Universitário, Ciudad de México (Mexico); Referee: Alberto Monard de Gama Malcher (Brazil)

**CHI:** Misael Escuti (13/0), Manuel Alvarez (34/0), Rodolfo Almeyda (16/0), Isaac Carrasco (20/0) [Carlos Huerta (1/0)], Ramiro Cortés (34/0), Carlos Cubillos (9/0), Jaime Caupolicán Ramírez Banda (15/4), Enrique Daniel Hormazábal Silva (34/15), Jorge Robledo (19/6) [José Fernández (13/1)], Carlos Tello (8/2), Leonel Guillermo Sánchez Lineros (9/2). Trainer: Luis Tirado (49).

**Goal**: Carlos Tello (36).

**129.** 11.03.1956 **ARGENTINA - CHILE** **3-0(1-0)** Panamerican Championship

Estadio Olímpico de Centro Universitário, Ciudad de México (Mexico); Referee: Alberto Monard de Gama Malcher (Brazil); Attendance: 40,000

**CHI:** Misael Escuti (14/0), Manuel Alvarez (35/0), Rodolfo Almeyda (17/0), Carlos Huerta (2/0), Ramiro Cortés (35/0), Carlos Cubillos (10/0), Braulio Musso (3/1) [Mario Ortíz (2/0)], Enrique Daniel Hormazábal Silva (35/15), René Meléndez (29/9) [Jorge Robledo (20/6)] Manuel Muñoz (26/8) [José Fernández (14/1)], Leonel Guillermo Sánchez Lineros (10/2) [Guillermo Díaz Zambrano (14/5)]. Trainer: Luis Tirado (50).

**130.** 15.03.1956 **PERU - CHILE** **2-2(2-2)** Panamerican Championship

Estadio Olímpico de Centro Universitário, Ciudad de México (Mexico); Referee: Danilo Alfaro (Costa Rica)

**CHI:** Carlos Espinoza (3/0), Sergio Goity (3/0), Carlos Carmona (1/0), Carlos Huerta (3/0), Ramón Climent (1/0) [Ramiro Cortés (36/1)], Mario Ortíz (3/0), Jaime Caupolicán Ramírez Banda (16/4), Carlos Tello (9/2), Jorge Robledo (21/6), José Fernández (15/1) [Enrique Daniel Hormazábal Silva (36/15)], Guillermo Díaz Zambrano (15/6) [René Meléndez (30/9)]. Trainer: Luis Tirado (51).

**Goals**: Guillermo Díaz Zambrano (18), Ramiro Cortés (40).

**131.** 18.03.1956 **MEXICO - CHILE** **2-1(1-1)** Panamerican Championship

Estadio Olímpico de Centro Universitário, Ciudad de México; Referee: Danilo Alfaro (Costa Rica)

**CHI:** Carlos Espinoza (4/0), Sergio Goity (4/0), Carlos Carmona (2/0), Carlos Huerta (4/0), Ramón Climent (2/0) [46.Ramiro Cortés (37/1)], Mario Ortíz (4/0), Jaime Caupolicán Ramírez Banda (17/4), Jorge Robledo (22/6), René Meléndez (31/9) [75.Guillermo Díaz Zambrano (16/6)], Carlos Tello (10/3) Leonel Guillermo Sánchez Lineros (11/2) [70.José Fernández (16/1)].Trainer: Luis Tirado (52).

**Goal**: Carlos Tello (40).

**132.** 26.08.1956 **CHILE - CZECHOSLOVAKIA** **3-0(2-0)**

Estadio Nacional, Santiago; Referee: Ronald Lynch (England); Attendance: 50,000

**CHI:** Misael Escuti (15/0), Caupolicán Peña (2/0), Mario Torres (3/0), Isaac Carrasco (21/0), Ramiro Cortés (38/1), Mario Ortíz (5/0), Jaime Caupolicán Ramírez Banda (18/4), Enrique Daniel Hormazábal Silva (37/16), Jorge Robledo (23/8), Carlos Tello (11/3), Raúl Aguila (1/0). Trainer: José Salerno (1).

**Goals**: Enrique Hormzazábal (37), Jorge Robledo (70, 78).

**133.** 13.03.1957 **BRAZIL - CHILE** **4-2(3-1)** 25th Copa América

Estadio Nacional, Lima (Peru); Referee: Bertley Cross (England); Attendance: 42,000

**CHI:** Misael Escuti (16/0), Mario Torres (4/0), Mario Ortíz (6/0), Caupolicán Peña (3/0), Ramiro Cortés (39/1) [Gonzalo Carrasco (1/0)], Isaac Carrasco (22/0), Jaime Caupolicán Ramírez Banda (19/5), Jesús Picó (1/0), Sergio Espinoza (6/0), Carlos Tello (12/3) [José Fernández (17/2)], Leonel Guillermo Sánchez Lineros (12/2). Trainer: José Salerno (2).

**Goals**: Jaime Caupolicán Ramírez Banda (13), José Fernández (89).

**134.** 16.03.1957 **PERU - CHILE** **1-0(0-0)** 25th Copa América

Estadio Nacional, Lima; Referee: Ronald Lynch (England); Attendance: 60,000

**CHI:** Misael Escuti (17/0), Mario Torres (5/0), Carlos Cubillos (11/0), Caupolicán Peña (4/0), Gonzalo Carrasco (2/0), Isaac Carrasco (23/0), Jaime Caupolicán Ramírez Banda (20/5), Andrés Prieto (15/8) [Jesús Picó (2/0)], Jorge Robledo (24/8), José Fernández (18/2), Leonel Guillermo Sánchez Lineros (13/2) [Raúl Aguila (2/0)]. Trainer: José Salerno (3).

**135.** 21.03.1957 **CHILE - COLOMBIA** **3-2(1-0)** 25th Copa América
Estadio Nacional, Lima (Peru); Referee: Erwin Hieger (Austria); Attendance: 45,000
**CHI:** Misael Escuti (18/0), Mario Torres (6/0) [Rodolfo Almeyda (18/0)], Carlos Cubillos (12/0), Caupolicán Peña (5/0), Gonzalo Carrasco (3/0), Sergio Valdés (1/0), Jaime Caupolicán Ramírez Banda (21/5), Sergio Espinoza (7/1) [Jorge Robledo 25/8)], Carlos Verdejo (1/2), Carlos Tello (13/3), Raúl Aguila (3/0). Trainer: José Salerno (4).
**Goals**: Carlos Verdejo (35), Sergio Espinoza (62), Carlos Verdejo (70).

**136.** 24.03.1957 **CHILE - ECUADOR** **2-2(2-1)** 25th Copa América
Estadio Nacional, Lima (Peru); Referee: Erwin Hieger (Austria); Attendance: 45,000
**CHI:** Misael Escuti (19/0), Rodolfo Almeyda (19/0), Carlos Cubillos (13/0), Caupolicán Peña (6/0), Gonzalo Carrasco (4/0), Sergio Valdés (2/0) [Daniel Morales (2/0)], Jaime Caupolicán Ramírez Banda (22/7) [Leonel Guillermo Sánchez Lineros (14/2)], Jesús Picó (3/0) [Andrés Prieto (16/8)], Carlos Verdejo (2/2), Carlos Tello (14/3), Raúl Aguila (4/0). Trainer: José Salerno (5).
**Goals**: Jaime Caupolicán Ramírez Banda (18, 26)

**137.** 28.03.1957 **ARGENTINA - CHILE** **6-2(2-2)** 25th Copa América
Estadio Nacional, Lima (Peru); Referee: Robert Turner (England); Attendance: 50,000
**CHI:** Misael Escuti (20/0), Rodolfo Almeyda (20/0), Carlos Cubillos (14/0), Caupolicán Peña (7/0), Mario Ortíz (7/0), Daniel Morales (3/0), Jaime Caupolicán Ramírez Banda (23/7) [Leonel Guillermo Sánchez Lineros (15/2)], Jesús Picó (4/0), Jorge Robledo (26/8), José Fernández (19/4), Raúl Aguila (5/0). Trainer: José Salerno (6).
**Goals**: José Fernández (14, 28).

**138.** 01.04.1957 **URUGUAY - CHILE** **2-0(2-0)** 25th Copa América
Estadio Nacional, Lima (Peru); Referee: Erwin Hieger (Austria); Attendance: 40,000
**CHI:** Francisco Nitsche (1/0), Caupolicán Peña (8/0), Rodolfo Almeyda (21/0), Mario Ortíz (8/0), Sergio Valdés (3/0), Gonzalo Carrasco (5/0), Raúl Aguila (6/0), Jesús Picó (5/0), Jorge Robledo (27/8), José Fernández (20/4), Jaime Caupolicán Ramírez Banda (24/7). Trainer: José Salerno (7).

**139.** 15.09.1957 **CHILE - BRAZIL** **1-0** Copa Bernardo O'Higgins
Estadio Nacional, Santiago; Referee: W. Manning (England); Attendance: 32,458
**CHI:** René Quitral (2/0) [Mario Ojeda (1/0)], Caupolicán Peña (9/0), Raúl Salazar (1/0), Luis Vera (4/0), Vicente Astorga (1/0), Antonio Morales (1/0), Jaime Caupolicán Ramírez Banda (25/7), Jorge Robledo (28/8), René Meléndez (32/10), José Fernández (21/4), Guillermo Díaz Zambrano (17/6). Trainer: László Pákozdi (1).
**Goal**: René Meléndez.

**140.** 18.09.1957 **CHILE - BRAZIL** **1-1(0-0,0-1)** Copa Bernardo O'Higgins
Estadio Nacional, Santiago; Referee: Danor Morales (Chile); Attendance: 41,024
**CHI:** René Quitral (3/0), Sergio Navarro (1/0), Juan Héctor Rojas (1/0), Néstor Bello (1/0) [Mario Torres (7/0)], Salvador Arenas (1/0), Osvaldo Díaz (1/0), Mario Ortíz (9/0), Braulio Musso (4/1), René Meléndez (33/10), Enrique Daniel Hormazábal Silva (38/16) [José Fernández (22/5)], Leonel Guillermo Sánchez Lineros (16/2) [Jaime Caupolicán Ramírez Banda (26/7)]. Trainer: László Pákozdi (2).
**Goals**: José Fernández.

**141.** 22.09.1957 **CHILE - BOLIVIA** **2-1(1-1)** 6th FIFA WC. Qualifiers
Estadio Nacional, Santiago; Referee: Paul Wyssling (Switzerland); Attendance: 37,071
**CHI:** René Quitral (4/0), Caupolicán Peña (10/0), Raúl Salazar (2/0), Antonio Morales (2/0), Luis Vera (5/0), Vicente Astorga (2/0), Jaime Caupolicán Ramírez Banda (27/8), Enrique Daniel Hormazábal Silva (39/16), Jorge Robledo (29/8), José Fernández (23/5), Guillermo Díaz Zambrano (18/7). Trainer: László Pákozdi (3).
**Goals**: Guillermo Díaz Zambrano (17), Jaime Caupolicán Ramírez Banda (67).

**142.** 29.09.1957 **BOLIVIA - CHILE** **3-0(1-0)** 6th FIFA WC. Qualifiers
Estadio „Hernando Siles Zuazo", La Paz; Referee: Paul Wyssling (Switzerland); Attendance: 30,000
**CHI:** René Quitral (5/0), Caupolicán Peña (11/0), Luis Vera (6/0), Mario Torres (8/0), Juan Toro (1/0), Osvaldo Díaz (2/0), Mario Ortíz (10/0), Raúl Aguila (7/0), Jorge Robledo (30/8), Jaime Caupolicán Ramírez Banda (28/8), Leonel Guillermo Sánchez Lineros (17/2). Trainer: László Pákozdi (4).

**143.** 13.10.1957 **CHILE - ARGENTINA** **0-2(0-1)** 6th FIFA WC. Qualifiers
Estadio Nacional, Santiago; Referee: Paul Wyssling (Switzerland); Attendance: 45,000
**CHI:** René Quitral (6/0), Caupolicán Peña (12/0), Luis Vera (7/0), Mario Torres (9/0), Juan Toro (2/0), Juan Héctor Rojas (2/0), Jaime Caupolicán Ramírez Banda (29/8), Jorge Robledo (31/8), René Meléndez (34/10), José Fernández (24/5), Guillermo Díaz Zambrano (19/7). Trainer: László Pákozdi (5).

**144.** 20.10.1957 **ARGENTINA - CHILE** **4-0(4-0)** 6th FIFA WC. Qualifiers
Estadio „Alberto Armando", Buenos Aires; Referee: Paul Wyssling (Switzerland); Attendance: 70,000
**CHI:** René Quitral (7/0), Sergio Navarro (2/0), Vicente Astorga (3/0), Luis Vera (8/0), Raúl Salazar (3/0), Juan Héctor Rojas (3/0), Oscar Carrasco (7/0), Enrique Daniel Hormazábal Silva (40/16), Juan Soto Mura (1/0), Jaime Caupolicán Ramírez Banda (30/8), Leonel Guillermo Sánchez Lineros (18/2). Trainer: László Pákozdi (6).

**145.** 07.03.1959 **ARGENTINA - CHILE** **6-1(4-1)** 26th Copa América
Estadio Monumental „Antonio Vespucio Liberti", Buenos Aires; Referee: Washington Rodríguez (Uruguay); Attendance: 70,000
**CHI:** Raúl Coloma (1/0), Sergio Valdés (4/0), Mario Torres (10/0 [Raúl Sánchez (1/0)], Sergio Navarro (3/0), Luis Vera (9/0), Hernán Rodríguez (2/0), Mario Soto (1/0), Luis Hernán Alvarez (1/1), Armando Tobar (1/0) [Eladio Rojas (1/0)], Leonel Guillermo Sánchez Lineros (19/2), Jorge Luis Toro Sánchez (1/0). Trainer: Fernando Riera Bauza (1).
**Goals**: Luis Hernán Alvarez (25).

**146.** 11.03.1959 **PARAGUAY - CHILE** **2-1** 26th Copa América
Estadio Monumental „Antonio Vespucio Liberti", Buenos Aires (Argentina); Referee: Luis Antonio Ventre (Argentina); Attendance: 45,000
**CHI:** Raúl Coloma (2/0), Sergio Valdés (5/0), Raúl Sánchez (2/0), Sergio Navarro (4/0), Luis Vera (10/0), Hernán Rodríguez (3/0), Mario Soto (2/0), Luis Hernán Alvarez (2/1), Juan Soto Mura (2/0) [Eladio Rojas (2/0)], Leonel Guillermo Sánchez Lineros (20/3), Jorge Luis Toro Sánchez (2/0). Trainer: Fernando Riera Bauza (2).
**Goals**: Leonel Guillermo Sánchez Lineros (45 penalty).

**147.** 15.03.1959 **BRAZIL - CHILE** **3-0(2-0)** 26th Copa América
Estadio Monumental „Antonio Vespucio Liberti", Buenos Aires (Argentina); Referee: Alberto Tejada Burga (Peru); Attendance: 40,000
**CHI:** Raúl Coloma (3/0), Sergio Valdés (6/0), Raúl Sánchez (3/0), Sergio Navarro (5/0), Luis Vera (11/0), Hernán Rodríguez (4/0), Mario Soto (3/0), Luis Hernán Alvarez (3/1) [Eladio Rojas (3/0)], Juan Soto Mura (3/0) [Carlos Verdejo (3/2)], Leonel Guillermo Sánchez Lineros (21/3), Mario Moreno (1/0). Trainer: Fernando Riera Bauza (3).

**148.** 21.03.1959 **CHILE - PERU** **1-1(0-1)** 26th Copa América
Estadio Monumental „Antonio Vespucio Liberti", Buenos Aires (Argentina); Referee: Washington Rodríguez (Uruguay); Attendance: 50,000
**CHI:** Raúl Coloma (4/0), Sergio Valdés (7/0), Raúl Sánchez (4/0), Sergio Navarro (6/0), Luis Vera (12/0), Hernán Rodríguez (5/0) [Juan Héctor Rojas (4/0)], Mario Soto (4/0), Jorge Luis Toro Sánchez (3/0) [Carlos Hoffmann (1/0)], Juan Soto Mura (4/0), Leonel Guillermo Sánchez Lineros (22/3) [Armando Tobar (2/0)], Mario Moreno (2/1). Trainer: Fernando Riera Bauza (4).
**Goal**: Mario Moreno (80).

**149.** 26.03.1959 **CHILE - BOLIVIA** **5-2** 26th Copa América
Estadio Monumental „Antonio Vespucio Liberti", Buenos Aires (Argentina); Referee: Luis Antonio Ventre (Argentina); Attendance: 70,000
**CHI:** Raúl Coloma (5/0), Sergio Valdés (8/0), Raúl Sánchez (5/0), Sergio Navarro (7/0) [Luis Armando Eyzaguirre (1/0)], Luis Vera (13/0) [Juan Héctor Rojas (5/0)], Hernán Rodríguez (6/0), Mario Moreno (3/1) [Eladio Rojas (4/0)], Mario Soto (5/2), Juan Soto Mura (5/2), Leonel Guillermo Sánchez Lineros (23/4), Carlos Hoffmann (2/0). Trainer: Fernando Riera Bauza (5).
**Goals**: Juan Soto Mura 2, Mario Soto 2, Leonel Guillermo Sánchez Lineros.

**150.** 02.04.1959 **CHILE - URUGUAY** **1-0(0-0)** 26th Copa América
Estadio Monumental „Antonio Vespucio Liberti", Buenos Aires (Argentina); Referee: Alberto Tejada Burga (Peru); Attendance: 5,000
**CHI:** Raúl Coloma (6/0), Sergio Valdés (9/0), Raúl Sánchez (6/0), Sergio Navarro (8/0), Luis Vera (14/0), Hernán Rodríguez (7/0), Mario Soto (6/2), Mario Moreno (4/2), Juan Soto Mura (6/2), Leonel Guillermo Sánchez Lineros (24/4) [Eladio Rojas (5/0)], Carlos Hoffmann (3/0) [Armando Tobar (3/0)]. Trainer: Fernando Riera Bauza (6).
**Goal**: Mario Moreno (88 ).

**151.** 17.09.1959 **BRAZIL - CHILE** **7-0** Copa Bernardo O'Higgins
Estádio „Jornalista Mario Filho" (Maracanã), Rio de Janeiro; Referee: Alberto Monard da Gama Malcher (Brazil); Attendance: 70,000
**CHI:** Francisco Fernández (1/0), Adelmo Yori (8/0), Raúl Sánchez (7/0), Sergio Navarro (9/0) [Luis Armando Eyzaguirre (2/0)], Gonzalo Carrasco (6/0) [Jorge Luco (1/0)], Hernán Rodríguez (8/0), Mario Moreno (5/2), Armando Tobar (4/0), Juan Soto Mura (7/2), Leonel Guillermo Sánchez Lineros (25/4) [Mario Soto (7/2)], Bernardo Bello (2/0). Trainer: Fernando Riera Bauza (7).

**152.** 20.09.1959 **BRAZIL - CHILE** **1-0** Copa Bernardo O'Higgins
Estádio Pacaembú, São Paulo; Referee: João Etzel Filho (Brazil); Attendance: 60,000
**CHI:** Raúl Coloma (7/0), Adelmo Yori (9/0), Mario Torres (11/0), Sergio Navarro (10/0), Hernán Rodríguez (9/0), Jorge Luco (2/0), Mario Moreno (6/2), Mario Soto (8/2) [Sergio Valdés (10/0)], Juan Soto Mura (8/2) [Armando Tobar (5/0)] Leonel Guillermo Sánchez Lineros (26/4) [Francisco Molina (7/7)] Bernardo Bello (3/0). Trainer: Fernando Riera Bauza (8).

**153.** 18.11.1959 **CHILE - ARGENTINA** **4-2(1-1)**
Estadio Nacional, Santiago; Referee: Juan Carlos Robles (Chile); Attendance: 36,581
**CHI:** Raúl Coloma (8/0), Luis Armando Eyzaguirre (3/0), Jorge Luco (3/0) [Carlos Contreras (1/0)], Sergio Navarro (11/0), Raúl Sánchez (8/0), René Meléndez (35/10) [Mario Soto (9/2)], Hernán Rodríguez (10/0), Mario Moreno (7/2), Armando Tobar (6/0) [José Benito Ríos (1/0)], Leonel Guillermo Sánchez Lineros (27/5), Bernardo Bello (4/2). Trainer: Fernando Riera Bauza (9).
**Goals**: José Benito Ríos (42), Bernardo Bello (55), Leonel Guillermo Sánchez Lineros (58), Bernardo Bello (70).

**154.** 16.03.1960. **FRANCE - CHILE** **6-0(1-0)**
Stade Parc des Princes, Paris; Referee: Gérard Versyp (Belgium); Attendance: 36,094
**CHI:** Raúl Coloma (9/0), Luis Armando Eyzaguirre (4/0), Jorge Luco (4/0), Raúl Sánchez (9/0), Sergio Navarro (12/0) [40.Isaac Carrasco (24/0)], Hernán Rodríguez (11/0), Leonel Guillermo Sánchez Lineros (28/5), Mario Moreno (8/2), Armando Tobar (7/0), Juan Soto Mura (9/2), Bernardo Bello (5/2). Trainer: Fernando Riera Bauza (10).

**155.** 23.03.1960 **WEST GERMANY - CHILE** **2-1(0-1)**
Neckarstadion, Stuttgart; Referee: Gottfried Dienst (Switzerland); Attendance: 72,500
**CHI:** Raúl Coloma (10/0), Luis Armando Eyzaguirre (5/0), Jorge Luco (5/0), Raúl Sánchez (10/0), Sergio Navarro (13/0), Leonel Guillermo Sánchez Lineros (29/5) [Mario Soto (10/2)], Hernán Rodríguez (12/0), Mario Moreno (9/2), Braulio Musso (5/1), Juan Soto Mura (10/3) [Armando Tobar (8/0)], Alberto Jorge Fouilloux Ahumada (1/0). Trainer: Fernando Riera Bauza (11).
**Goal**: Juan Soto Mura (22).

**156.** 30.03.1960 **REPUBLIC OF IRELAND - CHILE** **2-0(1-0)**
Dalymount Park, Dublin; Referee: Kenneth Aston (England); Attendance: 17,000
**CHI:** Raúl Coloma (11/0), Luis Armando Eyzaguirre (6/0), Sergio Navarro (14/0), Jorge Luco (6/0), Raúl Sánchez (11/0), Hernán Rodríguez (13/0), Mario Moreno (10/2), Alberto Jorge Fouilloux Ahumada (2/0), Juan Soto Mura (11/3), Leonel Guillermo Sánchez Lineros (30/5), Braulio Musso (6/1). Trainer: Fernando Riera Bauza (12).

**157.** 06.04.1960 **SWITZERLAND - CHILE** **4-2(1-1)**
St.Jakob Stadion, Basel; Referee: Leopold Sylvain Horn (Holland)
**CHI:** Raúl Coloma (12/0), Luis Armando Eyzaguirre (7/0), Jorge Luco (7/0), Raúl Sánchez (12/0), Sergio Navarro (15/0), Hernán Rodríguez (14/0), Leonel Guillermo Sánchez Lineros (31/5), Mario Moreno (11/2), Juan Soto Mura (12/4) [René Meléndez (36/10)], Alberto Jorge Fouilloux Ahumada (3/0), Bernardo Bello (6/2) [Armando Tobar (9/1)]. Trainer: Fernando Riera Bauza (13).
**Goals**: Juan Soto Mura (62), Armando Tobar (76).

**158.** 13.04.1960 **BELGIUM - CHILE** **1-1(0-0)**
Stade Heysel, Bruxelles; Referee: Michel Devillers (France); Attendance: 11,702
**CHI:** Manuel Astorga (1/0), Luis Armando Eyzaguirre (8/0), Jorge Luco (8/0), Raúl Sánchez (13/0), Sergio Navarro (16/0), Hernán Rodríguez (15/0), Mario Moreno (12/2), Juan Soto Mura (13/4) [René Meléndez (37/10)], Leonel Guillermo Sánchez Lineros (32/5), Braulio Musso (7/2), Armando Tobar (10/1) [Bernardo Bello (7/2)]. Trainer: Fernando Riera Bauza (14).
**Goal**: Braulio Musso (87).

**159.** 01.06.1960 **CHILE – URUGUAY** **2-3(1-0)**
Estadio Nacional, Santiago; Referee: Juan Carlos Robles (Chile); Attendance: 45,000
**CHI:** Manuel Astorga (2/0), Luis Armando Eyzaguirre (9/0), Jorge Luco (9/0) [Ramiro Cortés (40/1)], Raúl Sánchez (14/0), Sergio Navarro (17/0), Jaime Caupolicán Ramírez Banda (31/8) [Alberto Jorge Fouilloux Ahumada (4/1)], Hernán Rodríguez (16/0), Mario Moreno (13/3), Armando Tobar (11/1), Leonel Guillermo Sánchez Lineros (33/5), Bernardo Bello (8/2) [Braulio Musso (8/2)]. Trainer: Fernando Riera Bauza (15).
**Goals**: Mario Moreno (1), Alberto Jorge Fouilloux Ahumada (77).

**160.** 05.06.1960 **URUGUAY - CHILE** **2-2(0-1)**
Estadio Centenario, Montevideo; Referee: Estebán Marino (Uruguay); Attendance: 45,000
**CHI:** Manuel Astorga (3/0), Luis Armando Eyzaguirre (10/0), Ramiro Cortés (41/1), Raúl Sánchez (15/0), Sergio Navarro (18/0) [Sergio Valdés (11/0)], Alberto Jorge Fouilloux Ahumada (5/1) [René Meléndez (38/10)], Hernán Rodríguez (17/0), Mario Moreno (14/3), Armando Tobar (12/1), Leonel Guillermo Sánchez Lineros (34/7), Braulio Musso (9/2) [Constantino Mohor (1/0)]. Trainer: Fernando Riera Bauza (16).
**Goals**: Leonel Guillermo Sánchez Lineros (30, 75).

**161.** 29.06.1960 **BRAZIL - CHILE** **4-0**
Estádio „Jornalista Mario Filho“ (Maracanã), Rio de Janeiro; Referee: Alberto Monard da Gama Malcher (Brazil); Attendance:
**CHI:** Manuel Astorga (4/0), Luis Armando Eyzaguirre (11/0), Sergio Navarro (19/0) [Sergio Valdés (12/0)], Rodolfo Almeyda (22/0), Ramiro Cortés (42/1), Hernán Rodríguez (18/0), Alberto Jorge Fouilloux Ahumada (6/1), Mario Moreno (15/3) [René Meléndez (39/10)], Armando Tobar (13/1) [Jaime Caupolicán Ramírez Banda (32/8)], Leonel Guillermo Sánchez Lineros (35/7) [Carlos Hoffmann (4/0)], Braulio Musso (10/2). Trainer: Fernando Riera Bauza (17).

**162.** 14.07.1960 **CHILE - SPAIN** **0-4(0-3)**
Estadio Nacional, Santiago; Referee: José Luis Praddaude (Argentina); Attendance: 50,000
**CHI:** Misael Escuti (21/0), Luis Armando Eyzaguirre (12/0), Ramiro Cortés (43/1) [60.Jorge Luco (10/0)], Fernando Navarro (1/0), Sergio Valdés (13/0), Braulio Musso (11/2), Hernán Rodríguez (19/0), Mario Moreno (16/3), Jaime Caupolicán Ramírez Banda (33/8), Alberto Jorge Fouilloux Ahumada (7/1) [65.Jorge Luis Toro Sánchez (4/0)], Leonel Guillermo Sánchez Lineros (36/7). Trainer: Fernando Riera Bauza (18).

**163.** 17.07.1960 **CHILE - SPAIN** **1-4(0-4)**
Estadio Nacional, Santiago; Referee: Luis Antonio Ventre (Argentina); Attendance: 50,000
**CHI:** Misael Escuti (22/0), Sergio Valdés (14/0), Fernando Navarro (2/0) [46.Hernán Martínez (1/0)], Sergio Navarro (20/0), Ramiro Cortés (44/1), Hernán Rodríguez (20/0), Mario Moreno (17/3), Braulio Musso (12/3), Jaime Caupolicán Ramírez Banda (34/8), Jorge Luis Toro Sánchez (5/0), Leonel Guillermo Sánchez Lineros (37/7) [86.Alberto Jorge Fouilloux Ahumada (8/1)]. Trainer: Fernando Riera Bauza (19).
**Goal**: Braulio Musso (85).

**164.** 18.12.1960 **CHILE - PARAGUAY** **4-1**
Estadio Nacional, Santiago; Attendance: 50,000
**CHI:** Misael Escuti (23/0) [Constantino Zazzali (1/0)], Alberto Aldo Valentini (1/0), Juan Abello (1/1), Reinaldo Gallardo (1/0), Carlos Contreras (2/0) [Mario Soto (11/2)], Hernán Martínez (2/0), Carlos Campos (1/1), Jorge Luis Toro Sánchez (6/0), Ricardo Díaz (1/1), Rómulo Betta (1/0), Aldo Droguett (1/1). Trainer: Fernando Riera Bauza (20).
**Goal**: Juan Abello, Ricardo Díaz, Aldo Droguett, Carlos Campos.

**165.** 21.12.1960 **CHILE - PARAGUAY** **3-1**
Valparaíso; Attendance: 40,000
**CHI:** Misael Escuti (24/0), Luis Armando Eyzaguirre (13/0), Ramiro Cortés (45/1), Fernando Navarro (3/0), Sergio Valdés (15/0), Mario Ortíz (11/0), Alberto Jorge Fouilloux Ahumada (9/1), Jorge Luis Toro Sánchez (7/0), Mario Moreno (18/4), Ricardo Cabrera (1/2), Bernardo Bello (9/2) [Braulio Musso (13/3)]. Trainer: Fernando Riera Bauza (21).
**Goals**: Mario Moreno, Ricardo Cabrera 2.

**166.** 10.03.1961 **CHILE - PERU** **5-2(1-2)**
Estadio Nacional, Santiago; Referee: Juan Regis Brozzi (Argentina); Attendance: 24,735
**CHI:** Manuel Astorga (5/0), Luis Armando Eyzaguirre (14/0), Carlos Contreras (3/0), Fernando Navarro (4/0), Sergio Navarro (21/0), Jorge Luis Toro Sánchez (8/1), Mario Ortíz (12/0) [Eladio Rojas (6/0)], Mario Moreno (19/4) [Rómulo Betta (2/1)], Juan Soto Mura (14/5), Alberto Jorge Fouilloux Ahumada (10/1) [Jaime Caupolicán Ramírez Banda (35/8)], Leonel Guillermo Sánchez Lineros (38/9). Trainer: Fernando Riera Bauza (22).
**Goals**: Jorge Luis Toro Sánchez (40), Rómulo Betta (69), Juan Soto Mura (75), Leonel Guillermo Sánchez Lineros (82, 85).

**167.** 26.03.1961 **CHILE – WEST GERMANY** **3-1(2-1)**
Estadio Nacional, Santiago; Referee: José Luis Praddaude (Argentina); Attendance: 47,816
**CHI:** Misael Escuti (25/0), Luis Armando Eyzaguirre (15/0), Sergio Navarro (22/0), Carlos Contreras (4/0), Raúl Sánchez (16/0), Jorge Luis Toro Sánchez (9/1), Eladio Rojas (7/1), Rómulo Betta (3/1) [Mario Moreno (20/4)], Juan Soto Mura (15/5), Jaime Caupolicán Ramírez Banda (36/8), Leonel Guillermo Sánchez Lineros (39/11). Trainer: Fernando Riera Bauza (23).
**Goals**: Leonel Guillermo Sánchez Lineros (9, 37), Eladio Rojas (79).

**168.** 07.05.1961 **CHILE - BRAZIL** **1-2(0-2)** Copa Bernardo O'Higgins
Estadio Nacional, Santiago; Referee: Juan Carlos Robles (Chile); Attendance: 51,030
**CHI:** Misael Escuti (26/0), Luis Armando Eyzaguirre (16/0), Raúl Sánchez (17/0), Sergio Navarro (23/0), Carlos Contreras (5/0), Eladio Rojas (8/1), Alberto Jorge Fouilloux Ahumada (11/1) [Rómulo Betta (4/1)], Leonel Guillermo Sánchez Lineros (40/11) [Armando Tobar (14/1)], Jorge Luis Toro Sánchez (10/1), Juan Soto Mura (16/6), Carlos Hoffmann (5/0). Trainer: Fernando Riera Bauza (24).
**Goal**: Juan Soto Mura (88).

**169.** 11.05.1961 **CHILE - BRAZIL** **0-1(0-1)** Copa Bernardo O'Higgins
Estadio Nacional, Santiago; Referee: Juan Carlos Robles (Chile); Attendance: 46,252
**CHI:** Misael Escuti (27/0), Luis Armando Eyzaguirre (17/0), Raúl Sánchez (18/0), Sergio Navarro (24/0), Carlos Contreras (6/0), Eladio Rojas (9/1), Rómulo Betta (5/1) [Jaime Caupolicán Ramírez Banda (37/8)], Jorge Luis Toro Sánchez (11/1), Armando Tobar (15/1), Leonel Guillermo Sánchez Lineros (41/11) [Juan Soto Mura (17/6)], Carlos Hoffmann (6/0) [Braulio Musso (14/3)]. Trainer: Fernando Riera Bauza (25).

**170.** 12.10.1961 **CHILE - URUGUAY** **2-3(2-2)**
Estadio Nacional, Santiago; Referee: Alberto Tejada Burga (Peru); Attendance: 40,000
**CHI:** Misael Escuti (28/0), Luis Armando Eyzaguirre (18/0), Carlos Contreras (7/0), Raúl Sánchez (19/0), Sergio Navarro (25/0), Jorge Luis Toro Sánchez (12/1), Eladio Rojas (10/1), Honorino Landa (1/0), Mario Moreno (21/5), Armando Tobar (16/1), Leonel Guillermo Sánchez Lineros (42/11), Alberto Jorge Fouilloux Ahumada (12/2) [Jaime Caupolicán Ramírez Banda (38/8)]. Trainer: Fernando Riera Bauza (26).
**Goals**: Alberto Jorge Fouilloux Ahumada (30), Mario Moreno (38).

**171.** 22.11.1961 **CHILE – SOVIET UNION** **0-1(0-0)**
Estadio Nacional, Santiago; Referee: Juan Carlos Armental (Uruguay); Attendance: 45,000
**CHI:** Misael Escuti (29/0), Luis Armando Eyzaguirre (19/0), Carlos Contreras (8/0), Raúl Sánchez (20/0), Sergio Navarro (26/0), Jorge Luis Toro Sánchez (13/1), Eladio Rojas (11/1), Mario Moreno (22/5) [Alberto Jorge Fouilloux Ahumada (13/2)], Honorino Landa (2/0) [Carlos Campos (2/1)], Leonel Guillermo Sánchez Lineros (43/11), Jaime Caupolicán Ramírez Banda (39/8) [Bernardo Bello (10/2)]. Trainer: Fernando Riera Bauza (27).

**172.** 09.12.1961 **CHILE – HUNGARY** **5-1(2-0)**
Estadio Nacional, Santiago; Referee: Juan Carlos Armental (Uruguay); Attendance: 55,000
**CHI:** Misael Escuti (30/0), Humberto Cruz (1/0) [Hernán Rodríguez (21/0)], Hugo Lepe (1/0), Manuel Rodríguez Araneda (1/0), Sergio Valdés (16/0), Mario Moreno (23/5), Jorge Luis Toro Sánchez (14/1), Honorino Landa (3/2), Alberto Jorge Fouilloux Ahumada (14/2), Alfonso Sepúlveda (1/1), Leonel Guillermo Sánchez Lineros (44/13). Trainer: Fernando Riera Bauza (28).
**Goals**: Honorino Landa (23, 34), Leonel Guillermo Sánchez Lineros (49, 58 penalty), Alfonso Sepúlveda (69).

**173.** 13.12.1961 **CHILE – HUNGARY** **0-0**
Estadio Nacional, Santiago; Referee: Estebán Moreno (Uruguay); Attendance: 42,000
**CHI:** Misael Escuti (31/0), Sergio Valdés (17/0), Raúl Sánchez (21/0), Manuel Rodríguez Araneda (2/0) [75.Isaac Carrasco (25/0)], Humberto Cruz (2/0), Alfonso Sepúlveda (2/1), Mario Moreno (24/5) [75.Armando Tobar (17/1)], Jorge Luis Toro Sánchez (15/1), Honorino Landa (4/2) [Carlos Campos (3/1)], Alberto Jorge Fouilloux Ahumada (15/2), Leonel Guillermo Sánchez Lineros (45/13). Trainer: Fernando Riera Bauza (29).

**174.** 30.05.1962 **CHILE - SWITZERLAND** **3-1(1-1)** 7th FIFA WC. Group Stage.
Estadio Nacional, Santiago; Referee: Kenneth Aston (England); Attendance: 65,000
**CHI:** Misael Escuti (32/0), Luis Armando Eyzaguirre (20/0), Raúl Sánchez (22/0), Sergio Navarro (27/0), Carlos Contreras (9/0), Eladio Rojas (12/1), Jaime Caupolicán Ramírez Banda (40/9), Jorge Luis Toro Sánchez (16/1), Honorino Landa (5/2), Alberto Jorge Fouilloux Ahumada (16/2), Leonel Guillermo Sánchez Lineros (46/15). Trainer: Fernando Riera Bauza (30).
**Goals**: Leonel Guillermo Sánchez Lineros (44), Jaime Caupolicán Ramírez Banda (52), Leonel Guillermo Sánchez Lineros (55).

**175.** 02.06.1962 **CHILE - ITALY** **2-0(0-0)** 7th FIFA WC. Group Stage.
Estadio Nacional, Santiago; Referee: Kenneth Aston (England); Attendance: 65,057
**CHI:** Misael Escuti (33/0), Luis Armando Eyzaguirre (21/0), Raúl Sánchez (23/0), Sergio Navarro (28/0), Carlos Contreras (10/0), Eladio Rojas (13/1), Jaime Caupolicán Ramírez Banda (41/10), Jorge Luis Toro Sánchez (17/2), Honorino Landa (6/2), Alberto Jorge Fouilloux Ahumada (17/2), Leonel Guillermo Sánchez Lineros (47/15). Trainer: Fernando Riera Bauza (31).
**Goals**: Jaime Caupolicán Ramírez Banda (73), Jorge Luis Toro Sánchez (88).

**176.** 06.06.1962 **CHILE – WEST GERMANY** **0-2(0-1)** 7th FIFA WC. Group Stage.
Estadio Nacional, Santiago; Referee: Robert Davidson (Scotland); Attendance: 67,224
**CHI:** Misael Escuti (34/0), Luis Armando Eyzaguirre (22/0), Raúl Sánchez (24/0), Sergio Navarro (29/0), Carlos Contreras (11/0), Eladio Rojas (14/1), Mario Moreno (25/5), Jaime Caupolicán Ramírez Banda (42/10), Armando Tobar (18/1), Honorino Landa (7/2), Leonel Guillermo Sánchez Lineros (48/15). Trainer: Fernando Riera Bauza (32).

**177.** 10.06.1962 **CHILE – SOVIET UNION** **2-1(2-1)** 7th FIFA WC. Quarter-Finals.
Estadio „Carlos Dittborn“, Arica; Referee: Leopold Sylvain Horn (Holland); Attendance: 17,268
**CHI:** Misael Escuti (35/0), Luis Armando Eyzaguirre (23/0), Carlos Contreras (12/0), Raúl Sánchez (25/0), Sergio Navarro (30/0), Eladio Rojas (15/2), Jaime Caupolicán Ramírez Banda (43/10), Jorge Luis Toro Sánchez (18/2), Honorino Landa (8/2), Armando Tobar (19/1), Leonel Guillermo Sánchez Lineros (49/16). Trainer: Fernando Riera Bauza (33).
**Goals**: Leonel Guillermo Sánchez Lineros (11), Eladio Rojas (28).

**178.** 13.06.1962 **CHILE - BRAZIL** **2-4(1-2)** 7th FIFA WC. Semi-Finals.
Estadio Nacional, Santiago; Referee: Arturo Maximo Yamasaki Maldonado (Peru); Attendance: 76,594
**CHI:** Misael Escuti (36/0), Luis Armando Eyzaguirre (24/0), Raúl Sánchez (26/0), Manuel Rodríguez Araneda (3/0), Carlos Contreras (13/0), Eladio Rojas (16/2), Jaime Caupolicán Ramírez Banda (44/10), Jorge Luis Toro Sánchez (19/3), Honorino Landa (9/2), Armando Tobar (20/1), Leonel Guillermo Sánchez Lineros (50/17). Trainer: Fernando Riera Bauza (34).
**Goals**: Jorge Luis Toro Sánchez (42), Leonel Guillermo Sánchez Lineros (62 penalty).

**179.** 16.06.1962 **CHILE - YUGOSLAVIA** **1-0(0-0)** 7th FIFA WC. Bronze Medal.
Estadio Nacional, Santiago; Referee: Juan Gardeazabál Garay (Spain); Attendance: 66,697
**CHI:** Adán Godoy (1/0), Luis Armando Eyzaguirre (25/0), Raúl Sánchez (27/0), Manuel Rodríguez Araneda (4/0), Humberto Cruz (3/0), Eladio Rojas (17/3), Jaime Caupolicán Ramírez Banda (45/10), Jorge Luis Toro Sánchez (20/3), Carlos Campos (4/1), Armando Tobar (21/1), Leonel Guillermo Sánchez Lineros (51/17). Trainer: Fernando Riera Bauza (35).
**Goal**: Eladio Rojas (90).

**180.** 07.11.1962 **CHILE - ARGENTINA** **1-1(1-1)** Copa Carlos Dittborn
Estadio Nacional, Santiago; Referee: Juan Carlos Robles (Chile); Attendance: 51,000
**CHI:** Misael Escuti (37/0) [Adán Godoy (2/0)], Luis Armando Eyzaguirre (26/0), Raúl Sánchez (28/0), Manuel Rodríguez Araneda (5/0), Carlos Contreras (14/0), Eladio Rojas (18/3), Alberto Jorge Fouilloux Ahumada (18/2), Orlando Ramírez (1/0), Honorino Landa (10/3) [Carlos Verdejo (4/2)], Francisco Valdés Muñoz (1/0), Fernando Ibáñez (1/0) [Enrique Daniel Hormazábal Silva (41/16)]. Trainer: Luis Alamos Luque (1).
**Goal**: Honorino Landa (2).

**181.** 21.11.1962 **ARGENTINA - CHILE** **1-0(0-0)** Copa Carlos Dittborn
Estadio Monumental „Antonio Vespucio Liberti“, Buenos Aires; Referee: Roberto Héctor Goicoechea (Argentina); Attendance: 30,000
**CHI:** Misael Escuti (38/0), Alberto Aldo Valentini (2/0), Raúl Sánchez (29/0), Sergio Navarro (31/0), Carlos Contreras (15/0), Eladio Rojas (19/3), Alberto Jorge Fouilloux Ahumada (19/2), Orlando Ramírez (2/0) [Enrique Daniel Hormazábal Silva (42/16)], Honorino Landa (11/3) [Ricardo Cabrera (2/2)], Francisco Valdés Muñoz (2/0) [Carlos Verdejo (5/2)], Leonel Guillermo Sánchez Lineros (52/17). Trainer: Luis Alamos Luque (2).

**182.** 23.03.1963 **URUGUAY - CHILE** **3-2(2-0)** Copa Pinto Durán
Estadio Centenario, Montevideo; Referee: Paterlini (Uruguay); Attendance: 30,000
**CHI:** Misael Escuti (39/0), Luis Armando Eyzaguirre (27/0), Raúl Sánchez (30/0) [Humberto Donoso (1/0)], Manuel Rodríguez Araneda (6/0), Carlos Contreras (16/0) [Humberto Cruz (4/0)], Ernesto Alvarez (1/0), Alfonso Sepúlveda (3/1), Rómulo Betta (6/1) [Rubén Marcos (1/0)], Honorino Landa (12/3), Orlando Ramírez (3/2), Leonel Guillermo Sánchez Lineros (53/17). Trainer: Luis Alamos Luque (3).
**Goals**: Orlando Ramírez (58 penalty,84).

**183.** 24.07.1963 **CHILE - URUGUAY** **0-0** Copa Pinto Durán
Estadio Nacional, Santiago; Referee: Domingo Massaro (Chile); Attendance: 40,000
**CHI:** Misael Escuti (40/0), Oscar Montalva (1/0), Raúl Sánchez (31/0), José González (1/0), Humberto Cruz (5/0), Alberto Jorge Fouilloux Ahumada (20/2), Mario Ortíz (13/0), Orlando Ramírez (4/2), Armando Tobar (22/1) [Luis Hernán Alvarez (4/1)], Francisco Valdés Muñoz (3/0), Bernardo Bello (11/2) [Enrique Daniel Hormazábal Silva (43/16)]. Trainer: Francisco Hormazábal (1).

**184.** 24.09.1964 **ARGENTINA - CHILE** **5-0(3-0)** Copa Carlos Dittborn
Estadio Monumental „Antonio Vespucio Liberti", Buenos Aires; Referee: Aurelio Domingo Bossolino (Argentina); Attendance: 30,000
**CHI:** Manuel Astorga (6/0), Luis Armando Eyzaguirre (28/0), Raúl Sánchez (32/0), Hugo Villanueva (1/0), Carlos Contreras (17/0) [Humberto Cruz (6/0)], Orlando Aravena (1/0) [Alfonso Sepúlveda (4/1)], Alberto Jorge Fouilloux Ahumada (21/2), Mario Moreno (26/5) [Eugenio Méndez (1/0)], Armando Tobar (23/1), Rubén Marcos (2/0), Leonel Guillermo Sánchez Lineros (54/17). Trainer: Francisco Hormazábal (2).

**185.** 14.10.1964 **CHILE - ARGENTINA** **1-1(1-1)** Copa Carlos Dittborn
Estadio Nacional, Santiago; Referee: Juan Carlos Robles (Chile); Attendance: 52,160
**CHI:** Adán Godoy (3/0), Luis Armando Eyzaguirre (29/0), Raúl Sánchez (33/0), Alberto Aldo Valentini (3/0), Carlos Contreras (18/0), Carlos Verdejo (6/3), Orlando Aravena (2/0) [Roberto Hodge (1/0)], Pedro Damián Araya Toro (1/0), Honorino Landa (13/3), Rubén Marcos (3/0) [Guillermo Yávar (1/0)], Leonel Guillermo Sánchez Lineros (55/17) [Orlando Ramírez (5/2)]. Trainer: Francisco Hormazábal (3).
**Goal**: Carlos Verdejo (23).

**186.** 15.04.1965 **CHILE - PERU** **4-1(3-1)** Copa del Pacífico
Estadio Nacional, Santiago; Referee: Cláudio Vicuña Larrain (Chile); Attendance: 47,589
**CHI:** Adán Godoy (4/0) [Juan Carlos Olivares Sánchez (1/0)], Luis Armando Eyzaguirre (30/0), Humberto Donoso (2/0) [Hugo Berly (1/0)], Hugo Villanueva (2/0), Carlos Contreras (19/0), Ignacio Prieto (1/0), Roberto Hodge (2/0), Pedro Damián Araya Toro (2/2), Honorino Landa (14/5) [Ricardo Cabrera (3/2)], Rubén Marcos (4/0) [Francisco Valdés Muñoz (4/0)], Carlos Hoffmann (7/0) [Alberto Jorge Fouilloux Ahumada (22/2)]. Trainer: Francisco Hormazábal (4).
**Goals**: Honorino Landa (11 penalty,18), Pedro Damián Araya Toro (20, 76).

**187.** 28.04.1965 **PERU - CHILE** **0-1(0-0)** Copa del Pacífico
Estadio Nacional, Lima; Referee: Arturo Maximo Yamasaki Maldonado (Peru); Attendance: 45,000
**CHI:** Francisco Nitsche (2/0), Alberto Aldo Valentini (4/0), Carlos Contreras (20/0), Humberto Donoso (3/0), Hugo Villanueva (3/0), Ignacio Prieto (2/0) [Eugenio Méndez (2/0)], Orlando Aravena (3/0), Pedro Damián Araya Toro (3/3) [Leonel Guillermo Sánchez Lineros (56/17)], Honorino Landa (15/5), Alberto Jorge Fouilloux Ahumada (23/2) [Guillermo Yávar (2/0)], Carlos Hoffmann (8/0). Trainer: Francisco Hormazábal (5).
**Goal**: Pedro Damián Araya Toro (54).

**188.** 09.05.1965 **CHILE - URUGUAY** **0-0** Copa Pinto Durán
Estadio Nacional, Santiago; Referee: Pardiñas (Uruguay); Attendance: 59,316
**CHI:** Adán Godoy (5/0), Alberto Aldo Valentini (5/0), Carlos Contreras (21/0), Humberto Donoso (4/0), Hugo Villanueva (4/0), Ignacio Prieto (3/0) [Francisco Valdés Muñoz (5/0)], Orlando Aravena (4/0), Pedro Damián Araya Toro (4/3), Honorino Landa (16/5), Guillermo Yávar (3/0) [Rubén Marcos (5/0)], Carlos Hoffmann (9/0) [Leonel Guillermo Sánchez Lineros (57/17)]. Trainer: Francisco Hormazábal (6).

**189.** 16.05.1965 **URUGUAY - CHILE** **1-1(1-1)** Copa Pinto Durán
Estadio Centenario, Montevideo; Referee: Domingo Massaro (Chile); Attendance: 16,991
**CHI:** Adán Godoy (6/0), Luis Armando Eyzaguirre (31/0) [Alberto Aldo Valentini (6/0)], Carlos Contreras (22/0), Humberto Donoso (5/0), Hugo Villanueva (5/0), Ignacio Prieto (4/0) [Guillermo Yávar (4/0)], Orlando Aravena (5/0), Pedro Damián Araya Toro (5/3), Honorino Landa (17/5) [Ricardo Cabrera (4/2)], Rubén Marcos (6/0), Leonel Guillermo Sánchez Lineros (58/18). Trainer: Francisco Hormazábal (7).
**Goal**: Leonel Guillermo Sánchez Lineros (7).

**190.** 14.07.1965 **ARGENTINA - CHILE** **1-0(1-0)** Copa Carlos Dittborn
Estadio Monumental „Antonio Vespucio Liberti", Buenos Aires; Referee: Roberto Héctor Goicoechea (Argentina); Attendance: 25,000
**CHI:** Francisco Nitsche (3/0), Alberto Aldo Valentini (7/0), Carlos Contreras (23/0), Humberto Donoso (6/0), Hugo Villanueva (6/0) [Leonel Ramírez (1/0)], Ignacio Prieto (5/0), Roberto Hodge (3/0), Pedro Damián Araya Toro (6/3), Ricardo Cabrera (5/2) [Carlos Campos (5/1)], Alberto Jorge Fouilloux Ahumada (24/2) [Rubén Marcos (7/0)], Leonel Guillermo Sánchez Lineros (59/18). Trainer: Francisco Hormazábal (8).

**191.** 21.07.1965 **CHILE - ARGENTINA** **1-1(1-0)** Copa Carlos Dittborn
Estadio Nacional, Santiago; Referee: Rafael Hormazábal Díaz (Chile); Attendance: 30,000
**CHI:** Francisco Nitsche (4/0) [Manuel Astorga (7/0)], Alberto Aldo Valentini (8/0), Carlos Contreras (24/0), Humberto Donoso (7/0), José González (2/0), Ignacio Prieto (6/0), Roberto Hodge (4/0), Pedro Damián Araya Toro (7/3), Carlos Campos (6/1) [Honorino Landa (18/5)], Alberto Jorge Fouilloux Ahumada (25/2) [Rubén Marcos (8/0)], Leonel Guillermo Sánchez Lineros (60/19). Trainer: Francisco Hormazábal (9).
**Goal**: Leonel Guillermo Sánchez Lineros (45).

**192.** 01.08.1965 **CHILE - COLOMBIA** **7-2(4-0)** 8th FIFA WC. Qualifiers
Estadio Nacional, Santiago; Referee: E. Montes (Peru); Attendance: 70,052
**CHI:** Francisco Nitsche (5/0), Alberto Aldo Valentini (9/0), Humberto Donoso (8/0), José González (3/0), Carlos Contreras (25/0), Ignacio Prieto (7/1), Eugenio Méndez (3/2), Roberto Hodge (5/0), Carlos Campos (7/2), Alberto Jorge Fouilloux Ahumada (26/4), Leonel Guillermo Sánchez Lineros (61/20). Trainer: Francisco Hormazábal (10).
**Goals**: Leonel Guillermo Sánchez Lineros (11), Eugenio Méndez (15), Alberto Jorge Fouilloux Ahumada (25), Carlos Campos (42), Ignacio Prieto (58), Alberto Jorge Fouilloux Ahumada (65), Eugenio Méndez (70).

**193.** 07.08.1965 **COLOMBIA - CHILE** **2-0(0-0)** 8th FIFA WC. Qualifiers
Estadio Municipal, Barranquilla; Referee: Rodolfo Isasía Rica (Venezuela); Attendance: 4,401
**CHI:** Francisco Nitsche (6/0), Alberto Aldo Valentini (10/0), Humberto Donoso (9/0), José González (4/0), Carlos Contreras (26/0), Ignacio Prieto (8/1), Eugenio Méndez (4/2), Roberto Hodge (6/0), Honorino Landa (19/5), Alberto Jorge Fouilloux Ahumada (27/4), Leonel Guillermo Sánchez Lineros (62/20). Trainer: Francisco Hormazábal (11).

**194.** 15.08.1965 **ECUADOR - CHILE** **2-2(1-1)** 8th FIFA WC. Qualifiers
Estadio Modelo, Guayaquil; Referee: Eunápio Gouveia de Queiroz (Brazil); Attendance: 50,041
**CHI:** Manuel Astorga (8/0), Alberto Aldo Valentini (11/0), Humberto Donoso (10/0), José González (5/0), Carlos Contreras (27/0), Orlando Aravena (6/0), Rubén Marcos (9/0), Ignacio Prieto (9/2), Carlos Campos (8/3), Alberto Jorge Fouilloux Ahumada (28/4), Leonel Guillermo Sánchez Lineros (63/20). Trainer: Francisco Hormazábal (12).
**Goals**: Carlos Campos (38), Ignacio Prieto (57).

**195.** 22.08.1965 **CHILE - ECUADOR** **3-1(1-1)** 8th FIFA WC. Qualifiers

Estadio Nacional, Santiago; Referee: José María Codesal (Uruguay); Attendance: 70,602

**CHI:** Manuel Astorga (9/0), Alberto Aldo Valentini (12/0), Humberto Donoso (11/0), José González (6/0), Carlos Contreras (28/0), Roberto Hodge (7/0), Rubén Marcos (10/1), Ignacio Prieto (10/2), Ricardo Cabrera (6/2), Alberto Jorge Fouilloux Ahumada (29/5), Leonel Guillermo Sánchez Lineros (64/21). Trainer: Francisco Hormazábal (13).

**Goals**: Leonel Guillermo Sánchez Lineros (10 penalty), Rubén Marcos (61), Alberto Jorge Fouilloux Ahumada (74).

**196.** 12.10.1965 **CHILE - ECUADOR** **2-1(2-0)** 8th FIFA WC. Qualifiers (Play-off)

Estadio Nacional, Lima; Referee: Roberto Héctor Goicoechea (Argentina); Attendance: 44,864

**CHI:** Adán Godoy (7/0), Luis Armando Eyzaguirre (32/0), Humberto Donoso (12/0), José González (7/0), Humberto Cruz (7/0), Ignacio Prieto (11/2), Pedro Damián Araya Toro (8/3), Rubén Marcos (11/2), Carlos Campos (9/3), Alberto Jorge Fouilloux Ahumada (30/5), Leonel Guillermo Sánchez Lineros (65/22). Trainer: Luis Alamos Luque (4).

**Goals**: Leonel Guillermo Sánchez Lineros (16), Rubén Marcos (40).

**197.** 23.02.1966 **CHILE – SOVIET UNION** **0-2(0-1)**

Estadio Nacional, Santiago; Referee: Cláudio Vicuña Larrain (Chile); Attendance: 40,000

**CHI:** Adán Godoy (8/0), Alberto Aldo Valentini (13/0), José González (8/0), Elías Ricardo Figueroa Brander (1/0), Carlos Contreras (29/0), Guillermo Yávar (5/0), Roberto Hodge (8/0), Pedro Damián Araya Toro (9/3) [58.Pedro Arancibia (1/0)], Francisco Valdés Muñoz (6/0) [Orlando Ramírez (6/2)], Honorino Landa (20/5), Leonel Guillermo Sánchez Lineros (66/22) [75.Leonardo Véliz Díaz (1/0)]. Trainer: Luis Alamos Luque (5).

**198.** 17.04.1966 **CHILE - BRAZIL** **0-1(0-1)** Copa Bernardo O'Higgins

Estadio Nacional, Santiago; Referee: Ralph Howley (England); Attendance: 30,000

**CHI:** Juan Carlos Olivares Sánchez (2/0), Luis Armando Eyzaguirre (33/0), Humberto Cruz (8/0), Elías Ricardo Figueroa Brander (2/0), José González (9/0) [Hugo Villanueva (7/0)], Guillermo Yávar (6/0) [Francisco Valdés Muñoz (7/0)], Eladio Rojas (20/3), Pedro Damián Araya Toro (10/3), Honorino Landa (21/5), Orlando Ramírez (7/2), Leonardo Véliz Díaz (2/0) [Leonel Guillermo Sánchez Lineros (67/22)]. Trainer: Luis Alamos Luque (6).

**199.** 20.04.1966 **CHILE - BRAZIL** **2-1(1-0)** Copa Bernardo O'Higgins

Estadio Nacional, Santiago; Referee: Ralph Howley (England); Attendance: 42,000

**CHI:** Juan Carlos Olivares Sánchez (3/0), Alberto Aldo Valentini (14/0), Humberto Donoso (13/0), Hugo Villanueva (8/0), Carlos Contreras (30/0), Carlos Reinoso (1/0), Roberto Hodge (9/0) [Eladio Rojas (21/3)], Francisco Valdés Muñoz (8/1), Pedro Damián Araya Toro (11/4), Carlos Campos (10/3) [Honorino Landa (22/5)], Leonel Guillermo Sánchez Lineros (68/22). Trainer: Luis Alamos Luque (7).

**Goals**: Pedro Damián Araya Toro (26), Francisco Valdés Muñoz (76).

**200.** 11.05.1966 **MEXICO - CHILE** **1-0(1-0)**

Estadio Olímpico de Centro Universitário, Ciudad de México; Referee: Ralph Howley (England); Attendance: 55,000

**CHI:** Adán Godoy (9/0), Alberto Aldo Valentini (15/0), Humberto Donoso (14/0), Hugo Villanueva (9/0), Humberto Cruz (9/0), Eladio Rojas (22/3) [46.Leonel Guillermo Sánchez Lineros (69/22)], Alberto Jorge Fouilloux Ahumada (31/5), Guillermo Yávar (7/0) [62.Pedro Damián Araya Toro (12/4)], Armando Tobar (24/1), Orlando Ramírez (8/2) [82.Francisco Valdés Muñoz (9/1)], Rubén Marcos (12/2). Trainer: Luis Alamos Luque (8).

**201.** 15.05.1966 **BRAZIL - CHILE** **1-1(1-0)**

Estádio Pacaembú, São Paulo; Referee: William Syme (England); Attendance: 17,558

**CHI:** Adán Godoy (10/0), Luis Armando Eyzaguirre (34/0), Elías Ricardo Figueroa Brander (3/0), Humberto Cruz (10/0), Hugo Villanueva (10/0), Rubén Marcos (13/2), Guillermo Yávar (8/1), Pedro Damián Araya Toro (13/4), Armando Tobar (25/1) [Leonel Guillermo Sánchez Lineros (70/22)], Orlando Ramírez (9/2), Alberto Jorge Fouilloux Ahumada (32/5). Trainer: Luis Alamos Luque (9).

**Goal**: Guillermo Yávar (80).

**202.** 19.05.1966 **BRAZIL - CHILE** **1-0(0-0)**

Estádio „Jornalista Mario Filho" (Maracanã), Rio de Janeiro; Referee: Thomas Wharton (Scotland); Attendance: 90,000

**CHI:** Adán Godoy (11/0), Luis Armando Eyzaguirre (35/0), Elías Ricardo Figueroa Brander (4/0), Humberto Cruz (11/0), Hugo Villanueva (11/0), Guillermo Yávar (9/1) [Carlos Reinoso (2/0)], Rubén Marcos (14/2), Pedro Damián Araya Toro (14/4) [Orlando Ramírez (10/2)], Armando Tobar (26/1), Alberto Jorge Fouilloux Ahumada (33/5), Leonel Guillermo Sánchez Lineros (71/22). Trainer: Luis Alamos Luque (10).

**203.** 22.05.1966 **CHILE - WALES** **2-0(1-0)**

Estadio Nacional, Santiago; Referee: Sérgio Bustamante González (Chile); Attendance: 32,000

**CHI:** Adán Godoy (12/0), Luis Armando Eyzaguirre (36/0), Humberto Cruz (12/0), Elías Ricardo Figueroa Brander (5/0), Hugo Villanueva (12/0), Guillermo Yávar (10/1), Rubén Marcos (15/3), Pedro Damián Araya Toro (15/4) [Francisco Valdés Muñoz (10/1)], Armando Tobar (27/2) [Orlando Ramírez (11/2)], Alberto Jorge Fouilloux Ahumada (34/5), Leonel Guillermo Sánchez Lineros (72/22). Trainer: Luis Alamos Luque (11).

**Goals**: Rubén Marcos (9), Armando Tobar (51).

**204.** 29.05.1966 **CHILE - MEXICO** **0-1(0-1)**

Estadio Nacional, Santiago; Referee: Ralph Howley (England); Attendance: 71,630

**CHI:** Adán Godoy (13/0), Luis Armando Eyzaguirre (37/0) [55.Alberto Aldo Valentini (16/0)], Elías Ricardo Figueroa Brander (6/0), Hugo Villanueva (13/0), Humberto Cruz (13/0), Rubén Marcos (16/3), Guillermo Yávar (11/1) [46.Eladio Rojas (23/3)], Alberto Jorge Fouilloux Ahumada (35/5), Armando Tobar (28/2) [46.Orlando Ramírez (12/2)], Francisco Valdés Muñoz (11/1) [78.Pedro Damián Araya Toro (16/4)], Leonel Guillermo Sánchez Lineros (73/22). Trainer: Luis Alamos Luque (12).

**205.** 02.07.1966 **EAST GERMANY - CHILE** **5-2(2-0)**

Zentralstadion, Leipzig; Referee: Per Engblom (Finland); Attendance: 45,000

**CHI:** Adán Godoy (14/0), Luis Armando Eyzaguirre (38/0) [81.Alberto Aldo Valentini (17/0)], Elías Ricardo Figueroa Brander (7/0), Hugo Villanueva (14/0), Humberto Cruz (14/0), Ignacio Prieto (12/2), Alberto Jorge Fouilloux Ahumada (36/5) [70.Pedro Damián Araya Toro (17/4)], Rubén Marcos (17/4), Armando Tobar (29/3), Orlando Ramírez (13/2) [37.Honorino Landa (23/5)], Leonel Guillermo Sánchez Lineros (74/22). Trainer: Luis Alamos Luque (13).

**Goals**: Armando Tobar (62 penalty), Rubén Marcos (81).

**206.** 13.07.1966 **ITALY - CHILE** **2-0(1-0)** 8th FIFA WC. Group Stage.

Roker Park, Sunderland (England); Referee: Gottfried Dienst (Switzerland); Attendance: 27,199

**CHI:** Juan Carlos Olivares Sánchez (4/0), Luis Armando Eyzaguirre (39/0), Humberto Cruz (15/0), Elías Ricardo Figueroa Brander (8/0), Hugo Villanueva (15/0), Ignacio Prieto (13/2), Rubén Marcos (18/4), Alberto Jorge Fouilloux Ahumada (37/5), Pedro Damián Araya Toro (18/4), Armando Tobar (30/3), Leonel Guillermo Sánchez Lineros (75/22). Trainer: Luis Alamos Luque (14).

**207.** 15.07.1966 **NORTH KOREA - CHILE** **1-1(0-1)** 8th FIFA WC. Group Stage.
Ayresome Park, Middlesbrough (England); Referee: Ali Kandil (United Arab Republic); Attendance: 13,792
**CHI:** Juan Carlos Olivares Sánchez (5/0), Alberto Aldo Valentini (18/0), Humberto Cruz (16/0), Elías Ricardo Figueroa Brander (9/0), Hugo Villanueva (16/0), Ignacio Prieto (14/2), Rubén Marcos (19/5), Alberto Jorge Fouilloux Ahumada (38/5), Pedro Damián Araya Toro (19/4), Honorino Landa (24/5), Leonel Guillermo Sánchez Lineros (76/22). Trainer: Luis Alamos Luque (15).
**Goal**: Rubén Marcos (26 penalty).

**208.** 20.07.1966 **SOVIET UNION - CHILE** **2-1(1-1)** 8th FIFA WC. Group Stage.
Roker Park, Sunderland (England); Referee: John Adair (Northern Ireland); Attendance: 22,590
**CHI:** Juan Carlos Olivares Sánchez (6/0), Alberto Aldo Valentini (19/0), Humberto Cruz (17/0), Elías Ricardo Figueroa Brander (10/0), Hugo Villanueva (17/0), Ignacio Prieto (15/2), Rubén Marcos (20/6), Guillermo Yávar (12/1), Pedro Damián Araya Toro (20/4), Honorino Landa (25/5), Leonel Guillermo Sánchez Lineros (77/22). Trainer: Luis Alamos Luque (16).
**Goal**: Rubén Marcos (32).

**209.** 30.11.1966 **CHILE - COLOMBIA** **5-2(3-0)** 29th Copa América (Qualifiers)
Estadio Nacional, Santiago; Referee: Arturo Maximo Yamasaki Maldonado (Peru); Attendance: 69,066
**CHI:** Juan Carlos Olivares Sánchez (7/0), Víctor Adriazola (1/0), Humberto Cruz (18/0), Hugo Villanueva (18/0), Elías Ricardo Figueroa Brander (11/0), Roberto Hodge (10/0), Ignacio Prieto (16/3), Pedro Damián Araya Toro (21/5), Rubén Marcos (21/6) [9.Osvaldo Castro (1/2)], Carlos Campos (11/3) [Julio Gallardo (1/0)], Manuel Saavedra (1/1). Trainer: Alejandro Scopelli Casanova (1).
**Goals**: Pedro Damián Araya Toro (7), Osvaldo Castro (23), Ignacio Prieto (40 penalty), Osvaldo Castro (49), Manuel Saavedra (61).

**210.** 11.12.1966 **COLOMBIA - CHILE** **0-0** 29th Copa América (Qualifiers)
Estadio „Nemesio Camacho“ 'El Campín', Bogotá; Referee: Arturo Maximo Yamasaki Maldonado (Peru); Attendance: 31,303
**CHI:** Juan Carlos Olivares Sánchez (8/0), Víctor Adriazola (2/0), Humberto Cruz (19/0), Hugo Villanueva (19/0), Elías Ricardo Figueroa Brander (12/0), Roberto Hodge (11/0), Ignacio Prieto (17/3), Pedro Damián Araya Toro (22/5), Julio Gallardo (2/0) [*sent off 76*], Armando Tobar (31/3) [Carlos Reinoso (3/0)], Osvaldo Castro (2/2) [Nélson Torres (1/0)]. Trainer: Alejandro Scopelli Casanova (2).

**211.** 18.01.1967 **CHILE - VENEZUELA** **2-0(2-0)** 29th Copa América
Estadio Centenario, Montevideo (Uruguay); Referee: Isidro Ramírez Alvarez (Paraguay); Attendance: 15,000
**CHI:** Juan Carlos Olivares Sánchez (9/0), Víctor Adriazola (3/0), Humberto Cruz (20/0), Elías Ricardo Figueroa Brander (13/0), Hugo Villanueva (20/0), Roberto Hodge (12/0), Ignacio Prieto (18/3), Pedro Damián Araya Toro (23/5), Rubén Marcos (22/8), Carlos Campos (12/3) [Julio Gallardo (3/0)], Manuel Saavedra (2/1) [Osvaldo Castro (3/2)]. Trainer: Alejandro Scopelli Casanova (3).
**Goals**: Rubén Marcos (15, 40).

**212.** 22.01.1967 **CHILE - PARAGUAY** **4-2** 29th Copa América
Estadio Centenario, Montevideo (Uruguay); Referee: Roberto Héctor Goicoechea (Argentina); Attendance: 6,000
**CHI:** Juan Carlos Olivares Sánchez (10/0), Víctor Adriazola (4/0), Humberto Cruz (21/0), Hugo Villanueva (21/0) [Eduardo Herrera (1/0)], Elías Ricardo Figueroa Brander (14/0), Roberto Hodge (13/0), Pedro Damián Araya Toro (24/7), Ignacio Prieto (19/3), Julio Gallardo (4/2), Rubén Marcos (23/8), Osvaldo Castro (4/2). Trainer: Alejandro Scopelli Casanova (4).
**Goals**: Julio Gallardo (9, 44), Pedro Damián Araya Toro (72, 81).

**213.** 26.01.1967 **URUGUAY - CHILE** **2-2(1-2)** 29th Copa América
Estadio Centenario, Montevideo; Referee: Isidro Ramírez Alvarez (Paraguay); Attendance: 30,000
**CHI:** Juan Carlos Olivares Sánchez (11/0), Víctor Adriazola (5/0), Humberto Cruz (22/0), Eduardo Herrera (2/0), Elías Ricardo Figueroa Brander (15/0), Roberto Hodge (14/0), Ignacio Prieto (20/3), Pedro Damián Araya Toro (25/7), Julio Gallardo (5/3), Rubén Marcos (24/9) [Armando Tobar (32/3)], Osvaldo Castro (5/2). Trainer: Alejandro Scopelli Casanova (5).
**Goals**: Julio Gallardo (2), Rubén Marcos (37).

**214.** 28.01.1967 **ARGENTINA - CHILE** **2-0(1-0)** 29th Copa América
Estadio Centenario, Montevideo (Uruguay); Referee: Isidro Ramírez Álvarez (Paraguay); Attendance: 14,000
**CHI:** Juan Carlos Olivares Sánchez (12/0), Víctor Adriazola (6/0), Humberto Cruz (23/0), Eduardo Herrera (3/0), Elías Ricardo Figueroa Brander (16/0), Roberto Hodge (15/0) [José Moris (1/0)], Ignacio Prieto (21/3), Pedro Damián Araya Toro (26/7), Julio Gallardo (6/3), Rubén Marcos (25/9), Osvaldo Castro (6/2). Trainer: Alejandro Scopelli Casanova (6).

**215.** 01.02.1967 **CHILE - BOLIVIA** **0-0** 29th Copa América
Estadio Centenario, Montevideo (Uruguay); Referee: Roberto Héctor Goicoechea (Argentina); Attendance: 1,500
**CHI:** Juan Carlos Olivares Sánchez (13/0), Víctor Adriazola (7/0) [Víctor Castañeda (1/0)], Humberto Cruz (24/0), Eduardo Herrera (4/0), Elías Ricardo Figueroa Brander (17/0), Roberto Hodge (16/0) [Armando Tobar (33/3)], Ignacio Prieto (22/3), Pedro Damián Araya Toro (27/7), Julio Gallardo (7/3), Rubén Marcos (26/9), Osvaldo Castro (7/2). Trainer: Alejandro Scopelli Casanova (7).

**216.** 15.08.1967 **CHILE - ARGENTINA** **1-0(0-0)**
Estadio Nacional, Santiago; Referee: Rafael Hormazábal Díaz (Chile); Attendance: 60,000
**CHI:** Juan Carlos Olivares Sánchez (14/0), Hugo Berly (2/0), Humberto Cruz (25/0), Alberto Fernando Ralph Quintano (1/0), Eduardo Herrera (5/0), Ignacio Prieto (23/3) [Francisco Valdés Muñoz (12/1)], Roberto Hodge (17/0), Pedro Damián Araya Toro (28/8), Carlos Reinoso (4/0) [Osvaldo Castro (8/2)], Alberto Jorge Fouilloux Ahumada (39/5), Leonel Guillermo Sánchez Lineros (78/22). Trainer: Alejandro Scopelli Casanova (8).
**Goal**: Pedro Damián Araya Toro (31).

**217.** 19.09.1967 **CHILE - BRAZIL** **0-1(0-1)**
Estadio Nacional, Santiago; Referee: Rafael Hormazabal Díaz (Chile); Attendance: 50,000
**CHI:** Juan Carlos Olivares Sánchez (15/0), Eduardo Herrera (6/0), Víctor Adriazola (8/0), Alberto Fernando Ralph Quintano (2/0), Hugo Berly (3/0), Roberto Hodge (18/0) [Pedro García (1/0)], Ignacio Prieto (24/3) [Roberto Ampuero (1/0)], Pedro Damián Araya Toro (29/8), Carlos Reinoso (5/0), Leonel Guillermo Sánchez Lineros (79/22), Alberto Jorge Fouilloux Ahumada (40/5). Trainer: Alejandro Scopelli Casanova (9).

**218.** 08.11.1967 **CHILE - ARGENTINA** **3-1(2-0)**
Estadio Nacional, Santiago; Referee: Cláudio Vicuña Larrain (Chile); Attendance: 43,232
**CHI:** Juan Carlos Olivares Sánchez (16/0), Hugo Berly (4/0), Humberto Cruz (26/0), Alberto Fernando Ralph Quintano (3/0), Eduardo Herrera (7/0), Ignacio Prieto (25/3), Rubén Marcos (27/9) [Roberto Hodge (19/0)], Pedro Damián Araya Toro (30/8), Carlos Reinoso (6/1) [Pedro García (2/0)], Alberto Jorge Fouilloux Ahumada (41/7), Leonel Guillermo Sánchez Lineros (80/22) [Osvaldo Castro (9/2)]. Trainer: Alejandro Scopelli Casanova (10).
**Goals**: Alberto Jorge Fouilloux Ahumada (5, 8 penalty), Carlos Reinoso (71).

**219.** 13.12.1967 **CHILE - HUNGARY** **4-5(2-0)**
Estadio Nacional, Santiago; Referee: Cláudio Vicuña Larrain (Chile); Attendance: 43,232
**CHI:** Juan Carlos Olivares Sánchez (17/0), Hugo Berly (5/0), Víctor Adriazola (9/0) [Humberto Cruz (27/0)], Alberto Fernando Ralph Quintano (4/0), Eduardo Herrera (8/0) [Juan Rodríguez Vega (1/0)], Ignacio Prieto (26/3), Roberto Hodge (20/1), Alberto Jorge Fouilloux Ahumada (42/7), Carlos Reinoso (7/2), Osvaldo Castro (10/3) [Nélson Torres (2/0)], Leonel Guillermo Sánchez Lineros (81/23). Trainer: Alejandro Scopelli Casanova (11).
**Goals**: Leonel Guillermo Sánchez Lineros, Osvaldo Castro, Carlos Reinoso, Roberto Hodge.

**220.** 17.12.1967 **CHILE – SOVIET UNION** **1-4(0-1)**
Estadio Nacional, Santiago; Referee: Cláudio Vicuña Larrain (Chile); Attendance: 30,000
**CHI:** Juan Carlos Olivares Sánchez (18/0), Hugo Berly (6/0), Humberto Cruz (28/0) [Víctor Adriazola (10/0)], Alberto Fernando Ralph Quintano (5/0), Eduardo Herrera (9/0) [Juan Rodríguez Vega (2/0)], Ignacio Prieto (27/3) [Francisco Valdés Muñoz (13/1)], José Moris (2/0) [Roberto Ampuero (2/0)], Alberto Jorge Fouilloux Ahumada (43/7), Carlos Reinoso (8/3), Osvaldo Castro (11/3) [Ricardo Díaz (2/1)], Leonel Guillermo Sánchez Lineros (82/23). Trainer: Alejandro Scopelli Casanova (12).
**Goals**: Carlos Reinoso.

**221.** 18.08.1968 **PERU - CHILE** **1-2** Copa del Pacífico
Estadio Nacional, Lima; Attendance: 40,000
**CHI:** Leopoldo Manuel Vallejos Bravo (1/0), Juan Rodríguez Vega (3/0), Humberto Cruz (29/0), Alberto Fernando Ralph Quintano (6/0), Antonio Arias Mújica (1/0), Francisco Valdés Muñoz (14/3), Roberto Hodge (21/1), Pedro Damián Araya Toro (31/8), Carlos Reinoso (9/3), Rubén Marcos (28/9), Leonel Guillermo Sánchez Lineros (83/23) [Alberto Jorge Fouilloux Ahumada (44/7)]. Trainer: Salvador Nocetti (1).
**Goals**: Francisco Valdés Muñoz 2.

**222.** 21.08.1968 **PERU - CHILE** **0-0** Copa del Pacífico
Estadio Nacional, Lima; Attendance: 40,000
**CHI:** Efraín Santander (1/0), Juan Rodríguez Vega (4/0), Humberto Cruz (30/0), Alberto Fernando Ralph Quintano (7/0), Eduardo Herrera (10/0), Francisco Valdés Muñoz (15/3), Roberto Hodge (22/1), Pedro Damián Araya Toro (32/8) [Ricardo Cuevas (1/0)], Carlos Reinoso (10/3), Rubén Marcos (29/9), Leonel Guillermo Sánchez Lineros (84/23) [Alberto Jorge Fouilloux Ahumada (45/7)]. Trainer: Salvador Nocetti (2).

**223.** 28.08.1968 **MEXICO - CHILE** **3-1(3-1)**
Estadio Azteca, Ciudad de México; Referee: Abel Aguilar (Mexico); Attendance: 52,000
**CHI:** Juan Carlos Olivares Sánchez (19/0), Juan Rodríguez Vega (5/0), Alberto Fernando Ralph Quintano (8/0) [69.Antonio Arias Mújica (2/0)], Humberto Cruz (31/0), Eduardo Herrera (11/0), Roberto Hodge (23/1), Pedro Damián Araya Toro (33/8) [79.Adolfo Olivares (1/0)], Francisco Valdés Muñoz (16/3) [54.Alberto Jorge Fouilloux Ahumada (46/7)], Carlos Reinoso (11/3), Rubén Marcos (30/9), Leonel Guillermo Sánchez Lineros (85/24) [Hugo Berly (7/0)]. Trainer: Salvador Nocetti (3).
**Goal**: Leonel Guillermo Sánchez Lineros (5).

**224.** 23.10.1968 **CHILE - MEXICO** **3-1(3-0)**
Estadio Nacional, Santiago; Referee: Domingo Massaro (Chile); Attendance: 35,000
**CHI:** Juan Carlos Olivares Sánchez (20/0), Hugo Berly (8/0), Eduardo Herrera (12/0) [Raúl Angulo (1/0)], Alberto Fernando Ralph Quintano (9/0), Humberto Cruz (32/0), Roberto Hodge (24/1), Pedro Damián Araya Toro (34/9), Carlos Reinoso (12/3), Julio Gallardo (8/3) [Adolfo Olivares (2/2)], Rubén Marcos (31/9), Fabián Capot (1/0) [Alberto Jorge Fouilloux Ahumada (47/7)]. Trainer: Salvador Nocetti (4).
**Goals**: Pedro Damián Araya Toro (10), Adolfo Olivares (25, 37).

**225.** 27.11.1968 **ARGENTINA - CHILE** **4-0(2-0)** Copa Carlos Dittborn
Estadio Central, Rosario; Referee: Aurelio Domingo Bossolino (Argentina); Attendance: 20,000
**CHI:** Juan Carlos Olivares Sánchez (21/0), Juan Rodríguez Vega (6/0), Humberto Cruz (33/0), Raúl Angulo (2/0), Hugo Berly (9/0), Francisco Valdés Muñoz (17/3) [Adolfo Olivares (3/2)], Alfonso Lara Madrid (1/0), Orlando Ramírez (14/2), Carlos Reinoso (13/3), Alberto Jorge Fouilloux Ahumada (48/7), Osvaldo Castro (12/3) [Ricardo Cuevas (2/0)]. Trainer: Salvador Nocetti (5).

**226.** 04.12.1968 **CHILE - ARGENTINA** **2-1(1-1)** Copa Carlos Dittborn
Estadio Nacional, Santiago; Referee: Jaime Amor (Chile); Attendance: 30,000
**CHI:** Juan Carlos Olivares Sánchez (22/0) [Leopoldo Manuel Vallejos Bravo (2/0)], Hugo Berly (10/0) [Nélson Gallardo (1/0)], Humberto Cruz (34/0), Raúl Angulo (3/0), Eduardo Herrera (13/0), Carlos Reinoso (14/3), Alfonso Lara Madrid (2/0), Pedro Damián Araya Toro (35/9), Francisco Valdés Muñoz (18/3) [Nélson Torres (3/0)], Osvaldo Castro (13/3) [Adolfo Olivares (4/3)], Alberto Jorge Fouilloux Ahumada (49/8). Trainer: Salvador Nocetti (6).
**Goals**: Alberto Jorge Fouilloux Ahumada (35), Adolfo Olivares (58).

**227.** 18.12.1968 **CHILE – WEST GERMANY** **2-1(0-1)**
Estadio Nacional, Santiago; Referee: Juan Carlos Robles (Chile); Attendance: 50,000
**CHI:** Juan Carlos Olivares Sánchez (23/0), Juan Rodríguez Vega (7/0), Humberto Cruz (35/0), Raúl Angulo (4/0), Antonio Arias Mújica (3/0), Carlos Reinoso (15/3), Roberto Hodge (25/1), Alfonso Lara Madrid (3/0), Pedro Damián Araya Toro (36/10), Adolfo Olivares (5/3) [Nélson Torres (4/0)], Alberto Jorge Fouilloux Ahumada (50/9). Trainer: Salvador Nocetti (7).
**Goals**: Pedro Damián Araya Toro (61), Alberto Jorge Fouilloux Ahumada (77).

**228.** 28.05.1969 **CHILE - ARGENTINA** **1-1(1-0)**
Estadio Nacional, Santiago; Referee: Alberto Boullosa (Uruguay); Attendance: 30,000
**CHI:** Adolfo Nef Sanhueza (1/0), Juan Rodríguez Vega (8/0), Gustavo Laube (1/0), Alberto Fernando Ralph Quintano (10/0), Daniel Díaz (1/0), Francisco Valdés Muñoz (19/3), Roberto Hodge (26/1), Alberto Jorge Fouilloux Ahumada (51/9) [Carlos Humberto Caszely Garrido (1/0)], Adolfo Olivares (6/3) [Alfonso Lara Madrid (4/0)], Rubén Marcos (32/9), Leonardo Véliz Díaz (3/1). Trainer: Salvador Nocetti (8).
**Goal**: Leonardo Véliz Díaz (13).

**229.** 08.06.1969 **PARAGUAY - CHILE** **0-1(0-0)**
Estadio Defensores del Chaco, Asunción; Referee: Ángel Norberto Coerezza (Argentina); Attendance: 20,000
**CHI:** Adolfo Nef Sanhueza (2/0), Juan Rodríguez Vega (9/0), Gustavo Laube (2/0), Alberto Fernando Ralph Quintano (11/0), Daniel Díaz (2/0), Francisco Valdés Muñoz (20/3), Roberto Hodge (27/1), Rubén Marcos (33/9) [Pedro Damián Araya Toro (37/11)], Alberto Jorge Fouilloux Ahumada (52/9), Adolfo Olivares (7/3), Leonardo Véliz Díaz (4/1). Trainer: Salvador Nocetti (9).
**Goal**: Pedro Damián Araya Toro (68).

**230.** 11.06.1969 **ARGENTINA - CHILE** **2-1(0-0)**
Estadio Parque Independencia, La Plata; Referee: Rodolfo Pérez Osorio (Paraguay); Attendance: 25,000
**CHI:** Adolfo Nef Sanhueza (3/0), Juan Rodríguez Vega (10/0), Gustavo Laube (3/0), Alberto Fernando Ralph Quintano (12/0), Daniel Díaz (3/0), Francisco Valdés Muñoz (21/3), Roberto Hodge (28/1), Guillermo Yávar (13/1) [Carlos Reinoso (16/3)], Alberto Jorge Fouilloux Ahumada (53/9), Adolfo Olivares (8/4), Leonardo Véliz Díaz (5/1) [Alfonso Lara Madrid (5/0)]. Trainer: Salvador Nocetti (10).
**Goal**: Adolfo Olivares (78).

**231.** 15.06.1969 **COLOMBIA - CHILE** **3-3(0-2)**
Estadio „Nemesio Camacho" 'El Campín', Bogotá; Referee: Gómez (Colombia); Attendance: 30,000
**CHI:** Adolfo Nef Sanhueza (4/0), Juan Rodríguez Vega (11/0), Gustavo Laube (4/1), Alberto Fernando Ralph Quintano (13/0), Daniel Díaz (4/0) [Eduardo Herrera (14/0)], Francisco Valdés Muñoz (22/3) [Alfonso Lara Madrid (6/0)], Roberto Hodge (29/1), Carlos Reinoso (17/4) [Guillermo Yávar (14/1)], Pedro Damián Araya Toro (38/11), Adolfo Olivares (9/4), Alberto Jorge Fouilloux Ahumada (54/10). Trainer: Salvador Nocetti (11).
**Goals**: Alberto Jorge Fouilloux Ahumada (10), Carlos Reinoso (37), Gustavo Laube (64).

**232.** 22.06.1969 **EAST GERMANY - CHILE** **0-1(0-0)**
Ernst-Grube-Stadion, Magdeburg; Referee: Karlo Kruashvili (Soviet Union); Attendance: 20,000
**CHI:** Adolfo Nef Sanhueza (5/0), Juan Rodríguez Vega (12/0), Alberto Fernando Ralph Quintano (14/0), Gustavo Laube (5/1), Daniel Díaz (5/0), Roberto Hodge (30/1), Pedro Damián Araya Toro (39/11), Francisco Valdés Muñoz (23/3), Adolfo Olivares (10/4), Carlos Reinoso (18/4) [69.Guillermo Yávar (15/2)], Alberto Jorge Fouilloux Ahumada (55/10). Trainer: Salvador Nocetti (12).
**Goal**: Guillermo Yávar (90).

**233.** 25.06.1969 **EAST GERMANY - CHILE** **2-1(2-0)**
„Kurt Wabbe" Stadion, Halle; Referee: Helmuth Bader (East Germany); Attendance: 25,000
**CHI:** Adolfo Nef Sanhueza (6/0), Juan Rodríguez Vega (13/0), Alberto Fernando Ralph Quintano (15/0), Gustavo Laube (6/1), Daniel Díaz (6/0), Roberto Hodge (31/1) [Alfonso Lara Madrid (7/0)], Guillermo Yávar (16/2), Pedro Damián Araya Toro (40/11), Francisco Valdés Muñoz (24/3), Julio Gallardo (10/4), Alberto Jorge Fouilloux Ahumada (56/10). Trainer: Salvador Nocetti (13).
**Goal**: Julio Gallardo (90).

**234.** 06.07.1969 **CHILE - PARAGUAY** **0-0**
Estadio Nacional, Santiago; Referee: Aurelio Domingo Bossolino (Argentina); Attendance: 54,402
**CHI:** Adolfo Nef Sanhueza (7/0), Juan Rodríguez Vega (14/0), Gustavo Laube (7/1), Alberto Fernando Ralph Quintano (16/0), Daniel Díaz (7/0), Francisco Valdés Muñoz (25/3) [Guillermo Yávar (17/2)], Roberto Hodge (32/1), Pedro Damián Araya Toro (41/11), Julio Gallardo (10/4) [Adolfo Olivares (11/4)], Carlos Reinoso (19/4), Alberto Jorge Fouilloux Ahumada (57/10). Trainer: Salvador Nocetti (14).

**235.** 13.07.1969 **CHILE - URUGUAY** **0-0** 9th FIFA WC. Qualifiers
Estadio Nacional, Santiago; Referee: Aurelio Domingo Bossolino (Argentina); Attendance: 71,982
**CHI:** Adolfo Nef Sanhueza (8/0), Juan Rodríguez Vega (15/0), Gustavo Laube (8/1), Alberto Fernando Ralph Quintano (17/0), Daniel Díaz (8/0), Roberto Hodge (33/1), Francisco Valdés Muñoz (26/3), Pedro Damián Araya Toro (42/11), Carlos Reinoso (20/4), Adolfo Olivares (12/4), Alberto Jorge Fouilloux Ahumada (58/10) [36.Guillermo Yávar (18/2)]. Trainer: Salvador Nocetti (15).

**236.** 27.07.1969 **CHILE - ECUADOR** **4-1(0-0)** 9th FIFA WC. Qualifiers
Estadio Nacional, Santiago; Referee: Guillermo Velázquez Ramírez (Colombia); Attendance: 71,948
**CHI:** Adolfo Nef Sanhueza (9/0), Juan Rodríguez Vega (16/0), Gustavo Laube (9/1), Alberto Fernando Ralph Quintano (18/0), Daniel Díaz (9/0), Roberto Hodge (34/1), Francisco Valdés Muñoz (27/5), Pedro Damián Araya Toro (43/11), Adolfo Olivares (13/5) [84.Rubén Marcos (34/9)], Carlos Reinoso (21/4), Leonardo Véliz Díaz (6/1). Trainer: Salvador Nocetti (16).
**Goals**: Adolfo Olivares (55), Francisco Valdés Muñoz (62), Enrique Portilla (77 own goal), Francisco Valdés Muñoz (84).

**237.** 03.08.1969 **ECUADOR - CHILE** **1-1(1-0)** 9th FIFA WC. Qualifiers
Estadio Modelo, Guayaquil; Referee: Carlos Riveros (Peru); Attendance: 11,565
**CHI:** Adolfo Nef Sanhueza (10/0), Juan Rodríguez Vega (17/0), Gustavo Laube (10/1), Alberto Fernando Ralph Quintano (19/0), Daniel Díaz (10/0), Roberto Hodge (35/1), Rubén Marcos (35/9) [46.Guillermo Yávar (19/2)], Pedro Damián Araya Toro (44/11) [Reinaldo Hoffmann (1/0)], Adolfo Olivares (14/6), Carlos Reinoso (22/4), Leonardo Véliz Díaz (7/1). Trainer: Salvador Nocetti (17).
**Goal**: Adolfo Olivares (58).

**238.** 10.08.1969 **URUGUAY - CHILE** **2-0(1-0)** 9th FIFA WC. Qualifiers
Estadio Centenario, Montevideo; Referee: Armando Nunes Castanheiras da Rosa Marques (Brazil); Attendance: 62,693
**CHI:** Adolfo Nef Sanhueza (11/0), Juan Rodríguez Vega (18/0), Gustavo Laube (11/1), Alberto Fernando Ralph Quintano (20/0), Daniel Díaz (11/0), Roberto Hodge (36/1), Leonardo Véliz Díaz (8/1) [60.Alfonso Lara Madrid (8/0)], Carlos Reinoso (23/4), Adolfo Olivares (15/6), Guillermo Yávar (20/2), Reinaldo Hoffmann (2/0). Trainer: Salvador Nocetti (18).

**239.** 22.03.1970 **BRAZIL - CHILE** **5-0(4-0)**
Estádio „Cicero Pompeu de Toledo" Morumbi, São Paulo; Referee: Armando Nunes Castanheiras da Rosa Marques (Brazil); Attendance: 60,000
**CHI:** Manuel Astorga (10/0) [Leopoldo Manuel Vallejos Bravo (3/0)], Daniel Díaz (12/0), Gustavo Laube (12/1), Humberto Cruz (36/0), Eduardo Herrera (15/0), Luis Acevedo (1/0), Alberto Jorge Fouilloux Ahumada (59/10), Carlos Humberto Caszely Garrido (2/0) [*sent off*], Víctor Zelada (1/0) [Sergio Messen (1/0)], Osvaldo Castro (14/3), Reinaldo Hoffmann (3/0) [Moisés Silva (1/0)]. Trainer: Francisco Hormazábal (14).

**240.** 26.03.1970 **BRAZIL - CHILE** **2-1(0-1)**
Estádio „Jornalista Mario Filho" (Maracanã), Rio de Janeiro; Referee: Aírton Vieira de Moraes (Brazil); Attendance: 70,000
**CHI:** Leopoldo Manuel Vallejos Bravo (4/0), Daniel Díaz (13/0), Humberto Cruz (37/0), Gustavo Laube (13/1), Eduardo Herrera (16/0), Luis Acevedo (2/0), Moisés Silva (2/0), Eduardo Cortázar (1/0), Sergio Messen (2/0) [Víctor Zelada (2/0)], Osvaldo Castro (15/4), Carlos Humberto Caszely Garrido (3/0) [Hugo Berly (11/0)]. Trainer: Francisco Hormazábal (15).
**Goal**: Osvaldo Castro (18).

**241.** 04.10.1970 **CHILE - BRAZIL** **1-5**
Estadio Nacional, Santiago; Referee: Luis Pestarino (Argentina); Attendance: 73,000
**CHI:** Juan Carlos Olivares Sánchez (24/0), Juan Rodríguez Vega (19/0), Alberto Fernando Ralph Quintano (21/0), Gustavo Laube (14/1) [Antonio Arias Mújica (4/0)], Daniel Díaz (14/0), Roberto Hodge (37/1), Francisco Valdés Muñoz (28/5), Alberto Jorge Fouilloux Ahumada (60/10), Sergio Messen (3/1), Osvaldo Castro (16/4) [Esteban Aránguiz (1/0)], Leonardo Véliz Díaz (9/1) [Pedro Damián Araya Toro (45/11)]. Trainer: Fernando Riera Bauza (36).
**Goal**: Sergio Messen.

**242.** 14.07.1971 **CHILE - PARAGUAY** **3-2(2-0)**
Estadio Nacional, Santiago; Referee: Roberto Osvaldo Barreiro (Argentina); Attendance: 29,255
**CHI:** Juan Carlos Olivares Sánchez (25/0), Rolando Moisés García Jiménez (1/0), Juan Rodríguez Vega (20/0), Alberto Fernando Ralph Quintano (22/0), Francisco Pinochet (1/0), Carlos Pacheco (1/0), Gustavo Viveros (1/0), Pedro Damián Araya Toro (46/11), Alberto Jorge Fouilloux Ahumada (61/10) [Nelson Vásquez (1/0)], Osvaldo Castro (17/6), Fernando Osorio (1/1). Trainer: Luis Vera – Raúl Pino (1).
**Goals**: Fernando Osorio (2), Osvaldo Castro (39, 87).

**243.** 21.07.1971 **CHILE - ARGENTINA** **2-2(0-1)** Copa Carlos Dittborn
Estadio Nacional, Santiago; Referee: Arturo Andrés Ithurralde (Argentina); Attendance: 50,000
**CHI:** Leopoldo Manuel Vallejos Bravo (5/0), Rolando Moisés García Jiménez (2/0), Juan Rodríguez Vega (21/0), Alberto Fernando Ralph Quintano (23/0), Antonio Arias Mújica (5/0), Carlos Pacheco (2/0) [Nelson Vásquez (2/1)], Gustavo Viveros (2/1), Alberto Jorge Fouilloux Ahumada (62/10) [Claudio Gallegos (1/0)], Sergio Messen (4/1), Osvaldo Castro (18/6), Fernando Osorio (2/1). Trainer: Luis Vera – Raúl Pino (2).
**Goals**: Gustavo Viveros (54), Nelson Vásquez (89).

**244.** 04.08.1971 **ARGENTINA - CHILE** **1-0(0-0)** Copa Carlos Dittborn
Estadio „Alberto Armando“, Buenos Aires; Referee: Cantillana (Chile); Attendance: 30,000
**CHI:** Adolfo Nef Sanhueza (12/0), Rolando Moisés García Jiménez (3/0), Juan Rodríguez Vega (22/0) [Leonel Herrera (1/0)], Alberto Fernando Ralph Quintano (24/0), Francisco Pinochet (2/0), Eduardo Peralta (1/0), Gustavo Viveros (3/1), Carlos Pacheco (3/0), Pedro Damián Araya Toro (47/11) [Nelson Vásquez (3/1)], Osvaldo Castro (19/6), Fernando Osorio (3/1). Trainer: Luis Vera – Raúl Pino (3).

**245.** 08.08.1971 **PARAGUAY - CHILE** **2-0(2-0)**
Estadio Defensores del Chaco, Asunción; Attendance: 30,000
**CHI:** Leopoldo Manuel Vallejos Bravo (6/0), Rolando Moisés García Jiménez (4/0), Leonel Herrera (2/0), Alberto Fernando Ralph Quintano (25/0), Francisco Pinochet (3/0) [Antonio Arias Mújica (6/0)], Eduardo Peralta (2/0), Gustavo Viveros (4/1), Carlos Pacheco (4/0) [Sergio Messen (5/1)], Pedro Damián Araya Toro (48/11), Osvaldo Castro (20/6) [Claudio Gallegos (2/0)], Fernando Osorio (4/1). Trainer: Luis Vera – Raúl Pino (4).

**246.** 11.08.1971 **PERU - CHILE** **1-0(0-0)** Copa del Pacífico
Estadio Nacional, Lima; Attendance: 40,000
**CHI:** Adolfo Nef Sanhueza (13/0), Rolando Moisés García Jiménez (5/0), Leonel Herrera (3/0), Alberto Fernando Ralph Quintano (26/0), Antonio Arias Mújica (7/0), Eduardo Peralta (3/0) [Nelson Vásquez (4/1)], Gustavo Viveros (5/1), Carlos Pacheco (5/0), Pedro Damián Araya Toro (49/11), Sergio Messen (6/1) [Claudio Gallegos (3/0)], Fernando Osorio (5/1). Trainer: Luis Vera – Raúl Pino (5).

**247.** 18.08.1971 **CHILE - PERU** **1-0(0-0)** Copa del Pacífico
Estadio Nacional, Santiago; Attendance: 55,000
**CHI:** Adolfo Nef Sanhueza (14/0), Rolando Moisés García Jiménez (6/0), Leonel Herrera (4/0), Alberto Fernando Ralph Quintano (27/0), Francisco Pinochet (4/0), Nelson Vásquez (5/1), Gustavo Viveros (6/2) [Julián Urrizola (1/0)], Eduardo Peralta (4/0), Pedro Damián Araya Toro (50/11), Sergio Messen (7/1), Fernando Osorio (6/1) [Osvaldo Castro (21/6)]. Trainer: Luis Vera – Raúl Pino (6).
**Goal**: Gustavo Viveros (83).

**248.** 27.10.1971 **URUGUAY - CHILE** **3-0(2-0)** Copa Pinto Durán
Estadio Centenario, Montevideo; Referee: Peña Rocha (Uruguay); Attendance: 30,000
**CHI:** Adolfo Nef Sanhueza (15/0), Rolando Moisés García Jiménez (7/0), Juan Rodríguez Vega (23/0), Alberto Fernando Ralph Quintano (28/0), Antonio Arias Mújica (8/0), Eduardo Peralta (5/0), Gustavo Viveros (7/2), Carlos Pacheco (6/0) [Luis Pino (1/0)], Pedro Damián Araya Toro (51/11), Julio Crisosto (1/0) [Claudio Gallegos (4/0)], Fernando Osorio (7/1). Trainer: Luis Vera – Raúl Pino (7).

**249.** 03.11.1971 **CHILE - URUGUAY** **5-0(3-0)** Copa Pinto Durán
Estadio Nacional, Santiago; Referee: Juan Ambrosio Silvagno Cavanna (Chile); Attendance: 27,564
**CHI:** Adolfo Nef Sanhueza (16/0), Rolando Moisés García Jiménez (8/0), Juan Rodríguez Vega (24/0) [Leonel Herrera (5/0)], Alberto Fernando Ralph Quintano (29/0), Antonio Arias Mújica (9/0), Carlos Pacheco (7/1), Gustavo Viveros (8/2) [Nelson Vásquez (6/2)], Alberto Jorge Fouilloux Ahumada (63/10), Pedro Damián Araya Toro (52/12), Julio Crisosto (2/1), Fernando Osorio (8/2) [Luis Pino (2/0)]. Trainer: Luis Vera – Raúl Pino (8).
**Goals**: Fernando Osorio (22), Carlos Pacheco (27), Pedro Damián Araya Toro (37), Julio Crisosto (71), Nelson Vásquez (86).

**250.** 26.01.1972 **MEXICO – CHILE** **2-0(0-0)**
Estadio Monumental Jalisco, Guadalajara; Referee: Abel Aguilar (Mexico); Attendance: 55,000
**CHI:** Adolfo Nef Sanhueza (17/0), Rolando Moisés García Jiménez (9/0), Leonel Herrera (6/0), Rafael González Córdova (1/0), Eduardo Herrera (17/0), Alberto Jorge Fouilloux Ahumada (64/10) [77.Luis Pino (3/0)], Carlos Pacheco (8/1) [72.Guillermo Páez Cepeda (1/0)], Gustavo Viveros (9/2) [65.Alfonso Lara Madrid (9/0)], Rogelio Farías Salvador (1/0) [65.Fernando Espinoza (1/0)], Julio Crisosto (3/1), Fernando Osorio (9/2). Trainer: Raúl Pino (1).

**251.** 31.05.1972 **CHILE - ARGENTINA** **3-4(1-1)** Copa Carlos Dittborn
Estadio Nacional, Santiago; Referee: Humberto Oreste Dellacasa (Argentina); Attendance: 45,000
**CHI:** Adolfo Nef Sanhueza (18/0), Juan Salvador Machuca Valdéz (1/0), Gustavo Laube (15/1), Raúl Angulo (5/0) [Guillermo Azócar (1/0)], Antonio Arias Mújica (10/0), Francisco Valdés Muñoz (29/7), Alfonso Lara Madrid (10/0), Eduardo Peralta (6/0), Carlos Humberto Caszely Garrido (4/1), Julio Crisosto (4/1) [Rogelio Farías Salvador (2/0)], Alberto Jorge Fouilloux Ahumada (65/10). Trainer: Rudolf Guttendorf (1).
**Goals**: Francisco Valdés Muñoz (23, 48), Carlos Humberto Caszely Garrido (67).

**252.** 14.06.1972 **CHILE - ECUADOR** **2-1(0-0)** Brazil Independence Cup
Estádio „President Castelo Branco“, Natal (Brazil); Referee: Romualdo Arppi Filho (Brazil); Attendance: 10,000
**CHI:** Leopoldo Manuel Vallejos Bravo (7/0), Juan Salvador Machuca Valdéz (2/0), Guillermo Azócar (2/0), Raúl Angulo (6/0), Antonio Arias Mújica (11/0), Francisco Valdés Muñoz (30/7), Alfonso Lara Madrid (11/0), Eduardo Peralta (7/0), Alberto Jorge Fouilloux Ahumada (66/10) [Manuel Gaete (1/0)], Carlos Humberto Caszely Garrido (5/2), Leonardo Véliz Díaz (10/1) [Julio Crisosto (5/2)]. Trainer: Rudolf Guttendorf (2).
**Goals**: Julio Crisosto (51), Carlos Humberto Caszely Garrido (57).

**253.** 18.06.1972 **PORTUGAL - CHILE** **4-1(1-0)** Brazil Independence Cup
Estádio „José de Rego Maciel“, Recife (Brazil); Referee: Aurelio Angonese (Italy)
**CHI:** Leopoldo Manuel Vallejos Bravo (8/0), Juan Salvador Machuca Valdéz (3/0), Guillermo Azócar (3/0), Raúl Angulo (7/0), Antonio Arias Mújica (12/0), Francisco Valdés Muñoz (31/7) [Manuel Gaete (2/0)], Alfonso Lara Madrid (12/0), Eduardo Peralta (8/0), Carlos Humberto Caszely Garrido (6/3), Julio Crisosto (6/2) [Rogelio Farías Salvador (3/0)], Alberto Jorge Fouilloux Ahumada (Cap) (67/10). Trainer: Rudolf Guttendorf (3).
**Goal**: Carlos Humberto Caszely Garrido (56).

**254.** 21.06.1972 **CHILE – REPUBLIC OF IRELAND** **2-1(0-0)** Brazil Independence Cup
Estádio „José de Rego Maciel", Recife (Brazil); Referee: Romualdo Arppi Filho (Brazil)
**CHI:** Adolfo Nef Sanhueza (19/0), Juan Salvador Machuca Valdéz (4/0), Guillermo Azócar (4/0), Raúl Angulo (8/0), Antonio Arias Mújica (13/0), Alfonso Lara Madrid (13/0), Eduardo Peralta (9/0), Fernando Carvallo (1/0), Julio Crisosto (7/2) [Fernando Espinoza (2/0)], Carlos Humberto Caszely Garrido (7/4), Leonardo Véliz Díaz (11/1) [Alberto Jorge Fouilloux Ahumada (68/11)]. Trainer: Rudolf Guttendorf (4).
**Goals**: Carlos Humberto Caszely Garrido (60), Alberto Jorge Fouilloux Ahumada (68).

**255.** 25.06.1972 **CHILE - IRAN** **2-1** Brazil Independence Cup
Estádio „José de Rego Maciel", Recife (Brazil)
**CHI:** Adolfo Nef Sanhueza (20/0), Juan Salvador Machuca Valdéz (5/0), Guillermo Azócar (5/0), Raúl Angulo (9/0), Antonio Arias Mújica (14/0), Fernando Carvallo (2/0), Alfonso Lara Madrid (14/0), Eduardo Peralta (10/0), Fernando Espinoza (3/0) [Rogelio Farías Salvador (4/0)], Carlos Humberto Caszely Garrido (8/6), Alberto Jorge Fouilloux Ahumada (69/11). Trainer: Rudolf Guttendorf (5).
**Goals**: Carlos Humberto Caszely Garrido 2.

**256.** 16.08.1972 **CHILE - MEXICO** **0-2(0-1)**
Estadio Nacional, Santiago; Referee: Juan Ambrosio Silvagno Cavanna (Chile); Attendance: 35,000
**CHI:** Adolfo Sanhueza Nef (21/0) [Leopoldo Manuel Vallejos Bravo (9/0)], Juan Salvador Machuca Valdéz (6/0), Raúl Angulo (10/0), Francisco Pinochet (5/0), Guillermo Azócar (6/0), Alfonso Lara Madrid (15/0) [Guillermo Yávar (21/2)], Alberto Jorge Fouilloux Ahumada (70/11) [Fernando Espinoza (4/0)], Francisco Valdés Muñoz (32/7), Carlos Humberto Caszely Garrido (9/6), Eduardo Peralta (11/0), Víctor Manuel González (1/0) [Alejandro Trujillo (1/0)]. Trainer: Rudolf Guttendorf (6).

**257.** 27.09.1972 **ARGENTINA - CHILE** **2-0(1-0)** Copa Carlos Dittborn
Estadio „José Amalfitani", Buenos Aires; Referee: Alberto Martínez González (Chile); Attendance: 20,000
**CHI:** Juan Carlos Olivares Sánchez (26/0), Juan Salvador Machuca Valdéz (7/0) [Mario Enrique Galindo Calixto (1/0)], Leonel Herrera (7/0), Fernando Astudillo (1/0), Francisco Pinochet (6/0), Fernando Carvallo (3/0), Alfonso Lara Madrid (16/0), Hugo Solís (1/0), Estebán Aránguiz (2/0), Carlos Humberto Caszely Garrido (10/6), Sergio Messen (9/1) [Julio Crisosto (8/2)]. Trainer: Rudolf Guttendorf (7).

**258.** 14.04.1973 **HAITI - CHILE** **1-1**
Stade „François Duvalier", Port-au-Prince
**CHI:** Juan Carlos Olivares Sánchez (27/0), Juan Salvador Machuca Valdéz (8/0), Leonel Herrera (8/0), Rafael González Córdova (2/0), Antonio Arias Mújica (15/0), Francisco Valdés Muñoz (33/7) [Carlos Humberto Caszely Garrido (11/7)], Alfonso Lara Madrid (17/0) [Guillermo Páez Cepeda (2/0)], Jorge Luis Toro Sánchez (21/3), Gabriel Galleguillos González (1/0), Sergio Ahumada Bacho (1/0), Guillermo Muñoz (1/0). Trainer: Luis Alamos Luque (17).
**Goal**: Carlos Humberto Caszely Garrido.

**259.** 24.04.1973 **ECUADOR - CHILE** **1-1(0-1)**
Estadio Modelo, Guayaquil; Referee: Eduardo Rendón (Ecuador); Attendance: 30,000
**CHI:** Adolfo Nef Sanhueza (22/0), Mario Enrique Galindo Calixto (2/0) [Juan Salvador Machuca Valdéz (9/0)], Rafael González Córdova (3/0), Leonel Herrera (9/0), Antonio Arias Mújica (16/0), Francisco Valdés Muñoz (34/7), Alfonso Lara Madrid (18/0), Sergio Messen (10/1), Carlos Humberto Caszely Garrido (12/8), Sergio Ahumada Bacho (2/0) [Jorge Luis Toro Sánchez (22/3)], Guillermo Muñoz (2/0). Trainer: Luis Alamos Luque (18).
**Goal**: Carlos Humberto Caszely Garrido (5).

**260.** 29.04.1973 **PERU - CHILE** **2-0(1-0)** 10th FIFA WC. Qualifiers
Estadio Nacional, Lima; Referee: Armando Nunes Castanheiras da Rosa Marques (Brazil); Attendance: 42,947
**CHI:** Adolfo Nef Sanhueza (23/0), Juan Salvador Machuca Valdéz (10/0), Leonel Herrera (10/0), Alberto Fernando Ralph Quintano (30/0), Antonio Arias Mújica (17/0), Francisco Valdés Muñoz (35/7) [Jorge Luis Toro Sánchez (23/3)], Alfonso Lara Madrid (19/0), Sergio Messen (11/1) [*sent off 65*], Carlos Humberto Caszely Garrido (13/8), Sergio Ahumada Bacho (3/0) [Osvaldo Castro (22/6)], Guillermo Muñoz (3/0). Trainer: Luis Alamos Luque (19).

**261.** 13.05.1973 **CHILE - PERU** **2-0(0-0)** 10th FIFA WC. Qualifiers
Estadio Nacional, Santiago; Referee: Ramón Ivannoe Barreto Ruíz (Uruguay); Attendance: 69,881
**CHI:** Adolfo Nef Sanhueza (24/0), Mario Enrique Galindo Calixto (3/0), Alfonso Lara Madrid (20/0), Alberto Fernando Ralph Quintano (31/0), Antonio Arias Mújica (18/0), Francisco Valdés Muñoz (36/7), Guillermo Páez Cepeda (3/0), Guillermo Muñoz (4/0) [Osvaldo Castro (23/6)], Carlos Humberto Caszely Garrido (14/8) [Julio Crisosto (9/3)], Sergio Ahumada Bacho (4/1), Leonardo Véliz Díaz (12/1). Trainer: Luis Alamos Luque (20).
**Goals**: Julio Crisosto (68), Sergio Ahumada Bacho (71).

**262.** 13.07.1973 **ARGENTINA - CHILE** **5-4(3-2)** Copa Carlos Dittborn
Estadio „Alberto Armando", Buenos Aires; Referee: Armando Nunes Castanheiras da Rosa Marques (Brazil); Attendance: 25,000
**CHI:** Adolfo Nef Sanhueza (25/0), Mario Enrique Galindo Calixto (4/0) [Juan Salvador Machuca Valdéz (11/0)], Alfonso Lara Madrid (21/0), Rafael González Córdova (4/0), Antonio Arias Mújica (19/0), Francisco Valdés Muñoz (37/7), Guillermo Páez Cepeda (4/0) [Leonel Herrera (11/0)], Guillermo Muñoz (5/0), Carlos Humberto Caszely Garrido (15/9), Sergio Ahumada Bacho (5/3), Julio Crisosto (10/4). Trainer: Luis Alamos Luque (21).
**Goals**: Julio Crisosto (8), Carlos Humberto Caszely Garrido (15), Sergio Ahumada Bacho (18, 78).

**263.** 18.07.1973 **CHILE - ARGENTINA** **3-1(2-1)** Copa Carlos Dittborn
Estadio Nacional, Santiago; Referee: Ángel Eduardo Pazos Bianchi (Uruguay); Attendance: 35,000
**CHI:** Leopoldo Manuel Vallejos Bravo (10/0), Juan Salvador Machuca Valdéz (12/0), Leonel Herrera (12/0), Rafael González Córdova (5/0), Antonio Arias Mújica (20/0), Francisco Valdés Muñoz (38/7), Guillermo Páez Cepeda (5/0), Sergio Ahumada Bacho (6/3), Carlos Humberto Caszely Garrido (16/11) [Rogelio Farías Salvador (5/0)], Julio Crisosto (11/5), Leonardo Véliz Díaz (13/1) [Guillermo Muñoz (6/0)]. Trainer: Luis Alamos Luque (22).
**Goals**: Julio Crisosto (14), Carlos Humberto Caszely Garrido (34, 56).

**264.** 24.07.1973 **CHILE - BOLIVIA** **3-0(1-0)** Copa Leoncio Proveste
Estadio Nacional, Santiago; Referee: Arturo Maximo Yamasaki Maldonado (Peru); Attendance: 33,060
**CHI:** Juan Carlos Olivares Sánchez (28/0), Mario Enrique Galindo Calixto (5/0), Leonel Herrera (13/0) [Guillermo Azócar (7/0)], Rafael González Córdova (6/0), Eduardo Herrera (18/0), Nelson Vásquez (7/2), Alfonso Lara Madrid (22/0), Guillermo Muñoz (7/1), Rogelio Farías Salvador (6/1), Julio Crisosto (12/5), Hugo Solís (2/1). Trainer: Luis Alamos Luque (23).
**Goals**: Rogelio Farías Salvador (34), Guillermo Muñoz (56), Hugo Solís (77).

**265.** 05.08.1973 **CHILE - PERU** **2-1(1-1)** 10th FIFA WC. Qualifiers (Play-Off)
Estadio Centenario, Montevideo; Referee: Néstor Gregorio Da Rosa Caraballo (Uruguay); Attendance: 57,933
**CHI:** Juan Carlos Olivares Sánchez (29/0), Juan Salvador Machuca Valdéz (13/0), Juan Rodríguez Vega (25/0), Alberto Fernando Ralph Quintano (32/0), Antonio Arias Mújica (21/0), Francisco Valdés Muñoz (39/8), Alfonso Lara Madrid (23/0), Carlos Reinoso (24/4), Carlos Humberto Caszely Garrido (17/11), Sergio Ahumada Bacho (7/3) [46.Rogelio Farías Salvador (7/2)], Julio Crisosto (13/5). Trainer: Luis Alamos Luque (24).
**Goals**: Francisco Valdés Muñoz (45), Rogelio Farías Salvador (57).

**266.** 20.09.1973 **MEXICO - CHILE** **1-2(1-0)**
Estadio Azteca, Ciudad de México; Referee: Arturo Maximo Yamasaki Maldonado (Peru); Attendance: 100,000
**CHI:** Juan Carlos Olivares Sánchez (30/0), Juan Salvador Machuca Valdéz (14/0) [Mario Enrique Galindo Calixto (6/0)], Rafael González Córdova (7/0), Antonio Arias Mújica (22/0), Leonel Herrera (14/0), Guillermo Páez Cepeda (6/0), Francisco Valdés Muñoz (40/8), Sergio Ahumada Bacho (8/3), Rogelio Farías Salvador (8/2), Julio Crisosto (14/5) [Carlos Humberto Caszely Garrido (18/13)], Leonardo Véliz Díaz (14/1) [81.Alfonso Lara Madrid (24/0)]. Trainer: Luis Alamos Luque (25).
**Goals**: Carlos Humberto Caszely Garrido (68, 81).

**267.** 26.09.1973 **SOVIET UNION - CHILE** **0-0** 10th FIFA WC. Qualifiers (Play-Off)
Lenin Stadium, Moskva; Referee: Armando Nunes Castanheiras da Rosa Marques (Brazil); Attendance: 48,891
**CHI:** Juan Carlos Olivares Sánchez (31/0), Juan Salvador Machuca Valdéz (15/0), Alberto Fernando Ralph Quintano (33/0), Elías Ricardo Figueroa Brander (18/0), Antonio Arias Mújica (23/0), Juan Rodríguez Vega (26/0), Guillermo Páez Cepeda (7/0), Francisco Valdés Muñoz (41/8), Sergio Ahumada Bacho (9/3), Leonardo Véliz Díaz (15/1) [57.Julio Crisosto (15/5)], Carlos Humberto Caszely Garrido (19/13). Trainer: Luis Alamos Luque (26).
*The Soviet Union refused to send a team for the second leg to play in Santiago due to political reasons. After this withdraw, Chile qualified for the FIFA WC finals.*

**268.** 24.04.1974 **HAITI - CHILE** **0-1**
Stade „François Duvalier", Port-au-Prince
**CHI:** Juan Carlos Olivares Sánchez (32/0), Rolando Moisés García Jiménez (10/1), Alfonso Lara Madrid (25/0), Rafael González Córdova (8/0), Antonio Arias Mújica (24/0), Francisco Valdés Muñoz (42/8), Guillermo Páez Cepeda (8/0), Guillermo Yávar (22/2) [Jorge Socías Tuset (1/0)], Rogelio Farías Salvador (9/2), Sergio Ahumada Bacho (10/3), Leonardo Véliz Díaz (16/1) [Miguel Angel Gamboa Pedemonte (1/0)]. Trainer: Luis Alamos Luque (27).
**Goal**: Rolando Moisés García Jiménez.

**269.** 26.04.1974 **HAITI - CHILE** **0-0**
Stade „Silvio Cator", Port-au-Prince
**CHI:** Juan Carlos Olivares Sánchez (33/0), Juan Salvador Machuca Valdéz (16/0), Hugo Berly (12/0), Leonel Herrera (15/0), Vladimir David Bigorra López (1/0), Francisco Valdés Muñoz (43/8) [Rolando Moisés García Jiménez (11/1)], Guillermo Páez Cepeda (9/0) [Alfonso Lara Madrid (26/0)], Sergio Ahumada Bacho (11/3), Jorge Socías Tuset (2/0) [Guillermo Yávar (23/2)], Miguel Angel Gamboa Pedemonte (2/0), Leonardo Véliz Díaz (17/1). Trainer: Luis Alamos Luque (28).

**270.** 12.05.1974 **CHILE – REPUBLIC OF IRELAND** **1-2(1-1)**
Estadio Nacional, Santiago; Referee: Mario Líra González (Chile); Attendance: 50,000
**CHI:** Leopoldo Manuel Vallejos Bravo (11/0), Juan Salvador Machuca Valdéz (17/0), Rafael González Córdova (9/0), Alfonso Lara Madrid (27/0), Rolando Moisés García Jiménez (12/1), Francisco Valdés Muñoz (44/9), Guillermo Páez Cepeda (10/0), Carlos Reinoso (25/4) [*sent off 60*], Carlos Humberto Caszely Garrido (20/13), Osvaldo Castro (24/6) [Julio Crisosto (16/5)], Guillermo Yávar (24/2) [Leonardo Véliz Díaz (18/1)]. Trainer: Luis Alamos Luque (29).
**Goal**: Francisco Valdés Muñoz (40).

**271.** 14.06.1974 **WEST GERMANY - CHILE** **1-0(1-0)** 10th FIFA WC. Group Stage.
Olympiastadion, West-Berlin; Referee: Dogan Babaçan (Turkey); Attendance: 81,100
**CHI:** Leopoldo Manuel Vallejos Bravo (12/0), Rolando Moisés García Jiménez (13/1), Alberto Fernando Ralph Quintano (34/0), Elías Ricardo Figueroa Brander (19/0), Antonio Arias Mújica (25/0), Juan Rodríguez Vega (27/0) [84.Alfonso Lara Madrid (28/0)], Guillermo Páez Cepeda (11/0), Francisco Valdés Muñoz (45/9) [76.Leonardo Véliz Díaz (19/1)], Carlos Reinoso (26/4), Sergio Ahumada Bacho (12/3), Carlos Humberto Caszely Garrido (21/13) [*sent off 67*]. Trainer: Luis Alamos Luque (30).

**272.** 18.06.1974 **EAST GERMANY - CHILE** **1-1(0-0)** 10th FIFA WC. Group Stage.
Olympiastadion, West-Berlin (West Germany); Referee: Aurelio Angonese (Italy); Attendance: 28,300
**CHI:** Leopoldo Manuel Vallejos Bravo (13/0), Rolando Moisés García Jiménez (14/1), Alberto Fernando Ralph Quintano (35/0), Elías Ricardo Figueroa Brander (20/0), Antonio Arias Mújica (26/0), Guillermo Páez Cepeda (12/0), Francisco Valdés Muñoz (46/9) [46.Guillermo Yávar (25/2)], Carlos Reinoso (27/4), Jorge Socías Tuset (3/0) [66.Rogelio Farías Salvador (10/2)], Sergio Ahumada Bacho (13/4), Leonardo Véliz Díaz (20/1). Trainer: Luis Alamos Luque (31).
**Goal**: Sergio Ahumada Bacho (69).

**273.** 22.06.1974 **CHILE - AUSTRALIA** **0-0** 10th FIFA WC. Group Stage.
Olympiastadion, West-Berlin (West Germany); Referee: Jaffar Namdar (Iran); Attendance: 17,400
**CHI:** Leopoldo Manuel Vallejos Bravo (14/0), Rolando Moisés García Jiménez (15/1), Alberto Fernando Ralph Quintano (36/0), Elías Ricardo Figueroa Brander (21/0), Antonio Arias Mújica (27/0), Guillermo Páez Cepeda (13/0), Francisco Valdés Muñoz (47/9) [58.Rogelio Farías Salvador (11/2)], Carlos Reinoso (28/4), Sergio Ahumada Bacho (14/4), Leonardo Véliz Díaz (21/1) [72.Guillermo Yávar (26/2)], Carlos Humberto Caszely Garrido (22/13). Trainer: Luis Alamos Luque (32).

**274.** 06.11.1974 **CHILE - ARGENTINA** **0-2(0-0)** Copa Carlos Dittborn
Estadio Nacional, Santiago; Referee: Alberto Ducatelli (Argentina); Attendance: 45,000
**CHI:** Adolfo Nef Sanhueza (26/0), Juan Salvador Machuca Valdéz (18/0), Leonel Herrera (16/0), Rafael González Córdova (10/0), Francisco Pinochet (7/0), Javier Méndez (1/0), Sergio Ramírez (1/0), Manuel Gaete (3/0) [Miguel Angel Gamboa Pedemonte (3/0); Leonardo Véliz Díaz (22/1)], Luis Antonio Araneda Jorquera (1/0) [Alejandro Trujillo (2/0)], Sergio Ahumada Bacho (15/4), Pedro Pinto (1/0). Trainer: Pedro Morales (1).

**275.** 20.11.1974 **ARGENTINA - CHILE** **1-1(1-1)** Copa Carlos Dittborn
Estadio „José Amalfitani", Buenos Aires; Referee: Juan Ambrosio Silvagno Cavanna (Chile); Attendance: 20,000
**CHI:** Adolfo Nef Sanhueza (27/0), Mario Enrique Galindo Calixto (7/0), Leonel Herrera (17/0), Rafael González Córdova (11/0), Francisco Pinochet (8/0), Javier Méndez (2/1) [Francisco Valdés Muñoz (48/9)], Eddio Victorino Inostroza Ibacache (1/0), Sergio Ramírez (2/0), Alejandro Trujillo (3/0) [Héctor Pinto (1/0)], Sergio Ahumada Bacho (16/4), Leonardo Véliz Díaz (23/1). Trainer: Pedro Morales (2).
**Goal**: Javier Méndez (15).

**276.** 22.12.1974 **CHILE - PARAGUAY** **1-0**
Estadio Nacional, Santiago
**CHI:** Adolfo Nef Sanhueza (28/0), Mario Enrique Galindo Calixto (8/0), Elías Ricardo Figueroa Brander (22/0), Rafael González Córdova (12/0), Rolando Moisés García Jiménez (16/1), Javier Méndez (3/1) [Francisco Valdés Muñoz (49/9)], Eddio Victorino Inostroza Ibacache (2/0), Sergio Ramírez (3/0), Julio Crisosto (17/5), Sergio Ahumada Bacho (17/4) [Héctor Pinto (2/0)], Miguel Angel Gamboa Pedemonte (4/1) [Pedro Pinto (2/0)]. Trainer: Pedro Morales (3).
**Goal**: Miguel Angel Gamboa Pedemonte.

**277.** 04.06.1975 **URUGUAY - CHILE** **1-0(0-0)** Copa Pinto Durán
Estadio Centenario, Montevideo; Referee: José Luis Martínez Bazán (Uruguay); Attendance: 23,000
**CHI:** Adolfo Nef Sanhueza (29/0), Daniel Díaz (15/0), Leonel Herrera (18/0), Rafael González Córdova (13/0), Francisco Pinochet (9/0), Carlos Humberto Rivas Torres (1/0), Julián Urrizola (2/0), Sergio Ramírez (4/0), Patricio Ponce (1/0) [Alberto Hidalgo (1/0)], Héctor Pinto (3/0) [Víctor Pizarro (1/0)], Pedro Pinto (3/0). Trainer: Pedro Morales (4).

**278.** 25.06.1975 **CHILE - URUGUAY** **1-3(1-2)** Copa Pinto Durán
Estadio „Santa Laura", Santiago; Referee: Víctor Sergio Vásquez Sánchez (Chile); Attendance: 16,473
**CHI:** Adolfo Nef Sanhueza (30/0), Rolando Moisés García Jiménez (17/1), Leonel Herrera (19/0), Rafael González Córdova (14/0), Daniel Díaz (16/0), Carlos Humberto Rivas Torres (2/0), Julián Urrizola (3/0), Sergio Ramírez (5/0) [Alberto Hidalgo (2/0)], Héctor Pinto (4/1) [Víctor Pizarro (2/0)], Julio Crisosto (18/5), Pedro Pinto (4/0). Trainer: Pedro Morales (5).
**Goal**: Héctor Pinto (40).

**279.** 17.07.1975 **CHILE - PERU** **1-1(1-0)** 30th Copa América. Group Stage
Estadio Nacional, Santiago; Referee: Omar Delgado Piedrahita (Colombia); Attendance: 13,651
**CHI:** Leopoldo Manuel Vallejos Bravo (15/0), Mario del Transito Soto Benavides (1/0), Mario Enrique Galindo Calixto (9/0), Rafael González Córdova (15/0), Daniel Díaz (17/0), Francisco Las Heras (1/0), Alfonso Lara Madrid (29/0) [Francisco Valdés Muñoz (50/9)], Leonardo Véliz Díaz (24/1), Julio Crisosto (19/6) [Jorge Américo Spedaletti González (1/0)], Sergio Ahumada Bacho (18/4), Miguel Angel Gamboa Pedemonte (5/1). Trainer: Pedro Morales (6).
**Goal**: Julio Crisosto (10).

**280.** 20.07.1975 **BOLIVIA - CHILE** **2-1** 30th Copa América. Group Stage
Estadio „Jesús Bermúdez", Oruro; Referee: Héctor Ortíz (Paraguay); Attendance: 18,000
**CHI:** Leopoldo Manuel Vallejos Bravo (16/0), Mario Enrique Galindo Calixto (10/0), Mario del Transito Soto Benavides (2/0), Rafael González Córdova (16/0), Daniel Díaz (18/0), Javier Méndez (4/1), Eddio Victorino Inostroza Ibacache (3/0), Francisco Las Heras (2/0) [Leonel Herrera (20/0)], Leonardo Véliz Díaz (25/1) [Sergio Ahumada Bacho (19/4)], Jorge Américo Spedaletti González (2/0), Miguel Angel Gamboa Pedemonte (6/2). Trainer: Pedro Morales (7).
**Goal**: Miguel Angel Gamboa Pedemonte (41).

**281.** 13.08.1975 **CHILE - BOLIVIA** **4-0(1-0)** 30th Copa América. Group Stage
Estadio Nacional, Santiago; Referee: Arturo Andrés Ithurralde (Argentina); Attendance: 15,000
**CHI:** Adolfo Nef Sanhueza (31/0), Juan Salvador Machuca Valdéz (19/0), Mario del Transito Soto Benavides (3/0), Rafael González Córdova (17/0), Daniel Díaz (19/0), Carlos Reinoso (29/4), Eddio Victorino Inostroza Ibacache (4/0) [Jorge Américo Spedaletti González (3/0)], Francisco Las Heras (3/0), Luis Antonio Araneda Jorquera (2/2), Sergio Ahumada Bacho (20/5), Miguel Angel Gamboa Pedemonte (7/3). Trainer: Pedro Morales (8).
**Goals**: Luis Antonio Araneda Jorquera (40), Sergio Ahumada Bacho (61), Miguel Angel Gamboa Pedemonte (71), Luis Antonio Araneda Jorquera (87).

**282.** 20.08.1975 **PERU - CHILE** **3-1(3-0)** 30th Copa América. Group Stage
Estadio Nacional, Santiago; Referee: Juan José Fortunato (Uruguay); Attendance: 40,000
**CHI:** Adolfo Nef Sanhueza (32/0), Juan Salvador Machuca Valdéz (20/0), Mario del Transito Soto Benavides (4/0), Rafael González Córdova (18/0), Daniel Díaz (20/0), Carlos Reinoso (30/5), Eddio Victorino Inostroza Ibacache (5/0) [Jorge Américo Spedaletti González (4/0)], Francisco Las Heras (4/0), Luis Antonio Araneda Jorquera (3/2), Sergio Ahumada Bacho (21/5), Miguel Angel Gamboa Pedemonte (8/3) [Leonardo Véliz Díaz (26/1)]. Trainer: Pedro Morales (9).
**Goals**: Carlos Reinoso (76).

**283.** 06.10.1976 **CHILE - URUGUAY** **0-0** Copa Pinto Durán
Estadio Nacional, Santiago; Referee: Carvajal (Chile); Attendance: 35,000
**CHI:** Adolfo Nef Sanhueza (33/0), Enzo Sergio Escobar Olivares (1/0), Leonel Herrera (21/0), Mario del Transito Soto Benavides (5/0), Antonio Arias Mújica (28/0), Mario Salinas (1/0), Nélson Sanhueza Graavendaal (1/0), Miguel Angel Neira Pincheira (1/0), Leonardo Véliz Díaz (27/1) [Luis Antonio Araneda Jorquera (4/2)], Víctor Pizarro (3/0) [Julio Crisosto (20/6)], Gustavo Segundo Moscoso Huencho (1/0). Trainer: Caupolicán Peña (1).

**284.** 13.10.1976 **ARGENTINA - CHILE** **2-0(1-0)** Copa Carlos Dittborn
Estadio „José Amalfitani", Buenos Aires; Referee: Ramón Ivannoe Barreto Ruíz (Uruguay); Attendance: 40,000
**CHI:** Adolfo Nef Sanhueza (34/0), Enzo Sergio Escobar Olivares (2/0), Leonel Herrera (22/0), Rafael González Córdova (19/0), Antonio Arias Mújica (29/0), Nélson Sanhueza Graavendaal (2/0), Mario del Transito Soto Benavides (6/0), Miguel Angel Neira Pincheira (2/0), Leonardo Véliz Díaz (28/1) [Luis Miranda (1/0)], Julio Crisosto (21/6) [Mario Salinas (2/0)], Gustavo Segundo Moscoso Huencho (2/0). Trainer: Caupolicán Peña (2).

**285.** 26.01.1977 **CHILE - PARAGUAY** **4-0(3-0)**
Estadio Nacional, Santiago; Referee: Alberto Martínez (Chile); Attendance: 20,557
**CHI:** Adolfo Nef Sanhueza (35/0), Mario Enrique Galindo Calixto (11/0), Mario del Transito Soto Benavides (7/0), Alberto Fernando Ralph Quintano (37/0) [Leonel Herrera (23/0)], Enzo Sergio Escobar Olivares (3/0), Manuel Antonio Rojas Zuniga (1/1), Rodolfo del Rosario Dubó Segovia (1/0), Sergio Ahumada Bacho (22/5) [Héctor Pinto (5/1)], Luis Miranda (2/0) [Leonardo Véliz Díaz (29/1)], Julio Crisosto (22/9), Juan Carlos Orellana Jara (1/0). Trainer: Caupolicán Peña (3).
**Goals**: Julio Crisosto (9), Manuel Antonio Rojas Zuniga (19), Julio Crisosto (35, 75).

**286.** 30.01.1977 **URUGUAY - CHILE** **3-0(0-0)** Copa Pinto Durán
Estadio Centenario, Montevideo; Referee: Ángel Norberto Coerezza (Argentina); Attendance: 20,000
**CHI:** Leopoldo Manuel Vallejos Bravo (17/0), Mario Enrique Galindo Calixto (12/0), Alberto Fernando Ralph Quintano (38/0), Leonel Herrera (24/0), Enzo Sergio Escobar Olivares (4/0), Manuel Antonio Rojas Zuniga (2/1) [Mario del Transito Soto Benavides (8/0)], Rodolfo del Rosario Dubó Segovia (2/0), Héctor Pinto (6/1), Luis Miranda (3/0), Julio Crisosto (23/9), Juan Carlos Orellana Jara (2/0) [Sergio Ahumada Bacho (23/5)]. Trainer: Caupolicán Peña (4).

**287.** 02.02.1977 **PARAGUAY - CHILE** **2-0(1-0)**
Estadio Defensores del Chaco, Asunción; Referee: Artémio Martínez (Paraguay); Attendance: 15,037
**CHI:** Adolfo Nef Sanhueza (36/0), Mario Enrique Galindo Calixto (13/0) [Antonio Arias Mújica (30/0)], Alberto Fernando Ralph Quintano (39/0), Mario del Transito Soto Benavides (9/0), Enzo Sergio Escobar Olivares (5/0), Manuel Antonio Rojas Zuniga (3/1) [Mario Salinas (3/0)], Rodolfo del Rosario Dubó Segovia (3/0), Héctor Pinto (7/1), Sergio Ahumada Bacho (24/5), Julio Crisosto (24/9), Juan Carlos Orellana Jara (3/0). Trainer: Caupolicán Peña (5).

**288.** 27.02.1977 **ECUADOR - CHILE** **0-1(0-1)** 11th FIFA WC. Qualifiers
Estadio Modelo, Guayaquil; Referee: Jorge Eduardo Romero (Argentina); Attendance: 51,200
**CHI:** Adolfo Nef Sanhueza (37/0), Daniel Díaz (21/0), Elías Ricardo Figueroa Brander (23/0), Alberto Fernando Ralph Quintano (40/0), Enzo Sergio Escobar Olivares (6/0), Carlos Reinoso (31/5), Roberto Hodge (38/1), Ignacio Prieto (28/3) [Mario del Transito Soto Benavides (10/0)], Sergio Ahumada Bacho (25/5), Osvaldo Castro (25/6), Miguel Angel Gamboa Pedemonte (9/4). Trainer: Caupolicán Peña (6).
**Goal**: Miguel Angel Gamboa Pedemonte (33).

**289.** 06.03.1977 **CHILE - PERU** **1-1(1-0)** 11th FIFA WC. Qualifiers
Estadio Nacional, Santiago; Referee: José Faville Neto (Brazil); Attendance: 67,983
**CHI:** Adolfo Nef Sanhueza (38/0), Daniel Díaz (22/0), Elías Ricardo Figueroa Brander (24/0), Alberto Fernando Ralph Quintano (41/0), Enzo Sergio Escobar Olivares (7/0), Carlos Reinoso (32/5), Roberto Hodge (39/1), Ignacio Prieto (29/3) [40.Sergio Ahumada Bacho (26/6)], Luis Miranda (4/0) [67.Mario del Transito Soto Benavides (11/0)], Osvaldo Castro (26/6), Miguel Angel Gamboa Pedemonte (10/4). Trainer: Caupolicán Peña (7).
**Goal**: Sergio Ahumada Bacho (42).

**290.** 20.03.1977 **CHILE - ECUADOR** **3-0(2-0)** 11th FIFA WC. Qualifiers
Estadio Nacional, Santiago; Referee: Vicente Llobregat Vicedo (Venezuela); Attendance: 15,571
**CHI:** Adolfo Nef Sanhueza (39/0), Mario Enrique Galindo Calixto (14/0), Elías Ricardo Figueroa Brander (25/2), Alberto Fernando Ralph Quintano (42/0), Enzo Sergio Escobar Olivares (8/0), Manuel Antonio Rojas Zuniga (4/1) [Sergio Ahumada Bacho (27/6)], Rodolfo del Rosario Dubó Segovia (4/0), Héctor Pinto (8/1), Carlos Reinoso (33/5), Osvaldo Castro (27/7) [Julio Crisosto (25/9)], Pedro Pinto (5/0). Trainer: Caupolicán Peña (8).
**Goals**: Elías Ricardo Figueroa Brander (29), Osvaldo Castro (40), Elías Ricardo Figueroa Brander (55).

**291.** 26.03.1977 **PERU - CHILE** **2-0(0-0)** 11th FIFA WC. Qualifiers
Estadio Nacional, Lima; Referee: Arnaldo David César Coelho (Brazil); Attendance: 40,000
**CHI:** Leopoldo Manuel Vallejos Bravo (18/0), Daniel Díaz (23/0), Elías Ricardo Figueroa Brander (26/2), Alberto Fernando Ralph Quintano (43/0), Enzo Sergio Escobar Olivares (9/0), Héctor Pinto (9/1), Eddio Victorino Inostroza Ibacache (6/0), Rodolfo del Rosario Dubó Segovia (5/0) [Sergio Ahumada Bacho (28/6)], Carlos Reinoso (34/5), Jorge Américo Spedaletti González (5/0), Osvaldo Castro (28/7) [Pedro Pinto (6/0)]. Trainer: Caupolicán Peña (9).

**292.** 15.06.1977 **CHILE - SCOTLAND** **2-4(0-3)**
Estadio Nacional, Santiago; Referee: Juan Amrosio Silvagno Cavanna (Chile); Attendance: 60,000
**CHI:** Adolfo Nef Sanhueza (40/0), Juan Salvador Machuca Valdéz (21/0), Alberto Fernando Ralph Quintano (44/0), Elías Ricardo Figueroa Brander (27/2), Enzo Sergio Escobar Olivares (10/0), Waldo Quiróz (1/0), Eddio Victorino Inostroza Ibacache (7/0), Héctor Pinto (10/1), Juan Soto Quintana (1/0) [37.Julio Crisosto (26/11)], Rogelio Farías Salvador (12/2) [79.Gustavo Segundo Moscoso Huencho (3/0)], Leonardo Véliz Díaz (30/1). Trainer: Oscar Luis Santibáñez Díaz (1).
**Goals**: Julio Crisosto (48, 72).

**293.** 13.06.1979 **CHILE - ECUADOR** **0-0**
Estadio Nacional, Santiago; Referee: Jorge Eduardo Romero (Argentina); Attendance: 19,105
**CHI:** Manuel Araya (1/0), Mario Enrique Galindo Calixto (15/0), Elías Ricardo Figueroa Brander (28/2), Alberto Fernando Ralph Quintano (45/0), René Serrano (1/0), Manuel Antonio Rojas Zuniga (5/1) [Víctor Alejandro Merello Escobar (1/0)], Eduardo Guillermo Bonvallet Godoy (1/0), Miguel Angel Neira Pincheira (3/0), Jorge Neumann (1/0) [Patricio Nazario Yáñez Candia (1/0)], Juan Carlos Letelier Pizarro (1/0), Gustavo Segundo Moscoso Huencho (4/0). Trainer: Oscar Luis Santibáñez Díaz (2).

**294.** 21.06.1979 **ECUADOR - CHILE** **2-1(1-1)**
Estadio Modelo, Guayaquil; Referee: José Ramírez (Peru); Attendance: 35,000
**CHI:** Manuel Araya (2/0), Mario Enrique Galindo Calixto (16/0), Elías Ricardo Figueroa Brander (29/2), Alberto Fernando Ralph Quintano (46/0), René Serrano (2/0), Víctor Alejandro Merello Escobar (2/0) [Manuel Antonio Rojas Zuniga (6/1)], Eduardo Guillermo Bonvallet Godoy (2/0), Miguel Angel Neira Pincheira (4/0), Patricio Nazario Yáñez Candia (2/0), Juan Carlos Letelier Pizarro (2/0), Gustavo Segundo Moscoso Huencho (5/1). Trainer: Oscar Luis Santibáñez Díaz (3).
**Goal**: Gustavo Segundo Moscoso Huencho (42).

**295.** 11.07.1979 **CHILE - URUGUAY** **1-0(1-0)** Copa Pinto Durán
Estadio Nacional, Santiago; Referee: José Luis Martínez Bazán (Uruguay); Attendance: 23,000
**CHI:** Mario Ignacio Osbén Méndez (1/0), Raúl González (1/0), Leonel Herrera (25/0), Elías Ricardo Figueroa Brander (30/3), Enzo Sergio Escobar Olivares (11/0), Carlos Humberto Rivas Torres (3/0) [Waldo Quiróz (2/0)], Rodolfo del Rosario Dubó Segovia (6/0), Miguel Angel Neira Pincheira (5/0), Jorge Neumann (2/0), Víctor Estay (1/0) [Patricio Nazario Yáñez Candia (3/0)], Pedro Pinto (7/0) [Gustavo Segundo Moscoso Huencho (6/1)]. Trainer: Oscar Luis Santibáñez Díaz (4).
**Goal**: Elías Ricardo Figueroa Brander (23).

**296.** 18.07.1979 **URUGUAY - CHILE** **2-1(0-0)** Copa Pinto Durán
Estadio Centenario, Montevideo; Referee: Alberto Martínez (Chile); Attendance: 31,000
**CHI:** Mario Ignacio Osbén Méndez (2/0), Raúl González (2/0), Eduardo René Valenzuela Becker (1/0), Elías Ricardo Figueroa Brander (31/3), Enzo Sergio Escobar Olivares (12/0), Carlos Humberto Rivas Torres (4/0), Rodolfo del Rosario Dubó Segovia (7/0), Miguel Angel Neira Pincheira (6/0) [Waldo Quiróz (3/1)], Jorge Neumann (3/0) [Patricio Nazario Yáñez Candia (4/0)], Víctor Estay (2/0), Pedro Pinto (8/0). Trainer: Oscar Luis Santibáñez Díaz (5).
**Goal**: Waldo Quiróz (88).

**297.** 08.08.1979 **VENEZUELA - CHILE** **1-1(0-0)** 31st Copa América. Group Stage
Estadio Pueblo Nuevo, San Cristóbal; Referee: César Humberto Pagano Trucios (Peru); Attendance: 14,000
**CHI:** Mario Ignacio Osbén Méndez (3/0), Raúl González (3/0), Eduardo René Valenzuela Becker (2/0), Mario del Transito Soto Benavides (12/0), Enzo Sergio Escobar Olivares (13/0), Carlos Humberto Rivas Torres (5/0) [Waldo Quiróz (4/1)], Rodolfo del Rosario Dubó Segovia (8/0), Miguel Angel Neira Pincheira (7/0), Patricio Nazario Yáñez Candia (5/0), Jorge Sigfrido Peredo Gutiérrez (1/1), Leonardo Véliz Díaz (31/1). Trainer: Oscar Luis Santibáñez Díaz (6).
**Goal**: Jorge Sigfrido Peredo Gutiérrez (82).

**298.** 15.08.1979 **COLOMBIA - CHILE** **1-0(1-0)** 31st Copa América. Group Stage
Estadio „Nemesio Camacho" 'El Campín', Bogotá; Referee: Romualdo Arppi Filho (Brazil); Attendance: 40,000
**CHI:** Mario Ignacio Osbén Méndez (4/0), Raúl González (4/0), Eduardo René Valenzuela Becker (3/0), Alberto Fernando Ralph Quintano (47/0), Mario del Transito Soto Benavides (13/0), Enzo Sergio Escobar Olivares (14/0), Eduardo Guillermo Bonvallet Godoy (3/0), Carlos Humberto Rivas Torres (6/0), Waldo Quiróz (5/1), Miguel Angel Neira Pincheira (8/0), Víctor Estay (3/0) [Jorge Sigfrido Peredo Gutiérrez (2/1)]. Trainer: Oscar Luis Santibáñez Díaz (7).

**299.** 29.08.1979 **CHILE - VENEZUELA** **7-0(3-0)** 31st Copa América. Group Stage
Estadio Nacional, Santiago; Referee: Enrique Labó Revoredo (Peru); Attendance: 67,491
**CHI:** Mario Ignacio Osbén Méndez (5/0), Mario Enrique Galindo Calixto (17/0), Eduardo René Valenzuela Becker (4/0), Mario del Transito Soto Benavides (14/1), Enzo Sergio Escobar Olivares (15/0), Carlos Humberto Rivas Torres (7/2), Manuel Antonio Rojas Zuniga (7/1) [Miguel Angel Neira Pincheira (9/0)], Patricio Nazario Yáñez Candia (6/1), Jorge Sigfrido Peredo Gutiérrez (3/3), Carlos Humberto Caszely Garrido (23/13), Leonardo Véliz Díaz (32/2). Trainer: Oscar Luis Santibáñez Díaz (8).
**Goals**: Jorge Sigfrido Peredo Gutiérrez (5), Leonardo Véliz Díaz (31), Carlos Humberto Rivas Torres (38, 54), Jorge Sigfrido Peredo Gutiérrez (60), Mario del Transito Soto Benavides (72), Patricio Nazario Yáñez Candia (80).

**300.** 05.09.1979 **CHILE - COLOMBIA** **2-0(1-0)** 31st Copa América. Group Stage
Estadio Nacional, Santiago; Referee: Wilfredo Cáceres (Paraguay); Attendance: 78,494
**CHI:** Mario Ignacio Osbén Méndez (6/0), Mario Enrique Galindo Calixto (18/0), Eduardo René Valenzuela Becker (5/0), Mario del Transito Soto Benavides (15/1), Enzo Sergio Escobar Olivares (16/0), Carlos Humberto Rivas Torres (8/2), Manuel Antonio Rojas Zuniga (8/1) [Miguel Angel Neira Pincheira (10/0)], Patricio Nazario Yáñez Candia (7/1) [Eduardo Guillermo Bonvallet Godoy (4/0)], Jorge Sigfrido Peredo Gutiérrez (4/4), Carlos Humberto Caszely Garrido (24/14), Leonardo Véliz Díaz (33/2). Trainer: Oscar Luis Santibáñez Díaz (9).
**Goals**: Carlos Humberto Caszely Garrido (14), Jorge Sigfrido Peredo Gutiérrez (58).

**301.** 17.10.1979 **PERU - CHILE** **1-2(0-1)** 31st Copa América. Semi-Finals.
Estadio Nacional, Lima; Referee: Romualdo Arppi Filho (Brazil); Attendance: 43,724
**CHI:** Mario Ignacio Osbén Méndez (7/0), Mario Enrique Galindo Calixto (19/0), Eduardo René Valenzuela Becker (6/0), Elías Ricardo Figueroa Brander (32/3), Enzo Sergio Escobar Olivares (17/0), Carlos Humberto Rivas Torres (9/2), Rodolfo del Rosario Dubó Segovia (9/0), Mario del Transito Soto Benavides (16/1), Manuel Antonio Rojas Zuniga (9/1), Carlos Humberto Caszely Garrido (25/16) [81.Eduardo Guillermo Bonvallet Godoy (5/0)], Jorge Sigfrido Peredo Gutiérrez (5/4). Trainer: Oscar Luis Santibáñez Díaz (10).
**Goals**: Carlos Humberto Caszely Garrido (36, 76).

**302.** 24.10.1979 **CHILE - PERU** **0-0** 31st Copa América. Semi-Finals.
Estadio Nacional, Santiago; Referee: Juan Daniel Cardellino de San Vicente (Uruguay); Attendance: 75,681
**CHI:** Mario Ignacio Osbén Méndez (8/0), Mario Enrique Galindo Calixto (20/0), Eduardo René Valenzuela Becker (7/0), Elías Ricardo Figueroa Brander (33/3), Enzo Sergio Escobar Olivares (18/0), Carlos Humberto Rivas Torres (10/2), Rodolfo del Rosario Dubó Segovia (10/0) [63.Eduardo Guillermo Bonvallet Godoy (6/0)], Manuel Antonio Rojas Zuniga (10/1), Patricio Nazario Yáñez Candia (8/1), Carlos Humberto Caszely Garrido (26/16), Leonardo Véliz Díaz (34/2) [46.Mario del Transito Soto Benavides (17/1)]. Trainer: Oscar Luis Santibáñez Díaz (11).

**303.** 28.11.1979 **PARAGUAY - CHILE** **3-0(2-0)** 31st Copa América.Final.
Estadio Defensores del Chaco, Asunción; Referee: José Luis da Rosa Barbosa (Uruguay); Attendance: 36,684
**CHI:** Mario Ignacio Osbén Méndez (9/0), Mario Enrique Galindo Calixto (21/0), Eduardo René Valenzuela Becker (8/0), Alberto Fernando Ralph Quintano (48/0), Enzo Sergio Escobar Olivares (19/0), Carlos Humberto Rivas Torres (11/2), Mario del Transito Soto Benavides (18/1), Eduardo Guillermo Bonvallet Godoy (7/0) [46.Víctor Estay (4/0)], Manuel Antonio Rojas Zuniga (11/1), Carlos Humberto Caszely Garrido (27/16), Oscar Roberto Fabbiani Venturelli (1/0). Trainer: Oscar Luis Santibáñez Díaz (12).

**304.** 05.12.1979 **CHILE - PARAGUAY** **1-0(1-0)** 31st Copa América.Final.
Estadio Nacional, Santiago; Referee: Ramón Ivannoe Barreto Ruíz (Uruguay); Attendance: 51,193
**CHI:** Mario Ignacio Osbén Méndez (10/0), Mario Enrique Galindo Calixto (22/0), Eduardo René Valenzuela Becker (9/0), Elías Ricardo Figueroa Brander (34/3), Enzo Sergio Escobar Olivares (20/0), Carlos Humberto Rivas Torres (12/3), Eduardo Guillermo Bonvallet Godoy (8/0) [*sent off 17*], Manuel Antonio Rojas Zuniga (12/1) [85.Miguel Angel Neira Pincheira (11/0)], Carlos Humberto Caszely Garrido (28/16), Oscar Roberto Fabbiani Venturelli (2/0) [56.Víctor Estay (5/0)], Leonardo Véliz Díaz (35/2). Trainer: Oscar Luis Santibáñez Díaz (13).
**Goal**: Carlos Humberto Rivas Torres (10).

**305.** 11.12.1979 **PARAGUAY - CHILE** **0-0 a.e.t.** 31st Copa América.Final.
Estadio „José Amalfitani", Buenos Aires; Referee: Arnaldo César David Coelho (Brazil); Attendance: 6,000
**CHI:** Mario Ignacio Osbén Méndez (11/0), Mario Enrique Galindo Calixto (23/0), Elías Ricardo Figueroa Brander (35/3), Eduardo René Valenzuela Becker (10/0), Enzo Sergio Escobar Olivares (21/0), Carlos Humberto Rivas Torres (13/3), Rodolfo del Rosario Dubó Segovia (11/0) [90.Víctor Estay (6/0)], Manuel Antonio Rojas Zuniga (13/1), Carlos Humberto Caszely Garrido (29/16), Oscar Roberto Fabbiani Venturelli (3/0) [61.Patricio Nazario Yáñez Candia (9/1)], Leonardo Véliz Díaz (36/2). Trainer: Oscar Luis Santibáñez Díaz (14).

**306.** 24.06.1980 **BRAZIL - CHILE** **2-1(2-0)**
Estádio Mineirão, Belo Horizonte; Referee: Oscar Scolfaro (Brazil); Attendance: 60,000
**CHI:** Oscar Raúl Wirth Lafuente (1/0), Enzo Sergio Escobar Olivares (22/0), Eduardo René Valenzuela Becker (11/0), Elías Ricardo Figueroa Brander (36/3), Mario del Transito Soto Benavides (19/1), Vladimir David Bigorra López (2/0), Luis Rojas (1/0) [Jorge Socías Tuset (4/0)], Manuel Antonio Rojas Zuniga (14/1) [Juan Carlos Orellana Jara (4/0)], Eddio Victorino Inostroza Ibacache (8/0), Carlos Humberto Rivas Torres (14/3), Patricio Nazario Yáñez Candia (10/2). Trainer: Oscar Luis Santibáñez Díaz (15).
**Goal**: Patricio Nazario Yáñez Candia (65).

**307.** 21.08.1980 **URUGUAY - CHILE** **0-0**
Estadio Centenario, Montevideo; Referee: Teodoro Nitti (Argentina); Attendance: 18,000
**CHI:** Oscar Raúl Wirth Lafuente (2/0), Luis Rojas (2/0), Santiago Gatica (1/0), Mario del Transito Soto Benavides (20/1), Osvaldo Vargas (1/0), Vladimir David Bigorra López (3/0), Carlos Humberto Rivas Torres (15/3), Rodolfo del Rosario Dubó Segovia (12/0), Eduardo Guillermo Bonvallet Godoy (9/0), Patricio Nazario Yáñez Candia (11/2), Carlos Humberto Caszely Garrido (30/16). Trainer: Oscar Luis Santibáñez Díaz (16).

**308.** 18.09.1980 **ARGENTINA - CHILE** **2-2(2-1)**
Estadio Municipal, Mendoza; Referee: Claudio Aquiles Busca (Argentina); Attendance: 35,000
**CHI:** Oscar Raúl Wirth Lafuente (3/0), Luis Rojas (3/0), Osvaldo Vargas (2/1), Elías Ricardo Figueroa Brander (37/3), Mario del Transito Soto Benavides (21/1, Vladimir David Bigorra López (4/0), Manuel Antonio Rojas Zuniga (15/1), Rodolfo del Rosario Dubó Segovia (13/0), Eduardo Guillermo Bonvallet Godoy (10/0), Patricio Nazario Yáñez Candia (12/2) [78.Orlando Alberto Mondaca Reyes (1/0)], Sandrino Castec Martínez (1/1). Trainer: Oscar Luis Santibáñez Díaz (17).
**Goals**: Osvaldo Vargas (44), Sandrino Castec Martínez (66).

**309.** 10.03.1981 **CHILE - COLOMBIA** **1-0(1-0)**
Estadio Nacional, Santiago; Referee: Gilberto Aristizábal Murcia (Colombia); Attendance: 18,639
**CHI:** Oscar Raúl Wirth Lafuente (4/0), Lizardo Antonio Garrido Bustamante (1/0), Santiago Gatica (2/0), Mario del Transito Soto Benavides (22/1), Vladimir David Bigorra López (5/0) [Enzo Sergio Escobar Olivares (23/0)], Manuel Antonio Rojas Zuniga (16/1), Eduardo Guillermo Bonvallet Godoy (11/0), Miguel Angel Neira Pincheira (12/0), Patricio Nazario Yáñez Candia (13/2), Sandrino Castec Martínez (2/1), Oscar Herrera Hernández (1/1). Trainer: Oscar Luis Santibáñez Díaz (18).
**Goal**: Oscar Herrera Hernández (28).

**310.** 14.03.1981 **BRAZIL - CHILE** **2-1(1-0)**
Estádio Santa Cruz, Ribeirão Preto; Referee: Romualdo Arppi Filho (Brazil); Attendance: 58,000
**CHI:** Mario Ignacio Osbén Méndez (12/0), Lizardo Antonio Garrido Bustamante (2/0), Santiago Gatica (3/0) [Carlos Humberto Rivas Torres (16/3)], Eduardo René Valenzuela Becker (12/0), Mario del Transito Soto Benavides (23/1), Vladimir David Bigorra López (6/0), Rodolfo del Rosario Dubó Segovia (14/0), Manuel Antonio Rojas Zuniga (17/1), Eduardo Guillermo Bonvallet Godoy (12/0), Carlos Humberto Caszely Garrido (31/17) [Oscar Herrera Hernández (2/1)], Patricio Nazario Yáñez Candia (14/2). Trainer: Oscar Luis Santibáñez Díaz (19).
**Goal**: Carlos Humberto Caszely Garrido (49).

**311.** 19.03.1981 **COLOMBIA - CHILE** **1-2(0-2)**
Estadio „Nemesio Camacho" 'El Campín', Bogotá; Referee: Hernán Silva Arce (Chile); Attendance: 36,000
**CHI:** Mario Ignacio Osbén Méndez (13/0), Lizardo Antonio Garrido Bustamante (3/0), Santiago Gatica (4/0), Eduardo René Valenzuela Becker (13/0), Enzo Sergio Escobar Olivares (24/0), Carlos Humberto Rivas Torres (17/3), Rodolfo del Rosario Dubó Segovia (15/0), Eduardo Guillermo Bonvallet Godoy (13/0) [Osvaldo Vargas (3/1)], Manuel Antonio Rojas Zuniga (18/1), Patricio Nazario Yáñez Candia (15/2) [Oscar Herrera Hernández (3/1)], Carlos Humberto Caszely Garrido (32/19). Trainer: Oscar Luis Santibáñez Díaz (20).
**Goals**: Carlos Humberto Caszely Garrido (15, 19).

**312.** 19.04.1981 **CHILE - PERU** **3-0(1-0)**
Estadio Nacional, Santiago; Referee: Arturo Andrés Ithurralde (Argentina); Attendance: 20,692
**CHI:** Mario Ignacio Osbén Méndez (14/0), Mario Enrique Galindo Calixto (24/0), Eduardo René Valenzuela Becker (14/0) [79.Santiago Gatica (5/0)], Mario del Transito Soto Benavides (24/1), Lizardo Antonio Garrido Bustamante (4/0), Eduardo Guillermo Bonvallet Godoy (14/0), Miguel Angel Neira Pincheira (13/0) [60.Carlos Humberto Rivas Torres (18/3)], Oscar Herrera Hernández (4/1) [70.Patricio Nazario Yáñez Candia (16/2)], Carlos Humberto Caszely Garrido (33/20), Sandrino Castec Martínez (3/1) [60.Manuel Antonio Rojas Zuniga (19/1)], Gustavo Segundo Moscoso Huencho (7/3). Trainer: Oscar Luis Santibáñez Díaz (21).
**Goals**: Gustavo Segundo Moscoso Huencho (30), Carlos Humberto Caszely Garrido (65 penalty), Gustavo Segundo Moscoso Huencho (75).

**313.** 29.04.1981 **CHILE - URUGUAY** **1-2(0-0)** Copa Pinto Durán
Estadio Nacional, Santiago; Referee: Teodoro Nitti (Argentina); Attendance: 27,105
**CHI:** Oscar Raúl Wirth Lafuente (5/0), Eduardo René Valenzuela Becker (15/0), Mario del Transito Soto Benavides (25/1), Mario Enrique Galindo Calixto (25/0), Lizardo Antonio Garrido Bustamante (5/0), Eduardo Guillermo Bonvallet Godoy (15/0) [Rodolfo del Rosario Dubó Segovia (16/0)], Manuel Antonio Rojas Zuniga (20/2), Carlos Humberto Rivas Torres (19/3), Gustavo Segundo Moscoso Huencho (8/3), Oscar Herrera Hernández (5/1) [Patricio Nazario Yáñez Candia (17/2)], José Luis Alvarez (1/0). Trainer: Oscar Luis Santibáñez Díaz (22).
**Goal**: Manuel Antonio Rojas Zuniga (57).

**314.** 24.05.1981 **ECUADOR - CHILE** **0-0** 12th FIFA WC. Qualifiers
Estadio Modelo, Guayaquil; Referee: Juan Daniel Cardellino de San Vicente (Uruguay); Attendance: 55,000
**CHI:** Mario Ignacio Osbén Méndez (15/0), Lizardo Antonio Garrido Bustamante (6/0) [33.Enzo Sergio Escobar Olivares (25/0)], Eduardo René Valenzuela Becker (16/0), Mario del Transito Soto Benavides (26/1), Vladimir David Bigorra López (7/0), Carlos Humberto Rivas Torres (20/3), Rodolfo del Rosario Dubó Segovia (17/0), Eduardo Guillermo Bonvallet Godoy (16/0), Manuel Antonio Rojas Zuniga (21/2) [42.Miguel Angel Neira Pincheira (14/0)], Carlos Humberto Caszely Garrido (34/20), Gustavo Segundo Moscoso Huencho (9/3). Trainer: Oscar Luis Santibáñez Díaz (23).

**315.** 07.06.1981 **PARAGUAY - CHILE** **0-1(0-0)** 12th FIFA WC. Qualifiers
Estadio Defensores del Chaco, Asunción; Referee: Carlos Espósito (Argentina); Attendance: 46,178
**CHI:** Mario Ignacio Osbén Méndez (16/0), Lizardo Antonio Garrido Bustamante (7/0), Eduardo René Valenzuela Becker (17/0), Elías Ricardo Figueroa Brander (38/3), Mario del Transito Soto Benavides (27/1), Vladimir David Bigorra López (8/0), Eduardo Guillermo Bonvallet Godoy (17/0) [Miguel Angel Neira Pincheira (15/0)], Rodolfo del Rosario Dubó Segovia (18/0), Gustavo Segundo Moscoso Huencho (10/3), Patricio Nazario Yáñez Candia (18/3) [Manuel Antonio Rojas Zuniga (22/2)], Sandrino Castec Martínez (4/1). Trainer: Oscar Luis Santibáñez Díaz (24).
**Goal**: Patricio Nazario Yáñez Candia (71).

**316.** 14.06.1981 **CHILE - ECUADOR** **2-0(1-0)** 12th FIFA WC. Qualifiers
Estadio Nacional, Santiago; Referee: Gilberto Aristizábal Murcia (Colombia); Attendance: 72,290
**CHI:** Mario Ignacio Osbén Méndez (17/0), Lizardo Antonio Garrido Bustamante (8/0), Eduardo René Valenzuela Becker (18/0), Elías Ricardo Figueroa Brander (39/3), Vladimir David Bigorra López (9/0), Carlos Humberto Rivas Torres (21/4), Sandrino Castec Martínez (5/1) [75.Rodolfo del Rosario Dubó Segovia (19/0)], Manuel Antonio Rojas Zuniga (23/2), Patricio Nazario Yáñez Candia (19/3) [81.Oscar Herrera Hernández (6/1)], Carlos Humberto Caszely Garrido (35/21), Gustavo Segundo Moscoso Huencho (11/3). Trainer: Oscar Luis Santibáñez Díaz (25).
**Goals**: Carlos Humberto Rivas Torres (10), Carlos Humberto Caszely Garrido (85).

**317.** 21.06.1981 **CHILE - PARAGUAY** **3-0(3-0)** 12th FIFA WC. Qualifiers
Estadio Nacional, Santiago; Referee: Romualdo Arrpi Filho (Brazil); Attendance: 75,075
**CHI:** Mario Ignacio Osbén Méndez (18/0), Lizardo Antonio Garrido Bustamante (9/0), Eduardo René Valenzuela Becker (19/0), Mario del Transito Soto Benavides (28/1), Vladimir David Bigorra López (10/0), Miguel Angel Neira Pincheira (16/1), Manuel Antonio Rojas Zuniga (24/2), Rodolfo del Rosario Dubó Segovia (20/0), Patricio Nazario Yáñez Candia (20/4) [25.Oscar Herrera Hernández (7/1)], Carlos Humberto Caszely Garrido (36/22), Gustavo Segundo Moscoso Huencho (12/3). Trainer: Oscar Luis Santibáñez Díaz (26).
**Goals**: Carlos Humberto Caszely Garrido (10), Patricio Nazario Yáñez Candia (11), Miguel Angel Neira Pincheira (28).

**318.** 05.07.1981 **CHILE - SPAIN** **1-1(1-1)**
Estadio Nacional, Santiago; Referee: Jorge Eduardo Romero (Argentina); Attendance: 15,000
**CHI:** Mario Ignacio Osbén Méndez (19/0), Lizardo Antonio Garrido Bustamante (10/0), Eduardo René Valenzuela Becker (20/0), Mario del Transito Soto Benavides (29/1), Vladimir David Bigorra López (11/0), Carlos Humberto Rivas Torres (22/4) [66.Orlando Alberto Mondaca Reyes (2/0)], Rodolfo del Rosario Dubó Segovia (21/0), Miguel Angel Neira Pincheira (17/1), Patricio Nazario Yáñez Candia (21/4) [79.Oscar Herrera Hernández (8/1)], Carlos Humberto Caszely Garrido (37/23), Gustavo Segundo Moscoso Huencho (13/3). Trainer: Oscar Luis Santibáñez Díaz (27).
**Goal**: Carlos Humberto Caszely Garrido (8).

**319.** 15.07.1981 **URUGUAY - CHILE** **0-0** Copa Pinto Durán
Estadio Centenario, Montevideo; Referee: Abel Gnecco (Argentina); Attendance: 18,000
**CHI:** Mario Ignacio Osbén Méndez (20/0), Lizardo Antonio Garrido Bustamante (11/0), Santiago Gatica (6/0), Mario del Transito Soto Benavides (30/1), Vladimir David Bigorra López (12/0), Manuel Antonio Rojas Zuniga (25/2), Rodolfo del Rosario Dubó Segovia (22/0), Miguel Angel Neira Pincheira (18/1), Oscar Herrera Hernández (9/1) [Leonardo Véliz Díaz (37/2)], Carlos Humberto Caszely Garrido (38/23), Gustavo Segundo Moscoso Huencho (14/3). Trainer: Oscar Luis Santibáñez Díaz (28).

**320.** 05.08.1981 **PERU - CHILE** **1-2(0-2)**
Estadio Nacional, Lima; Referee: Sérgio Leiblinger (Peru); Attendance: 45,000
**CHI:** Mario Ignacio Osbén Méndez (21/0), Lizardo Antonio Garrido Bustamante (12/0), Eduardo René Valenzuela Becker (21/0) [71.Santiago Gatica (7/0)], Mario del Transito Soto Benavides (31/1), Vladimir David Bigorra López (13/0), Eduardo Guillermo Bonvallet Godoy (18/0), Rodolfo del Rosario Dubó Segovia (23/0), Miguel Angel Neira Pincheira (19/1), Oscar Herrera Hernández (10/1) [80.Orlando Alberto Mondaca Reyes (3/0)], Carlos Humberto Caszely Garrido (39/25) [77.Sandrino Castec Martínez (6/1)], Gustavo Segundo Moscoso Huencho (15/3) [46.Leonardo Véliz Díaz (38/2)]. Trainer: Oscar Luis Santibáñez Díaz (29).
**Goals**: Carlos Humberto Caszely Garrido (3, 19).

**321.** 26.08.1981 **CHILE - BRAZIL** **0-0**
Estadio Nacional, Santiago; Referee: Augusto Lamo Castillo (Spain); Attendance: 33,000
**CHI:** Mario Ignacio Osbén Méndez (22/0), Lizardo Antonio Garrido Bustamante (13/0), Santiago Gatica (8/0), Mario del Transito Soto Benavides (32/1), Vladimir David Bigorra López (14/0), Rodolfo del Rosario Dubó Segovia (24/0), Manuel Antonio Rojas Zuniga (26/2), Miguel Angel Neira Pincheira (20/1), Oscar Herrera Hernández (11/1) [Rodrígo Santander (1/0)], Carlos Humberto Caszely Garrido (40/25), Leonardo Véliz Díaz (39/2) [Eduardo Guillermo Bonvallet Godoy (19/0)]. Trainer: Oscar Luis Santibáñez Díaz (30).

**322.** 23.03.1982 **CHILE - PERU** **2-1(2-1)**
Estadio Nacional, Santiago; Referee: Edison Pérez Nuñez (Peru); Attendance: 49,800
**CHI:** Mario Ignacio Osbén Méndez (23/0), Mario Enrique Galindo Calixto (26/0), Elías Ricardo Figueroa Brander (40/3), Mario del Transito Soto Benavides (33/1), Vladimir David Bigorra López (15/0), Carlos Humberto Rivas Torres (23/4) [70.Armando Alarcón Rivera (1/0)], Rodolfo del Rosario Dubó Segovia (25/0), Miguel Angel Neira Pincheira (21/2), Juan Carlos Letelier Pizarro (3/1), Miguel Angel Gamboa Pedemonte (11/4) [46.Patricio Nazario Yáñez Candia (22/4)], Gustavo Segundo Moscoso Huencho (16/3). Trainer: Oscar Luis Santibáñez Díaz (31).
**Goals**: Juan Carlos Letelier Pizarro (10), Miguel Angel Neira Pincheira (24).

**323.** 30.03.1982 **PERU - CHILE** **1-0(1-0)** Copa del Pacífico
Estadio Nacional, Lima; Referee: Víctor Ojeda (Chile); Attendance: 38,000
**CHI:** Mario Ignacio Osbén Méndez (24/0), Mario Enrique Galindo Calixto (27/0), Oscar Vladimír Rojas Giacomozzi (1/0), Elías Ricardo Figueroa Brander (41/3), Enzo Sergio Escobar Olivares (26/0), Orlando Alberto Mondaca Reyes (4/0) [56.Carlos Humberto Caszely Garrido (41/25)], Rodolfo del Rosario Dubó Segovia (26/0), Eduardo Guillermo Bonvallet Godoy (20/0), Miguel Angel Neira Pincheira (22/2), Juan Carlos Letelier Pizarro (4/1), Miguel Angel Gamboa Pedemonte (12/4). Trainer: Oscar Luis Santibáñez Díaz (32).

**324.** 19.05.1982 **CHILE - ROMANIA** **2-3(0-3)**
Estadio Nacional, Santiago; Referee: Guillermo Budge Aguirre (Chile); Attendance: 9,166
**CHI:** Mario Ignacio Osbén Méndez (25/0), Lizardo Antonio Garrido Bustamante (14/0), Eduardo René Valenzuela Becker (22/0), Elías Ricardo Figueroa Brander (42/3), Vladimir David Bigorra López (16/1), Orlando Alberto Mondaca Reyes (5/0) [Elías Raúl Ormeño Pacheco (1/0)], Armando Alarcón Rivera (2/0) [Eduardo Guillermo Bonvallet Godoy (21/0)], Manuel Antonio Rojas Zuniga (27/2) [Miguel Angel Neira Pincheira (23/2)], Carlos Humberto Caszely Garrido (42/26), Miguel Angel Gamboa Pedemonte (13/5), Gustavo Segundo Moscoso Huencho (17/3). Trainer: Oscar Luis Santibáñez Díaz (33).
**Goals**: Miguel Angel Gamboa Pedemonte (55), Carlos Humberto Caszely Garrido (62).

**325.** 22.05.1982 **CHILE – REPUBLIC OF IRELAND** **1-0(1-0)**
Estadio Nacional, Santiago; Referee: Víctor Ojeda (Chile); Attendance: 25,000
**CHI:** Mario Ignacio Osbén Méndez (26/0), Lizardo Antonio Garrido Bustamante (15/0) [Mario Enrique Galindo Calixto (28/0)], Elías Ricardo Figueroa Brander (43/3), Eduardo René Valenzuela Becker (23/0), Mario del Transito Soto Benavides (34/1), Vladimir David Bigorra López (17/1), Carlos Humberto Rivas Torres (24/4), Rodolfo del Rosario Dubó Segovia (27/0), Patricio Nazario Yáñez Candia (23/4), Miguel Angel Gamboa Pedemonte (14/6) [Juan Carlos Letelier Pizarro (5/1)], Gustavo Segundo Moscoso Huencho (18/3). Trainer: Oscar Luis Santibáñez Díaz (34).
**Goal**: Miguel Angel Gamboa Pedemonte (1).

**326.** 17.06.1982 **AUSTRIA - CHILE** **1-0(1-0)** 12th FIFA WC. Group Stage.
Estadio „Carlos Tartiere“, Oviedo (Spain); Referee: Juan Daniel Cardellino de San Vicente (Uruguay); Attendance: 23,000
**CHI:** Mario Ignacio Osbén Méndez (27/0), Lizardo Antonio Garrido Bustamante (16/0), Eduardo René Valenzuela Becker (24/0), Elías Ricardo Figueroa Brander (44/3), Vladimir David Bigorra López (18/1), Miguel Angel Neira Pincheira (24/2) [72.Manuel Antonio Rojas Zuniga (28/2)], Rodolfo del Rosario Dubó Segovia (28/0), Eduardo Guillermo Bonvallet Godoy (22/0), Gustavo Segundo Moscoso Huencho (19/3) [69.Miguel Angel Gamboa Pedemonte (15/6)], Carlos Humberto Caszely Garrido (43/26), Patricio Nazario Yáñez Candia (24/4). Trainer: Oscar Luis Santibáñez Díaz (35).

**327.** 20.06.1982 **WEST GERMANY - CHILE** **4-1(1-0)** 12th FIFA WC. Group Stage.
Estadio El Molinón, Gijón (Spain); Referee: Bruno Galler (Switzerland); Attendance: 42,000
**CHI:** Mario Ignacio Osbén Méndez (28/0), Lizardo Antonio Garrido Bustamante (17/0), Eduardo René Valenzuela Becker (25/0), Elías Ricardo Figueroa Brander (45/3), Vladimir David Bigorra López (19/1), Mario del Transito Soto Benavides (35/1) [46.Juan Carlos Letelier Pizarro (6/1)], Rodolfo del Rosario Dubó Segovia (29/0), Eduardo Guillermo Bonvallet Godoy (23/0), Gustavo Segundo Moscoso Huencho (20/4), Patricio Nazario Yáñez Candia (25/4), Miguel Angel Gamboa Pedemonte (16/6) [66.Miguel Angel Neira Pincheira (25/2)]. Trainer: Oscar Luis Santibáñez Díaz (36).
**Goal**: Gustavo Segundo Moscoso Huencho (90).

**328.** 24.06.1982 **ALGERIA - CHILE** **3-2(3-0)** 12th FIFA WC. Group Stage.
Estadio „Carlos Tartiere", Oviedo (Spain); Referee: Romulo Méndez Molina (Guatemala); Attendance: 16,000
**CHI:** Mario Ignacio Osbén Méndez (29/0), Mario Enrique Galindo Calixto (29/0), Eduardo René Valenzuela Becker (26/0), Elías Ricardo Figueroa Brander (46/3), Vladimir David Bigorra López (20/1), Rodolfo del Rosario Dubó Segovia (30/0), Eduardo Guillermo Bonvallet Godoy (24/0) [37.Mario del Transito Soto Benavides (36/1)], Miguel Angel Neira Pincheira (26/3), Carlos Humberto Caszely Garrido (44/26) [58.Juan Carlos Letelier Pizarro (7/2)], Patricio Nazario Yáñez Candia (26/4), Gustavo Segundo Moscoso Huencho (21/4). Trainer: Oscar Luis Santibáñez Díaz (37).
**Goals**: Miguel Angel Neira Pincheira (59 penalty), Juan Carlos Letelier Pizarro (73).

**329.** 28.04.1983 **BRAZIL - CHILE** **3-2(2-1)**
Estádio „Jornalista Mario Filho" (Maracanã), Rio de Janeiro; Referee: Gabriel González Roa (Paraguay); Attendance: 53,648
**CHI:** Oscar Raúl Wirth Lafuente (6/0), Rubén Alberto Espinoza Molina (1/0) [Óscar Patricio Reyes Sánchez (1/0)], Marcelo Pacheco (1/0) [Luis Alberto Mosquera Rivera (1/0)], Héctor Díaz (1/0), Luis Valenzuela (1/0), Rodolfo del Rosario Dubó Segovia (31/0), Miguel Angel Neira Pincheira (27/3) [Juan Soto Quintana (2/0)], Juan Rojas (1/0), Osvaldo Heriberto Hurtado Galeguillo (1/0), Miguel Angel Gamboa Pedemonte (17/6), Juan Carlos Orellana Jara (5/2). Trainer: Luis Ibarra Castillo (1).
**Goals**: Juan Carlos Orellana Jara (36 penalty,61).

**330.** 12.05.1983 **CHILE - ARGENTINA** **2-2(1-0)**
Estadio Nacional, Santiago; Referee: Juan Daniel Cardellino de San Vicente (Uruguay); Attendance: 19,615
**CHI:** Oscar Raúl Wirth Lafuente (7/0), Rubén Alberto Espinoza Molina (2/0), Marcelo Pacheco (2/0), Eduardo René Valenzuela Becker (27/0), Luis Valenzuela (2/0), Juan Soto Quintana (3/0), Rodolfo del Rosario Dubó Segovia (32/1), Juan Rojas (2/0), Sandrino Castec Martínez (7/1), Miguel Angel Gamboa Pedemonte (18/6), Juan Carlos Orellana Jara (6/3). Trainer: Luis Ibarra Castillo (2).
**Goals**: Juan Carlos Orellana Jara (36), Rodolfo del Rosario Dubó Segovia (62).

**331.** 23.06.1983 **ARGENTINA - CHILE** **1-0(0-0)**
Estadio „José Amalfitani", Buenos Aires; Referee: Juan Francisco Escobar Váldez (Paraguay); Attendance: 18,000
**CHI:** Roberto Antonio Rojas Saavedra (1/0), Alejandro Manuel Hisis Araya (1/0), Leonel Herrera (26/0), Oscar Vladimír Rojas Giacomozzi (2/0), Luis Valenzuela (3/0), Juan Soto Quintana (4/0), Rodolfo del Rosario Dubó Segovia (33/1), Osvaldo Heriberto Hurtado Galeguillo (2/0) [79.Oscar Arriaza (1/0)], Jorge Orlando Aravena Plaza (1/0), Juan Rojas (3/0), Juan Carlos Letelier Pizarro (8/2) [79.Oscar Herrera Hernández (12/1)]. Trainer: Luis Ibarra Castillo (3).

**332.** 14.07.1983 **COLOMBIA - CHILE** **2-2(1-0)**
Estadio „Nemesio Camacho" 'El Campín', Bogotá; Referee: Gilberto Aristizábal Murcia (Colombia); Attendance: 40,000
**CHI:** Roberto Antonio Rojas Saavedra (2/0), Alejandro Manuel Hisis Araya (2/0), Eduardo René Valenzuela Becker (28/0), Leonel Herrera (27/0), Luis Valenzuela (4/0), Juan Soto Quintana (5/0), Rodolfo del Rosario Dubó Segovia (34/1), Osvaldo Heriberto Hurtado Galeguillo (3/1), Jorge Orlando Aravena Plaza (2/1), Juan Carlos Letelier Pizarro (9/2) [Oscar Herrera Hernández (13/1)], Juan Rojas (4/0). Trainer: Luis Ibarra Castillo (4).
**Goals**: Jorge Orlando Aravena Plaza (52 penalty), Osvaldo Heriberto Hurtado Galeguillo (56).

**333.** 19.07.1983 **BOLIVIA - CHILE** **1-2**
Estadio „Hernando Siles Zuazo", La Paz; Referee: Jorge Pabón (Bolivia); Attendance: 20,156
**CHI:** Marco Antonio Cornéz (1/0), Alejandro Manuel Hisis Araya (3/0), Eduardo René Valenzuela Becker (29/0), Leonel Herrera (28/0), Luis Valenzuela (5/0), Rodolfo del Rosario Dubó Segovia (35/1), Luis Rojas (4/0), Juan Soto Quintana (6/0), Jorge Orlando Aravena Plaza (3/2) [Oscar Herrera Hernández (14/1)], Juan Carlos Letelier Pizarro (10/3) [Juan Rojas (5/0)], Osvaldo Heriberto Hurtado Galeguillo (4/1) [Oscar Arriaza (2/0)]. Trainer: Luis Ibarra Castillo (5).
**Goals**: Jorge Orlando Aravena Plaza, Juan Carlos Letelier Pizarro.

**334.** 21.07.1983 **PERU - CHILE** **0-1(0-1)** Copa del Pacífico
Estadio Nacional, Lima; Referee: Enrique Labó Revoredo (Peru); Attendance: 20,000
**CHI:** Roberto Antonio Rojas Saavedra (3/0), Alejandro Manuel Hisis Araya (4/0), Eduardo René Valenzuela Becker (30/0), Leonel Herrera (29/0), Luis Valenzuela (6/0), Luis Rojas (5/0), Rodolfo del Rosario Dubó Segovia (36/1), Juan Soto Quintana (7/1) [61.Marcelo Pacheco (3/0)], Juan Rojas (6/0) [53.Juan Carlos Letelier Pizarro (11/3)], Osvaldo Heriberto Hurtado Galeguillo (5/1) [80.Oscar Arriaza (3/0)], Jorge Orlando Aravena Plaza (4/2). Trainer: Luis Ibarra Castillo (6).
**Goals**: Juan Soto Quintana (44).

**335.** 24.07.1983 **PARAGUAY - CHILE** **1-0(1-0)**
Estadio Defensores del Chaco, Asunción; Referee: Claudio Aquiles Busca (Argentina); Attendance: 20,000
**CHI:** Marco Antonio Cornéz (2/0), Alejandro Manuel Hisis Araya (5/0), Eduardo René Valenzuela Becker (31/0), Edgardo Enrique Fuentes Silva (1/0), Luis Valenzuela (7/0), Luis Rojas (6/0), Juan Soto Quintana (8/1), Marcelo Pacheco (4/0), Jorge Orlando Aravena Plaza (5/2), Juan Rojas (7/0) [Juan Carlos Letelier Pizarro (12/3)], Osvaldo Heriberto Hurtado Galeguillo (6/1). Trainer: Luis Ibarra Castillo (7).

**336.** 28.07.1983 **CHILE - BRAZIL** **0-0**
Estadio Nacional, Santiago; Referee: Abel Gnecco (Argentina); Attendance: 29,020
**CHI:** Roberto Antonio Rojas Saavedra (4/0), Alejandro Manuel Hisis Araya (6/0), Marcelo Pacheco (5/0), Leonel Herrera (30/0), Luis Valenzuela (8/0), Luis Rojas (7/0), Rodolfo del Rosario Dubó Segovia (37/1), Juan Soto Quintana (9/1), Jorge Orlando Aravena Plaza (6/2), Juan Rojas (8/0), Osvaldo Heriberto Hurtado Galeguillo (7/1) [Oscar Arriaza (4/0)]. Trainer: Luis Ibarra Castillo (8).

**337.** 03.08.1983 **CHILE - PERU** **2-0(2-0)** Copa del Pacífico
Estadio „Carlos Dittborn", Arica; Referee: Juan Ambrosio Silvagno Cavanna (Chile); Attendance: 18,802
**CHI:** Marco Antonio Cornéz (3/0), Alejandro Manuel Hisis Araya (7/0), Marcelo Pacheco (6/0), Eduardo René Valenzuela Becker (32/0), Luis Valenzuela (9/0), Juan Soto Quintana (10/1), Luis Rojas (8/0), Jorge Orlando Aravena Plaza (7/2), Juan Carlos Letelier Pizarro (13/5) [83.Oscar Herrera Hernández (15/1)], Oscar Arriaza (5/0) [60.Leonel Herrera (31/0)], Juan Carlos Orellana Jara (7/3) [50.Jorge Alejandro Contreras Lira (1/0)]. Trainer: Luis Ibarra Castillo (9).
**Goals**: Juan Carlos Letelier Pizarro (15, 36).

**338.** 17.08.1983 **CHILE - PARAGUAY** **3-2(1-1)**
Estadio Regional, Antofagasta; Referee: Jorge Eduardo Romero (Argentina); Attendance: 23,407
**CHI:** Roberto Antonio Rojas Saavedra (5/0), Rubén Alberto Espinoza Molina (3/0), Marcelo Pacheco (7/0), Leonel Herrera (32/0), Marco Opazo (1/0), Luis Rojas (9/0), Rodolfo del Rosario Dubó Segovia (38/1), Osvaldo Heriberto Hurtado Galeguillo (8/2), Jorge Orlando Aravena Plaza (8/3), Juan Rojas (9/0), Juan Carlos Letelier Pizarro (14/6). Trainer: Luis Ibarra Castillo (10).
**Goals**: Jorge Orlando Aravena Plaza (35 penalty), Juan Carlos Letelier Pizarro (70), Osvaldo Heriberto Hurtado Galeguillo (87).

**339.** 24.08.1983 **CHILE - BOLIVIA** **4-2(4-1)**
Estadio „Carlos Dittborn", Arica; Referee: Víctor Ojeda (Chile); Attendance: 18,000
**CHI:** Marco Antonio Cornéz (4/0), Rubén Alberto Espinoza Molina (4/0), Marcelo Pacheco (8/0), Eduardo René Valenzuela Becker (33/0), Alejandro Manuel Hisis Araya (8/0), Juan Soto Quintana (11/1), Rodolfo del Rosario Dubó Segovia (39/1), Jorge Alejandro Contreras Lira (2/0) [Oscar Arriaza (6/0)], Jorge Orlando Aravena Plaza (9/6) [Luis Valenzuela (10/0)], Juan Carlos Letelier Pizarro (15/7), Osvaldo Heriberto Hurtado Galeguillo (9/2) [Juan Rojas (10/0)]. Trainer: Luis Ibarra Castillo (11).
**Goals**: Juan Carlos Letelier Pizarro (10), Jorge Orlando Aravena Plaza (15, 22, 42).

**340.** 01.09.1983 **URUGUAY - CHILE** **2-1(1-0)** 32nd Copa América. Group Stage
Estadio Centenario, Montevideo; Referee: Arnaldo David César Coelho (Brazil); Attendance: 30,000
**CHI:** Marco Antonio Cornéz (5/0), Rubén Alberto Espinoza Molina (5/0), Eduardo René Valenzuela Becker (34/0), Leonel Herrera (33/0) [Juan Carlos Orellana Jara (8/4)], Alejandro Manuel Hisis Araya (9/0), Rodolfo del Rosario Dubó Segovia (40/1), Marcelo Pacheco (9/0), Luis Rojas (10/0), Jorge Orlando Aravena Plaza (10/6), Juan Carlos Letelier Pizarro (16/7), Osvaldo Heriberto Hurtado Galeguillo (10/2) [Juan Rojas (11/0) [*sent off 76*]]. Trainer: Luis Ibarra Castillo (12).
**Goal**: Juan Carlos Orellana Jara (76).

**341.** 08.09.1983 **CHILE - VENEZUELA** **5-0(3-0)** 32nd Copa América. Group Stage
Estadio Nacional, Santiago; Referee: Enrique Labó Revoredo (Peru); Attendance: 11,372
**CHI:** Roberto Antonio Rojas Saavedra (6/0), Rubén Alberto Espinoza Molina (6/1), Eduardo René Valenzuela Becker (35/0), Marcelo Pacheco (10/0), Alejandro Manuel Hisis Araya (10/0), Luis Rojas (11/0) [Juan Soto Quintana (12/1)], Rodolfo del Rosario Dubó Segovia (41/2), Jorge Orlando Aravena Plaza (11/8), Oscar Herrera Hernández (16/1) [Juan Carlos Letelier Pizarro (17/7)], Oscar Arriaza (7/1), Juan Carlos Orellana Jara (9/4). Trainer: Luis Ibarra Castillo (13).
**Goals**: Oscar Arriaza (23), Rodolfo del Rosario Dubó Segovia (25), Jorge Orlando Aravena Plaza (36), Rubén Alberto Espinoza Molina (75), Jorge Orlando Aravena Plaza (83).

**342.** 11.09.1983 **CHILE - URUGUAY** **2-0(1-0)** 32nd Copa América. Group Stage
Estadio Nacional, Santiago; Referee: Teodoro Nitti (Argentina); Attendance: 47,403
**CHI:** Roberto Antonio Rojas Saavedra (7/0), Rubén Alberto Espinoza Molina (7/1), Eduardo René Valenzuela Becker (36/0), Leonel Herrera (34/0), Alejandro Manuel Hisis Araya (11/0), Rodolfo del Rosario Dubó Segovia (42/3), Juan Soto Quintana (13/1), Luis Rojas (12/0), Juan Carlos Letelier Pizarro (18/8), Oscar Arriaza (8/1) [73.Juan Carlos Orellana Jara (10/4)], Jorge Orlando Aravena Plaza (12/8). Trainer: Luis Ibarra Castillo (14).
**Goals**: Rodolfo del Rosario Dubó Segovia (9), Juan Carlos Letelier Pizarro (80).

**343.** 21.09.1983 **VENEZUELA - CHILE** **0-0** 32nd Copa América. Group Stage
Estadio „Brígido Iriarte", Caracas; Referee: Elías Victoriano Jácome Guerreiro (Ecuador); Attendance: 3,000
**CHI:** Roberto Antonio Rojas Saavedra (8/0), Rubén Alberto Espinoza Molina (8/1) [Juan Soto Quintana (14/1)], Eduardo René Valenzuela Becker (37/0), Leonel Herrera (35/0), Alejandro Manuel Hisis Araya (12/0), Rodolfo del Rosario Dubó Segovia (43/3), Luis Rojas (13/0), Juan Carlos Letelier Pizarro (19/8), Jorge Orlando Aravena Plaza (13/8), Oscar Arriaza (9/1) [Juan Carlos Orellana Jara (11/4)], Juan Rojas (12/0). Trainer: Luis Ibarra Castillo (15).

**344.** 17.06.1984 **CHILE - ENGLAND** **0-0**
Estadio Nacional, Santiago; Referee: Luís Carlos Félix Ferrara (Brazil); Attendance: 9,876
**CHI:** Roberto Antonio Rojas Saavedra (9/0), Hugo del Carmen Tabilo Avilés (1/0), Eduardo Gómez (1/0), Manuel Araya (1/0), Luis Orlando Hormazábal Gavilan (1/0), Alejandro Manuel Hisis Araya (13/0), Juan Soto Quintana (15/1) [Luis Rodríguez (1/0)], Claudio Toro (1/0) [Eduardo Gino Cofré (1/0)], Jorge Orlando Aravena Plaza (14/8), Luis Venegas (1/0), Juan Covarrubias (1/0) [Héctor Eduardo Puebla (1/0)]. Trainer: Luis Ibarra Castillo (16).

**345.** 28.10.1984 **CHILE - MEXICO** **1-0(1-0)**
Estadio Nacional, Santiago; Referee: Juan Carlos Loustau (Argentina); Attendance: 25,000
**CHI:** Roberto Antonio Rojas Saavedra (10/0), Lizardo Antonio Garrido Bustamante (18/0), Eduardo René Valenzuela Becker (38/0), Eduardo Gómez (2/0), Luis Orlando Hormazábal Gavilan (2/0), Víctor Alejandro Merello Escobar (3/0) [Jorge García (1/0)], Alejandro Manuel Hisis Araya (14/0), Jorge Orlando Aravena Plaza (15/9), Juan Carlos Letelier Pizarro (20/8), Osvaldo Heriberto Hurtado Galeguillo (11/2), Hugo Eduardo Rubio Montecinos (1/0) [Oscar Herrera Hernández (17/1)]. Trainer: Vicente Cantatore Socci (1).
**Goal**: Jorge Orlando Aravena Plaza (25).

**346.** 06.02.1985 **CHILE - PARAGUAY** **1-0(1-0)**
Estadio Sausalito, Viña del Mar; Referee: Víctor Sergio Vásquez Sánchez (Chile); Attendance: 21,010
**CHI:** Roberto Antonio Rojas Saavedra (11/0), Lizardo Antonio Garrido Bustamante (19/0), Eduardo René Valenzuela Becker (39/0), Eduardo Gómez (3/0), Luis Orlando Hormazábal Gavilan (3/0), Miguel Angel Neira Pincheira (28/3), Alejandro Manuel Hisis Araya (15/0), Jorge Orlando Aravena Plaza (16/10) [Luis Rojas (14/0)], Hugo Eduardo Rubio Montecinos (2/0) [Oscar Herrera Hernández (18/1)], Osvaldo Heriberto Hurtado Galeguillo (12/2), Héctor Eduardo Puebla (2/0) [Juan Carlos Letelier Pizarro (21/8)]. Trainer: Pedro Morales (10).
**Goal**: Jorge Orlando Aravena Plaza (3 penalty).

**347.** 08.02.1985 **CHILE - FINLAND** **2-0(1-0)**
Estadio Sausalito, Viña del Mar; Referee: Guillermo Budge Aguirre (Chile); Attendance: 8,220
**CHI:** Oscar Raúl Wirth Lafuente (8/0), Rubén Alberto Espinoza Molina (9/1), Eduardo René Valenzuela Becker (40/0), Eduardo Gómez (4/0) [Oscar Vladimír Rojas Giacomozzi (3/0)], Luis Orlando Hormazábal Gavilan (4/0), Luis Rojas (15/0), Patricio Mardones Díaz (1/0), Jorge Orlando Aravena Plaza (17/11) [Miguel Angel Neira Pincheira (29/3)], Juan Carlos Letelier Pizarro (22/9), Osvaldo Heriberto Hurtado Galeguillo (13/2), Jorge Cabrera (1/0). Trainer: Pedro Morales (11).
**Goals**: Juan Carlos Letelier Pizarro (30), Jorge Orlando Aravena Plaza (60).

**348.** 21.02.1985 **CHILE - COLOMBIA** **1-1(0-1)**
Estadio Nacional, Santiago; Referee: Víctor Ojeda (Chile); Attendance: 22,245
**CHI:** Roberto Antonio Rojas Saavedra (12/0), Lizardo Antonio Garrido Bustamante (20/0), Eduardo René Valenzuela Becker (41/0), Eduardo Gómez (5/0), Luis Orlando Hormazábal Gavilan (5/0) [Hugo del Carmen Tabilo Avilés (2/0)], Miguel Angel Neira Pincheira (30/3) [Patricio Mardones Díaz (2/0)], Luis Rojas (16/0), Jorge Orlando Aravena Plaza (18/11), Hugo Eduardo Rubio Montecinos (3/0), Juan Carlos Letelier Pizarro (23/10), Héctor Eduardo Puebla (3/0) [Osvaldo Heriberto Hurtado Galeguillo (14/2)]. Trainer: Pedro Morales (12).
**Goal**: Juan Carlos Letelier Pizarro (90).

**349.** 24.02.1985 **CHILE - PERU** **1-2(0-1)**
Estadio Nacional, Santiago; Referee: Mario Líra González (Chile); Attendance: 61,294
**CHI:** Roberto Antonio Rojas Saavedra (13/0), Lizardo Antonio Garrido Bustamante (21/0), Eduardo Gómez (6/0), Oscar Vladimír Rojas Giacomozzi (4/0), Alejandro Manuel Hisis Araya (16/0), Luis Rojas (17/0), Patricio Mardones Díaz (3/0), Jorge Orlando Aravena Plaza (19/11) [57.Hugo Eduardo Rubio Montecinos (4/1)], Patricio Nazario Yáñez Candia (27/4), Osvaldo Heriberto Hurtado Galeguillo (15/2), Juan Carlos Letelier Pizarro (24/10) [60.Miguel Angel Neira Pincheira (31/3)]. Trainer: Pedro Morales (13).
**Goal**: Hugo Eduardo Rubio Montecinos (77).

**350.** 03.03.1985 **ECUADOR - CHILE** **1-1(1-1)** 13th FIFA WC.Qualifier
Estádio Olímpico „Atahualpa", Quito; Referee: José Roberto Ramiz Wright (Brazil); Attendance: 40,000
**CHI:** Roberto Antonio Rojas Saavedra (14/0), Lizardo Antonio Garrido Bustamante (22/0), Eduardo Gómez (7/0), Mario del Transito Soto Benavides (37/1), Luis Orlando Hormazábal Gavilan (6/0), Miguel Angel Neira Pincheira (32/3), Patricio Mardones Díaz (4/0) [Leonel Herrera (36/0)], Alejandro Manuel Hisis Araya (17/0), Jorge Orlando Aravena Plaza (20/11), Patricio Nazario Yáñez Candia (28/4), Juan Carlos Letelier Pizarro (25/11) [*sent off*]. Trainer: Pedro Morales (14).
**Goal**: Juan Carlos Letelier Pizarro (31).

**351.** 09.03.1985 **PERU - CHILE** **1-1(1-0)**
Estadio Nacional, Lima; Referee: José Francisco Ramírez Calle (Peru); Attendance: 50,000
**CHI:** Roberto Antonio Rojas Saavedra (15/0), Lizardo Antonio Garrido Bustamante (23/0), Eduardo Gómez (8/0), Mario del Transito Soto Benavides (38/1), Luis Orlando Hormazábal Gavilan (7/0), Miguel Angel Neira Pincheira (33/3), Patricio Mardones Díaz (5/0) [64.Héctor Eduardo Puebla (4/0)], Alejandro Manuel Hisis Araya (18/0), Jorge Orlando Aravena Plaza (21/12), Hugo Eduardo Rubio Montecinos (5/1), Osvaldo Heriberto Hurtado Galeguillo (16/2). Trainer: Pedro Morales (15).
**Goal**: Jorge Orlando Aravena Plaza (90).

**352.** 17.03.1985 **CHILE - ECUADOR** **6-2(4-2)** 13th FIFA WC.Qualifier
Estadio Nacional, Santiago; Referee: Orázio Di Rosa (Venezuela); Attendance: 60,892
**CHI:** Roberto Antonio Rojas Saavedra (16/0), Lizardo Antonio Garrido Bustamante (24/0), Eduardo Gómez (9/0), Mario del Transito Soto Benavides (39/1), Luis Orlando Hormazábal Gavilan (8/0), Miguel Angel Neira Pincheira (34/3), Alejandro Manuel Hisis Araya (19/1), Jorge Orlando Aravena Plaza (22/14), Hugo Eduardo Rubio Montecinos (6/1) [Oscar Herrera Hernández (19/1)], Carlos Humberto Caszely Garrido (45/28) [Patricio Mardones Díaz (6/0)], Héctor Eduardo Puebla (5/1). Trainer: Pedro Morales (16).
**Goals**: Héctor Eduardo Puebla (21), Carlos Humberto Caszely Garrido (29), Alejandro Manuel Hisis Araya (34), Carlos Humberto Caszely Garrido (40), Jorge Orlando Aravena Plaza (51, 89).

**353.** 24.03.1985 **CHILE - URUGUAY** **2-0(1-0)** 13th FIFA WC.Qualifier
Estadio Nacional, Santiago; Referee: Jesús Díaz Palacios (Colombia); Attendance: 79,911
**CHI:** Roberto Antonio Rojas Saavedra (17/0), Eduardo Gómez (10/0), Mario del Transito Soto Benavides (40/1), Lizardo Antonio Garrido Bustamante (25/0), Luis Orlando Hormazábal Gavilan (9/0), Alejandro Manuel Hisis Araya (20/1), Miguel Angel Neira Pincheira (35/3), Jorge Orlando Aravena Plaza (23/15), Hugo Eduardo Rubio Montecinos (7/2), Carlos Humberto Caszely Garrido (46/28), Héctor Eduardo Puebla (6/1). Trainer: Pedro Morales (17).
**Goals**: Hugo Eduardo Rubio Montecinos (28), Jorge Orlando Aravena Plaza (54).

**354.** 07.04.1985 **URUGUAY - CHILE** **2-1(1-1)** 13th FIFA WC.Qualifier
Estadio Centenario, Montevideo; Referee: Carlos Alfonso Espósito (Argentina); Attendance: 66,500
**CHI:** Roberto Antonio Rojas Saavedra (18/0), Hugo del Carmen Tabilo Avilés (3/0), Eduardo René Valenzuela Becker (42/0), Eduardo Gómez (11/0) [62.Juan Carlos Letelier Pizarro (26/11)], Mario del Transito Soto Benavides (41/1), Alejandro Manuel Hisis Araya (21/1), Luis Orlando Hormazábal Gavilan (10/0), Miguel Angel Neira Pincheira (36/3), Hugo Eduardo Rubio Montecinos (8/2), Carlos Humberto Caszely Garrido (47/28), Jorge Orlando Aravena Plaza (24/16). Trainer: Pedro Morales (18).
**Goals**: Jorge Orlando Aravena Plaza (28 penalty).

**355.** 14.05.1985 **ARGENTINA - CHILE** **2-0(1-0)**
Estadio Monumental „Antonio Vespucio Liberti", Buenos Aires; Referee: Carlos Alberto Maciel (Paraguay); Attendance: 36,000
**CHI:** Marco Antonio Cornéz (6/0), Rubén Alberto Espinoza Molina (10/1), Eduardo René Valenzuela Becker (43/0), Mario del Transito Soto Benavides (42/1), René Serrano (3/0), Miguel Angel Neira Pincheira (37/3), Patricio Mardones Díaz (7/0) [46.Mario Lepe (1/0)], Jorge Orlando Aravena Plaza (25/16), Hugo Eduardo Rubio Montecinos (9/2), Juan Carlos Letelier Pizarro (27/11) [70.Osvaldo Heriberto Hurtado Galeguillo (17/2)], Héctor Eduardo Puebla (7/1). Trainer: Pedro Morales (19).

**356.** 21.05.1985 **CHILE - BRAZIL** **2-1(2-0)**
Estadio Nacional, Santiago; Referee: Juan Oscar Ortubé Vargas (Bolivia); Attendance: 20,274
**CHI:** Roberto Antonio Rojas Saavedra (19/0), Lizardo Antonio Garrido Bustamante (26/0), Eduardo René Valenzuela Becker (44/0), Leonel Herrera (37/0), Luis Orlando Hormazábal Gavilan (11/0), Mario Lepe (2/0), Miguel Angel Neira Pincheira (38/3), Jorge Orlando Aravena Plaza (26/16) [Patricio Mardones Díaz (8/0)], Hugo Eduardo Rubio Montecinos (10/3) [Juan Carlos Letelier Pizarro (28/11)], Carlos Humberto Caszely Garrido (48/29) [Osvaldo Heriberto Hurtado Galeguillo (18/2)], Héctor Eduardo Puebla (8/1). Trainer: Pedro Morales (20).
**Goals**: Hugo Eduardo Rubio Montecinos (8), Carlos Humberto Caszely Garrido (43).

**357.** 08.06.1985 **BRAZIL - CHILE** **3-1(2-0)**
Estádio Beira Rio, Porto Alegre; Referee: Ricardo Calabria (Argentina); Attendance: 62,000
**CHI:** Roberto Antonio Rojas Saavedra (20/0), Lizardo Antonio Garrido Bustamante (27/0), Eduardo René Valenzuela Becker (45/0), Eduardo Gómez (12/0), Luis Orlando Hormazábal Gavilan (12/0) [René Serrano (4/0)], Mario Lepe (3/0), Miguel Angel Neira Pincheira (39/3) [Rodolfo del Rosario Dubó Segovia (44/3)], Jorge Orlando Aravena Plaza (27/16), Juan Carlos Letelier Pizarro (29/11) [Alfredo Núñez (1/1)], Osvaldo Heriberto Hurtado Galeguillo (19/2), Héctor Eduardo Puebla (9/1). Trainer: Pedro Morales (21).
**Goal**: Alfredo Núñez (77).

**358.** 09.10.1985 **PARAGUAY - CHILE** **0-0**
Estadio Defensores del Chaco, Asunción; Referee: Carlos Alberto Maciel (Paraguay); Attendance: 17,219
**CHI:** Roberto Antonio Rojas Saavedra (21/0), Lizardo Antonio Garrido Bustamante (28/0), Eduardo Gómez (13/0), Mario del Transito Soto Benavides (43/1), Luis Orlando Hormazábal Gavilan (13/0), Miguel Angel Neira Pincheira (40/3), Patricio Mardones Díaz (9/0) [Rodolfo del Rosario Dubó Segovia (45/3)], Mario Lepe (4/0), Jorge Muñoz (1/0), Juan Carlos Letelier Pizarro (30/11), Héctor Eduardo Puebla (10/1). Trainer: Pedro Morales (22).

**359.** 17.10.1985 **CHILE - URUGUAY** **1-0(1-0)**
Estadio Nacional, Santiago; Referee: Víctor Ojeda (Chile); Attendance: 25,000
**CHI:** Oscar Raúl Wirth Lafuente (9/0), Rubén Alberto Espinoza Molina (11/1), Leonel Contreras (1/0), Eduardo Gómez (14/0), Luis Orlando Hormazábal Gavilan (14/0), Miguel Angel Neira Pincheira (41/4) [Luis Arturo Jáuregui Peña (1/0)], Mario Lepe (5/0), Patricio Mardones Díaz (10/0), Jorge Muñoz (2/0), Juan Carlos Letelier Pizarro (31/11), Héctor Eduardo Puebla (11/1). Trainer: Pedro Morales (23).
**Goal**: Miguel Angel Neira Pincheira (33).

**360.** 19.10.1985 **CHILE - PARAGUAY** **0-0**
Estadio Nacional, Santiago; Referee: Enrique Marín Gallo (Chile); Attendance: 10,000
**CHI:** Roberto Antonio Rojas Saavedra (22/0), Lizardo Antonio Garrido Bustamante (29/0), Leonel Herrera (38/0), Mario del Transito Soto Benavides (44/1), René Serrano (5/0), Rodolfo del Rosario Dubó Segovia (46/3) [Miguel Angel Neira Pincheira (42/4)], Mario Lepe (6/0) [Alejandro Manuel Hisis Araya (22/1)], Luis Arturo Jáuregui Peña (2/0), Sergio Mario Salgado Cofré (1/0) [Jorge Muñoz (3/0)], Juan Carlos Letelier Pizarro (32/11), Héctor Eduardo Puebla (12/1). Trainer: Pedro Morales (24).

**361.** 27.10.1985 **CHILE - PERU** **4-2(3-0)** 13th FIFA WC.Qualifier
Estadio Nacional, Santiago; Referee: José Luis Martínez Bazán (Uruguay); Attendance: 40,340
**CHI:** Roberto Antonio Rojas Saavedra (23/0), Lizardo Antonio Garrido Bustamante (30/0) [80.Rubén Alberto Espinoza Molina (12/1)], Eduardo Gómez (15/0), Mario del Transito Soto Benavides (45/1), Luis Orlando Hormazábal Gavilan (15/0), Miguel Angel Neira Pincheira (43/4) [67.Mario Lepe (7/0)], Alejandro Manuel Hisis Araya (23/2), Jorge Orlando Aravena Plaza (28/18), Patricio Nazario Yáñez Candia (29/4), Hugo Eduardo Rubio Montecinos (11/4), Héctor Eduardo Puebla (13/1). Trainer: Pedro Morales (25).
**Goals**: Jorge Orlando Aravena Plaza (7), Hugo Eduardo Rubio Montecinos (9), Alejandro Manuel Hisis Araya (15), Jorge Orlando Aravena Plaza (65 penalty).

**362.** 03.11.1985 **PERU - CHILE** **0-1(0-0)** 13th FIFA WC.Qualifier
Estadio Nacional, Lima; Referee: Arnaldo David César Coelho (Brazil); Attendance: 45,244
**CHI:** Roberto Antonio Rojas Saavedra (24/0), Lizardo Antonio Garrido Bustamante (31/0), Eduardo Gómez (16/0), Mario del Transito Soto Benavides (46/1), Luis Orlando Hormazábal Gavilan (16/0), Alejandro Manuel Hisis Araya (24/2), Mario Lepe (8/0), Jorge Orlando Aravena Plaza (29/19), Patricio Nazario Yáñez Candia (30/4) [65.Rubén Alberto Espinoza Molina (13/1)], Hugo Eduardo Rubio Montecinos (12/4), Héctor Eduardo Puebla (14/1). Trainer: Pedro Morales (26).
**Goal**: Jorge Orlando Aravena Plaza (64).

**363.** 10.11.1985 **PARAGUAY - CHILE** **3-0(1-0)** 13th FIFA WC.Qualifier
Estadio Defensores del Chaco, Asunción; Referee: Arnaldo David César Coelho (Brazil); Attendance: 45,000
**CHI:** Roberto Antonio Rojas Saavedra (25/0), Lizardo Antonio Garrido Bustamante (32/0), Eduardo Gómez (17/0), Mario del Transito Soto Benavides (47/1), Luis Orlando Hormazábal Gavilan (17/0), Alejandro Manuel Hisis Araya (25/2), Mario Lepe (9/0) [Miguel Angel Neira Pincheira (44/4)], Jorge Orlando Aravena Plaza (30/19), Hugo Eduardo Rubio Montecinos (13/4), Juan Carlos Letelier Pizarro (33/11), Héctor Eduardo Puebla (15/1). Trainer: Pedro Morales (27).

**364.** 17.11.1985 **CHILE - PARAGUAY** **2-2(1-2)** 13th FIFA WC.Qualifier
Estadio Nacional, Santiago; Referee: Juan Daniel Cardellino de San Vicente (Uruguay); Attendance: 62,592
**CHI:** Roberto Antonio Rojas Saavedra (26/0), Rubén Alberto Espinoza Molina (14/1), Leonel Herrera (39/0) [Juan Carlos Letelier Pizarro (34/11)], Mario del Transito Soto Benavides (48/1), Luis Orlando Hormazábal Gavilan (18/0), Miguel Angel Neira Pincheira (45/4), Alejandro Manuel Hisis Araya (26/2) [*sent off 78*], Jorge Orlando Aravena Plaza (31/19), Patricio Nazario Yáñez Candia (31/4), Hugo Eduardo Rubio Montecinos (14/5) [Jorge Muñoz (4/1)], Héctor Eduardo Puebla (16/1). Trainer: Pedro Morales (28).
**Goals**: Hugo Eduardo Rubio Montecinos (21), Jorge Muñoz (77).

**365.** 07.05.1986 **BRAZIL - CHILE** **1-1(0-1)**
Estádio „Antônio de Couto Pereira" ‚Pinheirão', Curitiba; Referee: Carlos Martins (Brazil); Attendance: 30,000
**CHI:** Roberto Antonio Rojas Saavedra (27/0), Rubén Alberto Espinoza Molina (15/1), Luis Alejandro Valenzuela (1/0), Manuel Araya (2/0), Manuel Pellegrini (1/0), Óscar Patricio Reyes Sánchez (2/0), Jaime Andrés Vera (1/0) [78.Jaime Augusto Pizarro Herrera (1/0)], Juan Soto Quintana (16/1), Ivo Alexis Basay (1/0), Marco Antonio Figueroa Montero (1/0) [76.Fernando Astengo (1/0)], Mariano Puyol (1/1). Trainer: Luis Ibarra Castillo (17).
**Goal**: Mariano Puyol (26).

**366.** 19.06.1987 **PERU - CHILE** **1-3(0-0)**
Estadio Nacional, Lima; Referee: Samuel Alarcón (Peru); Attendance: 2,223
**CHI:** Marco Antonio Cornéz (7/0), Óscar Patricio Reyes Sánchez (3/0), Ricardo Toro (1/0), Carlos Soto Sandoval (1/1), Alex Martínez (1/0), Orlando Alberto Mondaca Reyes (6/0) [70.Iván Luis Zamorano Zamora (1/1)], Luis Rodríguez (2/0), Patricio Mardones Díaz (11/0), Sergio Mario Salgado Cofré (2/0), Osvaldo Heriberto Hurtado Galeguillo (20/2), Ivo Alexis Basay (2/1). Trainer: Orlando Aravena (1).
**Goals**: Carlos Soto Sandoval (70), Ivo Alexis Basay (72), Iván Luis Zamorano Zamora (74).

**367.** 21.06.1987 **PERU - CHILE** **2-0(1-0)**
Estadio Nacional, Lima; Referee: José Francisco Ramírez Calle (Peru); Attendance: 12,000
**CHI:** Marco Antonio Cornéz (8/0), Óscar Patricio Reyes Sánchez (4/0), Ricardo Toro (2/0), Carlos Soto Sandoval (2/1), Alex Martínez (2/0), Patricio Mardones Díaz (12/0), Luis Rodríguez (3/0), Osvaldo Heriberto Hurtado Galeguillo (21/2), Sergio Mario Salgado Cofré (3/0), Iván Luis Zamorano Zamora (2/1), Ivo Alexis Basay (3/1) [69.Orlando Alberto Mondaca Reyes (7/0)]. Trainer: Orlando Aravena (2).

**368.** 24.06.1987 **CHILE - PERU** **1-0(1-0)**
Estadio Nacional, Santiago; Referee: Víctor Ojeda (Chile); Attendance: 3,583
**CHI:** Roberto Antonio Rojas Saavedra (28/0), Rubén Alberto Espinoza Molina (16/1), Ricardo Toro (3/0), Eduardo Gómez (18/0), Luis Orlando Hormazábal Gavilan (19/0), Patricio Mardones Díaz (13/0), Jaime Augusto Pizarro Herrera (2/0), Osvaldo Heriberto Hurtado Galeguillo (22/3) [66.Iván Luis Zamorano Zamora (3/1)], Hugo Eduardo Rubio Montecinos (15/5) [59.Sergio Mario Salgado Cofré (4/0)], Jorge Alejandro Contreras Lira (3/0) [85.Jaime Andrés Vera (2/0)], Juan Carlos Letelier Pizarro (35/11) [73.Héctor Eduardo Puebla (17/1)]. Trainer: Orlando Aravena (3).
**Goal**: Osvaldo Heriberto Hurtado Galeguillo (18).

**369.** 30.06.1987 **CHILE - VENEZUELA** **3-1(1-1)** 33rd Copa América. Group Stage.
Estadio Chateau Carreras, Córdoba (Argentina); Referee: Luis Barrancos Álvarez (Bolivia); Attendance: 532
**CHI:** Roberto Antonio Rojas Saavedra (29/0), Rubén Alberto Espinoza Molina (17/1), Eduardo Gómez (19/0) [*sent off 56*], Fernando Astengo (2/0), Alex Martínez (3/0), Jaime Augusto Pizarro Herrera (3/0), Patricio Mardones Díaz (14/0), Osvaldo Heriberto Hurtado Galeguillo (23/3) [64.Jaime Andrés Vera (3/0)], Juan Carlos Letelier Pizarro (36/12) [46.Sergio Mario Salgado Cofré (5/1)], Ivo Alexis Basay (4/1), Jorge Alejandro Contreras Lira (4/1). Trainer: Orlando Aravena (4).
**Goals**: Juan Carlos Letelier Pizarro (17), Jorge Alejandro Contreras Lira (70), Sergio Mario Salgado Cofré (83).

**370.** 03.07.1987 **CHILE - BRAZIL** **4-0(1-0)** 33rd Copa América. Group Stage.
Estadio Chateau Carreras, Córdoba (Argentina); Referee: Juan Daniel Cardellino de San Vicente (Uruguay); Attendance: 15,000
**CHI:** Roberto Antonio Rojas Saavedra (30/0), Óscar Patricio Reyes Sánchez (5/0), Fernando Astengo (3/0), Ricardo Toro (4/0), Luis Orlando Hormazábal Gavilan (20/0), Patricio Mardones Díaz (15/0), Jaime Augusto Pizarro Herrera (4/0), Jorge Alejandro Contreras Lira (5/1), Héctor Eduardo Puebla (18/1), Ivo Alexis Basay (5/3) [80.Iván Luis Zamorano Zamora (4/1)], Juan Carlos Letelier Pizarro (37/14) [76.Sergio Mario Salgado Cofré (6/1)]. Trainer: Orlando Aravena (5).
**Goals**: Ivo Alexis Basay (41), Juan Carlos Letelier Pizarro (48), Ivo Alexis Basay (66), Juan Carlos Letelier Pizarro (75).

**371.** 08.07.1987 **CHILE - COLOMBIA** **2-1(0-0,0-0)** 33rd Copa América. Semi-Finals.
Estadio Chateau Carreras, Córdoba (Argentina); Referee: Romualdo Arppi Filho (Brazil); Attendance: 10,000
**CHI:** Roberto Antonio Rojas Saavedra (31/0), Óscar Patricio Reyes Sánchez (6/0), Fernando Astengo (4/1), Eduardo Gómez (20/0), Luis Orlando Hormazábal Gavilan (21/0), Patricio Mardones Díaz (16/0), Jaime Augusto Pizarro Herrera (5/0), Héctor Eduardo Puebla (19/1) [81.Jaime Andrés Vera (4/1)], Jorge Alejandro Contreras Lira (6/1), Ivo Alexis Basay (6/3) [54.Sergio Mario Salgado Cofré (7/1)], Juan Carlos Letelier Pizarro (38/14). Trainer: Orlando Aravena (6).
**Goals**: Fernando Astengo (106), Jaime Andrés Vera (108).

**372.** 12.07.1987 **URUGUAY - CHILE** **1-0(0-0)** 33rd Copa América. Final.
Estadio Monumental „Antonio Vespucio Liberti“, Buenos Aires (Argentina); Referee: Romualdo Arppi Filho (Brazil); Attendance: 35,000
**CHI:** Roberto Antonio Rojas Saavedra (32/0), Óscar Patricio Reyes Sánchez (7/0), Eduardo Gómez (21/0) [*sent off 14*], Fernando Astengo (5/1) [*sent off 88*], Luis Orlando Hormazábal Gavilan (22/0), Patricio Mardones Díaz (17/0), Jaime Augusto Pizarro Herrera (6/0), Héctor Eduardo Puebla (20/1) [19.Ricardo Toro (5/0); 65.Hugo Eduardo Rubio Montecinos (16/5)], Jorge Alejandro Contreras Lira (7/1), Juan Carlos Letelier Pizarro (39/14), Ivo Alexis Basay (7/3). Trainer: Orlando Aravena (7).

**373.** 09.12.1987 **BRAZIL - CHILE** **2-1(0-1)**
Estádio Parque do Sabiá, Uberlândia; Referee: Juan Escobar Váldez (Paraguay); Attendance: 40,000
**CHI:** Mario Ignacio Osbén Méndez (30/0), Óscar Patricio Reyes Sánchez (8/0), Gustavo Huerta (1/0) [Vladimir David Bigorra López (21/1)], Juan Rivera (1/0), Leonel Pedreros (1/0), Jaime Augusto Pizarro Herrera (7/0), Julio Suazo (1/0), Manuel Pedreros Guevara (1/0) [Francisco Ugarte (1/0)], Sergio Mario Salgado Cofré (8/1) [Iván Luis Zamorano Zamora (5/1)], Osvaldo Heriberto Hurtado Galeguillo (24/3), Rubén Martínez (1/1). Trainer: Manuel Rodríguez Araneda (1).
**Goal**: Rubén Martínez (36).

**374.** 23.05.1988 **GREECE - CHILE** **1-0(0-0)** Stanley Matthews Cup
Varsity Stadium, Toronto (Canada); Referee: Antonio Evangelista (Canada); Attendance: 11,106
**CHI:** Marco Antonio Cornéz (9/0), Óscar Patricio Reyes Sánchez (9/0), Claudio Tello (1/0), Oscar Vladimír Rojas Giacomozzi (5/0), Roberto Reynero (1/0), Nélson Enríquez (1/0) [Sergio Mario Salgado Cofré (9/1)], Jaime Augusto Pizarro Herrera (8/0), Francisco Ugarte (2/0), Hugo Eduardo Rubio Montecinos (17/5), Osvaldo Heriberto Hurtado Galeguillo (25/3), Iván Luis Zamorano Zamora (6/1). Trainer: Orlando Aravena (8).

**375.** 25.05.1988 **CANADA - CHILE** **1-0(1-0)** Stanley Matthews Cup
Varsity Stadium, Toronto; Referee: Carlo Longhi (Italy); Attendance: 4,178
**CHI:** Marco Antonio Cornéz (10/0), Óscar Patricio Reyes Sánchez (10/0), Claudio Tello (2/0), Oscar Vladimír Rojas Giacomozzi (6/0), Roberto Reynero (2/0), Nélson Enríquez (2/0) [Juan Soto Quintana (17/1)], Jaime Augusto Pizarro Herrera (9/0), Francisco Ugarte (3/0), Hugo Eduardo Rubio Montecinos (18/5), Osvaldo Heriberto Hurtado Galeguillo (26/3), Iván Luis Zamorano Zamora (7/1). Trainer: Orlando Aravena (9).

**376.** 01.06.1988 **UNITED STATES - CHILE** **1-1(0-0)**
Pacific University Stadium, Stockton; Referee: Núñez (Mexico); Attendance: 9,600
**CHI:** Marco Antonio Cornéz (11/0), Roberto Reynero (3/0), Claudio Tello (3/0), Oscar Vladimír Rojas Giacomozzi (7/0), Óscar Patricio Reyes Sánchez (11/0), Nélson Enríquez (3/0) [Francisco Ugarte (4/0)], Jaime Augusto Pizarro Herrera (10/0), Hugo Eduardo Rubio Montecinos (19/5), Juan Soto Quintana (18/1), Osvaldo Heriberto Hurtado Galeguillo (27/4), Iván Luis Zamorano Zamora (8/1) [Sergio Mario Salgado Cofré (10/1)]. Trainer: Orlando Aravena (10).
**Goal**: Osvaldo Heriberto Hurtado Galeguillo (49).

**377.** 03.06.1988 **UNITED STATES - CHILE** **1-3(1-2)**
San Diego; Referee: Couret (Mexico); Attendance: 6,000
**CHI:** Marco Antonio Cornéz (12/0), Marco Opazo (2/0), Claudio Tello (4/0), Oscar Vladimír Rojas Giacomozzi (8/1), Óscar Patricio Reyes Sánchez (12/0), Nélson Enríquez (4/0), Jaime Augusto Pizarro Herrera (11/0), Hugo Eduardo Rubio Montecinos (20/5), Juan Soto Quintana (19/1) [Francisco Ugarte (5/0)], Osvaldo Heriberto Hurtado Galeguillo (28/5) [Fernando Pérez (1/0)], Sergio Mario Salgado Cofré (11/2) [Iván Luis Zamorano Zamora (9/1)]. Trainer: Orlando Aravena (11).
**Goals**: Osvaldo Heriberto Hurtado Galeguillo (22), Sergio Mario Salgado Cofré (34), Oscar Vladimír Rojas Giacomozzi (53).

**378.** 05.06.1988 **UNITED STATES - CHILE** **0-3(0-1)**
Bulldog Stadium, Fresno; Referee: Couret (Mexico); Attendance: 4,610
**CHI:** Marco Antonio Cornéz (13/0), Marco Opazo (3/0), Claudio Tello (5/0), Oscar Vladimír Rojas Giacomozzi (9/1), Óscar Patricio Reyes Sánchez (13/0), Jaime Augusto Pizarro Herrera (12/0), Juan Soto Quintana (20/1) [Nélson Enríquez (5/0)], Francisco Ugarte (6/0), Hugo Eduardo Rubio Montecinos (21/7), Osvaldo Heriberto Hurtado Galeguillo (29/6) [Iván Luis Zamorano Zamora (10/1)], Sergio Mario Salgado Cofré (12/2) [Aníbal Segundo González (1/0)]. Trainer: Orlando Aravena (12).
**Goals**: Osvaldo Heriberto Hurtado Galeguillo (1), Hugo Eduardo Rubio Montecinos (51, 66).

**379.** 13.09.1988 **CHILE - ECUADOR** **3-1(1-0)**
Estadio La Portada, La Serena; Referee: Pedro Roa (Chile); Attendance: 6,345
**CHI:** Mario Ignacio Osbén Méndez (31/0), Daniel Ahumada Gaete (1/0), Eduardo René Valenzuela Becker (46/0), Claudio Tello (6/0), Héctor Eduardo Puebla (21/1), Luis Rodríguez (4/0), Nélson Enríquez (6/0), Jaime Patricio Ramírez (1/0) [83.Mario Cruz (1/0)], Sergio Mario Salgado Cofré (13/3), Ramón Pérez (1/0), Rubén Martínez (2/1) [63.Marcelo Alvarez (1/1)]. Trainer: Orlando Aravena (13).
**Goals**: Sergio Mario Salgado Cofré (7), Marcelo Alvarez (66), Kléber Fajardo (88 own goal).

**380.** 27.09.1988 **PARAGUAY - CHILE** **2-0(2-0)** Copa Boquerón

Estadio Defensores del Chaco, Asunción; Referee: Luís Carlos Félix Ferrara (Brazil); Attendance: 22,000

**CHI:** Mario Ignacio Osbén Méndez (32/0), Óscar Patricio Reyes Sánchez (14/0), Claudio Tello (7/0), Leonel Contreras (2/0), Héctor Eduardo Puebla (22/1) [46.Roberto Reynero (4/0)], Fernando Pérez (2/0), Mario Cruz (2/0) [46.Sergio Mario Salgado Cofré (14/3)], Luis Rodríguez (5/0), Jaime Patricio Ramírez (2/0), Ramón Pérez (2/0), Rubén Martínez (3/1). Trainer: Orlando Aravena (14).

**381.** 29.09.1988 **CHILE - ECUADOR** **0-0; 2-3 on penalties** Copa Boquerón

Estadio Defensores del Chaco, Asunción; Referee: Artemio Martínez (Paraguay); Attendance: 25,000

**CHI:** Mario Ignacio Osbén Méndez (33/0), Óscar Patricio Reyes Sánchez (15/0) [46.Daniel Ahumada Gaete (2/0)], Claudio Tello (8/0), Leonel Contreras (3/0), Roberto Reynero (5/0), Fernando Pérez (3/0), Luis Rodríguez (6/0), Jaime Patricio Ramírez (3/0), Sergio Mario Salgado Cofré (15/3), Ramón Pérez (3/0), Marcelo Alvarez (2/1) [67.Rubén Martínez (4/1)]. Trainer: Orlando Aravena (15).

**Penalties**: Sergio Mario Salgado Cofré, Leonel Contreras (both scored); Ramón Pérez, Rubén Martínez, Jaime Patricio Ramírez (all missed).

**382.** 25.10.1988 **CHILE - PERU** **2-0(1-0)** Copa del Pacífico

Estadio „Carlos Dittborn“, Arica; Referee: Juan Pablo Torrens (Chile); Attendance: 7,656

**CHI:** Mario Ignacio Osbén Méndez (34/0), Rubén Alberto Espinoza Molina (18/2), Hugo Armando González (1/1), Leonel Contreras (4/0), Roberto Reynero (6/0), Jaime Patricio Ramírez (4/0) [46.Patricio Mardones Díaz (18/0)], Jaime Augusto Pizarro Herrera (13/0), Mario Lepe (10/0), Oscar Herrera Hernández (20/1), Aníbal Segundo González (2/0) [66.Alfredo Núñez (2/1)], Marcelo Alvarez (3/1) [77.Juan Covarrubias (2/0)]. Trainer: Orlando Aravena (16).

**Goals**: Rubén Alberto Espinoza Molina (39 penalty), Hugo Armando González (85).

**383.** 01.11.1988 **CHILE - URUGUAY** **1-1(0-0)** Copa Pinto Durán

Estadio Regional, Concepción; Referee: Carlos Manuel Robles Mella (Chile); Attendance: 16,301

**CHI:** Mario Ignacio Osbén Méndez (35/0), Rubén Alberto Espinoza Molina (19/3), Hugo Armando González (2/1), Leonel Contreras (5/0), Roberto Reynero (7/0) [46.Lester Lacroix (1/0)], Patricio Mardones Díaz (19/0), Mario Lepe (11/0), Jaime Augusto Pizarro Herrera (14/0), Oscar Herrera Hernández (21/1), Alfredo Núñez (3/1) [65.Aníbal Segundo González (3/0)], Marcelo Alvarez (4/1). Trainer: Orlando Aravena (17).

**Goal**: Rubén Alberto Espinoza Molina (89 penalty).

**384.** 09.11.1988 **URUGUAY - CHILE** **3-1(0-0)** Copa Pinto Durán

Estadio Centenario, Montevideo; Referee: Juan Daniel Cardellino de San Vicente (Uruguay); Attendance: 6,470

**CHI:** Mario Ignacio Osbén Méndez (36/0), Rubén Alberto Espinoza Molina (20/4), Hugo Armando González (3/1), Leonel Contreras (6/0), Alex Martínez (4/0), Patricio Mardones Díaz (20/0), Jaime Augusto Pizarro Herrera (15/0), Mario Lepe (12/0), Jorge García (2/0), Oscar Herrera Hernández (22/1) [62.Juan Covarrubias (3/0)], Marcelo Alvarez (5/1). Trainer: Orlando Aravena (18).

**Goal**: Rubén Alberto Espinoza Molina (90).

**385.** 23.11.1988 **PERU - CHILE** **1-1(0-1)** Copa del Pacífico

Estadio Nacional, Lima; Referee: Walter Barrios (Peru); Attendance: 30,000

**CHI:** Marco Antonio Cornéz (14/0), Rubén Alberto Espinoza Molina (21/4), Hugo Armando González (4/1), Leonel Contreras (7/0), Héctor Eduardo Puebla (23/1), Patricio Mardones Díaz (21/1), Jaime Augusto Pizarro Herrera (16/0), Mario Lepe (13/0), Jorge García (3/0), Lukas Nicolás Túdor (1/0), Marcelo Alvarez (6/1) [78.Oscar Herrera Hernández (23/1)]. Trainer: Orlando Aravena (19).

**Goal**: Patricio Mardones Díaz (29).

**386.** 29.01.1989 **ECUADOR - CHILE** **1-0(1-0)**

Estadio Monumental „Isidro Romero Carbo“, Guayaquil; Referee: Alfredo Rodas (Ecuador); Attendance: 13,000

**CHI:** Oscar Raúl Wirth Lafuente (10/0), Daniel Ahumada Gaete (3/0), Jorge Carrasco (1/0), Leonel Contreras (8/0), Lester Lacroix (2/0) [62.Juan Carlos Hernández (1/0)], Carlos Ramos (1/0) [62.Rubén Martínez (5/1)], Iván Valdés (1/0), Marco Antonio Figueroa Montero (2/0), Jaime Patricio Ramírez (5/0), Ramón Pérez (4/0) [46.Marcelo Alvarez (7/1)], Cristián Olguín (1/0) [46.Guillermo Carreño (1/0)]. Trainer: Orlando Aravena (20).

**387.** 01.02.1989 **PERU - CHILE** **0-0**

Estadio Centenario, Arménia (Colombia); Referee: Armando Pérez Hoyos (Colombia); Attendance: 13,000

**CHI:** Oscar Raúl Wirth Lafuente (11/0), Daniel Ahumada Gaete (4/0) [*sent off 55*], Jorge Carrasco (2/0) [*sent off 50*], Leonel Contreras (9/0) [*sent off 87*], Juan Carlos Hernández (2/0), Iván Valdés (2/0), Luis Rodríguez (7/0), Claudio Figueroa (1/0), Jaime Patricio Ramírez (6/0) [46.José Cantillana (1/0)], Juan Carlos Letelier Pizarro (40/14), Marcelo Alvarez (8/1) [60.Rubén Martínez (6/1)]. Trainer: Orlando Aravena (21).

**388.** 05.02.1989 **COLOMBIA - CHILE** **1-0(0-0)**

Estadio Centenario, Arménia; Referee: Jesús Díaz Palacios (Colombia); Attendance: 12,000

**CHI:** Oscar Raúl Wirth Lafuente (12/0), Jorge Carrasco (3/0), José Cantillana (2/0), Leonel Contreras (10/0), Claudio Figueroa (2/0), Juan Carlos Hernández (3/0), Iván Valdés (3/0) [60.Rubén Martínez (7/1)], Luis Rodríguez (8/0), Jaime Patricio Ramírez (7/0) [56.Carlos Ramos (2/0)], Juan Carlos Letelier Pizarro (41/14), Marcelo Alvarez (9/1) [72.Guillermo Carreño (2/0)]. Trainer: Orlando Aravena (22).

**389.** 20.04.1989 **CHILE - ARGENTINA** **1-1(0-1)**

Estadio Nacional, Santiago; Referee: Octavio Sierra (Colombia); Attendance: 11,663

**CHI:** Marco Antonio Cornéz (15/0), Rubén Alberto Espinoza Molina (22/5), Hugo Armando González (5/1), Fernando Astengo (6/1), Juan Carlos Hernández (4/0), Elías Raúl Ormeño Pacheco (2/0), Jaime Augusto Pizarro Herrera (17/0), Claudio Figueroa (3/0), Jaime Patricio Ramírez (8/0), Sergio Mario Salgado Cofré (16/3) [62.Lukas Nicolás Túdor (2/0)], Juan Carlos Letelier Pizarro (42/14). Trainer: Orlando Aravena (23).

**Goal**: Rubén Alberto Espinoza Molina (69 penalty).

**390.** 05.05.1989 **CHILE - GUATEMALA** **1-0(0-0)** Copa Interamericana

Memorial Coliseum, Los Angeles; Referee: Majid Jay Abutalebi (United States); Attendance: 18,700

**CHI:** Roberto Antonio Rojas Saavedra (33/0), Óscar Patricio Reyes Sánchez (16/0), Hugo Armando González (6/1), Fernando Astengo (7/1) [46.Leonel Contreras (11/0)], Claudio Figueroa (4/0), Elías Raúl Ormeño Pacheco (3/0), Jaime Augusto Pizarro Herrera (18/0), Juvenal Mario Olmos Rojas (1/0), Jaime Patricio Ramírez (9/0) [34.Sergio Mario Salgado Cofré (17/3)], Juan Carlos Letelier Pizarro (43/14) [86.Luis Pérez (1/0)], Rubén Martínez (8/2). Trainer: Orlando Aravena (24).

**Goals**: Rubén Martínez (67).

**391.** 07.05.1989 **CHILE – EL SALVADOR** **1-0(0-0)** Copa Interamericana

Memorial Coliseum, Los Angeles; Referee: Edward Bellion (United States); Attendance: 10,997

**CHI:** Roberto Antonio Rojas Saavedra (34/0), Óscar Patricio Reyes Sánchez (17/0), Hugo Armando González (7/1), Leonel Contreras (12/0), Juan Carlos Hernández (5/0), Elías Raúl Ormeño Pacheco (4/1), Jaime Augusto Pizarro Herrera (19/0), Luis Arturo Jáuregui Peña (3/0), Luis Pérez (2/0), Lukas Nicolás Túdor (3/0), Rubén Martínez (9/2) [Juan Carlos Letelier Pizarro (44/14)]. Trainer: Orlando Aravena (25).

**Goals**: Elías Raúl Ormeño Pacheco (80).

**392.** 23.05.1989 **ENGLAND - CHILE** **0-0** Stanley Rous Cup

Wembley Stadium, London; Referee: Erik Fredriksson (Sweden); Attendance: 15,628

**CHI:** Roberto Antonio Rojas Saavedra (35/0), Leonel Contreras (13/0), Rubén Alberto Espinoza Molina (23/5), Hugo Armando González (8/1), Fernando Astengo (8/1), Óscar Patricio Reyes Sánchez (18/0), Elías Raúl Ormeño Pacheco (5/1), Jaime Augusto Pizarro Herrera (20/0), Osvaldo Heriberto Hurtado Galeguillo (30/6) [55.Jaime Andrés Vera (5/1)], Hugo Eduardo Rubio Montecinos (22/7), Juan Covarrubias (4/0) [46.Juan Carlos Letelier Pizarro (45/14)]. Trainer: Orlando Aravena (26).

**393.** 26.05.1989 **NORTHERN IRELAND - CHILE** **0-1(0-1)**

Windsor Park, Belfast; Referee: George Smith (Scotland); Attendance: 6,850

**CHI:** Roberto Antonio Rojas Saavedra (36/0), Leonel Contreras (14/0), Rubén Alberto Espinoza Molina (24/5), Hugo Armando González (9/1), Fernando Astengo (9/2) [46.Juvenal Mario Olmos Rojas (2/0)], Óscar Patricio Reyes Sánchez (19/0), Jaime Andrés Vera (6/1), Alejandro Manuel Hisis Araya (27/2), Jaime Augusto Pizarro Herrera (21/0), Osvaldo Heriberto Hurtado Galeguillo (31/6) [85.Luis Pérez (3/0)], Juan Carlos Letelier Pizarro (46/14) [46.Juan Covarrubias (5/0)]. Trainer: Orlando Aravena (27).

**Goal**: Fernando Astengo (44).

**394.** 30.05.1989 **SCOTLAND - CHILE** **2-0(1-0)** Stanley Rous Cup

Hampden Park, Glasgow; Referee: Alexis Ponnet (Belgium); Attendance: 9,006

**CHI:** Roberto Antonio Rojas Saavedra (37/0), Leonel Contreras (15/0), Óscar Patricio Reyes Sánchez (20/0), Hugo Armando González (10/1), Héctor Eduardo Puebla (24/1), Jaime Andrés Vera (7/1), Alejandro Manuel Hisis Araya (28/2), Jaime Augusto Pizarro Herrera (22/0), Juvenal Mario Olmos Rojas (3/0) [65.Jaime Patricio Ramírez (10/0)], Hugo Eduardo Rubio Montecinos (23/7), Juan Covarrubias (6/0) [46.Juan Carlos Letelier Pizarro (47/14)]. Trainer: Orlando Aravena (28).

**395.** 03.06.1989 **EGYPT - CHILE** **2-0(2-0)**

Nasser Stadium, Cairo; Referee: Mohamed Hussam El-Din (Egypt); Attendance: 22,000

**CHI:** Roberto Antonio Rojas Saavedra (38/0), Leonel Contreras (16/0), Óscar Patricio Reyes Sánchez (21/0), Hugo Armando González (11/1), Héctor Eduardo Puebla (25/1) [Rubén Alberto Espinoza Molina (25/5)], Jaime Andrés Vera (8/1), Alejandro Manuel Hisis Araya (29/2), Jaime Augusto Pizarro Herrera (23/0), Jaime Patricio Ramírez (11/0) [Luis Pérez (4/0)], Lukas Nicolás Túdor (4/0) [Osvaldo Heriberto Hurtado Galeguillo (32/6)], Rubén Martínez (10/2) [Juan Covarrubias (7/0)]. Trainer: Orlando Aravena (29).

**396.** 19.06.1989 **URUGUAY - CHILE** **2-2(0-1)**

Estadio Centenario, Montevideo; Referee: Ernesto Filippi Cavani (Uruguay); Attendance: 20,982

**CHI:** Roberto Antonio Rojas Saavedra (39/0), Jorge Carrasco (4/0), Hugo Armando González (12/2), Fernando Astengo (10/2), Óscar Patricio Reyes Sánchez (22/0), Elías Raúl Ormeño Pacheco (6/1), Alejandro Manuel Hisis Araya (30/2), Jaime Augusto Pizarro Herrera (24/1), Jaime Andrés Vera (9/1), Osvaldo Heriberto Hurtado Galeguillo (33/6) [Juan Carlos Letelier Pizarro (48/14)], Juan Covarrubias (8/0) [Juvenal Mario Olmos Rojas (4/0)]. Trainer: Orlando Aravena (30).

**Goals**: Hugo Armando González (34), Jaime Augusto Pizarro Herrera (66 penalty).

**397.** 22.06.1989 **BOLIVIA - CHILE** **0-1(0-1)**

Estadio „Ramón 'Tahuichi' Aguilera", Santa Cruz; Referee: Armando Aliaga (Bolivia); Attendance: 25,000

**CHI:** Roberto Antonio Rojas Saavedra (40/0), Jorge Carrasco (5/0), Hugo Armando González (13/2), Fernando Astengo (11/2), Óscar Patricio Reyes Sánchez (23/0), Jaime Andrés Vera (10/1) [Juvenal Mario Olmos Rojas (5/0)], Elías Raúl Ormeño Pacheco (7/1), Alejandro Manuel Hisis Araya (31/2), Jaime Augusto Pizarro Herrera (25/1), Juan Carlos Letelier Pizarro (49/14) [Lukas Nicolás Túdor (5/0)], Juan Covarrubias (9/1) [Jaime Patricio Ramírez (12/0)]. Trainer: Orlando Aravena (31).

**Goal**: Juan Covarrubias (18).

**398.** 27.06.1989 **CHILE - BOLIVIA** **2-1(2-0)**

Estadio Nacional, Santiago; Referee: Salvador Imperatore (Chile); Attendance: 16,092

**CHI:** Roberto Antonio Rojas Saavedra (41/0), Jorge Carrasco (6/0), Hugo Armando González (14/2) [46.Leonel Contreras (17/0)], Fernando Astengo (12/2), Óscar Patricio Reyes Sánchez (24/0), Jaime Andrés Vera (11/1), Alejandro Manuel Hisis Araya (32/2), Jaime Augusto Pizarro Herrera (26/2), Osvaldo Heriberto Hurtado Galeguillo (34/6) [75.Jaime Patricio Ramírez (13/0)], Juan Carlos Letelier Pizarro (50/14), Juan Covarrubias (10/2). Trainer: Orlando Aravena (32).

**Goals**: Juan Covarrubias (1), Jaime Augusto Pizarro Herrera (40 penalty).

**399.** 02.07.1989 **ARGENTINA - CHILE** **1-0(0-0)** 34th Copa América. Group Stage.

Estádio Serra Dourada, Goiânia (Brazil); Referee: Arnaldo David César Coelho (Brazil); Attendance: 40,000

**CHI:** Roberto Antonio Rojas Saavedra (42/0), Óscar Patricio Reyes Sánchez (25/0), Hugo Armando González (15/2), Leonel Contreras (18/0), Jaime Augusto Pizarro Herrera (27/2), Alejandro Manuel Hisis Araya (33/2), Elías Raúl Ormeño Pacheco (8/1) [63.Osvaldo Heriberto Hurtado Galeguillo (35/6)], Juvenal Mario Olmos Rojas (6/0), Héctor Eduardo Puebla (26/1), Jaime Andrés Vera (12/1) [55.Juan Carlos Letelier Pizarro (51/14)], Juan Covarrubias (11/2). Trainer: Orlando Aravena (33).

**400.** 06.07.1989 **URUGUAY - CHILE** **3-0(1-0)** 34th Copa América. Group Stage.

Estádio Serra Dourada, Goiânia (Brazil); Referee: José Ramírez Calle (Peru); Attendance: 2,029

**CHI:** Roberto Antonio Rojas Saavedra (43/0), Óscar Patricio Reyes Sánchez (26/0), Hugo Armando González (16/2), Leonel Contreras (19/0) [70.Jaime Andrés Vera (13/1)], Héctor Eduardo Puebla (27/1), Alejandro Manuel Hisis Araya (34/2), Juvenal Mario Olmos Rojas (7/0), Jaime Augusto Pizarro Herrera (28/2), Juan Covarrubias (12/2), Juan Carlos Letelier Pizarro (52/14) [*sent off 27*], Osvaldo Heriberto Hurtado Galeguillo (36/6). Trainer: Orlando Aravena (34).

**401.** 08.07.1989 **CHILE - BOLIVIA** **5-0(2-0)** 34th Copa América. Group Stage.

Estádio Serra Dourada, Goiânia (Brazil); Referee: Arnaldo David César Coelho (Brazil); Attendance: 3,000

**CHI:** Roberto Antonio Rojas Saavedra (44/0) [46.Marco Antonio Cornéz (16/0)], Óscar Patricio Reyes Sánchez (27/1), Hugo Armando González (17/2), Fernando Astengo (13/3), Héctor Eduardo Puebla (28/1), Alejandro Manuel Hisis Araya (35/2), Juvenal Mario Olmos Rojas (8/1), Jaime Augusto Pizarro Herrera (29/3), Juan Covarrubias (13/2), Jaime Patricio Ramírez (14/1), Osvaldo Heriberto Hurtado Galeguillo (37/6) [60.Jaime Andrés Vera (14/1)]. Trainer: Orlando Aravena (35).

**Goals**: Juvenal Mario Olmos Rojas (9), Jaime Patricio Ramírez (12), Fernando Astengo (52), Jaime Augusto Pizarro Herrera (67 penalty), Óscar Patricio Reyes Sánchez (86).

**402.** 10.07.1989 **CHILE - ECUADOR** **2-1(1-0)** 34th Copa América. Group Stage.
Estádio Serra Dourada, Goiânia (Brazil); Referee: Carlos Alberto Maciel (Paraguay); Attendance:
**CHI:** Marco Antonio Cornéz (17/0), Óscar Patricio Reyes Sánchez (28/1), Hugo Armando González (18/2), Fernando Astengo (14/3), Héctor Eduardo Puebla (29/1), Alejandro Manuel Hisis Araya (36/2), Juvenal Mario Olmos Rojas (9/2) [62.Jaime Andrés Vera (15/1)], Jaime Augusto Pizarro Herrera (30/3), Osvaldo Heriberto Hurtado Galeguillo (38/6) [72.Juan Covarrubias (14/2)], Jaime Patricio Ramírez (15/1), Juan Carlos Letelier Pizarro (53/15). Trainer: Orlando Aravena (36).
**Goal**: Juvenal Mario Olmos Rojas (10), Juan Carlos Letelier Pizarro (88).

**403.** 25.07.1989 **CHILE - PERU** **2-1(1-0)**
Estadio „Carlos Dittborn“, Arica; Referee: Juan Oscar Ortubé Vargas (Bolivia); Attendance: 10,430
**CHI:** Roberto Antonio Rojas Saavedra (45/0), Óscar Patricio Reyes Sánchez (29/1), Hugo Armando González (19/2) [87.Leonel Contreras (20/0)], Fernando Astengo (15/3), Héctor Eduardo Puebla (30/1), Jaime Augusto Pizarro Herrera (31/3), Alejandro Manuel Hisis Araya (37/2), Jorge Orlando Aravena Plaza (32/20), Juan Carlos Letelier Pizarro (54/15) [87.Jaime Patricio Ramírez (16/1)], Lukas Nicolás Túdor (6/1), Juan Covarrubias (15/2). Trainer: Orlando Aravena (37).
**Goals**: Lukas Nicolás Túdor (42), Jorge Orlando Aravena Plaza (61).

**404.** 06.08.1989 **VENEZUELA - CHILE** **1-3(0-2)** 14th FIFA WC. Qualifiers
Estadio „Brígido Iriarte“, Caracas; Referee: Carlos Montalván (Peru); Attendance: 13,000
**CHI:** Roberto Antonio Rojas Saavedra (46/0), Alejandro Manuel Hisis Araya (38/2), Hugo Armando González (20/2), Fernando Astengo (16/3), Héctor Eduardo Puebla (31/1), Elías Raúl Ormeño Pacheco (9/1), Jaime Augusto Pizarro Herrera (32/3), Jorge Orlando Aravena Plaza (33/22), Patricio Nazario Yáñez Candia (32/4), Hugo Eduardo Rubio Montecinos (24/7), Ivo Alexis Basay (8/3) [60.Iván Luis Zamorano Zamora (11/2)]. Trainer: Orlando Aravena (38).
**Goals**: Jorge Orlando Aravena Plaza (5, 33), Iván Luis Zamorano Zamora (71).

**405.** 13.08.1989 **CHILE - BRAZIL** **1-1(0-0)** 14th FIFA WC. Qualifiers
Estadio Nacional, Santiago; Referee: Jesús Díaz Palacios (Colombia); Attendance: 60,697
**CHI:** Roberto Antonio Rojas Saavedra (47/0), Alejandro Manuel Hisis Araya (39/2), Fernando Astengo (17/3), Hugo Armando González (21/2), Héctor Eduardo Puebla (32/1), Jaime Augusto Pizarro Herrera (33/3), Elías Raúl Ormeño Pacheco (10/1) [*sent off 13*], Hugo Eduardo Rubio Montecinos (25/7) [57.Ivo Alexis Basay (9/4)], Jorge Orlando Aravena Plaza (34/22), Patricio Nazario Yáñez Candia (33/4), Iván Luis Zamorano Zamora (12/2) [85.Juan Carlos Letelier Pizarro (55/15)]. Trainer: Orlando Aravena (39).
**Goal**: Ivo Alexis Basay (81).

**406.** 27.08.1989 **CHILE - VENEZUELA** **5-0(3-0)** 14th FIFA WC. Qualifiers
Estadio Malvinas Argentinas, Mendoza (Argentina); Referee: Elías Victoriano Jácome Guerreiro (Ecuador); Attendance: 19,000
**CHI:** Roberto Antonio Rojas Saavedra (48/0), Alejandro Manuel Hisis Araya (40/2), Hugo Armando González (22/2), Fernando Astengo (18/3) [46.Leonel Contreras (21/0)], Héctor Eduardo Puebla (33/1), Jaime Andrés Vera (16/2), Jaime Augusto Pizarro Herrera (34/3), Jorge Orlando Aravena Plaza (35/22), Patricio Nazario Yáñez Candia (34/5) [75.Juan Covarrubias (16/2)], Juan Carlos Letelier Pizarro (56/18), Ivo Alexis Basay (10/4). Trainer: Orlando Aravena (40).
**Goals**: Juan Carlos Letelier Pizarro (14, 34), Patricio Nazario Yáñez Candia (44), Juan Carlos Letelier Pizarro (69), Jaime Andrés Vera (84).

**407.** 03.09.1989 **BRAZIL - CHILE** **1-0(0-0)*** 14th FIFA WC. Qualifiers
Estádio „Jornalista Mario Filho“ (Maracanã), Rio de Janeiro; Referee: Juan Carlos Loustau (Argentina); Attendance: 141,072
**CHI:** Roberto Antonio Rojas Saavedra (49/0), Óscar Patricio Reyes Sánchez (30/1) [62.Ivo Alexis Basay (11/4)], Fernando Astengo (19/3), Hugo Armando González (23/2), Héctor Eduardo Puebla (34/1), Alejandro Manuel Hisis Araya (41/2), Jaime Augusto Pizarro Herrera (35/3), Jaime Andrés Vera (17/2), Jorge Orlando Aravena Plaza (36/22), Patricio Nazario Yáñez Candia (35/5), Juan Carlos Letelier Pizarro (57/18). Trainer: Orlando Aravena (41).
*The match was broken after 69 mins due to the incidents on the pitch (firework landed near chilean goalkeeper Rojas, who failed out with head injurie. The Chilean team refused to continue the match, but videos showed later that keeper Rojas has inflicted the injuries on himself! The FIFA awarded the match 2-0 for Brazil and banned Chile from the World Cup Qualifiers 1994 also Rojas for life).*

**408.** 17.10.1990 **CHILE - BRAZIL** **0-0** Copa Teixeira
Estadio Nacional, Santiago; Referee: Enrique Marín Gallo (Chile); Attendance: 32,358
**CHI:** Marco Antonio Cornéz (18/0), Rubén Alberto Espinoza Molina (26/5), Eduardo Enrique Vilches Arriagada (1/0), Lizardo Antonio Garrido Bustamante (33/0), Javier Luciano Margas Loyola (1/0), Fabián Raphael Estay Silva (1/0), Jaime Augusto Pizarro Herrera (36/3), Jorge Alejandro Contreras Lira (8/1) [Luis Pérez (5/0)], Jorge Orlando Aravena Plaza (37/22), Juan Ramón Garrido (1/0), Rubén Martínez (11/2) [Aníbal Segundo González (4/0)]. Trainer: Arturo Salah Cassani (1).

**409.** 08.11.1990 **BRAZIL - CHILE** **0-0** Copa Teixeira
Estádio Mangueirão, Belém; Referee: Luís Carlos Félix Ferrara (Brazil); Attendance: 58,676
**CHI:** Marco Antonio Cornéz (19/0), Andrés Antonio Romero (1/0), Lizardo Antonio Garrido Bustamante (34/0), Eduardo Enrique Vilches Arriagada (2/0), Javier Luciano Margas Loyola (2/0), Jaime Augusto Pizarro Herrera (37/3), Elías Raúl Ormeño Pacheco (11/1), Fabián Raphael Estay Silva (2/0), Jorge Alejandro Contreras Lira (9/1) [64.Héctor Eduardo Puebla (35/1)], Aníbal Segundo González (5/0) [46.Richard Zambrano (1/0)], Rubén Martínez (12/2) [46.Luis Guarda (1/0)]. Trainer: Arturo Salah Cassani (2).

**410.** 09.04.1991 **MEXICO - CHILE** **1-0(1-0)**
Estadio „Luis Alberto Fuentes Rodríguez“, Veracruz; Referee: Dave Bruner (Canada); Attendance: 7,000
**CHI:** Patricio Armando Toledo (1/0), Andrés Antonio Romero (2/0), Luis Abarca Aravena (1/0), Ronald Hugo Fuentes Núñez (1/0), Miguel Ponce Torres (1/0) [Fabián Guevara Arredondo (1/0)], Fabián Raphael Estay Silva (3/0) [Fernando Andrés Cornejo Jiménez (1/0)], Luis Eduardo Musrri Saravia (1/0) [Rodrígo Vicente Gómez (1/0)], Nelson Rodrigo Parraguez Riveros (1/0), Juan Carlos Vera (1/0) [José Luis Sierra Pando (1/0)], Luis Guarda (2/0), Francisco Marcelo Vega (1/0) [Cristián Bravo (1/0)]. Trainer: Arturo Salah Cassani (3).

**411.** 22.05.1991 **REPUBLIC OF IRELAND - CHILE** **1-1(0-0)**
Lansdowne Road, Dublin; Referee: Daniel Roduit (Switzerland); Attendance: 32,230
**CHI:** Patricio Armando Toledo (2/0), Andrés Antonio Romero (3/0), Luis Abarca Aravena (2/0), Ronald Hugo Fuentes Núñez (2/0), Fabián Guevara Arredondo (2/0) [15.Marcelo Miranda (1/0)], Jaime Andrés Vera (18/2) [63.Jorge Alejandro Contreras Lira (10/1)], Rodrígo Vicente Gómez (2/0), Nelson Rodrigo Parraguez Riveros (2/0), Fabián Raphael Estay Silva (4/1), Luis Guarda (3/0) [78.Aníbal Segundo González (6/0)], Hugo Eduardo Rubio Montecinos (26/7). Trainer: Arturo Salah Cassani (4).
**Goal**: Fabián Raphael Estay Silva (76).

**412.** 30.05.1991 **CHILE - URUGUAY** **2-1(1-0)**
Estadio „Santa Laura", Santiago; Referee: Iván Enrique Guerrero Levancini (Chile); Attendance: 4,500
**CHI:** Patricio Armando Toledo (3/0), Andrés Antonio Romero (4/0), Ronald Hugo Fuentes Núñez (3/0), Luis Abarca Aravena (3/0), Marcelo Miranda (2/0), Fernando Andrés Cornejo Jiménez (2/0) [80.Juan Rivera (2/0)], Fabián Raphael Estay Silva (5/1), Jorge Alejandro Contreras Lira (11/1), Rodrígo Vicente Gómez (3/0), Luis Guarda (4/0) [61.Aníbal Segundo González (7/1)], Francisco Marcelo Vega (2/1). Trainer: Arturo Salah Cassani (5).
**Goals**: Francisco Marcelo Vega (28), Aníbal Segundo González (80).

**413.** 19.06.1991 **ECUADOR - CHILE** **2-1(1-1)**
Estadio Modelo, Guayaquil; Referee: Luis Naranjo (Ecuador); Attendance: 25,000
**CHI:** Marco Antonio Cornéz (20/0), Andrés Antonio Romero (5/0), Miguel Mauricio Ramírez Pérez (1/0), Lizardo Antonio Garrido Bustamante (35/0), Javier Luciano Margas Loyola (3/0), Jaime Andrés Vera (19/3) [Jorge Alejandro Contreras Lira (12/1)], Eduardo Enrique Vilches Arriagada (3/0), Jaime Augusto Pizarro Herrera (38/3), Fabián Raphael Estay Silva (6/1), Hugo Eduardo Rubio Montecinos (27/7), Ivo Alexis Basay (12/4) [Aníbal Segundo González (8/1)]. Trainer: Arturo Salah Cassani (6).
**Goal**: Jaime Andrés Vera (10 penalty).

**414.** 26.06.1991 **URUGUAY - CHILE** **2-1(1-1)**
Estadio Centenario, Montevideo; Referee: Jorge Luis Nieves Parra (Uruguay); Attendance: 6,000
**CHI:** Patricio Armando Toledo (4/0), Lizardo Antonio Garrido Bustamante (36/0), Andrés Antonio Romero (6/0) [78.Aníbal Segundo González (9/1)], Miguel Mauricio Ramírez Pérez (2/0), Rodrígo Vicente Gómez (4/0), Rubén Alberto Espinoza Molina (27/5), Eduardo Enrique Vilches Arriagada (4/0), Jaime Augusto Pizarro Herrera (39/3), Jorge Alejandro Contreras Lira (13/1) [71.Fabián Raphael Estay Silva (7/1)], Hugo Eduardo Rubio Montecinos (28/8), Ivo Alexis Basay (13/4) [46.Iván Luis Zamorano Zamora (13/2)].Trainer: Arturo Salah Cassani (7).
**Goal**: Hugo Eduardo Rubio Montecinos (15).

**415.** 30.06.1991 **CHILE - ECUADOR** **3-1(3-0)**
Estadio Nacional, Santiago; Referee: Carlos Manuel Robles Mella (Chile); Attendance: 25,000
**CHI:** Patricio Armando Toledo (5/0), Andrés Antonio Romero (7/0), Miguel Mauricio Ramírez Pérez (3/0), Lizardo Antonio Garrido Bustamante (37/0), Rodrígo Vicente Gómez (5/0) [Patricio Nazario Yáñez Candia (36/5)], Rubén Alberto Espinoza Molina (28/5), Eduardo Enrique Vilches Arriagada (5/0), Jaime Augusto Pizarro Herrera (40/3), Jorge Alejandro Contreras Lira (14/1) [Jaime Andrés Vera (20/3)], Hugo Eduardo Rubio Montecinos (29/10) [Aníbal Segundo González (10/1)], Iván Luis Zamorano Zamora (14/3) [Fabián Raphael Estay Silva (8/1)]. Trainer: Arturo Salah Cassani (8).
**Goals**: Hugo Eduardo Rubio Montecinos (17), Iván Luis Zamorano Zamora (36), Hugo Eduardo Rubio Montecinos (41).

**416.** 06.07.1991 **CHILE - VENEZUELA** **2-0(2-0)** 35th Copa América. Group Stage.
Estadio Nacional, Santiago; Referee: Armando Pérez Hoyos (Colombia); Attendance: 45,000
**CHI:** Patricio Armando Toledo (6/0), Gabriel Rafael Mendoza Ibarra (1/0), Lizardo Antonio Garrido Bustamante (38/0), Eduardo Enrique Vilches Arriagada (6/1), Rodrígo Vicente Gómez (6/0), Nelson Rodrigo Parraguez Riveros (3/0), Rubén Alberto Espinoza Molina (29/5) [*sent off 88*], Jaime Augusto Pizarro Herrera (41/3), Jorge Alejandro Contreras Lira (15/1) [67.Jaime Andrés Vera (21/3)], Hugo Eduardo Rubio Montecinos (30/10), Iván Luis Zamorano Zamora (15/4). Trainer: Arturo Salah Cassani (9).
**Goals**: Eduardo Enrique Vilches Arriagada (22), Iván Luis Zamorano Zamora (34).

**417.** 08.07.1991 **CHILE - PERU** **4-2(1-0)** 35th Copa América. Group Stage.
Estadio Municipal, Concepción; Referee: Ernesto Filippi Cavani (Uruguay); Attendance: 21,520
**CHI:** Patricio Armando Toledo (7/0), Gabriel Rafael Mendoza Ibarra (2/0), Lizardo Antonio Garrido Bustamante (39/0), Javier Luciano Margas Loyola (4/0), Eduardo Enrique Vilches Arriagada (7/1), Nelson Rodrigo Parraguez Riveros (4/0), Jaime Augusto Pizarro Herrera (42/3) [83.Miguel Mauricio Ramírez Pérez (4/0)], Jorge Alejandro Contreras Lira (16/2), Fabián Raphael Estay Silva (9/1), Iván Luis Zamorano Zamora (16/6), Hugo Eduardo Rubio Montecinos (31/11) [57.Patricio Nazario Yáñez Candia (37/5)]. Trainer: Arturo Salah Cassani (10).
**Goals**: Hugo Eduardo Rubio Montecinos (16), Jorge Alejandro Contreras Lira (51 penalty), Iván Luis Zamorano Zamora (61, 74).

**418.** 10.07.1991 **CHILE - ARGENTINA** **0-1(0-0)** 35th Copa América. Group Stage.
Estadio Nacional, Santiago; Referee: José Roberto Ramiz Wright (Brazil); Attendance: 70,000
**CHI:** Patricio Armando Toledo (8/0), Gabriel Rafael Mendoza Ibarra (3/0), Lizardo Antonio Garrido Bustamante (40/0), Eduardo Enrique Vilches Arriagada (8/1), Javier Luciano Margas Loyola (5/0), Nelson Rodrigo Parraguez Riveros (5/0) [18.Miguel Mauricio Ramírez Pérez (5/0)], Jaime Augusto Pizarro Herrera (43/3), Jorge Alejandro Contreras Lira (17/2), Fabián Raphael Estay Silva (10/1), Iván Luis Zamorano Zamora (17/6), Hugo Eduardo Rubio Montecinos (32/11) [59.Patricio Nazario Yáñez Candia (38/5)]. Trainer: Arturo Salah Cassani (11).

**419.** 14.07.1991 **CHILE - PARAGUAY** **4-0(2-0)** 35th Copa América. Group Stage.
Estadio Nacional, Santiago; Referee: José Roberto Ramiz Wright (Brazil); Attendance: 76,000
**CHI:** Patricio Armando Toledo (9/0), Gabriel Rafael Mendoza Ibarra (4/0), Lizardo Antonio Garrido Bustamante (41/0), Eduardo Enrique Vilches Arriagada (9/1), Javier Luciano Margas Loyola (6/0), Miguel Mauricio Ramírez Pérez (6/0), Jaime Augusto Pizarro Herrera (44/3) [70.Jaime Andrés Vera (22/4)], Fabián Raphael Estay Silva (11/2), Patricio Nazario Yáñez Candia (39/5), Iván Luis Zamorano Zamora (18/7), Hugo Eduardo Rubio Montecinos (33/12) [77.Ivo Alexis Basay (14/4)]. Trainer: Arturo Salah Cassani (12).
**Goals**: Hugo Eduardo Rubio Montecinos (12), Iván Luis Zamorano Zamora (15), Fabián Raphael Estay Silva (63), Jaime Andrés Vera (68).

**420.** 17.07.1991 **CHILE - COLOMBIA** **1-1(0-1)** 35th Copa América. Final Round.
Estadio Nacional, Santiago; Referee: Ernesto Filippi Cavani (Uruguay); Attendance: 65,000
**CHI:** Patricio Armando Toledo (10/0), Gabriel Rafael Mendoza Ibarra (5/0), Lizardo Antonio Garrido Bustamante (42/0), Eduardo Enrique Vilches Arriagada (10/1), Javier Luciano Margas Loyola (7/0), Miguel Mauricio Ramírez Pérez (7/0), Jaime Augusto Pizarro Herrera (45/3) [75.Jaime Andrés Vera (23/4)], Fabián Raphael Estay Silva (12/2), Patricio Nazario Yáñez Candia (40/5), Iván Luis Zamorano Zamora (19/8), Hugo Eduardo Rubio Montecinos (34/12) [62.Jorge Alejandro Contreras Lira (18/2)]. Trainer: Arturo Salah Cassani (13).
**Goal**: Iván Luis Zamorano Zamora (74).

**421.** 19.07.1991 **CHILE - ARGENTINA** **0-0** 35th Copa América. Final Round.
Estadio Nacional, Santiago; Referee: Ernesto Filippi Cavani (Uruguay); Attendance: 50,000
**CHI:** Patricio Armando Toledo (11/0), Rubén Alberto Espinoza Molina (30/5) [77.Ivo Alexis Basay (15/4)], Lizardo Antonio Garrido Bustamante (43/0), Eduardo Enrique Vilches Arriagada (11/1), Javier Luciano Margas Loyola (8/0), Miguel Mauricio Ramírez Pérez (8/0), Jaime Augusto Pizarro Herrera (46/3), Fabián Raphael Estay Silva (13/2) [67.Jorge Alejandro Contreras Lira (19/2)], Patricio Nazario Yáñez Candia (41/5), Iván Luis Zamorano Zamora (20/8), Hugo Eduardo Rubio Montecinos (35/12). Trainer: Arturo Salah Cassani (14).

**422.** 21.07.1991 **CHILE - BRAZIL** **0-2(0-1)** 35th Copa América. Final Round.
Estadio Nacional, Santiago; Referee: Juan Oscar Ortubé Vargas (Bolivia); Attendance: 50,000
**CHI:** Patricio Armando Toledo (12/0), Gabriel Rafael Mendoza Ibarra (6/0), Lizardo Antonio Garrido Bustamante (44/0), Eduardo Enrique Vilches Arriagada (12/1), Javier Luciano Margas Loyola (9/0), Miguel Mauricio Ramírez Pérez (9/0) [70.Jaime Andrés Vera (24/4)], Jaime Augusto Pizarro Herrera (47/3), Fabián Raphael Estay Silva (14/2) [46.Ivo Alexis Basay (16/4)], Jorge Alejandro Contreras Lira (20/2), Iván Luis Zamorano Zamora (21/8), Hugo Eduardo Rubio Montecinos (36/12). Trainer: Arturo Salah Cassani (15).

**423.** 31.03.1993 **CHILE - BOLIVIA** **2-1(0-0)**
Estadio Nacional, Santiago; Referee: Enrique Marín Gallo (Chile); Attendance: 9,580
**CHI:** Marcelo Antonio Ramírez Gormaz (1/0), Gabriel Rafael Mendoza Ibarra (7/0), Miguel Mauricio Ramírez Pérez (10/0), Eduardo Enrique Vilches Arriagada (13/1), Javier Luciano Margas Loyola (10/0), Fabián Raphael Estay Silva (15/3) [64.Fabián Guevara Arredondo (3/0)], Luis Eduardo Musrri Saravia (2/0), Jaime Augusto Pizarro Herrera (48/3), Francisco Marcelo Vega (3/1) [60.José Luis Sierra Pando (2/1)], Juan Castillo (1/0), Richard Zambrano (2/0) [67.Marcelo Antonio Jara Valdés (1/0)]. Trainer: Arturo Salah Cassani (16).
**Goals**: Fabián Raphael Estay Silva (59 penalty), José Luis Sierra Pando (70).

**424.** 30.05.1993 **CHILE - COLOMBIA** **1-1(0-0)**
Estadio Nacional, Santiago; Referee: Salvador Imperatore (Chile); Attendance: 5,000
**CHI:** Patricio Armando Toledo (13/0), Gabriel Rafael Mendoza Ibarra (8/0), Miguel Mauricio Ramírez Pérez (11/0), Eduardo Enrique Vilches Arriagada (14/1), Javier Luciano Margas Loyola (11/0), Luis Eduardo Musrri Saravia (3/0), Fabián Raphael Estay Silva (16/3), Fabián Guevara Arredondo (4/1), José Luis Sierra Pando (3/1) [73.Pedro González Vera (1/0)], Richard Zambrano (3/0) [83.Marco Antonio Figueroa Montero (3/0)], Francisco Marcelo Vega (4/1). Trainer: Arturo Salah Cassani (17).
**Goal**: Fabián Guevara Arredondo (48).

**425.** 06.06.1993 **COLOMBIA - CHILE** **1-0(0-0)**
Estadio „Nemesio Camacho" 'El Campín', Bogotá; Referee: Zuluaga Vasco (Colombia); Attendance: 35,000
**CHI:** Marcelo Antonio Ramírez Gormaz (2/0), Gabriel Rafael Mendoza Ibarra (9/0), Miguel Mauricio Ramírez Pérez (12/0), Eduardo Enrique Vilches Arriagada (15/1), Javier Luciano Margas Loyola (12/0) [84.Fabián Guevara Arredondo (5/1)], Mario Lepe (14/0), Fabián Raphael Estay Silva (17/3) [74.Marco Antonio Figueroa Montero (4/0)], Nelson Rodrigo Parraguez Riveros (6/0), Francisco Marcelo Vega (5/1) [62.José Luis Sierra Pando (4/1)], Richard Zambrano (4/0), Juan Castillo (2/0) [46.Rodrígo Hernán Barrera Funes (1/0)]. Trainer: Arturo Salah Cassani (18).

**426.** 09.06.1993 **ECUADOR - CHILE** **1-2(1-2)**
Estadio Olímpico „Atahualpa", Quito; Referee: José Carpio Guevara (Ecuador); Attendance: 45,000
**CHI:** Patricio Armando Toledo (14/0), Gabriel Rafael Mendoza Ibarra (10/0), Miguel Mauricio Ramírez Pérez (13/0), Eduardo Enrique Vilches Arriagada (16/1), Javier Luciano Margas Loyola (13/0), Fabián Raphael Estay Silva (18/3) [José Luis Sierra Pando (5/1)], Mario Lepe (15/0), Jaime Augusto Pizarro Herrera (49/4), Francisco Marcelo Vega (6/1) [Fabián Guevara Arredondo (6/1)], Richard Zambrano (5/0) [Marco Antonio Figueroa Montero (5/0)], Rodrígo Hernán Barrera Funes (2/1). Trainer: Arturo Salah Cassani (19).
**Goals**: Jaime Augusto Pizarro Herrera (23), Rodrígo Hernán Barrera Funes (25).

**427.** 13.06.1993 **BOLIVIA - CHILE** **1-3(0-2)**
Estadio „Hernando Siles Zuazo", La Paz; Referee: Juan Oscar Ortubé Vargas (Bolivia); Attendance: 17,165
**CHI:** Marcelo Antonio Ramírez Gormaz (3/0), Gabriel Rafael Mendoza Ibarra (11/0) [85.Fernando Andrés Cornejo Jiménez (3/0)], Miguel Mauricio Ramírez Pérez (14/0), Eduardo Enrique Vilches Arriagada (17/1), Javier Luciano Margas Loyola (14/0), Jaime Augusto Pizarro Herrera (50/4) [83.Fabián Raphael Estay Silva (19/3)], Fabián Guevara Arredondo (7/1) [46.Nelson Rodrigo Parraguez Riveros (7/0)], Mario Lepe (16/0) [70.Luis Eduardo Musrri Saravia (4/0)], José Luis Sierra Pando (6/2), Marco Antonio Figueroa Montero (6/1), Juan Castillo (3/1) [60.Richard Zambrano (6/0)]. Trainer: Arturo Salah Cassani (20).
**Goals**: José Luis Sierra Pando (16), Marco Antonio Figueroa Montero (31), Juan Castillo (56).

**428.** 18.06.1993 **PARAGUAY - CHILE** **1-0(1-0)** 36th Copa América. Group Stage.
Estadio „Alejandro Serrano Aguillar", Cuenca (Ecuador); Referee: José Joaquín Torres Cadena (Colombia); Attendance: 22,000
**CHI:** Patricio Armando Toledo (15/0), Gabriel Rafael Mendoza Ibarra (12/0), Eduardo Enrique Vilches Arriagada (18/1), Miguel Mauricio Ramírez Pérez (15/0), Javier Luciano Margas Loyola (15/0) [*sent off 81*], Fabián Raphael Estay Silva (20/3), Mario Lepe (17/0) [80.Francisco Marcelo Vega (7/1)], Jaime Augusto Pizarro Herrera (51/4), José Luis Sierra Pando (7/2), Marco Antonio Figueroa Montero (7/1), Juan Castillo (4/1) [46.Rodrígo Hernán Barrera Funes (3/1)]. Trainer: Arturo Salah Cassani (21).

**429.** 21.06.1993 **CHILE - BRAZIL** **3-2(1-1)** 36th Copa América. Group Stage.
Estadio „Alejandro Serrano Aguillar", Cuenca (Ecuador); Referee: Alfredo Rodas Iñiguez (Ecuador); Attendance: 20,000
**CHI:** Patricio Armando Toledo (16/0), Gabriel Rafael Mendoza Ibarra (13/0), Eduardo Enrique Vilches Arriagada (19/1), Miguel Mauricio Ramírez Pérez (16/0), Fabián Guevara Arredondo (8/1), Fabián Raphael Estay Silva (21/3) [67.Nelson Rodrigo Parraguez Riveros (8/0)], Mario Lepe (18/0), Jaime Augusto Pizarro Herrera (52/4), José Luis Sierra Pando (8/3), Marco Antonio Figueroa Montero (8/1) [46.Richard Zambrano (7/2)], Rodrígo Hernán Barrera Funes (4/1). Trainer: Arturo Salah Cassani (22).
**Goals**: José Luis Sierra Pando (15), Richard Zambrano (51, 59).

**430.** 24.06.1993 **PERU - CHILE** **1-0(1-0)** 36th Copa América. Group Stage.
Estadio „Alejandro Serrano Aguillar", Cuenca (Ecuador); Referee: José Joaquín Torres Cadena (Colombia); Attendance: 25,000
**CHI:** Patricio Armando Toledo (17/0), Gabriel Rafael Mendoza Ibarra (14/0), Eduardo Enrique Vilches Arriagada (20/1), Miguel Mauricio Ramírez Pérez (17/0), Javier Luciano Margas Loyola (16/0), Fabián Raphael Estay Silva (22/3), Mario Lepe (19/0) [58.Rodrígo Hernán Barrera Funes (5/1)], Jaime Augusto Pizarro Herrera (53/4), José Luis Sierra Pando (9/3) [69.Francisco Marcelo Vega (8/1)], Iván Luis Zamorano Zamora (22/8), Richard Zambrano (8/2). Trainer: Arturo Salah Cassani (23).

**431.** 08.09.1993 **SPAIN - CHILE** **2-0(0-0)**
Estadio „José Rico Pérez", Alicante; Referee: Vítor Manuel Melo Pereira (Portugal); Attendance: 28,000
**CHI:** Marcelo Antonio Ramírez Gormaz (4/0), Gabriel Rafael Mendoza Ibarra (15/0), Juan Carlos González (1/0), Hugo Armando González (24/2) [*sent off 88*], Ricardo González (1/0) [71.Rodrígo Ruíz De Barbieri (1/0)], Fabián Raphael Estay Silva (23/3), Mario Alfredo Salas Saieg (1/0), Mario Lepe (20/0), Fabián Guevara Arredondo (9/1) [46.José Luis Sierra Pando (10/3)], Juan Enrique Carreño (1/0), Raimundo Tupper (1/0). Trainer: Nelson Bonifacio Acosta López (1).

**432.** 22.03.1994 **FRANCE - CHILE** **3-1(2-1)**
Stade Gerland, Lyon; Referee: Juan Manuel Brito Arceo (Spain); Attendance: 35,000
**CHI:** Nelson Antonio Tapia Rios (1/0), Ronald Hugo Fuentes Núñez (4/0), Daniel López (1/0), Carlos Fuentes (1/0), Pedro Jaque (1/0), Raimundo Tupper (2/0) [60.Marcelo Alvarez (10/1)], Mario Lepe (21/0), Nelson Rodrigo Parraguez Riveros (9/0), Fabián Raphael Estay Silva (24/3) [82.Lukas Nicolás Túdor (7/1)], Iván Luis Zamorano Zamora (23/9), Pedro González Vera (2/0) [74.Wilson Rojas (1/0)]. Trainer: Mirko Jožić (1).
**Goal**: Iván Luis Zamorano Zamora (11).

**433.** 27.03.1994 **SAUDI ARABIA - CHILE** **0-2(0-1)**
„King Fahd" International Stadium, Riyad; Referee: Abdul Aziz Ibrahim Al Aidan (Saudi Arabia); Attendance: 20,000
**CHI:** Nelson Antonio Tapia Rios (2/0), Ronald Hugo Fuentes Núñez (5/0), Pedro Jaque (2/0), Wilson Rojas (2/0) [53.Carlos Fuentes (2/0)], Cristián Castañeda Vargas (1/0) [80.Daniel López (2/0)], Nelson Rodrigo Parraguez Riveros (10/0), Mario Lepe (22/0), Fabián Guevara Arredondo (10/1), Fabián Raphael Estay Silva (25/3) [Marcelo Alvarez (11/1)], Lukas Nicolás Túdor (8/2) [88.Miguel Latín (1/0)], Pedro González Vera (3/0) [78.Raimundo Tupper (3/1)]. Trainer: Mirko Jožić (2).
**Goals**: Lukas Nicolás Túdor (18 penalty), Raimundo Tupper (85).

**434.** 29.03.1994 **SAUDI ARABIA - CHILE** **2-2(0-1)**
„King Fahd" International Stadium, Riyad; Referee: Hasan Antijaimin (Saudi Arabia); Attendance: 18,000
**CHI:** Nelson Antonio Tapia Rios (3/0) [46.Aníbal Pinto (1/0)], Ronald Hugo Fuentes Núñez (6/0), Pedro Jaque (3/0), Carlos Fuentes (3/0), Wilson Rojas (3/0), Miguel Latín (2/0) [46.Cristián Castañeda Vargas (2/0)], Daniel López (3/0), Mario Lepe (23/1), Fabián Guevara Arredondo (11/1) [75.Raimundo Tupper (4/1)], Fabián Raphael Estay Silva (26/3) [72.Pedro González Vera (4/0)], Marcelo Alvarez (12/1) [46.Lukas Nicolás Túdor (9/2)]. Trainer: Mirko Jožić (3).
**Goals**: Mario Lepe (29 penalty), Mohammed Al Qarni (47 own goal).

**435.** 30.04.1994 **UNITED STATES - CHILE** **0-2(0-1)**
University of New Mexico Stadium, Albuquerque; Referee: Raúl Gutiérrez (Costa Rica); Attendance: 15,610
**CHI:** Patricio Armando Toledo (18/0), Ronald Hugo Fuentes Núñez (7/0), Javier Luciano Margas Loyola (17/0), Pedro Antonio Reyes González (1/0), Eduardo Enrique Vilches Arriagada (21/1), Miguel Mauricio Ramírez Pérez (18/0), Gabriel Rafael Mendoza Ibarra (16/0), Esteban Andrés Valencia Bascuñán (1/0) [46.Mario Lepe (24/1)], Fabián Raphael Estay Silva (27/3), Rodrígo Hernán Barrera Funes (6/2), Patricio Nazario Yáñez Candia (42/5) [79.Pedro González Vera (5/1)]. Trainer: Mirko Jožić (4).
**Goals**: Rodrígo Hernán Barrera Funes (45), Pedro González Vera (89).

**436.** 18.05.1994 **CHILE - ARGENTINA** **3-3(1-1)**
Estadio Nacional, Santiago; Referee: Eduardo Dluzniewski (Uruguay); Attendance: 51,193
**CHI:** Patricio Armando Toledo (19/0), Ronald Hugo Fuentes Núñez (8/0), Miguel Ardiman (1/0), Javier Luciano Margas Loyola (18/0), Gabriel Rafael Mendoza Ibarra (17/0) [46.Cristián Castañeda Vargas (3/0)], Nelson Rodrigo Parraguez Riveros (11/0), Miguel Mauricio Ramírez Pérez (19/0), Fabián Guevara Arredondo (12/1) [67.José Marcelo Salas Melinao (1/1)], José Luis Sierra Pando (11/3) [83.Pedro Antonio Reyes González (2/0)], Juan Enrique Carreño (2/0), Rodrígo Hernán Barrera Funes (7/4). Trainer: Mirko Jožić (5).
**Goals**: Rodrígo Hernán Barrera Funes (33), José Marcelo Salas Melinao (75), Rodrígo Hernán Barrera Funes (79).

**437.** 25.05.1994 **CHILE - PERU** **2-1(2-1)**
Estadio Nacional, Santiago; Referee: Sabino Fariña (Paraguay); Attendance: 23,892
**CHI:** Marcelo Antonio Ramírez Gormaz (5/0), Ronald Hugo Fuentes Núñez (9/0), Miguel Ardiman (2/0), Javier Luciano Margas Loyola (19/0), Gabriel Rafael Mendoza Ibarra (18/1) [73.Juan Silva (1/0)], Nelson Rodrigo Parraguez Riveros (12/0), Miguel Mauricio Ramírez Pérez (20/0), Raimundo Tupper (5/1) [50.Pedro González Vera (6/1)], Esteban Andrés Valencia Bascuñán (2/0) [53.José Luis Sierra Pando (12/3)], Iván Luis Zamorano Zamora (24/10), Rodrígo Hernán Barrera Funes (8/4) [60.José Marcelo Salas Melinao (2/1)]. Trainer: Mirko Jožić (6).
**Goals**: Gabriel Rafael Mendoza Ibarra (14), Iván Luis Zamorano Zamora (45).

**438.** 21.09.1994 **CHILE - BOLIVIA** **1-2(0-1)**
Estadio Nacional, Santiago; Referee: Francisco Oscar Lamolina (Argentina); Attendance: 12,072
**CHI:** Nelson Antonio Tapia Rios (4/0), Ronald Hugo Fuentes Núñez (10/0) [46.Pedro Antonio Reyes González (3/0)], Miguel Ardiman (3/0), Juan Carlos González (2/0) [46.Cristián Castañeda Vargas (4/0)], Wilson Contreras (1/0) [46.Raimundo Tupper (6/1)], Gabriel Rafael Mendoza Ibarra (19/1), Miguel Mauricio Ramírez Pérez (21/0), Fabián Guevara Arredondo (13/1), Francisco Marcelo Vega (9/1), Pedro González Vera (7/1) [46.Lukas Nicolás Túdor (10/3)], José Marcelo Salas Melinao (3/1) [46.Rodrígo Hernán Barrera Funes (9/4)]. Trainer: Mirko Jožić (7).
**Goal**: Lukas Nicolás Túdor (54 penalty).

**439.** 16.11.1994 **CHILE - ARGENTINA** **0-3(0-2)**
Estadio Nacional, Santiago; Referee: José Joaquín Torres Cadena (Colombia); Attendance: 21,842
**CHI:** Marcelo Antonio Ramírez Gormaz (6/0), Miguel Ardiman (4/0), Ricardo Francisco Rojas Trujillo (1/0) [66.Pedro Antonio Reyes González (4/0)], Javier Luciano Margas Loyola (20/0), Nelson Rodrigo Parraguez Riveros (13/0) [46.Gabriel Rafael Mendoza Ibarra (20/1)], Miguel Mauricio Ramírez Pérez (22/0) [85.Juan Silva (2/0)], Mario Lepe (25/1) [46.Raimundo Tupper (7/1)], Fabián Raphael Estay Silva (28/3), Pedro González Vera (8/1) [46.Miguel Rojas (1/0)], Patricio Nazario Yáñez Candia (43/5), Rodrígo Hernán Barrera Funes (10/4). Trainer: Mirko Jožić (8).

**440.** 29.03.1995 **CHILE - MEXICO** **2-1(1-1)**
Memorial Coliseum, Los Angeles (United States); Referee: Arturo A. Angeles (United States); Attendance: 59,188
**CHI:** Alex Fabián Varas (1/0), Gabriel Rafael Mendoza Ibarra (21/1), Cristián Castañeda Vargas (5/0) [46.Pedro Jaque (4/0)], Javier Luciano Margas Loyola (21/0) [57.Clarence Acuña Donoso (1/0)], Eduardo Enrique Vilches Arriagada (22/1), Fabián Guevara Arredondo (14/1) [46.Francisco Marcelo Vega (10/1)], Esteban Andrés Valencia Bascuñán (3/0), Nelson Rodrigo Parraguez Riveros (14/0), José Luis Sierra Pando (13/3), Iván Luis Zamorano Zamora (25/11) [79.Ian MacNiven (1/0)], José Marcelo Salas Melinao (4/2). Trainer: Francisco Xabier Azcargorta Uriarte (1).
**Goals**: José Marcelo Salas Melinao (14), Iván Luis Zamorano Zamora (77 penalty).

**441.** 19.04.1995 **PERU - CHILE** **6-0(4-0)**
Estadio Nacional, Lima; Referee: Juan Carlos Lugones (Bolivia); Attendance: 15,000
**CHI:** Alex Fabián Varas (2/0), Gabriel Rafael Mendoza Ibarra (22/1), Clarence Acuña Donoso (2/0) [Pablo Galdames Díaz (1/0)], Javier Luciano Margas Loyola (22/0), Cristián Castañeda Vargas (6/0) [Francisco Ulises Rojas (1/0)], Esteban Andrés Valencia Bascuñán (4/0), Nelson Rodrigo Parraguez Riveros (15/0), Ian MacNiven (2/0) [Patricio Mardones Díaz (22/1)], Rodrígo Antonio Pérez Albornoz (1/0), Lukas Nicolás Túdor (11/3) [Rodrígo Goldberg (1/0)], José Marcelo Salas Melinao (5/2). Trainer: Francisco Xabier Azcargorta Uriarte (2).

**442.** 22.04.1995 **CHILE - ICELAND** **1-1(0-1)**
Estadio Municipal „Germán Becker", Temuco; Referee: Ernesto Filippi Cavani (Uruguay); Attendance: 12,779
**CHI:** Alex Fabián Varas (3/0), Gabriel Rafael Mendoza Ibarra (23/1), Clarence Acuña Donoso (3/0), Miguel Mauricio Ramírez Pérez (23/0) [67.Pablo Galdames Díaz (2/0)], Javier Luciano Margas Loyola (23/0), Nelson Rodrigo Parraguez Riveros (16/0), Rodrígo Antonio Pérez Albornoz (2/0), Esteban Andrés Valencia Bascuñán (5/0), Patricio Mardones Díaz (23/1), Lukas Nicolás Túdor (12/3) [46.Rodrígo Goldberg (2/0)], José Marcelo Salas Melinao (6/3). Trainer: Francisco Xabier Azcargorta Uriarte (3).
**Goal**: José Marcelo Salas Melinao (51).

**443.** 25.05.1995 **CHILE – NORTHERN IRELAND** **2-1(0-1)** Canada Cup
Commonwealth Stadium, Edmonton (Canada); Referee: Michael Seifert (Canada); Attendance: 6,124
**CHI:** Marco Antonio Cornéz (21/0), Miguel Mauricio Ramírez Pérez (24/0), Ronald Hugo Fuentes Núñez (11/0), Clarence Acuña Donoso (4/0), Gabriel Rafael Mendoza Ibarra (24/1), Patricio Mardones Díaz (24/2), Luis Eduardo Musrri Saravia (5/0) [46.Esteban Andrés Valencia Bascuñán (6/1)], Fabián Guevara Arredondo (15/1), Rodrígo Antonio Pérez Albornoz (3/0) [46.Fabián Raphael Estay Silva (29/3)], Rodrígo Goldberg (3/0) [46.Sebastián Rozental Igualt (1/0)], José Marcelo Salas Melinao (7/3). Trainer: Francisco Xabier Azcargorta Uriarte (4).
**Goals**: Esteban Andrés Valencia Bascuñán (74), Patricio Mardones Díaz (81).

**444.** 28.05.1995 **CANADA - CHILE** **1-2(1-1)** Canada Cup
Commonwealth Stadium, Edmonton; Referee: Timothy Weyland (United States); Attendance: 17,047
**CHI:** Marco Antonio Cornéz (22/0), Clarence Acuña Donoso (5/0), Ronald Hugo Fuentes Núñez (12/0), Miguel Mauricio Ramírez Pérez (25/0), Gabriel Rafael Mendoza Ibarra (25/1), Esteban Andrés Valencia Bascuñán (7/2) [Rodrígo Antonio Pérez Albornoz (4/0)], Patricio Mardones Díaz (25/2), Fabián Guevara Arredondo (16/1), Fabián Raphael Estay Silva (30/3), Sebastián Rozental Igualt (2/0) [Rodrígo Goldberg (4/0)], José Marcelo Salas Melinao (8/4). Trainer: Francisco Xabier Azcargorta Uriarte (5).
**Goals**: Esteban Andrés Valencia Bascuñán (32), José Marcelo Salas Melinao (87).

**445.** 16.06.1995 **CHILE – NEW ZEALAND** **3-1(2-1)** Copa Centenario
Estadio Regional, Antofagasta; Referee: Ubaldo Aquino Valenzano (Paraguay); Attendance: 28,325
**CHI:** Marcelo Antonio Ramírez Gormaz (7/0), Ronald Hugo Fuentes Núñez (13/1), Eduardo Enrique Vilches Arriagada (23/1), Miguel Mauricio Ramírez Pérez (26/1), Gabriel Rafael Mendoza Ibarra (26/1), Esteban Andrés Valencia Bascuñán (8/2) [83.Pablo Galdames Díaz (3/0)], Patricio Mardones Díaz (26/2), Fabián Guevara Arredondo (17/1), Fabián Raphael Estay Silva (31/3), Rodrígo Ruíz De Barbieri (2/1) [85.Ivo Alexis Basay (17/4)], José Marcelo Salas Melinao (9/4) [63.Sebastián Rozental Igualt (3/0)]. Trainer: Francisco Xabier Azcargorta Uriarte (6).
**Goals**: Miguel Mauricio Ramírez Pérez (21), Ronald Hugo Fuentes Núñez (36), Rodrígo Ruíz De Barbieri (68).

**446.** 18.06.1995 **CHILE - PARAGUAY** **0-1(0-1)** Copa Centenario
Estadio La Portada, La Serena; Referee: Kenneth Wallace (New Zealand); Attendance: 14,799
**CHI:** Marcelo Antonio Ramírez Gormaz (8/0), Ronald Hugo Fuentes Núñez (14/1), Eduardo Enrique Vilches Arriagada (24/1), Miguel Mauricio Ramírez Pérez (27/1), Gabriel Rafael Mendoza Ibarra (27/1), Esteban Andrés Valencia Bascuñán (9/2), Patricio Mardones Díaz (27/2), Fabián Raphael Estay Silva (32/3), Fabián Guevara Arredondo (18/1), Rodrígo Ruíz De Barbieri (3/1) [Sebastián Rozental Igualt (4/0)], José Marcelo Salas Melinao (10/4) [Ivo Alexis Basay (18/4)]. Trainer: Francisco Xabier Azcargorta Uriarte (7).

**447.** 22.06.1995 **CHILE - TURKEY** **0-0** Copa Centenario
Estadio Nacional, Santiago; Referee: Saúl Mario Feldman Apelbaun (Uruguay); Attendance: 5,000
**CHI:** Marcelo Antonio Ramírez Gormaz (9/0), Eduardo Enrique Vilches Arriagada (25/1), Javier Luciano Margas Loyola (24/0), Miguel Mauricio Ramírez Pérez (28/1), Gabriel Rafael Mendoza Ibarra (28/1), Fabián Raphael Estay Silva (33/3), Patricio Mardones Díaz (28/2) [Pablo Galdames Díaz (4/0)], José Luis Sierra Pando (14/3) [Esteban Andrés Valencia Bascuñán (10/2)], Fabián Guevara Arredondo (19/1), Sebastián Rozental Igualt (5/0) [José Marcelo Salas Melinao (11/4)], Ivo Alexis Basay (19/4). Trainer: Francisco Xabier Azcargorta Uriarte (8).

**448.** 08.07.1995 **UNITED STATES - CHILE** **2-1(2-0)** 37th Copa América. Group Stage.
Estadio „Parque General Artigas", Paysandú (Uruguay); Referee: Alberto Tejada Noriega (Peru); Attendance: 18,000
**CHI:** Marcelo Antonio Ramírez Gormaz (10/0), Eduardo Enrique Vilches Arriagada (26/1), Gabriel Rafael Mendoza Ibarra (29/1), Javier Luciano Margas Loyola (25/0) [*sent off 55*], Miguel Mauricio Ramírez Pérez (29/1), Fabián Guevara Arredondo (20/1), Nelson Rodrigo Parraguez Riveros (17/0), Esteban Andrés Valencia Bascuñán (11/2) [77.Rodrígo Hernán Barrera Funes (11/4)], Fabián Raphael Estay Silva (34/3) [46.José Luis Sierra Pando (15/3)], Ivo Alexis Basay (20/4), José Marcelo Salas Melinao (12/4) [46.Sebastián Rozental Igualt (6/1)]. Trainer: Francisco Xabier Azcargorta Uriarte (9).
**Goal**: Sebastián Rozental Igualt (63).

**449.** 11.07.1995 **ARGENTINA - CHILE** **4-0(2-0)** 37th Copa América. Group Stage.
Estadio „Parque General Artigas", Paysandú (Uruguay); Referee: Arturo Pablo Brizio Carter (Mexico); Attendance: 16,000
**CHI:** Marcelo Antonio Ramírez Gormaz (11/0), Gabriel Rafael Mendoza Ibarra (30/1), Eduardo Enrique Vilches Arriagada (27/1), Rodrígo Antonio Pérez Albornoz (5/0), Miguel Mauricio Ramírez Pérez (30/1), Esteban Andrés Valencia Bascuñán (12/2), Patricio Mardones Díaz (29/2), Nelson Rodrigo Parraguez Riveros (18/0), Fabián Raphael Estay Silva (35/3) [60.Pablo Galdames Díaz (5/0)], Ivo Alexis Basay (21/4) [78.José Marcelo Salas Melinao (13/4)], Rodrígo Ruíz De Barbieri (4/1) [46.Sebastián Rozental Igualt (7/1)]. Trainer: Francisco Xabier Azcargorta Uriarte (10).

**450.** 14.07.1995 **BOLIVIA - CHILE** **2-2(0-0)** 37th Copa América. Group Stage.
Estadio „Parque General Artigas", Paysandú (Uruguay); Referee: Alberto Tejada Noriega (Peru); Attendance: 12,000
**CHI:** Marcelo Antonio Ramírez Gormaz (12/0), Eduardo Enrique Vilches Arriagada (28/1), Javier Luciano Margas Loyola (26/0), Miguel Mauricio Ramírez Pérez (31/1), Rodrígo Antonio Pérez Albornoz (6/0) [46.José Marcelo Salas Melinao (14/4)], Gabriel Rafael Mendoza Ibarra (31/1), Nelson Rodrigo Parraguez Riveros (19/0), Clarence Acuña Donoso (6/0) [34.Esteban Andrés Valencia Bascuñán (13/2)], Pablo Galdames Díaz (6/0), Ivo Alexis Basay (22/6), Sebastián Rozental Igualt (8/1) [80.Rodrígo Hernán Barrera Funes (12/4)]. Trainer: Francisco Xabier Azcargorta Uriarte (11).
**Goals**: Ivo Alexis Basay (55, 61).

**451.** 11.10.1995 **CHILE - CANADA** **2-0(0-0)**
Estadio Regional, Concepción; Referee: Javier Alberto Castrilli (Argentina); Attendance: 11,700
**CHI:** Nelson Antonio Tapia Rios (5/0), Javier Luciano Margas Loyola (27/0), Gabriel Rafael Mendoza Ibarra (32/1) [46.Jaime Lopresti Travanic (1/0)], Ronald Hugo Fuentes Núñez (15/1) [75.Claudio Lizama (1/0)], Clarence Acuña Donoso (7/0), Francisco Ulises Rojas (2/0), Nelson Rodrigo Parraguez Riveros (20/0), Pablo Galdames Díaz (7/0) [46.Esteban Andrés Valencia Bascuñán (14/2)], Sebastián Rozental Igualt (9/2), José Marcelo Salas Melinao (15/5) [56.Moisés Avila (1/0)], Fabián Raphael Estay Silva (36/3) [79.César Muena (1/0)]. Trainer: Francisco Xabier Azcargorta Uriarte (12).
**Goals**: Sebastián Rozental Igualt (47 penalty), José Marcelo Salas Melinao (68).

**452.** 03.02.1996 **BOLIVIA - CHILE** **1-1(1-0)**
Estadio „Félix Capriles", Cochabamba; Referee: Armando Aliaga (Bolivia); Attendance: 24,130
**CHI:** Nelson Antonio Tapia Rios (6/0), Fernando Andrés Cornejo Jiménez (4/0), Miguel Ardiman (5/0), Ronald Hugo Fuentes Núñez (16/1) [Juan Carlos González (3/0)], Javier Luciano Margas Loyola (28/1) [Marcelo Miranda (3/0)], Esteban Andrés Valencia Bascuñán (15/2), Nelson Rodrigo Parraguez Riveros (21/0), Luis Eduardo Musrri Saravia (6/0), Gustavo Poirrier (1/0) [Jaime Patricio Ramírez (17/1)], Franz Arancibia Unger (1/0) [Claudio Patricio Núñez Camaño (1/0)], José Marcelo Salas Melinao (16/5) [Sebastián Rozental Igualt (10/2)]. Trainer: Francisco Xabier Azcargorta Uriarte (13).
**Goal**: Javier Luciano Margas Loyola (49).

**453.** 07.02.1996 **CHILE - MEXICO** **2-1(1-1)**
Estadio Sausalito, Viña del Mar; Referee: Julio Alcides Matto Estoceres (Uruguay); Attendance: 21,500
**CHI:** Nelson Antonio Tapia Rios (7/0), Fernando Andrés Cornejo Jiménez (5/0), Ronald Hugo Fuentes Núñez (17/1), Juan Carlos González (4/0) [Miguel Ardiman (6/0)], Marcelo Miranda (4/0), Esteban Andrés Valencia Bascuñán (16/2) [Pablo Galdames Díaz (8/0)], Nelson Rodrigo Parraguez Riveros (22/0), Luis Eduardo Musrri Saravia (7/0), Fabián Raphael Estay Silva (37/3) [Jaime Patricio Ramírez (18/2)], Rodrígo Goldberg (5/1) [Claudio Patricio Núñez Camaño (2/0)], José Marcelo Salas Melinao (17/5) [Sebastián Rozental Igualt (11/2)]. Trainer: Francisco Xabier Azcargorta Uriarte (14).
**Goals**: Rodrígo Goldberg (45), Jaime Patricio Ramírez (75).

**454.** 14.02.1996 **CHILE - PERU** **4-0(2-0)**
Estadio „Francisco Sánchez Rumoroso", Coquimbo; Referee: Luis Héctor Olivetto (Argentina); Attendance: 14,000
**CHI:** Nelson Antonio Tapia Rios (8/0), Fernando Andrés Cornejo Jiménez (6/0), Ronald Hugo Fuentes Núñez (18/1), Miguel Ardiman (7/0), Javier Luciano Margas Loyola (29/1) [65.Marcelo Miranda (5/0)], Nelson Rodrigo Parraguez Riveros (23/0), Luis Eduardo Musrri Saravia (8/0) [21.Pablo Galdames Díaz (9/1)], Esteban Andrés Valencia Bascuñán (17/2) [46.Gustavo Poirrier (2/0)], Jaime Patricio Ramírez (19/2) [62.Claudio Patricio Núñez Camaño (3/0)], Rodrígo Goldberg (6/3), José Marcelo Salas Melinao (18/6) [46.Sebastián Rozental Igualt (12/2)]. Trainer: Francisco Xabier Azcargorta Uriarte (15).
**Goals**: José Marcelo Salas Melinao (5), Pablo Galdames Díaz (22 penalty), Rodrígo Goldberg (47, 60).

**455.** 23.04.1996 **CHILE - AUSTRALIA** **3-0(0-0)**
Estadio Regional, Antofagasta; Referee: Roberto Rubén Ruscio (Argentina); Attendance: 30,000
**CHI:** Nelson Antonio Tapia Rios (9/0), Gabriel Rafael Mendoza Ibarra (33/1), Ronald Hugo Fuentes Núñez (19/1), Miguel Mauricio Ramírez Pérez (32/1), Javier Luciano Margas Loyola (30/1), Nelson Rodrigo Parraguez Riveros (24/0) [46.Pablo Galdames Díaz (10/1)], Luis Eduardo Musrri Saravia (9/0) [46.Esteban Andrés Valencia Bascuñán (18/3)], Fabián Raphael Estay Silva (38/3), Francisco Marcelo Vega (11/1) [63.José Marcelo Salas Melinao (19/6)], Iván Luis Zamorano Zamora (26/13) [85.Claudio Patricio Núñez Camaño (4/0)], Sebastián Rozental Igualt (13/2) [46.Rodrígo Goldberg (7/3)]. Trainer: Francisco Xabier Azcargorta Uriarte (16).
**Goals**: Iván Luis Zamorano Zamora (52), Esteban Andrés Valencia Bascuñán (61), Iván Luis Zamorano Zamora (82).

**456.** 26.05.1996 **CHILE - BOLIVIA** **2-0(2-0)**
Estadio Nacional, Santiago; Referee: Luis Héctor Olivetto (Argentina); Attendance: 24,307
**CHI:** Nelson Antonio Tapia Rios (10/0), Gabriel Rafael Mendoza Ibarra (34/1) [46.Francisco Ulises Rojas (3/0)], Miguel Mauricio Ramírez Pérez (33/1) [71.Clarence Acuña Donoso (8/0)], Ronald Hugo Fuentes Núñez (20/1), Javier Luciano Margas Loyola (31/1), Eduardo Enrique Vilches Arriagada (29/1), Fabián Raphael Estay Silva (39/3), Francisco Marcelo Vega (12/1), Esteban Andrés Valencia Bascuñán (19/3) [66.Sebastián Rozental Igualt (14/2)], Iván Luis Zamorano Zamora (27/13) [46.Claudio Patricio Núñez Camaño (5/0)], José Marcelo Salas Melinao (20/8) [84.Marcelo Miranda (6/0)]. Trainer: Francisco Xabier Azcargorta Uriarte (17).
**Goals**: José Marcelo Salas Melinao (32, 38).

**457.** 02.06.1996 **VENEZUELA - CHILE** **1-1(1-0)** 16th FIFA WC. Qualifiers
Estadio La Carolina, Barinas; Referee: Epifanio González Chávez (Paraguay); Attendance: 8,074
**CHI:** Nelson Antonio Tapia Rios (11/0), Gabriel Rafael Mendoza Ibarra (35/1), Ronald Hugo Fuentes Núñez (21/1), Javier Luciano Margas Loyola (32/2), Miguel Mauricio Ramírez Pérez (34/1), Fabián Raphael Estay Silva (40/3), Eduardo Enrique Vilches Arriagada (30/1) [75.Claudio Patricio Núñez Camaño (6/0)], Esteban Andrés Valencia Bascuñán (20/3) [46.Luis Eduardo Musrri Saravia (10/0)], Francisco Marcelo Vega (13/1) [46.Sebastián Rozental Igualt (15/2)], Iván Luis Zamorano Zamora (28/13), José Marcelo Salas Melinao (21/8). Trainer: Francisco Xabier Azcargorta Uriarte (18).
**Goal**: Javier Luciano Margas Loyola (89).

**458.** 06.07.1996 **CHILE - ECUADOR** **4-1(1-0)** 16th FIFA WC. Qualifiers
Estadio Nacional, Santiago; Referee: Pablo Peña Durán (Bolivia); Attendance: 74,905
**CHI:** Nelson Antonio Tapia Rios (12/0), Cristián Castañeda Vargas (7/0), Javier Luciano Margas Loyola (33/2), Marcelo Miranda (7/0), Juan Carlos González (5/0), Luis Eduardo Musrri Saravia (11/0), Esteban Andrés Valencia Bascuñán (21/3) [62.Fabián Raphael Estay Silva (41/4)], Francisco Marcelo Vega (14/1) [76.José Luis Sierra Pando (16/3)], Víctor Hugo Castañeda Vargas (1/0) [68.Cristián Mora Tejo (1/0)], Iván Luis Zamorano Zamora (29/15), José Marcelo Salas Melinao (22/9). Trainer: Nelson Bonifacio Acosta López (2).
**Goals**: Iván Luis Zamorano Zamora (27), José Marcelo Salas Melinao (75), Fabián Raphael Estay Silva (83), Iván Luis Zamorano Zamora (86).

**459.** 26.08.1996 **COSTA RICA - CHILE** **1-1(0-0)**
Estadio „Edgardo Baltonado", Liberia; Referee: Rodrigo Badilla Sequeira (Costa Rica); Attendance: 7,000
**CHI:** Marcelo Antonio Ramírez Gormaz (13/0) [Nelson Antonio Tapia Rios (13/0)], Clarence Acuña Donoso (9/0) [Cristián Romero Godoy (1/0)], Ricardo Francisco Rojas Trujillo (2/0), Agustín Alex Salvatierra Concha (1/0), Marcelo Miranda (8/0), Cristián Mora Tejo (2/0), Luis Eduardo Musrri Saravia (12/0), Víctor Hugo Castañeda Vargas (2/0) [José Luis Sierra Pando (17/3)], Francisco Marcelo Vega (15/1), Juan Enrique Carreño (3/0) [Iván Luis Zamorano Zamora (30/15)], Sebastián Rozental Igualt (16/2) [José Marcelo Salas Melinao (23/10)]. Trainer: Nelson Bonifacio Acosta López (3).
**Goal**: José Marcelo Salas Melinao (80).

**460.** 01.09.1996 **COLOMBIA - CHILE** **4-1(3-0)** 16th FIFA WC. Qualifiers
Estadio Metropolitano „Roberto Meléndez", Barranquilla; Referee: Marinho dos Santos Sidrack (Brazil); Attendance: 34,000
**CHI:** Nelson Antonio Tapia Rios (14/0), Ricardo Francisco Rojas Trujillo (3/0) [46.José Luis Sierra Pando (18/3) [*sent off 89*]], Juan Carlos González (6/0), Javier Luciano Margas Loyola (34/2), Cristián Mora Tejo (3/0), Luis Eduardo Musrri Saravia (13/0), Fabián Raphael Estay Silva (42/4) [86.Víctor Hugo Castañeda Vargas (3/0)], Francisco Marcelo Vega (16/1) [67.Sebastián Rozental Igualt (17/2)], Iván Luis Zamorano Zamora (31/16), José Marcelo Salas Melinao (24/10), Cristián Romero Godoy (2/0). Trainer: Nelson Bonifacio Acosta López (4).
**Goal**: Iván Luis Zamorano Zamora (56 penalty).

**461.** 09.10.1996 **PARAGUAY - CHILE** **2-1(1-1)** 16th FIFA WC. Qualifiers
Estadio Defensores del Chaco, Asunción; Referee: Oscar Julián Ruíz Acosta (Colombia); Attendance: 45,000
**CHI:** Marcelo Antonio Ramírez Gormaz (14/0), Cristián Castañeda Vargas (8/0), Pedro Antonio Reyes González (5/0), Ronald Hugo Fuentes Núñez (22/1), Javier Luciano Margas Loyola (35/3) [80.Fabián Raphael Estay Silva (43/4)], Marcelo Miranda (9/0), Fernando Andrés Cornejo Jiménez (7/0), Luis Eduardo Musrri Saravia (14/0), Jorge Alejandro Contreras Lira (21/2) [67.Sebastián Rozental Igualt (18/2)], Iván Luis Zamorano Zamora (32/16), Luis Fernando Vergara Meylan (1/0) [75.Rodrígo Goldberg (8/3)]. Trainer: Nelson Bonifacio Acosta López (5).

**Goal**: Javier Luciano Margas Loyola (22).

**462.** 12.11.1996 **CHILE - URUGUAY** **1-0(0-0)** 16th FIFA WC. Qualifiers
Estadio Nacional, Santiago; Referee: Ángel Guevara (Ecuador); Attendance: 73,547
**CHI:** Nelson Antonio Tapia Rios (15/0), Pedro Antonio Reyes González (6/0), Ronald Hugo Fuentes Núñez (23/1), Javier Luciano Margas Loyola (36/3), Luis Eugenio Chavarría Andrade (1/0), Cristián Castañeda Vargas (9/0), Víctor Hugo Castañeda Vargas (4/0) [70.Jorge Alejandro Contreras Lira (22/2)], Fernando Andrés Cornejo Jiménez (8/0), Luis Pérez (6/0) [46.Ivo Alexis Basay (23/6)], Sebastián Rozental Igualt (19/2) [77.Cristián Mora Tejo (4/0)], José Marcelo Salas Melinao (25/11). Trainer: Nelson Bonifacio Acosta López (6).
**Goal**: José Marcelo Salas Melinao (60).

**463.** 15.12.1996 **ARGENTINA - CHILE** **1-1(0-0)** 16th FIFA WC. Qualifiers
Estadio Monumental „Antonio Vespucio Liberti“, Buenos Aires; Referee: Ubaldo Aquino Valenzano (Paraguay); Attendance: 59,870
**CHI:** Nelson Antonio Tapia Rios (16/0), Cristián Castañeda Vargas (10/0) [65.Wilson Contreras (2/0)], Pedro Antonio Reyes González (7/0), Ronald Hugo Fuentes Núñez (24/1), Javier Luciano Margas Loyola (37/3), Fernando Andrés Cornejo Jiménez (9/1), Cristián Mora Tejo (5/0), Luis Eugenio Chavarría Andrade (2/0), Víctor Hugo Castañeda Vargas (5/0), Sebastián Rozental Igualt (20/2) [46.Marcelo Miranda (10/0)], José Marcelo Salas Melinao (26/11) [71.Iván Luis Zamorano Zamora (33/16)]. Trainer: Nelson Bonifacio Acosta López (7).
**Goal**: Fernando Andrés Cornejo Jiménez (53).

**464.** 04.01.1997 **CHILE - ARMENIA** **7-0(3-0)**
Estadio Sausalito, Viña del Mar; Referee: Mario Fernando Sánchez Yanten (Chile); Attendance: 17,726
**CHI:** Nelson Orlando Cossio Riquelme (1/0) [71.Nelson Antonio Tapia Rios (17/0)], Cristián Castañeda Vargas (11/1), Pedro Antonio Reyes González (8/0), Ronald Hugo Fuentes Núñez (25/1) [71.Dante Eugenio Poli García (1/0)], Marcelo Miranda (11/0), Fernando Andrés Cornejo Jiménez (10/2), Juan Carlos González (7/0) [74.Luis Eugenio Chavarría Andrade (3/0)], Jaime Eduardo Riveros Valenzuela (1/2), Jorge Alejandro Contreras Lira (23/2) [67.Pedro González Vera (9/2)], Rodrígo Goldberg (9/3), Luis Fernando Vergara Meylan (2/2) [67.Cristián Mora Tejo (6/0)]. Trainer: Nelson Bonifacio Acosta López (8).
**Goals**: Luis Fernando Vergara Meylan (5), Cristián Castañeda Vargas (20), Luis Fernando Vergara Meylan (44), Jaime Eduardo Riveros Valenzuela (68, 73), Fernando Andrés Cornejo Jiménez (80), Pedro González Vera (87).

**465.** 12.01.1997 **PERU - CHILE** **2-1(2-0)** 16th FIFA WC. Qualifiers
Estadio Nacional, Lima; Referee: José Luis Da Rosa Varela (Uruguay); Attendance: 35,373
**CHI:** Nelson Antonio Tapia Rios (18/0), Cristián Castañeda Vargas (12/1), Pedro Antonio Reyes González (9/0), Juan Carlos González (8/0), Marcelo Miranda (12/0), Fernando Andrés Cornejo Jiménez (11/2), Luis Eduardo Musrri Saravia (15/0) [57.Jaime Eduardo Riveros Valenzuela (2/2)], Cristián Mora Tejo (7/0), Sebastián Rozental Igualt (21/2) [81.Jorge Alejandro Contreras Lira (24/2)], Luis Fernando Vergara Meylan (3/2) [63.Pedro González Vera (10/2)], Iván Luis Zamorano Zamora (34/17). Trainer: Nelson Bonifacio Acosta López (9).
**Goal**: Iván Luis Zamorano Zamora (89).

**466.** 12.02.1997 **BOLIVIA - CHILE** **1-1(1-1)** 16th FIFA WC. Qualifiers
Estadio „Hernando Siles Zuazo“, La Paz; Referee: Alberto Tejada Noriega (Peru); Attendance: 41,908
**CHI:** Nelson Antonio Tapia Rios (19/0), Cristián Castañeda Vargas (13/1), Pedro Antonio Reyes González (10/0), Ronald Hugo Fuentes Núñez (26/1), Marcelo Miranda (13/0), Luis Eugenio Chavarría Andrade (4/0), Jaime Eduardo Riveros Valenzuela (3/2) [76.Jorge Alejandro Contreras Lira (25/2)], Víctor Hugo Castañeda Vargas (6/0) [60.Cristián Flores (1/0)], Mario Alfredo Salas Saieg (2/0), Iván Luis Zamorano Zamora (35/17) [87.Oscar Lee Chong (1/0)], Pedro González Vera (11/3). Trainer: Nelson Bonifacio Acosta López (10).
**Goal**: Pedro González Vera (45).

**467.** 02.04.1997 **BRAZIL - CHILE** **4-0(2-0)**
Estádio „Mané Garrincha“, Brasília; Referee: Carlos Eugênio Simon (Brazil); Attendance: 45,000
**CHI:** Nelson Antonio Tapia Rios (20/0), Gabriel Rafael Mendoza Ibarra (36/1), Javier Luciano Margas Loyola (38/3) [Raúl Andrés Muñoz Mardones (1/0)], Pedro Antonio Reyes González (11/0), Ronald Hugo Fuentes Núñez (27/1), Mario Alfredo Salas Saieg (3/0), Luis Eduardo Musrri Saravia (16/0), Víctor Hugo Castañeda Vargas (7/0) [46.Esteban Andrés Valencia Bascuñán (22/3)], José Luis Sierra Pando (19/3) [62.Jaime Eduardo Riveros Valenzuela (4/2)], Ivo Alexis Basay (24/6) [46.Rodrígo Goldberg (10/3)], Claudio Patricio Núñez Camaño (7/0) [81.Pedro González Vera (12/3)]. Trainer: Nelson Bonifacio Acosta López (11).

**468.** 29.04.1997 **CHILE - VENEZUELA** **6-0(3-0)** 16th FIFA WC. Qualifiers
Estadio Nacional, Santiago; Referee: Gilberto Alcalá Piñeda (Mexico); Attendance: 42,034
**CHI:** Nelson Antonio Tapia Rios (21/0), Cristián Mora Tejo (8/0), Juan Carlos González (9/0), Pedro Antonio Reyes González (12/1), Miguel Ponce Torres (2/0), Clarence Acuña Donoso (10/0), Luis Eduardo Musrri Saravia (17/0), Francisco Marcelo Vega (17/1) [81.Moisés Fermín Villarroel Ayala (1/0)], José Luis Sierra Pando (20/3) [68.Víctor Hugo Castañeda Vargas (8/0)], Claudio Patricio Núñez Camaño (8/0) [68.Rodrígo Goldberg (11/3)], Iván Luis Zamorano Zamora (36/22). Trainer: Nelson Bonifacio Acosta López (12).
**Goals**: Iván Luis Zamorano Zamora (19, 26, 31, 47), Pedro Antonio Reyes González (66), Iván Luis Zamorano Zamora (85).

**469.** 08.06.1997 **ECUADOR - CHILE** **1-1(1-0)** 16th FIFA WC. Qualifiers
Estadio Olímpico „Atahualpa“, Quito; Referee: Benito Armando Archundia Téllez (Mexico); Attendance: 42,225
**CHI:** Marcelo Antonio Ramírez Gormaz (15/0), Cristián Castañeda Vargas (14/1), Javier Luciano Margas Loyola (39/3), Juan Carlos González (10/0), Marcelo Miranda (14/0), Pedro Antonio Reyes González (13/1), Clarence Acuña Donoso (11/0), Luis Eduardo Musrri Saravia (18/0) [57.Fernando Andrés Cornejo Jiménez (12/2)], José Luis Sierra Pando (21/3) [71.Jaime Eduardo Riveros Valenzuela (5/2)], Pedro González Vera (13/3) [52.Claudio Patricio Núñez Camaño (9/0)], José Marcelo Salas Melinao (27/12). Trainer: Nelson Bonifacio Acosta López (13).
**Goal**: José Marcelo Salas Melinao (53).

**470.** 11.06.1997 **PARAGUAY - CHILE** **1-0(1-0)** 38th Copa América. Group Stage.
Estadio „Félix Capriles“, Cochabamba (Bolivia); Referee: René M. Ortubé Betancourt (Bolivia); Attendance: 17,000
**CHI:** Nelson Orlando Cossio Riquelme (2/0), Jorge Gómez (1/0), Raúl Andrés Muñoz Mardones (2/0) [60.Miguel Ponce Torres (3/0)], Nelson Rodrigo Parraguez Riveros (25/0), Ricardo Francisco Rojas Trujillo (4/0), Mario Alfredo Salas Saieg (4/0), Jaime Eduardo Riveros Valenzuela (6/2) [66.Clarence Acuña Donoso (12/0)], Esteban Andrés Valencia Bascuñán (23/3) [66.Juan Castillo (5/1)], Fernando Andrés Cornejo Jiménez (13/2), Claudio Patricio Núñez Camaño (10/0), Luis Fernando Vergara Meylan (4/2). Trainer: Nelson Bonifacio Acosta López (14).

**471.** 14.06.1997 **ARGENTINA - CHILE** **2-0(0-0)** 38th Copa América. Group Stage.
Estadio „Félix Capriles“, Cochabamba (Bolivia); Referee: Antônio Pereira Da Silva (Brazil); Attendance: 9,000
**CHI:** Nelson Orlando Cossio Riquelme (3/0), Jorge Gómez (2/0), Ricardo Francisco Rojas Trujillo (5/0), Nelson Rodrigo Parraguez Riveros (26/0), Miguel Ponce Torres (4/0) [68.Marcelo Miranda (15/0)], Mario Alfredo Salas Saieg (5/0), Moisés Fermín Villarroel Ayala (2/0) [54.Fernando Andrés Cornejo Jiménez (14/2)], Clarence Acuña Donoso (13/0), Esteban Andrés Valencia Bascuñán (24/3) [81.Jaime Eduardo Riveros Valenzuela (7/2)], Pedro González Vera (14/3), Luis Fernando Vergara Meylan (5/2). Trainer: Nelson Bonifacio Acosta López (15).

**472.** 17.06.1997 **ECUADOR - CHILE** **2-1(1-0)** 38th Copa América. Group Stage.
Estadio „Félix Capriles", Cochabamba (Bolivia); Referee: Rafael Sanabria Díaz (Colombia); Attendance: 8,000
**CHI:** Nelson Orlando Cossio Riquelme (4/0), Jorge Gómez (3/0), Dante Eugenio Poli García (2/0), Miguel Ponce Torres (5/0), Ricardo Francisco Rojas Trujillo (6/0), Fernando Andrés Cornejo Jiménez (15/2), Esteban Andrés Valencia Bascuñán (25/3), Luis Alejandro Osorio González (1/0) [63.Moisés Fermín Villarroel Ayala (3/0)], Clarence Acuña Donoso (14/0) [73.Juan Castillo (6/1)], Claudio Patricio Núñez Camaño (11/0), Luis Fernando Vergara Meylan (6/3) [80.Pedro González Vera (15/3)]. Trainer: Nelson Bonifacio Acosta López (16).
**Goal**: Luis Fernando Vergara Meylan (51).

**473.** 05.07.1997 **CHILE - COLOMBIA** **4-1(3-0)** 16th FIFA WC. Qualifiers
Estadio Nacional, Santiago; Referee: Paolo Borgosano (Venezuela); Attendance: 75,617
**CHI:** Nelson Antonio Tapia Rios (22/0), Cristián Castañeda Vargas (15/1), Ronald Hugo Fuentes Núñez (28/1), Javier Luciano Margas Loyola (40/3), Miguel Ponce Torres (6/0), Luis Eduardo Musrri Saravia (19/0), Clarence Acuña Donoso (15/0), Francisco Marcelo Vega (18/1) [75.Esteban Andrés Valencia Bascuñán (26/3)], Víctor Hugo Castañeda Vargas (9/0) [85.Fernando Andrés Cornejo Jiménez (16/2)], Iván Luis Zamorano Zamora (37/23), José Marcelo Salas Melinao (28/15). Trainer: Nelson Bonifacio Acosta López (17).
**Goals**: José Marcelo Salas Melinao (16, 27, 41), Iván Luis Zamorano Zamora (90).

**474.** 20.07.1997 **CHILE - PARAGUAY** **2-1(1-0)** 16th FIFA WC. Qualifiers
Estadio Nacional, Santiago; Referee: Rafael Torrealba (Venezuela); Attendance: 75,143
**CHI:** Nelson Antonio Tapia Rios (23/0), Cristián Castañeda Vargas (16/1), Ronald Hugo Fuentes Núñez (29/1), Javier Luciano Margas Loyola (41/3), Miguel Ponce Torres (7/0), Luis Eduardo Musrri Saravia (20/0), Clarence Acuña Donoso (16/0) [81.Fernando Andrés Cornejo Jiménez (17/2)], Francisco Marcelo Vega (19/1) [70.Esteban Andrés Valencia Bascuñán (27/3)], Víctor Hugo Castañeda Vargas (10/0) [*sent off 65*], Iván Luis Zamorano Zamora (38/25), José Marcelo Salas Melinao (29/15) [86.Claudio Patricio Núñez Camaño (12/0)]. Trainer: Nelson Bonifacio Acosta López (18).
**Goals**: Iván Luis Zamorano Zamora (8 penalty,51).

**475.** 20.08.1997 **URUGUAY - CHILE** **1-0(1-0)** 16th FIFA WC. Qualifiers
Estadio Centenario, Montevideo; Referee: Antônio Pereira Da Silva (Brazil); Attendance: 40,000
**CHI:** Nelson Antonio Tapia Rios (24/0), Cristián Castañeda Vargas (17/1) [88.Fernando Andrés Cornejo Jiménez (18/2)], Ronald Hugo Fuentes Núñez (30/1) [*sent off 60*], Javier Luciano Margas Loyola (42/3), Miguel Ponce Torres (8/0), Pedro Antonio Reyes González (14/1), Luis Eduardo Musrri Saravia (21/0) [81.Rodrígo Ruíz De Barbieri (5/1)], Claudio Patricio Núñez Camaño (13/0), Clarence Acuña Donoso (17/0), Francisco Marcelo Vega (20/1) [72.Esteban Andrés Valencia Bascuñán (28/3)], José Marcelo Salas Melinao (30/15). Trainer: Nelson Bonifacio Acosta López (19).

**476.** 10.09.1997 **CHILE - ARGENTINA** **1-2(1-1)** 16th FIFA WC. Qualifiers
Estadio Nacional, Santiago; Referee: Francisco Mourão Dacildo (Brazil); Attendance: 73,644
**CHI:** Nelson Antonio Tapia Rios (25/0), Cristián Castañeda Vargas (18/1), Pedro Antonio Reyes González (15/1), Javier Luciano Margas Loyola (43/3), Miguel Ponce Torres (9/0), Luis Eduardo Musrri Saravia (22/0), Nelson Rodrigo Parraguez Riveros (27/0), Wilson Contreras (3/0), José Luis Sierra Pando (22/3), Francisco Marcelo Vega (21/1) [80.Rodrígo Goldberg (12/3)], José Marcelo Salas Melinao (31/16). Trainer: Nelson Bonifacio Acosta López (20).
**Goal**: José Marcelo Salas Melinao (33).

**477.** 12.10.1997 **CHILE - PERU** **4-0(1-0)** 16th FIFA WC. Qualifiers
Estadio Nacional, Santiago; Referee: Márcio Rezende de Freitas (Brazil); Attendance: 74,219
**CHI:** Nelson Antonio Tapia Rios (26/0), Francisco Ulises Rojas (4/0), Pedro Antonio Reyes González (16/2), Ronald Hugo Fuentes Núñez (31/1), Miguel Ponce Torres (10/0) [46.Nelson Rodrigo Parraguez Riveros (28/0)], Clarence Acuña Donoso (18/0), Fernando Andrés Cornejo Jiménez (19/2), José Luis Sierra Pando (23/3), Francisco Marcelo Vega (22/1) [50.Víctor Hugo Castañeda Vargas (11/0)], Rodrígo Hernán Barrera Funes (13/4) [71.Juan Enrique Carreño (4/0)], José Marcelo Salas Melinao (32/19). Trainer: Nelson Bonifacio Acosta López (21).
**Goals**: José Marcelo Salas Melinao (13), Pedro Antonio Reyes González (69), José Marcelo Salas Melinao (83, 87).

**478.** 07.11.1997 **CHILE - GUATEMALA** **4-1(3-0)**
Estadio Regional, Antofagasta; Referee: Cristián Lemus (Chile); Attendance: 18,000
**CHI:** Nelson Antonio Tapia Rios (27/0), Fernando Andrés Cornejo Jiménez (20/2), Javier Luciano Margas Loyola (44/4), Ronald Hugo Fuentes Núñez (32/1) [75.Ricardo Francisco Rojas Trujillo (7/0)], Miguel Ponce Torres (11/0), Clarence Acuña Donoso (19/0) [75.Jorge Gómez (4/0)], Luis Eduardo Musrri Saravia (23/0) [63.Wilson Contreras (4/0)], Esteban Andrés Valencia Bascuñán (29/3), Francisco Marcelo Vega (23/1) [50.Cristián Castañeda Vargas (19/1)], Claudio Patricio Núñez Camaño (14/3), Rodrígo Hernán Barrera Funes (14/4). Trainer: Nelson Bonifacio Acosta López (22).
**Goals**: Javier Luciano Margas Loyola (26), Claudio Patricio Núñez Camaño (28, 30, 71).

**479.** 16.11.1997 **CHILE - BOLIVIA** **3-0(2-0)** 16th FIFA WC. Qualifiers
Estadio Nacional, Santiago; Referee: Wilson Mendonça Souza (Brazil); Attendance: 74,777
**CHI:** Nelson Antonio Tapia Rios (28/0), Cristián Castañeda Vargas (20/1), Javier Luciano Margas Loyola (45/4), Pedro Antonio Reyes González (17/2), Francisco Ulises Rojas (5/0), Clarence Acuña Donoso (20/0), Luis Eduardo Musrri Saravia (24/0), Francisco Marcelo Vega (24/1) [46.Esteban Andrés Valencia Bascuñán (30/3)], José Luis Sierra Pando (24/3) [82.Juan Enrique Carreño (5/1)], Rodrígo Hernán Barrera Funes (15/5) [74.Claudio Patricio Núñez Camaño (15/3)], José Marcelo Salas Melinao (33/20). Trainer: Nelson Bonifacio Acosta López (23).
**Goals**: Rodrígo Hernán Barrera Funes (24), José Marcelo Salas Melinao (41), Juan Enrique Carreño (85).

**480.** 31.01.1998 **IRAN - CHILE** **1-1(1-1,1-1); 4-2 on penalties** Carlsberg Cup
Government Stadium, Hong Kong; Referee: Peter Mikkelsen (Denmark); Attendance: 30,000
**CHI:** Marcelo Antonio Ramírez Gormaz (16/0), Jorge Gómez (5/0), Ronald Hugo Fuentes Núñez (33/1), Luis Alberto Fuentes Rodríguez (1/0), Rafael Andrés Olarra Guerrero (1/0), Moisés Fermín Villarroel Ayala (4/0), Nelson Rodrigo Parraguez Riveros (29/0), Paolo Vivar (1/0) [73.Clarence Acuña Donoso (21/0)], Francisco Marcelo Vega (25/1) [78.José Luis Sierra Pando (25/3)], Juan Enrique Carreño (6/1) [65.Rodrígo Hernán Barrera Funes (16/5)], Manuel Alejandro Neira Díaz (1/1). Trainer: Nelson Bonifacio Acosta López (24).
**Goal**: Manuel Alejandro Neira Díaz (6).
**Penalties**: Nelson Rodrigo Parraguez Riveros, Rodrígo Hernán Barrera Funes, José Luis Sierra Pando (miss), Rafael Andrés Olarra Guerrero (miss).

**481.** 04.02.1998 **NEW ZEALAND - CHILE** **0-0**
Ericsson Stadium, Auckland; Referee: Brian Precious (New Zealand); Attendance: 8,000
**CHI:** Marcelo Antonio Ramírez Gormaz (17/0), Ronald Hugo Fuentes Núñez (34/1), Pedro Antonio Reyes González (18/2), Javier Luciano Margas Loyola (46/4), Moisés Fermín Villarroel Ayala (5/0) [70.Fernando Andrés Cornejo Jiménez (21/2)], Clarence Acuña Donoso (22/0), Nelson Rodrigo Parraguez Riveros (30/0) [54.Pablo Galdames Díaz (11/1)], Francisco Ulises Rojas (6/0), Francisco Marcelo Vega (26/1) [63.José Luis Sierra Pando (26/3)], Manuel Alejandro Neira Díaz (2/1), Rodrígo Hernán Barrera Funes (17/5) [70.Claudio Patricio Núñez Camaño (16/3)]. Trainer: Nelson Bonifacio Acosta López (25).

**482.** 07.02.1998 **AUSTRALIA - CHILE** **0-1(0-1)**
Olympic Park, Melbourne; Referee: Gerard Connolly (Australia); Attendance: 12,000
**CHI:** Nelson Antonio Tapia Rios (29/0), Pedro Antonio Reyes González (19/2) [*sent off 84*], Ronald Hugo Fuentes Núñez (35/1), Javier Luciano Margas Loyola (47/4), Francisco Ulises Rojas (7/0), Pablo Galdames Díaz (12/1) [65.Fernando Andrés Cornejo Jiménez (22/2)], Clarence Acuña Donoso (23/1), Nelson Rodrigo Parraguez Riveros (31/0), José Luis Sierra Pando (27/3) [82.Francisco Marcelo Vega (27/1)], Juan Enrique Carreño (7/1) [78.Manuel Alejandro Neira Díaz (3/1)], Rodrígo Hernán Barrera Funes (18/5) [87.Jorge Gómez (6/0)]. Trainer: Nelson Bonifacio Acosta López (26).
**Goal**: Clarence Acuña Donoso (19).

**483.** 11.02.1998 **ENGLAND - CHILE** **0-2(0-1)**
Wembley Stadium, London; Referee: Ryszard Wójcik (Poland); Attendance: 65,228
**CHI:** Nelson Antonio Tapia Rios (30/0), Pedro Antonio Reyes González (20/2), Ronald Hugo Fuentes Núñez (36/1), Javier Luciano Margas Loyola (48/4), Moisés Fermín Villarroel Ayala (6/0), Nelson Rodrigo Parraguez Riveros (32/0), Clarence Acuña Donoso (24/1), Francisco Ulises Rojas (8/0), José Luis Sierra Pando (28/3) [88.Rodrígo Ignacio Valenzuela Avíles (1/0)], Rodrígo Hernán Barrera Funes (19/5) [77.Juan Enrique Carreño (8/1)], José Marcelo Salas Melinao (34/22). Trainer: Nelson Bonifacio Acosta López (27).
**Goals**: José Marcelo Salas Melinao (45, 79 penalty).

**484.** 22.04.1998 **CHILE - COLOMBIA** **2-2(1-0)**
Estadio Nacional, Santiago; Referee: Horacio Marcelo Elizondo (Argentina); Attendance: 34,127
**CHI:** Nelson Antonio Tapia Rios (31/0), Ronald Hugo Fuentes Núñez (37/1) [*sent off 31*], Javier Luciano Margas Loyola (49/5) [80.Ricardo Francisco Rojas Trujillo (8/0)], Miguel Mauricio Ramírez Pérez (35/1), Moisés Fermín Villarroel Ayala (7/0) [82.Fernando Andrés Cornejo Jiménez (23/2)], Francisco Ulises Rojas (9/0), Nelson Rodrigo Parraguez Riveros (33/0), Clarence Acuña Donoso (25/1), José Luis Sierra Pando (29/3) [76.Esteban Andrés Valencia Bascuñán (31/3)], Manuel Alejandro Neira Díaz (4/1) [61.Héctor Santiago Tapia Urdile (1/0)], José Marcelo Salas Melinao (35/23). Trainer: Nelson Bonifacio Acosta López (28).
**Goals**: Javier Luciano Margas Loyola (21), José Marcelo Salas Melinao (84).

**485.** 29.04.1998 **CHILE - LITHUANIA** **1-0(0-0)**
Estadio Nacional, Santiago; Referee: Daniel Bello Rotunno (Uruguay); Attendance: 7,671
**CHI:** Marcelo Antonio Ramírez Gormaz (18/0), Pablo Galdames Díaz (13/1) [46.Jorge Gómez (7/0)], Miguel Mauricio Ramírez Pérez (36/1), Javier Luciano Margas Loyola (50/5), Mauricio Fernando Aros (1/0), Clarence Acuña Donoso (26/1), Nelson Rodrigo Parraguez Riveros (34/0) [46.Fernando Andrés Cornejo Jiménez (24/2)], Esteban Andrés Valencia Bascuñán (32/3) [70.Juan Enrique Carreño (9/1)], Fabián Raphael Estay Silva (44/4), Rodrígo Hernán Barrera Funes (20/5) [70.Rodolfo Antonio Moya Spuler (1/0)], Héctor Santiago Tapia Urdile (2/0) [46.Claudio Patricio Núñez Camaño (17/4)]. Trainer: Nelson Bonifacio Acosta López (29).
**Goal**: Claudio Patricio Núñez Camaño (89).

**486.** 19.05.1998 **ARGENTINA - CHILE** **1-0(0-0)**
Estadio Malvinas Argentinas, Mendoza; Referee: Ubaldo Aquino Valenzano (Paraguay); Attendance: 43,864
**CHI:** Nelson Antonio Tapia Rios (32/0), Ronald Hugo Fuentes Núñez (38/1), Ricardo Francisco Rojas Trujillo (9/0) [77.Juan Enrique Carreño (10/1)], Miguel Mauricio Ramírez Pérez (37/1), Cristián Castañeda Vargas (21/1), Francisco Ulises Rojas (10/0), Luis Eduardo Musrri Saravia (25/0) [61.Fernando Andrés Cornejo Jiménez (25/2)], Nelson Rodrigo Parraguez Riveros (35/0), Fabián Raphael Estay Silva (45/4) [61.José Luis Sierra Pando (30/3)], Iván Luis Zamorano Zamora (39/25), José Marcelo Salas Melinao (36/23). Trainer: Nelson Bonifacio Acosta López (30).

**487.** 24.05.1998 **CHILE - URUGUAY** **2-2(2-0)**
Estadio Nacional, Santiago; Referee: José Antonio Arana Villamonte (Peru); Attendance: 61,528
**CHI:** Nelson Antonio Tapia Rios (33/0), Pedro Antonio Reyes González (21/2) [66.Mauricio Fernando Aros (2/0)], Ronald Hugo Fuentes Núñez (39/1), Javier Luciano Margas Loyola (51/5), Moisés Fermín Villarroel Ayala (8/0), Clarence Acuña Donoso (27/1), Nelson Rodrigo Parraguez Riveros (36/0), Francisco Ulises Rojas (11/0) [66.José Luis Sierra Pando (31/3)], Fabián Raphael Estay Silva (46/4) [46.Francisco Marcelo Vega (28/1)], Iván Luis Zamorano Zamora (40/26), José Marcelo Salas Melinao (37/24) [72.Rodrígo Hernán Barrera Funes (21/5)]. Trainer: Nelson Bonifacio Acosta López (31).
**Goals**: Iván Luis Zamorano Zamora (9), José Marcelo Salas Melinao (24).

**488.** 31.05.1998 **CHILE - TUNISIA** **3-2(0-0)**
Stade „Alexandre Tropenas“, Montélimar (France); Referee: Rémi Harrel (France); Attendance: 6,000
**CHI:** Nelson Antonio Tapia Rios (34/0), Ronald Hugo Fuentes Núñez (40/1), Pedro Antonio Reyes González (22/2), Javier Luciano Margas Loyola (52/5) [*sent off 90*], Moisés Fermín Villarroel Ayala (9/0) [80.Cristián Castañeda Vargas (22/1)], Luis Eduardo Musrri Saravia (26/0), Nelson Rodrigo Parraguez Riveros (37/0) [74.Fernando Andrés Cornejo Jiménez (26/2)], Francisco Ulises Rojas (12/0) [46.Mauricio Fernando Aros (3/0)], Fabián Raphael Estay Silva (47/4) [67.José Luis Sierra Pando (32/4)], José Marcelo Salas Melinao (38/25) [90.Miguel Mauricio Ramírez Pérez (38/1)], Iván Luis Zamorano Zamora (41/27). Trainer: Nelson Bonifacio Acosta López (32).
**Goals**: José Marcelo Salas Melinao (60), José Luis Sierra Pando (85), Iván Luis Zamorano Zamora (90).

**489.** 04.06.1998 **CHILE - MOROCCO** **1-1(0-0)**
Stade „Pierre de Coubertin“, Avignon (France); Referee: Bernard Saules (France); Attendance: 6,000
**CHI:** Marcelo Antonio Ramírez Gormaz (19/0), Pedro Antonio Reyes González (23/2), Ronald Hugo Fuentes Núñez (41/1), Miguel Mauricio Ramírez Pérez (39/1), Cristián Castañeda Vargas (23/1) [64.Moisés Fermín Villarroel Ayala (10/0)], Clarence Acuña Donoso (28/1) [83.Fabián Raphael Estay Silva (48/4)], Fernando Andrés Cornejo Jiménez (27/2), Mauricio Fernando Aros (4/0), José Luis Sierra Pando (33/4) [46.Francisco Marcelo Vega (29/1)], Manuel Alejandro Neira Díaz (5/1) [64.José Marcelo Salas Melinao (39/26)], Rodrígo Hernán Barrera Funes (22/5) [64.Iván Luis Zamorano Zamora (42/27)]. Trainer: Nelson Bonifacio Acosta López (33).
**Goal**: José Marcelo Salas Melinao (88).

**490.** 11.06.1998 **CHILE - ITALY** **2-2(1-1)** 16th FIFA WC. Group Stage.
Parc Lescure, Bordeaux (France); Referee: Lucien Bouchardeau (Niger); Attendance: 31,800
**CHI:** Nelson Antonio Tapia Rios (35/0), Moisés Fermín Villarroel Ayala (11/0), Pedro Antonio Reyes González (24/2), Ronald Hugo Fuentes Núñez (42/1), Javier Luciano Margas Loyola (53/5) [62.Miguel Mauricio Ramírez Pérez (40/1)], Francisco Ulises Rojas (13/0), Nelson Rodrigo Parraguez Riveros (38/0), Clarence Acuña Donoso (29/1) [81.Fernando Andrés Cornejo Jiménez (28/2)], Fabián Raphael Estay Silva (49/4) [80.José Luis Sierra Pando (34/4)], Iván Luis Zamorano Zamora (43/27), José Marcelo Salas Melinao (40/28). Trainer: Nelson Bonifacio Acosta López (34).
**Goals**: José Marcelo Salas Melinao (45, 49).

**491.** 17.06.1998 **CHILE - AUSTRIA** **1-1(0-0)** 16th FIFA WC. Group Stage.
Stade „Geoffroy-Guichard", Saint-Etienne (France); Referee: Gamal Al-Ghandour (Egypt); Attendance: 30,392
**CHI:** Nelson Antonio Tapia Rios (36/0), Pedro Antonio Reyes González (25/2), Ronald Hugo Fuentes Núñez (43/1), Javier Luciano Margas Loyola (54/5), Francisco Ulises Rojas (14/0), Nelson Rodrigo Parraguez Riveros (39/0), Clarence Acuña Donoso (30/1), Moisés Fermín Villarroel Ayala (12/0) [67.Cristián Castañeda Vargas (24/1)], Fabián Raphael Estay Silva (50/4) [57.José Luis Sierra Pando (35/4)], Iván Luis Zamorano Zamora (44/27), José Marcelo Salas Melinao (41/29). Trainer: Nelson Bonifacio Acosta López (35).
**Goal**: José Marcelo Salas Melinao (70).

**492.** 23.06.1998 **CHILE - CAMEROON** **1-1(1-0)** 16th FIFA WC. Group Stage.
Stade La Beaujoire, Nantes (France); Referee: László Vágner (Hungary); Attendance: 45,000
**CHI:** Nelson Antonio Tapia Rios (37/0), Ronald Hugo Fuentes Núñez (44/1), Javier Luciano Margas Loyola (55/5), Pedro Antonio Reyes González (26/2), Moisés Fermín Villarroel Ayala (13/0) [71.Fernando Andrés Cornejo Jiménez (29/2)], Francisco Ulises Rojas (15/0) [77.Miguel Mauricio Ramírez Pérez (41/1)], Clarence Acuña Donoso (31/1), Nelson Rodrigo Parraguez Riveros (40/0), José Luis Sierra Pando (36/5) [71.Fabián Raphael Estay Silva (51/4)], Iván Luis Zamorano Zamora (45/27), José Marcelo Salas Melinao (42/29). Trainer: Nelson Bonifacio Acosta López (36).
**Goal**: José Luis Sierra Pando (20).

**493.** 27.06.1998 **BRAZIL - CHILE** **4-1(3-0)** 16th FIFA WC. 2nd Round.
Stade Parc des Princes, Paris (France); Referee: Marc Batta (France); Attendance: 48,000
**CHI:** Nelson Antonio Tapia Rios (38/0), Pedro Antonio Reyes González (27/2), Ronald Hugo Fuentes Núñez (45/1), Javier Luciano Margas Loyola (56/5), Fernando Andrés Cornejo Jiménez (30/2), Clarence Acuña Donoso (32/1) [80.Luis Eduardo Musrri Saravia (27/0)], Miguel Mauricio Ramírez Pérez (42/1) [46.Fabián Raphael Estay Silva (52/4)], José Luis Sierra Pando (37/5) [46.Francisco Marcelo Vega (30/1)], Mauricio Fernando Aros (5/0), José Marcelo Salas Melinao (43/30), Iván Luis Zamorano Zamora (46/27). Trainer: Nelson Bonifacio Acosta López (37).
**Goal**: José Marcelo Salas Melinao (68).

**494.** 17.02.1999 **GUATEMALA - CHILE** **1-1(0-0)**
Estadio „Mateo Flores", Ciudad de Guatemala; Referee: Carlos Alberto Batres (Guatemala); Attendance: 12,000
**CHI:** Marcelo Antonio Ramírez Gormaz (20/0), Pablo Andrés Contreras Fica (1/0), Nelson Rodrigo Parraguez Riveros (41/0), Miguel Mauricio Ramírez Pérez (43/1), Moisés Fermín Villarroel Ayala (14/0), Clarence Acuña Donoso (33/1), Roberto Rodrigo Cartes Contreras (1/0), Francisco Ulises Rojas (16/0) [89.Mauricio Fernando Aros (6/0)], David Marcelo Pizarro Cortés (1/0), Rodolfo Antonio Moya Spuler (2/0) [66.Cristián Roberto Uribe Lara (1/0)], Manuel Alejandro Neira Díaz (6/2) [88.Reinaldo Marcelino Navia Amador (1/0)]. Trainer: Nelson Bonifacio Acosta López (38).
**Goal**: Manuel Alejandro Neira Díaz (46).

**495.** 21.02.1999 **UNITED STATES - CHILE** **2-1(0-0)**
Lockhart Stadium, Fort Lauderdale; Referee: Pascual Rebolledo Cardénas (Mexico); Attendance: 14,896
**CHI:** Marcelo Antonio Ramírez Gormaz (21/0), Pablo Andrés Contreras Fica (2/0), Francisco Ulises Rojas (17/0) [80.Mauricio Fernando Aros (7/0)], Miguel Mauricio Ramírez Pérez (44/1), Luis Arturo Mena Irarrázabal (1/0), Cristián Roberto Uribe Lara (2/0) [70.Patricio Enrique Neira Muñoz (1/0)], Clarence Acuña Donoso (34/1), David Marcelo Pizarro Cortés (2/0), Roberto Rodrigo Cartes Contreras (2/1), Manuel Alejandro Neira Díaz (7/2), Reinaldo Marcelino Navia Amador (2/0) [74.Rodolfo Antonio Moya Spuler (3/0)]. Trainer: Nelson Bonifacio Acosta López (39).
**Goal**: Roberto Rodrigo Cartes Contreras (64).

**496.** 28.04.1999 **BOLIVIA - CHILE** **1-1(1-0)**
Estadio „Félix Capriles", Cochabamba; Referee: José Antonio Arana Villamonte (Peru); Attendance: 3,000
**CHI:** Marcelo Antonio Ramírez Gormaz (22/0), Pablo Andrés Contreras Fica (3/0) [*sent off 26*], Jorge Francisco Vargas Palacios (1/0), Luis Alberto Fuentes Rodríguez (2/0), Mauricio Fernando Aros (8/0) [46. César Elías Santis Santander (1/0)], Clarence Acuña Donoso (35/1), Marcos Antonio Villaseca (1/0), David Marcelo Pizarro Cortés (3/1) [68.Mauricio Alejandro Donoso Pérez (1/0)], Esteban Andrés Valencia Bascuñán (33/3) [78.Raúl Alejandro Palacios Gamboa (1/0)], Pedro González Vera (16/3) [88.Moisés Fermín Villarroel Ayala (15/0)], Manuel Alejandro Neira Díaz (8/2) [18.Carlos Reyes (1/0)]. Trainer: Nelson Bonifacio Acosta López (40).
**Goal**: David Marcelo Pizarro Cortés (65).

**497.** 29.05.1999 **CHILE – COSTA RICA** **3-0(1-0)**
Estadio Municipal, Concepción; Referee: Guido Aros Alvarado (Chile); Attendance: 19,076
**CHI:** Nelson Antonio Tapia Rios (39/0), Raúl Alejandro Palacios Gamboa (2/0), Jorge Francisco Vargas Palacios (2/0), Miguel Mauricio Ramírez Pérez (45/1) [17.Pablo Andrés Contreras Fica (4/0)], Francisco Ulises Rojas (18/0) [83.Miguel Ponce Torres (12/0)], Marcos Antonio Villaseca (2/0), Clarence Acuña Donoso (36/2), Esteban Andrés Valencia Bascuñán (34/4) [73.Roberto Rodrigo Cartes Contreras (3/1)], David Marcelo Pizarro Cortés (4/1) [80.Moisés Fermín Villarroel Ayala (16/0)], Pedro González Vera (17/4), José Marcelo Salas Melinao (44/30) [69.Claudio Patricio Núñez Camaño (18/4)]. Trainer: Nelson Bonifacio Acosta López (41).
**Goals**: Clarence Acuña Donoso (44), Esteban Andrés Valencia Bascuñán (60), Pedro González Vera (79).

**498.** 20.06.1999 **CHILE - BOLIVIA** **1-0(1-0)**
Estadio Nacional, Santiago; Referee: Jorge Larrionda Pietrafiesa (Uruguay); Attendance: 25,000
**CHI:** Marcelo Antonio Ramírez Gormaz (23/0), Raúl Alejandro Palacios Gamboa (3/1), Pedro Antonio Reyes González (28/2), Miguel Mauricio Ramírez Pérez (46/1) [55.Javier Luciano Margas Loyola (57/5)], Francisco Ulises Rojas (19/0), Nelson Rodrigo Parraguez Riveros (42/0) [74.Roberto Rodrigo Cartes Contreras (4/1)], Clarence Acuña Donoso (37/2), David Marcelo Pizarro Cortés (5/1) [56.José Luis Sierra Pando (38/5)], Esteban Andrés Valencia Bascuñán (35/4) [55.Fabián Raphael Estay Silva (53/4)], Claudio Patricio Núñez Camaño (19/4) [57.Iván Luis Zamorano Zamora (47/27)], Cristian Antonio Montecinos González (1/0). Trainer: Nelson Bonifacio Acosta López (42).
**Goal**: Raúl Alejandro Palacios Gamboa (14).

**499.** 23.06.1999 **CHILE - ECUADOR** **0-0**
Estadio Nacional, Santiago; Referee: Daniel Orlando Giménez (Argentina); Attendance: 23,282
**CHI:** Marcelo Antonio Ramírez Gormaz (24/0), Pedro Antonio Reyes González (29/2), Jorge Francisco Vargas Palacios (3/0), Miguel Mauricio Ramírez Pérez (47/1), Moisés Fermín Villarroel Ayala (17/0) [68.David Marcelo Pizarro Cortés (6/1)], Miguel Ponce Torres (13/0) [30.Francisco Ulises Rojas (20/0)], Clarence Acuña Donoso (38/2), Roberto Rodrigo Cartes Contreras (5/1) [46.Raúl Alejandro Palacios Gamboa (4/1)], José Luis Sierra Pando (39/5) [46.Fabián Raphael Estay Silva (54/4)], Iván Luis Zamorano Zamora (48/27) [46.Pedro González Vera (18/4)], José Marcelo Salas Melinao (45/30). Trainer: Nelson Bonifacio Acosta López (43).

**500.** 30.06.1999 **MEXICO - CHILE** **1-0(0-0)** 39th Copa América. Group Stage.
Estadio „Antonio Oddone Sarubbi", Ciudad del Este (Paraguay); Referee: Horacio Marcelo Elizondo (Argentina); Attendance: 20,000
**CHI:** Marcelo Antonio Ramírez Gormaz (25/0), Pedro Antonio Reyes González (30/2), Jorge Francisco Vargas Palacios (4/0), Miguel Mauricio Ramírez Pérez (48/1), Francisco Ulises Rojas (21/0), Nelson Rodrigo Parraguez Riveros (43/0), Clarence Acuña Donoso (39/2) [74.Pedro González Vera (19/4)], Esteban Andrés Valencia Bascuñán (36/4) [77.Raúl Alejandro Palacios Gamboa (5/1)], David Marcelo Pizarro Cortés (7/1) [65.Fabián Raphael Estay Silva (55/4)], Iván Luis Zamorano Zamora (49/27), José Marcelo Salas Melinao (46/30). Trainer: Nelson Bonifacio Acosta López (44).

**501.** 03.07.1999 **CHILE - VENEZUELA** **3-0(2-0)** 39th Copa América. Group Stage.
Estadio „Antonio Oddone Sarubbi", Ciudad del Este (Paraguay); Referee: Juan Luna Humérez (Bolivia); Attendance: 5,000
**CHI:** Marcelo Antonio Ramírez Gormaz (26/0), Pedro Antonio Reyes González (31/2), Jorge Francisco Vargas Palacios (5/0), Miguel Mauricio Ramírez Pérez (49/1), Raúl Alejandro Palacios Gamboa (6/1), Clarence Acuña Donoso (40/2), Mauricio Fernando Aros (9/0), Fabián Raphael Estay Silva (56/4), José Luis Sierra Pando (40/6) [46.Nelson Rodrigo Parraguez Riveros (44/0)], Iván Luis Zamorano Zamora (50/28) [75.Pedro González Vera (20/4)], José Marcelo Salas Melinao (47/30). Trainer: Nelson Bonifacio Acosta López (45).
**Goals**: Iván Luis Zamorano Zamora (5), José Luis Sierra Pando (21), Edson Tortolero (66 own goal).

**502.** 06.07.1999 **BRAZIL - CHILE** **1-0(1-0)** 39th Copa América. Group Stage.
Estadio „Antonio Oddone Sarubbi", Ciudad del Este (Paraguay); Referee: Horacio Marcelo Elizondo (Argentina); Attendance: 10,000
**CHI:** Marcelo Antonio Ramírez Gormaz (27/0), Moisés Fermín Villarroel Ayala (18/0) [70.Mauricio Fernando Aros (10/0)], Pablo Andrés Contreras Fica (5/0), Miguel Mauricio Ramírez Pérez (50/1), Javier Luciano Margas Loyola (58/5), Francisco Ulises Rojas (22/0), Roberto Rodrigo Cartes Contreras (6/1), Nelson Rodrigo Parraguez Riveros (45/0) [46.Raúl Alejandro Palacios Gamboa (7/1)], José Luis Sierra Pando (41/6), Iván Luis Zamorano Zamora (51/28) [46.Claudio Patricio Núñez Camaño (20/4)], Pedro González Vera (21/4). Trainer: Nelson Bonifacio Acosta López (46).

**503.** 11.07.1999 **CHILE - COLOMBIA** **3-2(1-2)** 39th Copa América. Quarter-Finals.
Estadio „Feliciano Cáceres", Luque (Paraguay); Referee: Benito Armando Archundia Téllez (Mexico); Attendance: 3,000
**CHI:** Marcelo Antonio Ramírez Gormaz (28/0), Pedro Antonio Reyes González (32/4), Jorge Francisco Vargas Palacios (6/0), Raúl Alejandro Palacios Gamboa (8/1), Miguel Mauricio Ramírez Pérez (51/1), Mauricio Fernando Aros (11/0), Clarence Acuña Donoso (41/2), Fabián Raphael Estay Silva (57/4) [78.Roberto Rodrigo Cartes Contreras (7/1)], José Luis Sierra Pando (42/6) [65.David Marcelo Pizarro Cortés (8/1)], Iván Luis Zamorano Zamora (52/29), Pedro González Vera (22/4) [86.Claudio Patricio Núñez Camaño (21/4)]. Trainer: Nelson Bonifacio Acosta López (47).
**Goals**: Pedro Antonio Reyes González (25, 50), Iván Luis Zamorano Zamora (64).

**504.** 13.07.1999 **URUGUAY - CHILE** **1-1(1-0,1-1); 5-3 on penalties** 39th Copa América. Semi-Finals.
Estadio Defensores del Chaco, Asunción (Paraguay); Referee: Ubaldo Aquino Valenzano (Paraguay); Attendance: 7,000
**CHI:** Marcelo Antonio Ramírez Gormaz (29/0), Raúl Alejandro Palacios Gamboa (9/1), Pedro Antonio Reyes González (33/4), Miguel Mauricio Ramírez Pérez (52/1), Jorge Francisco Vargas Palacios (7/0), Clarence Acuña Donoso (42/2), Mauricio Fernando Aros (12/0), Fabián Raphael Estay Silva (58/4), José Luis Sierra Pando (43/6) [73.David Marcelo Pizarro Cortés (9/1)], Iván Luis Zamorano Zamora (53/30) [88.Pedro González Vera (23/4)], José Marcelo Salas Melinao (48/30). Trainer: Nelson Bonifacio Acosta López (48).
**Goal**: Iván Luis Zamorano Zamora (73).
**Penalties**: Jorge Francisco Vargas Palacios, Mauricio Fernando Aros (save), David Marcelo Pizarro Cortés, Pedro Antonio Reyes González.

**505.** 17.07.1999 **MEXICO - CHILE** **2-1(1-0)** 39th Copa América. Bronze Medal.
Estadio Defensores del Chaco, Asunción (Paraguay); Referee: Horacio Marcelo Elizondo (Argentina); Attendance: 2,500
**CHI:** Marcelo Antonio Ramírez Gormaz (30/0), Pedro Antonio Reyes González (34/4), Jorge Francisco Vargas Palacios (8/0) [61.Esteban Andrés Valencia Bascuñán (37/4)], Miguel Mauricio Ramírez Pérez (53/1) [37.Pablo Andrés Contreras Fica (6/0)], Raúl Alejandro Palacios Gamboa (10/2), Clarence Acuña Donoso (43/2), Mauricio Fernando Aros (13/0), Fabián Raphael Estay Silva (59/4), José Luis Sierra Pando (44/6), Iván Luis Zamorano Zamora (54/30), Pedro González Vera (24/4) [65.Claudio Patricio Núñez Camaño (22/4)]. Trainer: Nelson Bonifacio Acosta López (49).
**Goal**: Raúl Alejandro Palacios Gamboa (80).

**506.** 29.01.2000 **CHILE – UNITED STATES** **1-2(0-0)**
Estadio „Francisco Sánchez Rumoroso", Coquimbo; Referee: Pedro Saucedo Rodríguez (Bolivia); Attendance: 7,000
**CHI:** Marcelo Antonio Ramírez Gormaz (31/0), Raúl Alejandro Palacios Gamboa (11/2), Miguel Mauricio Ramírez Pérez (54/1) [46.Alex Christian von Schwedler Vasquez (1/0)], Mauricio Fernando Aros (14/0), Cristián Flores (2/0), Clarence Acuña Donoso (44/2), Marco Antonio Villaseca (3/0), Esteban Andrés Valencia Bascuñán (38/4) [37.Joel Antonio Reyes Zúñiga (1/0)], Jaime Eduardo Riveros Valenzuela (8/3), Mario Núñez (1/0) [65.Pedro González Vera (25/4)], Sebastian Rozental (22/2) [80.Ricardo Antonio Queraltó Alvarado (1/0)]. Trainer: Nelson Bonifacio Acosta López (50).
**Goal**: Jaime Eduardo Riveros Valenzuela (57).

**507.** 02.02.2000 **COSTA RICA - CHILE** **1-0(0-0)**
Estadio „Ricardo Saprissa", San José; Referee: Rafael Rodríguez (El Salvador); Attendance: 15,000
**CHI:** Marcelo Antonio Ramírez Gormaz (32/0), Raúl Alejandro Palacios Gamboa (12/2) [46.Jaime Eduardo Riveros Valenzuela (9/3)], Cristián Flores (3/0), Miguel Ponce Torres (14/0) [77.Mauricio Fernando Aros (15/0)], Alex Christian von Schwedler Vasquez (2/0) [21.Pedro Antonio Reyes González (35/4)], Nelson Rodrigo Parraguez Riveros (46/0), Clarence Acuña Donoso (45/2), Marco Antonio Villaseca (4/0), José Luis Sierra Pando (45/6) [73.Esteban Andrés Valencia Bascuñán (39/4)], Ricardo Antonio Queraltó Alvarado (2/0) [73.Mario Núñez (2/0)], Sebastián Rozental Igualt (23/2). Trainer: Nelson Bonifacio Acosta López (51).

**508.** 05.02.2000 **GUATEMALA - CHILE** **2-1(2-0)**
Estadio „Mateo Flores", Ciudad de Guatemala; Referee: Neftali Recinos Alvarenga (El Salvador); Attendance: 30,000
**CHI:** Marcelo Antonio Ramírez Gormaz (33/0), Pedro Antonio Reyes González (36/4), Miguel Mauricio Ramírez Pérez (55/1) [46.Cristián Flores (4/0)], Marco Antonio Villaseca (5/0), Nelson Rodrigo Parraguez Riveros (47/0), Mauricio Fernando Aros (16/0), Clarence Acuña Donoso (46/2), Esteban Andrés Valencia Bascuñán (40/4) [46.Mario Núñez (3/0)], José Luis Sierra Pando (46/6) [77.Jaime Eduardo Riveros Valenzuela (10/3)], Ricardo Antonio Queraltó Alvarado (3/1) [75.Miguel Ponce Torres (15/0)], Pedro González Vera (26/4). Trainer: Nelson Bonifacio Acosta López (52).
**Goal**: Ricardo Antonio Queraltó Alvarado (54).

**509.** 09.02.2000 **CHILE - AUSTRALIA** **2-1(1-1)** Copa Valparaíso
Estadio Playa Ancha, Valparaíso; Referee: Eduardo Gamboa Martínez (Chile); Attendance: 5,000
**CHI:** Marcelo Antonio Ramírez Gormaz (34/0), Francisco Fernández (1/0), Miguel Mauricio Ramírez Pérez (56/1) [61.Rodrigo Fabián Núñez Ortiz (1/0)], Nelson Rodrigo Parraguez Riveros (48/0), Jorge Francisco Vargas Palacios (9/0), Marco Antonio Villaseca (6/0), Mauricio Fernando Aros (17/0), Clarence Acuña Donoso (47/2), José Luis Sierra Pando (47/6) [81.Raúl Alejandro Palacios Gamboa (13/2)], Mario Núñez (4/0) [61.Julio Brian Gutiérrez González (1/0)], Pedro González Vera (27/5) [72.Reinaldo Marcelino Navia Amador (3/1)]. Trainer: Nelson Bonifacio Acosta López (53).
**Goals**: Pedro González Vera (10), Reinaldo Marcelino Navia Amador (90).

**510.** 12.02.2000 **CHILE - BULGARIA** **3-2(2-1)** Copa Valparaíso

Estadio Playa Ancha, Valparaíso; Referee: Braulio Antonio Arenas Miranda (Chile); Attendance: 5,000

**CHI:** Miguel Rodrígo Pinto (1/0), Francisco Fernández (2/0), Miguel Mauricio Ramírez Pérez (57/1), Nelson Rodrigo Parraguez Riveros (49/0) [46.Claudio Andrés Maldonado Rivera (1/0)], Mauricio Fernando Aros (18/0) [63.Rafael Andrés Olarra Guerrero (2/0)], Marco Antonio Villaseca (7/0), Clarence Acuña Donoso (48/3), José Luis Sierra Pando (48/7) [71.Rodrígo Alvaro Tello Valenzuela (1/0)], David Marcelo Pizarro Cortés (10/1) [63.Esteban Andrés Valencia Bascuñán (41/4)], Mario Núñez (5/1) [78.Reinaldo Marcelino Navia Amador (4/1)], Pedro González Vera (28/5). Trainer: Nelson Bonifacio Acosta López (54).

**Goals**: Clarence Acuña Donoso (31), José Luis Sierra Pando (45), Mario Núñez (54).

**511.** 15.02.2000 **CHILE - SLOVAKIA** **0-2(0-2)** Copa Valparaíso

Estadio Playa Ancha, Valparaíso; Referee: Guido Aros Alvarado (Chile); Attendance: 3,000

**CHI:** Marcelo Antonio Ramírez Gormaz (35/0), Nelson Rodrigo Parraguez Riveros (50/0), Miguel Mauricio Ramírez Pérez (58/1) [29.Claudio Andrés Maldonado Rivera (2/0)], Javier Luciano Margas Loyola (59/5), Raúl Alejandro Palacios Gamboa (14/2) [29.David Marcelo Pizarro Cortés (11/1)], Clarence Acuña Donoso (49/3) [46.Rodrigo Fabián Núñez Ortiz (2/0)], Marco Antonio Villaseca (8/0), Rafael Andrés Olarra Guerrero (3/0), José Luis Sierra Pando (49/7) [65.Rodrígo Alvaro Tello Valenzuela (2/0)], Mario Núñez (6/1), Reinaldo Marcelino Navia Amador (5/1) [64.Julio Brian Gutiérrez González (2/0)]. Trainer: Nelson Bonifacio Acosta López (55).

**512.** 22.03.2000 **CHILE - HONDURAS** **5-2(3-2)**

Estadio Nacional, Santiago; Referee: Ubaldo Aquino Valenzano (Paraguay); Attendance: 5,000

**CHI:** Nelson Antonio Tapia Rios (40/0), Jorge Francisco Vargas Palacios (10/0) [46.Claudio Andrés Maldonado Rivera (3/0)], Pedro Antonio Reyes González (37/4), Javier Luciano Margas Loyola (60/5), Mauricio Fernando Aros (19/0), Marcos Antonio Villaseca (9/0) [63.Luis Patricio Ormazábal Moya (1/0)], Clarence Acuña Donoso (50/3), José Luis Sierra Pando (50/8) [58.David Marcelo Pizarro Cortés (12/2)], Rodrígo Alvaro Tello Valenzuela (3/1) [80.Rodrigo Fabián Núñez Ortiz (3/0)], Mario Núñez (7/2), Héctor Santiago Tapia Urdile (3/1). Trainer: Nelson Bonifacio Acosta López (56).

**Goals**: Rodrígo Alvaro Tello Valenzuela (10), José Luis Sierra Pando (34), Héctor Santiago Tapia Urdile (42), David Marcelo Pizarro Cortés (80), Mario Núñez (88).

**513.** 29.03.2000 **ARGENTINA - CHILE** **4-1(2-1)** 17th FIFA WC. Qualifiers

Estadio Monumental „Antonio Vespucio Liberti“, Buenos Aires; Referee: Byron Aldemar Moreno Ruales (Ecuador); Attendance: 46,374

**CHI:** Marcelo Antonio Ramírez Gormaz (36/0), Claudio Andrés Maldonado Rivera (4/0), Pedro Antonio Reyes González (38/4), Javier Luciano Margas Loyola (61/5), Pablo Andrés Contreras Fica (7/0), Luis Patricio Ormazábal Moya (2/0) [83.Mauricio Fernando Aros (20/0)], Clarence Acuña Donoso (51/3), Rodrígo Alvaro Tello Valenzuela (4/2), David Marcelo Pizarro Cortés (13/2) [70.José Luis Sierra Pando (51/8)], Iván Luis Zamorano Zamora (55/30), José Marcelo Salas Melinao (49/30). Trainer: Nelson Bonifacio Acosta López (57).

**Goal**: Rodrígo Alvaro Tello Valenzuela (29).

**514.** 26.04.2000 **CHILE - PERU** **1-1(1-1)** 17th FIFA WC. Qualifiers

Estadio Nacional, Santiago; Referee: Epifanio González Chávez (Paraguay); Attendance: 44,979

**CHI:** Nelson Antonio Tapia Rios (41/0), Claudio Andrés Maldonado Rivera (5/0) [71.Claudio Patricio Núñez Camaño (23/4)], Pedro Antonio Reyes González (39/4), Javier Luciano Margas Loyola (62/6), Francisco Ulises Rojas (23/0) [71.Rodrigo Fabián Núñez Ortiz (4/0)], Jorge Francisco Vargas Palacios (11/0), Clarence Acuña Donoso (52/3), Rodrígo Alvaro Tello Valenzuela (5/2), David Marcelo Pizarro Cortés (14/2) [58.José Luis Sierra Pando (52/8)], Iván Luis Zamorano Zamora (56/30), José Marcelo Salas Melinao (50/30). Trainer: Nelson Bonifacio Acosta López (58).

**Goal**: Javier Luciano Margas Loyola (42).

**515.** 03.06.2000 **URUGUAY - CHILE** **2-1(2-1)** 17th FIFA WC. Qualifiers

Estadio Centenario, Montevideo; Referee: Robert Troxler Ayala (Paraguay); Attendance: 60,000

**CHI:** Nelson Antonio Tapia Rios (42/0), Ricardo Francisco Rojas Trujillo (10/0), Jorge Francisco Vargas Palacios (12/0), Pedro Antonio Reyes González (40/4), Rafael Andrés Olarra Guerrero (4/0) [68.Sebastián Rozental Igualt (24/2)], Pablo Galdames Díaz (14/1), Marcos Antonio Villaseca (10/0), Fabián Raphael Estay Silva (60/4) [87.Claudio Patricio Núñez Camaño (24/4)], Rodrígo Alvaro Tello Valenzuela (6/2), Iván Luis Zamorano Zamora (57/31), José Marcelo Salas Melinao (51/30). Trainer: Nelson Bonifacio Acosta López (59).

**Goal**: Iván Luis Zamorano Zamora (39 penalty).

**516.** 29.06.2000 **CHILE - PARAGUAY** **3-1(2-0)** 17th FIFA WC. Qualifiers

Estadio Nacional, Santiago; Referee: Claudio Mario Martín (Argentina); Attendance: 53,970

**CHI:** Nelson Antonio Tapia Rios (43/0), Ronald Hugo Fuentes Núñez (46/1), Pedro Antonio Reyes González (41/4), Ricardo Francisco Rojas Trujillo (11/0), Moisés Fermín Villarroel Ayala (19/0), Rodrígo Alvaro Tello Valenzuela (7/2), Fabián Raphael Estay Silva (61/4), Claudio Andrés Maldonado Rivera (6/0), Claudio Patricio Núñez Camaño (25/4) [58.David Marcelo Pizarro Cortés (15/2)], José Marcelo Salas Melinao (52/31) [*sent off 72*], Iván Luis Zamorano Zamora (58/32). Trainer: Nelson Bonifacio Acosta López (60).

**Goals**: Denis Caniza (19 own goal), José Marcelo Salas Melinao (35), Iván Luis Zamorano Zamora (80 penalty).

**517.** 19.07.2000 **BOLIVIA - CHILE** **1-0(0-0)**

Estadio „Hernando Siles Zuazo“, La Paz; Referee: John Jairo Toro Rendón (Colombia); Attendance: 35,412

**CHI:** Nelson Antonio Tapia Rios (44/0), Moisés Fermín Villarroel Ayala (20/0), Pedro Antonio Reyes González (42/4), Ronald Hugo Fuentes Núñez (47/1), Ricardo Francisco Rojas Trujillo (12/0), Rodrígo Alvaro Tello Valenzuela (8/2), Fernando Andrés Cornejo Jiménez (31/2), Claudio Andrés Maldonado Rivera (7/0), Fabián Raphael Estay Silva (62/4) [72.David Marcelo Pizarro Cortés (16/2)], Iván Luis Zamorano Zamora (59/32) [83.Reinaldo Marcelino Navia Amador (6/1)], Sebastián Rozental Igualt (25/2) [72.Héctor Santiago Tapia Urdile (4/1)]. Trainer: Nelson Bonifacio Acosta López (61).

**518.** 25.07.2000 **VENEZUELA - CHILE** **0-2(0-0)** 17th FIFA WC. Qualifiers

Estadio Pueblo Nuevo, San Cristóbal; Referee: Héctor Baldassi (Argentina); Attendance: 14,880

**CHI:** Nelson Antonio Tapia Rios (45/0), Ricardo Francisco Rojas Trujillo (13/0), Javier Luciano Margas Loyola (63/6), Ronald Hugo Fuentes Núñez (48/1), Francisco Ulises Rojas (24/0), Claudio Andrés Maldonado Rivera (8/0), Rodrígo Alvaro Tello Valenzuela (9/2), Fabián Raphael Estay Silva (63/4) [73.Fernando Andrés Cornejo Jiménez (32/2)], José Luis Sierra Pando (53/8) [66.David Marcelo Pizarro Cortés (17/2)], Iván Luis Zamorano Zamora (60/33), Sebastián Rozental Igualt (26/2) [46.Héctor Santiago Tapia Urdile (5/2)]. Trainer: Nelson Bonifacio Acosta López (62).

**Goals**: Héctor Santiago Tapia Urdile (70), Iván Luis Zamorano Zamora (89).

**519.** 15.08.2000 **CHILE - BRAZIL** **3-0(2-0)** 17th FIFA WC. Qualifiers

Estadio Nacional, Santiago; Referee: Epifanio González Chávez (Paraguay); Attendance: 64,671

**CHI:** Nelson Antonio Tapia Rios (46/0), Ronald Hugo Fuentes Núñez (49/1), Francisco Ulises Rojas (25/0), Pedro Antonio Reyes González (43/4), Ricardo Francisco Rojas Trujillo (14/0), Pablo Galdames Díaz (15/1), Marco Antonio Villaseca (11/0) [13.David Marcelo Pizarro Cortés (18/2) [*sent off 89*]], Rodrígo Alvaro Tello Valenzuela (10/2), Fabián Raphael Estay Silva (64/5), José Marcelo Salas Melinao (53/32) [84.Moisés Fermín Villarroel Ayala (21/0)], Iván Luis Zamorano Zamora (61/34) [86.Héctor Santiago Tapia Urdile (6/2)]. Trainer: Nelson Bonifacio Acosta López (63).

**Goals**: Fabián Raphael Estay Silva (26), Iván Luis Zamorano Zamora (44), José Marcelo Salas Melinao (74).

**520.** 02.09.2000 **CHILE - COLOMBIA** **0-1(0-0)** 17th FIFA WC. Qualifiers

Estadio Nacional, Santiago; Referee: Gustavo Adolfo Gallesio Greco (Uruguay); Attendance: 63,946

**CHI:** Nelson Antonio Tapia Rios (47/0), Pedro Antonio Reyes González (44/4), Ronald Hugo Fuentes Núñez (50/1), Ricardo Francisco Rojas Trujillo (15/0) [31.Pablo Andrés Contreras Fica (8/0)], Francisco Ulises Rojas (26/0), Pablo Galdames Díaz (16/1), Rodrígo Alvaro Tello Valenzuela (11/2), Fabián Raphael Estay Silva (65/5) [63.Esteban Andrés Valencia Bascuñán (42/4)], José Luis Sierra Pando (54/8) [63.Fernando Andrés Cornejo Jiménez (33/2)], José Marcelo Salas Melinao (54/32), Iván Luis Zamorano Zamora (62/34). Trainer: Nelson Bonifacio Acosta López (64).

**521.** 08.10.2000 **ECUADOR - CHILE** **1-0(0-0)** 17th FIFA WC. Qualifiers

Estadio Olímpico „Atahualpa“, Quito; Referee: John Jairo Toro Rendón (Colombia); Attendance: 28,556

**CHI:** Nelson Antonio Tapia Rios (48/0), Cristián Andrés Álvarez Valenzuela (1/0), Pablo Andrés Contreras Fica (9/0), Jorge Francisco Vargas Palacios (13/0), Rafael Andrés Olarra Guerrero (5/0), Claudio Andrés Maldonado Rivera (9/0), Fabián Raphael Estay Silva (66/5) [78.Sebastián Rozental Igualt (27/2)], Rodrígo Alvaro Tello Valenzuela (12/2), David Marcelo Pizarro Cortés (19/2) [81.Esteban Andrés Valencia Bascuñán (43/4)], Iván Luis Zamorano Zamora (63/34), Reinaldo Marcelino Navia Amador (7/1) [46.Claudio Patricio Núñez Camaño (26/4)]. Trainer: Nelson Bonifacio Acosta López (65).

**522.** 15.11.2000 **CHILE - ARGENTINA** **0-2(0-1)** 17th FIFA WC. Qualifiers

Estadio Nacional, Santiago; Referee: Carlos Amarilla Demarqui (Paraguay); Attendance: 56,529

**CHI:** Nelson Antonio Tapia Rios (49/0), Ricardo Francisco Rojas Trujillo (16/0), Pedro Antonio Reyes González (45/4), Pablo Andrés Contreras Fica (10/0) [77.Reinaldo Marcelino Navia Amador (8/1)], Claudio Andrés Maldonado Rivera (10/0) [72.Moisés Fermín Villarroel Ayala (22/0)], Pablo Galdames Díaz (17/1), Francisco Ulises Rojas (27/0), Fabián Raphael Estay Silva (67/5) [63.Esteban Andrés Valencia Bascuñán (44/4)], David Marcelo Pizarro Cortés (20/2), Iván Luis Zamorano Zamora (64/34), José Marcelo Salas Melinao (55/32). Trainer: Nelson Bonifacio Acosta López (66).

**523.** 22.03.2001 **HONDURAS - CHILE** **3-1(2-1)**

Estadio Olímpico Metropolitano, San Pedro Sula; Referee: Vivian Antonio Rodríguez (Honduras); Attendance: 30,000

**CHI:** Marcelo Antonio Ramírez Gormaz (37/0) [*sent off 35*], Miguel Mauricio Ramírez Pérez (59/1), Pedro Antonio Reyes González (46/4), Ricardo Francisco Rojas Trujillo (17/0), Rafael Andrés Olarra Guerrero (6/0) [46.Miguel Ponce Torres (16/0)], Nelson Rodrigo Parraguez Riveros (51/0), Joel Antonio Reyes Zúñiga (2/0) [69.Jorge Francisco Vargas Palacios (14/0)], Milovan Petar Mirošević Albornoz (1/0) [35.Carlos Antonio Toro Coronado (1/0)], Luis Alejandro Osorio González (2/0), Sebastián Ignacio González Valdés (1/1) [54.Rodrígo Ruíz De Barbieri (6/1)], Iván Luis Zamorano Zamora (65/34). Trainer: Pedro García Barros (1).

**Goal**: Sebastián Ignacio González Valdés (32).

**524.** 27.03.2001 **PERU - CHILE** **3-1(0-0)** 17th FIFA WC. Qualifiers

Estadio Nacional, Lima; Referee: Ángel Osvaldo Sánchez (Argentina); Attendance: 38,901

**CHI:** Nelson Antonio Tapia Rios (50/0), Jorge Francisco Vargas Palacios (15/0), Ricardo Francisco Rojas Trujillo (18/0), Miguel Mauricio Ramírez Pérez (60/1) [*sent off 82*], Claudio Andrés Maldonado Rivera (11/0), Miguel Ponce Torres (17/0), Luis Alejandro Osorio González (3/0), Nelson Rodrigo Parraguez Riveros (52/0) [25.Milovan Petar Mirošević Albornoz (2/0); 76.Rodrígo Ruíz De Barbieri (7/1)], Rodrígo Alvaro Tello Valenzuela (13/2) [Héctor Santiago Tapia Urdile (7/2) 46], Reinaldo Marcelino Navia Amador (9/2), Iván Luis Zamorano Zamora (66/34). Trainer: Pedro García Barros (2).

**Goal**: Reinaldo Marcelino Navia Amador (61).

**525.** 11.04.2001 **MEXICO - CHILE** **1-0(0-0)**

Estadio Tecnológico, Monterrey; Referee: Ricardo A. Valenzuela (United States); Attendance: 40,000

**CHI:** Carlos Antonio Toro Coronado (2/0), Italo Andrés Díaz Muñoz (1/0), Pedro Antonio Reyes González (47/4), David Andrés Henríquez Espinoza (1/0), Mauricio Andrés Pozo Quinteros (1/0), Marco Antonio Villaseca (12/0) [90.Jorge Andrés Ormeño Guerra (1/0)], Eros Roque Pérez Salas (1/0), Fabián Raphael Estay Silva (68/5) [86.Luis Alberto Fuentes Rodríguez (3/0)], Héctor Santiago Tapia Urdile (8/2) [70.Joel Antonio Reyes Zúñiga (3/0)], Iván Luis Zamorano Zamora (67/34) [65.Sebastián Ignacio González Valdés (2/1)], Reinaldo Marcelino Navia Amador (10/2) [46.Mauricio Alejandro Donoso Pérez (2/0)]. Trainer: Pedro García Barros (3).

**526.** 24.04.2001 **CHILE - URUGUAY** **0-1(0-1)** 17th FIFA WC. Qualifiers

Estadio Nacional, Santiago; Referee: Horacio Marcelo Elizondo (Argentina); Attendance: 45,676

**CHI:** Sergio Bernabé Vargas Buscalia (1/0), Italo Andrés Díaz Muñoz (2/0) [56.Jaime Andrés Valdés Zapata (1/0)], Pedro Antonio Reyes González (48/4), Pablo Andrés Contreras Fica (11/0), Claudio Andrés Maldonado Rivera (12/0), Rodrígo Alvaro Tello Valenzuela (14/2), Pablo Galdames Díaz (18/1), Luis Alejandro Osorio González (4/0) [74.Sebastián Ignacio González Valdés (3/1)], Fabián Raphael Estay Silva (69/5), Iván Luis Zamorano Zamora (68/34), Héctor Santiago Tapia Urdile (9/2) [46.Claudio Patricio Núñez Camaño (27/4)]. Trainer: Pedro García Barros (4).

**527.** 02.06.2001 **PARAGUAY - CHILE** **1-0(0-0)** 17th FIFA WC. Qualifiers

Estadio Defensores del Chaco, Asunción; Referee: Rodrigo Badilla Sequeira (Costa Rica); Attendance: 35,000

**CHI:** Sergio Bernabé Vargas Buscalia (2/0), Pedro Antonio Reyes González (49/4), Jorge Francisco Vargas Palacios (16/0), Pablo Andrés Contreras Fica (12/0), Mauricio Andrés Pozo Quinteros (2/0), Eros Roque Pérez Salas (2/0) [78.Rodrígo Ignacio Valenzuela Avíles (2/0)], Marco Antonio Villaseca (13/0), Luis Alejandro Osorio González (5/0), Rodrígo Alvaro Tello Valenzuela (15/2), Cristian Antonio Montecinos González (2/0), Reinaldo Marcelino Navia Amador (11/2) [63.Manuel Alejandro Neira Díaz (9/2)]. Trainer: Pedro García Barros (5).

**528.** 11.07.2001 **CHILE - ECUADOR** **4-1(1-0)** 40th Copa América. Group Stage.

Estadio Metropolitano „Roberto Meléndez“, Barranquilla (Colombia); Referee: René M. Ortubé Betancourt (Bolivia); Attendance: 33,511

**CHI:** Sergio Bernabé Vargas Buscalia (3/0), Luis Alberto Fuentes Rodríguez (4/0), Pedro Antonio Reyes González (50/4), Ricardo Francisco Rojas Trujillo (19/0), Moisés Fermín Villarroel Ayala (23/0) [79.David Andrés Henríquez Espinoza (2/0)], Claudio Andrés Maldonado Rivera (13/0) [65.Rodrígo Ignacio Valenzuela Avíles (3/0)], Marco Antonio Villaseca (14/0), Mauricio Fernando Aros (21/0), Luis Alejandro Osorio González (6/0), Cristian Antonio Montecinos González (3/2), Reinaldo Marcelino Navia Amador (12/3) [73.Marcelo Enrique Corrales García (1/1)]. Trainer: Pedro García Barros (6).

**Goals**: Reinaldo Marcelino Navia Amador (29), Cristian Antonio Montecinos González (73), Marcelo Enrique Corrales García (85), Cristian Antonio Montecinos González (90).

**529.** 14.07.2001 **CHILE - VENEZUELA** **1-0(0-0)** 40th Copa América. Group Stage.

Estadio Metropolitano „Roberto Meléndez“, Barranquilla (Colombia); Referee: Gilberto Alcalá Piñeda (Mexico); Attendance: 26,150

**CHI:** Sergio Bernabé Vargas Buscalia (4/0), Luis Alberto Fuentes Rodríguez (5/0), Pedro Antonio Reyes González (51/4), Ricardo Francisco Rojas Trujillo (20/0), Moisés Fermín Villarroel Ayala (24/0) [28.David Andrés Henríquez Espinoza (3/0)], Pablo Galdames Díaz (19/1), Marco Antonio Villaseca (15/0), Mauricio Fernando Aros (22/0) [46.Eros Roque Pérez Salas (3/0)], Luis Alejandro Osorio González (7/0) [66.Rodrígo Ignacio Valenzuela Avíles (4/0)], Cristian Antonio Montecinos González (4/3), Reinaldo Marcelino Navia Amador (13/3). Trainer: Pedro García Barros (7).

**Goal**: Cristian Antonio Montecinos González (78).

**530.** 17.07.2001 **COLOMBIA - CHILE** **2-0(1-0)** 40th Copa América. Group Stage.
Estadio Metropolitano „Roberto Meléndez", Barranquilla; Referee: Jorge Larrionda Pietrafiesa (Uruguay); Attendance: 21,818
**CHI:** Sergio Bernabé Vargas Buscalia (5/0), Claudio Andrés Maldonado Rivera (14/0), Ricardo Francisco Rojas Trujillo (21/0), Pedro Antonio Reyes González (52/4), Mauricio Andrés Pozo Quinteros (3/0), Pablo Galdames Díaz (20/1), Marco Antonio Villaseca (16/0), Eros Roque Pérez Salas (4/0), Rodrígo Ignacio Valenzuela Avíles (5/0) [63.Manuel Alejandro Neira Díaz (10/2)], Cristian Antonio Montecinos González (5/3), Reinaldo Marcelino Navia Amador (14/3) [46.Marcelo Enrique Corrales García (2/1); 71.Rodrigo Fabián Núñez Ortiz (5/0)]. Trainer: Pedro García Barros (8).

**531.** 22.07.2001 **MEXICO - CHILE** **2-0(1-0)** 40th Copa América. Quarter-Finals.
Estadio „Hernán Ramírez Villegas", Pereira (Colombia); Referee: Carlos Eugênio Simon (Brazil); Attendance: 11,239
**CHI:** Sergio Bernabé Vargas Buscalia (6/0), Luis Alberto Fuentes Rodríguez (6/0), Pedro Antonio Reyes González (53/4), Ricardo Francisco Rojas Trujillo (22/0), Claudio Andrés Maldonado Rivera (15/0) [75.David Andrés Henríquez Espinoza (4/0)], Eros Roque Pérez Salas (5/0) [66.Manuel Alejandro Neira Díaz (11/2)], Marco Antonio Villaseca (17/0), Luis Alejandro Osorio González (8/0), Rodrigo Fabián Núñez Ortiz (6/0) [41.Rodrígo Ignacio Valenzuela Avíles (6/0)], Reinaldo Marcelino Navia Amador (15/3), Cristian Antonio Montecinos González (6/3). Trainer: Pedro García Barros (9).

**532.** 14.08.2001 **CHILE - BOLIVIA** **2-2(1-1)** 17th FIFA WC. Qualifiers
Estadio Nacional, Santiago; Referee: Daniel Orlando Giménez (Argentina); Attendance: 34,657
**CHI:** Sergio Bernabé Vargas Buscalia (7/0), Mauricio Andrés Pozo Quinteros (4/0) [33. Fernando Esteban Solís Núñez (1/0)], Jorge Francisco Vargas Palacios (17/0), Pedro Antonio Reyes González (54/4), Mauricio Fernando Aros (23/0), Luis Eugenio Chavarría Andrade (5/0), Marco Antonio Villaseca (18/0), Esteban Andrés Valencia Bascuñán (45/4) [82.Axel Ahumada (1/0)], Claudio Patricio Núñez Camaño (28/4) [69.Miguel Angel Castillo (1/0)], José Marcelo Salas Melinao (56/34), Cristian Antonio Montecinos González (7/3). Trainer: Pedro García Barros (10).
**Goals**: José Marcelo Salas Melinao (35, 75).

**533.** 01.09.2001 **CHILE - FRANCE** **2-1(1-0)**
Estadio Nacional, Santiago; Referee: Daniel Orlando Giménez (Argentina); Attendance: 72,728
**CHI:** Sergio Bernabé Vargas Buscalia (8/0) [72.Nelson Antonio Tapia Rios (51/0)], Pedro Antonio Reyes González (55/4), Jorge Francisco Vargas Palacios (18/0), Ricardo Francisco Rojas Trujillo (23/0) [77.Luis Alberto Fuentes Rodríguez (7/0)], Francisco Ulises Rojas (28/0), Mauricio Fernando Aros (24/0) [64.Rodrígo Antonio Pérez Albornoz (7/0)], Pablo Galdames Díaz (21/2), Clarence Acuña Donoso (53/3), Rodrígo Alvaro Tello Valenzuela (16/2) [81.Esteban Andrés Valencia Bascuñán (46/4)], Iván Luis Zamorano Zamora (69/34) [87.Claudio Patricio Núñez Camaño (29/4)], Reinaldo Marcelino Navia Amador (16/4) [55.Cristian Antonio Montecinos González (8/3)]. Trainer: Pedro García Barros (11).
**Goals**: Pablo Galdames Díaz (4), Reinaldo Marcelino Navia Amador (51).

**534.** 04.09.2001 **CHILE - VENEZUELA** **0-2(0-0)** 17th FIFA WC. Qualifiers
Estadio Nacional, Santiago; Referee: René M. Ortubé Betancourt (Bolivia); Attendance: 25,000
**CHI:** Nelson Antonio Tapia Rios (52/0), Francisco Ulises Rojas (29/0), Jorge Francisco Vargas Palacios (19/0), Luis Alberto Fuentes Rodríguez (8/0), Mauricio Fernando Aros (25/0) [72.Rodrígo Antonio Pérez Albornoz (8/0)], Pablo Galdames Díaz (22/2), Clarence Acuña Donoso (54/3), Rodrígo Alvaro Tello Valenzuela (17/2), Claudio Patricio Núñez Camaño (30/4) [64.Esteban Andrés Valencia Bascuñán (47/4)], Cristian Antonio Montecinos González (9/3), Reinaldo Marcelino Navia Amador (17/4). Trainer: Pedro García Barros (12).

**535.** 07.10.2001 **BRAZIL - CHILE** **2-0(0-0)** 17th FIFA WC. Qualifiers
Estádio „Couto Pereira", Curitiba; Referee: Horacio Marcelo Elizondo (Argentina); Attendance: 52,000
**CHI:** Carlos Antonio Toro Coronado (3/0), Jorge Francisco Vargas Palacios (20/0), Héctor Robles Fuentes (1/0), Raúl Andrés Muñoz Mardones (3/0), Víctor Antonio Cancino Araneda (1/0), Marco Antonio Villaseca (19/0), Luis Patricio Ormazábal Moya (3/0), Rodrígo Antonio Pérez Albornoz (9/0) [78.Rodrigo David Meléndez Araya (1/0)], David Marcelo Pizarro Cortés (21/2) [83.Jaime Eduardo Riveros Valenzuela (11/3)], Rodrígo Ignacio Valenzuela Avíles (7/0) [55.Reinaldo Marcelino Navia Amador (18/4)], José Marcelo Salas Melinao (57/34). Trainer: Jorge Luis Garcés Rojas (1).

**536.** 07.11.2001 **COLOMBIA - CHILE** **3-1(1-1)** 17th FIFA WC. Qualifiers
Estadio „Nemesio Camacho" 'El Campín', Bogotá; Referee: Daniel Orlando Giménez (Argentina); Attendance: 16,050
**CHI:** Sergio Bernabé Vargas Buscalia (9/0), Jorge Francisco Vargas Palacios (21/0), Héctor Robles Fuentes (2/0), Raúl Andrés Muñoz Mardones (4/0), Moisés Fermín Villarroel Ayala (25/0) [*sent off 65*], Marco Antonio Villaseca (20/0) [*sent off 90*], Luis Patricio Ormazábal Moya (4/0), Víctor Antonio Cancino Araneda (2/0), Jaime Eduardo Riveros Valenzuela (12/4) [72.Luis Medina (1/0)], Reinaldo Marcelino Navia Amador (19/4) [72.Fernando Patricio Martel Helo (1/0)], Arturo Andrés Norambuena Ardiles (1/0) [77.Patricio Antonio Almendra Cifuentes (1/0)]. Trainer: Jorge Luis Garcés Rojas (2).
**Goal**: Jaime Eduardo Riveros Valenzuela (39).

**537.** 14.11.2001 **CHILE - ECUADOR** **0-0** 17th FIFA WC. Qualifiers
Estadio Nacional, Santiago; Referee: Juan Paniagua Arandia (Bolivia); Attendance: 19,237
**CHI:** Sergio Bernabé Vargas Buscalia (10/0), Jorge Torres (1/0), Héctor Robles Fuentes (3/0), Cristián Alejandro Gómez Chandía (1/0) [65.Patricio Antonio Almendra Cifuentes (2/0)], Darwin Eduardo Pérez Curiñanco (1/0), Luis Medina (2/0) [46.Axel Ahumada (2/0)], Héctor Arturo Sanhueza Medel (1/0) [46.Jorge Andrés Ormeño Guerra (2/0)], Raúl Andrés Muñoz Mardones (5/0), Jaime Eduardo Riveros Valenzuela (13/4), Julio Brian Gutiérrez González (3/0), Fernando Patricio Martel Helo (2/0). Trainer: Jorge Luis Garcés Rojas (3).

**538.** 17.04.2002 **TURKEY - CHILE** **2-0(1-0)**
Parkstad Limburg Stadion, Kerkrade (Holland); Referee: René J. Temmink (Holland); Attendance: 2,500
**CHI:** Johnny Cristian Herrera Muñoz (1/0), Pablo Andrés Contreras Fica (13/0), Alex Christian von Schwedler Vasquez (3/0), Rafael Andrés Olarra Guerrero (7/0), Gamadiel Adrián García Sánchez (1/0) [78.Héctor Arturo Sanhueza Medel (2/0)], Marcos Andrés González Salazar (1/0), Clarence Acuña Donoso (55/3), Rodrígo Javier Millar Carvajal (1/0), Rodrígo Alvaro Tello Valenzuela (18/2), Sebastián Eduardo Pardo Campos (1/0), Héctor Santiago Tapia Urdile (10/2) [68.Joel Antonio Torres Soto (1/0)]. Trainer: César Vaccia (1).

**539.** 30.03.2003 **CHILE - PERU** **2-0(1-0)**
Estadio Nacional, Santiago; Referee: Carlos Amarilla Demarqui (Paraguay); Attendance: 39,662
**CHI:** Nicolás Miroslav Peric Villarreal (1/0), Pablo Andrés Contreras Fica (14/0), Jorge Francisco Vargas Palacios (22/0), Ricardo Francisco Rojas Trujillo (24/0), Claudio Andrés Maldonado Rivera (16/0) [71.David Marcelo Pizarro Cortés (22/2)], Clarence Acuña Donoso (56/3), Raúl Andrés Muñoz Mardones (6/0) [46.Rodrígo Alvaro Tello Valenzuela (19/2)], Milovan Petar Mirošević Albornoz (3/1), Fernando Patricio Martel Helo (3/0) [86.Cristián Andrés Álvarez Valenzuela (2/0)], Sebastián Ignacio González Valdés (4/1) [60.Mauricio Ricardo Pinilla Ferrera (1/1)], Joel Antonio Torres Soto (2/0) [46.Reinaldo Marcelino Navia Amador (20/4)]. Trainer: Juvenal Mario Olmos Rojas (1).
**Goals**: Milovan Petar Mirošević Albornoz (45), Mauricio Ricardo Pinilla Ferrera (65).

**540.** 02.04.2003 **PERU - CHILE** **3-0(1-0)**
Estadio Nacional, Lima; Referee: Oscar Julián Ruíz Acosta (Colombia); Attendance: 25,000
**CHI:** Nicolás Miroslav Peric Villarreal (2/0), Cristián Andrés Álvarez Valenzuela (3/0), Pablo Andrés Contreras Fica (15/0), Ricardo Francisco Rojas Trujillo (25/0), Rodrígo Antonio Pérez Albornoz (10/0), Rodrígo Alvaro Tello Valenzuela (20/2) [81.Rodrigo David Meléndez Araya (2/0)], Clarence Acuña Donoso (57/3) [67.Claudio Andrés Maldonado Rivera (17/0)], Luis Patricio Ormazábal Moya (5/0) [46.Milovan Petar Mirošević Albornoz (4/1)], Fernando Patricio Martel Helo (4/0) [81.Joel Antonio Torres Soto (3/0)], Reinaldo Marcelino Navia Amador (21/4), Mauricio Ricardo Pinilla Ferrera (2/1) [55.Sebastián Ignacio González Valdés (5/1)]. Trainer: Juvenal Mario Olmos Rojas (2).

**541.** 30.04.2003 **CHILE – COSTA RICA** **1-0(0-0)**
Estadio Nacional, Santiago; Referee: Ubaldo Aquino Valenzano (Paraguay); Attendance: 8,618
**CHI:** Alex Fabián Varas (4/0), Cristián Andrés Álvarez Valenzuela (4/0), Jorge Francisco Vargas Palacios (23/0), Pablo Andrés Contreras Fica (16/1), Fernando Patricio Martel Helo (5/0) [69.Boris Igor González Garrido (1/0)], Jorge Cristián Acuña Concha (1/0) [69.Nicolás Andrés Córdova San Cristóbal (1/0)], Clarence Acuña Donoso (58/3) [46.Rodrigo David Meléndez Araya (3/0)], Rodrígo Alvaro Tello Valenzuela (21/2) [46.Rodrígo Antonio Pérez Albornoz (11/0)], Milovan Petar Mirošević Albornoz (5/1), Reinaldo Marcelino Navia Amador (22/4), Mauricio Ricardo Pinilla Ferrera (3/1) [52.Joel Antonio Torres Soto (4/0)]. Trainer: Juvenal Mario Olmos Rojas (3).
**Goal**: Pablo Andrés Contreras Fica (61).

**542.** 08.06.2003 **COSTA RICA - CHILE** **1-0(0-0)**
Estadio „Ricardo Saprissa“, San José; Referee: José Benigno Piñeda Fernández (Honduras); Attendance: 18,000
**CHI:** Nelson Antonio Tapia Rios (53/0), Cristián Andrés Álvarez Valenzuela (5/0) [*sent off 47*], Ricardo Francisco Rojas Trujillo (26/0), Pablo Andrés Contreras Fica (17/1), Rodrígo Antonio Pérez Albornoz (12/0), Boris Igor González Garrido (2/0) [76.Marcos Andrés González Salazar (2/0)], Claudio Andrés Maldonado Rivera (18/0), Jorge Cristián Acuña Concha (2/0), Milovan Petar Mirošević Albornoz (6/1) [46.Claudio Patricio Núñez Camaño (31/4)], Fernando Patricio Martel Helo (6/0), Héctor Santiago Tapia Urdile (11/2). Trainer: Juvenal Mario Olmos Rojas (4).

**543.** 11.06.2003 **HONDURAS - CHILE** **1-2(1-1)**
Estadio Olímpico Metropolitano, San Pedro Sula; Referee: Freddy Burgos Escobar (Guatemala); Attendance: 25,000
**CHI:** Nelson Antonio Tapia Rios (54/0), Jorge Cristián Acuña Concha (3/0), Ricardo Francisco Rojas Trujillo (27/0), Pablo Andrés Contreras Fica (18/1), Rodrígo Antonio Pérez Albornoz (13/0), Boris Igor González Garrido (3/0), Claudio Andrés Maldonado Rivera (19/0) [46.Joel Antonio Torres Soto (5/0)], Mark Dennis González Hoffmann (1/1), Milovan Petar Mirošević Albornoz (7/1) [46.Nicolás Andrés Córdova San Cristóbal (2/0)], Héctor Santiago Tapia Urdile (12/3), Fernando Patricio Martel Helo (7/0) [87.Rafael Andrés Olarra Guerrero (8/0)]. Trainer: Juvenal Mario Olmos Rojas (5).
**Goals**: Héctor Santiago Tapia Urdile (44 penalty), Mark Dennis González Hoffmann (60).

**544.** 20.08.2003 **CHINA P.R. - CHILE** **0-0**
Minyuan Stadium, Tianjin; Referee: Hwan Yunye (China P.R.); Attendance: 15,000
**CHI:** Nelson Antonio Tapia Rios (55/0), Cristián Andrés Álvarez Valenzuela (6/0), Luis Alberto Fuentes Rodríguez (9/0), David Andrés Henríquez Espinoza (5/0), Rodrígo Antonio Pérez Albornoz (14/0), Héctor Arturo Sanhueza Medel (3/0) [60.Boris Igor González Garrido (4/0)], Marcos Andrés González Salazar (3/0), Mark Dennis González Hoffmann (2/1), Rodrígo Javier Millar Carvajal (2/0) [80.José Luis Jérez Cerna (1/0)], Arturo Andrés Norambuena Ardiles (2/0) [60.José Luis Villanueva Ahumada (1/0)], Manuel Alejandro Neira Díaz (12/2) [80.Daniel Pérez (1/0)]. Trainer: Juvenal Mario Olmos Rojas (6).

**545.** 06.09.2003 **ARGENTINA - CHILE** **2-2(2-0)** 18th FIFA WC. Qualifiers
Estadio Monumental „Antonio Vespucio Liberti“, Buenos Aires; Referee: Ubaldo Aquino Valenzano (Paraguay); Attendance: 35,372
**CHI:** Nelson Antonio Tapia Rios (56/0), Cristián Andrés Álvarez Valenzuela (7/0) [*sent off 86*], Rafael Andrés Olarra Guerrero (9/0), Pablo Andrés Contreras Fica (19/1), Rodrígo Antonio Pérez Albornoz (15/0), Marcos Andrés González Salazar (4/0), Rodrigo David Meléndez Araya (4/0) [38.Milovan Petar Mirošević Albornoz (8/2)], Fernando Patricio Martel Helo (8/0), Mark Dennis González Hoffmann (3/1) [57.Jorge Cristián Acuña Concha (4/0)], Reinaldo Marcelino Navia Amador (23/5) [*sent off 90*], Héctor Santiago Tapia Urdile (13/3) [57.Mauricio Ricardo Pinilla Ferrera (4/1)]. Trainer: Juvenal Mario Olmos Rojas (7).
**Goals**: Milovan Petar Mirošević Albornoz (60), Reinaldo Marcelino Navia Amador (77).

**546.** 09.09.2003 **CHILE - PERU** **2-1(1-0)** 18th FIFA WC. Qualifiers
Estadio Nacional, Santiago; Referee: Horacio Marcelo Elizondo (Argentina); Attendance: 54,303
**CHI:** Nelson Antonio Tapia Rios (57/0), Pablo Andrés Contreras Fica (20/1), Ricardo Francisco Rojas Trujillo (28/0), Rafael Andrés Olarra Guerrero (10/0), Rodrígo Antonio Pérez Albornoz (16/0), Jorge Cristián Acuña Concha (5/0), Fernando Patricio Martel Helo (9/0) [46.David Marcelo Pizarro Cortés (23/2)], Marcos Andrés González Salazar (5/0) [46.Boris Igor González Garrido (5/0)], Milovan Petar Mirošević Albornoz (9/2), Mauricio Ricardo Pinilla Ferrera (5/2), Héctor Santiago Tapia Urdile (14/3) [67.Arturo Andrés Norambuena Ardiles (3/1)]. Trainer: Juvenal Mario Olmos Rojas (8).
**Goals**: Mauricio Ricardo Pinilla Ferrera (35), Arturo Andrés Norambuena Ardiles (70).

**547.** 15.11.2003 **URUGUAY - CHILE** **2-1(1-1)** 18th FIFA WC. Qualifiers
Estadio Centenario, Montevideo; Referee: Claudio Mario Martín (Argentina); Attendance: 70,000
**CHI:** Nelson Antonio Tapia Rios (58/0), Ricardo Francisco Rojas Trujillo (29/0), Rafael Andrés Olarra Guerrero (11/0), Miguel Mauricio Ramírez Pérez (61/1), Rodrígo Antonio Pérez Albornoz (17/0), Fernando Patricio Martel Helo (10/0) [53.Luis Patricio Ormazábal Moya (6/0)], Rodrigo David Meléndez Araya (5/1), Raúl Andrés Muñoz Mardones (7/0), Mark Dennis González Hoffmann (4/1) [53.Milovan Petar Mirošević Albornoz (10/2)], Reinaldo Marcelino Navia Amador (24/5) [74.Arturo Andrés Norambuena Ardiles (4/1)], Mauricio Ricardo Pinilla Ferrera (6/2). Trainer: Juvenal Mario Olmos Rojas (9).
**Goal**: Rodrigo David Meléndez Araya (21).

**548.** 18.11.2003 **CHILE - PARAGUAY** **0-1(0-1)** 18th FIFA WC. Qualifiers
Estadio Nacional, Santiago; Referee: Gustavo Méndez González (Uruguay); Attendance: 61,923
**CHI:** Nelson Antonio Tapia Rios (59/0), Pablo Andrés Contreras Fica (21/1), Rafael Andrés Olarra Guerrero (12/0), Miguel Mauricio Ramírez Pérez (62/1), Cristián Andrés Álvarez Valenzuela (8/0) [46.Luis Patricio Ormazábal Moya (7/0)], Marcos Andrés González Salazar (6/0) [46.Rodrigo David Meléndez Araya (6/1)], Rodrígo Antonio Pérez Albornoz (18/0), David Marcelo Pizarro Cortés (24/2), Milovan Petar Mirošević Albornoz (11/2), Reinaldo Marcelino Navia Amador (25/5) [63.Arturo Andrés Norambuena Ardiles (5/1)], Mauricio Ricardo Pinilla Ferrera (7/2). Trainer: Juvenal Mario Olmos Rojas (10).

**549.** 18.02.2004 **MEXICO - CHILE** **1-1(0-1)**
Home Depot Center, Carson (United States); Referee: Arkadiusz Prus (United States); Attendance: 26,000
**CHI:** Nelson Antonio Tapia Rios (60/0), Jorge Francisco Vargas Palacios (24/0), Ricardo Francisco Rojas Trujillo (30/0) [72.Moisés Fermín Villarroel Ayala (26/0)], Rafael Andrés Olarra Guerrero (13/0), Luis Pedro Figueroa Sepúlveda (1/0), Rodrigo David Meléndez Araya (7/1), Rodrígo Antonio Pérez Albornoz (19/0), Nicolás Andrés Córdova San Cristóbal (3/0) [46.Jorge Luis Valdivia Toro (1/0)], Jean André Emanuel Beausejour Coliqueo (1/0) [46.Mauricio Ricardo Pinilla Ferrera (8/2)], Reinaldo Marcelino Navia Amador (26/6), Fernando Patricio Martel Helo (11/0) [46.Mark Dennis González Hoffmann (5/1)]. Trainer: Juvenal Mario Olmos Rojas (11).
**Goal**: Reinaldo Marcelino Navia Amador (45).

**550.** 30.03.2004 **BOLIVIA - CHILE** **0-2(0-1)** 18th FIFA WC. Qualifiers
Estadio „Hernando Siles Zuazo", La Paz; Referee: Claudio Mario Martín (Argentina); Attendance: 40,000
**CHI:** Nelson Antonio Tapia Rios (61/0), Ricardo Francisco Rojas Trujillo (31/0), Jorge Francisco Vargas Palacios (25/0), Rafael Andrés Olarra Guerrero (14/0), Rodrígo Antonio Pérez Albornoz (20/0), Fernando Patricio Martel Helo (12/0) [75.Rodrígo Ignacio Valenzuela Avíles (8/0)], Moisés Fermín Villarroel Ayala (27/1) [56.Claudio Andrés Maldonado Rivera (20/0)], Rodrigo David Meléndez Araya (8/1), Mark Dennis González Hoffmann (6/2), Patricio Sebastián Galaz Sepulveda (1/0) [56.Mauricio Ricardo Pinilla Ferrera (9/2)], José Marcelo Salas Melinao (58/34). Trainer: Juvenal Mario Olmos Rojas (12).
**Goals**: Moisés Fermín Villarroel Ayala (37), Mark Dennis González Hoffmann (59).

**551.** 28.04.2004 **CHILE - PERU** **1-1(0-0)**
Estadio Nacional, Santiago; Referee: Carlos Amarilla Demarqui (Paraguay); Attendance: 23,000
**CHI:** Alex Fabián Varas (5/0), Cristián Andrés Álvarez Valenzuela (9/0) [46.Boris Igor González Garrido (6/0)], Luis Alberto Fuentes Rodríguez (10/1), Pablo Andrés Contreras Fica (22/1), Rodrígo Antonio Pérez Albornoz (21/0), Rodrígo Javier Millar Carvajal (3/0), Claudio Andrés Maldonado Rivera (21/0), Rodrigo David Meléndez Araya (9/1) [65.Luis Pedro Figueroa Sepúlveda (2/0)], Luis Antonio Jiménez Garcés (1/0) [77.Jean André Emanuel Beausejour Coliqueo (2/0)], Patricio Sebastián Galaz Sepulveda (2/0) [87.Jonathan Josué Cisternas (1/0)], Mauricio Ricardo Pinilla Ferrera (10/2). Trainer: Juvenal Mario Olmos Rojas (13).
**Goal**: Luis Alberto Fuentes Rodríguez (56).

**552.** 01.06.2004 **VENEZUELA – CHILE** **0-1(0-0)** 18th FIFA WC. Qualifiers
Estadio Pueblo Nuevo, San Cristóbal; Referee: Carlos Torres (Paraguay); Attendance: 23,040
**CHI:** Nelson Antonio Tapia Rios (62/0), Ricardo Francisco Rojas Trujillo (32/0), Jorge Francisco Vargas Palacios (26/0), Rafael Andrés Olarra Guerrero (15/0), Rodrígo Antonio Pérez Albornoz (22/0), David Marcelo Pizarro Cortés (25/2) [80.Rodrígo Ignacio Valenzuela Avíles (9/0)], Claudio Andrés Maldonado Rivera (22/0), Rodrigo David Meléndez Araya (10/1), Mark Dennis González Hoffmann (7/2) [58.Milovan Petar Mirošević Albornoz (12/2)], Patricio Sebastián Galaz Sepulveda (3/0) [46.Mauricio Ricardo Pinilla Ferrera (11/3)], Reinaldo Marcelino Navia Amador (27/6). Trainer: Juvenal Mario Olmos Rojas (14).
**Goal**: Mauricio Ricardo Pinilla Ferrera (84).

**553.** 06.06.2004 **CHILE - BRAZIL** **1-1(0-1)** 18th FIFA WC. Qualifiers
Estadio Nacional, Santiago; Referee: Horacio Marcelo Elizondo (Argentina); Attendance: 62,503
**CHI:** Nelson Antonio Tapia Rios (63/0), Ricardo Francisco Rojas Trujillo (33/0) [46.Cristián Andrés Álvarez Valenzuela (10/0)], Luis Alberto Fuentes Rodríguez (11/1), Rafael Andrés Olarra Guerrero (16/0), Rodrígo Antonio Pérez Albornoz (23/0), Fernando Patricio Martel Helo (13/0) [46.Patricio Sebastián Galaz Sepulveda (4/0)], Claudio Andrés Maldonado Rivera (23/0), Rodrigo David Meléndez Araya (11/1), Mark Dennis González Hoffmann (8/2) [56.Milovan Petar Mirošević Albornoz (13/2)], David Marcelo Pizarro Cortés (26/2), Reinaldo Marcelino Navia Amador (28/7). Trainer: Juvenal Mario Olmos Rojas (15).
**Goal**: Reinaldo Marcelino Navia Amador (89 penalty).

**554.** 08.07.2004 **BRAZIL - CHILE** **1-0(0-0)** 41st Copa América. Group Stage.
Estadio Universidad Nacional San Agustín, Arequipa (Peru); Referee: Marco Rodríguez (Mexico); Attendance: 35,000
**CHI:** Alex Fabián Varas (6/0), Moisés Fermín Villarroel Ayala (28/1), Luis Alberto Fuentes Rodríguez (12/1), Rafael Andrés Olarra Guerrero (17/0), Rodrígo Antonio Pérez Albornoz (24/0), Rodrígo Ignacio Valenzuela Avíles (10/0), Clarence Acuña Donoso (59/3), Rodrigo David Meléndez Araya (12/1), Jonathan Josué Cisternas (2/0) [46.Luis Antonio Jiménez Garcés (2/0)], Milovan Petar Mirošević Albornoz (14/2) [86.Patricio Sebastián Galaz Sepulveda (5/0)], Sebastián Ignacio González Valdés (6/1) [66.Héctor Raúl Mancilla Garcés (1/0)]. Trainer: Juvenal Mario Olmos Rojas (16).

**555.** 11.07.2004 **PARAGUAY - CHILE** **1-1(0-0)** 41st Copa América. Group Stage.
Estadio Universidad Nacional San Agustín, Arequipa (Peru); Referee: Gustavo Méndez González (Uruguay); Attendance: 35,000
**CHI:** Claudio Andrés Bravo Muñoz (1/0), Ismael Ignacio Fuentes Castro (1/0), Luis Alberto Fuentes Rodríguez (13/1), Rafael Andrés Olarra Guerrero (18/0), Rodrígo Antonio Pérez Albornoz (25/0) [46.Mauricio Fernando Aros (26/0)], Clarence Acuña Donoso (60/3) [64.Rodrígo Javier Millar Carvajal (4/0)], Milovan Petar Mirošević Albornoz (15/2), Rodrigo David Meléndez Araya (13/1), Rodrígo Ignacio Valenzuela Avíles (11/0), Patricio Sebastián Galaz Sepulveda (6/0) [46.Héctor Raúl Mancilla Garcés (2/0)], Sebastián Ignacio González Valdés (7/2). Trainer: Juvenal Mario Olmos Rojas (17).
**Goal**: Sebastián Ignacio González Valdés (72).

**556.** 14.07.2004 **COSTA RICA - CHILE** **2-1(0-1)** 41st Copa América. Group Stage.
Estadio Modelo „Jorge Basadre", Tacna (Peru); Referee: René M. Ortubé Betancourt (Bolivia); Attendance: 20,000
**CHI:** Alex Fabián Varas (7/0), Ismael Ignacio Fuentes Castro (2/0), Luis Alberto Fuentes Rodríguez (14/1), Rafael Andrés Olarra Guerrero (19/1), Rodrígo Antonio Pérez Albornoz (26/0) [71.Mauricio Fernando Aros (27/0)], Rodrígo Ignacio Valenzuela Avíles (12/0), Clarence Acuña Donoso (61/3) [46.Rodrigo David Meléndez Araya (14/1)], Luis Antonio Jiménez Garcés (3/0), Rodrígo Javier Millar Carvajal (5/0) [71.Milovan Petar Mirošević Albornoz (16/2)], Sebastián Ignacio González Valdés (8/2), Héctor Raúl Mancilla Garcés (3/0). Trainer: Juvenal Mario Olmos Rojas (18).
**Goal**: Rafael Andrés Olarra Guerrero (40).

**557.** 05.09.2004 **CHILE - COLOMBIA** **0-0** 18th FIFA WC. Qualifiers
Estadio Nacional, Santiago; Referee: Wilson Souza Mendonça (Brazil); Attendance: 62,523
**CHI:** Nelson Antonio Tapia Rios (64/0), Moisés Fermín Villarroel Ayala (29/1), Luis Alberto Fuentes Rodríguez (15/1), Rafael Andrés Olarra Guerrero (20/1), Rodrígo Antonio Pérez Albornoz (27/0) [*sent off 71*], David Marcelo Pizarro Cortés (27/2) [60.Rodrígo Ignacio Valenzuela Avíles (13/0)], Jorge Cristián Acuña Concha (6/0), Claudio Andrés Maldonado Rivera (24/0) [*sent off 17*], Milovan Petar Mirošević Albornoz (17/2) [60.Rodrígo Alvaro Tello Valenzuela (22/2)], Reinaldo Marcelino Navia Amador (29/7) [46.José Marcelo Salas Melinao (59/34)], Mauricio Ricardo Pinilla Ferrera (12/3). Trainer: Juvenal Mario Olmos Rojas (19).

**558.** 10.10.2004 **ECUADOR - CHILE** **2-0(0-0)** 18th FIFA WC. Qualifiers
Estadio Olímpico „Atahualpa", Quito; Referee: René M. Ortubé Betancourt (Bolivia); Attendance: 27,956
**CHI:** Nelson Antonio Tapia Rios (65/0), Ricardo Francisco Rojas Trujillo (34/0), Luis Alberto Fuentes Rodríguez (16/1), Rafael Andrés Olarra Guerrero (21/1), Pablo Andrés Contreras Fica (23/1), Fernando Patricio Martel Helo (14/0) [46.Jean André Emanuel Beausejour Coliqueo (3/0)], Juan Luis González (1/0), Rodrigo David Meléndez Araya (15/1), Rodrígo Ignacio Valenzuela Avíles (14/0) [58.Milovan Petar Mirošević Albornoz (18/2)], Patricio Sebastián Galaz Sepulveda (7/0) [78.Luis Ignacio Quinteros (1/0)], José Marcelo Salas Melinao (60/34). Trainer: Juvenal Mario Olmos Rojas (20).

**559.** 13.10.2004 **CHILE - ARGENTINA** **0-0** 18th FIFA WC. Qualifiers
Estadio Nacional, Santiago; Referee: Carlos Amarilla Demarqui (Paraguay); Attendance: 57,671
**CHI:** Nelson Antonio Tapia Rios (66/0), Cristián Andrés Álvarez Valenzuela (11/0), Luis Alberto Fuentes Rodríguez (17/1), Ricardo Francisco Rojas Trujillo (35/0) [46.Rafael Andrés Olarra Guerrero (22/1)], Jorge Francisco Vargas Palacios (27/0), Pablo Andrés Contreras Fica (24/1), Jorge Luis Valdivia Toro (2/0) [72.Luis Ignacio Quinteros (2/0)], Rodrigo David Meléndez Araya (16/1) [60.Milovan Petar Mirošević Albornoz (19/2)], Rodrígo Ignacio Valenzuela Avíles (15/0), José Marcelo Salas Melinao (61/34), Reinaldo Marcelino Navia Amador (30/7). Trainer: Juvenal Mario Olmos Rojas (21).

**560.** 17.11.2004 **PERU - CHILE** **2-1(0-0)** 18th FIFA WC. Qualifiers
Estadio Nacional, Lima; Referee: Héctor Baldassi (Argentina); Attendance: 39,752
**CHI:** Nelson Antonio Tapia Rios (67/0), Cristián Andrés Álvarez Valenzuela (12/0), Luis Alberto Fuentes Rodríguez (18/1), Pablo Andrés Contreras Fica (25/1), Rafael Andrés Olarra Guerrero (23/1) [62.Sebastián Ignacio González Valdés (9/3)], Rodrígo Ignacio Valenzuela Avíles (16/0) [46.Juan Luis González (2/0)], Claudio Andrés Maldonado Rivera (25/0) [76.Jorge Luis Valdivia Toro (3/0)], Rodrigo David Meléndez Araya (17/1) [*sent off 41*], Mark Dennis González Hoffmann (9/2), David Marcelo Pizarro Cortés (28/2), Mauricio Ricardo Pinilla Ferrera (13/3). Trainer: Juvenal Mario Olmos Rojas (22).
**Goal**: Sebastián Ignacio González Valdés (90).

**561.** 09.02.2005 **CHILE - ECUADOR** **3-0(2-0)**
Estadio Sausalito, Viña del Mar; Referee: Gabriel Favale (Argentina); Attendance: 17,171
**CHI:** Nelson Antonio Tapia Rios (68/0), Luis Alberto Fuentes Rodríguez (19/1), Ricardo Francisco Rojas Trujillo (36/0), Pablo Andrés Contreras Fica (26/1) [65.Rafael Andrés Olarra Guerrero (24/1)], Cristián Andrés Álvarez Valenzuela (13/0) [67.Luis Pedro Figueroa Sepúlveda (3/0)], Claudio Andrés Maldonado Rivera (26/1), David Marcelo Pizarro Cortés (29/2), Mark Dennis González Hoffmann (10/3) [46.Rodrígo Ignacio Valenzuela Avíles (17/0)], Jorge Luis Valdivia Toro (4/0) [82.Juan Luis González (3/0)], Sebastián Ignacio González Valdés (10/3) [82.Humberto Andrés Suazo Pontivo (1/0)], Daniel Pérez (2/0) [46.Mauricio Ricardo Pinilla Ferrera (14/4)]. Trainer: Juvenal Mario Olmos Rojas (23).
**Goals**: Claudio Andrés Maldonado Rivera (25), Mark Dennis González Hoffmann (35), Mauricio Ricardo Pinilla Ferrera (83).

**562.** 26.03.2005 **CHILE - URUGUAY** **1-1(0-1)** 18th FIFA WC. Qualifiers
Estadio Nacional, Santiago; Referee: Oscar Julián Ruíz Acosta (Colombia); Attendance: 55,000
**CHI:** Nelson Antonio Tapia Rios (69/0), Luis Alberto Fuentes Rodríguez (20/1), Ricardo Francisco Rojas Trujillo (37/0), Pablo Andrés Contreras Fica (27/1) [46.Jorge Luis Valdivia Toro (5/0)], Cristián Andrés Álvarez Valenzuela (14/0), Claudio Andrés Maldonado Rivera (27/1), David Marcelo Pizarro Cortés (30/2), Milovan Petar Mirošević Albornoz (20/3) [78.Rodrígo Ignacio Valenzuela Avíles (18/0)], Mark Dennis González Hoffmann (11/3) [78.Sebastián Ignacio González Valdés (11/3)], Mauricio Ricardo Pinilla Ferrera (15/4), José Marcelo Salas Melinao (62/34). Trainer: Juvenal Mario Olmos Rojas (24).
**Goal**: Milovan Petar Mirošević Albornoz (47).

**563.** 30.03.2005 **PARAGUAY - CHILE** **2-1(1-0)** 18th FIFA WC. Qualifiers
Estadio Defensores del Chaco, Asunción; Referee: Horacio Marcelo Elizondo (Argentina); Attendance: 10,000
**CHI:** Nelson Antonio Tapia Rios (70/0), Luis Alberto Fuentes Rodríguez (21/1), Ricardo Francisco Rojas Trujillo (38/0), Rafael Andrés Olarra Guerrero (25/1), Rodrígo Antonio Pérez Albornoz (28/0) [46.Cristián Andrés Álvarez Valenzuela (15/0)], Rodrigo David Meléndez Araya (18/1) [53.David Marcelo Pizarro Cortés (31/2)], Claudio Andrés Maldonado Rivera (28/1), Milovan Petar Mirošević Albornoz (21/3) [65.Sebastián Ignacio González Valdés (12/3)], Mark Dennis González Hoffmann (12/3), Mauricio Ricardo Pinilla Ferrera (16/5), José Marcelo Salas Melinao (63/34). Trainer: Juvenal Mario Olmos Rojas (25).
**Goal**: Mauricio Ricardo Pinilla Ferrera (72).

**564.** 04.06.2005 **CHILE - BOLIVIA** **3-1(2-0)** 18th FIFA WC. Qualifiers
Estadio Nacional, Santiago; Referee: Márcio Rezende de Freitas (Brazil); Attendance: 46,729
**CHI:** Nelson Antonio Tapia Rios (71/0), Moisés Fermín Villarroel Ayala (30/1), Ricardo Francisco Rojas Trujillo (39/0), Luis Alberto Fuentes Rodríguez (22/3), Francisco Ulises Rojas (30/0), Rodrigo David Meléndez Araya (19/1) [14.Jorge Cristián Acuña Concha (7/0)], Claudio Andrés Maldonado Rivera (29/1), Luis Antonio Jiménez Garcés (4/0) [72.Rodrígo Alvaro Tello Valenzuela (23/2)], David Marcelo Pizarro Cortés (32/2), Sebastián Ignacio González Valdés (13/3) [*sent off 31*], José Marcelo Salas Melinao (64/35) [70.Patricio Sebastián Galaz Sepulveda (8/0)]. Trainer: Nelson Bonifacio Acosta López (67).
**Goals**: Luis Alberto Fuentes Rodríguez (8, 34), José Marcelo Salas Melinao (66).

**565.** 08.06.2005 **CHILE - VENEZUELA** **2-1(1-0)** 18th FIFA WC. Qualifiers
Estadio Nacional, Santiago; Referee: Carlos Torres (Paraguay); Attendance: 35,506
**CHI:** Nelson Antonio Tapia Rios (72/0), Moisés Fermín Villarroel Ayala (31/1), Ricardo Francisco Rojas Trujillo (40/0), Luis Alberto Fuentes Rodríguez (23/3), Pablo Andrés Contreras Fica (28/1), Francisco Ulises Rojas (31/0), Claudio Andrés Maldonado Rivera (30/1), Jorge Cristián Acuña Concha (8/0), David Marcelo Pizarro Cortés (33/2) [88.Juan Luis González (4/0)], Luis Antonio Jiménez Garcés (5/2) [81.Jorge Luis Valdivia Toro (6/0)], Patricio Sebastián Galaz Sepulveda (9/0) [62.José Luis Villanueva Ahumada (2/0)]. Trainer: Nelson Bonifacio Acosta López (68).
**Goals**: Luis Antonio Jiménez Garcés (31, 60).

**566.** 17.08.2005 **PERU - CHILE** **3-1(1-1)**
Estadio Modelo „Jorge Basadre", Tacna; Referee: René M. Ortubé Betancourt (Bolivia)
**CHI:** Johnny Cristian Herrera Muñoz (2/0) [72.Claudio Andrés Bravo Muñoz (2/0)], Moisés Fermín Villarroel Ayala (32/1), Luis Alberto Fuentes Rodríguez (24/4), Ricardo Francisco Rojas Trujillo (41/0), Rodrígo Antonio Pérez Albornoz (29/0), Joel Antonio Reyes Zúñiga (4/0) [46.Juan Luis González (5/0)], Rodrigo David Meléndez Araya (20/1), Matías Ariel Fernández Fernández (1/0) [67.Rodrígo Toloza (1/0)], Jorge Luis Valdivia Toro (7/0) [67.Manuel Rolando Iturra Urrutia (1/0)], Patricio Sebastián Galaz Sepulveda (10/0) [67.Eduardo Javier Rubio Köstner (1/0)], Reinaldo Marcelino Navia Amador (31/7) [67.Humberto Andrés Suazo Pontivo (2/0)]. Trainer: Nelson Bonifacio Acosta López (69).
**Goal**: Luis Alberto Fuentes Rodríguez (37).

**567.** 04.09.2005 **BRAZIL - CHILE** **5-0(4-0)** 18th FIFA WC. Qualifiers
Estádio „Mané Garrincha", Brasília; Referee: Carlos Amarilla Demarqui (Paraguay); Attendance: 39,000
**CHI:** Nelson Antonio Tapia Rios (73/0), Luis Alberto Fuentes Rodríguez (25/4), Ricardo Francisco Rojas Trujillo (42/0), Pablo Andrés Contreras Fica (29/1) [59.Luis Antonio Jiménez Garcés (6/2)], Cristián Andrés Álvarez Valenzuela (16/0), Rodrigo David Meléndez Araya (21/1), Claudio Andrés Maldonado Rivera (31/1), Rodrígo Alvaro Tello Valenzuela (24/2) [59.Rodrígo Antonio Pérez Albornoz (30/0)], David Marcelo Pizarro Cortés (34/2), Mauricio Ricardo Pinilla Ferrera (17/5) [59.Jorge Cristián Acuña Concha (9/0)], Eduardo Javier Rubio Köstner (2/0). Trainer: Nelson Bonifacio Acosta López (70).

**568.** 08.10.2005 **COLOMBIA - CHILE** **1-1(1-0)** 18th FIFA WC. Qualifiers
Estadio Metropolitano „Roberto Meléndez", Barranquilla; Referee: Wilson Souza Mendonça (Brazil)
**CHI:** Claudio Andrés Bravo Muñoz (3/0), Luis Alberto Fuentes Rodríguez (26/4), Ricardo Francisco Rojas Trujillo (43/1), Pablo Andrés Contreras Fica (30/1) [57.Reinaldo Marcelino Navia Amador (32/7)], Rodrígo Antonio Pérez Albornoz (31/0), Moisés Fermín Villarroel Ayala (33/1), Jorge Cristián Acuña Concha (10/0), Luis Antonio Jiménez Garcés (7/2) [57.Milovan Petar Mirošević Albornoz (22/3)], Claudio Andrés Maldonado Rivera (32/1), David Marcelo Pizarro Cortés (35/2), Mauricio Ricardo Pinilla Ferrera (18/5) [80.Jorge Luis Valdivia Toro (8/0)]. Trainer: Nelson Bonifacio Acosta López (71).
**Goal**: Ricardo Francisco Rojas Trujillo (64).

**569.** 12.10.2005 **CHILE - ECUADOR** **0-0** 18th FIFA WC. Qualifiers
Estadio Nacional, Santiago; Referee: Horacio Marcelo Elizondo (Argentina); Attendance: 49,530
**CHI:** Claudio Andrés Bravo Muñoz (4/0), Luis Alberto Fuentes Rodríguez (27/4), Ricardo Francisco Rojas Trujillo (44/1), Rodrígo Antonio Pérez Albornoz (32/0), Moisés Fermín Villarroel Ayala (34/1) [59.Milovan Petar Mirošević Albornoz (23/3)], Claudio Andrés Maldonado Rivera (33/1), Rodrigo David Meléndez Araya (22/1), David Marcelo Pizarro Cortés (36/2), Jorge Luis Valdivia Toro (9/0) [54.Humberto Andrés Suazo Pontivo (3/0)], Luis Antonio Jiménez Garcés (8/2) [69.Matías Ariel Fernández Fernández (2/0)], Reinaldo Marcelino Navia Amador (33/7). Trainer: Nelson Bonifacio Acosta López (72).

**570.** 25.04.2006 **CHILE- NEW ZEALAND** **4-1(2-1)**
Estadio El Teniente, Rancagua; Referee: Jorge Osorio (Chile); Attendance: 10,171
**CHI:** Claudio Andrés Bravo Muñoz (5/0), Gonzalo Alejandro Jara Reyes (1/0), Mauricio Alejandro Zenteno Morales (1/0), Sebastián Alejandro Rocco Melgarejo (1/1), Roberto Andrés Cereceda Guajardo (1/0) [55.José Raúl Contreras Arrau (1/0)], Manuel Rolando Iturra Urrutia (2/0), Héctor Arturo Sanhueza Medel (4/0), Matías Ariel Fernández Fernández (3/0), Jorge Luis Valdivia Toro (10/0), Humberto Andrés Suazo Pontivo (4/1) [64.Eduardo Javier Rubio Köstner (3/1)], Juan Gonzalo Lorca Donoso (1/0). Trainer: Nelson Bonifacio Acosta López (73).
**Goals**: Humberto Andrés Suazo Pontivo (36), Jeremy Christie (39 own goal), Sebastián Alejandro Rocco Melgarejo (60), Eduardo Javier Rubio Köstner (66).

**571.** 28.04.2006 **CHILE- NEW ZEALAND** **1-0(1-0)**
Estadio „Nicolás Chahuan Nazar", La Calera; Referee: n/a; Attendance: 6,171
**CHI:** Miguel Ángel Pinto Jérez (1/0), Gonzalo Alejandro Jara Reyes (2/0) [46.Manuel Rolando Iturra Urrutia (3/0)], Waldo Alonso Ponce Carrizo (1/0) [58.Mauricio Alejandro Zenteno Morales (2/0)], Claudio Muñoz Camilo (1/0), José Raúl Contreras Arrau (2/0), Jorge Andrés Ormeño Guerra (3/0), Dagoberto Currimilla Gómez (1/0), Rodrígo Javier Millar Carvajal (6/0), Jorge Luis Valdivia Toro (11/0), Juan Gonzalo Lorca Donoso (2/0) [58.Alexis Alejandro Sánchez Sánchez (1/0)], Eduardo Javier Rubio Köstner (4/2) [69.Mathias Leonardo Vidangossy Rebolledo (1/0)]. Trainer: Nelson Bonifacio Acosta López (74).
**Goal**: Eduardo Javier Rubio Köstner (35).

**572.** 24.05.2006 **REPUBLIC OF IRELAND - CHILE** **0-1(0-0)**
Lansdowne Road, Dublin; Referee: Martin Ingvarsson (Sweden); Attendance: 36,171
**CHI:** Claudio Andrés Bravo Muñoz (6/0), Gonzalo Alejandro Jara Reyes (3/0), Jorge Francisco Vargas Palacios (28/0), Pablo Andrés Contreras Fica (31/1), Rafael Andrés Olarra Guerrero (26/1), Manuel Rolando Iturra Urrutia (4/1), Jorge Cristián Acuña Concha (11/0), Luis Antonio Jiménez Garcés (9/2), Mark Dennis González Hoffmann (13/3) [90.Mauricio Alejandro Zenteno Morales (3/0)], Humberto Andrés Suazo Pontivo (5/1) [79.Patricio Sebastián Galaz Sepulveda (11/0)], Reinaldo Marcelino Navia Amador (34/7) [75.Alexis Alejandro Sánchez Sánchez (2/0)]. Trainer: Nelson Bonifacio Acosta López (75).
**Goal**: Manuel Rolando Iturra Urrutia (48).

**573.** 30.05.2006 **IVORY COAST - CHILE** **1-1(0-0)**
Stade „Jean-Bouloumie", Vittel (France); Referee: Olivier Lamerre (France); Attendance: 10,000
**CHI:** Miguel Ángel Pinto Jérez (2/0), José Raúl Contreras Arrau (3/0), Ricardo Francisco Rojas Trujillo (45/1), Luis Alberto Fuentes Rodríguez (28/4), Rafael Andrés Olarra Guerrero (27/1) [46.Gonzalo Alejandro Jara Reyes (4/0)], Mauricio Alejandro Zenteno Morales (4/0), Jorge Cristián Acuña Concha (12/0) [46.Manuel Rolando Iturra Urrutia (5/1); Pablo Andrés Contreras Fica (32/1)], Jonathan Josué Cisternas (3/0) [53.Jorge Luis Valdivia Toro (12/0)], Jaime Andrés Valdés Zapata (2/0) [59.Jorge Francisco Vargas Palacios (29/0)], Luis Antonio Jiménez Garcés (10/2) [67.Humberto Andrés Suazo Pontivo (6/2)], Patricio Sebastián Galaz Sepulveda (12/0) [71.Alexis Alejandro Sánchez Sánchez (3/0)]. Trainer: Nelson Bonifacio Acosta López (76).
**Goal**: Humberto Andrés Suazo Pontivo (77 penalty).

**574.** 02.06.2006 **SWEDEN - CHILE** **1-1(1-0)**
Råsundastadion, Stockholm; Referee: Wolfgang Stark (Germany); Attendance: 34,735
**CHI:** Claudio Andrés Bravo Muñoz (7/0), Gonzalo Alejandro Jara Reyes (5/0), Jorge Francisco Vargas Palacios (30/0), Pablo Andrés Contreras Fica (33/1), Rafael Andrés Olarra Guerrero (28/1), Jorge Luis Valdivia Toro (13/0), Jorge Cristián Acuña Concha (13/0), Mauricio Alejandro Zenteno Morales (5/0), Luis Antonio Jiménez Garcés (11/2), Alexis Alejandro Sánchez Sánchez (4/0), Humberto Andrés Suazo Pontivo (7/3) [86.José Raúl Contreras Arrau (4/0)]. Trainer: Nelson Bonifacio Acosta López (77).
**Goal**: Humberto Andrés Suazo Pontivo (51).

**575.** 16.08.2006 **CHILE - COLOMBIA** **1-2(0-0)**
Estadio Nacional, Santiago; Referee: Jorge Luis Larrionda Pietrafiesa (Uruguay); Attendance: 15,000
**CHI:** Claudio Andrés Bravo Muñoz (8/0), Gonzalo Alejandro Jara Reyes (6/0) [78.Gonzalo Antonio Fierro Caniullán (1/0)], Rafael Andrés Olarra Guerrero (29/1), Mauricio Alejandro Zenteno Morales (6/0), Ricardo Francisco Rojas Trujillo (46/1), Claudio Andrés Maldonado Rivera (34/1) [68.Manuel Rolando Iturra Urrutia (6/1)], Héctor Arturo Sanhueza Medel (5/0), Matías Ariel Fernández Fernández (4/0), Luis Antonio Jiménez Garcés (12/2) [61.Alexis Alejandro Sánchez Sánchez (5/0)], Jorge Luis Valdivia Toro (14/0) [71.Esteban Efraín Paredes Quintanilla (1/0)], Humberto Andrés Suazo Pontivo (8/4). Trainer: Nelson Bonifacio Acosta López (78).
**Goal**: Humberto Andrés Suazo Pontivo (82 penalty).

**576.** 07.10.2006 **CHILE - PERU** **3-2(1-1)** Copa del Pacífico
Estadio Sausalito, Viña del Mar; Referee: Olivier Viera (Uruguay); Attendance: 20,000
**CHI:** Miguel Ángel Pinto Jérez (3/0), Boris Alexis Rieloff Venegas (1/0) [70.Sebastián Alejandro Rocco Melgarejo (2/1)], Jorge Francisco Vargas Palacios (Cap) (31/0), Pablo Andrés Contreras Fica (34/1), Rafael Andrés Olarra Guerrero (30/1) [*sent off 41*], Luis Pedro Figueroa Sepúlveda (4/0), Manuel Rolando Iturra Urrutia (7/1), Héctor Arturo Sanhueza Medel (6/0) [83.Jorge Cristián Acuña Concha (14/0)], Matías Ariel Fernández Fernández (5/2) [63.Esteban Efraín Paredes Quintanilla (2/0)], Mauricio Ricardo Pinilla Ferrera (19/5) [69.José Luis Villanueva Ahumada (3/0)], Reinaldo Marcelino Navia Amador (35/8) [83.Eduardo Javier Rubio Köstner (5/2)]. Trainer: Nelson Bonifacio Acosta López (79).
**Goals**: Matías Ariel Fernández Fernández (28, 50), Reinaldo Marcelino Navia Amador (71).

**577.** 11.10.2006 **PERU - CHILE** **0-1(0-1)** Copa del Pacífico
Estadio „José Basadre", Tacna; Referee: Samuel Haro (Ecuador); Attendance: 12,000
**CHI:** Claudio Andrés Bravo Muñoz (9/0), Pablo Andrés Contreras Fica (35/1), Waldo Alonso Ponce Carrizo (2/0), Jorge Francisco Vargas Palacios (Cap) (32/0), Luis Pedro Figueroa Sepúlveda (5/0), Manuel Rolando Iturra Urrutia (8/1) [90.Gonzalo Alejandro Jara Reyes (7/0)], Jorge Cristián Acuña Concha (15/0), Eros Roque Pérez Salas (6/0), Jorge Luis Valdivia Toro (15/0), Mauricio Ricardo Pinilla Ferrera (20/5) [90.Esteban Efraín Paredes Quintanilla (3/0)], Reinaldo Marcelino Navia Amador (36/9) [78.José Luis Villanueva Ahumada (4/0)]. Trainer: Nelson Bonifacio Acosta López (80).
**Goal**: Reinaldo Marcelino Navia Amador (25).

**578.** 15.11.2006 **CHILE - PARAGUAY** **3-2(1-0)**
Estadio Sausalito, Viña del Mar; Referee: Héctor Walter Baldassi (Argentina); Attendance: 8,000
**CHI:** Miguel Ángel Pinto Jérez (4/0), Waldo Alonso Ponce Carrizo (3/1), Jorge Francisco Vargas Palacios (Cap) (33/0), Sebastián Alejandro Rocco Melgarejo (3/1), Luis Pedro Figueroa Sepúlveda (6/1), Manuel Rolando Iturra Urrutia (9/1), Jorge Cristián Acuña Concha (16/0) [90.Mauricio Alejandro Zenteno Morales (7/0)], Hugo Patricio Droguett Diocares (1/0) [85.José Raúl Contreras Arrau (5/0)], Jorge Luis Valdivia Toro (16/1) [85.Esteban Efraín Paredes Quintanilla (4/0)], Leonardo Esteban Monje Valenzuela (1/0) [90.Eduardo Javier Rubio Köstner (6/2)], Mauricio Ricardo Pinilla Ferrera (21/5) [46.Manuel Alejandro Neira Díaz (13/2)]. Trainer: Nelson Bonifacio Acosta López (81).
**Goals**: Waldo Alonso Ponce Carrizo (40), Jorge Luis Valdivia Toro (51), Luis Pedro Figueroa Sepúlveda (63 penalty).

**579.** 07.02.2007 **VENEZUELA - CHILE** **0-1(0-1)**

Estadio „José Encarnación 'Pachenco' Romero", Maracaibo; Referee: José Hernando Buitrago Arango (Colombia); Attendance: 9,000

**CHI:** Claudio Andrés Bravo Muñoz (10/0), Ismael Ignacio Fuentes Castro (3/0), Jorge Francisco Vargas Palacios (34/0), Pablo Andrés Contreras Fica (36/1), Luis Pedro Figueroa Sepúlveda (7/1), Manuel Rolando Iturra Urrutia (10/1), Héctor Arturo Sanhueza Medel (7/0), Mark Dennis González Hoffmann (14/3) [81.Hugo Patricio Droguett Diocares (2/0)], Matías Ariel Fernández Fernández (6/3) [73.Carlos Andrés Villanueva Roland (1/0)], Reinaldo Marcelino Navia Amador (37/9) [73.Alexis Alejandro Sánchez Sánchez (6/0)], Humberto Andrés Suazo Pontivo (9/4) [90.Arturo Erasmo Vidal Pardo (1/0)]. Trainer: Nelson Bonifacio Acosta López (82).

**Goal**: Matías Ariel Fernández Fernández (44).

**580.** 24.03.2007 **BRAZIL - CHILE** **4-0(2-0)**

Ullevi Stadion, Göteborg (Sweden); Referee: Espen Berntsen (Norway); Attendance: 30,122

**CHI:** Claudio Andrés Bravo Muñoz (11/0), Ismael Ignacio Fuentes Castro (4/0), Jorge Francisco Vargas Palacios (35/0), Alex Christian von Schwedler Vasquez (4/0) [46.Reinaldo Marcelino Navia Amador (38/9)], Luis Pedro Figueroa Sepúlveda (8/1), Claudio Andrés Maldonado Rivera (35/1), Héctor Arturo Sanhueza Medel (8/0), Mark Dennis González Hoffmann (15/3) [79.Manuel Rolando Iturra Urrutia (11/1)], Matías Ariel Fernández Fernández (7/3) [46.Jorge Luis Valdivia Toro (17/1)], Luis Antonio Jiménez Garcés (13/2) [79.Rodrigo Álvaro Tello Valenzuela (25/2)], Humberto Andrés Suazo Pontivo (10/4). Trainer: Nelson Bonifacio Acosta López (83).

**581.** 28.03.2007 **CHILE – COSTA RICA** **1-1(1-0)**

Estadio Fiscal, Talca; Referee: René Ortubé Betancourt (Bolivia); Attendance: 8,000

**CHI:** Miguel Ángel Pinto Jérez (5/0), Ismael Ignacio Fuentes Castro (5/0), Waldo Alonso Ponce Carrizo (4/1), Boris Alexis Rieloff Venegas (2/0) [69.Luis Pedro Figueroa Sepúlveda (9/1)], Rodrigo Álvaro Tello Valenzuela (26/2) [62.Hugo Patricio Droguett Diocares (3/0)], Héctor Arturo Sanhueza Medel (9/0), Claudio Andrés Maldonado Rivera (36/1) [62.Manuel Rolando Iturra Urrutia (12/1)], Luis Antonio Jiménez Garcés (14/2) [78.José Raúl Contreras Arrau (6/0)], Jorge Luis Valdivia Toro (18/1), Humberto Andrés Suazo Pontivo (11/4) [62.Luis Patricio Núñez Blanco (1/0)], Reinaldo Marcelino Navia Amador (39/10). Trainer: Nelson Bonifacio Acosta López (84).

**Goal**: Reinaldo Marcelino Navia Amador (33).

**582.** 18.04.2007 **ARGENTINA - CHILE** **0-0**

Estadio Malvinas Argentinas, Mendoza; Referee: Martín Emilio Vázquez Broquetas (Uruguay); Attendance: 38,000

**CHI:** Miguel Ángel Pinto Jérez (6/0), Boris Alexis Rieloff Venegas (3/0), Sebastián Alejandro Rocco Melgarejo (4/1), Miguel Augusto Riffo Garay (1/0), Arturo Erasmo Vidal Pardo (2/0), Gonzalo Antonio Fierro Caniullán (2/0), Héctor Arturo Sanhueza Medel (10/0), Manuel Rolando Iturra Urrutia (13/1) [62.Gary Alexis Medel Soto (1/0)], Jorge Luis Valdivia Toro (19/1), Humberto Andrés Suazo Pontivo (12/4), Alexis Alejandro Sánchez Sánchez (7/0) [73.Rodolfo Antonio Moya Spuler (4/0)]. Trainer: Nelson Bonifacio Acosta López (85).

**583.** 09.05.2007 **CHILE - CUBA** **3-0(2-0)**

Estadio Parque Schott, Osorno; Referee: Fernando Cabrera (Uruguay); Attendance: 1,800

**CHI:** Francisco Javier Prieto Caroca (1/0), Boris Alexis Rieloff Venegas (4/0) [79.José Luis Cabión Dianta (1/0)], Rodrigo Osvaldo Rivera Godoy (1/0) [58.Mauricio Alejandro Zenteno Morales (8/0)], Sebastián Alejandro Rocco Melgarejo (5/1), José Manuel Rojas Bahamondes (1/1) [58.José Raúl Contreras Arrau (7/0)], Daniel Felipe González Calvo (1/0) [70.Fernando Andrés Meneses Cornejo (1/0)], Fernando Alejandro Manríquez Hernández (1/0), Christian Jorge Martínez Muñoz (1/0) [58.Francisco Andrés Silva Gajardo (1/0)], Carlos Andrés Villanueva Roland (2/0) [79.Mathias Leonardo Vidangossy Rebolledo (2/0)], Roberto Carlos Gutiérrez Gamboa (1/1), Luis Reinaldo Flores Abarca (1/1). Trainer: Nelson Bonifacio Acosta López (86).

**Goals**: Roberto Carlos Gutiérrez Gamboa (6), José Manuel Rojas Bahamondes (26), Luis Reinaldo Flores Abarca (88).

**584.** 16.05.2007 **CHILE - CUBA** **2-0(1-0)**

Estadio Municipal „Germán Becker", Temuco; Referee: Ricardo Grance (Paraguay); Attendance: 3,500

**CHI:** Fernando Javier Hurtado Pérez (1/0) [85.Javier Eduardo di Gregorio (1/0)], Fernando Andrés Meneses Cornejo (2/0), Mauricio Alejandro Zenteno Morales (9/0), Mauricio Antonio Arias González (1/0), Claudio Andrés Muñoz Carrillo (1/0), Carlos Patricio Cisternas Tobar (1/0) [60.Fernando Alejandro Manríquez Hernández (2/0)], José Luis Cabión Dianta (2/0), Daniel Felipe González Calvo (2/1), Pedro Andrés Morales Flores (1/0) [60.José Raúl Contreras Arrau (8/0)], Jean Paul Jesús Pineda Cortés (1/0) [61.Mathias Leonardo Vidangossy Rebolledo (3/0)], Roberto Carlos Gutiérrez Gamboa (2/2) [61.Luis Reinaldo Flores Abarca (2/1)]. Trainer: Nelson Bonifacio Acosta López (87).

**Goals**: Roberto Carlos Gutiérrez Gamboa (40), Daniel Felipe González Calvo (72).

**585.** 23.05.2007 **HAITI - CHILE** **0-0**

Stade "Sylvio Cator", Port au Prince; Referee: Guidner Edouard (Haiti); Attendance: 12,000

**CHI:** Nicolás Miroslav Peric Villarreal (3/0), Boris Alexis Rieloff Venegas (5/0) [24.Boris Igor González Garrido (7/0)], Mauricio Alejandro Zenteno Morales (10/0), Sebastián Alejandro Rocco Melgarejo (6/1), Roberto Andrés Cereceda Guajardo (2/0), Fernando Alejandro Manríquez Hernández (3/0), José Luis Cabión Dianta (3/0), Carlos Andrés Villanueva Roland (3/0) [46.José Raúl Contreras Arrau (9/0)], Daniel Felipe González Calvo (3/1) [82.Christian Jorge Martínez Muñoz (2/0)], Roberto Carlos Gutiérrez Gamboa (3/2) [46.Juan Gonzalo Lorca Donoso (3/0)], Rodolfo Antonio Moya Spuler (5/0) [17.Mathias Leonardo Vidangossy Rebolledo (4/0)]. Trainer: Nelson Bonifacio Acosta López (88).

**586.** 02.06.2007 **COSTA RICA - CHILE** **2-0(1-0)**

Estadio "Ricardo Saprissa", San José; Referee: Manuel Glower (Mexico); Attendance: 25,000

**CHI:** Claudio Andrés Bravo Muñoz (12/0), Alvaro Andrés Ormeño Salazar (1/0), Pablo Andrés Contreras Fica (37/1) [*sent off 40*], Mauricio Alejandro Zenteno Morales (11/0) [67.Ismael Ignacio Fuentes Castro (6/0)], Arturo Erasmo Vidal Pardo (3/0) [76.José Luis Cabión Dianta (4/0)], Rodrigo David Meléndez Araya (23/1) [83.Manuel Rolando Iturra Urrutia (14/1)], Héctor Arturo Sanhueza Medel (11/0), Jorge Luis Valdivia Toro (20/1), Matías Ariel Fernández Fernández (8/3) [46.Roberto Andrés Cereceda Guajardo (3/0)], Luis Antonio Jiménez Garcés (15/2) [62.Juan Gonzalo Lorca Donoso (4/0)], Roberto Carlos Gutiérrez Gamboa (4/2) [76.Julio Brian Gutiérrez González (4/0)]. Trainer: Nelson Bonifacio Acosta López (89).

**587.** 05.06.2007 **JAMAICA - CHILE** **0-1(0-1)**

Independence Park, Kingston; Referee: José Guerrero (Nicaragua); Attendance: 15,000

**CHI:** Nicolás Miroslav Peric Villarreal (4/0), Gonzalo Antonio Fierro Caniullán (3/0) [77.Carlos Andrés Villanueva Roland (4/0)], Ismael Ignacio Fuentes Castro (7/0), Jorge Francisco Vargas Palacios (36/0) [59.Rodrigo David Meléndez Araya (24/1)], Arturo Erasmo Vidal Pardo (4/0), José Luis Cabión Dianta (5/0), Héctor Arturo Sanhueza Medel (12/0), Matías Ariel Fernández Fernández (9/3), Jorge Luis Valdivia Toro (21/1), Julio Brian Gutiérrez González (5/0) [64.Alvaro Andrés Ormeño Salazar (2/0)], Juan Gonzalo Lorca Donoso (5/1) [89.Manuel Rolando Iturra Urrutia (15/1)]. Trainer: Nelson Bonifacio Acosta López (90).

**Goal**: Juan Gonzalo Lorca Donoso (18).

**588.** 27.06.2007 **ECUADOR - CHILE** **2-3(2-1)** 42nd Copa América. Group Stage.
Estadio Polideportivo Cachamay, Puerto Ordaz (Venezuela); Referee: Óscar Julián Ruiz Acosta (Colombia); Attendance: 25,000
**CHI:** Claudio Andrés Bravo Muñoz (13/0), Alvaro Andrés Ormeño Salazar (3/0), Jorge Francisco Vargas Palacios (37/0), Pablo Andrés Contreras Fica (38/1), Mark Dennis González Hoffmann (16/3), Matías Ariel Fernández Fernández (10/3) [46.Miguel Augusto Riffo Garay (2/0)], Rodrigo David Meléndez Araya (25/1) [73.Carlos Andrés Villanueva Roland (5/1)], Héctor Arturo Sanhueza Medel (13/0), Jorge Luis Valdivia Toro (22/1), Reinaldo Marcelino Navia Amador (40/10) [46.Juan Gonzalo Lorca Donoso (6/1)], Humberto Andrés Suazo Pontivo (13/6). Trainer: Nelson Bonifacio Acosta López (91).
**Goals**: Humberto Andrés Suazo Pontivo (20, 80), Carlos Andrés Villanueva Roland (86).

**589.** 01.07.2007 **BRAZIL - CHILE** **3-0(1-0)** 42nd Copa América. Group Stage.
Estadio Monumental, Maturín (Venezuela); Referee: Carlos Manuel Torres (Paraguay); Attendance: 42,000
**CHI:** Claudio Andrés Bravo Muñoz (14/0), Alvaro Andrés Ormeño Salazar (4/0), Ismael Ignacio Fuentes Castro (8/0), Miguel Augusto Riffo Garay (3/0) [54.Jorge Francisco Vargas Palacios (38/0)], Pablo Andrés Contreras Fica (39/1), Gonzalo Alejandro Jara Reyes (8/0) [46.Juan Gonzalo Lorca Donoso (7/1)], Rodrigo David Meléndez Araya (26/1) [19.Manuel Rolando Iturra Urrutia (16/1)], Héctor Arturo Sanhueza Medel (14/0), Mark Dennis González Hoffmann (17/3), Jorge Luis Valdivia Toro (23/1), Humberto Andrés Suazo Pontivo (14/6).Trainer: Nelson Bonifacio Acosta López (92).

**590.** 04.07.2007 **MEXICO - CHILE** **0-0** 42nd Copa América. Group Stage.
Estadio Olímpico „Luis Ramos“, Puerto la Cruz (Venezuela); Referee: Carlos Arecio Amarilla Demarqui (Paraguay); Attendance: 38,000
**CHI:** Claudio Andrés Bravo Muñoz (15/0), Ismael Ignacio Fuentes Castro (9/0), Pablo Andrés Contreras Fica (40/1), Sebastián Alejandro Rocco Melgarejo (7/1), Gonzalo Antonio Fierro Caniullán (4/0), Manuel Rolando Iturra Urrutia (17/1), Héctor Arturo Sanhueza Medel (15/0), Rodrigo Álvaro Tello Valenzuela (27/2), Carlos Andrés Villanueva Roland (6/1) [70.Matías Ariel Fernández Fernández (11/3)], Humberto Andrés Suazo Pontivo (15/6), Juan Gonzalo Lorca Donoso (8/1) [77.Mark Dennis González Hoffmann (18/3)]. Trainer: Nelson Bonifacio Acosta López (93).

**591.** 07.07.2007 **BRAZIL - CHILE** **6-1(3-0)** 42nd Copa América.Quarter-Finals.
Estadio “General José Antonio Anzoátegui”, Puerto La Cruz (Venezuela); Referee: Jorge Luis Larrionda Pietrafiesa (Uruguay); Attendance: 25,000
**CHI:** Claudio Andrés Bravo Muñoz (16/0), Alvaro Andrés Ormeño Salazar (5/0), Ismael Ignacio Fuentes Castro (10/0), Pablo Andrés Contreras Fica (41/1), Gonzalo Alejandro Jara Reyes (9/0) [56.José Luis Cabión Dianta (6/0)], Gonzalo Antonio Fierro Caniullán (5/0) [46.Jorge Luis Valdivia Toro (24/1)], Manuel Rolando Iturra Urrutia (18/1), Héctor Arturo Sanhueza Medel (16/0), Mark Dennis González Hoffmann (19/3) [66.Matías Ariel Fernández Fernández (12/3)], Juan Gonzalo Lorca Donoso (9/1), Humberto Andrés Suazo Pontivo (16/7). Trainer: Nelson Bonifacio Acosta López (94).
**Goal**: Humberto Andrés Suazo Pontivo (76).

**592.** 07.09.2007 **SWITZERLAND - CHILE** **2-1(1-1)** International Tournament
“Ernst Happel” Stadion, Wien (Austria); Referee: Fritz Stuchlik (Austria); Attendance: 2,500
**CHI:** Claudio Andrés Bravo Muñoz (17/0), Cristián Andrés Álvarez Valenzuela (17/0) [87.Gonzalo Antonio Fierro Caniullán (6/0)], Miguel Augusto Riffo Garay (4/0), Ismael Ignacio Fuentes Castro (11/0), Arturo Erasmo Vidal Pardo (5/0) [66.Marco Andrés Estrada Quinteros (1/0)], Manuel Rolando Iturra Urrutia (19/1), Mauricio Aníbal Isla Isla (1/0) [66.Luis Antonio Jiménez Garcés (16/2)], Matías Ariel Fernández Fernández (13/3), Alexis Alejandro Sánchez Sánchez (8/1), Humberto Andrés Suazo Pontivo (17/7) [86.José Marcelo Salas Melinao (65/35)], Eduardo Javier Rubio Köstner (7/2). Trainer: Marcelo Alberto Bielsa Caldera (1).
**Goal**: Alexis Alejandro Sánchez Sánchez (44).

**593.** 11.09.2007 **AUSTRIA - CHILE** **0-2(0-0)** International Tournament
„Ernst Happel“ Stadion, Wien; Referee: Jacek Granat (Poland); Attendance: 12,000
**CHI:** Nicolás Miroslav Peric Villarreal (5/0), Waldo Alonso Ponce Carrizo (5/1), Gary Alexis Medel Soto (2/0), Miguel Augusto Riffo Garay (5/0), Gonzalo Antonio Fierro Caniullán (7/0) [67.Manuel Rolando Iturra Urrutia (20/1)], Claudio Andrés Maldonado Rivera (37/1), Hugo Patricio Droguett Diocares (4/1) [85.Marco Andrés Estrada Quinteros (2/0)], Luis Antonio Jiménez Garcés (17/2) [57.Matías Ariel Fernández Fernández (14/3)], Alexis Alejandro Sánchez Sánchez (9/1) [88.Carlos Andrés Villanueva Roland (7/1)], José Marcelo Salas Melinao (66/35) [71.Humberto Andrés Suazo Pontivo (18/7)], Mark Dennis González Hoffmann (20/3) [78.Eduardo Javier Rubio Köstner (8/3)]. Trainer: Marcelo Alberto Bielsa Caldera (2).
**Goals**: Hugo Patricio Droguett Diocares (66), Eduardo Javier Rubio Köstner (84).

**594.** 13.10.2007 **ARGENTINA - CHILE** **2-0(2-0)** 19th FIFA WC. Qualifiers
Estadio Monumental „Antonio Vespucio Liberti“, Buenos Aires; Referee: Martín Emilio Vázquez Broquetas (Uruguay); Attendance: 55,000
**CHI:** Claudio Andrés Bravo Muñoz (18/0), Cristián Andrés Álvarez Valenzuela (18/0) [*sent off 54*], Waldo Alonso Ponce Carrizo (6/1), Miguel Augusto Riffo Garay (6/0), Gonzalo Antonio Fierro Caniullán (8/0) [37.Hugo Patricio Droguett Diocares (5/1)], Manuel Rolando Iturra Urrutia (21/1) [63.Claudio Andrés Maldonado Rivera (38/1)], Arturo Erasmo Vidal Pardo (6/0), Eduardo Javier Rubio Köstner (9/3) [46.José Marcelo Salas Melinao (67/35)], Matías Ariel Fernández Fernández (15/3), Mark Dennis González Hoffmann (21/3), Humberto Andrés Suazo Pontivo (19/7). Trainer: Marcelo Alberto Bielsa Caldera (3).

**595.** 17.10.2007 **CHILE - PERU** **2-0(1-0)** 19th FIFA WC. Qualifiers
Estadio Nacional, Santiago; Referee: Óscar Julián Ruiz Acosta (Colombia); Attendance: 60,000
**CHI:** Claudio Andrés Bravo Muñoz (19/0), Waldo Alonso Ponce Carrizo (7/1), Miguel Augusto Riffo Garay (7/0), Arturo Erasmo Vidal Pardo (7/0), Gonzalo Antonio Fierro Caniullán (9/0) [89.Ismael Ignacio Fuentes Castro (12/0)], Manuel Rolando Iturra Urrutia (22/1), Hugo Patricio Droguett Diocares (6/1), Matías Ariel Fernández Fernández (16/4), Humberto Andrés Suazo Pontivo (20/8) [84.Eduardo Javier Rubio Köstner (10/3)], José Marcelo Salas Melinao (68/35) [88.Luis Antonio Jiménez Garcés (18/2)], Mark Dennis González Hoffmann (22/3). Trainer: Marcelo Alberto Bielsa Caldera (4).
**Goals**: Humberto Andrés Suazo Pontivo (11), Matías Ariel Fernández Fernández (51).

**596.** 18.11.2007 **URUGUAY - CHILE** **2-2(1-0)** 19th FIFA WC. Qualifiers
Estadio Centenario, Montevideo; Referee: Sergio Fabián Pezzotta (Argentina); Attendance: 43,000
**CHI:** Claudio Andrés Bravo Muñoz (20/0), Cristián Andrés Álvarez Valenzuela (19/0) [60.Ismael Ignacio Fuentes Castro (13/0)], Miguel Augusto Riffo Garay (8/0), Waldo Alonso Ponce Carrizo (8/1), Gonzalo Alejandro Jara Reyes (10/0), Arturo Erasmo Vidal Pardo (8/0), Hugo Patricio Droguett Diocares (7/1), Humberto Andrés Suazo Pontivo (21/8) [72.Rodolfo Antonio Moya Spuler (6/0)], Matías Ariel Fernández Fernández (17/4), Eduardo Javier Rubio Köstner (11/3) [46.Carlos Andrés Villanueva Roland (8/1)], José Marcelo Salas Melinao (69/37). Trainer: Marcelo Alberto Bielsa Caldera (5).
**Goals**: José Marcelo Salas Melinao (59, 69 penalty).

**597.** 21.11.2007 **CHILE - PARAGUAY** **0-3(0-2)** 19th FIFA WC. Qualifiers
Estadio Nacional, Santiago; Referee: Óscar Julián Ruiz Acosta (Colombia); Attendance: 60,000
**CHI:** Claudio Andrés Bravo Muñoz (21/0), Cristián Andrés Álvarez Valenzuela (20/0), Waldo Alonso Ponce Carrizo (9/1), Miguel Augusto Riffo Garay (9/0), Manuel Rolando Iturra Urrutia (23/1) [46.Luis Antonio Jiménez Garcés (19/2)], Claudio Andrés Maldonado Rivera (39/1), Hugo Patricio Droguett Diocares (8/1), Matías Ariel Fernández Fernández (18/4), Humberto Andrés Suazo Pontivo (22/8), José Marcelo Salas Melinao (70/37), Eduardo Javier Rubio Köstner (12/3) [46.Carlos Andrés Villanueva Roland (9/1)]. Trainer: Marcelo Alberto Bielsa Caldera (6).

**598.** 26.01.2008 **JAPAN - CHILE** **0-0**
National Stadium, Tokyo; Referee: Lee Min-Hui (South Korea); Attendance: 37,261
**CHI:** Miguel Ángel Pinto Jérez (7/0), Gary Alexis Medel Soto (3/0), Gonzalo Alejandro Jara Reyes (11/0), Hans Alexis Martínez Cabrera (1/0), Roberto Andrés Cereceda Guajardo (4/0), Manuel Rolando Iturra Urrutia (Cap) (24/1), Marco Andrés Estrada Quinteros (3/0), Pedro Andrés Morales Flores (2/0), Gonzalo Antonio Fierro Caniullán (10/0), Eduardo Javier Rubio Köstner (13/3), Jean André Emanuel Beausejour Coliqueo (4/0). Trainer: Marcelo Alberto Bielsa Caldera (7).

**599.** 30.01.2008 **SOUTH KOREA - CHILE** **0-1(0-0)**
Seoul World Cup Stadium, Seoul; Referee: Hajime Matsudo (Japan); Attendance: 15,012
**CHI:** Miguel Ángel Pinto Jérez (8/0), Gary Alexis Medel Soto (4/0), Gonzalo Alejandro Jara Reyes (12/0), Hans Alexis Martínez Cabrera (2/0), Roberto Andrés Cereceda Guajardo (5/0), Manuel Rolando Iturra Urrutia (25/1), Marco Andrés Estrada Quinteros (4/0), Pedro Andrés Morales Flores (3/0) [89.Boris Alexis Sagredo Romero (1/0)], Gonzalo Antonio Fierro Caniullán (11/1), Eduardo Javier Rubio Köstner (14/3) [90+2.Osvaldo Alexis González Sepúlveda (1/0)], Jean André Emanuel Beausejour Coliqueo (5/0). Trainer: Marcelo Alberto Bielsa Caldera (8).
**Goal**: Gonzalo Antonio Fierro Caniullán (55).

**600.** 26.03.2008 **ISRAEL - CHILE** **1-0(1-0)**
National Stadium, Ramat Gan, Tel Aviv; Referee: Carlos Velasco Carballo (Spain); Attendance: 24,463
**CHI:** Eduardo Eugenio Lobos Landaeta (1/0), Arturo Erasmo Vidal Pardo (9/0) [68.Mauricio Aníbal Isla Isla (2/0)], Waldo Alonso Ponce Carrizo (10/1), Ismael Ignacio Fuentes Castro (14/0), Cristián Andrés Álvarez Valenzuela (21/0), Claudio Andrés Maldonado Rivera (40/1), Hugo Patricio Droguett Diocares (9/1) [46.Luis Antonio Jiménez Garcés (20/2)], Matías Ariel Fernández Fernández (19/4), Alexis Alejandro Sánchez Sánchez (10/1), Humberto Andrés Suazo Pontivo (23/8) [75.Juan Gonzalo Lorca Donoso (10/1)], Mark Dennis González Hoffmann (23/3). Trainer: Marcelo Alberto Bielsa Caldera (9).

**601.** 04.06.2008 **CHILE - GUATEMALA** **2-0(2-0)**
Estadio El Teniente, Rancagua; Referee: Antonio Arias Alvarenga (Paraguay); Attendance: 7,000
**CHI:** Claudio Andrés Bravo Muñoz (22/0), Rafael Antonio Caroca Cordero (1/0), Osvaldo Alexis González Sepúlveda (2/0), Ismael Ignacio Fuentes Castro (15/0) [46.Waldo Alonso Ponce Carrizo (11/1)], Hugo Patricio Droguett Diocares (10/1) [46.Roberto Andrés Cereceda Guajardo (6/0)], Manuel Rolando Iturra Urrutia (26/1), Carlos Emilio Carmona Tello (1/0) [46.Gary Alexis Medel Soto (5/0)], Carlos Andrés Villanueva Roland (10/1), Alexis Alejandro Sánchez Sánchez (11/3) [46.Humberto Andrés Suazo Pontivo (24/8); 74.José Pedro Fuenzalida Gana (1/0)], Daúd Jared Gazale Álvarez (1/0), Jean André Emanuel Beausejour Coliqueo (6/0) [46.Mark Dennis González Hoffmann (24/3)]. Trainer: Marcelo Alberto Bielsa Caldera (10).
**Goals**: Alexis Alejandro Sánchez Sánchez (2, 35).

**602.** 07.06.2008 **CHILE - PANAMA** **0-0**
Estadio Chiledeportes de Valparaiso; Referee: Sálvio Spínola Fagundes Filho); Attendance: 6,000
**CHI:** Claudio Andrés Bravo Muñoz (23/0), Gary Alexis Medel Soto (6/0), Ismael Ignacio Fuentes Castro (16/0) [46.Waldo Alonso Ponce Carrizo (12/1)], Gonzalo Alejandro Jara Reyes (13/0), Manuel Rolando Iturra Urrutia (27/1), Carlos Emilio Carmona Tello (2/0) [46.Roberto Andrés Cereceda Guajardo (7/0)], Hugo Patricio Droguett Diocares (11/1) [46.Fabián Ariel Orellana Valenzuela (1/0)], Pedro Andrés Morales Flores (4/0) [73.Carlos Andrés Villanueva Roland (11/1)], José Pedro Fuenzalida Gana (2/0), Daúd Jared Gazale Álvarez (2/0), Jean André Emanuel Beausejour Coliqueo (7/0). Trainer: Marcelo Alberto Bielsa Caldera (11).

**603.** 15.06.2008 **BOLIVIA - CHILE** **0-2(0-1)** 19th FIFA WC. Qualifiers
Estadio "Hernándo Siles Zuazo", La Paz; Referee: Victor Hugo Rivera (Peru); Attendance: 27,722
**CHI:** Claudio Andrés Bravo Muñoz (24/0), Gary Alexis Medel Soto (7/2), Ismael Ignacio Fuentes Castro (17/0), Gonzalo Alejandro Jara Reyes (14/0), José Pedro Fuenzalida Gana (3/0) [46.Marco Andrés Estrada Quinteros (5/0)], Carlos Emilio Carmona Tello (3/0), Roberto Andrés Cereceda Guajardo (8/0), Pedro Andrés Morales Flores (5/0) [55.Carlos Andrés Villanueva Roland (12/1)], Alexis Alejandro Sánchez Sánchez (12/3), Humberto Andrés Suazo Pontivo (25/8), Jean André Emanuel Beausejour Coliqueo (8/0) [58.Mark Dennis González Hoffmann (25/3)]. Trainer: Marcelo Alberto Bielsa Caldera (12).
**Goals**: Gary Alexis Medel Soto (28, 76).

**604.** 19.06.2008 **VENEZUELA - CHILE** **2-3(0-0)** 19th FIFA WC. Qualifiers
Estadio Olímpico "Luis Ramos", Puerto la Cruz; Referee: Roberto Carlos Silvera (Uruguay); Attendance: 38,000
**CHI:** Claudio Andrés Bravo Muñoz (25/0), Gonzalo Alejandro Jara Reyes (15/1), Ismael Ignacio Fuentes Castro (18/0), Marco Andrés Estrada Quinteros (6/0), Gary Alexis Medel Soto (8/2), Carlos Emilio Carmona Tello (4/0), Roberto Andrés Cereceda Guajardo (9/0) [76.Waldo Alonso Ponce Carrizo (13/1)], Pedro Andrés Morales Flores (6/0) [60.Daúd Jared Gazale Álvarez (3/0)], Alexis Alejandro Sánchez Sánchez (13/3), Humberto Andrés Suazo Pontivo (26/10), Jean André Emanuel Beausejour Coliqueo (9/0) [59.Mark Dennis González Hoffmann (26/3)]. Trainer: Marcelo Alberto Bielsa Caldera (13).
**Goals**: Humberto Andrés Suazo Pontivo (65 penalty), Gonzalo Alejandro Jara Reyes (72), Humberto Andrés Suazo Pontivo (90+2).

**605.** 20.08.2008 **TURKEY - CHILE** **1-0(0-0)**
Kocaeli İsmetpaşa Stadı, Izmit; Referee: Anastasios Kakkos (Greece); Attendance: n/a
**CHI:** Claudio Andrés Bravo Muñoz (26/0), Arturo Erasmo Vidal Pardo (10/0), Gonzalo Alejandro Jara Reyes (16/1), Pablo Andrés Contreras Fica (42/1), Roberto Andrés Cereceda Guajardo (10/0), Carlos Emilio Carmona Tello (5/0) [76.Gonzalo Antonio Fierro Caniullán (12/1)], Marco Andrés Estrada Quinteros (7/0), Matías Ariel Fernández Fernández (20/4) [46.Jorge Luis Valdivia Toro (25/1)], Alexis Alejandro Sánchez Sánchez (14/3), Humberto Andrés Suazo Pontivo (27/10), Mark Dennis González Hoffmann (27/3) [76.Jean André Emanuel Beausejour Coliqueo (10/0)]. Trainer: Marcelo Alberto Bielsa Caldera (14).

**606.** 07.09.2008 **CHILE - BRAZIL** **0-3(0-2)** 19th FIFA WC. Qualifiers
Estadio Nacional „Julio Martínez Prádanos", Santiago; Referee: Carlos Manuel Torres (Paraguay); Attendance: 60,239
**CHI:** Claudio Andrés Bravo Muñoz (27/0), Gary Alexis Medel Soto (9/2), Gonzalo Alejandro Jara Reyes (17/1), Marco Andrés Estrada Quinteros (8/0), Carlos Emilio Carmona Tello (6/0), Arturo Erasmo Vidal Pardo (11/0) [46.Jean André Emanuel Beausejour Coliqueo (11/0)], Hugo Patricio Droguett Diocares (12/1) [34.Jorge Luis Valdivia Toro (26/1) [*sent off 62*]], Matías Ariel Fernández Fernández (21/4), Alexis Alejandro Sánchez Sánchez (15/3), Humberto Andrés Suazo Pontivo (28/10), Mark Dennis González Hoffmann (28/3) [46.Roberto Andrés Cereceda Guajardo (11/0)]. Trainer: Marcelo Alberto Bielsa Caldera (15).

**607.** 10.09.2008 **CHILE - COLOMBIA** **4-0(2-0)** 19th FIFA WC. Qualifiers
Estadio Nacional „Julio Martínez Prádanos", Santiago; Referee: Jorge Luis Larrionda Pietrafesa (Uruguay); Attendance: 47,459
**CHI:** Claudio Andrés Bravo Muñoz (28/0), Gary Alexis Medel Soto (10/2), Gonzalo Alejandro Jara Reyes (18/2), Ismael Ignacio Fuentes Castro (19/1), Arturo Erasmo Vidal Pardo (12/0), Marco Andrés Estrada Quinteros (9/0), Roberto Andrés Cereceda Guajardo (12/0) [78.Pablo Andrés Contreras Fica (43/1)], Matías Ariel Fernández Fernández (22/5), Alexis Alejandro Sánchez Sánchez (16/3) [81.Gonzalo Antonio Fierro Caniullán (13/1)], Humberto Andrés Suazo Pontivo (29/11) [85.Pedro Andrés Morales Flores (7/0)], Mark Dennis González Hoffmann (29/3). Trainer: Marcelo Alberto Bielsa Caldera (16).
**Goals**: Gonzalo Alejandro Jara Reyes (26), Humberto Andrés Suazo Pontivo (38), Ismael Ignacio Fuentes Castro (48), Matías Ariel Fernández Fernández (71).

**608.** 24.09.2008 **MEXICO - CHILE** **0-1(0-0)**
Estadio Nacional „Julio Martínez Prádanos“, Santiago; Referee: Kevin Stott (United States); Attendance: 32,924
**CHI:** Miguel Ángel Pinto Jérez (9/0), Hans Alexis Martínez Cabrera (3/0), Osvaldo Alexis González Sepúlveda (3/0), Marco Andrés Estrada Quinteros (10/0), Fernando Andrés Meneses Cornejo (3/0), Manuel Rolando Iturra Urrutia (28/1), Roberto Andrés Cereceda Guajardo (13/0), Emilio Exequiel Hernández Hernández (1/0) [89.Matías Jesús Celis Contreras (1/0)], José Pedro Fuenzalida Gana (4/0), Fabián Ariel Orellana Valenzuela (2/0) [86.Francisco Javier Pizarro Cartes (1/0)], Boris Alexis Sagredo Romero (2/0) [79.Luis Pedro Figueroa Sepúlveda (10/1)]. Trainer: Marcelo Alberto Bielsa Caldera (17).
**Goal**: Juan Carlos Valenzuela (75 own goal).

**609.** 12.10.2008 **ECUADOR - CHILE** **1-0(0-0)** 19th FIFA WC. Qualifiers
Estadio Olimpico “Atahualpa”, Quito; Referee: Martín Emilio Vázquez Broquetas (Uruguay); Attendance: 33,079
**CHI:** Claudio Andrés Bravo Muñoz (29/0), Gary Alexis Medel Soto (11/2), Gonzalo Alejandro Jara Reyes (19/2) [*sent off 82*], Ismael Ignacio Fuentes Castro (20/1) [*sent off 20*], Arturo Erasmo Vidal Pardo (13/0), Carlos Emilio Carmona Tello (7/0), Roberto Andrés Cereceda Guajardo (14/0) [53.Marco Andrés Estrada Quinteros (11/0)], Matías Ariel Fernández Fernández (23/5) [23.Pablo Andrés Contreras Fica (44/1)], Mark Dennis González Hoffmann (30/3), Alexis Alejandro Sánchez Sánchez (17/3), Humberto Andrés Suazo Pontivo (30/11) [58.Pedro Andrés Morales Flores (8/0)]. Trainer: Marcelo Alberto Bielsa Caldera (18).

**610.** 15.10.2008 **CHILE - ARGENTINA** **1-0(1-0)** 19th FIFA WC. Qualifiers
Estadio Nacional „Julio Martínez Prádanos“, Santiago; Referee: Óscar Julián Ruiz Acosta (Colombia); Attendance: 65,000
**CHI:** Claudio Andrés Bravo Muñoz (30/0), Gary Alexis Medel Soto (12/2), Marco Andrés Estrada Quinteros (12/0), Waldo Alonso Ponce Carrizo (14/1) [87.Arturo Erasmo Vidal Pardo (14/0)], Pablo Andrés Contreras Fica (45/1), Carlos Emilio Carmona Tello (8/0), Matías Ariel Fernández Fernández (24/5), Mark Dennis González Hoffmann (31/3) [20.Hugo Patricio Droguett Diocares (13/1)], Jean André Emanuel Beausejour Coliqueo (12/0), Fabián Ariel Orellana Valenzuela (3/1) [85.Hans Alexis Martínez Cabrera (4/0)], Humberto Andrés Suazo Pontivo (31/11). Trainer: Marcelo Alberto Bielsa Caldera (19).
**Goal**: Fabián Ariel Orellana Valenzuela (35).

**611.** 19.11.2008 **SPAIN - CHILE** **3-0(1-0)**
Estadio El Madrigal, Villarreal; Referee: Giorgi Vadachkoria (Georgia); Attendance: 30,000
**CHI:** Claudio Andrés Bravo Muñoz (31/0), Cristián Andrés Álvarez Valenzuela (22/0), Waldo Alonso Ponce Carrizo (15/1), Ismael Ignacio Fuentes Castro (21/1), Rodrigo Álvaro Tello Valenzuela (28/2), Carlos Emilio Carmona Tello (9/0), Matías Ariel Fernández Fernández (25/5), Mauricio Aníbal Isla Isla (3/0), Alexis Alejandro Sánchez Sánchez (18/3), Humberto Andrés Suazo Pontivo (32/11) [87.Jorge Luis Valdivia Toro (27/1)], Fabián Ariel Orellana Valenzuela (4/1). Trainer: Marcelo Alberto Bielsa Caldera (20).

**612.** 18.01.2009 **CHILE - HONDURAS** **0-2(0-0)**
Lockhart Stadium, Fort Lauderdale (United States); Referee: Shane Moody (United States); Attendance: 12,282
**CHI:** Miguel Ángel Pinto Jérez (10/0), Hans Alexis Martínez Cabrera (5/0), Roberto Andrés Cereceda Guajardo (15/0), Albert Alejandro Acevedo Vergara (1/0) [81.Cristóbal Andrés Jorquera Torres (1/0)], Marco Andrés Estrada Quinteros (13/0), Manuel Rolando Iturra Urrutia (29/1), Luis Pedro Figueroa Sepúlveda (11/1) [31.José Pedro Fuenzalida Gana (5/0) [*sent off 34*]], Rodrigo Javier Millar Carvajal (7/0), Fabián Ariel Orellana Valenzuela (5/1), Daúd Jared Gazale Álvarez (4/0) [64.Fernando Andrés Meneses Cornejo (4/0)], Emilio Exequiel Hernández Hernández (2/0). Trainer: Marcelo Alberto Bielsa Caldera (21).

**613.** 11.02.2009 **SOUTH AFRICA - CHILE** **0-2(0-1)**
„Peter Mokaba“ Stadium, Polokwane; Referee: Wilson Mpanisi (Zambia); Attendance: 16,300
**CHI:** Claudio Andrés Bravo Muñoz (32/0), Mauricio Aníbal Isla Isla (4/0), Waldo Alonso Ponce Carrizo (16/1), Marco Andrés Estrada Quinteros (14/0), Arturo Erasmo Vidal Pardo (15/0), Rodrigo Álvaro Tello Valenzuela (29/2) [46.Gonzalo Alejandro Jara Reyes (20/2)], Carlos Emilio Carmona Tello (10/0) [86.Manuel Rolando Iturra Urrutia (30/1)], Jorge Luis Valdivia Toro (28/2) [58.Matías Ariel Fernández Fernández (26/5)], Alexis Alejandro Sánchez Sánchez (19/4), Humberto Andrés Suazo Pontivo (33/11) [90+1.Emilio Exequiel Hernández Hernández (3/0)], Mark Dennis González Hoffmann (32/3) [46.Fabián Ariel Orellana Valenzuela (6/1)]. Trainer: Marcelo Alberto Bielsa Caldera (22).
**Goals**: Jorge Luis Valdivia Toro (45+1), Alexis Alejandro Sánchez Sánchez (67).

**614.** 29.03.2009 **PERU - CHILE** **1-3(1-2)** 19th FIFA WC. Qualifiers
Estadio Monumental, Lima; Referee: Carlos Arecio Amarilla Demarqui (Paraguay); Attendance: 48,700
**CHI:** Claudio Andrés Bravo Muñoz (33/0), Gonzalo Alejandro Jara Reyes (21/2), Waldo Alonso Ponce Carrizo (17/1), Roberto Andrés Cereceda Guajardo (16/0), Mauricio Aníbal Isla Isla (5/0) [63.Pablo Andrés Contreras Fica (46/1)], Carlos Emilio Carmona Tello (11/0) [75.Marco Andrés Estrada Quinteros (15/0)], Matías Ariel Fernández Fernández (27/6) [72.Rodrigo Álvaro Tello Valenzuela (30/2)], Mark Dennis González Hoffmann (33/3), Alexis Alejandro Sánchez Sánchez (20/5), Humberto Andrés Suazo Pontivo (34/12), Jean André Emanuel Beausejour Coliqueo (13/0). Trainer: Marcelo Alberto Bielsa Caldera (23).
**Goals**: Alexis Alejandro Sánchez Sánchez (2), Humberto Andrés Suazo Pontivo (32 penalty), Matías Ariel Fernández Fernández (70).

**615.** 01.04.2009 **CHILE - URUGUAY** **0-0** 19th FIFA WC. Qualifiers
Estadio Nacional „Julio Martínez Prádanos“, Santiago; Referee: Héctor Walter Baldassi (Argentina); Attendance: 55,000
**CHI:** Claudio Andrés Bravo Muñoz (34/0), Pablo Andrés Contreras Fica (47/1), Gonzalo Alejandro Jara Reyes (22/2), Waldo Alonso Ponce Carrizo (18/1), Mauricio Aníbal Isla Isla (6/0) [*sent off 33*], Carlos Emilio Carmona Tello (12/0), Matías Ariel Fernández Fernández (28/6) [60.Fabián Ariel Orellana Valenzuela (7/1)], Mark Dennis González Hoffmann (34/3), Alexis Alejandro Sánchez Sánchez (21/5), Humberto Andrés Suazo Pontivo (35/12), Jean André Emanuel Beausejour Coliqueo (14/0) [38.Manuel Rolando Iturra Urrutia (31/1); 46.Roberto Andrés Cereceda Guajardo (17/0)]. Trainer: Marcelo Alberto Bielsa Caldera (24).

**616.** 27.05.2009 **JAPAN - CHILE** **4-0(2-0)** Kirin Cup
Nagai Stadium, Osaka; Referee: Anders Hermansen (Denmark); Attendance: 43,531
**CHI:** Miguel Ángel Pinto Jérez (11/0), Ismael Ignacio Fuentes Castro (22/1), Gonzalo Alejandro Jara Reyes (23/2), Gary Alexis Medel Soto (13/2) [46.José Pedro Fuenzalida Gana (6/0)], Roberto Andrés Cereceda Guajardo (18/0) [67.José Manuel Rojas Bahamondes (2/1)], Marco Andrés Estrada Quinteros (16/0), Rodrigo Javier Millar Carvajal (8/0), Esteban Efraín Paredes Quintanilla (5/0), Jorge Luis Valdivia Toro (29/2), Fabián Ariel Orellana Valenzuela (8/1) [46.Edson Raúl Puch Cortéz (1/0)], Jean André Emanuel Beausejour Coliqueo (15/0). Trainer: Marcelo Alberto Bielsa Caldera (25).

**617.** 29.05.2009 **BELGIUM - CHILE** **1-1(1-1)** Kirin Cup
Fukuda Denshi Arena, Chiba (Japan); Referee: Minoru Tojo (Japan); Attendance: 6,050
**CHI:** Miguel Ángel Pinto Jérez (12/0), Gonzalo Alejandro Jara Reyes (24/2), Gary Alexis Medel Soto (14/3) [57.José Pedro Fuenzalida Gana (7/0)], Roberto Andrés Cereceda Guajardo (19/0), Marco Andrés Estrada Quinteros (17/0), Manuel Rolando Iturra Urrutia (32/1) [30.Ismael Ignacio Fuentes Castro (23/1)], Rodrigo Javier Millar Carvajal (9/0), Esteban Efraín Paredes Quintanilla (6/0) [80.Daúd Jared Gazale Álvarez (5/0)], Jorge Luis Valdivia Toro (30/2) [55.Braulio Antonio Leal Salvo (1/0)], Fabián Ariel Orellana Valenzuela (9/1), Edson Raúl Puch Cortéz (2/0) [46.Jean André Emanuel Beausejour Coliqueo (16/0)]. Trainer: Marcelo Alberto Bielsa Caldera (26).
**Goal**: Gary Alexis Medel Soto (23).

**618.** 06.06.2009 **PARAGUAY - CHILE** **0-2(0-1)** 19th FIFA WC. Qualifiers
Estadio Defensores del Chaco, Asunción; Referee: Sergio Fabián Pezzotta (Argentina); Attendance: 34,000
**CHI:** Claudio Andrés Bravo Muñoz (35/0), Gonzalo Alejandro Jara Reyes (25/2), Waldo Alonso Ponce Carrizo (19/1), Gary Alexis Medel Soto (15/3), Carlos Emilio Carmona Tello (13/0), Marco Andrés Estrada Quinteros (18/0), Matías Ariel Fernández Fernández (29/7), Mark Dennis González Hoffmann (35/3) [46.Rodrigo Javier Millar Carvajal (10/0)], Alexis Alejandro Sánchez Sánchez (22/5) [88.Fabián Ariel Orellana Valenzuela (10/1)], Humberto Andrés Suazo Pontivo (36/13) [72.Héctor Raúl Mancilla Garcés (4/0)], Jean André Emanuel Beausejour Coliqueo (17/0). Trainer: Marcelo Alberto Bielsa Caldera (27).
**Goals**: Matías Ariel Fernández Fernández (13), Humberto Andrés Suazo Pontivo (50).

**619.** 10.06.2009 **CHILE - BOLIVIA** **4-0(1-0)** 19th FIFA WC. Qualifiers
Estadio Nacional „Julio Martínez Prádanos“, Santiago; Referee: Roberto Carlos Silvera (Uruguay); Attendance: 60,124
**CHI:** Claudio Andrés Bravo Muñoz (36/0), Gonzalo Alejandro Jara Reyes (26/2), Waldo Alonso Ponce Carrizo (20/1), Gary Alexis Medel Soto (16/3), Marco Andrés Estrada Quinteros (19/1), Rodrigo Javier Millar Carvajal (11/0) [84.Mauricio Aníbal Isla Isla (7/0)], Matías Ariel Fernández Fernández (30/7) [68.Jorge Luis Valdivia Toro (31/2)], Mark Dennis González Hoffmann (36/3), Alexis Alejandro Sánchez Sánchez (23/7), Humberto Andrés Suazo Pontivo (37/13) [84.Héctor Raúl Mancilla Garcés (5/0)], Jean André Emanuel Beausejour Coliqueo (18/1). Trainer: Marcelo Alberto Bielsa Caldera (28).
**Goals**: Jean André Emanuel Beausejour Coliqueo (43), Marco Andrés Estrada Quinteros (74), Alexis Alejandro Sánchez Sánchez (78, 88).

**620.** 12.08.2009 **DENMARK - CHILE** **1-2(0-0)**
Brøndby Stadium, København; Referee: Kristinn Jakobson (Iceland); Attendance: 8,700
**CHI:** Miguel Ángel Pinto Jérez (13/0), Gonzalo Alejandro Jara Reyes (27/2), Gary Alexis Medel Soto (17/3), Mauricio Aníbal Isla Isla (8/0), Arturo Erasmo Vidal Pardo (16/0), Carlos Emilio Carmona Tello (14/0), Rodrigo Álvaro Tello Valenzuela (31/2) [60.Roberto Andrés Cereceda Guajardo (20/0)], Matías Ariel Fernández Fernández (31/7), Héctor Raúl Mancilla Garcés (6/0) [40.Esteban Efraín Paredes Quintanilla (7/1)], Alexis Alejandro Sánchez Sánchez (24/8), Jean André Emanuel Beausejour Coliqueo (19/1). Trainer: Marcelo Alberto Bielsa Caldera (29).
**Goals**: Esteban Efraín Paredes Quintanilla (61), Alexis Alejandro Sánchez Sánchez (69).

**621.** 05.09.2009 **CHILE - VENEZUELA** **2-2(1-2)** 19th FIFA WC. Qualifiers
Estadio Monumental „David Arellano“, Santiago; Referee: René Ortubé Betancourt (Bolivia); Attendance: 44,000
**CHI:** Claudio Andrés Bravo Muñoz (37/0), Gonzalo Alejandro Jara Reyes (28/2), Gary Alexis Medel Soto (18/3), Roberto Andrés Cereceda Guajardo (21/0) [46.Rodrigo Javier Millar Carvajal (12/1)], Mauricio Aníbal Isla Isla (9/0), Arturo Erasmo Vidal Pardo (17/1), Carlos Emilio Carmona Tello (15/0) [46.Fabián Ariel Orellana Valenzuela (11/1)], Matías Ariel Fernández Fernández (32/7), Alexis Alejandro Sánchez Sánchez (25/8), Humberto Andrés Suazo Pontivo (38/13) [62.Jorge Luis Valdivia Toro (32/2)], Jean André Emanuel Beausejour Coliqueo (20/1). Trainer: Marcelo Alberto Bielsa Caldera (30).
**Goals**: Arturo Erasmo Vidal Pardo (11), Rodrigo Javier Millar Carvajal (53).

**622.** 09.09.2009 **BRAZIL - CHILE** **4-2(2-1)** 19th FIFA WC. Qualifiers
Estádio Metropolitano „Roberto Santos“, Salvador; Referee: Jorge Luis Larrionda Pietrafesa (Uruguay); Attendance: 30,000
**CHI:** Claudio Andrés Bravo Muñoz (38/0), Gonzalo Alejandro Jara Reyes (29/2), Waldo Alonso Ponce Carrizo (21/1), Gary Alexis Medel Soto (19/3), Arturo Erasmo Vidal Pardo (18/1) [46.Roberto Andrés Cereceda Guajardo (22/0)], Carlos Emilio Carmona Tello (16/0), Rodrigo Javier Millar Carvajal (13/1) [68.Mauricio Aníbal Isla Isla (10/0)], Matías Ariel Fernández Fernández (33/7) [68.Jorge Luis Valdivia Toro (33/2)], Alexis Alejandro Sánchez Sánchez (26/8) [*sent off 77*], Humberto Andrés Suazo Pontivo (39/15), Jean André Emanuel Beausejour Coliqueo (21/1). Trainer: Marcelo Alberto Bielsa Caldera (31).
**Goals**: Humberto Andrés Suazo Pontivo (45+1 penalty, 52).

**623.** 10.10.2009 **COLOMBIA - CHILE** **2-4(1-2)** 19th FIFA WC. Qualifiers
Estadio „Atanasio Girardot“, Medellín; Referee: Víctor Hugo Rivera (Peru); Attendance: 18,000
**CHI:** Claudio Andrés Bravo Muñoz (39/0), Waldo Alonso Ponce Carrizo (22/2), Gary Alexis Medel Soto (20/3), Arturo Erasmo Vidal Pardo (19/1), Carlos Emilio Carmona Tello (17/0), Rodrigo Javier Millar Carvajal (14/1), Matías Ariel Fernández Fernández (34/7) [31.Jorge Luis Valdivia Toro (34/3)], Mark Dennis González Hoffmann (37/3) [63.Gonzalo Antonio Fierro Caniullán (14/1)], Fabián Ariel Orellana Valenzuela (12/2) [*sent off 90+2*], Humberto Andrés Suazo Pontivo (40/16), Jean André Emanuel Beausejour Coliqueo (22/1) [46.Ismael Ignacio Fuentes Castro (24/1)]. Trainer: Marcelo Alberto Bielsa Caldera (32).
**Goals**: Waldo Alonso Ponce Carrizo (34), Humberto Andrés Suazo Pontivo (35), Jorge Luis Valdivia Toro (71), Fabián Ariel Orellana Valenzuela (78).

**624.** 14.10.2009 **CHILE - ECUADOR** **1-0(0-0)** 19th FIFA WC. Qualifiers
Estadio Monumental „David Arellano“, Santiago; Referee: Carlos Arecio Amarilla Demarqui (Paraguay); Attendance: 47,000
**CHI:** Claudio Andrés Bravo Muñoz (40/0), Waldo Alonso Ponce Carrizo (23/2), Gary Alexis Medel Soto (21/3), Roberto Andrés Cereceda Guajardo (23/0) [76.Ismael Ignacio Fuentes Castro (25/1)], Arturo Erasmo Vidal Pardo (20/1) [67.Gonzalo Alejandro Jara Reyes (30/2)], Manuel Rolando Iturra Urrutia (33/1), Rodrigo Javier Millar Carvajal (15/1), Jorge Luis Valdivia Toro (35/3), Alexis Alejandro Sánchez Sánchez (27/8), Humberto Andrés Suazo Pontivo (41/17), Jean André Emanuel Beausejour Coliqueo (23/1) [31.Esteban Efraín Paredes Quintanilla (8/1)]. Trainer: Marcelo Alberto Bielsa Caldera (33).
**Goal**: Humberto Andrés Suazo Pontivo (53).

**625.** 04.11.2009 **CHILE - PARAGUAY** **2-1(0-0)**
Estadio CAP, Talcahuano; Referee: Héctor Walter Baldassi (Argentina); Attendance: n/a
**CHI:** Nery Alexis Veloso Espinoza (1/0), Pablo Andrés Contreras Fica (48/1), Hans Alexis Martínez Cabrera (6/0), Roberto Andrés Cereceda Guajardo (24/0), Charles Mariano Aránguiz Sandoval (1/0), José Pedro Fuenzalida Gana (8/0), Rodrigo Javier Millar Carvajal (16/1), Esteban Efraín Paredes Quintanilla (9/2), Boris Alexis Sagredo Romero (3/0) [46.Paulo Cezar Magalhaes Lobos (1/0)], Juan Gonzalo Lorca Donoso (11/1), Eduardo Jesús Vargas Rojas (1/0) [60.Renato Patricio González De La Hoz (1/1)]. Trainer: Marcelo Alberto Bielsa Caldera (34).
**Goals**: Esteban Efraín Paredes Quintanilla (72), Renato Patricio González De La Hoz (90+1).

**626.** 17.11.2009 **SLOVAKIA - CHILE** **1-2(1-1)**
Štadión Pod Dubňom, Žilina; Referee: István Vad (Hungary); Attendance: 11,072
**CHI:** Claudio Andrés Bravo Muñoz (41/0), Pablo Andrés Contreras Fica (49/1), Gonzalo Alejandro Jara Reyes (31/3), Roberto Andrés Cereceda Guajardo (25/0), Arturo Erasmo Vidal Pardo (21/1), Claudio Andrés del Tránsito Maldonado Rivera (41/1) [71.Carlos Emilio Carmona Tello (18/0)], Rodrigo Javier Millar Carvajal (17/1), Rodrigo Álvaro Tello Valenzuela (32/2) [46.Fabián Ariel Orellana Valenzuela (13/2)], Jorge Luis Valdivia Toro (36/3) [15.Matías Ariel Fernández Fernández (35/7)], Gonzalo Antonio Fierro Caniullán (15/1), Esteban Efraín Paredes Quintanilla (10/3) [68.Edson Raúl Puch Cortéz (3/0)]. Trainer: Marcelo Alberto Bielsa Caldera (35).
**Goals**: Gonzalo Alejandro Jara Reyes (9), Esteban Efraín Paredes Quintanilla (55).

**627.** 20.01.2010 **CHILE - PANAMA** **2-1(0-0)**
Estadio „Francisco Sánchez Rumoroso“, Coquimbo; Referee: Martín Emilio Vázquez Broquetas (Uruguay); Attendance: 15,000
**CHI:** Cristopher Benjamín Toselli Ríos (1/0), Hans Alexis Martínez Cabrera (7/0), Marco Andrés Estrada Quinteros (20/1), Roberto Andrés Cereceda Guajardo (26/0) [73.José Víctor Martínez Díaz (1/0)], Charles Mariano Aránguiz Sandoval (2/0), José Pedro Fuenzalida Gana (9/0), Edson Raúl Puch Cortéz (4/0) [82.Eduardo Jesús Vargas Rojas (2/0)], Rodrigo Javier Millar Carvajal (18/1), Daúd Jared Gazale Álvarez (6/0), Esteban Efraín Paredes Quintanilla (11/5), Emilio Exequiel Hernández Hernández (4/0) [85.Francisco Fernando Castro Gamboa (1/0)]. Trainer: Marcelo Alberto Bielsa Caldera (36).
**Goals**: Esteban Efraín Paredes Quintanilla (51, 53).

**628.** 31.03.2010 **CHILE - VENEZUELA** **0-0**
Estadio Municipal „Germán Becker“, Temuco; Referee: Roberto Carlos Silvera (Uruguay); Attendance: 18,000
**CHI:** Luis Antonio Marín Barahona (1/0), Hans Alexis Martínez Cabrera (8/0), Gary Alexis Medel Soto (22/3), Charles Mariano Aránguiz Sandoval (3/0), José Pedro Fuenzalida Gana (10/0) [78.Juan René Abarca Fuentes (1/0)], Felipe Ignacio Seymour Dobud (1/0), Rodrigo Javier Millar Carvajal (19/1), Esteban Efraín Paredes Quintanilla (12/5) [32.Ronald Damián González Tabilo (1/0); 78.Carlos Esteban Ross Cotal (1/0)], Emilio Exequiel Hernández Hernández (5/0), Gonzalo Antonio Fierro Caniullán (16/1), Eduardo Jesús Vargas Rojas (3/0). Trainer: Marcelo Alberto Bielsa Caldera (37).

**629.** 05.05.2010 **CHILE – TRINIDAD & TOBAGO** **2-0(1-0)**
Estadio Tierra de Campeones, Iquique; Referee: Jorge Joaquín Antequera (Bolivia); Attendance: 8,500
**CHI:** Luis Antonio Marín Barahona (2/0), Carlos Alfredo Labrín Candia (1/0) [46.Kevin Andrew Harbottle Carrasco (1/0)], Hans Alexis Martínez Cabrera (9/0), Roberto Andrés Cereceda Guajardo (27/0), Fernando Andrés Meneses Cornejo (5/0), Sebastián Patricio Toro Hormazábal (1/1), Gary Alexis Medel Soto (23/3), José Pedro Fuenzalida Gana (11/0) [69.Juan Carlos Espinoza (1/0)], Emilio Exequiel Hernández Hernández (6/0), Pedro Andrés Morales Flores (9/1) [83.Rafael Antonio Caroca Cordero (2/0)], Daúd Jared Gazale Álvarez (7/0) [76.Francisco Javier Pizarro Cartes (2/0)]. Trainer: Marcelo Alberto Bielsa Caldera (38).
**Goals**: Pedro Andrés Morales Flores (2), Sebastián Patricio Toro Hormazábal (49).

**630.** 16.05.2010 **MEXICO - CHILE** **1-0(1-0)**
Estadio Azteca, Ciudad de México“, Santiago; Referee: Mark Geiger (United States); Attendance: 85,000
**CHI:** Luis Antonio Marín Barahona (3/0), Ismael Ignacio Fuentes Castro (26/1), Waldo Alonso Ponce Carrizo (24/2), Roberto Andrés Cereceda Guajardo (28/0) [46.Gonzalo Alejandro Jara Reyes (32/3)], Arturo Erasmo Vidal Pardo (22/1), José Pedro Fuenzalida Gana (12/0) [75.Francisco Fernando Castro Gamboa (2/0)], Rodrigo Javier Millar Carvajal (20/1), Matías Ariel Fernández Fernández (36/7), Pedro Andrés Morales Flores (10/1) [58.Manuel Rolando Iturra Urrutia (34/1) [*sent off 60*]], Jorge Luis Valdivia Toro (37/3), Jaime Andrés Valdés Zapata (3/0) [46.Jean André Emanuel Beausejour Coliqueo (24/1)]. Trainer: Marcelo Alberto Bielsa Caldera (39).

**631.** 26.05.2010 **CHILE - ZAMBIA** **3-0(0-0)**
Estadio Municipal, Calama; Referee: Gabriel Norberto Favale (Argentina); Attendance: 12,000
**CHI:** Claudio Andrés Bravo Muñoz (42/0), Pablo Andrés Contreras Fica (50/1), Ismael Ignacio Fuentes Castro (27/1) [46.Mauricio Aníbal Isla Isla (11/0)], Gonzalo Alejandro Jara Reyes (33/3) [46.Marco Andrés Estrada Quinteros (21/1)], Roberto Andrés Cereceda Guajardo (29/0) [46.Alexis Alejandro Sánchez Sánchez (28/10)], Carlos Emilio Carmona Tello (19/0), Esteban Efraín Paredes Quintanilla (13/5) [46.Jean André Emanuel Beausejour Coliqueo (25/1)], Rodrigo Álvaro Tello Valenzuela (33/2), Jorge Luis Valdivia Toro (38/4), Gonzalo Antonio Fierro Caniullán (17/1), Fabián Ariel Orellana Valenzuela (14/2). Trainer: Marcelo Alberto Bielsa Caldera (40).
**Goals**: Alexis Alejandro Sánchez Sánchez (52, 83), Jorge Luis Valdivia Toro (85).

**632.** 30.05.2010 **CHILE – NORTHERN IRELAND** **1-0(1-0)**
Estadio Bicentenario „Nelson Oyarzún Arenas“, Chillán; Referee: Líber Tabaré Prudente González (Uruguay); Attendance: 12,000
**CHI:** Miguel Ángel Pinto Jérez (14/0), Pablo Andrés Contreras Fica (51/1), Ismael Ignacio Fuentes Castro (28/1), Roberto Andrés Cereceda Guajardo (30/0), Mauricio Aníbal Isla Isla (12/0), Arturo Erasmo Vidal Pardo (23/1) [75.Carlos Esteban Ross Cotal (2/0)], Marco Andrés Estrada Quinteros (22/1), Matías Ariel Fernández Fernández (37/7) [90.Felipe Alejandro Gutiérrez Leiva (1/0)], Esteban Efraín Paredes Quintanilla (14/6), Gonzalo Antonio Fierro Caniullán (18/1), Mark Dennis González Hoffmann (38/3) [63.Fabián Ariel Orellana Valenzuela (15/2)]. Trainer: Marcelo Alberto Bielsa Caldera (41).
**Goal**: Esteban Efraín Paredes Quintanilla (30).

**633.** 31.05.2010 **CHILE - ISRAEL** **3-0(1-0)**
Estadio Municipal, Concepción; Referee: Antonio Arias Alvarenga (Paraguay); Attendance: 25,000
**CHI:** Claudio Andrés Bravo Muñoz (43/0), Waldo Alonso Ponce Carrizo (25/2), Gonzalo Alejandro Jara Reyes (34/3), Gary Alexis Medel Soto (24/3) [79.José Víctor Martínez Díaz (2/0)], Rodrigo Álvaro Tello Valenzuela (34/3), Carlos Emilio Carmona Tello (20/0), Rodrigo Javier Millar Carvajal (21/1) [77.Luis Ignacio Casanova Sandoval (1/0)], Jorge Luis Valdivia Toro (39/4) [46.Felipe Alejandro Gutiérrez Leiva (2/0)], Alexis Alejandro Sánchez Sánchez (29/11) [70.Bernardo Andrés Campos Araniba (1/0)], Jean André Emanuel Beausejour Coliqueo (26/1), Humberto Andrés Suazo Pontivo (42/18) [46.Fabián Ariel Orellana Valenzuela (16/2)]. Trainer: Marcelo Alberto Bielsa Caldera (42).
**Goals**: Humberto Andrés Suazo Pontivo (19), Alexis Alejandro Sánchez Sánchez (49), Rodrigo Álvaro Tello Valenzuela (90).

**634.** 16.06.2010 **HONDURAS - CHILE** **0-1(0-1)** 19th FIFA WC. Group Stage.
Mbombela Stadium, Nelspruit (South Africa); Referee: Eddy Allen Maillet Guyto (Seychelles); Attendance: 32,664
**CHI:** Claudio Andrés Bravo Muñoz (Cap) (44/0), Mauricio Aníbal Isla Isla (13/0), Gary Alexis Medel Soto (25/3), Waldo Alonso Ponce Carrizo (26/2), Arturo Erasmo Vidal Pardo (24/1) [81.Pablo Andrés Contreras Fica (52/1)], Rodrigo Javier Millar Carvajal (22/1) [52.Gonzalo Alejandro Jara Reyes (35/3)], Carlos Emilio Carmona Tello (21/0), Matías Ariel Fernández Fernández (38/7), Jorge Luis Valdivia Toro (40/4) [87.Mark Dennis González Hoffmann (39/3)], Alexis Alejandro Sánchez Sánchez (30/11), Jean André Emanuel Beausejour Coliqueo (27/2). Trainer: Marcelo Alberto Bielsa Caldera (43).
**Goal**: Jean André Emanuel Beausejour Coliqueo (34).

**635.** 21.06.2010 **CHILE - SWITZERLAND** **1-0(0-0)** 19th FIFA WC. Group Stage.
„Nelson Mandela“ Bay Stadium, Port Elizabeth (South Africa); Referee: Khalil Ibrahim Al Ghamdi (Saudi Arabia); Attendance: 34,872
**CHI:** Claudio Andrés Bravo Muñoz (Cap) (45/0), Mauricio Aníbal Isla Isla (14/0), Gary Alexis Medel Soto (26/3), Waldo Alonso Ponce Carrizo (27/2), Gonzalo Alejandro Jara Reyes (36/3), Arturo Erasmo Vidal Pardo (25/1) [46.Jorge Luis Valdivia Toro (41/4)], Carlos Emilio Carmona Tello (22/0), Matías Ariel Fernández Fernández (39/7) [65.Esteban Efraín Paredes Quintanilla (15/6)], Alexis Alejandro Sánchez Sánchez (31/11), Humberto Andrés Suazo Pontivo (43/18) [46.Mark Dennis González Hoffmann (40/4)], Jean André Emanuel Beausejour Coliqueo (28/2). Trainer: Marcelo Alberto Bielsa Caldera (44).
**Goal**: Mark Dennis González Hoffmann (75).

**636.** 25.06.2010 **CHILE - SPAIN** **1-2(0-2)** 19th FIFA WC. Group Stage.
Loftus Versfeld Stadium, Pretoria (South Africa); Referee: Marco Antonio Rodríguez Moreno (Mexico); Attendance: 41,958
**CHI:** Claudio Andrés Bravo Muñoz (Cap) (46/0), Mauricio Aníbal Isla Isla (15/0), Gary Alexis Medel Soto (27/3), Waldo Alonso Ponce Carrizo (28/2), Gonzalo Alejandro Jara Reyes (37/3), Arturo Erasmo Vidal Pardo (26/1), Marco Andrés Estrada Quinteros (23/1) [*sent off 37*], Mark Dennis González Hoffmann (41/4) [46.Rodrigo Javier Millar Carvajal (23/2)], Jorge Luis Valdivia Toro (42/4) [46.Esteban Efraín Paredes Quintanilla (16/6)], Alexis Alejandro Sánchez Sánchez (32/11) [65.Fabián Ariel Orellana Valenzuela (17/2)], Jean André Emanuel Beausejour Coliqueo (29/2). Trainer: Marcelo Alberto Bielsa Caldera (45).
**Goal**: Rodrigo Javier Millar Carvajal (47).

**637.** 28.06.2010 **BRAZIL - CHILE** **3-0(2-0)** 19th FIFA WC. 2nd Round.
Ellis Park Stadium, Johannesburg (South Africa); Referee: Howard Melton Webb (England); Attendance: 54,096
**CHI:** Claudio Andrés Bravo Muñoz (Cap) (47/0), Mauricio Aníbal Isla Isla (16/0) [62.Rodrigo Javier Millar Carvajal (24/2)], Pablo Andrés Contreras Fica (53/1) [46.Jorge Luis Valdivia Toro (43/4)], Gonzalo Alejandro Jara Reyes (38/3), Ismael Ignacio Fuentes Castro (29/1), Arturo Erasmo Vidal Pardo (27/1), Carlos Emilio Carmona Tello (23/0), Jean André Emanuel Beausejour Coliqueo (30/2), Alexis Alejandro Sánchez Sánchez (33/11), Humberto Andrés Suazo Pontivo (44/18), Mark Dennis González Hoffmann (42/4) [46.Rodrigo Álvaro Tello Valenzuela (35/3)]. Trainer: Marcelo Alberto Bielsa Caldera (46).

**638.** 07.09.2010 **UKRAINE - CHILE** **2-1(1-0)**
„Valeriy Lobanovskiy“ Stadium, Kyiv; Referee: Vital Sevastsyanik (Belarus); Attendance: 10,000
**CHI:** Luis Antonio Marín Barahona (4/0), Carlos Alfredo Labrín Candia (2/0), Osvaldo Alexis González Sepúlveda (4/0), Mauricio Aníbal Isla Isla (17/1), Rodrigo Álvaro Tello Valenzuela (36/3) [46.Eugenio Esteban Mena Reveco (1/0)], Marco Andrés Estrada Quinteros (24/1) [73.Charles Mariano Aránguiz Sandoval (4/0)], Rodrigo Javier Millar Carvajal (25/2), Fernando Andrés Meneses Cornejo (6/0) [57.José Pedro Fuenzalida Gana (13/0)], Pedro Andrés Morales Flores (11/1), Emilio Exequiel Hernández Hernández (7/0), Héctor Raúl Mancilla Garcés (7/0). Trainer: Marcelo Alberto Bielsa Caldera (47).
**Goal**: Mauricio Aníbal Isla Isla (86).

**639.** 09.10.2010 **UNITED ARAB EMIRATES - CHILE** **0-2(0-2)**
Zayed Sport City, Abu Dhabi; Referee: Khalil Ibrahim Al Ghamdi (Saudi Arabia); Attendance: 600
**CHI:** Luis Antonio Marín Barahona (5/0), Hans Alexis Martínez Cabrera (10/0), Roberto Andrés Cereceda Guajardo (31/1), Osvaldo Alexis González Sepúlveda (5/0), José Pedro Fuenzalida Gana (14/0), Claudio Andrés del Tránsito Maldonado Rivera (42/1) [73.Sebastián Patricio Toro Hormazábal (2/1)], Rodrigo Javier Millar Carvajal (26/2), Mark Dennis González Hoffmann (43/4) [58.Carlos Andrés Villanueva Roland (13/1)], Pedro Andrés Morales Flores (12/2) [46.Esteban Efraín Paredes Quintanilla (17/6)], Emilio Exequiel Hernández Hernández (8/0) [46.Fernando Andrés Meneses Cornejo (7/0)], Héctor Raúl Mancilla Garcés (8/0) [68.Paulo Cezar Magalhaes Lobos (2/0)]. Trainer: Marcelo Alberto Bielsa Caldera (48).
**Goals**: Roberto Andrés Cereceda Guajardo (6), Pedro Andrés Morales Flores (37).

**640.** 12.10.2010 **OMAN - CHILE** **0-1(0-1)**
Sultan Qaboos Sports Complex, Muscat; Referee: Abdullah Al Bloushi (Qatar); Attendance: 8,000
**CHI:** Luis Antonio Marín Barahona (6/0), Hans Alexis Martínez Cabrera (11/0), Roberto Andrés Cereceda Guajardo (32/1), Osvaldo Alexis González Sepúlveda (6/0), Claudio Andrés del Tránsito Maldonado Rivera (43/1), Rodrigo Javier Millar Carvajal (27/2), Fernando Andrés Meneses Cornejo (8/0), Pedro Andrés Morales Flores (13/3) [46.Esteban Efraín Paredes Quintanilla (18/6)], Mark Dennis González Hoffmann (44/4), Emilio Exequiel Hernández Hernández (9/0) [88.Paulo Cezar Magalhaes Lobos (3/0)], Héctor Raúl Mancilla Garcés (9/0) [66.José Pedro Fuenzalida Gana (15/0)]. Trainer: Marcelo Alberto Bielsa Caldera (49).
**Goal**: Pedro Andrés Morales Flores (21).

**641.** 17.11.2010 **CHILE - URUGUAY** **2-0(1-0)**
Estadio Monumental „David Arellano“, Santiago; Referee: Carlos Manuel Torres (Paraguay), Attendance: 45,017
**CHI:** Claudio Andrés Bravo Muñoz (48/0), Gonzalo Alejandro Jara Reyes (39/3), Waldo Alonso Ponce Carrizo (29/2), Gary Alexis Medel Soto (28/3) [90.Claudio Andrés del Tránsito Maldonado Rivera (44/1)], Mauricio Aníbal Isla Isla (18/1) [77.Rodrigo Javier Millar Carvajal (28/2)], Arturo Erasmo Vidal Pardo (28/2), Marco Andrés Estrada Quinteros (25/1) [65.Carlos Emilio Carmona Tello (24/0)], Mark Dennis González Hoffmann (45/4) [76.Jean André Emanuel Beausejour Coliqueo (31/2)], Fabián Ariel Orellana Valenzuela (18/2) [71.Pedro Andrés Morales Flores (14/3)], Alexis Alejandro Sánchez Sánchez (34/12), Humberto Andrés Suazo Pontivo (45/18) [61.Esteban Efraín Paredes Quintanilla (19/6)]. Trainer: Marcelo Alberto Bielsa Caldera (50).
**Goals**: Alexis Alejandro Sánchez Sánchez (38), Arturo Erasmo Vidal Pardo (75).

**642.** 22.01.2011 **UNITED STATES - CHILE** **1-1(0-0)**
The Home Depot Center, Carson; Referee: Francisco Chacón Gutiérrez (Mexico); Attendance: 18,580
**CHI:** Paulo Andrés Garcés Contreras (1/0), Juan René Abarca Fuentes (2/0), Eugenio Esteban Mena Reveco (2/0), Sebastián Patricio Toro Hormazábal (3/1), Luis Pedro Figueroa Sepúlveda (12/1) [46.Felipe Ignacio Seymour Dobud (2/0)], Paulo Cezar Magalhaes Lobos (4/0), Francisco Andrés Silva Gajardo (2/0), Fernando Andrés Meneses Cornejo (9/0), Esteban Efraín Paredes Quintanilla (20/7), Daúd Jared Gazale Álvarez (8/0) [71.Lucas Domínguez Irarrázabal (1/0)], Edson Raúl Puch Cortés (5/0). Trainer: Marcelo Alberto Bielsa Caldera (51).
**Goal**: Esteban Efraín Paredes Quintanilla (53).

**643.** 26.03.2011 **PORTUGAL - CHILE** **1-1(1-1)**
Estádio „Dr. Magalhães Pessoa“, Leiria; Referee: Kevin Blom (Holland); Attendance: 10,694
**CHI:** Claudio Andrés Bravo Muñoz (49/0), Pablo Andrés Contreras Fica (54/1), Waldo Alonso Ponce Carrizo (30/2), Gonzalo Alejandro Jara Reyes (40/3), Gary Alexis Medel Soto (29/3), Mauricio Aníbal Isla Isla (19/1) [83.Fabián Ariel Orellana Valenzuela (19/2)], Arturo Erasmo Vidal Pardo (29/2), Carlos Emilio Carmona Tello (25/0), Matías Ariel Fernández Fernández (40/8), Jean André Emanuel Beausejour Coliqueo (32/2) [67.Gonzalo Antonio Fierro Caniullán (19/1)], Alexis Alejandro Sánchez Sánchez (35/12). Trainer: Claudio Daniel Borghi Bidos (1).
**Goal**: Matías Ariel Fernández Fernández (42).

**644.** 29.03.2011 **CHILE - COLOMBIA** **2-0(2-0)**
Kyocera Stadion, Den Haag (Holland); Referee: Pieter Vink (Holland); Attendance: 4,000
**CHI:** Claudio Andrés Bravo Muñoz (50/0), Pablo Andrés Contreras Fica (55/1) [87.Osvaldo Alexis González Sepúlveda (7/0)], Waldo Alonso Ponce Carrizo (31/2), Gonzalo Alejandro Jara Reyes (41/3), Gary Alexis Medel Soto (30/3), Mauricio Aníbal Isla Isla (20/1), Arturo Erasmo Vidal Pardo (30/2) [81.Marco Andrés Estrada Quinteros (26/1)], Matías Ariel Fernández Fernández (41/9), Jean André Emanuel Beausejour Coliqueo (33/3) [76.Cristóbal Andrés Jorquera Torres (2/0)], Héctor Raúl Mancilla Garcés (10/0) [63.Carlos Andrés Muñoz Rojas (1/0)], Alexis Alejandro Sánchez Sánchez (36/12). Trainer: Claudio Daniel Borghi Bidos (2).
**Goals**: Matías Ariel Fernández Fernández (6), Jean André Emanuel Beausejour Coliqueo (30).

**645.** 19.06.2011 **CHILE - ESTONIA** **4-0(3-0)**
Estadio Monumental „David Arellano“, Santiago; Referee: Martín Emilio Vázquez Broquetas (Uruguay); Attendance: 18,000
**CHI:** Claudio Andrés Bravo Muñoz (51/0) [69.Miguel Ángel Pinto Jérez (15/0)], Pablo Andrés Contreras Fica (56/1), Waldo Alonso Ponce Carrizo (32/3), Mauricio Aníbal Isla Isla (21/1) [73.Gonzalo Antonio Fierro Caniullán (20/1)], Gonzalo Alejandro Jara Reyes (42/3), Carlos Emilio Carmona Tello (26/0) [60.Jorge Luis Valdivia Toro (44/4)], Marco Andrés Estrada Quinteros (27/1), Matías Ariel Fernández Fernández (42/10) [67.Luis Antonio Jiménez Garcés (21/2)], Jean André Emanuel Beausejour Coliqueo (34/3) [75.Felipe Alejandro Gutiérrez Leiva (3/0)], Humberto Andrés Suazo Pontivo (46/19), Alexis Alejandro Sánchez Sánchez (37/13) [71.Esteban Efraín Paredes Quintanilla (21/7)]. Trainer: Claudio Daniel Borghi Bidos (3).
**Goals**: Matías Ariel Fernández Fernández (21), Waldo Alonso Ponce Carrizo (41), Humberto Andrés Suazo Pontivo (45 penalty), Alexis Alejandro Sánchez Sánchez (50).

**646.** 23.06.2011 **PARAGUAY - CHILE** **0-0**
Estadio Defensores del Chaco, Asunción; Referee: Paulo César Oliveira (Brazil); Attendance: 2,865
**CHI:** Claudio Andrés Bravo Muñoz (52/0), Pablo Andrés Contreras Fica (57/1), Waldo Alonso Ponce Carrizo (33/3), Gonzalo Alejandro Jara Reyes (43/3) [75.Francisco Andrés Silva Gajardo (3/0)], Gary Alexis Medel Soto (31/3) [75.Arturo Erasmo Vidal Pardo (31/2)], Marco Andrés Estrada Quinteros (28/1) [82.Carlos Emilio Carmona Tello (27/0)], Gonzalo Antonio Fierro Caniullán (21/1) [62.Fernando Andrés Meneses Cornejo (10/0)], Luis Antonio Jiménez Garcés (22/2) [70.Felipe Alejandro Gutiérrez Leiva (4/0)], Esteban Efraín Paredes Quintanilla (22/7), Jean André Emanuel Beausejour Coliqueo (35/3), Diego Iván Rubio Köstner (1/0) [63.Carlos Andrés Muñoz Rojas (2/0)]. Trainer: Claudio Daniel Borghi Bidos (4).

**647.** 04.07.2011 **CHILE - MEXICO** **2-1(0-1)** 43rd Copa América. Group Stage.
Estadio del Bicentenario, San Juan (Argentina); Referee: Juan Ernesto Soto Arevalo (Venezuela); Attendance: n/a
**CHI:** Claudio Andrés Bravo Muñoz (53/0), Pablo Andrés Contreras Fica (58/1), Waldo Alonso Ponce Carrizo (34/3), Gonzalo Alejandro Jara Reyes (44/3), Mauricio Aníbal Isla Isla (22/1), Arturo Erasmo Vidal Pardo (32/3), Gary Alexis Medel Soto (32/3), Jean André Emanuel Beausejour Coliqueo (36/3) [60.Esteban Efraín Paredes Quintanilla (23/8)], Matías Ariel Fernández Fernández (43/10) [83.Carlos Emilio Carmona Tello (28/0)], Alexis Alejandro Sánchez Sánchez (38/13), Humberto Andrés Suazo Pontivo (47/19) [90+2.Marco Andrés Estrada Quinteros (29/1)]. Trainer: Claudio Daniel Borghi Bidos (5).
**Goals**: Esteban Efraín Paredes Quintanilla (66), Arturo Erasmo Vidal Pardo (72).

**648.** 08.07.2011 **URUGUAY - CHILE** **1-1(0-0)** 43rd Copa América. Group Stage.
Estadio Malvinas Argentinas, Mendoza (Argentina); Referee: Carlos Arecio Amarilla Demarqui (Paraguay); Attendance: 38,000
**CHI:** Claudio Andrés Bravo Muñoz (54/0), Pablo Andrés Contreras Fica (59/1), Waldo Alonso Ponce Carrizo (35/3), Gonzalo Alejandro Jara Reyes (45/3) [60.Jorge Luis Valdivia Toro (45/4)], Mauricio Aníbal Isla Isla (23/1), Gary Alexis Medel Soto (33/3), Arturo Erasmo Vidal Pardo (33/3), Jean André Emanuel Beausejour Coliqueo (37/3) [74.Carlos Emilio Carmona Tello (29/0)], Luis Antonio Jiménez Garcés (23/2), Alexis Alejandro Sánchez Sánchez (39/14), Humberto Andrés Suazo Pontivo (48/19) [74.Esteban Efraín Paredes Quintanilla (24/8)]. Trainer: Claudio Daniel Borghi Bidos (6).
**Goal**: Alexis Alejandro Sánchez Sánchez (50).

**649.** 12.07.2011 **CHILE - PERU** **1-0(0-0)** 43rd Copa América. Group Stage.
Estadio Malvinas Argentinas, Mendoza (Argentina); Referee: Sálvio Spínola Fagundes Filho (Brazil); Attendance: n/a
**CHI:** Miguel Ángel Pinto Jérez (16/0), Gonzalo Alejandro Jara Reyes (46/3), Waldo Alonso Ponce Carrizo (36/3), Marco Andrés Estrada Quinteros (30/1), Gonzalo Antonio Fierro Caniullán (22/1) [58.Jorge Luis Valdivia Toro (46/4)], Francisco Andrés Silva Gajardo (4/0) [78.Gary Alexis Medel Soto (34/3)], Carlos Emilio Carmona Tello (30/0), Jean André Emanuel Beausejour Coliqueo (38/3) [*sent off 62*], Luis Antonio Jiménez Garcés (24/2), Esteban Efraín Paredes Quintanilla (25/8) [58.Alexis Alejandro Sánchez Sánchez (40/14)], Humberto Andrés Suazo Pontivo (49/19). Trainer: Claudio Daniel Borghi Bidos (7).
**Goal**: André Martín Carrillo Díaz (90+2 own goal).

**650.** 17.07.2011 **CHILE - VENEZUELA** **1-2(0-1)** 43rd Copa América. Quarter-Finals.
Estadio del Bicentenario, San Juan (Argentina); Referee: Carlos Alfredo Vera Rodríguez (Ecuador); Attendance: n/a
**CHI:** Claudio Andrés Bravo Muñoz (55/0), Pablo Andrés Contreras Fica (60/1), Waldo Alonso Ponce Carrizo (37/3), Gonzalo Alejandro Jara Reyes (47/3) [62.Esteban Efraín Paredes Quintanilla (26/8)], Mauricio Aníbal Isla Isla (24/1), Gary Alexis Medel Soto (35/3) [*sent off 82*], Carlos Emilio Carmona Tello (31/0) [46.Jorge Luis Valdivia Toro (47/4)], Arturo Erasmo Vidal Pardo (34/3), Luis Antonio Jiménez Garcés (25/2) [83.Carlos Andrés Muñoz Rojas (3/0)], Alexis Alejandro Sánchez Sánchez (41/14), Humberto Andrés Suazo Pontivo (50/20). Trainer: Claudio Daniel Borghi Bidos (8).
**Goals**: Humberto Andrés Suazo Pontivo (69).

**651.** 10.08.2011 **FRANCE - CHILE** **1-1(1-0)**
Stade de la Mosson, Montpellier; Referee: Stuart Steven Attwell (England); Attendance: 30,000
**CHI:** Claudio Andrés Bravo Muñoz (56/0), Pablo Andrés Contreras Fica (61/1) [90.Gonzalo Alejandro Jara Reyes (48/3)], Waldo Alonso Ponce Carrizo (38/3), Arturo Erasmo Vidal Pardo (35/3), Mauricio Aníbal Isla Isla (25/1), Carlos Emilio Carmona Tello (32/0) [85.Marco Andrés Estrada Quinteros (31/1)], Gary Alexis Medel Soto (36/3) [46.Felipe Ignacio Seymour Dobud (3/0)], Jean André Emanuel Beausejour Coliqueo (39/3) [81.Fabián Ariel Orellana Valenzuela (20/2)], Jorge Luis Valdivia Toro (48/4), Luis Antonio Jiménez Garcés (26/2) [46.Alexis Alejandro Sánchez Sánchez (42/14)], Diego Iván Rubio Köstner (2/0) [65.Nicolás Andrés Córdova San Cristóbal (4/1)]. Trainer: Claudio Daniel Borghi Bidos (9).
**Goal**: Nicolás Andrés Córdova San Cristóbal (77).

**652.** 02.09.2011 **SPAIN - CHILE** **3-2(0-2)**
AFG-Arena, St. Gallen (Switzerland); Referee: Jerome Laperrier (Switzerland); Attendance: 14,605
**CHI:** Claudio Andrés Bravo Muñoz (57/0), Pablo Andrés Contreras Fica (62/1) [*sent off 82*], Arturo Erasmo Vidal Pardo (36/3), Gonzalo Alejandro Jara Reyes (49/3), Gary Alexis Medel Soto (37/3) [88.Marco Andrés Estrada Quinteros (32/1)], Mauricio Aníbal Isla Isla (26/2) [83.Fernando Andrés Meneses Cornejo (11/0)], Carlos Emilio Carmona Tello (33/0), Jean André Emanuel Beausejour Coliqueo (40/3) [78.Felipe Alejandro Gutiérrez Leiva (5/0)], Jorge Luis Valdivia Toro (49/4) [85.Fabián Ariel Orellana Valenzuela (21/2)], Alexis Alejandro Sánchez Sánchez (43/14), Eduardo Jesús Vargas Rojas (4/1) [57.Felipe Ignacio Seymour Dobud (4/0)]. Trainer: Claudio Daniel Borghi Bidos (10).
**Goals**: Mauricio Aníbal Isla Isla (10), Eduardo Jesús Vargas Rojas (20).

**653.** 04.09.2011 **MEXICO - CHILE** **1-0(0-0)**
Estadi Cornellà-El Prat, Barcelona (Spain); Referee: César Muñiz Fernández (Spain); Attendance: 7,210
**CHI:** Claudio Andrés Bravo Muñoz (58/0) [46.Miguel Ángel Pinto Jérez (17/0)], Gerson Elías Acevedo Rojas (1/0) [46.Gary Alexis Medel Soto (38/3)], Miguel Ángel Aceval Muñoz (1/0), Christian Alberto Vilches González (1/0), Charles Mariano Aránguiz Sandoval (5/0) [67.Mauricio Aníbal Isla Isla (27/2)], Arturo Erasmo Vidal Pardo (37/3), Felipe Ignacio Seymour Dobud (5/0) [62.Jean André Emanuel Beausejour Coliqueo (41/3)], Marco Andrés Estrada Quinteros (33/1), Nicolás Andrés Córdova San Cristóbal (5/1), Fabián Ariel Orellana Valenzuela (22/2) [62.Eduardo Jesús Vargas Rojas (5/1)], Diego Iván Rubio Köstner (3/0) [39.Alexis Alejandro Sánchez Sánchez (44/14)]. Trainer: Claudio Daniel Borghi Bidos (11).

**654.** 07.10.2011 **ARGENTINA - CHILE** **4-1(2-0)** 20th FIFA WC. Qualifiers
Estadio Monumental „Antonio Vespucio Liberti", Buenos Aires; Referee: Wilmar Alexander Roldán Pérez (Colombia); Attendance: 26,161
**CHI:** Claudio Andrés Bravo Muñoz (59/0), Waldo Alonso Ponce Carrizo (39/3), Mauricio Aníbal Isla Isla (28/2), Gonzalo Alejandro Jara Reyes (50/3), Carlos Emilio Carmona Tello (34/0), Arturo Erasmo Vidal Pardo (38/3), Matías Ariel Fernández Fernández (44/11) [81.Cristóbal Andrés Jorquera Torres (3/0)], Jorge Luis Valdivia Toro (50/4), Jean André Emanuel Beausejour Coliqueo (42/3) [55.Marcos Andrés González Salazar (7/0)], Mauricio Ricardo Pinilla Ferrera (22/5) [55.Eduardo Jesús Vargas Rojas (6/1)], Humberto Andrés Suazo Pontivo (51/20). Trainer: Claudio Daniel Borghi Bidos (12).
**Goal**: Matías Ariel Fernández Fernández (59).

**655.** 11.10.2011 **CHILE - PERU** **4-2(2-0)** 20th FIFA WC. Qualifiers
Estadio Monumental „David Arellano", Santiago; Referee: Raúl Orosco Delgadillo (Bolivia); Attendance: 39,000
**CHI:** Claudio Andrés Bravo Muñoz (60/0), Marcos Andrés González Salazar (8/0), Waldo Alonso Ponce Carrizo (40/4), Mauricio Aníbal Isla Isla (29/2), Gonzalo Alejandro Jara Reyes (51/3), Gary Alexis Medel Soto (39/4), Arturo Erasmo Vidal Pardo (39/3), Jorge Luis Valdivia Toro (51/4) [90.Carlos Emilio Carmona Tello (35/0)], Jean André Emanuel Beausejour Coliqueo (43/3), Humberto Andrés Suazo Pontivo (52/21) [72.Esteban Efraín Paredes Quintanilla (27/8)], Eduardo Jesús Vargas Rojas (7/2) [84.Matías Ariel Fernández Fernández (45/11)]. Trainer: Claudio Daniel Borghi Bidos (13).
**Goals**: Waldo Alonso Ponce Carrizo (2), Eduardo Jesús Vargas Rojas (18), Gary Alexis Medel Soto (47), Humberto Andrés Suazo Pontivo (63 penalty).

**656.** 11.11.2011 **URUGUAY - CHILE** **4-0(2-0)** 20th FIFA WC. Qualifiers
Estadio Centenario, Montevideo; Referee: Héctor Walter Baldassi (Argentina); Attendance: 40,500
**CHI:** Claudio Andrés Bravo Muñoz (61/0), Pablo Andrés Contreras Fica (63/1), Marcos Andrés González Salazar (9/0), Waldo Alonso Ponce Carrizo (41/4), Matías Daniel Campos Toro (1/0), Marcelo Alfonso Díaz Rojas (1/0) [61.Esteban Efraín Paredes Quintanilla (28/8)], Mauricio Aníbal Isla Isla (30/2), Gary Alexis Medel Soto (40/4), Matías Ariel Fernández Fernández (46/11), Humberto Andrés Suazo Pontivo (53/21) [61.Milovan Petar Mirošević Albornoz (24/3)], Eduardo Jesús Vargas Rojas (8/2) [73.Gustavo Javier Canales (1/0)]. Trainer: Claudio Daniel Borghi Bidos (14).

**657.** 15.11.2011 **CHILE - PARAGUAY** **2-0(1-0)** 20th FIFA WC. Qualifiers
Estadio Nacional „Julio Martínez Prádanos", Santiago; Referee: Héber Roberto Lopes (Brazil); Attendance: 44,726
**CHI:** Claudio Andrés Bravo Muñoz (62/0), Pablo Andrés Contreras Fica (64/2), Marcos Andrés González Salazar (10/0), Waldo Alonso Ponce Carrizo (42/4), Mauricio Aníbal Isla Isla (31/2), Gary Alexis Medel Soto (41/4), Charles Mariano Aránguiz Sandoval (6/0), Matías Ariel Fernández Fernández (47/11) [86.Milovan Petar Mirošević Albornoz (25/3)], Alexis Alejandro Sánchez Sánchez (45/14), Humberto Andrés Suazo Pontivo (54/21) [70.Matías Daniel Campos Toro (2/1)], Eduardo Jesús Vargas Rojas (9/2) [78.Esteban Efraín Paredes Quintanilla (29/8)]. Trainer: Claudio Daniel Borghi Bidos (15).
**Goals**: Pablo Andrés Contreras Fica (28), Matías Daniel Campos Toro (86).

**658.** 21.12.2011 **CHILE - PARAGUAY** **3-2(1-0)**
Estadio La Portada, La Serena; Referee: Raúl Orosco Delgadillo (Bolivia); Attendance: 9,000
**CHI:** Luis Antonio Marín Barahona (7/0), Leandro Javier Delgado Plenkovich (1/0) [73.Eric Orlando Godoy Zepeda (1/0)], Luis Ignacio Casanova Sandoval (2/0), Lucas Domínguez Irarrázabal (2/0), Michael Contreras Araya (1/0) [*sent off 51*], Christian Jorge Martínez Muñoz (3/0), Lorenzo Enrique Reyes Vicencio (1/0) [83.Matías Ignacio Gutiérrez Breve (1/0)], Matías Daniel Campos Toro (3/1), Mathias Leonardo Vidangossy Rebolledo (5/0) [73.Jorge Israel Romo Salinas (1/0)], Antenor Junior Fernandes da Silva Vitoria (1/0) [86.Sebastián Andrés Ubilla Cambón (1/0)], Sebastián Andrés Pinto Perurena (1/3) [76.Leonardo Esteban Monje Valenzuela (2/0)]. Trainer: Claudio Daniel Borghi Bidos (16).
**Goals**: Sebastián Andrés Pinto Perurena (19, 62, 74).

**659.** 15.02.2012 **PARAGUAY - CHILE** **2-0(1-0)**
Estadio „Feliciano Cáceres", Luque; Referee: Leandro Pedro Vuaden (Brazil); Attendance: 10,000
**CHI:** Luis Antonio Marín Barahona (8/0), Enzo Pablo Andía Roco (1/0), Luis Ignacio Casanova Sandoval (3/0), Lucas Domínguez Irarrázabal (3/0) Matías Daniel Campos Toro (4/1), Francisco Andrés Silva Gajardo (5/0), José Pedro Fuenzalida Gana (16/0) [86.Bryan Paul Carrasco Santos (1/0)], Felipe Alejandro Gutiérrez Leiva (6/0) [86.Mathias Leonardo Vidangossy Rebolledo (6/0)], Lorenzo Enrique Reyes Vicencio (2/0) [69.Boris Alexis Sagredo Romero (4/0)], Nicolás Sebastián Canales Calas (1/0) [69.Joseph Aníbal Carvallo Torres (1/0)], Carlos Andrés Muñoz Rojas (4/0) [56.Francisco Javier Pizarro Cartes (3/0)]. Trainer: Claudio Daniel Borghi Bidos (17).

**660.** 29.02.2012 **CHILE - GHANA** **1-1(0-1)**
PPL Park, Chester (United States); Referee: Elías Bazakos (United States); Attendance: 6,000
**CHI:** Claudio Andrés Bravo Muñoz (63/0), Marcos Andrés González Salazar (11/0), José Manuel Rojas Bahamondes (3/1) [58.Lucas Domínguez Irarrázabal (4/0)], Matías Daniel Campos Toro (5/1) [*sent off 69*], Marcelo Alfonso Díaz Rojas (2/0), Osvaldo Alexis González Sepúlveda (8/0), Gary Alexis Medel Soto (42/4) [88.Braulio Antonio Leal Salvo (2/0)], Charles Mariano Aránguiz Sandoval (7/0) [55.Eduardo Jesús Vargas Rojas (10/2)], Matías Ariel Fernández Fernández (48/12), Alexis Alejandro Sánchez Sánchez (46/14), Humberto Andrés Suazo Pontivo (55/21) [72.Antenor Junior Fernandes da Silva Vitoria (2/0)]. Trainer: Claudio Daniel Borghi Bidos (18).
**Goals**: Matías Ariel Fernández Fernández (74).

**661.** 21.03.2012 **CHILE - PERU** **3-1(2-1)** Copa del Pacífico
Estadio „Carlos Dittborn", Arica; Referee: Julio César Quintana Rodríguez (Paraguay); Attendance: 12,000
**CHI:** Cristopher Benjamín Toselli Ríos (2/0), Enzo Pablo Andía Roco (2/1) [62.Sebastián Patricio Toro Hormazábal (4/1)], Lucas Domínguez Irarrázabal (5/0) [89.Marko Andrés Biskupović Venturino (1/0)], Luis Ignacio Casanova Sandoval (4/0), Charles Mariano Aránguiz Sandoval (8/0) [82.Bryan Paul Carrasco Santos (2/0)], Braulio Antonio Leal Salvo (3/0), Marcelo Alfonso Díaz Rojas (3/0), Eugenio Esteban Mena Reveco (3/1), Rodrigo Javier Millar Carvajal (29/2) [64.Felipe Alejandro Gutiérrez Leiva (7/0)], Esteban Efraín Paredes Quintanilla (30/9) [60.Felipe Ignacio Flores Chandía (1/0)], Antenor Junior Fernandes da Silva Vitoria (3/0) [56.Edson Raúl Puch Cortés (6/0)]. Trainer: Claudio Daniel Borghi Bidos (19).
**Goals**: Esteban Efraín Paredes Quintanilla (5), Enzo Pablo Andía Roco (43), Eugenio Esteban Mena Reveco (87).

**662.** 11.04.2012 **PERU - CHILE** **0-3(0-0)** Copa del Pacífico
Estadio „Jorge Basadre", Tacna; Referee: Enrique Cáceres (Paraguay); Attendance: 15,000
**CHI:** Cristopher Benjamín Toselli Ríos (3/0), Enzo Pablo Andía Roco (3/1) [75.Marko Andrés Biskupović Venturino (2/0)], Luis Ignacio Casanova Sandoval (5/0), Lucas Domínguez Irarrázabal (6/0) [76.Sebastián Patricio Toro Hormazábal (5/1)], Luis Pedro Figueroa Sepúlveda (13/1) [66.Bryan Paul Carrasco Santos (3/1)], Charles Mariano Aránguiz Sandoval (9/0), Marcelo Alfonso Díaz Rojas (4/0), Eugenio Esteban Mena Reveco (4/2) [70.Matías Daniel Campos Toro (6/1)], Felipe Alejandro Gutiérrez Leiva (8/0) [74.Bryan Martín Rabello Mella (1/0)], Carlos Andrés Muñoz Rojas (5/0) [63.Felipe Ignacio Flores Chandía (2/1)], Antenor Junior Fernandes da Silva Vitoria (4/0). Trainer: Claudio Daniel Borghi Bidos (20).
**Goals**: Eugenio Esteban Mena Reveco (46), Felipe Ignacio Flores Chandía (64), Bryan Paul Carrasco Santos (72).

**663.** 02.06.2012 **BOLIVIA - CHILE** **0-2(0-1)** 20th FIFA WC. Qualifiers
Estadio „Hernándo Siles Zuazo", La Paz; Referee: Alfredo Stalin Intriago Ortega (Ecuador); Attendance: 34,389
**CHI:** Claudio Andrés Bravo Muñoz (64/0), Pablo Andrés Contreras Fica (65/2), Osvaldo Alexis González Sepúlveda (9/0), José Manuel Rojas Bahamondes (4/1), Marcelo Alfonso Díaz Rojas (5/0), Eugenio Esteban Mena Reveco (5/2), Matías Ariel Fernández Fernández (49/12) [74.Luis Pedro Figueroa Sepúlveda (14/1)], Arturo Erasmo Vidal Pardo (40/4), Charles Mariano Aránguiz Sandoval (10/1) [88.Braulio Antonio Leal Salvo (4/0)], Alexis Alejandro Sánchez Sánchez (47/14), Humberto Andrés Suazo Pontivo (56/21) [78.Eduardo Jesús Vargas Rojas (11/2)]. Trainer: Claudio Daniel Borghi Bidos (21).
**Goals**: Charles Mariano Aránguiz Sandoval (45+3), Arturo Erasmo Vidal Pardo (83).

**664.** 09.06.2012 **VENEZUELA - CHILE** **0-2(0-0)** 20th FIFA WC. Qualifiers
Estadio „José Antonio Anzoátegui", Puerto La Cruz; Referee: José Hernando Buitrago Arango (Colombia); Attendance: 35,000
**CHI:** Claudio Andrés Bravo Muñoz (65/0), Pablo Andrés Contreras Fica (66/2) [65.Luis Pedro Figueroa Sepúlveda (15/1)], Osvaldo Alexis González Sepúlveda (10/0), José Manuel Rojas Bahamondes (5/1) [30.Marcos Andrés González Salazar (12/0)], Marcelo Alfonso Díaz Rojas (6/0), Eugenio Esteban Mena Reveco (6/2), Matías Ariel Fernández Fernández (50/13), Arturo Erasmo Vidal Pardo (41/4), Charles Mariano Aránguiz Sandoval (11/2), Alexis Alejandro Sánchez Sánchez (48/14), Humberto Andrés Suazo Pontivo (57/21) [79.Sebastián Andrés Pinto Perurena (2/3)]. Trainer: Claudio Daniel Borghi Bidos (22).
**Goals**: Matías Ariel Fernández Fernández (85), Charles Mariano Aránguiz Sandoval (90+1).

**665.** 15.08.2012 **ECUADOR - CHILE** **3-0(2-0)**
Citi Field, New York (United States); Referee: Terry Vaughn (United States); Attendance: 31,901
**CHI:** Miguel Ángel Pinto Jérez (18/0), Eugenio Esteban Mena Reveco (7/2) [65.César Alexis Cortés Pinto (1/0)], Marcos Andrés González Salazar (13/0), José Manuel Rojas Bahamondes (6/1), Carlos Alfredo Labrín Candia (3/0), Gary Alexis Medel Soto (43/4), Charles Mariano Aránguiz Sandoval (12/2), Fernando Andrés Meneses Cornejo (12/0) [46.Braulio Antonio Leal Salvo (5/0)], Alexis Alejandro Sánchez Sánchez (49/14), Humberto Andrés Suazo Pontivo (58/21), Eduardo Jesús Vargas Rojas (12/2) [46.Cristóbal Andrés Jorquera Torres (4/0)]. Trainer: Claudio Daniel Borghi Bidos (23).

**666.** 11.09.2012 **CHILE - COLOMBIA** **1-3(1-0)** 20th FIFA WC. Qualifiers
Estadio Monumental "David Arellano", Santiago; Referee: Víctor Hugo Carrillo (Peru); Attendance: 38,000
**CHI:** Claudio Andrés Bravo Muñoz (66/0), Marcos Andrés González Salazar (14/0), Eugenio Esteban Mena Reveco (8/2), Gonzalo Alejandro Jara Reyes (52/3), Mauricio Aníbal Isla Isla (32/2) [67.Antenor Junior Fernándes da Silva Vitoria (5/0)], Matías Ariel Fernández Fernández (51/14), Arturo Erasmo Vidal Pardo (42/4), Marcelo Alfonso Díaz Rojas (7/0), Gary Alexis Medel Soto (44/4) [*sent off 34*], Alexis Alejandro Sánchez Sánchez (50/14) [82.Mauricio Ricardo Pinilla Ferrera (23/5)], Humberto Andrés Suazo Pontivo (59/21) [71.Sebastián Andrés Pinto Perurena (3/3)]. Trainer: Claudio Daniel Borghi Bidos (24).
**Goal**: Matías Ariel Fernández Fernández (41).

**667.** 12.10.2012 **ECUADOR - CHILE** **3-1(1-1)** 20th FIFA WC. Qualifiers
Estadio Olímpico Atahualpa, Quito; Referee: Héber Roberto Lopes (Brazil); Attendance: 32,600
**CHI:** Miguel Ángel Pinto Jérez (19/0), Gonzalo Alejandro Jara Reyes (53/3), Pablo Andrés Contreras Fica (67/2) [*sent off 54*], Mauricio Aníbal Isla Isla (33/2), Osvaldo Alexis González Sepúlveda (11/0), Matías Ariel Fernández Fernández (52/14) [60.Antenor Junior Fernándes da Silva Vitoria (6/0)], Arturo Erasmo Vidal Pardo (43/4) [*sent off 86*], Marcelo Alfonso Díaz Rojas (8/0), Felipe Ignacio Seymour Dobud (6/0) [68.Mark Dennis González Hoffmann (46/4)], Jean André Emanuel Beausejour Coliqueo (44/3) [78.Eduardo Jesús Vargas Rojas (13/2)], Alexis Alejandro Sánchez Sánchez (51/14). Trainer: Claudio Daniel Borghi Bidos (25).
**Goal**: Juan Carlos Paredes Reasco (25 own goal).

**668.** 16.10.2012 **CHILE - ARGENTINA** **1-2(0-2)** 20th FIFA WC. Qualifiers
Estadio Nacional „Julio Martínez Prádanos", Santiago; Referee: Antonio Javier Arias Alvarenga (Paraguay); Attendance: 45,000
**CHI:** Miguel Ángel Pinto Jérez (20/0), Marcos Andrés González Salazar (15/0), Gonzalo Alejandro Jara Reyes (54/3), Mauricio Aníbal Isla Isla (34/2), Mark Dennis González Hoffmann (47/4) [75.Felipe Alejandro Gutiérrez Leiva (9/1)], Matías Ariel Fernández Fernández (53/14), Marcelo Alfonso Díaz Rojas (9/0), Gary Alexis Medel Soto (45/4), Jean André Emanuel Beausejour Coliqueo (45/3), Alexis Alejandro Sánchez Sánchez (52/14), Sebastián Andrés Pinto Perurena (4/3) [55.Eduardo Jesús Vargas Rojas (14/2)]. Trainer: Claudio Daniel Borghi Bidos (26).
**Goal**: Felipe Alejandro Gutiérrez Leiva (90+1).

**669.** 14.11.2012 **SERBIA - CHILE** **3-1(1-0)**
AFG Arena, St. Gallen (Switzerland); Referee: Sascha Kever (Switzerland); Attendance: 2,116
**CHI:** Miguel Ángel Pinto Jérez (21/0), Gonzalo Alejandro Jara Reyes (55/3), Osvaldo Alexis González Sepúlveda (12/0) [74.Marcos Andrés González Salazar (16/0)], José Manuel Rojas Bahamondes (7/1), Manuel Rolando Iturra Urrutia (35/1) [46.Yerson Flavio Opazo Riquelme (1/0)], Matías Ariel Fernández Fernández (54/14), Arturo Erasmo Vidal Pardo (44/4) [*sent off 78*], Gary Alexis Medel Soto (46/4), Jean André Emanuel Beausejour Coliqueo (46/3) [70.Eugenio Esteban Mena Reveco (9/2)], Alexis Alejandro Sánchez Sánchez (53/14) [20.Ángelo José Henríquez Iturra (1/1)], Eduardo Jesús Vargas Rojas (15/2) [56.Felipe Alejandro Gutiérrez Leiva (10/1)]. Trainer: Claudio Daniel Borghi Bidos (27).
**Goal**: Ángelo José Henríquez Iturra (87).

**670.** 15.01.2013 **CHILE - SENEGAL** **2-1(0-1)**
Estadio La Portada, La Serena; Referee: Germán Delfino (Argentina); Attendance: 10,000
**CHI:** Johnny Cristián Herrera Muñoz (3/0), Paulo Cezar Magalhães Lobos (5/0), Albert Alejandro Acevedo Vergara (2/0), José Manuel Rojas Bahamondes (8/1), Eugenio Esteban Mena Reveco (10/2), Francisco Andrés Silva Gajardo (6/0), Fernando Andrés Meneses Cornejo (13/1), César Alexis Cortés Pinto (2/0), Michael Fabián Ríos Ripoll (1/0) [46.Patricio Rodolfo Rubio Pulgar (1/0)], Sebastián Andrés Ubilla Cambón (2/0) [84.Boris Alexis Sagredo Romero (5/0)], Carlos Andrés Muñoz Rojas (6/1) [88.José Pedro Fuenzalida Gana (17/0)]. Trainer: Jorge Luis Sampaoli Moya (1).
**Goals**: Carlos Andrés Muñoz Rojas (52), Fernando Andrés Meneses Cornejo (65 penalty).

**671.** 19.01.2013 **CHILE - HAITI** **3-0(0-0)**
Estadio Municipal "Alcaldesa Ester Roa Rebolledo", Concepción; Referee: Óscar Maldonado Urey (Bolivia); Attendance: 22,000
**CHI:** Johnny Cristián Herrera Muñoz (4/0), Paulo Cezar Magalhães Lobos (6/0), Eugenio Esteban Mena Reveco (11/2), José Manuel Rojas Bahamondes (9/1), Albert Alejandro Acevedo Vergara (3/0), José Pedro Fuenzalida Gana (18/1) [73.Patricio Rodolfo Rubio Pulgar (2/1)], Francisco Andrés Silva Gajardo (7/0) [87.Michael Fabián Ríos Ripoll (2/0)], Fernando Andrés Meneses Cornejo (14/1), César Alexis Cortés Pinto (3/0) [82.Manuel Arturo Villalobos Salvos (1/0)], Sebastián Andrés Ubilla Cambón (3/0) [70.Boris Alexis Sagredo Romero (6/0)], Carlos Andrés Muñoz Rojas (7/2) [82.Lorenzo Enrique Reyes Vicencio (3/0)]. Trainer: Jorge Luis Sampaoli Moya (2).
**Goals**: Carlos Andrés Muñoz Rojas (48), José Pedro Fuenzalida Gana (57), Patricio Rodolfo Rubio Pulgar (76).

**672.** 06.02.2013 **CHILE - EGYPT** **2-1(0-0)**
Estadio "Vicente Calderón", Madrid (Spain); Referee: Fernando Teixeira Vitienes (Spain); Attendance: 3,000
**CHI:** Claudio Andrés Bravo Muñoz (67/0), Gonzalo Alejandro Jara Reyes (56/3), Mauricio Aníbal Isla Isla (35/2), José Manuel Rojas Bahamondes (10/1), Arturo Erasmo Vidal Pardo (45/4) [79.Felipe Alejandro Gutiérrez Leiva (11/1)], Gary Alexis Medel Soto (47/4), Jean André Emanuel Beausejour Coliqueo (47/3) [79.Fabián Ariel Orellana Valenzuela (23/2)], Carlos Emilio Carmona Tello (36/1), Bryan Martín Rabello Mella (2/0) [46.Marcelo Alfonso Díaz Rojas (10/0)], Alexis Alejandro Sánchez Sánchez (54/14), Humberto Andrés Suazo Pontivo (60/21) [46.Eduardo Jesús Vargas Rojas (16/3)]. Trainer: Jorge Luis Sampaoli Moya (3).
**Goals**: Eduardo Jesús Vargas Rojas (60), Carlos Emilio Carmona Tello (66).

**673.** 22.03.2013 **PERU - CHILE** **1-0(0-0)** 20th FIFA WC. Qualifiers
Estadio Nacional, Lima; Referee: Diego Hernán Abal (Argentina); Attendance: 43,000
**CHI:** Claudio Andrés Bravo Muñoz (68/0), Marcos Andrés González Salazar (17/0), Eugenio Esteban Mena Reveco (12/2), Mauricio Aníbal Isla Isla (36/2), José Manuel Rojas Bahamondes (11/1), Gary Alexis Medel Soto (48/4), Charles Mariano Aránguiz Sandoval (13/2) [54.Francisco Andrés Silva Gajardo (8/0)], Jean André Emanuel Beausejour Coliqueo (48/3) [70.Nicolás Ignacio Castillo Mora (1/0)], Carlos Emilio Carmona Tello (37/1), Alexis Alejandro Sánchez Sánchez (55/14), Eduardo Jesús Vargas Rojas (17/3) [75.Antenor Junior Fernándes da Silva Vitoria (7/0)]. Trainer: Jorge Luis Sampaoli Moya (4).

**674.** 26.03.2013 **CHILE - URUGUAY** **2-0(1-0)** 20th FIFA WC. Qualifiers
Estadio Nacional „Julio Martínez Prádanos“, Santiago; Referee: Néstor Fabián Pitana (Argentina); Attendance: 43,816
**CHI:** Claudio Andrés Bravo Muñoz (69/0), Gonzalo Alejandro Jara Reyes (57/3), Eugenio Esteban Mena Reveco (13/2), Mauricio Aníbal Isla Isla (37/2) [85.Marcos Andrés González Salazar (18/0)], José Manuel Rojas Bahamondes (12/1), Marcelo Alfonso Díaz Rojas (11/0), Gary Alexis Medel Soto (49/4), Charles Mariano Aránguiz Sandoval (14/2) [59.Matías Ariel Fernández Fernández (55/14)], Jean André Emanuel Beausejour Coliqueo (49/3) [70.Carlos Emilio Carmona Tello (38/1)], Esteban Efraín Paredes Quintanilla (31/10), Eduardo Jesús Vargas Rojas (18/4). Trainer: Jorge Luis Sampaoli Moya (5).
**Goals**: Esteban Efraín Paredes Quintanilla (10), Eduardo Jesús Vargas Rojas (77).

**675.** 24.04.2013 **BRAZIL - CHILE** **2-2(1-1)**
Estádio "Governador Magalhães Pinto", Belo Horizonte; Referee: Carlos Arecio Amarilla Demarqui (Paraguay); Attendance: 53,331
**CHI:** Johnny Cristián Herrera Muñoz (5/0), Marcos Andrés González Salazar (19/1), Eugenio Esteban Mena Reveco (14/2), José Manuel Rojas Bahamondes (13/1), Cristián Andrés Álvarez Valenzuela (23/0), Braulio Antonio Leal Salvo (6/0) [*sent off 90*], Fernando Andrés Meneses Cornejo (15/1) [69.Carlos Andrés Muñoz Rojas (8/2)], Lorenzo Enrique Reyes Vicencio (4/0), Eduardo Jesús Vargas Rojas (19/5) [90+1.Andrés Sebastián Robles Fuentes (1/0)], César Alexis Cortés Pinto (4/0) [60.José Pedro Fuenzalida Gana (19/1)], Patricio Rodolfo Rubio Pulgar (3/1) [78.Luis Pedro Figueroa Sepúlveda (16/1)]. Trainer: Jorge Luis Sampaoli Moya (6).
**Goals**: Marcos Andrés González Salazar (8), Eduardo Jesús Vargas Rojas (64).

**676.** 07.06.2013 **PARAGUAY - CHILE** **1-2(0-1)** 20th FIFA WC. Qualifiers
Estadio Defensores del Chaco, Asunción; Referee: Leandro Pedro Vuaden (Brazil); Attendance: 30,000
**CHI:** Claudio Andrés Bravo Muñoz (70/0), Marcos Andrés González Salazar (20/1), Eugenio Esteban Mena Reveco (15/2), Mauricio Aníbal Isla Isla (38/2), José Manuel Rojas Bahamondes (14/1), Arturo Erasmo Vidal Pardo (46/5), Marcelo Alfonso Díaz Rojas (12/0), Gary Alexis Medel Soto (50/4), Esteban Efraín Paredes Quintanilla (32/10) [59.Matías Ariel Fernández Fernández (56/14)], Alexis Alejandro Sánchez Sánchez (56/14) [90+3.Sebastián Andrés Pinto Perurena (5/3)], Eduardo Jesús Vargas Rojas (20/7) [85.Felipe Alejandro Gutiérrez Leiva (12/1)]. Trainer: Jorge Luis Sampaoli Moya (7).
**Goals**: Eduardo Jesús Vargas Rojas (41), Arturo Erasmo Vidal Pardo (56).

**677.** 11.06.2013 **CHILE - BOLIVIA** **3-1(2-1)** 20th FIFA WC. Qualifiers
Estadio Nacional „Julio Martínez Prádanos“, Santiago; Referee: Darío Agustín Ubriaco (Uruguay); Attendance: 45,000
**CHI:** Claudio Andrés Bravo Muñoz (71/0), Marcos Andrés González Salazar (21/1), José Manuel Rojas Bahamondes (15/1), Gary Alexis Medel Soto (51/4), David Marcelo Pizarro Cortés (37/2), Arturo Erasmo Vidal Pardo (47/6), Marcelo Alfonso Díaz Rojas (13/0), Eugenio Esteban Mena Reveco (16/2) [75.Jean André Emanuel Beausejour Coliqueo (50/3)], Esteban Efraín Paredes Quintanilla (33/10) [54.Gonzalo Alejandro Jara Reyes (58/3)], Alexis Alejandro Sánchez Sánchez (57/15), Eduardo Jesús Vargas Rojas (21/7). Trainer: Jorge Luis Sampaoli Moya (8).
**Goals**: Eduardo Jesús Vargas Rojas (16), Alexis Alejandro Sánchez Sánchez (18), Arturo Erasmo Vidal Pardo (90+3).

**678.** 14.08.2013 **CHILE - IRAQ** **6-0(5-0)**
Brøndby Stadion, København (Denmark); Referee: Michael Johansen (Denmark); Attendance: 7,000
**CHI:** Claudio Andrés Bravo Muñoz (72/0), José Manuel Rojas Bahamondes (16/1), Eugenio Esteban Mena Reveco (17/3), Mauricio Aníbal Isla Isla (39/2) [61.Gonzalo Alejandro Jara Reyes (59/3)], Arturo Erasmo Vidal Pardo (48/6) [69.David Marcelo Pizarro Cortés (38/2)], Marcelo Alfonso Díaz Rojas (14/0) [72.Carlos Emilio Carmona Tello (39/1)], Gary Alexis Medel Soto (52/4), Charles Mariano Aránguiz Sandoval (15/2) [62.Felipe Alejandro Gutiérrez Leiva (13/1)], Jean André Emanuel Beausejour Coliqueo (51/5) [62.Bryan Martín Rabello Mella (3/0)], Alexis Alejandro Sánchez Sánchez (58/17) [62.Antenor Junior Fernandes da Silva Vitoria (8/0)], Ángelo José Henríquez Iturra (2/2). Trainer: Jorge Luis Sampaoli Moya (9).
**Goals**: Eugenio Esteban Mena Reveco (8), Alexis Alejandro Sánchez Sánchez (22, 29), Jean André Emanuel Beausejour Coliqueo (37, 45+1), Ángelo José Henríquez Iturra (80).

**679.** 07.09.2013 **CHILE - VENEZUELA** **3-0(2-0)** 20th FIFA WC. Qualifiers
Estadio Nacional „Julio Martínez Prádanos“, Santiago; Referee: Sandro Meira Ricci (Brazil); Attendance: 46,500
**CHI:** Claudio Andrés Bravo Muñoz (73/0), Marcos Andrés González Salazar (22/2), Eugenio Esteban Mena Reveco (18/3), Jorge Luis Valdivia Toro (52/4) [73.Jean André Emanuel Beausejour Coliqueo (52/5)], Arturo Erasmo Vidal Pardo (49/7), Mauricio Aníbal Isla Isla (40/2), Marcelo Alfonso Díaz Rojas (15/0), Gary Alexis Medel Soto (53/4), Charles Mariano Aránguiz Sandoval (16/2) [58.David Marcelo Pizarro Cortés (39/2)], Alexis Alejandro Sánchez Sánchez (59/17), Eduardo Jesús Vargas Rojas (22/8) [84.Ángelo José Henríquez Iturra (3/2)]. Trainer: Jorge Luis Sampaoli Moya (10).
**Goals**: Eduardo Jesús Vargas Rojas (10), Marcos Andrés González Salazar (30), Arturo Erasmo Vidal Pardo (85).

**680.** 10.09.2013 **SPAIN - CHILE** **2-2(1-2)**
Stade de Genève, Genève (Switzerland); Referee: Adrien Jaccottet (Switzerland); Attendance:
**CHI:** Claudio Andrés Bravo Muñoz (74/0), Marcos Andrés González Salazar (23/2), Gonzalo Alejandro Jara Reyes (60/3), Eugenio Esteban Mena Reveco (19/3), David Marcelo Pizarro Cortés (40/2) [46.Francisco Andrés Silva Gajardo (9/0)], Arturo Erasmo Vidal Pardo (50/7), Mauricio Aníbal Isla Isla (41/2), Marcelo Alfonso Díaz Rojas (16/0), Gary Alexis Medel Soto (54/4), Alexis Alejandro Sánchez Sánchez (60/17) [90+3.Antenor Junior Fernandes da Silva Vitoria (9/0)], Eduardo Jesús Vargas Rojas (23/10) [86.Jean André Emanuel Beausejour Coliqueo (53/5)]. Trainer: Jorge Luis Sampaoli Moya (11).
**Goals**: Eduardo Jesús Vargas Rojas (5, 44).

**681.** 11.10.2013 **COLOMBIA - CHILE** **3-3(0-3)** 20th FIFA WC. Qualifiers
Estadio Metropolitano "Roberto Meléndez", Barranquilla; Referee: Paulo César de Oliveira (Brazil); Attendance: 40,388
**CHI:** Claudio Andrés Bravo Muñoz (75/0), Marcos Andrés González Salazar (24/2), Gonzalo Alejandro Jara Reyes (61/3), Eugenio Esteban Mena Reveco (20/3), Jorge Luis Valdivia Toro (53/4) [61.Jean André Emanuel Beausejour Coliqueo (54/5)], Arturo Erasmo Vidal Pardo (51/8), Mauricio Aníbal Isla Isla (42/2) [53.José Manuel Rojas Bahamondes (17/1)], Gary Alexis Medel Soto (55/4), Carlos Emilio Carmona Tello (40/1) [*sent off 66*], Alexis Alejandro Sánchez Sánchez (61/19), Eduardo Jesús Vargas Rojas (24/10) [69.Francisco Andrés Silva Gajardo (10/0)]. Trainer: Jorge Luis Sampaoli Moya (12).
**Goals**: Arturo Erasmo Vidal Pardo (19 penalty), Alexis Alejandro Sánchez Sánchez (22, 29).

**682.** 16.10.2013 **CHILE - ECUADOR** **2-1(2-0)** 20th FIFA WC. Qualifiers
Estadio Nacional „Julio Martínez Prádanos", Santiago; Referee: Leandro Pedro Vuaden (Brazil); Attendance: 47,458
**CHI:** Claudio Andrés Bravo Muñoz (76/0), Marcos Andrés González Salazar (25/2), Eugenio Esteban Mena Reveco (21/3), Jorge Luis Valdivia Toro (54/4) [89.Mauricio Ricardo Pinilla Ferrera (24/5)], Arturo Erasmo Vidal Pardo (52/8), Mauricio Aníbal Isla Isla (43/2), Marcelo Alfonso Díaz Rojas (17/0), Gary Alexis Medel Soto (56/5), Charles Mariano Aránguiz Sandoval (17/2) [76.Matías Ariel Fernández Fernández (57/14)], Alexis Alejandro Sánchez Sánchez (62/20), Eduardo Jesús Vargas Rojas (25/10) [86.Jean André Emanuel Beausejour Coliqueo (55/5)]. Trainer: Jorge Luis Sampaoli Moya (13).
**Goals**: Alexis Alejandro Sánchez Sánchez (35), Gary Alexis Medel Soto (38).

**683.** 15.11.2013 **ENGLAND - CHILE** **0-2(0-1)**
The National Stadium, Wembley, London; Referee: Florian Meyer (Germany); Attendance: 62,953
**CHI:** Claudio Andrés Bravo Muñoz (77/0), Marcos Andrés González Salazar (26/2), Eugenio Esteban Mena Reveco (22/3), Matías Ariel Fernández Fernández (58/14) [46.Felipe Alejandro Gutiérrez Leiva (14/1)], Mauricio Aníbal Isla Isla (44/2) [59.Gonzalo Alejandro Jara Reyes (62/3)], Marcelo Alfonso Díaz Rojas (18/0), Gary Alexis Medel Soto (57/5), Charles Mariano Aránguiz Sandoval (18/2) [46.Carlos Emilio Carmona Tello (41/1)], Jean André Emanuel Beausejour Coliqueo (56/5) [82.José Pedro Fuenzalida Gana (20/1)], Alexis Alejandro Sánchez Sánchez (63/22), Eduardo Jesús Vargas Rojas (26/10) [72.Carlos Andrés Muñoz Rojas (9/2)]. Trainer: Jorge Luis Sampaoli Moya (14).
**Goals**: Alexis Alejandro Sánchez Sánchez (7, 90+4).

**684.** 20.11.2013 **BRAZIL - CHILE** **2-1(1-0)**
Rogers Centre, Toronto (Canada); Attendance: Silviu Petrescu (Canada); Attendance: 38,514
**CHI:** Claudio Andrés Bravo Muñoz (78/0), Marcos Andrés González Salazar (27/2), Gonzalo Alejandro Jara Reyes (63/3), Eugenio Esteban Mena Reveco (23/3), Marcelo Alfonso Díaz Rojas (19/0) [8.Jean André Emanuel Beausejour Coliqueo (57/5)], José Pedro Fuenzalida Gana (21/1) [22.Jorge Luis Valdivia Toro (55/4); 59.Matías Ariel Fernández Fernández (59/14)], Gary Alexis Medel Soto (58/5), Carlos Emilio Carmona Tello (42/1), Felipe Alejandro Gutiérrez Leiva (15/1) [86.Carlos Andrés Muñoz Rojas (10/2)], Alexis Alejandro Sánchez Sánchez (64/22), Eduardo Jesús Vargas Rojas (27/11). Trainer: Jorge Luis Sampaoli Moya (15).
**Goal**: Eduardo Jesús Vargas Rojas (71).

# INTERNATIONAL PLAYERS

| FM/Nr | Name | DOB | Caps | Goals | Period, Club |
|---|---|---|---|---|---|
| (410/527) | ABARCA ARAVENA Luis | 20.08.1965 | 3 | 0 | 1991, CD Cobreloa Calama (1/0). |
| (628/761) | ABARCA FUENTES Juan René | 07.12.1988 | 2 | 0 | 2010-2011, CFP de la Universidad de Chile Santiago (2/0). |
| (25/073) | ABARZÚA Heriberto | | 3 | 0 | 1924, Primero de Mayo Santiago (3/0). |
| (5/029) | ABELLO Enrique | | 10 | 0 | 1916-1922, CD Magallanes Santiago (10/0). |
| (164/292) | ABELLO Juan | | 1 | 1 | 1960, CD San Luis Quillota (1/1). |
| (653/775) | ACEVAL MUÑOZ Miguel Ángel | 08.01.1983 | 1 | 0 | 2011, CD Universidad de Concepción (1/0). |
| (239/354) | ACEVEDO Luis | | 2 | 0 | 1970, CD Huachipato Talcahuano (2/0). |
| (653/774) | ACEVEDO ROJAS Gerson Elías | 05.04.1988 | 1 | 0 | 2011, FK Mordovia Saransk (1/0). |
| (612/744) | ACEVEDO VERGARA Albert Alejandro | 06.05.1983 | 3 | 0 | 2009-2013, CD O'Higgins Rancagua (1/0), CFP de la Universidad de Chile Santiago (2/0). |
| (1/007) | ACUÑA Arturo | | 2 | 0 | 1910, CD Santiago Wanderers Valparaíso (2/0). |
| (541/666) | ACUÑA CONCHA Jorge Cristián | 31.07.1978 | 16 | 0 | 2003-2006, SC Feyenoord Rotterdam (5/0), CD Universidad Católica Santiago (1/0), SC Feyenoord Rotterdam (2/0), RBC Roosendaal (5/0), *unattached* (3/0). |
| (440/570) | ACUÑA DONOSO Clarence | 08.02.1975 | 61 | 3 | 1995-2004, CD O'Higgins Rancagua (9/0), CF de la Universidad de Chile Santiago (43/3), Newcastle United FC (6/0), CA Rosario Central (3/0). |
| (74/194) | ACUÑA Juan Manuel | | 6 | 0 | 1947, Audax CS Italiano Santiago (6/0). |
| (209/328) | ADRIAZOLA Víctor | | 10 | 0 | 1966-1967, CD Universidad Católica Santiago (10/0). |
| (132/255) | AGUILA Raúl | | 7 | 0 | 1956-1957, Audax CS Italiano Santiago (7/0). |
| (38/105) | AGUILERA Juan | | 1 | 0 | 1930, Audax CS Italiano Santiago (1/0). |
| (532/646) | AHUMADA Axel | 04.05.1977 | 2 | 0 | 2001, CD Coquimbo Unido (2/0). |
| (258/386) | AHUMADA BACHO Sergio | 02.02.1947 | 28 | 6 | 1973-1977, CSD Colo-Colo Santiago (9/3), Club Unión Española Santiago (12/2), CD Everton Viña del Mar (7/1). |
| (379/501) | AHUMADA GAETE Daniel | 02.02.1960 | 4 | 0 | 1988-1989, CD Huachipato Talcahuano (4/0). |
| (322/438) | ALARCÓN RIVERA Armando | 19.08.1955 | 2 | 0 | 1982, CD Cobreloa Calama (2/0). |
| (62/167) | ALCÁNTARA Juan | | 5 | 6 | 1945-1946, Audax CS Italiano Santiago (5/6). |
| (32/090) | ALFARO Oscar | | 4 | 4 | 1927-1928, CD Santiago Wanderers Valparaíso (1/2), CD San Luis Quillota (3/2). |
| (1/005) | ALLEN Henry | | 3 | 0 | 1910, Unión FC Santiago (3/0). |
| (536/653) | ALMENDRA CIFUENTES Patricio Antonio | 03.09.1977 | 2 | 0 | 2001, Club Deportes Concepción (2/0). |
| (111/241) | ALMEYDA Rodolfo | | 22 | 0 | 1954-1960, CD Palestino Santiago (22/0). |
| (11/048) | ALVARADO Juan | | 3 | 0 | 1917, CD Santiago Wanderers Valparaíso (3/0). |
| (182/309) | ALVAREZ Ernesto | 10.08.1928 | 1 | 0 | 1963, CF de la Universidad de Chile Santiago (1/0). |
| (313/436) | ALVAREZ José Luis | | 1 | 0 | 1981, CSD Colo-Colo Santiago (1/0). |
| (145/274) | ALVAREZ Luis Hernán | | 4 | 1 | 1959-1963, CSD Colo-Colo Santiago (4/1). |
| (73/187) | ALVAREZ Manuel | 23.05.1928 | 35 | 0 | 1947-1956, CD Universidad Católica Santiago (35/0). |
| (379/504) | ALVAREZ Marcelo | 16.01.1967 | 12 | 1 | 1988-1994, CDFA Arturo Fernández Vial Concepción (6/1), CD Cobreloa Calama (6/0). |
| (105/232) | ALVAREZ Sergio | | 1 | 0 | 1953, CD Everton Viña del Mar (1/0). |
| (521/632) | ÁLVAREZ VALENZUELA Cristián Andrés | 20.01.1980 | 23 | 0 | 2000-2013, CD Universidad Católica Santiago (16/0), Beitar Jerusalem FC (6/0), CD Universidad Católica Santiago (1/0). |
| (217/338) | AMPUERO Roberto | | 2 | 0 | 1967, CD Magallanes Santiago (2/0). |
| (659/789) | ANDÍA ROCO Enzo Pablo | 16.08.1992 | 3 | 1 | 2012, CD Universidad Católica Santiago (3/1). |
| (223/345) | ANGULO Raúl | | 10 | 0 | 1968-1972, CD Palestino Santiago (4/0), Club Unión Española Santiago (6/0). |
| (658/783) | Antenor Junior FERNANDES da Silva Vitoria | 04.10.1988 | 9 | 0 | 2011-2013, CD Palestino Santiago (1/0), CFP de la Universidad de Chile Santiago (3/0), TSV Bayer 04 Leverkusen (3/0), GNK Dinamo Zagreb (2/0). |
| (56/159) | ARANCIBIA Carlos | | 3 | 0 | 1942, Green Cross Santiago (3/0). |
| (44/127) | ARANCIBIA Manuel | | 6 | 3 | 1937-1942, Bádminton FC Santiago (3/2), Green Cross Santiago (3/1). |
| (197/326) | ARANCIBIA Pedro | | 1 | 0 | 1966, CD Everton Viña del Mar (1/0). |
| (452/582) | ARANCIBIA UNGER Franz | 07.04.1967 | 1 | 0 | 1996, Club de Deportes Temuco (1/0). |
| (39/110) | ARANDA Andrés Carlos | | 3 | 0 | 1935, Audax CS Italiano Santiago (3/0). |
| (39/109) | ARANEDA Enrique | | 3 | 0 | 1935, Audax CS Italiano Santiago (3/0). |
| (274/393) | ARANEDA JORQUERA Luis Antonio | | 4 | 2 | 1974-1976, CSD Colo-Colo Santiago (4/2). |
| (241/359) | ARÁNGUIZ Esteban | | 2 | 0 | 1970-1972, CF de la Universidad de Chile Santiago (2/0). |
| (625/750) | ARÁNGUIZ SANDOVAL Charles Mariano | 17.04.1989 | 18 | 2 | 2009-2013, CSD Colo-Colo Santiago (3/0), Quilmes AC (1/0), CFP de la Universidad de Chile Santiago (14/2). |
| (184/315) | ARAVENA Orlando | | 6 | 0 | 1964-1965, Club de Deportes La Serena (2/0), CD Palestino Santiago (4/0). |
| (331/451) | ARAVENA PLAZA Jorge Orlando | 22.04.1958 | 37 | 22 | 1983-1990, CD Universidad Católica Santiago (27/16), Real Valladolid CF (4/3), Associação Portuguesa de Desportos São Paulo (6/3). |
| (68/177) | ARAYA Jorge | | 8 | 2 | 1946-1947, Green Cross Santiago (8/2). |
| (293/415) | ARAYA Manuel | | 2 | 0 | 1979, CD Palestino Santiago (2/0). |
| (344/459) | ARAYA Manuel | | 2 | 0 | 1984-1986, CD Cobresal El Salvador (2/0). |
| (185/317) | ARAYA TORO Pedro Damián | 23.01.1942 | 52 | 12 | 1964-1971, CF de la Universidad de Chile Santiago (52/12). |
| (436/563) | ARDIMAN Miguel | 10.06.1967 | 7 | 0 | 1994-1996, CD Universidad Católica Santiago (7/0). |
| (26/078) | ARELLANO David | | 6 | 7 | 1924-1926, CD Magallanes Santiago (2/0), CSD Colo-Colo Santiago (4/7). |
| (25/071) | ARELLANO Francisco | | 3 | 0 | 1924, CD Magallanes Santiago (3/0). |
| (38/104) | ARELLANO Guillermo | 21.08.1908 | 1 | 1 | 1930, CSD Colo-Colo Santiago (1/1). |
| (99/224) | ARENAS Augusto | | 1 | 0 | 1953, CD Everton Viña del Mar (1/0). |

| | | | | | |
|---|---|---|---|---|---|
| (140/268) | ARENAS Salvador | | **1** | **0** | 1957, CF de la Universidad de Chile Santiago (1/0). |
| (584/723) | ARIAS GONZÁLEZ Mauricio Antonio | 27.10.1984 | **1** | **0** | 2007, CD Huachipato Talcahuano (1/0). |
| (34/098) | ARIAS José del Carmen | | **2** | **0** | 1928, The Commercial Talcahuano (2/0). |
| (221/341) | ARIAS MÚJICA Antonio | 09.10.1944 | **30** | **0** | 1968-1977, CD Magallanes Santiago (3/0), Club Unión Española Santiago (27/0). |
| (56/156) | ARMINGOL Benito | | **8** | **1** | 1942-1945, Club Unión Española Santiago (8/0). |
| (485/605) | AROS Mauricio Fernando | 09.03.1976 | **27** | **0** | 1998-2004, CF de la Universidad de Chile Santiago (25/0), CD Huachipato Talcahuano (2/0). |
| (87/204) | ARRIAGADA Manuel | | **2** | **0** | 1950, CD Universidad Católica Santiago (2/0). |
| (331/452) | ARRIAZA Oscar | | **9** | **0** | 1983, CD Naval Talcahuano (9/0). |
| (2/012) | ASHE E.F. | | **2** | **0** | 1910, Bádminton FC Valparaíso (2/0). |
| (365/483) | ASTENGO Fernando | 08.01.1960 | **19** | **3** | 1986-1989, CSD Colo-Colo Santiago (1/0), Grêmio Foot-ball Porto-Alegrense (18/3). |
| (158/287) | ASTORGA Manuel | | **10** | **0** | 1960-1970, CF de la Universidad de Chile Santiago (9/0), CD Huachipato Talcahuano (1/0). |
| (139/262) | ASTORGA Vicente | | **3** | **0** | 1957, Audax CS Italiano Santiago (3/0). |
| (257/382) | ASTUDILLO Fernando | | **1** | **0** | 1972, CD Universidad Católica Santiago (1/0). |
| (62/164) | ATAGLICH Carlos | | **4** | **0** | 1945, Bádminton FC Santiago (4/0). |
| (40/115) | AVENDAÑO José | | **12** | **3** | 1935-1941, CD Magallanes Santiago (12/3). |
| (451/578) | AVILA Moisés | 13.04.1974 | **1** | **0** | 1995, CD O'Higgins Rancagua (1/0). |
| (39/113) | AVILÉS Moisés | | **3** | **0** | 1935-1937, Audax CS Italiano Santiago (3/0). |
| (251/377) | AZÓCAR Guillermo | | **7** | **0** | 1972-1973, CD Huachipato Talcahuano (7/0). |
| (40/116) | AZZERMAN Isaías | | **1** | **0** | 1935, Audax CS Italiano Santiago (1/0). |
| (6/035) | BÁEZ Ángel | | **4** | **1** | 1916, Thunder FC Coquimbo (4/1). |
| (14/054) | BÁEZ Telésforo Segundo | | **3** | **0** | 1919, CD Santiago Wanderers Valparaíso (3/0). |
| (10/041) | BAEZA Héctor | | **5** | **0** | 1917-1919, Loma Blanca FC Santiago (2/0), Rancagua FC (3/0). |
| (42/124) | BAEZA Mario | | **4** | **0** | 1936-1947, CD Magallanes Santiago (2/0), CF de la Universidad de Chile Santiago (2/0). |
| (21/066) | BALBONTÍN René | | **2** | **0** | 1922, Bádminton FC Valparaíso (2/0). |
| (75/195) | BALBUENA José | | **1** | **0** | 1947, CF de la Universidad de Chile Santiago (1/0). |
| (57/160) | BARRERA Florencio | | **10** | **0** | 1942-1945, CD Magallanes Santiago (10/0). |
| (425/546) | BARRERA FUNES Rodrígo Hernán | 30.03.1970 | **22** | **5** | 1993-1998, CD Universidad Católica Santiago (12/4), CF de la Universidad de Chile Santiago (10/1). |
| (1/003) | BARRIGA Luis | | **1** | **0** | 1910, Santiago National (1/0). |
| (365/480) | BASAY HATIBOVIC Ivo Alexis | 13.04.1966 | **24** | **6** | 1986-1997, CD Everton Viña del Mar (7/3), Stade de Reims (4/1), CID Necaxa Ciudad de México (11/2), CSD Colo-Colo Santiago (2/0). |
| (549/674) | BEAUSEJOUR COLIQUEO Jean André Emanuel | 01.06.1984 | **57** | **5** | 2004-2013, CD Universidad Católica Santiago (2/0), Servette FC Genève (1/0), CD Cobreloa Calama (2/0), CD O'Higgins Rancagua (7/0), Club América Ciudad de México (18/2), Birmingham City FC (13/1), Wigan Athletic FC (14/2). |
| (110/240) | BELLO Bernardo | | **11** | **2** | 1954-1963, CSD Colo-Colo Santiago (11/2). |
| (140/267) | BELLO Néstor | | **1** | **0** | 1957, CD Rangers Talca (1/0). |
| (101/228) | BEPERET Valentín | | **1** | **0** | 1953, Club Unión Española Santiago (1/0). |
| (186/321) | BERLY Hugo | 31.12.1941 | **12** | **0** | 1967-1974, Audax CS Italiano Santiago (11/0), Club Unión Española Santiago (1/0). |
| (20/062) | BERNAL Guillermo | | **3** | **0** | 1922, Jorge V Valparaíso (3/0). |
| (164/296) | BETTA Rómulo | | **6** | **1** | 1960-1963, CD Everton Viña del Mar (6/1). |
| (269/390) | BIGORRA LÓPEZ Vladimir David | 09.08.1954 | **21** | **0** | 1974-1987, CF de la Universidad de Chile Santiago (20/0), CD Cobresal El Salvador (1/0). |
| (661/794) | BISKUPOVIĆ VENTURINO Marko Andrés | 30.06.1989 | **2** | **0** | 2012, CD Universidad Católica Santiago (2/0). |
| (11/050) | BOLADOS Hernando | | **5** | **2** | 1917-1920, Unión Marítimo FC Taltal (3/0), CD Santiago Wanderers Valparaíso (2/2). |
| (293/417) | BONVALLET GODOY Eduardo Guillermo | 13.01.1955 | **24** | **0** | 1979-1982, CD O'Higgins Rancagua (8/0), CD Universidad Católica Santiago (16/0). |
| (410/538) | BRAVO Cristián | 07.12.1968 | **1** | **0** | 1991, CD Cobresal El Salvador (1/0). |
| (20/065) | BRAVO Manuel | | **5** | **2** | 1922-1928, CD Unión Coquimbo (4/1), CD Santiago Wanderers Valparaíso (1/1). |
| (555/680) | BRAVO MUÑOZ Claudio Andrés | 13.04.1983 | **78** | **0** | 2004-2013, CSD Colo-Colo Santiago (7/0), Real Sociedad de Fútbol San Sebastián (71/0). |
| (4/023) | BRITO Primedio | | **1** | **0** | 1913, La Cruz FC Quillota Valparaíso (1/0). |
| (63/170) | BUSQUETS Miguel | 15.10.1920 | **18** | **0** | 1945-1950, CF de la Universidad de Chile Santiago (18/0). |
| (583/721) | CABIÓN DIANTA José Luis | 14.11.1983 | **6** | **0** | 2007, Club de Deportes Melipilla (6/0). |
| (347/470) | CABRERA Jorge | | **1** | **0** | 1985, Club de Deportes Arica (1/0). |
| (42/119) | CABRERA Luis | | **5** | **0** | 1936-1937, Audax CS Italiano Santiago (5/0). |
| (165/299) | CABRERA Ricardo | | **6** | **2** | 1960-1965, CD Magallanes Santiago (1/2), CD O'Higgins Rancagua (1/0), CD Santiago Wanderers Valparaíso (4/0). |
| (52/140) | CABRERA Roberto | | **8** | **0** | 1941-1942, Audax CS Italiano Santiago (8/0). |
| (1/009) | CAMPBELL Colin | | **3** | **1** | 1910, Santiago National (3/1). |
| (633/767) | CAMPOS ARANIBA Bernardo Andrés | 07.04.1988 | **1** | **0** | 2010, CD Universidad Católica Santiago (1/0). |
| (164/294) | CAMPOS Carlos | 14.02.1937 | **12** | **3** | 1960-1967, CF de la Universidad de Chile Santiago (12/3). |
| (76/196) | CAMPOS Fernando Iván | 1921 | **5** | **3** | 1947-1950, CD Santiago Wanderers Valparaíso (5/3). |
| (656/777) | CAMPOS TORO Matías Daniel | 22.06.1989 | **6** | **1** | 2011-2012, Audax Italiano La Florida (3/1), CD Universidad Católica Santiago (3/0). |
| (659/790) | CANALES CALAS Nicolás Sebastián | 27.06.1985 | **1** | **0** | 2012, CD Palestino Santiago (1/0). |
| (656/779) | CANALES Gustavo Javier | 30.03.1982 | **1** | **0** | 2011, CFP de la Universidad de Chile Santiago (1/0). |
| (535/648) | CANCINO ARANEDA Víctor Antonio | 27.06.1972 | **2** | **0** | 2001, Club Deportes Concepción (2/0). |
| (387/516) | CANTILLANA José | | **2** | **0** | 1989, Club de Deportes Iquique (2/0). |

| | | | | | |
|---|---|---|---|---|---|
| (224/346) | CAPOT Fabián | | **1** | **0** | 1968, CD Santiago Morning (1/0). |
| (33/096) | CARBONELL Alejandro | | **2** | **1** | 1928, Valparaíso Ferroviarios FC (2/1). |
| (4/018) | CÁRDENAS Enrique | | **9** | **0** | 1913-1917, CD Santiago Wanderers Valparaíso (9/0). |
| (39/112) | CARMONA Arturo | | **8** | **1** | 1935-1937, CD Magallanes Santiago (8/1). |
| (130/253) | CARMONA Carlos | | **2** | **0** | 1956, Ferrobádminton Santiago (2/0). |
| (601/737) | CARMONA TELLO Carlos Emilio | 21.02.1987 | **42** | **1** | 2008-2013, CD O'Higgins Rancagua (4/0), Reggina Calcio Reggio Emilia (19/0), Atalanta Bergamasca Calcio (19/1). |
| (601/736) | CAROCA CORDERO Rafael Antonio | 19.07.1989 | **2** | **0** | 2008-2010, CSD Colo-Colo Santiago (2/0). |
| (133/257) | CARRASCO Gonzalo | | **6** | **0** | 1957-1959, Green Cross Santiago (6/0). |
| (109/236) | CARRASCO Isaac | | **25** | **0** | 1954-1961, Audax CS Italiano Santiago (4/0), CSD Colo-Colo Santiago (20/0), CD Santiago Morning (1/0). |
| (386/509) | CARRASCO Jorge | 03.11.1961 | **6** | **0** | 1989, CD Huachipato Talcahuano (6/0). |
| (99/226) | CARRASCO Oscar | | **7** | **0** | 1953-1957, Audax CS Italiano Santiago (7/0). |
| (659/792) | CARRASCO SANTOS Bryan Paul | 31.01.1991 | **3** | **1** | 2012, Audax Italiano La Serena (3/1). |
| (386/513) | CARREÑO Guillermo | 06.02.1963 | **2** | **0** | 1989, Club de Deportes Iquique (2/0). |
| (431/550) | CARREÑO Juan Enrique | 16.11.1968 | **10** | **1** | 1993-1998, Club Unión Española Santiago (2/0), Club Deportes Concepción (6/1), CD Huachipato Talcahuano (2/0). |
| (494/608) | CARTES CONTRERAS Roberto Rodrigo | 16.03.1972 | **7** | **1** | 1999, AA Argentinos Juniors Buenos Aires (7/1). |
| (52/142) | CARVAJAL Osvaldo | | **4** | **0** | 1941, Green Cross Santiago (4/0). |
| (47/131) | CARVAJAL Voltaire | | **2** | **0** | 1939, Club Unión Española Santiago (2/0). |
| (68/176) | CARVALLO CASTRO Hernán | 19.08.1922 | **7** | **0** | 1946-1950, CD Universidad Católica Santiago (7/0). |
| (254/379) | CARVALLO Fernando | 24.09.1948 | **3** | **0** | 1972, CD Universidad Católica Santiago (3/0). |
| (659/791) | CARVALLO TORRES Joseph Aníbal | 01.05.1990 | **1** | **0** | 2012, CD Universidad de Concepción (1/0). |
| (56/157) | CASANOVA Guillermo | | **5** | **0** | 1942, CD Santiago Morning (5/0). |
| (633/768) | CASANOVA SANDOVAL Luis Ignacio | 01.07.1992 | **5** | **0** | 2010-2012, CD O'Higgins Rancagua (5/0). |
| (433/558) | CASTAÑEDA VARGAS Cristián | 18.09.1968 | **24** | **1** | 1994-1998, CF de la Universidad de Chile Santiago (24/1). |
| (458/584) | CASTAÑEDA VARGAS Víctor Hugo | 06.07.1962 | **11** | **0** | 1996-1997, CF de la Universidad de Chile Santiago (11/0). |
| (215/335) | CASTAÑEDA Víctor | | **1** | **0** | 1967, CD Palestino Santiago (1/0). |
| (308/432) | CASTEC MARTÍNEZ Sandrino | 18.06.1960 | **7** | **1** | 1980-1983, CF de la Universidad de Chile Santiago (7/1). |
| (423/543) | CASTILLO Juan | 29.10.1970 | **6** | **1** | 1993-1997, Club Unión Española Santiago (4/1), Club de Deportes Temuco (2/0). |
| (532/645) | CASTILLO Miguel Angel | 25.08.1972 | **1** | **0** | 2001, CD Palestino Santiago (1/0). |
| (673/802) | CASTILLO MORA Nicolás Ignacio | 14.02.1993 | **1** | **0** | 2013, CD Universidad Católica Santiago (1/0). |
| (627/756) | CASTRO GAMBOA Francisco Fernando | 04.09.1990 | **2** | **0** | 2010, CD Cobreloa Calama (2/0). |
| (66/173) | CASTRO Mario | | **13** | **0** | 1945-1953, CD Santiago Morning (6/0), CSD Colo-Colo Santiago (7/0). |
| (209/330) | CASTRO Osvaldo | 14.04.1947 | **28** | **7** | 1966-1977, Club Unión La Calera (13/3), Club Deportes Concepción (8/3), CF América SA Ciudad de México (7 |
| (228/352) | CASZELY GARRIDO Carlos Humberto | 05.07.1950 | **48** | **29** | 1969-1985, CSD Colo-Colo Santiago (19/13), UD Levante Valencia (3/0), CSD Colo-Colo Santiago (26/16). |
| (20/063) | CATALÁN Alberto | | **5** | **0** | 1922, Fábrica de Vidrios Santiago (5/0). |
| (608/743) | CELIS CONTRERAS Matías Jesús | 09.01.1989 | **1** | **0** | 2008, CF de la Universidad de Chile Santiago (1/0). |
| (570/692) | CERECEDA GUAJARDO Roberto Andrés | 10.10.1984 | **32** | **1** | 2006-2010, Audax CS Italiano Santiago (3/0), CSD Colo-Colo Santiago (29/1). |
| (33/094) | CHAPARRO ESQUIVEL Ernesto | 04.01.1901 | **5** | **0** | 1928-1930, CSD Colo-Colo Santiago (5/0). |
| (462/589) | CHAVARRÍA ANDRADE Luis Eugenio | 26.03.1970 | **5** | **0** | 1996-2001, Club Deportes Concepción (4/0), CF de la Universidad de Chile Santiago (1/0). |
| (10/042) | CISTERNAS Guillermo | | **2** | **0** | 1917, Maestranza FC Iquique (2/0). |
| (108/235) | CISTERNAS Horacio | | **1** | **0** | 1953, CD Universidad Católica Santiago (1/0). |
| (551/678) | CISTERNAS Jonathan Josué | 16.06.1980 | **3** | **0** | 2004-2006, CD Cobreloa Calama (3/0). |
| (584/725) | CISTERNAS TOBAR Carlos Patricio | 27.09.1985 | **1** | **0** | 2007, Deportivo Ñublense Chillán (1/0). |
| (68/179) | CLAVERÍA Rodolfo | | **2** | **0** | 1946, CD Universidad Católica Santiago (2/0). |
| (62/166) | CLAVERO Guillermo | | **6** | **3** | 1945, CD Everton Viña del Mar (6/3). |
| (130/254) | CLIMENT Ramón | | **2** | **0** | 1956, CD Rangers Talca (2/0). |
| (344/465) | COFRÉ Eduardo Gino | 23.07.1962 | **1** | **0** | 1984, CD Santiago Wanderers Valparaíso (1/0). |
| (145/272) | COLOMA Raúl | | **12** | **0** | 1959-1960, Ferrobádminton Santiago (12/0). |
| (658/781) | CONTRERAS ARAYA Michael | 10.02.1993 | **1** | **0** | 2011, CD Iquique (1/0). |
| (52/143) | CONTRERAS Armando | | **14** | **2** | 1941-1945, CSD Colo-Colo Santiago (14/2). |
| (570/694) | CONTRERAS ARRAU José Raúl | 23.03.1982 | **9** | **0** | 2006-2007, CD Santiago Wanderers Valparaíso (5/0), CD Huachipato Talcahuano (4/0). |
| (153/284) | CONTRERAS Carlos | 02.10.1938 | **30** | **0** | 1959-1966, CF de la Universidad de Chile Santiago (30/0). |
| (494/607) | CONTRERAS FICA Pablo Andrés | 11.09.1978 | **67** | **2** | 1999-2012, CSD Colo-Colo Santiago (6/0), AS Monaco (4/0), Racing Club Avellaneda (2/0), CA Osasuna Pamplona (1/0), Sporting Clube de Portugal Lisboa (5/1), Real Club Celta de Vigo (23/0), PAOK Thessaloníki (23/1), CSD Colo Colo Santiago (2/0), PAE Olympiacos Peiraiás (1/0). |
| (32/093) | CONTRERAS Humberto | | **2** | **0** | 1927-1928, CD Santiago Wanderers Valparaíso (1/0), Unión Deportiva Española Santiago (1/0). |
| (359/474) | CONTRERAS Leonel | 30.08.1962 | **21** | **0** | 1985-1989, CD Everton Viña del Mar (10/0), Club de Deportes La Serena (11/0). |
| (337/455) | CONTRERAS LIRA Jorge Alejandro | 03.07.1960 | **25** | **2** | 1983-1997, CD Palestino Santiago (2/0), UD Las Palmas (5/1), CD Universidad Católica Santiago (13/1), Club Deportes Concepción (2/0), CD Santiago Wanderers Valparaíso (3/0). |
| (438/566) | CONTRERAS Wilson | 05.10.1967 | **4** | **0** | 1994-1997, CD Regional Atacama (1/0), CD Huachipato Talcahuano (3/0). |
| (42/120) | CÓRDOVA Jorge | | **10** | **0** | 1936-1939, CD Magallanes Santiago (10/0). |
| (47/132) | CÓRDOVA Julio | | **4** | **0** | 1939, CD Magallanes Santiago (4/0). |

| | | | | | |
|---|---|---|---|---|---|
| (541/668) | CÓRDOVA SAN CRISTÓBAL Nicolás Andrés | 09.02.1979 | **5** | **1** | 2003-2011, AS Bari (3/0), Brescia Calcio (2/1). |
| (410/535) | CORNEJO JIMÉNEZ Fernando Andrés | 28.01.1969 | **33** | **2** | 1991-2000, CD O'Higgins Rancagua (2/0), CD Cobreloa Calama (18/2), CD Universidad Católica Santiago (10/0), CD Cobreloa Calama (3/0). |
| (333/453) | CORNÉZ Marco Antonio | 15.10.1957 | **22** | **0** | 1983-1995, CD Palestino Santiago (5/0), CD Universidad Católica Santiago (14/0), Club de Deportes Antofagasta (1/0), CD Everton Viña del Mar (2/0). |
| (528/643) | CORRALES GARCÍA Marcelo Enrique | 05.01.1970 | **2** | **1** | 2001, CD Unión San Felipe (2/1). |
| (240/358) | CORTÁZAR Eduardo | | **1** | **0** | 1970, Green Cross Temuco (1/0). |
| (39/107) | CORTÉS Ascanio | | **13** | **0** | 1935-1941, Audax CS Italiano Santiago (13/0). |
| (665/796) | CORTÉS PINTO César Alexis | 09.01.1984 | **4** | **0** | 2012-2013, CFP de la Universidad de Chile Santiago (4/0). |
| (94/221) | CORTÉS Ramiro | | **45** | **1** | 1952-1960, Audax CS Italiano Santiago (45/1). |
| (29/086) | CORTÉS Roberto | 02.02.1905 | **9** | **0** | 1926-1935, Chilex Chiquicamata (3/0), CSD Colo-Colo Santiago (6/0). |
| (464/590) | COSSIO RIQUELME Nelson Orlando | 14.06.1966 | **4** | **0** | 1997, Audax CS Italiano Santiago (4/0). |
| (344/463) | COVARRUBIAS Juan | 15.01.1961 | **16** | **2** | 1984-1989, CD Cobreloa Calama (16/2). |
| (64/171) | CREMASCHI Atilio | 08.03.1923 | **32** | **10** | 1945-1954, Club Unión Española Santiago (29/10), CSD Colo-Colo Santiago (3/0). |
| (248/370) | CRISOSTO Julio | | **26** | **11** | 1971-1977, CD Universidad Católica Santiago (15/5), CSD Colo-Colo Santiago (11/6). |
| (172/301) | CRUZ Humberto | 08.12.1939 | **37** | **0** | 1961-1970, CD Santiago Morning (4/0), CSD Colo-Colo Santiago (33/0). |
| (379/505) | CRUZ Mario | 25.03.1966 | **2** | **0** | 1988, CD Everton Viña del Mar (2/0). |
| (114/246) | CUBILLOS Carlos | | **14** | **0** | 1954-1957, Club Unión Española Santiago (14/0). |
| (222/343) | CUEVAS Ricardo | | **2** | **0** | 1968, CD Santiago Morning (2/0). |
| (571/698) | CURRIMILLA GÓMEZ Dagoberto | 26.12.1987 | **1** | **0** | 2006, CD Huachipato Talcahuano (1/0). |

| | | | | | |
|---|---|---|---|---|---|
| (1/010) | DAVIDSON J.P. | | **2** | **0** | 1910, Bádminton FC Valparaíso (2/0). |
| (4/020) | DEAN Harold | | **1** | **0** | 1913, Vaparaíso FC (1/0). |
| (15/056) | DEL RÍO Carlos | | **2** | **0** | 1919, Liceo de Concepción (2/0). |
| (658/780) | DELGADO PLANKOVICH Leandro Javier | 15.07.1982 | **1** | **0** | 2011, Unión Española Santiago (1/0). |
| (584/728) | DI GREGORIO Javier Eduardo | 23.01.1977 | **1** | **0** | 2007, Club de Deportes Temuco (1/0). |
| (94/222) | DÍAZ CARMONA Guillermo | 29.12.1930 | **11** | **4** | 1952-1955, CD Santiago Morning (11/4). |
| (228/351) | DÍAZ Daniel | | **23** | **0** | 1969-1977, CD Universidad Católica Santiago (14/0), CD Huachipato Talcahuano (6/0), CSD Colo-Colo Santiago (3/0). |
| (329/443) | DÍAZ Héctor | | **1** | **0** | 1983, Audax CS Italiano Santiago (1/0). |
| (525/636) | DÍAZ MUÑOZ Italo Andrés | 21.06.1971 | **2** | **0** | 2001, CD Cobreloa Calama (2/0). |
| (140/269) | DÍAZ Osvaldo | | **2** | **0** | 1957, CF de la Universidad de Chile Santiago (2/0). |
| (164/295) | DÍAZ Ricardo | | **2** | **1** | 1960-1967, CD Santiago Wanderers Valparaíso (1/1), CD Santiago Morning (1/0). |
| (656/778) | DÍAZ ROJAS Marcelo Alfonso | 30.12.1986 | **19** | **0** | 2011-2013, CFP de la Universidad de Chile Santiago (6/0), FC Basel (13/0). |
| (87/206) | DÍAZ ZAMBRANO Guillermo | | **19** | **7** | 1950-1957, CD Santiago Wanderers Valparaíso (13/5), CD Palestino Santiago (6/2). |
| (47/130) | DOMÍNGUEZ Alfonso | | **12** | **3** | 1939-1942, Club Unión Española Santiago (4/1), CSD Colo-Colo Santiago (8/2). |
| (14/053) | DOMÍNGUEZ Aurelio | | **14** | **1** | 1919-1924, Artillero de Costa FC Talcahuano (14/1). |
| (642/771) | DOMÍNGUEZ IRARRÁZABAL Lucas | 27.10.1989 | **6** | **0** | 2011-2012, Audax Italiano La Florida (6/0). |
| (182/310) | DONOSO Humberto | 09.10.1938 | **14** | **0** | 1963-1966, CF de la Universidad de Chile Santiago (14/0). |
| (496/618) | DONOSO PÉREZ Mauricio Alejandro | 30.04.1976 | **2** | **0** | 1999-2001, CD Cobreloa Calama (1/0), Club Universidad Nacional Autonoma de México (1/0). |
| (164/297) | DROGUETT Aldo | | **1** | **1** | 1960, CD O'Higgins Rancagua (1/1). |
| (578/704) | DROGUETT DIOCARES Hugo Patricio | 02.09.1982 | **13** | **1** | 2006-2008, CF Estudiantes Tecos Guadalajara (11/1), CA Monarcas Morélia (2/0). |
| (285/411) | DUBÓ SEGOVIA Rodolfo del Rosario | 11.09.1953 | **46** | **3** | 1977-1985, CD Palestino Santiago (32/1), CF de la Universidad de Chile (11/2), CD Palestino Santiago (3/0). |

| | | | | | |
|---|---|---|---|---|---|
| (4/021) | ELGUETA Agustín | | **1** | **0** | 1913, Eleuterio Ramírez FC Santiago (1/0). |
| (17/059) | ELGUETA Humberto | | **10** | **0** | 1920-1930, Gold Cross FC Talcahuano (8/0), CD Santiago Wanderers Valparaíso (1/0), CD Naval Talcahuano (1/0). |
| (52/139) | ELLIS Oscar | | **1** | **0** | 1941, CD Santiago Morning (1/0). |
| (10/045) | ENCINA Luis | | **5** | **0** | 1917-1922, Norteamérica Iquique (5/0). |
| (374/498) | ENRÍQUEZ Nélson | 17.06.1961 | **6** | **0** | 1988, CD Cobreloa Calama (5/0), Club de Deportes La Serena (1/0). |
| (4/017) | ERNST Otto | | **4** | **0** | 1913-1924, Santiago National (1/0), CD Magallanes Santiago (3/0). |
| (283/404) | ESCOBAR OLIVARES Enzo Sergio | 10.11.1951 | **26** | **0** | 1976-1982, Club Unión Española Santiago (21/0), CD Cobreloa Calama (5/0). |
| (106/233) | ESCUTI Misael | 20.12.1926 | **40** | **0** | 1953-1963, CSD Colo-Colo Santiago (40/0). |
| (125/249) | ESPINOZA Carlos | | **4** | **0** | 1956, CD Everton Viña del Mar (4/0). |
| (250/374) | ESPINOZA Fernando | | **4** | **0** | 1972, CD Magallanes Santiago (4/0). |
| (629/765) | ESPINOZA Juan Carlos | 05.07.1991 | **1** | **0** | 2010, CD Huachipato Talcahuano (1/0). |
| (329/441) | ESPINOZA MOLINA Rubén Alberto | 01.06.1961 | **30** | **5** | 1983-1991, CD Universidad Católica Santiago (21/4), CSD Colo-Colo Santiago (9/1). |
| (101/229) | ESPINOZA Sergio | | **7** | **1** | 1954-1957, Audax CS Italiano Santiago (7/1). |
| (408/521) | ESTAY SILVA Fabián Raphael | 05.10.1968 | **69** | **5** | 1990-2001, CD Universidad Católica Santiago (14/2), CF de la Universidad de Chile Santiago (9/1), Olympiakos SFP Peiraiás (5/0), CSD Colo-Colo Santiago (8/0), CD Toluca AC (23/1), CF América SA Ciudad de México (10/1). |

| | | | | | |
|---|---|---|---|---|---|
| (295/424) | ESTAY Víctor | | **6** | **0** | 1979, Club Unión Española Santiago (6/0). |
| (592/731) | ESTRADA QUINTEROS Marco Andrés | 28.05.1983 | **33** | **1** | 2007-2011, CF de la Universidad de Chile Santiago (23/1), Montpellier Hérault SC (10/0). |
| (149/281) | EYZAGUIRRE Luis Armando | 22.07.1941 | **39** | **0** | 1959-1966, CF de la Universidad de Chile Santiago (39/0). |
| (303/427) | FABBIANI VENTURELLI Oscar Roberto | 17.12.1950 | **3** | **0** | 1979, Tampa Bay Rowdies (3/0). |
| (87/208) | FARÍAS Arturo | 01.11.1927 | **24** | **0** | 1950-1954, CSD Colo-Colo Santiago (24/0). |
| (250/373) | FARÍAS SALVADOR Rogelio | 13.08.1949 | **12** | **2** | 1972-1977, Club Unión Española (12/2). |
| (566/685) | FERNÁNDEZ FERNÀNDEZ Matías Ariel | 15.05.1986 | **59** | **14** | 2005-2013, CSD Colo-Colo Santiago (5/2), Villarreal CF (25/5), Sporting Clube de Portugal Lisboa (20/6), AC Fiorentina Firenze (9/1). |
| (151/282) | FERNÁNDEZ Francisco | | **1** | **0** | 1959, Audax CS Italiano Santiago (1/0). |
| (509/625) | FERNÁNDEZ Francisco | 19.08.1975 | **2** | **0** | 2000, CD Universidad Católica Santiago (2/0). |
| (56/158) | FERNÁNDEZ Hernán | | **10** | **0** | 1942-1952, Club Unión Española Santiago (10/0). |
| (87/209) | FERNÁNDEZ José | | **24** | **5** | 1950-1957, CD Santiago Wanderers Valparaíso (6/0), CD Palestino Santiago (18/5). |
| (575/702) | FIERRO CANIULLÁN Gonzalo Antonio | 21.03.1983 | **22** | **1** | 2006-2011, CSD Colo-Colo Santiago (12/1), CR Flamengo Rio de Janeiro (10/0). |
| (197/324) | FIGUEROA BRANDER Elías Ricardo | 25.10.1946 | **46** | **3** | 1966-1982, CD Santiago Wanderers Valparaíso (17/0), SC Internacional Porto Alegre (5/0), CD Palestino Santiago (15/3), Fort Lauderdale Strikers (2/0), CSD Colo-Colo Santiago (7/0). |
| (387/515) | FIGUEROA Claudio | 20.04.1960 | **4** | **0** | 1989, CDFA Arturo Fernández Vial Concepción (4/0). |
| (31/087) | FIGUEROA Manuel | | **1** | **0** | 1926, CDFA Arturo Fernández Vial Concepción (1/0). |
| (365/481) | FIGUEROA MONTERO Marco Antonio | 21.02.1962 | **8** | **1** | 1986-1993, CD Everton Viña del Mar (1/0), 1989 (1/0), CD Cobreloa Calama (6/1). |
| (549/673) | FIGUEROA SEPÚLVEDA Luis Pedro | 14.05.1983 | **16** | **1** | 2004-2013, CD Universidad de Concepción (3/0), CF de la Universidad de Chile Santiago (3/1), Arsenal FC de Sarandí (3/0), CSD Colo-Colo Santiago (2/0), Club Unión Española Santiago (1/0), CD O'Higgins Rancagua (4/0). |
| (583/718) | FLORES ABARCA Luis Reinaldo | 03.05.1982 | **2** | **1** | 2007, Deportivo Ñublense Chillán (2/1). |
| (661/793) | FLORES CHANDÍA Felipe Ignacio | 09.01.1987 | **2** | **1** | 2012, CD Cobreloa Calama (2/1). |
| (466/593) | FLORES Cristián | 05.03.1972 | **4** | **0** | 1997-2000, CD Santiago Wanderers Valparaíso (1/0), CSD Colo-Colo Santiago (3/0). |
| (81/201) | FLORES Miguel | | **3** | **0** | 1949, CD Magallanes Santiago (3/0). |
| (53/147) | FLORES Segundo | | **3** | **0** | 1941, CSD Colo-Colo Santiago (3/0). |
| (155/286) | FOUILLOUX AHUMADA Alberto Jorge | 22.11.1940 | **70** | **11** | 1960-1972, CD Universidad Católica Santiago (58/10), CD Huachipato Talcahuano (6/0), Club Unión Española Santiago (6/1). |
| (6/036) | FRANCE Alfredo | | **10** | **2** | 1916-1920, CD Estrella del Mar Talcahuano (4/1), Gold Cross FC Talcahuano (6/1). |
| (16/057) | FREZ Guillermo | | **1** | **0** | 1919, La Cruz FC Quillota Valparaíso (1/0). |
| (432/555) | FUENTES Carlos | 09.04.1968 | **3** | **0** | 1994, CD Cobreloa Calama (3/0). |
| (555/681) | FUENTES CASTRO Ismael Ignacio | 04.08.1981 | **29** | **1** | 2004-2010, CD Rangers Talca (2/0), Club Jaguares de Chiapas Tuxtla Gutiérrez (19/1), CD Atlas Guadalajara (4/0), CD Universidad Católica Santiago (4/0). |
| (5/032) | FUENTES Eufemio | | **6** | **0** | 1916-1919, La Cruz FC Quillota Valparaíso (3/0), CD Estrella del Mar Talcahuano (3/0). |
| (410/528) | FUENTES NÚÑEZ Ronald Hugo | 22.06.1969 | **50** | **1** | 1991-2000, CD Cobresal El Salvador (3/0), CF de la Universidad de Chile Santiago (47/1). |
| (480/599) | FUENTES RODRÍGUEZ Luis Alberto | 14.08.1971 | **28** | **4** | 1998-2006, CD Coquimbo Unido (1/0), CD Cobreloa Calama (26/4). |
| (335/454) | FUENTES SILVA Edgardo Enrique | 18.08.1958 | **1** | **0** | 1983, CD Palestino Santiago (1/0). |
| (601/739) | FUENZALIDA GANA José Pedro | 22.02.1985 | **21** | **1** | 2008-2013, CSD Colo-Colo Santiago (3/0), CD O'Higgins Rancagua (5/0), CSD Colo-Colo Santiago (12/1). |
| (69/182) | FUENZALIDA Guillermo | | **2** | **0** | 1946, CSD Colo-Colo Santiago (2/0). |
| (252/378) | GAETE Manuel | | **3** | **0** | 1972-1974, CD Unión San Felipe (2/0), Club Unión Española Santiago (1/0). |
| (550/676) | GALAZ SEPULVEDA Patricio Sebastián | 31.12.1976 | **12** | **0** | 2004-2006, CD Cobreloa Calama (7/0), CD Atlante Ciudad de México (5/0). |
| (441/573) | GALDAMES DÍAZ Pablo | 26.06.1974 | **22** | **2** | 1995-2001, Club Unión Española Santiago (7/0), CF de la Universidad de Chile Santiago (10/1), CDS y Cultual Cruz Azul Ciudad de México (5/1). |
| (257/384) | GALINDO CALIXTO Mario Enrique | 10.08.1951 | **29** | **0** | 1972-1982, CSD Colo-Colo Santiago (29/0). |
| (209/331) | GALLARDO Julio | | **10** | **4** | 1966-1969, CD Universidad Católica Santiago (8/3), CD Palestino Santiago (2/1). |
| (226/348) | GALLARDO Nélson | | **1** | **0** | 1968, CF de la Universidad de Chile Santiago (1/0). |
| (164/293) | GALLARDO Reinaldo | | **1** | **0** | 1960, CD Everton Viña del Mar (1/0). |
| (243/366) | GALLEGOS Claudio | | **4** | **0** | 1971, CD Everton Viña del Mar (4/0). |
| (258/385) | GALLEGUILLOS Gabriel | 19.11.1944 | **1** | **0** | 1973, Club Deportes Concepción (1/0). |
| (268/389) | GAMBOA PEDEMONTE Miguel Ángel | 21.06.1951 | **18** | **6** | 1974-1983, CSD Colo-Colo Santiago (8/3), CF América SA Ciudad de México (2/1), CF de la Universidad de Chile Santiago (8/2). |
| (642/770) | GARCÉS CONTRERAS Paulo Andrés | 02.08.1984 | **1** | **0** | 2011, CD Universidad Católica Santiago (1/0). |
| (28/083) | GARCÍA Carlos Luis | | **3** | **0** | 1926-1927, CD Everton Viña del Mar (3/0). |
| (242/360) | GARCÍA JIMÉNEZ Rolando Moisés | 15.12.1942 | **17** | **1** | 1971-1975, Club Deportes Concepción (9/0), CSD Colo-Colo Santiago (8/1). |
| (345/468) | GARCÍA Jorge | | **3** | **0** | 1984-1988, CD Everton Viña del Mar (1/0), CD Cobreloa Calama (2/0). |
| (10/040) | GARCÍA Luis Alberto | | **4** | **0** | 1917-1926, Thunder FC Coquimbo (4/0). |
| (217/337) | GARCÍA Pedro | | **2** | **0** | 1967, Club Unión Española Santiago (2/0). |
| (538/659) | GARCÍA SÁNCHEZ Gamadiel Adrián | 20.07.1979 | **1** | **0** | 2002, CF de la Universidad de Chile Santiago (1/0). |

| | | | | | |
|---|---|---|---|---|---|
| (309/434) | GARRIDO BUSTAMANTE Antonio Lizardo | 25.08.1957 | **44** | **0** | 1981-1991, CSD Colo-Colo Santiago (44/0). |
| (408/522) | GARRIDO Juan Ramón | | **1** | **0** | 1990, CD Palestino Santiago (1/0). |
| (10/039) | GATICA Francisco | | **5** | **0** | 1917-1919, CD Santiago Wanderers Valparaíso (5/0). |
| (14/051) | GATICA Pedro | | **2** | **0** | 1919, Eleuterio Ramírez FC Santiago (2/0). |
| (307/430) | GATICA Santiago | | **8** | **0** | 1980-1981, CD O'Higgins Rancagua (8/0). |
| (601/738) | GAZALE ÁLVAREZ Daúd Jared | 10.08.1984 | **8** | **0** | 2008-2011, CD Concepción (3/0), CSD Colo-Colo Santiago (2/0), CD Huachipato Talcahuano (2/0), CSD Colo-Colo Santiago (1/0). |
| (4/022) | GELDES Manuel | | **7** | **0** | 1913-1917, CD Santiago Wanderers Valparaíso (6/0). |
| (1/001) | GIBSON L.C. | | **3** | **0** | 1910, Valparaíso FC (3/0). |
| (39/111) | GIUDICE Carlos | | **3** | **1** | 1935, Audax CS Italiano Santiago (3/1). |
| (179/305) | GODOY Adán | 26.11.1936 | **14** | **0** | 1962-1966, CD Santiago Morning (3/0), CD Universidad Católica Santiago (11/0). |
| (658/785) | GODOY ZEPEDA Eric Orlando | 26.03.1987 | **1** | **0** | 2011, CD Santiago Wanderers Valparaíso (1/0). |
| (125/250) | GOITY Sergio | | **4** | **0** | 1956, CD Palestino Santiago (4/0). |
| (441/575) | GOLDBERG Rodrígo | 09.08.1971 | **12** | **3** | 1995-1997, CF de la Universidad de Chile Santiago (11/3), Maccabi Tel Aviv FC (1/0). |
| (537/655) | GÓMEZ CHANDÍA Cristián Alejandro | 14.01.1978 | **1** | **0** | 2001, CD Coquimbo Unido (1/0). |
| (344/458) | GÓMEZ Eduardo | 02.06.1958 | **21** | **0** | 1984-1987, CD Cobreloa Calama (21/0). |
| (470/597) | GÓMEZ Jorge | 14.09.1968 | **7** | **0** | 1997-1998, Club de Deportes Temuco (4/0), CD Cobreloa Calama (3/0). |
| (410/536) | GÓMEZ Rodrígo Vicente | 25.01.1968 | **6** | **0** | 1991, CD Palestino Santiago (6/0). |
| (378/500) | GONZÁLEZ Aníbal Segundo | 13.03.1964 | **10** | **1** | 1988-1991, CD O'Higgins Rancagua (5/0), Club Unión Española Santiago (5/1). |
| (583/714) | GONZÁLEZ CALVO Daniel Felipe | 30.01.1984 | **3** | **1** | 2007, CD O'Higgins Rancagua (3/1). |
| (4/019) | GONZÁLEZ Carlos | | **4** | **0** | 1913-1919, CD Santiago Wanderers Valparaíso (1/0), Artillero de Costa FC Talcahuano (3/0). |
| (250/372) | GONZÁLEZ CÓRDOVA Rafael | 24.04.1950 | **19** | **0** | 1972-1976, CSD Colo-Colo Santiago (18/0), 1976 (1/0). |
| (625/753) | GONZÁLEZ DE LA HOZ Renato Patricio | 19.02.1990 | **1** | **1** | 2009, CD Palestino Santiago (1/1). |
| (541/667) | GONZÁLEZ GARRIDO Boris Igor | 22.05.1980 | **7** | **0** | 2003-2007, CD Cobreloa Calama (6/0), CSD Colo-Colo Santiago (1/0). |
| (543/669) | GONZÁLEZ HOFFMANN Mark Dennis | 10.07.1984 | **47** | **4** | 2003-2012, CD Universidad Católica Santiago (8/2), Albacete Balompié (4/1), Real Sociedad de Fútbol San Sebastián (1/0), Real Betis Balompié Sevilla (23/0), FK CSKA Moskva (11/1). |
| (382/506) | GONZÁLEZ Hugo Armando | 11.03.1963 | **24** | **2** | 1988-1993, CSD Colo-Colo Santiago (23/2), CD Cobreloa Calama (1/0). |
| (183/313) | GONZÁLEZ José | | **9** | **0** | 1963-1966, CSD Colo-Colo Santiago (9/0). |
| (431/547) | GONZÁLEZ Juan Carlos | 13.11.1968 | **10** | **0** | 1993-1997, Club Unión Española Santiago (2/0), CSD Colo-Colo Santiago (8/0). |
| (558/682) | GONZÁLEZ Juan Luis | 16.06.1974 | **5** | **0** | 2004-2005, CD Cobreloa Calama (5/0). |
| (20/064) | GONZÁLEZ Oscar "Tránsito" | | **8** | **0** | 1922-1926, La Cruz FC Quillota Valparaíso (8/0). |
| (1/006) | GONZÁLEZ Próspero | | **5** | **0** | 1910-1916, Arco Iris FC Santiago (3/0), CD Santiago Wanderers Valparaíso (2/0). |
| (295/423) | GONZÁLEZ Raúl | | **4** | **0** | 1979, CD Palestino Santiago (4/0). |
| (431/548) | GONZÁLEZ Ricardo | 31.08.1965 | **1** | **0** | 1993, Club Unión Española Santiago (1/0). |
| (538/660) | GONZÁLEZ SALAZAR Marcos Andrés | 09.06.1980 | **27** | **2** | 2002-2013, CD Rangers Talca (1/0), CF de la Universidad de Chile Santiago (9/0), CR Flamengo Rio de Janeiro (17/2). |
| (599/734) | GONZÁLEZ SEPÚLVEDA Osvaldo Alexis | 10.08.1984 | **12** | **0** | 2008-2012, CD Universidad de Concepción (2/0), CF de la Universidad de Chile Santiago (1/0), Deportivo Toluca FC (4/0), CFP de la Universidad de Chile Santiago (5/0). |
| (628/759) | GONZÁLEZ TABILO Ronald Damián | 17.10.1990 | **1** | **0** | 2010, CD Antofagasta (1/0). |
| (523/634) | GONZÁLEZ VALDÉS Sebastián Ignacio | 14.12.1978 | **13** | **3** | 2001-2005, CSD Colo-Colo Santiago (4/1), CD Atlante Ciudad de México (10/2). |
| (424/545) | GONZÁLEZ VERA Pedro | 17.10.1967 | **28** | **5** | 1993-2000, CD Cobreloa Calama (15/3), CF de la Universidad de Chile Santiago (13/2). |
| (256/380) | GONZÁLEZ Víctor Manuel | | **1** | **0** | 1972, Green Cross Temuco (1/0). |
| (39/108) | GORNALL Guillermo | | **4** | **0** | 1935, Audax CS Italiano Santiago (4/0). |
| (409/525) | GUARDA Luis | 11.07.1968 | **4** | **0** | 1990-1991, CD Everton Viña del Mar (1/0), CD Cobreloa Calama (3/0). |
| (5/027) | GUERRERO Manuel | | **12** | **0** | 1916-1920, La Cruz FC Quillota Valparaíso (12/0). |
| (410/534) | GUEVARA ARREDONDO Fabián | 22.06.1968 | **20** | **1** | 1991-1995, CD Palestino Santiago (2/0), CF de la Universidad de Chile Santiago (11/1), CF Monterrey (7/0). |
| (11/047) | GUEVARA Norberto | | **2** | **0** | 1917, Gold Cross FC Valparaíso (2/0). |
| (658/787) | GUTIÉRREZ BREVE Matías Ignacio | 04.10.1994 | **1** | **0** | 2011, CSD Colo-Colo Santiago (1/0). |
| (5/033) | GUTIÉRREZ Enrique | | **2** | **0** | 1916, CD Magallanes Santiago (2/0). |
| (583/717) | GUTIÉRREZ GAMBOA Roberto Carlos | 18.04.1983 | **4** | **2** | 2007, CD Universidad Católica Santiago (4/2). |
| (509/627) | GUTIÉRREZ GONZÁLEZ Julio Brian | 14.09.1979 | **5** | **0** | 2000-2007, Club Unión Española Santiago (2/0), AC Messina (1/0), CD Universidad Católica Santiago (2/0). |
| (632/766) | GUTIÉRREZ LEIVA Felipe Alejandro | 08.10.1990 | **15** | **1** | 2010-2013, CD Universidad Católica Santiago (8/0), FC Twente Enschede (7/1). |

| | | | | | |
|---|---|---|---|---|---|
| (25/070) | HAMABLET Jorge | | **3** | **0** | 1924, Ferroviarios San Bernardo (3/0). |
| (1/011) | HAMILTON J. | | **3** | **0** | 1910, Valparaíso FC (3/0). |
| (629/764) | HARBOTTLE CARRASCO Kevin Andrew | 08.06.1990 | **1** | **0** | 2010, CD O'Higgins Rancagua (1/0). |
| (525/637) | HENRÍQUEZ ESPINOZA David Andrés | 12.07.1977 | **5** | **0** | 2001-2003, CSD Colo-Colo Santiago (5/0). |

| | | | | | |
|---|---|---|---|---|---|
| (669/797) | HENRÍQUEZ ITURRA Ángelo José | 13.04.1994 | 3 | 2 | 2012-2013, Manchester United FC (1/1), Wigan Athletic FC (1/1), Real Zaragoza (1/0). |
| (608/741) | HERNÁNDEZ HERNÁNDEZ Emilio Exequiel | 14.09.1984 | 9 | 0 | 2008-2010, CFP de la Universidad de Chile Santiago (3/0), AA Argentinos Juniors (6/0). |
| (386/514) | HERNÁNDEZ Juan Carlos | 10.10.1959 | 5 | 0 | 1989, CD Palestino Santiago (5/0). |
| (212/333) | HERRERA Eduardo | | 18 | 0 | 1967-1973, CD Santiago Wanderers Valparaíso (18/0). |
| (309/435) | HERRERA HERNÁNDEZ Oscar | | 23 | 1 | 1981-1988, CD Naval Talcahuano (23/1). |
| (244/368) | HERRERA Leonel | | 39 | 0 | 1971-1985, CSD Colo-Colo Santiago (20/0), Club Unión Española Santiago (4/0), CSD Colo-Colo Santiago (15/0). |
| (538/658) | HERRERA MUÑOZ Johnny Cristian | 09.05.1981 | 5 | 0 | 2002-2013, CF de la Universidad de Chile Santiago (2/0). |
| (277/399) | HIDALGO Alberto | | 2 | 0 | 1975, CD Palestino Santiago (2/0). |
| (28/079) | HILL Carlos | | 1 | 0 | 1926, CD Santiago Wanderers Valparaíso (1/0). |
| (331/450) | HISIS ARAYA Alejandro Manuel | 16.02.1962 | 41 | 2 | 1983-1989, CSD Colo-Colo Santiago (26/2), OF Iráklion (15/0). |
| (185/318) | HODGE Roberto | 30.07.1944 | 39 | 1 | 1964-1977, CF de la Universidad de Chile Santiago (37/1), CD Palestino Santiago (2/0). |
| (148/280) | HOFFMANN Carlos | | 9 | 0 | 1959-1965, CD Santiago Wanderers Valparaíso (6/0), Green Cross Temuco (3/0). |
| (237/353) | HOFFMANN Reinaldo | | 3 | 0 | 1969-1970, CD Santiago Wanderers Valparaíso (3/0). |
| (1/002) | HORMAZÁBAL Carlos | | 3 | 0 | 1910, CD Magallanes Santiago (3/0). |
| (62/163) | HORMAZÁBAL Francisco | | 4 | 1 | 1945, CSD Colo-Colo Santiago (4/1). |
| (344/460) | HORMAZÁBAL Luis Orlando | 13.02.1959 | 22 | 0 | 1984-1987, CSD Colo-Colo Santiago (22/0). |
| (84/203) | HORMAZÁBAL Pablo | | 2 | 0 | 1949, Green Cross Santiago (2/0). |
| (87/211) | HORMAZÁBAL SILVA Enrique Daniel | | 43 | 16 | 1950-1963, CD Santiago Morning (27/11), CSD Colo-Colo Santiago (16/6). |
| (1/004) | HOYL Andrés | | 1 | 0 | 1910, Bádminton FC Valparaíso (1/0). |
| (128/252) | HUERTA Carlos | | 4 | 0 | 1956, Ferrobádminton Santiago (4/0). |
| (373/489) | HUERTA Gustavo | 15.10.1957 | 1 | 0 | 1987, CD Cobresal El Salvador (1/0). |
| (100/227) | HURTADO Fernando | | 3 | 0 | 1953, CD Everton Viña del Mar (3/0). |
| (329/446) | HURTADO GALEGUILLO Osvaldo Heriberto | 02.11.1957 | 38 | 6 | 1983-1989, CD Universidad Católica Santiago (29/6), Charleroi SC (9/0). |
| (584/722) | HURTADO PÉREZ Fernando Javier | 05.04.1983 | 1 | 0 | 2007, CD Cobreloa Calama (1/0). |
| (32/088) | IBACACHE Juan | | 4 | 0 | 1927-1928, CSD Colo-Colo Santiago (4/0). |
| (93/220) | IBÁÑEZ Carlos | 30.11.1931 | 1 | 0 | 1950, CD Magallanes Santiago (1/0). |
| (180/308) | IBÁÑEZ Fernando | | 1 | 0 | 1962, CD Universidad Católica Santiago (1/0). |
| (56/152) | IBÁÑEZ Mario | | 1 | 0 | 1942, CF de la Universidad de Chile Santiago (1/0). |
| (73/193) | INFANTE Ricardo Raimundo | | 12 | 5 | 1947-1950, CD Universidad Católica Santiago (12/5). |
| (275/395) | INOSTROZA IBACACHE Eddio Victorino | 03.09.1946 | 8 | 0 | 1974-1980, CD Huachipato Talcahuano (2/0), Club Unión Española Santiago (3/0), CSD Colo-Colo Santiago (3/0). |
| (592/730) | ISLA ISLA Mauricio Aníbal | 12.06.1988 | 44 | 2 | 2007-2013, Udinese Calcio (31/2), Juventus FC Torino (13/0). |
| (566/687) | ITURRA URRUTIA Manuel Rolando | 23.06.1984 | 35 | 1 | 2005-2012, CF de la Universidad de Chile Santiago (34/1), Málaga CF (1/0). |
| (432/556) | JAQUE Pedro | 01.10.1963 | 4 | 0 | 1994-1995, CD Cobreloa Calama (3/0), Club Atlético Morelia AC (1/0). |
| (570/689) | JARA REYES Gonzalo Alejandro | 29.08.1985 | 63 | 3 | 2006-2013, CD Huachipato Talcahuano (7/0), CSD Colo-Colo Santiago (19/2), West Bromwich Albion FC (29/1), Nottingham Forest FC (8/0). |
| (423/544) | JARA VALDÉS Marcelo Antonio | 13.08.1972 | 1 | 0 | 1993, CF de la Universidad de Chile Santiago (1/0). |
| (359/475) | JÁUREGUI PEÑA Luis Arturo | 1956 | 3 | 0 | 1985-1989, Club Unión Española Santiago (2/0), CD Naval Talcahuano (1/0). |
| (544/671) | JÉREZ CERNA José Luis | 26.06.1978 | 1 | 0 | 2003, Club Unión Española Santiago (1/0). |
| (551/677) | JIMÉNEZ GARCÉS Luis Antonio | 17.06.1984 | 26 | 2 | 2004-2011, Ternana Calcio Polisportiva (8/2), AC Fiorentina Firenze (3/0), Ternana Calcio Polisportiva (1/0), SS Lazio Roma (3/0), Internazionale FC Milano (5/0), AC Cesena (2/0), Al-Ahli Club Dubai (4/0). |
| (4/026) | JOHNSTON J. | | 1 | 0 | 1913, Valparaíso FC (1/0). |
| (612/745) | JORQUERA TORRES Cristóbal Andrés | 04.08.1988 | 4 | 0 | 2009-2012, CD O'Higgins Rancagua (1/0), CSD Colo-Colo Santiago (1/0), Genoa CFC (2/0). |
| (62/162) | KLEIN Víctor | | 1 | 0 | 1945, CD Santiago Morning (1/0). |
| (629/762) | LABRÍN CANDIA Carlos Alfredo | 02.09.1990 | 3 | 0 | 2010-2012, CD Huachipato Talcahuano (2/0), US Città di Palermo (1/0). |
| (383/507) | LACROIX Lester | 18.03.1965 | 2 | 0 | 1988-1989, Club Deportes Concepción (2/0). |
| (170/300) | LANDA Honorino | 01.06.1942 | 24 | 5 | 1961-1966, Club Unión Española Santiago (20/5), Green Cross Temuco (5/0). |
| (225/347) | LARA MADRID Alfonso | 27.04.1946 | 29 | 0 | 1968-1975, CD Magallanes Santiago (8/0), Lota Schwager Coronel (8/0), CSD Colo-Colo Santiago (13/0). |
| (56/154) | LAS HERAS Francisco | | 13 | 0 | 1942-1946, CF de la Universidad de Chile Santiago (2/0), CD Magallanes Santiago (11/0). |
| (279/402) | LAS HERAS Francisco | | 4 | 0 | 1975, Club Unión Española Santiago (4/0). |
| (433/559) | LATÍN Miguel | 27.07.1968 | 2 | 0 | 1994, Club de Deportes Temuco (2/0). |
| (228/350) | LAUBE Gustavo | | 15 | 1 | 1969-1972, CD Universidad Católica Santiago (14/1), CD Magallanes Santiago (1/0). |
| (617/747) | LEAL SALVO Braulio Antonio | 22.11.1981 | 6 | 0 | 2009-2013, Unión Española Santiago (4/0), CD O'Higgins Rancagua (2/0). |
| (466/594) | LEE CHONG Oscar | 20.03.1965 | 1 | 0 | 1997, CD Palestino Santiago (1/0). |
| (172/302) | LEPE Hugo | | 1 | 0 | 1961, CD Santiago Morning (1/0). |
| (355/471) | LEPE Mario | 25.03.1965 | 25 | 1 | 1985-1994, CD Universidad Católica Santiago (25/1). |
| (4/016) | LESTER Roy | | 1 | 0 | 1913, CD Santiago Wanderers Valparaíso (1/0). |

| | | | | | |
|---|---|---|---|---|---|
| (293/419) | LETELIER PIZARRO Juan Carlos | 20.05.1959 | **57** | **18** | 1979-1989, CD Santiago Wanderers Valparaíso (2/0), CD Cobreloa Calama (37/14), CD Independiente Medellin (2/0), Club de Deportes La Serena (16/4). |
| (35/099) | LINFORD Jorge | | **1** | **0** | 1928, CSD Colo-Colo Santiago (1/0). |
| (52/138) | LIVINGSTONE POHLHAMMER Sergio Roberto | 26.03.1920 | **52** | **0** | 1941-1954, CD Universidad Católica Santiago (52/0). |
| (451/579) | LIZAMA Claudio | 21.03.1973 | **1** | **0** | 1995, CD Universidad Católica Santiago (1/0). |
| (48/134) | LOBOS Augusto | | **3** | **0** | 1939, CD Santiago Morning (3/0). |
| (600/735) | LOBOS LANDAETA Eduardo Eugenio | 30.07.1981 | **1** | **0** | 2008, FK Krylya Sovetov Samara (1/0). |
| (432/554) | LÓPEZ Daniel | 06.03.1969 | **3** | **0** | 1994, CD Universidad Católica Santiago (3/0). |
| (69/181) | LÓPEZ José | | **6** | **0** | 1946-1950, CD Magallanes Santiago (6/0). |
| (81/202) | LÓPEZ Luis | | **3** | **0** | 1949, CD Magallanes Santiago (3/0). |
| (73/191) | LÓPEZ Pedro Hugo | | **16** | **5** | 1947-1952, CSD Colo-Colo Santiago (7/3), CF de la Universidad de Chile Santiago (7/2), Club Unión Española Santiago (2/0). |
| (451/577) | LOPRESTI TRAVANIC Jaime | 27.01.1974 | **1** | **0** | 1995, CD Coquimbo Unido (1/0). |
| (570/693) | LORCA DONOSO Juan Gonzalo | 15.01.1985 | **11** | **1** | 2006-2009, CD Huachipato Talcahuano (2/0), CSD Colo-Colo Santiago Santiago (9/1). |
| (87/205) | LORCA Mario | | **8** | **0** | 1950-1954, Club Unión Española Santiago (6/0), Ferrobádminton Santiago (2/0). |
| (151/283) | LUCO Jorge | | **10** | **0** | 1959-1960, CD Universidad Católica Santiago (10/0). |
| (47/133) | LUCO Roberto | | **3** | **1** | 1939, CSD Colo-Colo Santiago (3/1). |

| | | | | | |
|---|---|---|---|---|---|
| (73/188) | MACHUCA BERRÍOS Manuel | 1924 | **19** | **0** | 1947-1950, CSD Colo-Colo Santiago (19/0). |
| (251/376) | MACHUCA VALDÉZ Juan Salvador | 07.03.1951 | **21** | **0** | 1972-1977, Club Unión Española Santiago (21/0). |
| (440/571) | MacNIVEN Ian | 25.10.1971 | **2** | **0** | 1995, CD Universidad Católica Santiago (2/0). |
| (625/752) | MAGALHAES LOBOS Paulo Cezar | 14.12.1989 | **6** | **0** | 2009-2013, CSD Colo-Colo Santiago (4/0), CFP de la Universidad de Chile Santiago (2/0). |
| (510/629) | MALDONADO RIVERA Claudio Andrés | 03.01.1980 | **44** | **1** | 2000-2010, São Paulo FC (17/0), Cruzeiro EC Belo Horizonte (16/1), Santos FC (6/0), Fenerbahçe SK Istanbul (1/0), CR Flamengo Rio de Janeiro (4/0). |
| (554/679) | MANCILLA GARCÉS Héctor Raúl | 12.11.1980 | **3** | **0** | 2004-2010, CD Huachipato Talcahuano (3/0), Deportivo Toluca FC (6/0). |
| (618/748) | MANCILLA GARCÉS Héctor Raúl | 12.11.1980 | **10** | **0** | 2009-2011, Deportivo Toluca FC (9/0), Universidad Autónoma de Nuevo León (1/0). |
| (583/715) | MANRÍQUEZ HERNÁNDEZ Fernando Alejandro | 01.02.1984 | **3** | **0** | 2007, CD Santiago Morning (3/0). |
| (69/183) | MANSILLA Luis Víctor | | **3** | **0** | 1946, CD Universidad Católica Santiago (3/0). |
| (182/311) | MARCOS Rubén | 06.12.1942 | **35** | **9** | 1963-1969, CF de la Universidad de Chile Santiago (35/8). |
| (347/469) | MARDONES DÍAZ Patricio | 17.07.1962 | **29** | **2** | 1985-1995, CD Universidad Católica Santiago (21/1), CF de la Universidad de Chile Santiago (8/1). |
| (408/520) | MARGAS LOYOLA Javier Luciano | 10.05.1969 | **63** | **6** | 1990-2000, CSD Colo-Colo Santiago (33/2), CF América SA Ciudad de México (4/1), CD Universidad Católica Santiago (19/2), West Ham United FC London (7/1). |
| (628/757) | MARÍN BARAHONA Luis Antonio | 18.05.1983 | **8** | **0** | 2010-2012, Unión Española Santiago (6/0), CD O'Higgins Rancagua (2/0). |
| (536/652) | MARTEL HELO Fernando Patricio | 02.10.1975 | **14** | **0** | 2001-2004, CD Santiago Morning (2/0), CD Cobreloa Calama (5/0), Club Jaguares de Chiapas Tuxtla Gutiérrez (3/0), CD Atlante Ciudad de México (4/0). |
| (366/487) | MARTÍNEZ Alex | 26.10.1960 | **4** | **0** | 1987-1988, CD Universidad Católica Santiago (4/0). |
| (598/732) | MARTÍNEZ CABRERA Hans Alexis | 04.01.1987 | **11** | **0** | 2008-2010, CD Universidad Católica Santiago (11/0). |
| (627/755) | MARTÍNEZ DÍAZ José Víctor | 18.03.1991 | **2** | **0** | 2010, CD Universidad Católica Santiago (2/0). |
| (163/290) | MARTÍNEZ Hernán | | **2** | **0** | 1960, CD Everton Viña del Mar (2/0). |
| (583/716) | MARTÍNEZ MUÑOZ Christian Jorge | 18.06.1983 | **3** | **0** | 2007-2011, CF de la Universidad de Chile Santiago (2/0), Audax Italiano La Florida (1/0). |
| (373/494) | MARTÍNEZ Rubén | | **12** | **2** | 1987-1990, CD Cobresal El Salvador (10/2), CSD Colo-Colo Santiago (2/0). |
| (91/218) | MAYANÉS Luis Lindorfo | | **1** | **0** | 1950, CD Universidad Católica Santiago (1/0). |
| (2/013) | McWILLIAMS J. | | **2** | **0** | 1910, Bádminton FC Valparaíso (2/0). |
| (582/710) | MEDEL SOTO Gary Alexis | 03.08.1987 | **58** | **5** | 2007-2013, CD Universidad Católica Santiago (16/3), CA Boca Juniors Buenos Aires (12/0), Sevilla FC (23/1), Cardiff City FC (7/1). |
| (48/135) | MEDIAVILLA Felipe | | **3** | **0** | 1939, Club Unión Española Santiago (3/0). |
| (54/150) | MEDINA Desiderio | | **12** | **5** | 1941-1946, Club Deportivo Viña del Mar (1/0), Santiago National (11/5). |
| (536/651) | MEDINA Luis | 11.05.1970 | **2** | **0** | 2001, Club Unión Española Santiago (2/0). |
| (56/155) | MEDINA Oscar | | **6** | **0** | 1942, CSD Colo-Colo Santiago (6/0). |
| (535/649) | MELÉNDEZ ARAYA Rodrigo David | 03.10.1977 | **26** | **1** | 2001-2007, CD Cobreloa Calama (3/0), Quilmes AC (11/1), Club Estudiantes de La Plata (8/0), CSD Colo-Colo Santiago (4/0). |
| (89/214) | MELÉNDEZ René | | **39** | **10** | 1950-1960, CD Everton Viña del Mar (31/9), CF de la Universidad de Chile Santiago (3/1), CD O'Higgins Rancagua (5/0). |
| (495/612) | MENA IRARRÁZABAL Luis Arturo | 28.08.1979 | **1** | **0** | 1999, CSD Colo-Colo Santiago (1/0). |
| (638/769) | MENA REVECO Eugenio Esteban | 18.07.1988 | **23** | **3** | 2010-2013, CFP de la Universidad de Chile Santiago (16/2), Santos FC (6/1). |
| (184/316) | MÉNDEZ Eugenio | | **4** | **2** | 1964-1965, CD Santiago Wanderers Valparaíso (4/2). |
| (274/391) | MÉNDEZ Javier | | **4** | **1** | 1974-1975, Aviación Santiago (4/1). |
| (416/541) | MENDOZA IBARRA Gabriel Rafael | 22.05.1968 | **36** | **1** | 1991-1997, CSD Colo-Colo Santiago (35/1), São Paulo FC (1/0). |
| (583/720) | MENESES CORNEJO Fernando Andrés | 27.09.1985 | **15** | **1** | 2007-2013, CD O'Higgins Rancagua (4/0), CD Universidad Católica Santiago (11/1). |
| (293/420) | MERELLO ESCOBAR Víctor Alejandro | 21.12.1952 | **3** | **0** | 1979-1984, CD Cobreloa Calama (3/0). |

| | | | | | |
|---|---|---|---|---|---|
| (239/356) | MESSEN Sergio | | 10 | 2 | 1970-1973, CD Universidad Católica Santiago (3/1), CSD Colo-Colo Santiago (7/0). |
| (538/661) | MILLAR CARVAJAL Rodrígo Javier | 03.11.1981 | 29 | 2 | 2002-2012, CD Huachipato Talcahuano (6/0), CSD Colo-Colo Santiago (23/2). |
| (284/409) | MIRANDA Luis | | 4 | 0 | 1976-1977, Club Unión Española Santiago (4/0). |
| (411/539) | MIRANDA Marcelo | 29.01.1967 | 15 | 0 | 1991-1997, Club Deportes Concepción (2/0), CD Cobreloa Calama (13/0). |
| (523/633) | MIROŠEVIC ALBORNOZ Milovan Petar | 20.06.1980 | 25 | 3 | 2001-2005, CD Universidad Católica Santiago (2/0), Racing Club Avellaneda (21/3), CD Universidad Católica Santiago (2/0). |
| (160/288) | MOHOR Constantino | | 1 | 0 | 1960, CD Palestino Santiago (1/0). |
| (99/225) | MOLINA Francisco | | 7 | 7 | 1953-1959, CD Universidad Católica Santiago (6/7), Audax CS Italiano Santiago (1/0). |
| (25/075) | MOLINA Oscar | | 1 | 0 | 1924, Ferroviarios San Bernardo (1/0). |
| (308/433) | MONDACA REYES Orlando Alberto | 24.06.1961 | 7 | 0 | 1980-1987, CF de la Universidad de Chile Santiago (7/0). |
| (578/705) | MONJE VALENZUELA Leonardo Esteban | 16.03.1981 | 2 | 0 | 2006-2011, Club Deportes Concepción (1/0), Unión Española Santiago (1/0). |
| (183/312) | MONTALVA Oscar | | 1 | 0 | 1963, CSD Colo-Colo Santiago (1/0). |
| (498/620) | MONTECINOS GONZÁLEZ Cristian Antonio | 19.12.1970 | 9 | 3 | 1999-2001, CSD Colo-Colo Santiago (1/0), Club Deportes Concepción (5/3), Al Wasl Sports (3/0). |
| (42/121) | MONTERO Juan | | 7 | 0 | 1936-1939, CSD Colo-Colo Santiago (7/0). |
| (458/585) | MORA TEJO Cristián | 21.12.1968 | 8 | 0 | 1996-1997, CF de la Universidad de Chile Santiago (8/0). |
| (139/263) | MORALES Antonio | | 2 | 0 | 1957, CD Everton Viña del Mar (2/0). |
| (89/213) | MORALES Daniel | | 3 | 0 | 1950-1957, CD Magallanes Santiago (3/0). |
| (584/726) | MORALES FLORES Pedro Andrés | 25.05.1985 | 14 | 3 | 2007-2010, CD Huachipato Talcahuano (1/0), CF de la Universidad de Chile Santiago (5/0), NK Dinamo Zagreb (8/3). |
| (25/072) | MORALES SALES Víctor | 10.05.1905 | 10 | 0 | 1924-1930, Camilo Henríquez Santiago (3/0), CSD Colo-Colo Santiago (7/0). |
| (28/085) | MORENO Humberto | | 3 | 1 | 1926, CSD Colo-Colo Santiago (3/1). |
| (147/279) | MORENO Mario | | 26 | 5 | 1959-1964, CSD Colo-Colo Santiago (26/5). |
| (5/034) | MORENO Rubén | | 3 | 0 | 1916, Instituto Nacional Santiago (3/0). |
| (214/334) | MORIS José | | 2 | 0 | 1967, CD Palestino Santiago (2/0). |
| (283/408) | MOSCOSO HUENCHO Gustavo Segundo | 10.08.1955 | 21 | 4 | 1976-1982, CD Universidad Católica Santiago (21/4). |
| (329/448) | MOSQUERA RIVERA Luis Alberto | 03.10.1959 | 1 | 0 | 1983, CF de la Universidad de Chile Santiago (1/0). |
| (486/606) | MOYA SPULER Rodolfo Antonio | 27.07.1979 | 6 | 0 | 1998-2007, CD Universidad Católica Santiago (3/0), Audax CS Italiano Santiago (3/0). |
| (451/580) | MUENA César | 30.09.1967 | 1 | 0 | 1995, CD Cobreloa Calama (1/0). |
| (10/044) | MUÑOZ Bartolomé | | 4 | 1 | 1917, CDFA Arturo Fernández Vial Concepción (4/1). |
| (571/697) | MUÑOZ CAMILO Claudio | 02.12.1984 | 1 | 0 | 2006, CD Universidad Católica Santiago (1/0). |
| (584/724) | MUÑOZ CARRILLO Claudio Andrés | 02.12.1984 | 1 | 0 | 2007, CD Universidad Católica Santiago (1/0). |
| (80/198) | MUÑOZ Gilberto | | 6 | 0 | 1949, CSD Colo-Colo Santiago (6/0). |
| (258/387) | MUÑOZ Guillermo | | 7 | 1 | 1973, CD Santiago Wanderers Valparaíso (7/1). |
| (11/049) | MUÑOZ Horacio | | 9 | 0 | 1917-1926, CDFA Arturo Fernández Vial Concepción (9/0). |
| (358/473) | MUÑOZ Jorge | 21.12.1961 | 4 | 1 | 1985, CD Huachipato Talcahuano (4/1). |
| (55/151) | MUÑOZ Juan | | 1 | 0 | 1941, Bádminton FC Santiago (1/0). |
| (90/216) | MUÑOZ Manuel | 28.04.1928 | 26 | 8 | 1950-1956, CSD Colo-Colo Santiago (26/8). |
| (467/595) | MUÑOZ MARDONES Raúl Andrés | 27.05.1975 | 7 | 0 | 1997-2003, CSD Colo-Colo Santiago (6/0), Club Real San Luis (1/0). |
| (48/137) | MUÑOZ Raúl | | 4 | 1 | 1939, CD Magallanes Santiago (4/1). |
| (644/772) | MUÑOZ ROJAS Carlos Andrés | 21.04.1989 | 10 | 2 | 2011-2013, CD Santiago Wanderers (3/0), CSD Colo-Colo Santiago (5/2), Baniyas Sports Club Abu Dhabi (2/0). |
| (410/530) | MUSRRI SARAVIA Luis Eduardo | 24.12.1969 | 27 | 0 | 1991-1998, CF de la Universidad de Chile Santiago (27/0). |
| (113/244) | MUSSO Braulio | | 14 | 3 | 1954-1961, CF de la Universidad de Chile Santiago (14/3). |

| | | | | | |
|---|---|---|---|---|---|
| (162/289) | NAVARRO Fernando | | 4 | 0 | 1960-1961, CSD Colo-Colo Santiago (4/0). |
| (140/265) | NAVARRO Sergio | 20.11.1936 | 31 | 0 | 1957-1962, CF de la Universidad de Chile Santiago (31/0). |
| (494/611) | NAVIA AMADOR Reinaldo Marcelino | 10.05.1978 | 36 | 9 | 1999-2007, CD Santiago Wanderers Valparaíso (8/1), Club Universidád Autonoma de Guadalajara (11/3), Club Atlético Morelia (6/1), CF América Ciudad de México (9/2), San Luis FC (2/2), CD Atlas Guadalajara (4/1). |
| (228/349) | NEF SANHUEZA Adolfo | 18.01.1946 | 41 | 0 | 1969-1977, CF de la Universidad de Chile Santiago (21/0), CSD Colo-Colo Santiago (19/0). |
| (73/192) | NEGRI Juan | | 16 | 0 | 1947-1950, CF de la Universidad de Chile Santiago (16/0). |
| (480/602) | NEIRA DÍAZ Manuel Alejandro | 12.10.1977 | 13 | 2 | 1998-2006, CSD Colo-Colo Santiago (8/2), Club Unión Española Santiago (3/0), CSD Colo-Colo Santiago (1/0), Club Unión Española Santiago (1/0). |
| (495/613) | NEIRA MUÑOZ Patricio Enrique | 18.04.1979 | 1 | 0 | 1999, CD Huachipato Talcahuano (1/0). |
| (283/407) | NEIRA PINCHEIRA Miguel Angel | 09.10.1954 | 45 | 4 | 1976-1985, Club Unión Española Santiago (2/0), CD O'Higgins Rancagua (10/0), CD Universidad Católica Santiago (33/4). |
| (293/418) | NEUMANN Jorge | | 3 | 0 | 1979, Club Unión Española Santiago (3/0). |
| (138/260) | NITSCHE Francisco | | 6 | 0 | 1957-1965, Club Unión Española Santiago (6/0). |
| (536/650) | NORAMBUENA ARDILES Arturo Andrés | 24.11.1971 | 5 | 1 | 2001-2003, CD Universidad Católica Santiago (5/1). |
| (357/472) | NÚÑEZ Alfredo | | 3 | 1 | 1985-1988, CD Palestino Santiago (3/1). |
| (581/708) | NÚÑEZ BLANCO Luis Patricio | 20.01.1980 | 1 | 0 | 2007, CD Universidad Católica Santiago (1/0). |
| (452/583) | NÚÑEZ CAMAÑO Claudio Patricio | 16.10.1975 | 31 | 4 | 1996-2003, CD Santiago Wanderers Valparaíso (6/0), CD Universidad Autonoma de Nuevo León Monterrey (24/4), CF Puebla de la Franja (1/0). |
| (506/621) | NÚÑEZ Mario | 02.03.1976 | 7 | 2 | 2000, CD Universidad Católica Santiago (6/2). |
| (509/626) | NÚÑEZ ORTIZ Rodrigo Fabián | 05.02.1977 | 6 | 0 | 2000-2001, CD Santiago Wanderers Valparaíso (6/0). |
| (105/231) | NÚÑEZ Rogelio | | 2 | 0 | 1953, CSD Colo-Colo Santiago (2/0). |

| | | | | | |
|---|---|---|---|---|---|
| (139/264) | OJEDA Mario | | 1 | 0 | 1957, CD Magallanes Santiago (1/0). |
| (36/100) | OJEDA Tomás | 20.04.1910 | 7 | 0 | 1930-1937, Boca Juniors Antofagasta (2/0), Audax CS Italiano Santiago (5/0). |
| (480/600) | OLARRA GUERRERO Rafael Andrés | 26.05.1978 | 30 | 1 | 1998-2006, CF de la Universidad de Chile Santiago (6/0), CA Osasuna Pamplona (1/0), CF de la Universidad de Chile Santiago (1/0), CA Independiente Avellaneda (11/1), CF de la Universidad de Chile Santiago (6/0), Maccabi Haifa FC (5/0). |
| (386/512) | OLGUÍN Cristián | 05.12.1963 | 1 | 0 | 1989, CF de la Universidad de Chile Santiago (1/0). |
| (25/076) | OLGUÍN José Miguel | | 8 | 0 | 1924-1928, Escuela Normal Santiago (3/0), CSD Colo-Colo Santiago (5/0). |
| (223/344) | OLIVARES Adolfo | | 15 | 6 | 1968-1969, CD Santiago Morning (15/7). |
| (186/322) | OLIVARES SÁNCHEZ Juan Carlos | 20.02.1941 | 33 | 0 | 1965-1974, CD Santiago Wanderers Valparaíso (23/0), Club Unión Española Santiago (8/0), CD Magallanes Santiago (2/0). |
| (103/230) | OLIVOS Alfredo | | 1 | 0 | 1953, Audax CS Italiano Santiago (1/0). |
| (390/517) | OLMOS ROJAS Juvenal Mario | 04.10.1962 | 9 | 2 | 1989, CD Universidad Católica Santiago (9/2). |
| (338/456) | OPAZO Marco | 27.04.1962 | 3 | 0 | 1983-1988, CD Palestino Santiago (3/0). |
| (669/798) | OPAZO RIQUELME Yerson Flavio | 02.12.1984 | 1 | 0 | 2012, CD O`Higgins Rancagua (1/0). |
| (285/412) | ORELLANA JARA Juan Carlos | 21.06.1955 | 11 | 4 | 1977-1983, CSD Colo-Colo Santiago (4/0), CD O'Higgins Rancagua (7/4). |
| (602/740) | ORELLANA VALENZUELA Fabián Ariel | 27.01.1986 | 23 | 2 | 2008-2013, Audax CS Italiano Santiago (5/1), Audax Italiano La Florida (5/0), CD Xerez (7/1), Granada CF (3/0), RC Celta de Vigo (3/0). |
| (512/631) | ORMAZÁBAL MOYA Luis Patricio | 12.02.1979 | 7 | 0 | 2000-2003, CD Universidad Católica Santiago (5/0), CA San Lorenzo de Almagro (2/0). |
| (525/640) | ORMEÑO GUERRA Jorge Andrés | 14.06.1977 | 3 | 0 | 2001-2006, CD Santiago Wanderers Valparaíso (2/0), CD Universidad Católica Santiago (1/0). |
| (324/440) | ORMEÑO PACHECO Elías Raúl | 21.06.1958 | 11 | 1 | 1982-1990, CSD Colo-Colo Santiago (11/1). |
| (586/729) | ORMEÑO SALAZAR Alvaro Andrés | 04.04.1979 | 5 | 0 | 2007, Club Gymnasia y Esgrima La Plata (5/0). |
| (125/251) | ORTÍZ Mario | | 13 | 0 | 1956-1963, CD Palestino Santiago (10/0), CSD Colo-Colo Santiago (3/0). |
| (295/422) | OSBÉN MÉNDEZ Mario Ignacio | 14.07.1955 | 36 | 0 | 1979-1988, Club Unión Española Santiago (11/0), CSD Colo-Colo Santiago (18/0), CD Cobreloa Calama (7/0). |
| (242/364) | OSORIO Fernando | | 9 | 2 | 1971-1972, Lota Schwager Coronel (9/2). |
| (472/598) | OSORIO GONZÁLEZ Luis Alejandro | 24.09.1976 | 8 | 0 | 1997-2001, CD Universidad Católica Santiago (1/0), Club Estudiantes de La Plata (7/0). |

| | | | | | |
|---|---|---|---|---|---|
| (242/362) | PACHECO Carlos | | 8 | 1 | 1971-1972, Club Unión Española Santiago (8/1). |
| (329/442) | PACHECO Marcelo | | 10 | 0 | 1983, CD Naval Talcahuano (10/0). |
| (250/375) | PÁEZ CEPEDA Guillermo | 18.04.1945 | 13 | 0 | 1972-1974, Lota Schwager Coronel (1/0), CSD Colo-Colo Santiago (12/0). |
| (496/619) | PALACIOS GAMBOA Raúl Alejandro | 30.10.1976 | 14 | 2 | 1999-2000, CD Santiago Morning (10/2), CSD Colo-Colo Santiago (4/0). |
| (538/662) | PARDO CAMPOS Sebastián Eduardo | 01.01.1982 | 1 | 0 | 2002, CF de la Universidad de Chile Santiago (1/0). |
| (8/037) | PAREDES Jorge | | 2 | 0 | 1916, Nacional FC Talca (2/0). |
| (10/046) | PAREDES Julio | | 4 | 0 | 1917, América FC Valparaíso (4/0). |
| (575/701) | PAREDES QUINTANILLA Esteban Efraín | 01.08.1980 | 33 | 10 | 2006-2013, CD Santiago Morning (6/0), CSD Colo-Colo Santiago (24/9), CF Atlante Cancún (3/1). |
| (17/061) | PARRA Blas | | 1 | 0 | 1920, Artillero de Costa FC Talcahuano (1/0). |
| (410/531) | PARRAGUEZ RIVEROS Nelson Rodrigo | 05.04.1971 | 52 | 0 | 1991-2001, CD Universidad Católica Santiago (50/0), CID Necaxa Ciudad de México (2/0). |
| (52/141) | PASTENE José | | 14 | 0 | 1941-1945, CSD Colo-Colo Santiago (14/0). |
| (373/493) | PEDREROS GUEVARA Manuel | 1955 | 1 | 0 | 1987, CD Cobresal El Salvador (1/0). |
| (373/491) | PEDREROS Leonel | 12.04.1962 | 1 | 0 | 1987, CDFA Arturo Fernández Vial Concepción (1/0). |
| (365/478) | PELLEGRINI Manuel | 16.09.1953 | 1 | 0 | 1986, CF de la Universidad de Chile Santiago (1/0). |
| (110/239) | PEÑA Caupolicán | | 12 | 0 | 1954-1957, CSD Colo-Colo Santiago (12/0). |
| (70/184) | PEÑALOZA Jorge | | 8 | 1 | 1946-1947, CSD Colo-Colo Santiago (8/1). |
| (244/367) | PERALTA Eduardo | | 11 | 0 | 1971-1972, CF de la Universidad de Chile Santiago (11/0). |
| (297/426) | PEREDO GUTIÉRREZ Jorge Sigfrido | | 5 | 4 | 1979, Club Unión Española Santiago (5/4). |
| (441/572) | PÉREZ ALBORNOZ Rodrígo Antonio | 19.08.1973 | 32 | 0 | 1995-2001, CD O'Higgins Rancagua (6/0), CD Cobreloa Calama (26/0). |
| (537/656) | PÉREZ CURIÑANCO Darwin Eduardo | 08.05.1977 | 1 | 0 | 2001, Club Deportes Concepción (1/0). |
| (544/672) | PÉREZ Daniel | 11.08.1975 | 2 | 0 | 2003-2005, CD Universidad Católica Santiago (1/0), CD Cobreloa Calama (1/0). |
| (377/499) | PÉREZ Fernando | 29.05.1963 | 3 | 0 | 1988, CD Huachipato Talcahuano (3/0). |
| (390/518) | PÉREZ Luis | 17.04.1965 | 6 | 0 | 1989-1996, CD Universidad Católica Santiago (1/0). |
| (379/503) | PÉREZ Ramón | 28.06.1963 | 4 | 0 | 1988-1989, CD Palestino Santiago (4/0). |
| (52/144) | PÉREZ Raúl | | 4 | 1 | 1941-1942, River Plate Pedro de Valdivia (4/1). |
| (525/639) | PÉREZ SALAS Eros Roque | 03.06.1976 | 6 | 0 | 2001-2006, Club Colón Santa Fé (5/0), CD Universidad Católica Santiago (1/0). |
| (539/664) | PERIC VILLARREAL Nicolás Miroslav | 19.10.1978 | 5 | 0 | 2003-2007, CD Rangers Talca (2/0), Audax CS Italiano (3/0). |
| (133/256) | PICÓ Jesús | | 5 | 0 | 1957, CD Santiago Wanderers Valparaíso (5/0). |
| (584/727) | PINEDA CORTÉS Jean Paul Jesús | 24.02.1989 | 1 | 0 | 2007, CD Palestino Santiago (1/0). |
| (62/165) | PIÑEIRO Manuel | | 6 | 1 | 1945, Audax CS Italiano Santiago (6/1). |
| (539/665) | PINILLA FERRERA Mauricio Ricardo | 04.02.1984 | 24 | 5 | 2003-2013, CF de la Universidad de Chile Santiago (3/1), AC Chievo Verona (4/1), Real Club Celta de Vigo (6/1), Sporting Clube de Portugal Lisboa (5/2), Heart of Midlothian FC Edinburgh (3/0), US Città de Palermo (1/0), Cagliari Calcio (2/0). |
| (68/174) | PINO Domingo | | 1 | 0 | 1946, CD Magallanes Santiago (1/0). |
| (248/371) | PINO Luis | | 3 | 0 | 1971-1972, CD O'Higgins Rancagua (3/0). |

| | | | | | |
|---|---|---|---|---|---|
| (242/361) | PINOCHET Francisco | | 9 | 0 | 1971-1975, Club Deportes Concepción (6/0), CD Huachipato Talcahuano (3/0). |
| (434/560) | PINTO Aníbal | 20.02.1971 | 1 | 0 | 1994, Club de Deportes Melipilla (1/0). |
| (275/396) | PINTO Héctor | | 10 | 1 | 1974-1977, CF de la Universidad de Chile Santiago (4/1), CSD Colo-Colo Santiago (6/0). |
| (571/695) | PINTO JÉREZ Miguel Ángel | 04.07.1983 | 21 | 0 | 2006-2012, CF de la Universidad de Chile Santiago (14/0), CSD Atlas de Guadalajara (7/0). |
| (510/628) | PINTO Miguel Rodrígo | 04.10.1973 | 3 | 0 | 2000, CD Santiago Morning (1/0). |
| (274/394) | PINTO Pedro | | 8 | 0 | 1974-1979, CD Palestino Santiago (8/0). |
| (658/784) | PINTO PERURENA Sebastián Andrés | 05.02.1986 | 5 | 3 | 2011-2013, CD O'Higgins Rancagua (1/3), Bursaspor Kulübü (4/0). |
| (608/742) | PIZARRO CARTES Francisco Javier | 10.05.1989 | 3 | 0 | 2008-2012, CD Universidad Católica Santiago (3/0). |
| (494/609) | PIZARRO CORTÉS David Marcelo | 11.02.1979 | 40 | 2 | 1999-2013, CD Santiago Wanderers Valparaíso (2/0), Udinese Calcio (31/2), Internazionale FC Milano (3/0), AC Fiorentina Firenze (4/0). |
| (48/136) | PIZARRO Gustavo | | 4 | 0 | 1939, Bádminton FC Santiago (4/0). |
| (365/484) | PIZARRO HERRERA Jaime Augusto | 02.03.1964 | 53 | 4 | 1986-1993, CSD Colo-Colo Santiago (53/4). |
| (277/400) | PIZARRO Víctor | | 3 | 0 | 1975-1976, CD Santiago Morning (2/0), Club Unión Española Santiago (1/0). |
| (14/052) | POIRIER Ulises | 02.02.1897 | 16 | 0 | 1919-1930, La Cruz FC Quillota Valparaíso (16/0). |
| (452/581) | POIRRIER Gustavo | 27.05.1965 | 2 | 0 | 1996, Club de Deportes Temuco (2/0). |
| (464/592) | POLI GARCÍA Dante Eugenio | 15.08.1976 | 2 | 0 | 1997, CD Universidad Católica Santiago (2/0). |
| (571/696) | PONCE CARRIZO Waldo Alonso | 04.12.1982 | 42 | 4 | 2006-2011, CF de la Universidad de Chile Santiago (9/1), CA Vélez Sarsfield (14/1), CD Universidad Católica Santiago (5/0), Real Racing Club de Santander (1/0), CDSC Cruz Azul Ciudad de México (13/2). |
| (44/126) | PONCE Luis | | 8 | 0 | 1937-1939, CD Magallanes Santiago (8/0). |
| (277/398) | PONCE Patricio | | 1 | 0 | 1975, Lota Schwager Coronel (1/0). |
| (410/529) | PONCE TORRES Miguel | 18.08.1971 | 17 | 0 | 1991-2001, CD Universidad Católica Santiago (1/0), CF de la Universidad de Chile Santiago (10/0), CD Universidad Católica Santiago (6/0). |
| (525/638) | POZO QUINTEROS Mauricio Andrés | 16.08.1970 | 4 | 0 | 2001, CD Cobreloa Calama (4/0). |
| (73/190) | PRIETO Andrés | 19.12.1928 | 16 | 8 | 1947-1957, CD Universidad Católica Santiago (16/8). |
| (583/711) | PRIETO CAROCA Francisco Javier | 01.07.1983 | 1 | 0 | 2007, CD Santiago Wanderers (1/0). |
| (186/320) | PRIETO Ignacio | 23.09.1943 | 29 | 3 | 1965-1977, CD Universidad Católica Santiago (27/3), CDS y Cultural Cruz Azul Ciudad de México (2/0). |
| (616/746) | PUCH CORTÉZ Edson Raúl | 04.09.1986 | 6 | 0 | 2009-2012, CD Municipal Iquique (2/0), CFP de la Universidad de Chile Santiago (3/0), CD Iquique (1/0). |
| (344/466) | PUEBLA Héctor Eduardo | 10.07.1955 | 35 | 1 | 1984-1990, CD Cobreloa Calama (35/1). |
| (365/482) | PUYOL Mariano | 03.06.1959 | 1 | 1 | 1986, CF de la Universidad de Chile Santiago (1/1). |

| | | | | | |
|---|---|---|---|---|---|
| (506/624) | QUERALTÓ ALVARADO Ricardo Antonio | 12.01.1976 | 3 | 1 | 2000, Club Unión Española Santiago (3/1). |
| (216/336) | QUINTANO Alberto Fernando Ralph | 26.04.1946 | 48 | 0 | 1967-1979, CF de la Universidad de Chile Santiago (29/0), CDS y Cultural Cruz Azul Ciudad de México (7/0), CF de la Universidad de Chile Santiago (12/0). |
| (558/683) | QUINTEROS Luis Ignacio | 23.04.1979 | 2 | 0 | 2004, CF Puebla de la Franja (2/0). |
| (292/413) | QUIROZ Waldo | | 5 | 1 | 1977-1979, Club Unión Española Santiago (1/0), CD O'Higgins Rancagua (4/1). |
| (90/215) | QUITRAL René | | 7 | 0 | 1950-1957, CD Santiago Wanderers Valparaíso (1/0), CD San Luis Quillota (6/0). |

| | | | | | |
|---|---|---|---|---|---|
| (662/795) | RABELLO MELLA Bryan Martín | 16.05.1994 | 3 | 0 | 2012-2013, CSD Colo-Colo Santiago (1/0), Sevilla FC (2/0). |
| (25/069) | RAMÍREZ Aníbal | | 2 | 0 | 1924, Gold Cross FC Santiago (2/0). |
| (113/245) | RAMÍREZ BANDA Jaime Caupolicán | 14.08.1931 | 45 | 10 | 1954-1962, CSD Colo-Colo Santiago (30/8), CD O'Higgins Rancagua (4/0), CF de la Universidad de Chile Santiago (11/2). |
| (423/542) | RAMÍREZ GORMAZ Marcelo Antonio | 29.05.1965 | 37 | 0 | 1993-2001, CSD Colo-Colo Santiago (37/0). |
| (379/502) | RAMÍREZ Jaime Patricio | 03.03.1968 | 19 | 2 | 1988-1996, Club Unión Española Santiago (19/2). |
| (190/323) | RAMÍREZ Leonel | | 1 | 0 | 1965, CD Santiago Morning (1/0). |
| (22/067) | RAMÍREZ Manuel | | 7 | 3 | 1922-1927, Centro de Torneros Talcahuano (3/0), The Commercial Talcahuano (4/3). |
| (180/306) | RAMÍREZ Orlando | 07.05.1943 | 14 | 2 | 1962-1968, CD Universidad Católica Santiago (5/2), CD Palestino Santiago (9/0). |
| (413/540) | RAMÍREZ PÉREZ Miguel Mauricio | 11.06.1970 | 62 | 1 | 1991-2003, CSD Colo-Colo Santiago (34/1), CD Universidad Católica Santiago (28/0). |
| (274/392) | RAMÍREZ Sergio | | 5 | 0 | 1974-1975, CD Palestino Santiago (5/0). |
| (386/510) | RAMOS Carlos | | 2 | 0 | 1989, Club de Deportes Iquique (2/0). |
| (80/197) | RAMOS Ulises | | 6 | 1 | 1949, CF de la Universidad de Chile Santiago (6/1). |
| (87/210) | REBELLO Reinaldo | | 1 | 0 | 1950, CD Santiago Morning (1/0). |
| (199/327) | REINOSO Carlos | 07.03.1945 | 34 | 5 | 1966-1977, Audax CS Italiano Santiago (23/4), CF América SA Ciudad de México (11/1). |
| (496/616) | REYES Carlos | 21.08.1973 | 1 | 0 | 1999, Audax CS Italiano Santiago (1/0). |
| (25/074) | REYES Germán | | 3 | 0 | 1924, Liceo de Concepción (3/0). |
| (435/561) | REYES GONZÁLEZ Pedro Antonio | 13.11.1972 | 55 | 4 | 1994-2001, CSD Colo-Colo Santiago (27/2), AJ Auxerre (28/2). |
| (329/447) | REYES SÁNCHEZ Óscar Patricio | 16.12.1957 | 30 | 1 | 1983-1989, CF de la Universidad de Chile (29/1), Club de Deportes La Serena (1/0). |
| (658/782) | REYES VICENCIO Lorenzo Enrique | 13.06.1991 | 4 | 0 | 2011-2013, CD Huachipato Talcahuano (2/0), Real Betis Balompié Sevilla (2/0). |
| (506/622) | REYES ZÚÑIGA Joel Antonio | 08.04.1972 | 4 | 0 | 2000-2005, CD Santiago Morning (3/0), Club Unión Española Santiago (1/0). |
| (374/497) | REYNERO Roberto | 01.01.1965 | 7 | 0 | 1988, CF de la Universidad de Chile Santiago (7/0). |
| (576/703) | RIELOFF VENEGAS Boris Alexis | 08.01.1984 | 5 | 0 | 2006-2007, Audax CS Italiano Santiago (5/0). |

| | | | | | |
|---|---|---|---|---|---|
| (58/161) | RIERA BAUZA Fernando | 27.06.1920 | 16 | 4 | 1942-1950, CD Universidad Católica Santiago (16/4). |
| (582/709) | RIFFO GARAY Miguel Augusto | 21.06.1981 | 9 | 0 | 2007, CSD Colo-Colo Santiago (9/0). |
| (153/285) | RÍOS José Benito | | 1 | 0 | 1959, CD O'Higgins Rancagua (1/0). |
| (670/799) | RÍOS RIPOLL Michael Fabián | 24.04.1985 | 2 | 0 | 2013, CD Universidad Católica Santiago (2/0). |
| (277/397) | RIVAS TORRES Carlos Humberto | 24.05.1953 | 24 | 4 | 1975-1982, Regional Antofagasta (2/0), CSD Colo-Colo Santiago (22/4). |
| (583/712) | RIVERA GODOY Rodrigo Osvaldo | 03.12.1983 | 1 | 0 | 2007, CF de la Universidad de Chile Santiago (1/0). |
| (373/490) | RIVERA Juan | | 2 | 0 | 1987-1991, CD Cobresal El Salvador (1/0), Club Unión Española Santiago (1/0). |
| (34/097) | RIVEROS Guillermo Arturo | 10.02.1902 | 14 | 1 | 1928-1939, La Cruz FC Quillota Valparaíso (3/0), Audax CS Italiano Santiago (11/1). |
| (464/591) | RIVEROS VALENZUELA Jaime Eduardo | 27.11.1970 | 13 | 4 | 1997-2001, CD Cobreloa Calama (10/3), CD Santiago Wanderers Valparaíso (3/1). |
| (47/129) | ROA Humberto | | 12 | 0 | 1939-1945, Audax CS Italiano Santiago (12/0). |
| (109/237) | ROBLEDO Eduardo | 26.08.1928 | 9 | 0 | 1954-1955, CSD Colo-Colo Santiago (9/0). |
| (91/219) | ROBLEDO Jorge | 14.04.1926 | 31 | 8 | 1950-1957, Newcastle United FC (3/1), CSD Colo-Colo Santiago (28/7). |
| (26/077) | ROBLES Alberto | | 1 | 0 | 1924, CDFA Arturo Fernández Vial Concepción (1/0). |
| (675/803) | ROBLES FUENTES Andrés Sebastián | 07.05.1994 | 1 | 0 | 2013, CD Santiago Wanderers (1/0). |
| (535/647) | ROBLES FUENTES Héctor | 07.09.1971 | 3 | 0 | 2001, CD Santiago Wanderers Valparaíso (3/0). |
| (2/014) | ROBSON Joseph | | 2 | 0 | 1910, English FC Santiago (2/0). |
| (570/691) | ROCCO MELGAREJO Sebastián Alejandro | 26.06.1983 | 7 | 1 | 2006-2007, CD Santiago Wanderers Valparaíso (7/1). |
| (172/303) | RODRÍGUEZ ARANEDA Manuel | 18.01.1938 | 6 | 0 | 1961-1963, Club Unión Española Santiago (6/0). |
| (115/247) | RODRÍGUEZ Hernán | | 21 | 0 | 1955-1961, CSD Colo-Colo Santiago (20/0), Ferrobádminton Santiago (1/0). |
| (344/464) | RODRÍGUEZ Luis | 16.03.1961 | 8 | 0 | 1984-1989, CF de la Universidad de Chile Santiago (8/0). |
| (219/339) | RODRÍGUEZ VEGA Juan | 16.01.1944 | 27 | 0 | 1967-1974, CF de la Universidad de Chile Santiago (18/0), Club Unión Española Santiago (6/0), Club Atlético Español Ciudad de México (3/0). |
| (583/713) | ROJAS BAHAMONDES José Manuel | 23.06.1983 | 17 | 1 | 2007-2013, CF de la Universidad de Chile Santiago (17/1). |
| (80/200) | ROJAS Carlos Rodolfo | 1928 | 17 | 1 | 1949-1954, Club Unión Española Santiago (12/1), CD Palestino Santiago (5/0). |
| (145/278) | ROJAS Eladio | 08.11.1934 | 23 | 3 | 1959-1966, CD Everton Viña del Mar (19/3), CSD Colo-Colo Santiago (4/0). |
| (441/574) | ROJAS Francisco Ulises | 22.07.1974 | 31 | 0 | 1995-2005, CSD Colo-Colo Santiago (27/0), SK Sturm Graz (4/0). |
| (323/439) | ROJAS GIACOMOZZI Oscar Vladimír | 15.11.1958 | 9 | 1 | 1982-1988, CSD Colo-Colo Santiago (9/1). |
| (329/445) | ROJAS Juan | | 12 | 0 | 1983, CD Magallanes Santiago (3/0), CSD Colo-Colo Santiago (9/0). |
| (140/266) | ROJAS Juan Héctor | | 5 | 0 | 1957-1959, CD Magallanes Santiago (3/0), Club de Deportes La Serena (2/0). |
| (306/429) | ROJAS Luis | | 17 | 0 | 1980-1985, Club Unión Española Santiago (17/0). |
| (439/568) | ROJAS Miguel | 28.05.1968 | 1 | 0 | 1994, CD Cobreloa Calama (1/0). |
| (10/043) | ROJAS Rodolfo | | 4 | 0 | 1917, Loma Blanco FC Santiago (4/0). |
| (331/449) | ROJAS SAAVEDRA Roberto Antonio | 08.08.1957 | 49 | 0 | 1983-1989, CSD Colo-Colo Santiago (32/0), São Paulo FC (17/0). |
| (439/567) | ROJAS TRUJILLO Ricardo | 07.05.1974 | 46 | 1 | 1994-2006, Club Unión Española Santiago (3/0), CF de la Universidad de Chile Santiago (13/0), CF América Ciudad de México (17/0), CF de la Universidad de Chile Santiago (2/0), CF América SA Ciudad de México (11/1). |
| (432/557) | ROJAS Wilson | 11.11.1966 | 3 | 0 | 1994, CD O'Higgins Rancagua (3/0). |
| (285/410) | ROJAS ZUNIGA Manuel Antonio | 13.06.1954 | 28 | 2 | 1977-1982, CD Palestino Santiago (15/1), CD Universidad Católica Santiago (13/1). |
| (91/217) | ROLDÁN Fernando | | 17 | 0 | 1950-1954, CD Universidad Católica Santiago (17/0). |
| (32/092) | ROMÁN Carlos Eduardo | | 1 | 0 | 1927, CD Everton Viña del Mar (1/0). |
| (87/207) | ROMÁN Mariano | | 2 | 0 | 1950, Bádminton FC Santiago (2/0). |
| (409/523) | ROMERO Andrés Antonio | 11.05.1967 | 7 | 0 | 1990-1991, CD Universidad Católica Santiago (7/0). |
| (459/587) | ROMERO GODOY Cristián | 26.12.1963 | 2 | 0 | 1996, CF de la Universidad de Chile Santiago (2/0). |
| (68/180) | ROMO Domingo | | 2 | 0 | 1946, Audax CS Italiano Santiago (2/0). |
| (658/786) | ROMO SALINAS Jorge Israel | 09.01.1990 | 1 | 0 | 2011, CD Everton Viña del Mar (1/0). |
| (628/760) | ROSS COTAL Carlos Esteban | 10.05.1987 | 2 | 0 | 2010, Audax Italiano La Florida (2/0). |
| (443/576) | ROZENTAL IGUALT Sebastián | 01.09.1975 | 27 | 2 | 1995-2000, CD Universidad Católica Santiago (20/2), Glasgow Rangers FC (6/0), CA Independiente Avellaneda (1/0). |
| (646/773) | RUBIO KÖSTNER Diego Javier | 17.05.1993 | 3 | 0 | 2011, CSD Colo-Colo Santiago (1/0), Sporting Clube de Portugal Lisboa (2/0). |
| (566/688) | RUBIO KÖSTNER Eduardo Javier | 07.11.1983 | 14 | 3 | 2005-2008, CD Universidad Católica Santiago (6/2), CSD Colo-Colo Santiago (8/1). |
| (345/467) | RUBIO MONTECINOS Hugo Eduardo | 05.07.1960 | 36 | 12 | 1984-1991, CD Cobreloa Calama (14/5), CSD Colo-Colo Santiago (7/2), FC St.Gallen (15/5). |
| (670/800) | RUBIO PULGAR Patricio Rodolfo | 18.07.1989 | 3 | 1 | 2013, Club Unión Española Santiago (3/1). |
| (53/149) | RUÍZ David | | 2 | 0 | 1941, Audax CS Italiano Santiago (2/0). |
| (431/552) | RUÍZ DE BARBIERI Rodrígo | 10.05.1972 | 7 | 1 | 1993-2001, Club Unión Española Santiago (1/0), CF Puebla de la Franja (3/1), CD Toros de Neza Nezahualcoyotl (1/0), Club Santos Laguna Torreon (2/0). |
| (72/185) | RUÍZ Francisco | | 1 | 0 | 1946, Green Cross Santiago (1/0). |

| | | | | | |
|---|---|---|---|---|---|
| (209/329) | SAAVEDRA Manuel | | 2 | 1 | 1966-1967, Club Unión La Calera (2/1). |
| (28/082) | SAAVEDRA TAPIA Guillermo | 05.11.1903 | 9 | 1 | 1926-1930, Caupolicán FC Rancagua (4/1), CSD Colo-Colo Santiago (5/0). |
| (68/178) | SÁEZ Osvaldo | | 22 | 3 | 1946-1954, CD Santiago Wanderers Valparaíso (8/3), CSD Colo-Colo Santiago (14/0). |

| | | | | | |
|---|---|---|---|---|---|
| (599/733) | SAGREDO ROMERO Boris Alexis | 21.03.1989 | 6 | 0 | 2008-2013, CSD Colo-Colo Santiago (1/0), CD Palestino Santiago (1/0), CD Municipal Iquique (1/0), CD O'Higgins Rancagua (3/0). |
| (80/199) | SALAMANCA Manuel | | 3 | 1 | 1949, CD Magallanes Santiago (3/1). |
| (436/564) | SALAS MELINAO José Marcelo | 24.12.1974 | 70 | 37 | 1994-2007, CF de la Universidad de Chile Santiago (24/10), CA River Plate Buenos Aires (19/20), SS Lazio Roma (13/4), FC Juventus Torino (1/0), CA River Plate Buenos Aires (4/0), CF de la Universidad de Chile Santiago (9/3). |
| (431/549) | SALAS SAIEG Mario Alfredo | 11.10.1967 | 5 | 0 | 1993-1997, Club Unión Española Santiago (1/0), CSD Colo-Colo Santiago (4/0). |
| (5/031) | SALAZAR Enrique Hernando | | 2 | 1 | 1916, Thunder FC Coquimbo (2/1). |
| (139/261) | SALAZAR Raúl | | 3 | 0 | 1957, CD O'Higgins Rancagua (3/0). |
| (56/153) | SALFATE Santiago | | 11 | 1 | 1942-1946, CSD Colo-Colo Santiago (6/0), Green Cross Santiago (5/1). |
| (360/476) | SALGADO COFRÉ Sergio Mario | 12.09.1958 | 17 | 3 | 1985-1989, CD Cobresal El Salvador (15/3), CSD Colo-Colo Santiago (2/0). |
| (283/405) | SALINAS Mario | | 3 | 0 | 1976-1977, CD Everton Viña del Mar (3/0). |
| (459/586) | SALVATIERRA CONCHA Agustín Alex | 07.12.1970 | 1 | 0 | 1996, CD Palestino Santiago (1/0). |
| (28/081) | SÁNCHEZ Francisco | | 3 | 0 | 1926-1927, CDFA Arturo Fernández Vial Concepción (3/0). |
| (116/248) | SÁNCHEZ LINEROS Leonel Guillermo | 25.04.1936 | 85 | 24 | 1955-1968, CF de la Universidad de Chile Santiago (85/24). |
| (52/145) | SÁNCHEZ Oscar | | 2 | 0 | 1941, CF de la Universidad de Chile Santiago (2/0). |
| (145/277) | SÁNCHEZ Raúl | 26.10.1933 | 33 | 0 | 1959-1964, CD Santiago Wanderers Valparaíso (33/0). |
| (571/699) | SÁNCHEZ SÁNCHEZ Alexis Alejandro | 19.12.1988 | 64 | 22 | 2006-2013, Udinese Calcio (4/0), CSD Colo-Colo Santiago (3/0), CF River Plate Buenos Aires (6/3), Udinese Calcio (28/11), FC Barcelona (23/8). |
| (283/406) | SANHUEZA GRAAVENDAAL Nélson | 01.05.1952 | 2 | 0 | 1976, CD Universidad Católica Santiago (2/0). |
| (537/657) | SANHUEZA MEDEL Héctor Arturo | 11.03.1979 | 16 | 0 | 2001-2007, CD Santiago Wanderers Valparaíso (3/0), CSD Colo-Colo Santiago (13/0). |
| (222/342) | SANTANDER Efraín | | 1 | 0 | 1968, CSD Colo-Colo Santiago (1/0). |
| (321/437) | SANTANDER Rodrigo | 1959 | 1 | 0 | 1981, CSD Colo-Colo Santiago (1/0). |
| (496/617) | SANTIS SANTANDER César Elías | 05.02.1979 | 1 | 0 | 1999, Club Unión Española Santiago (1/0). |
| (32/091) | SCHNEEBERGER Carlos | 21.06.1902 | 5 | 0 | 1927-1930, CSD Colo-Colo Santiago (5/0). |
| (41/118) | SCHNEEBERGER Eduardo | | 3 | 0 | 1935-1937, CSD Colo-Colo Santiago (3/0). |
| (172/304) | SEPÚLVEDA Alfonso | | 4 | 1 | 1961-1964, CF de la Universidad de Chile Santiago (4/1). |
| (68/175) | SEPÚLVEDA José | | 10 | 0 | 1946-1947, CF de la Universidad de Chile Santiago (10/0). |
| (293/416) | SERRANO René | 02.08.1955 | 5 | 0 | 1979-1985, CD O'Higgins Rancagua (5/0). |
| (628/758) | SEYMOUR DOBUD Felipe Ignacio | 23.07.1988 | 6 | 0 | 2010-2012, CFP de la Universidad de Chile Santiago (2/0), Genoa CFC (4/0). |
| (410/537) | SIERRA PANDO José Luis | 05.12.1968 | 54 | 8 | 1991-2000, Club Unión Española Santiago (12/3), São Paulo FC (3/0), CSD Colo-Colo Santiago (22/2), no club (2/0), CD Universitario de Nuevo Leon Monterrey (5/1), CSD Colo-Colo Santiago (10/2). |
| (583/719) | SILVA GAJARDO Francisco Andrés | 11.02.1986 | 10 | 0 | 2007-2013, CD Provincial Osorno (1/0), CD Universidad Católica Santiago (4/0), CA Osasuna Pamplona (5/0). |
| (437/565) | SILVA Juan | 18.06.1970 | 2 | 0 | 1994, CD Cobreloa Calama (2/0). |
| (239/357) | SILVA Moisés | | 2 | 0 | 1970, Green Cross Temuco (2/0). |
| (47/128) | SIMIÁN Eduardo | | 3 | 0 | 1939, CF de la Universidad de Chile Santiago (3/0). |
| (1/008) | SIMMONS Frank | | 2 | 1 | 1910, Bádminton FC Valparaíso (2/1). |
| (4/024) | SKEWES Alexander | | 1 | 0 | 1913, Bádminton FC Valparaíso (1/0). |
| (268/388) | SOCÍAS TUSET Jorge | 06.10.1951 | 4 | 0 | 1974-1980, CF de la Universidad de Chile Santiago (4/0). |
| (257/383) | SOLÍS Hugo | | 2 | 1 | 1972-1973, CD Universidad Católica Santiago (2/1). |
| (532/644) | SOLÍS NÚÑEZ Fernando Esteban | 28.06.1976 | 1 | 0 | 2001, Club Unión Española Santiago (1/0). |
| (39/114) | SORREL Enrique | | 10 | 5 | 1935-1941, CSD Colo-Colo Santiago (10/5). |
| (279/401) | SOTO BENAVIDES Mario del Transito | 10.07.1950 | 48 | 1 | 1975-1985, Club Unión Española Santiago (11/0), CD Cobreloa Calama (37/1). |
| (43/125) | SOTO Eugenio | | 1 | 0 | 1937, CD Magallanes Santiago (1/0). |
| (145/273) | SOTO Mario | | 11 | 2 | 1959-1960, CD Universidad Católica Santiago (11/2). |
| (144/271) | SOTO MURA Juan | | 17 | 6 | 1957-1961, CSD Colo-Colo Santiago (17/6). |
| (292/414) | SOTO QUINTANA Juan | | 20 | 1 | 1977-1988, CF de la Universidad de Chile Santiago (1/0), CD Naval Talcahuano (15/1), CSD Colo-Colo Santiago (4/0). |
| (366/486) | SOTO SANDOVAL Carlos | | 2 | 1 | 1987, CD Palestino Santiago (2/1). |
| (279/403) | SPEDALETTI GONZÁLEZ Jorge Américo | 24.09.1947 | 5 | 0 | 1975-1977, Club Unión Española Santiago (4/0), CD Everton Viña del Mar (1/0). |
| (3/015) | STURGESS Heriberto | | 1 | 0 | 1910, Talca FC (1/0). |
| (373/492) | SUAZO Julio | 1955 | 1 | 0 | 1987, CD Cobresal El Salvador (1/0). |
| (561/684) | SUAZO PONTIVO Humberto Andrés | 10.05.1981 | 60 | 21 | 2005-2013, Audax CS Italiano Santiago (3/0), CSD Colo-Colo Santiago (13/7), CF Monterrey (25/10), Real Zaragoza (4/1), CF Monterrey (15/3). |
| (28/084) | SUBIABRE ASTORGA Guillermo | 25.02.1902 | 10 | 6 | 1926-1930, CD Santiago Wanderers Valparaíso (4/2), CSD Colo-Colo Santiago (6/4). |
| (344/457) | TABILO Hugo | 15.09.1956 | 3 | 0 | 1984-1985, CD Cobreloa Calama (3/0). |
| (432/553) | TAPIA RIOS Nelson Antonio | 22.09.1966 | 73 | 0 | 1994-2005, CD Universidad Católica Santiago (49/0), CA Vélez Sarsfield Buenos Aires (1/0), CD Puerto Montt (2/0), CD Cobreloa Calama (11/0), Santos FC (4/0), CD Cobreloa Calama (5/0), CPD Atlético Junior Barranquilla (1/0). |
| (484/604) | TAPIA URDILE Héctor Santiago | 30.09.1977 | 14 | 3 | 1998-2003, CSD Colo-Colo Santiago (2/0), AC Perugia (4/2), CSD Colo-Colo Santiago (3/0), CD Palestino Santiago (1/0), OSC Lille (4/1). |

| | | | | | |
|---|---|---|---|---|---|
| (95/223) | TELLO Carlos | | 14 | 3 | 1952-1957, Audax CS Italiano Santiago (14/3). |
| (374/496) | TELLO Claudio | 28.09.1962 | 8 | 0 | 1988, CD Cobreloa Calama (8/0). |
| (510/630) | TELLO VALENZUELA Rodrígo Alvaro | 14.10.1979 | 36 | 3 | 2000-2010, CF de la Universidad de Chile Santiago (12/2), Sporting Clube de Portugal Lisboa (14/0) , Beşiktaş JK Istanbul (9/1), Eskişehirspor Kulübü (1/0). |
| (4/025) | TEUCHE Enrique | | 6 | 0 | 1913-1916, 5 de Abril FC Santiago (1/0), CD Magallanes Santiago (5/0). |
| (145/275) | TOBAR Armando | 07.06.1938 | 33 | 3 | 1959-1967, CD Santiago Wanderers Valparaíso (17/1), CD Universidad Católica Santiago (16/2). |
| (410/526) | TOLEDO Patricio Armando | 14.07.1962 | 19 | 0 | 1991-1994, CD Universidad Católica Santiago (19/0). |
| (566/686) | TOLOZA Rodrígo | 03.05.1984 | 1 | 0 | 2005, CD Palestino Santiago (1/0). |
| (344/461) | TORO Claudio | | 1 | 0 | 1984, CD Magallanes Santiago (1/0). |
| (523/635) | TORO CORONADO Carlos Antonio | 04.02.1976 | 3 | 0 | 2001, CD Santiago Morning (3/0). |
| (629/763) | TORO HORMAZÁBAL Sebastián Patricio | 02.02.1990 | 5 | 1 | 2010-2012, CSD Colo-Colo Santiago (3/1), CD Iquique (2/0). |
| (142/270) | TORO Juan | | 2 | 0 | 1957, CD Palestino Santiago (2/0). |
| (42/123) | TORO Raúl Julio | | 13 | 12 | 1936-1941, CD Santiago Wanderers Valparaíso (5/7), CD Santiago Morning (8/5). |
| (366/485) | TORO Ricardo | | 5 | 0 | 1987, CD Palestino Santiago (5/0). |
| (145/276) | TORO SÁNCHEZ Jorge Luis | 10.01.1939 | 23 | 3 | 1959-1973, CSD Colo-Colo Santiago (20/3), Club Unión Española Santiago (3/0). |
| (17/060) | TORO Víctor | | 7 | 0 | 1920-1926, CDFA Arturo Fernández Vial Concepción (3/0), Diez de Julio Concepción (4/0). |
| (33/095) | TORRES CARRASCO Arturo | 20.10.1906 | 8 | 0 | 1928-1935, CD Everton Viña del Mar (3/0), CSD Colo-Colo Santiago (3/0), CD Magallanes Santiago (2/0). |
| (37/103) | TORRES Casimiro Luis | 1906 | 2 | 0 | 1930, CD Everton Viña del Mar (2/0). |
| (42/122) | TORRES Guillermo | | 9 | 1 | 1936-1942, CD Santiago Wanderers Valparaíso (9/1). |
| (537/654) | TORRES Jorge | 27.09.1969 | 1 | 0 | 2001, Club Deportes Concepción (1/0). |
| (113/242) | TORRES Mario | | 11 | 0 | 1954-1959, Audax CS Italiano Santiago (11/0). |
| (210/332) | TORRES Nélson | | 4 | 0 | 1966-1968, CD Palestino Santiago (4/0). |
| (538/663) | TORRES SOTO Joel Antonio | 09.04.1982 | 5 | 0 | 2002-2003, CD Santiago Wanderers Valparaíso (5/0). |
| (627/754) | TOSELLI RÍOS Cristopher Benjamín | 15.06.1988 | 3 | 0 | 2010-2012, CD Universidad Católica Santiago (3/0). |
| (53/148) | TREJOS Héctor | | 3 | 0 | 1941, Audax CS Italiano Santiago (3/0). |
| (256/381) | TRUJILLO Alejandro | | 3 | 0 | 1972-1974, Club Unión Española Santiago (1/0), CD O'Higgins Rancagua (2/0). |
| (385/508) | TÚDOR Lukas Nicolás | 22.02.1969 | 12 | 3 | 1988-1995, CD Universidad Católica Santiago (12/3). |
| (431/551) | TUPPER Raimundo | 07.01.1969 | 7 | 1 | 1993-1994, CD Universidad Católica Santiago (7/1). |
| (658/788) | UBILLA CAMBÓN Sebastián Andrés | 09.08.1990 | 3 | 0 | 2011-2013, CD Santiago Wanderers (1/0), CFP de la Universidad de Chil3 Santiago (2/0). |
| (373/495) | UGARTE Francisco | 21.03.1961 | 6 | 0 | 1987-1988, Club Unión Española Santiago (1/0), 1988 (5/0). |
| (5/030) | UNZAGA Ramón | | 8 | 0 | 1916-1920, CD Estrella del Mar Talcahuano (8/0). |
| (494/610) | URIBE LARA Cristián Roberto | 01.08.1976 | 2 | 0 | 1999, CSD Colo-Colo Santiago (2/0). |
| (32/089) | URREJOLA Víctor | | 1 | 0 | 1927, CD Santiago Wanderers Valparaíso (1/0). |
| (247/369) | URRIZOLA Julián | | 3 | 0 | 1971-1975, Club Deportes Concepción (1/0), CD Huachipato Talcahuano (2/0). |
| (73/186) | URROZ Francisco | | 11 | 0 | 1947-1950, CSD Colo-Colo Santiago (11/0). |
| (386/511) | VALDÉS Iván | | 3 | 0 | 1989, Club de Deportes Valdivia (1/0). |
| (109/238) | VALDÉS José | | 2 | 0 | 1954, CD Magallanes Santiago (2/0). |
| (180/307) | VALDÉS MUÑOZ Francisco | 19.03.1943 | 50 | 9 | 1962-1975, CSD Colo-Colo Santiago (27/5), Club Unión Española Santiago (1/0), CSD Colo-Colo Santiago (22/4). |
| (135/258) | VALDÉS Sergio | | 17 | 0 | 1957-1961, CD Magallanes Santiago (10/0), CD Universidad Católica Santiago (7/0). |
| (526/642) | VALDÉS ZAPATA Jaime Andrés | 11.01.1981 | 2 | 0 | 2001-2010, AS Bari (1/0), US Lecce (1/0), Atalanta Bergamasca calcio (1/0). |
| (549/675) | VALDIVIA TORO Jorge Luis | 19.01.1983 | 55 | 4 | 2004-2013, AD Rayo Vallecano Vallecas (1/0), Servette FC Genève (3/0), CSD Colo-Colo Santiago (9/0), SE Palmeiras São Paulo (11/1), Al-Ain Sports and Cultural Club (19/3), SE Palmeiras São Paulo (12/0). |
| (435/562) | VALENCIA BASCUÑÁN Esteban Andrés | 08.01.1972 | 47 | 4 | 1994-2001, CF de la Universidad de Chile Santiago (41/4), Club Colón de Santa Fé (3/0), no club (1/0), CD Puerto Montt (2/0). |
| (164/291) | VALENTINI Alberto Aldo | 25.11.1938 | 19 | 0 | 1960-1966, CD Santiago Wanderers Valparaíso (13/0), CSD Colo-Colo Santiago (6/0). |
| (483/603) | VALENZUELA AVÍLES Rodrígo Ignacio | 27.11.1975 | 18 | 0 | 1998-2005, Club Unión Española Santiago (1/0), CD Santiago Wanderers Valparaíso (1/0), CSD Leon AC (5/0), CD Atlas Guadalajara (5/0), CF América Ciudad de México (6/0). |
| (296/425) | VALENZUELA BECKER Eduardo René | 20.04.1955 | 46 | 0 | 1979-1988, CD O'Higgins Rancagua (10/0), CD Universidad Católica Santiago (35/0), Club Unión Española Santiago (1/0). |
| (329/444) | VALENZUELA Luis | | 10 | 0 | 1983, CD Naval Talcahuano (10/0). |
| (365/477) | VALENZUELA Luis Alejandro | | 1 | 0 | 1986, CD Cobresal El Salvador (1/0). |
| (106/234) | VALJALO Antonio | | 2 | 0 | 1953-1955, CSD Colo-Colo Santiago (2/0). |
| (221/340) | VALLEJOS BRAVO Leopoldo Manuel | 16.07.1944 | 18 | 0 | 1968-1977, CD Universidad Católica Santiago (4/0), Club Unión Española Santiago (12/0), CD Everton Viña del Mar (2/0). |
| (440/569) | VARAS Alex Fabián | 26.03.1976 | 7 | 0 | 1995-2004, CD Universidad Católica Santiago (3/0), CD Santiago Wanderers Valparaíso (4/0). |
| (14/055) | VARAS Víctor | | 10 | 0 | 1919-1922, Artillero de Costa FC Talcahuano (10/0). |
| (65/172) | VARELA Carlos | | 12 | 1 | 1947-1949, Audax CS Italiano Santiago (12/1). |
| (526/641) | VARGAS BUSCALIA Sergio Bernabé | 17.08.1965 | 10 | 0 | 2001, CF de la Universidad de Chile Santiago (10/0). |
| (307/431) | VARGAS Osvaldo | | 3 | 1 | 1980-1981, CD O'Higgins Rancagua (3/1). |

| | | | | | |
|---|---|---|---|---|---|
| (496/614) | VARGAS PALACIOS Jorge Francisco | 08.02.1976 | **38** | **0** | 1999-2007, CD Universidad Católica Santiago (8/0), Reggina Calcio Reggio Calabria (15/0), Empoli FC (3/0), AS Livorno Calcio (4/0), FC Red Bull Salzburg (8/0). |
| (41/117) | VARGAS Quintín | | **1** | **0** | 1935, CD Magallanes Santiago (1/0). |
| (625/751) | VARGAS ROJAS Eduardo Jesús | 20.11.1989 | **27** | **11** | 2009-2013, CD Cobreloa Calama (1/0), CFP de la Universidad de Chile Santiago (8/2), SSC Napoli (6/0), Grêmio Foot-Ball Porto Alegrense (12/9). |
| (8/038) | VÁSQUEZ Erasmo | | **1** | **0** | 1916, La Cruz FC Quillota Valparaíso (1/0). |
| (63/169) | VÁSQUEZ Jorge | | **5** | **0** | 1945, CSD Colo-Colo Santiago (5/0). |
| (242/365) | VÁSQUEZ Nelson | | **7** | **2** | 1971-1973, CD Everton Viña del Mar (6/2), Club Deportes Concepción (1/0). |
| (410/533) | VEGA Francisco Marcelo | 12.08.1971 | **30** | **1** | 1991-1998, Club Unión Española Santiago (9/1), CSD Colo-Colo Santiago (1/0), CD Regional Atacama (6/0), CD Santiago Wanderers Valparaíso (11/0), New York/New Jersey Metro Stars (3/0). |
| (197/325) | VÉLIZ DÍAZ Leonardo | 03.09.1945 | **39** | **2** | 1966-1981, CD Everton Viña del Mar (2/0), Club Unión Española Santiago (7/1), CSD Colo-Colo Santiago (14/0), Club Unión Española Santiago (7/0), CSD Colo-Colo Santiago (9/1). |
| (625/749) | VELOSO ESPINOZA Nery Alexis | 01.03.1987 | **1** | **0** | 2009, CD Huachipato Talcahuano (1/0). |
| (28/080) | VELOSO Leoncio | | **3** | **0** | 1926, Bádminton FC Santiago (3/0). |
| (344/462) | VENEGAS Luis | | **1** | **0** | 1984, CD Magallanes Santiago (1/0). |
| (62/168) | VERA Erasmo | | **9** | **1** | 1945-1946, CD Santiago Morning (9/1). |
| (365/479) | VERA Jaime Andrés | 25.03.1963 | **24** | **4** | 1986-1991, CSD Colo-Colo Santiago (4/1), OF Iráklion (20/3). |
| (410/532) | VERA Juan Carlos | 06.07.1960 | **1** | **0** | 1991, Club UNAM Ciudad de México (1/0). |
| (113/243) | VERA Luis | | **14** | **0** | 1954-1959, Audax CS Italiano Santiago (14/0). |
| (135/259) | VERDEJO Carlos | | **6** | **3** | 1957-1964, Club de Deportes La Serena (5/2), CD Palestino Santiago (1/0). |
| (461/588) | VERGARA MEYLAN Luis Fernando | 13.05.1970 | **6** | **3** | 1996-1997, CSD Colo-Colo Santiago (6/3). |
| (17/058) | VERGARA Pedro | | **7** | **0** | 1920-1922, CD Santiago Wanderers Valparaíso (3/0), Eleuterio Ramírez FC Santiago (4/0). |
| (36/102) | VIDAL Carlos | 24.02.1902 | **6** | **2** | 1930-1935, CD Lota Schwager (3/2), CD Magallanes Santiago (3/0). |
| (53/146) | VIDAL Luis | | **3** | **0** | 1941, CD Universidad Católica Santiago (3/0). |
| (579/707) | VIDAL PARDO Arturo Erasmo | 22.05.1987 | **52** | **8** | 2007-2013, CSD Colo-Colo Santiago (4/0), TSV Bayer 04 Leverkusen (30/3), FC Juventus Torino (18/5). |
| (571/700) | VIDANGOSSY REBOLLEDO Mathias Leonardo | 25.05.1987 | **6** | **0** | 2006-2012, Club Unión Española Santiago (4/0), CD La Serena (1/0), CSD Colo-Colo Santiago (1/0). |
| (408/519) | VILCHES ARRIAGADA Eduardo Enrique | 21.04.1963 | **30** | **1** | 1990-1996, CSD Colo-Colo Santiago (21/1), CID Necaxa Ciudad de México (9/0). |
| (653/776) | VILCHES GONZÁLEZ Christian Alberto | 27.10.1983 | **1** | **0** | 2011, CSD Colo-Colo Santiago (1/0). |
| (36/101) | VILLALOBOS Eberardo | 01.04.1908 | **3** | **0** | 1930, Rangers FC Osorno (3/0). |
| (671/801) | VILLALOBOS SALVOS Manuel Arturo | 15.10.1980 | **1** | **0** | 2013, CD Iquique (1/0). |
| (544/670) | VILLANUEVA AHUMADA José Luis | 05.11.1981 | **4** | **0** | 2003-2006, CD Palestino Santiago (1/0), CD Universidad Católica Santiago (1/0), Club Atlético Morelia (2/0). |
| (184/314) | VILLANUEVA Hugo | 09.04.1939 | **21** | **0** | 1964-1967, CF de la Universidad de Chile Santiago (21/0). |
| (579/706) | VILLANUEVA ROLAND Carlos Andrés | 05.02.1986 | **13** | **1** | 2007-2010, Audax CS Italiano Santiago (12/1), Al-Shabab Al-Arabi Club Dubai (1/0). |
| (468/596) | VILLARROEL AYALA Moisés Fermín | 12.02.1976 | **34** | **1** | 1997-2005, CD Santiago Wanderers Valparaíso (27/1), CSD Colo-Colo Santiago (7/0). |
| (496/615) | VILLASECA Marcos Antonio | 15.03.1975 | **20** | **0** | 1999-2001, CSD Colo-Colo Santiago (20/0). |
| (480/601) | VIVAR Paolo | 11.03.1977 | **1** | **0** | 1998, CD Cobreloa Calama (1/0). |
| (242/363) | VIVEROS Gustavo | | **9** | **2** | 1971-1972, Club Deportes Concepción (9/2). |
| (506/623) | VON SCHWEDLER VASQUEZ Alex Christian | 17.02.1980 | **4** | **0** | 2000-2007, CF de la Universidad de Chile Santiago (3/0), CS Marítimo Funchal (1/0). |
| (39/106) | WELSH Conrado | | **3** | **0** | 1935, CSD Colo-Colo Santiago (3/0). |
| (306/428) | WIRTH LAFUENTE Oscar Raúl | 05.11.1955 | **12** | **0** | 1980-1989, CD Cobreloa Calama (5/0), CD Everton Viña del Mar (2/0), no club (5/0). |
| (5/028) | WITTKE Marcos | | **5** | **0** | 1916, CD Magallanes Santiago (5/0). |
| (73/189) | WOOD Freddy | | **2** | **0** | 1947, CD Santiago Morning (2/0). |
| (293/421) | YÁÑEZ CANDIA Patricio Nazario | 20.01.1961 | **43** | **5** | 1979-1994, CD San Luis Quillota (26/4), Real Valladolid CF (2/0), Real Zaragoza CD (3/0), Real Betis Balompié Sevilla (4/1), CSD Colo-Colo Santiago (8/0). |
| (185/319) | YÁVAR Guillermo | 26.03.1943 | **26** | **2** | 1964-1974, CD Magallanes Santiago (5/0), CF de la Universidad de Chile Santiago (15/2), Club Unión Española Santiago (1/0), CF de la Universidad de Chile Santiago (5/1). |
| (88/212) | YORI Adelmo | | **9** | **0** | 1950-1959, Audax CS Italiano Santiago (9/0). |
| (409/524) | ZAMBRANO Richard | 20.05.1967 | **8** | **2** | 1990-1993, Club Unión Española Santiago (1/0), CF de la Universidad de Chile Santiago (7/2). |
| (366/488) | ZAMORANO ZAMORA Iván Luis | 18.01.1967 | **69** | **34** | 1987-2001, CD Cobresal El Salvador (10/1), FC St.Gallen (2/1), Sevilla CF (9/6), Real Madrid CF (8/7), Internazional FC Milano (35/19), CF América Ciudad de México (5/0). |
| (23/068) | ZAVALA Víctor | | **1** | **0** | 1922, Linares FC (1/0). |
| (164/298) | ZAZZALI Constantino | | **1** | **0** | 1960, CD San Luis Quillota (1/0). |
| (239/355) | ZELADA Víctor | | **2** | **0** | 1970, CSD Colo-Colo Santiago (2/0). |
| (570/690) | ZENTENO MORALES Mauricio Alejandro | 21.04.1984 | **11** | **0** | 2006-2007, CD Universidad Católica Santiago (11/0). |

**Player who won caps for another countries:**

| Name | Country | Period | Caps | Goals |
|---|---|---|---|---|
| INFANTE Ricardo Raimundo | Argentina | 1952-1958 | 4 | 2 |

## NATIONAL COACHES

| Name | Period | Matches | P | W | D | L | GF | - | GA | |
|---|---|---|---|---|---|---|---|---|---|---|
| Carlos FANTA TOMASZEWSKI | 02.07.1916 – 14.07.1916 | [5-9] | 5 | 0 | 1 | 4 | 3 | - | 16 | 10.00 % |
| Julián BERTOLA | 30.09.1917 – 21.10.1917 | [10-13] | 4 | 0 | 1 | 3 | 1 | - | 11 | 12.50 % |
| Héctor PARRA | 11.05.1919 – 22.05.1919 | [14-16] | 3 | 0 | 0 | 3 | 1 | - | 12 | 0.00 % |
| Juan Carlos BERTONE (*Uruguay*) | 11.09.1920 – 05.10.1922 | [17-23] | 7 | 0 | 2 | 5 | 3 | - | 14 | 14.28 % |
| Carlos ACUÑA | 22.10.1922 – 01.11.1924 | [24-27] | 4 | 0 | 0 | 4 | 1 | - | 11 | 0.00 % |
| José ROSETTI (*Italy*) | 12.10.1926 – 10.12.1927 | [28-32] | 5 | 2 | 1 | 2 | 16 | - | 9 | 50.00 % |
| Frank POWELL (*England*) | 27.05.1928 – 08.06.1928 | [33-35] | 3 | 1 | 1 | 1 | 7 | - | 7 | 50.00 % |
| György ORTH (*Hungary*) | 16.07.1930 – 22.07.1930 | [36-38] | 3 | 2 | 0 | 1 | 5 | - | 3 | 66.66 % |
| Joaquín MORALES | 06.01.1935 – 26.01.1935 | [39-41] | 3 | 0 | 0 | 3 | 2 | - | 7 | 0.00 % |
| Pedro MAZULLO (*Uruguay*) | 30.12.1936 – 26.02.1939 | [42-51] | 10 | 3 | 1 | 6 | 24 | - | 27 | 35.00 % |
| Máximo GARAY (*Hungary*) | 02.02.1941 – 04.03.1941 | [52-55] | 4 | 2 | 0 | 2 | 6 | - | 3 | 50.00 % |
| Ferenc PLATKÓ (*Hungary*) | 10.01.1942 – 28.02.1945 | [56-67] | 12 | 5 | 3 | 4 | 19 | - | 20 | 54.16 % |
| Luis TIRADO | 16.01.1946 – 08.05.1949 | [68-86] | 19 | 8 | 2 | 9 | 32 | - | 38 | 47.36 % |
| Ferenc PLATKÓ (*Hungary*) | 26.02.1950 – 09.04.1950 | [87-90] | 4 | 2 | 0 | 2 | 8 | - | 8 | 50.00 % |
| Alberto BUCCICARDI | 25.06.1950 – 02.07.1950 | [91-93] | 3 | 1 | 0 | 2 | 5 | - | 6 | 33.33 % |
| Luis TIRADO | 16.03.1952 – 24.05.1953 | [94-105] | 12 | 6 | 2 | 4 | 26 | - | 18 | 58.33 % |
| Ferenc PLATKÓ (*Hungary*) | 12.07.1953 – 28.07.1953 | [106-108] | 3 | 1 | 0 | 2 | 3 | - | 8 | 33.33 % |
| Luis TIRADO | 14.02.1954 – 14.03.1954 | [109-112] | 4 | 0 | 0 | 4 | 1 | - | 10 | 0.00 % |
| Selection Comittee | 17.09.1954 – 19.09.1954 | [113-114] | 2 | 1 | 0 | 1 | 4 | - | 5 | 50.00 % |
| Luis TIRADO | 27.02.1955 – 18.03.1956 | [115-131] | 17 | 6 | 3 | 8 | 37 | - | 30 | 44.11 % |
| José SALERNO (*Argentina*) | 26.08.1956 – 01.04.1957 | [132-138] | 7 | 2 | 1 | 4 | 12 | - | 17 | 35.71 % |
| László PÁKOZDI (*Hungary*) | 15.09.1957 – 20.10.1957 | [139-144] | 6 | 2 | 1 | 3 | 4 | - | 11 | 41.66 % |
| Fernando RIERA BAUZA | 07.03.1959 – 16.06.1962 | [145-179] | 35 | 12 | 4 | 19 | 55 | - | 77 | 40.00 % |
| Luis ALAMOS LUQUE | 07.11.1962 – 23.03.1963 | [180-182] | 3 | 0 | 1 | 2 | 3 | - | 5 | 16.66 % |
| Francisco HORMAZÁBAL | 24.07.1963 – 22.08.1965 | [183-195] | 13 | 4 | 6 | 3 | 20 | - | 17 | 53.84 % |
| Luis ALAMOS LUQUE | 12.10.1965 – 20.07.1966 | [196-208] | 13 | 3 | 2 | 8 | 11 | - | 19 | 30.76 % |
| Alejandro SCOPELLI Casanova (*Argentina*) | 30.11.1966 – 17.12.1967 | [209-220] | 12 | 5 | 3 | 4 | 22 | - | 19 | 54.16 % |
| Salvador NOCETTI (*Argentina*) | 18.08.1968 – 10.08.1969 | [221-238] | 18 | 7 | 6 | 5 | 23 | - | 23 | 55.55 % |
| Francisco HORMAZÁBAL | 22.03.1970 – 26.03.1970 | [239-240] | 2 | 0 | 0 | 2 | 1 | - | 7 | 0.00 % |
| Fernando RIERA | 04.10.1970 | [241] | 1 | 0 | 0 | 1 | 1 | - | 5 | 0.00 % |
| Luis VERA – Raúl PINO | 14.07.1971 – 03.11.1971 | [242-249] | 8 | 3 | 1 | 4 | 11 | - | 11 | 43.75 % |
| Raúl PINO | 26.01.1972 | [250] | 1 | 0 | 0 | 1 | 0 | - | 2 | 0.00 % |
| Rudolf GUTTENDORF (*West Germany*) | 31.05.1972 – 27.09.1972 | [251-257] | 7 | 3 | 0 | 4 | 10 | - | 15 | 42.85 % |
| Luis ALAMOS LUQUE | 14.04.1973 – 22.06.1974 | [258-273] | 16 | 6 | 6 | 4 | 21 | - | 16 | 56.25 % |
| Pedro MORALES | 06.11.1974 – 20.08.1975 | [274-282] | 9 | 2 | 2 | 5 | 10 | - | 13 | 33.33 % |
| Caupolicán PEÑA | 06.10.1976 – 26.03.1977 | [283-291] | 9 | 3 | 2 | 4 | 9 | - | 10 | 44.44 % |
| Oscar Luis SANTIBÁÑEZ DÍAZ | 15.06.1977 – 24.06.1982 | [292-328] | 37 | 14 | 10 | 13 | 46 | - | 38 | 51.35 % |
| Luis IBARRA CASTILLO | 28.04.1983 – 17.06.1984 | [329-344] | 16 | 7 | 5 | 4 | 26 | - | 16 | 59.37 % |
| Vicente CANTATORE SOCCI | 28.10.1984 | [345] | 1 | 1 | 0 | 0 | 1 | - | 0 | 100.00 % |
| Pedro MORALES | 06.02.1985 – 17.11.1985 | [346-364] | 19 | 8 | 6 | 5 | 27 | - | 22 | 57.89 % |
| Luis IBARRA CASTILLO | 07.05.1986 | [365] | 1 | 0 | 1 | 0 | 1 | - | 1 | 50.00 % |
| Orlando ARAVENA | 19.06.1987 – 12.07.1987 | [366-372] | 7 | 5 | 0 | 2 | 13 | - | 6 | 71.42 % |
| Manuel RODRÍGUEZ ARANEDA | 09.12.1987 | [373] | 1 | 0 | 0 | 1 | 1 | - | 2 | 0.00 % |
| Orlando ARAVENA | 23.05.1988 – 03.09.1989 | [374-407] | 34 | 14 | 9 | 11 | 42 | - | 31 | 54.41 % |
| Arturo SALAH CASSANI | 17.10.1990 – 24.06.1993 | [408-430] | 23 | 9 | 6 | 8 | 30 | - | 23 | 52.17 % |
| Nelson Bonifacio ACOSTA LÓPEZ | 08.09.1993 | [431] | 1 | 0 | 0 | 1 | 0 | - | 2 | 0.00 % |
| Mirko JOŽIĆ (Croatia) | 22.03.1994 – 16.11.1994 | [432-439] | 8 | 3 | 2 | 3 | 13 | - | 14 | 50.00 % |
| Francisco Xabier AZCARGORTA URIARTE (*Spain*) | 29.03.1995 – 02.06.1996 | [440-457] | 18 | 9 | 5 | 4 | 28 | - | 23 | 63.88 % |
| Nelson Bonifacio ACOSTA LÓPEZ | 06.07.1996 – 15.11.2000 | [458-522] | 65 | 25 | 17 | 23 | 102 | - | 79 | 51.53 % |
| Pedro GARCÍA BARROS | 22.03.2001 – 04.09.2001 | [523-534] | 12 | 3 | 1 | 8 | 11 | - | 19 | 29.16 % |
| Jorge Luis GARCÉS ROJAS | 07.10.2001 – 14.11.2001 | [535-537] | 3 | 0 | 1 | 2 | 1 | - | 5 | 16.66 % |
| César VACCIA | 17.04.2002 | [538] | 1 | 0 | 0 | 1 | 0 | - | 2 | 0.00 % |
| Juvenal Mario OLMOS ROJAS | 30.03.2003 – 30.03.2005 | [539-563] | 25 | 7 | 9 | 9 | 24 | - | 25 | 46.00 % |
| Nelson Bonifacio ACOSTA LÓPEZ | 04.06.2005 – 07.07.2007 | [564-591] | 28 | 13 | 8 | 7 | 35 | - | 38 | 60.71 % |
| Marcelo Alberto BIELSA CALDERA (*Argentina*) | 07.09.2007 – 22.01.2011 | [592-642] | 51 | 27 | 8 | 16 | 69 | - | 49 | 60.78 % |
| Claudio Daniel BORGHI BIDOS (*Argentina*) | 26.03.2011 – 14.11.2012 | [643-669] | 27 | 11 | 5 | 11 | 38 | - | 40 | 50.00 % |
| Jorge Luis SAMPAOLI Moya (*Argentina*) | 15.01.2013 -> | [670-> | 15 | 10 | 3 | 2 | 35 | - | 15 | |

Chile played without national coach in following matches: [1-4].

**National coaches several times in charge:**

| Name | How often | Matches | M | W | D | L | GF | - | GA | |
|---|---|---|---|---|---|---|---|---|---|---|
| Ferenc PLATKÓ (*Hungary*) | 3x | [56-67],[87-90],[106-108] | 19 | 8 | 3 | 8 | 30 | - | 36 | 50.00 % |
| Luis TIRADO | 4x | [68-86],[94-105],[109-112],[115-131] | 52 | 20 | 7 | 25 | 96 | - | 96 | 45.19 % |
| Luis ALAMOS LUQUE | 3x | [180-182],[196-208],[258-273] | 32 | 9 | 9 | 14 | 35 | - | 40 | 42.18 % |
| Francisco HORMAZÁBAL | 2x | [183-195],[239-240] | 15 | 4 | 6 | 5 | 21 | - | 24 | 46.66 % |
| Fernando RIERA BAUZA | 2x | [145-179],[241] | 36 | 12 | 4 | 20 | 56 | - | 82 | 38.88 % |
| Pedro MORALES | 2x | [274-282],[346-364] | 28 | 10 | 8 | 10 | 37 | - | 35 | 50.00 % |
| Luis IBARRA CASTILLO | 2x | [329-344],[365] | 17 | 7 | 6 | 4 | 27 | - | 17 | 58.82 % |
| Orlando ARAVENA | 2x | [366-372],[374-407] | 41 | 19 | 9 | 13 | 55 | - | 37 | 57.31 % |
| Nelson Bonifacio ACOSTA LÓPEZ | 3x | [431],[458-522],[564-574] | 94 | 38 | 25 | 31 | 135 | - | 119 | 53.72 % |

# HEAD-TO-HEAD STATISTICS

| | HOME | | | | | AWAY | | | | | NEUTRAL | | | | | TOTAL | | | | |
|---|---|---|---|---|---|---|---|---|---|---|---|---|---|---|---|---|---|---|---|---|
| Algeria | | | | | | | | | | | 1 | 0 | 0 | 1 | 2 : 3 | 1 | 0 | 0 | 1 | 2 : 3 |
| Argentina | 30 | 6 | 13 | 11 | 34 : 42 | 30 | 0 | 6 | 24 | 20 : 75 | 15 | 0 | 2 | 13 | 6 : 39 | 75 | 6 | 21 | 48 | 60 : 156 |
| Armenia | 1 | 1 | 0 | 0 | 7 : 0 | | | | | | | | | | | 1 | 1 | 0 | 0 | 7 : 0 |
| Australia | 2 | 2 | 0 | 0 | 5 : 1 | 1 | 1 | 0 | 0 | 1 : 0 | 1 | 0 | 1 | 0 | 0 : 0 | 4 | 3 | 1 | 0 | 6 : 1 |
| Austria | | | | | | 1 | 1 | 0 | 0 | 2 : 0 | 2 | 0 | 1 | 1 | 1 : 2 | 3 | 1 | 1 | 1 | 3 : 2 |
| Belgium | | | | | | 1 | 0 | 1 | 0 | 1 : 1 | 1 | 0 | 1 | 0 | 1 : 1 | 2 | 0 | 2 | 0 | 2 : 2 |
| Bolivia | 17 | 15 | 1 | 1 | 53 : 13 | 12 | 6 | 3 | 3 | 16 : 11 | 9 | 4 | 3 | 2 | 24 : 15 | 38 | 25 | 7 | 6 | 93 : 39 |
| Brazil | 22 | 4 | 6 | 12 | 15 : 30 | 27 | 0 | 6 | 21 | 17 : 69 | 19 | 3 | 1 | 15 | 26 : 58 | 68 | 7 | 13 | 48 | 58 : 157 |
| Bulgaria | 1 | 1 | 0 | 0 | 3 : 2 | | | | | | | | | | | 1 | 1 | 0 | 0 | 3 : 2 |
| Cameroon | | | | | | | | | | | 1 | 0 | 1 | 0 | 1 : 1 | 1 | 0 | 1 | 0 | 1 : 1 |
| Canada | 1 | 1 | 0 | 0 | 2 : 0 | 2 | 1 | 0 | 1 | 2 : 2 | | | | | | 3 | 2 | 0 | 1 | 4 : 2 |
| China P.R. | | | | | | 1 | 0 | 1 | 0 | 0 : 0 | | | | | | 1 | 0 | 1 | 0 | 0 : 0 |
| Colombia | 15 | 7 | 5 | 3 | 32 : 16 | 14 | 2 | 5 | 7 | 17 : 26 | 6 | 5 | 1 | 0 | 15 : 7 | 35 | 14 | 11 | 10 | 64 : 49 |
| Costa Rica | 3 | 2 | 1 | 0 | 5 : 1 | 4 | 0 | 1 | 3 | 1 : 5 | 2 | 0 | 0 | 2 | 2 : 4 | 9 | 2 | 2 | 5 | 8 : 10 |
| Cuba | 2 | 2 | 0 | 0 | 5 : 0 | | | | | | | | | | | 2 | 2 | 0 | 0 | 5 : 0 |
| Czechoslovakia | 1 | 1 | 0 | 0 | 3 : 0 | | | | | | | | | | | 1 | 1 | 0 | 0 | 3 : 0 |
| Denmark | | | | | | 1 | 1 | 0 | 0 | 2 : 1 | | | | | | 1 | 1 | 0 | 0 | 2 : 1 |
| East Germany | | | | | | 3 | 1 | 0 | 2 | 4 : 7 | 1 | 0 | 1 | 0 | 1 : 1 | 4 | 1 | 1 | 2 | 5 : 8 |
| Ecuador | 18 | 14 | 4 | 0 | 52 : 12 | 16 | 3 | 6 | 7 | 15 : 19 | 13 | 9 | 2 | 2 | 26 : 15 | 47 | 26 | 12 | 9 | 93 : 46 |
| Egypt | | | | | | 1 | 0 | 0 | 1 | 0 : 2 | 1 | 1 | 0 | 0 | 2 : 1 | 2 | 1 | 0 | 1 | 2 : 3 |
| El Salvador | | | | | | | | | | | 1 | 1 | 0 | 0 | 1 : 0 | 1 | 1 | 0 | 0 | 1 : 0 |
| England | 2 | 0 | 1 | 1 | 1 : 2 | 3 | 2 | 1 | 0 | 4 : 0 | 1 | 0 | 0 | 1 | 0 : 2 | 6 | 2 | 2 | 2 | 5 : 4 |
| Estonia | 1 | 1 | 0 | 0 | 4 : 0 | | | | | | | | | | | 1 | 1 | 0 | 0 | 4 : 0 |
| Finland | 1 | 1 | 0 | 0 | 2 : 0 | | | | | | | | | | | 1 | 1 | 0 | 0 | 2 : 0 |
| France | 1 | 1 | 0 | 0 | 2 : 1 | 3 | 0 | 1 | 2 | 2 : 10 | 1 | 1 | 0 | 0 | 1 : 0 | 5 | 2 | 1 | 2 | 5 : 11 |
| Germany | 3 | 2 | 0 | 1 | 5 : 4 | 2 | 0 | 0 | 2 | 1 : 3 | 1 | 0 | 0 | 1 | 1 : 4 | 6 | 2 | 0 | 4 | 7 : 11 |
| Ghana | | | | | | | | | | | 1 | 0 | 1 | 0 | 1 : 1 | 1 | 0 | 1 | 0 | 1 : 1 |
| Greece | | | | | | | | | | | 1 | 0 | 0 | 1 | 0 : 1 | 1 | 0 | 0 | 1 | 0 : 1 |
| Guatemala | 2 | 2 | 0 | 0 | 6 : 1 | 2 | 0 | 1 | 1 | 2 : 3 | 1 | 1 | 0 | 0 | 1 : 0 | 5 | 3 | 1 | 1 | 9 : 4 |
| Haiti | 1 | 1 | 0 | 0 | 3 : 0 | 4 | 1 | 3 | 0 | 2 : 1 | | | | | | 5 | 2 | 3 | 0 | 5 : 1 |
| Holland | | | | | | 1 | 0 | 0 | 1 | 0 : 2 | | | | | | 1 | 0 | 0 | 1 | 0 : 2 |
| Honduras | 1 | 1 | 0 | 0 | 5 : 2 | 2 | 1 | 0 | 1 | 3 : 4 | 2 | 1 | 0 | 1 | 1 : 2 | 5 | 3 | 0 | 2 | 9 : 8 |
| Hungary | 3 | 1 | 1 | 1 | 9 : 6 | | | | | : | | | | | | 3 | 1 | 1 | 1 | 9 : 6 |
| Iceland | 1 | 0 | 1 | 0 | 1 : 1 | | | | | | | | | | | 1 | 0 | 1 | 0 | 1 : 1 |
| Iran | | | | | | | | | | | 2 | 1 | 1 | 0 | 3 : 2 | 2 | 1 | 1 | 0 | 3 : 2 |
| Iraq | | | | | | | | | | | 1 | 1 | 0 | 0 | 6 : 0 | 1 | 1 | 0 | 0 | 6 : 0 |
| Israel | 1 | 1 | 0 | 0 | 3 : 0 | 1 | 0 | 0 | 1 | 0 : 1 | | | | | | 2 | 1 | 0 | 1 | 3 : 1 |
| Italy | 1 | 1 | 0 | 0 | 2 : 0 | | | | | | 2 | 0 | 1 | 1 | 2 : 4 | 3 | 1 | 1 | 1 | 4 : 4 |
| Ivory Coast | | | | | | | | | | | 1 | 0 | 1 | 0 | 1 : 1 | 1 | 0 | 1 | 0 | 1 : 1 |
| Jamaica | | | | | | 1 | 1 | 0 | 0 | 1 : 0 | | | | | | 1 | 1 | 0 | 0 | 1 : 0 |
| Japan | | | | | | 2 | 0 | 1 | 1 | 0 : 4 | | | | | | 2 | 0 | 1 | 1 | 0 : 4 |
| Lithuania | 1 | 1 | 0 | 0 | 1 : 0 | | | | | | | | | | | 1 | 1 | 0 | 0 | 1 : 0 |
| Mexico | 6 | 4 | 0 | 2 | 10 : 5 | 9 | 2 | 0 | 7 | 5 : 12 | 10 | 4 | 2 | 4 | 12 : 10 | 25 | 10 | 2 | 13 | 27 : 27 |
| Morocco | | | | | | | | | | | 1 | 0 | 1 | 0 | 1 : 1 | 1 | 0 | 1 | 0 | 1 : 1 |
| New Zealand | 3 | 3 | 0 | 0 | 8 : 2 | 1 | 0 | 1 | 0 | 0 : 0 | | | | | | 4 | 3 | 1 | 0 | 8 : 2 |
| North Korea | | | | | | | | | | | 1 | 0 | 1 | 0 | 1 : 1 | 1 | 0 | 1 | 0 | 1 : 1 |
| Northern Ireland | 1 | 1 | 0 | 0 | 1 : 0 | 1 | 1 | 0 | 0 | 1 : 0 | 1 | 1 | 0 | 0 | 2 : 1 | 3 | 3 | 0 | 0 | 4 : 1 |
| Oman | | | | | | 1 | 1 | 0 | 0 | 1 : 0 | | | | | | 1 | 1 | 0 | 0 | 1 : 0 |
| Panama | 3 | 2 | 1 | 0 | 8 : 2 | | | | | | | | | | | 3 | 2 | 1 | 0 | 8 : 2 |
| Paraguay | 26 | 19 | 3 | 4 | 59 : 26 | 17 | 4 | 2 | 11 | 8 : 25 | 16 | 3 | 2 | 11 | 16 : 32 | 59 | 26 | 7 | 26 | 83 : 83 |
| Peru | 32 | 25 | 5 | 2 | 76 : 32 | 32 | 11 | 4 | 17 | 29 : 49 | 11 | 4 | 5 | 2 | 14 : 14 | 75 | 40 | 14 | 21 | 119 : 95 |
| Portugal | | | | | | 1 | 0 | 1 | 0 | 1 : 1 | 2 | 0 | 0 | 2 | 3 : 8 | 3 | 0 | 1 | 2 | 4 : 9 |
| Rep of Ireland | 2 | 1 | 0 | 1 | 2 : 2 | 3 | 1 | 1 | 1 | 2 : 3 | 1 | 1 | 0 | 0 | 2 : 1 | 6 | 3 | 1 | 2 | 6 : 6 |
| Romania | 1 | 0 | 0 | 1 | 2 : 3 | | | | | | | | | | | 1 | 0 | 0 | 1 | 2 : 3 |
| Saudi Arabia | | | | | | 2 | 1 | 1 | 0 | 4 : 2 | | | | | | 2 | 1 | 1 | 0 | 4 : 2 |
| Scotland | 1 | 0 | 0 | 1 | 2 : 4 | 1 | 0 | 0 | 1 | 0 : 2 | | | | | | 2 | 0 | 0 | 2 | 2 : 6 |
| Senegal | 1 | 1 | 0 | 0 | 2 : 1 | | | | | | | | | | | 1 | 1 | 0 | 0 | 2 : 1 |
| Serbia | 1 | 1 | 0 | 0 | 1 : 0 | | | | | | 1 | 0 | 0 | 1 | 1 : 3 | 2 | 1 | 0 | 1 | 2 : 3 |
| Slovakia | 1 | 0 | 0 | 1 | 0 : 2 | 1 | 1 | 0 | 0 | 2 : 1 | | | | | | 2 | 1 | 0 | 1 | 2 : 3 |
| South Africa | | | | | | 1 | 1 | 0 | 0 | 2 : 0 | | | | | | 1 | 1 | 0 | 0 | 2 : 0 |
| South Korea | | | | | | 1 | 1 | 0 | 0 | 1 : 0 | | | | | | 1 | 1 | 0 | 0 | 1 : 0 |
| Soviet Union | 4 | 1 | 0 | 3 | 3 : 8 | 1 | 0 | 1 | 0 | 0 : 0 | 1 | 0 | 0 | 1 | 1 : 2 | 6 | 1 | 1 | 4 | 4 : 10 |
| Spain | 4 | 0 | 1 | 3 | 3 : 11 | 2 | 0 | 0 | 2 | 0 : 5 | 4 | 0 | 1 | 3 | 5 : 9 | 10 | 0 | 2 | 8 | 8 : 25 |
| Switzerland | | | | | | 1 | 0 | 1 | 0 | 1 : 1 | | | | | | 1 | 0 | 1 | 0 | 1 : 1 |
| Sweden | 1 | 1 | 0 | 0 | 3 : 1 | 1 | 0 | 0 | 1 | 2 : 4 | 2 | 1 | 0 | 1 | 2 : 2 | 4 | 2 | 0 | 2 | 7 : 7 |
| Trinidad & Tob. | 1 | 1 | 0 | 0 | 2 : 0 | | | | | | | | | | | 1 | 1 | 0 | 0 | 2 : 0 |
| Tunisia | | | | | | | | | | | 1 | 1 | 0 | 0 | 3 : 2 | 1 | 1 | 0 | 0 | 3 : 2 |
| Turkey | 1 | 0 | 1 | 0 | 0 : 0 | 1 | 0 | 0 | 1 | 0 : 1 | 1 | 0 | 0 | 1 | 0 : 2 | 3 | 0 | 1 | 2 | 0 : 3 |
| Ukraine | | | | | | 1 | 0 | 0 | 1 | 1 : 2 | | | | | | 1 | 0 | 0 | 1 | 1 : 2 |
| U. A. Emirates | | | | | | 1 | 1 | 0 | 0 | 2 : 0 | | | | | | 1 | 1 | 0 | 0 | 2 : 0 |
| United States | 1 | 0 | 0 | 1 | 1 : 2 | 6 | 3 | 2 | 1 | 11 : 5 | 2 | 1 | 0 | 1 | 6 : 4 | 9 | 4 | 2 | 3 | 18 : 11 |
| Uruguay | 31 | 12 | 9 | 10 | 40 : 35 | 25 | 0 | 7 | 18 | 20 : 60 | 18 | 4 | 2 | 12 | 16 : 36 | 74 | 16 | 18 | 40 | 76 : 131 |
| Venezuela | 9 | 5 | 2 | 1 | 27 : 5 | 9 | 6 | 3 | 0 | 14 : 5 | 6 | 5 | 0 | 1 | 15 : 3 | 24 | 16 | 5 | 2 | 56 : 13 |
| Wales | 1 | 1 | 0 | 0 | 2 : 0 | | | | | | | | | | | 1 | 1 | 0 | 0 | 2 : 0 |
| Zambia | 1 | 1 | 0 | 0 | 3 : 0 | | | | | | | | | | | 1 | 1 | 0 | 0 | 3 : 0 |
| **TOTAL** | **264** | **148** | **55** | **60** | **515 : 275** | **254** | **55** | **60** | **139** | **220 : 424** | **166** | **53** | **32** | **81** | **225 : 295** | **684** | **256** | **147** | **280** | **960 : 994** |